POCKET

SCRABBLE®

DICTIONARY

POCKET

SCRABBLE®

DICTIONARY

Collins

first edition 2004

This edition produced for Premier Direct Group Plc in 2004

© HarperCollins Publishers 2004

HarperCollins Publishers
Westerhill Road, Bishopbriggs
Glasgow G64 2QT
Great Britain

www.collins.co.uk

Collins® is a registered trademark of
HarperCollins Publishers Limited

Scrabble® is a registered trademark of
J. W. Spear & Sons Ltd., a subsidiary of Mattel, Inc
© 2004 Mattel, Inc.

ISBN 0-00-772155-2

All rights reserved. No part of this book may be reproduced, stored
in a retrieval system, or transmitted in any form or by any means,
electronic, mechanical, photocopying, recording or otherwise,
without the prior permission in writing of the Publisher.

A catalogue record for this book is available from the British Library

This book is set in CollinsFedra, a typeface specifically
created for Collins dictionaries by Peter Bil'ak.

Printed and bound in England by Clays Ltd, St Ives plc

Contributors

Editors
Sandra Anderson
Kay Cullen
Penny Hands
Andrew Holmes
Mike Munro

Project Manager
Justin Crozier

For the Publisher
Morven Dooner
Elaine Higgleton

Computing Support
Thomas Callan

Collins Corpus Programmer
Nigel Rochford

Typesetting
Wordcraft

Contents

Introduction

Collins Pocket Scrabble Dictionary – Every Word Counts

The *Collins Pocket Scrabble Dictionary* is the ideal reference book for people who play Scrabble for enjoyment, in a social or family setting. This dictionary doesn't include every word eligible for Scrabble, but does contain the most commonly used of the 260,000 words in *Collins Scrabble Words 2005*, the definitive Scrabble wordlist. The concise definitions in the *Pocket Scrabble Dictionary* allow players to check the meaning of words, as well as using the book for settling arguments during games.

The *Collins Pocket Scrabble Dictionary* contains only words of up to 15 letters in length, as longer words cannot be used in Scrabble. Because the dictionary is designed for family play, it does not include offensive terms. Such words are included in *Collins Scrabble Words 2005*, the complete wordlist for tournaments and club competitions.

Word order
In the *Collins Pocket Scrabble Dictionary*, words are listed in alphabetical order, rather than being grouped at the base form as in a conventional dictionary. Where words are inflections of a base form, only the base form has a definition, but the inflections are listed alphabetically as individual entries for easy reference during a game.

Special Scrabble Words
To help family players learn and use some of the rarer and higher-scoring words in the game, the Collins Pocket Scrabble Dictionary includes a number of special panel entries. These are unusual words which are particularly useful in Scrabble, either because they use the high-scoring 'power tiles' (J, Q, X,

and Z), or because they have only two or three letters. There are also panel entries at the start of every letter section, which offer advice on useful words beginning with that letter.

The *Collins Pocket Scrabble Dictionary* is designed to be useful to new players and Scrabble veterans alike – we hope you enjoy using it!

Forming Words

The key to successful Scrabble is constant awareness of the opportunities for forming words on the board. The obvious way to play a new word is to place it so that it intersects a word already on the board through a common letter:

			D_2		
			O_1		
	L_1	U_1	C_3	K_5	
			T_1		
			O_1		
			R_1		

Other methods of forming words, however, create more than one new word in the process, giving a higher score. The two main ways of doing this are 'hooking' and 'tagging'.

Hooking
Hooking involves 'hanging' one word on another – the word already on the board acts as a 'hook' on which the other word can be hung – changing the first word in the process. When you form a word by hooking, you add a letter to the beginning or end of a word on the board, transforming it into a longer word as you do so:

C_3	O_1	M_3	E_1	T_1	

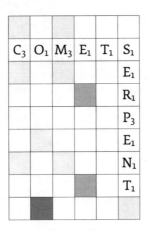

In this example, you get the points for COMETS as well as for SERPENTS. Plurals ending in S provide some of the most obvious – and useful – end-hooks. But there are plenty of other end-hooks as well. There are also lots of useful front-hooks. Consider the following example:

If you happened to have CEFIKL among the letters on your rack, you could play the following, taking full advantage of the valuable X played by your opponent:

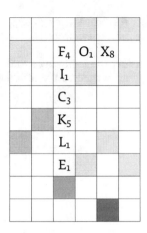

Here you get the 13 points for FOX as well as those for FICKLE. So you can see that hooking is generally a much more profitable method of word-formation than simply playing a word through one that is already on the board.

Obviously, only certain words can act as hooks. Some words cannot form other words by having a letter added to their front or back; these are known as 'blockers', as they prevent other players from adding words by hooking.

Tagging

Playing a word parallel to one already on the board, so that one or more tiles are in contact, is known as tagging. Tagging is more difficult than hooking because you need to form one additional word for each tile in contact with the word on the board. In most circumstances, these will be two-letter words, which is why short words are so vital to the game. The more two-letter words you know, the greater your opportunities for fitting words onto the board through tagging – and of running up some impressive scores!

For example, consider the following situation (your opponent has started the game with SHAM, and you have EEHISTX on your rack):

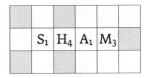

You could play HEXES so that it also forms SH, HE, AX and ME (all valid two-letter words), thus adding the scores for these three words to the points you make from HEXES:

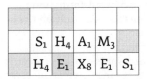

A particular advantage of tagging is that it allows you to benefit from valuable tiles twice in one go, as in the example above where X is used in both HEXES and AX.

Two-letter words are very important for tagging. The panel sections of this dictionary contain a number of unusual two-letter words: learning these is a good method of improving your game immediately!

ABBREVIATIONS USED IN THIS DICTIONARY

AD	anno Domini	Meteorol	Meteorology
adj	adjective	Mil	Military
adv	adverb	n	noun
Anat	Anatomy	N	North
Archit	Architecture	Naut	Nautical
Astrol	Astrology	NZ	New Zealand
Aust	Australia(n)	Obs	Obsolete
BC	before Christ	Offens	Offensive
Biol	Biology	orig.	originally
Brit	British	Photog	Photography
Chem	Chemistry	pl	plural
C of E	Church of England	prep	preposition
conj	conjunction	pron	pronoun
E	East	Psychol	Psychology
e.g.	for example	®	Trademark
esp.	especially	RC	Roman Catholic
etc.	et cetera	S	South
fem	feminine	S Afr	South Africa(n)
foll.	followed	Scot	Scottish
Geom	Geometry	sing	singular
Hist	History	US	United States
interj	interjection	usu.	usually
Lit	Literary	v	verb
masc	masculine	W	West
Med	Medicine	Zool	Zoology

Aa

A forms a two-letter word when followed by any one of A, B, D, E, G, H, I, M, N, R, S, T, W, X and Y – 15 letters out of 26 – so it's a really useful tile. There are also a number of short high-scoring words beginning with A. **Axe** (10 points) and **adze** (14 points) are good examples, but don't forget their US variants, **ax** (9 points) and **adz** (13 points). Also remember their plurals and the verb form **axed** (12 points). **Aye** (6) and **ay** (5) are handy for tight corners.

a *adj* indefinite article, used before a noun being mentioned for the first time

aa aa *n* (**aas**). Aa is a type of volcanic rock. Aa scores 2 points and is a good way of getting rid of annoying multiples of A.

aah *interj*. Aah is a sound people make when they're pleased or amazed. Aah scores 6 points.

aal *adj* Aal is a Scots word for **all**. Aal scores 3 points.

aardvark *n* (*pl* **-s**) S African anteater with long ears and snout

aardvarks *n* ▷ **aardvark**

ab *n* (*pl* **-s**) (*Informal*) (usually plural) abdominal muscle

aba *noun* (**abas**). Cloth made from goat or camel hair. This is a useful word to remember for when you have more than one A on your rack. Aba scores 5 points.

aback *adv* startled or disconcerted

abacus (*pl* **-es**) *n* beads on a wire frame, used for doing calculations

abacuses *n* ▷ **abacus**

abalone (*pl* **-s**) *n* edible sea creature with a shell lined with mother of pearl

abalones *n* ▷ **abalone**

abandon *v* (**-s, -ing, -ed**) desert or leave (one's wife, children, etc.) ▶ *n* lack of inhibition > **abandonment** *n* (*pl* **-s**)

abandoned *adj* deserted ▶ *v* ▷ **abandon**

abandoning *v* ▷ **abandon**

abandonment *n* ▷ **abandon**

abandonments *n* ▷ **abandon**

abandons *v* ▷ **abandon**

abase *v* (**-ses, -sing, -sed**) humiliate or degrade

(oneself) > **abasement** *n* (*pl* **-s**)

abased *v* ▷ **abase**

abasement *n* ▷ **abase**

abasements *n* ▷ **abase**

abases *v* ▷ **abase**

abashed *adj* embarrassed and ashamed

abasing *v* ▷ **abase**

abate *v* (**-tes, -ting, -ted**) make or become less strong > **abatement** *n* (*pl* **-s**)

abated *v* ▷ **abate**

abatement *n* ▷ **abate**

abatements *n* ▷ **abate**

abates *v* ▷ **abate**

abating *v* ▷ **abate**

abattoir [ab-a-twahr] *n* place where animals are killed for food (*pl* **-s**)

abattoirs *n* ▷ **abattoir**

abb *noun* (**abbs**). Abb is yarn used in weaving. Remember this word for when you have two Bs on your rack, as there will probably already be an A on the board that you can use. Abb scores 7 points.

abbess *n* (*pl* **-es**) nun in charge of a convent

abbesses *n* ▷ **abbess**

abbey *n* (*pl* **-s**) dwelling place of, or a church belonging to, a community of monks or nuns

abbeys *n* ▷ **abbey**

abbot *n* (*pl* **-s**) head of an abbey of monks

abbots *n* ▷ **abbot**

abbreviate *v* (**-tes, -ting, -ted**) shorten (a word) by leaving out some letters

abbreviated *v* ▷ **abbreviate**

abbreviates *v* ▷ **abbreviate**

abbreviating *v* ▷ **abbreviate**

abbreviation *n* (*pl* **-s**) shortened form of a word or words

abbreviations *n* ▷ **abbreviation**

abdicate v (-tes, -ting, -ted) give up (the throne or a responsibility) > **abdication** n (pl -s)
  abdicated v ▷ abdicate
  abdicates v ▷ abdicate
  abdicating v ▷ abdicate
  abdication n ▷ abdicate
  abdications n ▷ abdicate
abdomen n (pl -s) part of the body containing the stomach and intestines > **abdominal** adj
  abdomens n ▷ abdomen
  abdominal adj ▷ abdomen
abduct v (-s, -ting, -ed) carry off, kidnap > **abduction** n (pl -s) > **abductor** n (pl -s)
  abducted v ▷ abduct
  abducting v ▷ abduct
  abduction n ▷ abduct
  abductions n ▷ abduct
  abductor n ▷ abduct
  abductors n ▷ abduct
  abducts v ▷ abduct
aberrant adj showing aberration
aberration n (pl -s) sudden change from what is normal, accurate, or correct
  aberrations n ▷ aberration
abet v (-s, -ting, -ted) help or encourage in wrongdoing > **abettor** n (pl -s)
  abets v ▷ abet
  abetted v ▷ abet
  abetting v ▷ abet
  abettor n ▷ abet
  abettors n ▷ abet
abeyance n (pl -s) not in use
  abeyances n ▷ abeyance
abhor v (-s, -horring, -horred) detest utterly > **abhorrence** n (pl -s)
  abhorred v ▷ abhor
  abhorrence n ▷ abhor
  abhorrences n ▷ abhor
abhorrent adj hateful, loathsome
  abhorring v ▷ abhor
  abhors v ▷ abhor
abide v (-des, -ding, -ded) endure, put up with
  abided v ▷ abide
  abides v ▷ abide
  abiding adj lasting ► v ▷ abide
  abilities n ▷ ability
ability n (pl -ties) competence, power
abject adj utterly miserable > **abjectly** adv
  abjectly adv ▷ abject
abjure v (-res, -ring, -red) deny or renounce on oath
  abjured v ▷ abjure
  abjures v ▷ abjure
  abjuring v ▷ abjure

ablative n (pl -s) case of nouns in Latin and other languages, indicating source, agent, or instrument of action
  ablatives n ▷ ablative
ablaze adj burning fiercely
able adj (-r, -st) capable, competent > **ably** adv
  abler adj ▷ able
  ablest adj ▷ able
ablution n (pl -s) (usually plural) act of washing
  ablutions n ▷ ablution
  ably adv ▷ able
abnormal adj not normal or usual > **abnormally** adv > **abnormality** n (pl -ties)
  abnormalities n ▷ abnormal
  abnormality n ▷ abnormal
  abnormally adv ▷ abnormal
aboard adv, prep on, in, onto, or into (a ship, train, or plane)
abode n (pl -s) home, dwelling
  abodes n ▷ abode
abolish v (-shes, -shing, -shed) do away with > **abolition** n (pl -s)
  abolished v ▷ abolish
  abolishes v ▷ abolish
  abolishing v ▷ abolish
  abolition n ▷ abolish
abolitionist n (pl -s) person who wishes to do away with something, esp. slavery
  abolitionists n ▷ abolitionist
  abolitions n ▷ abolish
abominable adj detestable, very bad > **abominably** adv
  abominably adv ▷ abominable
abomination n (pl -s) someone or something that is detestable
  abominations n ▷ abomination
aboriginal n, adj ▷ aborigine
  aboriginals n ▷ aborigine
aborigine, aboriginal [ab-or-rij-in-ee] n (pl -s) original inhabitant of a country or region, esp. (A-) Australia > **aboriginal** adj
  aborigines n ▷ aborigine
abort v (-s, -ing, -ed) have an abortion or perform an abortion on
  aborted v ▷ abort
  aborting v ▷ abort
abortion n (pl -s) operation to end a pregnancy
abortionist n (pl -s) person who performs abortions, esp. illegally
  abortionists n ▷ abortionist
  abortions n ▷ abortion
abortive adj unsuccessful
  aborts v ▷ abort
abound v (-s, -ing, -ed) be plentiful

> **abounding** *adj*
abounded *v* ▷ abound
abounding *v, adj* ▷ abound
abounds *v* ▷ abound
about *prep* concerning, on the subject of ▶ *adv* nearly, approximately
above *adv, prep* over or higher (than)
abracadabra *n* (*pl* -s) supposedly magic word
abracadabras *n* ▷ abracadabra
abrasion *n* (*pl* -s) scraped area on the skin
abrasions *n* ▷ abrasion
abrasive *adj* harsh and unpleasant in manner ▶ *n* (*pl* -s) substance for cleaning or polishing by rubbing
abrasives *n* ▷ abrasive
abreast *adv, adj* side by side
abridge *v* (-ges, -ging, -ged) shorten by using fewer words > **abridgment, abridgement** *n* (*pl* -s)
abridged *v* ▷ abridge
abridgement *n* ▷ abridge
abridgements *n* ▷ abridge
abridges *v* ▷ abridge
abridging *v* ▷ abridge
abridgment *n* ▷ abridge
abridgments *n* ▷ abridge
abroad *adv* to or in a foreign country
abrogate *v* (-tes, -ting, -ted) cancel (a law or agreement) formally > **abrogation** *n* (*pl* -s)
abrogated *v* ▷ abrogate
abrogates *v* ▷ abrogate
abrogating *v* ▷ abrogate
abrogation *n* ▷ abrogate
abrogations *n* ▷ abrogate
abrupt *adj* (-er, -est) sudden, unexpected > **abruptly** *adv* > **abruptness** *n* (*pl* -es)
abrupter *adj* ▷ abrupt
abruptest *adj* ▷ abrupt
abruptly *adv* ▷ abrupt
abruptness *n* ▷ abrupt
abruptnesses *n* ▷ abrupt
abs *n* ▷ ab
abscess *n* (*pl* abscesses) inflamed swelling containing pus
abscesses *n* ▷ abscess
abscond *v* (-s, -ing, -ed) leave secretly
absconded *v* ▷ abscond
absconding *v* ▷ abscond
absconds *v* ▷ abscond
abseil [ab-sale] *v* (-s, -ing, -ed) go down a steep drop by a rope fastened at the top and tied around one's body
abseiled *v* ▷ abseil
abseiling *v* ▷ abseil
abseils *v* ▷ abseil

absence *n* (*pl* -s) being away
absences *n* ▷ absence
absent *adj* not present ▶ *v* (-s, -ing, -ed) stay away > **absently** *adv*
absented *v* ▷ absent
absentee *n* (*pl* -s) person who should be present but is not
absenteeism *n* (*pl* -s) persistent absence from work or school
absenteeisms *n* ▷ absenteeism
absentees *n* ▷ absentee
absenting *v* ▷ absent
absently *adv* ▷ absent
absents *v* ▷ absent
absinthe *n* (*pl* -s) strong green aniseed-flavoured liqueur
absinthes *n* ▷ absinthe
absolute *adj* complete, perfect
absolutely *adv* completely ▶ *interj* certainly, yes
absolution *n* ▷ absolve
absolutions *n* ▷ absolve
absolutism *n* (*pl* -s) government by a ruler with unrestricted power
absolutisms *n* ▷ absolutism
absolve *v* (-ves, -ving, -ved) declare to be free from blame or sin > **absolution** *n* (*pl* -s)
absolved *v* ▷ absolve
absolves *v* ▷ absolve
absolving *v* ▷ absolve
absorb *v* (-s, -ing, -ed) soak up (a liquid) > **absorption** *n* (*pl* -s) > **absorbency** *n* (*pl* -s)
absorbed *v* ▷ absorb
absorbencies *n* ▷ absorb
absorbency *n* ▷ absorb
absorbent *adj* able to absorb liquid
absorbing *v* ▷ absorb
absorbs *v* ▷ absorb
absorption *n* ▷ absorb
absorptions *n* ▷ absorb
abstain *v* (-s, -ing, -ed) choose not to do something > **abstainer** *n* (*pl* -s)
abstained *v* ▷ abstain
abstainer *n* ▷ abstain
abstainers *n* ▷ abstain
abstaining *v* ▷ abstain
abstains *v* ▷ abstain
abstemious *adj* taking very little alcohol or food > **abstemiousness** *n* (*pl* -es)
abstemiousness *n* ▷ abstemious
abstemiousnesses *n* ▷ abstemious
abstention *n* (*pl* -s) abstaining, esp. from voting
abstentions *n* ▷ abstention
abstinence *n* (*pl* -s) abstaining, esp. from

drinking alcohol > **abstinent** *adj*
abstinences *n* ▷ **abstinence**
abstinent *adj* ▷ **abstinence**
abstract *adj* (**-er, -est**) existing as a quality
or idea rather than a material object ▶ *n* (*pl*
-s) summary ▶ *v* (**-s, -ing, -ed**) summarize
> **abstraction** *n* (*pl* -s)
abstracted *adj* lost in thought *v* ▷ **abstract**
abstracter *adj* ▷ **abstract**
abstractest *adj* ▷ **abstract**
abstracting *adj* ▷ **abstract**
abstraction *n* ▷ **abstract**
abstractions *n* ▷ **abstract**
abstracts *n, v* ▷ **abstract**
abstruse *adj* (**-er, -est**) not easy to understand
abstruser *adj* ▷ **abstruse**
abstrusest *adj* ▷ **abstruse**
absurd *adj* (**-er, -est**) incongruous or ridiculous
> **absurdly** *adv* > **absurdity** *n* (*pl* -ties)
absurder *adj* ▷ **absurd**
absurdest *adj* ▷ **absurd**
absurdities *n* ▷ **absurd**
absurdity *n* ▷ **absurd**
absurdly *adv* ▷ **absurd**
abundance *n* ▷ **abundant**
abundances *n* ▷ **abundant**
abundant *adj* plentiful > **abundantly** *adv*
> **abundance** *n* (*pl* -s)
abundantly *adv* ▷ **abundant**
abuse *v* (**-ses, -sing, -sed**) use wrongly ▶ *n* (*pl*
-s) prolonged ill-treatment > **abuser** *n* (*pl* -s)
> **abusive** *adj* > **abusively** *adv* > **abusiveness**
n (*pl* -es)
abused *v* ▷ **abuse**
abuser *n* ▷ **abuse**
abusers *n* ▷ **abuse**
abuses *v, n* ▷ **abuse**
abusing *v* ▷ **abuse**
abusive *adj* ▷ **abuse**
abusively *adv* ▷ **abuse**
abusiveness *n* ▷ **abuse**
abusivenesses *n* ▷ **abuse**
abut *v* (**-s, abutting, abutted**) be next to or
touching
abuts *v* ▷ **abut**
abutted *v* ▷ **abut**
abutting *v* ▷ **abut**

> **aby** *verb* (**abys abying abought**). Aby is
> an old word meaning to pay a penalty.
> If someone plays this word, remember
> that it can be expanded to **baby**,
> **abysmal** or **abyss**. Aby scores 8 points.

abysmal *adj* (*Informal*) extremely bad, awful
> **abysmally** *adv*
abysmally *adv* ▷ **abysmal**

abyss *n* (*pl* -es) very deep hole or chasm
abysses *n* ▷ **abyss**
acacia [a-**kay**-sha] *n* (*pl* -s) tree or shrub with
yellow or white flowers
acacias *n* ▷ **acacia**
academic *adj* of an academy or university ▶ *n*
(*pl* -s) lecturer or researcher at a university
> **academically** *adv*
academically *adv* ▷ **academic**
academician *n* (*pl* -s) member of an academy
academicians *n* ▷ **academician**
academics *n* ▷ **academician**
academies *n* ▷ **academy**
academy *n* (*pl* -mies) society to advance arts
or sciences
acanthus *n* (*pl* -es) prickly plant
acanthuses *n* ▷ **acanthus**
accede *v* (**-des, -ding, -ded**) consent or agree
(to)
acceded *v* ▷ **accede**
accedes *v* ▷ **accede**
acceding *v* ▷ **accede**
accelerate *v* (**-tes, -ting, -ted**) (cause to) move
faster > **acceleration** *n* (*pl* -s)
accelerated *v* ▷ **accelerate**
accelerates *v* ▷ **accelerate**
accelerating *v* ▷ **accelerate**
acceleration *n* ▷ **accelerate**
accelerations *n* ▷ **accelerate**
accelerator *n* (*pl* -s) pedal in a motor vehicle to
increase speed
accelerators *n* ▷ **accelerator**
accent *n* (*pl* -s) distinctive style of
pronunciation of a local, national, or social
group ▶ *v* (**-s, -ing, -ed**) place emphasis on
accented *v* ▷ **accent**
accenting *v* ▷ **accent**
accents *n, v* ▷ **accent**
accentuate *v* (**-tes, -ting, -ted**) stress,
emphasize > **accentuation** *n* (*pl* -s)
accentuated *v* ▷ **accentuate**
accentuates *v* ▷ **accentuate**
accentuating *v* ▷ **accentuate**
accentuation *n* ▷ **accentuate**
accentuations *n* ▷ **accentuate**
accept *v* (**-s, -ing, -ed**) receive willingly
> **acceptance** *n* (*pl* -s)
acceptabilities *n* ▷ **acceptable**
acceptability *n* ▷ **acceptable**
acceptable *adj* tolerable > **acceptably** *adv*
> **acceptability** *n* (*pl* -ties)
acceptably *adv* ▷ **acceptable**
acceptance *n* ▷ **accept**
acceptances *n* ▷ **accept**
accepted *v* ▷ **accept**

accepting v ▷ accept
accepts v ▷ accept
access n (pl -es) means of or right to approach or enter ▶ v (-es, -ing, -ed) obtain (data) from a computer
accessed v ▷ access
accesses n, v ▷ access
accessibilities n ▷ accessible
accessibility n ▷ accessible
accessible adj easy to reach > **accessibility** n (pl -ties)
accessing v ▷ access
accession n (pl -s) taking up of an office or position
accessions n ▷ accession
accessories n ▷ accessory
accessory n (pl -ries) supplementary part or object
accident n (pl -s) mishap, often causing injury
accidental adj happening by chance or unintentionally ▶ n (pl -s) (MUSIC) symbol indicating that a sharp, flat, or natural note is not a part of the key signature > **accidentally** adv
accidentally adv ▷ accidental
accidentals n ▷ accidental
accidents n ▷ accident
acclaim v (-s, -ing, -ed) applaud, praise ▶ n (pl -s) enthusiastic approval > **acclamation** n (pl -s)
acclaimed v ▷ acclaim
acclaiming v ▷ acclaim
acclaims v, n ▷ acclaim
acclamation n ▷ acclaim
acclamations n ▷ acclaim
acclimatization n ▷ acclimatize
acclimatizations n ▷ acclimatize
acclimatize v (-zes, -zing, -zed) adapt to a new climate or environment > **acclimatization** n (pl -s)
acclimatized v ▷ acclimatize
acclimatizes v ▷ acclimatize
acclimatizing v ▷ acclimatize
accolade n (pl -s) award, honour, or praise
accolades n ▷ accolade
accommodate v (-tes, -ting, -ted) provide with lodgings
accommodated v ▷ accommodate
accommodates v ▷ accommodate
accommodating adj obliging ▶ v ▷ accommodate
accommodation n (pl -s) house or room for living in
accommodations n ▷ accommodation
accompanied v ▷ accompany

accompanies v ▷ accompany
accompaniment n (pl -s) something that accompanies
accompaniments n ▷ accompaniment
accompanist n ▷ accompany
accompanists n ▷ accompany
accompany v (-nies, -nying, -nied) go along with > **accompanist** n (pl -s)
accompanying v ▷ accompany
accomplice n (pl -s) person who helps another to commit a crime
accomplices n ▷ accomplice
accomplish v (-es, -ing, -ed) manage to do
accomplished adj expert, proficient ▶ v ▷ accomplish
accomplishes v ▷ accomplish
accomplishing v ▷ accomplish
accomplishment n (pl -s) completion
accomplishments n ▷ accomplishment
accord n (pl -s) agreement, harmony ▶ v (-s, -ing, -ed) fit in with
accordance n (pl -s) conforming to or according to
accordances n ▷ accordance
accorded v ▷ accord
according adv as stated by ▶ v ▷ accord
accordingly adv in an appropriate manner
accordion n (pl -s) portable musical instrument played by moving the two sides apart and together, and pressing a keyboard or buttons to produce the notes > **accordionist** n
accordionist n (pl -s) ▷ accordion
accordionists n ▷ accordion
accordions n ▷ accordion
accords v ▷ accord
accost v (-s, -ing, -ed) approach and speak to, often aggressively
accosted v ▷ accost
accosting v ▷ accost
accosts v ▷ accost
account n (pl -s) report, description ▶ v (-s, -ing, -ed) judge to be
accountabilities n ▷ accountable
accountability n ▷ accountable
accountable adj responsible to someone or for something > **accountability** n (pl -ties)
accountancies n ▷ accountant
accountancy n ▷ accountant
accountant n (pl -s) person who maintains and audits business accounts > **accountancy** n (pl -cies)
accountants n ▷ accountant
accounted v ▷ account
accounting n (pl -s) skill or practice of

maintaining and auditing business accounts
▶ v ▷ **account**
accountings n ▷ **accounting**
accounts n, v ▷ **account**
accoutrement n (pl -s) an item of clothing and equipment for a particular activity
accoutrements n ▷ **accoutrement**
accredited adj authorized, officially recognized
accretion [ak-**kree**-shun] n (pl -s) gradual growth
accretions n ▷ **accretion**
accrual n ▷ **accrue**
accruals n ▷ **accrue**
accrue v (-crues, -cruing, -crued) increase gradually > **accrual** n (pl -s)
accrued v ▷ **accrue**
accrues v ▷ **accrue**
accruing v ▷ **accrue**
accumulate v (-tes, -ting, -ted) gather together in increasing quantity
> **accumulation** n (pl -s) > **accumulative** adj
accumulated v ▷ **accumulate**
accumulates v ▷ **accumulate**
accumulating v ▷ **accumulate**
accumulation n ▷ **accumulate**
accumulations n ▷ **accumulate**
accumulative adj ▷ **accumulate**
accumulator n (pl -s) (BRIT & AUST) rechargeable electric battery
accumulators n ▷ **accumulator**
accuracies n ▷ **accurate**
accuracy n ▷ **accurate**
accurate adj exact, correct > **accurately** adv
> **accuracy** n (pl -cies)
accurately adv ▷ **accurate**
accursed adj under a curse
accusation n ▷ **accuse**
accusations n ▷ **accuse**
accusative n (pl -s) grammatical case indicating the direct object
accusatives n ▷ **accusative**
accusatory adj ▷ **accuse**
accuse v (-ses, -sing, -sed) charge with wrongdoing > **accused** n > **accuser** n (pl -s) > **accusing** adj > **accusation** n (pl -s)
> **accusatory** adj
accused v ▷ **accuse**
accused n ▷ **accuse**
accuser n ▷ **accuse**
accusers n ▷ **accuse**
accuses v ▷ **accuse**
accusing v, adj ▷ **accuse**
accusing adj ▷ **accuse**
accustom v (-s, -ing, -ed) make used to

accustomed adj usual v ▷ **accustom**
accustoming v ▷ **accustom**
accustoms v ▷ **accustom**
ace n (pl -s) playing card with one symbol on it
▶ adj (Informal) excellent
acerbic [ass-**sir**-bik] adj harsh or bitter
> **acerbity** n (pl -ties)
acerbities n ▷ **acerbic**
acerbity n ▷ **acerbic**
aces n ▷ **ace**
acetate [**ass**-it-tate] n (pl -s) (CHEM) salt or ester of acetic acid
acetates n ▷ **acetate**
acetic [ass-**see**-tik] adj of or involving vinegar
acetone [**ass**-it-tone] n (pl -s) colourless liquid used as a solvent
acetones n ▷ **acetone**
acetylene [ass-**set**-ill-een] n (pl -s) colourless flammable gas used in welding metals
acetylenes n ▷ **acetylene**
ache n (pl -s) dull continuous pain ▶ v (-ches, -ching, -ched) be in or cause continuous dull pain
ached n ▷ **ache**
aches v, n ▷ **ache**
achieve v (-ves, -ving, -ved) gain by hard work or ability
achieved v ▷ **achieve**
achievement n (pl -s) something accomplished
achievements n ▷ **achievement**
achieves v ▷ **achieve**
achieving v ▷ **achieve**
aching v ▷ **ache**
achromatic adj colourless
acid n (pl -s) (CHEM) one of a class of compounds, corrosive and sour when dissolved in water, that combine with a base to form a salt ▶ adj containing acid > **acidic** adj > **acidify** v > **acidity** n (pl -ties)
acidic adj ▷ **acid**
acidify v ▷ **acid**
acidities n ▷ **acid**
acidity n ▷ **acid**
acids n ▷ **acid**
acknowledge v (-ges, -ging, -ged) admit, recognize > **acknowledgment, acknowledgement** n (pl -s)
acknowledged v ▷ **acknowledge**
acknowledgement n ▷ **acknowledge**
acknowledgements n ▷ **acknowledge**
acknowledges v ▷ **acknowledge**
acknowledging v ▷ **acknowledge**
acknowledgment n ▷ **acknowledge**
acknowledgments n ▷ **acknowledge**

acme [ak-mee] n (pl -s) highest point of achievement or excellence
  acmes n ▷ acme
acne [ak-nee] n (pl -s) pimply skin disease
  acnes n ▷ acne
acolyte n (pl -s) follower or attendant
  acolytes n ▷ acolyte
aconite n (pl -s) poisonous plant with hoodlike flowers
  aconites n ▷ aconite
acorn n (pl -s) nut of the oak tree
  acorns n ▷ acorn
acoustic adj of sound and hearing
  > acoustically adv
  acoustically adv ▷ acoustic
acoustics n science of sounds
acquaint v (-s, -ing, -ed) make familiar, inform
  > acquainted adj
acquaintance n (pl -s) person known
  acquaintances n ▷ acquaintance
  acquainted v, adj ▷ acquaint
  acquainting v ▷ acquaint
  acquaints v ▷ acquaint
acquiesce [ak-wee-ess] v (-sces, -scing, -sced) agree to what someone wants
  > acquiescence n (pl -s) > acquiescent adj
  acquiesced v ▷ acquiesce
  acquiescence n ▷ acquiesce
  acquiescences n ▷ acquiesce
  acquiescent adj ▷ acquiesce
  acquiesces v ▷ acquiesce
  acquiescing v ▷ acquiesce
acquire v (-res, -ring, -red) gain, get
  acquired v ▷ acquire
  acquires v ▷ acquire
  acquiring v ▷ acquire
acquisition n (pl -s) thing acquired
  acquisitions n ▷ acquisition
acquisitive adj eager to gain material possessions > acquisitiveness n (pl -es)
  acquisitiveness n ▷ acquisitive
  acquisitivenesses n ▷ acquisitive
acquit v (-s, -quitting, -quitted) pronounce (someone) innocent > acquittal n (pl -s)
  acquits v ▷ acquit
  acquittal n ▷ acquit
  acquittals n ▷ acquit
  acquitted v ▷ acquit
  acquitting v ▷ acquit
acre n (pl -s) measure of land, 4840 square yards (4046.86 square metres)
acreage [ake-er-rij] n (pl -s) land area in acres
  acreages n ▷ acreage
  acres n ▷ acre
acrid [ak-rid] adj (-er, -est) pungent, bitter

acrider adj ▷ acrid
acridest adj ▷ acrid
acrimonies n ▷ acrimonious
acrimonious adj bitter in speech or manner
  > acrimony n (pl -ies)
  acrimony n ▷ acrimonious
acrobat n (pl -s) person skilled in gymnastic feats requiring agility and balance
  > acrobatic adj
  acrobatic adj ▷ acrobatic
acrobatics pl n acrobatic feats
  acrobats n ▷ acrobat
acronym n (pl -s) word formed from the initial letters of other words, such as NASA
  acronyms n ▷ acronym
across adv, prep from side to side (of)
acrostic n (pl -s) lines of writing in which the first or last letters of each line spell a word or saying
  acrostics n ▷ acrostic
acrylic n (pl -s) ▶ adj (synthetic fibre, paint, etc.) made from acrylic acid
  acrylics n ▷ acrylic
act n (pl -s) thing done ▶ v (-s, -ing, -ed) do something
  acted v ▷ act
acting n (pl -s) art of an actor ▶ adj temporarily performing the duties of ▶ v ▷ act
  actings n ▷ acting
actinium n (pl -s) (CHEM) radioactive chemical element
  actiniums n ▷ actinium
action n (pl -s) process of doing something
actionable adj giving grounds for a lawsuit
  actions n ▷ action
activate v (-tes, -ting, -ted) make active
  > activation n (pl -s) > activator n (pl -s)
  activated v ▷ activate
  activates v ▷ activate
  activating v ▷ activate
  activation n ▷ activate
  activations n ▷ activate
  activator n ▷ activate
  activators n ▷ activate
active adj moving, working > actively adv
  actively adv ▷ active
  activism n ▷ activist
  activisms n ▷ activist
activist n (pl -s) person who works energetically to achieve political or social goals > activism n (pl -s)
  activists n ▷ activist
  activities n ▷ activity
activity n (pl -ties) state of being active
actor n (pl -s) person who acts in a play, film,

etc.
actors n ▷ actor
actress n (pl -es) woman who acts in a play, film, etc.
actresses n ▷ actress
acts n, v ▷ act
actual adj existing in reality > **actuality** n (pl -ties)
actualities n ▷ actual
actuality n ▷ actual
actually adv really, indeed
actuarial adj ▷ actuary
actuaries n ▷ actuary
actuary n (pl -ries) statistician who calculates insurance risks > **actuarial** adj
actuate v (-tes, -ting, -ted) start up (a device)
actuated v ▷ actuate
actuates v ▷ actuate
actuating v ▷ actuate
acuities n ▷ acuity
acuity [ak-**kew**-it-ee] n (pl -ties) keenness of vision or thought
acumen [ak-yew-men] n (pl -s) ability to make good judgments
acumens n ▷ acumen
acupuncture n (pl -s) medical treatment involving the insertion of needles at various points on the body > **acupuncturist** n (pl -s)
acupunctures n ▷ acupuncture
acupuncturist n ▷ acupuncture
acupuncturists n ▷ acupuncture
acute adj (-r, -st) severe ▶ n (pl -s) accent (´) over a letter to indicate the quality or length of its sound, as in café > **acutely** adv > **acuteness** n
acutely adv ▷ acute
acuteness n ▷ acute
acuter adj ▷ acute
acutes n ▷ acute
acutest adj ▷ acute
ad n (pl -s) (Informal) advertisement
adage n (pl -s) wise saying, proverb
adages n ▷ adage
adagio n (pl -gios) ▶ adv (MUSIC) (piece to be played) slowly and gracefully
adagios n ▷ adagio
adamant adj unshakable in determination or purpose > **adamantly** adv
adamantly adv ▷ adamant
adapt v (-s, -ing, -ed) alter for new use or new conditions > **adaptable** adj > **adaptability** n (pl -ties)
adaptabilities n ▷ adapt
adaptability n ▷ adapt
adaptable adj ▷ adapt

adaptation n (pl -s) thing produced by adapting something
adaptations n ▷ adaptation
adapted v ▷ adapt
adapter n ▷ adaptor
adapters n ▷ adaptor
adapting v ▷ adapt
adaptor, adapter n (pl -s) device for connecting several electrical appliances to a single socket
adaptors n ▷ adaptor
adapts v ▷ adapt
add v (-s, -ing, -ed) combine (numbers or quantities)
added v ▷ add
addenda n ▷ addendum
addendum n (pl -da) addition
adder n (pl -s) small poisonous snake
adders n ▷ adder
addict n (pl -s) person who is unable to stop taking drugs > **addicted** adj > **addiction** n (pl -s)
addicted adj ▷ addict
addiction n ▷ addict
addictions n ▷ addict
addictive adj causing addiction
addicts n ▷ addict
adding v ▷ add
addition n (pl -s) adding > **additional** adj > **additionally** adv
additional adj ▷ addition
additionally adv ▷ addition
additions n ▷ addition
additive n (pl -s) something added, esp. to a foodstuff, to improve it or prevent deterioration
additives n ▷ additive
addled adj confused or unable to think clearly
address n (pl -es) place where a person lives ▶ v (-es, -ing, -ed) mark the destination, as on an envelope
addressed v ▷ address
addressee n (pl -s) person addressed
addressees n ▷ addressee
addresses n, v ▷ address
addressing v ▷ address
adds v ▷ add
adduce v (-ces, -cing, -uced) mention something as evidence or proof
adduced v ▷ adduce
adduces v ▷ adduce
adducing v ▷ adduce
adenoid [ad-in-oid] n (pl -s) (usually plural) mass of tissue at the back of the throat
adenoidal adj having a nasal voice caused by

swollen adenoids
adenoids n ▷ adenoid
adept adj (-er, -est) ▶ n (pl -s) very skilful (person)
adepter adj ▷ adept
adeptest adj ▷ adept
adepts n ▷ adept
adequacies n ▷ adequate
adequacy n ▷ adequate
adequate adj sufficient, enough > **adequately** adv > **adequacy** n (pl -ies)
adequately adv ▷ adequate
adhere v (-res, -ring, -red) stick (to) > **adherence** n (pl -ces)
adhered v ▷ adhere
adherence n ▷ adhere
adherences n ▷ adhere
adherent n (pl -s) devotee, follower
adherents n ▷ adherent
adheres v ▷ adhere
adhering v ▷ adhere
adhesion n (pl -s) sticking (to)
adhesions n ▷ adhesion
adhesive n (pl -s) substance used to stick things together ▶ adj able to stick to things
adhesives n ▷ adhesive
adieu [a-dew] interj (Lit) farewell, goodbye
adipose adj of or containing fat
adjacent adj near or next (to)
adjectival adj ▷ adjective
adjective n (pl -es) word that adds information about a noun or pronoun > **adjectival** adj
adjectives n ▷ adjective
adjoin v (-s, -ing, -ed) be next to ▶ **adjoining** adj
adjoined v ▷ adjoin
adjoining v, adj ▷ adjoin
adjoins v ▷ adjoin
adjourn v (-s, -ing, -ed) close (a court) at the end of a session > **adjournment** n (pl -s)
adjourned v ▷ adjourn
adjourning v ▷ adjourn
adjournment n ▷ adjourn
adjournments n ▷ adjourn
adjourns v ▷ adjourn
adjudge v (-ges, -ging, -ged) declare (to be)
adjudged v ▷ adjudge
adjudges v ▷ adjudge
adjudging v ▷ adjudge
adjudicate v (-tes, -ting, -ted) give a formal decision on (a dispute) > **adjudication** n (pl -s) > **adjudicator** n (pl -s)
adjudicated v ▷ adjudicate
adjudicates v ▷ adjudicate
adjudicating v ▷ adjudicate
adjudication n ▷ adjudicate

adjudications n ▷ adjudicate
adjudicator n ▷ adjudicate
adjudicators n ▷ adjudicate
adjunct n (pl -s) subordinate or additional person or thing
adjuncts n ▷ adjunct
adjure v (-res, -ring, -red) command (to do)
adjured v ▷ adjure
adjures v ▷ adjure
adjuring v ▷ adjure
adjust v (-s, -ing, -ted) adapt to new conditions > **adjustable** adj > **adjuster** n (pl -s) > **adjustment** n (pl -s)
adjustable adj ▷ adjust
adjusted v ▷ adjust
adjuster n ▷ adjust
adjusters n ▷ adjust
adjustment n ▷ adjust
adjustments n ▷ adjust
adjusts v ▷ adjust
adjutant [aj-oo-tant] n (pl -s) army officer in charge of routine administration
adjutants n ▷ adjutant
admin n (pl -s) (Informal) administration
administer v (-s, -ing, -ed) manage (business affairs)
administered v ▷ administer
administering v ▷ administer
administers v ▷ administer
administrate v (-tes, -ting, -ated) manage (an organization) > **administrator** n (pl -s)
administrated v ▷ administrate
administrates v ▷ administrate
administrating v ▷ administrate
administration n (pl -s) management of an organization
administrations n ▷ administration
administrative adj of the management of an organization
administrator n ▷ administrate
administrators n ▷ administrate
admins n ▷ admin
admirable adj ▷ admire
admirably adv ▷ admire
admiral n (pl -s) highest naval rank
admirals n ▷ admiral
admiralties n ▷ admiralty
admiralty n (pl -ties) the office or jurisdiction of an admiral
admiration n ▷ admire
admirations n ▷ admire
admire v (-res, -ring, -red) regard with esteem and approval > **admirable** adj > **admirably** adv > **admiration** n (pl -s) > **admirer** n (pl -s) > **admiring** adj > **admiringly** adv

admired v ▷ admire
admirer n ▷ admire
admirers n ▷ admire
admires v ▷ admire
admiring v, adj ▷ admire
admiringly adv ▷ admire
admissibilities n ▷ admissible
admissibility n ▷ admissible
admissible adj allowed to be brought in as evidence in court > **admissibility** n (pl -ties)
admission n (pl -s) permission to enter
admissions n ▷ admission
admit v (-mits, -mitting, -mitted) confess, acknowledge
admits v ▷ admit
admittance n (pl -s) permission to enter
admittances n ▷ admittance
admitted v ▷ admit
admittedly adv it must be agreed
admitting v ▷ admit
admixture n (pl -s) mixture
admixtures n ▷ admixture
admonish v (-es, -ing, -ed) reprove sternly > **admonition** n (pl -s)
admonished v ▷ admonish
admonishes v ▷ admonish
admonishing v ▷ admonish
admonition n ▷ admonish
admonitions n ▷ admonish
ado n (pl -s) (Lit) fuss, trouble
adobe [ad-oh-bee] n (pl -s) sun-dried brick
adobes n ▷ adobe
adolescence n (pl -s) period between puberty and adulthood
adolescences n ▷ adolescence
adolescent n (pl -s), adj (person) between puberty and adulthood
adolescents n ▷ adolescent
adopt v (-s, -ing, -ed) take (someone else's child) as one's own > **adoption** n (pl -s)
adopted v ▷ adopt
adopting v ▷ adopt
adoption n ▷ adopt
adoptions n ▷ adopt
adoptive adj related by adoption
adopts v ▷ adopt
adorable adj ▷ adore
adoration n ▷ adore
adorations n ▷ adore
adore v (-res, -ring, -red) love intensely > **adorable** adj > **adoration** n (pl -s) > **adoring** adj > **adoringly** adv
adored v ▷ adore
adores v ▷ adore
adoring v, adj ▷ adore

adoringly adv ▷ adore
adorn v (-s, -ing, -ed) decorate, embellish > **adornment** n (pl -s)
adorned v ▷ adorn
adorning v ▷ adorn
adornment n ▷ adorn
adornments n ▷ adorn
adorns v ▷ adorn
ados n ▷ ado
adrenal [ad-reen-al] adj near the kidneys
adrenalin, adrenaline n (pl -s) hormone secreted by the adrenal glands in response to stress
adrenaline n ▷ adrenalin
adrenalines n ▷ adrenalin
adrenalins n ▷ adrenalin
adrift adj, adv drifting
adroit adj quick and skilful > **adroitly** adv > **adroitness** n
adroitly adv ▷ adroit
adroitness n ▷ adroit
ads n ▷ ad
adsorb v (-s, -ing, -ed) (of a gas or vapour) condense and form a thin film on a surface > **adsorption** n (pl -s)
adsorbed v ▷ adsorb
adsorbing v ▷ adsorb
adsorbs v ▷ adsorb
adsorption n ▷ adsorb
adsorptions n ▷ adsorb
adulation n (pl -s) uncritical admiration
adulations n ▷ adulation
adult adj fully grown, mature ▶ n (pl -s) adult person or animal > **adulthood** n (pl -s)
adulterate v (-tes, -ting, -ted) spoil something by adding inferior material > **adulteration** n (pl -s)
adulterated v ▷ adulterate
adulterates v ▷ adulterate
adulterating v ▷ adulterate
adulteration n ▷ adulterate
adulterations n ▷ adulterate
adulterer n ▷ adultery
adulterers n ▷ adultery
adulteress n ▷ adultery
adulteresses n ▷ adultery
adulteries n ▷ adultery
adulterous adj ▷ adultery
adultery n (pl -teries) sexual unfaithfulness of a husband or wife > **adulterer** n (pl -s) > **adulteress** n (pl -es) > **adulterous** adj
adulthood n ▷ adult
adulthoods n ▷ adult
adults n ▷ adult
advance v (-ces, -cing, -ced) go or bring

forward ▶ n (pl -s) forward movement ▶ adj done or happening before an event

advanced adj at a late stage in development ▶ v ▷ advance

advancement n (pl advancements) promotion

advancements n ▷ advancement

advances v, n ▷ advance

advancing v ▷ advance

advantage n (pl -s) more favourable position or state > advantageous adj > advantageously adv

advantageous adj ▷ advantage

advantageously adv ▷ advantage

advantages n ▷ advantage

advent n (pl -s) arrival

adventitious adj added or appearing accidentally

advents n ▷ advent

adventure n (pl -s) exciting and risky undertaking or exploit > adventurous adj

adventurer n (pl -s) person who unscrupulously seeks money or power

adventurers n ▷ adventurer

adventures n ▷ adventure

adventuress n (pl -es) woman who unscrupulously seeks money or power

adventuresses n ▷ adventuress

adventurous adj ▷ adventure

adverb n (pl -s) word that adds information about a verb, adjective, or other adverb > adverbial adj

adverbial adj ▷ adverb

adverbs n ▷ adverb

adversaries n ▷ adversary

adversary [ad-verse-er-ree] n (pl -ries) opponent or enemy

adverse adj unfavourable > adversely adv

adversely adv ▷ adverse

adversities n ▷ adversity

adversity n (pl -ties) very difficult or hard circumstances

advert n (pl -s) (Informal) advertisement

advertise v (-ses, -sing, -sed) present or praise (goods or services) to the public in order to encourage sales > advertiser n (pl -s) > advertising adj, n (pl -s)

advertised v ▷ advertise

advertisement n (pl -s) public announcement to sell goods or publicize an event

advertisements n ▷ advertisement

advertiser n ▷ advertise

advertises v ▷ advertise

advertising v, adj n ▷ advertise

advertisings n ▷ advertise

adverts n ▷ advert

advice n (pl -s) recommendation as to what to do

advices n ▷ advice

advisabilities n ▷ advisable

advisability n ▷ advisable

advisable adj prudent, sensible > advisability n (pl -ties)

advise v (-ses, -sing, -sed) offer advice to

advised adj considered, thought-out ▶ v ▷ advise

advisedly adv deliberately

adviser, advisor n (pl -s) person who offers advice, e.g. on careers to students or school pupils

advisers n ▷ adviser

advises v ▷ advise

advising v ▷ advise

advisor n ▷ adviser

advisors n ▷ adviser

advisory adj giving advice

advocaat n (pl -s) liqueur with a raw egg base

advocaats n ▷ advocaat

advocacies n ▷ advocate

advocacy n ▷ advocate

advocate v (-tes, -ting, -ted) propose or recommend ▶ n (pl -s) person who publicly supports a cause > advocacy n (pl -cies)

advocated v ▷ advocate

advocates v, n ▷ advocate

advocating v ▷ advocate

adz n ▷ adze

adze, adz n (pl adzes) tool with an arched blade at right angles to the handle

adzes n ▷ adze

> **ae** adj. Ae is a Scots word that means **one**. This is a useful word to remember when you want to form words in two directions at once. Ae scores 2 points.

aegis [ee-jiss] n (pl -es) sponsorship, protection

aegises n ▷ aegis

aeon [ee-on] n (pl -s) immeasurably long period of time

aeons n ▷ aeon

aerate v (-tes, -ting, -ted) put gas into (a liquid), as when making a fizzy drink > aeration n (pl -s)

aerated v ▷ aerate

aerates v ▷ aerate

aerating v ▷ aerate

aeration n ▷ aerate

aerations n ▷ aerate

aerial adj in, from, or operating in the air ▶ n (pl -ls) metal pole, wire, etc., for receiving or transmitting radio or TV signals

aerials n ▷ aerial
aerobatic adj ▷ aerobatics
aerobatics pl n stunt flying ▷ aerobatic adj
aerobic adj ▷ aerobics
aerobics n exercises designed to increase the
amount of oxygen in the blood ▷ aerobic adj
aerodrome n (pl -s) small airport
aerodromes n ▷ aerodrome
aerodynamic adj ▷ aerodynamics
aerodynamics n study of how air flows
around moving solid objects ▷ aerodynamic
adj
aerofoil n (pl -s) part of an aircraft, such as the
wing, designed to give lift
aerofoils n ▷ aerofoil
aerogram n (pl -s) airmail letter on a single
sheet of paper that seals to form an envelope
aerograms n ▷ aerogram
aeronautical adj ▷ aeronautics
aeronautics n study or practice of aircraft
flight ▷ aeronautical adj
aeroplane n (pl -s) powered flying vehicle with
fixed wings
aeroplanes n ▷ aeroplane
aerosol n (pl -s) pressurized can from which a
substance can be dispensed as a fine spray
aerosols n ▷ aerosol
aerospace n (pl -s) earth's atmosphere and
space beyond
aerospaces n ▷ aerospace
aesthete [eess-theet] n (pl -s) person who
has or affects an extravagant love of art
▷ aestheticism n (pl -s)
aesthetes n ▷ aesthete
aesthetic [iss-thet-ik] adj relating to
the appreciation of art and beauty
▷ aesthetically adv
aesthetically adv ▷ aesthetic
aestheticism n ▷ aesthete
aestheticisms n ▷ aesthete
aesthetics n study of art, beauty, and good
taste
aether n (pl -s) ▷ ether
aethers n ▷ aether
aetiologies n ▷ aetiology
aetiology [ee-tee-ol-a-jee] n (pl -gies) ▷ etiology
afar adv from or at a great distance
affabilities n ▷ affable
affability n ▷ affable
affable adj friendly and easy to talk to ▷ affably
adv ▷ affability n (pl -ties)
affably adv ▷ affable
affair n (pl -s) event or happening
affairs n ▷ affair
affect[1] v (-s, -ing, -ed) act on, influence

affect[2] v (-s, -ing, -ed) put on a show of
affectation n (pl -s) attitude or manner put on
to impress
affectations n ▷ affectation
affected adj displaying affectation ▶ v
▷ affect[1, 2]
affecting v ▷ affect[1, 2]
affection n (pl -s) fondness or love
affectionate adj loving ▷ affectionately adv
affectionately adv ▷ affectionate
affections n ▷ affection
affects v ▷ affect[1, 2]
affianced [af-fie-anst] adj (Old-fashioned)
engaged to be married
affidavit [af-fid-dave-it] n (pl -s) written
statement made on oath
affidavits n ▷ affidavit
affiliate v (-tes, -ting, -ted) (of a group) link up
with a larger group ▷ affiliation n (pl -s)
affiliated v ▷ affiliate
affiliates v ▷ affiliate
affiliating v ▷ affiliate
affiliation n ▷ affiliate
affiliations n ▷ affiliate
affinities n ▷ affinity
affinity n (pl -ties) close connection or liking
affirm v (-s, -ing, -ed) declare to be true
▷ affirmation n (pl -s)
affirmation n ▷ affirm
affirmations n ▷ affirm
affirmative n (pl -s), adj (word or phrase)
indicating agreement
affirmatives n ▷ affirmative
affirmed v ▷ affirm
affirming v ▷ affirm
affirms v ▷ affirm
affix v (-fixes, -fixing, -fixed) attach or fasten
▶ n (pl -fixes) word or syllable added to a word
to change its meaning
affixed v ▷ affix
affixes v, n ▷ affix
affixing v ▷ affix
afflict v (-s, -ing, -ed) give pain or grief to
▷ affliction n (pl -s)
afflicted v ▷ afflict
afflicting v ▷ afflict
affliction n ▷ afflict
afflictions n ▷ afflict
afflicts v ▷ afflict
affluence n (pl -s) wealth
affluences n ▷ affluence
affluent adj having plenty of money
afford v (-s, -ing, -ed) have enough money to
buy ▷ affordable adj
affordable adj ▷ afford

afforded v ▷ afford
affording v ▷ afford
affords v ▷ afford
afforest v (-s, -ing, -ed) plant trees on > **afforestation** n (pl -s)
afforestation n ▷ afforest
afforestations n ▷ afforest
afforested v ▷ afforest
afforesting v ▷ afforest
afforests v ▷ afforest
affray n (pl -s) (BRIT, AUST & NZ) (LAW) noisy fight, brawl
affrays n ▷ affray
affront v (-s, -ing, -ed), n (pl -s) insult
affronted v ▷ affront
affronting v ▷ affront
affronts v, n ▷ affront
afghan adj of Afghanistan or its language
aficionado [af-fish-yo-**nah**-do] n (pl -dos) enthusiastic fan of something or someone
aficionados n ▷ aficionado
afield adv far away
aflame adj burning
afloat adv, adj floating
afoot adv, adj happening, in operation
aforementioned adj referred to previously
aforesaid adj referred to previously
aforethought adj premeditated
afraid adj frightened
afresh adv again, anew
aft adv at or towards the rear of a ship or aircraft
after prep following in time or place ▶ conj at a later time than ▶ adv at a later time
afterbirth n (pl -s) material expelled from the womb after childbirth
afterbirths n ▷ afterbirth
aftercare n (pl -s) support given to a person discharged from a hospital or prison
aftercares n ▷ aftercare
aftereffect n (pl -s) result occurring some time after its cause
aftereffects n ▷ aftereffect
afterglow n (pl -s) glow left after a source of light has gone
afterglows n ▷ afterglow
afterlife n (pl -lives) life after death
afterlives n ▷ afterlife
aftermath n (pl -s) results of an event considered together
aftermaths n ▷ aftermath
afternoon n (pl -s) time between noon and evening
afternoons n ▷ afternoon
afters pl n (BRIT) (Informal) dessert

aftershave n (pl -s) lotion applied to the face after shaving
aftershaves n ▷ aftershave
afterthought n (pl -s) idea occurring later
afterthoughts n ▷ afterthought
afterward adv ▷ afterwards
afterwards, afterward adv later

> **ag** adj. Ag means to do with **agriculture**. This is a good short word to remember, as it can come in handy when you need to form words in more than one direction. Ag scores 3 points.

again adv once more
against prep in opposition or contrast to
agape adj (of the mouth) wide open
agaric n (pl -s) fungus with gills on the underside of the cap, such as a mushroom
agarics n ▷ agaric
agate [ag-git] n (pl -s) semiprecious form of quartz with striped colouring
agates n ▷ agate
age n (pl -s) length of time a person or thing has existed ▶ v (-s, ageing or aging, -d) make or grow old ▶ **ageing, aging** n, adj
aged adj [ay-jid] old ▷ age
ageing v, n, adj ▷ age
ageless adj apparently never growing old
agencies n ▷ agency
agency n (pl -cies) organization providing a service
agenda n (pl -s) list of things to be dealt with, esp. at a meeting
agendas n ▷ agenda
agent n (pl -s) person acting on behalf of another
agents n ▷ agent
ages n, v ▷ age
agglomeration n (pl -s) confused mass or cluster
agglomerations n ▷ agglomeration
aggrandize v (-zes, -zing, -zed) make greater in size, power, or rank > **aggrandizement** n (pl -s)
aggrandized v ▷ aggrandize
aggrandizement n ▷ aggrandize
aggrandizements n ▷ aggrandize
aggrandizes v ▷ aggrandize
aggrandizing v ▷ aggrandize
aggravate v (-tes, -ting, -ted) make worse > **aggravating** adj > **aggravation** n (pl -s)
aggravated v ▷ aggravate
aggravates v ▷ aggravate
aggravating v, adj ▷ aggravate
aggravation n ▷ aggravate
aggravations n ▷ aggravate

aggregate n (pl -s) total ▶ adj gathered into a mass ▶ v (-tes, -ting, -ted) combine into a whole > **aggregation** n (pl -s)
  aggregated v ▷ aggregate
  aggregates n, v ▷ aggregate
  aggregating v ▷ aggregate
  aggregation n ▷ aggregate
  aggregations n ▷ aggregate
aggression n (pl -s) hostile behaviour > **aggressor** n (pl -s)
  aggressions n ▷ aggression
aggressive adj showing aggression > **aggressively** adv > **aggressiveness** n
  aggressively adv ▷ aggressive
  aggressiveness n ▷ aggressive
  aggressor n ▷ aggression
  aggressors n ▷ aggression
aggrieved adj upset and angry
aggro n (pl -s) (BRIT, AUST & NZ) (Slang) aggressive behaviour
  aggros n ▷ aggro
aghast adj overcome with amazement or horror
agile adj (-r, -st) nimble, quick-moving > **agility** n (pl -ties)
  agiler adj ▷ agile
  agilest adj ▷ agile
  agilities n ▷ agile
  agility n ▷ agile
  aging v, n, adj ▷ age
agitate v (-tes, -ting, -ted) disturb or excite > **agitation** n (pl -s) > **agitator** n (pl -s)
  agitated v ▷ agitate
  agitates v ▷ agitate
  agitating v ▷ agitate
  agitation n ▷ agitate
  agitations n ▷ agitate
  agitator n ▷ agitate
  agitators n ▷ agitate
aglow adj glowing
agnostic n (pl -s) person who believes that it is impossible to know whether God exists ▶ adj of agnostics > **agnosticism** n (pl -s)
  agnosticism n ▷ agnostic
  agnosticisms n ▷ agnostic
  agnostics n ▷ agnostic
ago adv in the past
agog adj eager or curious
  agonies n ▷ agony
agonize v (-zes, -zing, -zed) worry greatly > **agonizing** adj
  agonized v ▷ agonize
  agonizes v ▷ agonize
  agonizing v, adj ▷ agonize
agony n (pl -nies) extreme physical or mental pain

agoraphobia n (pl -s) fear of open spaces > **agoraphobic** n (pl -s), adj
  agoraphobias n ▷ agoraphobia
  agoraphobic n, adj ▷ agoraphobia
  agoraphobics n ▷ agoraphobic
agrarian adj of land or agriculture
agree v (-s, -ing, -d) be of the same opinion
agreeable adj pleasant and enjoyable > **agreeably** adv
  agreeably adv ▷ agreeable
  agreed v ▷ agree
  agreeing v ▷ agree
agreement n (pl agreements) agreeing
  agreements n ▷ agreement
  agrees v ▷ agree
agricultural adj ▷ agriculture
  agriculturalist n ▷ agriculture
  agriculturalists n ▷ agriculture
agriculture n (pl -s) raising of crops and livestock > **agricultural** adj > **agriculturalist** n (pl -s)
  agricultures n ▷ agriculture
  agronomies n ▷ agronomy
  agronomist n ▷ agronomy
  agronomists n ▷ agronomy
agronomy [ag-ron-om-mee] n (pl -mies) science of soil management and crop production > **agronomist** n (pl -s)
aground adv onto the bottom of shallow water
ague [aig-yew] n (pl -s) (Old-fashioned) periodic fever with shivering
  agues n ▷ ague

> **ah** interj. Ah is a sound people make to show pleasure or pain. Ah scores 5 points, and is a good word to form as a result of playing a longer word.

ahead adv in front
ahoy interj shout used at sea to attract attention

> **ai** n (**ais**). An ai is a three-toed sloth. Although ai only scores 2 points, it's a useful word to remember when you're trying to form several words at once.

aid v (-s, -ing, -ed) ▶ n (pl -s) (give) assistance or support
aide n (pl -s) assistant
  aided v ▷ aid
  aides n ▷ aide
  aiding v ▷ aid
  aids v, n ▷ aid
ail v (-s, -ing, -ed) trouble, afflict
  ailed v ▷ ail
aileron n (pl -s) movable flap on an aircraft

wing which controls rolling
ailerons n ▷ aileron
ailing adj sickly ▶ v ▷ ail
ailment n (pl -s) illness
ailments n ▷ ailment
ails v ▷ ail
aim v (-s, -ing, -ed) point (a weapon or missile) or direct (a blow or remark) at a target ▶ n (pl -s) aiming
aimed v ▷ aim
aiming v ▷ aim
aimless adj having no purpose > **aimlessly** adv
aimlessly adv ▷ aimless
aims v, n ▷ aim
air n (pl -s) mixture of gases forming the earth's atmosphere ▶ v (-s, -ing, -ed) make known publicly
airborne adj carried by air
airbrush n (pl -es) atomizer spraying paint by compressed air
airbrushes n ▷ airbrush
aircraft n any machine that flies, such as an aeroplane
aired v ▷ air
airfield n (pl -s) place where aircraft can land and take off
airfields n ▷ airfield
airier adj ▷ airy
airiest adj ▷ airy
airily adv ▷ airy
airing n (pl -s) exposure to air for drying or ventilation ▶ v ▷ air
airings n ▷ airing
airless adj stuffy
airlift n (pl -s) transport of troops or cargo by aircraft when other routes are blocked ▶ v (-s, -ing, -ed) transport by airlift
airlifted v ▷ airlift
airlifting v ▷ airlift
airlifts n, v ▷ airlift
airline n (pl -s) company providing scheduled flights for passengers and cargo
airliner n (pl -s) large passenger aircraft
airliners n ▷ airliner
airlines n ▷ airline
airlock n (pl -s) air bubble blocking the flow of liquid in a pipe
airlocks n ▷ airlock
airmail n system of sending mail by aircraft
airman n (pl -men) member of the air force
airmen n ▷ airman
airplay n (pl -s) broadcast performances of a record on radio
airplays n ▷ airplay
airport n (pl -s) airfield for civilian aircraft,

with facilities for aircraft maintenance and passengers
airports n ▷ airport
airs n, v ▷ air
airship n (pl -s) lighter-than-air self-propelled aircraft
airships n ▷ airship
airspace n (pl -s) atmosphere above a country, regarded as its territory
airspaces n ▷ airspace
airstrip n (pl -s) cleared area where aircraft can take off and land
airstrips n ▷ airstrip
airtight adj sealed so that air cannot enter
airworthiness n ▷ airworthy
airworthinesses n ▷ airworthy
airworthy adj (of aircraft) fit to fly
  > **airworthiness** n ▷ airworthy
airy adj (-rier, -riest) well-ventilated > **airily** adv
aisle [rhymes with **mile**] n (pl -s) passageway separating seating areas in a church, theatre, etc., or row of shelves in a supermarket
aisles n ▷ aisle
ajar adj, adv (of a door) partly open
akimbo adv with hands on hips and elbows outwards
akin adj similar, related
    al conj. Al is an old word for **if** or **although**. Al scores 2 points.
alabaster n (pl -s) soft white translucent stone
alabasters n ▷ alabaster
alacrities n ▷ alacrity
alacrity n (pl -ies) speed, eagerness
alarm n (pl -s) sudden fear caused by awareness of danger ▶ v (-s, -ing, -med) fill with fear > **alarming** adj
alarmed v ▷ alarm
alarming v, adj ▷ alarm
alarmist n (pl -s) person who alarms others needlessly
alarmists n ▷ alarmist
alarms n, v ▷ alarm
alas adv unfortunately, regrettably
albatross n (pl -es) large sea bird with very long wings
albatrosses n ▷ albatross
albeit conj even though
albino n (pl -nos) person or animal with white skin and hair and pink eyes
albinos n ▷ albino
album n (pl -s) book with blank pages for keeping photographs or stamps in
albumen n (pl -s) egg white
albumens n ▷ albumen
albumin n (pl -s) protein found in blood

plasma, egg white, milk, and muscle
albumins n ▷ **albumin**
albums n ▷ **album**
alchemies n ▷ **alchemy**
alchemist n ▷ **alchemy**
alchemists n ▷ **alchemy**
alchemy n (pl -ies) medieval form of chemistry concerned with trying to turn base metals into gold and to find the elixir of life
> **alchemist** n (pl -s)
alcohol n (pl -s) colourless flammable liquid present in intoxicating drinks
alcoholic adj of alcohol ▶ n (pl -s) person addicted to alcohol
alcoholics n ▷ **alcoholic**
alcoholism n (pl -s) addiction to alcohol
alcoholisms n ▷ **alcoholism**
alcohols n ▷ **alcohol**
alcopop n (pl -s) (BRIT, AUST & S AFR) (Informal) alcoholic drink that tastes like a soft drink
alcopops n ▷ **alcopop**
alcove n (pl -s) recess in the wall of a room
alcoves n ▷ **alcove**
aldehyde n (pl -s) one of a group of chemical compounds derived from alcohol by oxidation
aldehydes n ▷ **aldehyde**
alder n (pl -s) tree related to the birch
alderman n (pl -men) formerly, senior member of a local council
aldermen n ▷ **alderman**
alders n ▷ **alder**
ale n (pl -s) kind of beer
alert adj (-er, -est) watchful, attentive ▶ n (pl -s) warning of danger ▶ v (-s, -ing, -ed) warn of danger > **alertness** n (pl -es)
alerted v ▷ **alert**
alerter adj ▷ **alert**
alertest adj ▷ **alert**
alerting v ▷ **alert**
alertness n ▷ **alert**
alertnesses n ▷ **alert**
alerts n, v ▷ **alert**
ales n ▷ **ale**
alfalfa n (pl -s) kind of plant used to feed livestock
alfalfas n ▷ **alfalfa**
alfresco adv, adj in the open air
alga n (pl -e) (usually plural) plant which lives in or near water and has no true stems, leaves, or roots
algae [al-jee] n ▷ **alga**
algebra n (pl -s) branch of mathematics using symbols to represent numbers > **algebraic** adj
algebraic adj ▷ **algebra**

algebras n ▷ **algebra**
algorithm n (pl -s) logical arithmetical or computational procedure for solving a problem
algorithms n ▷ **algorithm**
alias adv also known as ▶ n (pl -ses) false name
aliases n ▷ **alias**
alibi n (pl -s) plea of being somewhere else when a crime was committed
alibis n ▷ **alibi**
alien adj foreign ▶ n (pl -s) foreigner
alienate v (-tes, -ting, -ted) cause to become hostile > **alienation** n (pl -s)
alienated v ▷ **alienate**
alienates v ▷ **alienate**
alienating v ▷ **alienate**
alienation n ▷ **alienate**
alienations n ▷ **alienate**
aliens n ▷ **alien**
alight¹ v (-s, -ing, -ed) step out of (a vehicle)
alight² adj on fire
alighted v ▷ **alight¹**
alighting v ▷ **alight¹**
alights v ▷ **alight¹**
align [a-line] v (-s, -ing, -ed) bring (a person or group) into agreement with the policy of another > **alignment** n (pl -s)
aligned v ▷ **align**
aligning v ▷ **align**
alignment n ▷ **align**
alignments n ▷ **align**
aligns v ▷ **align**
alike adj like, similar ▶ adv in the same way
alimentary adj of nutrition
alimonies n ▷ **alimony**
alimony n (pl -nies) allowance paid under a court order to a separated or divorced spouse
aliquot (MATHS) adj of or denoting an exact divisor of a number ▶ n (pl -s) exact divisor
aliquots n ▷ **aliquot**
alive adj living, in existence
alkali [alk-a-lie] n (pl -s) substance which combines with acid and neutralizes it to form a salt > **alkaline** adj > **alkalinity** n (pl -ties)
alkaline adj ▷ **alkali**
alkalinities n ▷ **alkali**
alkalinity n ▷ **alkali**
alkalis n ▷ **alkali**
alkaloid n (pl -s) any of a group of organic compounds containing nitrogen
alkaloids n ▷ **alkaloid**
all adj whole quantity or number (of) ▶ adv wholly, entirely
allay v (-s, -ing, -ed) reduce (fear or anger)
allayed v ▷ **allay**

allaying v ▷ allay

allays v ▷ allay

allegation n (pl -s) unproved accusation

allegations n ▷ allegation

allege v (-ges, -ging, -ged) state without proof > alleged adj > allegedly adv

alleged v, adj ▷ allege

allegedly adv ▷ allege

alleges v ▷ allege

allegiance n (pl -s) loyalty to a person, country, or cause

allegiances n ▷ allegiance

alleging v ▷ allege

allegorical adj ▷ allegory

allegories n ▷ allegory

allegory n (pl -ries) story with an underlying meaning as well as the literal one > allegorical adj

allegretto n (pl -s) ▶ adv (MUSIC) (piece to be played) fairly quickly or briskly

allegrettos n ▷ allegretto

allegro n (pl -s) ▶ adv (MUSIC) (piece to be played) in a brisk lively manner

allegros n ▷ allegro

alleluia interj ▷ hallelujah

allergen n (pl -s) substance capable of causing an allergic reaction

allergens n ▷ allergen

allergic adj having or caused by an allergy

allergies n ▷ allergy

allergy n (pl -gies) extreme sensitivity to a substance, which causes the body to react to it

alleviate v (-tes, -ting, -ted) lessen (pain or suffering) > alleviation n (pl -s)

alleviated v ▷ alleviate

alleviates v ▷ alleviate

alleviating v ▷ alleviate

alleviation n ▷ alleviate

alleviations n ▷ alleviate

alley n (pl -s) narrow street or path

alleys n ▷ alley

alliance n (pl -s) state of being allied

alliances n ▷ alliance

allied v, adj ▷ ally

allies n, v ▷ ally

alligator n (pl -s) reptile of the crocodile family, found in the southern US and China

alligators n ▷ alligator

alliteration n (pl -s) use of the same sound at the start of words occurring together, e.g. moody music > alliterative adj

alliterations n ▷ alliteration

alliterative adj ▷ alliteration

allocate v (-tes, -ting, -ted) assign to someone

or for a particular purpose > allocation n (pl -s)

allocated v ▷ allocate

allocates v ▷ allocate

allocating v ▷ allocate

allocation n ▷ allocate

allocations n ▷ allocate

allot v (-lots, -lotting, -lotted) assign as a share or for a particular purpose

allotment n (pl -s) distribution

allotments n ▷ allotment

allotrope n (pl -s) any of two or more physical forms in which an element can exist

allotropes n ▷ allotrope

allots v ▷ allot

allotted v ▷ allot

allotting v ▷ allot

allow v (-s, -ing, -ed) permit > allowable adj

allowable adj ▷ allow

allowance n (pl -s) amount of money given at regular intervals

allowances n ▷ allowance

allowed v ▷ allow

allowing v ▷ allow

allows v ▷ allow

alloy n (pl -s) mixture of two or more metals ▶ v (-s, -ing, -ed) mix (metals)

alloyed v ▷ alloy

alloying v ▷ alloy

alloys n, v ▷ alloy

allspice n (pl -s) spice made from the berries of a tropical American tree

allspices n ▷ allspice

allude v (-des, -ding, -ded) (foll. by to) refer indirectly to

alluded v ▷ allude

alludes v ▷ allude

alluding v ▷ allude

allure n (pl -s) attractiveness ▶ v (-s, -ing, -ed) entice or attract > alluring adj

allured v ▷ allure

allures n, v ▷ allure

alluring v, adj ▷ allure

allusion n (pl -s) indirect reference > allusive adj

allusions n ▷ allusion

allusive adj ▷ allusion

alluvial adj ▷ alluvium

alluvium n (pl -s) fertile soil deposited by flowing water > alluvial adj

alluviums n ▷ alluvium

ally n (pl -lies) country, person, or group with an agreement to support another ▶ v (-lies, -lying, -lied) > allied adj

allying v ▷ ally

almanac n (pl -s) yearly calendar with detailed information on anniversaries, phases of the moon, etc.
　almanacs n ▷ almanac
almighty adj having absolute power
almond n (pl -s) edible oval-shaped nut which grows on a small tree
　almonds n ▷ almond
almoner n (pl -s) (BRIT) formerly, a hospital social worker
　almoners n ▷ almoner
almost adv very nearly
alms [ahmz] pl n (Old-fashioned) gifts to the poor
aloe n (pl -s) plant with fleshy spiny leaves
　aloes n ▷ aloe
aloft adv in the air
alone adj, adv without anyone or anything else
along prep over part or all the length of ▶ adv forward
alongside prep, adv beside (something)
aloof adj distant or haughty in manner
　> **aloofness** n (pl -es)
　aloofness n ▷ aloof
　aloofnesses n ▷ aloof
alopecia [al-loh-pee-sha] n (pl -s) loss of hair
　alopecias n ▷ alopecia
aloud adv in an audible voice
alpaca n (pl -s) Peruvian llama
　alpacas n ▷ alpaca
alpenstock n (pl -s) iron-tipped stick used by climbers
　alpenstocks n ▷ alpenstock
alpha n (pl -s) first letter in the Greek alphabet
alphabet n (pl -s) set of letters used in writing a language
alphabetical adj in the conventional order of the letters of an alphabet > **alphabetically** adv
　alphabetically adv ▷ alphabetical
alphabetize v (-zes, -zing, -zed) put in alphabetical order
　alphabetized v ▷ alphabetize
　alphabetizes v ▷ alphabetize
　alphabetizing v ▷ alphabetize
　alphabets n ▷ alphabet
　alphas n ▷ alpha
alpine adj of high mountains ▶ n (pl -s) mountain plant
　alpines n ▷ alpine
already adv before the present time
alright adj, interj all right
also adv in addition, too
altar n (pl -s) table used for Communion in Christian churches
altarpiece n (pl -s) work of art above and

behind the altar in some Christian churches
　altarpieces n ▷ altarpiece
　altars n ▷ altar
alter v (-s, -ing, -ed) make or become different
　> **alteration** n (pl -s)
　alteration n ▷ alter
　alterations n ▷ alter
altercation n (pl -s) heated argument
　altercations n ▷ altercation
　altered v ▷ alter
　altering v ▷ alter
alternate v (-tes, -ting, -ted) (cause to) occur by turns ▶ adj occurring by turns
　> **alternately** adv > **alternation** n (pl -s)
　alternated v ▷ alternate
　alternately adv ▷ alternate
　alternates v ▷ alternate
　alternating v ▷ alternate
　alternation n ▷ alternate
　alternations n ▷ alternate
alternative n (pl -s) one of two choices ▶ adj able to be done or used instead of something else > **alternatively** adv
　alternatively adv ▷ alternative
　alternatives n ▷ alternative
alternator n (pl -s) electric generator for producing alternating current
　alternators n ▷ alternator
　alters v ▷ alter
although conj despite the fact that
altimeter [al-tim-it-er] n (pl -s) instrument that measures altitude
　altimeters n ▷ altimeter
altitude n (pl -s) height above sea level
　altitudes n ▷ altitude
alto n (pl -s) (MUSIC) (singer with) the highest adult male voice
altogether adv entirely
　altos n ▷ alto
altruism n (pl -s) unselfish concern for the welfare of others > **altruist** n (pl -s) > **altruistic** adj > **altruistically** adv
　altruisms n ▷ altruism
　altruist n ▷ altruism
　altruists n ▷ altruism
　altruistic adj ▷ altruism
　altruistically adv ▷ altruism
aluminium n (pl -s) (CHEM) light silvery-white metal that does not rust
　aluminiums n ▷ aluminium
　alumna n ▷ alumnus
　alumnae n ▷ alumnus
　alumni n ▷ alumnus
alumnus [al-lumm-nuss] n (pl -ni) [-nie] graduate of a college > **alumna** [al-lumm-na]

▶ n fem (pl -**nae**) [-nee]
always adv at all times
alyssum n (pl -s) garden plant with small yellow or white flowers
  alyssums n ▷ alyssum
am v ▷ be
amalgam n (pl -s) blend or combination
amalgamate v (-tes, -ting, -ted) combine or unite > **amalgamation** n (pl -s)
  amalgamated v ▷ amalgamate
  amalgamates v ▷ amalgamate
  amalgamating v ▷ amalgamate
  amalgamation n ▷ amalgamate
  amalgamations n ▷ amalgamate
  amalgams n ▷ amalgam
amandla [ah-**mand**-lah] n (S AFR) political slogan calling for power to the Black population
  amanuenses n ▷ amanuensis
amanuensis [am-man-yew-en-siss] n (pl -ses) [-seez] person who writes from dictation
amaranth n (pl -s) imaginary flower that never fades
  amaranths n ▷ amaranth
amaryllis n (pl -ses) lily-like plant with large red, pink, or white flowers
  amaryllises n ▷ amaryllis
amass v (-ses, -sing, -sed) collect or accumulate
  amassed v ▷ amass
  amasses v ▷ amass
  amassing v ▷ amass
amateur n (pl -s) person who engages in a sport or activity as a pastime rather than as a profession
amateurish adj lacking skill > **amateurishly** adv
  amateurishly adv ▷ amateurish
  amateurs n ▷ amateur
amatory adj relating to romantic or sexual love
amaze v (-zes, -zing, -zed) surprise greatly, astound > **amazing** adj > **amazingly** adv > **amazement** n (pl -s)
  amazed v ▷ amaze
  amazement n ▷ amaze
  amazements n ▷ amaze
  amazes v ▷ amaze
  amazing v, adj ▷ amaze
  amazingly adv ▷ amaze
amazon n (pl -s) strong and powerful woman > **amazonian** adj
  amazonian adj ▷ amazon
  amazons n ▷ amazon
ambassador n (pl -s) senior diplomat who

represents his or her country in another country > **ambassadorial** adj
  ambassadorial adj ▷ ambassador
  ambassadors n ▷ ambassador
amber n (pl -s) clear yellowish fossil resin ▶ adj brownish-yellow
ambergris [am-ber-greece] n (pl -es) waxy substance secreted by the sperm whale, used in making perfumes
  ambergrises n ▷ ambergris
  ambers n ▷ amber
ambidextrous adj able to use both hands with equal ease
ambience n (pl -s) atmosphere of a place
  ambiences n ▷ ambience
ambient adj surrounding
  ambiguities n ▷ ambiguous
  ambiguity n ▷ ambiguous
ambiguous adj having more than one possible meaning > **ambiguously** adv > **ambiguity** n (pl -ties)
  ambiguously adv ▷ ambiguous
ambit n (pl -s) limits or boundary
ambition n (pl -s) desire for success > **ambitious** adj > **ambitiously** adv
  ambitions n ▷ ambition
  ambitious adj ▷ ambition
  ambitiously adv ▷ ambition
  ambits n ▷ ambit
ambivalence n (pl -s) state of feeling two conflicting emotions at the same time > **ambivalent** adj > **ambivalently** adv
  ambivalences n ▷ ambivalence
  ambivalent adj ▷ ambivalence
  ambivalently adv ▷ ambivalence
amble v (-les, -ling, -led) walk at a leisurely pace ▶ n (pl -s) leisurely walk or pace
  ambled v ▷ amble
  ambles v, n ▷ amble
  ambling v ▷ amble
ambrosia n (pl -s) (MYTH) food of the gods > **ambrosial** adj
  ambrosial adj ▷ ambrosia
  ambrosias n ▷ ambrosia
ambulance n (pl -s) motor vehicle designed to carry sick or injured people
  ambulances n ▷ ambulance
ambush n (pl -es) act of waiting in a concealed position to make a surprise attack ▶ v (-shes, -shing, -shed) attack from a concealed position
  ambushed v ▷ ambush
  ambushes n, v ▷ ambush
  ambushing v ▷ ambush
ameliorate [am-**meal**-yor-rate] v (-tes,

-ting, -ted) make (something) better
> **amelioration** n (pl -s)
ameliorated v ▷ ameliorate
ameliorates v ▷ ameliorate
ameliorating v ▷ ameliorate
amelioration n ▷ ameliorate
ameliorations n ▷ ameliorate
amen interj so be it: used at the end of a prayer
amenable adj likely or willing to cooperate
amend v (-s, -ing, -ed) make small changes
to correct or improve (something)
> **amendment** n (pl -s)
amended v ▷ amend
amending v ▷ amend
amendment n ▷ amend
amends pl n compensation for ▶ v ▷ amend
amenities n ▷ amenity
amenity n (pl -ties) useful or enjoyable feature
amethyst [am-myth-ist] n (pl -s) bluish-violet
variety of quartz used as a gemstone
amethysts n ▷ amethyst
amiabilities n ▷ amiable
amiability n ▷ amiable
amiable adj friendly, pleasant-natured
> **amiably** adv > **amiability** n (pl -ties)
amiably adv ▷ amiable
amicable adj friendly > **amicably** adv
amicably adv ▷ amicable
amid, amidst prep in the middle of, among
amidships adv at or towards the middle of
a ship
amidst prep ▷ amid
amiss adv wrongly, badly ▶ adj wrong, faulty
amities n ▷ amity
amity n (pl -ties) friendship
ammeter n (pl -s) instrument for measuring
electric current
ammeters n ▷ ammeter
ammonia n (pl -s) strong-smelling alkaline gas
containing hydrogen and nitrogen
ammonias n ▷ ammonia
ammonite n (pl -s) fossilized spiral shell of an
extinct sea creature
ammonites n ▷ ammonite
ammunition n (pl -s) bullets, bombs, and
shells that can be fired from or as a weapon
ammunitions n ▷ ammunition
amnesia n (pl -s) loss of memory > **amnesiac**
adj, n (pl -s)
amnesiac adj, n ▷ amnesia
amnesiacs n ▷ amnesia
amnesias n ▷ amnesia
amnesties n ▷ amnesty
amnesty n (pl -ties) general pardon for
offences against a government

amniocenteses n ▷ amniocentesis
amniocentesis n (pl -ses) removal of
some amniotic fluid to test for possible
abnormalities in a fetus
amoeba [am-mee-ba] n (pl -bae, -bas)
microscopic single-celled animal able to
change its shape
amoebae n ▷ amoeba
amoebas n ▷ amoeba
amok [a-muck, a-mock] adv in a violent frenzy
among, amongst prep in the midst of
amongst prep ▷ among
amoral [aim-mor-ral] adj without moral
standards > **amorality** n (pl -ties)
amoralities n ▷ amoral
amorality n ▷ amoral
amorous adj feeling, showing, or relating to
sexual love > **amorously** adv
amorously adv ▷ amorous
amorphous adj without distinct shape
amortize v (-zes, -zing, -zed) pay off (a debt)
gradually by periodic transfers to a sinking
fund
amortized v ▷ amortize
amortizes v ▷ amortize
amortizing v ▷ amortize
amount n (pl -s) extent or quantity ▶ v (-s, -ing,
-ed) (foll. by to) be equal or add up to
amounted v ▷ amount
amounting v ▷ amount
amounts n, v ▷ amount
amour n (pl -s) (secret) love affair
amours n ▷ amour
amp n (pl -s) ampere
ampere [am-pair] n (pl -s) basic unit of electric
current
amperes n ▷ ampere
ampersand n (pl -s) the character (&) meaning
and
ampersands n ▷ ampersand
amphetamine [am-fet-am-mean] n (pl -s) drug
used as a stimulant
amphetamines n ▷ amphetamine
amphibian n (pl -s) animal that lives on land
but breeds in water
amphibians n ▷ amphibian
amphibious adj living or operating both on
land and in water
amphitheatre n (pl -s) open oval or circular
building with tiers of seats rising round an
arena
amphitheatres n ▷ amphitheatre
amphora [am-for-ra] n (pl -phorae) two-
handled ancient Greek or Roman jar
amphorae n ▷ amphora

ample *adj* (**-r, -st**) more than sufficient ▷ **amply** *adv*
ampler *adj* ▷ ample
amplest *adj* ▷ ample
amplification *n* ▷ amplify
amplifications *n* ▷ amplify
amplified *v* ▷ amplify
amplifier *n* (*pl* **-s**) device used to amplify a current or sound signal
amplifiers *n* ▷ amplifier
amplifies *v* ▷ amplify
amplify *v* (**-fies, -fying, -fied**) increase the strength of (a current or sound signal) of ▷ **amplification** *n* (*pl* **-s**)
amplifying *v* ▷ amplify
amplitude *n* (*pl* **-s**) greatness of extent
amplitudes *n* ▷ amplitude
amply *adv* ▷ ample
ampoule *n* (*pl* **-s**) small sealed glass vessel containing liquid for injection
ampoules *n* ▷ ampoule
amps *n* ▷ amp
amputate *v* (**-tes, -ting, -ted**) cut off (a limb or part of a limb) for medical reasons ▷ **amputation** *n* (*pl* **-s**)
amputated *v* ▷ amputate
amputates *v* ▷ amputate
amputating *v* ▷ amputate
amputation *n* ▷ amputate
amputations *n* ▷ amputate
amuck *adv* ▷ amok
amulet *n* (*pl* **-s**) something carried or worn as a protection against evil
amulets *n* ▷ amulet
amuse *v* (**-ses, -sing, -sed**) cause to laugh or smile ▷ **amusing** *adj*
amused *v* ▷ amuse
amusement *n* (*pl* **-s**) state of being amused
amusements *n* ▷ amusement
amuses *v* ▷ amuse
amusing *v, adj* ▷ amuse
an *adj* form of a used before vowels, and sometimes before h
anachronism [an-nak-kron-iz-zum] *n* (*pl* **-s**) person or thing placed in the wrong historical period or seeming to belong to another time ▷ **anachronistic** *adj*
anachronisms *n* ▷ anachronism
anachronistic *adj* ▷ anachronism
anaconda *n* (*pl* **-s**) large S American snake which kills by constriction
anacondas *n* ▷ anaconda
anaemia [an-neem-ee-a] *n* (*pl* **-s**) deficiency in the number of red blood cells
anaemias *n* ▷ anaemia

anaemic *adj* having anaemia
anaesthesia [an-niss-theez-ee-a] *n* (*pl* **-s**) loss of bodily feeling
anaesthesias *n* ▷ anaesthesia
anaesthetic [an-niss-thet-ik] *n* (*pl* **-s**), *adj* (substance) causing loss of bodily feeling
anaesthetics *n* ▷ anaesthetic
anaesthetist [an-neess-thet-ist] *n* (*pl* **-s**) doctor trained to administer anaesthetics ▷ **anaesthetize** *v* (**-zes, -zing, -zed**)
anaesthetists *n* ▷ anaesthetist
anaesthetize *v* ▷ anaesthetist
anaesthetized *v* ▷ anaesthetist
anaesthetizes *v* ▷ anaesthetist
anaesthetizing *v* ▷ anaesthetist
anagram *n* (*pl* **-s**) word or phrase made by rearranging the letters of another word or phrase
anagrams *n* ▷ anagram
anal [ain-al] *adj* of the anus
analgesia *n* (*pl* **-s**) absence of pain
analgesias *n* ▷ analgesia
analgesic [an-nal-jeez-ik] *n* (*pl* **-s**) ▶ *adj* (drug) relieving pain
analgesics *n* ▷ analgesic
analogical *adj* ▷ analogy
analogies *n* ▷ analogy
analogous *adj* similar in some respects
analogue *n* (*pl* **-s**) something that is similar in some respects to something else ▶ *adj* displaying information by means of a dial
analogues *n* ▷ analogue
analogy *n* (*pl* **-gies**) similarity in some respects ▷ **analogical** *adj*
analyse *v* (**-ses, -sing, -sed**) make an analysis of (something)
analysed *v* ▷ analyse
analyses *v* ▷ analyse ▶ *n* ▷ analysis
analysing *v* ▷ analyse
analysis *n* (*pl* **-ses**) separation of a whole into its parts for study and interpretation ▷ **analytical, analytic** *adj* ▷ **analytically** *adv*
analyst *n* (*pl* **-s**) person skilled in analysis
analysts *n* ▷ analyst
analytic *adj* ▷ analysis
analytical *adj* ▷ analysis
analytically *adv* ▷ analysis
anarchic *adj* ▷ anarchy
anarchies *n* ▷ anarchy
anarchism *n* (*pl* **-s**) doctrine advocating the abolition of government
anarchisms *n* ▷ anarchy
anarchist *n* (*pl* **-s**) person who advocates the abolition of government ▷ **anarchistic** *adj*
anarchistic *adj* ▷ anarchist

anarchists n ▷ **anarchist**

anarchy [an-ark-ee] n (pl -ies) lawlessness and disorder > **anarchic** adj

anathema [an-nath-im-a] n (pl -s) detested person or thing

anathemas n ▷ **anathema**

anatomical adj ▷ **anatomy**

anatomically adv ▷ **anatomy**

anatomies n ▷ **anatomy**

anatomist n (pl -s) expert in anatomy

anatomists n ▷ **anatomist**

anatomy n (pl -mies) science of the structure of the body > **anatomical** adj > **anatomically** adv

ancestor n (pl -s) person from whom one is descended > **ancestral** adj

ancestors n ▷ **ancestor**

ancestral adj ▷ **ancestor**

ancestries n ▷ **ancestry**

ancestry n (pl -ries) lineage or descent

anchor n (pl -s) heavy hooked device attached to a boat by a cable and dropped overboard to fasten the ship to the sea bottom ▶ v (-s, -ing, -ed) fasten with or as if with an anchor

anchorage n (pl -s) place where boats can be anchored

anchorages n ▷ **anchorage**

anchored v ▷ **anchor**

anchoring v ▷ **anchor**

anchorite n (pl -s) religious recluse

anchorites n ▷ **anchorite**

anchorman n (pl -men) broadcaster in a central studio who links up and presents items from outside camera units and other studios

anchormen n ▷ **anchorman**

anchors n, v ▷ **anchor**

anchorwoman n (pl -women) female broadcaster in a central studio who links up and presents items from outside camera units and other studios

anchorwomen n ▷ **anchorwoman**

anchovies n ▷ **anchovy**

anchovy [an-chov-ee] n (pl -vies) small strong-tasting fish

ancient adj dating from very long ago

ancients pl n people who lived very long ago

ancillary adj supporting the main work of an organization

and conj in addition to

andante [an-dan-tay] n (pl -s) ▶ adv (MUSIC) (piece to be played) moderately slowly

andantes n ▷ **andante**

andiron n (pl -s) iron stand for supporting logs in a fireplace

andirons n ▷ **andiron**

androgynous adj having both male and female characteristics

android n (pl -s) robot resembling a human

androids n ▷ **android**

anecdotal adj ▷ **anecdote**

anecdote n (pl -s) short amusing account of an incident > **anecdotal** adj

anecdotes n ▷ **anecdote**

anemometer n (pl -s) instrument for recording wind speed

anemometers n ▷ **anemometer**

anemone [an-nem-on-ee] n (pl -s) plant with white, purple, or red flowers

anemones n ▷ **anemone**

aneurism n ▷ **aneurysm**

aneurisms n ▷ **aneurysm**

aneurysm, aneurism [an-new-riz-zum] n (pl -s) permanent swelling of a blood vessel

aneurysms n ▷ **aneurysm**

anew adv once more

angel n (pl -s) spiritual being believed to be an attendant or messenger of God > **angelic** adj > **angelically** adv

angelic adj ▷ **angel**

angelica n (pl -s) aromatic plant

angelically adv ▷ **angel**

angelicas n ▷ **angelica**

angels n ▷ **angel**

angelus [an-jell-uss] n (pl -es) (in the Roman Catholic Church) prayers recited in the morning, at midday, and in the evening

angeluses n ▷ **angelus**

anger n (pl -s) fierce displeasure or extreme annoyance ▶ v (-s, -ing, -ed) make (someone) angry

angered v ▷ **anger**

angering v ▷ **anger**

angers n, v ▷ **anger**

angina [an-jine-a] n (pl -s) heart disorder causing sudden severe chest pains

anginas n ▷ **angina**

angle¹ n (pl -s) space between or shape formed by two lines or surfaces that meet ▶ v (-s, -ing, -ed) bend or place (something) at an angle

angle² v (-s, -ing, -ed) fish with a hook and line > **angling** n (pl -s)

angled v ▷ **angle¹, ²**

angler n (pl -s) person who fishes with a hook and line

anglers n ▷ **angler**

angles n ▷ **angle¹** ▶ v ▷ **angle¹, ²**

anglicize v (-zes, -zing, -zed) make or become English in outlook, form, etc.

anglicized v ▷ **anglicize**

anglicizes v ▷ anglicize

anglicizing v ▷ anglicize

angling n ▷ angle² ▸ v ▷¹, ²

anglings n ▷ angle²

angophora n (pl -s) Australian tree related to the eucalyptus

angophoras n ▷ angophora

angora n (pl -s) variety of goat, cat, or rabbit with long silky hair

angoras n ▷ angora

angrier adj ▷ angry

angriest adj ▷ angry

angrily adv ▷ angry

angry adj (-grier, -griest) full of anger > **angrily** adv

angst n feeling of anxiety

angstrom n (pl angstroms) unit of length used to measure wavelengths

angstroms n ▷ angstrom

anguish n (pl -es) great mental pain > **anguished** adj

anguished adj ▷ anguish

anguishes n ▷ anguish

angular adj (of a person) lean and bony > **angularity** n (pl -ties)

angularities n ▷ angular

angularity n ▷ angular

anhydrous adj (CHEM) containing no water

aniline n (pl -s) colourless oily liquid obtained from coal tar and used for making dyes, plastics, and explosives

anilines n ▷ aniline

animal n (pl -s) living creature with specialized sense organs and capable of voluntary motion, esp. one other than a human being ▸ adj of animals

animals n ▷ animal

animate v (-tes, -ting, -ted) give life to ▸ adj having life > **animated** adj > **animator** n (pl -s)

animated v, adj ▷ animate

animates v ▷ animate

animating v ▷ animate

animation n (pl -s) technique of making cartoon films

animations n ▷ animation

animator n ▷ animate

animators n ▷ animate

animism n (pl -s) belief that natural objects possess souls > **animist** n (pl -s) adj > **animistic** adj

animisms n ▷ animism

animist n, adj ▷ animism

animistic adj ▷ animism

animists n ▷ animism

animosities n ▷ animosity

animosity n (pl -ties) hostility, hatred

animus n (pl -es) hatred, animosity

animuses n ▷ animus

anion [an-eye-on] n (pl -s) ion with negative charge

anions n ▷ anion

anise [an-niss] n (pl -s) plant with liquorice-flavoured seeds

aniseed n (pl -s) liquorice-flavoured seeds of the anise plant

aniseeds n ▷ aniseed

anises n ▷ anise

ankle n (pl -s) joint between the foot and leg

ankles n ▷ ankle

anklet n (pl -s) ornamental chain worn round the ankle

anklets n ▷ anklet

annal n (usually plural) yearly record of events

annals n ▷ annal

anneal v (-s, -ing, -ed) toughen (metal or glass) by heating and slow cooling

annealed v ▷ anneal

annealing v ▷ anneal

anneals v ▷ anneal

annelid n (pl -s) worm with a segmented body, such as an earthworm

annelids n ▷ annelid

annex v (-es, -ing, -ed) seize (territory) > **annexation** n (pl -s)

annexation n ▷ annex

annexations n ▷ annex

annexe n (pl -s) extension to a building

annexed v ▷ annex

annexes v ▷ annex ▸ n ▷ annexe

annexing v ▷ annex

annihilate v (-tes, -ting, -ted) destroy utterly > **annihilation** n (pl -s)

annihilated v ▷ annihilate

annihilates v ▷ annihilate

annihilating v ▷ annihilate

annihilation n ▷ annihilate

annihilations n ▷ annihilate

anniversaries n ▷ anniversary

anniversary n (pl -ries) date on which something occurred in a previous year

annotate v (-tes, -ting, -ted) add notes to (a written work) > **annotation** n (pl -s)

annotated v ▷ annotate

annotates v ▷ annotate

annotating v ▷ annotate

annotation n ▷ annotate

annotations n ▷ annotate

announce v (-ces, -cing, -ced) make known publicly > **announcement** n (pl -s)

announced v ▷ announce

announcement n ▷ announce
announcements n ▷ announce
announcer n (pl -s) person who introduces radio or television programmes
announcers n ▷ announcer
announces v ▷ announce
announcing v ▷ announce
annoy v (-s, -ing, -ed) irritate or displease > **annoyance** n (pl -s)
annoyance n ▷ annoy
annoyances n ▷ annoy
annoyed v ▷ annoy
annoying v ▷ annoy
annoys v ▷ annoy
annual adj happening once a year ▶ n (pl -s) plant that completes its life cycle in a year > **annually** adv
annually adv ▷ annual
annuals n ▷ annual
annuities n ▷ annuity
annuity n (pl -ties) fixed sum paid every year
annul v (-ls, -lling, -lled) declare (something, esp. a marriage) invalid > **annulment** n (pl -s)
annular [an-new-lar] adj ring-shaped
annulled v ▷ annul
annulling v ▷ annul
annulment n ▷ annul
annulments n ▷ annul
annuls v ▷ annul
anode n (pl -s) (ELECTRICITY) positive electrode in a battery, valve, etc.
anodes n ▷ anode
anodize v (-zes, -zing, -zed) coat (metal) with a protective oxide film by electrolysis
anodized v ▷ anodize
anodizes v ▷ anodize
anodizing v ▷ anodize
anodyne n (pl -s) something that relieves pain or distress ▶ adj relieving pain or distress
anodynes n ▷ anodyne
anoint v (-s, -ing, -ed) smear with oil as a sign of consecration
anointed v ▷ anoint
anointing v ▷ anoint
anoints v ▷ anoint
anomalies n ▷ anomaly
anomalous adj ▷ anomaly
anomaly [an-nom-a-lee] n (pl -lies) something that deviates from the normal, irregularity > **anomalous** adj
anon adv (Obs) in a short time, soon
anonymity n ▷ anonymous
anonymous adj by someone whose name is unknown or withheld > **anonymously** adv > **anonymity** n

anonymously adv ▷ anonymous
anorak n (pl -s) light waterproof hooded jacket
anoraks n ▷ anorak
anorexia n (pl -s) psychological disorder characterized by fear of becoming fat and refusal to eat > **anorexic** adj, n
anorexias n ▷ anorexia
anorexic adj, n ▷ anorexia
another adj, pron one more
answer n (pl -s) reply to a question, request, letter, etc. ▶ v (-s, -ing, -ed) give an answer (to)
answerable adj (foll. by for or to) responsible for or accountable to
answered v ▷ answer
answering v ▷ answer
answers n, v ▷ answer
ant n (pl -s) small insect living in highly organized colonies
antacid n (pl -s) substance that counteracts acidity, esp. in the stomach
antacids n ▷ antacid
antagonism n (pl -s) open opposition or hostility
antagonisms n ▷ antagonism
antagonist n (pl -s) opponent or adversary > **antagonistic** adj
antagonistic adj ▷ antagonist
antagonists n ▷ antagonist
antagonize v (-zes, -zing, -zed) arouse hostility in, annoy
antagonized v ▷ antagonize
antagonizes v ▷ antagonize
antagonizing v ▷ antagonize
antarctic n area around the South Pole ▶ adj of this region
ante n (pl -s) player's stake in poker ▶ v (-tes, -teing, -ted or -teed) place (one's stake) in poker
anteater n (pl -s) mammal which feeds on ants by means of a long snout
anteaters n ▷ anteater
antecedent n (pl -s) event or circumstance happening or existing before another ▶ adj preceding, prior
antecedents n ▷ antecedent
anted v ▷ ante
antedate v (-tes, -ting, -ted) precede in time
antedated v ▷ antedate
antedates v ▷ antedate
antedating v ▷ antedate
antediluvian adj of the time before the biblical Flood
anteed v ▷ ante
anteing v ▷ ante
antelope n (pl -s) deerlike mammal with long

legs and horns
antelopes n ▷ antelope
antenatal adj during pregnancy, before birth
antenna n (pl -e) insect's feeler; (pl -s) aerial
antennae n ▷ antenna
antennas n ▷ antenna
anterior adj to the front
anteroom n (pl -s) small room leading into a
larger one, often used as a waiting room
anterooms n ▷ anteroom
antes n, v ▷ ante
anthem n (pl -s) song of loyalty, esp. to a
country
anthems n ▷ anthem
anther n (pl -s) part of a flower's stamen
containing pollen
anthers n ▷ anther
anthologies n ▷ anthology
anthologist n ▷ anthology
anthologists n ▷ anthology
anthology n (pl -gies) collection of poems
or other literary pieces by various authors
> **anthologist** n (pl -s)
anthraces n ▷ anthrax
anthracite n (pl -s) hard coal burning slowly
with little smoke or flame but intense heat
anthracites n ▷ anthracite
anthrax n (pl -thraces) dangerous disease of
cattle and sheep, communicable to humans
anthropoid adj like a human ▶ n (pl -s) ape,
such as a chimpanzee, that resembles a
human
anthropoids n ▷ anthropoid
anthropological adj ▷ anthropology
anthropologies n ▷ anthropology
anthropologist n ▷ anthropology
anthropologists n ▷ anthropology
anthropology n (pl -ies) study of human
origins, institutions, and beliefs
> **anthropological** adj > **anthropologist** n
(pl -s)
anthropomorphic adj attributing human
form or personality to a god, animal, or
object > **anthropomorphism** n (pl -s)
anthropomorphism n ▷ anthropomorphic
anthropomorphisms n ▷ anthropomorphic
antibiotic n (pl -s) chemical substance capable
of destroying bacteria ▶ adj of antibiotics
antibiotics n ▷ antibiotic
antibodies n ▷ antibody
antibody n (pl -dies) protein produced in the
blood, which destroys bacteria
anticipate v (-tes, -ting, -ted) foresee and
act in advance of > **anticipation** n (pl -s)
> **anticipatory** adj

anticipated v ▷ anticipate
anticipates v ▷ anticipate
anticipating v ▷ anticipate
anticipation n ▷ anticipate
anticipations n ▷ anticipate
anticipatory adj ▷ anticipate
anticlimax n (pl -es) disappointing conclusion
to a series of events
anticlimaxes n ▷ anticlimax
anticlockwise adv, adj in the opposite
direction to the rotation of the hands of a
clock
antics pl n absurd acts or postures
anticyclone n (pl -s) area of moving air of high
pressure in which the winds rotate outwards
anticyclones n ▷ anticyclone
antidote n (pl -s) substance that counteracts
a poison
antidotes n ▷ antidote
antifreeze n (pl -s) liquid added to water to
lower its freezing point, used esp. in car
radiators
antifreezes n ▷ antifreeze
antigen [an-tee-jen] n (pl -s) substance,
usu. a toxin, causing the blood to produce
antibodies
antigens n ▷ antigen
antihero n (pl -roes) central character in a
book, film, etc., who lacks the traditional
heroic virtues
antiheroes n ▷ antihero
antihistamine n (pl -s) drug used to treat
allergies
antihistamines n ▷ antihistamine
antimacassar n (pl -s) cloth put over a chair-
back to prevent soiling
antimacassars n ▷ antimacassar
antimonies n ▷ antimony
antimony n (pl -ies) (CHEM) brittle silvery-
white metallic element
antipathetic adj ▷ antipathy
antipathies n ▷ antipathy
antipathy [an-tip-a-thee] n (pl -thies) dislike,
hostility > **antipathetic** adj
antiperspirant n (pl -s) substance used to
reduce or prevent sweating
antiperspirants n ▷ antiperspirant
antiphon n (pl -s) hymn sung in alternate parts
by two groups of singers > **antiphonal** adj
antiphonal adj ▷ antiphon
antiphons n ▷ antiphon
antipodean adj ▷ antipodes
antipodes [an-tip-pod-deez] pl n any two places
diametrically opposite one another on the
earth's surface > **antipodean** adj

antipyretic adj reducing fever ▶ n (pl -s) drug that reduces fever
  antipyretics n ▷ antipyretic
antiquarian adj of or relating to antiquities or rare books ▶ n (pl -s) antiquary
  antiquarians n ▷ antiquarian
  antiquaries n ▷ antiquary
antiquary n (pl -ries) student or collector of antiques or ancient works of art
antiquated adj out-of-date
antique n (pl -s) object of an earlier period, valued for its beauty, workmanship, or age ▶ adj made in an earlier period
  antiques n ▷ antique
antiquities pl n objects dating from ancient times ▶ n ▷ antiquity
antiquity n (pl -ties) great age
antiracism n (pl -s) policy of challenging racism and promoting racial tolerance
  antiracisms n ▷ antiracism
antirrhinum n (pl -s) two-lipped flower of various colours
  antirrhinums n ▷ antirrhinum
antiseptic adj preventing infection by killing germs ▶ n (pl -s) antiseptic substance
  antiseptics n ▷ antiseptic
antisocial adj avoiding the company of other people
antistatic adj reducing the effects of static electricity
  antitheses n ▷ antithesis
antithesis [an-tith-iss-iss] n (pl -ses) [-seez] exact opposite > **antithetical** adj
  antithetical adj ▷ antithesis
antitoxin n (pl -s) (serum containing) an antibody that acts against a toxin
  antitoxins n ▷ antitoxin
antitrust adj (AUST & S AFR) (of laws) opposing business monopolies
antler n (pl -s) branched horn of male deer
  antlers n ▷ antler
antonym n (pl -s) word that means the opposite of another
  antonyms n ▷ antonym
  ants n ▷ ant
anus [ain-uss] n (pl -es) opening at the end of the alimentary canal, through which faeces are discharged
  anuses n ▷ anus
anvil n (pl -s) heavy iron block on which metals are hammered into particular shapes
  anvils n ▷ anvil
  anxieties n ▷ anxiety
anxiety n (pl -ties) state of being anxious
anxious adj worried and tense > **anxiously** adv

  anxiously adv ▷ anxious
any adj, pron one or some, no matter which ▶ adv at all > **anything** pron
anybody pron anyone
anyhow adv anyway
anyone pron any person
  anything pron ▷ any
anyway adv at any rate, nevertheless
anywhere adv in, at, or to any place
aorta [eh-or-ta] n (pl -s) main artery of the body, carrying oxygen-rich blood from the heart
  aortas n ▷ aorta
apace adv (Lit) swiftly
  apalled v ▷ appal
apart adv to or in pieces
apartheid n (pl -s) former official government policy of racial segregation in S Africa
  apartheids n ▷ apartheid
apartment n (pl -s) room in a building
  apartments n ▷ apartment
apathetic adj ▷ apathy
apathy n (pl -thies) lack of interest or enthusiasm > **apathetic** adj
  apethies n ▷ apathy
ape n (pl -s) tailless monkey such as the chimpanzee or gorilla ▶ v (apes, aping, aped) imitate
  aped v ▷ ape
aperient [ap-peer-ee-ent] adj having a mild laxative effect ▶ n (pl -s) mild laxative
  aperients n ▷ aperient
aperitif [ap-per-rit-teef] n (pl -s) alcoholic drink taken before a meal
  aperitifs n ▷ aperitif
aperture n (pl -s) opening or hole
  apertures n ▷ aperture
  apes n, v ▷ ape
apex n (pl -es) highest point
  apexes n ▷ apex
aphasia n disorder of the central nervous system that affects the ability to speak and understand words
aphid [eh-fid], **aphis** [eh-fiss] n (pl aphids) small insect which sucks the sap from plants
  aphids n ▷ aphid
  aphis n ▷ aphid
aphorism n (pl -s) short clever saying expressing a general truth
  aphorisms n ▷ aphorism
aphrodisiac [af-roh-diz-zee-ak] n (pl -s) substance that arouses sexual desire ▶ adj arousing sexual desire
  aphrodisiacs n ▷ aphrodisiac
  apiaries n ▷ apiary
apiary n (pl -ries) place where bees are kept

apiculture n (pl -s) breeding and care of bees
  apicultures n ▷ apiculture
apiece adv each
  aping v ▷ ape
aplomb n (pl -s) calm self-possession
  aplombs n ▷ aplomb
apocalypse n (pl -s) end of the world
  > **apocalyptic** adj
  apocalypses n ▷ apocalypse
  apocalyptic adj ▷ apocalypse
apocryphal [ap-pok-rif-al] adj (of a story) of
  questionable authenticity
apogee [ap-oh-jee] n (pl -s) point of the moon's
  or a satellite's orbit that is farthest from
  the earth
  apogees n ▷ apogee
apologetic adj showing or expressing regret
  > **apologetically** adv
  apologetically adv ▷ apologetic
apologetics n branch of theology concerned
  with the reasoned defence of Christianity
  apologies n ▷ apology
apologist n (pl -s) person who formally
  defends a cause
  apologists n ▷ apologist
apologize v (-zes, -zing, -zed) make an apology
  apologized v ▷ apologize
  apologizes v ▷ apologize
  apologizing v ▷ apologize
apology n (pl -gies) expression of regret for
  wrongdoing
apoplectic adj of apoplexy
  apoplexies n ▷ apoplexy
apoplexy n (pl -xies) (MED) stroke
  apostasies n ▷ apostasy
apostasy [ap-poss-stass-ee] n (pl -sies)
  abandonment of one's religious faith or other
  belief > **apostate** n (pl -s) adj
  apostate n, adj ▷ apostasy
  apostates n ▷ apostasy
apostle n (pl -s) ardent supporter of a cause or
  movement > **apostolic** adj
  apostles n ▷ apostle
  apostolic adj ▷ apostle
apostrophe [ap-poss-trof-fee] n (pl -s)
  punctuation mark (') showing the omission
  of a letter or letters in a word, e.g. don't, or
  forming the possessive, e.g. Jill's car
  apostrophes n ▷ apostrophe
  apothecaries n ▷ apothecary
apothecary n (pl -ries) (Obs) chemist
  apotheoses n ▷ apotheosis
apotheosis [ap-poth-ee-oh-siss] n (pl -ses)
  [-seez] perfect example
appal v (-s, -lling, -lled) dismay, terrify

appalled v ▷ appal
appalling adj dreadful, terrible ▶ v ▷ appal
  appals v ▷ appal
apparatus n (pl -es) equipment for a particular
  purpose
  apparatuses n ▷ apparatus
apparel n (pl -s) (Old-fashioned) clothing
  apparels n ▷ apparel
apparent adj readily seen, obvious
  > **apparently** adv
  apparently adv ▷ apparent
apparition n (pl -s) ghost or ghostlike figure
  apparitions n ▷ apparition
appeal v (-s, -ing, -ed) make an earnest request
  ▶ n (pl -s) earnest request > **appealing** adj
  appealed v ▷ appeal
  appealing v, adj ▷ appeal
  appeals v, n ▷ appeal
appear v (-s, -ing, -ed) become visible or
  present
appearance n (pl -s) appearing
  appearances n ▷ appearance
  appeared v ▷ appear
  appearing v ▷ appear
  appears v ▷ appear
appease v (-s, -ing, -ed) pacify (a person)
  by yielding to his or her demands
  > **appeasement** n (pl -s)
  appeased v ▷ appease
  appeasement n ▷ appeal
  appeasements n ▷ appeal
  appeases v ▷ appease
  appeasing v ▷ appease
appellant n (pl -s) person who makes an
  appeal to a higher court
  appellants n ▷ appellant
appellation n (pl -s) (Formal) name, title
  appellations n ▷ appellation
append v (-s, -ing, -ed) join on, add
appendage n (pl -s) thing joined on or added
  appendages n ▷ appendage
  appended v ▷ append
  appendices n ▷ appendix
appendicitis n (pl -es) inflammation of the
  appendix
  appendicitises n ▷ appendicitis
  appending v ▷ append
appendix n (pl -dices, -dixes) separate
  additional material at the end of a book
  appendixes n ▷ appendix
  appends v ▷ append
appertain v (-s, -ing, -ed) (foll. by to) belong to
  appertained v ▷ appertain
  appertaining v ▷ appertain
  appertains v ▷ appertain

appetite n (pl -s) desire for food or drink
  appetites n ▷ appetite
appetizer n (pl -s) thing eaten or drunk to stimulate the appetite > **appetizing** adj stimulating the appetite
  appetizers n ▷ appetizer
  appetizing adj ▷ appetizer
applaud v (-s, -ing, -ed) show approval of by clapping one's hands
  applauded v ▷ applaud
  applauding v ▷ applaud
  applauds v ▷ applaud
applause n (pl -s) approval shown by clapping one's hands
  applauses n ▷ applause
apple n (pl -s) round firm fleshy fruit that grows on trees
  apples n ▷ apple
appliance n (pl -s) device with a specific function
  appliances n ▷ appliance
  applicabilities n ▷ applicable
  applicability n ▷ applicable
applicable adj relevant, appropriate > **applicability** n (pl -ties)
applicant n (pl -s) person who applies for something
  applicants n ▷ applicant
application n (pl -s) formal request
  applications n ▷ application
applied adj (of a skill, science, etc.) put to practical use ▷ v ▷ apply
  applies v ▷ apply
appliqué [ap-plee-kay] n (pl -s) kind of decoration in which one material is cut out and attached to another
  appliqués n ▷ appliqué
apply v (-plies, -plying, -plied) make a formal request
  applying v ▷ apply
appoint v (-s, -ing, -ed) assign to a job or position
  appointed v ▷ appoint
  appointing v ▷ appoint
appointment n (pl -s) arrangement to meet a person
  appointments n ▷ appointment
  appoints v ▷ appoint
apportion v (-s, -ing, -ed) divide out in shares
  apportioned v ▷ apportion
  apportioning v ▷ apportion
  apportions v ▷ apportion
apposite adj suitable, apt
apposition n (pl -s) grammatical construction in which two nouns or phrases referring to

the same thing are placed one after another without a conjunction
  appositions n ▷ apposition
appraisal n ▷ appraise
  appraisals n ▷ appraise
appraise v (-ses, -sing, -sed) estimate the value or quality of > **appraisal** n (pl -s)
  appraised v ▷ appraise
  appraises v ▷ appraise
  appraising v ▷ appraise
appreciable adj enough to be noticed > **appreciably** adv
  appreciably adv ▷ appreciable
appreciate v (-tes, -ting, -ted) value highly > **appreciation** n (pl -s)
  appreciated v ▷ appreciate
  appreciates v ▷ appreciate
  appreciating v ▷ appreciate
  appreciation n ▷ appreciate
  appreciations n ▷ appreciate
appreciative adj feeling or showing appreciation
apprehend v (-s, -ing, -ed) arrest and take into custody
  apprehended v ▷ apprehend
  apprehending v ▷ apprehend
  apprehends v ▷ apprehend
apprehension n (pl -s) dread, anxiety
  apprehensions n ▷ apprehension
apprehensive adj fearful or anxious
apprentice n (pl -s) someone working for a skilled person for a fixed period in order to learn his or her trade ▶ v (-ces, -cing, -ced) take or place (someone) as an apprentice > **apprenticeship** n (pl -s)
  apprenticed v ▷ apprentice
  apprentices n, v ▷ apprentice
  apprenticing v ▷ apprentice
apprise v (-ses, -sing, -sed) make aware (of)
  apprised v ▷ apprise
  apprises v ▷ apprise
  apprising v ▷ apprise
appro n (pl -s) (BRIT, AUST, NZ & S AFR) (Informal) on approval
approach v (-ches, -ching, -ched) come near or nearer (to) ▶ n (pl -es) approaching or means of approaching > **approachable** adj
  approachable adj ▷ approach
  approached v ▷ approach
  approaches v, n ▷ approach
  approaching v ▷ approach
approbation n (pl -s) approval
  approbations n ▷ approbation
appropriate adj suitable, fitting ▶ v (-tes, -ting, -ted) take for oneself > **appropriately**

adv ▷ **appropriateness** *n* ▷ **appropriation** *n* (*pl* **-s**)

appropriated *v* ▷ **appropriate**

appropriately *adv* ▷ **appropriate**

appropriateness *n* ▷ **appropriate**

appropriates *v* ▷ **appropriate**

appropriating *v* ▷ **appropriate**

appropriation *n* ▷ **appropriate**

appropriations *n* ▷ **appropriate**

appros *n* ▷ **appro**

approval *n* (*pl* **-s**) consent

approvals *n* ▷ **approval**

approve *v* (**-ves, -ving, -ved**) consider good or right

approved *v* ▷ **approve**

approves *v* ▷ **approve**

approving *v* ▷ **approve**

approximate *adj* almost but not quite exact ▶ *v* (**-tes, -ting, -ted**) (foll. by **to**) come close to ▷ **approximately** *adv* ▷ **approximation** *n* (*pl* **-s**)

approximated *v* ▷ **approximate**

approximately *adv* ▷ **approximate**

approximates *v* ▷ **approximate**

approximating *v* ▷ **approximate**

approximation *n* ▷ **approximate**

approximations *n* ▷ **approximate**

appurtenance *n* (*pl* **-s**) a minor or additional feature

appurtenances *n* ▷ **appurtenance**

apricot *n* (*pl* **-s**) yellowish-orange juicy fruit like a small peach ▶ *adj* yellowish-orange

apricots *n* ▷ **apricot**

apron *n* (*pl* **-s**) garment worn over the front of the body to protect the clothes

aprons *n* ▷ **apron**

apropos [ap-prop-**poh**] *adj*, *adv* appropriate(ly)

apse *n* (*pl* **-s**) arched or domed recess, esp. in a church

apses *n* ▷ **apse**

apt *adj* having a specified tendency ▷ **aptly** *adv* ▷ **aptness** *n* (*pl* **-es**)

aptitude *n* (*pl* **-s**) natural ability

aptitudes *n* ▷ **aptitude**

aptly *adv* ▷ **apt**

aptness *n* ▷ **apt**

aptnesses *n* ▷ **apt**

aqualung *n* (*pl* **-s**) mouthpiece attached to air cylinders, worn for underwater swimming

aqualungs *n* ▷ **aqualung**

aquamarine *n* (*pl* **-s**) greenish-blue gemstone ▶ *adj* greenish-blue

aquamarines *n* ▷ **aquamarine**

aquaplane *n* (*pl* **-s**) board on which a person stands to be towed by a motorboat ▶ *v* (**-nes, -ning, -ned**) ride on an aquaplane

aquaplaned *v* ▷ **aquaplane**

aquaplanes *n*, *v* ▷ **aquaplane**

aquaplaning *v* ▷ **aquaplane**

aquaria *n* ▷ **aquarium**

aquarium *n* (*pl* **-s, -ria**) tank in which fish and other underwater creatures are kept

aquariums *n* ▷ **aquarium**

aquatic *adj* living in or near water

aquatics *pl n* water sports

aquatint *n* (*pl* **-s**) print like a watercolour, produced by etching copper

aquatints *n* ▷ **aquatint**

aqueduct *n* (*pl* **-s**) structure carrying water across a valley or river

aqueducts *n* ▷ **aqueduct**

aqueous *adj* of, like, or containing water

aquiline *adj* (of a nose) curved like an eagle's beak

> **ar** *n* (**ars**). Ar is the letter R. This is a good two-letter word to remember because it uses two very common tiles, and so is easy to fit on the board. Ar scores 2 points.

arabesque [ar-ab-**besk**] *n* (*pl* **-s**) ballet position in which one leg is raised behind and the arms are extended

arabesques *n* ▷ **arabesque**

arable *adj* suitable for growing crops on

arachnid [ar-**rak**-nid] *n* (*pl* **-s**) eight-legged invertebrate, such as a spider, scorpion, tick, or mite

arachnids *n* ▷ **arachnid**

arbiter *n* (*pl* **-s**) person empowered to judge in a dispute

arbiters *n* ▷ **arbiter**

arbitrarily *adv* ▷ **arbitrary**

arbitrary *adj* based on personal choice or chance, rather than reason ▷ **arbitrarily** *adv*

arbitrate *v* ▷ **arbitration**

arbitrated *v* ▷ **arbitration**

arbitrates *v* ▷ **arbitration**

arbitrating *v* ▷ **arbitration**

arbitration *n* (*pl* **-s**) hearing and settling of a dispute by an impartial referee chosen by both sides ▷ **arbitrate** *v* (**-tes, -ting, -ted**) ▷ **arbitrator** *n* (*pl* **-s**)

arbitrations *n* ▷ **arbitration**

arbitrator *n* ▷ **arbitration**

arbitrators *n* ▷ **arbitration**

arboreal *adj* of or living in trees

arboreta *n* ▷ **arboretum**

arboretum [ahr-bore-**ee**-tum] *n* (*pl* **-ta**) place where rare trees or shrubs are cultivated

arboriculture *n* (*pl* **-s**) cultivation of trees or shrubs

arboricultures n ▷ arboriculture
arbour n (pl -s) glade sheltered by trees
arbours n ▷ arbour
arc n (pl -s) part of a circle or other curve ▶ v (-s, -ing, -ed) form an arc
arcade n (pl -s) covered passageway lined with shops
arcades n ▷ arcade
arcane adj mysterious and secret
arced v ▷ arc
arch[1] n (pl -es) curved structure supporting a bridge or roof ▶ v (-es, -ing, -ed) (cause to) form an arch
arch[2] adj (-er, -est) superior, knowing > **archly** adv > **archness** n (pl -es)
archaeological adj ▷ archaeology
archaeologies n ▷ archaeology
archaeologist n ▷ archaeology
archaeologists n ▷ archaeology
archaeology n (pl -ies) study of ancient cultures from their physical remains > **archaeological** adj > **archaeologist** n (pl -s)
archaic [ark-kay-ik] adj ancient > **archaism** [ark-kay-iz-zum] ▶ n (pl -s) archaic word or phrase
archaism n ▷ archaic
archaisms n ▷ archaic
archangel [ark-ain-jell] n (pl -s) chief angel
archangels n ▷ archangel
archbishop n (pl -s) chief bishop
archbishops n ▷ archbishop
archdeacon n (pl -s) priest ranking just below a bishop
archdeacons n ▷ archdeacon
archdiocese n (pl -es) diocese of an archbishop
archdioceses n ▷ archdiocese
arched v ▷ arch[1]
archer n (pl -s) person who shoots with a bow and arrow ▶ adj ▷ arch[2] > **archery** n (pl -ries)
archeries n ▷ archer
archers n ▷ archer
archery n ▷ archer
arches n, v ▷ arch[1]
archest adj ▷ arch[2]
archetypal adj ▷ archetype
archetype [ark-ee-type] n (pl -s) perfect specimen > **archetypal** adj
archetypes n ▷ archetype
arching v ▷ arch[1]
archipelago [ark-ee-pel-a-go] n (pl -gos) group of islands
archipelagos n ▷ archipelago
architect n (pl -s) person qualified to design and supervise the construction of buildings
architects n ▷ architect

architectural adj ▷ architecture
architecture n (pl -s) style in which a building is designed and built > **architectural** adj
architectures n ▷ architecture
architrave n (pl -s) (ARCHIT) beam that rests on columns
architraves n ▷ architrave
archival adj ▷ archive
archive [ark-ive] n (pl -s) (often pl collection of records or documents > **archival** adj
archives n ▷ archive
archivist [ark-iv-ist] n (pl -s) person in charge of archives
archivists n ▷ archivist
archly adv ▷ arch[2]
archness n ▷ arch[2]
archnesses n ▷ arch[2]
archway n (pl -s) passageway under an arch
archways n ▷ archway
arcing v ▷ arc
arcs n, v ▷ arc
arctic n (pl -s) area around the North Pole ▶ adj of this region
arctics n ▷ arctic
ardent adj passionate > **ardently** adv
ardently adv ▷ ardent
ardour n (pl -s) passion
ardours n ▷ ardour
arduous adj hard to accomplish, strenuous > **arduously** adv
arduously adv ▷ arduous
are[1] v ▷ be
are[2] n (pl -s) unit of measure, 100 square metres
area n (pl -s) part or region
areas n ▷ area
arena n (pl -s) seated enclosure for sports events
arenas n ▷ arena
areola n (pl -lae, -las) small circular area, such as the coloured ring around the human nipple
areolae n ▷ areola
areolas n ▷ areola
ares n ▷ are[2]
argon n (pl -s) (CHEM) inert gas found in the air
argons n ▷ argon
argot [ahr-go] n (pl -s) slang or jargon
argots n ▷ argot
arguable adj ▷ argue
arguably adv ▷ argue
argue v (-gues, -guing, -gued) try to prove by giving reasons > **arguable** adj > **arguably** adv
argued v ▷ argue
argues v ▷ argue

arguing v ▷ argue
argument n (pl -s) quarrel
argumentation n (pl -s) process of reasoning methodically
  argumentations n ▷ argumentation
argumentative adj given to arguing
  arguments n ▷ argument
aria [ah-ree-a] n (pl -s) elaborate song for solo voice, esp. one from an opera
  arias n ▷ aria
arid adj parched, dry ▶ **aridity** n (pl -ties)
  aridities n ▷ arid
  aridity n ▷ arid
aright adv rightly
arise v (arises, arising, arose, arisen) come about
  arisen v ▷ arise
  arises v ▷ arise
  arising v ▷ arise
  aristocracies n ▷ aristocracy
aristocracy n (pl -cies) highest social class
aristocrat n (pl -s) member of the aristocracy ▷ **aristocratic** adj
  aristocratic adj ▷ aristocrat
  aristocrats n ▷ aristocrat
arithmetic n (pl -s) calculation by or of numbers ▶ adj of arithmetic ▷ **arithmetical** adj ▷ **arithmetically** adv
  arithmetical adj ▷ arithmetic
  arithmetically adv ▷ arithmetic
  arithmetics n ▷ arithmetic
ark n (pl -s) (OLD TESTAMENT) boat built by Noah, which survived the Flood
  arks n ▷ ark
arm¹ n (pl -s) either of the upper limbs from the shoulder to the wrist
arm² v (-s, -ing, -ed) supply with weapons
armada n (pl -s) large number of warships
  armadas n ▷ armada
armadillo n (pl -s) small S American mammal covered in strong bony plates
  armadillos n ▷ armadillo
armament n (pl -s) military weapons
  armaments n ▷ armament
armature n (pl -s) revolving structure in an electric motor or generator, wound with coils carrying the current
  armatures n ▷ armature
armchair n (pl -s) upholstered chair with side supports for the arms
  armchairs n ▷ armchair
  armed v ▷ arm²
armful n (pl -s) as much as can be held in the arms
  armfuls n ▷ armful
armhole n (pl -s) opening in a garment

through which the arm passes
  armholes n ▷ armhole
  armies n ▷ army
  arming v ▷ arm²
armistice [arm-miss-stiss] n (pl -s) agreed suspension of fighting
  armistices n ▷ armistice
armour n (pl -s) metal clothing formerly worn to protect the body in battle
armourer n (pl -s) maker, repairer, or keeper of arms or armour
  armourers n ▷ armourer
  armouries n ▷ armoury
  armours n ▷ armour
armoury n (pl -ries) place where weapons are stored
armpit n (pl -s) hollow under the arm at the shoulder
  armpits n ▷ armpit
arms pl n weapons ▶ n ▷ arm¹ ▶ v ▷ arm²
army n (pl -mies) military land forces of a nation
aroma n (pl -s) pleasant smell ▶ **aromatic** adj
  aromas n ▷ aroma
  aromatherapies n ▷ aromatherapy
aromatherapy n (pl -pies) massage with fragrant oils to relieve tension
aromatic adj ▷ aroma
arose v ▷ arise
around prep, adv on all sides (of)
arouse v (-ses, -sing, -sed) stimulate, make active
  aroused v ▷ arouse
  arouses v ▷ arouse
  arousing v ▷ arouse
arpeggio [arp-pej-ee-oh] n (pl -s) (MUSIC) notes of a chord played or sung in quick succession
  arpeggios n ▷ arpeggio
arraign [ar-rain] v (-s, -ing, -ed) bring (a prisoner) before a court to answer a charge ▷ **arraignment** n (pl -s)
  arraigned v ▷ arraign
  arraigning v ▷ arraign
  arraignment n ▷ arraign
  arraignments n ▷ arraign
  arraigns v ▷ arraign
arrange v (-ges, -ging, -ged) plan ▷ **arrangement** n (pl -s)
  arranged v ▷ arrange
  arrangement n ▷ arrange
  arrangements n ▷ arrange
  arranges v ▷ arrange
  arranging v ▷ arrange
arrant adj utter, downright
arras n (pl -es) tapestry wall-hanging
  arrases n ▷ arras
array n (pl -s) impressive display or collection

(*Poetic*) ► v (**-s, -ing, -ed**) arrange in order
arrayed v ▷ array
arraying v ▷ array
arrays n, v ▷ array
arrear n (p **-s**) (usually plural) money owed
arrears n ▷ arrear
arrest v (**-s, -ing, -ed**) take (a person) into
custody ► n (pl **-s**) act of taking a person into
custody
arrested v ▷ arrest
arresting adj attracting attention, striking
► v ▷ arrest
arrests v, n ▷ arrest
arrival n (pl **-s**) arriving
arrivals n ▷ arrival
arrive v (**-ves, -ving, -ved**) reach a place or
destination
arrived v ▷ arrive
arrives v ▷ arrive
arriving v ▷ arrive
arrogance n ▷ arrogant
arrogances n ▷ arrogant
arrogant adj proud and overbearing
> **arrogantly** adv > **arrogance** n (pl **-s**)
arrogantly adv ▷ arrogant
arrogate v (**-tes, -ting, -ted**) claim or seize
without justification
arrogated v ▷ arrogate
arrogates v ▷ arrogate
arrogating v ▷ arrogate
arrow n (pl **-s**) pointed shaft shot from a bow
arrowhead n (pl **-s**) pointed tip of an arrow
arrowheads n ▷ arrowhead
arrowroot n (pl **-s**) nutritious starch obtained
from the root of a W Indian plant
arrowroots n ▷ arrowroot
arrows n ▷ arrow
arsenal n (pl **-s**) place where arms and
ammunition are made or stored
arsenals n ▷ arsenal
arsenic n (pl **-s**) toxic grey element > **arsenical**
adj
arsenical adj ▷ arsenic
arsenics n ▷ arsenic
arson n (pl **-s**) crime of intentionally setting
property on fire > **arsonist** n (pl **-s**)
arsonist n ▷ arson
arsonists n ▷ arson
arsons n ▷ arson
art n (pl **-s**) creation of works of beauty, esp.
paintings or sculpture
artefact n (pl **-s**) something made by human
beings
artefacts n ▷ artefact
arterial adj of an artery

arteries n ▷ artery
artery n (pl **-ries**) one of the tubes carrying
blood from the heart
artful adj cunning, wily > **artfully** adv
> **artfulness** n (pl **-es**)
artfully adv ▷ artful
artfulness n ▷ artful
artfulnesses n ▷ artful
arthritic adj, n ▷ arthritis
arthritics n ▷ arthritis
arthritis n (pl **-es**) painful inflammation of a
joint or joints > **arthritic** adj, n (pl **-s**)
arthritises n ▷ arthritis
arthropod n (pl **-s**) animal, such as a spider or
insect, with jointed limbs and a segmented
body
arthropods n ▷ arthropod
artichoke n (pl **-s**) flower head of a thistle-like
plant, cooked as a vegetable
artichokes n ▷ artichoke
article n (pl **-s**) written piece in a magazine or
newspaper
articled adj bound (as an apprentice) by a
written contract
articles n ▷ article
articulate adj able to express oneself clearly
and coherently ► v (**-tes, -ting, -ted**) speak or
say clearly and coherently > **articulately** adv
> **articulation** n (pl **-s**)
articulated adj jointed ► v ▷ articulate
articulates v ▷ articulate
articulating v ▷ articulate
articulation n ▷ articulate
articulations n ▷ articulate
artier adj ▷ arty
artiest adj ▷ arty
artifice n (pl **-s**) clever trick
artificer [art-**tiff**-iss-er] n (pl **-s**) craftsman
artificers n ▷ artificer
artifices n ▷ artifice
artificial adj man-made, not occurring
naturally > **artificially** adv > **artificiality** n
(pl **-ties**)
artificialities n ▷ artificial
artificiality n ▷ artificial
artificially adv ▷ artificial
artilleries n ▷ artillery
artillery n (pl **-ies**) large-calibre guns
artisan n (pl **-s**) skilled worker, craftsman
artisans n ▷ artisan
artist n (pl **-s**) person who produces works of
art, esp. paintings or sculpture
> **artistic** adj
> **artistically** adv
artiste n (pl **-s**) professional entertainer such
as a singer or dancer

artistes n ▷ artiste
artistic adj ▷ artist
artistically adv ▷ artist
artistries n ▷ artistry
artistry n (pl -ries) artistic skill
artists n ▷ artist
artless adj free from deceit or cunning
> **artlessly** adv
artlessly adv ▷ artless
arts n ▷ art
arty adj (-tier, -tiest) (Informal) having an affected interest in art
arvie n (pl -s) (S AFR) (Informal) afternoon
arvies n ▷ arvie
as conj while, when ▶ adv, conj used to indicate amount or extent in comparisons ▶ prep in the role of, being
asafoetida n (pl -s) strong-smelling plant resin used as a spice in Eastern cookery
asafoetidas n ▷ asafoetida
asbestos n (pl -es) fibrous mineral which does not burn
asbestoses n ▷ asbestos, asbestosis
asbestosis n (pl -ses) lung disease caused by inhalation of asbestos fibre
ascend v (-s, -ing, -ed) go or move up
ascendancies n ▷ ascendancy
ascendancy n (pl -cies) condition of being dominant
ascendant adj dominant or influential
ascended v ▷ ascend
ascending v ▷ ascend
ascends v ▷ ascend
ascent n (pl -s) ascending
ascents n ▷ ascent
ascertain v (-s, -ing, -ed) find out definitely
> **ascertainable** adj > **ascertainment** n (pl -s)
ascertainable adj ▷ ascertain
ascertained v ▷ ascertain
ascertaining v ▷ ascertain
ascertainment n ▷ ascertain
ascertainments n ▷ ascertain
ascertains v ▷ ascertain
ascetic [ass-set-tik] n (pl -s) ▶ adj (person) abstaining from worldly pleasures and comforts > **asceticism** n (pl -s)
asceticism n ▷ ascetic
asceticisms n ▷ ascetic
ascetics n ▷ ascetic
ascribe v (-bes, -bing, -bed) attribute, as to a particular origin > **ascription** n (pl -s)
ascribed v ▷ ascribe
ascribes v ▷ ascribe
ascribing v ▷ ascribe
ascription n ▷ ascribe

ascriptions n ▷ ascribe
aseptic [eh-sep-tik] adj free from harmful bacteria
asexual [eh-sex-yew-al] adj without sex
> **asexually** adv
asexually adv ▷ asexual
ash[1] n (pl -es) powdery substance left when something is burnt
ash[2] n (pl -es) tree with grey bark
ashamed adj feeling shame
ashen adj pale with shock
ashes n ▷ ash[1, 2]
ashlar n (pl -s) square block of hewn stone used in building
ashlars n ▷ ashlar
ashore adv towards or on land
ashram n (pl -s) religious retreat where a Hindu holy man lives
ashrams n ▷ ashram
ashtray n (pl -s) receptacle for tobacco ash and cigarette butts
ashtrays n ▷ ashtray
aside adv to one side ▶ n (pl -s) remark not meant to be heard by everyone present
asides n ▷ aside
asinine adj stupid, idiotic
ask v (-s, -ing, -ed) say or write (something) in a form that requires an answer
askance [ass-kanss] adv with an oblique glance
asked v ▷ ask
askew adv, adj to one side, crooked
asking v ▷ ask
asks v ▷ ask
aslant adv, prep at a slant (to), slanting (across)
asleep adj sleeping
asp n (pl -s) small poisonous snake
asparagus n (pl -es) plant whose shoots are cooked as a vegetable
asparaguses n ▷ asparagus
aspect n (pl -s) feature or element
aspects n ▷ aspect
aspen n (pl -s) kind of poplar tree
aspens n ▷ aspen
asperities n ▷ asperity
asperity n (pl -ties) roughness of temper
aspersion n (pl -s) derogatory remark
aspersions n ▷ aspersion
asphalt n (pl -s) black hard tarlike substance used for road surfaces etc.
asphalts n ▷ asphalt
asphodel n (pl -s) plant with clusters of yellow or white flowers
asphodels n ▷ asphodel
asphyxia [ass-fix-ee-a] n (pl -s) suffocation
asphyxiate v (-tes, -ting, -ted) suffocate

> **asphyxiation** n (pl -s)
asphyxiated v ▷ asphyxiate
asphyxiates v ▷ asphyxiate
asphyxiating v ▷ asphyxiate
asphyxiation n ▷ asphyxiate
asphyxiations n ▷ asphyxiate

aspic n (pl -s) savoury jelly used to coat meat, eggs, fish, etc.
aspics n ▷ aspic

aspidistra n (pl -s) plant with long tapered leaves
aspidistras n ▷ aspidistra

aspirant n (pl -s) person who aspires
aspirants n ▷ aspirant

aspirate (PHONETICS) v (-tes, -ting, -ted) pronounce with an h sound ▶ n (pl -s) h sound
aspirated v ▷ aspirate
aspirates v, n ▷ aspirate
aspirating v ▷ aspirate

aspiration n (pl -s) strong desire or aim
aspirations n ▷ aspiration

aspire v (-res, -ring, -red) (foll. by to) yearn (for), hope (to do or be)
aspired v ▷ aspire
aspires v ▷ aspire

aspirin n (pl -s) drug used to relieve pain and fever
aspiring v ▷ aspire
aspirins n ▷ aspirin
asps n ▷ asp

ass n (pl -es) donkey

assail v (-s, -ing, -ed) attack violently
> **assailant** n (pl -s)
assailant n ▷ assail
assailants n ▷ assail
assailed v ▷ assail
assailing v ▷ assail
assails v ▷ assail

assassin n (pl -s) person who murders a prominent person
assassinate v (-tes, -ting, -ted) murder (a prominent person) > **assassination** n (pl -s)
assassinated v ▷ assassinate
assassinates v ▷ assassinate
assassinating v ▷ assassinate
assassination n ▷ assassinate
assassinations n ▷ assassinate
assassins n ▷ assassin

assault n (pl -ts) violent attack ▶ v (-s, -ing, -ed) attack violently
assaulted v ▷ assault
assaulting v ▷ assault
assaults n, v ▷ assault

assay n (pl -s) analysis of a substance, esp. a metal, to ascertain its purity ▶ v (-s, -ing, -ed)

assayed v ▷ assay
assaying v ▷ assay
assays n, v ▷ assay

assegai [ass-a-guy] n (pl -s) slender spear used in S Africa
assegais n ▷ assegai

assemblage n (pl -s) collection or group
assemblages n ▷ assemblage

assemble v (-bles, -bling, -bled) collect or congregate
assembled v ▷ assemble
assembles v ▷ assemble
assemblies n ▷ assembly
assembling v ▷ assemble

assembly n (pl -blies) assembled group

assent n (pl -s) agreement or consent ▶ v (-s, -ing, -ed) agree or consent
assented v ▷ assent
assenting v ▷ assent
assents n, v ▷ assent

assert v (-s, -ing, -ed) declare forcefully
> **assertion** n (pl -s) > **assertive** adj
> **assertively** adv
asserted v ▷ assert
asserting v ▷ assert
assertion n ▷ assert
assertions n ▷ assert
assertive adj ▷ assert
assertively adv ▷ assert
asserts v ▷ assert
asses n ▷ ass

assess v (-es, -ing, -ed) judge the worth or importance of > **assessment** n (pl -s)
> **assessor** n (pl -s)
assessed v ▷ assess
assesses v ▷ assess
assessing v ▷ assess
assessment n ▷ assess
assessments n ▷ assess
assessor n ▷ assess
assessors n ▷ assess

asset n (pl -s) valuable or useful person or thing
assets n ▷ asset

asseverate v (-tes, -ting, -ted) declare solemnly
asseverated v ▷ asseverate
asseverates v ▷ asseverate
asseverating v ▷ asseverate
assiduities n ▷ assiduous
assiduity n ▷ assiduous

assiduous adj hard-working > **assiduously** adv
> **assiduity** n (pl -ties)
assiduously adv ▷ assiduous

assign v (-s, -ing, -ed) appoint (someone) to a job or task

assignation n (pl **-s**) assigning
  assignations n ▷ assignation
  assigned v ▷ assign
  assigning v ▷ assign
assignment n (pl **-s**) task assigned
  assignments n ▷ assignment
  assigns v ▷ assign
  assimilable adj ▷ assimilate
assimilate v (**-tes, -ting, -ted**) learn and
understand (information) > **assimilable** adj
> **assimilation** n (pl **-s**)
  assimilated v ▷ assimilate
  assimilates v ▷ assimilate
  assimilating v ▷ assimilate
  assimilation n ▷ assimilate
  assimilations n ▷ assimilate
assist v (**-s, -ing, -ed**) give help or support
> **assistance** n (pl **-s**)
  assistance n ▷ assist
  assistances n ▷ assist
assistant n (pl **-s**) helper ▶ adj junior or deputy
  assistants n ▷ assistant
  assisted v ▷ assist
  assisting v ▷ assist
  assists v ▷ assist
assizes pl n (BRIT) court sessions formerly held
in each county of England and Wales
associate v (**-tes, -ting, -ted**) connect in the
mind ▶ n (pl **-s**) partner in business ▶ adj
having partial rights or subordinate status
  associated v ▷ associate
  associates v, n ▷ associate
  associating v ▷ associate
association n (pl **-s**) society or club
  associations n ▷ association
assonance n (pl **-s**) rhyming of vowel sounds
but not consonants, as in *time* and *light*
  assonances n ▷ assonance
assorted adj consisting of various types mixed
together
assortment n (pl **-s**) assorted mixture
  assortments n ▷ assortment
assuage [ass-**wage**] v (**-ges, -ging, -ged**) relieve
(pain, grief, thirst, etc.)
  assuaged v ▷ assuage
  assuages v ▷ assuage
  assuaging v ▷ assuage
assume v (**-mes, -ming, -med**) take to be true
without proof
  assumed v ▷ assume
  assumes v ▷ assume
  assuming v ▷ assume
assumption n (pl **-s**) thing assumed
  assumptions n ▷ assumption
assurance n (pl **-s**) assuring or being assured

assurances n ▷ assurance
assure v (**-res, -ring, -red**) promise or
guarantee
assured adj confident ▶ v ▷ assure
assuredly adv definitely
  assures v ▷ assure
  assuring v ▷ assure
astatine n (pl **-s**) (CHEM) radioactive
nonmetallic element
  astatines n ▷ astatine
aster n (pl **-s**) plant with daisy-like flowers
asterisk n (pl **-s**) star-shaped symbol (°) used
in printing or writing to indicate a footnote
etc. ▶ v (**-s, -ing, -ed**) mark with an asterisk
  asterisked v ▷ asterisk
  asterisking v ▷ asterisk
  asterisks n, v ▷ asterisk
astern adv at or towards the stern of a ship
asteroid n (pl **-s**) any of the small planets that
orbit the sun between Mars and Jupiter
  asteroids n ▷ asteroid
  asters n ▷ aster
asthma [ass-ma] n (pl **-s**) illness causing
difficulty in breathing > **asthmatic** adj, n
(pl **-s**)
  asthmas n ▷ asthma
  asthmatic adj, n ▷ asthma
  asthmatics n ▷ asthma
astigmatism [eh-**stig**-mat-tiz-zum] n (pl **-s**)
inability of a lens, esp. of the eye, to focus
properly
  astigmatisms n ▷ astigmatism
astir adj (Old-fashioned) out of bed
astonish v (**-es, -ing, -ed**) surprise greatly
> **astonishment** n (pl **-s**)
  astonished v ▷ astonish
  astonishes v ▷ astonish
  astonishing v ▷ astonish
  astonishment n ▷ astonish
  astonishments n ▷ astonish
astound v (**-s, -ing, -ed**) overwhelm with
amazement > **astounding** adj
  astounded v ▷ astound
  astounding v, adj ▷ astound
  astounds v ▷ astound
astrakhan n (pl **-s**) dark curly fleece of lambs
from Astrakhan in Russia
  astrakhans n ▷ astrakhan
astral adj of stars
astray adv off the right path
astride adv, prep with a leg on either side (of)
  astringencies n ▷ astringent
  astringency n ▷ astringent
astringent adj causing contraction of body
tissue ▶ n (pl **-s**) astringent substance

> **astringency** n (pl **-cies**)
astringents n ▷ astringent
astrolabe n (pl **-s**) instrument formerly used to measure the altitude of stars and planets
astrolabes n ▷ astrolabe
astrologer n ▷ astrology
astrologers n ▷ astrology
astrological adj ▷ astrology
astrologies n ▷ astrology
astrology n (pl **-gies**) study of the alleged influence of the stars, planets, and moon on human affairs > **astrologer** n (pl **-s**)
> **astrological** adj
astronaut n (pl **-s**) person trained for travelling in space
astronautical adj ▷ astronautics
astronautics n science and technology of space flight > **astronautical** adj
astronauts n ▷ astronaut
astronomer n ▷ astronomy
astronomers n ▷ astronomy
astronomical adj very large > **astronomically** adv
astronomically adv ▷ astronomical
astronomies n ▷ astronomy
astronomy n (pl **-mies**) scientific study of heavenly bodies > **astronomer** n (pl **-s**)
astrophysical adj ▷ astrophysics
astrophysicist n ▷ astrophysics
astrophysicists n ▷ astrophysics
astrophysics n science of the physical and chemical properties of stars, planets, etc.
> **astrophysical** adj > **astrophysicist** n (pl **-s**)
astute adj perceptive or shrewd > **astutely** adv
> **astuteness** n (pl **-es**)
astutely adv ▷ astute
astuteness n ▷ astute
astutenesses n ▷ astute
asunder adv (Obs or poetic) into parts or pieces
asylum n (pl **-s**) refuge or sanctuary
asylums n ▷ asylum
asymmetric adj ▷ asymmetry
asymmetrical adj ▷ asymmetry
asymmetries n ▷ asymmetry
asymmetry n (pl **-tries**) lack of symmetry
> **asymmetrical, asymmetric** adj
asymptote [ass-im-tote] n (pl **-s**) straight line closely approached but never met by a curve
asymptotes n ▷ asymptote
at prep indicating position in space or time, movement towards an object, etc.
atavism [at-a-viz-zum] n (pl **-s**) recurrence of a trait present in distant ancestors > **atavistic** adj
atavisms n ▷ atavism
atavistic adj ▷ atavism

ate v ▷ eat
atheism [aith-ee-iz-zum] n (pl **-s**) belief that there is no God > **atheist** n (pl **-s**) > **atheistic** adj
atheisms n ▷ atheism
atheist n ▷ atheism
atheistic adj ▷ atheism
atheists n ▷ atheism
atherosclerosis n disease in which deposits of fat cause the walls of the arteries to thicken
athlete n (pl **-s**) person trained in or good at athletics
athletes n ▷ athlete
athletic adj physically fit or strong
> **athletically** adv > **athleticism** n (pl **-s**)
athletically adv ▷ athletic
athleticism n ▷ athletic
athleticisms n ▷ athletic
athletics pl n track-and-field sports such as running, jumping, throwing, etc.
athwart prep across ▶ adv transversely
atlas n (pl **-es**) book of maps
atlases n ▷ atlas
atmosphere n (pl **-s**) mass of gases surrounding a heavenly body, esp. the earth
> **atmospheric** adj
atmospheres n ▷ atmosphere
atmospheric adj ▷ atmosphere
atmospherics pl n radio interference due to electrical disturbance in the atmosphere
atoll n (pl **-s**) ring-shaped coral reef enclosing a lagoon
atolls n ▷ atoll
atom n (pl **-s**) smallest unit of matter which can take part in a chemical reaction
atomic adj of or using atomic bombs or atomic energy
atomize v (**-zes, -zing, -zed**) reduce to atoms or small particles
atomized v ▷ atomize
atomizer n (pl **-s**) device for discharging a liquid in a fine spray
atomizers n ▷ atomizer
atomizes v ▷ atomize
atomizing v ▷ atomize
atoms n ▷ atom
atonal [eh-tone-al] adj (of music) not written in an established key
atone v (**-nes, -ning, -ned**) make amends (for sin or wrongdoing) > **atonement** n (pl **-s**)
atoned v ▷ atone
atonement n ▷ atone
atonements n ▷ atone
atones v ▷ atone
atoning v ▷ atone

atop *prep* (*Lit*) on top of
 atria *n* ▷ **atrium**
atrium *n* (*pl* **atria**) upper chamber of either half of the heart
atrocious *adj* extremely cruel or wicked > **atrociously** *adv*
 atrociously *adv* ▷ **atrocious**
 atrocities *n* ▷ **atrocity**
atrocity *n* (*pl* **-ties**) wickedness
 atrophied *v* ▷ **atrophy**
 atrophies *n, v* ▷ **atrophy**
atrophy [at-trof-fee] *n* (*pl* **-phies**) wasting away of an organ or part ▶ *v* (**-phies, -phying, -phied**) (cause to) waste away
 atrophying *v* ▷ **atrophy**
attach *v* (**-es, -ing, -ed**) join, fasten, or connect > **attached** *adj* (*foll. by* **to**) fond of > **attachment** *n* (*pl* **-s**)
attaché [at-tash-shay] *n* (*pl* **-s**) specialist attached to a diplomatic mission
 attached *v, adj* ▷ **attach**
 attaches *v* ▷ **attach**
 attachés *n* ▷ **attaché**
 attaching *v* ▷ **attach**
attack *v* (**-s, -ing, -ed**) launch a physical assault (against) ▶ *n* (*pl* **-s**) act of attacking > **attacker** *n* (*pl* **-s**)
 attacked *v* ▷ **attack**
 attacker *n* ▷ **attack**
 attackers *n* ▷ **attack**
 attacking *v* ▷ **attack**
 attacks *v, n* ▷ **attack**
attain *v* (**-s, -ing, -ed**) achieve or accomplish (a task or aim) > **attainable** *adj*
 attainable *adj* ▷ **attain**
 attained *v* ▷ **attain**
 attaining *v* ▷ **attain**
attainment *n* (*pl* **-s**) accomplishment
 attainments *n* ▷ **attainment**
 attains *v* ▷ **attain**
attar *n* (*pl* **-s**) fragrant oil made from roses
 attars *n* ▷ **attar**
attempt *v* (**-s, -ing, -ed**) try, make an effort ▶ *n* (*pl* **-s**) effort or endeavour
 attempted *v* ▷ **attempt**
 attempting *v* ▷ **attempt**
 attempts *v, n* ▷ **attempt**
attend *v* (**-s, -ing, -ed**) be present at
attendance *n* (*pl* **-s**) attending
 attendances *n* ▷ **attendance**
attendant *n* (*pl* **-s**) person who assists, guides, or provides a service ▶ *adj* accompanying
 attendants *n* ▷ **attendant**
 attended *v* ▷ **attend**
 attending *v* ▷ **attend**

 attends *v* ▷ **attend**
attention *n* (*pl* **-s**) concentrated direction of the mind
 attentions *n* ▷ **attention**
attentive *adj* giving attention > **attentively** *adv* > **attentiveness** *n* (*pl* **-es**)
 attentively *adv* ▷ **attentive**
 attentiveness *n* ▷ **attentive**
 attentivenesses *n* ▷ **attentive**
attenuated *adj* weakened > **attenuation** *n* (*pl* **-s**)
 attenuation *n* ▷ **attenuated**
 attenuations *n* ▷ **attenuated**
attest *v* (**-s, -ing, -ed**) affirm the truth of, be proof of > **attestation** *n* (*pl* **-s**)
 attestation *n* ▷ **attest**
 attestations *n* ▷ **attest**
 attested *v* ▷ **attest**
 attesting *v* ▷ **attest**
 attests *v* ▷ **attest**
attic *n* (*pl* **-s**) space or room within the roof of a house
 attics *n* ▷ **attic**
attire *n* (*pl* **-s**) (*Formal*) fine or formal clothes
attired *adj* dressed in a specified way
 attires *n* ▷ **attire**
attitude *n* (*pl* **-s**) way of thinking and behaving
 attitudes *n* ▷ **attitude**
attorney *n* (*pl* **-s**) person legally appointed to act for another (US & S AFR)
 attorneys *n* ▷ **attorney**
attract *v* (**-s, -ing, -ed**) arouse the interest or admiration of
 attracted *v* ▷ **attract**
 attracting *v* ▷ **attract**
attraction *n* (*pl* **-s**) power to attract > **attractive** *adj* > **attractively** *adv* > **attractiveness** *n*
 attractions *n* ▷ **attraction**
 attractive *adj* ▷ **attraction**
 attractively *adv* ▷ **attraction**
 attractiveness *n* ▷ **attraction**
 attracts *v* ▷ **attract**
 attributable *adj* ▷ **attribute**
attribute *v* (**-tes, -ting, -ted**) (*usu. foll. by* **to**) regard as belonging to or produced by ▶ *n* (*pl* **-s**) quality or feature representative of a person or thing > **attributable** *adj* > **attribution** *n* (*pl* **-s**)
 attributed *v* ▷ **attribute**
 attributes *v, n* ▷ **attribute**
 attributing *v* ▷ **attribute**
attributive *adj* (GRAMMAR) (of an adjective) preceding the noun modified
attrition *n* (*pl* **-s**) constant wearing down to weaken or destroy

attritions n ▷ attrition
attune v (-nes, -ning, -ned) adjust or accustom (a person or thing)
attuned v ▷ attune
attunes v ▷ attune
attuning v ▷ attune
atypical [eh-**tip**-ik-al] adj not typical
aubergine [oh-bur-**zheen**] n (pl -s) (BRIT) dark purple tropical fruit, cooked and eaten as a vegetable
aubergines n ▷ aubergine
aubrietia [aw-**bree**-sha] n (pl -s) trailing plant with purple flowers
aubrietias n ▷ aubrietia
auburn adj (of hair) reddish-brown
auction n (pl -s) public sale in which articles are sold to the highest bidder ▶ v (-s, -ing, -ed) sell by auction
auctioned v ▷ auction
auctioneer n (pl -s) person who conducts an auction
auctioneers n ▷ auctioneer
auctioning v ▷ auction
auctions n, v ▷ auction
audacious adj recklessly bold or daring > **audaciously** adv > **audacity** n (pl -ties)
audaciously adv ▷ audacious
audacities n ▷ audacious
audacity n ▷ audacious
audibilities n ▷ audible
audibility n ▷ audible
audible adj loud enough to be heard > **audibly** adv > **audibility** n (pl -ties)
audibly adv ▷ audible
audience n (pl -s) group of spectators or listeners
audiences n ▷ audience
audio adj of sound or hearing > **audiovisual** adj (esp. of teaching aids) involving both sight and hearing
audiovisual adj ▷ audio
audit n (pl -s) official examination of business accounts ▶ v (-s, -ing, -ted) examine (business accounts) officially > **auditor** n (pl -s)
audited v ▷ audit
auditing v ▷ audit
audition n (pl -s) test of a performer's ability for a particular role or job ▶ v (-s, -ing, -ed) test or be tested in an audition
auditioned v ▷ audition
auditioning v ▷ audition
auditions n, v ▷ audition
auditor n ▷ audit
auditoria n ▷ auditorium
auditorium n (pl -riums, -ria) area of a concert hall or theatre where the audience sits

auditoriums n ▷ auditorium
auditors n ▷ audit
auditory adj of or relating to hearing
audits n, v ▷ audit

■ **auf** n (aufs). An auf is an elf-child left in place of a human baby. Auf scores 6 points.

auger n (pl -s) tool for boring holes
augers n ▷ auger
aught pron (Obs) anything whatever
augment v (-s, -ing, -ed) increase or enlarge > **augmentation** n (pl -s)
augmentation n ▷ augment
augmentations n ▷ augment
augmented v ▷ augment
augmenting v ▷ augment
augments v ▷ augment
augur v (-s, -ing, -ed) be a sign of (future events)
augured v ▷ augur
auguries n ▷ augury
auguring v ▷ augur
augurs v ▷ augur
augury n (pl -ries) foretelling of the future
august [aw-**gust**] adj dignified and imposing
auk n (pl -s) northern sea bird with short wings and black-and-white plumage
auks n ▷ auk
aunt n (pl -s) father's or mother's sister
auntie, aunty n (pl -ties) (Informal) aunt
aunties n ▷ auntie
aunts n ▷ aunt
aunty n ▷ auntie
aura n (pl -s) distinctive air or quality of a person or thing
aural adj of or using the ears or hearing
auras n ▷ aura
aureola n ▷ aureole
aureolas n ▷ aureole
aureole, aureola n (pl -s) halo
aureoles n ▷ aureole
auricle n (pl -s) upper chamber of the heart > **auricular** adj
auricles n ▷ auricle
auricular adj ▷ auricle
aurochs n (pl aurochs) recently extinct European wild ox
aurora n (pl -ras, -rae) bands of light sometimes seen in the sky in polar regions
aurorae n ▷ aurora
auroras n ▷ aurora
auscultation n (pl -s) listening to the internal sounds of the body, usu. with a stethoscope, to help with diagnosis
auscultations n ▷ auscultation

auspice [aw-spiss] n (pl -s) (usually plural) patronage or guidance
auspices n ▷ auspice
auspicious adj showing signs of future success, favourable > **auspiciously** adv
auspiciously adv ▷ auspicious
austere adj (-r, -st) stern or severe > **austerely** adv > **austerity** n (pl -ties)
austerely adv ▷ austere
austerer adj ▷ austere
austerest adj ▷ austere
austerities n ▷ austere
austerity n ▷ austere
autarchies n ▷ autarchy
autarchy [aw-tar-kee] n (pl -chies) absolute power or autocracy
autarkies n ▷ autarky
autarky [aw-tar-kee] n (pl -kies) policy of economic self-sufficiency
authentic adj known to be real, genuine
> **authentically** adv > **authenticity** n (pl -ties)
authentically adv ▷ authentic
authenticate v (-tes, -ting, -ted) establish as genuine > **authentication** n (pl -s)
authenticated v ▷ authenticate
authenticates v ▷ authenticate
authenticating n ▷ authenticate
authentication n ▷ authenticate
authentications n ▷ authenticate
authenticities n ▷ authentic
authenticity n ▷ authentic
author n (pl -s) writer of a book etc.
> **authorship** n (pl -s)
authoritarian n (pl -s) ▶ adj (person) insisting on strict obedience to authority
authoritarians n ▷ authoritarian
authoritative adj recognized as being reliable
> **authoritatively** adv
authoritatively adv ▷ authoritative
authorities n ▷ authority
authority n (pl -ties) power to command or control others
authorization n ▷ authorize
authorizations n ▷ authorize
authorize v (-zes, -zing, -zed) give authority to
> **authorization** n (pl -s)
authorized v ▷ authorize
authorizes v ▷ authorize
authorizing v ▷ authorize
authors n ▷ author
authorship n ▷ author
authorships n ▷ author
autism n (pl -s) (PSYCHIATRY) disorder, usu. of children, characterized by lack of response to people and limited ability to communicate

> **autistic** adj
autisms n ▷ autism
autistic adj ▷ autism
autobiographical adj ▷ autobiography
autobiographically adv ▷ autobiography
autobiographies n ▷ autobiography
autobiography n (pl -phies) account of a person's life written by that person
> **autobiographical** adj > **autobiographically** adv
autocracies n ▷ autocracy
autocracy n (pl -cies) government by an autocrat
autocrat n (pl -s) ruler with absolute authority
> **autocratic** adj > **autocratically** adv
autocratic adj ▷ autocrat
autocratically adv ▷ autocrat
autocrats n ▷ autocrat
autocross n (pl -es) motor-racing over a rough course
autocrosses n ▷ autocross
autocue n (pl autocues) ® electronic television prompting device displaying a speaker's script, unseen by the audience
autocues n ▷ autocue
autogiro, autogyro n (pl -ros) self-propelled aircraft resembling a helicopter but with an unpowered rotor
autogiros n ▷ autogiro
autograph n (pl -s) handwritten signature of a (famous) person ▶ v (-s, -ing, -ed) write one's signature on or in
autographed v ▷ autograph
autographing v ▷ autograph
autographs n, v ▷ autograph
autogyro n ▷ autogiro
autogyros n ▷ autogiro
automat n (pl -s) (US) vending machine
automate v (-tes, -ting, -ted) make (a manufacturing process) automatic
> **automation** n (pl -s)
automated v ▷ automate
automates v ▷ automate
automatic adj (of a device) operating mechanically by itself ▶ n (pl -s) self-loading firearm > **automatically** adv
automatically adv ▷ automatic
automatics n ▷ automatic
automating v ▷ automate
automation n ▷ automate
automations n ▷ automate
automaton n (pl -s) robot
automatons n ▷ automaton
automats n ▷ automat
automobile n (pl -s) (US) motor car

automobiles n ▷ automobile

autonomies n ▷ autonomy

autonomous adj ▷ autonomy

autonomy n (pl -**mies**) self-government
> **autonomous** adj

autopsies n ▷ autopsy

autopsy n (pl -**sies**) examination of a corpse to determine the cause of death

autosuggestion n (pl -**s**) process in which a person unconsciously influences his or her own behaviour or beliefs

autosuggestions n ▷ autosuggestion

autumn n (pl -**s**) season between summer and winter > **autumnal** adj

autumnal adj ▷ autumn

autumns n ▷ autumn

auxiliaries n ▷ auxiliary

auxiliary adj secondary or supplementary ▶ n (pl -**ries**) person or thing that supplements or supports

avail v (-**s**, -**ing**, -**ed**) be of use or advantage (to) ▶ n (pl -**s**) use or advantage

availabilities n ▷ available

availability n ▷ available

available adj obtainable or accessible
> **availability** n (pl -**ties**)

availed v ▷ avail

availing v ▷ avail

avails v, n ▷ avail

avalanche n (pl -**s**) mass of snow or ice falling down a mountain

avalanches n ▷ avalanche

avarice [av-a-riss] n (pl -**s**) greed for wealth
> **avaricious** adj

avarices n ▷ avarice

avaricious adj ▷ avarice

avast interj (NAUT) stop

avatar n (pl -**s**) (HINDUISM) appearance of a god in animal or human form

avatars n ▷ avatar

avenge v (-**ges**, -**ging**, -**ged**) take revenge in retaliation for (harm done) or on behalf of (a person harmed) > **avenger** n (pl -**s**)

avenged v ▷ avenge

avenger n ▷ avenge

avengers n ▷ avenge

avenges n ▷ avenge

avenging v ▷ avenge

avenue n (pl -**s**) wide street

avenues n ▷ avenue

aver [av-**vur**] v (**avers**, **averring**, **averred**) state to be true

average n (pl -**s**) typical or normal amount or quality ▶ adj usual or typical ▶ v (-**ges**, -**ging**, -**ged**) calculate the average of

averaged v ▷ average

averages n, v ▷ average

averred v ▷ aver

averring v ▷ aver

avers v ▷ aver

averages n, v ▷ average

averse adj (usu. foll. by **to**) disinclined or unwilling

aversion n (pl -**s**) strong dislike

aversions n ▷ aversion

avert v (-**s**, -**ing**, -**ed**) turn away

averted v ▷ avert

averting v ▷ avert

averts v ▷ avert

aviaries n ▷ aviary

aviary n (pl -**ries**) large cage or enclosure for birds

aviation n (pl -**s**) art of flying aircraft > **aviator** n (pl -**s**)

aviations n ▷ aviation

aviator n ▷ aviation

aviators n ▷ aviation

avid adj (-**er**, -**est**) keen or enthusiastic > **avidly** adv > **avidity** n (pl -**ties**)

avider adj ▷ avid

avidest adj ▷ avid

avidities n ▷ avid

avidity n ▷ avid

avidly adv ▷ avid

avocado n (pl -**dos**) pear-shaped tropical fruit with a leathery green skin and yellowish-green flesh

avocados n ▷ avocado

avocation n (pl -**s**) (Old-fashioned) occupation

avocations n ▷ avocation

avocet n (pl -**s**) long-legged wading bird with a long slender upward-curving bill

avocets n ▷ avocet

avoid v (-**s**, -**ing**, -**ed**) prevent from happening
> **avoidable** adj > **avoidance** n (pl -**s**)

avoidable adj ▷ avoid

avoidance n ▷ avoid

avoidances n ▷ avoid

avoided v ▷ avoid

avoiding v ▷ avoid

avoids v ▷ avoid

avoirdupois [av-er-de-**poise**] n (pl -**es**) system of weights based on pounds and ounces

avoirdupoises n ▷ avoirdupois

avow v (-**s**, -**ing**, -**ed**) state or affirm > **avowal** n (pl -**s**) > **avowed** adj > **avowedly** adv

avowal n ▷ avow

avowals n ▷ avow

avowed v, adj ▷ avow

avowedly adv ▷ avow

avowing v ▷ avow

avows v ▷ avow

avuncular adj (of a man) friendly, helpful, and caring towards someone younger

aw interj. A sound people make when they're feeling sorry for someone. Aw scores 5 points.

await v (-s, -ing, -ed) wait for

awaited v ▷ await

awaiting v ▷ await

awaits v ▷ await

awake v (awakes, awaking, awoke, awoken) emerge or rouse from sleep ▶ adj not sleeping

awaken v (-s, -ing, -ed) awake

awakened v ▷ awaken

awakening v ▷ awaken

awakens v ▷ awaken

awakes v ▷ awake

awaking v ▷ awake

award v (-s, -ing, -ed) give (something, such as a prize) formally ▶ n (pl -es) something awarded, such as a prize

awarded v ▷ award

awarding v ▷ award

awards v, n ▷ award

aware adj having knowledge, informed
> **awareness** n (pl -es)

awareness n ▷ aware

awarenesses n ▷ aware

awash adv washed over by water

away adv from a place ▶ adj not present

awe n (pl -s) wonder and respect mixed with dread ▶ v (awes, awing, awed) fill with awe

awed v ▷ awe

awes n, v ▷ awe

awesome adj inspiring awe

awestruck adj filled with awe

awful adj (-ller, -llest) very bad or unpleasant

awfuller adj ▷ awful

awfullest adj ▷ awful

awfully adv in an unpleasant way

awhile adv for a brief time

awing v ▷ awe

awkward adj (-er, -est) clumsy or ungainly
> **awkwardly** adv ▷ **awkwardness** n (pl -es)

awkwarder adj ▷ awkward

awkwardest adj ▷ awkward

awkwardly adv ▷ awkward

awkwardness n ▷ awkward

awkwardnesses n ▷ awkward

awl n (pl -s) pointed tool for piercing wood, leather, etc.

awls n ▷ awl

awning n (pl -s) canvas roof supported by a frame to give protection against the weather

awnings n ▷ awning

awoke v ▷ awake

awoken v ▷ awake

awry [a-rye] adv, adj with a twist to one side, askew

ax n ▷ axe

axe, ax n (pl axes) tool with a sharp blade for felling trees or chopping wood (Informal)
▶ v (axes, axing, axed) (Informal) dismiss (employees), restrict (expenditure), or terminate (a project)

axed v ▷ axe

axes n, v ▷ axe, axis

axial adj ▷ axis

axil n (pl -s) angle where the stalk of a leaf joins a stem

axils n ▷ axil

axing v ▷ axe

axiom n (pl -s) generally accepted principle

axiomatic adj self-evident

axioms n ▷ axiom

axis n (pl axes) (imaginary) line round which a body can rotate or about which an object or geometrical figure is symmetrical > **axial** adj

axle n (pl -s) shaft on which a wheel or pair of wheels turns

axles n ▷ axle

axolotl n (pl -s) aquatic salamander of central America

axolotls n ▷ axolotl

ay interj ▷ aye

ayatollah n (pl -s) Islamic religious leader in Iran

ayatollahs n ▷ ayatollah

aye, ay interj yes ▶ n (pl -s) affirmative vote or voter

ayes n ▷ aye

azalea [az-zale-ya] n (pl -s) garden shrub grown for its showy flowers

azaleas n ▷ azalea

azimuth n (pl -s) arc of the sky between the zenith and the horizon

azimuths n ▷ azimuth

azo adj. Azo describes a kind of chemical. Azo scores 12 points, and so is a very high-scoring word for only three letters.

azulejo n (azulejos). An azulejo is a painted and glazed tile. Azulejo scores 23 points, and if you are lucky enough to have all seven letters needed for it, you'll get the 50-point bonus for using all of your tiles.

azure adj, n (pl -s) (of) the colour of a clear blue sky

azures n ▷ azure

Bb

B forms a two-letter word with every vowel except U – and with Y as well. With a B in your rack, you can play lots of short everyday words that will give you relatively high scores. The best of these is **box** (12 points), but don't forget **bay** (8), **by** (7), **bow** (8), **boy** (8), **buy** (8) and **bye** (8).

ba n (**bas**). A ba is the human soul in Egyptian mythology, shown in paintings as a bird with a human head. Ba scores 4 points.

baa v (**-s, -ing, -ed**) make the characteristic bleating sound of a sheep ▶ n (pl **-s**) cry made by a sheep
  baaed v ▷ **baa**
  baaing v ▷ **baa**
  baas v, n ▷ **baa**

babble v (**-les, -ling, -led**) talk excitedly or foolishly ▶ n (pl **-s**) muddled or foolish speech
  babbled v ▷ **babble**
  babbles v, n ▷ **babble**
  babbling v ▷ **babble**

babe n (pl **-s**) baby

babel n (pl **-s**) confused mixture of noises or voices
  babels n ▷ **babel**
  babes n ▷ **babe**
  babies n ▷ **baby**

baboon n (pl **-s**) large monkey with a pointed face and a long tail
  baboons n ▷ **baboon**

baby n (pl **-bies**) very young child or animal
  ▶ adj comparatively small of its type
  > **babyish** adj
  babyish adj ▷ **baby**

babysitter n (pl **-s**) someone who looks after children when the parents are out
  babysitters n ▷ **babysitter**

baccarat [back-a-rah] n (pl **-s**) card game involving gambling
  baccarats n ▷ **baccarat**

bacchanalia [back-a-**nail**-ee-a] n (pl **-s**) wild drunken party or orgy
  bacchanalias n ▷ **bacchanalia**

bach [batch] (NZ) n (pl **-es**) small holiday cottage
  ▶ v (**-es, -ing, -ed**) look after oneself when one's spouse is away

bached v ▷ **bach**

bachelor n (pl **-s**) unmarried man
  bachelors n ▷ **bachelor**
  baches n, v ▷ **bach**
  baching v ▷ **bach**
  bacilli n ▷ **bacillus**

bacillus [bass-ill-luss] n (pl **-li**) [-lie] rod-shaped bacterium

back n (pl **-s**) rear part of the human body, from the neck to the pelvis ▶ v (**-s, -ing, -ed**) (cause to) move backwards ▶ adv at, to, or towards the rear

backbencher n (pl **-s**) Member of Parliament who does not hold office in the government or opposition
  backbenchers n ▷ **backbencher**

backbiting n (pl **-s**) spiteful talk about an absent person
  backbitings n ▷ **backbiting**

backbone n (pl **-s**) spinal column
  backbones n ▷ **backbone**

backchat n (pl **-s**) (Informal) impudent replies
  backchats n ▷ **backchat**

backcloth n (pl **-s**) painted curtain at the back of a stage set
  backcloths n ▷ **backcloth**

backdate v (**-tes, -ting, -ted**) make (a document) effective from a date earlier than its completion
  backdated v ▷ **backdate**
  backdates v ▷ **backdate**
  backdating v ▷ **backdate**

backdrop n (pl **-s**) painted curtain at the back of a stage set
  backdrops n ▷ **backdrop**
  backed v ▷ **back**

backer n (pl **-s**) person who gives financial support
  backers n ▷ **backer**

backfire v (**-res, -ring, -red**) (of a plan) fail to

have the desired effect
backfired v ▷ **backfire**
backfires v ▷ **backfire**
backfiring v ▷ **backfire**
backgammon n (pl -s) game played with counters and dice
backgammons n ▷ **backgammon**
background n (pl -s) events or circumstances that help to explain something
backgrounds n ▷ **background**
backhand n (pl -s) (TENNIS ETC.) stroke played with the back of the hand facing the direction of the stroke
backhanded adj ambiguous or implying criticism
backhander n (pl -s) (Slang) bribe
backhanders n ▷ **backhander**
backhands n ▷ **backhand**
backing n (pl -s) support ▶ v ▷ **back**
backings n ▷ **backing**
backlash n (pl -es) sudden and adverse reaction
backlashes n ▷ **backlash**
backlog n (pl -s) accumulation of things to be dealt with
backlogs n ▷ **backlog**
backpack n (pl -s) large pack carried on the back
backpacks n ▷ **backpack**
backs n, v ▷ **back**
backside n (pl -s) (Informal) buttocks
backsides n ▷ **backside**
backslid v ▷ **backslide**
backslide v (-slides, -sliding, -slid) relapse into former bad habits > **backslider** n (pl -s)
backslider n ▷ **backslide**
backsliders n ▷ **backslide**
backslides v ▷ **backslide**
backsliding v ▷ **backslide**
backstage adv, adj behind the stage in a theatre
backstroke n (pl -s) swimming stroke performed on the back
backstrokes n ▷ **backstroke**
backtrack v (-s, -ing, -ed) return by the same route by which one has come
backtracked v ▷ **backtrack**
backtracking v ▷ **backtrack**
backtracks v ▷ **backtrack**
backup n (pl -s) support or reinforcement
backups n ▷ **backup**
backward adj directed towards the rear > **backwardness** n (pl -es)
backwardness n ▷ **backward**
backwardnesses n ▷ **backwardness**

backwards adv towards the rear
backwash n (pl -es) water washed backwards by the motion of a boat
backwashes n ▷ **backwash**
backwater n (pl -s) isolated or backward place or condition
backwaters n ▷ **backwater**
backwood n (pl -s) (usually plural) remote sparsely populated area
backwoods n ▷ **backwood**
bacon n (pl -s) salted or smoked pig meat
bacons n ▷ **bacon**
bacteria pl n (sing -rium) large group of microorganisms, many of which cause disease > **bacterial** adj
bacterial adj ▷ **bacteria**
bacteriologist n ▷ **bacteriology**
bacteriologists n ▷ **bacteriology**
bacteriology n study of bacteria > **bacteriologist** n (pl -s)
bacterium n ▷ **bacteria**
bad adj (worse, worst) of poor quality > **badly** adv > **badness** n (pl -es)
bade v ▷ **bid**
badge n (pl -s) emblem worn to show membership, rank, etc.
badger n (pl -s) nocturnal burrowing mammal of Europe, Asia, and N America with a black and white head ▶ v (-s, -ing, -ed) pester or harass
badgered v ▷ **badger**
badgering v ▷ **badger**
badgers n, v ▷ **badger**
badges n ▷ **badge**
badinage [bad-in-nahzh] n (pl -s) playful and witty conversation
badinages n ▷ **badinage**
badly adv ▷ **bad**
badminton n (pl -s) game played with rackets and a shuttlecock, which is hit back and forth over a high net
badmintons n ▷ **badminton**
badness n ▷ **bad**
badnesses n ▷ **bad**
baffle v (-les, -ling, -led) perplex or puzzle ▶ n (pl -s) device to limit or regulate the flow of fluid, light, or sound > **bafflement** n
baffled v ▷ **baffle**
bafflement n ▷ **baffle**
baffles v, n ▷ **baffle**
baffling v ▷ **baffle**
bag n (pl -s) flexible container with an opening at one end ▶ v (**bags, bagging, bagged**) put into a bag
bagatelle n (pl -s) something of little value

bagatelles n ▷ bagatelle

bagel n (pl -s) hard ring-shaped bread roll

bagels n ▷ bagel

baggage n (pl -s) suitcases packed for a journey

baggages n ▷ baggage

bagged n ▷ bag

baggier adj ▷ baggy

baggiest adj ▷ baggy

bagging n ▷ bag

baggy adj (-gier, -ggiest) (of clothes) hanging loosely

bagpipes pl n musical wind instrument with reed pipes and an inflatable bag

bags n, v ▷ bag

bah interj. Bah is something people say when they are annoyed or disgusted. Bah scores 8 points.

bail¹ n (pl -s) (LAW) money deposited with a court as security for a person's reappearance in court ▶ v (-s, -ing, -ed) pay bail for (a person)

bail², **bale** v (-s, -ing, -ed) (foll. by out) remove (water) from (a boat) (Informal)

bail³ n (pl -s) (CRICKET) either of two wooden bars across the tops of the stumps

bailed v ▷ bail¹, ²

bailey n (pl -s) outermost wall or court of a castle

baileys n ▷ bailey

bailiff n (pl -s) sheriff's officer who serves writs and summonses

bailiffs n ▷ bailiff

bailing v ▷ bail¹, ²

bails n ▷ bail¹, ³, ² v ▷ bail¹, ²

bairn n (pl -s) (SCOT) child

bairns n ▷ bairn

bait n (pl -s) piece of food on a hook or in a trap to attract fish or animals ▶ v (-s, -ing, -ed) put a piece of food on or in (a hook or trap)

baited v ▷ bait

baiting v ▷ bait

baits n, v ▷ bait

baize n (pl -s) woollen fabric used to cover billiard and card tables

baizes n ▷ baize

bake v (-kes, -king, -ked) cook by dry heat as in an oven

baked v ▷ bake

baker n (pl -s) person whose business is to make or sell bread, cakes, etc.

bakeries n ▷ bakery

bakers n ▷ baker

bakery n (pl -eries) place where bread, cakes, etc. are baked or sold

bakes v ▷ bake

baking v ▷ bake

bakkie n (pl -s) (S AFR) small truck

bakkies n ▷ bakkie

balaclava n (pl -s) close-fitting woollen hood that covers the ears and neck

balaclavas n ▷ balaclava

balalaika n (pl -s) guitar-like musical instrument with a triangular body

balalaikas n ▷ balalaika

balance n (pl -s) state in which a weight or amount is evenly distributed ▶ v (-ces, -cing, -ced) weigh in or by a balance

balanced v ▷ balance

balances n, v ▷ balance

balancing v ▷ balance

balconies n ▷ balcony

balcony n (pl -nies) platform on the outside of a building with a rail along the outer edge

bald adj (-er, -est) having little or no hair on the scalp > **baldness** n (pl -es)

balder adj ▷ bald

balderdash n (pl -es) stupid talk

balderdashes n ▷ balderdash

baldest adj ▷ bald

balding adj becoming bald

baldness n ▷ bald

baldnesses n ▷ bald

bale¹ n (pl -s) large bundle of hay or goods tightly bound together ▶ v (-les, -ling, -led) make or put into bales

bale² v ▷ bail²

baled v ▷ bale¹, ²

baleful adj vindictive or menacing > **balefully** adv

balefully adv ▷ baleful

bales n, v ▷ bale¹, ²

baling v ▷ bale¹, ²

balk, **baulk** v (-s, -ing, -ed) be reluctant to (do something)

balked v ▷ balk

balking v ▷ balk

balks v ▷ balk

ball¹ n (pl -s) round or nearly round object, esp. one used in games ▶ v (-lls, -lling, -lled) form into a ball

ball² n (pl -s) formal social function for dancing > **ballroom** n (pl -s)

ballad n (pl -s) narrative poem or song

ballads n ▷ ballad

ballast n (pl -s) substance, such as sand, used to stabilize a ship when it is not carrying cargo

ballasts n ▷ ballast

balled v ▷ ball¹

ballerina n (pl -s) female ballet dancer
  ballerinas n ▷ ballerina
ballet n (pl -s) classical style of expressive dancing based on conventional steps
  ballets n ▷ ballet
  balling v ▷ ball¹
  ballistic adj ▷ ballistics
ballistics n study of the flight of projectiles, such as bullets > **ballistic** adj
balloon n (pl -s) inflatable rubber bag used as a plaything or decoration ▶ v (-s, -ing, -ed) fly in a balloon > **balloonist** n (pl -s)
  ballooned v ▷ balloon
  ballooning v ▷ balloon
  balloonist n ▷ balloon
  balloonists n ▷ balloon
  balloons n, v ▷ balloon
ballot n (pl -s) method of voting ▶ v (-lots, -loting, -loted) vote or ask for a vote from
  balloted v ▷ ballot
  balloting v ▷ ballot
  ballots n, v ▷ ballot
ballpoint n (pl -s) pen with a tiny ball bearing as a writing point
  ballpoints n ▷ ballpoint
  ballroom n ▷ ball²
  ballrooms n ▷ ball²
  balls n ▷ ball¹, ² v ▷ ball¹
ballyhoo n (pl -s) exaggerated fuss
  ballyhoos n ▷ ballyhoo
balm n (pl -s) aromatic substance used for healing and soothing
  balmier adj ▷ balmy
  balmiest adj ▷ balmy
  balms n ▷ balm
balmy adj (-mier, -miest) (of weather) mild and pleasant
baloney, boloney n (pl -s) (Informal) nonsense
  baloneys n ▷ baloney
balsa [bawl-sa] n (pl -s) very light wood from a tropical American tree
balsam n (pl -s) soothing ointment
  balsams n ▷ balsam
  balsas n ▷ balsa
baluster n (pl -s) set of posts supporting a rail
  balusters n ▷ baluster
balustrade n (pl -s) ornamental rail supported by balusters
  balustrades n ▷ balustrade
bamboo n (pl -s) tall treelike tropical grass with hollow stems
  bamboos n ▷ bamboo
bamboozle v (-zles, -zling, -zled) (Informal) cheat or mislead
  bamboozled v ▷ bamboozle

  bamboozles v ▷ bamboozle
  bamboozling v ▷ bamboozle
ban v (-s, -nning, -nned) prohibit or forbid officially ▶ n (pl -s) official prohibition
banal [ban-nahl] adj (-er, -est) ordinary and unoriginal > **banality** n (pl -ties)
  banaler adj ▷ banal
  banalest adj ▷ banal
  banalities n ▷ banal
  banality n ▷ banal
banana n (pl -s) yellow crescent-shaped fruit
  bananas n ▷ banana
band¹ n (pl -s) group of musicians playing together > **bandsman** n (pl -men)
band² n (pl -s) strip of some material, used to hold objects
bandage n (pl -s) piece of material used to cover a wound or wrap an injured limb ▶ v (-ges, -ging, -ged) cover with a bandage
  bandaged v ▷ bandage
  bandages n, v ▷ bandage
  bandaging v ▷ bandage
  bandana n ▷ bandanna
  bandanas n ▷ bandanna
bandanna, bandana n (pl -s) large brightly coloured handkerchief or neckerchief
  bandannas n ▷ bandanna
bandicoot n (pl -s) ratlike Australian marsupial
  bandicoots n ▷ bandicoot
  bandied v ▷ bandy
  bandier adj ▷ bandy
  bandies v ▷ bandy
  bandiest n ▷ bandy
bandit n (pl -s) robber, esp. a member of an armed gang > **banditry** n
  banditry n ▷ bandit
  bandits n ▷ bandit
bandolier n (pl -s) shoulder belt for holding cartridges
  bandoliers n ▷ bandolier
  bands n ▷ band¹, ²
  bandsman n ▷ band¹
  bandsmen n ▷ band¹
bandstand n (pl -s) roofed outdoor platform for a band
  bandstands n ▷ bandstand
bandwagon n (pl -s) a party or movement that seems assured of success
  bandwagons n ▷ bandwagon
bandy adj (-dier, -diest) ▶ v (-dies, -dying, -died) exchange (words) in a heated manner
  bandying v ▷ bandy
bane n (pl -s) person or thing that causes misery or distress > **baneful** adj

baneful adj ▷ bane

banes n ▷ bane

bang n (pl -s) short loud explosive noise ▶ v (-s, -ging, -ged) hit or knock, esp. with a loud noise ▶ adv precisely

banged v ▷ bang

banger n (pl -s) (Informal) (BRIT & AUST) old decrepit car

bangers n ▷ banger

banging v ▷ bang

bangle n (pl -s) bracelet worn round the arm or the ankle

bangles n ▷ bangle

bangs n, v ▷ bang

banish v (-es, -ing, -ed) send (someone) into exile ▷ **banishment** n (pl -s)

banished v ▷ banish

banishes v ▷ banish

banishing v ▷ banish

banishment n ▷ banish

banishments n ▷ banish

banisters, bannisters pl n railing supported by posts on a staircase

banjax v (banjaxes, banjaxing, banjaxed). If you banjax something, you wreck or ruin it. This is a great word to remember, with its high-scoring combination of J and X. Look out for chances to form it from either **ban** or **ax**. Banjax scores 22 points.

banjo n (pl -jos, -joes) guitar-like musical instrument with a circular body

banjoes n ▷ banjo

banjos n ▷ banjo

bank¹ n (pl -s) institution offering services such as the safekeeping and lending of money ▶ v (-s, -ing, -ed) deposit (cash or cheques) in a bank ▷ **banking** n

bank² n (pl -s) raised mass, esp. of earth ▶ v (-s, -ing, -ed) form into a bank

bank³ n (pl -s) arrangement of switches, keys, oars, etc. in a row or in tiers

banked v ▷ bank¹,²

banker n (pl -s) manager or owner of a bank

bankers n ▷ banker

banking v ▷ bank¹,² ▶ n ▷ bank¹

banknote n (pl -s) piece of paper money

banknotes n ▷ banknote

bankrupt n (pl -s) person declared by a court to be unable to pay his or her debts ▶ adj financially ruined ▶ v (-s, -ing, -ed) make bankrupt ▷ **bankruptcy** n (pl -cies)

bankruptcies n ▷ bankrupt

bankruptcy n ▷ bankrupt

bankrupted v ▷ bankrupt

bankrupting v ▷ bankrupt

bankrupts n, v ▷ bankrupt

banks n ▷ bank¹,²,³ ▶ v ▷ bank¹,²

banksia n (pl -s) Australian evergreen tree or shrub

banksias n ▷ banksia

banned v ▷ ban

banner n (pl -s) long strip of cloth displaying a slogan, advertisement, etc.

banners n ▷ banner

banning v ▷ ban

bannisters pl n ▷ banisters

banns pl n public declaration, esp. in a church, of an intended marriage

banquet n (pl -s) elaborate formal dinner

banquets n ▷ banquet

bans v, n ▷ ban

banshee n (pl -s) (in Irish folklore) female spirit whose wailing warns of a coming death

banshees n ▷ banshee

bantam n (pl -s) small breed of chicken

bantams n ▷ bantam

bantamweight n (pl -s) boxer weighing up to 118lb (professional) or 54kg (amateur)

bantamweights n ▷ bantamweight

banter v (-s, -ing, -ed) tease jokingly ▶ n (pl -s) teasing or joking conversation

bantered v ▷ banter

bantering v ▷ banter

banters v, n ▷ banter

baobab [bay-oh-bab] n (pl -s) African tree with a thick trunk and angular branches

baobabs n ▷ baobab

baptism n (pl -s) Christian religious ceremony in which a person is immersed in or sprinkled with water as a sign of being cleansed from sin and accepted into the Church ▷ **baptismal** adj

baptismal adj ▷ baptism

baptisms n ▷ baptism

baptist n (pl -s) member of a Protestant denomination that believes in adult baptism by immersion

baptists n ▷ baptist

baptize v (-zes, -zing, -zed) perform baptism on

baptized v ▷ baptize

baptizes v ▷ baptize

baptizing v ▷ baptize

bar¹ n (pl -s) rigid length of metal, wood, etc. ▶ v (bars, barring, barred) secure with a bar ▷ **barman** (pl -men), **barmaid** (pl -s) ▶ n

bar² n (pl -s) unit of atmospheric pressure

barb n (pl -s) cutting remark ▷ **barbed** adj

barbarian n (pl -s) member of a primitive or

uncivilized people

barbarians n ▷ barbarian

barbaric adj cruel or brutal

barbarism n (pl -s) condition of being backward or ignorant

barbarisms n ▷ barbarism

barbarities n ▷ barbarity

barbarity n (pl -ties) state of being barbaric or barbarous

barbarous adj uncivilized

barbecue n (pl -s) grill on which food is cooked over hot charcoal, usu. outdoors ▶ v (-cues, -cuing, -cued) cook (food) on a barbecue

barbecued v ▷ barbecue

barbecues n, v ▷ barbecue

barbecuing v ▷ barbecue

barbed adj ▷ barb

barber n (pl -s) person who cuts men's hair and shaves beards

barbers n ▷ barber

barbiturate n (pl -s) drug used as a sedative

barbiturates n ▷ barbiturate

barbs n ▷ barb

bard n (pl -s) (Lit) poet

bards n ▷ bard

bare adj (-r, -st) unclothed, naked ▶ v (-res, -ring, -red) uncover > **bareness** n (pl -es)

bareback adj, adv (of horse-riding) without a saddle

bared v ▷ bare

barefaced adj shameless or obvious

barely adv only just

bareness n ▷ bare

barenesses n ▷ bare

barer adj ▷ bare

bares v ▷ bare

barest adj ▷ bare

bargain n (pl -s) agreement establishing what each party will give, receive, or perform in a transaction ▶ v (-s, -ing, -ed) negotiate the terms of an agreement

bargained v ▷ bargain

bargaining v ▷ bargain

bargains n, v ▷ bargain

barge n (pl -s) flat-bottomed boat used to transport freight ▶ v (-ges, -ging, -ged) (Informal) push violently

barged v ▷ barge

barges n, v ▷ barge

barging v ▷ barge

baring v ▷ bare

barista [bar-ee-sta] n (pl -s) person who makes and sells coffee in a coffee bar

baristas n ▷ barista

baritone n (pl -s) (singer with) the second

lowest adult male voice

baritones n ▷ baritone

barium n (pl -s) (CHEM) soft white metallic element

bariums n ▷ barium

bark¹ n (pl -s) loud harsh cry of a dog ▶ v (-s, -ing, -ed) (of a dog) make its typical cry

bark² n (pl -s) tough outer layer of a tree

barked v ▷ bark¹

barking v ▷ bark¹

barks n, v ▷ bark¹ ▶ n ▷ bark²

barley n (pl -s) tall grasslike plant cultivated for grain

barleys n ▷ barley

barmaid n ▷ bar¹

barmaids n ▷ bar¹

barman n ▷ bar¹

barmen n ▷ bar¹

barmier adj ▷ barmy

barmiest adj ▷ barmy

barmy adj (-mier, -miest) (Slang) insane

barn n (pl -s) large building on a farm used for storing grain

barnacle n (pl -s) shellfish that lives attached to rocks, ship bottoms, etc.

barnacles n ▷ barnacle

barney n (pl -s) (Informal) noisy fight or argument

barneys n ▷ barney

barns n ▷ barn

barometer n (pl -s) instrument for measuring atmospheric pressure > **barometric** adj

barometers n ▷ barometer

barometric adj ▷ barometer

baron n (pl -s) member of the lowest rank of nobility > **baroness** n (pl -es) **baronial** adj

baroness n ▷ baron

baronesses n ▷ baron

baronet n (pl baronets) commoner who holds the lowest hereditary British title

baronets n ▷ baronet

baronial adj ▷ baron

barons n ▷ baron

baroque [bar-rock] n (pl -s) highly ornate style of art, architecture, or music from the late 16th to the early 18th century ▶ adj ornate in style

baroques n ▷ baroque

barque [bark] n (pl -s) sailing ship, esp. one with three masts

barques n ▷ barque

barra n (pl -s) (AUST) (Informal) ▷ barramundi

barrack v (-s, -ing, -ed) criticize loudly or shout against (a team or speaker)

barracked v ▷ barrack

barracking v ▷ barrack
barracks v ▷ barrack ▶ pl n building used to accommodate military personnel
barracouta n (pl -s) large Pacific fish with a protruding lower jaw and strong teeth
barracoutas n ▷ barracouta
barracuda n (pl barracuda) tropical sea fish
barrage [bar-rahzh] n (pl -s) continuous delivery of questions, complaints, etc.
barrages n ▷ barrage
barramundi n (pl -s) edible Australian fish
barramundis n ▷ barramundi
barras n ▷ barra
barred v ▷ bar¹
barrel n (pl -s) cylindrical container with rounded sides and flat ends
barrels n ▷ barrel
barren adj (-er, -est) (of a woman or female animal) incapable of producing offspring
> **barrenness** n (pl -es)
barrener adj ▷ barren
barrenest adj ▷ barren
barrenness n ▷ barren
barrennesses n ▷ barren
barricade n (pl -s) barrier, esp. one erected hastily for defence ▶ v (-des, -ding, -ded) erect a barricade across (an entrance)
barricaded v ▷ barricade
barricades n, v ▷ barricade
barricading v ▷ barricade
barrier n (pl -s) anything that prevents access, progress, or union
barriers n ▷ barrier
barring v ▷ bar¹ ▶ prep except for
barrister n (pl -s) (BRIT, AUST & NZ) lawyer qualified to plead in a higher court
barristers n ▷ barrister
barrow¹ n (pl -s) wheelbarrow
barrow² n (pl -s) mound of earth over a prehistoric tomb
barrows n ▷ barrow¹, ²
bars n ▷ bar¹, ², v ▷ bar¹
barter v (-s, -ing, -ed) trade (goods) in exchange for other goods ▶ n (pl -s) trade by the exchange of goods
bartered v ▷ barter
bartering v ▷ barter
barters v, n ▷ barter
basalt [bass-awlt] n (pl -s) dark volcanic rock
> **basaltic** adj
basaltic adj ▷ basalt
basalts n ▷ basalt
base¹ n (pl -s) bottom or supporting part of anything ▶ v (bases, basing, based) (foll. by on or upon) use as a basis (for) > **baseless** adj

base² adj (-r, -st) dishonourable or immoral
> **baseness** n
baseball n (pl -s) team game in which runs are scored by hitting a ball with a bat then running round four bases
baseballs n ▷ baseball
based v ▷ base¹
baseless adj ▷ base¹
basement n (pl -s) partly or wholly underground storey of a building
basements n ▷ basement
baseness n ▷ base²
baser adj ▷ base²
bases n ▷ base¹, basis v ▷ base¹
basest adj ▷ base²
bash (Informal) v (-es, -ing, -ed) hit violently or forcefully ▶ n (pl bashes) heavy blow
bashed v ▷ bash
bashes v, n ▷ bash
bashful adj shy or modest > **bashfully** adv
> **bashfulness** n
bashfully adv ▷ bash
bashfulness n ▷ bash
bashing v ▷ bash
basic adj of or forming a base or basis
> **basically** adv
basically adv ▷ basic
basics pl n fundamental principles, facts, etc.
basil n (pl -s) aromatic herb used in cooking
basilica n (pl -s) rectangular church with a rounded end and two aisles
basilicas n ▷ basilica
basilisk n (pl -s) legendary serpent said to kill by its breath or glance
basilisks n ▷ basilisk
basils n ▷ basil
basin n (pl -s) round open container
basing v ▷ base¹
basins n ▷ basin
basis n (pl -ses) fundamental principles etc. from which something is started or developed
bask v (-s, -ing, -ed) lie in or be exposed to something, esp. pleasant warmth
basked v ▷ bask
basket n (pl -s) container made of interwoven strips of wood or cane > **basketwork** n (pl -s)
basketball n (pl -s) team game in which points are scored by throwing the ball through a high horizontal hoop
basketballs n ▷ basketball
baskets n ▷ basket
basketwork n ▷ basket
basketworks n ▷ basket
basking v ▷ bask

basks v ▷ bask

bass¹ [base] n (pl -es) (singer with) the lowest adult male voice ▶ adj of the lowest range of musical notes

bass² n (pl bass) edible sea fish
  basses n ▷ bass¹

bassoon n (pl -s) low-pitched woodwind instrument
  bassoons n ▷ bassoon

bastard n (pl -s) (Offens) obnoxious or despicable person
  bastards n ▷ bastard

baste¹ v (bastes, basting, basted) moisten (meat) during cooking with hot fat

baste² v (bastes, basting, basted) sew with loose temporary stitches
  basted v ▷ baste¹, ²
  bastes v ▷ baste¹, ²
  basting v ▷ baste¹, ²

bastion n (pl -s) projecting part of a fortification
  bastions n ▷ bastion

bat¹ n (pl -s) any of various types of club used to hit the ball in certain sports ▶ v (bats, batting, batted) strike with or as if with a bat

bat² n (pl -s) nocturnal mouselike flying animal

batch n (pl -es) group of people or things dealt with at the same time
  batches n ▷ batch

bath n (pl -s) large container in which to wash the body ▶ pl public swimming pool ▶ v (-s, -ing, -ed) wash in a bath

bathe v (-thes, -thing, -thed) swim in open water for pleasure > bather n (pl -s)
  bathed v ▷ bath ▷ bathe
  bather n ▷ bathe
  bathers n ▷ bathe
  bathes v ▷ bath ▷ bathe
  bathing v ▷ bath ▷ bathe

bathos [bay-thoss] n (pl -es) sudden ludicrous change in speech or writing from a serious subject to a trivial one
  bathoses n ▷ bathos

bathroom n (pl -s) room with a bath, sink, and usu. a toilet
  bathrooms n ▷ bathe
  baths n, v ▷ bath

batik [bat-teek] n (pl -s) process of printing fabric using wax to cover areas not to be dyed
  batiks n ▷ batik

batman n (pl -men) officer's servant in the armed forces
  batmen n ▷ batman

baton n (pl -s) thin stick used by the conductor of an orchestra

batons n ▷ baton

bats n ▷ bat¹, ² ▶ v ▷ bat¹

batsman n (pl -men) (CRICKET) person who bats or specializes in batting
  batsmen n ▷ batsman

battalion n (pl -s) army unit consisting of three or more companies
  battalions n ▷ battalion

batted v ▷ bat¹

batten n (pl -s) strip of wood fixed to something, esp. to hold it in place
  battens n ▷ batten

batter¹ v (-s, -ing, -ed) hit repeatedly

batter² n (pl -s) mixture of flour, eggs, and milk, used in cooking
  battered v ▷ batter¹
  batteries n ▷ battery
  battering v ▷ batter¹
  batters v, n ▷ batter¹, ²

battery n (pl -teries) device that produces electricity in a torch, radio, etc. ▶ adj kept in series of cages for intensive rearing
  battier adj ▷ batty
  battiest adj ▷ batty
  batting adj ▷ bat¹

battle n (pl -s) fight between large armed forces ▶ v (battles, battling, battled) struggle
  battled v ▷ battle

battlement n (pl -s) wall with gaps along the top for firing through
  battlements n ▷ battlement
  battles n, v ▷ battle

battleship n (pl -s) large heavily armoured warship
  battleships n ▷ battleship
  battling v ▷ battle

batty adj (-tier, -tiest) (Slang) eccentric or crazy

bauble n (pl -s) trinket of little value
  baubles n ▷ bauble

bauera n (pl -s) small evergreen Australian shrub
  baueras n ▷ bauera

baulk v (-s, -ing, -ed) ▷ balk
  baulked v ▷ baulk
  baulking v ▷ baulk
  baulks v ▷ baulk

bauxite n (pl -s) claylike substance that is the chief source of aluminium
  bauxites n ▷ bauxite
  bawdier adj ▷ bawdy
  bawdiest adj ▷ bawdy

bawdy adj (-ier, -iest) (of writing etc.) containing humorous references to sex

bawl v (-s, -ing, -ed) shout or weep noisily
  bawled v ▷ bawl

bawling v ▷ **bawl**

bawls v ▷ **bawl**

bay[1] n (pl -s) stretch of coastline that curves inwards

bay[2] n (pl -s) recess in a wall

bay[3] v (-s, -ing, -ed) howl in deep prolonged tones

bay[4] n (pl -s) Mediterranean laurel tree

bay[5] adj, n (pl -s) reddish-brown (horse)

bayed v ▷ **bay**[3]

baying v ▷ **bay**[3]

bayonet n (pl -s) sharp blade that can be fixed to the end of a rifle ▶ v (-nets, -neting, -neted) stab with a bayonet

bayoneted v ▷ **bayonet**

bayoneting v ▷ **bayonet**

bayonets n, v ▷ **bayonet**

bays n ▷ **bay**[1, 2, 4, 5] ▶ v[3]

bazaar n (pl -s) sale in aid of charity

bazaars n ▷ **bazaar**

bazooka n (pl -s) portable rocket launcher that fires an armour-piercing projectile

bazookas n ▷ **bazooka**

be v (present sing (1st person **am**) (2nd person **are**) (3rd person **is**) (present pl **are**) (past sing (1st person **was**) (2nd person **were**) (3rd person **was**) (past pl **were**) (present participle **being**) (past participle **been**) exist or live

beach n (pl -es) area of sand or pebbles on a shore ▶ v (-es, -ing, -ed) run or haul (a boat) onto a beach

beached v ▷ **beach**

beaches n, v ▷ **beach**

beachhead n (pl -s) beach captured by an attacking army on which troops can be landed

beachheads v ▷ **beachhead**

beaching v ▷ **beach**

beacon n (pl -s) fire or light on a hill or tower, used as a warning

beacons n ▷ **beacon**

bead n (pl -s) small piece of plastic, wood, etc., pierced for threading on a string to form a necklace etc. > **beaded** adj

beaded n ▷ **bead**

beadier adj ▷ **beady**

beadiest adj ▷ **beady**

beading n strip of moulding used for edging furniture

beads n ▷ **bead**

beady adj (-ier, -iest) small, round, and glittering

beagle n (pl -s) small hound with short legs and drooping ears

beagles n ▷ **beagle**

beak[1] n (pl -s) projecting horny jaws of a bird > **beaky** adj (-ier, -iest)

beak[2] n (pl -s) (BRIT, AUST & NZ) (Slang) judge, magistrate, or headmaster

beaker n (pl -s) large drinking cup

beakers n ▷ **beaker**

beakier adj ▷ **beak**[1]

beakiest adj ▷ **beak**[1]

beaks n ▷ **beak**[1, 2]

beaky adj ▷ **beak**[1]

beam n (pl -s) broad smile ▶ v (-s, -ing, -ed) smile broadly

beamed v ▷ **beam**

beaming v ▷ **beam**

beams n, v ▷ **beam**

bean n (pl -s) seed or pod of various plants, eaten as a vegetable or used to make coffee etc.

beanie n (pl -s) close-fitting woollen hat

beanies n ▷ **beanie**

beans n ▷ **bean**

bear[1] v (**bears, bearing, bore, borne**) support or hold up (passive **born**) > **bearable** adj

bear[2] n (pl -s) large heavy mammal with a shaggy coat

bearable adj ▷ **bear**[1]

beard n (pl -s) hair growing on the lower parts of a man's face > **bearded** adj

bearded adj ▷ **beard**

beards n ▷ **beard**

bearer n (pl -s) person who carries, presents, or upholds something

bearers n ▷ **bearer**

bearing n (pl -s) relevance (to) ▶ pl sense of one's own relative position ▶ v ▷ **bear**[1]

bearings n ▷ **bearing**

bears v ▷ **bear**[1] ▶ n ▷ **bear**[2]

bearskin n (pl -s) tall fur helmet worn by some British soldiers

bearskins n ▷ **bearskin**

beast n (pl -s) large wild animal

beastliness n ▷ **beastly**

beastly adj unpleasant or disagreeable > **beastliness** n

beasts n ▷ **beast**

beat v (**beats, beating, beat, beaten** or **beat**) hit hard and repeatedly ▶ n (pl **beats**) regular throb

beaten v ▷ **beat**

beatific adj displaying great happiness

beatification n ▷ **beatify**

beatifications n ▷ **beatify**

beatified v ▷ **beatify**

beatifies v ▷ **beatify**

beatify [bee-at-if-fie] v (-fies, -fying, -fied) (RC

CHURCH) declare (a dead person) to be among the blessed in heaven: the first step towards canonization > **beatification** n (pl -s)
  beatifying v ▷ beatify
  beating v ▷ beat
beatitude n (pl -s) (CHRISTIANITY) any of the blessings on the poor, meek, etc., in the Sermon on the Mount
  beatitudes n ▷ beatitude
  beats v, n ▷ beat
beau [boh] n (pl **beaux, beaus**) boyfriend or admirer
  beaus n ▷ beau
beautician n (pl -s) person who gives beauty treatments professionally
  beauticians n ▷ beautician
  beauties n ▷ beauty
  beautification n ▷ beautify
  beautified v ▷ beautify
  beautifies v ▷ beautify
beautiful adj very attractive to look at
  > **beautifully** adv
  beautifully adv ▷ beautiful
beautify v (-fies, -fying, -fied) make beautiful
  > **beautification** n
  beautifying v ▷ beautify
beauty n (pl -ties) combination of all the qualities of a person or thing that delight the senses and mind
  beaus n ▷ beau
beaver n (pl -s) amphibious rodent with a big flat tail
  beavers n ▷ beaver
becalmed adj (of a sailing ship) motionless through lack of wind
  became v ▷ become
because conj on account of the fact that
beck n (pl -s) (N ENGLISH) stream
beckon v (-s, -ing, -ed) summon with a gesture
  beckoned v ▷ beckon
  beckoning v ▷ beckon
  beckons v ▷ beckon
  becks n ▷ beck
become v (-coming, -came, -come) come to be
becoming adj attractive or pleasing
bed n (pl -s) piece of furniture on which to sleep
  > **bedroom** n (pl -s)
bedding n (pl -s) sheets and covers that are used on a bed
  beddings n ▷ bedding
bedevil v (-s, -illing, -illed) harass, confuse, or torment
  bedevilled v ▷ bedevil
  bedevilling v ▷ bedevil
  bedevils v ▷ bedevil

bedlam n (pl -s) noisy confused situation
  bedlams n ▷ bedlam
bedpan n (pl -s) shallow bowl used as a toilet by bedridden people
  bedpans n ▷ bedpan
bedraggled adj untidy, wet, or dirty
bedridden adj confined to bed because of illness or old age
bedrock n (pl -s) solid rock beneath the surface soil
  bedrocks n ▷ bedrock
  bedroom n ▷ bed
  bedrooms n ▷ bed
  beds n ▷ bed
bedsit, bedsitter n (pl -s) furnished sitting room with a bed
  bedsits n ▷ bedsit
  bedsitters n ▷ bedsit
bee n (pl -s) insect that makes wax and honey
beech n (pl -es) tree with a smooth greyish bark
  beeches n ▷ beech
beef n (pl **beeves**) flesh of a cow, bull, or ox
beefburger n (pl -s) flat grilled or fried cake of minced beef
  beefburgers n ▷ beefburger
beefeater n (pl -s) yeoman warder at the Tower of London
  beefeaters n ▷ beefeater
  beefier adj ▷ beefy
  beefiest adj ▷ beefy
beefy adj (-fier, -fiest) like beef
beehive n (pl -s) structure in which bees live
  beehives n ▷ beehive
  been v ▷ be
beep n (pl -s) high-pitched sound, like that of a car horn ▶ v (-s, -ing, -ed) (cause to) make this noise
  beeped v ▷ beep
  beeping v ▷ beep
  beeps n, v ▷ beep
beer n (pl -s) alcoholic drink brewed from malt and hops > **beery** (-ier, -iest) ▶ adj
  beerier adj ▷ beer
  beeriest adj ▷ beer
  beers n ▷ beer
  beery adj ▷ beer
  bees n ▷ bee
beeswax n (pl -es) wax secreted by bees, used in polishes etc.
  beeswaxes n ▷ beeswax
beet n (pl -s) plant with an edible root and leaves
beetle n (pl -s) insect with a hard wing cover on its back

beetles n ▷ beetle

beetroot n (pl -s) type of beet plant with a dark red root

beetroots n ▷ beetroot

beets n ▷ beet

beeves n ▷ beef

befall v (-falls, -falling, -fell, -fallen) (Old-fashioned) happen to (someone)

befallen v ▷ befall

befalling v ▷ befall

befalls v ▷ befall

befell v ▷ befall

befit v (-fits, -fitting, -fitted) be appropriate or suitable for > befitting adj

befits v ▷ befit

befitted v ▷ befit

befitting v, adj ▷ befit

before conj, prep adv indicating something earlier in time, in front of, or preferred to

beforehand adv in advance

befriend v (-s, -ing, -ed) become friends with

befriended v ▷ befriend

befriending v ▷ befriend

befriends v ▷ befriend

beg v (begs, begging, begged) solicit (for money or food), esp. in the street

began v ▷ begin

begat v ▷ beget

beget v (-gets, -getting, -got or -gat; -gotten or -got) (Old-fashioned) cause or create

begets v ▷ beget

begetting v ▷ beget

beggar n (pl s) person who lives by begging > beggarly adj > beggarliness n

beggarliness n ▷ beggar

beggarly adj ▷ beggar

beggars n ▷ beggar

begged v ▷ beg

begging v ▷ beg

begin v (-gins, -ginning, -gan, -gun) start > beginning n (pl -s)

beginner n (pl -s) person who has just started learning to do something

beginners n ▷ begin

beginning v, n ▷ begin

begins v ▷ begin

begonia n (pl -s) tropical plant with waxy flowers

begonias n ▷ begonia

begot v ▷ beget

begotten v ▷ beget

begrudge v (-grudges, -grudging, -grudged) envy (someone) the possession of something

begrudged v ▷ begrudge

begrudges v ▷ begrudge

begrudging v ▷ begrudge

begs v ▷ beg

beguile [big-gile] v (-guiles, -guiling, -guiled) cheat or mislead > beguiling adj

beguiled v ▷ beguile

beguiles v ▷ beguile

beguiling v, adj ▷ beguile

begun v ▷ begin

behalf n in the interest of or for the benefit of

behave v (-haves, -having, -haved) act or function in a particular way

behaved v ▷ behave

behaves v ▷ behave

behaving v ▷ behave

behaviour n (pl -s) manner of behaving

behaviours n ▷ behaviour

behead v (-s, -ing, -ed) remove the head from

beheaded v ▷ behead

beheading v ▷ behead

beheads v ▷ behead

beheld v ▷ behold

behest n (pl -s) order or earnest request

behests n ▷ behest

behind prep, adv indicating position to the rear, lateness, responsibility, etc. ▶ n (pl -s) (Informal) buttocks

behinds n ▷ behind

behold v (-holds, -holding, -held) (Old-fashioned) look (at) > beholder n (pl -s)

beholden adj indebted or obliged

beholder n ▷ behold

beholders n ▷ behold

beholding v ▷ behold

beholds v ▷ behold

behove v (-hoves, -hoving, -hoved) (Old-fashioned) be necessary or fitting for

behoved v ▷ behove

behoves v ▷ behove

behoving v ▷ behove

beige adj pale brown

being n (pl -s) state or fact of existing ▶ v ▷ be

beings n ▷ being

belabour v (-s, -ing, -ed) attack verbally or physically

belaboured v ▷ belabour

belabouring v ▷ belabour

belabours v ▷ belabour

belated adj late or too late > belatedly adv

belatedly adv ▷ belated

belch v (-es, -ing, -ed) expel wind from the stomach noisily through the mouth ▶ n (pl belches) act of belching

belched v ▷ belch

belches v, n ▷ belch

belching v ▷ belch

beleaguered adj struggling against difficulties or criticism
 belfries n ▷ **belfry**
belfry n (pl -**fries**) part of a tower where bells are hung
belie v (**belies, belying, belied**) show to be untrue
 belied v ▷ **belie**
belief n (pl -s) faith or confidence
 beliefs n ▷ **belief**
 belies v ▷ **belie**
 believable adj ▷ **believe**
believe v (-**lieves, -lieving, -lieved**) accept as true or real > **believable** adj > **believer** n (pl -s)
 believed v ▷ **believe**
 believer n ▷ **believe**
 believers n ▷ **believe**
 believes v ▷ **believe**
 believing v ▷ **believe**
belittle v (-**ttles, -ttling, -ttled**) treat as having little value or importance
 belittled v ▷ **belittle**
 belittles v ▷ **belittle**
 belittling v ▷ **belittle**
bell n (pl -s) hollow, usu. metal, cup-shaped instrument that emits a ringing sound when struck
belladonna n (pl -s) (drug obtained from) deadly nightshade
 belladonnas n ▷ **belladonna**
bellbird n (pl -s) Australasian bird with bell-like call
 bellbirds n ▷ **bellbird**
belle n (pl -s) beautiful woman, esp. the most attractive woman at a function
 belles n ▷ **belle**
bellicose adj warlike and aggressive
 bellied v ▷ **belly**
 bellies n, v ▷ **belly**
 belligerence n ▷ **belligerent**
belligerent adj hostile and aggressive ▶ n (pl -s) person or country engaged in war > **belligerence** n
 belligerents n ▷ **belligerent**
bellow v (-s, -ing, -ed) make a low deep cry like that of a bull ▶ n (pl -s) loud deep roar
 bellowed v ▷ **bellow**
 bellowing v ▷ **bellow**
bellows v, n ▷ **bellow** ▶ pl n instrument for pumping a stream of air into something
 bells n ▷ **bell**
belly n (pl -**lies**) part of the body of a vertebrate which contains the intestines ▶ v (-**lies, -lying, -lied**) (cause to) swell out
bellyful n (pl -s) (Slang) more than one can

tolerate
 bellyfuls n ▷ **bellyful**
 bellying v ▷ **belly**
belong v (-s, -ing, -ed) (foll. by **to**) be the property of
 belonged v ▷ **belong**
 belonging v ▷ **belong**
belongings pl n personal possessions
 belongs v ▷ **belong**
beloved adj dearly loved ▶ n (pl -s) person dearly loved
 beloveds n ▷ **beloved**
below prep, adv at or to a position lower than, under
belt n (pl -s) band of cloth, leather, etc., worn usu. around the waist ▶ v (-s, -ing, -ed) fasten with a belt
 belted v ▷ **belt**
 belting v ▷ **belt**
 belts n, v ▷ **belt**
 belying v ▷ **belie**
bemoan v (-s, -ing, -ed) express sorrow or dissatisfaction about
 bemoaned v ▷ **bemoan**
 bemoaning v ▷ **bemoan**
 bemoans v ▷ **bemoan**
bemused adj puzzled or confused
bench n (pl -es) long seat
 benches n ▷ **bench**
benchmark n (pl -s) criterion by which to measure something
 benchmarks n ▷ **benchmark**
bend v (-s, -ing, bent) (cause to) form a curve ▶ n curved part > **bendy** adj (-**dier, -diest**) > **bendiness** n (pl -es)
 bendier adj ▷ **bend**
 bendiest adj ▷ **bend**
 bendiness n ▷ **bend**
 bendinesses n ▷ **bend**
 bending v ▷ **bend**
 bends v ▷ **bend** ▶ pl n (Informal) decompression sickness
 bendy adj ▷ **bend**
beneath adv, prep below
benediction n (pl -s) prayer for divine blessing
 benedictions n ▷ **benediction**
 benefaction n ▷ **benefactor**
 benefactions n ▷ **benefactor**
benefactor, benefactress n (pl -s, -esses) someone who supports a person or institution by giving money > **benefaction** n (pl -s)
 benefactors n ▷ **benefactor**
 benefactress n ▷ **benefactor**
 benefactresses n ▷ **benefactor**

beneficence n ▷ **beneficent**
beneficent [bin-**eff**-iss-ent] adj charitable or generous > **beneficence** n
beneficial adj helpful or advantageous
beneficiaries n ▷ **beneficiary**
beneficiary n (pl -ciaries) person who gains or benefits
benefit n (pl -s) something that improves or promotes ▶ v (-s, -fiting, -fited) do or receive good
benefited v ▷ **benefit**
benefiting v ▷ **benefit**
benefits n, v ▷ **benefit**
benevolence n (pl -s) inclination to do good > **benevolently** adv
benevolences n ▷ **benevolence**
benevolent adj ▷ **benevolence**
benevolently adv ▷ **benevolence**
benighted adj ignorant or uncultured
benign [bin-**nine**] adj showing kindliness > **benignly** adv
benignly adv ▷ **benign**
bent v ▷ **bend** ▶ adj curved ▶ n (pl -s) personal inclination or aptitude
bento n (pl -s) thin lightweight box divided into compartments, which contain small separate dishes comprising a Japanese meal
bentos n ▷ **bento**
bents n ▷ **bent**
benzene n (pl -s) flammable poisonous liquid used as a solvent, insecticide, etc.
benzenes n ▷ **benzene**
bequeath v (-s, -ing, -ed) dispose of (property) as in a will
bequeathed v ▷ **bequeath**
bequeathing v ▷ **bequeath**
bequeaths v ▷ **bequeath**
bequest n (pl -s) legal gift of money or property by someone who has died
bequests v ▷ **bequest**
berate v (-ates, -ating, -ated) scold harshly
berated v ▷ **berate**
berates v ▷ **berate**
berating v ▷ **berate**
bereaved adj having recently lost a close friend or relative through death > **bereavement** n (pl -s)
bereavements n ▷ **bereavement**
bereft adj (foll. by of) deprived
beret [**ber**-ray] n (pl -s) round flat close-fitting brimless cap
berets n ▷ **beret**
berg[1] n (pl -s) iceberg
berg[2] n (pl -s) (S AFR) mountain
bergamot n (pl -s) small Asian tree, the fruit of

which yields an oil used in perfumery
bergamots n ▷ **bergamot**
bergs n ▷ **berg**[1, 2]
beriberi n (pl -s) disease caused by vitamin B deficiency
beriberis n ▷ **beriberi**
berk n (pl -s) (BRIT, AUST & NZ) (Slang) stupid person
berks n ▷ **berk**
berm n (pl -s) (NZ) narrow grass strip between the road and the footpath in a residential area
berms n ▷ **berm**
berries n ▷ **berry**
berry n (pl -ries) small soft stoneless fruit
berserk adj violent or destructive
berth n (pl -s) bunk in a ship or train ▶ v (-s, -ing, -ed) dock (a ship)
berthed v ▷ **berth**
berthing v ▷ **berth**
berths n, v ▷ **berth**
beryl n (pl -s) hard transparent mineral
beryllium n (pl -s) (CHEM) toxic silvery-white metallic element
berylliums n ▷ **beryllium**
beryls n ▷ **beryl**
beseech v (-seeches, -seeching, -sought or -seeched) ask earnestly; beg
beseeched v ▷ **beseech**
beseeches v ▷ **beseech**
beseeching v ▷ **beseech**
beset v (-sets, -setting, -set) trouble or harass constantly
besets v ▷ **beset**
besetting v ▷ **beset**
beside prep at, by, or to the side of
besides adv, prep in addition
besiege v (-sieges, -sieging, -sieged) surround with military forces
besieged v ▷ **besiege**
besieges v ▷ **besiege**
besieging v ▷ **besiege**
besotted adj infatuated
besought v ▷ **beseech**
bespeak v (-speaks, -speaking, -spoke, -spoken) indicate or suggest
bespeaking v ▷ **bespeak**
bespeaks v ▷ **bespeak**
bespoke v ▷ **bespeak** ▶ adj (esp. of a suit) made to the customer's specifications
bespoken v ▷ **bespeak**
best adj most excellent of a particular group etc. ▶ adv in a manner surpassing all others ▶ n (pl -s) most outstanding or excellent person, thing, or group in a category

bestial adj brutal or savage ▷ **bestiality** n (pl -ities)
  bestialities n ▷ bestial
  bestiality n ▷ bestial
bestir v (-stirs, -stirring, -stirred) cause (oneself) to become active
  bestirred v ▷ bestir
  bestirring v ▷ bestir
  bestirs v ▷ bestir
bestow v (-s, -ing, -ed) present (a gift) or confer (an honour) ▷ **bestowal** n (pl -s)
  bestowal n ▷ bestow
  bestowals n ▷ bestow
  bestowed v ▷ bestow
  bestowing v ▷ bestow
  bestows v ▷ bestow
  bestridden v ▷ bestride
bestride v (-strides, -striding, -strode, -stridden) have or put a leg on either side of
  bestrides v ▷ bestride
  bestriding v ▷ bestride
  bestrode v ▷ bestride
  bests n ▷ best
bestseller n (pl -s) book or other product that has sold in great numbers
  bestsellers n ▷ bestseller
bet n (pl -s) the act of staking a sum of money or other stake on the outcome of an event ▷ v (bets, betting, bet or betted) make or place (a bet)
betel [bee-tl] n (pl -s) Asian climbing plant, the leaves and nuts of which can be chewed
  betels n ▷ betels
betide v (-tides, -tiding, -tided) happen (to)
  betided v ▷ betide
  betides v ▷ betide
  betiding v ▷ betide
betoken v (-s, -ing, -ed) indicate or signify
  betokened v ▷ betoken
  betokening v ▷ betoken
  betokens v ▷ betoken
betray v (-s, -ing, -ed) hand over or expose (one's nation, friend, etc.) treacherously to an enemy ▷ **betrayal** n (pl -s) ▷ **betrayer** n (pl -s)
  betrayal n ▷ betray
  betrayals n ▷ betray
  betrayed v ▷ betray
  betrayer n ▷ betray
  betrayers n ▷ betray
  betraying v ▷ betray
  betrays v ▷ betray
betrothal n ▷ betrothed
  betrothals n ▷ betrothed
betrothed adj engaged to be married
  ▷ **betrothal** n (pl -s)

bets n, v ▷ bet
  betted v ▷ bet
better adj more excellent than others ▷ adv in a more excellent manner ▷ pl n one's superiors ▷ v (-s, -ing, -ed) improve upon
  bettered v ▷ better
  bettering v ▷ better
  betters n, v ▷ better
  betting v ▷ bet
bettong n (pl -s) short-nosed rat kangaroo
  bettongs n ▷ bettong
between prep, adv indicating position in the middle, alternatives, etc.
betwixt prep, adv (Old-fashioned) between
bevel n (pl -s) slanting edge ▷ v (-els, -elling, -elled) cut a bevel on (a piece of timber etc.)
  bevelled v ▷ bevel
  bevelling v ▷ bevel
  bevels n, v ▷ bevel
beverage n (pl -s) drink
  beverages n ▷ beverage
  bevies n ▷ bevy
bevy n (pl bevies) flock or group
bewail v (-s, -ing, -ed) express great sorrow over
  bewailed v ▷ bewail
  bewailing v ▷ bewail
  bewails v ▷ bewail
beware v (-wares, -waring, -wared) be on one's guard (against)
  bewared v ▷ beware
  bewares v ▷ beware
  bewaring v ▷ beware
bewilder v (-s, -ing, -ed) confuse utterly ▷ **bewildering** adj ▷ **bewilderment** n (pl -s)
  bewildered v ▷ bewilder
  bewildering v, adj ▷ bewilder
  bewilderment n ▷ bewilder
  bewilderments n ▷ bewilder
  bewilders v ▷ bewilder
bewitch v (-es, -ing, -ed) attract and fascinate ▷ **bewitching** adj
  bewitched v ▷ bewitch
  bewitches v ▷ bewitch
  bewitching v, adj ▷ bewitch
      bey n (beys). A bey was an official in the Ottoman empire, and scores 8 points.
beyond prep at or to a point on the other side of ▷ adv at or to the far side of something
      bez n (bezes). A bez is the second spike of a deer's antler. This is a really handy word when you have Z on your rack. Bez scores 14 points.
      bezique n (beziques). Bezique is a card game; if you're lucky enough to be able

…… to play it, you'll score 27 points.

bi *adj, n (pl -s)* short for bisexual

biannual *adj* occurring twice a year
> **biannually** *adv*
  biannually *adv* ▷ **biannual**

bias *n (pl -es)* mental tendency, esp. prejudice
▶ *v (-ases, -asing, -ased or -asses or -assing or -assed)* cause to have a bias > **biased, biassed** *adj*
  biased *v* ▷ **bias**
  biases *n, v* ▷ **bias**
  biasing *v* ▷ **bias**
  biassed *v* ▷ **bias**
  biasses *n, v* ▷ **bias**
  biassing *v* ▷ **bias**

bib *n (pl -s)* piece of cloth or plastic worn to protect a young child's clothes when eating

bible *n (pl -s)* book regarded as authoritative
> **biblical** *adj*
  bibles *n* ▷ **bible**
  biblical *n* ▷ **bible**
  bibliographer *n* ▷ **bibliography**
  bibliographers *n* ▷ **bibliography**
  bibliographies *n* ▷ **bibliography**

bibliography *n (pl -phies)* list of books on a subject > **bibliographer** *n (pl -s)*

bibliophile *n (pl -s)* person who collects or is fond of books
  bibliophiles *n* ▷ **bibliophile**
  bibs *n* ▷ **bib**

bibulous *adj* addicted to alcohol

bicarbonate *n (pl -s)* salt of carbonic acid
  bicarbonates *n* ▷ **bicarbonate**
  bicentenaries *n* ▷ **bicentenary**

bicentenary *n (pl -naries)* 200th anniversary

biceps *n (pl -es)* muscle with two origins, esp. the muscle that flexes the forearm

bicker *v (-s, -ing, -ed)* argue over petty matters
  bickered *v* ▷ **bicker**
  bickering *v* ▷ **bicker**
  bickers *v* ▷ **bicker**

bicycle *n (pl -s)* vehicle with two wheels, one behind the other, pedalled by the rider
  bicycles *n* ▷ **bicycle**

bid *v (bids, bidding, bade, bidden)* say (a greeting) *(past bid)* ▶ *n (pl -s)* offer of a specified amount > **bidder** *n (pl -s)*

biddable *adj* obedient
  bidden *v* ▷ **bid**
  bidder *n* ▷ **bid**
  bidders *n* ▷ **bid**

bidding *n (pl -s)* command ▶ *v* ▷ **bid**

bide *v (bides, biding, bided)* wait patiently for an opportunity
  bided *v* ▷ **bide**

  bides *v* ▷ **bide**

bidet [**bee**-day] *n (pl -s)* low basin for washing the genital area
  bidets *n* ▷ **bidet**
  biding *v* ▷ **bide**
  bids *v, n* ▷ **bid**

biennial *adj* occurring every two years ▶ *n (pl -s)* plant that completes its life cycle in two years
  biennials *n* ▷ **biennial**

bier *n (pl -s)* stand on which a corpse or coffin rests before burial
  biers *n* ▷ **bier**

bifocals *pl n* spectacles with lenses permitting near and distant vision

big *adj (bigger, biggest)* of considerable size, height, number, or capacity ▶ *adv* on a grand scale
  bigamies *n* ▷ **bigamy**
  bigamist *n* ▷ **bigamy**
  bigamists *n* ▷ **bigamy**
  bigamous *adj* ▷ **bigamy**
  bigamously *adv* ▷ **bigamy**

bigamy *n (pl -mies)* crime of marrying a person while still legally married to someone else > **bigamist** *n (pl -s)* > **bigamous** *adj*
> **bigamously** *adv*
  bigger *adj* ▷ **big**
  biggest *adj* ▷ **big**

bighead *n (pl -s)* (*Informal*) conceited person
> **bigheaded** *adj*
  bigheaded *n* ▷ **bighead**
  bigheads *n* ▷ **bighead**

bigot *n (pl -s)* person who is intolerant, esp. regarding religion or race > **bigoted** *adj*
> **bigotry** *n (pl -tries)*
  bigoted *adj* ▷ **bigot**
  bigotries *n* ▷ **bigot**
  bigotry *n* ▷ **bigot**
  bigots *n* ▷ **bigot**

bigwig *n (pl -s)* (*Informal*) important person
  bigwigs *n* ▷ **bigwig**

    bijou *n* (**bijoux**). A bijou is an intricate trinket. The plural form, bijoux, uses an X and allows you to score 22 points.

bike *n (pl -s)* (*Informal*) bicycle or motorcycle
  bikes *n* ▷ **bike**

bikini *n (pl -s)* woman's brief two-piece swimming costume
  bikinis *n* ▷ **bikini**

bilateral *adj* affecting or undertaken by two parties > **bilaterally** *adv*
  bilaterally *adv* ▷ **bilateral**
  bilberries *n* ▷ **bilberry**

bilberry *n (pl -berries)* bluish-black edible berry

bilbies n ▷ **bilby**

bilby n (pl -**bies**) Australian marsupial with long pointed ears and grey fur

bile n (pl -**s**) bitter yellow fluid secreted by the liver

biles n ▷ **bile**

bilge n (pl -**s**) (Informal) nonsense

bilges n ▷ **bilge**

bilingual adj involving or using two languages

bilious adj sick, nauseous > **biliousness** n

biliousness n ▷ **bilious**

bill[1] n (pl -**s**) statement of money owed for goods or services supplied ▶ v (-**s**, -**ing**, -**ed**) send or present a bill to

bill[2] n (pl -**s**) bird's beak

billabong n (pl -**s**) (AUST) stagnant pool in an intermittent stream

billabongs n ▷ **billabong**

billed v ▷ **bill**[1]

billet v (-**lets**, -**leting**, -**leted**) assign a lodging to (a soldier) ▶ n (pl -**s**) accommodation for a soldier in civil lodgings

billeted v ▷ **billet**

billeting v ▷ **billet**

billets v, n ▷ **billet**

billhook n (pl -**s**) tool with a hooked blade, used for chopping etc.

billhooks n ▷ **billhook**

billiards n game played on a table with balls and a cue

billies n ▷ **billy**

billing v ▷ **bill**[1]

billion n (pl -**s**) one thousand million > **billionth** adj

billions n ▷ **billion**

billionth adj ▷ **billion**

billow n (pl -**s**) large sea wave ▶ v (-**s**, -**ing**, -**ed**) rise up or swell out > **billowy**, **billowing** adj

billowed v ▷ **billow**

billowing v, adj ▷ **billow**

billows n, v ▷ **billow**

billowy adj ▷ **billow**

bills n ▷ **bill**[1, 2] ▶ v ▷ **bill**[1]

billy, **billycan** n (pl -**lies**, -**s**) metal can or pot for cooking on a camp fire

billycan n ▷ **billy**

billycans n ▷ **billy**

biltong n (pl -**s**) (S AFR) strips of dried meat

biltongs n ▷ **biltong**

bimbo n (pl -**s**) (Slang) attractive but empty-headed young person, esp. a woman

bimbos n ▷ **bimbo**

bin n (pl -**s**) container for rubbish or for storing grain, coal, etc.

binary adj composed of two parts (MATHS)

(COMPUTERS)

bind v (**binds**, **binding**, **bound**) make secure with or as if with a rope ▶ n (pl -**s**) (Informal) annoying situation

binder n (pl -**s**) firm cover for holding loose sheets of paper together

binders n ▷ **binder**

binding n (pl -**s**) anything that binds or fastens ▶ n ▷ **bind**

bindings n ▷ **binding**

bindweed n (pl -**s**) plant that twines around a support

bindweeds n ▷ **bindweed**

binge n (pl -**s**) (Informal) bout of excessive indulgence, esp. in drink

binges n ▷ **binge**

bingo n (pl -**s**) gambling game in which numbers are called out and covered by the players on their individual cards

bingos n ▷ **bingo**

binoculars pl n optical instrument consisting of two small telescopes joined together

binomial n (pl -**s**), adj (mathematical expression) consisting of two terms

binomials n ▷ **binomial**

bins n ▷ **bin**

biochemistries n ▷ **biochemistry**

biochemistry n (pl -**ries**) study of the chemistry of living things > **biochemist** n (pl -**s**)

biochemists n ▷ **biochemistry**

biodegradable adj capable of being decomposed by natural means

biodiversities n ▷ **biodiversity**

biodiversity n (pl -**s**) existence of a wide variety of species in their natural environment

biographer n (pl -**s**) person who writes an account of another person's life

biographers n ▷ **biographer**

biographical n ▷ **biography**

biographies n ▷ **biography**

biography n (pl -**phies**) account of a person's life by another person > **biographical** adj

biological adj of or relating to biology > **biologically** adv

biologically adv ▷ **biological**

biologies n ▷ **biology**

biologist n ▷ **biology**

biologists n ▷ **biology**

biology n (pl -**ogies**) study of living organisms > **biologist** n ▷ **biology**

biometric adj of any automated system using physiological or behavioural traits as a means of identification.

bionic adj having a part of the body that is operated electronically

biopsies n ▷ **biopsy**

biopsy n (pl -**sies**) examination of tissue from a living body

biotechnologies n ▷ **biotechnology**

biotechnology n (pl -**ologies**) use of microorganisms, such as cells or bacteria, in industry and technology

bioterrorism n (pl -**s**) use of viruses, bacteria, etc., by terrorists > **bioterrorist** n (pl -**s**)

bioterrorisms n ▷ **bioterrorism**

bioterrorists n ▷ **bioterrorism**

biped [bye-ped] n (pl -**s**) animal with two feet

bipeds n ▷ **biped**

biplane n (pl -**s**) aeroplane with two sets of wings, one above the other

biplanes n ▷ **biplane**

birch n (pl -**es**) tree with thin peeling bark

birches n ▷ **birch**

bird n (pl -**s**) creature with feathers and wings, most types of which can fly

birdie n (pl -**s**) (GOLF) score of one stroke under par for a hole

birdies n ▷ **birdie**

birds n ▷ **bird**

biretta n (pl -**s**) stiff square cap worn by the Catholic clergy

birettas n ▷ **biretta**

birth n (pl -**s**) process of bearing young; childbirth

birthday n (pl -**s**) anniversary of the day of one's birth

birthdays n ▷ **birthday**

birthmark n (pl -**s**) blemish on the skin formed before birth

birthmarks n ▷ **birthmark**

birthright n (pl -**s**) privileges or possessions that someone is entitled to as soon as he or she is born

birthrights n ▷ **birthright**

births n ▷ **birth**

bis n ▷ **bi**

biscuit n (pl -**s**) small flat dry sweet or plain cake

biscuits n ▷ **biscuit**

bisect v (-**s**, -**ing**, -**ed**) divide into two equal parts

bisected v ▷ **bisect**

bisecting v ▷ **bisect**

bisects v ▷ **bisect**

bisexual adj sexually attracted to both men and women > **bisexuality** n (pl -**ties**)

bisexualities n ▷ **bisexual**

bisexuality n ▷ **bisexual**

bishop n (pl -**s**) clergyman who governs a diocese

bishopric n (pl -**s**) diocese or office of a bishop

bishoprics n ▷ **bishopric**

bishops n ▷ **bishop**

bismuth n (pl -**s**) (CHEM) pinkish-white metallic element

bismuths n ▷ **bismuth**

bison n (pl -**bison**) large hairy animal of the cattle family, native to N America and Europe

bistro n (pl -**s**) small restaurant

bistros n ▷ **bistro**

bit¹ n (pl -**s**) small piece, portion, or quantity

bit² n (pl -**s**) metal mouthpiece on a bridle

bit³ v ▷ **bite**

bit³ n (pl -**s**) (MATHS) (COMPUTERS) single digit of binary notation, either 0 or 1

bitch n (pl -**es**) female dog, fox, or wolf ▶ v (-**es**, -**ing**, -**ed**) (Informal) complain or grumble > **bitchy** adj (-**ier**, -**iest**) > **bitchiness** n

bitched v ▷ **bitch**

bitches n, v ▷ **bitch**

bitchier adj ▷ **bitch**

bitchiest adj ▷ **bitch**

bitching v ▷ **bitch**

bitchy adj ▷ **bitch**

bite v (**bites**, **biting**, **bit**, **bitten**) grip, tear, or puncture the skin, as with the teeth or jaws ▶ n (pl -**s**) act of biting > **biter** n (pl -**s**)

biter n ▷ **bite**

biters n ▷ **bite**

bites v, n ▷ **bite**

biting adj piercing or keen ▶ v ▷ **bite**

bits n ▷ **bit¹, ², ⁴**

bitten v ▷ **bite**

bitter adj (-**er**, -**est**) having a sharp unpleasant taste ▶ n (pl -**s**) beer with a slightly bitter taste ▶ pl bitter-tasting alcoholic drink > **bitterly** adv > **bitterness** n (pl -**es**)

bitterer adj ▷ **bitter**

bitterest adj ▷ **bitter**

bitterly adv ▷ **bitter**

bittern n (pl -**s**) wading marsh bird with a booming call

bitterness n ▷ **bitter**

bitternesses n ▷ **bitter**

bitterns n ▷ **bittern**

bitters n ▷ **bitter**

bitumen n (pl -**s**) black sticky substance obtained from tar or petrol

bitumens n ▷ **bitumen**

bivalve n (pl -**s**) ▶ adj (marine mollusc) with two hinged segments to its shell

bivalves n ▷ **bivalve**

bivouac n (pl -**s**) temporary camp in the

open air ▶ v (-acs, -acking, -acked) camp in a bivouac
bivouacked v ▷ bivouac
bivouacking v ▷ bivouac
bivouacs n, v ▷ bivouac

bizarre adj odd or unusual > **bizarrely** adv > **bizarreness** n
bizarrely adv ▷ bizarre
bizarreness n ▷ bizarre

blab v (blabs, blabbing, blabbed) reveal (secrets) indiscreetly
blabbed v ▷ blab
blabbing v ▷ blab
blabs v ▷ blab

black adj (-er, -est) of the darkest colour, like coal ▶ n (pl -s) darkest colour ▶ v (-s, -ing, -ed) make black > **blackness** n

blackball v (-balls, -balling, -balled) exclude from a group ▶ n (pl -balls) (NZ) hard boiled sweet with black-and-white stripes
blackballed v ▷ blackball
blackballing v ▷ blackball
blackballs v, n ▷ blackball
blackberries n ▷ blackberry

blackberry n (pl -ries) small blackish edible fruit

blackbird n (pl -s) common European thrush
blackbirds n ▷ blackbird

blackboard n (pl -s) hard black surface used for writing on with chalk
blackboards n ▷ blackboard

blackboy n (pl -s) Australian plant with grasslike leaves and a spike of small white flowers
blackboys n ▷ blackboy

blackbutt n (pl -s) Australian eucalyptus tree with hard wood used as timber
blackbutts n ▷ blackbutt

blackcurrant n (pl -s) very small blackish edible fruit that grows in bunches
blackcurrants n ▷ blackcurrant
blacked v ▷ black

blacken v (-s, -ing, -ed) make or become black
blackened v ▷ blacken
blackening v ▷ blacken
blackens v ▷ blacken
blacker adj ▷ black
blackest adj ▷ black

blackfish n (pl blackfish) small dark Australian estuary fish

blackguard [blag-gard] n (pl -s) unprincipled person
blackguards n ▷ blackguard

blackhead n (pl -s) black-tipped plug of fatty matter clogging a skin pore

blackheads n ▷ blackhead
blacking v ▷ black

blackleg n (pl -s) person who continues to work during a strike
blacklegs n ▷ blackleg

blacklist n (pl -s) list of people or organizations considered untrustworthy etc.
blacklists n ▷ blacklist

blackmail n (pl -s) act of attempting to extort money by threats ▶ v (-s, -ing, -ed) (attempt to) obtain money by blackmail
blackmailed v ▷ blackmail
blackmailing v ▷ blackmail
blackmails n, v ▷ blackmail
blackness n ▷ black

blackout n (pl -s) extinguishing of all light as a precaution against an air attack
blackouts n ▷ blackout
blacks n, v ▷ black

blacksmith n (pl -s) person who works iron with a furnace, anvil, etc.
blacksmiths n ▷ blacksmith

bladder n (pl -s) sac in the body where urine is held
bladders n ▷ bladder

blade n (pl -s) cutting edge of a weapon or tool
blades n ▷ blade

blame v (-mes, -ming, -med) consider (someone) responsible for ▶ n (pl -s) responsibility for something that is wrong > **blameless** adj
blamed v ▷ blame
blameless adj ▷ blame
blames v, n ▷ blame

blameworthy adj deserving blame
blaming v ▷ blame

blanch v (-es, -ing, -ed) become white or pale
blanched v ▷ blanch
blanches v ▷ blanch
blanching v ▷ blanch

blancmange [blam-monzh] n (pl -s) jelly-like dessert made with milk
blancmanges n ▷ blancmange

bland adj (-er, -est) dull and uninteresting > **blandly** adv
blander adj ▷ bland
blandest adj ▷ bland

blandishments pl n flattery intended to coax or persuade
blandly adj ▷ bland

blank adj not written on ▶ n (pl -s) empty space > **blankly** adv

blanket n (pl -s) large thick cloth used as covering for a bed ▶ v (-s, -ing, -ed) cover as with a blanket

blanketed v ▷ blanket
blanketing v ▷ blanket
blankets n, v ▷ blanket
blankly adv ▷ blank
blanks n ▷ blank
blare v (**blares, blaring, blared**) sound loudly and harshly ▶ n (pl **-s**) loud harsh noise
blared v ▷ blare
blares v, n ▷ blare
blaring v ▷ blare
blarney n (pl **-s**) flattering talk
blarneys n ▷ blarney
blasé [blah-zay] adj indifferent or bored through familiarity
blaspheme v (**-phemes, -pheming, -phemed**) speak disrespectfully of (God or sacred things) > **blasphemy** n (pl **-phemies**) > **blasphemous** adj > **blasphemously** adv > **blasphemer** n (pl **-s**)
blasphemed v ▷ blaspheme
blasphemer n ▷ blaspheme
blasphemers n ▷ blaspheme
blasphemes v ▷ blaspheme
blasphemies n ▷ blaspheme
blaspheming v ▷ blaspheme
blasphemous v ▷ blaspheme
blasphemously v ▷ blaspheme
blast n (pl **-s**) explosion ▶ v (**-s, -ing, -ed**) blow up (a rock etc.) with explosives
blasted v ▷ blast
blasting v ▷ blast
blastoff n (pl **-s**) launching of a rocket
blastoffs n ▷ blastoff
blasts n, v ▷ blast
blatant adj glaringly obvious > **blatantly** adv
blatantly adv ▷ blatant
blaze¹ n (pl **-s**) strong fire or flame ▶ v (**-s, -ing, -d**) burn or shine brightly
blaze² n (pl **-s**) mark made on a tree to indicate a route
blazed v ▷ blaze¹
blazer n (pl **-s**) lightweight jacket, often in the colours of a school etc.
blazers n ▷ blazer
blazes n ▷ blaze¹, ² ▶ v ▷ blaze¹
blazing v ▷ blaze¹
blazon v (**-s, -ing, -ed**) proclaim publicly
blazoned v ▷ blazon
blazoning v ▷ blazon
blazons v ▷ blazon
bleach v (**-es, -ing, -ed**) make or become white or colourless ▶ n (pl **-es**) bleaching agent
bleached v ▷ bleach
bleaches v, n ▷ bleach
bleaching v ▷ bleach

bleak adj (**-er, -est**) exposed and barren > **bleakly** adv > **bleakness** n (pl **-es**)
bleaker adj ▷ bleak
bleakest adj ▷ bleak
bleakly adv ▷ bleak
bleakness n ▷ bleak
bleaknesses n ▷ bleak
blearier adj ▷ bleary
bleariest adj ▷ bleary
blearily adv ▷ bleary
bleariness n ▷ bleary
blearinesses n ▷ bleary
bleary adj (**-rier, -riest**) with eyes dimmed, as by tears or tiredness > **blearily** adv > **bleariness** n (pl **-es**)
bleat v (**-s, -ing, -ed**) (of a sheep, goat, or calf) utter its plaintive cry ▶ n (pl **-s**) cry of sheep, goats, and calves
bleated v ▷ bleat
bleating v ▷ bleat
bleats v, n ▷ bleat
bled v ▷ bleed
bleed v (**-s, -ing, bled**) lose or emit blood
bleeding v ▷ bleed
bleeds v ▷ bleed
bleep n (pl **-s**) short high-pitched sound made by an electrical device ▶ v (**-s, -ing, -ed**) make a bleeping sound
bleeped v ▷ bleep
bleeper n (pl **-s**) small portable radio receiver that makes a bleeping signal
bleepers n ▷ bleeper
bleeping v ▷ bleep
bleeps n, v ▷ bleep
blemish n (pl **-es**) defect or stain ▶ v (**-es, -ing, -ed**) spoil or tarnish
blemished v ▷ blemish
blemishes n, v ▷ blemish
blemishing v ▷ blemish
blench v (**-es, -ing, -ed**) shy away, as in fear
blenched v ▷ blench
blenches v ▷ blench
blenching v ▷ blench
blend v (**-s, -ing, -ed**) mix or mingle (components or ingredients) ▶ n (pl **-s**) mixture
blended v ▷ blend
blender n (pl **-s**) electrical appliance for puréeing vegetables etc.
blenders n ▷ blender
blending v ▷ blend
blends v, n ▷ blend
bless v (**-es, -ing, -ed**) make holy by means of a religious rite
blessed adj holy ▶ v ▷ blessed > **blessedness** n

blessedness n ▷ blessed
blesses v ▷ bless
blessing n (pl **-s**) invoking of divine aid ▶ v ▷ bless
blessings n ▷ blessing
blether (Scot) v (**-s, -ing, -ed**) talk, esp. foolishly or at length ▶ n (pl **-s**) conversation
blethered v ▷ blether
blethering v ▷ blether
blethers v, n ▷ blether
blew v ▷ blow¹
blight n (pl **-s**) person or thing that spoils or prevents growth ▶ v (**-s, -ing, -ed**) frustrate or disappoint
blighted v ▷ blight
blighter n (pl **-s**) (Informal) irritating person
blighters n ▷ blighter
blighting v ▷ blight
blights n, v ▷ blight
blimp n (pl **-s**) small airship
blimps n ▷ blimp
blind adj (**-er, -est**) unable to see ▶ v (**-s, -ing, -ed**) deprive of sight ▶ n (pl **-s**) covering for a window ▶ **blindly** adv ▷ **blindness** n (pl **-es**)
blinded v ▷ blind
blinder adj ▷ blind
blindest adj ▷ blind
blindfold v (**-s, -ing, -ed**) prevent (a person) from seeing by covering the eyes ▶ n (pl **-s**) piece of cloth used to cover the eyes
blindfolded v ▷ blindfold
blindfolding v ▷ blindfold
blindfolds v, n ▷ blindfold
blinding adj, v ▷ blind
blindly adv ▷ blind
blindness n ▷ blind
blindnesses n ▷ blind
blinds v, n ▷ blind
blink v (**-s, -ing, -ed**) close and immediately reopen (the eyes) ▶ n (pl **-s**) act of blinking
blinked v ▷ blink
blinkers pl n leather flaps on a horse's bridle to prevent sideways vision
blinking v ▷ blink
blinks v, n ▷ blink
blip n (pl **-s**) spot of light on a radar screen indicating the position of an object
blips n ▷ blip
bliss n (pl **-es**) perfect happiness > **blissful** adj > **blissfully** adv
blisses n ▷ bliss
blissful adj ▷ bliss
blissfully adv ▷ bliss
blister n (pl **-s**) small bubble on the skin ▶ v (**-s, -ing, -ed**) (cause to) have blisters

blistered v ▷ blister
blistering adj (of weather) very hot ▶ v ▷ blister > **blisteringly** adv
blisteringly adv ▷ blistering
blisters n, v ▷ blister
blithe adj (**-r, -st**) casual and indifferent > **blithely** adv > **blitheness** n (pl **-es**)
blithely adv ▷ blithe
blitheness n ▷ blithe
blithenesses n ▷ blithe
blither adj ▷ blithe
blithest adj ▷ blithe
blitz n (pl **-es**) violent and sustained attack by aircraft ▶ v (**-es, -ing, -ed**) attack suddenly and intensively
blitzed v ▷ blitz
blitzes n, v ▷ blitz
blitzing v ▷ blitz
blizzard n (pl **-s**) blinding storm of wind and snow
blizzards n ▷ blizzard
bloat v (**-s, -ing, -ed**) cause to swell, as with liquid or air
bloated v ▷ bloat
bloater n (pl **-s**) (BRIT) salted smoked herring
bloaters n ▷ bloater
bloating v ▷ bloat
bloats v ▷ bloat
blob n (pl **-s**) soft mass or drop
blobs n ▷ blob
bloc n (pl **-s**) people or countries combined by a common interest
block n (pl **-s**) large solid piece of wood, stone, etc. ▶ v (**-s, -ing, -ed**) obstruct or impede by introducing an obstacle > **blockage** n (pl **-s**)
blockade n (pl **-s**) sealing off of a place to prevent the passage of goods ▶ v (**-ades, -ading, -aded**) impose a blockade on
blockaded n ▷ blockade
blockades n, v ▷ blockade
blockading v ▷ blockade
blockage n ▷ block
blockages n ▷ block
blocked v ▷ block
blockhead n (pl **-s**) stupid person
blockheads n ▷ blockhead
blockie n (pl **-s**) (AUST) owner of a small property, esp. a farm
blockies n ▷ blockie
blocking v ▷ block
blocks n, v ▷ block
blocs n ▷ bloc
blog n (pl **-s**) ▷ weblog
blogs n ▷ blog
bloke n (pl **-s**) (Informal) man

blokes n ▷ bloke

blonde, *masc* **blond** *adj, n (pl* **-es, -s)** fair-haired (person)

blondes n ▷ blonde

blonds n ▷ blonde

blood n (pl **-s**) red fluid that flows around the body > **bloodless** *adj* > **bloodlessness** n

bloodhound n (pl **-s**) large dog formerly used for tracking

bloodhounds n ▷ bloodhound

bloodied v ▷ bloody

bloodies v ▷ bloody

bloodily *adv* ▷ bloody

bloodiness n ▷ bloody

bloodless *adj* ▷ blood

bloodlessness n ▷ blood

bloods n ▷ blood

bloodshed n (pl **-s**) slaughter or killing

bloodsheds n ▷ bloodshed

bloodshot *adj* (of an eye) inflamed

bloodstream n (pl **-s**) flow of blood round the body

bloodstreams n ▷ bloodstream

bloodsucker n (pl **-s**) animal that sucks blood

bloodsuckers n ▷ bloodsucker

bloodthirstily *adv* ▷ bloodthirsty

bloodthirstiness n ▷ bloodthirsty

bloodthirsty *adj* taking pleasure in violence > **bloodthirstily** *adv* > **bloodthirstiness** n

bloody *adj* covered with blood ▶ *adj, adv* (Slang) extreme or extremely ▶ v (**-dies, -dying, -died**) stain with blood > **bloodily** *adv* > **bloodiness** n

bloodying v ▷ bloody

bloom n (pl **-s**) blossom on a flowering plant ▶ v (**-s, -ing, -ed**) bear flowers

bloomed v ▷ bloom

bloomer n (pl **-s**) (BRIT) (Informal) stupid mistake

bloomers n ▷ bloomer ▶ *pl* n woman's baggy knickers

blooming v ▷ bloom

blooms n, v ▷ bloom

blooper n (pl **-s**) (CHIEFLY US) (Informal) stupid mistake

bloopers n ▷ blooper

blossom n (pl **-s**) flowers of a plant ▶ v (**-s, -ing, -ed**) (of plants) flower

blossomed v ▷ blossom

blossoming v ▷ blossom

blossoms n, v ▷ blossom

blot n (pl **-s**) spot or stain ▶ v (**-s, -tting, -tted**) cause a blemish in or on > **blotter** n (pl **-s**)

blotch n (pl **-es**) discoloured area or stain > **blotchy** *adj*

blotches n ▷ blotch

blotchy *adj* ▷ blotch

blots n, v ▷ blot

blotted v ▷ blot

blotter n ▷ blot

blotters n ▷ blot

blotting v ▷ blot

blotto *adj* (BRIT, AUST & NZ) (Slang) extremely drunk

blouse n (pl **-s**) woman's shirtlike garment

blouses n ▷ blouse

blow¹ v (**-s, -ing, blew, blown**) (of air, the wind, etc.) move > **blower** n (pl **-s**)

blow² n (pl **-s**) hard hit

blower n ▷ blow¹

blowers n ▷ blow¹

blowie n (pl **blowies**) (AUST) (Informal) bluebottle

blowier n ▷ blowy

blowies n ▷ blowie

blowiest n ▷ blowy

blowing v ▷ blow¹

blown v ▷ blow¹

blowout n (pl **-s**) sudden loss of air in a tyre

blowouts n ▷ blowout

blows v ▷ blow¹ ▶ n ▷ blow²

blowsier n ▷ blowsy

blowsiest n ▷ blowsy

blowsy *adj* (**-sier, -siest**) fat, untidy, and red-faced

blowy *adj* (**-wier, -wiest**) windy

blubber n (pl **-s**) fat of whales, seals, etc. ▶ v (**-s, -ing, -ed**) sob without restraint

blubbered v ▷ blubber

blubbering v ▷ blubber

blubbers n, v ▷ blubber

bludge (Informal) v (**-s, -ging, -d**) evade work (AUST & NZ) ▶ n (pl **-s**) (AUST) easy task

bludged v ▷ bludge

bludgeon n (pl **-s**) short thick club ▶ v (**-s, -ing, -ed**) hit with a bludgeon

bludgeoned v ▷ bludgeon

bludgeoning v ▷ bludgeon

bludgeons n, v ▷ bludgeon

bludger n (pl **-s**) person who scrounges

bludgers n ▷ bludger

bludges v, n ▷ bludge

bludging v ▷ bludge

blue n (pl **-s**) colour of a clear unclouded sky ▶ *pl* feeling of depression ▶ *adj* (**bluer, bluest**) of the colour blue > **bluish** *adj*

bluebell n (pl **-s**) flower with blue bell-shaped flowers

bluebells n ▷ bluebell

bluebottle n (pl **-s**) large fly with a dark-blue body

bluebottles n ▷ bluebottle

blueprint n (pl -s) photographic print of a plan
  blueprints n ▷ blueprint
  bluer adj ▷ blue
  blues n ▷ blue
  bluest adj ▷ blue
bluetongue n (pl -s) Australian lizard with a
  blue tongue
  bluetongues n ▷ bluetongue
bluff¹ v (-s, -ing, -ed) pretend to be confident
  in order to influence (someone) ▶ n (pl -s) act
  of bluffing
bluff² n (pl -s) steep cliff or bank ▶ adj good-
  naturedly frank and hearty
  bluffed v ▷ bluff¹
  bluffing v ▷ bluff¹
  bluffs v, n ▷ bluff¹,²
  bluish adj ▷ blue
blunder n (pl -s) clumsy mistake ▶ v (-s, -ing,
  -ed) make a blunder
blunderbuss n (pl -es) obsolete gun with a
  wide flared muzzle
  blunderbusses n ▷ blunderbuss
  blundered v ▷ blunder
  blundering v ▷ blunder
  blunders n, v ▷ blunder
blunt adj (blunter, bluntest) not having a sharp
  edge or point ▶ v (-s, -ing, -ed) make less
  sharp > **bluntly** adv > **bluntness** n
  blunted v ▷ blunt
  blunter adj ▷ blunt
  bluntest adj ▷ blunt
  blunting v ▷ blunt
  bluntly adv ▷ blunt
  bluntness n ▷ blunt
  blunts v ▷ blunt
blur v (-s, -rring, -rred) make or become vague
  or less distinct ▶ n (pl -s) something vague,
  hazy, or indistinct > **blurry** adj (-rrier, -rriest)
blurb n (pl -s) promotional description, as on
  the jacket of a book
  blurbs n ▷ blurb
  blurred v ▷ blur
  blurrier adj ▷ blur
  blurriest adj ▷ blur
  blurring v ▷ blur
  blurry adj ▷ blur
  blurs v, n ▷ blur
blurt v (-s, -ing, -ed) (foll. by **out**) utter suddenly
  and involuntarily
  blurted v ▷ blurt
  blurting v ▷ blurt
  blurts v ▷ blurt
blush v (-es, -ing, -ed) become red in the face,
  esp. from embarrassment or shame ▶ n (pl
  -es) reddening of the face

blushed v ▷ blush
blushes v, n ▷ blush
blushing v ▷ blush
bluster v (-s, -ing, -ed) speak loudly or in a
  bullying way ▶ n (pl -s) empty threats or
  protests
  blustered v ▷ bluster
  blusteriness n ▷ blustery
  blustering v ▷ bluster
  blusters v, n ▷ bluster
blustery adj (of weather) rough and windy
  > **blusteriness** n

  bo or **boh** interjection. Bo is an
  exclamation used to startle someone.
  Bo scores 4 points, while boh scores 8.

boa n (pl -s) large nonvenomous snake
boab [boh-ab] n (pl -s) (AUST) (Informal) ▷ baobab
  boabs n ▷ boab
boar n (pl -s) uncastrated male pig
board n (pl -s) long flat piece of sawn timber ▶ v
  (-s, -ing, -ed) go aboard (a train, aeroplane,
  etc.)
  boarded v ▷ board
boarder n (pl -s) person who pays rent in return
  for accommodation in someone else's home
  boarders n ▷ boarder
  boarding v ▷ board
boardroom n (pl -s) room where the board of a
  company meets
  boardrooms n ▷ boardroom
  boards n, v ▷ board
  boars n ▷ boar
  boas n ▷ boa
boast v (-s, -ing, -ed) speak too proudly
  about one's talents etc. ▶ n (pl -s) bragging
  statement > **boastful** adj > **boastfully** adv
  > **boastfulness** n
  boasted v ▷ boast
  boastful adj ▷ boast
  boastfully adv ▷ boast
  boastfulness n ▷ boast
  boasting v ▷ boast
  boasts v, n ▷ boast
boat n (pl -s) small vehicle for travelling across
  water > **boating** n
boater n (pl -s) flat straw hat
  boaters n ▷ boater
  boating v ▷ boat
  boats n ▷ boat
boatswain n (pl -s) ▷ bosun
  boatswains n ▷ boatswain
bob¹ v (bobs, bobbing, bobbed) move up and
  down repeatedly ▶ n (pl -s) short abrupt
  movement
bob² n (pl -s) hairstyle in which the hair is cut

short evenly all round the head ▶ v (**bobs, bobbing, bobbed**) cut (the hair) in a bob
bobbed v ▷ bob[1,2]
bobbies n ▷ bobby
bobbin n (pl -s) reel on which thread is wound
bobbing v ▷ bob[1,2]
bobbins n ▷ bobbin
bobble n (pl -s) small ball of material, usu. for decoration
bobbles n ▷ bobble
bobby n (pl -bies) (BRIT) (Informal) policeman
bobotie [ba-boot-ee] n (pl -s) (S AFR) dish of curried mince
boboties n ▷ bobotie
bobs v ▷ bob[1,2] ▶ n[1,2]
bobsleigh n (pl -s) sledge for racing down an icy track ▶ v (-s, -ing, -ed) ride on a bobsleigh
bobsleighed v ▷ bobsleigh
bobsleighing v ▷ bobsleigh
bobsleighs n, v ▷ bobsleigh
bode v (-s, -ding, -ed) be an omen of (good or ill)
boded v ▷ bode
bodes v ▷ bode
bodice n (pl -s) upper part of a dress
bodices n ▷ bodice
bodies n ▷ body
bodily adj relating to the body ▶ adv by taking hold of the body
boding v ▷ bode
bodkin n (pl -s) blunt large-eyed needle
bodkins n ▷ bodkin
body n (pl -dies) entire physical structure of an animal or human
bodyboard n (pl -s) small polystyrene surfboard
bodyboards n ▷ bodyboard
bodyguard n (pl -s) person or group of people employed to protect someone
bodyguards n ▷ bodyguard
bodywork n (pl -s) outer shell of a motor vehicle
bodyworks n ▷ bodywork
boerewors n (S AFR) spiced sausage
boffin n (pl -s) (BRIT, AUST, NZ & S AFR) (Informal) scientist or expert
boffins n ▷ boffin
bog n (pl -s) wet spongy ground > **boggy** adj (**boggier, boggiest**)
bogan n (pl -s) (AUST DATED & NZ) (Slang) youth who dresses and behaves rebelliously
bogans n ▷ bogan
bogey, bogy n (pl bogeys, bogies) something that worries or annoys
bogeys n ▷ bogey

boggier adj ▷ bog
boggiest adj ▷ bog
boggle v (**boggles, boggling, boggled**) be surprised, confused, or alarmed
boggled v ▷ boggle
boggles v ▷ boggle
boggling v ▷ boggle
boggy adj ▷ bog
bogies n ▷ bogey
bogong, bugong n (pl -s, -s) large nocturnal Australian moth
bogongs n ▷ bogong
bogs n ▷ bog
bogus adj not genuine
bogy n (pl -gies) ▷ bogey
bohemian n (pl -s) ▶ adj (person) leading an unconventional life
bohemians n ▷ bohemian
boil[1] v (-s, -ing, -ed) (cause to) change from a liquid to a vapour so quickly that bubbles are formed ▶ n (pl -s) state or action of boiling
boil[2] n (pl -s) red pus-filled swelling on the skin
boiled v ▷ boil[1]
boiler n (pl -s) piece of equipment which provides hot water
boilers n ▷ boiler
boiling v ▷ boil[1]
boils v, n ▷ boil[1,2]
boisterous adj noisy and lively > **boisterously** adv > **boisterousness** n
boisterously adv ▷ boisterous
boisterousness n ▷ boisterous

bok n (boks). A bok is a goat or antelope. Bok scores 9 points.

bold adj (-er, -est) confident and fearless > **boldly** adv> **boldness** n (pl -es)
bolder adj ▷ bold
boldest adj ▷ bold
boldly adv ▷ bold
boldness n ▷ bold
boldnesses n ▷ bold
bole n (pl -s) tree trunk
bolero n (pl -s) (music for) traditional Spanish dance
boleros n ▷ bolero
boles n ▷ bole
bollard n (pl -s) short thick post used to prevent the passage of motor vehicles
bollards n ▷ bollard
boloney n (pl -s) ▷ baloney
boloneys n ▷ boloney
bolshie, bolshy adj (Informal) difficult or rebellious
bolshy n ▷ bolshie
bolster v (-s, -ing, -ed) support or strengthen

▶ *n (pl* **-s**) long narrow pillow

bolstered *v* ▷ **bolster**

bolstering *v* ▷ **bolster**

bolsters *v, n* ▷ **bolster**

bolt *n (pl* **-s**) sliding metal bar for fastening a door etc. ▶ *v* (**-s, -ing, -ed**) run away suddenly

bolted *v* ▷ **bolt**

bolting *v* ▷ **bolt**

bolts *n, v* ▷ **bolt**

bomb *n (pl* **-s**) container fitted with explosive material ▶ *v* (**-s, -ing, -ed**) attack with bombs

bombard *v* (**-s, -ing, -ed**) attack with heavy gunfire or bombs ▷ **bombardment** *n (pl* **-s**)

bombarded *v* ▷ **bombard**

bombarding *v* ▷ **bombard**

bombardment *n* ▷ **bombard**

bombardments *n* ▷ **bombard**

bombards *n* ▷ **bombard**

bombast *n (pl* **-s**) pompous language > **bombastic** *adj*

bombastic *adj* ▷ **bombast**

bombasts *n* ▷ **bombast**

bombed *v* ▷ **bomb**

bomber *n (pl* **-s**) aircraft that drops bombs

bombers *n* ▷ **bomber**

bombing *v* ▷ **bomb**

bombs *n, v* ▷ **bomb**

bombshell *n (pl* **-s**) shocking or unwelcome surprise

bombshells *n* ▷ **bombshell**

bonanza *n (pl* **-s**) sudden good luck or wealth

bonanzas *n* ▷ **bonanza**

bond *n (pl* **-s**) something that binds, fastens or holds together ▶ *pl* something that restrains or imprisons ▶ *v* (**-s, -ing, -ed**) bind > **bonded** *adj*

bondage *n (pl* **-s**) slavery

bondages *n* ▷ **bondage**

bonded *v, adj* ▷ **bond**

bonding *v* ▷ **bond**

bonds *n, v* ▷ **bond**

bone *n (pl* **-s**) any of the hard parts in the body that form the skeleton ▶ *v* (**-s, -ing, -d**) remove the bones from (meat for cooking etc.) > **boneless** *adj*

boned *v* ▷ **bone**

boneless *adj* ▷ **bone**

bones *n, v* ▷ **bone**

bonfire *n (pl* **-s**) large outdoor fire

bonfires *n* ▷ **bonfire**

bongo *n (pl* **-gos, -goes**) small drum played with the fingers

bongoes *n* ▷ **bongo**

bongos *n* ▷ **bongo**

bonhomie [bon-om-ee] *n (pl* **-s**) cheerful friendliness

bonhomies *n* ▷ **bonhomie**

boning *v* ▷ **bone**

bonito [ba-nee-toh] *n (pl* **-s**) small tunny-like marine food fish

bonitos *n* ▷ **bonito**

bonnet *n (pl* **-s**) metal cover over a vehicle's engine

bonnets *n* ▷ **bonnet**

bonnier *adj* ▷ **bonny**

bonniest *adj* ▷ **bonny**

bonnily *adv* ▷ **bonny**

bonny *adj* (**-nier, -niest**) (Scot) beautiful > **bonnily** *adv*

bonsai *n (pl* **bonsai**) ornamental miniature tree or shrub

bonus *n (pl* **-es**) something given, paid, or received above what is due or expected

bonuses *n* ▷ **bonus**

bony *adj* having many bones

boo *interj* shout of disapproval ▶ *v* (**-s, -ing, -ed**) shout 'boo' to show disapproval

boob (Slang) *n (pl* **-s**) foolish mistake

boobies *n* ▷ **booby**

boobook [boo-book] *n (pl* **-s**) small spotted Australian brown owl

boobooks *n* ▷ **boobook**

boobs *n* ▷ **boob**

booby *n (pl* **-bies**) foolish person

booed *v* ▷ **boo**

boogie *v* (**-s, -ing, -ied**) (Informal) dance to fast pop music

boogied *v* ▷ **boogie**

boogieing *v* ▷ **boogie**

boogies *v* ▷ **boogie**

booing *v* ▷ **boo**

book *n (pl* **-s**) number of pages bound together between covers ▶ *pl* record of transactions of a business or society ▶ *v* (**-s, -ing, -ed**) reserve (a place, passage, etc.) in advance

booked *n* ▷ **book**

booking *v* ▷ **book**

booklet *n (pl* **-s**) thin book with paper covers

booklets *v* ▷ **booklet**

bookmaker *n (pl* **-s**) person whose occupation is taking bets

bookmakers *n* ▷ **bookmaker**

bookmark *n (pl* **-s**) strip of material used to mark a place in a book ▶ *v* (**-s, -ing, -ed**) (COMPUTERS) identify and store (a website) so that one can return to it quickly and easily

bookmarked *v* ▷ **bookmark**

bookmarking *v* ▷ **bookmark**

bookmarks *n, v* ▷ **bookmark**

books *n, v* ▷ **book**

bookworm n (pl -s) person devoted to reading
  bookworms n ▷ **bookworm**
boom[1] v (-s, -ing, -ed) make a loud deep
  echoing sound ▶ n (pl -s) loud deep echoing
  sound
boom[2] n (pl -s) pole to which the foot of a sail
  is attached
  boomed v ▷ **boom**[1]
boomer n (pl -s) (AUST) large male kangaroo
boomerang n (pl -s) curved wooden missile
  which can be made to return to the
  thrower ▶ v (-s, -ing, -ed) (of a plan) recoil
  unexpectedly
  boomeranged n ▷ **boomerang**
  boomeranging v ▷ **boomerang**
  boomerangs n, v ▷ **boomerang**
  boomers n ▷ **boomer**
  booming v ▷ **boom**[1]
  booms v, n ▷ **boom**[1, 2]
boon n (pl -s) something helpful or beneficial
  boongaries n ▷ **boongary**
boongary [boong-gar-ree] n (pl -garies) tree
  kangaroo of NE Queensland, Australia
  boons n ▷ **boon**
boor n (pl -s) rude or insensitive person
  > **boorish** adj > **boorishly** adv > **boorishness** n
  boorishly adv ▷ **boor**
  boorishness n ▷ **boor**
  boors n ▷ **boor**
  boos v ▷ **boo**
boost n (pl -s) encouragement or help ▶ v (-s,
  -ing, -ed) improve
  boosted v ▷ **boost**
booster n (pl -s) small additional injection of
  a vaccine
  boosters n ▷ **booster**
  boosting v ▷ **boost**
  boosts n, v ▷ **boost**
boot n (pl -s) outer covering for the foot that
  extends above the ankle ▶ v (-s, -ing, -ed)
  (Informal) kick
  booted v ▷ **boot**
bootee n (pl -s) baby's soft shoe
  bootees n ▷ **bootee**
booth n (pl -s) small partly enclosed cubicle
  booths n ▷ **booth**
  booties n ▷ **booty**
  booting v ▷ **boot**
bootleg adj produced, distributed, or sold
  illicitly ▶ v (-legs, -legging, -legged) make,
  carry, or sell (illicit goods) > **bootlegger** n
  (pl -s)
  bootlegged v ▷ **bootleg**
  bootlegger n ▷ **bootleg**
  bootleggers n ▷ **bootleg**

bootlegging v ▷ **bootleg**
  bootlegs v ▷ **bootleg**
  boots n ▶ v ▷ **boot**
booty n (pl -ties) valuable articles obtained
  as plunder
booze v (-zes, -zing, -zed) ▶ n (pl -s) (Informal)
  (consume) alcoholic drink > **boozy** adj (-zier,
  -ziest) > **boozily** adv
  boozed v ▷ **booze**
boozer n (pl -s) (Informal) person who is fond
  of drinking
  boozers n ▷ **booze**
  boozes v, n ▷ **booze**
  boozier adj ▷ **booze**
  booziest adj ▷ **booze**
  boozily adv ▷ **booze**
  boozing v ▷ **booze**
  boozy adj ▷ **booze**
bop v (-s, -pping, -pped) (Informal) dance to
  pop music
  bopped v ▷ **bop**
  bopping v ▷ **bop**
  bops v ▷ **bop**
bora n (pl -s) (AUST) Aboriginal ceremony
  boras n ▷ **bora**
borax n (pl -es) white mineral used in making
  glass
  boraxes n ▷ **borax**
border n (pl -s) dividing line between political
  or geographical regions ▶ v (-s, -ing, -ed)
  provide with a border
  bordered v ▷ **border**
  bordering v ▷ **border**
  borders n, v ▷ **border**
bore[1] v (-s, -ring, -ed) make (a hole) with a drill
  etc. ▶ n (pl -s) (diameter of) the hollow of a
  gun barrel or other tube
bore[2] v (-s, -ring, -ed) make weary by being dull
  or repetitious ▶ n dull or repetitious person or
  thing > **bored** adj > **boredom** n
bore[3] n (pl -s) high wave in a narrow estuary,
  caused by the tide
bore[4] ▷ **bear**[1]
bored v, n ▷ **bore**[1, 2]
boree [baw-ree] n (pl -s) (AUST) ▷ **myall**
  borees n ▷ **boree**
bores n ▷ **bore**[1, 2, 3] ▶ v ▷ **bore**[1, 2]
  boring v ▷ **bore**[1, 2]
born v ▷ **bear**[1] ▶ adj possessing certain
  qualities from birth
  borne v ▷ **bear**[1]
boron n (pl -s) (CHEM) element used in
  hardening steel
boronia n (pl -s) Australian aromatic flowering
  shrub

boronias n ▷ boronia

borons n ▷ boron

borough n (pl -s) (CHIEFLY BRIT) town or district with its own council

boroughs n ▷ borough

borrow v (-s, -ing, -ed) obtain (something) temporarily > borrower n (pl -s)

borrowed v ▷ borrow

borrower n ▷ borrow

borrowers n ▷ borrow

borrowing v ▷ borrow

borrows v ▷ borrow

borstal n (pl -s) (formerly in Britain) prison for young criminals

borstals n ▷ borstal

borzoi n (pl -s) tall dog with a long silky coat

borzois n ▷ borzoi

bosh n (pl -es) (BRIT, AUST & NZ) (Informal) empty talk, nonsense

boshes n ▷ bosh

bosom n (pl -es) chest of a person, esp. the female breasts ▶ adj very dear

bosoms n ▷ bosom

boss¹ n (pl -es) person in charge of or employing others ▶ v (-es, -ing, -ed) be domineering towards > bossy adj > bossiness n

boss² n (pl -es) raised knob or stud

bossed v ▷ boss¹

bosses n ▷ boss¹, ² ▶ v ▷ boss¹

bossiness n ▷ boss¹

bossing v ▷ boss¹

bossy adj ▷ boss¹

bosun n (pl -s) officer responsible for the maintenance of a ship

bosuns n ▷ bosun

botanic adj ▷ botany

botanical adj ▷ botany

botanies n ▷ botany

botanist n ▷ botany

botanists n ▷ botany

botany n (pl -ies) study of plants > botanical, botanic adj > botanist n (pl -s)

botch v (-es, -ing, -ed) spoil through clumsiness ▶ n (pl -es) (also botch-up) (pl -s) badly done piece of work or repair

botched v ▷ botch

botches v, n ▷ botch

botching v ▷ botch

both adj, pron two considered together

bother v (-s, -ing, -ed) take the time or trouble ▶ n (pl -s) trouble, fuss, or difficulty > bothersome adj

bothered v ▷ bother

bothering v ▷ bother

bothers v, n ▷ bother

bothersome adj ▷ bother

bottle n (pl -s) container for holding liquids ▶ v (-s, -ttling, -d) put in a bottle

bottled v ▷ bottle

bottleneck n (pl -s) narrow stretch of road where traffic is held up

bottlenecks n ▷ bottleneck

bottles n, v ▷ bottle

bottling v ▷ bottle

bottom n (pl -s) lowest, deepest, or farthest removed part of a thing ▶ adj lowest or last > bottomless adj

bottomless adj ▷ bottom

bottoms n ▷ bottom

botulism n (pl -s) severe food poisoning

botulisms n ▷ botulism

boudoir [boo-dwahr] n (pl -s) woman's bedroom or private sitting room

boudoirs n ▷ boudoir

bougainvillea n (pl -s) climbing plant with red or purple flowers

bougainvilleas n ▷ bougainvillea

bough n (pl -s) large branch of a tree

boughs n ▷ bough

bought v ▷ buy

boulder n (pl -s) large rounded rock

boulders n ▷ boulder

boulevard n (pl -s) wide, usu. tree-lined, street

boulevards n ▷ boulevard

bounce v (-s, -cing, -d) (of a ball etc.) rebound from an impact (Slang) ▶ n (pl -s) act of rebounding

bounced v ▷ bounce

bouncer n (pl -s) person employed at a disco etc. to remove unwanted people

bouncers n ▷ bouncer

bounces v, n ▷ bounce

bouncing v ▷ bounce ▶ adj vigorous and robust

bound¹ v (-s, -ing, -ed) ▷ bind ▶ adj destined or certain

bound² v (-s, -ing, -ed) move forwards by jumps ▶ n (pl -s) jump upwards or forwards

bound³ v (-s, -ing, -ed) form a boundary of ▶ pl n limit

bound⁴ adj going or intending to go towards

boundaries n ▷ boundary

boundary n (pl -aries) dividing line that indicates the farthest limit

bounded v ▷ bound², ³

bounding v ▷ bound², ³

bounds v, n ▷ bound², ³

bounteous adj ▷ bounty

bounties n ▷ bounty

bountiful adj ▷ bounty

bounty n (pl -ties) generosity > **bountiful, bounteous** adj

bouquet n (pl -s) bunch of flowers

bouquets n ▷ bouquet

bourbon [bur-bn] n (pl -s) whiskey made from maize

bourbons n ▷ bourbon

bourgeois [boor-zhwah] adj, n (pl bourgeois) middle-class (person)

bout n (pl -s) period of activity or illness

boutique n (pl -s) small clothes shop

boutiques n ▷ boutique

bouts n ▷ bout

bovine adj relating to cattle

bow¹ [rhymes with now] v (-s, -ing, -ed) lower (one's head) or bend (one's knee or body) as a sign of respect or shame ▶ n (pl -s) movement made when bowing

bow² [rhymes with go] n (pl -s) knot with two loops and loose ends

bow³ [rhymes with now] n (pl -s) front end of a ship

bowdlerize v (-zes, -zing, -zed) remove words regarded as indecent from (a play, novel, etc.)

bowdlerized v ▷ bowdlerize

bowdlerizes v ▷ bowdlerize

bowdlerizing v ▷ bowdlerize

bowed v ▷ bow¹

bowel n (pl -s) intestine, esp. the large intestine ▶ pl innermost part

bowels n ▷ bowel

bower n (pl -s) shady leafy shelter

bowerbird n (pl -s) songbird of Australia and New Guinea, the males of which build bower-like display grounds to attract females

bowerbirds n ▷ bowerbird

bowers n ▷ bower

bowing v ▷ bow¹

bowl¹ n (pl -s) round container with an open top

bowl² n (pl -s) large heavy ball ▶ pl game played on smooth grass with wooden bowls ▶ v (-s, -ing, -ed) (CRICKET) send (a ball) towards the batsman

bowled v ▷ bowl²

bowlegged adj having legs that curve outwards at the knees

bowler¹ n (pl -s) (CRICKET) player who sends (a ball) towards the batsman

bowler² n (pl -s) stiff felt hat with a rounded crown

bowlers n ▷ bowler¹,²

bowling n game in which bowls are rolled at a group of pins ▶ v ▷ bowl²

bowls n ▷ bowl¹,² ▶ v ▷ bowl²

bows v ▷ bow¹ ▶ n ▷ bow¹,²,³

box¹ n (pl -es) container with a firm flat base and sides ▶ v (-es, -ing, -ed) put into a box

box² v (-es, -ing, -ed) fight (an opponent) in a boxing match

box³ n (pl -es) evergreen tree with shiny leaves bark

boxed v ▷ box¹,²

boxer n (pl -s) person who participates in the sport of boxing

boxers n ▷ boxer

boxes v ▷ box¹,² ▶ n ▷ box¹,²,³

boxing n sport of fighting with the fists ▶ v ▷ box¹,²

boy n (pl -s) male child > **boyish** adj > **boyhood** n (pl -s)

boycott v (-cotts, -cotting, -cotted) refuse to deal with (an organization or country) ▶ n (pl -s) instance of boycotting

boycotted v ▷ boycott

boycotting v ▷ boycott

boycotts v, n ▷ boycott

boyfriend n (pl -s) male friend with whom a person is romantically or sexually involved

boyfriends n ▷ boyfriend

boyhood n ▷ boy

boyhoods n ▷ boy

boyish n ▷ boy

boys n ▷ boy

bra n (pl -s) woman's undergarment for supporting the breasts

braai n ▷ braaivlies

braaied v ▷ braaivlies

braaiing v ▷ braaivlies

braais n, v ▷ braaivlies

braaivlies [brye-flayss], **braai** (S AFR) n (pl braais) grill on which food is cooked over hot charcoal, usu. outdoors ▶ v (braais, braaiing, braaied) cook (food) in this way

brace n (pl -s) object fastened to something to straighten or support it ▶ pl straps worn over the shoulders to hold up trousers ▶ v (-ces, -cing, -ced) steady or prepare (oneself) for something unpleasant

braced n, v ▷ brace

bracelet n (pl -s) ornamental chain or band for the wrist

bracelets n ▷ bracelet

braces n, v ▷ brace

bracing adj refreshing and invigorating ▶ v ▷ brace

bracken n (pl -s) large fern

brackens n ▷ bracken

bracket n (pl -s) either of a pair of characters

used to enclose a section of writing ▶ v (-ets, -eting, -eted) put in brackets
  bracketed v ▷ bracket
  bracketing v ▷ bracket
  brackets n, v ▷ bracket
brackish adj (of water) slightly salty > **brackishness** n
  brackishness n ▷ bracket
bract n (pl -s) leaf at the base of a flower
  bracts n ▷ bract
brag v (-s, -gging, -gged) speak arrogantly and boastfully > **braggart** n (pl -s)
  braggart n ▷ brag
  braggarts n ▷ brag
  bragged v ▷ brag
  bragging v ▷ brag
  brags v ▷ brag
braid v (-s, -ing, -ed) interweave (hair, thread, etc.) ▶ n (pl -s) length of hair etc. that has been braided
  braided v ▷ braid
  braiding v ▷ braid
  braids v, n ▷ braid
braille n (pl -s) system of writing for the blind, consisting of raised dots interpreted by touch
  brailles n ▷ braille
brain n (pl -s) soft mass of nervous tissue in the head ▶ v (-s, -ing, -ed) hit (someone) hard on the head
brainchild n (pl -children) idea produced by creative thought
  brainchildren n ▷ brainchild
  brained v ▷ brain
  brainier adj ▷ brainy
  brainiest adj ▷ brainy
  braininess n ▷ brainy
  braininesses n ▷ brainy
  braining v ▷ brain
brainless adj stupid
  brains n, v ▷ brain
brainwash v (-es, -ing, -ed) cause (a person) to alter his or her beliefs, esp. by methods based on isolation, sleeplessness, etc.
  brainwashed v ▷ brainwash
  brainwashes v ▷ brainwash
  brainwashing v ▷ brainwash
brainwave n (pl -s) sudden idea
  brainwaves v ▷ brainwave
brainy adj (-nier, -niest) (Informal) clever > **braininess** n (pl -es)
braise v (-ses, -sing, -sed) cook slowly in a covered pan with a little liquid
  braised v ▷ braise
  braises v ▷ braise

braising v ▷ braise
brake n (pl -s) device for slowing or stopping a vehicle ▶ v (-kes, -king, -ked) slow down or stop by using a brake
  braked v ▷ brake
  brakes n, v ▷ brake
  braking v ▷ brake
bramble n (pl -s) prickly shrub that produces blackberries
  brambles n ▷ bramble
bran n (pl -s) husks of cereal grain
branch n (pl -es) secondary stem of a tree ▶ v (-es, -ing, -ed) (of stems, roots, etc.) divide, then develop in different directions
  branched v ▷ branch
  branches n, v ▷ branch
  branching v ▷ branch
brand n (pl -s) particular product ▶ v (-s, -ing, -ed) mark with a brand
  branded v ▷ brand
  brandies n ▷ brandy
  branding v ▷ brand
brandish v (-es, -ing, -ed) wave (a weapon etc.) in a threatening way
  brandished v ▷ brandish
  brandishes v ▷ brandish
  brandishing v ▷ brandish
  brands n, v ▷ brand
brandy n (pl -dies) alcoholic spirit distilled from wine
  brans n ▷ bran
  bras n ▷ bra
brash adj offensively loud, showy, or self-confident > **brashness** n
  brashness n ▷ brash
brass n (pl -es) alloy of copper and zinc
  brasses n ▷ brass
  brassier adj ▷ brassy
brassiere n (pl -s) bra
  brassieres n ▷ brassiere
  brassiest adj ▷ brassy
  brassiness adj ▷ brassy
  brassinesses adj ▷ brassy
brassy adj (-ssier, -ssiest) brazen or flashy > **brassiness** n (pl -es)
brat n (pl -s) unruly child
  brats n ▷ brat
bravado n (pl -oes) showy display of self-confidence
  bravadoes n ▷ bravado
brave adj (-r, -st) having or showing courage, resolution, and daring ▶ n (pl -s) Native American warrior ▶ v (-ves, -ving, -ved) confront with resolution or courage > **bravery** n (pl -ies)

braved v ▷ **brave**

braver adj ▷ **brave**

braveries n ▷ **brave**

bravery n ▷ **brave**

braves n, v ▷ **brave**

bravest adj ▷ **brave**

braving v ▷ **brave**

bravo interj well done!

brawl n (pl -s) noisy fight ▶ v (-s, -ing, -ed) fight noisily

brawled v ▷ **brawl**

brawling v ▷ **brawl**

brawls n, v ▷ **brawl**

brawn n (pl -s) physical strength > **brawny** (-nier, -niest) adj

brawnier adj ▷ **brawn**

brawniest adj ▷ **brawn**

brawns n ▷ **brawn**

brawny adj ▷ **brawn**

bray v (-s, -ing, -ed) (of a donkey) utter its loud harsh sound ▶ n (pl -s) donkey's loud harsh sound

brayed v ▷ **bray**

braying v ▷ **bray**

brays v, n ▷ **bray**

brazen adj shameless and bold ▶ v (-s, -ing, -ed) > **brazenly** adv > **brazenness** n

brazened v ▷ **brazen**

brazening v ▷ **brazen**

brazenly adv ▷ **brazen**

brazenness n ▷ **brazen**

brazens v ▷ **brazen**

brazier [bray-zee-er] n (pl -s) portable container for burning charcoal or coal

braziers n ▷ **brazier**

breach n (pl -es) breaking of a promise, obligation, etc. ▶ v (-es, -ing, -ed) break (a promise, law, etc.)

breached v ▷ **breach**

breaches n, v ▷ **breach**

breaching v ▷ **breach**

bread n (pl -s) food made by baking a mixture of flour and water or milk

breads n ▷ **bread**

breadth n (pl -s) extent of something from side to side

breadths n ▷ **breadth**

breadwinner n (pl -s) person whose earnings support a family

breadwinners n ▷ **breadwinner**

break v (breaks, breaking, broke, broken) separate or become separated into two or more pieces ▶ n (pl -s) act or result of breaking > **breakable** adj > **breakage** n (pl -s)

breakable adj ▷ **break**

breakage n ▷ **break**

breakages n ▷ **break**

breakdown n (pl -s) act or instance of breaking down

breakdowns n ▷ **breakdown**

breaker n (pl -s) large wave

breakers n ▷ **breaker**

breakfast v (-s, -ing, -ed) ▶ n (pl -s) (eat) the first meal of the day

breakfasted v ▷ **breakfast**

breakfasting v ▷ **breakfast**

breakfasts v, n ▷ **breakfast**

breaking v ▷ **break**

breakneck adj fast and dangerous

breaks v, n ▷ **break**

breakthrough n (pl -s) important development or discovery

breakthroughs n ▷ **breakthrough**

breakwater n (pl -s) wall that extends into the sea to protect a harbour or beach from the force of waves

breakwaters n ▷ **breakwater**

bream n (pl **bream**) freshwater fish with silvery scales

breast n (pl -s) either of the two soft fleshy milk-secreting glands on a woman's chest

breastbone n (pl -s) long flat bone in the front of the body, to which most of the ribs are attached

breastbones n ▷ **breastbone**

breasts n ▷ **breast**

breaststroke n (pl -s) swimming stroke in which the arms are extended in front of the head and swept back on either side

breaststrokes n ▷ **breaststroke**

breath n (pl -s) taking in and letting out of air during breathing > **breathless** adj > **breathlessly** adv > **breathlessness** n

breathalysed v ▷ **breathalyser**

breathalyser n (pl -s) ® device for estimating the amount of alcohol in the breath > **breathalyse** (-ses, -sing, -sed)

breathalysers n ▷ **breathalyser**

breathalyses v ▷ **breathalyser**

breathalysing v ▷ **breathalyser**

breathe v (-thes, -thing, -thed) take in oxygen and give out carbon dioxide > **breathing** n

breathed v ▷ **breathe**

breather n (pl -s) (Informal) short rest

breathers n ▷ **breathe**

breathes v ▷ **breathe**

breathing v, n ▷ **breathe**

breathless adj ▷ **breath**

breathlessly adv ▷ **breath**

breathlessness n ▷ **breath**

breaths n ▷ breath

breathtaking adj causing awe or excitement
bred v ▷ breed

breech n (pl -es) buttocks

breeches pl n trousers extending to just below
the knee ▶ n ▷ breech

breed v (-s, -ding, bred) produce new or
improved strains of (domestic animals or
plants) ▶ n (pl -s) group of animals etc. within
a species that have certain clearly defined
characteristics > breeder n (pl -s)
breeder n ▷ breed
breeders n ▷ breed

breeding n (pl -s) result of good upbringing or
training ▶ v ▷ breed
breedings n ▷ breeding
breeds v, n ▷ breed

breeze n (pl -s) gentle wind ▶ v (-zes, -zing,
-zed) move quickly or casually
breezed v ▷ breeze
breezes n, v ▷ breeze
breezier adj ▷ breezy
breeziest adj ▷ breezy
breezily adj ▷ breezy
breezing v ▷ breeze

breezy adj (-zier, -ziest) windy > breezily adv

brethren pl n (Old-fashioned) (used in religious
contexts) brothers

brevities n ▷ brevity

brevity n (pl -ities) shortness

brew v (-s, -ing, -ed) make (beer etc.) by
steeping, boiling, and fermentation ▶ n (pl -s)
beverage produced by brewing
brewed v ▷ brew

brewer n (pl -s) person or company that brews
beer
breweries n ▷ brewery
brewers n ▷ brewer

brewery n (pl -eries) place where beer etc. is
brewed
brewing v ▷ brew
brews v, n ▷ brew

briar¹, brier n (pl -s) European shrub with a
hard woody root
briar2 n (pl -s) ▷ brier¹
briars n ▷ briar¹, ²

bribe v (bribes, bribing, bribed) offer or give
something to someone to gain favour,
influence, etc. ▶ n (pl -s) something given or
offered as a bribe > bribery n
bribed v ▷ bribe
bribes v, n ▷ bribe
bribing v ▷ bribe

brick n (pl -s) (rectangular block of) baked clay
used in building ▶ v (-s, -ing, -ed) (foll. by up or

over) build, enclose, or fill with bricks
bricked v ▷ brick
bricking v ▷ brick

bricklayer n (pl -s) person who builds with
bricks
bricklayers n ▷ bricklayer
bricks n, v ▷ brick
bridal adj ▷ bride

bride n (pl -s) woman who has just been or is
about to be married > bridal adj

bridegroom n (pl -s) man who has just been or
is about to be married
bridegrooms n ▷ bridegroom
brides n ▷ bride

bridesmaid n (pl -s) girl or woman who
attends a bride at her wedding
bridesmaids n ▷ bridesmaid

bridge¹ n (pl -s) structure for crossing a river
etc. ▶ v (-dges, -dging, -dged) build a bridge
over (something)

bridge² n (pl -s) card game based on whist,
played between two pairs
bridged v ▷ bridge¹

bridgehead n (pl -s) fortified position at the
end of a bridge nearest the enemy
bridgeheads n ▷ bridgehead
bridges n ▷ bridge¹, ² ▶ v ▷ bridge¹
bridging v ▷ bridge¹

bridle n (pl -s) headgear for controlling a
horse ▶ v (-dles, -dling, -dled) show anger or
indignation
bridled v ▷ bridle
bridles n, v ▷ bridle
bridling v ▷ bridle

brief adj (-er, -est) short in duration ▶ n (pl -s)
condensed statement or written synopsis
(also briefing) (pl -s) ▶ pl men's or women's
underpants ▶ v (-s, -ing, -ed) give information
and instructions to (a person) > briefly adv
briefcase n (pl -s) small flat case for carrying
papers, books, etc.
briefcases n ▷ briefcase
briefed v ▷ brief
briefer adj ▷ brief
briefest adj ▷ brief
briefing v, n ▷ brief
briefings n ▷ brief
briefly adv ▷ brief
briefs n, v ▷ brief

brier¹, briar n (pl -s) wild rose with long thorny
stems
brier² n (pl -s) ▷ briar¹
briers n ▷ brier¹, ²

brig n (pl -s) two-masted square-rigged ship

brigade n (pl -s) army unit smaller than a

division

brigades n ▷ brigade

brigadier n (pl -s) high-ranking army officer

brigadiers n ▷ brigadier

brigalow n (pl -s) (AUST) type of acacia tree

brigalows n ▷ brigalow

brigand n (pl -s) (Lit) bandit

brigands n ▷ brigand

brigantine n (pl -s) two-masted sailing ship

brigantines n ▷ brigantine

bright adj (-er, -est) emitting or reflecting
much light ▸ **brightly** adv ▸ **brightness** n
▸ **brighten** v (-s, -ing, -ed)

brighten v ▷ bright

brightened v ▷ bright

brightening v ▷ bright

brightens v ▷ bright

brighter adj ▷ bright

brightest adj ▷ bright

brightly adj ▷ bright

brigs n ▷ brig

brilliance n ▷ brilliant

brilliancy n ▷ brilliant

brilliant adj shining with light ▸ **brilliance,
brilliancy** n ▸ **brilliantly** adv

brilliantly adv ▷ brilliant

brim n (pl -s) upper rim of a cup etc. ▸ v (brims,
brimming, brimmed) be full to the brim

brimmed v ▷ brim

brimming v ▷ brim

brims n, v ▷ brim

brimstone n (pl -s) (Obs) sulphur

brimstones n ▷ brimstone

brine n (pl -s) salt water

brines n ▷ brine

bring v (-s, -ing, brought) carry, convey, or take
to a designated place or person

bringing v ▷ bring

brings v ▷ bring

brinier adj ▷ briny

briniest adj ▷ briny

brinjal n (pl -s) (S AFR) aubergine

brinjals n ▷ brinjal

brink n (pl -s) edge of a steep place

brinks n ▷ brink

briny (brinier, briniest) adj very salty

brisk adj (-er, -est) lively and quick ▸ **briskly** adv

brisker adj ▷ brisk

briskest adj ▷ brisk

brisket n (pl -s) beef from the breast of a cow

briskets n ▷ brisket

briskly adv ▷ brisk

bristle n (pl -s) short stiff hair ▸ v (-les, -ling,
-led) (cause to) stand up like bristles ▸ **bristly**
adj (-lier, -liest)

bristled v ▷ bristle

bristles n, v ▷ bristle

bristlier adj ▷ bristle

bristliest adj ▷ bristle

bristling v ▷ bristle

bristly adj ▷ bristle

brit n (pl -s) (Informal) British person

brits n ▷ brit

brittle adj (-r, -st) hard but easily broken
▸ **brittleness** n (pl -es)

brittleness n ▷ brittle

brittlenesses n ▷ brittle

brittler adj ▷ brittle

brittlest adj ▷ brittle

broach v (-es, -ing, -ed) introduce (a topic) for
discussion

broached v ▷ broach

broaches v ▷ broach

broaching v ▷ broach

broad adj (-er, -est) having great breadth or
width ▸ **broadly** adv ▸ **broaden** v (-s, -ing, -ed)

broadband n (pl -s) telecommunication
transmission technique using a wide range
of frequencies

broadbands n ▷ broadband

broadcast n (pl -s) programme or
announcement on radio or television ▸ v
(-s, -ing, broadcast) transmit (a programme
or announcement) on radio or television
▸ **broadcaster** n (pl -s) ▸ **broadcasting** n

broadcaster n ▷ broadcast

broadcasters n ▷ broadcast

broadcasting v, n ▷ broadcast

broadcasts n, v ▷ broadcast

broaden v ▷ broad

broadened v ▷ broad

broadening v ▷ broad

broadens v ▷ broad

broader adj ▷ broad

broadest adj ▷ broad

broadly adv ▷ broad

broadminded adj tolerant

broadside n (pl -s) strong verbal or written
attack

broadsides n ▷ broadside

brocade n (pl -s) rich fabric woven with a
raised design

brocades n ▷ brocade

broccoli n (pl -s) type of cabbage with greenish
flower heads

broccolis n ▷ broccoli

brochure n (pl -s) booklet that contains
information about a product or service

brochures n ▷ brochure

broekies [brook-eez] pl n (S AFR) (Informal)

underpants

brogue[1] n (pl -s) sturdy walking shoe

brogue[2] n (pl -s) strong accent, esp. Irish

brogues n ▷ brogue[1, 2]

broil v (-s, -ing, -ed) (AUST, NZ, US & CANADIAN) cook by direct heat under a grill

broiled v ▷ broil

broiling v ▷ broil

broils v ▷ broil

broke v ▷ break ▶ adj (Informal) having no money

broken v ▷ break ▶ adj fractured or smashed

brokenhearted adj overwhelmed by grief

broker n (pl -s) agent who buys or sells goods, securities, etc.

brokers n ▷ broker

brolga n (pl -s) large grey Australian crane with a trumpeting call

brolgas n ▷ brolga

brollies n ▷ brolly

brolly n (pl -lies) (Informal) umbrella

bromide n (pl -s) chemical compound used in medicine and photography

bromides n ▷ bromide

bromine n (pl -s) (CHEM) dark red liquid element that gives off a pungent vapour

bromines n ▷ bromine

bronchi n ▷ bronchus

bronchial [bronk-ee-al] adj of the bronchi

bronchitis [bronk-**eye**-tiss] n inflammation of the bronchi

bronchus [bronk-uss] n (pl bronchi) [bronk-eye] either of the two branches of the windpipe

bronco n (pl -s) (in the US) wild or partially tamed pony

broncos n ▷ bronco

brontosaurus n (pl -es) very large plant-eating four-footed dinosaur

brontosauruses n ▷ brontosaurus

bronze n (pl -s) alloy of copper and tin ▶ adj made of, or coloured like, bronze ▶ v (-zes, -zing, -zed) (esp. of the skin) make or become brown

bronzed v ▷ bronze

bronzes n, v ▷ bronze

bronzing v ▷ bronze

brooch n (pl -es) ornament with a pin, worn fastened to clothes

brooches n ▷ brooch

brood n (pl -s) number of birds produced at one hatching ▶ v (-s, -ing, -ed) think long and unhappily ▷ **broody** adj moody and sullen (Informal)

brooded v ▷ brood

brooding v ▷ brood

broods n, v ▷ brood

broody adj ▷ brood

brook[1] n (pl -s) small stream

brook[2] v (-s, -ing, -ed) bear or tolerate

brooked v ▷ brook[2]

brooking v ▷ brook[2]

brooks n ▷ brook[1] ▶ v ▷ brook[2]

broom n (pl -s) long-handled sweeping brush

brooms n ▷ broom

broomstick n (pl -s) handle of a broom

broomsticks n ▷ broomstick

broth n (pl -s) soup, usu. containing vegetables

brothel n (pl -s) house where men pay to have sex with prostitutes

brothels n ▷ brothel

brother n (pl -s) boy or man with the same parents as another person > **brotherly** adj

brotherhood n (pl -s) fellowship

brotherhoods n ▷ brotherhood

brotherly adj ▷ brother

brothers n ▷ brother

broths n ▷ broth

brought v ▷ bring

brow n (pl -s) part of the face from the eyes to the hairline

browbeat v (-s, -ing, browbeat, -en) frighten (someone) with threats

browbeaten v ▷ browbeat

browbeating v ▷ browbeat

browbeats v ▷ browbeat

brown n (pl -s) colour of earth or wood ▶ adj (-er, -est) of the colour brown ▶ v (-s, -ing, -ed) make or become brown > **brownish** adj

browned v ▷ brown

browner adj ▷ brown

brownest adj ▷ brown

browning v ▷ brown

brownish adj ▷ brown

browns n, v ▷ brown

brows n ▷ brow

browse v (-ses, -sing, -sed) look through (a book or articles for sale) in a casual manner ▶ n (pl -s) instance of browsing

browsed v ▷ browse

browser n (pl -s) (COMPUTERS) software package that enables a user to read hypertext, esp. on the Internet

browsers n ▷ browser

browses v, n ▷ browse

browsing v ▷ browse

bruise n (pl -s) discoloured area on the skin caused by an injury ▶ v (-ses, -sing, -sed) cause a bruise on

bruised v ▷ bruise

bruiser n (pl -s) strong tough person

bruisers n ▷ bruiser
bruises n, v ▷ bruise
bruising v ▷ bruise
brumbies n ▷ brumby
brumby n (pl -bies) (AUST) wild horse
brunch n (pl -es) (Informal) breakfast and lunch combined
brunches n ▷ brunch
brunette n (pl -s) girl or woman with dark brown hair
brunettes n ▷ brunette
brunt n (pl -s) main force or shock of a blow, attack, etc.
brunts n ▷ brunt
brush¹ n (pl -es) device made of bristles, wires, etc. used for cleaning, painting, etc. ▶ v (-es, -ing, -ed) clean, scrub, or paint with a brush
brush² n (pl -es) thick growth of shrubs
brushed v ▷ brush¹
brushes v ▷ brush¹ ▶ n ▷ brush¹, ²
brushing v ▷ brush¹
brusque adj (-r, -st) blunt or curt in manner or speech > **brusquely** adv > **brusqueness** n (pl -es)
brusquely adv ▷ brusque
brusqueness n ▷ brusque
brusquenesses n ▷ brusque
brusquer adj ▷ brusque
brusquest adj ▷ brusque
brutal adj cruel and vicious > **brutally** adv > **brutality** n (pl -alities) > **brutalize** v (-lizes, -lizing, -lized)
brutalities n ▷ brutal
brutality n ▷ brutal
brutalized v ▷ brutal
brutalizes v ▷ brutal
brutalizing v ▷ brutal
brutally adv ▷ brutal
brute n (pl -s) brutal person ▶ adj wholly instinctive or physical, like an animal
brutes n ▷ brute
brutish adj of or like an animal > **brutishly** adv > **brutishness** n
brutishly adv ▷ brutish
brutishness n ▷ brutish
bubble n (pl -s) ball of air in a liquid or solid ▶ v (-les, -ling, -led) form bubbles
bubbled v ▷ bubble
bubbles n, v ▷ bubble
bubblier adj ▷ bubbly
bubbliest adj ▷ bubbly
bubbling v ▷ bubble
bubbly adj (-lier, -liest) excited and lively
buccaneer n (pl -s) (HIST) pirate
buccaneers n ▷ buccaneer

buck¹ n (pl -s) male of the goat, hare, kangaroo, rabbit, and reindeer ▶ v (-s, -ing, -ed) (of a horse etc.) jump with legs stiff and back arched
buck² n (pl -s) (US, CANADIAN, AUST & NZ) (Slang) dollar
bucked v ▷ buck¹
bucket n (pl -s) open-topped round container with a handle ▶ v (-ets, -eting, -eted) rain heavily ▶ **bucketful** n (pl -s)
bucketed v ▷ bucket
bucketful n ▷ bucket
bucketfuls n ▷ bucket
bucketing v ▷ bucket
buckets n, v ▷ buck¹
bucking v ▷ buck¹
buckle n (pl -s) clasp for fastening a belt or strap ▶ v (-les, -ling, -led) fasten or be fastened with a buckle
buckled v ▷ buckle
buckles n, v ▷ buckle
buckling v ▷ buckle
bucks v ▷ buck¹, ² ▶ n ▷ buck¹, ²
buckshee adj (Slang) free
buckteeth pl n projecting upper front teeth > **buck-toothed** adj
buck-toothed adj ▷ buckteeth
buckwheat n (pl -s) small black grain used for making flour
buckwheats n ▷ buckwheat
bucolic [bew-koll-ik] adj of the countryside or country life
bud n (pl -s) swelling on a tree or plant that develops into a leaf or flower ▶ v (buds, budding, budded) produce buds
budded v ▷ bud
buddies n ▷ buddy
budding adj beginning to develop or grow ▶ v ▷ bud
buddleia n (pl -s) shrub with long spikes of purple flowers
buddleias n ▷ buddleia
buddy n (pl -dies) (Informal) friend
budge v (budges, budging, budged) move slightly
budged v ▷ budge
budgerigar n (pl -s) small cage bird bred in many different-coloured varieties
budgerigars n ▷ budgerigar
budges v ▷ budge
budget n (pl -s) financial plan for a period of time ▶ v (-ets, -eting, -eted) plan the expenditure of (money or time) ▶ adj cheap > **budgetary** adj
budgeted v ▷ budget

budgeting v ▷ budget

budgets n, v ▷ budget

budgie n (pl -s) (Informal) ▷ budgerigar

budgies n ▷ budgie

budging v ▷ budge

buds n, v ▷ bud

buff¹ adj dull yellowish-brown ▶ v (-s, -ing, -ed) clean or polish with soft material

buff² n (pl -s) (Informal) expert on or devotee of a given subject

buffalo n (pl -oes) type of cattle (us)

buffaloes n ▷ buffalo

buffed v ▷ buff¹

buffer n (pl -s) something that lessens shock or protects from damaging impact, circumstances, etc.

buffers n ▷ buffer

buffet¹ [boof-ay, buff-ay] n (pl -s) counter where drinks and snacks are served

buffet² [buff-it] v (-s, -feting, -feted) knock against or about

buffeted v ▷ buffet²

buffeting v ▷ buffet²

buffets n ▷ buffet¹ ▶ v ▷ buffet²

buffing v ▷ buff¹

buffoon n (pl -s) clown or fool ▷ buffoonery n (pl -ries)

buffooneries n ▷ buffoon

buffoonery n ▷ buffoon

buffoons n ▷ buffoon

buffs v ▷ buff¹ ▶ n ▷ buff²

bug n (pl -s) small insect ▶ v (bugs, bugging, bugged) (Informal) irritate (someone)

bugbear n (pl -s) thing that causes obsessive anxiety

bugbears n ▷ bugbear

bugged v ▷ bug

bugging v ▷ bug

bugle n (pl -s) instrument like a small trumpet > bugler n (pl -s)

bugler n ▷ bugle

buglers n ▷ bugle

bugles n ▷ bugle

bugong n ▷ bogong

bugongs n ▷ bogong

bugs n, v ▷ bug

build v (builds, building, built) make, construct, or form by joining parts or materials ▶ n (pl -s) shape of the body > builder n (pl -s)

builder n ▷ build

builders n ▷ build

building v ▷ build ▶ n (pl -s) structure with walls and a roof

buildings n ▷ building

builds v, n ▷ build

built v ▷ build

bulb n (pl -s) onion-shaped root which grows into a flower or plant

bulbous adj round and fat

bulbs n ▷ bulb

bulge n (pl -s) swelling on a normally flat surface ▶ v (bulges, bulging, bulged) swell outwards > bulging adj

bulged v ▷ bulge

bulges n, v ▷ bulge

bulging v, adj ▷ bulge

bulimia n (pl -s) disorder characterized by compulsive overeating followed by vomiting > bulimic adj, n (pl -s)

bulimias n ▷ bulimia

bulimic adj, n ▷ bulimia

bulimics n ▷ bulimia

bulk n (pl -s) size or volume, esp. when great > bulky adj (-ier, -iest)

bulkhead n (pl -s) partition in a ship or aeroplane

bulkheads n ▷ bulkhead

bulkier adj ▷ bulk

bulkiest adj ▷ bulk

bulks n ▷ bulk

bulky adj ▷ bulk

bull¹ n (pl -s) male of some animals, such as cattle, elephants, and whales

bull² n (pl -s) (Informal) complete nonsense

bull³ n (pl -s) papal decree

bulldog n (pl -s) thickset dog with a broad head and a muscular body

bulldogs n ▷ bulldog

bulldoze v ▷ bulldozer

bulldozed v ▷ bulldozer

bulldozer n (pl -s) powerful tractor for moving earth ▷ bulldoze v (-zes, -zing, -zed)

bulldozers n ▷ bulldozer

bulldozes v ▷ bulldozer

bulldozing v ▷ bulldozer

bullet n (pl -s) small piece of metal fired from a gun

bulletin n (pl -s) short official report or announcement

bulletins n ▷ bulletin

bullets n ▷ bullet

bullfight n (pl -s) public show in which a matador kills a bull > bullfighter n (pl -s)

bullfighter n ▷ bullfight

bullfighters n ▷ bullfight

bullfights n ▷ bullfight

bullied v ▷ bully

bullies n, v ▷ bully

bullion n (pl -s) gold or silver in the form of bars
  bullions n ▷ bullion
bullock n (pl -s) castrated bull
  bullocks n ▷ bullock
  bulls n ▷ bull¹, ², ³
bullswool n (AUST DATED & NZ) (Slang) nonsense
bully n (pl -lies) person who hurts, persecutes,
  or intimidates a weaker person ▶ v (-lies,
  -lying, -lied) hurt, intimidate, or persecute (a
  weaker person)
  bullying v ▷ bully
bulrush n (pl -es) tall stiff reed
  bulrushes n ▷ bulrush
bulwark n (pl -s) wall used as a fortification
  bulwarks n ▷ bulwark
bum¹ n (pl -s) (Slang) buttocks or anus
bum² (Informal) n (pl -s) disreputable idler ▶ adj
  of poor quality
bumble v (-bles, -bling, -bled) speak, do, or
  move in a clumsy way ▶ **bumbling** adj, n
bumblebee n (pl -s) large hairy bee
  bumblebees n ▷ bumblebee
  bumbled v ▷ bumble
  bumbles v ▷ bumble
  bumbling v, adj n ▷ bumble
bumf, bumph n (pl -s) (Informal) official
  documents or forms
  bumfs n ▷ bumf
bump v (-s, -ing, -ed) knock or strike with a jolt
  ▶ n (pl -s) dull thud from an impact or collision
  ▶ **bumpy** adj (-ier, -iest)
  bumped v ▷ bump
bumper¹ n (pl -s) bar on the front and back of a
  vehicle to protect against damage
bumper² adj unusually large or abundant
  bumpers n ▷ bumper¹
  bumph n ▷ bumf
  bumphs n ▷ bumf
  bumpier adj ▷ bump
  bumpiest adj ▷ bump
  bumping v ▷ bump
bumpkin n (pl -s) awkward simple country
  person
  bumpkins n ▷ bumpkin
  bumps v, n ▷ bump
bumptious adj offensively self-assertive
  ▶ **bumptiously** adv ▶ **bumptiousness** n
  bumptiously adj ▷ bumptious
  bumptiousness adj ▷ bumptious
  bumpy adj ▷ bump
  bums n ▷ bum¹, ²
bun n (pl -s) small sweet bread roll or cake
bunch n (pl -es) number of things growing,
  fastened, or grouped together ▶ v (-es, -ing,
  -ed) group or be grouped together in a bunch

  bunched v ▷ bunch
  bunches n, v ▷ bunch
  bunching v ▷ bunch
bundle n (pl -s) number of things gathered
  loosely together ▶ v (-dles, -dling, -dled) cause
  to go roughly or unceremoniously
  bundled v ▷ bundle
  bundles n, v ▷ bundle
  bundling v ▷ bundle
bung n (pl -s) stopper for a cask etc. ▶ v (-s, -ing,
  -ed) (foll. by up) (Informal) close with a bung
bungalow n (pl -s) one-storey house
  bungalows n ▷ bungalow
  bunged v ▷ bung
  bunging v ▷ bung
bungle v (-gles, -gling, -gled) spoil through
  incompetence ▶ **bungler** n (pl -s) ▶ **bungling**
  adj, n
  bungled v ▷ bungle
  bungler n ▷ bungle
  bunglers n ▷ bungle
  bungles n ▷ bungle
  bungling v, adj n ▷ bungle
  bungs n, v ▷ bung
bunion n (pl -s) inflamed swelling on the big
  toe
  bunions n ▷ bunion
bunk¹ n (pl -s) narrow shelflike bed
bunk² n (pl -s) ▷ bunkum
bunk³ (Slang) n (pl -s) (BRIT) make a hurried and
  secret departure ▶ v (-s, -ing, -ed) (BRIT, NZ & S
  AFR) be absent without permission
  bunked v ▷ bunk³
bunker n (pl -s) sand-filled hollow forming an
  obstacle on a golf course
  bunkers n ▷ bunker
  bunking v ▷ bunk³
  bunks n ▷ bunk¹, ², ³ ▶ v ▷ bunk³
bunkum n (pl -s) nonsense
  bunkums n ▷ bunkum
  bunnies n ▷ bunny
bunny n (pl -nies) child's word for a rabbit
  buns n ▷ bun
bunting n (pl -s) decorative flags
  buntings n ▷ bunting
bunya n (pl -s) tall dome-shaped Australian
  coniferous tree
  bunyas n ▷ bunya
bunyip n (pl -s) (AUST) legendary monster said
  to live in swamps and lakes
  bunyips n ▷ bunyip
buoy n (pl -s) floating marker anchored in the
  sea ▶ v (-s, -ing, -ed) prevent from sinking
  buoyancy n ▷ buoyant
buoyant adj able to float ▶ **buoyancy** n

buoyed v ▷ buoy

buoying v ▷ buoy

buoys n, v ▷ buoy¹

bur n (pl -s) ▷ burr¹

burble v (-bles, -bling, -bled) make a bubbling sound

burbled v ▷ burble

burbles v ▷ burble

burbling v ▷ burble

burden¹ n (pl -s) heavy load ▶ v (-s, -ing, -ed) put a burden on > burdensome adj

burden² n (pl -s) theme of a speech etc.

burdened v ▷ burden¹

burdening v ▷ burden¹

burdens v ▷ burden¹ ▶ n ▷ burden¹, ²

burdensome adj ▷ burden¹

bureau n (pl -reaus, -reaux) office that provides a service

bureaucracies n ▷ bureaucracy

bureaucracy n (pl -cies) administrative system based on complex rules and procedures > bureaucrat n (pl -s) > bureaucratic adj

bureaucrat n ▷ bureaucracy

bureaucratic adj ▷ bureaucracy

bureaucrats n ▷ bureaucracy

bureaus n ▷ bureau

bureaux n ▷ bureau

burgeon v (-s, -ing, -ed) develop or grow rapidly

burgeoned v ▷ burgeon

burgeoning v ▷ burgeon

burgeons v ▷ burgeon

burgh n (pl -s) Scottish borough

burghs n ▷ burgh

burglar n (pl -s) person who enters a building to commit a crime, esp. theft > burglary n (pl -glaries) > burgle v (burgles, burgling, burgled)

burglaries n ▷ burglar

burglars n ▷ burglar

burglary n ▷ burglar

burgled v ▷ burglar

burgles v ▷ burglar

burgling v ▷ burglar

burgundy adj dark-purplish red

burial n (pl -s) burying of a dead body

burials n ▷ burial

buried v ▷ bury

buries v ▷ bury

burlesque n (pl -s) artistic work which satirizes a subject by caricature

burlesques n ▷ burlesque

burlier adj ▷ burly

burliest adj ▷ burly

burly adj (-lier, -liest) (of a person) broad and strong

burn¹ v (-s, -ing, -t or -ed) be or set on fire ▶ n (pl burns) injury or mark caused by fire or exposure to heat

burn² n (pl -s) (Scot) small stream

burned v ▷ burn¹

burning adj intense ▶ v ▷ burn¹

burnish v (-es, -ing, -ed) make smooth and shiny by rubbing

burnished v ▷ burnish

burnishes v ▷ burnish

burnishing v ▷ burnish

burns n ▷ burn¹, ² v ▷ burn¹

burnt v ▷ burn¹

burp v (-s, -ing, -ed) ▶ n (pl -s) (Informal) belch

burped v ▷ burp

burping v ▷ burp

burps v, n ▷ burp

burr¹, bur n (pl -s) head of a plant with prickles or hooks

burr² n (pl -s) soft trilling sound given to the letter r in some dialects

burrawang n (pl -s) Australian plant with fernlike leaves and an edible nut

burrawangs n ▷ burrawang

burrow n (pl -s) hole dug in the ground by a rabbit etc. ▶ v (-s, -ing, -ed) dig holes in the ground

burrowed v ▷ burrow

burrowing v ▷ burrow

burrows n, v ▷ burrow

burrs n ▷ burr¹, ²

burs n ▷ bur

bursar n (pl -s) treasurer of a school, college, or university

bursaries n ▷ bursary

bursars n ▷ bursar

bursary n (pl -ries) scholarship

burst v (-s, -ing, burst) (cause to) break open or apart noisily and suddenly ▶ n (pl -s) instance of breaking open suddenly

bursting v ▷ burst

bursts v, n ▷ burst

bury v (buries, burying, buried) place in a grave

burying v ▷ bury

bus n (pl buses) large motor vehicle for carrying passengers ▶ v (busses, bussing, bussed) travel or transport by bus

busbies n ▷ busby

busby n (pl -bies) tall fur hat worn by some soldiers

buses n ▷ bus

bush n (pl -es) dense woody plant, smaller than a tree

bushbabies n ▷ bushbaby

bushbaby n (pl -**babies**) small African tree-living mammal with large eyes

bushel n (pl -s) obsolete unit of measure equal to 8 gallons (36.4 litres)
bushels n ▷ bushel
bushes n ▷ bush
bushier adj ▷ bushy
bushiest adj ▷ bushy

bushy adj (-**shier**, -**shiest**) (of hair) thick and shaggy
busied v ▷ busy
busier adj ▷ busy
busies v ▷ busy
busiest adj ▷ busy

business n (pl -es) purchase and sale of goods and services > **businessman** n (pl -men), **businesswoman** (pl -women)
businesses n ▷ business

businesslike adj efficient and methodical
businessman n ▷ business
businessmen n ▷ business
businesswoman n ▷ business
businesswomen n ▷ business

busk v (-s, -ing, -ed) act as a busker
busked v ▷ busk

busker n (pl -s) street entertainer
buskers n ▷ busker
busking v ▷ busk
busks v ▷ busk
bussed v ▷ bus
busses v ▷ bus
bussing v ▷ bus

bust[1] n (pl -s) woman's bosom

bust[2] (Informal) v (**busts**, **busting**, **bust** or **busted**) burst or break ▶ adj broken

bustard n (pl -s) bird with long strong legs, a heavy body, a long neck, and speckled plumage
bustards n ▷ bustard
busted v ▷ bust[2]
busting v ▷ bust[2]

bustle[1] v (-**les**, -**ling**, -**led**) hurry with a show of activity or energy ▶ n (pl -s) energetic and noisy activity > **bustling** adj

bustle[2] n (pl -s) cushion or framework formerly worn under the back of a woman's skirt to hold it out
bustled v ▷ bustle[1]
bustles v ▷ bustle[1] ▶ n ▷ bustle[1, 2]
bustling v, adj ▷ bustle[1]
busts n ▷ bust[1] ▶ v ▷ bust[2]

busy adj (**busier**, **busiest**) actively employed ▶ v (**busies**, **busying**, **busied**) keep (someone, esp. oneself) busy > **busily** adv
busybodies n ▷ busybody

busybody n (pl -**bodies**) meddlesome or nosy person
busying v ▷ busy

but conj contrary to expectation ▶ prep except ▶ adv only

butane n (pl -s) gas used for fuel
butanes n ▷ butane

butch adj (-**er**, -**est**) (Slang) markedly or aggressively masculine

butcher n (pl -s) person who slaughters animals or sells their meat ▶ v (-s, -ing, -ed) kill and prepare (animals) for meat > **butchery** n (pl -ries) adj ▷ butch

butcherbird n (pl -s) Australian magpie that impales its prey on thorns
butcherbirds n ▷ butcherbird
butchered v ▷ butcher
butcheries n ▷ butcher
butchering v ▷ butcher
butchers n, v ▷ butcher
butchery n ▷ butcher
butchest adj ▷ butch

butler n (pl -s) chief male servant
butlers n ▷ butler

butt[1] n (pl -s) thicker end of something

butt[2] n (pl -s) person or thing that is the target of ridicule

butt[3] v (-s, -ing, -ed) strike with the head or horns

butt[4] n (pl -s) large cask
butted v ▷ butt[3]

butter n (pl -s) edible fatty solid made by churning cream ▶ v (-s, -ing, -ed) put butter on > **buttery** adj

buttercup n (pl -s) small yellow flower
buttercups n ▷ buttercup
buttered v ▷ butter

butterfingers n (pl -s) (Informal) person who drops things by mistake
butterflies n ▷ butterfly

butterfly n (pl -**flies**) insect with brightly coloured wings
buttering v ▷ butter

buttermilk n (pl -s) sourish milk that remains after the butter has been separated from milk
buttermilks n ▷ buttermilks
butters n, v ▷ butter

butterscotch n (pl -es) kind of hard brittle toffee
butterscotches n ▷ butterscotch
buttery adj ▷ butter
butting v ▷ butt[3]

buttock n (pl -s) either of the two fleshy masses that form the human rump
buttocks n ▷ buttock

button n (pl -s) small disc or knob sewn to clothing, which can be passed through a slit in another piece of fabric to fasten them ▶ v (-s, -ing, -ed) fasten with buttons
buttoned v ▷ **button**
buttonhole n (pl -s) slit in a garment through which a button is passed ▶ v (-holes, -holing, -holed) detain (someone) in conversation
buttonholed v ▷ **buttonhole**
buttonholes n, v ▷ **buttonhole**
buttonholing v ▷ **buttonhole**
buttoning v ▷ **button**
buttons n, v ▷ **button**
buttress n (pl -es) structure to support a wall ▶ v (-es, -ing, -ed) support with, or as if with, a buttress
buttressed v ▷ **buttress**
buttresses n, v ▷ **buttress**
buttressing v ▷ **buttress**
butts n ▷ **butt**[1, 2, 4] ▶ v ▷ **butt**[3]
buxom adj (-er, -est) (of a woman) healthily plump and full-bosomed
buxomer adj ▷ **buxom**
buxomest adj ▷ **buxom**
buy v (-s, -ing, bought) acquire by paying money for ▶ n (pl -s) thing acquired through payment
buyer n (pl -s) customer
buyers n ▷ **buyer**
buying v ▷ **buy**
buys v, n ▷ **buy**
buzz n (pl -es) rapidly vibrating humming sound (Informal) ▶ v (-es, -ing, -ed) make a humming sound > **buzzer** n (pl -s)
buzzard n (pl -s) bird of prey of the hawk family

buzzards n ▷ **buzzard**
buzzed v ▷ **buzz**
buzzer n ▷ **buzz**
buzzers n ▷ **buzz**
buzzes n, v ▷ **buzz**
buzzing v ▷ **buzz**
by prep indicating the doer of an action, nearness, movement past, time before or during which, etc. ▶ adv near
bye interj (Informal) goodbye
byelaw n ▷ **bylaw**
byelaws n ▷ **bylaw**
bygone adj past or former
bylaw, byelaw n (pl -s) rule made by a local authority
bylaws n ▷ **bylaw**
bypass n (pl -es) main road built to avoid a city ▶ v (-es, -ing, -ed) go round or avoid
bypassed v ▷ **bypass**
bypasses n, v ▷ **bypass**
bypassing v ▷ **bypass**
byre n (pl -s) (BRIT) shelter for cows
byres n ▷ **byre**
bystander n (pl -s) person present but not involved
bystanders n ▷ **bystander**
byte n (pl -s) (COMPUTERS) group of bits processed as one unit of data
bytes n ▷ **byte**
byway n (pl -s) minor road
byways n ▷ **byway**
byword n (pl -s) person or thing regarded as a perfect example of something
bywords n ▷ **byword**

Cc

C can be a tricky letter to use, especially as it only forms a single two-letter word **ch**. But if you remember this, you won't waste time racking your brains for two-letter words. There are, however, plenty of good three-letter words beginning with C. **Cox** scores 12 points, while **caw, cow** and **coy** are each worth 8. It's also a good idea to remember the short words starting with C that don't contain any vowels: **cly** and **cwm** as well as **ch**.

cab n (pl **-s**) taxi

cabal [kab-**bal**] n (pl **-s**) small group of political plotters
   cabals n ▷ **cabal**

cabaret [kab-a-ray] n (pl **-s**) dancing and singing show in a nightclub
   cabarets n ▷ **cabaret**

cabbage n (pl **-s**) vegetable with a large head of green leaves
   cabbages n ▷ **cabbage**

cabbie, cabby n (pl **-bies**) (Informal) taxi driver
   cabbies n ▷ **cabbie**
   cabby v ▷ **cabbie**

caber n (pl **-s**) tree trunk tossed in competition at Highland games
   cabers n ▷ **caber**

cabin n (pl **-s**) compartment in a ship or aircraft

cabinet n (pl **-s**) piece of furniture with drawers or shelves

cabinetmaker n (pl **-s**) person who makes fine furniture
   cabinetmakers n ▷ **cabinetmaker**
   cabinets n ▷ **cabinet**
   cabins n ▷ **cabin**

cable n (pl **-s**) strong thick rope ▶ v (**-les, -ling, -led**) send (someone) a message by cable
   cabled v ▷ **cable**
   cables n, v ▷ **cable**
   cabling v ▷ **cable**

caboodle n (Informal) the whole lot

cabriolet [kab-ree-oh-**lay**] n (pl **-s**) small horse-drawn carriage with a folding hood
   cabriolets n ▷ **cabriolet**
   cabs n ▷ **cab**

cacao [kak-**kah**-oh] n (pl **-s**) tropical tree with seed pods from which chocolate and cocoa are made
   cacaos n ▷ **cacao**

cache [kash] n (pl **-s**) hidden store of weapons or treasure
   caches n ▷ **cache**

cachet [kash-shay] n (pl **-s**) prestige, distinction
   cachets n ▷ **cachet**

cackle v (**-les, -ling, -led**) laugh shrilly ▶ n (pl **-s**) cackling noise
   cackled v ▷ **cackle**
   cackles v, n ▷ **cackle**
   cackling v ▷ **cackle**

cacophonies n ▷ **cacophony**

cacophonous adj ▷ **cacophony**

cacophony [kak-**koff**-on-ee] n (pl **-phonies**) harsh discordant sound > **cacophonous** adj

cacti n ▷ **cactus**

cactus n (pl **-tuses, -ti**) fleshy desert plant with spines but no leaves
   cactuses n ▷ **cactus**

cad n (pl **-s**) (Old-fashioned) dishonourable man > **caddish** adj

cadaver [kad-**dav**-ver] n (pl **-s**) corpse

cadaverous adj pale, thin, and haggard
   cadavers n ▷ **cadaver**

caddie, caddy n (pl **-dies**) person who carries a golfer's clubs ▶ v (**-dies, -dying, -died**) act as a caddie
   caddies n ▷ **caddie, caddy** ▶ v ▷ **caddie**
   caddish adj ▷ **cad**

caddy n (pl **-dies**) small container for tea
   ▷ **caddie**

cadence [kade-enss] n (pl **-s**) rise and fall in the pitch of the voice
   cadences n ▷ **cadence**

cadenza n (pl **-s**) complex solo passage in a piece of music
   cadenzas n ▷ **cadenza**

cadet n (pl **-s**) young person training for the armed forces or police

cadets n ▷ cadet

cadge v (**cadges, cadging, cadged**) (*Informal*) get (something) by taking advantage of someone's generosity > **cadger** n (pl -**s**)

  cadged v ▷ cadge

  cadger n ▷ cadge

  cadgers n ▷ cadge

  cadges v ▷ cadge

  cadging v ▷ cadge

cadmium n (pl -**s**) (CHEM) bluish-white metallic element used in alloys

  cadmiums n ▷ cadmium

cadre [kah-der] n (pl -**s**) small group of people selected and trained to form the core of a political organization or military unit

  cadres n ▷ cadre

  cads n ▷ cad

  caeca n ▷ caecum

caecum [seek-um] n (pl -**ca**) [-ka] pouch at the beginning of the large intestine

caesium n (pl -**s**) (CHEM) silvery-white metallic element used in photocells

  caesiums n ▷ caesium

café n (pl -**s**) small or inexpensive restaurant serving light refreshments

  cafés n ▷ café

cafeteria n (pl -**s**) self-service restaurant

  cafeterias n ▷ cafeteria

caffeine n (pl -**s**) stimulant found in tea and coffee

  caffeines n ▷ caffeine

caftan n (pl -**s**) ▷ kaftan

  caftans n ▷ caftan

cage n (pl -**s**) enclosure of bars or wires, for keeping animals or birds

caged adj kept in a cage

  cages n ▷ cage

cagey adj (**cagier, cagiest**) (*Informal*) reluctant to go into details

  cagier adj ▷ cagey

  cagiest adj ▷ cagey

cagoule n (pl -**s**) (BRIT) lightweight hooded waterproof jacket

  cagoules n ▷ cagoule

cahoots pl n (*Informal*) conspiring together

cairn n (pl -**s**) mound of stones erected as a memorial or marker

  cairns n ▷ cairn

cajole v (-**les, -ling, -led**) persuade by flattery > **cajolery** n

  cajoled v ▷ cajole

  cajolery n ▷ cajole

  cajoles v ▷ cajole

  cajoling v ▷ cajole

cake n (pl -**s**) sweet food baked from a mixture of flour, eggs, etc. ▶ v (**cakes, caking, caked**) form into a hardened mass or crust

  caked v ▷ cake

  cakes n, v ▷ cake

  caking v ▷ cake

calamine n (pl -**s**) pink powder consisting chiefly of zinc oxide, used in skin lotions and ointments

  calamines n ▷ calamine

  calamities n ▷ calamity

  calamitous adj ▷ calamity

calamity n (pl -**ties**) disaster > **calamitous** adj

  calcification v ▷ calcify

  calcified v ▷ calcify

  calcifies v ▷ calcify

calcify v (-**fies, -fying, -fied**) harden by the depositing of calcium salts > **calcification** n

  calcifying v ▷ calcify

calcium n (pl -**s**) (CHEM) silvery-white metallic element found in bones, teeth, limestone, and chalk

  calciums n ▷ calcium

  calculable adj ▷ calculate

calculate v (-**lates, -lating, -lated**) solve or find out by a mathematical procedure or by reasoning > **calculable** adj > **calculation** n (pl -**s**)

  calculated v ▷ calculate

  calculates v ▷ calculate

calculating adj selfishly scheming ▶ v ▷ calculate

  calculation n ▷ calculate

  calculations n ▷ calculate

calculator n (pl -**s**) small electronic device for making calculations

  calculators n ▷ calculator

calculus n (pl -**es**) branch of mathematics dealing with infinitesimal changes to a variable number or quantity

  calculuses n ▷ calculus

calendar n (pl -**s**) chart showing a year divided up into months, weeks, and days

  calendars n ▷ calendar

calendula n (pl -**s**) marigold

  calendulas n ▷ calendula

calf¹ n (pl **calves**) young cow, bull, elephant, whale, or seal

calf² n (pl **calves**) back of the leg between the ankle and knee

calibrate v (-**brates, -brating, -brated**) mark the scale or check the accuracy of (a measuring instrument) > **calibration** n (pl -**s**)

  calibrated v ▷ calibrate

  calibrates v ▷ calibrate

  calibrating v ▷ calibrate

calibration n ▷ calibrate
calibrations n ▷ calibrate
calibre n (pl -s) person's ability or worth
calibres n ▷ calibre
calico n (pl -coes) white cotton fabric
calicoes n ▷ calico
caliph n (pl -s) (HIST) Muslim ruler
caliphs n ▷ caliph
call v (-s, -ing, -ed) name ▶ n (pl -s) cry, shout
▷ **caller** n (pl -s)
called v ▷ call
caller n ▷ call
callers n ▷ call
calligrapher n ▷ calligraphy
calligraphers n ▷ calligraphy
calligraphies n ▷ calligraphy
calligraphy n (pl -phies) (art of) beautiful
handwriting ▷ **calligrapher** n (pl -s)
calling n (pl -s) vocation, profession ▶ v ▷ call
callings n ▷ calling
calliper n (pl -s) metal splint for supporting
the leg
callipers n ▷ calliper
callisthenics pl n light keep-fit exercises
callous adj showing no concern for other
people's feelings ▷ **callously** adv ▷ **callousness**
n
calloused adj (of skin) thickened and hardened
callously adv ▷ callous
callousness n ▷ callous
callow adj (-er, -est) young and inexperienced
▷ **callowness** n (pl -es)
callower adj ▷ callow
callowest adj ▷ callow
callowness adv ▷ callow
callownesses adv ▷ callow
calls v, n ▷ call
callus n (pl -es) area of thick hardened skin
calluses n ▷ callus
calm adj (-er, -est) not agitated or excited ▶ n
(pl -s) peaceful state ▶ v (-s, -ing, -ed) (often
foll. by **down**) make or become calm ▷ **calmly**
adv ▷ **calmness** n (pl -es)
calmed v ▷ calm
calmer adj ▷ calm
calmest adj ▷ calm
calming v ▷ calm
calmly adv ▷ calm
calmness adv ▷ calm
calmnesses adv ▷ calm
calms n, v ▷ calm
calorie n (pl -s) unit of measurement for the
energy value of food
calories n ▷ calorie
calorific adj of calories or heat

calumnies n ▷ calumny
calumny n (pl -nies) false or malicious
statement
calve v (calves, calving, calved) give birth
to a calf
calved v ▷ calve
calves v ▷ calve ▶ n ▷ calf[1, 2]
calving v ▷ calve
calyces n ▷ calyx
calypso n (pl -s) West Indian song with
improvised topical lyrics
calypsos n ▷ calypso
calyx n (pl calyxes, calyces) outer leaves that
protect a flower bud
calyxes n ▷ calyx
cam n (pl -s) device that converts a circular
motion to a to-and-fro motion
camaraderie n (pl -s) comradeship
camaraderies n ▷ camaraderie
camber n (pl -s) slight upward curve to the
centre of a surface
cambers n ▷ camber
cambric n (pl -s) fine white linen fabric
cambrics n ▷ cambric
camcorder n (pl -s) combined portable video
camera and recorder
camcorders n ▷ camcorder
came v ▷ come
camel n (pl -s) humped mammal that can
survive long periods without food or water in
desert regions
camellia [kam-**meal**-ya] n (pl -s) evergreen
ornamental shrub with white, pink, or red
flowers
camellias n ▷ camellia
camels n ▷ camel
cameo n (pl -s) brooch or ring with a profile
head carved in relief
cameos n ▷ cameo
camera n (pl -s) apparatus used for taking
photographs or pictures for television or
cinema
cameraman n (pl -men) man who operates a
camera for television or cinema
cameramen n ▷ cameraman
cameras n ▷ camera
camiknickers pl n (BRIT) woman's
undergarment consisting of knickers
attached to a camisole
camisole n (pl -s) woman's bodice-like
garment
camisoles n ▷ camisole
camomile n (pl -s) aromatic plant, used to
make herbal tea
camomiles n ▷ camomile

camouflage [kam-moo-flahzh] n (pl -s) use of natural surroundings or artificial aids to conceal or disguise something ▶ (-lages, -flaging, -flaged) conceal by camouflage
camouflaged v ▷ camouflage
camouflages n, v ▷ camouflage
camouflaging v ▷ camouflage
camp[1] n (pl -s) (place for) temporary lodgings consisting of tents, huts, or cabins ▶ v (-s, -ing, -ed) stay in a camp > **camper** n (pl -s)
camp[2] adj (-er, -est) (Informal) effeminate or homosexual
campaign n (pl -s) series of coordinated activities designed to achieve a goal ▶ v (-s, -ing, -ed) take part in a campaign
campaigned v ▷ campaign
campaigning v ▷ campaign
campaigns n, v ▷ campaign
campanologies n ▷ campanology
campanology n (pl -gies) art of ringing bells
campanula n (pl -s) plant with blue or white bell-shaped flowers
campanulas n ▷ campanula
camped v ▷ camp[1]
camper n ▷ camp[1] ▶ adj ▷ camp[2]
campers n ▷ camp[1]
campest adj ▷ camp[2]
camphor n (pl -s) aromatic crystalline substance used medicinally and in mothballs
camphors n ▷ camphor
camping v ▷ camp[1]
campion n (pl -s) red, pink, or white wild flower
campions n ▷ campion
camps n, v ▷ camp[1]
campus n (pl -es) grounds of a university or college
campuses n ▷ campus
cams n ▷ cam
camshaft n (pl -s) part of an engine consisting of a rod to which cams are fixed
camshafts n ▷ camshaft
can[1] v (past could) be able to
can[2] n (pl -s) metal container for food or liquids ▶ v (cans, canning, canned) put (something) into a can
canal n (pl -s) artificial waterway
canals n ▷ canal
canapé [kan-nap-pay] n (pl -s) small piece of bread or toast with a savoury topping
canapés n ▷ canapé
canaries n ▷ canary
canary n (pl -ries) small yellow songbird often kept as a pet
canasta n (pl -s) card game like rummy, played

with two packs
canastas n ▷ canasta
cancan n (pl -s) lively high-kicking dance performed by a female group
cancans n ▷ cancan
cancel v (-cels, -celling, -celled) stop (something that has been arranged) from taking place > **cancellation** n (pl -s)
cancellation n ▷ cancel
cancellations n ▷ cancel
cancelled v ▷ cancel
cancelling v ▷ cancel
cancels v ▷ cancel
cancer n (pl -s) serious disease resulting from a malignant growth or tumour > **cancerous** adj
cancerous adj ▷ cancer
cancers n ▷ cancer
candela [kan-dee-la] n (pl -s) unit of luminous intensity
candelabra n ▷ candelabrum
candelabrum n (pl -bra) large branched candle holder
candelas n ▷ candela
candid adj (-er, -est) honest and straightforward > **candidly** adv > **candidness** n (pl -es)
candidacies n ▷ candidate
candidacy n ▷ candidate
candidate n (pl -s) person seeking a job or position > **candidacy** (pl -acies), **candidature** n (pl -s)
candidates n ▷ candidate
candidature n ▷ candidate
candidatures n ▷ candidate
candider adj ▷ candid
candidest adj ▷ candid
candidly adv ▷ candid
candidness n ▷ candid
candidnesses n ▷ candid
candied adj coated with sugar
candies n ▷ candy
candle n (pl -s) stick of wax enclosing a wick, which is burned to produce light
candles n ▷ candle
candlestick n (pl -s) holder for a candle
candlesticks n ▷ candlestick
candlewick n (pl -s) cotton fabric with a tufted surface
candlewicks n ▷ candlewick
candour n (pl -s) honesty and straightforwardness
candours n ▷ candour
candy n (pl -dies) (US) sweet or sweets
candyfloss n (pl -es) light fluffy mass of spun sugar on a stick

candyflosses n ▷ **candyfloss**
cane n (pl -s) stem of the bamboo or similar plant ▶ v (**canes, caning, caned**) beat with a cane
caned v ▷ **cane**
canes n, v ▷ **cane**
canine adj of or like a dog ▶ n (pl -s) sharp pointed tooth between the incisors and the molars
canines n ▷ **canine**
caning v ▷ **cane**
canister n (pl -s) metal container
canisters n ▷ **canister**
canker n (pl -s) ulceration, ulcerous disease
cankers n ▷ **canker**
cannabis n (pl -es) Asian plant with tough fibres
cannabises n ▷ **cannabis**
canned adj preserved in a can ▶ v ▷ **can²**
cannelloni pl n tubular pieces of pasta filled with meat etc.
canneries n ▷ **cannery**
cannery n (pl -ries) factory where food is canned
cannibal n (pl -s) person who eats human flesh > **cannibalism** n
cannibalize v (-lizes, -lizing, -lized) use parts from (one machine) to repair another
cannibalized v ▷ **cannibalize**
cannibalizes n ▷ **cannibalize**
cannibalizing v ▷ **cannibalize**
cannibals n ▷ **cannibal**
cannier adj ▷ **canny**
canniest adj ▷ **canny**
cannily adv ▷ **canny**
canning v ▷ **can²**
cannon n (pl -s) large gun on wheels
cannonade n (pl -s) continuous heavy gunfire
cannonades n ▷ **cannonade**
cannonball n (pl -s) heavy metal ball fired from a cannon
cannonballs n ▷ **cannonball**
cannons n ▷ **cannon**
cannot v can not
canny adj (-nier, -niest) shrewd, cautious > **cannily** adv
canoe n (pl -s) light narrow open boat propelled by a paddle or paddles > **canoeist** n (pl -s)
canoeing n sport of rowing in a canoe
canoeist n ▷ **canoe**
canoeists n ▷ **canoe**
canoes n ▷ **canoe**
canon¹ n (pl -s) priest serving in a cathedral
canon² n (pl -s) Church decree regulating morals or religious practices > **canonical** adj

canonical adj ▷ **canon²**
canonization n ▷ **canonize**
canonizations n ▷ **canonize**
canonize v (-izes, -izing, -ized) declare (a person) officially to be a saint > **canonization** n (pl -s)
canonized v ▷ **canonize**
canonizes v ▷ **canonize**
canonizing v ▷ **canonize**
canons n ▷ **canon¹, ²**
canoodle v (-les, -ling, -led) (Slang) kiss and cuddle
canoodled v ▷ **canoodle**
canoodles v ▷ **canoodle**
canoodling v ▷ **canoodle**
canopied adj covered with a canopy
canopies n ▷ **canopy**
canopy n (pl -pies) covering above a bed, door, etc
cans n, v ▷ **can²**
cant¹ n (pl -s) insincere talk
cant² n (pl -s) tilted position ▶ v (-s, -ing, -ed) tilt, overturn
cantaloupe, cantaloup n (pl -s) kind of melon with sweet orange flesh
cantaloupes n ▷ **cantaloupe**
cantaloups n ▷ **cantaloupe**
cantankerous adj quarrelsome, bad-tempered
cantata n (pl -s) musical work consisting of arias, duets, and choruses
cantatas n ▷ **cantata**
canted v ▷ **cant²**
canteen n (pl -s) restaurant attached to a workplace or school
canteens n ▷ **canteen**
canter n (pl -s) horse's gait between a trot and a gallop ▶ v (-s, -ing, -ed) move at a canter
cantered v ▷ **canter**
cantering v ▷ **canter**
canters n, v ▷ **canter**
canticle n (pl -s) short hymn with words from the Bible
canticles n ▷ **canticle**
cantilever n (pl -s) beam or girder fixed at one end only
cantilevers n ▷ **cantilever**
canting v ▷ **cant²**
canto n (pl -s) main division of a long poem
canton n (pl -s) political division of a country, esp. Switzerland
cantons n ▷ **canton**
cantor n (pl -s) man employed to lead services in a synagogue

cantors n ▷ cantor

cantos n ▷ canto

cants n ▷ cant¹, ² ▶ v ▷ cant²

canvas n (pl -es) heavy coarse cloth used for sails and tents, and for oil painting

canvases n ▷ canvas

canvass v (-es, -ing, -ed) try to get votes or support (from) ▶ n (pl -es) canvassing

canvassed v ▷ canvass

canvasses v, n ▷ canvass

canvassing v ▷ canvass

canyon n (pl -s) deep narrow valley

canyons n ▷ canyon

cap n (pl -s) soft close-fitting covering for the head ▶ v (caps, capping, capped) cover or top with something

capabilities n ▷ capable

capability n ▷ capable

capable adj (foll. by of) having the ability (for) > capably adv > capability n (pl -ties)

capably adv ▷ capable

capacious adj roomy

capacitance n (pl -s) (measure of) the ability of a system to store electrical charge

capacitances n ▷ capacit

capacities n ▷ capacity

capacitor n (pl -s) device for storing electrical charge

capacitors n ▷ capacitor

capacity n (pl -ties) ability to contain, absorb, or hold

caparisoned adj magnificently decorated

cape¹ n (pl -s) short cloak

cape² n (pl -s) large piece of land that juts out into the sea

caper n (pl -s) high-spirited prank ▶ v (-s, -ing, -ed) skip about

capercaillie, capercailzie [kap-per-kale-yee] n (pl -s) large black European grouse

capercaillies n ▷ capercaillie

capercailzie n ▷ capercaillie

capercailzies n ▷ capercaillie

capered v ▷ caper

capering v ▷ caper

capers pl n pickled flower buds of a Mediterranean shrub used in sauces ▶ n ▷ caper ▶ v ▷ caper

capes n ▷ cape¹, ²

capillaries n ▷ capillary

capillary n (pl -laries) very fine blood vessel

capital¹ n (pl -s) chief city of a country ▶ adj involving or punishable by death

capital² n (pl -s) top part of a pillar

capitalism n (pl -s) economic system based on the private ownership of industry

capitalisms n ▷ capitalism

capitalist adj of capitalists or capitalism ▶ n (pl -s) supporter of capitalism > capitalistic adj

capitalistic adj ▷ capitalist

capitalists n ▷ capitalist

capitalize v (-lizes, -lizing, -lized) write or print (words) in capitals

capitalized v ▷ capitalize

capitalizes v ▷ capitalize

capitalizing v ▷ capitalize

capitals n ▷ capital¹, ²

capitation n (pl -s) tax of a fixed amount per person

capitations n ▷ capitation

capitulate v (-lates, -lating, -lated) surrender on agreed terms > capitulation n (pl -s)

capitulated v ▷ capitulate

capitulates v ▷ capitulate

capitulating v ▷ capitulate

capitulation n ▷ capitulate

capitulations n ▷ capitulate

capon n (pl -s) castrated cock fowl fattened for eating

capons n ▷ capon

capped v ▷ cap

capping v ▷ cap

cappuccino [kap-poo-cheen-oh] n (pl -s) coffee with steamed milk, sprinkled with powdered chocolate

cappuccinos n ▷ cappuccino

caprice [kap-reess] n (pl -s) sudden change of attitude

caprices n ▷ caprice

capricious adj tending to have sudden changes of attitude > capriciously adv

capriciously adv ▷ capricious

caps n, v ▷ cap

capsicum n (pl -s) kind of pepper used as a vegetable or as a spice

capsicums n ▷ capsicum

capsize v (-sizes, -sizing, -sized) (of a boat) overturn accidentally

capsized v ▷ capsize

capsizes v ▷ capsize

capsizing v ▷ capsize

capstan n (pl -s) rotating cylinder round which a ship's rope is wound

capstans n ▷ capstan

capsule n (pl -s) soluble gelatine case containing a dose of medicine

capsules n ▷ capsule

captain n (pl -s) commander of a ship or civil aircraft ▶ v (-s, -ing, -ed) be captain of > captaincy n (pl -cies)

captaincies n ▷ captain

captaincy n ▷ **captain**
captained v ▷ **captain**
captaining v ▷ **captain**
captains n, v ▷ **captain**
caption n (pl -s) title or explanation accompanying an illustration ▶ v (-s, -ing, -ed) provide with a caption
captioned v ▷ **caption**
captioning v ▷ **caption**
captions n, v ▷ **caption**
captious adj tending to make trivial criticisms > **captiously** adv > **captiousness** n
captiously adv ▷ **captious**
captiousness n ▷ **captious**
captivate v (-ates, -ating, -ated) attract and hold the attention of > **captivating** adj
captivated v ▷ **captivate**
captivates v ▷ **captivate**
captivating adj, v ▷ **captivate**
captive n (pl -s) person kept in confinement ▶ adj kept in confinement > **captivity** n
captives n ▷ **captive**
captivity n ▷ **captive**
captor n (pl -s) person who captures a person or animal
captors n ▷ **captor**
capture v (-tures, -turing, -tured) take by force ▶ n (pl -s) capturing
captured v ▷ **capture**
captures v, n ▷ **capture**
capturing v ▷ **capture**
car n (pl -s) motor vehicle designed to carry a small number of people
carafe [kar-raff] n (pl -s) glass bottle for serving water or wine
carafes n ▷ **carafe**
caramel n (pl -s) chewy sweet made from sugar and milk
caramelize v (-izes, -izing, -ized) turn into caramel
caramelized v ▷ **caramelize**
caramelizes v ▷ **caramelize**
caramelizing v ▷ **caramelize**
caramels n ▷ **caramel**
carapace n (pl -s) hard upper shell of tortoises and crustaceans
carapaces n ▷ **carapace**
carat n (pl -s) unit of weight of precious stones
carats n ▷ **carat**
caravan n (pl -s) large enclosed vehicle for living in, designed to be towed by a car or horse
caravans n ▷ **caravan**
caraway n (pl -s) plant whose seeds are used as a spice

caraways n ▷ **caraway**
carbide n (pl -s) compound of carbon with a metal
carbides n ▷ **carbide**
carbine n (pl -s) light automatic rifle
carbines n ▷ **carbine**
carbohydrate n (pl -s) any of a large group of energy-producing compounds in food, such as sugars and starches
carbohydrates n ▷ **carbohydrate**
carbon n (pl -s) nonmetallic element occurring as charcoal, graphite, and diamond, found in all organic matter
carbonate n (pl -s) salt or ester of carbonic acid
carbonated adj (of a drink) containing carbon dioxide
carbonates n ▷ **carbonate**
carbonize v (-izes, -izing, -ized) turn into carbon as a result of heating
carbonized v ▷ **carbonize**
carbonizes v ▷ **carbonize**
carbonizing v ▷ **carbonize**
carbons n ▷ **carbon**
carbuncle n (pl -s) inflamed boil
carbuncles n ▷ **carbuncle**
carburettor n (pl -s) device which mixes petrol and air in an internal-combustion engine
carburettors n ▷ **carburettor**
carcase n ▷ **carcass**
carcases n ▷ **carcass**
carcass, carcase n (pl -es, -es) dead body of an animal
carcasses n ▷ **carcass**
carcinogen n (pl -s) substance that produces cancer > **carcinogenic** adj
carcinogenic adj ▷ **carcinogen**
carcinogens n ▷ **carcinogen**
carcinoma n (pl -s) malignant tumour
carcinomas n ▷ **carcinoma**
card n (pl -s) piece of thick stiff paper or cardboard used for identification, reference, or sending greetings or messages ▶ pl any card game, or card games in general
cardboard n (pl -s) thin stiff board made from paper pulp
cardboards n ▷ **cardboard**
cardiac adj of the heart
cardigan n (pl -s) knitted jacket
cardigans n ▷ **cardigan**
cardinal n (pl -s) any of the high-ranking clergymen of the RC Church who elect the Pope and act as his counsellors ▶ adj fundamentally important
cardinals n ▷ **cardinal**
cardiogram n (pl -s) electrocardiogram

cardiograms n ▷ cardiogram
cardiograph n (pl -s) electrocardiograph
cardiographs n ▷ cardiograph
cardiologist n ▷ cardiology
cardiologists n ▷ cardiology
cardiology n study of the heart and its diseases > **cardiologist** n (pl -s)
cardiovascular adj of the heart and the blood vessels
cards n ▷ card
cardsharp n (pl -s) professional card player who cheats
cardsharps n ▷ cardsharp
care v (cares, caring, cared) be concerned ▶ n (pl -s) careful attention, caution > **careful** adj (-ller, -llest) > **carefully** adv > **carefulness** n (pl -es) > **careless** adj > **carelessly** adv > **carelessness** n
cared v ▷ care
careen v (-s, -ing, -ed) tilt over to one side
careened v ▷ careen
careening v ▷ careen
careens v ▷ careen
career n (pl -s) series of jobs in a profession or occupation that a person has through their life ▶ v (-s, -ing, -ed) rush in an uncontrolled way
careered v ▷ career
careering v ▷ career
careerist n (pl -s) person who seeks advancement by any possible means
careerists n ▷ careerist
careers n, v ▷ careerist
carefree adj without worry or responsibility
careful adj ▷ care
carefuller adj ▷ care
carefullest adj ▷ care
carefully adv ▷ care
carefulness n ▷ care
carefulnesses n ▷ care
careless adj ▷ care
carelessly adv ▷ care
carelessness adv ▷ care
cares v, n ▷ care
caress n (pl -es) gentle affectionate touch or embrace ▶ v (-es, -ing, -ed) touch gently and affectionately
caressed v ▷ caress
caresses n, v ▷ caress
caressing v ▷ caress
caret [kar-rett] n (pl -s) symbol (∧) indicating a place in written or printed matter where something is to be inserted
caretaker n (pl -s) person employed to look after a place

caretakers n ▷ caretaker
carets n ▷ caret
careworn adj showing signs of worry
cargo n (pl -es) goods carried by a ship, aircraft, etc.
cargoes n ▷ cargo
caribou n (pl -bou or -bous) large N American reindeer
caribous n ▷ caribou
caricature n (pl -s) drawing or description of a person that exaggerates features for comic effect ▶ v (-tures, -turing, -tured) make a caricature of
caricatured v ▷ caricature
caricatures n, ▷ caricature
caricaturing v ▷ caricature
caries [care-reez] n (pl caries) tooth decay
carillon [kar-rill-yon] n (pl -s) set of bells played by keyboard or mechanically
carillons n ▷ carillon
caring v ▷ care
cark v (-s, -ing, -ed) (AUST & NZ) (Slang) die
carked v ▷ cark
carking v ▷ cark
carks v ▷ cark
carmine adj vivid red
carnage n (pl -s) extensive slaughter of people
carnages n ▷ carnage
carnal adj of a sexual or sensual nature > **carnally** adv
carnally adv ▷ carnal
carnation n (pl -s) cultivated plant with fragrant white, pink, or red flowers
carnations n ▷ carnation
carnival n (pl -s) festive period with processions, music, and dancing in the street
carnivals n ▷ carnival
carnivore n (pl -s) meat-eating animal > **carnivorous** adj
carnivores n ▷ carnivore
carnivorous adj ▷ carnivore
carob n (pl -s) pod of a Mediterranean tree, used as a chocolate substitute
carobs n ▷ carob
carol n (pl -s) joyful Christmas hymn ▶ v (-ls, -lling, -lled) sing carols
carolled v ▷ carol
carolling v ▷ carol
carols n, v ▷ carol
carotid adj, n (pl -s) (of) either of the two arteries supplying blood to the head
carotids n ▷ carotid
carouse v (-ouses, -ousing, -oused) have a merry drinking party
caroused v ▷ carouse

carousel [kar-roo-**sell**] n (pl -s) revolving conveyor belt for luggage or photographic slides
  carousels n ▷ carousel
  carouses v ▷ carouse
  carousing v ▷ carouse

carp¹ n (pl carp) large freshwater fish

carp² v (-s, -ing, -ed) complain, find fault
  carped v ▷ carp²

carpel n (pl -s) female reproductive organ of a flowering plant
  carpels n ▷ carpel

carpenter n (pl -s) person who makes or repairs wooden structures > **carpentry** n
  carpenters n ▷ carpenter
  carpentry n ▷ carpenter

carpet n (pl -s) heavy fabric for covering floors ▶ v (-s, -ing, -ed) cover with a carpet
  carpeted v ▷ carpet
  carpeting v ▷ carpet
  carpets n, v ▷ carpet
  carpi n ▷ carpus
  carping v ▷ carp²
  carps v ▷ carp²

carpus n (pl -pi) set of eight bones of the wrist

carriage n (pl -s) one of the sections of a train for passengers
  carriages n ▷ carriage

carriageway n (pl -s) (BRIT) part of a road along which traffic passes in one direction
  carriageways n ▷ carriageway
  carried v ▷ carry

carrier n (pl -s) person or thing that carries something
  carriers n ▷ carrier
  carries v ▷ carry

carrion n (pl -s) dead and rotting flesh
  carrions n ▷ carrion

carrot n (pl -s) long tapering orange root vegetable
  carrots n ▷ carrot

carroty adj (of hair) reddish-orange

carry v (-ries, -rying, -ried) take from one place to another
  carrying v ▷ carry
  cars n ▷ car

cart n (pl -s) open two-wheeled horse-drawn vehicle for carrying goods or passengers ▶ v (-s, -ing, -ed) carry, usu. with some effort
  carted v ▷ cart

cartel n (pl -s) association of competing firms formed to fix prices
  cartels n ▷ cartel

carthorse n (pl -s) large heavily built horse
  carthorses n ▷ carthorse

cartilage n (pl -s) strong flexible tissue forming part of the skeleton > **cartilaginous** adj
  cartilages n ▷ cartilage
  cartilaginous n ▷ cartilage
  carting v ▷ cart
  cartographer n ▷ cartography
  cartographers n ▷ cartography
  cartographic adj ▷ cartography
  cartographically adj ▷ cartography
  cartographies n ▷ cartography

cartography n (pl -ies) map making > **cartographer** n (pl -s) > **cartographic** adj > **cartographically** adv

carton n (pl -s) container made of cardboard or waxed paper
  cartons n ▷ carton

cartoon n (pl -s) humorous or satirical drawing > **cartoonist** n (pl -s)
  cartoonist n ▷ cartoon
  cartoonists n ▷ cartoon
  cartoons n ▷ cartoon

cartridge n (pl -s) casing containing an explosive charge and bullet for a gun
  cartridges n ▷ cartridge
  carts n, v ▷ cart

cartwheel n (pl -s) sideways somersault supported by the hands with legs outstretched
  cartwheels n ▷ cartwheel

carve v (carves, carving, carved) cut to form an object > **carving** n (pl -s)
  carved v ▷ carve
  carves v ▷ carve
  carving v, n ▷ carve
  carvings n ▷ carve

caryatid [kar-ree-**at**-id] n (pl -s) supporting column in the shape of a female figure
  caryatids n ▷ caryatid

casbah n (pl -s) citadel of a N African city
  casbahs n ▷ casbah

cascade n (pl -s) waterfall ▶ v (-cades, -cading, -caded) flow or fall in a cascade
  cascaded v ▷ cascade
  cascades n, v ▷ cascade
  cascading v ▷ cascade

case¹ n (pl -s) instance, example

case² n (pl -s) container, protective covering ▶ v (cases, casing, cased) (Slang) inspect (a building) with the intention of burgling it
  cased v ▷ case²

casement n (pl -s) window that is hinged on one side
  casements n ▷ casement
  cases n ▷ case¹, ² ▶ v ▷ case²

cash n banknotes and coins ▶ v (**-es, -ing, -ed**) obtain cash for
  cashed v ▷ **cash**
  cashes v ▷ **cash**
cashew n (pl **-s**) edible kidney-shaped nut
  cashews n ▷ **cashew**
cashier[1] n (pl **-s**) person responsible for handling cash in a bank, shop, etc.
cashier[2] v (**-s, -ing, -ed**) dismiss with dishonour from the armed forces
  cashiered v ▷ **cashier**[2]
  cashiering v ▷ **cashier**[2]
  cashiers n ▷ **cashier**[1] ▶ v ▷ **cashier**[2]
  cashing v ▷ **cash**
cashmere n (pl **-s**) fine soft wool obtained from goats
  cashmeres n ▷ **cashmere**
casing n (pl **-s**) protective case, covering ▶ v ▷ **case**[2]
  casings n ▷ **casing**
casino n (pl **-s**) public building or room where gambling games are played
  casinos n ▷ **casino**
cask n (pl **-s**) barrel used to hold alcoholic drink
casket n (pl **-s**) small box for valuables
  caskets n ▷ **casket**
  casks n ▷ **cask**
cassava n (pl **-s**) starch obtained from the roots of a tropical American plant, used to make tapioca
  cassavas n ▷ **cassava**
casserole n (pl **-s**) covered dish in which food is cooked slowly, usu. in an oven ▶ v (**-oles, -oling, -oled**) cook in a casserole
  casseroled v ▷ **casserole**
  casseroles n, v ▷ **casserole**
  casseroling v ▷ **casserole**
cassette n (pl **-s**) plastic case containing a reel of film or magnetic tape
  cassettes n ▷ **cassette**
cassock n (pl **-s**) long tunic, usu. black, worn by priests
  cassocks n ▷ **cassock**
  cassowaries n ▷ **cassowary**
cassowary n (pl **-waries**) large flightless bird of Australia and New Guinea
cast n (pl **-s**) actors in a play or film collectively ▶ v (**casts, casting, cast**) select (an actor) to play a part in a play or film
castanets pl n musical instrument, used by Spanish dancers, consisting of curved pieces of hollow wood clicked together in the hand
castaway n (pl **-s**) shipwrecked person
  castaways n ▷ **castaway**
caste n (pl **-s**) any of the hereditary classes into

which Hindu society is divided
castellated adj having battlements
  castes n ▷ **caste**
castigate v (**-gates, -gating, -gated**) reprimand severely > **castigation** n
  castigated v ▷ **castigate**
  castigates v ▷ **castigate**
  castigating v ▷ **castigate**
  castigation v ▷ **castigate**
  casting v ▷ **cast**
castle n (pl **-s**) large fortified building, often built as a ruler's residence
  castles n ▷ **castle**
castoff adj, n (pl **-s**) discarded (person or thing)
  castoffs n ▷ **castoff**
castor n (pl **-s**) small swivelling wheel fixed to the bottom of a piece of furniture for easy moving
  castors n ▷ **castor**
castrate v (**-tes, -ting, -ted**) remove the testicles of > **castration** n (pl **-s**)
  castrated v ▷ **castrate**
  castrates v ▷ **castrate**
  castrating v ▷ **castrate**
  castration n ▷ **castrate**
  castrations n ▷ **castrate**
  casts n, v ▷ **cast**
casual adj careless, nonchalant > **casually** adv
  casually adv ▷ **casual**
  casualties n ▷ **casualty**
casualty n (pl **-ties**) person killed or injured in an accident or war
casuarina [kass-yew-a-**reen**-a] n (pl **-s**) Australian tree with jointed green branches
  casuarinas n ▷ **casuarina**
  casuistries n ▷ **casuistry**
casuistry n (pl **-ries**) reasoning that is misleading or oversubtle
cat n (pl **-s**) small domesticated furry mammal
cataclysm [kat-a-kliz-zum] n (pl **-s**) violent upheaval > **cataclysmic** adj
  cataclysmic adj ▷ **cataclysm**
  cataclysms n ▷ **cataclysm**
catacombs [kat-a-**koomz**] pl n underground burial place consisting of tunnels with recesses for tombs
catafalque [kat-a-**falk**] n (pl **-s**) raised platform on which a body lies in state before or during a funeral
  catafalques n ▷ **catafalque**
  catalepsies n ▷ **catalepsy**
catalepsy n (pl **-sies**) trancelike state in which the body is rigid > **cataleptic** adj
  cataleptic adj ▷ **catalepsy**
catalogue n (pl **-s**) book containing details of

items for sale ► v (-logues, -loguing, -logued) make a systematic list of
catalogued v ▷ catalogue
catalogues n, v ▷ catalogue
cataloguing v ▷ catalogue
catalyse v (-lyses, -lysing, -lysed) speed up (a chemical reaction) by a catalyst
catalysed v ▷ catalyse
catalyses v ▷ catalyse
catalysing v ▷ catalyse
catalysis n ▷ catalyst
catalyst n (pl -s) substance that speeds up a chemical reaction without itself changing > **catalysis** n > **catalytic** adj > **catalytically** adv
catalysts n ▷ catalyst
catalytic adj ▷ catalyst
catalytically adv ▷ catalyst
catamaran n (pl -s) boat with twin parallel hulls
catamarans n ▷ catamaran
catapult n (pl -s) Y-shaped device with a loop of elastic, used by children for firing stones ► v (-s, -ing, -ed) shoot forwards or upwards violently
catapulted v ▷ catapult
catapulting v ▷ catapult
catapults n, v ▷ catapult
cataract n (pl -s) eye disease in which the lens becomes opaque
cataracts n ▷ cataract
catarrh [kat-tar] n (pl -s) excessive mucus in the nose and throat, during or following a cold > **catarrhal** adj
catarrhal adj ▷ catarrh
catarrhs n ▷ catarrh
catastrophe [kat-ass-trof-fee] n (pl -s) great and sudden disaster > **catastrophic** adj > **catastrophically** adv
catastrophes n ▷ catastrophe
catastrophic adj ▷ catastrophe
catastrophically adv ▷ catastrophe
catcall n (pl -s) derisive whistle or cry
catcalls n ▷ catcall
catch v (catches, catching, caught) seize, capture ► n (pl -es) device for fastening a door, window, etc.
catches v, n ▷ catch
catchier adj ▷ catchy
catchiest adj ▷ catchy
catchily adv ▷ catchy
catchiness n ▷ catchy
catchinesses n ▷ catchy
catching adj infectious ► v ▷ catch
catchword n (pl -s) well-known and frequently used phrase

catchwords n ▷ catchword
catchy adj (-chier, -chiest) (of a tune) pleasant and easily remembered > **catchily** adv > **catchiness** n (pl -es)
catechism [kat-ti-kiz-zum] n (pl -s) instruction on the doctrine of a Christian Church in a series of questions and answers
catechisms n ▷ catechism
categorical adj absolutely clear and certain > **categorically** adv
categorically adv ▷ categorical
categories n ▷ category
categorization n ▷ categorize
categorizations n ▷ categorize
categorize v (-izes, -izing, -ized) put in a category > **categorization** n (pl -s)
categorized v ▷ categorize
categorizes v ▷ categorize
categorizing v ▷ categorize
category n (pl -ries) class, group
cater v (-s, -ing, -ed) provide what is needed or wanted, esp. food or services > **caterer** n (pl -s)
catered v ▷ cater
caterer n ▷ cater
caterers n ▷ cater
catering v ▷ cater
caterpillar n (pl -s) wormlike larva of a moth or butterfly
caterpillars n ▷ caterpillar
caters v ▷ cater
caterwaul v (-s, -ing, -ed) wail, yowl
caterwauled v ▷ caterwaul
caterwauling v ▷ caterwaul
caterwauls v ▷ caterwaul
catfish n (pl catfish, catfishes) fish with whisker-like barbels round the mouth
catfishes n ▷ catfish
catgut n (pl -s) strong cord used to string musical instruments and sports rackets
catguts n ▷ catgut
catharses n ▷ catharsis
catharsis [kath-thar-siss] n (pl -ses) relief of strong suppressed emotions > **cathartic** adj
cathartic adj ▷ catharsis
cathedral n (pl -s) principal church of a diocese
cathedrals n ▷ cathedral
catheter [kath-it-er] n (pl -s) tube inserted into a body cavity to drain fluid
catheters n ▷ catheter
cathode n (pl -s) negative electrode, by which electrons leave a circuit
cathodes n ▷ cathode
catholic adj (of tastes or interests) covering a wide range > **catholicism** n (pl -s)
catholicism n ▷ catholic

catholicisms n ▷ **catholic**

cation [kat-eye-on] n (pl -s) positively charged ion

cations n ▷ **cation**

catkin n (pl -s) drooping flower spike of certain trees

catkins n ▷ **catkin**

catnap n (pl -s) ▶ v (-naps, -napping, -napped) doze

catnapped v ▷ **catnap**

catnapping v ▷ **catnap**

catnaps n, v ▷ **catnap**

cats n ▷ **cat**

cattier adj ▷ **catty**

cattiest adj ▷ **catty**

cattily adv ▷ **catty**

cattiness n ▷ **catty**

cattle pl n domesticated cows and bulls

catty adj (cattier, cattiest) (Informal) spiteful > **cattily** adv > **cattiness** n

catwalk n (pl -s) narrow pathway or platform

catwalks n ▷ **catwalk**

caucus n (pl -es) local committee or faction of a political party

caught v ▷ **catch**

cauldron n (pl -s) large pot used for boiling

cauldrons n ▷ **cauldron**

cauliflower n (pl -s) vegetable with a large head of white flower buds surrounded by green leaves

cauliflowers n ▷ **cauliflower**

caulk v (-s, -ing, -ed) fill in (cracks) with paste etc.

caulked v ▷ **caulk**

caulking v ▷ **caulk**

caulks v ▷ **caulk**

causal adj of or being a cause > **causally** adv

causality n ▷ **causation**

causally adv ▷ **causal**

causation, causality n relationship of cause and effect

cause n (pl -s) something that produces a particular effect ▶ v (causes, causing, caused) be the cause of

caused v ▷ **cause**

causes n, v ▷ **cause**

causeway n (pl -s) raised path or road across water or marshland

causeways n ▷ **causeway**

causing v ▷ **cause**

caustic adj capable of burning by chemical action > **caustically** adv

caustically adv ▷ **caustic**

cauterize v (-izes, -izing, -ized) burn (a wound) with heat or a caustic agent to prevent infection

cauterized v ▷ **cauterize**

cauterizes v ▷ **cauterize**

cauterizing v ▷ **cauterize**

caution n (pl -s) care, esp. in the face of danger ▶ v (-s, -ing, -ed) warn, advise

cautionary adj warning

cautioned v ▷ **caution**

cautioning v ▷ **caution**

cautions n, v ▷ **caution**

cautious adj showing caution > **cautiously** adv

cautiously adv ▷ **cautious**

cavalcade n (pl -s) procession of people on horseback or in cars

cavalcades n ▷ **cavalcade**

cavalier adj showing haughty disregard ▶ n (pl -s) (C-) supporter of Charles I in the English Civil War > **cavalierly** adv

cavalierly adv ▷ **cavalier**

cavaliers n ▷ **cavalier**

cavalries n ▷ **cavalry**

cavalry n (pl -ries) part of the army orig. on horseback, but now often using fast armoured vehicles

cave n (pl -s) hollow in the side of a hill or cliff

caveat [kav-vee-at] n (pl -s) warning

caveats n ▷ **caveat**

caveman n (pl -men) prehistoric cave dweller

cavemen n ▷ **caveman**

cavern n (pl -s) large cave > **cavernous** adj

cavernous adj ▷ **cavern**

caverns n ▷ **cavern**

caves n ▷ **cave**

caviar, caviare n (pl -s) salted sturgeon roe, regarded as a delicacy

caviare n ▷ **caviar**

caviares n ▷ **caviar**

caviars n ▷ **caviar**

cavil v (-ils, -illing, -illed) make petty objections ▶ n (pl -s) petty objection

cavilled v ▷ **cavil**

cavilling v ▷ **cavil**

cavils v, n ▷ **cavil**

caving n sport of exploring caves

cavities n ▷ **cavity**

cavity n (pl -ties) hollow space

cavort v (-s, -ing, -ed) skip about

cavorted v ▷ **cavort**

cavorting v ▷ **cavort**

cavorts v ▷ **cavort**

caw n (pl -s) cry of a crow, rook, or raven ▶ v (-s, -ing, -ed) make this cry

cawed v ▷ **caw**

cawing v ▷ **caw**

caws n, v ▷ **caw**

cay n (**cays**). A cay is a small low island. Cay scores 8 points.

cayman n (pl -**s**) S American reptile similar to an alligator

caymans n ▷ **cayman**

caz adj. Caz is a slang word for **casual**. It's a great word to have up your sleeve as it scores 14 points.

cazique n (**caziques**). A cazique is a chief among certain American Indian tribes. Cazique scores 27 points, and will earn you a 50-point bonus if you manage to use all of your tiles to form it.

cease v (**ceases, ceasing, ceased**) bring or come to an end > **ceaseless** adj > **ceaselessly** adv

ceased v ▷ **cease**

ceasefire n (pl -**s**) temporary truce

ceasefires n ▷ **ceasefire**

ceaseless adj ▷ **cease**

ceaselessly adv ▷ **cease**

ceases v ▷ **cease**

ceasing v ▷ **cease**

cedar n (pl -**s**) evergreen coniferous tree

cedars n ▷ **cedar**

cede v (**cedes, ceding, ceded**) surrender (territory or legal rights)

ceded v ▷ **cede**

cedes v ▷ **cede**

cedilla n (pl -**s**) character (.) placed under a c in some languages, to show that it is pronounced s, not k

cedillas n ▷ **cedilla**

ceding v ▷ **cede**

ceilidh [kay-lee] n (pl -**s**) informal social gathering for singing and dancing, esp. in Scotland

ceilidhs n ▷ **ceilidh**

ceiling n (pl -**s**) inner upper surface of a room

ceilings n ▷ **ceiling**

celandine n (pl -**s**) wild plant with yellow flowers

celandines n ▷ **celandine**

celebrant n (pl -**s**) person who performs a religious ceremony

celebrants n ▷ **celebrant**

celebrate v (-**rates, -rating, -rated**) hold festivities to mark (a happy event, anniversary, etc.) > **celebration** n (pl -**s**)

celebrated adj well known ▶ v ▷ **celebrate**

celebrates v ▷ **celebrate**

celebrating v ▷ **celebrate**

celebration n ▷ **celebrate**

celebrations n ▷ **celebrate**

celebrities n ▷ **celebrity**

celebrity n (pl -**rities**) famous person

celeriac [sill-**ler**-ee-ak] n (pl -**s**) variety of celery with a large turnip-like root

celeriacs n ▷ **celeriac**

celeries n ▷ **celery**

celerities n ▷ **celerity**

celerity [sill-**ler**-rit-tee] n (pl -**ties**) swiftness

celery n (pl -**ries**) vegetable with long green crisp edible stalks

celestial adj heavenly, divine > **celestially** adv

celestially adv ▷ **celestial**

celibacy n ▷ **celibate**

celibate adj unmarried or abstaining from sex, esp. because of a religious vow of chastity ▶ n (pl -**s**) celibate person > **celibacy** n

celibates n ▷ **celibate**

cell n (pl -**s**) smallest unit of an organism that is able to function independently

cellar n (pl -**s**) underground room for storage

cellars n ▷ **cellar**

cellist n ▷ **cello**

cellists n ▷ **cello**

cello [**chell**-oh] n (pl -**s**) large low-pitched instrument of the violin family > **cellist** n (pl -**s**)

cellophane n (pl -**s**)® thin transparent cellulose sheeting used as wrapping

cellophanes n ▷ **cellophane**

cellos n ▷ **cello**

cells n ▷ **cell**

cellular adj of or consisting of cells

celluloid n (pl -**s**) kind of plastic used to make toys and, formerly, photographic film

celluloids n ▷ **celluloid**

cellulose n (pl -**s**) main constituent of plant cell walls, used in making paper, plastics, etc.

celluloses n ▷ **cellulose**

cement n (pl -**s**) fine grey powder mixed with water and sand to make mortar or concrete ▶ v (-**s, -ing, -ed**) join, bind, or cover with cement

cemented v ▷ **cement**

cementing v ▷ **cement**

cements n, v ▷ **cement**

cemeteries n ▷ **cemetery**

cemetery n (pl -**ries**) place where dead people are buried

cenotaph n (pl -**s**) monument honouring soldiers who died in a war

cenotaphs n ▷ **cenotaph**

censer n (pl -**s**) container for burning incense

censers n ▷ **censer**

censor n (pl -**s**) person authorized to examine

films, books, etc., to ban or cut anything considered obscene or objectionable ▶ v (-s, -ing, -ed) ban or cut parts of (a film, book, etc.) > censorship n
censored v ▷ censor
censoring v ▷ censor
censorious adj harshly critical > censoriously adv
censoriously adv ▷ censorious
censors n, v ▷ censor
censorship n ▷ censor
censure n (pl -s) severe disapproval ▶ v (-sures, -suring, -sured) criticize severely
censured v ▷ censure
censures n, v ▷ censure
censuring v ▷ censure
census n (pl -es) official count of a population
censuses n ▷ census
cent n (pl -s) hundredth part of a monetary unit such as the dollar or euro
centaur n (pl -s) mythical creature with the head, arms, and torso of a man, and the lower body and legs of a horse
centaurs n ▷ centaur
centenarian n (pl -s) person at least 100 years old
centenarians n ▷ centenarian
centenaries n ▷ centenary
centenary [sen-teen-a-ree] n (CHIEFLY BRIT) (pl -naries) 100th anniversary or its celebration
centennial n (pl -s) 100th anniversary or its celebration
centennials n ▷ centennial
centigrade adj of the temperature in which water freezes at 0° and boils at 100°
centigram, centigramme n (pl -s) one hundredth of a gram
centigramme n ▷ centigram
centigrammes n ▷ centigram
centigrams n ▷ centigram
centilitre n (pl -s) one hundredth of a litre
centilitres n ▷ centilitre
centimetre n (pl -s) one hundredth of a metre
centimetres n ▷ centimetre
centipede n (pl -s) small wormlike creature with many legs
centipedes n ▷ centipede
central adj of, at, or forming the centre > centrally adv centrality n
centralism n principle of central control of a country or organization > centralist n (pl -s)
centralist n ▷ centralism
centralists n ▷ centralism
centrality n ▷ central
centralization n ▷ centralize

centralizations n ▷ centralize
centralize v (-izes, -izing, -ized) bring under central control > centralization n (pl -s)
centralized v ▷ centralize
centralizes v ▷ centralize
centralizing v ▷ centralize
centrally adv ▷ central
centre n (pl -s) middle point or part (SPORT) ▶ v (centres, centring, centred) put in the centre of something
centred v ▷ centre
centres n, v ▷ centre
centrifugal adj moving away from a centre > centrifugally adv
centrifugally adv ▷ centrifugal
centrifuge n (pl -s) machine that separates substances by centrifugal force
centrifuges n ▷ centrifuge
centring v ▷ centre
centripetal adj moving towards a centre > centripetally adv
centripetally adv ▷ centripetal
centrist n (pl -s) person favouring political moderation
centrists n ▷ centrist
cents n ▷ cent
centuries n ▷ century
centurion n (pl -s) (in ancient Rome) officer commanding 100 men
centurions n ▷ centurion
century n (pl -ries) period of 100 years
   cep n (ceps) A cep is an edible fungus. Cep scores 7 points.
cephalopod [seff-a-loh-pod] n (pl -s) sea mollusc with a head and tentacles, such as the octopus
cephalopods n ▷ cephalopod
ceramic n (pl -s) hard brittle material made by heating clay to a very high temperature ▶ pl art of producing ceramic objects ▶ adj made of ceramic
ceramics n ▷ ceramic
cereal n (pl -s) grass plant with edible grain, such as oat or wheat
cereals n ▷ cereal
cerebra n ▷ cerebrum
cerebral [ser-rib-ral, ser-reeb-ral] adj of the brain
cerebrum [serr-rib-rum] n (pl -brums, -bra) [-bra] main part of the brain
cerebrums n ▷ cerebrum
ceremonial adj ▷ ceremony
ceremonially adv ▷ ceremony
ceremonials n ▷ ceremony
ceremonies n ▷ ceremony
ceremonious adj excessively polite or formal

> **ceremoniously** adv
ceremoniously adv ▷ ceremonious
ceremony n (pl -nies) formal act or ritual
> **ceremonial** adj, n (pl -s) > **ceremonially** adv
cerise [ser-reess] adj cherry-red
certain adj (-er, -est) positive and confident
> **certainly** adv
certainer adj ▷ certain
certainest adj ▷ certain
certainly adv ▷ certain
certainties n ▷ certainty
certainty n (pl -ties) state of being sure
certifiable adj considered legally insane
> **certifiably** adv
certifiably n ▷ certifiable
certificate n (pl -s) official document stating
the details of a birth, academic course, etc.
certificates n ▷ certificate
certification n ▷ certify
certifications n ▷ certify
certified v ▷ certify
certifies v ▷ certify
certify v (-fies, -fying, -fied) confirm, attest to
> **certification** n (pl -s)
certifying v ▷ certify
certitude n (pl -s) confidence, certainty
certitudes n ▷ certitude
cervical adj ▷ cervix
cervices n ▷ cervix
cervix n (pl cervixes, cervices) narrow
entrance of the womb > **cervical** adj
cervixes n ▷ cervix
cessation n (pl -s) ceasing
cessations n ▷ cessation
cesspit, cesspool n (pl -s) covered tank or pit
for sewage
cesspits n ▷ cesspit
cesspool n ▷ cesspit
cesspools n ▷ cesspit
cetacean [sit-tay-shun] n (pl -s) fish-shaped sea
mammal such as a whale or dolphin
cetaceans n ▷ cetacean

ch pron. This is an old dialect form of **I**.
It's the only two-letter word that can
be formed with the letter C, and it's
a good word to remember because
it doesn't use any vowels. Ch scores
7 points.
cha n (**chas**). Cha is a slang word for
tea. Cha scores 8 points.

chafe v (chafes, chafing, chafed) make sore or
worn by rubbing
chafed v ▷ chafe
chafes v ▷ chafe
chaff¹ n (pl -s) grain husks

chaff² v (-s, -ing, -ed) (Old-fashioned) tease
good-naturedly
chaffed v ▷ chaff²
chaffinch n (pl -es) small European songbird
chaffinches n ▷ chaffinch
chaffing v ▷ chaff²
chaffs n ▷ chaff¹ ▶ v ▷ chaff²
chafing v ▷ chafe
chagrin [shag-grin] n (pl -s) annoyance and
disappointment
chagrined adj annoyed and disappointed
chagrins n ▷ chagrin
chain n (pl -s) flexible length of connected
metal links ▶ v (-s, -ing, -ed) restrict or fasten
with or as if with a chain
chained v ▷ chain
chaining v ▷ chain
chains n, v ▷ chain
chair n (pl -s) seat with a back, for one person
▶ v (-s, -ing, -ed) preside over (a meeting)
chaired v ▷ chair
chairing v ▷ chair
chairlift (pl -s) series of chairs suspended from
a moving cable for carrying people up a slope
chairlifts n ▷ chairlift
chairman, chairwoman n (pl -men, -women)
person in charge of a company's board of
directors or a meeting (also **chairperson**)
(pl -s)
chairmen n ▷ chairman
chairperson n ▷ chairman
chairpersons n ▷ chairman
chairs n, v ▷ chair
chairwoman n ▷ chairman
chairwomen n ▷ chairman
chaise [shaze] n (pl -s) (HIST) light horse-drawn
carriage
chaises n ▷ chaise
chalcedonies n ▷ chalcedony
chalcedony [kal-sed-don-ee] n (pl -nies) variety
of quartz
chalet n (pl -s) kind of Swiss wooden house
with a steeply sloping roof
chalets n ▷ chalet
chalice n (pl -s) large goblet
chalices n ▷ chalice
chalk n (pl -s) soft white rock consisting of
calcium carbonate ▶ v (-s, -ing, -ed) draw or
mark with chalk > **chalky** adj (-kier, -kiest)
chalked v ▷ chalk
chalkier adj ▷ chalk
chalkiest adj ▷ chalk
chalking v ▷ chalk
chalks n, v ▷ chalk
chalky adj ▷ chalk

challenge n (pl -s) demanding or stimulating situation ▸ v (-ges, -ging, -ged) issue a challenge to ▹ **challenger** n (pl -s)

challenged adj disabled as specified ▸ v ▹ **challenge**

challenger n ▹ **challenge**

challengers n ▹ **challenge**

challenges n, v ▹ **challenge**

challenging v ▹ **challenge**

chamber n (pl -s) hall used for formal meetings (Old-fashioned) ▸ pl set of rooms used as offices by a barrister

chamberlain n (pl -s) (HIST) officer who managed the household of a king or nobleman

chamberlains n ▹ **chamberlain**

chambermaid n (pl -s) woman employed to clean bedrooms in a hotel

chambermaids n ▹ **chambermaid**

chambers n ▹ **chamber**

chameleon [kam-**meal**-yon] n (pl -s) small lizard that changes colour to blend in with its surroundings

chameleons n ▹ **chameleon**

chamfer [cham-fer] v (-s, -ing, -ed) bevel the edge of

chamfered v ▹ **chamfer**

chamfering v ▹ **chamfer**

chamfers v ▹ **chamfer**

chamois [sham-wah] n (pl -ois) small mountain antelope

chamomile [kam-mo-mile] n (pl -s) ▹ **camomile**

chamomiles n ▹ **chamomile**

champ¹ v (-s, -ing, -ed) chew noisily

champ² n (pl -s) ▹ **champion**

champagne n (pl -s) sparkling white French wine

champagnes n ▹ **champagne**

champed v ▹ **champ¹**

champing v ▹ **champ¹**

champion n (pl -s) overall winner of a competition (foll. by of) ▸ v (-s, -ing, -ed) support ▸ adj (Dialect) excellent ▹ **championship** n (pl -s)

championed v ▹ **champion**

championing v ▹ **champion**

champions n, v ▹ **champion**

championship n ▹ **champion**

championships n ▹ **champion**

champs v ▹ **champ¹** ▸ n ▹ **champ²**

chance n (pl -s) likelihood, probability ▸ v (chances, chancing, chanced) risk, hazard

chanced v ▹ **chance**

chancel n (pl -s) part of a church containing the altar and choir

chancellor n (pl -s) head of government in some European countries ▹ **chancellorship** n (pl -s)

chancellors n ▹ **chancellor**

chancellorship n ▹ **chancellor**

chancellorships n ▹ **chancellor**

chancels n ▹ **chancel**

chances n, v ▹ **chance**

chancier adj ▹ **chancy**

chanciest adj ▹ **chancy**

chancing v ▹ **chance**

chancy adj (-cier, -ciest) uncertain, risky

chandelier [shan-dill-**eer**] n (pl -s) ornamental light with branches and holders for several candles or bulbs

chandeliers n ▹ **chandelier**

chandler n (pl -s) dealer, esp. in ships' supplies

chandlers n ▹ **chandler**

change n (pl -s) becoming different ▸ v (changes, changing, changed) make or become different

changeable adj changing often

changed v ▹ **change**

changeling n (pl -s) child believed to have been exchanged by fairies for another

changelings n ▹ **changeling**

changes n, v ▹ **change**

changing v ▹ **change**

channel n (pl -s) band of broadcasting frequencies ▸ v (-nels, -nelling, -nelled) direct or convey through a channel

channelled v ▹ **channel**

channelling v ▹ **channel**

channels n, v ▹ **channel**

chant v (-s, -ing, -ed) utter or sing (a slogan or psalm) ▸ n (pl -s) rhythmic or repetitive slogan

chanted v ▹ **chant**

chanter n (pl -s) (on bagpipes) pipe on which the melody is played

chanters n ▹ **chanter**

chanting v ▹ **chant**

chants v, n ▹ **chant**

chaos n complete disorder or confusion ▹ **chaotic** adj ▹ **chaotically** adv

chaotic adj ▹ **chaos**

chaotically adv ▹ **chaos**

chap n (pl -s) (Informal) man or boy

chapati, chapatti n (pl -s) (in Indian cookery) flat thin unleavened bread

chapatis n ▹ **chapati**

chapatti n ▹ **chapati**

chapattis n ▹ **chapati**

chapel n (pl -s) place of worship with its own altar, within a church chapels n ▷ chapel

chaperone [shap-per-rone] n (pl -s) older person who accompanies and supervises a young person or young people on a social occasion ▶ v (-ones, -oning, -oned) act as a chaperone to

chaperoned v ▷ chaperone

chaperones n, v ▷ chaperone

chaperoning v ▷ chaperone

chaplain n (pl -s) clergyman attached to a chapel, military body, or institution > chaplaincy n (pl -cies)

chaplaincies n ▷ chaplain

chaplaincy n ▷ chaplain

chaplains n ▷ chaplain

chaplet n (pl -s) garland for the head

chaplets n ▷ chaplet

chapped adj (of the skin) raw and cracked, through exposure to cold

chaps n ▷ chap

chapter n (pl -s) division of a book

chapters n ▷ chapter

char¹ v (chars, charring, charred) blacken by partial burning

char² (BRIT) (Informal) n (pl -s) charwoman ▶ v (chars, charring, charred) clean other people's houses as a job

char³ n (BRIT) (Old-fashioned slang) tea

charabanc [shar-rab-bang] n (pl -s) (Old-fashioned) coach for sightseeing

charabancs n ▷ charabanc

character n (pl -s) combination of qualities distinguishing a person, group, or place

characteristic n (pl -s) distinguishing feature or quality ▶ adj typical > characteristically adv

characteristically n ▷ characteristic

characteristics n ▷ characteristic

characterization n ▷ characterize

characterizations n ▷ characterize

characterize v (-rizes, -rizing, -rized) be a characteristic of (foll. by as) > characterization n (pl -s)

characterized v ▷ characterize

characterizes v ▷ characterize

characterizing v ▷ characterize

characters n ▷ character

charade [shar-rahd] n (pl -s) absurd pretence ▶ pl game in which one team acts out a word or phrase, which the other team has to guess

charades n ▷ charade

charcoal n (pl -s) black substance formed by partially burning wood

charcoals n ▷ charcoal

charge v (charges, charging, charged) ask as a

price ▶ n (pl -s) price charged > chargeable adj

chargeable adj ▷ charge

charged v ▷ charge

charger n (pl -s) device for charging an accumulator

chargers n ▷ charger

charges v, n ▷ charge

charging v ▷ charge

charier adj ▷ chary

chariest adj ▷ chary

chariot n (pl -s) two-wheeled horse-drawn vehicle used in ancient times in wars and races

charioteer n (pl -s) chariot driver

charioteers n ▷ charioteer

chariots n ▷ chariot

charisma [kar-rizz-ma] n (pl -s) person's power to attract or influence people > charismatic [kar-rizz-mat-ik] ▶ adj

charismas n ▷ charisma

charismatic adj ▷ charisma

charitable adj ▷ charity

charitably adv ▷ charity

charities n ▷ charity

charity n (pl -ties) organization that gives help, such as money or food, to those in need > charitable adj > charitably adv

charladies n ▷ charlady

charlady n (pl -ladies) (BRIT) (Informal) ▷ charwoman

charlatan [shar-lat-tan] n (pl -s) person who claims expertise that he or she does not have

charlatans n ▷ charlatan

charleston n (pl -s) lively dance of the 1920s

charlestons n ▷ charleston

charm n (pl -s) attractive quality ▶ v (-s, -ing, -ed) attract, delight > charmer n (pl -s)

charmed v ▷ charm

charmer n ▷ charm

charmers n ▷ charm

charming adj attractive ▶ v ▷ charm

charms n, v ▷ charm

charred v ▷ char¹, ²

charring v ▷ char¹, ²

chars v ▷ char¹, ², ▶ n ▷ char²

chart n (pl -s) graph, table, or diagram showing information ▶ v (-s, -ing, -ed) plot the course of

charted v ▷ chart

charter n (pl -s) document granting or demanding certain rights ▶ v (-s, -ing, -ed) hire by charter

chartered adj officially qualified to practise a profession ▶ v ▷ charter

chartering v ▷ charter

charters n, v ▷ charter

charting v ▷ chart

chartreuse [shar-trerz] n (pl -s) sweet-smelling green or yellow liqueur

chartreuses n ▷ chartreuse

charts n, v ▷ chart

charwoman n (pl charwomen) woman whose job is to clean other people's homes

charwomen n ▷ charwoman

chary [chair-ee] adj (-rier, -riest) wary, careful

chase¹ v (chases, chasing, chased) run after quickly in order to catch or drive away ▶ n (pl -s) chasing, pursuit

chase² v (chases, chasing, chased) engrave or emboss (metal)

chased v ▷ chase¹, ²

chaser n (pl -s) milder drink drunk after another stronger one

chasers n ▷ chaser

chases v ▷ chase¹, ² ▶ n ▷ chase¹

chasing v ▷ chase¹, ²

chasm [kaz-zum] n (pl -s) deep crack in the earth

chasms n ▷ chasm

chassis [shass-ee] n (pl -sis) frame, wheels, and mechanical parts of a vehicle

chaste adj (-r, -st) abstaining from sex outside marriage or altogether > chastely adv > chasteness n (pl -es) chastity n (pl -ties)

chastely adv ▷ chaste

chasten [chase-en] v (-s, -ing, -ed) subdue by criticism

chastened v ▷ chasten

chasteness n ▷ chaste

chastenesses n ▷ chaste

chastening v ▷ chasten

chastens v ▷ chasten

chaster adj ▷ chaste

chastest adj ▷ chaste

chastise v (-ises, -ising, -ised) scold severely > chastisement n (pl -s)

chastised v ▷ chastise

chastisement n ▷ chastise

chastisements n ▷ chastise

chastises v ▷ chastise

chastising v ▷ chastise

chastities n ▷ chaste

chastity n ▷ chaste

chat n (pl -s) informal conversation ▶ v (chats, chatting, chatted) have an informal conversation > chatty adj (-ttier, -ttiest) > chattily adv > chattiness n (pl -es)

chateau [shat-toe] n (pl -teaux, -teaus) French castle

chateaus n ▷ chateau

chateaux n ▷ chateau

chatelaine [shat-tell-lane] n (pl -s) (formerly) mistress of a large house or castle

chatelaines n ▷ chatelaine

chatroom n (pl -s) site on the Internet where users have group discussions by e-mail

chatrooms n ▷ chatroom

chats n, v ▷ chat

chatted v ▷ chat

chattel n (pl -s) (usually plural) possessions

chattels n ▷ chattel

chatter v (-s, -ing, -ed) speak quickly and continuously about unimportant things ▶ n (pl -s) idle talk

chatterbox n (pl -es) person who chatters a lot

chatterboxes n ▷ chatterbox

chattered v ▷ chatter

chattering v ▷ chatter

chatters v, n ▷ chatter

chattier adj ▷ chat

chattiest adj ▷ chat

chattily adv ▷ chat

chattiness n ▷ chat

chattinesses n ▷ chat

chatting v ▷ chat

chatty adj ▷ chat

chauffeur n (pl -s) person employed to drive a car for someone

chauffeurs n ▷ chauffeur

chauvinism [show-vin-iz-zum] n (pl -s) irrational belief that one's own country, race, group, or sex is superior > chauvinist n (pl -s) adj > chauvinistic adj > chauvinistically adv

chauvinisms n ▷ chauvinism

chauvinist n ▷ chauvinism

chauvinistic adj ▷ chauvinism

chauvinistically adv ▷ chauvinism

chauvinists n ▷ chauvinism

che pron. Like ch, che is an old dialect form of I. It scores 8 points.

cheap adj (-er, -est) costing relatively little > cheaply adv

cheapen v (-s, -ing, -ed) lower the reputation of

cheapened v ▷ cheapen

cheapening v ▷ cheapen

cheapens v ▷ cheapen

cheaper adj ▷ cheap

cheapest adj ▷ cheap

cheaply adv ▷ cheap

cheapskate n (pl -s) (Informal) miserly person

cheapskates n ▷ cheapskate

cheat v (-s, -ing, -ed) act dishonestly to gain profit or advantage ▶ n (pl -s) person who cheats

cheated v ▷ cheat

cheating v ▷ cheat

cheats v, n ▷ cheat

check v (-s, -ing, -ed) examine, investigate ▶ n (pl -s) test to ensure accuracy or progress

checked v ▷ check

checking v ▷ check

checkmate n (pl -s) (CHESS) winning position in which an opponent's king is under attack and unable to escape ▶ v (-mates, -mating, -mated) (CHESS) place the king of (one's opponent) in checkmate

checkmated v ▷ checkmate

checkmates n, v ▷ checkmate

checkmating v ▷ checkmate

checkout n (pl -s) counter in a supermarket, where customers pay

checkouts n ▷ checkout

checks v, n ▷ check

checkup n (pl -s) thorough medical examination

checkups n ▷ checkup

cheddar n (pl -s) firm orange or yellowy-white cheese

cheddars n ▷ cheddar

cheek n (pl -s) either side of the face below the eye (Informal) ▶ v (-s, -ing, -ed) (BRIT, AUST & NZ) (Informal) speak impudently to

cheeked v ▷ cheek

cheekier adj ▷ cheeky

cheekiest adj ▷ cheeky

cheekily adv ▷ cheeky

cheekiness n ▷ cheeky

cheekinesses n ▷ cheeky

cheeking v ▷ cheek

cheeks n, v ▷ cheek

cheeky adj (-kier, -kiest) impudent, disrespectful > **cheekily** adv > **cheekiness** n (pl -es)

cheep n (pl -s) young bird's high-pitched cry ▶ v (-s, -ing, -ed) utter a cheep

cheeped v ▷ cheep

cheeping v ▷ cheep

cheeps n, v ▷ cheep

cheer v (-s, -ing, -ed) applaud or encourage with shouts ▶ n (pl -s) shout of applause or encouragement > **cheerful** adj (-ller, -llest) > **cheerfully** adv > **cheerfulness** n > **cheery** adj (-rier, -riest) > **cheerily** adv

cheered v ▷ cheer

cheerful adj ▷ cheer

cheerfuller adj ▷ cheer

cheerfullest adj ▷ cheer

cheerfully adv ▷ cheer

cheerfulness n ▷ cheer

cheerier adj ▷ cheer

cheeriest adj ▷ cheer

cheerily adv ▷ cheer

cheering v ▷ cheer

cheerio interj (Informal) goodbye ▶ n (pl -s) (AUST & NZ) small red cocktail sausage

cheerios n ▷ cheerio

cheerless adj dreary, gloomy > **cheerlessly** adv > **cheerlessness** n

cheerlessly adv ▷ cheerless

cheerlessness n ▷ cheerless

cheers v, n ▷ cheer

cheery adj ▷ cheer

cheese n (pl -s) food made from coagulated milk curd > **cheesy** adj (pl -sier, -siest) > **cheesily** adv > **cheesiness** n

cheeseburger n (pl -s) hamburger topped with melted cheese

cheeseburgers n ▷ cheeseburger

cheesecake n (pl -s) dessert with a biscuit-crumb base covered with a sweet cream-cheese mixture

cheesecakes n ▷ cheesecake

cheesecloth n (pl -s) light cotton cloth

cheesecloths n ▷ cheesecloth

cheeses n ▷ cheese

cheesier adj ▷ cheese

cheesiest adj ▷ cheese

cheesily adv ▷ cheese

cheesiness n ▷ cheese

cheesy adj ▷ cheese

cheetah n (pl -s) large fast-running spotted African wild cat

cheetahs n ▷ cheetah

chef n (pl -s) cook in a restaurant

chefs n ▷ chef

chemical n (pl -s) substance used in or resulting from a reaction involving changes to atoms or molecules ▶ adj of chemistry or chemicals > **chemically** adv

chemically adv ▷ chemical

chemicals n ▷ chemical

chemise [shem-meez] n (pl -s) (Old-fashioned) woman's loose-fitting slip

chemises n ▷ chemise

chemist n (pl -s) shop selling medicines and cosmetics

chemistries n ▷ chemistry

chemistry n (pl -ries) science of the composition, properties, and reactions of substances

chemists n ▷ chemist

chemotherapies n ▷ chemotherapy

chemotherapy n (pl -apies) treatment of disease, often cancer, using chemicals

chenille [shen-neel] n (pl -s) (fabric of) thick tufty yarn

chenilles n ▷ chenille

cheque n (pl -s) written order to one's bank to pay money from one's account

chequer n (pl chequers) piece used in Chinese chequers ▶ pl game of draughts

chequered adj marked by varied fortunes

chequers n ▷ chequer

cheques n ▷ cheque

cherish v (-es, -ing, -ed) cling to (an idea or feeling)

cherished v ▷ cherish

cherishes v ▷ cherish

cherishing v ▷ cherish

cheroot [sher-root] n (pl -s) cigar with both ends cut flat

cheroots n ▷ cheroot

cherries n ▷ cherry

cherry n (pl -ries) small red or black fruit with a stone ▶ adj deep red

cherub n (pl -s, -ubim) angel, often represented as a winged child > **cherubic** [cher-rew-bik] ▶ adj

cherubic adj ▷ cherub

cherubim n ▷ cherub

cherubs n ▷ cherub

chervil n (pl -s) aniseed-flavoured herb

chervils n ▷ chervil

chess n (pl -es) game for two players with 16 pieces each, played on a chequered board of 64 squares

chesses n ▷ chess

chessman n (pl -men) piece used in chess

chessmen n ▷ chessman

chest n (pl -s) front of the body, from neck to waist

chesterfield n (pl -s) couch with high padded sides and back

chesterfields n ▷ chesterfield

chestnut n (pl -s) reddish-brown edible nut (Informal) ▶ adj (of hair or a horse) reddish-brown

chestnuts n ▷ chestnut

chests n ▷ chest

chevron [shev-ron] n (pl -s) V-shaped pattern, esp. on the sleeve of a military uniform to indicate rank

chevrons n ▷ chevron

chew v (-s, -ing, -ed) grind (food) between the teeth

chewed v ▷ chew

chewier adj ▷ chewy

chewiest adj ▷ chewy

chewiness n ▷ chewy

chewinesses n ▷ chewy

chewing v ▷ chew

chews v ▷ chew

chewy adj (-ier, -iest) requiring a lot of chewing > **chewiness** n (pl -es)

chi n (chis). Chi is a letter of the Greek alphabet, and is worth 8 points.

chianti [kee-ant-ee] n (pl -s) dry red Italian wine

chiantis n ▷ chianti

chiaroscuro [kee-ah-roh-skew-roh] n (pl -s) distribution of light and shade in a picture

chiaroscuros n ▷ chiaroscuro

chic [sheek] adj (-er, -est) stylish, elegant ▶ n (pl -s) stylishness, elegance

chicane [shik-kane] n (pl -s) obstacle in a motor-racing circuit

chicaneries n ▷ chicanery

chicanery n (pl -eries) trickery, deception

chicanes n ▷ chicane

chicer adj ▷ chic

chicest adj ▷ chic

chick n (pl -s) baby bird

chicken n (pl -s) domestic fowl ▶ adj (Slang) cowardly

chickenpox n (pl -es) infectious disease with an itchy rash

chickenpoxes n ▷ chickenpox

chickens n ▷ chicken

chickpea n (pl -s) edible yellow pealike seed

chickpeas n ▷ chickpea

chicks n ▷ chick

chickweed n (pl -s) weed with small white flowers

chickweeds n ▷ chickweed

chicories n ▷ chicory

chicory n (pl -ries) plant whose leaves are used in salads

chics n ▷ chic

chid v ▷ chide

chidden v ▷ chide

chide v (chiding, chided or chid) (chid or chidden) rebuke, scold

chided v ▷ chide

chiding v ▷ chide

chief n (pl -s) head of a group of people ▶ adj most important

chiefly adv especially

chiefs n ▷ chief

chieftain n (pl -s) leader of a tribe

chieftains n ▷ chieftain

chiffon [shif-fon] n (pl -s) fine see-through fabric

chiffons n ▷ chiffon

chignon [sheen-yon] n (pl -s) knot of hair pinned up at the back of the head chignons n ▷ chignon

chihuahua [chee-**wah**-wah] n (pl -s) tiny short-haired dog
chihuahuas n ▷ chihuahua

chilblain n (pl -s) inflammation of the fingers or toes, caused by exposure to cold
chilblains n ▷ chilblain

child n (pl children) young human being, boy or girl ▷ childhood n (pl -s) ▷ childless adj
> childlessness n

childbirth n (pl -s) giving birth to a child
childbirths n ▷ childbirth
childhood n ▷ child
childhoods n ▷ child

childish adj immature, silly > childishly adv
> childishness n
childishly adv ▷ childish
childishness n ▷ childish
childless adj ▷ child
childlessness n ▷ child

childlike adj innocent, trustful
children n ▷ child
chili n ▷ chilli
chilies n ▷ chilli

chill n (pl -s) feverish cold ▷ v (-s, -ing, -ed) make (something) cool or cold ▷ adj unpleasantly cold
chilled v ▷ chill

chilli, chili n (pl -es) small red or green hot-tasting capsicum pod, used in cooking
chillier adj ▷ chilly
chillies n ▷ chilli
chilliest adj ▷ chilly
chilliness n ▷ chilly
chillinesses n ▷ chilly
chilling v ▷ chill
chills n, v ▷ chill

chilly adj (-llier, -lliest) moderately cold
> chilliness n (pl -es)

chime n (pl -s) musical ringing sound of a bell or clock ▷ v (-mes, -ming, -med) make a musical ringing sound
chimed v ▷ chime

chimera [kime-**meer**-a] n (pl -s) unrealistic hope or idea
chimeras n ▷ chimera
chimes n, v ▷ chime
chiming v ▷ chime

chimney n (pl -s) hollow vertical structure for carrying away smoke from a fire
chimneys n ▷ chimney

chimp n (pl -s) (Informal) ▷ chimpanzee

chimpanzee n (pl -s) intelligent black African ape
chimpanzees n ▷ chimpanzee

chimps n ▷ chimp

chin n (pl -s) part of the face below the mouth

china n (pl -s) fine earthenware or porcelain
chinas n ▷ china

chinchilla n (pl -s) S American rodent bred for its soft grey fur
chinchillas n ▷ chinchilla

chine n (pl -s) cut of meat including part of the backbone
chines n ▷ chine

chink¹ n (pl -s) small narrow opening

chink² v (-s, -ing, -ed) ▷ n (pl -s) (make) a light ringing sound
chinked v ▷ chink²
chinking v ▷ chink²
chinks n ▷ chink¹, ² ▷ v ▷ chink²
chins n ▷ chin

chintz n (pl -es) printed cotton fabric with a glazed finish
chintzes n ▷ chintz

chinwag n (pl -s) (BRIT, AUST & NZ) (Informal) chat
chinwags n ▷ chinwag

chip n (pl -s) strip of potato, fried in deep fat ▷ v (chips, chipping, chipped) break small pieces from

chipboard n (pl -s) thin board made of compressed wood particles
chipboards n ▷ chipboard

chipmunk n (pl -s) small squirrel-like N American rodent with a striped back
chipmunks n ▷ chipmunk
chipped v ▷ chip

chippie n (pl -s) (BRIT, AUST & NZ) (Informal) carpenter
chippies n ▷ chippie
chipping v ▷ chip
chips n, v ▷ chip

chiropodist [kir-**rop**-pod-ist] n (pl -s) person who treats minor foot complaints
> chiropody n
chiropodists n ▷ chiropodist
chiropody n ▷ chiropodist

chiropractic [kire-oh-**prak**-tik] n (pl -s) system of treating bodily disorders by manipulation of the spine > chiropractor n (pl -s)
chiropractics n ▷ chiropractic
chiropractor n ▷ chiropractic
chiropractors n ▷ chiropractic

chirp v (-s, -ing, -ed) (of a bird or insect) make a short high-pitched sound ▷ n (pl -s) chirping sound
chirped v ▷ chirp
chirpier adj ▷ chirpy
chirpiest adj ▷ chirpy
chirpily adv ▷ chirpy

chirpiness n ▷ chirpy
chirping v ▷ chirp
chirps v, n ▷ chirp
chirpy adj (-pier, -piest) (Informal) lively and cheerful > **chirpily** adv > **chirpiness** n
chisel n (pl -s) metal tool with a sharp end for shaping wood or stone ▶ v (-els, -elling, -elled) carve or form with a chisel
chiselled v ▷ chisel
chiselling v ▷ chisel
chisels n, v ▷ chisel
chit¹ n (pl -s) short official note, such as a receipt
chit² n (pl -s) (BRIT, AUST & NZ) (old-fashioned) pert or impudent girl
chitchat n (pl -s) chat, gossip
chitchats n ▷ chitchat
chits n ▷ chit¹, ²
chitterlings pl n pig's intestines cooked as food
chivalries n ▷ chivalry
chivalrous adj ▷ chivalry
chivalrously adv ▷ chivalry
chivalry n (pl -ries) courteous behaviour, esp. by men towards women > **chivalrous** adj > **chivalrously** adv
chives pl n herb with a mild onion flavour
chivvied v ▷ chivvy
chivvies n ▷ chivvy
chivvy v (-vies, -vying, -vied) (Informal) harass, nag
chivvying v ▷ chivvy
chloride n (pl -s) compound of chlorine and another substance
chlorides n ▷ chloride
chlorinate v (-ates, -ating, -ated) disinfect (water) with chlorine > **chlorination** n
chlorinated v ▷ chlorinate
chlorinates v ▷ chlorinate
chlorinating v ▷ chlorinate
chlorination n ▷ chlorinate
chlorine n (pl -s) strong-smelling greenish-yellow gaseous element, used to disinfect water
chlorines n ▷ chlorine
chlorofluorocarbon n (pl -s) any of various gaseous compounds of carbon, hydrogen, chlorine, and fluorine, used in refrigerators and aerosol propellants, some of which break down the ozone in the atmosphere
chlorofluorocarbons n ▷ chlorofluorocarbon
chloroform n (pl -s) strong-smelling liquid formerly used as an anaesthetic
chloroforms n ▷ chloroform
chlorophyll n (pl -s) green colouring matter

of plants, which enables them to convert sunlight into energy
chlorophylls n ▷ chlorophyll
chock n (pl -s) block or wedge used to prevent a heavy object from moving
chockablock adj completely full
chocks n ▷ chock
chocolate n (pl -s) sweet food made from cacao seeds ▶ adj dark brown
chocolates n ▷ chocolate
choice n (pl -s) choosing ▶ adj (**choicer, choicest**) of high quality
choicer adj ▷ choice
choices n ▷ choice
choicest adj ▷ choice
choir n (pl -s) organized group of singers, esp. in church
choirs n ▷ choir
choke v (**chokes, choking, choked**) hinder or stop the breathing of (a person) by strangling or smothering ▶ n (pl -s) device controlling the amount of air that is mixed with the fuel in a petrol engine
choked v ▷ choke
choker n (pl -s) tight-fitting necklace
chokers n ▷ choker
chokes v, n ▷ choke
choking v ▷ choke
cholera [kol-ler-a] n (pl -s) serious infectious disease causing severe vomiting and diarrhoea
choleras n ▷ cholera
choleric [kol-ler-ik] adj bad-tempered
cholesterol [kol-**lest**-er-oll] n (pl -s) fatty substance found in animal tissue, an excess of which can cause heart disease
cholesterols n ▷ cholesterol
chomp v (-s, -ing, -ed) chew noisily
chomped v ▷ chomp
chomping v ▷ chomp
chomps v ▷ chomp
chook n (pl -s) (AUST & NZ) hen or chicken
chooks n ▷ chook
choose v (**chooses, choosing, chose, chosen**) select from a number of alternatives
chooses v ▷ choose
choosier adj ▷ choosy
choosiest adj ▷ choosy
choosing v ▷ choose
choosy adj (-sier, -siest) (Informal) fussy, hard to please
chop¹ v (**chops, chopping, chopped**) cut with a blow from an axe or knife (BOXING) (KARATE) ▶ n (pl -s) cutting or sharp blow
chop² v (**chops, chopping, chopped**) change

one's mind repeatedly
chopped v ▷ chop¹, ²
chopper n (pl -s) (Informal) helicopter
choppers n ▷ chopper
choppier adj ▷ choppy
choppiest adj ▷ choppy
choppiness n ▷ choppy
choppinesses n ▷ choppy
chopping v ▷ chop¹, ²
choppy adj (-pier, -piest) (of the sea) fairly
rough ▷ **choppiness** n (pl -es)
chops pl n (BRIT, AUST & NZ) (Informal) jaws,
cheeks ▶ v ▷ chop¹, ² ▶ n ▷ chop¹
chopsticks pl n pair of thin sticks used to eat
Chinese food
choral adj of a choir
chorale [kor-rahl] n (pl -s) slow stately hymn
tune
chorales n ▷ chorale
chord¹ n (pl -s) (MATHS) straight line joining two
points on a curve
chord² n (pl -s) simultaneous sounding of
three or more musical notes
chords n ▷ chord¹, ²
chore n (pl -s) routine task
choreographer n ▷ choreography
choreographers n ▷ choreography
choreographic adj ▷ choreography
choreographies n ▷ choreography
choreography n (pl -phies) composition
of steps and movements for dancing
▷ **choreographer** n (pl -s) ▷ **choreographic** adj
chores n ▷ chore
chorister n (pl -s) singer in a choir
choristers n ▷ chorister
chortle v (-tles, -tling, -tled) chuckle in
amusement ▶ n (pl -s) amused chuckle
chortled v ▷ chortle
chortles v, n ▷ chortle
chortling v ▷ chortle
chorus n (pl -es) large choir ▶ v (-es, -ing, -ed)
sing or say together
chorused v ▷ chorus
choruses n, v ▷ chorus
chorusing v ▷ chorus
chose v ▷ choose
chosen v ▷ choose
chow n (pl -s) thick-coated dog with a curled
tail, orig. from China
chowder n (pl -s) thick soup containing clams
or fish
chowders n ▷ chowder
chows n ▷ chow
christen v (-s, -ing, -ed) baptize ▷ **christening**
n (pl -s)

christened v ▷ christen
christening v, n ▷ christen
christenings n ▷ christen
christens v ▷ christen
chromatic adj of colour or colours
▷ **chromatically** adv
chromatically adv ▷ chromatic
chromatographies n ▷ chromatic
chromatography n (pl -phies) separation and
analysis of the components of a substance
by slowly passing it through an adsorbing
material
chrome n ▷ chromium
chromes n ▷ chromium
chromium, chrome n (pl -s) (CHEM) grey
metallic element used in steel alloys and for
electroplating
chromiums n ▷ chromium
chromosome n (pl -s) microscopic gene-
carrying body in the nucleus of a cell
chromosomes n ▷ chromosome
chronic adj (of an illness) lasting a long time
▷ **chronically** adv
chronically adv ▷ chronic
chronicle n (pl -s) record of events in order of
occurrence ▶ v (-les, -ing, -led) record in or as
if in a chronicle ▷ **chronicler** n (pl -s)
chronicled v ▷ chronicle
chronicler n ▷ chronicle
chroniclers n ▷ chronicle
chronicles v ▷ chronicle
chronicling v ▷ chronicle
chronological adj ▷ chronology
chronologically adv ▷ chronology
chronologies n ▷ chronology
chronology n (pl -gies) arrangement or list of
events in order of occurrence ▷ **chronological**
adj ▷ **chronologically** adv
chronometer n (pl -s) timepiece designed to
be accurate in all conditions
chronometers n ▷ chronometer
chrysalis [kriss-a-liss] n (pl -es) insect in the
stage between larva and adult, when it is in
a cocoon
chrysalises n ▷ chrysalis
chrysanthemum n (pl -s) garden flower with a
large head made up of thin petals
chrysanthemums n ▷ chrysanthemum
chub n (pl chub) European freshwater fish of
the carp family
chubbier adj ▷ chubby
chubbiest adj ▷ chubby
chubbiness n ▷ chubby
chubby adj (-bier, -biest) plump and round
▷ **chubbiness** n

chuck¹ v (-s, -ing, -ed) (*Informal*) throw

chuck² n (pl -s) cut of beef from the neck to the shoulder

chucked v ▷ chuck¹

chucking v ▷ chuck¹

chuckle v (-les, -ling, -led) laugh softly ▶ n (pl -s) soft laugh

chuckled v ▷ chuckle

chuckles v, n ▷ chuckle

chuckling v ▷ chuckle

chucks v ▷ chuck¹ ▶ n ▷ chuck²

chuffed adj (*Informal*) very pleased

chug n (pl -s) short dull sound like the noise of an engine ▶ v (chugs, chugging, chugged) operate or move with this sound

chugged v ▷ chug

chugging v ▷ chug

chugs n, v ▷ chug

chukka n (pl -s) period of play in polo

chukkas n ▷ chukka

chum (*Informal*) n (pl -s) close friend ▶ v (chums, chumming, chummed) form a close friendship with > **chummy** adj (-mmier, -mmiest) > **chumminess** n (pl -es)

chummed v ▷ chum

chummier adj ▷ chum

chummiest adj ▷ chum

chumminess n ▷ chum

chumminesses n ▷ chum

chumming v ▷ chum

chummy adj ▷ chum

chump n (pl -s) (*Informal*) stupid person

chumps n ▷ chump

chums n, v ▷ chump

chunk n (pl -s) thick solid piece

chunkier adj ▷ chunky

chunkiest adj ▷ chunky

chunkiness n ▷ chunky

chunkinesses n ▷ chunky

chunks n ▷ chunk

chunky adj (-kier, -kiest) (of a person) broad and heavy > **chunkiness** n (pl -es)

church n (pl -s) building for public Christian worship

churches n ▷ church

churchgoer n (pl -s) person who attends church regularly

churchgoers n ▷ churchgoer

churchwarden n (pl -s) member of a congregation who assists the vicar

churchwardens n ▷ churchwarden

churchyard n (pl -s) grounds round a church, used as a graveyard

churchyards n ▷ churchyard

churlish adj surly and rude > **churlishly** adv

> **churlishness** n

churlishly adv ▷ churlish

churlishness n ▷ churlish

churn n (pl -s) machine in which cream is shaken to make butter ▶ v (-s, -ing, -ed) stir (cream) vigorously to make butter

churned v ▷ churn

churning v ▷ churn

churns n, v ▷ churn

chute¹ [shoot] n (pl -s) steep slope down which things may be slid

chute² n (pl -s) (*Informal*) ▷ parachute

chutes n ▷ chute¹, ²

chutney n (pl -s) pickle made from fruit, vinegar, spices, and sugar

chutneys n ▷ chutney

cicada [sik-kah-da] n (pl -s) large insect that makes a high-pitched drone

cicadas n ▷ cicada

cicatrices n ▷ cicatrix

cicatrix [sik-a-trix] n (pl -trices) scar

   cid n (cids). A cid is a hero or commander. Cid scores 6 points.

cider n (pl -s) alcoholic drink made from fermented apple juice

ciders n ▷ cider

cigar n (pl -s) roll of cured tobacco leaves for smoking

cigarette n (pl -s) thin roll of shredded tobacco in thin paper, for smoking

cigarettes n ▷ cigarette

cigars n ▷ cigar

cinch [sinch] n (pl -es) (*Informal*) easy task

cinches n ▷ cinch

cinder n (pl -s) piece of material that will not burn, left after burning coal

cinders n ▷ cinder

cinema n (pl -s) place for showing films

> **cinematic** adj

cinemas n ▷ cinema

cinematic adj ▷ cinema

cinematographer n ▷ cinematography

cinematographers n ▷ cinematography

cinematography n technique of making films

> **cinematographer** n (pl -s)

cineraria n (pl -s) garden plant with daisy-like flowers

cinerarias n ▷ cineraria

cinnamon n (pl -s) spice obtained from the bark of an Asian tree

cinnamons n ▷ cinnamon

cipher, cypher [sife-er] n (pl -s) system of secret writing

ciphers n ▷ cipher

circa [sir-ka] prep (LATIN) approximately, about

circle n (pl -s) perfectly round geometric figure, line, or shape ▶ v (**circles, circling, circled**) move in a circle (round)
circled v ▷ circle
circles n, v ▷ circle

circlet n (pl -s) circular ornament worn on the head
circlets n ▷ circlet
circling v ▷ circle

circuit n (pl -s) complete route or course, esp. a circular one

circuitous [sir-kew-it-uss] adj indirect and lengthy > **circuitously** adv
circuitously adv ▷ circuitous

circuitry [sir-kit-tree] n electrical circuit(s)
circuits n ▷ circuit

circular adj in the shape of a circle ▶ n (pl -s) letter for general distribution > **circularity** n
circularity n ▷ circular
circulars n ▷ circular

circulate v (**-lates, -lating, -lated**) send, go, or pass from place to place or person to person > **circulatory** adj
circulated v ▷ circulate
circulates v ▷ circulate
circulating v ▷ circulate

circulation n flow of blood around the body
circulatory adj ▷ circulate

circumcise v (**-cises, -cising, -cised**) remove the foreskin of > **circumcision** n (pl -s)
circumcised v ▷ circumcise
circumcises v ▷ circumcise
circumcising v ▷ circumcise
circumcision n ▷ circumcise
circumcisions n ▷ circumcise

circumference n (pl -s) boundary of a specified area or shape, esp. of a circle
circumferences n ▷ circumference

circumflex n (pl -es) mark (^) over a vowel to show that it is pronounced in a particular way
circumflexes n ▷ circumflex

circumlocution n (pl -s) indirect way of saying something
circumlocutions n ▷ circumlocution

circumnavigate v (**-gates, -gating, -gated**) sail right round > **circumnavigation** n (pl -s)
circumnavigated v ▷ circumnavigate
circumnavigates v ▷ circumnavigate
circumnavigating v ▷ circumnavigate
circumnavigation n ▷ circumnavigate
circumnavigations n ▷ circumnavigate

circumscribe v (**-scribes, -scribing, -scribed**) limit, restrict > **circumscription** n (pl -s)
circumscribed v ▷ circumscribe

circumscribes v ▷ circumscribe
circumscribing v ▷ circumscribe
circumscription n ▷ circumscribe
circumscriptions n ▷ circumscribe

circumspect adj cautious and careful not to take risks > **circumspectly** adv > **circumspection** n
circumspection n ▷ circumspect
circumspectly adv ▷ circumspect

circumstance n (pl -s) (usu. pl) occurrence or condition that accompanies or influences a person or event
circumstances n ▷ circumstance

circumstantial adj (of evidence) strongly suggesting something but not proving it

circumvent v (**-s, -ing, -ed**) avoid or get round (a rule etc.) > **circumvention** n (pl -s)
circumvented v ▷ circumvent
circumventing v ▷ circumvent
circumvention n ▷ circumvent
circumventions n ▷ circumvent
circumvents v ▷ circumvent

circus n (pl -es) (performance given by) a travelling company of acrobats, clowns, performing animals, etc.
circuses n ▷ circus

cirrhosis [sir-roh-siss] n serious liver disease, often caused by drinking too much alcohol > **cirrhotic** adj
cirrhotic adj ▷ cirrhosis
cirri n ▷ cirrus

cirrus n (pl -ri) high wispy cloud

cistern n (pl -s) water tank, esp. one that holds water for flushing a toilet
cisterns n ▷ cistern

citadel n (pl -s) fortress in a city
citadels n ▷ citadel
citation n ▷ cite
citations n ▷ cite

cite v (**cites, citing, cited**) quote, refer to > **citation** n (pl -s)
cited v ▷ cite
cites v ▷ cite
cities n ▷ city
citing v ▷ cite

citizen n (pl -s) native or naturalized member of a state or nation > **citizenship** n (pl -s)
citizens n ▷ citizen
citizenship n ▷ citizen
citizenships n ▷ citizen

city n (pl -ties) large or important town

civet [siv-vit] n (pl -s) spotted catlike African mammal
civets n ▷ civet

civic adj of a city or citizens

civics n study of the rights and responsibilities of citizenship

civil adj relating to the citizens of a state as opposed to the armed forces or the Church > **civilly** adv

civilian n (pl -s) ▸ adj (person) not belonging to the armed forces

civilians n ▷ civilian

civilities n ▷ civility

civility n (pl -ities) polite or courteous behaviour

civilization n (pl -s) high level of human cultural and social development

civilizations n ▷ civilization

civilize v (-izes, -izing, -ized) refine or educate (a person)

civilized v ▷ civilize

civilizes v ▷ civilize

civilizing v ▷ civilize

civilly adv ▷ civil

civvies pl n (BRIT, AUST & NZ) (Slang) ordinary clothes that are not part of a uniform

clack n (pl -s) sound made by two hard objects striking each other ▸ v (-s, -ing, -ed) make this sound

clacked v ▷ clack

clacking v ▷ clack

clacks n, v ▷ clack

clad (clads, cladding, clad) ▷ clothe

cladding n (pl -s) material used to cover the outside of a building ▸ v ▷ clad

claddings n ▷ cladding

clads v ▷ clad

claim v (-s, -ing, -ed) assert as a fact ▸ n (pl -s) assertion that something is true > **claimant** n (pl -s)

claimant n ▷ claim

claimants n ▷ claim

claimed v ▷ claim

claiming v ▷ claim

claims v, n ▷ claim

clairvoyance n (pl -s) power of perceiving things beyond the natural range of the senses > **clairvoyant** n (pl -s) adj

clairvoyances n ▷ clairvoyance

clairvoyant n, adj ▷ clairvoyance

clairvoyants n ▷ clairvoyance

clam n (pl -s) edible shellfish with a hinged shell ▸ v (clams, clamming, clammed) (Informal) stop talking, esp. through nervousness

clamber v (-s, -ing, -ed) climb awkwardly

clambered v ▷ clamber

clambering v ▷ clamber

clambers v ▷ clamber

clammed v ▷ clam

clammier adj ▷ clammy

clammiest adj ▷ clammy

clamming v ▷ clam

clammy adj (-mier, -miest) unpleasantly moist and sticky

clamour n (pl -s) loud protest ▸ v (-s, -ing, -ed) make a loud noise or outcry > **clamorous** adj > **clamorously** adv > **clamorousness** n

clamoured v ▷ clamour

clamouring v ▷ clamour

clamourous adj ▷ clamour

clamourously adv ▷ clamour

clamourousness n ▷ clamour

clamours n, v ▷ clamour

clamp n (pl -s) tool with movable jaws for holding things together tightly ▸ v (-s, -ing, -ed) fasten with a clamp

clamped v ▷ clamp

clamping v ▷ clamp

clamps n, v ▷ clamp

clams v, n ▷ clam

clan n (pl -s) group of families with a common ancestor, esp. among Scottish Highlanders

clandestine adj secret and concealed > **clandestinely** adv

clandestinely adv ▷ clandestine

clang v (-s, -ing, -ed) make a loud ringing metallic sound ▸ n (pl -s) ringing metallic sound

clanged v ▷ clang

clanger n (pl -s) (Informal) obvious mistake

clangers n ▷ clanger

clanging v ▷ clang

clangour n (pl -s) loud continuous clanging sound

clangours n ▷ clangour

clangs v, n ▷ clang

clank n (pl -s) harsh metallic sound ▸ v (-s, -ing, -ed) make such a sound

clanked v ▷ clank

clanking v ▷ clank

clanks n, v ▷ clank

clannish adj (of a group) tending to exclude outsiders > **clannishness** n

clannishness n ▷ clannish

clans n ▷ clan

clap v (claps, clapping, clapped) applaud by hitting the palms of one's hands sharply together ▸ n (pl -s) act or sound of clapping

clapped v ▷ clap

clapper n (pl -s) piece of metal inside a bell, which causes it to sound when struck against the side

clapperboard n (pl -s) pair of hinged boards

clapped together during filming to help in synchronizing sound and picture
clapperboards n ▷ clapperboard
clappers n ▷ clapper
clapping v ▷ clap
claps v, n ▷ clap
claptrap n (pl -s) (Informal) foolish or pretentious talk
claptraps n ▷ claptrap
claret [klar-rit] n (pl -s) dry red wine from Bordeaux
clarets n ▷ claret
clarification n ▷ clarify
clarifications n ▷ clarify
clarified v ▷ clarify
clarifies v ▷ clarify
clarify v (-fies, -fying, -fied) make (a matter) clear and unambiguous > **clarification** n (pl -s)
clarifying v ▷ clarify
clarinet n (pl -s) keyed woodwind instrument with a single reed > **clarinettist** n (pl -s)
clarinets n ▷ clarinet
clarinettist n ▷ clarinet
clarinettists n ▷ clarinet
clarion n (pl -s) obsolete high-pitched trumpet
clarions n ▷ clarion
clarities n ▷ clarity
clarity n (pl -ities) clearness
clash v (-es, -ing, -ed) come into conflict ▶ n (pl -es) fight, argument
clashed v ▷ clash
clashes v, n ▷ clash
clashing v ▷ clash
clasp n (pl -s) device for fastening things ▶ v (-s, -ing, -ed) grasp or embrace firmly
clasped v ▷ clasp
clasping v ▷ clasp
clasps n, v ▷ clasp
class n (pl -es) group of people sharing a similar social position ▶ v (-es, -ing, -ed) place in a class
classed v ▷ class
classes n, v ▷ class
classic adj being a typical example of something ▶ n (pl -s) author, artist, or work of art of recognized excellence ▶ pl study of ancient Greek and Roman literature and culture
classical adj of or in a restrained conservative style > **classically** adv
classically adv ▷ classical
classicism n artistic style showing emotional restraint and regularity of form > **classicist** n (pl -s)

classicist n ▷ classicism
classicists n ▷ classicism
classics n ▷ classic
classier adj ▷ classy
classiest adj ▷ classy
classifiable adj ▷ classify
classification n ▷ classify
classifications n ▷ classify
classified v ▷ classify
classifies v ▷ classify
classify v (-fies, -fying, -fied) divide into groups with similar characteristics > **classifiable** adj > **classification** n (pl -s)
classifying v ▷ classify
classing v ▷ class
classy adj (classier, classiest) (Informal) stylish and elegant
clatter v (-s, -ing, -ed) ▶ n (pl -s) (make) a rattling noise
clattered v ▷ clatter
clattering v ▷ clatter
clatters v, n ▷ clatter
clause n (pl -s) section of a legal document
clauses n ▷ clause
claustrophobia n (pl -s) abnormal fear of confined spaces > **claustrophobic** adj
claustrophobia n ▷ claustrophobia
claustrophobias n ▷ claustrophobia
claustrophobic adj ▷ claustrophobia
clavichord n (pl -s) early keyboard instrument
clavichords n ▷ clavichord
clavicle n (pl -s) collarbone
clavicles n ▷ clavicle
claw n (pl -s) sharp hooked nail of a bird or beast ▶ v (-s, -ing, -ed) tear with claws or nails
clawed v ▷ claw
clawing v ▷ claw
claws n, v ▷ claw
clay n (pl -s) fine-grained earth, soft when moist and hardening when baked, used to make bricks and pottery > **clayey** adj
clayey adj ▷ clay
claymore n (pl -s) large two-edged sword formerly used by Scottish Highlanders
claymores n ▷ claymore
clays n ▷ clay
clean adj (-er, -est) free from dirt or impurities ▶ v (-s, -ing, -ed) make (something) free from dirt ▶ adv (Not standard) completely > **cleaner** n (pl -s) > **cleanly** adv > **cleanliness** n (pl -es)
cleaned v ▷ clean
cleaner n, adj ▷ clean
cleaners n ▷ clean
cleanest adj ▷ clean
cleaning v ▷ clean

cleanliness *n* ▷ clean
cleanlinesses *n* ▷ clean
cleanly *adv* ▷ clean
cleans *v* ▷ clean
cleanse *v* (-ses, -sing, -sed) make clean
▷ **cleanser** *n* (*pl* -s)
cleansed *v* ▷ cleanse
cleanser *n* ▷ cleanse
cleansers *n* ▷ cleanse
cleanses *v* ▷ cleanse
cleansing *v* ▷ cleanse
clear *adj* (-er, -est) free from doubt or confusion
▶ *adv* out of the way ▶ *v* (-s, -ing, -ed) make or
become clear ▷ **clearly** *adv*
clearance *n* (*pl* -s) clearing
clearances *n* ▷ clear
cleared *v* ▷ clear
clearer *adj* ▷ clear
clearest *adj* ▷ clear
clearing *n* (*pl* -s) treeless area in a wood ▶ *v*
▷ clear
clearings *n* ▷ clearing
clearly *adv* ▷ clear
clears *v* ▷ clear
clearway *n* (*pl* -s) stretch of road on which
motorists may stop in an emergency
clearways *n* ▷ clearway
cleat *n* (*pl* -s) wedge
cleats *n* ▷ cleat
cleavage *n* (*pl* -s) space between a woman's
breasts, as revealed by a low-cut dress
cleavages *n* ▷ cleavage
cleave¹ *v* (-ves, -ving, cleft, -ved *or* clove) (cleft,
cleaved *or* cloven) split apart
cleave² *v* (-ves, -ving, cleft, cleft) cling or stick
cleaved *v* ▷ cleave¹
cleaver *n* (*pl* -s) butcher's heavy knife with a
square blade
cleavers *n* ▷ cleaver
cleaves *v* ▷ cleave¹, ²
cleaving *v* ▷ cleave¹, ²
clef *n* (*pl* -s) (MUSIC) symbol at the beginning of
a stave to show the pitch
clefs *n* ▷ clef
cleft *n* (*pl* -s) narrow opening or crack ▶ *v*
▷ cleave¹, ²
clefted *v* ▷ cleft
clefting *v* ▷ cleft
clefts *n*, *v* ▷ cleft
clematis *n* climbing plant with large colourful
flowers
clemencies *n* ▷ clemency
clemency *n* (*pl* -cies) kind or lenient treatment
clement *adj* (of weather) mild
clementine *n* (*pl* -s) small orange citrus fruit

clementines *n* ▷ clementine
clench *v* (-es, -ing, -ed) close or squeeze (one's
teeth or fist) tightly
clenched *v* ▷ clench
clenches *v* ▷ clench
clenching *v* ▷ clench
clerestories *n* ▷ clerestory
clerestory [clear-store-ee] *n* (*pl* -ries) row
of windows at the top of a wall above an
adjoining roof
clergies *n* ▷ clergy
clergy *n* (*pl* clergies) priests and ministers as a
group > **clergyman** *n* (*pl* -men)
clergyman *n* ▷ clergy
clergymen *n* ▷ clergy
cleric *n* (*pl* -s) member of the clergy
clerical *adj* of clerks or office work
clerics *n* ▷ cleric
clerk *n* (*pl* -s) employee in an office, bank, or
court who keeps records, files, and accounts
clerks *n* ▷ clerk
clever *adj* (-er, -est) intelligent, quick at
learning > **cleverly** *adv* > **cleverness** *n* (*pl* -es)
cleverer *adj* ▷ clever
cleverest *adj* ▷ clever
cleverly *adv* ▷ clever
cleverness *n* ▷ clever
clevernesses *n* ▷ clever
clianthus [klee-anth-us] *n* (*pl* -es) Australian or
NZ plant with slender scarlet flowers
clianthuses *n* ▷ clianthus
cliché [klee-shay] *n* (*pl* -s) expression or idea
that is no longer effective because of overuse
> **clichéd** *adj*
clichéd *n* ▷ cliché
clichés *n* ▷ cliché
click *n* (*pl* -s) short sharp sound ▶ *v* (-s, -ing, -ed)
make this sound
clicked *v* ▷ click
clicking *v* ▷ click
clicks *n*, *v* ▷ click
client *n* (*pl* -s) person who uses the services of a
professional person or company
clientele [klee-on-tell] *n* (*pl* -s) clients
collectively
clienteles *n* ▷ clientele
clients *n* ▷ client
cliff *n* (*pl* -s) steep rock face, esp. along the
sea shore
cliffhanger *n* (*pl* -s) film, game, etc., that is
tense and exciting because its outcome is
uncertain
cliffhangers *n* ▷ cliffhanger
cliffs *n* ▷ cliff
climactic *adj* ▷ climax

climate n (pl -s) typical weather conditions of an area > **climatic** adj
climates n ▷ climate
climatic adj ▷ climate
climax n (pl -es) most intense point of an experience, series of events, or story > **climactic** adj
climaxes n ▷ climax
climb v (-s, -ing, -ed) go up, ascend ▶ n (pl -s) climbing > **climber** n (pl -s)
climbed v ▷ climb
climber n ▷ climb
climbers n ▷ climb
climbing v ▷ climb
climbs v, n ▷ climb
clime n (pl -s) (Poetic) place or its climate
climes n ▷ clime
clinch v (-es, -ing, -ed) settle (an argument or agreement) decisively
clinched v ▷ clinch
clincher n (pl -s) (Informal) something decisive
clinchers n ▷ clincher
clinches v ▷ clinch
clinching v ▷ clinch
cling v (clings, clinging, clung) hold tightly or stick closely
clingfilm n (pl -s) thin polythene material for wrapping food
clingfilms n ▷ clingfilm
clinging v ▷ cling
clings v ▷ cling
clinic n (pl -s) building where outpatients receive medical treatment or advice
clinical adj of a clinic > **clinically** adv
clinically adv ▷ clinic
clinics n ▷ clinic
clink¹ v (-s, -ing, -ed) ▶ n (pl -s) (make) a light sharp metallic sound
clink² n (pl -s) (BRIT, AUST & NZ) (Slang) prison
clinked v ▷ clink¹
clinker n (pl -s) fused coal left over in a fire or furnace
clinkers n ▷ clinker
clinking v ▷ clink¹
clinks n ▷ clink¹, ² ▶ v ▷ clink¹
clip¹ v (clips, clipping, clipped) cut with shears or scissors ▶ n (-s) short extract of a film
clip² n device for attaching or holding things together ▶ v (clips, clipping, clipped) attach or hold together with a clip
clipped v ▷ clip¹, ²
clipper n (pl -s) fast commercial sailing ship
clippers pl n tool for clipping ▶ n ▷ clipper
clipping n (-s) something cut out, esp. an article from a newspaper ▶ v ▷ clip¹, ²

clippings n ▷ clipping
clips n, v ▷ clip¹, ²
clique [kleek] n (pl -s) small exclusive group
cliques n ▷ clique
clitoral adj ▷ clitoris
clitoris [klit-or-iss] n (pl -es) small sexually sensitive organ at the front of the vulva > **clitoral** adj
clitorises n ▷ clitoris
cloak n (pl -s) loose sleeveless outer garment ▶ v (-s, -ing, -ed) cover or conceal
cloaked v ▷ cloak
cloaking v ▷ cloak
cloakroom n (pl -s) room where coats may be left temporarily
cloakrooms n ▷ cloakroom
cloaks n, v ▷ cloak
clobber¹ v (-s, -ing, -ed) (Informal) hit
clobber² n (pl -s) (BRIT, AUST & NZ) (Informal) belongings, esp. clothes
clobbered v ▷ clobber¹
clobbering v ▷ clobber¹
clobbers v ▷ clobber¹ ▶ n ▷ clobber²
cloche [klosh] n (pl -s) cover to protect young plants
cloches n ▷ cloche
clock n (pl -s) instrument for showing the time
clocks n ▷ clock
clockwise adv, adj in the direction in which the hands of a clock rotate
clockwork n mechanism similar to the kind in a clock, used in wind-up toys
clod n (pl -s) lump of earth
clods n ▷ clod
clog v (clogs, clogging, clogged) obstruct ▶ n (pl -s) wooden or wooden-soled shoe
clogged v ▷ clog
clogging v ▷ clog
clogs v, n ▷ clog
cloister n (pl -s) covered pillared arcade, usu. in a monastery
cloistered adj sheltered
cloisters n ▷ cloister
clone n (pl -s) animal or plant produced artificially from the cells of another animal or plant, and identical to the original (Informal) ▶ v (clones, cloning, cloned) produce as a clone
cloned v ▷ clone
clones n, v ▷ clone
cloning v ▷ clone
close¹ v (-ses, -sing, -sed) [rhymes with **nose**] shut ▶ n (pl -s) end, conclusion
close² adj (-r, -st) [rhymes with **dose**] near ▶ adv closely, tightly > **closely** adv > **closeness** n

(pl **-es**)

closed v ▷ close[1]

closely adv ▷ close[2]

closeness n ▷ close[2]

closenesses n ▷ close[2]

closer adj ▷ close[2]

closes v, n ▷ close[1]

closest adj ▷ close[2]

closet n (pl **-s**) (us) cupboard ▶ adj private, secret ▶ v (**-s, -ing, -ed**) shut (oneself) away in private

closeted v ▷ closet

closeting v ▷ closet

closets n, v ▷ closet

closing v ▷ close[1]

closure n (pl **-s**) closing

closures n ▷ closure

clot n (pl **-s**) soft thick lump formed from liquid ▶ v (**-s, -tting, -tted**) form soft thick lumps

cloth n (pl **-s**) (piece of) woven fabric

clothe v (**clothes, clothing, clothed** or **clad**) put clothes on

clothed v ▷ clothe

clothes pl n articles of dress ▶ v ▷ clothe

clothing n clothes collectively ▶ v ▷ clothe

cloths n ▷ cloth

clots n, v ▷ clot

clotted v ▷ clot

clotting v ▷ clot

cloud n (pl **-s**) mass of condensed water vapour floating in the sky ▶ v (**-s, -ing, -ed**) (foll. by **over**) become cloudy > **cloudless** adj

cloudburst n (pl **-s**) heavy fall of rain

cloudbursts n ▷ cloudburst

clouded v ▷ cloud

cloudier adj ▷ cloud

cloudiest adj ▷ cloud

cloudiness n ▷ cloudy

clouding v ▷ cloud

cloudless adj ▷ cloud

clouds n, v ▷ cloud

cloudy adj (**-dier, -diest**) having a lot of clouds > **cloudiness** n

clout (Informal) n (pl **-s**) hard blow ▶ v (**-s, -ed, -ing**) hit hard

clouted v ▷ clout

clouting v ▷ clout

clouts n, v ▷ clout

clove[1] n (pl **-s**) dried flower bud of a tropical tree, used as a spice

clove[2] n (pl **-s**) segment of a bulb of garlic

clove[3] v ▷ cleave[1]

cloven v ▷ cleave[1]

clover n (pl **-s**) plant with three-lobed leaves

clovers n ▷ clover

cloves n ▷ clove[1, 2]

clown n (pl **-s**) comic entertainer in a circus ▶ v (**-s, -ing, -ed**) behave foolishly > **clownish** adj > **clownishly** adv > **clownishness** n

clowned v ▷ clown

clowning v ▷ clown

clownish adj ▷ clown

clownishly adv ▷ clown

clownishness n ▷ clown

clowns n, v ▷ clown

club n (pl **-s**) association of people with common interests ▶ v (**clubs, clubbing, clubbed**) hit with a club

clubbed v ▷ club

clubbing v ▷ club

clubs n, v ▷ club

cluck n (pl **-s**) low clicking noise made by a hen ▶ v (**-s, -ing, -ed**) make this noise

clucked v ▷ cluck

clucking v ▷ cluck

clucks n, v ▷ cluck

clue n (pl **-s**) something that helps to solve a mystery or puzzle

clueless adj stupid > **cluelessly** adv > **cluelessness** n

cluelessly adv ▷ clueless

cluelessness n ▷ clueless

clues n ▷ clue

clump n (pl **-s**) small group of things or people ▶ v (**-s, -ing, -ed**) walk heavily

clumped v ▷ clump

clumping v ▷ clump

clumps n, v ▷ clump

clumsier adj ▷ clumsy

clumsiest adj ▷ clumsy

clumsily adv ▷ clumsy

clumsiness n ▷ clumsy

clumsy adj (**-sier, -siest**) lacking skill or physical coordination > **clumsily** adv > **clumsiness** n

clung v ▷ cling

clunk n (pl **-s**) dull metallic sound ▶ v (**-s, -ing, -ed**) make such a sound

clunked v ▷ clunk

clunking v ▷ clunk

clunks n, v ▷ clunk

cluster n (pl **-s**) small close group ▶ v (**-s, -ing, -ed**) gather in clusters

clustered v ▷ cluster

clustering v ▷ cluster

clusters n, v ▷ cluster

clutch[1] v (**-es, -ing, -ed**) grasp tightly (foll. by **at**) ▶ n (pl **-es**) device enabling two revolving shafts to be connected and disconnected, esp. in a motor vehicle

clutch² n (pl -es) set of eggs laid at the same time

clutched v ▷ clutch¹

clutches v ▷ clutch¹ ▶ n ▷ clutch¹, ²

clutching v ▷ clutch¹

clutter v (-s, -ing, -ed) scatter objects about (a place) untidily ▶ n (pl -s) untidy mess

cluttered v ▷ clutter

cluttering v ▷ clutter

clutters v, n ▷ clutter

> **cly** verb (**clys, clying, clyed**). Cly is an old word meaning steal. The various forms of this word can be useful when you are short of vowels. Cly scores 8 points.

coach n (pl -es) long-distance bus ▶ v (-es, -ing, -ed) train, teach

coached v ▷ coach

coaches n, v ▷ coach

coaching v ▷ coach

coagulant n (pl -s) substance causing coagulation

coagulants n ▷ coagulant

coagulate [koh-ag-yew-late] v (-lates, -lating, -lated) change from a liquid to a semisolid mass > **coagulation** n (pl -s)

coagulated v ▷ coagulate

coagulates v ▷ coagulate

coagulating v ▷ coagulate

coagulation n ▷ coagulate

coagulations n ▷ coagulate

coal n (pl -s) black rock consisting mainly of carbon, used as fuel

coalesce [koh-a-less] v (-lesces, -lescing, -lesced) come together, merge > **coalescence** n (pl -s)

coalesced v ▷ coalesce

coalescence n ▷ coalesce

coalescences n ▷ coalesce

coalesces v ▷ coalesce

coalescing v ▷ coalesce

coalfield n (pl -s) area with coal under the ground

coalfields n ▷ coalfield

coalition [koh-a-lish-un] n (pl -s) temporary alliance, esp. between political parties

coalitions n ▷ coalition

coals n ▷ coal

coarse adj (-r, -st) rough in texture > **coarsely** adv > **coarseness** n (pl -es) > **coarsen** v (-s, -ing, -ed)

coarsely adv ▷ coarse

coarsen v ▷ coarse

coarsened v ▷ coarse

coarseness n ▷ coarse

coarsenesses n ▷ coarse

coarsening v ▷ coarse

coarsens v ▷ coarse

coarser adj ▷ coarse

coarsest adj ▷ coarse

coast n (pl -s) place where the land meets the sea ▶ v (-s, -ing, -ed) move by momentum, without the use of power > **coastal** adj

coastal adj ▷ coast

coasted v ▷ coast

coaster n (pl -s) small mat placed under a glass

coasters n ▷ coaster

coastguard n (pl -s) organization that aids ships and swimmers in trouble and prevents smuggling

coastguards n ▷ coastguard

coasting v ▷ coast

coastline n (pl -s) outline of a coast

coastlines n ▷ coastline

coasts n, v ▷ coast

coat n (pl -s) outer garment with long sleeves ▶ v (-s, -ing, -ed) cover with a layer

coated v ▷ coat

coating n (pl -s) covering layer ▶ v ▷ coat

coatings n ▷ coating

coats n, v ▷ coat

coax v (-es, -ing, -ed) persuade gently

coaxed v ▷ coax

coaxes v ▷ coax

coaxial [koh-ax-ee-al] adj (of a cable) transmitting by means of two concentric conductors separated by an insulator

coaxing v ▷ coax

cob n (pl -s) stalk of an ear of maize

cobalt n (pl -s) (CHEM) brittle silvery-white metallic element

cobalts n ▷ cobalt

cobber n (pl -s) (AUST & OLD-FASHIONED NZ) (Informal) friend

cobbers n ▷ cobber

cobble n (pl -s) cobblestone

cobbler n (pl -s) shoe mender

cobblers n ▷ cobbler

cobbles n ▷ cobble

cobblestone n (pl -s) rounded stone used for paving

cobblestones n ▷ cobblestone

cobia [koh-bee-a] n (pl -s) large dark-striped game fish of tropical and subtropical seas

cobias n ▷ cobia

cobra n (pl -s) venomous hooded snake of Asia and Africa

cobras n ▷ cobra

cobs n ▷ cob

cobweb n (pl -s) spider's web

cobwebs n ▷ cobweb

cocaine n (pl -s) addictive drug used as a narcotic and as an anaesthetic
cocaines n ▷ cocaine
coccyges n ▷ coccyx
coccyx [kok-six] n (pl coccyges) [kok-**sije**-eez] bone at the base of the spinal column
cochineal n (pl -s) red dye obtained from a Mexican insect, used for food colouring
cochineals n ▷ cochineal
cock n (pl -s) male bird, esp. of domestic fowl ▶ v (-s, -ing, -ed) draw back (the hammer of a gun) to firing position
cockade n (pl -s) feather or rosette worn on a hat as a badge
cockades n ▷ cockade
cockateel n ▷ cockatiel
cockateels n ▷ cockatiel
cockatiel, cockateel n (pl -s) crested Australian parrot with a greyish-brown and yellow plumage
cockatiels n ▷ cockatiel
cockatoo n (pl -s) crested parrot of Australia or the East Indies
cockatoos n ▷ cockatoo
cocked v ▷ cock
cockerel n (pl -s) young domestic cock
cockerels n ▷ cockerel
cockeyed adj (Informal) crooked, askew
cockie, cocky n (pl -kies) (AUST & NZ) (Informal) farmer
cockier adj ▷ cocky
cockies n ▷ cockie
cockiest adj ▷ cocky
cockily adv ▷ cocky
cockiness n ▷ cocky
cocking v ▷ cock
cockle n (pl -s) edible shellfish
cockles n ▷ cockle
cockney n (pl -s) native of the East End of London
cockneys n ▷ cockney
cockpit n (pl -s) pilot's compartment in an aircraft
cockpits n ▷ cockpit
cockroach n (pl -es) beetle-like insect which is a household pest
cockroaches n ▷ cockroach
cocks n, v ▷ cock
cocksure adj overconfident, arrogant
cocktail n (pl -s) mixed alcoholic drink
cocktails n ▷ cocktail
cocky adj (cockier, cockiest) conceited and overconfident ▶ n ▷ cockie > **cockily** adv > **cockiness** n
cocoa n (pl -s) powder made from the seed of

the cacao tree
cocoas n ▷ cocoa
coconut n (pl -s) large hard fruit of a type of palm tree
coconuts n ▷ coconut
cocoon n (pl -s) silky protective covering of a silkworm ▶ v (-s, -ing, -ed) wrap up tightly for protection
cocooned v ▷ cocoon
cocooning v ▷ cocoon
cocoons n, v ▷ cocoon
cod n (pl cod) large food fish of the North Atlantic
coda n (pl -s) final part of a musical composition
codas n ▷ coda
coddle v (coddles, coddling, coddled) pamper, overprotect
coddled v ▷ coddle
coddles v ▷ coddle
coddling v ▷ coddle
code n (pl -s) system of letters, symbols, or prearranged signals by which messages can be communicated secretly or briefly ▶ v (codes, coding, coded) put into code
coded v ▷ code
codeine [kode-een] n (pl -s) drug used as a painkiller
codeines v ▷ codeine
codes n, v ▷ code
codex n (pl codices) volume of manuscripts of an ancient text
codger n (pl -s) (BRIT, AUST & NZ) (Informal) old man
codgers n ▷ codger
codices n ▷ codex
codicil [kode-iss-ill] n (pl -s) addition to a will
codicils n ▷ codicil
codification n ▷ codify
codifications n ▷ codify
codified v ▷ codify
codifies v ▷ codify
codify v (-fies, -fying, -fied) organize (rules or procedures) systematically > **codification** n (pl -s)
codifying v ▷ codify
coding v ▷ code
coeducation n education of boys and girls together > **coeducational** adj
coeducational adj ▷ coeducation
coefficient n (pl -s) (MATHS) number or constant placed before and multiplying a quantity
coefficients n ▷ coefficient
coelacanth [seel-a-kanth] n (pl -s) primitive marine fish

coelacanths n ▷ coelacanth

coerce [koh-**urss**] v (**-ces, -cing, -ced**) compel, force > **coercion** n > **coercive** adj

coerced v ▷ coerce

coerces v ▷ coerce

coercing v ▷ coerce

coercion n ▷ coerce

coercive adj ▷ coerce

coeval [koh-**eev**-al] adj, n (pl **-s**) contemporary

coevals n ▷ coeval

coexist v (**-s, -ing, -ed**) exist together, esp. peacefully despite differences > **coexistence** n

coexisted v ▷ coexist

coexistence n ▷ coexist

coexisting v ▷ coexist

coexists v ▷ coexist

coffee n (pl **-s**) drink made from the roasted and ground seeds of a tropical shrub ▶ adj medium-brown

coffees n ▷ coffee

coffer n (pl **-s**) chest for valuables ▶ pl store of money

coffers n ▷ coffer

coffin n (pl **-s**) box in which a corpse is buried or cremated

coffins n ▷ coffin

cog n (pl **-s**) one of the teeth on the rim of a gearwheel

cogency n ▷ cogent

cogent [koh-**jent**] adj forcefully convincing > **cogency** n > **cogently** adv

cogently n ▷ cogent

cogitate [koj-**it**-tate] v (**-tates, -tating, -tated**) think deeply about > **cogitation** n (pl **-s**)

cogitated v ▷ cogitate

cogitates v ▷ cogitate

cogitating v ▷ cogitate

cogitation n ▷ cogitate

cogitations n ▷ cogitate

cognac [kon-**yak**] n (pl **-s**) French brandy

cognacs n ▷ cognac

cognate adj derived from a common original form

cognition n (pl **-s**) act or experience of knowing or acquiring knowledge > **cognitive** adj

cognitions n ▷ cognition

cognitive adj ▷ cognition

cognizance n (pl **-s**) knowledge, understanding > **cognizant** adj

cognizances n ▷ cognizance

cognizant adj ▷ cognizance

cognoscenti [kon-yo-**shen**-tee] pl n connoisseurs

cogs n ▷ cog

cohabit v (**-s, -ing, -ed**) live together as husband and wife without being married > **cohabitation** n (pl **-s**)

cohabitation n ▷ cohabit

cohabitations n ▷ cohabit

cohabited v ▷ cohabit

cohabiting v ▷ cohabit

cohabits v ▷ cohabit

cohere v (**-heres, -hering, -hered**) hold or stick together

cohered v ▷ cohere

coherence n ▷ coherent

coherent adj logical and consistent > **coherence** n > **coherently** adv

coherently n ▷ coherent

coheres v ▷ cohere

cohering v ▷ cohere

cohesion n sticking together

cohesive adj sticking together to form a whole

cohort n (pl **-s**) band of associates

cohorts n ▷ cohort

coiffeur n ▷ coiffure

coiffeurs n ▷ coiffure

coiffeuse n ▷ coiffure

coiffeuses n ▷ coiffure

coiffure n (pl **-s**) hairstyle > **coiffeur, coiffeuse** n (pl **-s**) hairdresser

coiffures n ▷ coiffure

coil v (**-s, -ing, -ed**) wind in loops ▶ n (pl **-s**) something coiled

coiled v ▷ coil

coiling v ▷ coil

coils v, n ▷ coil

coin n (pl **-s**) piece of metal money ▶ v (**-s, -ing, -ed**) invent (a word or phrase)

coinage n (pl **-s**) coins collectively

coinages n ▷ coinage

coincide v (**-cides, -ciding, -cided**) happen at the same time

coincided v ▷ coincide

coincidence n (pl **-s**) occurrence of simultaneous or apparently connected events

coincidences n ▷ coincidence

coincident adj in agreement

coincidental adj resulting from coincidence > **coincidentally** adv

coincidentally adv ▷ coincidental

coincides v ▷ coincide

coinciding v ▷ coincide

coined v ▷ coin

coining v ▷ coin

coins n, v ▷ coin

coir n (pl **-s**) coconut fibre, used for matting

coirs n ▷ coir

coital adj ▷ coitus

coition n ▷ coitus

coitions n ▷ coitus

coitus [koh-it-uss], **coition** [koh-ish-un] n (pl -s) sexual intercourse > **coital** adj

coke¹ n (pl -s) solid fuel left after gas has been distilled from coal

coke² n (pl -s) (Slang) cocaine

cokes n ▷ coke¹·²

col n (pl -s) high mountain pass

cola n (pl -s) dark brown fizzy soft drink

colander n (pl -s) perforated bowl for straining or rinsing foods

colanders n ▷ colander

colas n ▷ cola

cold adj (-er, -est) lacking heat ▶ n (pl -s) lack of heat > **coldly** adv > **coldness** n (pl -es)

colder adj ▷ cold

coldest adj ▷ cold

coldly adv ▷ cold

coldness n ▷ cold

coldnesses n ▷ cold

colds n ▷ cold

coleslaw n (pl -s) salad dish of shredded raw cabbage in a dressing

coleslaws n ▷ coleslaw

coley n (pl -s) codlike food fish of the N Atlantic

coleys n ▷ coley

colic n (pl -s) severe pains in the stomach and bowels > **colicky** adj (-ckier, -ckiest)

colickier adj ▷ colic

colickiest adj ▷ colic

colicky adj ▷ colic

colics n ▷ colic

colitis [koh-**lie**-tiss] n inflammation of the colon

collaborate v (-ates, -ating, -ated) work with another on a project > **collaboration** n (pl -s) > **collaborative** adj > **collaboratively** adv > **collaborator** n (pl -s)

collaborated v ▷ collaborate

collaborates v ▷ collaborate

collaborating v ▷ collaborate

collaboration n ▷ collaborate

collaborations n ▷ collaborate

collaborative adj ▷ collaborate

collaboratively adv ▷ collaborate

collaborator n ▷ collaborate

collaborators n ▷ collaborate

collage [kol-**lahzh**] n (pl -s) art form in which various materials or objects are glued onto a surface

collages n ▷ collage

collapse v (-lapses, -lapsing, -lapsed) fall down suddenly ▶ n (pl -s) collapsing > **collapsible** adj

collapsed v ▷ collapse

collapses v, n ▷ collapse

collapsible adj ▷ collapse

collapsing v ▷ collapse

collar n (pl -s) part of a garment round the neck ▶ v (-s, -ing, -ed) (BRIT, AUST & NZ) (Informal) seize, arrest

collarbone n (pl -s) bone joining the shoulder blade to the breastbone

collarbones n ▷ collarbone

collared v ▷ collar

collaring v ▷ collar

collars n, v ▷ collar

collate v (-lates, -lating, -lated) gather together, examine, and put in order

collated v ▷ collate

collateral n (pl -s) security pledged for the repayment of a loan

collaterals n ▷ collateral

collates v ▷ collate

collating v ▷ collate

collation n (pl -s) collating

collations n ▷ collation

colleague n (pl -s) fellow worker, esp. in a profession

colleagues n ▷ colleague

collect¹ v (-s, -ing, -ed) gather together > **collector** n (pl -s)

collect² n (pl -s) short prayer

collected adj calm and controlled ▶ v ▷ collect¹ > **collectedly** adv > **collectedness** n

collectedly adv ▷ collected

collectedness n ▷ collected

collecting v ▷ collect¹

collection n (pl -s) things collected

collections n ▷ collection

collective adj of or done by a group ▶ n (pl -s) group of people working together on an enterprise and sharing the benefits from it > **collectively** adv

collectively adv ▷ collective

collectives n ▷ collective

collects v ▷ collect¹ ▶ n ▷ collect²

colleen n (pl -s) (IRISH) girl

colleens n ▷ colleen

college n (pl -s) place of higher education > **collegiate** adj

colleges n ▷ college

collegiate adj ▷ college

collide v (-lides, -liding, -lided) crash together violently > **collision** n (pl -s)

collided v ▷ collide

collides v ▷ collide

colliding v ▷ collide

collie n (pl -s) silky-haired sheepdog
collier n (pl -s) coal miner
  collieries n ▷ colliery
  colliers n ▷ collier
colliery n (pl -lieries) coal mine
  collies n ▷ collie
collision n ▷ collide
  collisions n ▷ collide
collocate v (-cates, -cating, -cated) (of words) occur together regularly > **collocation** n (pl -s)
  collocated v ▷ collocate
  collocates v ▷ collocate
  collocating v ▷ collocate
  collocation n ▷ collocate
  collocations n ▷ collocate
colloid n (pl -s) suspension of particles in a solution
  colloids n ▷ colloid
colloquial adj suitable for informal speech or writing > **colloquially** adv
colloquialism n (pl -s) colloquial word or phrase
  colloquialisms n ▷ colloquialism
  colloquially adv ▷ colloquial
collude v (-ludes, -luding, -luded) act in collusion
  colluded v ▷ collude
  colludes v ▷ collude
  colluding v ▷ collude
collusion n (pl -s) secret or illegal cooperation
  collusions n ▷ collusion
collywobbles pl n (Slang) nervousness
cologne n (pl -s) mild perfume
  colognes n ▷ cologne
colon¹ n (pl -s) punctuation mark (:)
colon² n (pl -s) part of the large intestine connected to the rectum
colonel n (pl -s) senior commissioned army or air-force officer
  colonels n ▷ colonel
colonial adj, n (pl -s) (inhabitant) of a colony
colonialism n policy of acquiring and maintaining colonies
  colonials n ▷ colonial
  colonies n ▷ colony
colonist n (pl -s) settler in a colony
  colonists n ▷ colonist
  colonization n ▷ colonize
  colonizations n ▷ colonize
colonize v (-izes, -izing, -ized) make into a colony > **colonization** n (pl -s)
  colonized v ▷ colonize
  colonizes v ▷ colonize
  colonizing v ▷ colonize
colonnade n (pl -s) row of columns

colonnades n ▷ colonnade
colons n ▷ colon¹, ²
colony n (pl -nies) group of people who settle in a new country but remain under the rule of their homeland
coloration n (pl -s) arrangement of colours
  colorations n ▷ coloration
  colosally adv ▷ colossal
colossal adj very large > **colossally** adv
  colossi n ▷ colossus
colossus n (pl -si, -suses) huge statue
  colossuses n ▷ colossus
  colostomies n ▷ colostomy
colostomy n (pl -mies) operation to form an opening from the colon onto the surface of the body, for emptying the bowel
colour n (pl -s) appearance of things as a result of reflecting light ▶ pl flag of a country or regiment (SPORT) ▶ v (-s, -ing, -ed) apply colour to > **colourless** adj > **colourlessly** adv
coloured adj having colour ▶ v ▷ colour
colourful adj with bright or varied colours > **colourfully** adv
  colourfully adv ▷ colourful
  colouring v ▷ colour
  colourless adj ▷ colour
  colourlessly adv ▷ colour
  colours n, v ▷ colour
  cols n ▷ col
colt n (pl -s) young male horse
  colts n ▷ colt
columbine n (pl -s) garden flower with five petals
  columbines n ▷ columbine
column n (pl -s) pillar
columnist n (pl -s) journalist who writes a regular feature in a newspaper
  columnists n ▷ columnist
  columns n ▷ column
coma n (pl -s) state of deep unconsciousness
  comas n ▷ coma
comatose adj in a coma
comb n (pl -s) toothed implement for arranging the hair ▶ v (-s, -ing, -ed) use a comb on
combat n (pl -s) ▶ v (-s, -ing, -ed) fight, struggle > **combatant** n (pl -s) > **combative** adj > **combativeness** n
  combatant n ▷ combat
  combatants n ▷ combat
  combated v ▷ combat
  combating v ▷ combat
  combats n, v ▷ combat
  combed v ▷ comb
combination n (pl -s) combining ▶ pl (BRIT) old-

fashioned undergarment with long sleeves and long legs

combinations n ▷ combination

combine v (-bines, -bining, -bined) join together ▶ n (pl -s) association of people or firms for a common purpose

combined v ▷ combine

combines v, n ▷ combine

combing v ▷ comb

combining v ▷ combine

combs n, v ▷ comb

combustible adj burning easily

combustion n (pl -s) process of burning

combustions n ▷ combustion

come v (comes, coming, came, come) move towards a place, arrive

comeback n (pl -s) (Informal) return to a former position

comebacks n ▷ comeback

comedian, comedienne n (pl -s) entertainer who tells jokes

comedians n ▷ comedian

comedienne n ▷ comedian

comediennes n ▷ comedian

comedies n ▷ comedy

comedown n (pl -s) decline in status

comedowns n ▷ comedown

comedy n (pl -dies) humorous play, film, or programme

comelier adj ▷ comely

comeliest adj ▷ comely

comeliness n ▷ comely

comely adj (-lier, -liest) (Old-fashioned) nice-looking > **comeliness** n

comes v ▷ come

comestibles pl n (Formal) food

comet n (pl -s) heavenly body with a long luminous tail

comets n ▷ comet

comeuppance n (Informal) deserved punishment

comfier adj ▷ comfy

comfiest adj ▷ comfy

comfit n (pl -s) (Old-fashioned) sugar-coated sweet

comfits n ▷ comfit

comfort n (pl -s) physical ease or wellbeing ▶ v (-s, -ing, -ed) soothe, console > **comforter** n (pl -s)

comfortable adj giving comfort > **comfortably** adv

comfortably adv ▷ comfortable

comforted v ▷ comfort

comforter n ▷ comfort

comforters n ▷ comfort

comforting v ▷ comfort

comforts n, v ▷ comfort

comfrey n (pl -s) tall plant with bell-shaped flowers

comfreys n ▷ comfrey

comfy adj (-fier, -fiest) (Informal) comfortable

comic adj humorous, funny ▶ n (pl -s) comedian

comical adj amusing > **comically** adv

comically adv ▷ comical

comics n ▷ comic

coming v ▷ come

comma n (pl -s) punctuation mark (,)

command v (-s, -ing, -ed) order ▶ n (pl -s) authoritative instruction that something must be done

commandant n (pl -s) officer commanding a military group

commandants n ▷ commandant

commanded v ▷ command

commandeer v (-s, -ing, -ed) seize for military use

commandeered v ▷ commandeer

commandeering v ▷ commandeer

commandeers v ▷ commandeer

commander n (pl -s) military officer in command of a group or operation

commanders n ▷ commander

commanding v ▷ command

commandment n (pl -s) command from God

commandments n ▷ commandment

commando n (pl -dos, -does) (member of) a military unit trained for swift raids in enemy territory

commandoes n ▷ commando

commandos n ▷ commando

commands v, n ▷ command

commas n ▷ comma

commemorate v (-rates, -rating, -rated) honour the memory of > **commemoration** n (pl -s) > **commemorative** adj

commemorated v ▷ commemorate

commemorates v ▷ commemorate

commemorating v ▷ commemorate

commemoration n ▷ commemorate

commemorations n ▷ commemorate

commemorative adj ▷ commemorate

commence v (-mences, -mencing, -menced) begin > **commencement** n (pl -s)

commenced v ▷ commence

commencement n ▷ commence

commencements n ▷ commence

commences v ▷ commence

commencing v ▷ commence

commend v (-s, -ing, -ed) praise

> commendable adj > commendably adv
> commendation n (pl -s)
commendable adj ▷ commend
commendably adv ▷ commend
commendation n ▷ commend
commendations n ▷ commend
commended v ▷ commend
commending v ▷ commend
commends v ▷ commend
commensurable adj measurable by the same standards
commensurate adj corresponding in degree, size, or value
comment n (pl -s) remark ▶ v (-s, -ing, -ed) make a comment
commentaries n ▷ commentary
commentary n (pl -taries) spoken accompaniment to a broadcast or film
commentate v (-tates, -tating, -tated) provide a commentary > commentator n (pl -s)
commentated v ▷ commentate
commentates v ▷ commentate
commentating v ▷ commentate
commentator n ▷ commentate
commentators n ▷ commentate
commented v ▷ comment
commenting v ▷ comment
comments n, v ▷ comment
commerce n (pl -s) buying and selling, trade
commerces n ▷ commerce
commercial adj of commerce ▶ n (pl -s) television or radio advertisement
commercialization n ▷ commercialize
commercialize v (-izes, -izing, -ized) make commercial > commercialization n
commercialized v ▷ commercialize
commercializes v ▷ commercialize
commercializing v ▷ commercialize
commercials n ▷ commercial
commiserate v (-rates, -rating, -rated) (foll. by with) express sympathy (for) > commiseration n (pl -s)
commiserated v ▷ commiserate
commiserates v ▷ commiserate
commiserating v ▷ commiserate
commiseration n ▷ commiserate
commiserations n ▷ commiserate
commissar n (pl -s) (BRIT, AUST & NZ) (formerly) official responsible for political education in Communist countries
commissariat n (pl -s) (BRIT, AUST & NZ) military department in charge of food supplies
commissariats n ▷ commissariat
commissars n ▷ commissar

commission n (pl -s) piece of work that an artist is asked to do (MIL) ▶ v (-s, -ing, -ed) place an order for
commissionaire n (pl -s) uniformed doorman at a hotel, theatre, etc.
commissionaires n ▷ commissionaire
commissioned v ▷ commission
commissioner n (pl -s) appointed official in a government department
commissioners n ▷ commissioner
commissioning v ▷ commission
commissions n, v ▷ commission
commit v (-mits, -mitting, -mitted) perform (a crime or error)
commitment n (pl -s) dedication to a cause
commitments n ▷ commitment
commits v ▷ commit
committal n (pl -s) sending someone to prison or hospital
committals n ▷ committal
committed v ▷ commit
committee n (pl -s) group of people appointed to perform a specified service or function
committees n ▷ committee
committing v ▷ commit
commode n (pl -s) seat with a hinged flap concealing a chamber pot
commodes n ▷ commode
commodious adj roomy
commodities n ▷ commodity
commodity n (pl -ities) something that can be bought or sold
commodore n (pl -s) senior commissioned officer in the navy
commodores n ▷ commodore
common adj (-er, -est) occurring often ▶ n (pl -s) area of grassy land belonging to a community > commonly adv
commoner n (pl -s) person who does not belong to the nobility ▶ adj ▷ common
commoners n ▷ commoner
commonest adj ▷ common
commonly adv ▷ common
commonplace adj ordinary, everyday ▶ n (pl -s) trite remark
commonplaces n ▷ commonplace
commons n ▷ common
commonwealth n (pl -s) state or nation viewed politically
commonwealths n ▷ commonwealth
commotion n (pl -s) noisy disturbance
commotions n ▷ commotion
communal adj shared > communally adv
communally n ▷ communal
commune¹ n (pl -s) group of people who live

together and share everything

commune² v (-munes, -muning, -muned) (foll. by with) feel very close (to)

communed v ▷ commune²

communes n ▷ commune¹ ▶ v ▷ commune²

communicable adj (of a disease) able to be passed on

communicant n (pl -s) person who receives Communion

communicants n ▷ communicant

communicate v (-cates, -cating, -cated) make known or share (information, thoughts, or feelings)

communicated v ▷ communicate

communicates v ▷ communicate

communicating adj (of a door) joining two rooms ▶ v ▷ communicate

communication n communicating ▶ pl (-s) means of travelling or sending messages

communications n ▷ communication

communicative adj talking freely

communing v ▷ commune²

communion n (pl -s) sharing of thoughts or feelings

communions n ▷ communion

communiqué [kom-mune-ik-kay] n (pl -s) official announcement

communiqués n ▷ communiqué

communism n belief that all property and means of production should be shared by the community > **communist** n (pl -s) adj

communists n ▷ communism

communities n ▷ community

community n (pl -ties) all the people living in one district

commutator n (pl -s) device used to change alternating electric current into direct current

commutators n ▷ commutator

commute v (-mutes, -muting, -muted) travel daily to and from work

commuted v ▷ commute

commuter n (pl -s) person who commutes to and from work

commuters n ▷ commuter

commutes v ▷ commute

commuting v ▷ commute

compact¹ adj (-er, -est) closely packed ▶ n (pl -s) small flat case containing a mirror and face powder ▶ v (-s, -ing, -ed) pack closely together > **compactly** adv > **compactness** n

compact² n (pl -s) contract, agreement

compacted v ▷ compact¹

compacter adj ▷ compact¹

compactest adj ▷ compact¹

compacting v ▷ compact¹

compactly adv ▷ compact¹

compactness n ▷ compact¹

compacts n ▷ compact¹,² ▶ v ▷ compact¹

companies n ▷ company

companion n (pl -s) person who associates with or accompanies someone > **companionship** n (pl -s)

companionable adj friendly > **companionably** adv

companionably adv ▷ companionable

companions n ▷ companion

companionship n ▷ companion

companionships n ▷ companion

companionway n (pl -s) ladder linking the decks of a ship

companionways n ▷ companionway

company n (pl -nies) business organization

comparability n ▷ compare

comparable adj ▷ compare

comparative adj relative ▶ n (pl -s) (GRAMMAR) comparative form of a word > **comparatively** adv

comparatively adv ▷ comparative

comparatives n ▷ comparative

compare v (-pares, -paring, -pared) examine (things) and point out the resemblances or differences (foll. by to) (foll. by with) > **comparable** adj > **comparability** n

compared v ▷ compare

compares v ▷ compare

comparing v ▷ compare

comparison n (pl -s) comparing

comparisons n ▷ comparison

compartment n (pl -s) section of a railway carriage

compartments n ▷ compartment

compass n (pl -es) instrument for showing direction, with a needle that points north ▶ pl hinged instrument for drawing circles

compasses n ▷ compass

compassion n pity, sympathy > **compassionate** adj > **compassionately** adv

compassionate adj ▷ compassion

compassionately adj ▷ compassion

compatibility n ▷ compatible

compatible adj able to exist, work, or be used together > **compatibility** n

compatriot n (pl -s) fellow countryman or countrywoman

compatriots n ▷ compatriot

compel v (-pels, -pelling, -pelled) force (to be or do)

compelled v ▷ compel

compelling v ▷ compel

compels v ▷ compel

compendia n ▷ compendium

compendious adj brief but comprehensive

compendium n (pl -diums, -dia) selection of board games in one box

compendiums n ▷ compendium

compensate v (-sates, -sating, -sated) make amends to (someone), esp. for injury or loss (foll. by for) > **compensatory** adj

compensated v ▷ compensate

compensates v ▷ compensate

compensating v ▷ compensate

compensation n (pl -s) payment to make up for loss or injury

compensations n ▷ compensation

compensatory adj ▷ compensation

compere n (pl -s) person who presents a stage, radio, or television show ▶ v (-peres, -pering, -pered) be the compere of

compered v ▷ compere

comperes n, v ▷ compere

compering v ▷ compere

compete v (-petes, -peting, -peted) try to win or achieve (a prize, profit, etc.) > **competitive** adj > **competitively** adv > **competitiveness** n > **competitor** n (pl -s)

competed v ▷ compete

competence n ▷ competent

competent adj having the skill or knowledge to do something well > **competence** n

competently adv ▷ competent

competes v ▷ compete

competing v ▷ compete

competition n (pl -s) competing

competitions n ▷ competition

competitive adj ▷ compete

competitively adv ▷ compete

competitiveness n ▷ compete

competitor n ▷ compete

competitors n ▷ compete

compilation n ▷ compile

compilations n ▷ compile

compile v (-piles, -piling, -piled) collect and arrange (information), esp. to make a book > **compilation** n (pl -s) > **compiler** n (pl -s)

compiled v ▷ compile

compiler n ▷ compile

compilers n ▷ compile

compiles v ▷ compile

compiling v ▷ compile

complacencies n ▷ complacent

complacency n ▷ complacent

complacent adj self-satisfied > **complacently** (pl -cies) adv > **complacency** n

complacently adv ▷ complacent

complain v (-s, -ing, -ed) express resentment or displeasure

complainant n (pl -s) (LAW) plaintiff

complainants n ▷ complainant

complained v ▷ complain

complaining v ▷ complain

complains v ▷ complain

complaint n (pl -s) complaining

complaints n ▷ complaint

complaisance n ▷ complaisant

complaisant [kom-**play**-zant] adj willing to please > **complaisance** n

complement n (pl -s) thing that completes something (GRAMMAR) ▶ v (-s, -ing, -ed) make complete > **complementary** adj

complementary adj ▷ complement

complemented v ▷ complement

complementing v ▷ complement

complements n, v ▷ complement

complete adj thorough, absolute ▶ v (-pletes, -pleting, -pleted) finish > **completely** adv > **completeness** n

completed v ▷ complete

completely adv ▷ complete

completeness n ▷ complete

completes v ▷ complete

completing v ▷ complete

completion n finishing

complex adj (-er, -est) made up of parts ▶ n (pl -es) whole made up of parts > **complexity** n (pl -ities)

complexer adj ▷ complex

complexes n ▷ complex

complexest adj ▷ complex

complexion n (pl -s) skin of the face

complexions n ▷ complexion

complexities n ▷ complex

complexity n ▷ complex

compliance n (pl -s) complying > **compliant** adj

compliances n ▷ compliance

compliant adj ▷ compliance

complicate v (-cates, -cating, -cated) make or become complex or difficult to deal with > **complication** n (pl -s)

complicated adj ▷ complicate

complicates v ▷ complicate

complicating v ▷ complicate

complication n ▷ complicate

complications n ▷ complicate

complicities n ▷ complicity

complicity n (pl -ities) fact of being an accomplice in a crime

complied v ▷ comply

complies v ▷ comply
compliment n (pl -s) expression of praise ▶ pl formal greetings ▶ v (-s, -ing, -ed) praise
complimentary adj expressing praise
complimented v ▷ compliment
complimenting v ▷ compliment
compliments n, v ▷ compliment
compline n (pl -s) last service of the day in the Roman Catholic Church
complines n ▷ compline
comply v (-plies, -plying, -plied) (foll. by with) act in accordance (with)
complying v ▷ comply
component n (pl -s) ▶ adj (being) part of a whole
components n ▷ component
comport v (-s, -ing, -ed) (Formal) behave (oneself) in a specified way
comported v ▷ comport
comporting v ▷ comport
comports v ▷ comport
compose v (-poses, -posing, -posed) put together
composed v ▷ compose
composer n (pl -s) person who writes music
composers n ▷ composer
composes v ▷ compose
composing v ▷ compose
composite n (pl -s) ▶ adj (something) made up of separate parts
composites n ▷ composite
composition n (pl -s) way that something is put together or arranged
compositions n ▷ composition
compositor n (pl -s) person who arranges type for printing
compositors n ▷ compositor
compost n (pl -s) decayed plants used as a fertilizer
composts n ▷ compost
composure n calmness
compote n (pl -s) fruit stewed with sugar
compotes n ▷ compote
compound¹ n (pl -s) ▶ adj (thing, esp. chemical) made up of two or more combined parts or elements ▶ v (-s, -ing, -ed) combine or make by combining
compound² n (pl -s) fenced enclosure containing buildings
compounded v ▷ compound¹
compounding v ▷ compound¹
compounds v ▷ compound¹ ▶ n ▷ compound¹, ²
comprehend v (-s, -ing, -ed) understand
> **comprehensible** adj > **comprehensibly** adv
> **comprehension** n (pl -s)

comprehended v ▷ comprehend
comprehending v ▷ comprehend
comprehends v ▷ comprehend
comprehensible adj ▷ comprehend
comprehensibly adv ▷ comprehend
comprehension n ▷ comprehend
comprehensions n ▷ comprehend
comprehensive adj of broad scope, fully inclusive ▶ n (pl -s) (BRIT) comprehensive school > **comprehensively** adv
> **comprehensiveness** n
comprehensively adv ▷ comprehensive
comprehensiveness n ▷ comprehensive
comprehensives n ▷ comprehensive
compress v (-es, -ing, -ed) [kum-press] squeeze together ▶ n (pl -es) [kom-press] pad applied to stop bleeding or cool inflammation
> **compression** n (pl -s)
compressed v ▷ compress
compresses v, n ▷ compress
compressing v ▷ compress
compression n ▷ compress
compressions n ▷ compress
compressor n (pl -s) machine that compresses gas or air
compressors n ▷ compressor
comprise v (-ises, -ising, -ised) be made up of or make up
comprised v ▷ comprise
comprises v ▷ comprise
comprising v ▷ comprise
compromise [kom-prom-mize] n (pl -s) settlement reached by concessions on each side ▶ v (-ises, -ising, -ised) settle a dispute by making concessions
compromised v ▷ compromise
compromises n, v ▷ compromise
compromising v ▷ compromise
comptroller n (pl -s) (in titles) financial controller
comptrollers n ▷ comptroller
compulsion n (pl -s) irresistible urge
> **compulsive** adj > **compulsively** adv
compulsions n ▷ compulsion
compulsive adj ▷ compulsion
compulsively adv ▷ compulsion
compulsorily adv ▷ compulsory
compulsoriness n ▷ compulsory
compulsory adj required by rules or laws
> **compulsorily** adv > **compulsoriness** n
compunction n (pl -s) feeling of guilt or shame
compunctions n ▷ compunction
computation n ▷ compute
computations n ▷ compute
compute v (-putes, -puting, -puted) calculate,

esp. using a computer > **computation** n (pl -s)
computed v ▷ compute
computer n (pl -s) electronic machine that
stores and processes data > **computerize** v
(-izes, -izing, -ized) adapt (a system) to be
handled by computer > **computerization**
n (pl -s)
computerization n ▷ computerize
computerizations v ▷ computerize
computerized v ▷ computerize
computerizes v ▷ computerize
computerizing v ▷ computerize
computers n ▷ computer
computes v ▷ compute
computing v ▷ compute
comrade n (pl -s) fellow member of a union or
socialist political party > **comradeship** n
comrades n ▷ comrade
comradeship n ▷ comrade
con¹ (Informal) n (pl -s) ▷ **confidence trick** ▶ v
(cons, conning, conned) deceive, swindle
con² n (pl -s) ▷ **pro¹**
concatenation n (pl -s) series of linked events
concatenations n ▷ concatenation
concave adj curving inwards
conceal v (-s, -ing, -ed) cover and hide
> **concealment** n
concealed v ▷ conceal
concealing v ▷ conceal
concealment n ▷ conceal
conceals v ▷ conceal
concede v (-cedes, -ceding, -ceded) admit to
be true
conceded v ▷ concede
concedes v ▷ concede
conceding v ▷ concede
conceit n (pl -s) too high an opinion of
oneself > **conceited** adj > **conceitedly** adv
> **conceitedness** n
conceited adj ▷ conceit
conceitedly adv ▷ conceit
conceitedness adv ▷ conceit
conceits n ▷ conceit
conceivable adj imaginable, possible
> **conceivably** adv
conceivably adv ▷ conceivable
conceive v (-ceives, -ceiving, -ceived) imagine,
think
conceived v ▷ conceive
conceives v ▷ conceive
conceiving v ▷ conceive
concentrate v (-rates, -rating, -rated) fix one's
attention or efforts on something ▶ n (pl -s)
concentrated liquid
concentrated v ▷ concentrate

concentrates v, n ▷ concentrate
concentrating v ▷ concentrate
concentration n (pl -s) concentrating
concentrations n ▷ concentration
concentric adj having the same centre
concept n (pl -s) abstract or general idea
conception n (pl -s) general idea
conceptions n ▷ conception
concepts n ▷ concept
conceptual adj of or based on concepts
> **conceptually** adv
conceptualize v (-izes, -izing, -ized) form a
concept of
conceptualized v ▷ conceptualize
conceptualizes v ▷ conceptualize
conceptualizing v ▷ conceptualize
conceptually adv ▷ conceptual
concern n (pl -s) anxiety, worry ▶ v (-s, -ing, -ed)
worry (someone)
concerned adj interested, involved ▶ v
▷ concern
concerning prep about, regarding ▶ v
▷ concern
concerns n, v ▷ concern
concert n (pl -s) musical entertainment
concerted adj done together
concerti n ▷ concerto
concertina n (pl -s) small musical instrument
similar to an accordion ▶ v (-nas, -naing,
-naed) collapse or fold up like a concertina
concertinaed v ▷ concertina
concertinaing v ▷ concertina
concertinas n, v ▷ concertina
concerto [kon-chair-toe] n (pl -tos, -ti) large-
scale composition for a solo instrument and
orchestra
concertos n ▷ concerto
concerts n ▷ concert
concession n (pl -s) grant of rights, land, or
property > **concessionary** adj
concessionary adj ▷ concession
concessions n ▷ concession
conch n (pl -s) shellfish with a large spiral shell
conchs n ▷ conch
concierge [kon-see-airzh] n (pl -s) (in France)
caretaker in a block of flats
concierges n ▷ concierge
conciliate v (-ates, -ating, -ated) try to end
a disagreement (with) > **conciliation** n
> **conciliator** n (pl -s)
conciliated v ▷ conciliate
conciliates v ▷ conciliate
conciliating v ▷ conciliate
conciliation n ▷ conciliate
conciliator n ▷ conciliate

conciliators *n* ▷ conciliate

conciliatory *adj* intended to end a disagreement

concise *adj* (**-r, -st**) brief and to the point > **concisely** *adv* > **concision, conciseness** *n* (*pl* **-s, -es**)

concisely *adv* ▷ concise

conciseness *n* ▷ concise

concisenesses *n* ▷ concise

conciser *adj* ▷ concise

concisest *adj* ▷ concise

concision *n* ▷ concise

concisions *n* ▷ concise

conclave *n* (*pl* **-s**) secret meeting

conclaves *n* ▷ conclave

conclude *v* (**-cludes, -cluding, -cluded**) decide by reasoning

concluded *v* ▷ conclude

concludes *v* ▷ conclude

concluding *v* ▷ conclude

conclusion *n* (*pl* **-s**) decision based on reasoning

conclusions *n* ▷ conclusion

conclusive *adj* ending doubt, convincing > **conclusively** *adv*

conclusively *adv* ▷ conclusive

concoct *v* (**-s, -ing, -ed**) make up (a story or plan) > **concoction** *n* (*pl* **-s**)

concocted *v* ▷ concoct

concocting *v* ▷ concoct

concoction *n* ▷ concoct

concoctions *n* ▷ concoct

concocts *v* ▷ concoct

concomitant *adj* existing along with something else

concord *n* (*pl* **-s**) state of peaceful agreement, harmony

concordance *n* (*pl* **-s**) similarity or consistency

concordances *n* ▷ concordance

concordant *adj* agreeing > **concordantly** *adv*

concordantly *adv* ▷ concordant

concords *n* ▷ concord

concourse *n* (*pl* **-s**) large open public place where people can gather

concourses *n* ▷ concourse

concrete *n* (*pl* **-s**) mixture of cement, sand, stone, and water, used in building ▶ *adj* made of concrete

concretes *n* ▷ concrete

concubine [kon-kew-bine] *n* (*pl* **-s**) (HIST) woman living in a man's house but not married to him and kept for his sexual pleasure

concubines *n* ▷ concubine

concupiscence [kon-kew-piss-enss] *n* (Formal) lust

concur *v* (**-curs, -curring, -curred**) agree > **concurrence** *n* (*pl* **-s**)

concurred *v* ▷ concur

concurrence *n* ▷ concur

concurrent *adj* happening at the same time or place

concurrently *adv* at the same time

concurring *v* ▷ concur

concurs *v* ▷ concur

concussed *adj* having concussion

concussion *n* (*pl* **-s**) period of unconsciousness caused by a blow to the head

concussions *n* ▷ concussion

condemn *v* (**-s, -ing, -ed**) express disapproval of > **condemnation** *n* (*pl* **-s**) > **condemnatory** *adj*

condemnation *n* ▷ condemn

condemnations *n* ▷ condemn

condemnatory *adj* ▷ condemn

condemned *v* ▷ condemn

condemning *v* ▷ condemn

condemns *v* ▷ condemn

condensation *n* ▷ condense

condense *v* (**-denses, -densing, -densed**) make shorter > **condensation** *n*

condensed *v* ▷ condense

condenser *n* (*pl* **-s**) (ELECTRICITY) capacitor

condensers *n* ▷ condenser

condenses *v* ▷ condense

condensing *v* ▷ condense

condescend *v* (**-s, -ing, -ed**) behave patronizingly towards someone > **condescension** *n*

condescended *v* ▷ condescend

condescending *v* ▷ condescend

condescends *v* ▷ condescend

condescension *n* ▷ condescend

condiment *n* (*pl* **-s**) seasoning for food, such as salt or pepper

condiments *n* ▷ condiment

condition *n* (*pl* **-s**) particular state of being ▶ *pl* circumstances ▶ *v* (**-s, -ed, -ing**) train or influence to behave in a particular way

conditional *adj* depending on circumstances > **conditionally** *adv*

conditionally *adv* ▷ conditional

conditioned *v* ▷ condition

conditioner *n* (*pl* **-s**) thick liquid used when washing to make hair or clothes feel softer

conditioning *v* ▷ condition

conditioners *n* ▷ condition

conditions *n, v* ▷ condition

condolence *n* (*pl* **-s**) sympathy ▶ *pl* expression of sympathy

condolences n ▷ condolence

condom n (pl -s) rubber sheath worn on the penis or in the vagina during sexual intercourse to prevent conception or infection

condominium n (pl -s) (AUST, US & CANADIAN) block of flats in which each flat is owned by the occupant

  condominiums n ▷ condominium

  condoms n ▷ condom

condone v (-dones, -doning, -doned) overlook or forgive (wrongdoing)

  condoned v ▷ condone

  condones v ▷ condone

  condoning v ▷ condone

condor n (pl -s) large vulture of S America

  condors n ▷ condor

conducive adj (foll. by **to**) likely to lead (to)

conduct n (pl -s) management of an activity ▶ v (-s, -ing, -ed) carry out (a task)

  conducted v ▷ conduct

  conducting v ▷ conduct

conduction n transmission of heat or electricity

  conductive adj ▷ conductivity

  conductivities n ▷ conductivity

conductivity n (pl -vities) ability to transmit heat or electricity > **conductive** adj

conductor n (pl -s) person who conducts musicians, fem **conductress** ▶ n (pl -es)

  conductors n ▷ conductor

  conductress n ▷ conductor

  conductresses n ▷ conductor

  conducts n, v ▷ conduct

conduit [kon-dew-it] n (pl -s) channel or tube for fluid or cables

  conduits n ▷ conduit

cone n (pl -s) object with a circular base, tapering to a point

  cones n ▷ cone

coney n (pl -s) ▷ cony

  coneys n ▷ coney

confab n (pl -s) (Informal) conversation (also **confabulation**)

  confabs n ▷ confab

  confabulation n ▷ confab

  confabulations n ▷ confab

confection n (pl -s) any sweet food (Old-fashioned)

confectioner n (pl -s) maker or seller of confectionery

  confectioneries n ▷ confectionery

  confectioners n ▷ confectioner

confectionery n (pl -eries) sweets

  confections n ▷ confection

confederacies n ▷ confederacy

confederacy n (pl -cies) union of states or people for a common purpose

confederate n (pl -s) member of a confederacy ▶ adj united, allied ▶ v (-rates, -rating, -rated) unite in a confederacy

  confederated v ▷ confederate

  confederates n, v ▷ confederate

  confederating v ▷ confederate

confederation n (pl -s) alliance of political units

  confederations n ▷ confederation

confer v (-fers, -ferring, -ferred) discuss together

conference n (pl -s) meeting for discussion

  conferences n ▷ conference

conferment n (pl -s) granting, giving

  conferments n ▷ conferment

  conferred v ▷ confer

  conferring v ▷ confer

  confers v ▷ confer

confess v (-es, -ing, -ed) admit (a fault or crime)

  confessed v ▷ confess

  confesses v ▷ confess

  confessing v ▷ confess

confession n (pl -s) something confessed

confessional n (pl -s) small stall in which a priest hears confessions

  confessionals n ▷ confessional

  confessions n ▷ confession

confessor n (pl -s) priest who hears confessions

  confessors n ▷ confessor

confetti n (pl -s) small pieces of coloured paper thrown at weddings

  confettis n ▷ confetti

confidant n (pl -s) person confided in > **confidante** n fem (pl -s)

  confidante n ▷ confidant

  confidantes n ▷ confidant

  confidants n ▷ confidant

confide v (-fides, -fiding, -fided) tell someone (a secret)

  confided v ▷ confide

confidence n (pl -s) trust

  confidences n ▷ confidence

confident adj sure, esp. of oneself > **confidently** adv

confidential adj private, secret > **confidentially** adv > **confidentiality** n

  confidentiality n ▷ confidential

  confidentially adv ▷ confidential

  confidently adv ▷ confident

  confides v ▷ confide

confiding v ▷ confide
configuration n (pl -s) arrangement of parts
configurations n ▷ configuration
confine v (-fines, -fining, -fined) keep within bounds
confined v ▷ confine
confinement n (pl -s) being confined
confines pl n boundaries, limits ▶ v ▷ confine
confining v ▷ confine
confirm v (-s, -ing, -ed) prove to be true
confirmation n (pl -s) confirming
confirmations n ▷ confirmation
confirmed adj firmly established in a habit or condition ▶ v ▷ confirm
confirming v ▷ confirm
confirms v ▷ confirm
confiscate v (-cates, -cating, -cated) seize (property) by authority ▶ **confiscation** n (pl -s)
confiscated v ▷ confiscate
confiscates v ▷ confiscate
confiscating v ▷ confiscate
confiscation n ▷ confiscate
confiscations n ▷ confiscate
conflagration n (pl -s) large destructive fire
conflagrations n ▷ conflagration
conflate v (-ates, -ating, -ated) combine or blend into a whole ▶ **conflation** n (pl -s)
conflated v ▷ conflate
conflates v ▷ conflate
conflating v ▷ conflate
conflation n ▷ conflate
conflations n ▷ conflate
conflict n (pl -s) disagreement ▶ v (-s, -ing, -ed) be incompatible
conflicted v ▷ conflict
conflicting v ▷ conflict
conflicts n, v ▷ conflict
confluence n (pl -s) place where two rivers join
confluences n ▷ confluence
conform v (-s, -ing, -ed) comply with accepted standards or customs (foll. by **to** or **with**)
conformed v ▷ conform
conforming v ▷ conform
conformist n (pl -s) ▶ adj (person) complying with accepted standards or customs
conformists n ▷ conformist
conformities n ▷ conformity
conformity n (pl -ities) compliance with accepted standards or customs
conforms v ▷ conform
confound v (-s, -ing, -ed) astound, bewilder
confounded adj (Old-fashioned) damned ▶ v ▷ confound ▶ **confoundedly** adv
confoundedly adv ▷ confounded
confounding v ▷ confound

confounds v ▷ confound
confront v (-s, -ing, -ed) come face to face with
confrontation n (pl -s) serious argument ▶ **confrontational** adj
confrontational adj ▷ confrontation
confrontations n ▷ confrontation
confronted v ▷ confront
confronting v ▷ confront
confronts v ▷ confront
confuse v (-fuses, -fusing, -fused) mix up ▶ **confusion** n (pl -s)
confused v ▷ confuse
confuses v ▷ confuse
confusing v ▷ confuse
confusion n ▷ confuse
confusions n ▷ confuse
confute v (-futes, -futing, -futed) prove wrong
confuted v ▷ confute
confutes v ▷ confute
confuting v ▷ confute
conga n (pl -s) dance performed by a number of people in single file
congas n ▷ conga
congeal v (-s, -ing, -ed) (of a liquid) become thick and sticky
congealed v ▷ congeal
congealing v ▷ congeal
congeals v ▷ congeal
congenial adj pleasant, agreeable ▶ **congeniality** n ▶ **congenially** adv
congeniality n ▷ congenial
congenially adv ▷ congenial
congenital adj (of a condition) existing from birth ▶ **congenitally** adv
congenitally adv ▷ congenital
conger n (pl -s) large sea eel
congers n ▷ conger
congested adj crowded to excess ▶ **congestion** n
congestion n ▷ congested
conglomerate n (pl -s) large corporation made up of many companies ▶ v (-rates, -rating, -rated) form into a mass ▶ adj made up of several different elements ▶ **conglomeration** n (pl -s)
conglomerated v ▷ conglomerate
conglomerates n, v ▷ conglomerate
conglomerating v ▷ conglomerate
conglomeration n ▷ conglomerate
conglomerations n ▷ conglomerate
congratulate v (-lates, -lating, -lated) express one's pleasure to (someone) at his or her good fortune or success ▶ **congratulations** pl n, interj ▶ **congratulatory** adj
congratulated v ▷ congratulate

congratulates v ▷ congratulate
congratulating v ▷ congratulate
congratulations n ▷ congratulate
congratulatory adj ▷ congratulate
congregate v (-gates, -gating, -gated) gather together in a crowd
congregated v ▷ congregate
congregates v ▷ congregate
congregating v ▷ congregate
congregation n (pl -s) people who attend a church > **congregational** adj
congregational adj ▷ congregation
congregations n ▷ congregation
congress n (pl congresses) formal meeting for discussion > **congressional** adj
congresses n ▷ congress
congressional n ▷ congress
congressman, congresswoman n (pl -men, -women) member of Congress
congressmen n ▷ congressman
congresswoman n ▷ congressman
congresswomen n ▷ congressman
congruence n ▷ congruent
congruent adj similar, corresponding > **congruence** n
conical adj cone-shaped
conies n ▷ cony
conifer n (pl -s) cone-bearing tree, such as the fir or pine > **coniferous** adj
coniferous adj ▷ conifer
conifers n ▷ conifer
conjectural adj ▷ conjecture
conjecture n (pl -s) ▶ v (-tures, -turing, -tured) guess > **conjectural** adj
conjectured v ▷ conjecture
conjectures n, v ▷ conjecture
conjecturing v ▷ conjecture
conjugal adj of marriage > **conjugally** adv
conjugally adv ▷ conjugal
conjugate v (-gates, -gating, -gated) give the inflections of (a verb)
conjugated v ▷ conjugate
conjugates v ▷ conjugate
conjugating v ▷ conjugate
conjugation n (pl -s) complete set of inflections of a verb
conjugations n ▷ conjugation
conjunction n (pl -s) combination
conjunctions n ▷ conjunction
conjunctiva n (pl -s) the membrane covering the eyeball and inner eyelid
conjunctivas n ▷ conjunctiva
conjunctivitis n inflammation of the conjunctiva
conjure v (-jures, -juring, -jured) perform

tricks that appear to be magic > **conjuror** n (pl -s)
conjured v ▷ conjure
conjures v ▷ conjure
conjuring v ▷ conjure
conjuror n ▷ conjure
conjurors n ▷ conjure
conk n (pl -s) (BRIT, AUST & NZ) (Slang) nose
conker n (pl -s) (Informal) nut of the horse chestnut
conkers n ▷ conker
conks n ▷ conk
connect v (-s, -ing, -ed) join together > **connection, connexion** n (pl -s) relationship, association > **connective** adj
connected v ▷ connect
connecting v ▷ connect
connection n ▷ connect
connections n ▷ connect
connective n ▷ connect
connects v ▷ connect
conned v ▷ con¹
connexion n ▷ connect
connexions n ▷ connect
conning v ▷ con¹
connivance n ▷ connive
connivances n ▷ connive
connive v (-nives, -niving, -nived) (foll. by **at**) allow (wrongdoing) by ignoring it > **connivance** n (pl -s)
connived v ▷ connive
connives v ▷ connive
conniving v ▷ connive
connoisseur [kon-noss-**sir**] n (pl -s) person with special knowledge of the arts, food, or drink
connoisseurs n ▷ connoisseur
connotation n (pl -s) associated idea conveyed by a word > **connote** v (-notes, -noting, -noted)
connotations n ▷ connotation
connoted v ▷ connotation
connotes v ▷ connotation
connoting v ▷ connotation
connubial adj (Formal) of marriage
conquer v (-s, -ing, -ed) defeat > **conqueror** n (pl -s)
conquered v ▷ conquer
conquering v ▷ conquer
conqueror n ▷ conquer
conquerors n ▷ conquer
conquers v ▷ conquer
conquest n (pl -s) conquering
conquests n ▷ conquest
cons n ▷ con¹, ²
conscience n (pl -s) sense of right or wrong as

regards thoughts and actions
consciences n ▷ conscience
conscientious adj painstaking
> **conscientiously** adv
conscientiously adv ▷ conscientious
conscious adj alert and awake > **consciously**
adv > **consciousness** n
consciously adv ▷ conscious
consciousness n ▷ conscious
conscript n (pl -s) person enrolled for
compulsory military service ▶ v (-s, -ing, -ed)
enrol (someone) for compulsory military
service > **conscription** n (pl -s)
conscripted v ▷ conscript
conscripting v ▷ conscript
conscription n ▷ conscript
conscriptions n ▷ conscript
conscripts n, v ▷ conscript
consecrate v (-rates, -rating, -rated) make
sacred > **consecration** n (pl -s)
consecrated v ▷ consecrate
consecrates v ▷ consecrate
consecrating v ▷ consecrate
consecration n ▷ consecrate
consecrations n ▷ consecrate
consecutive adj in unbroken succession
> **consecutively** adv
consecutively adv ▷ consecutive
consensus n general agreement
consent n (pl -s) agreement, permission ▶ v (-s,
-ing, -ed) (foll. by to) permit, agree to
consented v ▷ consent
consenting v ▷ consent
consents v, n ▷ consent
consequence n (pl -s) result, effect
consequences n ▷ consequence
consequent adj resulting
consequential adj important
consequently adv as a result, therefore
conservancies n ▷ conservancy
conservancy n (pl -cies) environmental
conservation
conservation n (pl -s) protection of
natural resources and the environment
> **conservationist** n (pl -s)
conservationist n ▷ conservation
conservationists n ▷ conservation
conservations n ▷ conservation
conservatism adv ▷ conservative
conservative adj opposing change ▶ n (pl -s)
conservative person > **conservatively** adv
> **conservatism** n
conservatively adv ▷ conservative
conservatives n ▷ conservative
conservatoire [kon-**serv**-a-twahr] n (pl -s)

school of music
conservatoires n ▷ conservatoire
conservatories n ▷ conservatory
conservatory n (pl -ries) room with glass walls
and a glass roof, attached to a house
conserve v (-serves, -serving, -served) protect
from harm, decay, or loss ▶ n (pl -s) jam
containing large pieces of fruit
conserved v ▷ conserve
conserves v, n ▷ conserve
conserving v ▷ conserve
consider v (-s, -ing, -ed) regard as
considerable adj large in amount or degree
> **considerably** adv
considerably adv ▷ considerable
considerate adj thoughtful towards others
> **considerately** adv
considerately adv ▷ considerate
consideration n (pl -s) careful thought
considerations n ▷ consideration
considered v ▷ consider
considering prep taking (a specified fact) into
account ▶ v ▷ consider
considers v ▷ consider
consign v (-s, -ing, -ed) put somewhere
consigned v ▷ consign
consigning v ▷ consign
consignment n (pl -s) shipment of goods
consignments n ▷ consignment
consigns v ▷ consign
consist v (-s, -ing, -ed) be made up of
consisted v ▷ consist
consistencies n ▷ consistency
consistency n (pl -cies) being consistent
consistent adj unchanging, constant (foll. by
with) > **consistently** adv
consistently adv ▷ consistent
consisting v ▷ consist
consists v ▷ consist
consolation n (pl -s) consoling
consolations n ▷ consolation
console[1] v (-soles, -soling, -soled) comfort in
distress
console[2] n (pl -s) panel of controls for
electronic equipment
consoled v ▷ console[1]
consoles v ▷ console[1] ▶ n ▷ console[2]
consolidate v (-dates, -dating, -dated)
make or become stronger or more stable
> **consolidation** n (pl -s)
consolidated v ▷ consolidate
consolidates v ▷ consolidate
consolidating v ▷ consolidate
consolidation n ▷ consolidate
consolidations n ▷ consolidate

consoling v ▷ **console¹**

consommé [kon-**som**-may] n (pl **-s**) thin clear meat soup

consommés n ▷ **consommé**

consonance n agreement, harmony

consonant n (pl **-s**) speech sound made by partially or completely blocking the breath stream, such as b or f ▶ adj (foll. by **with**) agreeing (with) > **consonantly** adv

consonantly adv ▷ **consonant**

consonants n ▷ **consonant**

consort v (**-s**, **-ing**, **-ed**) (foll. by **with**) keep company (with) ▶ n (pl **-s**) husband or wife of a monarch

consorted v ▷ **consort**

consortia n ▷ **consortium**

consorting v ▷ **consort**

consortium n (pl **-tia**) association of business firms

consorts v, n ▷ **consort**

conspectus n (pl **-es**) (Formal) survey or summary

conspectuses n ▷ **conspectus**

conspicuous adj clearly visible > **conspicuously** adv > **conspicuousness** n

conspicuously adv ▷ **conspectus**

conspicuousness n ▷ **conspectus**

conspiracies n ▷ **conspiracy**

conspiracy n (pl **-cies**) conspiring > **conspirator** n (pl **-s**) > **conspiratorial** adj

conspirator n ▷ **conspiracy**

conspiratorial adj ▷ **conspiracy**

conspirators n ▷ **conspiracy**

conspire v (**-spires**, **-spiring**, **-spired**) plan a crime together in secret

conspired v ▷ **conspire**

conspires v ▷ **conspire**

conspiring v ▷ **conspire**

constable n (pl **-s**) police officer of the lowest rank

constables n ▷ **constable**

constabularies n ▷ **constabulary**

constabulary n (pl **-laries**) police force of an area

constancy n ▷ **constant**

constant adj continuous ▶ n (pl **-s**) unvarying quantity > **constantly** adv > **constancy** n

constantly adv ▷ **constant**

constants n ▷ **constant**

constellation n (pl **-s**) group of stars

constellations n ▷ **constellation**

consternation n anxiety or dismay

constipated adj having constipation

constipation n difficulty in defecating

constituencies n ▷ **constituency**

constituency n (pl **-cies**) area represented by a Member of Parliament

constituent n (pl **-s**) member of a constituency ▶ adj forming part of a whole

constituents n ▷ **constituent**

constitute v (**-tutes**, **-tuting**, **-tuted**) form, make up

constituted v ▷ **constitute**

constitutes v ▷ **constitute**

constituting v ▷ **constitute**

constitution n (pl **-s**) principles on which a state is governed

constitutional adj of a constitution ▶ n (pl **-s**) walk taken for exercise > **constitutionally** adv

constitutionally adv ▷ **constitutional**

constitutionals n ▷ **constitutional**

constitutions n ▷ **constitution**

constrain v (**-s**, **-ing**, **-ed**) compel, force > **constraint** n (pl **-s**)

constrained v ▷ **constrain**

constraining v ▷ **constrain**

constrains v ▷ **constrain**

constraint n ▷ **constrain**

constraints n ▷ **constrain**

constrict v (**-s**, **-ing**, **-ed**) make narrower by squeezing > **constriction** n (pl **-s**) > **constrictive** adj

constricted v ▷ **constrict**

constricting v ▷ **constrict**

constriction n ▷ **constrict**

constrictions n ▷ **constrict**

constrictive adj ▷ **constrict**

constrictor n (pl **-s**) large snake that squeezes its prey to death

constrictors n ▷ **constrictor**

constricts v ▷ **constrict**

construct v (**-s**, **-ing**, **-ed**) build or put together

constructed v ▷ **construct**

constructing v ▷ **construct**

construction n (pl **-s**) constructing

constructions n ▷ **construction**

constructive adj (of advice, criticism, etc.) useful and helpful > **constructively** adv

constructively adv ▷ **constructive**

constructs v ▷ **construct**

construe v (**-strues**, **-struing**, **-strued**) interpret

construed v ▷ **construe**

construes v ▷ **construe**

construing v ▷ **construe**

consul n (pl **-s**) official representing a state in a foreign country > **consular** adj > **consulship** n (pl **-s**)

consular adj ▷ **consul**

consulate n (pl **-s**) workplace or position of

a consul

consulates n ▷ consulate

consuls n ▷ consul

consulship n ▷ consul

consulships n ▷ consul

consult v (-s, -ing, -ed) go to for advice or information

consultancies n ▷ consultancy

consultancy n (pl -cies) work or position of a consultant

consultant n (pl -s) specialist doctor with a senior position in a hospital

consultants n ▷ consultant

consultation n (pl -s) (meeting for) consulting

consultations n ▷ consultation

consultative adj giving advice

consulted v ▷ consult

consulting v ▷ consult

consults v ▷ consult

consume v (-sumes, -suming, -sumed) eat or drink

consumed v ▷ consume

consumer n (pl -s) person who buys goods or uses services

consumers n ▷ consumer

consumes v ▷ consume

consuming v ▷ consume

consummate [kon-sum-mate] v (-mates, -mating, -mated) make (a marriage) legal by sexual intercourse ▶ adj [kon-**sum**-mit] supremely skilled > **consummately** adv > **consummation** n (pl -s)

consummated v ▷ consummate

consummately adv ▷ consummate

consummates v ▷ consummate

consummating v ▷ consummate

consummation n ▷ consummate

consummations n ▷ consummate

consumption n (pl -s) amount consumed

consumptions n ▷ consumption

consumptive n (pl -s) ▶ adj (Old-fashioned) (person) having tuberculosis

consumptives n ▷ consumptive

contact n (pl -s) communicating ▶ v (-s, -ing, -ed) get in touch with

contacted v ▷ contact

contacting v ▷ contact

contacts n, v ▷ contact

contagion n (pl -s) passing on of disease by contact

contagions n ▷ contagion

contagious adj spreading by contact, catching

contain v (-s, -ing, -ed) hold or be capable of holding

contained v ▷ contain

container n (pl -s) object used to hold or store things in

containers n ▷ container

containing v ▷ contain

containment n prevention of the spread of something harmful

contains v ▷ contain

contaminant n (pl -s) contaminating substance

contaminants n ▷ contaminant

contaminate v (-nates, -nating, -nated) make impure, pollute > **contamination** n (pl -s)

contaminated v ▷ contaminate

contaminates v ▷ contaminate

contaminating v ▷ contaminate

contamination n ▷ contaminate

contaminations n ▷ contaminate

contemplate v (-lates, -lating, -lated) think deeply > **contemplation** n (pl -s) > **contemplative** adj

contemplated v ▷ contemplate

contemplates v ▷ contemplate

contemplating v ▷ contemplate

contemplation n ▷ contemplate

contemplations n ▷ contemplate

contemplative adj ▷ contemplate

contemporaneous adj happening at the same time

contemporaries n ▷ contemporary

contemporary adj present-day, modern ▶ n (pl -raries) person or thing living or occurring at the same time as another

contempt n (pl -s) dislike and disregard

contemptible adj deserving contempt > **contemptibly** adv

contemptibly adv ▷ contemptible

contempts n ▷ contempt

contemptuous adj showing contempt > **contemptuously** adv

contemptuously adv ▷ contemptuous

contend v (-s, -ing, -ed) (foll. by with) deal with

contended v ▷ contend

contender n (pl -s) competitor, esp. a strong one

contenders n ▷ contender

contending v ▷ contend

contends v ▷ contend

content¹ n (pl -s) meaning or substance of a piece of writing ▶ pl what something contains

content² adj satisfied with things as they are ▶ v (-s, -ing, -ed) make (someone) content ▶ n happiness and satisfaction > **contented** adj > **contentedly** adv > **contentment** n

contented v, adj ▷ content²
contentedly adv ▷ content²
contenting v ▷ content²
contention n (pl -s) disagreement or dispute
contentions n ▷ contention
contentious adj causing disagreement
> contentiously adv > contentiousness n
contentiously adv ▷ contentious
contentiousness n ▷ contentious
contentment n ▷ content²
contents n ▷ content¹ ▶ v ▷ content²
contest n (pl -s) competition or struggle ▶ v
(-s, -ing, -ed) dispute, object to ▷ contestant
n (pl -s)
contestant n ▷ contest
contestants n ▷ contest
contested v ▷ contest
contesting v ▷ contest
contests n, v ▷ contest
context n (pl -s) circumstances of an event or
fact > contextual adj
contexts n ▷ context
contextual adj ▷ context
contiguous adj very near or touching
> contiguously adv
contiguously adv ▷ contiguous
continence n ▷ continent²
continent¹ n (pl -s) one of the earth's
large masses of land > continental adj
> continentally adv
continent² adj able to control one's bladder
and bowels > continence n
continental adj ▷ continent¹
continentally adv ▷ continent¹
continents n ▷ continent¹
contingencies n ▷ contingency
contingency n (pl -cies) something that may
happen
contingent n (pl -s) group of people that
represents or is part of a larger group ▶ adj
(foll. by on) dependent on (something
uncertain)
contingents n ▷ contingent
continua n ▷ continuum
continual adj constant > continually adv
continually adv ▷ continual
continuance n continuing
continuation n (pl -s) continuing
continuations n ▷ continuation
continue v (-tinues, -tinuing, -tinued) (cause
to) remain in a condition or place
continued v ▷ continue
continues v ▷ continue
continuing v ▷ continue
continuities n ▷ continuity

continuity n (pl -ities) smooth development
or sequence
continuo n (pl -s) (MUSIC) continuous bass part,
usu. played on a keyboard instrument
continuos n ▷ continuo
continuous adj continuing uninterrupted
> continuously adv
continuously adv ▷ continuous
continuum n (pl -tinua, -tinuums) continuous
series
continuums n ▷ continuum
contort v (-s, -ing, -ed) twist out of shape
> contortion n (pl -s)
contorted v ▷ contort
contorting v ▷ contort
contortion n ▷ contort
contortionist n (pl -s) performer who contorts
his or her body to entertain
contortionists n ▷ contortionist
contortions n ▷ contort
contorts v ▷ contort
contour n (pl -s) outline
contours n ▷ contour
contraband n, adj smuggled (goods)
contraception n (pl -s) prevention of
pregnancy by artificial means
contraceptions n ▷ contraception
contraceptive n (pl -s) device used or pill
taken to prevent pregnancy ▶ adj preventing
pregnancy
contraceptives n ▷ contraceptive
contract n (pl -s) (document setting out) a
formal agreement ▶ v (-s, -ing, -ed) make
a formal agreement (to do something)
> contraction n (pl -s) > contractual adj
> contractually adv
contracted v ▷ contract
contracting v ▷ contract
contraction n ▷ contract
contractions n ▷ contract
contractor n (pl -s) firm that supplies
materials or labour
contractors n ▷ contractor
contracts n, v ▷ contract
contractual adj ▷ contract
contractually adv ▷ contract
contradict v (-s, -ing, -ed) declare the opposite
of (a statement) to be true > contradiction n
(pl -s) > contradictory adj
contradicted v ▷ contradict
contradicting v ▷ contradict
contradiction n ▷ contradict
contradictions n ▷ contradict
contradictory adj ▷ contradict
contradicts v ▷ contradict

contraflow n (pl -s) flow of traffic going alongside but in an opposite direction to the usual flow
  contraflows n ▷ contraflow
contralto n (pl -s) (singer with) the lowest female voice
  contraltos n ▷ contralto
contraption n (pl -s) strange-looking device
  contraptions n ▷ contraption
contrapuntal adj (MUSIC) of or in counterpoint
  > **contrapuntally** adv
  contrapuntally adv ▷ contrapuntal
  contraries n ▷ contrary
  contrarily adv ▷ contrary
  contrariness n ▷ contrary
  contrariwise adv ▷ contrary
contrary n (pl -aries) complete opposite
  ▶ adj opposed, completely different ▶ adv in opposition > **contrarily** adv > **contrariness** n
  > **contrariwise** adv
contrast n (pl -s) obvious difference ▶ v
  (-s, -ing, -ed) compare in order to show differences (foll. by **with**)
  contrasted v ▷ contrast
  contrasting v ▷ contrast
  contrasts n, v ▷ contrast
contravene v (-venes, -vening, -vened) break (a rule or law) > **contravention** n (pl -s)
  contravened v ▷ contravene
  contravenes v ▷ contravene
  contravening v ▷ contravene
  contravention n ▷ contravene
  contraventions n ▷ contravene
contretemps [kon-tra-tahn] n (pl -temps) embarrassing minor disagreement
contribute v (-butes, -buting, -buted) give for a common purpose or fund (foll. by **to**)
  > **contribution** n (pl -s) > **contributor** n (pl -s)
  > **contributory** adj
  contributed v ▷ contribute
  contributes v ▷ contribute
  contributing v ▷ contribute
  contribution n ▷ contribute
  contributions n ▷ contribute
  contributor n ▷ contribute
  contributors n ▷ contribute
  contributory adj ▷ contribute
contrite adj sorry and apologetic > **contritely** adv > **contrition** n
  contritely adv ▷ contrite
  contrition n ▷ contrite
contrivance n (pl -s) device
  contrivances n ▷ contrivance
contrive v (-trives, -triving, -trived) make happen

contrived adj planned or artificial ▶ v
  ▷ contrive
  contrives v ▷ contrive
  contriving v ▷ contrive
control n (pl -s) power to direct something ▶ pl instruments used to operate a machine ▶ v
  (-trols, -trolling, -trolled) have power over
  > **controllable** adj > **controller** n (pl -s)
  controllable adj ▷ control
  controlled v ▷ control
  controller n ▷ control
  controllers n ▷ control
  controlling v ▷ control
  controls n, v ▷ control
controversial adj causing controversy
  > **controversially** adv
  controversially adv ▷ controversial
  controversies n ▷ controversy
controversy n (pl -sies) fierce argument or debate
  contumelies n ▷ contumely
contumely [kon-tume-mill-ee] n (pl -melies)
  (Lit) scornful or insulting treatment
contusion n (pl -s) (Formal) bruise
  contusions n ▷ contusion
conundrum n (pl -s) riddle
  conundrums n ▷ conundrum
conurbation n (pl -s) large urban area formed by the growth and merging of towns
  conurbations n ▷ conurbation
convalesce v (-lesces, -lescing, -lesced) recover after an illness or operation
  > **convalescence** n (pl -s) > **convalescent** n
  (pl -s) adj
  convalesced v ▷ convalesce
  convalescence n ▷ convalesce
  convalescences n ▷ convalesce
  convalescent n ▷ convalesce
  convalescents n ▷ convalesce
  convalesces v ▷ convalesce
  convalescing v ▷ convalesce
convection n (pl -s) transmission of heat in liquids or gases by the circulation of currents
  convections n ▷ convection
convector n (pl -s) heater that gives out hot air
  convectors n ▷ convector
convene v (-venes, -vening, -vened) gather or summon for a formal meeting
  convened v ▷ convene
convener, convenor n (pl -s) person who calls a meeting
  conveners n ▷ convener
  convenes v ▷ convene
convenience n (pl -s) quality of being convenient

conveniences n ▷ convenience
convenient adj suitable or opportune
> **conveniently** adv
conveniently adv ▷ convenient
convening v ▷ convene
convenor n ▷ convener
convenors n ▷ convener
convent n (pl -s) building where nuns live
convention n (pl -s) widely accepted view of proper behaviour
conventional adj (unthinkingly) following the accepted customs > **conventionally** adv
> **conventionality** n
conventionality n ▷ conventional
conventionally adv ▷ conventional
conventions n ▷ convention
convents n ▷ convent
converge v (-verges, -verging, -verged) meet or join > **convergence** n
converged v ▷ converge
converges v ▷ converge
converging v ▷ converge
conversant adj having knowledge or experience of
conversation n (pl -s) informal talk
> **conversational** adj
conversational adj ▷ conversation
conversationalist n (pl -s) person with a specified ability at conversation
conversationalists n ▷ conversationalist
conversations n ▷ conversation
converse[1] v (-verses, -versing, versed) have a conversation
converse[2] adj, n (pl -s) opposite or contrary
> **conversely** adv
conversed v ▷ converse[1]
conversely adv ▷ converse[2]
converses v ▷ converse[1] ▷ n ▷ converse[2]
conversing v ▷ converse[1]
conversion n (pl -s) (thing resulting from) converting
conversions n ▷ conversion
convert v (-s, -ing, ed) change in form, character, or function ▶ n (pl -s) person who has converted to a different belief or religion
converted v ▷ convert
convertible adj capable of being converted ▶ (pl -s) car with a folding or removable roof
convertibles n ▷ convertible
converting v ▷ convert
converts v, n ▷ convert
convex adj curving outwards
convey v (-s, -ing, -ed) communicate (information)
conveyance n (pl -s) (Old-fashioned) vehicle

conveyances n ▷ conveyance
conveyancing n branch of law dealing with the transfer of ownership of property
conveyed v ▷ convey
conveying v ▷ convey
conveys v ▷ convey
convict v (-s, -ing, -ed) declare guilty ▶ n (pl -s) person serving a prison sentence
convicted v ▷ convict
convicting v ▷ convict
conviction n (pl -s) firm belief
convictions n ▷ conviction
convicts v, n ▷ convict
convince v (-vinces, -vincing, -vinced) persuade by argument or evidence
> **convincing** adj > **convincingly** adv
convinced v ▷ convince
convinces v ▷ convince
convincing v, adj ▷ convince
convincingly adv ▷ convince
convivial adj sociable, lively > **conviviality** n
> **convivially** adv
conviviality n ▷ convivial
convivially adv ▷ convivial
convocation n (pl -s) calling together
convocations n ▷ convocation
convoke v (-vokes, -voking, -voked) call together
convoked v ▷ convoke
convokes v ▷ convoke
convoking v ▷ convoke
convoluted adj coiled, twisted > **convolution** n (pl -s)
convolution n ▷ convoluted
convolutions n ▷ convoluted
convolvulus n (pl -es) twining plant with funnel-shaped flowers
convolvuluses n ▷ convolvulus
convoy n (pl -s) group of vehicles or ships travelling together
convoys n ▷ convoy
convulse v (-vulses, -vulsing, -vulsed) (of part of the body) undergo violent spasms (Informal) > **convulsive** adj > **convulsively** adv
convulsed v ▷ convulse
convulses v ▷ convulse
convulsing v ▷ convulse
convulsion n (pl -s) violent muscular spasm ▶ pl uncontrollable laughter
convulsions n ▷ convulsion
convulsive adj ▷ convulse
convulsively adv ▷ convulse
cony, coney n (pl conies, -s) (BRIT) rabbit
coo v (coos, cooing, cooed) (of a dove or pigeon) make a soft murmuring sound

cooed v ▷ coo

cooee interj (BRIT, AUST & NZ) call to attract attention

cooing v ▷ coo

cook v (-s, -ing, -ed) prepare (food) by heating ▶ n (pl -s) person who cooks food

cooked v ▷ cook

cooker n (pl -s) (CHIEFLY BRIT) apparatus for cooking heated by gas or electricity

cookers n ▷ cooker

cookery n art of cooking

cookie n (pl -s) (US) biscuit

cookies n ▷ cookie

cooking v ▷ cook

cooks v, n ▷ cook

cool adj (-er, -est) moderately cold (Informal) ▶ v (-s, -ing, -ed) make or become cool ▶ n (pl -s) coolness ▶ coolly adv > coolness n (pl -es)

coolant n (pl -s) fluid used to cool machinery while it is working

coolants n ▷ coolant

cooled v ▷ cool

cooler n (pl -s) container for making or keeping things cool ▶ adj ▷ cool

coolers n ▷ cooler

coolest adj ▷ cool

coolibah n (pl -s) Australian eucalypt that grows beside rivers

coolibahs n ▷ coolibah

cooling v ▷ cool

coolly adv ▷ cool

coolness n ▷ cool

coolnesses n ▷ cool

cools v, n ▷ cool

coomb, coombe n (pl -s) (S ENGLISH) short valley or deep hollow

coombe n ▷ coomb

coombes n ▷ coomb

coombs n ▷ coomb

coop¹ n (pl -s) cage or pen for poultry

coop² [koh-op] n (pl -s) (BRIT, US & AUST) (shop run by) a cooperative society

cooper n (pl -s) person who makes or repairs barrels

cooperate v (-rates, -rating, -rated) work or act together > cooperation n

cooperated v ▷ cooperate

cooperates v ▷ cooperate

cooperating v ▷ cooperate

cooperation n ▷ cooperate

cooperative adj willing to cooperate ▶ n (pl -s) cooperative organization

cooperatives n ▷ cooperative

coopers n ▷ cooper

coops n ▷ coop¹, ²

coopt [koh-opt] v (-s, -ing, -ed) add (someone) to a group by the agreement of the existing members

coopted v ▷ coopt

coopting v ▷ coopt

coopts v ▷ coopt

coordinate v (-nates, -nating, -nated) bring together and cause to work together efficiently ▶ n (pl -s) (MATHS) any of a set of numbers defining the location of a point ▶ pl clothes designed to be worn together > coordination n > coordinator n (pl -s)

coordinated v ▷ coordinate

coordinates v, n ▷ coordinate

coordinating v ▷ coordinate

coordination n ▷ coordinate

coordinator n ▷ coordinate

coordinators n ▷ coordinate

coos v ▷ coo

coot n (pl -s) small black water bird

coots n ▷ coot

cop (Slang) n (pl -s) policeman ▶ v (cops, copping, copped) take or seize

cope¹ v (copes, coping, coped) (often foll. by with) deal successfully (with)

cope² n (pl -s) large ceremonial cloak worn by some Christian priests

coped v ▷ cope¹

copes v ▷ cope¹ ▶ n ▷ cope²

copied v ▷ copy

copies n, v ▷ copy

coping v ▷ cope¹ ▶ n (pl -s) sloping top row of a wall

copings n ▷ coping

copious [kope-ee-uss] adj abundant, plentiful > copiously adv

copiously adv ▷ copious

copped v ▷ cop

copper¹ n (pl -s) soft reddish-brown metal

copper² n (pl -s) (BRIT) (Slang) policeman

copperplate n (pl -s) fine handwriting style

copperplates n ▷ copperplate

coppers n ▷ copper¹, ²

coppice, copse n (pl -s) small group of trees growing close together

coppices n ▷ coppice

copping v ▷ cop

copra n (pl -s) dried oil-yielding kernel of the coconut

copras n ▷ copra

cops n, v ▷ cop

copse n ▷ coppice

copses n ▷ coppice

copulate v (-lates, -lating, -lated) have sexual intercourse > copulation n (pl -s) copulated v ▷ copulate

copulates v ▷ copulate

copulating v ▷ copulate

copulation n ▷ copulate

copulations n ▷ copulate

copy n (pl copies) thing made to look exactly like another ▶ v (copies, copying, copied) make a copy of

copying v ▷ copy

copyright n (pl -s) exclusive legal right to reproduce and control a book, work of art, etc. ▶ v (-s, -ing, -ed) take out a copyright on ▶ adj protected by copyright

copyrighted v ▷ copyright

copyrighting v ▷ copyright

copyrights n, v ▷ copyright

copywriter n (pl -s) person who writes advertising copy

copywriters n ▷ copywriter

coquette n (pl -s) woman who flirts > coquettish adj

coquettes n ▷ coquette

coquettish adj ▷ coquette

coracle n (pl -s) small round boat of wicker covered with skins

coracles n ▷ coracle

coral n (pl -s) hard substance formed from the skeletons of very small sea animals ▶ adj orange-pink

corals n ▷ coral

cord n (pl -s) thin rope or thick string ▶ pl corduroy trousers

cordial adj warm and friendly ▶ n (pl -s) drink with a fruit base > cordially adv > cordiality n

cordiality n ▷ cordial

cordially adv ▷ cordial

cordials n ▷ cordial

cordite n (pl -s) explosive used in guns and bombs

cordites n ▷ cordite

cordon n (pl -s) chain of police, soldiers, etc., guarding an area

cordons n ▷ cordon

cords n ▷ cord

corduroy n (pl -s) cotton fabric with a velvety ribbed surface

corduroys n ▷ corduroy

core n (pl -s) central part of certain fruits, containing the seeds ▶ v (cores, coring, cored) remove the core from

cored v ▷ core

corella n (pl -s) white Australian cockatoo

corellas n ▷ corella

cores n, v ▷ core

corgi n (pl -s) short-legged sturdy dog

corgis n ▷ corgi

coriander n (pl -s) plant grown for its aromatic seeds and leaves

corianders n ▷ coriander

coring v ▷ core

cork n (pl -s) thick light bark of a Mediterranean oak ▶ v (-s, -ing, -ed) seal with a cork

corkage n (pl -s) restaurant's charge for serving wine bought elsewhere

corkages n ▷ corkage

corked v ▷ cork

corking v ▷ cork

corks n, v ▷ cork

corkscrew n (pl -s) spiral metal tool for pulling corks from bottles

corkscrews n ▷ corkscrew

corm n (pl -s) bulblike underground stem of certain plants

cormorant n (pl -s) large dark-coloured long-necked sea bird

cormorants n ▷ cormorant

corms n ▷ corm

corn¹ n (pl -s) cereal plant such as wheat or oats

corn² n (pl -s) painful hard skin on the toe

cornea [korn-ee-a] n (pl -neas, -neae) transparent membrane covering the eyeball > corneal adj

corneae n ▷ cornea

corneal adj ▷ cornea

corneas n ▷ cornea

corner n (pl -s) area or angle where two converging lines or surfaces meet (SPORT) ▶ v (-s, -ing, -ed) force into a difficult or inescapable position

cornered v ▷ corner

cornering v ▷ corner

corners n, v ▷ corner

cornerstone n (pl -s) indispensable part or basis

cornerstones n ▷ cornerstone

cornet n (pl -s) brass instrument similar to the trumpet

cornets n ▷ cornet

cornflakes pl n breakfast cereal made from toasted maize

cornflour n (pl -s) (CHIEFLY BRIT) fine maize flour

cornflours n ▷ cornflour

cornflower n (pl -s) plant with blue flowers

cornflowers n ▷ cornflower

cornice n (pl -s) decorative moulding round the top of a wall

cornices n ▷ cornice

cornier adj ▷ corny

corniest adj ▷ corny

corns n ▷ corn[1, 2]

cornucopia [korn-yew-**kope**-ee-a] n (pl -**s**) great abundance

cornucopias n ▷ cornucopia

corny (-nier, -niest) adj (Slang) unoriginal or oversentimental

corolla n (pl -**s**) petals of a flower collectively

corollaries n ▷ corollary

corollary n (pl -laries) idea, fact, or proposition which is the natural result of something else

corollas n ▷ corolla

corona n (pl -nas, -nae) ring of light round the moon or sun

coronae n ▷ corona

coronaries n ▷ coronary

coronary [kor-ron-a-ree] adj of the arteries surrounding the heart ▶ n (pl -naries)

coronas n ▷ corona

coronation n (pl -**s**) ceremony of crowning a monarch

coronations n ▷ coronation

coroner n (pl -**s**) (BRIT, AUST & NZ) official responsible for the investigation of violent, sudden, or suspicious deaths

coroners n ▷ coroner

coronet n (pl -**s**) small crown

coronets n ▷ coronet

corpora n ▷ corpus

corporal[1] n (pl -**s**) noncommissioned officer in an army

corporal[2] adj of the body > corporally adv

corporally adv ▷ corporal[2]

corporals n ▷ corporal[1]

corporate adj of business corporations

corporation n (pl -**s**) large business or company

corporations n ▷ corporation

corporeal [kore-**pore**-ee-al] adj physical or tangible

corps [kore] n (pl corps) military unit with a specific function

corpse n (pl -**s**) dead body

corpses n ▷ corpse

corpulence n ▷ corpulent

corpulent adj fat or plump > corpulence n

corpus n (pl corpora) collection of writings, esp. by a single author

corpuscle n (pl -**s**) red or white blood cell

corpuscles n ▷ corpuscle

corral (US) n (pl -**s**) enclosure for cattle or horses ▶ v (-rals, -ralling, -ralled) put in a corral

corralled v ▷ corral

corralling v ▷ corral

corrals n, v ▷ corral

correct adj free from error, true ▶ v (-**s**, -ing, -ed) put right > correctly adv > correctness n

corrected v ▷ correct

correcting v ▷ correct

correction n (pl -**s**) correcting

corrections n ▷ correction

corrective adj intended to put right something wrong

correctly adv ▷ correct

correctness n ▷ correct

corrects v ▷ correct

correlate v (-lates, -lating, -lated) place or be placed in a mutual relationship > correlation n (pl -**s**)

correlated v ▷ correlate

correlates v ▷ correlate

correlating v ▷ correlate

correlation n ▷ correlate

correlations n ▷ correlate

correspond v (-**s**, -ing, -ed) be consistent or compatible (with) > corresponding adj > correspondingly adv

corresponded v ▷ correspond

correspondence n communication by letters

correspondent n (pl -**s**) person employed by a newspaper etc. to report on a special subject or from a foreign country

correspondents n ▷ correspondent

corresponding v, adj ▷ correspond

correspondingly adv ▷ correspond

corresponds v ▷ correspond

corridor n (pl -**s**) passage in a building or train

corridors n ▷ corridor

corrigenda n ▷ corrigendum

corrigendum [kor-rij-**end**-um] n (pl -da) error to be corrected

corroborate v (-rates, -rating, -rated) support (a fact or opinion) by giving proof > corroboration n (pl -**s**) > corroborative adj

corroborated v ▷ corroborate

corroborates v ▷ corroborate

corroborating v ▷ corroborate

corroboration n ▷ corroborate

corroborations n ▷ corroborate

corroborative adj ▷ corroborate

corroboree n (pl -**s**) (AUST) Aboriginal gathering or dance

corroborees n ▷ corroboree

corrode v (-rodes, -roding, -roded) eat or be eaten away by chemical action or rust > corrosion n > corrosive adj > corrosively adv > corrosiveness n

corroded v ▷ corrode

corrodes v ▷ corrode

corroding v ▷ corrode

corrosion n ▷ corrode

corrosive v ▷ corrode

corrosively adv ▷ corrode

corrosiveness n ▷ corrode

corrugated adj folded into alternate grooves and ridges

corrupt adj (-er, -est) open to or involving bribery ▶ v (-s, -ing, -ed) make corrupt > **corruptly** adv > **corruption** n > **corruptible** adj

corrupted v ▷ corrupt

corrupter adj ▷ corrupt

corruptest adj ▷ corrupt

corruptible adj ▷ corrupt

corrupting v ▷ corrupt

corruption n ▷ corrupt

corruptly adv ▷ corrupt

corrupts v ▷ corrupt

corsage [kor-sahzh] n (pl -s) small bouquet worn on the bodice of a dress

corsages n ▷ corsage

corsair n (pl -s) pirate

corsairs n ▷ corsair

corset n (pl -s) women's close-fitting undergarment worn to shape the torso

corsets n ▷ corset

cortege [kor-tayzh] n (pl -s) funeral procession

corteges n ▷ cortege

cortex n (pl -tices) (ANAT) outer layer of the brain or other internal organ > **cortical** adj

cortical adj ▷ cortex

cortices n ▷ cortex

cortisone n (pl -s) steroid hormone used to treat various diseases

cortisones n ▷ cortisone

corundum n (pl -s) hard mineral used as an abrasive

corundums n ▷ corundum

coruscate v (-cates, -cating, -cated) (Formal) sparkle

coruscated v ▷ coruscate

coruscates v ▷ coruscate

coruscating v ▷ coruscate

corvette n (pl -s) lightly armed escort warship

corvettes n ▷ corvette

cosh n (pl -es) (BRIT) heavy blunt weapon ▶ v (-es, -ing, -ed) hit with a cosh

coshed v, n ▷ cosh

coshes v ▷ cosh

coshing v ▷ cosh

cosier adj ▷ cosy

cosies adj ▷ cosy

cosiest adj ▷ cosy

cosily adv ▷ cosy

cosine [koh-sine] n (pl -s) (in trigonometry) ratio of the length of the adjacent side to that of the hypotenuse in a right-angled triangle

cosines n ▷ cosine

cosiness n ▷ cosy

cosmetic n (pl -s) preparation used to improve the appearance of a person's skin ▶ adj improving the appearance only

cosmetics n ▷ cosmetic

cosmic adj of the whole universe > **cosmically** adv

cosmically adv ▷ cosmic

cosmological adj ▷ cosmology

cosmologist n ▷ cosmology

cosmologists n ▷ cosmology

cosmology n study of the origin and nature of the universe > **cosmological** adj > **cosmologist** n (pl -s)

cosmonaut n (pl -s) Russian name for an astronaut

cosmonauts n ▷ cosmonaut

cosmopolitan adj composed of people or elements from many countries ▶ n (pl -s) cosmopolitan person > **cosmopolitanism** n

cosmopolitanism n ▷ cosmopolitan

cosmopolitans n ▷ cosmopolitan

cosmos n (pl cosmos) the universe

cossack n (pl -s) member of a S Russian people famous as horsemen and dancers

cossacks n ▷ cossack

cosset v (-s, -ing, -ed) pamper

cosseted v ▷ cosset

cosseting v ▷ cosset

cossets v ▷ cosset

cost n (pl -s) amount of money, time, labour, etc., required for something ▶ pl expenses of a lawsuit ▶ v (costs, costing, cost) have as its cost

costermonger n (pl -s) (BRIT) person who sells fruit and vegetables from a street barrow

costermongers n ▷ costermonger

costing v ▷ cost

costlier adj ▷ costly

costliest adj ▷ costly

costliness n ▷ costly

costlinesses n ▷ costly

costly adj (-lier, -liest) expensive > **costliness** n (pl -es)

costs n, v ▷ cost

costume n (pl -s) style of dress of a particular place or time, or for a particular activity

costumes n ▷ costume

costumier n (pl -s) maker or seller of costumes

costumiers n ▷ costumier

cosy adj (-sier, -siest) warm and snug ▶ n (pl -sies) cover for keeping things warm > **cosily** adv > **cosiness** n

cot n (pl **-s**) baby's bed with high sides

cote n (pl **-s**) shelter for birds or animals

coterie [kote-er-ee] n (pl **-s**) exclusive group, clique
  coteries n ▷ coterie
  cotes n ▷ cote

cotoneaster [kot-tone-ee-**ass**-ter] n (pl **-s**) garden shrub with red berries
  cotoneasters n ▷ cotoneaster
  cots n ▷ cot

cottage n (pl **-s**) small house in the country
  cottages n ▷ cottage

cotter n (pl **-s**) pin or wedge used to secure machine parts
  cotters n ▷ cotter

cotton n (pl **-s**) white downy fibre covering the seeds of a tropical plant > **cottony** adj
  cottons n ▷ cotton
  cottony adj ▷ cotton

cotyledon [kot-ill-**ee**-don] n (pl **-s**) first leaf of a plant embryo
  cotyledons n ▷ cotyledon

couch n (pl **couches**) piece of upholstered furniture for seating more than one person ▶ v (**-es**, **-ing**, **-ed**) express in a particular way
  couched v ▷ couch
  couches n, v ▷ couch

couchette [koo-**shett**] n (pl **-s**) bed converted from seats on a train or ship
  couchettes n ▷ couchette
  couching v ▷ couch

cougan n (pl **-s**) (AUST) (Slang) drunk and rowdy person
  cougans n ▷ cougan

cougar n (pl **-s**) puma
  cougars n ▷ cougar

cough v (**-s**, **-ing**, **-ed**) expel air from the lungs abruptly and noisily ▶ n (pl **-s**) act or sound of coughing
  coughed v ▷ cough
  coughing v ▷ cough
  coughs v, n ▷ cough
  could v ▷ can[1]

coulomb [koo-lom] n (pl **-s**) SI unit of electric charge
  coulombs n ▷ coulomb

coulter n (pl **-s**) blade at the front of a ploughshare
  coulters n ▷ coulter

council n (pl **-s**) group meeting for discussion or consultation ▶ adj of or by a council

councillor n (pl **-s**) member of a council
  councillors n ▷ councillor
  councils n ▷ council

counsel n (pl **-s**) advice or guidance ▶ v (**-sels**, **-selling**, **-selled**) give guidance to
  > **counsellor** n (pl **-s**)
  counselled v ▷ counsel
  counselling v ▷ counsel
  counsellor n ▷ counsel
  counsellors n ▷ counsel
  counsels n, v ▷ counsel

count[1] v (**-s**, **-ing**, **-ed**) say numbers in order ▶ n (pl **-s**) counting

count[2] n (pl **-s**) European nobleman

countdown n (pl **-s**) counting backwards to zero of the seconds before an event
  countdowns n ▷ countdown
  counted v ▷ count[1]

countenance n (pl **-s**) (expression of) the face ▶ v (**-nances**, **-nancing**, **-nanced**) allow or tolerate
  countenanced v ▷ countenance
  countenances n, v ▷ countenance
  countenancing v ▷ countenance

counter[1] n (pl **-s**) long flat surface in a bank or shop, on which business is transacted

counter[2] v (**-s**, **-ing**, **-ed**) oppose, retaliate against ▶ adv in the opposite direction ▶ n (pl **-s**) opposing or retaliatory action

counteract v (**-s**, **-ing**, **-ed**) act against or neutralize > **counteraction** n
  counteracted v ▷ counteract
  counteracting v ▷ counteract
  counteraction n ▷ counteract
  counteracts v ▷ counteract

counterattack n (pl **-s**) ▶ v (**-s**, **-ing**, **-ed**) attack in response to an attack
  counterattacked v ▷ counterattack
  counterattacking v ▷ counterattack
  counterattacks n, v ▷ counterattack

counterbalance n (pl **-s**) weight or force balancing or neutralizing another ▶ v (**-ces**, **-cing**, **-ced**) act as a counterbalance to
  counterbalanced v ▷ counterbalance
  counterbalances n, v ▷ counterbalance
  counterbalancing v ▷ counterbalance

counterblast n (pl **-s**) aggressive response to a verbal attack
  counterblasts n ▷ counterblast
  countered v ▷ counter

counterfeit adj fake, forged ▶ n (pl **-s**) fake, forgery ▶ v (**-s**, **-ing**, **-ed**) fake, forge
  counterfeited v ▷ counterfeit
  counterfeiting v ▷ counterfeit
  counterfeits n, v ▷ counterfeit

counterfoil n (pl **-s**) part of a cheque or receipt kept as a record
  counterfoils n ▷ counterfoil
  countering v ▷ counter

countermand v (-s, -ing, -ed) cancel (a previous order)
  countermanded v ▷ countermand
  countermanding v ▷ countermand
  countermands v ▷ countermand
counterpane n (pl -s) bed covering
  counterpanes n ▷ counterpane
counterpart n (pl -s) person or thing complementary to or corresponding to another
  counterparts n ▷ counterpart
counterpoint n (pl -s) (MUSIC) technique of combining melodies
  counterpoints n ▷ counterpoint
counterpoise n (pl -s) ▶ v (-ses, -sing, -sed) counterbalance
  counterpoised v ▷ counterpoise
  counterpoises n, v ▷ counterpoise
  counterpoising v ▷ counterpoise
counterproductive adj having an effect opposite to the one intended
  counters n ▷ counter¹, ² ▶ v ▷ counter²
  countersank v ▷ countersink
countersign v (-s, -ing, -ed) sign (a document already signed by someone) as confirmation
  countersigned v ▷ countersign
  countersigning v ▷ countersign
  countersigns v ▷ countersign
countersink v (-sinks, -sinking, -sank, -sunk) drive (a screw) into a shaped hole so that its head is below the surface
  countersinking v ▷ countersink
  countersinks v ▷ countersink
  countersunk v ▷ countersink
countertenor n (pl -s) male alto
  countertenors n ▷ countertenor
counterterrorism n measures to prevent terrorist attacks or eradicate terrorist groups
countess n (pl -es) woman holding the rank of count or earl
  countesses n ▷ countess
  counties n ▷ county
  counting v ▷ count¹
countless adj too many to count
  countries n ▷ country
countrified adj rustic in manner or appearance
country n (pl -tries) nation
countryman, countrywoman n (pl -men, -women) person from one's native land
  countrymen n ▷ countryman
countryside n land away from cities
  countrywoman n ▷ countryman
  countrywomen n ▷ countryman
  counts v ▷ count¹ ▶ n ▷ count¹, ²

county n (pl -ties) (in some countries) division of a country
coup [koo] n (pl -s) successful action
coupé [koo-pay] n (pl -s) sports car with two doors and a sloping fixed roof
  coupés n ▷ coupé
couple n (pl -s) two people who are married or romantically involved ▶ v (-ples, -pling, -pled) connect, associate
  coupled v ▷ couple
  couples n, v ▷ couple
couplet n (pl -s) two consecutive lines of verse, usu. rhyming and of the same metre
  couplets n ▷ couplet
coupling n (pl -s) device for connecting things, such as railway carriages ▶ v ▷ couple
  couplings n ▷ coupling
coupon n (pl -s) piece of paper entitling the holder to a discount or gift
  coupons n ▷ coupon
  coups n ▷ coup
courage n ability to face danger or pain without fear > **courageous** adj > **courageously** adv
  courageous adj ▷ courage
  courageously adv ▷ courage
courgette n (pl -s) type of small vegetable marrow
  courgettes n ▷ courgette
courier n (pl -s) person employed to look after holiday-makers
  couriers n ▷ courier
course n (pl -s) series of lessons or medical treatment ▶ v (-ses, -sing, -sed) (of liquid) run swiftly
  coursed v ▷ course
  courses n, v ▷ course
  coursing v ▷ course
court n (pl -s) body which decides legal cases ▶ v (-s, -ing, -ed) (Old-fashioned) try to gain the love of
  courted v ▷ court
courteous adj polite > **courteously** adv
  courteously adv ▷ courteous
courtesan [kor-tiz-zan] n (pl -s) (HIST) mistress or high-class prostitute
  courtesans n ▷ courtesan
  courtesies n ▷ courtesy
courtesy n (pl -sies) politeness, good manners
courtier n (pl -s) attendant at a royal court
  courtiers n ▷ courtier
  courting v ▷ court
  courtlier adj ▷ courtly
  courtliest adj ▷ courtly
  courtliness n ▷ courtly

courtlinesses n ▷ courtly
courtly adj (-lier, -liest) ceremoniously polite
> **courtliness** n (pl -es)
courts n, v ▷ court
courtship n (pl -s) courting of an intended
spouse or mate
courtships n ▷ courtship
courtyard n (pl -s) paved space enclosed by
buildings or walls
courtyards n ▷ courtyard
cousin n (pl -s) child of one's uncle or aunt
cousins n ▷ cousin
couture [koo-**toor**] n (pl -s) high-fashion
designing and dressmaking
coutures n ▷ couture
couturier n (pl -s) person who designs
women's fashion clothes
couturiers n ▷ couturier
cove n (pl -s) small bay or inlet
coven [**kuv**-ven] n (pl -s) meeting of witches
covenant [**kuv**-ven-ant] n (pl -s) contract ▶ v (-s,
-ing, -ed) agree by a covenant
covenanted v ▷ covenant
covenanting v ▷ covenant
covenants n, v ▷ covenant
covens n ▷ coven
cover v (-s, -ing, -ed) place something over, to
protect or conceal ▶ n (pl -s) anything that
covers
coverage n amount or extent covered
covered v ▷ cover
covering v ▷ cover
coverlet n (pl -s) bed cover
coverlets v ▷ coverlet
covers v, n ▷ cover
covert adj concealed, secret ▶ n (pl -s) thicket
giving shelter to game birds or animals
> **covertly** adv
covertly adv ▷ covert
coverts n ▷ covert
coves n ▷ cove
covet v (-s, -ing, -ed) long to possess (what
belongs to someone else) > **covetous** adj
> **covetousness** n
coveted v ▷ covet
coveting v ▷ covet
covetous adj ▷ covet
covetousness n ▷ covet
covets v ▷ covet
covey [**kuv**-vee] n (pl -s) small flock of grouse
or partridge
coveys n ▷ covey
cow[1] n (pl -s) mature female of cattle and of
certain other mammals, such as the elephant
or seal

cow[2] v (-s, -ing, -ed) intimidate, subdue
coward n (pl -s) person who lacks courage
> **cowardly** adj > **cowardliness** n
cowardice n lack of courage
cowardliness n ▷ coward
cowardly adj ▷ coward
cowards n ▷ coward
cowboy n (pl -s) (in the US) ranch worker who
herds and tends cattle, usu. on horseback
cowboys n ▷ cowboy
cowed v ▷ cow[2]
cower v (-s, -ing, -ed) cringe in fear
cowered v ▷ cower
cowering v ▷ cower
cowers v ▷ cower
cowing v ▷ cow[2]
cowl n (pl -s) loose hood
cowling n (pl -s) cover on an engine
cowlings n ▷ cowling
cowls n ▷ cowl
cowrie n (pl -s) brightly-marked sea shell
cowries n ▷ cowrie
cows n ▷ cow[1] ▶ v ▷ cow[2]
cowslip n (pl -s) small yellow wild European
flower
cowslips n ▷ cowslip
cox n (pl -es) coxswain ▶ v (-es, -ing, -ed) act as
cox of (a boat)
coxed v ▷ cox
coxes n, v ▷ cox
coxing v ▷ cox
coxswain [**kok**-sn] n (pl -s) person who steers
a rowing boat
coxswains n ▷ coxswain
coy adj (-er, -est) affectedly shy or modest
> **coyly** adv > **coyness** n (pl -es)
coyer adj ▷ coy
coyest adj ▷ coy
coyly adv ▷ coy
coyness n ▷ coy
coynesses n ▷ coy
coyote [koy-**ote**-ee] n (pl -s) prairie wolf of N
America
coyotes n ▷ coyote
coypu n (pl -s) beaver-like aquatic rodent
native to S America, bred for its fur
coypus n ▷ coypu

> **coz** n (**cozes**) Coz is an old word for
> **cousin**, and a good one to know as it
> scores 14 points.

cozen v (-s, -ing, -ed) (Lit) cheat, trick
cozened v ▷ cozen
cozening v ▷ cozen
cozens v ▷ cozen
crab n (pl -s) edible shellfish with ten legs, the

first pair modified into pincers

crabbed adj (of handwriting) hard to read (also crabby) (crabbier, crabbiest)

crabbier adj ▷ crabbed

crabbiest adj ▷ crabbed

crabby adj ▷ crabbed

crabs n ▷ crab

crack v (-s, -ing, -ed) break or split partially ▶ n (pl -s) sudden sharp noise ▶ adj (Informal) first-rate, excellent

crackdown n (pl -s) severe disciplinary measures

crackdowns n ▷ crackdown

cracked v ▷ crack

cracker n (pl -s) thin dry biscuit

crackers n ▷ cracker ▶ adj (Slang) insane

cracking adj very good ▶ v ▷ crack

crackle v (-ckles, -ckling, -ckled) make small sharp popping noises ▶ n (pl -ckles) crackling sound

crackled v ▷ crackle

crackles v, n ▷ crackle

crackling n crackle ▶ v ▷ crackle

crackpot n (pl -s) ▶ adj (Informal) eccentric (person)

crackpots n ▷ crackpot

cracks v, n ▷ crack

cradle n (pl -s) baby's bed on rockers ▶ v (-dles, -dling, -dled) hold gently as if in a cradle

cradled v ▷ cradle

cradles n, v ▷ cradle

cradling v ▷ cradle

craft n (pl -s) occupation requiring skill with the hands

craftier adj ▷ crafty

craftiest adj ▷ crafty

craftily adv ▷ crafty

craftiness n ▷ crafty

craftinesses n ▷ crafty

crafts n ▷ craft

craftsman, craftswoman n (pl -men, -women) skilled worker > **craftsmanship** n (pl -s)

craftsmanship n ▷ craftsman

craftsmanships n ▷ craftsman

craftsmen n ▷ craftsman

craftswoman n ▷ craftsman

craftswomen n ▷ craftsman

crafty adj (-tier, -tiest) skilled in deception > **craftily** adv > **craftiness** n (pl -es)

crag n (pl -s) steep rugged rock > **craggy** adj (-ggier, -ggiest)

craggier adj ▷ crag

craggiest adj ▷ crag

craggy adj ▷ crag

crags n ▷ crag

cram v (-s, -mming, -mmed) force into too small a space

crammed v ▷ cram

cramming v ▷ cram

cramp¹ n (pl -s) painful muscular contraction

cramp² v (-s, -ing, -ed) confine, restrict

cramped v ▷ cramp²

cramping v ▷ cramp²

crampon n (pl -s) spiked plate strapped to a boot for climbing on ice

crampons n ▷ crampon

cramps n ▷ cramp¹ ▶ v ▷ cramp²

crams v ▷ cram

cranberries n ▷ cranberry

cranberry n (pl -berries) sour edible red berry

crane n (pl -s) machine for lifting and moving heavy weights ▶ v (cranes, craning, craned) stretch (one's neck) to see something

craned v ▷ crane

cranes n, v ▷ crane

crania n ▷ cranium

cranial adj ▷ cranium

craning v ▷ crane

cranium n (pl -niums, -nia) (ANAT) skull > **cranial** adj

craniums n ▷ cranium

crank n (pl -s) arm projecting at right angles from a shaft, for transmitting or converting motion (Informal) ▶ v (-s, -ing, -ed) start (an engine) with a crank

cranked v ▷ crank

crankier adj ▷ cranky

crankiest adj ▷ cranky

cranking v ▷ crank

cranks n, v ▷ crank

crankshaft n (pl -s) shaft driven by a crank

crankshafts n ▷ crankshaft

cranky adj (-kier, -kiest) (Informal) eccentric

crannies n ▷ cranny

cranny n (pl -nies) narrow opening

crape n (pl -s) ▷ crepe

crapes n ▷ crape

craps n gambling game played with two dice

crash n (pl -es) collision involving a vehicle or vehicles ▶ v (-es, -ing, -ed) (cause to) collide violently with a vehicle, a stationary object, or the ground

crashed v ▷ crash

crashes n, v ▷ crash

crashing v ▷ crash

crass adj (-er, -est) stupid and insensitive > **crassly** adv > **crassness** n (pl -es)

crasser adj ▷ crass

crassest adj ▷ crass

crassly adv ▷ crass

crassness n ▷ crass

crassnesses n ▷ crass

crate n (pl -s) large wooden container for packing goods

crater n (pl -s) very large hole in the ground or in the surface of the moon

craters n ▷ crater

crates n ▷ crate

cravat n (pl -s) man's scarf worn like a tie

cravats n ▷ cravat

crave v (craves, craving, craved) desire intensely > craving n (pl -s)

craved v ▷ crave

craven adj cowardly

cravens v ▷ crave

craving n, v ▷ crave

cravings n ▷ crave

crawfish n (pl crawfish) ▷ crayfish

crawl v (-s, -ing, -ed) move on one's hands and knees ► n (pl -s) crawling motion or pace > crawler n (pl -s)

crawled v ▷ crawl

crawler n ▷ crawl

crawlers n ▷ crawl

crawling v ▷ crawl

crawls v, n ▷ crawl

crayfish n (pl crayfish) edible shellfish like a lobster

crayon v (-s, -ing, -ed), n (pl -s) (draw or colour with) a stick or pencil of coloured wax or clay

crayoned v ▷ crayon

crayoning v ▷ crayon

crayons v, n ▷ crayon

craze n (pl -s) short-lived fashion or enthusiasm

crazed adj wild and uncontrolled

crazes n ▷ craze

crazier adj ▷ crazy

craziest adj ▷ crazy

crazily adv ▷ crazy

craziness n ▷ crazy

crazinesses n ▷ crazy

crazy adj (-zier, -ziest) ridiculous > crazily adv > craziness n (pl -es)

creak v, n (pl -s) (make) a harsh squeaking sound > creaky adj (-kier, -kiest)

creakier adj ▷ creak

creakiest adj ▷ creak

creaks n ▷ creak

creaky adj ▷ creak

cream n (pl -s) fatty part of milk ► adj yellowish-white ► v (-s, -ing, -ed) beat to a creamy consistency > creamy adj > creaminess n

creamed v ▷ cream

creaminess n ▷ cream

creaming v ▷ cream

creams n, v ▷ cream

creamy adj ▷ cream

crease n (pl -s) line made by folding or pressing ► v (creases, creasing, creased) crush or line

creased v ▷ crease

creases n, v ▷ crease

creasing v ▷ crease

create v (creates, creating, created) make, cause to exist > creation n (pl -s) > creator n (pl -s)

created v ▷ create

creates v ▷ create

creating v ▷ create

creation n ▷ create

creations n ▷ create

creative adj imaginative or inventive > creatively adv > creativity n

creatively adv ▷ creative

creativity n ▷ creative

creator n ▷ create

creators n ▷ create

creature n (pl -s) animal, person, or other being

creatures n ▷ creature

crèche n (pl -s) place where small children are looked after while their parents are working, shopping, etc.

crèches n ▷ crèche

credence n (pl -s) belief in the truth or accuracy of a statement

credences n ▷ credence

credentials pl n document giving evidence of a person's identity or qualifications

credibility n ▷ credible

credible adj believable > credibly adv > credibility n

credibly adv ▷ credible

credit n (pl -s) system of allowing customers to receive goods and pay later ► v (-s, -ing, -ed) enter as a credit in an account

creditable adj praiseworthy > creditably adv

creditably adv ▷ creditable

credited v ▷ credit

crediting v ▷ credit

creditor n (pl -s) person to whom money is owed

creditors n ▷ creditor

credits n, v ▷ credit

credulity n ▷ credulous

credulous adj too willing to believe > credulity n > credulously adv

credulously adv ▷ credulous

creed n (pl -s) statement or system of (Christian) beliefs or principles
creeds n ▷ **creed**

creek n (pl -s) narrow inlet or bay (AUST, NZ, US & CANADIAN)
creeks n ▷ **creek**

creel n (pl -s) wicker basket used by anglers
creels n ▷ **creel**

creep v (creeps, creeping, crept) move quietly and cautiously ▶ n (pl -s) (Slang) obnoxious or servile person

creeper n (pl -s) creeping plant
creepers n ▷ **creeper**
creepier adj ▷ **creepy**
creepiest adj ▷ **creepy**
creepily adv ▷ **creepy**
creepiness n ▷ **creepy**
creepinesses n ▷ **creepy**
creeping v ▷ **creep**
creeps v, n ▷ **creep**

creepy adj (-pier, -piest) (Informal) causing a feeling of fear or disgust > **creepily** adv > **creepiness** n (pl -es)

cremate v (-mates, -mating, -mated) burn (a corpse) to ash > **cremation** n (pl -s)
cremated v ▷ **cremate**
cremates v ▷ **cremate**
cremating v ▷ **cremate**
cremation n ▷ **cremate**
cremations n ▷ **cremate**
crematoria n ▷ **crematorium**

crematorium n (pl -iums, -ia) building where corpses are cremated
crematoriums n ▷ **crematorium**

crenellated adj having battlements

creole n (pl -s) language developed from a mixture of languages
creoles n ▷ **creole**

creosote n (pl -s) dark oily liquid made from coal tar and used for preserving wood ▶ v (-sotes, -soting, -soted) treat with creosote
creosoted v ▷ **creosote**
creosotes n, v ▷ **creosote**
creosoting v ▷ **creosote**

crepe, crape [krayp] n (pl -s) fabric or rubber with a crinkled texture
crepes n ▷ **crepe**
crept v ▷ **creep**

crepuscular adj (Lit) of or like twilight

crescendo [krish-end-oh] n (pl -s) gradual increase in loudness, esp. in music
crescendos n ▷ **creep**

crescent n (pl -s) (curved shape of) the moon as seen in its first or last quarter
crescents n ▷ **crescent**

cress n (pl -es) plant with strong-tasting leaves, used in salads
cresses n ▷ **cress**

crest n (pl -s) top of a mountain, hill, or wave > **crested** adj
crested adj ▷ **crest**
crestfallen adj disheartened
crests n ▷ **crest**

cretin n (pl -s) (Informal) stupid person > **cretinous** adj
cretinous adj ▷ **cretin**
cretins n ▷ **cretin**

crevasse n (pl -s) deep open crack in a glacier
crevasses n ▷ **crevasse**

crevice n (pl -s) narrow crack or gap in rock
crevices n ▷ **crevice**

crew n (pl -s) people who work on a ship or aircraft (Informal) ▶ v (-s, -ing, -ed) serve as a crew member (on)
crewed v ▷ **crew**

crewel n (pl -s) fine worsted yarn used in embroidery
crewels n ▷ **crewel**
crewing v ▷ **crew**
crews n, v ▷ **crew**

crib n (pl -s) piece of writing stolen from elsewhere ▶ v (cribs, cribbing, cribbed) copy (someone's work) dishonestly

cribbage n card game for two to four players
cribbed v ▷ **crib**
cribbing v ▷ **crib**
cribs n, v ▷ **crib**

crick n (pl -s) muscle spasm or cramp in the back or neck ▶ v (-s, -ing, -ed) cause a crick in
cricked v ▷ **crick**

cricket¹ n (pl -s) outdoor game played with bats, a ball, and wickets by two teams of eleven > **cricketer** n (pl -s)

cricket² n (pl -s) chirping insect like a grasshopper
cricketer n ▷ **cricket¹**
cricketers n ▷ **cricket¹**
crickets n ▷ **cricket¹, ²**
cricking v ▷ **crick**
cricks n, v ▷ **crick**
cried v ▷ **cry**
cries v ▷ **cry**

crime n (pl -s) unlawful act
crimes n ▷ **crime**

criminal n (pl -s) person guilty of a crime ▶ adj of crime > **criminally** adv > **criminality** n
criminality n ▷ **criminal**
criminally adv ▷ **criminal**
criminals n ▷ **criminal**
criminologist n ▷ **criminology**

criminologists n ▷ criminology
criminology n study of crime > **criminologist**
 n (pl -s)
crimp v (-s, -ing, -ed) fold or press into ridges
 crimped v ▷ crimp
 crimping v ▷ crimp
 crimps v ▷ crimp
crimson adj deep purplish-red
cringe v (cringes, cringing, cringed) flinch
 in fear
 cringed v ▷ cringe
 cringes v ▷ cringe
 cringing v ▷ cringe
crinkle v (-kles, -kling, -kled) ▶ n (pl -s) wrinkle,
 crease, or fold
 crinkled v ▷ crinkle
 crinkles v, n ▷ crinkle
 crinkling v ▷ crinkle
crinoline n (pl -s) hooped petticoat
 crinolines n ▷ crinoline
cripple n (pl -s) person who is lame or disabled
 ▶ v (-pples, -ppling, -ppled) make lame or
 disabled
 crippled v ▷ cripple
 cripples n, v ▷ cripple
 crippling v ▷ cripple
 crises n ▷ crisis
crisis n (pl -ses) crucial stage, turning point
crisp adj (-er, -est) fresh and firm ▶ n (pl -s) (BRIT)
 very thin slice of potato fried till crunchy
 > **crisply** adv > **crispness** n (pl -es)
crispbread n (pl -s) thin dry biscuit
 crispbreads n ▷ crispbread
 crisper adj ▷ crisp
 crispest adj ▷ crisp
 crispier adj ▷ crisp
 crispiest adj ▷ crisp
 crisply adv ▷ crisp
 crispness adv ▷ crisp
 crispnesses adv ▷ crisp
 crisps n ▷ crisp
crispy adj (-pier, -piest) hard and crunchy
crisscross v (-es, -ing, -ed) move in or mark
 with a crosswise pattern ▶ adj (of lines)
 crossing in different directions
 crisscrossed v ▷ crisscross
 crisscrosses v ▷ crisscross
 crisscrossing v ▷ crisscross
 criteria n ▷ criterion
criterion n (pl -ria) standard of judgment
critic n (pl -s) professional judge of any of
 the arts
critical adj very important or dangerous
 > **critically** adv
 critically adv ▷ critical

criticism n (pl -s) fault-finding
 criticisms n ▷ criticism
criticize v (-cizes, -cizing, -cized) find fault
 with
 criticized v ▷ criticize
 criticizes v ▷ criticize
 criticizing v ▷ criticize
 critics n ▷ critic
critique n (pl -s) critical essay
 critiques n ▷ critique
croak v (-s, -ing, -ed) (of a frog or crow) give a
 low hoarse cry ▶ n (pl -s) low hoarse sound
 croaked v ▷ croak
 croakiness n ▷ croaky
 croaking v ▷ croak
 croaks v, n ▷ croak
croaky adj hoarse > **croakiness** n
crochet [kroh-shay] v (-chets, -cheting,
 -cheted) make by looping and intertwining
 yarn with a hooked needle ▶ n (pl -s) work
 made in this way
 crocheted v ▷ crochet
 crocheting v ▷ crochet
 crochets v, n ▷ crochet
crock¹ n (pl -s) earthenware pot or jar
crock² n (pl -s) (BRIT, AUST & NZ) (Informal) old or
 decrepit person or thing
crockery n dishes
 crocks n ▷ crock¹, ²
crocodile n (pl -s) large amphibious tropical
 reptile
 crocodiles n ▷ crocodile
crocus n (pl -cuses) small plant with yellow,
 white, or purple flowers in spring
 crocuses n ▷ crocus
croft n (pl -s) small farm worked by one family
 in Scotland > **crofter** n (pl -s)
 crofter n ▷ croft
 crofters n ▷ croft
 crofts n ▷ croft
croissant [krwah-son] n (pl -s) rich flaky
 crescent-shaped roll
 croissants n ▷ croissant
cromlech n (pl -s) (BRIT) circle of prehistoric
 standing stones
 cromlechs n ▷ cromlech
crone n (pl -s) witchlike old woman
 crones n ▷ crone
 cronies n ▷ crony
crony n (pl -nies) close friend
crook n (pl -s) (Informal) criminal ▶ adj (AUST & NZ)
 (Slang) unwell, injured
crooked adj bent or twisted > **crookedly** adv
 > **crookedness** n
 crookedly adv ▷ crooked

crookedness n ▷ **crooked**

crooks n ▷ **crook**

croon v (-s, -ing, -ed) sing, hum, or speak in a soft low tone

  crooned v ▷ **croon**

crooner n (pl -s) male singer of sentimental ballads

  crooners n ▷ **crooner**

  crooning v ▷ **croon**

  croons v ▷ **croon**

crop n (pl -s) cultivated plant ▶ v (**crops, cropping, cropped**) cut very short > **cropper** n (pl -s)

  cropped v ▷ **crop**

  cropper n ▷ **crop**

  croppers n ▷ **crop**

  cropping v ▷ **crop**

  crops n, v ▷ **crop**

croquet [kroh-kay] n (pl -s) game played on a lawn in which balls are hit through hoops

  croquets n ▷ **croquet**

croquette [kroh-kett] n (pl -s) fried cake of potato, meat, or fish

  croquettes n ▷ **croquette**

crosier n (pl -s) ▷ **crozier**

  crosiers n ▷ **crosier**

cross v (-es, -ing, -ed) move or go across (something) ▶ n (pl -es) structure, symbol, or mark of two intersecting lines ▶ adj (-er, -est) angry, annoyed > **crossly** adv > **crossness** n (pl -es)

crossbar n (pl -s) horizontal bar across goalposts or on a bicycle

  crossbars n ▷ **crossbar**

crossbow n (pl -s) weapon consisting of a bow fixed across a wooden stock

  crossbows n ▷ **crossbow**

crossbred adj bred from two different types of animal or plant

crossbreed n (pl -s) crossbred animal or plant

  crossbreeds n ▷ **crossbreed**

  crossed v ▷ **cross**

  crosser adj ▷ **cross**

  crosses v, n ▷ **cross**

  crossest adj ▷ **cross**

crossfire n (pl -s) gunfire crossing another line of fire

  crossfires n ▷ **crossfire**

crossing n (pl -s) place where a street may be crossed safely ▶ v ▷ **cross**

  crossings n ▷ **crossing**

  crossly adv ▷ **cross**

  crossness n ▷ **cross**

  crossnesses n ▷ **cross**

crossroads n place where roads intersect

crosswise adj, adv across

crossword n (pl -s) puzzle in which words suggested by clues are written into a grid of squares

  crosswords n ▷ **crossword**

crotch n (pl -es) part of the body between the tops of the legs

  crotches n ▷ **crotch**

crotchet n (pl -s) musical note half the length of a minim

  crotchetier adj ▷ **crotchety**

  crotchetiest adj ▷ **crotchety**

  crotchets n ▷ **crotchet**

crotchety adj (-tier, -tiest) (Informal) bad-tempered

crouch v (-es, -ing, -ed) bend low with the legs and body close ▶ n (pl -es) this position

  crouched v ▷ **crouch**

  crouches v, n ▷ **crouch**

  crouching v ▷ **crouch**

croup¹ [kroop] n (pl -s) throat disease of children, with a cough

croup² [kroop] n (pl -s) hind quarters of a horse

croupier [kroop-ee-ay] n (pl -s) person who collects bets and pays out winnings at a gambling table in a casino

  croupiers n ▷ **croupier**

  croups n ▷ **croup¹, ²**

crouton n (pl -s) small piece of fried or toasted bread served in soup

  croutons n ▷ **crouton**

crow¹ n (pl -s) large black bird with a harsh call

crow² v (-s, -ing, -ed) (of a cock) make a shrill squawking sound

crowbar n (pl -s) iron bar used as a lever

  crowbars n ▷ **crowbar**

crowd n (pl -s) large group of people or things ▶ v (-s, -ing, -ed) gather together in large numbers

  crowded v ▷ **crowd**

  crowding v ▷ **crowd**

  crowds n, v ▷ **crowd**

  crowed v ▷ **crow²**

  crowing v ▷ **crow²**

crown n (pl -s) monarch's headdress of gold and jewels ▶ v (-s, -ing, -ed) put a crown on the head of (someone) to proclaim him or her monarch

  crowned v ▷ **crown**

  crowning v ▷ **crown**

  crowns n, v ▷ **crown**

  crows n ▷ **crow¹** ▶ v ▷ **crow²**

crozier, crosier n (pl -s) bishop's hooked staff

  croziers n ▷ **crozier**

crucial adj very important > **crucially** adv

crucially adv ▷ crucial
crucible n (pl -s) pot in which metals are melted
  crucibles n ▷ crucible
  crucified v ▷ crucify
  crucifies v ▷ crucify
crucifix n (pl -es) model of Christ on the Cross
  crucifixes n ▷ crucify
crucifixion n (pl -s) crucifying
  crucifixions n ▷ crucifixion
cruciform adj cross-shaped
crucify v (-fies, -fying, -fied) put to death by fastening to a cross
  crucifying v ▷ crucify
crude adj (-r, -st) rough and simple > **crudely** adv > **crudeness** n (pl -es) > **crudity** n (pl -ties)
  crudely adv ▷ crude
  crudeness n ▷ crude
  crudenesses n ▷ crude
  cruder adj ▷ crude
  crudest adj ▷ crude
  crudities n ▷ crude
  crudity n ▷ crude
cruel adj (-ller, -llest) delighting in others' pain > **cruelly** adv > **cruelty** n (pl -ties)
  crueller adj ▷ cruel
  cruellest adj ▷ cruel
  cruelly adv ▷ cruel
  cruelties n ▷ cruel
  cruelty n ▷ cruel
cruet n (pl -s) small container for salt, pepper, etc., at table
  cruets n ▷ cruet
cruise n (pl -s) sail for pleasure ▶ v (cruises, cruising, cruised) sail from place to place for pleasure
  cruised v ▷ cruise
cruiser n (pl -s) fast warship
  cruisers n ▷ cruiser
  cruises n, v ▷ cruise
  cruising v ▷ cruise
crumb n (pl -s) small fragment of bread or other dry food
crumble v (-bles, -bling, -bled) break into fragments ▶ n (pl -s) pudding of stewed fruit with a crumbly topping > **crumbly** adj (-blier, -bliest)
  crumbled v ▷ crumble
  crumbles v, n ▷ crumble
  crumblier adj ▷ crumble
  crumbliest adj ▷ crumble
  crumbling v ▷ crumble
  crumbly adj ▷ crumble
  crumbs n ▷ crumb
  crummier adj ▷ crummy

  crummiest adj ▷ crummy
crummy adj (-mier, -miest) (Slang) of poor quality
crumpet n (pl -s) round soft yeast cake, eaten buttered
  crumpets n ▷ crumpet
crumple v (-ples, -pling, -pled) crush, crease > **crumpled** adj
  crumpled v, adj ▷ crumple
  crumples v ▷ crumple
  crumpling v ▷ crumple
crunch v (-es, -ing, -ed) bite or chew with a noisy crushing sound ▶ n (pl -es) crunching sound (Informal) > **crunchy** adj (-chier, -chiest)
  crunched v ▷ crunch
  crunches v, n ▷ crunch
  crunchier adj ▷ crunch
  crunchiest adj ▷ crunch
  crunching v ▷ crunch
  crunchy adj ▷ crunch
crupper n (pl -s) strap that passes from the back of a saddle under a horse's tail
  cruppers n ▷ crupper
crusade n (pl -s) medieval Christian war to recover the Holy Land from the Muslims ▶ v (-sades, -sading, -saded) take part in a crusade
  crusaded v ▷ crusade
crusader n (pl -s) person who took part in the medieval Christian war to recover the Holy Land from the Muslims
  crusaders n ▷ crusader
  crusades n, v ▷ crusade
  crusading v ▷ crusade
crush v (-es, -ing, -ed) compress so as to injure, break, or crumple ▶ n (pl -es) dense crowd
  crushed v ▷ crush
  crushes v, n ▷ crush
  crushing v ▷ crush
crust n (pl -s) hard outer part of something, esp. bread ▶ v (-s, -ing, -ed) cover with or form a crust
crustacean n (pl -s) hard-shelled, usu. aquatic animal with several pairs of legs, such as the crab or lobster
  crustaceans n ▷ crustacean
  crusted v ▷ crust
  crustier adj ▷ crusty
  crustiest adj ▷ crusty
  crusting v ▷ crust
  crusts n, v ▷ crust
crusty adj (-tier, -tiest) having a crust
crutch n (pl -es) long sticklike support with a rest for the armpit, used by a lame person
  crutches n ▷ crutch

crux n (pl -es) crucial or decisive point
  cruxes n ▷ **crux**
cry v (**cries, crying, cried**) shed tears ▶ n (pl
  cries) fit of weeping
  crybabies n ▷ **crybaby**
crybaby n (pl -**babies**) person, esp. a child, who
  cries too readily
  crying v ▷ **cry**
  cryogenic adj ▷ **cryogenics**
cryogenics n branch of physics concerned
  with very low temperatures > **cryogenic** adj
crypt n (pl -**s**) vault under a church, esp. one
  used as a burial place
cryptic adj obscure in meaning, secret
  > **cryptically** adv
  cryptographer n ▷ **cryptography**
  cryptographers n ▷ **cryptography**
cryptography n art of writing in and
  deciphering codes > **cryptographer** n (pl -**s**)
  crypts n ▷ **crypt**
crystal n (pl -**s**) (single grain of) a
  symmetrically shaped solid formed naturally
  by some substances ▶ adj bright and clear
crystalline adj of or like crystal or crystals
  crystallization n ▷ **crystallize**
  crystallizations n ▷ **crystallize**
crystallize v (-**lizes, -lizing, -lized**) make or
  become definite > **crystallization** n (pl -**s**)
  crystallized v ▷ **crystallize**
  crystallizes v ▷ **crystallize**
  crystallizing v ▷ **crystallize**
  crystals n ▷ **crystal**
cub n (pl -**s**) young wild animal such as a bear
  or fox ▶ v (**cubs, cubbing, cubbed**) give birth
  to cubs
  cubbed v ▷ **cub**
  cubbing v ▷ **cub**
cubbyhole n (pl -**s**) small enclosed space or
  room
  cubbyholes n ▷ **cubbyhole**
cube n (pl -**s**) object with six equal square sides
  ▶ v (**cubes, cubing, cubed**) cut into cubes
  cubed v ▷ **cube**
  cubes n, v ▷ **cube**
cubic adj having three dimensions
cubicle n (pl -**s**) enclosed part of a large room,
  screened for privacy
  cubicles n ▷ **cubicle**
  cubing v ▷ **cube**
cubism n style of art in which objects are
  represented by geometrical shapes > **cubist**
  adj, n (pl -**s**)
  cubists n ▷ **cubist**
  cubs n, v ▷ **cub**
cuckold n (pl -**s**) man whose wife has been

  unfaithful ▶ v (-**s, -ing, -ed**) be unfaithful to
  (one's husband)
  cuckolded v ▷ **cuckold**
  cuckolding v ▷ **cuckold**
  cuckolds n, v ▷ **cuckold**
cuckoo n (pl -**s**) migratory bird with a
  characteristic two-note call, which lays its
  eggs in the nests of other birds ▶ adj (Informal)
  insane or foolish
  cuckoos n ▷ **cuckoo**
cucumber n (pl -**s**) long green-skinned fleshy
  fruit used in salads
  cucumbers n ▷ **cucumber**
cud n (pl -**s**) partially digested food which
  a ruminant brings back into its mouth to
  chew again
cuddle v (**cuddles, cuddling, cuddled**) ▶ n (pl -**s**)
  hug > **cuddly** adj (-**lier, -liest**)
  cuddled v ▷ **cuddle**
  cuddles v, n ▷ **cuddle**
  cuddlier adj ▷ **cuddle**
  cuddliest adj ▷ **cuddle**
  cuddling v ▷ **cuddle**
  cuddly adj ▷ **cuddle**
cudgel n (pl -**s**) short thick stick used as a
  weapon
  cudgels n ▷ **cudgel**
  cuds n ▷ **cud**
cue¹ n (pl -**s**) signal to an actor or musician to
  begin speaking or playing ▶ v (**cues, cueing,
  cued**) give a cue to
cue² n long tapering stick used in billiards,
  snooker, or pool ▶ v (**cues, cueing, cued**) hit (a
  ball) with a cue
  cued v ▷ **cue¹, ²**
  cueing v ▷ **cue¹, ²**
  cues n, v ▷ **cue¹, ²**
cuff¹ n (pl -**s**) end of a sleeve
cuff² (BRIT, AUST & NZ) v (-**s, -ing, -ed**) hit with an
  open hand ▶ n (pl -**s**) blow with an open hand
  cuffed v ▷ **cuff²**
  cuffing v ▷ **cuff²**
  cuffs n ▷ **cuff¹, ²** ▶ v ▷ **cuff²**
cuisine [quiz-zeen] n (pl -**s**) style of cooking
  cuisines n ▷ **cuisine**
culinary adj of kitchens or cookery
cull v (-**s, -ing, -ed**) choose, gather ▶ n (pl -**s**)
  culling
  culled v ▷ **cull**
  culling v ▷ **cull**
  culls v, n ▷ **cull**
culminate v (-**nates, -nating, -nated**) reach
  the highest point or climax > **culmination**
  n (pl -**s**)
  culminated v ▷ **culminate**

culminates *v* ▷ culminate
culminating *v* ▷ culminate
culmination *n* ▷ culminate
culminations *n* ▷ culminate
culottes *pl n* women's knee-length trousers cut to look like a skirt
culpabilities *n* ▷ culpable
culpability *n* ▷ culpable
culpable *adj* deserving blame > culpability *n* (*pl* -ties)> culpably *adv*
culpably *adv* ▷ culpable
culprit *n* (*pl* -s) person guilty of an offence or misdeed
culprits *n* ▷ culprit
cult *n* (*pl* -s) specific system of worship
cultivate *v* (-vates, -vating, -vated) prepare (land) to grow crops > cultivation *n*
cultivated *adj* well-educated ▶ *v* ▷ cultivate
cultivates *v* ▷ cultivate
cultivating *v* ▷ cultivate
cultivation *n* ▷ cultivate
cults *n* ▷ cult
cultural *adj* ▷ culture
culturally *adv* ▷ culture
culture *n* (*pl* -s) ideas, customs, and art of a particular society > cultural *adj* > culturally *adv*
cultured *adj* showing good taste or manners
cultures *n* ▷ culture
culvert *n* (*pl* -s) drain under a road or railway
culverts *n* ▷ culvert
cumbersome *adj* awkward because of size or shape
cumin, cummin *n* (*pl* -s) sweet-smelling seeds of a Mediterranean plant, used in cooking
cumins *n* ▷ cumin
cummerbund *n* (*pl* -s) wide sash worn round the waist
cummerbunds *n* ▷ cummerbund
cummin *n* ▷ cumin
cummins *n* ▷ cumin
cumulative *adj* increasing steadily > cumulatively *adv*
cumulatively *adv* ▷ cumulative
cumuli *n* ▷ cumulus
cumulus [kew-myew-luss] *n* (*pl* -li) thick white or dark grey cloud
cuneiform [kew-nif-form] *n*, *adj* (written in) an ancient system of writing using wedge-shaped characters
cunjevoi *n* (*pl* -s) (AUST) plant of tropical Asia and Australia with small flowers, cultivated for its edible rhizome
cunjevois *n* ▷ cunjevoi
cunning *adj* clever at deceiving ▶ *n* cleverness

at deceiving > cunningly *adv*
cunningly *adv* ▷ cunning
cup *n* (*pl* -s) small bowl-shaped drinking container with a handle ▶ *v* (cups, cupping, cupped) form (one's hands) into the shape of a cup > cupful *n* (*pl* -s)
cupboard *n* (*pl* -s) piece of furniture or alcove with a door, for storage
cupboards *n* ▷ cupboard
cupful *n* ▷ cup
cupfuls *n* ▷ cup
cupidity [kew-pid-it-ee] *n* greed for money or possessions
cupola [kew-pol-la] *n* (*pl* -s) domed roof or ceiling
cupolas *n* ▷ cupola
cupped *v* ▷ cup
cupping *v* ▷ cup
cups *n*, *v* ▷ cup
cur *n* (*pl* -s) (*Lit*) mongrel dog
curable *adj* ▷ cure
curaçao [kew-rah-so] *n* orange-flavoured liqueur
curacies *n* ▷ curacy
curacy [kew-rah-see] *n* (*pl* -cies) work or position of a curate
curare [kew-rah-ree] *n* (*pl* -s) poisonous resin of a S American tree, used as a muscle relaxant in medicine
curares *n* ▷ curare
curate *n* (*pl* -s) clergyman who assists a parish priest
curates *n* ▷ curate
curative *adj*, *n* (*pl* -s) (something) able to cure
curatives *n* ▷ curative
curator *n* (*pl* -s) person in charge of a museum or art gallery > curatorship *n* (*pl* -s)
curators *n* ▷ curator
curatorship *n* ▷ curator
curatorships *n* ▷ curator
curb *n* (*pl* -s) something that restrains ▶ *v* (-s, -ing, -ed) control, restrain
curbed *v* ▷ curb
curbing *v* ▷ curb
curbs *n*, *v* ▷ curb
curd *n* (*pl* -s) coagulated milk, used to make cheese
curdle *v* (-dles, -dling, -dled) turn into curd, coagulate
curdled *v* ▷ curdle
curdles *v* ▷ curdle
curdling *v* ▷ curdle
curds *n* ▷ curd
cure *v* (cures, curing, cured) get rid of (an illness or problem) ▶ *n* (*pl* -s) (treatment

causing) curing of an illness or person
> **curable** adj
cured v ▷ **cure**
cures v, n ▷ **cure**
curettage n ▷ **curette**
curettages n ▷ **curette**
curette n (pl -s) surgical instrument for
scraping tissue from body cavities ▶ v
(**curettes, curetting, curetted**) scrape with a
curette > **curettage** n (pl -s)
curetted v ▷ **curette**
curettes n, v ▷ **curette**
curetting v ▷ **curette**
curfew n (pl -s) law ordering people to stay
inside their homes after a specific time at
night
curfews n ▷ **curfew**
curie n (pl -s) standard unit of radioactivity
curies n ▷ **curie**
curing v ▷ **cure**
curio n (pl -s) rare or unusual object valued as a
collector's item
curios n ▷ **curio**
curiosities n ▷ **curiosity**
curiosity n eagerness to know or find out
(pl -**ties**)
curiously adv ▷ **curious**
curious adj eager to learn or know > **curiously**
adv
curl n (pl -s) curved piece of hair ▶ v (-s, -ing,
-ed) make (hair) into curls or (of hair) grow in
curls > **curler** n (pl -s) > **curly** adj (-**lier, -liest**)
curled v ▷ **curl**
curler n ▷ **curl**
curlers n ▷ **curl**
curlew n (pl -s) long-billed wading bird
curlews n ▷ **curlew**
curlier adj ▷ **curl**
curliest adj ▷ **curl**
curling n game like bowls, played with heavy
stones on ice ▶ v ▷ **curl**
curls n, v ▷ **curl**
curly adj ▷ **curl**
curmudgeon n (pl -s) bad-tempered person
> **curmudgeonly** adj
curmudgeonly adj ▷ **curmudgeon**
curmudgeons n ▷ **curmudgeon**
currajong n (pl -s) ▷ **kurrajong**
currajongs n ▷ **currajong**
currant n (pl -s) small dried grape
currants n ▷ **currant**
currawong n (pl -s) Australian songbird
currawongs n ▷ **currawong**
currencies n ▷ **currency**
currency n (pl -**cies**) money in use in a

particular country
current adj of the immediate present ▶ n
(pl -s) flow of water or air in one direction
> **currently** adv
currently adv ▷ **current**
currents n ▷ **current**
curricula n ▷ **curriculum**
curriculum n (pl -**la, -lums**) all the courses of
study offered by a school or college
curriculums n ▷ **curriculum**
curried v ▷ **curry**[1, 2]
curries n ▷ **curry**[1] ▶ v ▷ **curry**[1, 2]
curry[1] n (pl -**ries**) Indian dish of meat or
vegetables in a hot spicy sauce ▶ v (-**ries,
-rying, -ried**) prepare (food) with curry
powder
curry[2] v (-**ries, -rying, -ried**) groom (a horse)
currying v ▷ **curry**[1, 2]
curs n ▷ **cur**
curse v (**curses, cursing, cursed**) swear (at) ▶ n
(pl -s) swearword > **cursed** adj
cursed adj, v ▷ **curse**
curses v, n ▷ **curse**
cursing v ▷ **curse**
cursive adj, n (pl -s) (handwriting) done with
joined letters > **cursively** adv
cursively adv ▷ **cursive**
cursives n ▷ **cursive**
cursor n (pl -s) movable point of light that
shows a specific position on a visual display
unit
cursorily adv ▷ **cursory**
cursoriness n ▷ **cursory**
cursors n ▷ **cursor**
cursory adj quick and superficial > **cursorily**
adv > **cursoriness** n
curt adj (-**er, -est**) brief and rather rude > **curtly**
adv > **curtness** n (pl -**es**)
curtail v (-s, -ing, -ed) cut short > **curtailment**
n (pl -s)
curtailed v ▷ **curtail**
curtailing v ▷ **curtail**
curtailment n ▷ **curtail**
curtailments n ▷ **curtail**
curtails v ▷ **curtail**
curtain n (pl -s) piece of cloth hung at a
window or opening as a screen ▶ v (-s, -ing,
-ed) provide with curtains
curtained v ▷ **curtain**
curtaining v ▷ **curtain**
curtains n, v ▷ **curtain**
curter adj ▷ **curt**
curtest adj ▷ **curt**
curtly adv ▷ **curt**
curtness n ▷ **curt**

curtnesses n ▷ curt
curtsey n ▷ curtsy
curtseyed v ▷ curtsy
curtseying v ▷ curtsy
curtseys n, v ▷ curtsy
curtsied v ▷ curtsy
curtsies n, v ▷ curtsy
curtsy, curtsey n (pl -sies, -seys) woman's gesture of respect made by bending the knees and bowing the head ▶ v (-sies, -seys, -sying, -sied or -seying) (-seyed) make a curtsy
curtsying v ▷ curtsy
curvaceous adj (Informal) (of a woman) having a shapely body
curvature n (pl -s) curved shape
curvatures n ▷ curvature
curve n (pl -s) continuously bending line with no straight parts ▶ v (curves, curving, curved) form or move in a curve > **curvy** adj (-vier, -viest)
curved v ▷ curve
curves n, v ▷ curve
curvier adj ▷ curve
curviest adj ▷ curve
curvilinear adj consisting of or bounded by a curve
curving v ▷ curve
curvy adj ▷ curve
cuscus n (pl -ses) large Australian nocturnal possum
cuscuses n ▷ cuscus
cushier adj ▷ cushy
cushiest adj ▷ cushy
cushion n (pl -s) bag filled with soft material, to make a seat more comfortable ▶ v (-s, -ing, -ed) lessen the effects of
cushioned v ▷ cushion
cushioning v ▷ cushion
cushions n, v ▷ cushion
cushy adj (cushier, cushiest) (Informal) easy
cusp n (pl -s) pointed end, esp. on a tooth
cusps n ▷ cusp
cuss (Informal) n (pl -es) curse, oath ▶ v (-es, -ing, -ed) swear (at)
cussed [kuss-id] adj (Informal) obstinate ▶ v ▷ **cuss** > **cussedly** adv > **cussedness** n
cussedly adv ▷ cussed
cussedness n ▷ cussed
cusses n, v ▷ cuss
cussing v ▷ cuss
custard n (pl -s) sweet yellow sauce made from milk and eggs
custards n ▷ custard
custodial adj ▷ custody

custodian n (pl -s) person in charge of a public building
custodians n ▷ custodian
custodies n ▷ custody
custody n (pl -dies) protective care > **custodial** adj
custom n (pl -s) long-established activity or action ▶ pl duty charged on imports or exports
customarily adv ▷ customary
customary adj usual > **customarily** adv
customer n (pl s) person who buys goods or services
customers n ▷ customer
customs n ▷ custom
cut v (cuts, cutting, cut) open up, penetrate, wound, or divide with a sharp instrument ▶ n (pl -s) stroke or incision made by cutting
cutaneous [kew-tane-ee-uss] adj of the skin
cute adj (cuter, cutest) appealing or attractive > **cutely** adv > **cuteness** n
cutely adv ▷ cute
cuteness n ▷ cute
cuter adj ▷ cute
cutest adj ▷ cute
cuticle n (pl -s) skin at the base of a fingernail or toenail
cuticles n ▷ cuticle
cutlass n (pl -es) curved one-edged sword formerly used by sailors
cutlasses n ▷ cutlass
cutler n (pl -s) maker of cutlery
cutlers n ▷ cutler
cutlery n knives, forks, and spoons
cutlet n (pl -s) small piece of meat like a chop
cutlets n ▷ cutlet
cuts v, n ▷ cut
cutter n (pl -s) person or tool that cuts
cutters n ▷ cutter
cutting n (pl -s) article cut from a newspaper or magazine ▶ adj (of a remark) hurtful ▶ v ▷ **cut** > **cuttingly** adv
cuttingly adv ▷ cutting
cuttings n ▷ cutting
cuttlefish n (pl cuttlefish) squidlike sea mollusc

> **cuz** n (cuzzes) Like **coz**, cuz is an old word for **cousin**. You need a blank tile for the second Z if you're going to play the plural. Cuz scores 14 points.
> **cwm** n (cwms) Cwm is a Welsh word for a valley. It's a useful one to remember because it doesn't contain any vowels. Cwm scores 10 points.

cyanide n (pl -s) extremely poisonous chemical

compound

cyanides n ▷ cyanide

cybernetics n branch of science in which electronic and mechanical systems are studied and compared to biological systems

cyberspace n place said to contain all the data stored in computers

cyclamen [**sik**-la-men] n (pl **-s**) plant with red, pink, or white flowers

cyclamens n ▷ cyclamen

cycle v (cycles, cycling, cycled) ride a bicycle ▶ n (pl **-s**) (BRIT, AUST & NZ) bicycle

cycled v ▷ cycle

cycles v, n ▷ cycle

cyclic adj ▷ cyclical

cyclical, cyclic adj occurring in cycles > **cyclically** adv

cyclically adv ▷ cyclical

cycling v ▷ cycle

cyclist n (pl **-s**) person who rides a bicycle

cyclists n ▷ cyclist

cyclone n (pl **-s**) violent wind moving round a central area

cyclones n ▷ cyclone

cyclotron n (pl **-s**) apparatus that accelerates charged particles by means of a strong vertical magnetic field

cyclotrons n ▷ cyclotron

cygnet n (pl **-s**) young swan

cygnets n ▷ cygnet

cylinder n (pl **-s**) solid or hollow body with straight sides and circular ends > **cylindrical** adj

cylinders n ▷ cylinder

cylindrical adj ▷ cylinder

cymbal n (pl **-s**) percussion instrument consisting of a brass plate which is struck

against another or hit with a stick

cymbals n ▷ cymbal

cynic [**sin**-ik] n (pl **-s**) person who believes that people always act selfishly > **cynical** adj > **cynically** adv > **cynicism** n

cynical adj ▷ cynic

cynically adv ▷ cynic

cynicism n ▷ cynic

cynics n ▷ cynic

cynosure [**sin**-oh-zyure] n (pl **-s**) centre of attention

cynosures n ▷ cynosure

cypher n (pl **-s**) ▷ cipher

cyphers n ▷ cipher

cypress n (pl **-es**) evergreen tree with dark green leaves

cypresses n ▷ cypress

cyst [**sist**] n (pl **-s**) (abnormal) sac in the body containing fluid or soft matter > **cystic** adj

cystic adj ▷ cyst

cystitis [siss-**tite**-iss] n inflammation of the bladder

cysts n ▷ cyst

cytological adj ▷ cytology

cytologically adv ▷ cytology

cytologies n ▷ cytology

cytologist n ▷ cytology

cytologists n ▷ cytology

cytology [site-**ol**-a-jee] n (pl **-logies**) study of plant and animal cells > **cytological** adj > **cytologically** adv > **cytologist** n (pl **-s**)

czar [**zahr**] n (pl **-s**) ▷ tsar > **czarism** n > **czarist** adj, n (pl **-s**)

czarism n ▷ czar

czarist n ▷ czar

czarists n ▷ czar

czars n ▷ czar

Dd

D only starts a handful of two-letter words, but it does form a two-letter word before every vowel except U. There are plenty of good three-letter words beginning with D, particularly those with a Y or W: **day**, **dye** and **dew** are worth 7 points each, for example.

da n (**das**). A da is a Burmese knife. Da scores 3 points.

dab¹ v (**-s**, **-bbing**, **-bbed**) pat lightly ▷ n (pl **-s**) small amount of something soft or moist

  dab² n (pl **-s**) small European flatfish with rough scales

  dabbed v ▷ **dab**¹

  dabbing v ▷ **dab**¹

dabble v (**-les**, **-ling**, **-led**) be involved in something superficially ▷ **dabbler** n (pl **-s**)

  dabbled v ▷ **dabble**

  dabbler n ▷ **dabble**

  dabblers n ▷ **dabble**

  dabbles v ▷ **dabble**

  dabbling v ▷ **dabble**

  dabs n ▷ **dab**¹, ² v ▷ **dab**¹

dace n (pl **dace**) small European freshwater fish

dachshund n (pl **-s**) dog with a long body and short legs

  dachshunds n ▷ **dachshund**

dad n (pl **-s**) (Informal) father

  daddies n ▷ **daddy**

daddy n (pl **-dies**) (Informal) father

dado [day-doe] n (pl **-does**, **-dos**) lower part of an interior wall, below a rail, decorated differently from the upper part

  dadoes n ▷ **dado**

  dados n ▷ **dado**

  dads n ▷ **dad**

daffodil n (pl **-s**) yellow trumpet-shaped flower that blooms in spring

  daffodils n ▷ **daffodil**

daft adj (**-er**, **-est**) (Informal) foolish or crazy ▷ **daftness** n (pl **-es**)

  dafter adj ▷ **daft**

  daftest adj ▷ **daft**

  daftness n ▷ **daft**

  daftnesses n ▷ **daft**

dag (NZ) n (pl **-s**) dried dung on a sheep's rear (Informal) ▷ v (**-s**, **-gging**, **-gged**) remove the dags from a sheep

dagga n (pl **-s**) (S AFR) (Informal) cannabis

  daggas n ▷ **dagga**

  dagged v ▷ **dag**

dagger n (pl **-s**) short knifelike weapon with a pointed blade

  daggers n ▷ **dagger**

  daggier adj ▷ **daggy**

  daggiest adj ▷ **daggy**

  dagging v ▷ **dag**

daggy adj (**-ggier**, **-ggiest**) (NZ) (Informal) amusing

  dags n, v ▷ **dag**

daguerreotype [dag-**gair**-oh-type] n (pl **-s**) type of early photograph produced on chemically treated silver

  daguerreotypes n ▷ **daguerreotype**

dahlia [day-lya] n (pl **-s**) brightly coloured garden flower

  dahlias n ▷ **dahlia**

  dailies n ▷ **daily**

daily adj occurring every day or every weekday ▷ adv every day ▷ n (pl **-lies**) daily newspaper

  daintier adj ▷ **dainty**

  daintiest adj ▷ **dainty**

  daintily adv ▷ **dainty**

dainty adj (**-tier**, **-tiest**) delicate or elegant ▷ **daintily** adv

daiquiri [dak-**eer**-ee] n (pl **-s**) iced drink containing rum, lime juice, and sugar

  daiquiris n ▷ **daiquiri**

  dairies n ▷ **dairy**

dairy n (pl **-ies**) place for the processing or sale of milk and its products ▷ adj of milk or its products

dais [day-iss, dayss] n (pl **-es**) raised platform in a hall, used by a speaker

  daises n ▷ **dais**

  daisies n ▷ **daisy**

daisy n (pl **-sies**) small wild flower with a

yellow centre and white petals

dak *n* (**daks**). A dak is an old Indian mail or transport system. This is a good word to know if you have a K on your rack but can't think of a longer word in which to use it. Dak scores 8 points.

dale *n* (*pl* -**s**) (*esp. in N England*) valley
  dales *n* ▷ **dale**
dalliance *n* (*pl* -**s**) flirtation
  dalliances *n* ▷ **dalliance**
  dallied *v* ▷ **dally**
  dallies *v* ▷ **dally**
dally *v* (**-lies, -lying, -lied**) waste time
  dallying *v* ▷ **dally**
dalmatian *n* (*pl* -**s**) large dog with a white coat and black spots
  dalmatians *n* ▷ **dalmatian**
dam¹ *n* (*pl* -**s**) barrier built across a river to create a lake ▸ *v* (**dams, damming, dammed**) build a dam across (a river)
dam² *n* (*pl* -**s**) mother of an animal such as a sheep or horse
damage *v* (**-ages, -aging, -aged**) harm, spoil ▸ *n* (*pl* -**s**) harm to a person or thing ▸ *pl* money awarded as compensation for injury or loss
  damaged *v* ▷ **damage**
  damages *v, n* ▷ **damage**
  damaging *v* ▷ **damage**
damask *n* (*pl* -**s**) fabric with a pattern woven into it, used for tablecloths etc.
  damasks *n* ▷ **damask**
dame *n* (*pl* -**s**) (CHIEFLY US & CANADIAN) (*Slang*) woman
  dames *n* ▷ **dame**
  dammed *v* ▷ **dam¹**
  damming *v* ▷ **dam¹**
damn *interj* (*Slang*) exclamation of annoyance ▸ *adv, adj* (*also* **damned**) (*Slang*) extreme(ly) ▸ *v* (**-s, -ing, -ed**) condemn as bad or worthless > **damnation** *interj*, *n* (*pl* -**s**)
damnable *adj* annoying > **damnably** *adv*
  damnably *adv* ▷ **damnable**
  damnation *interj, n* ▷ **damn**
  damnations *n* ▷ **damn**
  damned *v* ▷ **damn**
damning *adj* proving or suggesting guilt ▸ *v* ▷ **damn**
  damns *v* ▷ **damn**
damp *adj* (**-er, -est**) slightly wet ▸ *n* (*pl* -**s**) slight wetness, moisture ▸ *v* (**-s, -ing, -ed**) (*also* **dampen**) (**-s, -ing, -ed**) make damp (foll. by down) > **damply** *adv* > **dampness** *n*
  damped *v* ▷ **damp**
  dampen *v* ▷ **dampen**
  dampened *v* ▷ **dampen**

  dampening *v* ▷ **dampen**
  dampens *v* ▷ **dampen**
damper *n* (*pl* -**s**) movable plate to regulate the draught in a fire ▸ *adj* ▷ **damp**
  dampers *n* ▷ **damper**
  dampest *adj* ▷ **damp**
  damping *v* ▷ **damp**
  damply *adv* ▷ **damp**
  dampness *n* ▷ **damp**
  damps *v, n* ▷ **damp**
  dams *n* ▷ **dam¹, ²** ▸ *v* ▷ **dam¹**
damsel *n* (*pl* -**s**) (*Old-fashioned*) young woman
  damsels *n* ▷ **damsel**
damson *n* (*pl* -**s**) small blue-black plumlike fruit
  damsons *n* ▷ **damson**
dance *v* (**dances, dancing, danced**) move the feet and body rhythmically in time to music ▸ *n* (*pl* -**s**) series of steps and movements in time to music > **dancer** *n* (*pl* -**s**)
  danced *v* ▷ **dance**
  dancer *n* ▷ **dance**
  dancers *n* ▷ **dance**
  dances *v, n* ▷ **dance**
  dancing *v* ▷ **dance**
dandelion *n* (*pl* -**s**) yellow-flowered wild plant
  dandelions *n* ▷ **dandelion**
dander *n* (*pl* -**s**) (*Slang*) anger
  danders *n* ▷ **dander**
  dandier *adj* ▷ **dandy**
  dandies *n* ▷ **dandy**
  dandiest *adj* ▷ **dandy**
  dandified *adj* ▷ **dandy**
dandle *v* (**-dles, -dling, -dled**) move (a child) up and down on one's knee
  dandled *v* ▷ **dandle**
  dandles *v* ▷ **dandle**
  dandling *v* ▷ **dandle**
dandruff *n* (*pl* -**s**) loose scales of dry dead skin shed from the scalp
  dandruffs *n* ▷ **dandruff**
dandy *n* (*pl* -**dies**) man who is overconcerned with the elegance of his appearance ▸ *adj* (**-dier, -diest**) (*Informal*) very good > **dandified** *adj*
danger *n* (*pl* -**s**) possibility of being injured or killed > **dangerous** *adj* > **dangerously** *adv*
  dangerous *adj* ▷ **danger**
  dangerously *adv* ▷ **danger**
  dangers *n* ▷ **danger**
dangle *v* (**-gles, -gling, -gled**) hang loosely
  dangled *v* ▷ **dangle**
  dangles *v* ▷ **dangle**
  dangling *v* ▷ **dangle**
dank *adj* (**-er, -est**) unpleasantly damp and

chilly > **dankly** adv > **dankness** n (pl -es)
danker adj ▷ dank
dankest adj ▷ dank
dankly adv ▷ dank
dankness n ▷ dank
danknesses n ▷ dank
dapper adj (-er, -est) (of a man) neat in appearance > **dapperly** adv > **dapperness** n (pl -es)
dapperer adj ▷ dapper
dapperest adj ▷ dapper
dapperly adv ▷ dapper
dapperness n ▷ dapper
dappernesses n ▷ dapper
dappled adj marked with spots of a different colour
dare v (dares, daring, dared) be courageous enough to try (to do something) ▶ n (pl -s) challenge to do something risky
dared v ▷ dare
daredevil adj, n (pl -s) recklessly bold (person)
daredevils n ▷ daredevil
dares v, n ▷ dare
daring adj willing to take risks ▶ n courage to do dangerous things ▶ v ▷ dare > **daringly** adv
daringly adv ▷ daring
dark adj (-er, -est) having little or no light ▶ n (pl -s) absence of light > **darkly** adv > **darkness** n (pl -es) > **darken** v (-s, -ing, -ed)
darken v ▷ dark
darkened v ▷ dark
darkening v ▷ dark
darkens v ▷ dark
darker adj ▷ dark
darkest adj ▷ dark
darkly adv ▷ dark
darkness n ▷ dark
darknesses n ▷ dark
darkroom n (pl -s) darkened room for processing photographic film
darkrooms n ▷ darkroom
darks n ▷ dark
darling n (pl -s) much-loved person ▶ adj much-loved
darlings n ▷ darling
darn[1] v (-s, -ing, -ed) mend (a garment) with a series of interwoven stitches ▶ n (pl -s) patch of darned work
darn[2] interj, adv, adj, v (-s, -ing, -ed) (Euphemistic) damn
darned v ▷ darn[1, 2]
darning v ▷ darn[1, 2]
darns v ▷ darn[1, 2] ▶ n ▷ darn[1]
dart n (pl -s) small narrow pointed missile that is thrown or shot, esp. in the game of

darts ▶ pl game in which darts are thrown at a circular numbered board ▶ v (-s, -ing, -ed) move or direct quickly and suddenly
darted v ▷ dart
darting v ▷ dart
darts n, v ▷ dart
dash v (-es, -ing, -ed) move quickly ▶ n (pl -es) sudden quick movement
dashboard n (pl -s) instrument panel in a vehicle
dashboards n ▷ dashboard
dashed v ▷ dash
dashes v, n ▷ dash
dashing adj stylish and attractive ▶ v ▷ dash > **dashingly** adv
dashingly adv ▷ dashing
dassie n (pl -s) (S AFR) type of hoofed rodent-like animal (also **hyrax**)
dassies n ▷ dassie
dastardliness n ▷ dastardly
dastardly adj wicked and cowardly > **dastardliness** n
dasyure [dass-ee-your] n (pl -s) small marsupial of Australia, New Guinea, and adjacent islands
dasyures n ▷ dasyure
data n information consisting of observations, measurements, or facts
date[1] n (pl -s) specified day of the month ▶ v (dates, dating, dated) mark with the date
date[2] n (pl -s) dark-brown sweet-tasting fruit of the date palm
dated adj old-fashioned ▶ v ▷ date[1]
dates n ▷ date[1, 2] ▶ v ▷ date[1]
dating v ▷ date[1]
dative n (pl -s) (in certain languages) the form of the noun that expresses the indirect object
datives n ▷ dative
datum n (pl data) single piece of information in the form of a fact or statistic
daub v (-s, -ing, -ed) smear or spread quickly or clumsily
daubed v ▷ daub
daubing v ▷ daub
daubs v ▷ daub
daughter n (pl -s) female child > **daughterly** adj
daughterly adj ▷ daughter
daughters n ▷ daughter
daunting adj intimidating or worrying > **dauntingly** adv
dauntingly adv ▷ daunting
dauntless adj fearless > **dauntlessly** adv > **dauntlessness** n
dauntlessly adv ▷ dauntless
dauntlessness n ▷ dauntless

dauphin [doe-fan] n (pl -s) (formerly) eldest son of the king of France
   dauphins n ▷ dauphin

davenport n (pl -s) (CHIEFLY BRIT) small writing table with drawers
   davenports n ▷ davenport

davit [dav-vit] n (pl -s) crane, usu. one of a pair, at a ship's side, for lowering and hoisting a lifeboat
   davits n ▷ davit

   daw n (daws). A daw is another name for a **jackdaw**. Daw scores 7 points.

dawdle v (-dles, -dling, -dled) walk slowly, lag behind
   dawdled v ▷ dawdle
   dawdles v ▷ dawdle
   dawdling v ▷ dawdle

dawn n (pl -s) daybreak ▶ v (-s, -ing, -ed) begin to grow light
   dawned v ▷ dawn
   dawning v ▷ dawn
   dawns n, v ▷ dawn

day n (pl -s) period of 24 hours

daybreak n time in the morning when light first appears

daydream n (pl -s) pleasant fantasy indulged in while awake ▶ v (-s, -ing, -ed) indulge in idle fantasy > **daydreamer** n (pl -s)
   daydreamed v ▷ daydream
   daydreamer n ▷ daydream
   daydreamers n ▷ daydream
   daydreaming v ▷ daydream
   daydreams n, v ▷ daydream

daylight n light from the sun
   days n ▷ day

daze v (dazes, dazing, dazed) stun, by a blow or shock ▶ n (pl -s) state of confusion or shock
   dazed v ▷ daze
   dazes v, n ▷ daze
   dazing v ▷ daze

dazzle v (-zles, -zling, -zled) impress greatly ▶ n (pl -s) bright light that dazzles > **dazzling** adj > **dazzlingly** adv
   dazzled v ▷ dazzle
   dazzles v, n ▷ dazzle
   dazzling v, adj ▷ dazzle
   dazzlingly adv ▷ dazzle

   de prep. De means of or from. This is a useful little word to fit in when trying to form several words at once. De scores 3 points.

deacon n (pl -s) (CHRISTIANITY) ordained minister ranking immediately below a priest
   deacons n ▷ deacon

dead adj (-er, -est) no longer alive ▶ n (pl -s)

period during which coldness or darkness is most intense ▶ adv extremely

deadbeat n (pl -s) (Informal) lazy useless person
   deadbeats n ▷ deadbeat

deaden v (-s, -ing, -ed) make less intense
   deadened v ▷ deaden
   deadening v ▷ deaden
   deadens v ▷ deaden
   deader adj ▷ dead
   deadest adj ▷ dead
   deadlier adj ▷ deadly
   deadliest adj ▷ deadly

deadline n (pl -s) time limit
   deadlines n ▷ deadline
   deadliness n ▷ deadly

deadlock n (pl -s) point in a dispute at which no agreement can be reached > **deadlocked** adj
   deadlocked adj ▷ deadlock
   deadlocks n ▷ deadlock

deadly adj (-lier, -liest) likely to cause death ▶ adv extremely > **deadliness** n

deadpan adj, adv showing no emotion or expression
   deads n ▷ dead

deaf adj (-er, -est) unable to hear > **deafness** n (pl -es)

deafen v (-s, -ing, -ed) make deaf, esp. temporarily
   deafened v ▷ deafen
   deafening v ▷ deafen
   deafens v ▷ deafen
   deafer adj ▷ deaf
   deafest adj ▷ deaf
   deafness n ▷ deaf
   deafnesses n ▷ deaf

deal¹ n (pl -s) agreement or transaction ▶ v (deals, dealing, dealt) inflict (a blow) on > **dealer** n (pl -s)

deal² n (pl -s) plank of fir or pine wood
   dealer n ▷ deal¹
   dealers n ▷ deal¹
   dealing v ▷ deal¹

dealings pl n transactions or business relations
   deals v ▷ deal¹ ▶ n ▷ deal¹, ²
   dealt v ▷ deal¹

dean n (pl -s) chief administrative official of a college or university faculty
   deaneries n ▷ deanery

deanery n (pl -eries) office or residence of a dean
   deans n ▷ dean

dear n (pl -s) someone regarded with affection ▶ adj (-er, -est) much-loved > **dearly** adv

> **dearness** n (pl -**es**) ▷ **dear**
dearer adj ▷ **dear**
dearest adj ▷ **dear**
dearly adv ▷ **dear**
dearness n ▷ **dear**
dearnesses n ▷ **dear**
dears n ▷ **dear**
dearth [dirth] n (pl -**s**) inadequate amount, scarcity
dearths n ▷ **dearth**
death n (pl -**s**) permanent end of life in a person or animal
deathly adj, adv like death
deaths n ▷ **death**
deb n (pl -**s**) (Informal) debutante
debacle [day-bah-kl] n (pl -**s**) disastrous failure
debacles n ▷ **debacle**
debar v (-**bars**, -**barring**, -**barred**) prevent, bar
debarred v ▷ **debar**
debarring v ▷ **debar**
debars v ▷ **debar**
debase v (-**bases**, -**basing**, -**based**) lower in value, quality, or character > **debasement** n (pl -**s**)
debased v ▷ **debase**
debasement n ▷ **debase**
debasements n ▷ **debase**
debases v ▷ **debase**
debasing v ▷ **debase**
debatable adj not absolutely certain > **debatably** adv
debate n (pl -**s**) discussion ▶ v (-**bates**, -**bating**, -**bated**) discuss formally
debated v ▷ **debate**
debates n, v ▷ **debate**
debating v ▷ **debate**
debauch [dib-bawch] v (-**es**, -**ing**, -**ed**) make (someone) bad or corrupt, esp. sexually > **debauchery** n (pl -**eries**)
debauched adj immoral, sexually corrupt ▶ v ▷ **debauch**
debaucheries n ▷ **debauch**
debauchery n ▷ **debauch**
debauches v ▷ **debauch**
debauching v ▷ **debauch**
debenture n (pl -**s**) long-term bond bearing fixed interest, issued by a company or a government agency
debentures n ▷ **debenture**
debilitate v (-**tates**, -**tating**, -**tated**) weaken, make feeble > **debilitation** n
debilitated v ▷ **debilitate**
debilitates v ▷ **debilitate**
debilitating v ▷ **debilitate**
debilitation n ▷ **debilitate**

debilities n ▷ **debility**
debility n (pl -**ities**) weakness, infirmity
debit n (pl -**s**) acknowledgment of a sum owing by entry on the left side of an account ▶ v (-**s**, -**ing**, -**ed**) charge (an account) with a debt
debited v ▷ **debit**
debiting v ▷ **debit**
debits n, v ▷ **debit**
debonair adj (of a man) charming and refined
debouch v (-**s**, -**ing**, -**ed**) move out from a narrow place to a wider one
debouched v ▷ **debouch**
debouches v ▷ **debouch**
debouching v ▷ **debouch**
debrief v (-**s**, -**ing**, -**ed**) receive a report from (a soldier, diplomat, etc.) after an event > **debriefing** n (pl -**s**)
debriefed v ▷ **debrief**
debriefing v, n ▷ **debrief**
debriefings n ▷ **debrief**
debriefs v ▷ **debrief**
debris [deb-ree] n fragments of something destroyed
debs n ▷ **deb**
debt n (pl -**s**) something owed, esp. money > **debtor** n (pl -**s**)
debtor n ▷ **debt**
debtors n ▷ **debt**
debts n ▷ **debt**
debunk v (-**s**, -**ing**, -**ed**) (Informal) expose the falseness of
debunked v ▷ **debunk**
debunking v ▷ **debunk**
debunks v ▷ **debunk**
debut [day-byoo] n (pl -**s**) first public appearance of a performer
debutante [day-byoo-tont] n (pl -**s**) young upper-class woman being formally presented to society
debutantes n ▷ **debutante**
debuts n ▷ **debut**
decade n (pl -**s**) period of ten years
decadence n (pl -**s**) deterioration in morality or culture > **decadent** adj > **decadently** adv
decadences n ▷ **decadence**
decadent adj ▷ **decadence**
decadently adv ▷ **decadence**
decades n ▷ **decade**
decaffeinated [dee-kaf-fin-ate-id] adj (of coffee, tea, or cola) with caffeine removed
decagon n (pl -**s**) geometric figure with ten faces > **decagonal** adj
decagonal adj ▷ **decagon**
decagons n ▷ **decagon**
decahedral adj ▷ **decahedron**

decahedron [deck-a-**heed**-ron] *n* (*pl* -**s**) solid figure with ten sides > **decahedral** *adj*
  decahedrons *n* ▷ **decahedron**
decamp *v* (-**s**, -**ing**, -**ed**) depart secretly or suddenly
  decamped *v* ▷ **decamp**
  decamping *v* ▷ **decamp**
  decamps *v* ▷ **decamp**
decant *v* (-**s**, -**ing**, -**ed**) pour (a liquid) from one container to another
  decanted *v* ▷ **decant**
decanter *n* (*pl* -**s**) stoppered bottle for wine or spirits
  decanters *n* ▷ **decanter**
  decanting *v* ▷ **decant**
  decants *v* ▷ **decant**
decapitate *v* (-**tates**, -**tating**, -**tated**) behead > **decapitation** *n* (*pl* -**s**)
  decapitated *v* ▷ **decapitate**
  decapitates *v* ▷ **decapitate**
  decapitating *v* ▷ **decapitate**
  decapitation *n* ▷ **decapitate**
  decapitations *n* ▷ **decapitate**
decathlete *n* ▷ **decathlon**
  decathletes *n* ▷ **decathlon**
decathlon *n* (*pl* -**s**) athletic contest with ten events > **decathlete** *n* (*pl* -**s**)
  decathlons *n* ▷ **decathlon**
decay *v* (-**s**, -**ing**, -**ed**) become weaker or more corrupt ▶ *n* (*pl* -**s**) process of decaying
  decayed *v* ▷ **decay**
  decaying *v* ▷ **decay**
  decays *v, n* ▷ **decay**
decease *n* (*pl* -**s**) (*Formal*) death
  deceases *n* ▷ **decease**
deceased *adj* (*Formal*) dead
deceit *n* (*pl* -**s**) behaviour intended to deceive > **deceitful** *adj* > **deceitfully** *adv*
  deceitful *adj* ▷ **deceit**
  deceitfully *adv* ▷ **deceit**
  deceits *n* ▷ **deceit**
deceive *v* (-**ceives**, -**ceiving**, -**ceived**) mislead by lying > **deceiver** *n* (*pl* -**s**)
  deceived *v* ▷ **deceive**
  deceiver *n* ▷ **deceive**
  deceivers *n* ▷ **deceive**
  deceives *v* ▷ **deceive**
  deceiving *v* ▷ **deceive**
decelerate *v* (-**rates**, -**rating**, -**rated**) slow down > **deceleration** *n* (*pl* -**s**)
  decelerated *v* ▷ **decelerate**
  decelerates *v* ▷ **decelerate**
  decelerating *v* ▷ **decelerate**
  deceleration *n* ▷ **decelerate**
  decelerations *n* ▷ **decelerate**

decencies *n* ▷ **decent**
decency *n* ▷ **decent**
decent *adj* (-**er**, -**est**) (of a person) polite and morally acceptable > **decently** *adv* > **decency** *n* (*pl* -**cies**)
  decenter *adj* ▷ **decent**
  decentest *adj* ▷ **decent**
  decently *adv* ▷ **decent**
decentralization *n* ▷ **decentralize**
decentralize *v* (-**lizes**, -**lizing**, -**lized**) reorganize into smaller local units > **decentralization** *n*
  decentralized *v* ▷ **decentralize**
  decentralizes *v* ▷ **decentralize**
  decentralizing *v* ▷ **decentralize**
deception *n* (*pl* -**s**) deceiving
  deceptions *n* ▷ **deception**
deceptive *adj* likely or designed to deceive > **deceptively** *adv* > **deceptiveness** *n*
  deceptively *adv* ▷ **deceptive**
  deceptiveness *n* ▷ **deceptive**
decibel *n* (*pl* -**s**) unit for measuring the intensity of sound
  decibels *n* ▷ **decibel**
decide *v* (-**cides**, -**ciding**, -**cided**) (cause to) reach a decision
decided *adj* unmistakable ▶ *v* ▷ **decide** > **decidedly** *adv*
  decidedly *adv* ▷ **decided**
  decides *v* ▷ **decide**
  deciding *v* ▷ **decide**
deciduous *adj* (of a tree) shedding its leaves annually
decimal *n* (*pl* -**s**) fraction written in the form of a dot followed by one or more numbers ▶ *adj* relating to or using powers of ten > **decimalization** *n* > **decimally** *adv*
  decimalization *n* ▷ **decimal**
  decimally *adv* ▷ **decimal**
  decimals *n* ▷ **decimal**
decimate *v* (-**mates**, -**mating**, -**mated**) destroy or kill a large proportion of > **decimation** *n* (*pl* -**s**)
  decimated *v* ▷ **decimate**
  decimates *v* ▷ **decimate**
  decimating *v* ▷ **decimate**
  decimation *n* ▷ **decimate**
  decimations *n* ▷ **decimate**
decipher *v* (-**s**, -**ing**, -**ed**) work out the meaning of (something illegible or in code) > **decipherable** *adj*
  decipherable *adj* ▷ **decipher**
  deciphered *v* ▷ **decipher**
  deciphering *v* ▷ **decipher**
  deciphers *v* ▷ **decipher**

decision n (pl -s) judgment, conclusion, or resolution
 decisions n ▷ decision
decisive adj having a definite influence
 > **decisively** adv > **decisiveness** n
 decisively adv ▷ decisive
 decisiveness n ▷ decisive
deck n (pl -s) area of a ship that forms a floor
decking n wooden platform in a garden
 decks n ▷ deck
declaim v (-s, -ing, -ed) speak loudly and dramatically > **declamation** n (pl -s)
 > **declamatory** adj
 declaimed v ▷ declaim
 declaiming v ▷ declaim
 declaims v ▷ declaim
 declamation n ▷ declaim
 declamations n ▷ declaim
 declamatory adj ▷ declaim
 declaration n ▷ declare
 declarations n ▷ declare
 declaratory adj ▷ declare
declare v (-clares, -claring, -clared) state firmly and forcefully > **declaration** n (pl -s)
 > **declaratory** adj
 declared v ▷ declare
 declares v ▷ declare
 declaring v ▷ declare
declension n (pl -s) (GRAMMAR) changes in the form of nouns, pronouns, or adjectives to show case, number, and gender
 declensions n ▷ declension
decline v (-clines, -clining, -clined) become smaller, weaker, or less important ▶ n (pl -s) gradual weakening or loss
 declined v ▷ decline
 declines v, n ▷ decline
 declining v ▷ decline
 declivities n ▷ declivity
declivity n (pl -ties) downward slope
declutch v (-es, -ing, -ed) disengage the clutch of a motor vehicle
 declutched v ▷ declutch
 declutches v ▷ declutch
 declutching v ▷ declutch
decoct v (-s, -ing, -ed) extract the essence from (a substance) by boiling > **decoction** n (pl -s)
 decocted v ▷ decoct
 decocting v ▷ decoct
 decoction n ▷ decoct
 decoctions n ▷ decoct
 decocts v ▷ decoct
decode v (-codes, -coding, -coded) convert from code into ordinary language > **decoder** n (pl -s)

decoded v ▷ decode
decoder n ▷ decode
decoders n ▷ decode
decodes v ▷ decode
decoding v ▷ decode
décolleté [day-kol-tay] adj (of a woman's garment) low-cut
decommission v (-s, -ing, -ed) dismantle (a nuclear reactor, weapon, etc.) which is no longer needed
 decommissioned v ▷ decommission
 decommissioning v ▷ decommission
 decommissions v ▷ decommission
decompose v (-poses, -posing, -posed) be broken down through chemical or bacterial action > **decomposition** n (pl -s)
 decomposed v ▷ decompose
 decomposes v ▷ decompose
 decomposing v ▷ decompose
 decomposition n ▷ decompose
 decompositions n ▷ decompose
decompress v (-presses, -pressing, -pressed) free from pressure > **decompression** n (pl -s)
 decompressed v ▷ decompress
 decompresses v ▷ decompress
 decompressing v ▷ decompress
 decompression n ▷ decompress
 decompressions n ▷ decompress
decongestant n (pl -s) medicine that relieves nasal congestion
 decongestants n ▷ decongestant
decontaminate v (-nates, -nating, -nated) make safe by removing poisons, radioactivity, etc. > **decontamination** n (pl -s)
 decontaminated v ▷ decontaminate
 decontaminates v ▷ decontaminate
 decontaminating v ▷ decontaminate
 decontamination n ▷ decontaminate
 decontaminations n ▷ decontaminate
decor [day-core] n (pl -s) style in which a room or house is decorated
decorate v (-rates, -rating, -rated) make more attractive by adding something ornamental > **decoration** n (pl -s) > **decorative** adj
 > **decorator** n (pl -s)
 decorated v ▷ decorate
 decorates v ▷ decorate
 decorating v ▷ decorate
 decoration n ▷ decorate
 decorations n ▷ decorate
 decorator n ▷ decorate
 decorators n ▷ decorate
decorous [dek-a-russ] adj polite, calm, and sensible in behaviour > **decorously** adv
 > **decorousness** n

decorously adv ▷ decorous

decorousness n ▷ decorous

decors n ▷ decor

decorum [dik-core-um] n (pl -s) polite and socially correct behaviour

decorums n ▷ decorum

decoy n (pl -s) person or thing used to lure someone into danger ▶ v (-s, -ing, -ed) lure away by means of a trick

decoyed v ▷ decoy

decoying v ▷ decoy

decoys n, v ▷ decoy

decrease v (-creases, -creasing, -creased) make or become less ▶ n (pl -s) lessening, reduction

decreased v ▷ decrease

decreases v, n ▷ decrease

decreasing v ▷ decrease

decree n (pl -s) law made by someone in authority ▶ v (-crees, -creeing, -creed) order by decree

decreed v ▷ decree

decreeing v ▷ decree

decrees n, v ▷ decree

decrepit adj weakened or worn out by age or long use > **decrepitude** n (pl -s)

decrepitude n ▷ decrepit

decrepitudes n ▷ decrepit

decried v ▷ decry

decries v ▷ decry

decry v (-cries, -crying, -cried) express disapproval of

decrying v ▷ decry

dedicate v (-cates, -cating, -cated) commit (oneself or one's time) wholly to a special purpose or cause > **dedication** n (pl -s)

dedicated adj devoted to a particular purpose or cause ▶ v ▷ dedicate

dedicates v ▷ dedicate

dedicating v ▷ dedicate

dedication n ▷ dedicate

dedications n ▷ dedicate

deduce v (-duces, -ducing, -duced) reach (a conclusion) by reasoning from evidence > **deducible** adj

deduced v ▷ deduce

deduces v ▷ deduce

deducible adj ▷ deduce

deducing v ▷ deduce

deduct v (-s, -ing, -ed) subtract

deducted v ▷ deduct

deducting v ▷ deduct

deduction n (pl -s) deducting > **deductive** adj

deductions n ▷ deduction

deductive adj ▷ deduction

deducts v ▷ deduct

deed n (pl -s) something that is done

deeds n ▷ deed

deem v (-s, -ing, -ed) consider, judge

deemed v ▷ deem

deeming v ▷ deem

deems v ▷ deem

deep adj (-er, -est) extending or situated far down, inwards, backwards, or sideways > **deepen** v (-s, -ing, -ed)

deepen v ▷ deep

deepened v ▷ deep

deepening v ▷ deep

deepens v ▷ deep

deeper adj ▷ deep

deepest adj ▷ deep

deepfreeze n (pl -s) ▷ freezer

deepfreezes n ▷ deepfreeze

deeply adv profoundly or intensely

deer n (pl deer) large wild animal, the male of which has antlers

deerstalker n (pl -s) cloth hat with peaks at the back and front and earflaps

deerstalkers n ▷ deerstalker

deface v (-faces, -facing, -faced) deliberately spoil the appearance of > **defacement** n (pl -s)

defaced v ▷ deface

defacement n ▷ deface

defacements n ▷ deface

defaces v ▷ deface

defacing v ▷ deface

defamation n ▷ defame

defamations n ▷ defame

defamatory adj ▷ defame

defame v (-fames, -faming, -famed) attack the good reputation of > **defamation** n (pl -s) > **defamatory** [dif-fam-a-tree] adj

defamed v ▷ defame

defames v ▷ defame

defaming v ▷ defame

default n (pl -s) failure to do something ▶ v (-s, -ing, -ed) fail to fulfil an obligation > **defaulter** n (pl -s)

defaulted v ▷ default

defaulter n ▷ default

defaulters n ▷ default

defaulting v ▷ default

defaults n, v ▷ default

defeat v (-s, -ing, -ed) win a victory over ▶ n (pl -s) defeating

defeated v ▷ defeat

defeating v ▷ defeat

defeatism n ready acceptance or expectation of defeat > **defeatist** adj, n (pl -s)

defeatist n, adj ▷ defeatism

defeatists n ▷ defeatism
defeats v, n ▷ defeat
defecate v (-cates, -cating, -cated) discharge waste from the body through the anus
> **defecation** n (pl -s)
  defecated v ▷ defecate
  defecates v ▷ defecate
  defecating v ▷ defecate
  defecation n ▷ defecate
  defecations n ▷ defecate
defect n (pl -s) imperfection, blemish ▶ v (-s, -ing, -ed) desert one's cause or country to join the opposing forces > **defection** n (pl -s)
> **defector** n (pl -s)
  defected v ▷ defect
  defecting v ▷ defect
  defection n ▷ defect
  defections n ▷ defect
defective adj imperfect, faulty
> **defectiveness** n
  defectiveness n ▷ defective
  defector n ▷ defect
  defectors n ▷ defect
  defects n, v ▷ defect
defence n (pl -s) resistance against attack
> **defenceless** adj
  defenceless adj ▷ defence
  defences n ▷ defence
defend v (-s, -ing, -ed) protect from harm or danger
defendant n (pl -s) person accused of a crime
  defendants n ▷ defendant
  defended v ▷ defend
defender n (pl -s) person who supports someone or something in the face of criticism
  defenders n ▷ defender
  defending v ▷ defend
  defends v ▷ defend
  defensibilities n ▷ defensible
  defensibility n ▷ defensible
defensible adj capable of being defended because believed to be right > **defensibility** n (pl -ities)
defensive adj intended for defence
> **defensively** adv
  defensively adv ▷ defensive
defer[1] v (-fers, -ferring, -ferred) delay (something) until a future time > **deferment**, **deferral** n (pl -s)
defer[2] v (-fers, -ferring, -ferred) (foll. by **to**) comply with the wishes (of)
deference n polite and respectful behaviour
> **deferential** adj > **deferentially** adv
  deferential adj ▷ deference

deferentially adv ▷ deference
deferment n ▷ defer[1]
deferments n ▷ defer[1]
deferral n ▷ defer[1]
deferrals n ▷ defer[1]
deferred v ▷ defer[1, 2]
deferring v ▷ defer[1, 2]
defers v ▷ defer[1, 2]
defiance n ▷ defy
defiances n ▷ defy
defiant adj ▷ defy
defiantly adv ▷ defy
deficiencies n ▷ deficiency
deficiency n (pl -cies) state of being deficient
deficient adj lacking some essential thing or quality > **deficiently** adv
  deficiently adv ▷ deficient
deficit n (pl -s) amount by which a sum of money is too small
  deficits n ▷ deficit
defied v ▷ defy
defies v ▷ defy
defile[1] v (-files, -filing, -filed) treat (something sacred or important) without respect
> **defilement** n (pl -s)
defile[2] n (pl -s) narrow valley or pass
  defiled v ▷ defile[1]
  defilement n ▷ defile[1]
  defilements n ▷ defile[1]
  defiles v ▷ defile[1] ▶ n ▷ defile[1, 2]
  defiling v ▷ defile[1]
  definable adj ▷ define
define v (-fines, -fining, -fined) state precisely the meaning of > **definable** adj
  defined v ▷ define
  defines v ▷ define
  defining v ▷ define
definite adj firm, clear, and precise > **definitely** adv
  definitely adv ▷ definite
definition n (pl -s) statement of the meaning of a word or phrase
  definitions n ▷ definition
definitive adj providing an unquestionable conclusion > **definitively** adv
  definitively adv ▷ definitive
deflate v (-flates, -flating, -flated) (cause to) collapse through the release of air
  deflated v ▷ deflate
  deflates v ▷ deflate
  deflating v ▷ deflate
deflation n (pl -s) (ECONOMICS) reduction in economic activity resulting in lower output and investment > **deflationary** adj
  deflationary adj ▷ deflation

deflations n ▷ deflation

deflect v (-flects, -flecting, -flected) (cause to) turn aside from a course > **deflection** n (pl -s) > **deflector** n (pl -s)
deflected v ▷ deflect
deflecting v ▷ deflect
deflection n ▷ deflect
deflections n ▷ deflect
deflector n ▷ deflect
deflectors n ▷ deflect
deflects v ▷ deflect

deflower v (-flowers, -flowering, -flowered) (Lit) deprive (a woman) of her virginity
deflowered v ▷ deflower
deflowering v ▷ deflower
deflowers v ▷ deflower

defoliant n ▷ defoliate
defoliants n ▷ defoliate

defoliate v (-ates, -ating, -ated) deprive (a plant) of its leaves > **defoliant** n (pl -s) > **defoliation** n (pl -s)
defoliated v ▷ defoliate
defoliates v ▷ defoliate
defoliating v ▷ defoliate
defoliation n ▷ defoliate
defoliations n ▷ defoliate

deforestation n (pl -s) destruction of all the trees in an area
deforestations n ▷ deforestation

deform v (-s, -ing, -ed) put out of shape or spoil the appearance of > **deformation** n (pl -s) > **deformity** n (pl -ties)
deformation n ▷ deform
deformations n ▷ deform
deformed v ▷ deform
deforming v ▷ deform
deformities n ▷ deform
deformity n ▷ deform
deforms v ▷ deform

defraud v (-s, -ing, -ed) cheat out of money, property, etc.
defrauded v ▷ defraud
defrauding v ▷ defraud
defrauds v ▷ defraud

defray v (-s, -ing, -ed) provide money for (costs or expenses)
defrayed v ▷ defray
defraying v ▷ defray
defrays v ▷ defray

defrock v (-s, -ing, -ed) deprive (a priest) of priestly status
defrocked v ▷ defrock
defrocking v ▷ defrock
defrocks v ▷ defrock

defrost v (-s, -ing, -ed) make or become free of ice

defrosted v ▷ defrost
defrosting v ▷ defrost
defrosts v ▷ defrost

deft adj quick and skilful in movement > **deftly** adv > **deftness** n (pl -es)
deftly adv ▷ deft
deftness n ▷ deft
deftnesses n ▷ deft

defunct adj no longer existing or operative

defuse v (-fuses, -fusing, -fused) remove the fuse of (an explosive device)
defused v ▷ defuse
defuses v ▷ defuse
defusing v ▷ defuse

defy v (-fies, -fying, -fied) resist openly and boldly > **defiance** n (pl -s) > **defiant** adj > **defiantly** adv
defying v ▷ defy

degeneracies n ▷ degeneracy

degeneracy n (pl -acies) degenerate behaviour

degenerate adj having deteriorated to a lower mental, moral, or physical level ▶ n (pl -s) degenerate person ▶ v (-ates, -ating, -ated) become degenerate > **degeneration** n (pl -s)
degenerated v ▷ degenerate
degenerates n, v ▷ degenerate
degenerating v ▷ degenerate
degeneration n ▷ degenerate
degenerations n ▷ degenerate

degradation n ▷ degrade
degradations n ▷ degrade

degrade v (-grades, -grading, -graded) reduce to dishonour or disgrace (CHEM) > **degradation** n (pl -s)
degraded v ▷ degrade
degrades v ▷ degrade
degrading v ▷ degrade

degree n (pl -s) stage in a scale of relative amount or intensity
degrees n ▷ degree

dehumanization n ▷ dehumanize
dehumanizations n ▷ dehumanize

dehumanize v (-izes, -izing, -ized) deprive of human qualities > **dehumanization** n (pl -s)
dehumanized v ▷ dehumanize
dehumanizes v ▷ dehumanize
dehumanizing v ▷ dehumanize

dehydrate v (-ates, -ating, -ated) remove water from (food) to preserve it > **dehydration** n (pl -s)
dehydrated v ▷ dehydrate
dehydrates v ▷ dehydrate
dehydrating v ▷ dehydrate
dehydration n ▷ dehydrate

dehydrations n ▷ **dehydrate**
deification n ▷ **deify**
deifications n ▷ **deify**
deified v ▷ **deify**
deifies v ▷ **deify**
deify [day-if-fie] v (**-fies, -fying, -fied**) treat or worship as a god > **deification** n (pl **-s**)
deifying v ▷ **deify**
deign [dane] v (**-s, -ing, -ed**) agree (to do something), but as if doing someone a favour
deigned v ▷ **deign**
deigning v ▷ **deign**
deigns v ▷ **deign**
deities n ▷ **deity**
deity [dee-it-ee, day-it-ee] n (pl **-ties**) god or goddess
dejected adj unhappy > **dejectedly** adv > **dejection** n (pl **-s**)
dejectedly adv ▷ **dejected**
dejection n ▷ **dejected**
dejections n ▷ **dejected**
dekko n (pl **-s**) (BRIT, AUST & NZ) (Slang) look
dekkos n ▷ **dekko**
delay v (**-s, -ing, -ed**) put off to a later time ▶ n (pl **-s**) act of delaying
delayed v ▷ **delay**
delaying v ▷ **delay**
delays v, n ▷ **delay**
delectable adj delightful, very attractive
delectation n (pl **-s**) (Formal) great pleasure
delectations n ▷ **delectation**
delegate n (pl **-s**) person chosen to represent others, esp. at a meeting ▶ v (**-gates, -gating, -gated**) entrust (duties or powers) to someone
delegated v ▷ **delegate**
delegates n, v ▷ **delegate**
delegating v ▷ **delegate**
delegation n (pl **-s**) group chosen to represent others
delegations n ▷ **delegation**
delete v (**-letes, -leting, -leted**) remove (something written or printed) > **deletion** n (pl **-s**)
deleted v ▷ **delete**
deleterious [del-lit-eer-ee-uss] adj harmful, injurious
deletes v ▷ **delete**
deleting v ▷ **delete**
deletion n ▷ **deletion**
deletions n ▷ **deletion**
deliberate adj planned in advance, intentional ▶ v (**-ates, -ating, -ated**) think something over > **deliberately** adv > **deliberation** n (pl **-s**) > **deliberative** adj

deliberated v ▷ **deliberate**
deliberately adv ▷ **deliberate**
deliberates v ▷ **deliberate**
deliberating v ▷ **deliberate**
deliberation n ▷ **deliberate**
deliberations n ▷ **deliberate**
deliberative adj ▷ **deliberate**
delicacies n ▷ **delicacy**
delicacy n (pl **-cies**) being delicate
delicate adj fine or subtle in quality or workmanship > **delicately** adv
delicately adv ▷ **delicate**
delicatessen n (pl **-s**) shop selling imported or unusual foods, often already cooked or prepared
delicatessens n ▷ **delicatessen**
delicious adj very appealing to taste or smell > **deliciously** adv > **deliciousness** n
deliciously adv ▷ **delicious**
deliciousness n ▷ **delicious**
delight n (pl **-s**) (source of) great pleasure ▶ v (**-s, -ing, -ed**) please greatly > **delightful** adj > **delightfully** adv
delighted v ▷ **delight**
delightful adj ▷ **delight**
delightfully adv ▷ **delight**
delighting v ▷ **delight**
delights n, v ▷ **delight**
delimit v (**-s, -ing, -ed**) mark or lay down the limits of > **delimitation** n (pl **-s**)
delimitation n ▷ **delimit**
delimitations n ▷ **delimit**
delimited v ▷ **delimit**
delimiting v ▷ **delimit**
delimits v ▷ **delimit**
delineate [dill-lin-ee-ate] v (**-ates, -ating, -ated**) show by drawing > **delineation** n (pl **-s**)
delineated v ▷ **delineate**
delineates v ▷ **delineate**
delineating v ▷ **delineate**
delineation n ▷ **delineate**
delineations n ▷ **delineate**
delinquencies n ▷ **delinquent**
delinquency n ▷ **delinquent**
delinquent n (pl **-s**) someone, esp. a young person, who repeatedly breaks the law ▶ adj repeatedly breaking the law > **delinquency** n (pl **-cies**)
delinquents n ▷ **delinquent**
delirious adj ▷ **delirium**
deliriously adv ▷ **delirium**
delirium n (pl **-s**) state of excitement and mental confusion, often with hallucinations > **delirious** adj > **deliriously** adv
deliriums n ▷ **delirium**

deliver v (-s, -ing, -ed) carry (goods etc.) to a
destination

deliverance n (pl -s) rescue from captivity
or evil

  deliverances n ▷ **deliverance**

  delivered v ▷ **deliver**

  deliveries n ▷ **delivery**

  delivering v ▷ **deliver**

  delivers v ▷ **deliver**

delivery n (pl -eries) delivering

dell n (pl -s) (CHIEFLY BRIT) small wooded hollow

  dells n ▷ **dell**

delphinium n (pl -s) large garden plant with
blue flowers

  delphiniums n ▷ **delphinium**

delta n (pl -s) fourth letter in the Greek
alphabet

  deltas n ▷ **delta**

delude v (-ludes, -luding, -luded) deceive

  deluded v ▷ **delude**

  deludes v ▷ **delude**

  deluding v ▷ **delude**

deluge [del-lyooj] n (pl -s) great flood ▶ v
(-luges, -luging, -luged) flood

  deluged v ▷ **deluge**

  deluges n, v ▷ **deluge**

  deluging v ▷ **deluge**

delusion n (pl -s) mistaken idea or belief
> **delusive** adj

  delusions n ▷ **delusion**

  delusive adj ▷ **delusion**

delve v (delves, delving, delved) research
deeply (for information)

  delved v ▷ **delve**

  delves v ▷ **delve**

  delving v ▷ **delve**

demagogic adj ▷ **demagogue**

  demagogies v ▷ **demagogue**

demagogue n (pl -s) political agitator who
appeals to the prejudice and passions of the
mob > **demagogic** adj > **demagogy** n (pl -gies)

  demagogues n ▷ **demagogue**

  demagogy n ▷ **demagogue**

demand v (-s, -ing, -ed) request forcefully ▶ n
(pl -s) forceful request

  demanded v ▷ **demand**

demanding adj requiring a lot of time or effort
▶ v ▷ **demand**

  demands v, n ▷ **demand**

demarcation n (pl -s) (Formal) establishing
limits or boundaries, esp. between the work
performed by different trade unions

  demarcations n ▷ **demarcation**

demean v (-s, -ing, -ed) do something
unworthy of one's status or character

  demeaned v ▷ **demean**

  demeaning v ▷ **demean**

demeanour n (pl -s) way a person behaves

  demeanours n ▷ **demeanour**

  demeans v ▷ **demean**

demented adj mad > **dementedly** adv

  dementedly adv ▷ **demented**

dementia [dim-men-sha] n (pl -s) state of
serious mental deterioration

  dementias n ▷ **dementia**

demerit n (pl -s) fault, disadvantage

  demerits n ▷ **demerit**

demesne [dim-mane] n (pl -s) land surrounding
a house

  demesnes n ▷ **demesne**

demijohn n (pl -s) large bottle with a short
neck, often encased in wicker

  demijohns n ▷ **demijohn**

  demilitarization n ▷ **demilitarize**

  demilitarizations n ▷ **demilitarize**

demilitarize v (-izes, -izing, -ized) remove
the military forces from > **demilitarization**
n (pl -s)

  demilitarized v ▷ **demilitarize**

  demilitarizes v ▷ **demilitarize**

  demilitarizing v ▷ **demilitarize**

demimonde n (pl -s) (esp. in the 19th century)
class of women considered to be outside
respectable society because of promiscuity

  demimondes n ▷ **demimonde**

demise n (pl -s) eventual failure (of something
successful)

  demises n ▷ **demise**

demo n (pl -s) (Informal) demonstration,
organized expression of public opinion

demob v (-mobs, -mobbing, -mobbed) (BRIT,
AUST & NZ) (Informal) demobilize

  demobbed v ▷ **demob**

  demobbing v ▷ **demob**

  demobilization n ▷ **demobilize**

  demobilizations n ▷ **demobilize**

demobilize v (-lizes, -lizing, -lized) release
from the armed forces > **demobilization** n
(pl -s)

  demobilized v ▷ **demobilize**

  demobilizes v ▷ **demobilize**

  demobilizing v ▷ **demobilize**

  demobs v ▷ **demob**

  democracies n ▷ **democracy**

democracy n (pl -cies) government by the
people or their elected representatives

democrat n (pl -s) advocate of democracy

democratic adj of democracy
> **democratically** adv

  democratically adv ▷ **democratic**

democrats n ▷ democrat
demographer n ▷ demography
demographers n ▷ demography
demographic adj ▷ demography
demographies n ▷ demography
demography n (pl -phies) study of population statistics, such as births and deaths
> **demographer** n (pl -s) > **demographic** adj
demolish v (-es, -ing, -ed) knock down or destroy (a building) > **demolition** n (pl -s)
demolished v ▷ demolish
demolishes v ▷ demolish
demolishing v ▷ demolish
demolition n ▷ demolish
demolitions n ▷ demolish
demon n (pl -s) evil spirit
demoniac adj ▷ demonic
demoniacal adj ▷ demonic
demoniacally adv ▷ demonic
demonic adj evil > **demoniac, demoniacal** adj appearing to be possessed by a devil
> **demoniacally** adv
demonologies n ▷ demonology
demonologist n ▷ demonology
demonologists n ▷ demonology
demonology n (pl -logies) study of demons
> **demonologist** n (pl -s)
demons n ▷ demon
demonstrable adj able to be proved
> **demonstrably** adv
demonstrably adv ▷ demonstrable
demonstrate v (-rates, -rating, -rated) show or prove by reasoning or evidence
demonstrated v ▷ demonstrate
demonstrates v ▷ demonstrate
demonstrating v ▷ demonstrate
demonstration n (pl -s) organized expression of public opinion
demonstrations n ▷ demonstration
demonstrative adj tending to show one's feelings unreservedly > **demonstratively** adv
demonstratively adv ▷ demonstrative
demonstrator n (pl -s) person who demonstrates how a device or machine works
demonstrators n ▷ demonstrator
demoralization n ▷ demoralize
demoralizations n ▷ demoralize
demoralize v (-lizes, -lizing, -lized) undermine the morale of > **demoralization** n (pl -s)
demoralized v ▷ demoralize
demoralizes v ▷ demoralize
demoralizing v ▷ demoralize
demos n ▷ demo
demote v (-motes, -moting, -moted) reduce in

status or rank > **demotion** n (pl -s)
demoted v ▷ demote
demotes v ▷ demote
demoting v ▷ demote
demotion n ▷ demote
demotions n ▷ demote
demur v (-murs, -murring, -murred) show reluctance
demure adj (-r, -st) quiet, reserved, and rather shy > **demurely** adv
demurely adv ▷ demure
demurer adj ▷ demure
demurest adj ▷ demure
demurred v ▷ demur
demurring v ▷ demur
demurs v ▷ demur
den n (pl -s) home of a wild animal
denationalization n ▷ denationalize
denationalizations n ▷ denationalize
denationalize v (-lizes, -lizing, -lized) transfer (an industry) from public to private ownership > **denationalization** n (pl -s)
denationalized v ▷ denationalize
denationalizes v ▷ denationalize
denationalizing v ▷ denationalize
denature v (-tures, -turing, -tured) change the nature of
denatured v ▷ denature
denatures v ▷ denature
denaturing v ▷ denature
deniable adj ▷ deny
deniably adv ▷ deny
denial n (pl -s) statement that something is not true
denials n ▷ denial
denied v ▷ deny
denier [den-yer] n (pl -s) unit of weight used to measure the fineness of nylon or silk
deniers n ▷ denier
denies v ▷ deny
denigrate v (-grates, -grating, -grated) criticize unfairly > **denigration** n (pl -s)
denigrated v ▷ denigrate
denigrates v ▷ denigrate
denigrating v ▷ denigrate
denigration n ▷ denigrate
denigrations n ▷ denigrate
denim n (pl -s) hard-wearing cotton fabric, usu. blue ▶ pl jeans made of denim
denims n ▷ denim
denizen n (pl -s) inhabitant
denizens n ▷ denizen
denominate v (-nates, -nating, -nated) give a specific name to
denominated v ▷ denominate

denominates v ▷ denominate
denominating v ▷ denominate
denomination n (pl -s) group having a distinctive interpretation of a religious faith > **denominational** adj
  denominational adj ▷ denomination
  denominations n ▷ denomination
denominator n (pl -s) number below the line in a fraction
  denominators n ▷ denominator
  denotation n ▷ denote
  denotations n ▷ denote
denote v (-notes, -noting, -noted) be a sign of > **denotation** n (pl -s)
  denoted v ▷ denote
  denotes v ▷ denote
  denoting v ▷ denote
denouement [day-noo-mon] n (pl -s) final outcome or solution in a play or book
  denouements n ▷ denouement
denounce v (-ces, -cing, -ced) speak vehemently against
  denounced v ▷ denounce
  denounces v ▷ denounce
  denouncing v ▷ denounce
  dens n ▷ den
dense adj (-r, -st) closely packed > **densely** adv
  densely adv ▷ dense
  denser adj ▷ dense
  densest adj ▷ dense
  densities n ▷ density
density n (pl -ties) degree to which something is filled or occupied
dent n (pl -s) hollow in the surface of something, made by hitting it ▶ v (-s, -ing, -ed) make a dent in
dental adj of teeth or dentistry
  dented v ▷ dent
dentine [den-teen] n (pl -s) hard dense tissue forming the bulk of a tooth
  dentines n ▷ dentine
  denting v ▷ dent
dentist n (pl -s) person qualified to practise dentistry
  dentistries n ▷ dentistry
dentistry n (pl -ries) branch of medicine concerned with the teeth and gums
  dentists n ▷ dentist
  dents n, v ▷ dent
denture n (pl -s) false tooth
  dentures n ▷ denture
denude v (-nudes, -nuding, -nuded) remove the covering or protection from
  denuded v ▷ denude
  denudes v ▷ denude

  denuding v ▷ denude
denunciation n (pl -s) open condemnation
  denunciations n ▷ denunciation
deny v (-nies, -nying, -nied) declare to be untrue > **deniable** adj > **deniably** adv
  denying v ▷ deny
deodorant n (pl -s) substance applied to the body to mask the smell of perspiration
  deodorants n ▷ deodorant
deodorize v (-izes, -izing, -ized) remove or disguise the smell of
  deodorized v ▷ deodorize
  deodorizes v ▷ deodorize
  deodorizing v ▷ deodorize
depart v (-s, -ing, -ed) leave > **departed** > **departure** n (pl -s)
departed adj (Euphemistic) dead ▶ v ▷ depart
  departing v ▷ depart
department n (pl -s) specialized division of a large organization > **departmental** adj
  departmental adj ▷ department
  departments n ▷ department
  departs v ▷ depart
  departure n ▷ depart
  departures n ▷ depart
depend v (-s, -ing, -ed) (foll. by on) put trust (in) > **dependable** adj > **dependably** adv > **dependability** n (pl -ities)
  dependabilities n ▷ depend
  dependability n ▷ depend
  dependable adj ▷ depend
  dependably adv ▷ depend
dependant n (pl -s) person who depends on another for financial support
  dependants n ▷ dependant
  depended v ▷ depend
dependence n (pl -s) state of being dependent
  dependences n ▷ dependence
  dependencies n ▷ dependency
dependency n (pl -cies) country controlled by another country
dependent adj depending on someone or something > **dependently** adv
  dependently adv ▷ dependent
  depending v ▷ depend
  depends v ▷ depend
depict v (-s, -ing, -ed) produce a picture of > **depiction** n (pl -s)
  depicted v ▷ depict
  depicting v ▷ depict
  depiction n ▷ depict
  depictions n ▷ depict
  depicts v ▷ depict
  depilatories n ▷ depilatory
depilatory [dip-pill-a-tree] n (pl -tories) ▶ adj

(substance) designed to remove unwanted hair

deplete v (-letes, -leting, -leted) use up
> **depletion** n (pl -s)
  depleted v ▷ deplete
  depletes v ▷ deplete
  depleting v ▷ deplete
  depletion n ▷ deplete
  depletions n ▷ deplete

deplorable adj very bad or unpleasant
> **deplorably** adv
  deplorably adv ▷ deplorable

deplore v (-lores, -loring, -lored) condemn strongly
  deplored v ▷ deplore
  deplores v ▷ deplore
  deploring v ▷ deplore

deploy v (-s, -ing, -ed) organize (troops or resources) into a position ready for immediate action > **deployment** n (pl -s)
  deployed v ▷ deploy
  deploying v ▷ deploy
  deployment n ▷ deploy
  deployments n ▷ deploy
  deploys v ▷ deploy

depopulate v (-lates, -lating, -lated) reduce the population of > **depopulation** n (pl -s)
  depopulated v ▷ depopulate
  depopulates v ▷ depopulate
  depopulating v ▷ depopulate
  depopulation n ▷ depopulate
  depopulations n ▷ depopulate

deport v (-s, -ing, -ed) remove forcibly from a country > **deportation** n (pl -s) > **deportee** n (pl -s)
  deportation n ▷ deport
  deportations n ▷ deport
  deported v ▷ deport
  deportee n ▷ deport
  deportees n ▷ deport
  deporting v ▷ deport

deportment n (pl -s) way in which a person moves or stands
  deportments n ▷ deportment
  deports v ▷ deport

depose v (-poses, -posing, -posed) remove from an office or position of power
  deposed v ▷ depose
  deposes v ▷ depose
  deposing v ▷ depose

deposit v (-s, -ing, -ed) put down ▶ n (pl -s) sum of money paid into a bank account
> **depositor** n (pl -s)
  depositaries n ▷ depositary

depositary n (pl -aries) person to whom

something is entrusted for safety
  deposited v ▷ deposit
  depositing v ▷ deposit

deposition n (pl -s) (LAW) sworn statement of a witness used in court in his or her absence
  depositions n ▷ deposition
  depositor n ▷ deposit
  depositories n ▷ deposit
  depositors n ▷ deposit

depository n (pl -ories) store for furniture etc.
  deposits v, n ▷ deposit

depot [dep-oh] n (pl -s) building where goods or vehicles are kept when not in use
  depots n ▷ depot

depraved adj morally bad > **depravity** n (pl -ities)
  depravities n ▷ depraved
  depravity n ▷ depraved

deprecate v (-cates, -cating, -cated) express disapproval of > **deprecation** n (pl -s)
> **deprecatory** adj
  deprecated v ▷ deprecate
  deprecates v ▷ deprecate
  deprecating v ▷ deprecate
  deprecation n ▷ deprecate
  deprecations n ▷ deprecate
  deprecatory adj ▷ deprecate

depreciate v (-ates, -ating, -ated) decline in value or price > **depreciation** n (pl -s)
  depreciated v ▷ depreciate
  depreciates v ▷ depreciate
  depreciating v ▷ depreciate
  depreciation n ▷ depreciate
  depreciations n ▷ depreciate

depredation n (pl -s) plundering
  depredations n ▷ depredation

depress v (-es, -ing, -ed) make sad
> **depressing** adj > **depressingly** adv

depressant n (pl -s) ▶ adj (drug) able to reduce nervous activity
  depressants n ▷ depressant
  depressed v ▷ depress
  depresses v ▷ depress
  depressing v, adj ▷ depress
  depressingly adv ▷ depress

depression n (pl -s) mental state in which a person has feelings of gloom and inadequacy
  depressions n ▷ depression

depressive adj tending to cause depression
▶ n (pl -s) person who suffers from depression
> **depressively** adv
  depressively adv ▷ depressive
  depressives n ▷ depressive
  deprivation n ▷ deprive
  deprivations n ▷ deprive

deprive v (-rives, -riving, -rived) (foll. by of) prevent from (having or enjoying) > **deprivation** n (pl -s)

deprived adj lacking adequate living conditions, education, etc. ▶ v ▷ **deprive**

deprives v ▷ **deprive**

depriving v ▷ **deprive**

depth n (pl -s) distance downwards, backwards, or inwards

depths n ▷ **depth**

deputation n (pl -s) body of people appointed to represent others

deputations n ▷ **deputation**

depute v (-putes, -puting, -puted) appoint (someone) to act on one's behalf

deputed v ▷ **depute**

deputes v ▷ **depute**

deputies n ▷ **deputy**

deputing v ▷ **depute**

deputize v (-izes, -izing, -ized) act as deputy

deputized v ▷ **deputize**

deputizes v ▷ **deputize**

deputizing v ▷ **deputize**

deputy n (pl -ties) person appointed to act on behalf of another

derail v (-s, -ing, -ed) cause (a train) to go off the rails > **derailment** n (pl -s)

derailed v ▷ **derail**

derailing v ▷ **derail**

derailment n ▷ **derail**

derailments n ▷ **derail**

derails v ▷ **derail**

deranged adj insane or uncontrolled > **derangement** n (pl -s)

derangement n ▷ **derange**

derangements n ▷ **derange**

derbies n ▷ **derby**

derby [dah-bee] n (pl -bies) sporting event between teams from the same area ▶ n any of various horse races

deregulate v (-ates, -ating, -ated) remove regulations or controls from > **deregulation** n (pl -s)

deregulated v ▷ **deregulate**

deregulates v ▷ **deregulate**

deregulating v ▷ **deregulate**

deregulation n ▷ **deregulate**

deregulations n ▷ **deregulate**

derelict adj unused and falling into ruins ▶ n (pl -s) social outcast, vagrant

dereliction n (pl -s) state of being abandoned

derelictions n ▷ **dereliction**

derelicts n ▷ **derelict**

deride v (-rides, -riding, -rided) treat with contempt or ridicule > **derision** n (pl -s)

derided v ▷ **deride**

derides v ▷ **deride**

deriding v ▷ **deride**

derision n ▷ **deride**

derisions n ▷ **deride**

derisive adj mocking, scornful > **derisively** adv > **derisiveness** n

derisively adv ▷ **derisive**

derisiveness n ▷ **derisive**

derisory adj too small or inadequate to be considered seriously

derivation n ▷ **derive**

derivations n ▷ **derive**

derivative adj word, idea, etc., derived from another > **derivatively** adv

derivatively adv ▷ **derivative**

derive v (-rives, -riving, -rived) (foll. by from) take or develop (from) > **derivation** n (pl -s)

derived v ▷ **derive**

derives v ▷ **derive**

deriving v ▷ **derive**

dermatitis n inflammation of the skin

dermatologies n ▷ **dermatology**

dermatologist n ▷ **dermatology**

dermatologists n ▷ **dermatology**

dermatology n (pl -ogies) branch of medicine concerned with the skin > **dermatologist** n (pl -s)

derogatorily adv ▷ **derogatory**

derogatory [dir-rog-a-tree] adj intentionally offensive > **derogatorily** adv

derrick n (pl -s) simple crane

derricks n ▷ **derrick**

derv n (pl -s) (BRIT) diesel oil, when used for road transport

dervish n (pl -es) member of a Muslim religious order noted for a frenzied whirling dance

dervishes n ▷ **dervish**

dervs n ▷ **derv**

descant n (pl -s) (MUSIC) tune played or sung above a basic melody

descants n ▷ **descant**

descend v (-s, -ing, -ed) move down (a slope etc.)

descendant n (pl -s) person or animal descended from an individual, race, or species

descendants n ▷ **descendant**

descended v ▷ **descend**

descendent adj descending

descending v ▷ **descend**

descends v ▷ **descend**

descent n (pl -s) descending

descents v ▷ **descent**

describe v (-ribes, -ribing, -ribed) give an account of (something or someone) in words
described v ▷ describe
describes v ▷ describe
describing v ▷ describe
descried v ▷ descry
descries v ▷ descry
description n (pl -s) statement that describes something or someone > **descriptive** adj > **descriptively** adv > **descriptiveness** n
descriptions n ▷ description
descriptive adj ▷ description
descriptively adv ▷ description
descriptiveness n ▷ description
descry v (-scries, -scrying, -scried) catch sight of
descrying v ▷ descry
desecrate v (-rates, -rating, -rated) damage or insult (something sacred) > **desecration** n (pl -s)
desecrated v ▷ desecrate
desecrates v ▷ desecrate
desecrating v ▷ desecrate
desecration n ▷ desecrate
desecrations n ▷ desecrate
desegregate v (-gates, -gating, -gated) end racial segregation in > **desegregation** n (pl -s)
desegregated v ▷ desegregate
desegregates v ▷ desegregate
desegregating v ▷ desegregate
desegregation n ▷ desegregate
desegregations n ▷ desegregate
deselect v (-s, -ing, -ed) (BRIT) (POLITICS) refuse to select (an MP) for re-election > **deselection** n (pl -s)
deselected v ▷ deselect
deselecting v ▷ deselect
deselection n ▷ deselect
deselections n ▷ deselect
deselects v ▷ deselect
desert[1] n (pl -s) region with little or no vegetation because of low rainfall
desert[2] v (-s, -ing, -ed) abandon (a person or place) without intending to return > **deserter** n (pl -s) > **desertion** n (pl -s)
deserted v ▷ desert[2]
deserter n ▷ desert[2]
deserters n ▷ desert[2]
deserting v ▷ desert[2]
desertion n ▷ desert[2]
desertions n ▷ desert[2]
deserts n ▷ desert[1] ▶ pl n the punishment one deserves ▶ v ▷ desert[2]
deserve v (-serves, -serving, -served) be entitled to or worthy of

deserved adj rightfully earned ▶ v ▷ deserve > **deservedly** adv
deservedly adv ▷ deserved
deserves v ▷ deserve
deserving adj worthy of help, praise, or reward ▶ v ▷ deserve
deshabille [day-zab-beel] n (pl -s) state of being partly dressed
deshabilles n ▷ deshabille
desiccate v (-siccates, -siccating, -siccated) remove most of the water from > **desiccation** n (pl -s)
desiccated v ▷ desiccate
desiccates v ▷ desiccate
desiccating v ▷ desiccate
desiccation n ▷ desiccate
desiccations n ▷ desiccate
design v (-s, -ing, -ed) work out the structure or form of (something), by making a sketch or plans ▶ n (pl -s) preliminary drawing
designate [dez-zig-nate] v (-nates, -nating, -nated) give a name to ▶ adj appointed but not yet in office
designated v ▷ designate
designates v ▷ designate
designating v ▷ designate
designation n (pl -s) name
designations v ▷ designation
designed v ▷ design
designedly [dee-zine-id-lee] adv intentionally
designer n (pl -s) person who draws up original sketches or plans from which things are made ▶ adj designed by a well-known designer
designers n ▷ designer
designing adj cunning and scheming ▶ v ▷ design
designs v, n ▷ design
desirabilities n ▷ desirable
desirability n ▷ desirable
desirable adj worth having > **desirability** n (pl -ities) > **desirably** adv
desirably adv ▷ desirable
desire v (-sires, -siring, -sired) want very much ▶ n (pl -s) wish, longing
desired v ▷ desire
desires v, n ▷ desire
desiring v ▷ desire
desist v (-s, -ing, -ed) (foll. by from) stop (doing something)
desisted v ▷ desist
desisting v ▷ desist
desists v ▷ desist
desk n (pl -s) piece of furniture with a writing surface and drawers

desks n ▷ desk

desktop adj (of a computer) small enough to use at a desk

desolate adj uninhabited and bleak ▶ v (-lates, -lating, -lated) deprive of inhabitants > desolately adv > desolateness n > desolation n (pl -s)

desolated v ▷ desolate

desolately adv ▷ desolate

desolateness n ▷ desolate

desolates v ▷ desolate

desolating v ▷ desolate

desolation n ▷ desolate

desolations n ▷ desolate

despair n (pl -s) total loss of hope ▶ v (-s, -ing, -ed) lose hope > despairingly adv

despaired v ▷ despair

despairing v ▷ despair

despairingly adv ▷ despair

despairs n, v ▷ despair

despatch v (-es, -ing, -ed) ▶ n (pl -es) ▷ dispatch

despatched v ▷ despatch

despatches v, n ▷ despatch

despatching v ▷ despatch

desperado n (pl -does, -dos) reckless person ready to commit any violent illegal act

desperadoes v ▷ desperado

desperados v ▷ desperado

desperate adj in despair and reckless > desperately adv > desperateness n > desperation n (pl -s)

desperately adv ▷ desperate

desperateness n ▷ desperate

desperation n ▷ desperate

desperations n ▷ desperate

despicable adj deserving contempt > despicably adv

despicably adv ▷ despicable

despise v (-pises, -pising, -pised) regard with contempt

despised v ▷ despise

despises v ▷ despise

despising v ▷ despise

despite prep in spite of

despoil v (-s, -ing, -ed) (Formal) plunder > despoliation n (pl -s)

despoiled v ▷ despoil

despoiling v ▷ despoil

despoils v ▷ despoil

despoliation n ▷ despoil

despoliations n ▷ despoil

despondencies n ▷ despondent

despondency n ▷ despondent

despondent adj unhappy > despondently adv > despondency n (pl -cies)

despondently adv ▷ despondent

despot n (pl -s) person in power who acts unfairly or cruelly > despotic adj > despotically adv

despotic adj ▷ despot

despotically adv ▷ despot

despotism n (pl -s) unfair or cruel government or behaviour

despotisms n ▷ despotism

despots n ▷ despot

dessert n (pl -s) sweet course served at the end of a meal

desserts n ▷ dessert

dessertspoon n (pl -s) spoon between a tablespoon and a teaspoon in size

dessertspoons n ▷ dessertspoon

destination n (pl -s) place to which someone or something is going

destinations n ▷ destination

destined adj certain to be or to do something

destinies n ▷ destiny

destiny n (pl -nies) future marked out for a person or thing

destitute adj having no money or possessions > destitution n

destitution n ▷ destitute

destroy v (-s, -ing, -ed) ruin, demolish

destroyed v ▷ destroy

destroyer n (pl -s) small heavily armed warship

destroyers n ▷ destroyer

destroying v ▷ destroy

destroys v ▷ destroy

destruction n (pl -s) destroying

destructions n ▷ destruction

destructive adj (capable of) causing destruction > destructively adv > destructiveness n

destructively adv ▷ destructive

destructiveness n ▷ destructive

desuetude [diss-syoo-it-tude] n (pl -s) condition of not being in use

desuetudes n ▷ desuetude

desultorily adv ▷ desultory

desultoriness n ▷ desultory

desultory [dez-zl-tree] adj jumping from one thing to another, disconnected > desultorily adv > desultoriness n

detach v (-es, -ing, -ed) disengage and separate > detachable adj

detachable adj ▷ detach

detached adj (BRIT, AUST & S AFR) (of a house) not joined to another house ▶ v ▷ detach

detaches v ▷ detach

detaching v ▷ detach

detachment n (pl -s) lack of emotional

involvement
detachments n ▷ **detachment**
detail n (pl -s) individual piece of information ▶ v (-s, -ing, -ed) list fully
detailed v ▷ **detail**
detailing v ▷ **detail**
details n, v ▷ **detail**
detain v (-s, -ing, -ed) delay (someone) > **detainee** n (pl -s)
detained v ▷ **detain**
detainee n ▷ **detain**
detainees n ▷ **detain**
detaining v ▷ **detain**
detains v ▷ **detain**
detect v (-s, -ing, -ed) notice > **detectable** adj > **detection** n (pl -ed)
detectable adj ▷ **detect**
detected v ▷ **detect**
detecting v ▷ **detect**
detection n ▷ **detect**
detections n ▷ **detect**
detective n (pl -s) policeman or private agent who investigates crime
detectives n ▷ **detective**
detector n (pl -s) instrument used to find something
detectors n ▷ **detector**
detects v ▷ **detect**
detente [day-tont] n (pl -s) easing of tension between nations
detentes n ▷ **detente**
detention n (pl -s) imprisonment
detentions n ▷ **detention**
deter v (-ters, -terring, -terred) discourage (someone) from doing something by instilling fear or doubt
detergent n (pl -s) chemical substance for washing clothes or dishes
detergents n ▷ **detergent**
deteriorate v (-rates, -rating, -rated) become worse > **deterioration** n (pl -s)
deteriorated v ▷ **deteriorate**
deteriorates v ▷ **deteriorate**
deteriorating v ▷ **deteriorate**
deterioration n ▷ **deteriorate**
deteriorations n ▷ **deteriorate**
determinant n (pl -s) factor that determines
determinants n ▷ **determinant**
determinate adj definitely limited or fixed > **determinateness** n
determinateness n ▷ **determinate**
determination n (pl -s) being determined or resolute
determinations n ▷ **determination**
determine v (-mines, -mining, -mined) settle

(an argument or a question) conclusively
determined adj firmly decided, unable to be dissuaded ▶ v ▷ **determine** > **determinedly** adv
determiner n (pl -s) (GRAMMAR) word that determines the object to which a noun phrase refers
determiners n ▷ **determiner**
determines v ▷ **determine**
determining v ▷ **determine**
determinism n theory that human choice is not free, but decided by past events > **determinist** n (pl -s) adj
determinist n ▷ **determinism**
determinists n ▷ **determinism**
deterred v ▷ **deter**
deterrent n (pl -s) something that deters ▶ adj tending to deter
deterrents n ▷ **deterrent**
deterring v ▷ **deter**
deters v ▷ **deter**
detest v (-s, -ing, -ed) dislike intensely > **detestable** adj > **detestably** adv > **detestation** n (pl -s)
detestable adj ▷ **detest**
detestably adv ▷ **detest**
detestation n ▷ **detest**
detestations n ▷ **detest**
detested v ▷ **detest**
detesting v ▷ **detest**
detests v ▷ **detest**
dethrone v (-rones, -roning, -roned) remove from a throne or position of power
dethroned v ▷ **dethrone**
dethrones v ▷ **dethrone**
dethroning v ▷ **dethrone**
detonate v (-nates, -nating, -nated) explode > **detonation** n (pl -s)
detonated v ▷ **detonate**
detonates v ▷ **detonate**
detonating v ▷ **detonate**
detonation n ▷ **detonate**
detonations n ▷ **detonate**
detonator n (pl -s) small amount of explosive, or a device, used to set off an explosion
detonators n ▷ **detonator**
detour n (pl -s) route that is not the most direct one
detours n ▷ **detour**
detract v (-s, -ing, -ed) (foll. by from) make (something) seem less good > **detractor** n (pl -s)
detracted v ▷ **detract**
detracting v ▷ **detract**
detractor n ▷ **detract**

detractors n ▷ detract
detracts v ▷ detract
detriment n (pl -s) disadvantage or damage > **detrimental** adj > **detrimentally** adv
detrimental adj ▷ detract
detrimentally adv ▷ detract
detriments n ▷ detract
detritus [dit-trite-uss] n loose mass of stones and silt worn away from rocks
deuce [dyewss] n (pl -s) (TENNIS) score of forty all
deuces n ▷ deuce

deus n (di). Deus is a Latin word for a god. Its plural, di, is a very handy word to know when trying to form several words at once. Di scores 3 points.

deuterium n (pl -s) isotope of hydrogen twice as heavy as the normal atom
deuteriums n ▷ deuterium

dev n (devs). A dev is a Hindu god. Dev scores 7 points.

devaluation n ▷ devalue
devaluations n ▷ devalue
devalue v (-lues, -luing, -lued) reduce the exchange value of (a currency) > **devaluation** n (pl -s)
devalued v ▷ devalue
devalues v ▷ devalue
devaluing v ▷ devalue
devastate v (-tates, -tating, -tated) destroy > **devastation** n (pl -s)
devastated adj shocked and extremely upset ▶ v ▷ devastate
devastates v ▷ devastate
devastating v ▷ devastate
devastation n ▷ devastate
devastations n ▷ devastate
develop v (-s, -ing, -ed) grow or bring to a later, more elaborate, or more advanced stage > **development** n (pl -s)
developed v ▷ develop
developer n (pl -s) person who develops property
developers n ▷ developer
developing v ▷ develop
development n ▷ develop
developments n ▷ develop
develops v ▷ develop
deviance n ▷ deviant
deviances n ▷ deviant
deviant n (pl -s) ▶ adj (person) deviating from what is considered acceptable behaviour > **deviance** n (pl -s)
deviants n ▷ deviant
deviate v (-ates, -ating, -ated) differ from others in belief or thought > **deviation** n (pl -s)

deviated v ▷ deviate
deviates v ▷ deviate
deviating v ▷ deviate
deviation n ▷ deviate
deviations n ▷ deviate
device n (pl -s) machine or tool used for a specific task
devices n ▷ device
devil n (pl -s) evil spirit ▶ (Informal) ▶ v (-ils, -illing, -illed) prepare (food) with a highly flavoured spiced mixture
devilish adj cruel or unpleasant ▶ adv (also **devilishly**) (Informal) extremely
devilishly adv ▷ devilish
devilled v ▷ devil
devilling v ▷ devil
devil-may-care adj carefree and cheerful
devilment n (pl -s) mischievous conduct
devilments n ▷ devilment
devilries n ▷ devilry
devilry n (pl -ries) mischievousness
devils n, v ▷ devil
devious adj insincere and dishonest > **deviously** adv > **deviousness** n
deviously adv ▷ devious
deviousness n ▷ devious
devise v (-vises, -vising, -vised) work out (something) in one's mind
devised v ▷ devise
devises v ▷ devise
devising v ▷ devise
devoid adj (foll. by of) completely lacking (in)
devolution n (pl -s) transfer of authority from a central government to regional governments
devolutions n ▷ devolution
devolve v (-volves, -volving, -volved) (foll. by on or to) pass (power or duties) or (of power or duties) be passed to a successor or substitute
devolved v ▷ devolve
devolves v ▷ devolve
devolving v ▷ devolve
devote v (-votes, -voting, -voted) apply or dedicate to a particular purpose
devoted adj showing loyalty or devotion ▶ v ▷ devote > **devotedly** adv
devotedly adv ▷ devoted
devotee n (pl -s) person who is very enthusiastic about something
devotees n ▷ devotee
devotes v ▷ devote
devoting v ▷ devote
devotion n (pl -s) strong affection for or loyalty to someone or something ▶ pl prayers > **devotional** adj

devotional adj ▷ **devotion**
devotions adj ▷ **devotion**
devour v (-s, -ing, -ed) eat greedily
devoured v ▷ **devour**
devouring v ▷ **devour**
devours v ▷ **devour**
devout adj deeply religious > **devoutly** adv
> **devoutness** n
devoutly adv ▷ **devout**
devoutness n ▷ **devout**
dew n (pl -s) drops of water that form on the
ground at night from vapour in the air > **dewy**
adj (-wier, -wiest)
dewier adj ▷ **dew**
dewiest adj ▷ **dew**
dewlap n (pl -s) loose fold of skin hanging
under the throat in dogs, cattle, etc.
dewlaps n ▷ **dewlap**
dews n ▷ **dew**
dewy adj ▷ **dew**

> **dex** n (**dexes**). Dex is a slang word for a
kind of amphetamine. This is an easy
way to pick up a some points after
another player has used an X. Dex
scores 11 points.

dexterities n ▷ **dexterity**
dexterity n (pl -ities) skill in using one's hands
> **dexterous** adj > **dexterously** adv
dexterous adj ▷ **dexterity**
dexterously adv ▷ **dexterity**
dextrose n (pl -s) glucose occurring in fruit,
honey, and the blood of animals
dextroses n ▷ **dextrose**

> **dey** n (**deys**). A dey is an Ottoman
governor. Dey scores 7 points.

diabetes [die-a-beet-eez] n disorder in which
an abnormal amount of urine containing
an excess of sugar is excreted > **diabetic** n
(pl -s) adj
diabetic n ▷ **diabetes**
diabetics n ▷ **diabetes**
diabolic adj of the Devil
diabolical adj (Informal) extremely bad
> **diabolically** adv > **diabolicalness** n
diabolically adv ▷ **diabolical**
diabolicalness n ▷ **diabolical**
diabolism n witchcraft, devil worship
> **diabolist** n (pl -s)
diabolist n ▷ **diabolism**
diabolists n ▷ **diabolism**
diaconate n (pl -s) position or period of office
of a deacon
diaconates n ▷ **diaconate**
diacritic n (pl -s) sign above or below a
character to indicate phonetic value or stress

diacritics n ▷ **diacritic**
diadem n (pl -s) (Old-fashioned) crown
diadems n ▷ **diadem**
diaereses n ▷ **diaeresis**
diaeresis n (pl -ses) mark (¨) placed over
a vowel to show that it is pronounced
separately from the preceding one, for
example in Noël
diagnosed v ▷ **diagnosis**
diagnoses n, v ▷ **diagnosis**
diagnosing v ▷ **diagnosis**
diagnosis [die-ag-no-siss] n (pl -ses) [-seez]
discovery and identification of diseases from
the examination of symptoms > **diagnose** v
(-noses, -nosing, -nosed) > **diagnostic** adj
diagnostic adj ▷ **diagnosis**
diagonal adj from corner to corner ▶ n (pl -s)
diagonal line > **diagonally** adv
diagonally adv ▷ **diagonal**
diagonals n ▷ **diagonal**
diagram n (pl -s) sketch showing the form or
workings of something > **diagrammatic** adj
diagrammatic adj ▷ **diagram**
diagrams n ▷ **diagram**
dial n (pl -s) face of a clock or watch ▶ v (**dials**,
dialling, **dialled**) operate the dial or buttons
on a telephone in order to contact (a number)
dialect n (pl -s) form of a language spoken in
a particular area > **dialectal** adj > **dialectally**
adv
dialectal adj ▷ **dialect**
dialectally adv ▷ **dialect**
dialectic n (pl -s) logical debate by question
and answer to resolve differences between
two views > **dialectical** adj > **dialectically** adv
dialectical adj ▷ **dialectic**
dialectically adv ▷ **dialectic**
dialectics n ▷ **dialectic**
dialects n ▷ **dialect**
dialled v ▷ **dial**
dialling v ▷ **dial**
dialogue n (pl -s) conversation between two
people, esp. in a book, film, or play
dialogues n ▷ **dialogue**
dials n, v ▷ **dial**
dialyses n ▷ **dialysis**
dialysis [die-al-iss-iss] n (pl -ses) (MED) filtering
of blood through a membrane to remove
waste products
diamanté [die-a-man-tee] adj decorated with
artificial jewels or sequins
diameter n (pl -s) (length of) a straight line
through the centre of a circle or sphere
diameters n ▷ **diameter**
diametric, diametrical adj of a diameter

> **diametrically** adv

diametrical adj ▷ **diametric**

diametrically adv ▷ **diametric**

diamond n (pl -s) exceptionally hard, usu. colourless, precious stone

diamonds n ▷ **diamond**

diaper n (pl -s) (US) nappy

diapers n ▷ **diaper**

diaphanous [die-af-an-ous] adj fine and almost transparent > **diaphanously** adv

diaphanously adv ▷ **diaphanous**

diaphragm [die-a-fram] n (pl -s) muscular partition that separates the abdominal cavity and chest cavity

diaphragms n ▷ **diaphragm**

diaries n ▷ **diary**

diarist n ▷ **diary**

diarists n ▷ **diary**

diarrhoea [die-a-ree-a] n (pl -s) frequent discharge of abnormally liquid faeces

diarrhoeas n ▷ **diarrhoea**

diary n (pl -ries) (book for) a record of daily events, appointments, or observations > **diarist** n (pl -s)

diatribe n (pl -s) bitter critical attack

diatribes n ▷ **diatribe**

dibble n (pl -s) small hand tool used to make holes in the ground for seeds or plants

dibbles n ▷ **dibble**

dice n (pl dice) small cube each of whose sides has a different number of spots (1 to 6), used in games of chance ▶ v (dices, dicing, diced) cut (food) into small cubes

diced v ▷ **dice**

dices v ▷ **dice**

dicey adj (dicier, diciest) (Informal) dangerous or risky

dichotomies n ▷ **dichotomy**

dichotomy [die-kot-a-mee] n (pl -mies) division into two opposed groups or parts

dicier adj ▷ **dice**

diciest adj ▷ **dice**

dicing v ▷ **dice**

dickier adj ▷ **dicky²**

dickies n ▷ **dicky¹**

dickiest adj ▷ **dicky²**

dicky¹ n (pl dickies) false shirt front

dicky² adj (dickier, dickiest) (Informal) shaky or weak

dickybird n (pl -s) child's word for a bird

dickybirds n ▷ **dickybird**

dicta n ▷ **dictum**

dictate v (-tes, -ting, -ted) say aloud for someone else to write down (foll. by to) ▶ n (pl -s) authoritative command > **dictation**

n (pl -s)

dictated v ▷ **dictate**

dictates v, n ▷ **dictate**

dictating v ▷ **dictate**

dictation n ▷ **dictate**

dictations n ▷ **dictate**

dictator n (pl -s) ruler who has complete power > **dictatorship** n (pl -s)

dictatorial adj like a dictator > **dictatorially** adv

dictatorially adv ▷ **dictatorial**

dictators n ▷ **dictator**

dictatorship n ▷ **dictator**

dictatorships n ▷ **dictator**

diction n (pl -s) manner of pronouncing words and sounds

dictionaries n ▷ **dictionary**

dictionary n (pl -aries) book consisting of an alphabetical list of words with their meanings

dictions n ▷ **diction**

dictum n (pl -tums, -ta) formal statement

dictums n ▷ **dictum**

did v ▷ **do**

didactic adj intended to instruct > **didactically** adv

didactically adv ▷ **didactic**

diddle v (-dles, -dling, -dled) (Informal) swindle

diddled v ▷ **diddle**

diddles v ▷ **diddle**

diddling v ▷ **diddle**

didgeridoo n (pl -s) Australian musical instrument made from a long hollow piece of wood

didgeridoos n ▷ **didgeridoo**

didn't did not

die¹ v (dies, dying, died) (of a person, animal, or plant) cease all biological activity permanently

die² n (pl -s) shaped block used to cut or form metal

died v ▷ **die¹**

diehard n (pl -s) person who resists change

diehards n ▷ **diehard**

diereses n ▷ **dieresis**

dieresis [die-air-iss-iss] n (pl -ses) [-seez] ▷ **diaeresis**

dies v ▷ **die¹** ▶ n ▷ **die²**

diesel n (pl -s) diesel engine

diesels n ▷ **diesel**

diet¹ n (pl -s) food that a person or animal regularly eats ▶ v (-s, -ing, -ed) follow a special diet so as to lose weight ▶ adj (of food) suitable for a weight-reduction diet > **dietary** adj > **dieter** n (pl -s)

diet² n (pl -s) parliament of some countries
  dietary adj ▷ diet
  dieted v ▷ diet
  dieter n ▷ diet
  dieters n ▷ diet
dietetic adj prepared for special dietary requirements
dietetics n study of diet and nutrition
dietician n (pl -s) person who specializes in dietetics
  dieticians n ▷ dietician
  dieting v ▷ diet
  diets v ▷ diet¹ ▶ n ▷ diet¹, ²
differ v (-s, -ing, -ed) be unlike
  differed v ▷ differ
difference n (pl -s) state of being unlike
  differences n ▷ difference
different adj unlike ▷ **differently** adv
differential adj of or using a difference ▶ n (pl -s) factor that differentiates between two comparable things ▷ **differentially** adv
  differentially adv ▷ differential
  differentials n ▷ differential
differentiate v, v (-te, -ting, -ted) perceive or show the difference (between) ▷ **differentiation** n (pl -s)
  differentiated v ▷ differentiate
  differentiates v ▷ differentiate
  differentiating v ▷ differentiate
  differentiation n ▷ differentiate
  differentiations n ▷ differentiate
  differently n ▷ different
  differing v ▷ differ
  differs v ▷ differ
difficult adj requiring effort or skill to do or understand ▷ **difficultly** adv ▷ **difficulty** n (pl -ties)
  difficulties n ▷ difficult
  difficultly adv ▷ difficult
  difficulty n ▷ difficult
  diffidence n ▷ diffident
  diffidences n ▷ diffident
diffident adj lacking self-confidence ▷ **diffidence** n (pl -s) ▷ **diffidently** adv
  diffidently adv ▷ diffident
diffraction n (pl -s) (PHYSICS) deviation in the direction of a wave at the edge of an obstacle in its path
  diffractions n ▷ diffraction
diffuse v (-fuses, -fusing, -fused) spread over a wide area ▶ adj widely spread ▷ **diffusely** adv ▷ **diffuseness** n ▷ **diffusion** n (pl -s)
  diffused v ▷ diffuse
  diffusely adv ▷ diffuse
  diffuseness n ▷ diffuse

diffuses v ▷ diffuse
  diffusing v ▷ diffuse
  diffusion n ▷ diffuse
  diffusions n ▷ diffuse
dig v (digs, digging, dug) cut into, break up, and turn over or remove (earth), esp. with a spade ▶ n (pl -s) digging ▶ pl (pl -s) (BRIT, AUST & S AFR) (Informal) lodgings
digest v (-s, -ing, -ed) subject to a process of digestion ▶ n (pl -s) shortened version of a book, report, or article ▷ **digestible** adj ▷ **digestibility** n ▷ **digestive** adj ▷ **digestively** adv
  digested v ▷ digest
  digestibility n ▷ digest
  digestible adj ▷ digest
  digesting v ▷ digest
digestion n (pl -s) (body's system for) breaking down food into easily absorbed substances
  digestions n ▷ digestion
  digestive adj ▷ digest
  digestively adv ▷ digest
  digests v, n ▷ digest
digger n (pl -s) machine used for digging
  diggers n ▷ digger
  digging v ▷ dig
  diggings n ▷ dig
digit [dij-it] n (pl -s) finger or toe
digital adj displaying information as numbers rather than with hands and a dial ▷ **digitally** adv
digitalis n drug made from foxglove leaves, used as a heart stimulant
  digitally adv ▷ digital
  digits n ▷ digit
  dignified n ▷ dignify
  dignifies n ▷ dignify
dignify v (-s, -ing, -ed) add distinction to
  dignifying v ▷ dignify
  dignitaries n ▷ dignitary
dignitary n (pl -aries) person of high official position
  dignities n ▷ dignity
dignity n (pl -ties) serious, calm, and controlled behaviour or manner
digress v (-es, -ing, -ed) depart from the main subject in speech or writing ▷ **digression** n (pl -s)
  digressed v ▷ digress
  digresses v ▷ digress
  digressing v ▷ digress
  digression n ▷ digress
  digressions n ▷ digress
  digs v, n ▷ dig
  dike n (pl -s) ▷ dyke

dikes n ▷ dike

dilapidated adj (of a building) having fallen into ruin ▷ **dilapidation** n (pl -s)

dilapidation n ▷ dilapidated

dilapidations n ▷ dilapidated

dilatation n ▷ dilate

dilatations n ▷ dilate

dilate v (-lates, -lating, -lated) make or become wider or larger ▷ **dilation, dilatation** n (pl -s)

dilated v ▷ dilate

dilates v ▷ dilate

dilating v ▷ dilate

dilation n ▷ dilate

dilations n ▷ dilate

dilatorily adv ▷ dilatory

dilatoriness n ▷ dilatory

dilatory [dill-a-tree] adj tending or intended to waste time ▷ **dilatorily** adv ▷ **dilatoriness** n

dilemma n (pl -s) situation offering a choice between two equally undesirable alternatives

dilemmas n ▷ dilemma

dilettante [dill-it-tan-tee] n (pl -tantes, -tanti) person whose interest in a subject is superficial rather than serious ▷ **dilettantism** n

dilettantes n ▷ dilettante

dilettanti n ▷ dilettante

dilettantism n ▷ dilettante

diligence n ▷ diligent

diligent adj careful and persevering in carrying out duties ▷ **diligently** adv ▷ **diligence** n

diligently adv ▷ diligent

dill n (pl -s) sweet-smelling herb

dills n ▷ dill

dilute v (-lutes, -luting, -luted) make (a liquid) less concentrated, esp. by adding water ▷ **dilution** n (pl -s)

diluted v ▷ dilute

dilutes v ▷ dilute

diluting v ▷ dilute

dilution n ▷ dilute

dilutions n ▷ dilute

diluvial, diluvian adj of a flood, esp. the great Flood described in the Old Testament

diluvian adj ▷ diluvial

dim adj (dimmer, dimmest) badly lit ▶ v (dims, dimming, dimmed) make or become dim ▷ **dimly** adv ▷ **dimness** n

dime n (pl -s) coin of the US and Canada, worth ten cents

dimension n (pl -s) measurement of the size of something in a particular direction

dimensions n ▷ dimension

dimes n ▷ dime

diminish v (-es, -ing, -ed) make or become smaller, fewer, or less ▷ **diminution** n (pl -s)

diminished v ▷ diminish

diminishes v ▷ diminish

diminishing v ▷ diminish

diminuendo n (pl -s) (MUSIC) gradual decrease in loudness

diminuendos n ▷ diminuendo

diminution n ▷ diminish

diminutions n ▷ diminish

diminutive adj very small ▶ n (pl -s) word or affix which implies smallness or unimportance ▷ **diminutively** adv ▷ **diminutiveness** n

diminutively adv ▷ diminutive

diminutiveness n ▷ diminutive

diminutives n ▷ diminutive

dimly adv ▷ dim

dimmed v ▷ dim

dimmer n (pl -s) device for dimming an electric light ▶ adj ▷ dim

dimmers n ▷ dimmer

dimmest adj ▷ dim

dimming v ▷ dim

dimness n ▷ dim

dimple n (pl -s) small natural dent, esp. in the cheeks or chin ▶ v (-ples, -pling, -pled) produce dimples by smiling

dimpled v ▷ dimple

dimples n, v ▷ dimple

dimpling v ▷ dimple

dims v ▷ dim

din n (pl -s) loud unpleasant confused noise ▶ v (dins, dinning, dinned) (foll. by into) instil (something) into someone by constant repetition

dinar [dee-nahr] n (pl -s) monetary unit of various Balkan, Middle Eastern, and North African countries

dinars n ▷ dinar

dine v (dines, dining, dined) eat dinner

dined v ▷ dine

diner n (pl -s) person eating a meal

diners n ▷ diner

dines v ▷ dine

ding n (pl -s) (AUST DATED & NZ) (Informal) small dent in a vehicle

dinghies n ▷ dinghy

dinghy [ding-ee] n (pl -ghies) small boat, powered by sails, oars, or a motor

dingier adj ▷ dingy

dingiest adj ▷ dingy

dinginess n ▷ dingy

dingo n (pl -goes) Australian wild dog

dingoes n ▷ dingo

dings n ▷ ding

dingy [din-jee] adj (-gier, -giest) (BRIT, AUST & NZ) dull and drab ▶ dinginess n

dining v ▷ dine

dinkier adj ▷ dinky

dinkiest adj ▷ dinky

dinkum adj (AUST & NZ) (Informal) genuine or right

dinky adj (-kier, -kiest) (BRIT, AUST & NZ) (Informal) small and neat

dinned v ▷ din

dinner n (pl -s) main meal of the day, eaten either in the evening or at midday

dinners n ▷ dinner

dinning v ▷ din

dinosaur n (pl -s) type of extinct prehistoric reptile, many of which were of gigantic size

dinosaurs n ▷ dinosaur

dins n, v ▷ din

dint n (pl -s) means

dints n ▷ dint

diocesan adj ▷ diocese

diocese [die-a-siss] n (pl -s) district over which a bishop has control ▷ diocesan adj

dioceses n ▷ diocese

diode n (pl -s) semiconductor device for converting alternating current to direct current

diodes n ▷ diode

dioptre [die-op-ter] n (pl -s) unit for measuring the refractive power of a lens

dioptres n ▷ dioptre

dioxide n (pl -s) oxide containing two oxygen atoms per molecule

dioxides n ▷ dioxide

dip v (dips, dipping, dipped) plunge quickly or briefly into a liquid ▶ n (pl -s) dipping

diphtheria [dif-theer-ya] n (pl -s) contagious disease producing fever and difficulty in breathing and swallowing

diphtherias n ▷ diphtheria

diphthong n (pl -s) union of two vowel sounds in a single compound sound

diphthongs n ▷ diphthong

diploma n (pl -s) qualification awarded by a college on successful completion of a course

diplomacies n ▷ diplomacy

diplomacy n (pl -macies) conduct of the relations between nations by peaceful means

diplomas n ▷ diploma

diplomat n (pl -s) official engaged in diplomacy

diplomatic adj of diplomacy > diplomatically adv

diplomatically adv ▷ diplomatic

diplomats n ▷ diplomat

dipped v ▷ dip

dipper n (pl -s) ladle used for dipping

dippers n ▷ dipper

dipping v ▷ dip

diprotodont [die-pro-toe-dont] n (pl -s) marsupial with fewer than three upper incisor teeth on each side of the jaw

diprotodonts n ▷ diprotodont

dips v, n ▷ dip

dipsomania n (pl -s) compulsive craving for alcohol > dipsomaniac n (pl -s) adj

dipsomaniac n, adj ▷ dipsomania

dipsomaniacs n ▷ dipsomania

dipsomanias n ▷ dipsomania

diptych [dip-tik] n (pl -s) painting on two hinged panels

diptychs n ▷ diptych

dire adj (-er, -est) disastrous, urgent, or terrible > direly adv > direness n (pl -es)

direct adj (of a route) shortest, straight ▶ adv in a direct manner ▶ v (-s, -ing, -ed) lead and organize > directness n

directed v ▷ direct

directing v ▷ direct

direction n (pl -s) course or line along which a person or thing moves, points, or lies ▶ pl instructions for doing something or for reaching a place > directional adj

directional adj ▷ direction

directions n ▷ direction

directive n (pl -s) instruction, order

directives n ▷ directive

directly adv in a direct manner ▶ conj as soon as

directness n ▷ direct

director n (pl -s) person or thing that directs or controls > directorial adj > directorship n (pl -s)

directorate n (pl -s) board of directors

directorates n ▷ directorate

directorial adj ▷ director

directories n ▷ directory

directors n ▷ director

directorship n ▷ director

directorships n ▷ director

directory n (pl -ries) book listing names, addresses, and telephone numbers

directs v ▷ direct

direly adv ▷ dire

direness n ▷ dire

direnesses n ▷ dire

direr adj ▷ dire

direst adj ▷ dire

dirge n (pl -s) slow sad song of mourning
  dirges n ▷ dirge

dirigible [dir-rij-jib-bl] adj able to be steered ▶ n
(pl -s) airship
  dirigibles n ▷ dirigible

dirk n (pl -s) dagger, formerly worn by Scottish
Highlanders
  dirks n ▷ dirk

dirndl n (pl -s) full gathered skirt originating
from Tyrolean peasant wear
  dirndls n ▷ dirndl

dirt n (pl -s) unclean substance, filth
  dirtied v ▷ dirty
  dirtier adj ▷ dirty
  dirties v ▷ dirty
  dirtiest adj ▷ dirty
  dirtily adv ▷ dirty
  dirtiness n ▷ dirty
  dirts n ▷ dirt

dirty adj (dirtier, dirtiest) covered or marked
with dirt ▶ v (dirties, dirtying, dirtied) make
dirty > **dirtily** adv > **dirtiness** n
  dirtying v ▷ dirty
  disabilities n ▷ disability

disability n (pl -ties) condition of being
disabled

disable v (-bles, -bling, -bled) make ineffective,
unfit, or incapable > **disablement** n

disabled adj lacking a physical power, such as
the ability to walk ▶ v ▷ disable
  disablement n ▷ disable
  disables v ▷ disable
  disabling v ▷ disable

disabuse v (-buses, -busing, -bused) (foll. by of)
rid (someone) of a mistaken idea
  disabused v ▷ disabuse
  disabuses v ▷ disabuse
  disabusing v ▷ disabuse

disadvantage n (pl -s) unfavourable or
harmful circumstance > **disadvantageous**
adj > **disadvantageously** adv
> **disadvantageousness** n

disadvantaged adj socially or economically
deprived
  disadvantageous adj ▷ disadvantage
  disadvantageously adv ▷ disadvantage
  disadvantageousness n ▷ disadvantage
  disadvantages n ▷ disadvantage

disaffected adj having lost loyalty to or
affection for someone or something
> **disaffectedly** adv > **disaffection** n (pl -s)
  disaffectedly adv ▷ disaffected
  disaffection n ▷ disaffected
  disaffections n ▷ disaffected

disagree v (-grees, -greeing, -greed) argue

or have different opinions > **disagreement**
n (pl -s)

disagreeable adj unpleasant
> **disagreeableness** n > **disagreeably** adv
  disagreeableness n ▷ disagreeable
  disagreeably adv ▷ disagreeable
  disagreed v ▷ disagree
  disagreeing v ▷ disagree
  disagreement n ▷ disagree
  disagreements n ▷ disagree
  disagrees v ▷ disagree

disallow v (-s, -ing, -ed) reject as untrue or
invalid
  disallowed v ▷ disallow
  disallowing v ▷ disallow
  disallows v ▷ disallow

disappear v (-s, -ing, -ed) cease to be visible
> **disappearance** n (pl -s)
  disappearance n ▷ disappear
  disappearances n ▷ disappear
  disappeared v ▷ disappear
  disappearing v ▷ disappear
  disappears v ▷ disappear

disappoint v (-s, -ing, -ed) fail to meet the
expectations or hopes of > **disappointingly**
adv
  disappointed v ▷ disappoint
  disappointing v ▷ disappoint
  disappointingly adv ▷ disappoint

disappointment n (pl -s) feeling of being
disappointed
  disappointments n ▷ disappointment
  disappoints v ▷ disappoint

disapprobation n (pl -s) disapproval
  disapprobations n ▷ disapprobation
  disapproval n ▷ disapprove
  disapprovals n ▷ disapprove

disapprove v (-proves, -proving, -proved) (foll
by of) consider wrong or bad > **disapproval**
n (pl -s)
  disapproved v ▷ disapprove
  disapproves v ▷ disapprove
  disapproving v ▷ disapprove

disarm v (-s, -ing, -ed) deprive of weapons
> **disarmament** n (pl -s)
  disarmament n ▷ disarm
  disarmaments n ▷ disarm
  disarmed v ▷ disarm

disarming adj removing hostility or suspicion
▶ v ▷ disarm > **disarmingly** adv
  disarmingly adv ▷ disarming
  disarms v ▷ disarm

disarrange v (-ranges, -ranging, -ranged)
throw into disorder
  disarranged v ▷ disarrange

disarranges v ▷ disarrange

disarranging v ▷ disarrange

disarray n (pl -s) confusion and lack of discipline

disarrays n ▷ disarray

disaster n (pl -s) occurrence that causes great distress or destruction > **disastrous** adj > **disastrously** adv

disasters n ▷ disaster

disastrous adj ▷ disaster

disastrously adv ▷ disaster

disavow v (-s, -ing, -ed) deny connection with or responsibility for > **disavowal** n (pl -s)

disavowal n ▷ disavow

disavowals n ▷ disavow

disavowed v ▷ disavow

disavowing v ▷ disavow

disavows v ▷ disavow

disband v (-s, -ing, -ed) (cause to) cease to function as a group

disbanded v ▷ disband

disbanding v ▷ disband

disbands v ▷ disband

disbelief n ▷ disbelieve

disbelieve v (-lieves, -lieving, -lieved) reject as false (foll. by **in**) > **disbelief** n

disbelieved v ▷ disbelieve

disbelieves v ▷ disbelieve

disbelieving v ▷ disbelieve

disburse v (-burses, -bursing, -bursed) pay out > **disbursement** n (pl -s)

disbursed v ▷ disburse

disbursement n ▷ disburse

disbursements n ▷ disburse

disburses v ▷ disburse

disbursing v ▷ disburse

disc n (pl -s) flat circular object ▷ **disk**

discard v (-s, -ing, -ed) get rid of (something or someone) as useless or undesirable

discarded v ▷ discard

discarding v ▷ discard

discards v ▷ discard

discern v (-s, -ing, -ed) see or be aware of (something) clearly > **discernible** adj > **discernibly** adv > **discernment** n (pl -s)

discerned v ▷ discern

discernible adj ▷ discern

discernibly adv ▷ discern

discerning adj having good judgment ▶ v ▷ discern

discernment n ▷ discern

discernments n ▷ discern

discerns v ▷ discern

discharge v (-charges, -charging, -charged) release, allow to go ▶ n (pl -s) substance that comes out from a place

discharged v ▷ discharge

discharges v, n ▷ discharge

discharging v ▷ discharge

disciple [diss-sipe-pl] n (pl -s) follower of the doctrines of a teacher, esp. Jesus Christ

disciples n ▷ disciple

disciplinarian n (pl -s) person who practises strict discipline

disciplinarians n ▷ disciplinarian

disciplinary adj ▷ discipline

discipline n (pl -s) practice of imposing strict rules of behaviour ▶ v (-plines, -plining, -plined) attempt to improve the behaviour of (oneself or another) by training or rules > **disciplinary** adj

disciplined adj able to behave and work in a controlled way ▶ v ▷ discipline

disciplines n, v ▷ discipline

disciplining v ▷ discipline

disclaimed v ▷ disclaim

disclaimer n (pl -s) statement denying responsibility > **disclaim** v (-s, -ing, -ed)

disclaimers n ▷ disclaimer

disclaiming v ▷ disclaimer

disclaims v ▷ disclaimer

disclose v (-closes, -closing, -closed) make known > **disclosure** n (pl -s)

disclosed v ▷ disclose

discloses v ▷ disclose

disclosing v ▷ disclose

disclosure n ▷ disclose

disclosures n ▷ disclose

disco n (pl -s) nightclub where people dance to amplified pop records

discoloration n ▷ discolour

discolorations n ▷ discolour

discolour v (-s, -ing, -ed) change in colour, fade > **discoloration** n (pl -s)

discoloured v ▷ discolour

discolouring v ▷ discolour

discolours v ▷ discolour

discomfit v (-s, -ing, -ed) make uneasy or confused > **discomfiture** n (pl -s)

discomfited v ▷ discomfit

discomfiting v ▷ discomfit

discomfits v ▷ discomfit

discomfiture n ▷ discomfit

discomfitures n ▷ discomfit

discomfort n (pl -s) inconvenience, distress, or mild pain

discomforts n ▷ discomfort

discommode v (-modes, -moding, -moded) cause inconvenience to

discommoded v ▷ discommode

discommodes v ▷ discommode
discommoding v ▷ discommode
disconcert v (-s, -ing, -ed) embarrass or upset
disconcerted v ▷ disconcert
disconcerting v ▷ disconcert
disconcerts v ▷ disconcert
disconnect v (-s, -ing, -ed) undo or break
the connection between (two things)
> **disconnection** n (pl -s)
disconnected adj (of speech or ideas) not
logically connected ▶ v ▷ disconnect
disconnecting v ▷ disconnect
disconnection n ▷ disconnect
disconnections n ▷ disconnect
disconnects v ▷ disconnect
disconsolate adj sad beyond comfort
> **disconsolately** adv
disconsolately adv ▷ disconsolate
discontent n (pl -s) lack of contentment
> **discontented** adj > **discontentedly** adv
discontented adj ▷ discontent
discontentedly adv ▷ discontent
discontents n ▷ discontent
discontinue v (-nues, -nuing, -nued) come or
bring to an end
discontinued v ▷ discontinue
discontinues v ▷ discontinue
discontinuing v ▷ discontinue
discontinuities n ▷ discontinuous
discontinuity n ▷ discontinuous
discontinuous adj characterized by
interruptions > **discontinuity** n (pl -nuities)
discord n (pl -s) lack of agreement or
harmony between people > **discordant** adj
> **discordantly** adv > **discordance** n (pl -s)
discordance n ▷ discord
discordances n ▷ discord
discordant adj ▷ discord
discordantly adv ▷ discord
discords n ▷ discord
discos n ▷ disco
discotheque n (pl -s) ▷ disco
discotheques n ▷ discotheque
discount v (-s, -ing, -ed) take no account of
(something) because it is considered to be
unreliable, prejudiced, or irrelevant ▶ n (pl -s)
deduction from the full price of something
discounted v ▷ discount
discounting v ▷ discount
discounts v, n ▷ discount
discourage v (-rages, -raging, -raged)
deprive of the will to persist in something
> **discouragement** n (pl -s)
discouraged v ▷ discourage
discouragement n ▷ discourage

discouragements n ▷ discourage
discourages v ▷ discourage
discouraging v ▷ discourage
discourse n (pl -s) conversation ▶ v (-ses, -sing,
-sed) (foll. by on) speak or write (about) at
length
discoursed v ▷ discourse
discourses n, v ▷ discourse
discoursing v ▷ discourse
discourteous adj showing bad manners
> **discourteously** adv > **discourtesy** n (pl
-esies)
discourteously adv ▷ discourteous
discourtesies n ▷ discourteous
discourtesy n ▷ discourteous
discover v (-s, -ing, -ed) be the first to find or to
find out about > **discoverer** n (pl -s)
discovered v ▷ discover
discoverer n ▷ discover
discoverers n ▷ discover
discoveries n ▷ discovery
discovering v ▷ discover
discovers v ▷ discover
discovery n (pl -eries) discovering
discredit v (-s, -ing, -ed) damage the
reputation of ▶ n (pl -s) damage to someone's
reputation
discreditable adj bringing shame
discredited v ▷ discredit
discrediting v ▷ discredit
discredits v, n ▷ discredit
discreet adj (-er, -est) careful to avoid
embarrassment, esp. by keeping confidences
secret > **discreetly** adv > **discreetness** n (pl -es)
discreeter adj ▷ discreet
discreetest adj ▷ discreet
discreetly adv ▷ discreet
discreetness n ▷ discreet
discreetnesses n ▷ discreet
discrepancies n ▷ discrepancy
discrepancy n (pl -cies) conflict or variation
between facts, figures, or claims
discrete adj (-r, -st) separate, distinct
> **discretely** adv > **discreteness** n (pl -es)
discretely adv ▷ discrete
discreteness n ▷ discrete
discretenesses n ▷ discrete
discreter adj ▷ discrete
discretest adj ▷ discrete
discretion n (pl -s) quality of behaving in a
discreet way > **discretionary** adj
discretionary adj ▷ discretion
discretions n ▷ discretion
discriminate v (-nates, -nating, -nated)
(foll. by against or in favour of) single

out (a particular person or group) for
worse or better treatment than others
> **discrimination** n (pl -s)
discriminated v ▷ discriminate
discriminates v ▷ discriminate
discriminating adj showing good taste and
judgment ▶ v ▷ discriminate
discrimination n ▷ discriminate
discriminations n ▷ discriminate
discriminatory adj based on prejudice
discs n ▷ disc
discursive adj passing from one topic to
another > **discursively** adv > **discursiveness** n
discursively adv ▷ discursive
discursiveness n ▷ discursive
discus n (pl -es) heavy disc-shaped object
thrown in sports competitions
discuses n ▷ discus
discuss v (-es, -ing, -ed) consider (something)
by talking it over > **discussion** n (pl -s)
discussed v ▷ discuss
discusses v ▷ discuss
discussing v ▷ discuss
discussion n ▷ discuss
discussions n ▷ discuss
disdain n feeling of superiority and dislike ▶ v
(-s, -ing, -ed) refuse with disdain > **disdainful**
adj > **disdainfully** adv
disdained v ▷ disdain
disdainful adj ▷ disdain
disdainfully adv ▷ disdain
disdaining v ▷ disdain
disdains v ▷ disdain
disease n (pl -s) illness, sickness > **diseased** adj
diseased v ▷ disease
diseases n ▷ disease
disembark v (-s, -ing, -ed) get off a ship,
aircraft, or bus > **disembarkation** n (pl -s)
disembarkation n ▷ disembark
disembarkations n ▷ disembark
disembarked v ▷ disembark
disembarking v ▷ disembark
disembarks v ▷ disembark
disembodied adj lacking a body
disembowel v (-els, -elling, -elled) remove the
entrails of
disembowelled v ▷ disembowel
disembowelling v ▷ disembowel
disembowels v ▷ disembowel
disenchanted adj disappointed and
disillusioned > **disenchantment** n (pl -s)
disenchantment n ▷ disenchant
disenchantments n ▷ disenchant
disenfranchise, disfranchise v (-ises,
-ising, -ised) deprive (someone) of the right

to vote or of other rights of citizenship
> **disenfranchisement** n (pl -s)
disenfranchised v ▷ disenfranchise
disenfranchisement n ▷ disenfranchise
disenfranchisements n ▷ disenfranchise
disenfranchises v ▷ disenfranchise
disenfranchising v ▷ disenfranchise
disengage v (-gages, -gaging, -gaged) release
from a connection > **disengagement** n (pl -s)
disengaged v ▷ disengage
disengagement n ▷ disengage
disengagements n ▷ disengage
disengages v ▷ disengage
disengaging v ▷ disengage
disentangle v (-tangles, -tangling, -tangled)
release from entanglement or confusion
disentangled v ▷ disentangle
disentangles v ▷ disentangle
disentangling v ▷ disentangle
disfavour n (pl -s) disapproval or dislike
disfavours v ▷ disfavour
disfigure v (-gures, -guring, -gured) spoil the
appearance of > **disfigurement** n (pl -s)
disfigured v ▷ disfigure
disfigurement n ▷ disfigure
disfigurements n ▷ disfigure
disfigures v ▷ disfigure
disfiguring v ▷ disfigure
disfranchise v (-ises, -ising, -ised)
▷ disenfranchise
disfranchised v ▷ disfranchise
disfranchises v ▷ disfranchise
disfranchising v ▷ disfranchise
disgorge v (-gorges, -gorging, -gorged) empty
out, discharge
disgorged v ▷ disgorge
disgorges v ▷ disgorge
disgorging v ▷ disgorge
disgrace n (pl -s) condition of shame, loss of
reputation, or dishonour ▶ v (-graces,
-gracing, -graced) bring shame upon (oneself
or others) > **disgraceful** adj > **disgracefully**
adv
disgraced v ▷ disgrace
disgraceful adj ▷ disgrace
disgracefully adv ▷ disgrace
disgraces n, v ▷ disgrace
disgracing v ▷ disgrace
disgruntled adj sulky or discontented
> **disgruntlement** n
disgruntlement n ▷ disgruntled
disguise v (-guises, -guising, -guised) change
the appearance or manner in order to conceal
the identity of (someone or something)
▶ n (pl -s) mask, costume, or manner that

disguises
disguised v ▷ disguise
disguises v, n ▷ disguise
disguising v ▷ disguise
disgust n (pl -s) great loathing or distaste ▶ v (-s, -ing, -ed) sicken, fill with loathing
disgusted v ▷ disgust
disgusting v ▷ disgust
disgusts v ▷ disgust
dish n (pl -es) shallow container used for holding or serving food
dishabille [diss-a-beel] n (pl -s) ▷ deshabille
dishabilles n ▷ deshabille
dishcloth n (pl -s) cloth for washing dishes
dishcloths n ▷ dishcloth
dishearten v (-s, -ing, -ed) weaken or destroy the hope, courage, or enthusiasm of
disheartened v ▷ dishearten
disheartening v ▷ dishearten
disheartens v ▷ dishearten
dishes n ▷ dish
dishevelled adj (of a person's hair, clothes, or general appearance) disordered and untidy
dishonest adj not honest or fair > **dishonestly** adv > **dishonesty** n (pl -ties)
dishonesties n ▷ dishonest
dishonestly adv ▷ dishonest
dishonesty n ▷ dishonest
dishonour v (-s, -ing, -ed) treat with disrespect ▶ n (pl -s) lack of respect > **dishonourable** adj > **dishonourably** adv
dishonourable adj ▷ dishonour
dishonourably adv ▷ dishonour
dishonoured v ▷ dishonour
dishonouring v ▷ dishonour
dishonours v, n ▷ dishonour
disillusion v (-s, -ing, -ed) destroy the illusions or false ideas of (also **disillusionment**) ▶ n (pl -s) state of being disillusioned
disillusioned v ▷ disillusion
disillusioning v ▷ disillusion
disillusionment n ▷ disillusion
disillusionments n ▷ disillusion
disillusions v, n ▷ disillusion
disincentive n (pl -s) something that acts as a deterrent
disincentives n ▷ disincentive
disinclination n ▷ disinclined
disinclinations n ▷ disinclined
disinclined adj unwilling, reluctant > **disinclination** n (pl -s)
disinfect v (-s, -ing, -ed) rid of harmful germs, chemically > **disinfection** n (pl -s)
disinfectant n (pl -s) substance that destroys harmful germs

disinfectants n ▷ disinfectant
disinfected v ▷ disinfect
disinfecting v ▷ disinfect
disinfection n ▷ disinfect
disinfections n ▷ disinfect
disinfects v ▷ disinfect
disinformation n false information intended to mislead
disingenuous adj not sincere > **disingenuously** adv > **disingenuousness** n
disingenuously adv ▷ disingenuous
disingenuousness n ▷ disingenuous
disinherit v (-s, -ing, -ed) (LAW) deprive (an heir) of inheritance > **disinheritance** n (pl -s)
disinheritance n ▷ disinherit
disinheritances n ▷ disinherit
disinherited v ▷ disinherit
disinheriting v ▷ disinherit
disinherits v ▷ disinherit
disintegrate v (-rates, -rating, -rated) break up > **disintegration** n (pl -s)
disintegrated v ▷ disintegrate
disintegrates v ▷ disintegrate
disintegrating v ▷ disintegrate
disintegration n ▷ disintegrate
disintegrations n ▷ disintegrate
disinter v (-ters, -terring, -terred) dig up
disinterest n ▷ disinterested
disinterested adj free from bias or involvement > **disinterest** n > **disinterestedly** adv > **disinterestedness** n
disinterestedly adv ▷ disinterested
disinterestedness n ▷ disinterested
disinterred v ▷ disinter
disinterring v ▷ disinter
disinters v ▷ disinter
disjointed adj having no coherence, disconnected > **disjointedly** adv
disjointedly adv ▷ disjointed
disk n (pl -s) (COMPUTERS) storage device, consisting of a stack of plates coated with a magnetic layer, which rotates rapidly as a single unit
disks n ▷ disk
dislike v (-likes, -liking, -liked) consider unpleasant or disagreeable ▶ n (pl -s) feeling of not liking something or someone
disliked v ▷ dislike
dislikes v, n ▷ dislike
disliking v ▷ dislike
dislocate v (-cates, -cating, -cated) displace (a bone or joint) from its normal position > **dislocation** n (pl -s)
dislocated v ▷ dislocate
dislocates v ▷ dislocate

dislocating v ▷ dislocate
dislocation n ▷ dislocate
dislocations n ▷ dislocate
dislodge v (-lodges, -lodging, -lodged) remove (something) from a previously fixed position
dislodged v ▷ dislodge
dislodges v ▷ dislodge
dislodging v ▷ dislodge
disloyal adj not loyal, deserting one's allegiance > **disloyalty** n (pl -ties)
disloyalties n ▷ disloyalty
dismal adj gloomy and depressing > **dismally** adv > **dismalness** n
dismally adv ▷ dismal
dismalness n ▷ dismal
dismantle v (-mantles, -mantling, -mantled) take apart piece by piece
dismantled v ▷ dismantle
dismantles v ▷ dismantle
dismantling v ▷ dismantle
dismay v (-s, -ing, -ed) fill with alarm or depression ▶ n (pl -s) alarm mixed with sadness
dismayed v ▷ dismay
dismaying v ▷ dismay
dismays v, n ▷ dismay
dismember v (-s, -ing, -ed) remove the limbs of > **dismemberment** n (pl -s)
dismembered v ▷ dismember
dismembering v ▷ dismember
dismemberment n ▷ dismember
dismemberments n ▷ dismember
dismembers v ▷ dismember
dismiss v (-es, -ing, -ed) remove (an employee) from a job > **dismissal** n (pl -s)
dismissal n ▷ dismiss
dismissals n ▷ dismiss
dismissed v ▷ dismiss
dismisses v ▷ dismiss
dismissing v ▷ dismiss
dismissive adj scornful, contemptuous
dismount v (-s, -ing, -ed) get off a horse or bicycle
dismounted v ▷ dismount
dismounting v ▷ dismount
dismounts v ▷ dismount
disobedience n ▷ disobey
disobedient adj ▷ disobey
disobediently adv ▷ disobey
disobey v (-s, -ing, -ed) neglect or refuse to obey > **disobedient** adj > **disobediently** adv > **disobedience** n
disobeyed v ▷ disobey
disobeying v ▷ disobey
disobeys v ▷ disobey

disobliging adj unwilling to help
disorder n (pl -s) state of untidiness and disorganization
disordered adj untidy
disorderliness n ▷ disorderly
disorderly adj untidy and disorganized > **disorderliness** n
disorders n ▷ disorder
disorganization n ▷ disorganize
disorganizations n ▷ disorganize
disorganize v (-nizes, -nizing, -nized) disrupt the arrangement or system of > **disorganization** n (pl -s)
disorganized v ▷ disorganize
disorganizes v ▷ disorganize
disorganizing v ▷ disorganize
disorientate, disorient v (-tates, -tating, -tated, -s, -ing, -ed) cause (someone) to lose his or her bearings > **disorientation** n (pl -s)
disorientated v ▷ disorientate
disorientates v ▷ disorientate
disorientating v ▷ disorientate
disorientation n ▷ disorientate
disorientations n ▷ disorientate
disoriented v ▷ disorientate
disorienting v ▷ disorientate
disorients v ▷ disorientate
disown v (-s, -ing, -ed) deny any connection with (someone)
disowned v ▷ disown
disowning v ▷ disown
disowns v ▷ disown
disparage v (-rages, -raging, -raged) speak contemptuously of > **disparagement** n (pl -s)
disparaged v ▷ disparage
disparagement n ▷ disparage
disparagements n ▷ disparage
disparages v ▷ disparage
disparaging v ▷ disparage
disparate adj completely different > **disparately** adv > **disparateness** n > **disparity** n (pl -ities)
disparately adv ▷ disparate
disparateness n ▷ disparate
disparities n ▷ disparate
disparity n ▷ disparate
dispassionate adj not influenced by emotion > **dispassionately** adv
dispassionately adv ▷ dispassionate
dispatch v (-es, -ing, -ed) send off to a destination or to perform a task ▶ n (pl -es) official communication or report, sent in haste
dispatched v ▷ dispatch
dispatches v, n ▷ dispatch

dispatching v ▷ dispatch
dispel v (-pels, -pelling, -pelled) destroy or remove
　dispelled v ▷ dispel
　dispelling v ▷ dispel
　dispels v ▷ dispel
　dispensability n ▷ dispensable
dispensable adj not essential > **dispensability** n
　dispensaries n ▷ dispensary
dispensary n (pl -saries) place where medicine is dispensed
dispensation n (pl -s) dispensing
　dispensations n ▷ dispensation
dispense v (-penses, -pensing, -pensed) distribute in portions > **dispenser** n (pl -s)
　dispensed v ▷ dispense
　dispenser n ▷ dispense
　dispensers n ▷ dispense
　dispenses v ▷ dispense
　dispensing v ▷ dispense
　dispersal n ▷ disperse
　dispersals n ▷ disperse
disperse v (-perses, -persing, -persed) scatter over a wide area > **dispersal, dispersion** n (pl -s)
　dispersed v ▷ disperse
　disperses v ▷ disperse
　dispersing v ▷ disperse
　dispersion n ▷ disperse
　dispersions n ▷ disperse
dispirit v (-s, -ing, -ed) make downhearted
　dispirited v ▷ dispirit
　dispiriting v ▷ dispirit
　dispirits v ▷ dispirit
displace v (-places, -placing, -placed) move from the usual location > **displacement** n (pl -s)
　displaced v ▷ displace
　displacement n ▷ displace
　displacements n ▷ displace
　displaces v ▷ displace
　displacing v ▷ displace
display v (-s, -ing, -ed) make visible or noticeable ▶ n (pl -s) displaying
　displayed v ▷ display
　displaying v ▷ display
　displays v, n ▷ display
displease v (-ses, -sing, -sed) annoy or upset > **displeasure** n (pl -s)
　displeased v ▷ displease
　displeases v ▷ displease
　displeasing v ▷ displease
　displeasure n ▷ displease
　displeasures n ▷ displease

disport v (-s, -ing, -ed) indulge oneself in pleasure
　disported v ▷ disport
　disporting v ▷ disport
　disports v ▷ disport
　disposability n ▷ disposable
disposable adj designed to be thrown away after use > **disposability** n
disposal n (pl -s) getting rid of something
　disposals n ▷ disposal
dispose v (-poses, -posing, -posed) place in a certain order
disposed adj willing or eager ▶ v ▷ dispose
　disposes v ▷ dispose
　disposing v ▷ dispose
disposition n (pl -s) person's usual temperament
　dispositions n ▷ disposition
dispossess v (-es, -ing, -ed) (foll. by of) deprive (someone) of (a possession) > **dispossession** n (pl -s)
　dispossessed v ▷ dispossess
　dispossesses v ▷ dispossess
　dispossessing v ▷ dispossess
　dispossession n ▷ dispossess
　dispossessions n ▷ dispossess
disproportion n (pl -s) lack of proportion or equality
disproportionate adj out of proportion > **disproportionately** adv
　disproportionately adv ▷ disproportionate
　disproportions n ▷ disproportion
disprove v (-proves, -proving, -proved) show (an assertion or claim) to be incorrect
　disproved v ▷ disprove
　disproves v ▷ disprove
　disproving v ▷ disprove
dispute n (pl -s) disagreement, argument ▶ v (-putes, -puting, -puted) argue about (something)
　disputed v ▷ dispute
　disputes n, v ▷ dispute
　disputing v ▷ dispute
　disqualification n ▷ disqualify
　disqualifications n ▷ disqualify
　disqualified v ▷ disqualify
　disqualifies v ▷ disqualify
disqualify v (-fies, -fying, -fied) stop (someone) officially from taking part in something for wrongdoing > **disqualification** n (pl -s)
　disqualifying v ▷ disqualify
disquiet n (pl -s) feeling of anxiety ▶ v (-s, -ing, -ed) make (someone) anxious > **disquietude** n (pl -s)

disquieted v ▷ disquiet
disquieting v ▷ disquiet
disquiets v, n ▷ disquiet
disquietude n ▷ disquiet
disquietudes n ▷ disquiet
disregard v (-s, -ing, -ed) give little or no attention to ▶ n (pl -s) lack of attention or respect
disregarded v ▷ disregard
disregarding v ▷ disregard
disregards v, n ▷ disregard
disrepair n (pl -s) condition of being worn out or in poor working order
disrepairs n ▷ disrepair
disreputable adj having or causing a bad reputation > disreputably adv
disreputably adv ▷ disreputable
disrepute n (pl -s) loss or lack of good reputation
disreputes n ▷ disrepute
disrespect n (pl -s) lack of respect
  > disrespectful adj > disrespectfully adv
disrespectful adj ▷ disrespect
disrespectfully adv ▷ disrespect
disrespects n ▷ disrespect
disrobe v (-robes, -robing, -robed) undress
disrobed v ▷ disrobe
disrobes v ▷ disrobe
disrobing v ▷ disrobe
disrupt v (-s, -ing, -ed) interrupt the progress of > disruption n (pl -s) > disruptive adj
disrupted v ▷ disrupt
disrupting v ▷ disrupt
disruption n ▷ disrupt
disruptions n ▷ disrupt
disruptive adj ▷ disrupt
disrupts v ▷ disrupt
dissatisfaction n ▷ dissatisfied
dissatisfactions n ▷ dissatisfied
dissatisfied adj not pleased or contented
  > dissatisfaction n (pl -s)
dissect v (-s, -ing, -ed) cut open (a corpse) to examine it > dissection n (pl -s)
dissected v ▷ dissect
dissecting v ▷ dissect
dissection n ▷ dissect
dissections n ▷ dissect
dissects v ▷ dissect
dissemble v (-bles, -bling, -bled) conceal one's real motives or emotions by pretence
dissembled v ▷ dissemble
dissembles v ▷ dissemble
dissembling v ▷ dissemble
disseminate v (-nates, -nating, -nated) spread (information) > dissemination n (pl -s)

disseminated v ▷ disseminate
disseminates v ▷ disseminate
disseminating v ▷ disseminate
dissemination n ▷ disseminate
disseminations n ▷ disseminate
dissension n ▷ dissent
dissensions n ▷ dissent
dissent v (-s, -ing, -ed) disagree ▶ n (pl -s) disagreement > dissension n (pl -s)
  > dissenter n (pl -s)
dissented v ▷ dissent
dissenter n ▷ dissent
dissenters n ▷ dissent
dissenting v ▷ dissent
dissents v ▷ dissent
dissertation n (pl -s) written thesis, usu. required for a higher university degree
dissertations n ▷ dissertation
disservice n (pl -s) harmful action
disservices n ▷ disservice
dissidence n ▷ dissident
dissidences n ▷ dissident
dissident n (pl -s) person who disagrees with and criticizes the government
  ▶ adj disagreeing with the government
  > dissidence n (pl -s)
dissidents n ▷ dissident
dissimilar adj not alike, different
  > dissimilarity n (pl -ities)
dissimilarities n ▷ dissimilar
dissimilarity n ▷ dissimilar
dissimulate v (-lates, -lating, -lated) conceal one's real feelings by pretence
  > dissimulation n (pl -s)
dissimulated v ▷ dissimulate
dissimulates v ▷ dissimulate
dissimulating v ▷ dissimulate
dissimulation n ▷ dissimulate
dissimulations n ▷ dissimulate
dissipate v (-pates, -pating, -pated) waste or squander > dissipation n (pl -s)
dissipated adj showing signs of overindulgence in alcohol and other physical pleasures ▶ v ▷ dissipate
dissipates v ▷ dissipate
dissipating v ▷ dissipate
dissipation n ▷ dissipate
dissipations n ▷ dissipate
dissociate v (-ciates, -ciating, -ciated) regard or treat as separate > dissociation n (pl -s)
dissociated v ▷ dissociate
dissociates v ▷ dissociate
dissociating v ▷ dissociate
dissociation n ▷ dissociate
dissociations n ▷ dissociate

dissolute *adj* leading an immoral life
> **dissolutely** *adv* > **dissoluteness** *n*
  dissolutely *adv* ▷ **dissolute**
  dissoluteness *n* ▷ **dissolute**
dissolution *n* (*pl* -**s**) official breaking up of an organization or institution, such as Parliament
  dissolutions *n* ▷ **dissolution**
dissolve *v* (-**solves**, -**solving**, -**solved**) (cause to) become liquid
  dissolved *v* ▷ **dissolve**
  dissolves *v* ▷ **dissolve**
  dissolving *v* ▷ **dissolve**
dissonance *n* (*pl* -**s**) lack of agreement or harmony > **dissonant** *adj*
  dissonances *n* ▷ **dissonance**
  dissonant *adj* ▷ **dissonance**
dissuade *v* (-**suades**, -**suading**, -**suaded**) deter (someone) by persuasion from doing something > **dissuasion** *n* (*pl* -**s**)
  dissuaded *v* ▷ **dissuade**
  dissuades *v* ▷ **dissuade**
  dissuading *v* ▷ **dissuade**
  dissuasion *n* ▷ **dissuade**
  dissuasions *n* ▷ **dissuade**
distaff *n* (*pl* -**s**) rod on which wool etc. is wound for spinning
  distaffs *n* ▷ **distaff**
distance *n* (*pl* -**s**) space between two points
  distances *n* ▷ **distance**
distant *adj* far apart > **distantly** *adv*
  distantly *adv* ▷ **distant**
distaste *n* (*pl* -**s**) dislike, disgust
distasteful *adj* unpleasant, offensive
> **distastefulness** *n*
  distastefulness *n* ▷ **distasteful**
  distastes *n* ▷ **distaste**
distemper[1] *n* (*pl* -**s**) highly contagious viral disease of dogs
distemper[2] *n* (*pl* -**s**) paint mixed with water, glue, etc., used for painting walls
  distempers *n* ▷ **distemper**[1, 2]
distend *v* (-**s**, -**ing**, -**ed**) (of part of the body) swell > **distension** *n* (*pl* -**s**)
  distended *v* ▷ **distend**
  distending *v* ▷ **distend**
  distends *v* ▷ **distend**
  distension *n* ▷ **distend**
  distensions *n* ▷ **distend**
distil *v* (-**tils**, -**tilling**, -**tilled**) subject to or obtain by distillation
  distillate *n* ▷ **distillation**
  distillates *n* ▷ **distillation**
distillation *n* (*pl* -**s**) process of evaporating a liquid and condensing its vapour (*also*

distillate) (*pl* -**s**)
  distillations *n* ▷ **distillation**
  distilled *v* ▷ **distil**
distiller *n* (*pl* -**s**) person or company that makes strong alcoholic drink, esp. whisky
  distilleries *n* ▷ **distillery**
  distillers *n* ▷ **distiller**
distillery *n* (*pl* -**leries**) place where a strong alcoholic drink, esp. whisky, is made
  distilling *v* ▷ **distil**
  distils *v* ▷ **distil**
distinct *adj* (-**er**, -**est**) not the same > **distinctly** *adv* > **distinctness** *n* (*pl* -**es**)
  distincter *adj* ▷ **distinct**
  distinctest *adj* ▷ **distinct**
distinction *n* (*pl* -**s**) act of distinguishing
  distinctions *n* ▷ **distinction**
distinctive *adj* easily recognizable
> **distinctively** *adv* > **distinctiveness** *n*
  distinctively *adv* ▷ **distinctive**
  distinctiveness *n* ▷ **distinctive**
  distinctly *adv* ▷ **distinct**
  distinctness *n* ▷ **distinct**
  distinctnesses *n* ▷ **distinct**
distinguish *v* (-**es**, -**ing**, -**ed**) (*usu.* foll. by **between**) make, show, or recognize a difference (between) > **distinguishable** *adj*
  distinguishable *adj* ▷ **distinguish**
distinguished *adj* dignified in appearance ▶ *v* ▷ **distinguish**
  distinguishes *v* ▷ **distinguish**
  distinguishing *v* ▷ **distinguish**
distort *v* (-**s**, -**ing**, -**ed**) misrepresent (the truth or facts) > **distortion** *n* (*pl* -**s**)
  distorted *v* ▷ **distort**
  distorting *v* ▷ **distort**
  distortion *n* ▷ **distort**
  distortions *n* ▷ **distort**
  distorts *v* ▷ **distort**
distract *v* (-**s**, -**ing**, -**ed**) draw the attention of (a person) away from something
> **distraction** *n* (*pl* -**s**)
distracted *adj* unable to concentrate, preoccupied ▶ *v* ▷ **distract** > **distractedly** *adv*
  distractedly *adv* ▷ **distracted**
  distracting *v* ▷ **distract**
  distraction *n* ▷ **distract**
  distractions *n* ▷ **distract**
  distracts *v* ▷ **distract**
distrait [diss-**tray**] *adj* absent-minded or preoccupied
distraught [diss-**trawt**] *adj* extremely anxious or agitated
distress *n* (*pl* -**es**) extreme unhappiness ▶ *v* (-**es**, -**ing**, -**ed**) upset badly > **distressing** *adj*

> **distressingly** adv

distressed adj extremely upset ▶ v ▷ **distress**
distresses n, v ▷ **distress**
distressing v, adj ▷ **distress**
distressingly adv ▷ **distress**

distribute v (-butes, -buting, -buted) hand out or deliver > **distributive** adj > **distributively** adv
distributed v ▷ **distribute**
distributes v ▷ **distribute**
distributing v ▷ **distribute**

distribution n (pl -s) distributing
distributions n ▷ **distribution**
distributive adj ▷ **distribute**
distributively adv ▷ **distribute**

distributor n (pl -s) wholesaler who distributes goods to retailers in a specific area
distributors n ▷ **distributor**

district n (pl -s) area of land regarded as an administrative or geographical unit
districts n ▷ **district**

distrust v (-s, -ing, -ed) regard as untrustworthy ▶ n (pl -s) feeling of suspicion or doubt > **distrustful** adj
distrusted v ▷ **distrust**
distrustful adj ▷ **distrust**
distrusting v ▷ **distrust**
distrusts v, n ▷ **distrust**

disturb v (-s, -ing, -ed) intrude on
> **disturbance** n (pl -s) > **disturbing** adj
> **disturbingly** adv
disturbance n ▷ **disturb**
disturbances n ▷ **disturb**

disturbed adj (PSYCHIATRY) emotionally upset or maladjusted ▶ v ▷ **disturb**
disturbing v, adj ▷ **disturb**
disturbingly adv ▷ **disturb**
disturbs v ▷ **disturb**

disunite v (-nites, -niting, -nited) cause disagreement among > **disunity** n (pl -ities)
disunited v ▷ **disunite**
disunites v ▷ **disunite**
disunities n ▷ **disunite**
disuniting v ▷ **disunite**
disunity n ▷ **disunite**

disuse n (pl -s) state of being no longer used
> **disused** adj
disused adj ▷ **disuse**
disuses n ▷ **disuse**

ditch n (pl -es) narrow channel dug in the earth for drainage or irrigation ▶ v (-es, -ing, -ed) (Slang) abandon
ditched v ▷ **ditch**
ditches n, v ▷ **ditch**

ditching v ▷ **ditch**

dither v (-s, -ing, -ed) be uncertain or indecisive ▶ n (pl -s) state of indecision or agitation > **ditherer** n (pl -s) > **dithery** adj
> **ditheriness** n
dithered v ▷ **dither**
ditheriness n ▷ **dither**
dithering v ▷ **dither**
dithers v, n ▷ **dither**
dithery adj ▷ **dither**
ditties n ▷ **ditty**

ditto n (pl -tos) the same ▶ adv in the same way
dittos n ▷ **ditto**

ditty n (pl -ties) short simple poem or song

diuretic [die-yoor-et-ik] n (pl -s) drug that increases the flow of urine
diuretics n ▷ **diuretic**

diurnal [die-urn-al] adj happening during the day or daily > **diurnally** adv
diurnally adv ▷ **diurnal**

diva n (pl -s) distinguished female singer

divan n (pl -s) low backless bed
divans n ▷ **divan**
divas n ▷ **diva**

dive v (dives, diving, dived) plunge headfirst into water (foll. by in or into) ▶ n (pl -s) diving
dived v ▷ **dive**

diver n (pl -s) person who works or explores underwater

diverge v (-verges, -verging, -verged) separate and go in different directions > **divergence** n (pl -s) > **divergent** adj
diverged v ▷ **diverge**
divergence n ▷ **diverge**
divergences n ▷ **diverge**
divergent adj ▷ **diverge**
diverges v ▷ **diverge**
diverging v ▷ **diverge**

divers adj (Old-fashioned) various ▶ n ▷ **diver**

diverse adj having variety, assorted
> **diversely** adv > **diversify** v (-fies, -fying, -fied) > **diversification** n (pl -s)
diversely adv ▷ **diverse**
diversification n ▷ **diverse**
diversifications n ▷ **diverse**
diversified v ▷ **diverse**
diversifies v ▷ **diverse**
diversify v ▷ **diverse**
diversifying v ▷ **diverse**

diversion n (pl -s) official detour used by traffic when a main route is closed > **diversionary** adj
diversionary adj ▷ **diversion**
diversions n ▷ **diversion**
diversities n ▷ **diversity**

diversity n (pl **-ties**) quality of being different or varied

divert v (**-s, -ing, -ed**) change the direction of
　diverted v ▷ divert
　diverting v ▷ divert
　diverts v ▷ divert
　dives v, n ▷ dive

divest v (**-s, -ing, -ed**) strip (of clothes)
　divested v ▷ divest
　divesting v ▷ divest
　divests v ▷ divest

divide v (**-vides, -viding, -vided**) separate into parts ▶ n (pl **-s**) division, split
　divided v ▷ divide

dividend n (pl **-s**) sum of money representing part of the profit made, paid by a company to its shareholders
　dividends n ▷ dividend

divider n (pl **-s**) screen used to divide a room into separate areas ▶ pl compasses with two pointed arms, used for measuring or dividing lines
　dividers n ▷ divider
　divides v, n ▷ divide
　dividing v ▷ divide

divination n (pl **-s**) art of discovering future events, as though by supernatural powers
　divinations n ▷ divine

divine adj (**-r, -st**) of God or a god ▶ v (**-nes, -ning, -ned**) discover (something) by intuition or guessing ▷ **divinely** adv
　divined v ▷ divine
　divinely adv ▷ divine
　diviner adj ▷ divine
　divines v ▷ divine
　divinest adj ▷ divine
　diving v ▷ dive
　divining v ▷ divine
　divinities n ▷ divinity

divinity n study of religion (pl **-ties**)
　divisibility n ▷ divisible
　divisible adj ▷ divisibility n

division n (pl **-s**) dividing, sharing out

divisional adj of a division in an organization ▷ **divisionally** adv
　divisionally adv ▷ divisional
　divisions n ▷ division

divisive adj tending to cause disagreement ▷ **divisively** adv ▷ **divisiveness** n
　divisively adv ▷ divisive
　divisiveness n ▷ divisive

divisor n (pl **-s**) number to be divided into another number
　divisors n ▷ divisor

divorce n (pl **-s**) legal ending of a marriage ▶ v (**-ces, -cing, -ced**) legally end one's marriage (to)
　divorcé n ▷ divorcée
　divorced v ▷ divorce

divorcée, masc **divorcé** n (pl **-s**) person who is divorced
　divorcées n ▷ divorcée
　divorces n, v ▷ divorce
　divorcés n ▷ divorcée
　divorcing v ▷ divorce

divulge v (**-ges, -ging, -ged**) make known, disclose ▷ **divulgence** n (pl **-s**)
　divulged v ▷ divulge
　divulgence n ▷ divulge
　divulgences n ▷ divulge
　divulges v ▷ divulge
　divulging v ▷ divulge
　dizzied v ▷ dizzy
　dizzier adj ▷ dizzy
　dizzies v ▷ dizzy
　dizziest adj ▷ dizzy
　dizzily adv ▷ dizzy
　dizziness n ▷ dizzy

dizzy adj (**-zier, -ziest**) having or causing a whirling sensation ▶ v (**-zies, -zying, -zied**) make dizzy ▷ **dizzily** adv ▷ **dizziness** n
　dizzying v ▷ dizzy

do v (**does, doing, did, done**) perform or complete (a deed or action) ▶ n (pl **dos, do's**) (Informal) party, celebration

docile adj (**-r, -st**) (of a person or animal) easily controlled ▷ **docilely** adv ▷ **docility** n (pl **-ties**)
　docilely adv ▷ docile
　dociler adj ▷ docile
　docilest adj ▷ docile
　docilities n ▷ docile
　docility n ▷ docile

dock¹ n (pl **-s**) enclosed area of water where ships are loaded, unloaded, or repaired ▶ v (**-s, -ing, -ed**) bring or be brought into dock

dock² v (**docks, docking, docked**) deduct money from (a person's wages)

dock³ n (pl **-s**) enclosed space in a court of law where the accused person sits or stands

dock⁴ n (pl **-s**) weed with broad leaves
　docked v ▷ dock

docker n (pl **-s**) (BRIT) person employed to load and unload ships
　dockers n ▷ docker

docket n (pl **dockets**) label on a package or other delivery, stating contents, delivery instructions, etc.
　dockets n ▷ docket
　docking v ▷ dock
　docks n ▷ dock¹, ³, ⁴ ▶ v ▷ dock¹, ²

dockyard n (pl -s) place where ships are built or repaired
   dockyards n ▷ dockyard
doctor n (pl -s) person licensed to practise medicine ▶ v (-s, -ing, -ed) alter in order to deceive > **doctoral** adj
   doctoral adj ▷ doctor
doctorate n (pl -s) highest academic degree in any field of knowledge
   doctorates n ▷ doctorate
   doctored v ▷ doctor
   doctoring v ▷ doctor
   doctors n, v ▷ doctor
doctrinaire adj stubbornly insistent on the application of a theory without regard to practicality
doctrinal adj of doctrines > **doctrinally** adv
   doctrinally adv ▷ doctrinal
doctrine n (pl -s) body of teachings of a religious, political, or philosophical group
   doctrines n ▷ doctrine
document n (pl -s) piece of paper providing an official record of something ▶ v (-s, -ing, -ed) record or report (something) in detail > **documentation** n (pl -s)
   documentaries n ▷ documentary
documentary n (pl -ries) film or television programme presenting the facts about a particular subject ▶ adj (of evidence) based on documents
   documentation n ▷ document
   documentations n ▷ document
   documented v ▷ document
   documenting v ▷ document
   documents n, v ▷ document
dodder v (-s, -ing, -ed) move unsteadily > **doddery** adj (-rier, -riest)
   doddered v ▷ dodder
   dodderier adj ▷ dodder
   dodderiest adj ▷ dodder
   doddering v ▷ dodder
   dodders v ▷ dodder
   doddery adj ▷ dodder
dodecagon [doe-deck-a-gon] n (pl -s) geometric figure with twelve sides
   dodecagons n ▷ dodecagon
dodge v (dodges, dodging, dodged) avoid (a blow, being seen, etc.) by moving suddenly ▶ n (pl -s) cunning or deceitful trick
   dodged v ▷ dodge
dodger n (pl -s) person who evades a responsibility or duty
   dodgers n ▷ dodger
   dodges v, n ▷ dodge
   dodgier adj ▷ dodgy

   dodgiest adj ▷ dodgy
   dodging v ▷ dodge
dodgy adj (-gier, -giest) (Informal) dangerous, risky
dodo n (pl -s, -es) large flightless extinct bird
   dodoes n ▷ dodo
   dodos n ▷ dodo
doe n (pl -s) female deer, hare, or rabbit
   does n ▷ doe ▶ v ▷ do
doesn't does not
doff v (-s, -ing, -ed) take off or lift (one's hat) in polite greeting
   doffed v ▷ doff
   doffing v ▷ doff
   doffs v ▷ doff
dog n (pl -s) domesticated four-legged mammal of many different breeds ▶ v (dogs, dogging, dogged) follow (someone) closely
dogcart n (pl -s) light horse-drawn two-wheeled cart
   dogcarts n ▷ dogcart
doge [doje] n (pl -s) (formerly) chief magistrate of Venice or Genoa
dogeared adj (of a book) having pages folded down at the corner
   doges n ▷ doge
dogfight n (pl -s) close-quarters combat between fighter aircraft
   dogfights n ▷ dogfight
dogfish n (pl -es) small shark
   dogfishes n ▷ dogfish
dogged [dog-gid] adj obstinately determined ▶ v ▷ dog > **doggedly** adv > **doggedness** n (pl -es)
   doggedly adv ▷ dogged
   doggedness n ▷ dogged
   doggednesses n ▷ dogged
doggerel n (pl -s) poorly written poetry, usu. comic
   doggerels n ▷ doggerel
   doggie n ▷ doggy
   doggies n ▷ doggy
   dogging v ▷ dog
doggo adv (Informal) in hiding and keeping quiet
doggy, doggie n (pl -gies) child's word for a dog
doghouse n (pl -s) (US) kennel
   doghouses n ▷ doghouse
dogleg n (pl -s) sharp bend
   doglegs n ▷ dogleg
dogma n (pl -s) doctrine or system of doctrines proclaimed by authority as true > **dogmatic** adj habitually stating one's opinions forcefully or arrogantly > **dogmatically** adv

> **dogmatism** n

dogmas n ▷ **dogma**

dogs n, v ▷ **dog**

dogsbodies n ▷ **dogsbody**

dogsbody n (pl -**bodies**) (Informal) person who carries out boring tasks for others

> **doh** interj. Doh is a sound people make when things go wrong. Doh scores 7 points.

doilies n ▷ **doily**

doily n (pl -**lies**) decorative lacy paper mat, laid on a plate

doing v ▷ **do**

doldrums pl n depressed state of mind

dole n (pl -**s**) (BRIT, AUST & NZ) (Informal) money received from the state while unemployed ▶ v (**doles, doling, doled**) (foll. by **out**) distribute in small quantities

doled v ▷ **dole**

doleful adj dreary, unhappy > **dolefully** adv > **dolefulness** n

dolefully adv ▷ **doleful**

dolefulness n ▷ **doleful**

doles v, n ▷ **dole**

doling v ▷ **dole**

doll n (pl -**s**) small model of a human being, used as a toy

dollar n (pl -**s**) standard monetary unit of many countries

dollars n ▷ **dollar**

dollies n ▷ **dolly**

dollop n (pl -**s**) (Informal) lump (of food)

dollops n ▷ **dollop**

dolls n ▷ **doll**

dolly n (pl -**lies**) child's word for a doll

dolmen n (pl -**s**) prehistoric monument consisting of a horizontal stone supported by vertical stones

dolmens n ▷ **dolmen**

dolomite n (pl -**s**) mineral consisting of calcium magnesium carbonate

dolomites n ▷ **dolomite**

dolorous adj sad, mournful > **dolorously** adv

dolorously adv ▷ **dolorous**

dolphin n (pl -**s**) sea mammal of the whale family, with a beaklike snout

dolphinaria n ▷ **dolphinarium**

dolphinarium n (pl -**ariums, -aria**) aquarium for dolphins

dolphinariums n ▷ **dolphinarium**

dolphins n ▷ **dolphin**

dolt n (pl -**s**) stupid person > **doltish** adj > **doltishness** n

doltish adj ▷ **dolt**

doltishness n ▷ **dolt**

dolts n ▷ **dolt**

domain n (pl -**s**) field of knowledge or activity

domains n ▷ **domain**

dome n (pl -**s**) rounded roof built on a circular base > **domed** adj

domes n ▷ **dome**

domestic adj of one's own country or a specific country ▶ n (pl -**s**) person whose job is to do housework in someone else's house > **domestically** adv > **domesticity** n

domestically adv ▷ **domestic**

domesticate v (-**cates, -cating, -cated**) bring or keep (a wild animal or plant) under control or cultivation > **domestication** n (pl -**s**)

domesticated v ▷ **domesticate**

domesticates v ▷ **domesticate**

domesticating v ▷ **domesticate**

domestication n ▷ **domesticate**

domestications n ▷ **domesticate**

domesticity n ▷ **domestic**

domestics n ▷ **domestic**

domicile [dom-miss-ile] n (pl -**s**) place where one lives

domiciles n ▷ **domicile**

dominance n ▷ **dominant**

dominances n ▷ **dominant**

dominant adj having authority or influence > **dominance** n

dominate v (-**nates, -nating, -nated**) control or govern > **domination** n (pl -**s**)

dominated v ▷ **dominate**

dominates v ▷ **dominate**

dominating v ▷ **dominate**

domination n ▷ **dominate**

dominations n ▷ **dominate**

domineering adj forceful and arrogant

dominion n (pl -**s**) control or authority

dominions n ▷ **dominion**

domino n (pl -**noes**) small rectangular block marked with dots, used in dominoes ▶ pl game in which dominoes with matching halves are laid together

dominoes n ▷ **domino**

don[1] v (**dons, donning, donned**) put on (clothing)

don[2] n (pl -**s**) (BRIT) member of the teaching staff at a university or college

donate v (-**nates, -nating, -nated**) give, esp. to a charity or organization

donated v ▷ **donate**

donates v ▷ **donate**

donating v ▷ **donate**

donation n (pl -**s**) donating

donations n ▷ **donation**

done v ▷ **do**

donga [dong-ga] n (pl **-s**) (S AFR, AUST & NZ) steep-sided gully created by soil erosion
  dongas n ▷ **donga**

donkey n (pl **-s**) long-eared member of the horse family
  donkeys n ▷ **donkey**

donkeywork n (pl **-s**) tedious hard work
  donkeyworks n ▷ **donkeywork**
  donned v ▷ **don¹**
  donning v ▷ **don¹**

donnish adj serious and academic
  > **donnishness** n (pl **-es**)
  donnishness n ▷ **donnish**
  donnishnesses n ▷ **donnish**

donor n (pl **-s**) (MED) person who gives blood or organs for use in the treatment of another person
  donors n ▷ **donor**
  dons v ▷ **don¹** ▶ n ▷ **don²**

doodle v (**-dles, -dling, -dled**) scribble or draw aimlessly ▶ n (pl **-s**) shape or picture drawn aimlessly
  doodled v ▷ **doodle**
  doodles v, n ▷ **doodle**
  doodling v ▷ **doodle**

doom n (pl **-s**) death or a terrible fate ▶ v (**-s, -ing, -ed**) destine or condemn to death or a terrible fate
  doomed v ▷ **doom**
  dooming v ▷ **doom**
  dooms n, v ▷ **doom**

doomsday n (pl **-s**) (CHRISTIANITY) day on which the Last Judgment will occur
  doomsdays n ▷ **doomsday**

door n (pl **-s**) hinged or sliding panel for closing the entrance to a building, room, etc.
  doormat n (pl **-s**) mat for wiping dirt from shoes before going indoors
  doormats n ▷ **doormat**
  doors n ▷ **door**

doorway n (pl **-s**) opening into a building or room
  doorways n ▷ **doorway**

dope n (pl **-s**) (Slang) illegal drug, usu. cannabis ▶ v (**dopes, doping, doped**) give a drug to, esp. in order to improve performance in a race
  doped v ▷ **dope**
  dopes n, v ▷ **dope**

dopey, dopy (**dopier, dopiest**) adj half-asleep, drowsy
  dopier adj ▷ **dopey**
  dopiest adj ▷ **dopey**
  doping v ▷ **dope**
  dopy adj ▷ **dopey**
  dorb n ▷ **dorba**

dorba n (pl **-s**) (AUST) (Slang) stupid, inept, or clumsy person (also **dorb**) (pl **-s**)
  dorbas n ▷ **dorba**
  dorbs n ▷ **dorba**
  dories n ▷ **dory**

dork n (pl **-s**) (Slang) stupid person
  dorks n ▷ **dork**
  dormancy n ▷ **dormant**

dormant adj temporarily quiet, inactive, or not being used > **dormancy** n

dormer n (pl **-s**) window that sticks out from a sloping roof
  dormers n ▷ **dormer**
  dormice n ▷ **dormouse**
  dormitories n ▷ **dormitory**

dormitory n (pl **-ries**) large room, esp. at a school, containing several beds

dormouse n (pl **-mice**) small mouselike rodent with a furry tail

dorp n (pl **-s**) (S AFR) small town
  dorps n ▷ **dorp**

dorsal adj of or on the back

dory n (pl **-ries**) spiny-finned edible sea fish
  dos n ▷ **do**
  do's n ▷ **do**

dosage n (pl **-s**) size of a dose
  dosages n ▷ **dosage**

dose n (pl **-s**) specific quantity of a medicine taken at one time ▶ v (**doses, dosing, dosed**) give a dose to
  dosed v ▷ **dose**
  doses n, v ▷ **dose**
  dosing v ▷ **dose**

doss v (**-es, -ing, -ed**) (Slang) sleep in an uncomfortable place
  dossed v ▷ **doss**
  dosses v ▷ **doss**

dosshouse n (pl **-s**) (BRIT & S AFR) (Slang) cheap lodging house for homeless people
  dosshouses n ▷ **dosshouse**

dossier [doss-ee-ay] n (pl **-s**) collection of documents about a subject or person
  dossiers n ▷ **dossier**
  dossing v ▷ **doss**

dot n (pl **-s**) small round mark ▶ v (**dots, dotting, dotted**) mark with a dot

dotage n (pl **-s**) weakness as a result of old age
  dotages n ▷ **dotage**

dotcom n (pl **-s**) company that does most of its business on the Internet
  dotcoms n ▷ **dotcom**

dote v (**dotes, doting, doted**) love to an excessive degree
  doted v ▷ **dote**
  dotes v ▷ **dote**

doting v ▷ dote

dots n, v ▷ dot

dotted v ▷ dot

dottier adj ▷ dotty

dottiest adj ▷ dotty

dottily adv ▷ dotty

dottiness n ▷ dotty

dottinesses n ▷ dotty

doting v ▷ dot

dotty adj (-ttier, -ttiest) (Slang) rather eccentric > dottily adv > dottiness n (pl -es)

double adj as much again in number, amount, size, etc. ▶ adv twice over ▶ n (pl -s) twice the number, amount, size, etc. ▶ pl game between two pairs of players ▶ v (-bles, -bling, -bled) make or become twice as much or as many > doubly adv

doubled v ▷ double

doubles n, v ▷ double

doublet [dub-lit] n (pl -s) (HIST) man's close-fitting jacket, with or without sleeves

doublets n ▷ doublet

doubling v ▷ double

doubloon n (pl -s) former Spanish gold coin

doubloons n ▷ doubloon

doubly adv ▷ double

doubt n (pl -s) uncertainty about the truth, facts, or existence of something ▶ v (-s, -ing, -ed) question the truth of > doubter n (pl -s)

doubted v ▷ doubt

doubter n ▷ doubt

doubters n ▷ doubt

doubtful adj unlikely > doubtfully adv

doubtfully adv ▷ doubtful

doubting v ▷ doubt

doubtless adv probably or certainly > doubtlessly adv

doubtlessly adv ▷ doubtless

doubts n, v ▷ doubt

douche [doosh] n (pl -s) (instrument for applying) a stream of water directed onto or into the body for cleansing or medical purposes ▶ v (-es, -ing, -ed) cleanse or treat by means of a douche

douched v ▷ douche

douches n, v ▷ douche

douching v ▷ douche

dough n (pl -s) thick mixture of flour and water or milk, used for making bread etc.

doughnut n (pl -s) small cake of sweetened dough fried in deep fat

doughnuts n ▷ doughnut

doughs n ▷ dough

doughtier adj ▷ doughty

doughtiest adj ▷ doughty

doughtily adv ▷ doughty

doughtiness n ▷ doughty

doughtinesses n ▷ doughty

doughty [dowt-ee] adj (-tier, -tiest) (Old-fashioned) brave and determined > doughtily adv > doughtiness n (pl -es)

dour [doo-er] adj (-er, -est) sullen and unfriendly > dourly adv > dourness n (pl -es)

dourer adj ▷ dour

dourest adj ▷ dour

dourly adv ▷ dour

dourness n ▷ dour

dournesses n ▷ dour

douse [rhymes with mouse] v (-ses, -sing, -sed) drench with water or other liquid

doused v ▷ douse

douses v ▷ douse

dousing v ▷ douse

dove n (pl -s) bird with a heavy body, small head, and short legs

dovecot n ▷ dovecote

dovecote, dovecot n (pl -s) structure for housing pigeons

dovecotes n ▷ dovecote

dovecots n ▷ dovecote

doves n ▷ dove

dovetail n (pl -s) joint containing wedge-shaped tenons ▶ v (-s, -ing, -ed) fit together neatly

dovetailed v ▷ dovetail

dovetailing v ▷ dovetail

dovetails v ▷ dovetail

dow n (dows). A dow is an Arab ship. Dow scores 7 points.

dowager n (pl -s) widow possessing property or a title obtained from her husband

dowagers n ▷ dowager

dowdier adj ▷ dowdy

dowdiest adj ▷ dowdy

dowdily adv ▷ dowdy

dowdiness n ▷ dowdy

dowdy adj (-dier, -diest) dull and old-fashioned > dowdily adv > dowdiness n

dowel n (pl -s) wooden or metal peg that fits into two corresponding holes to join two adjacent parts

dowels n ▷ dowel

dower n (pl -s) life interest in a part of her husband's estate allotted to a widow by law

dowers n ▷ dower

down¹ prep, adv indicating movement to or position in a lower place ▶ adv indicating completion of an action, lessening of intensity, etc. ▶ adj depressed, unhappy ▶ v (-s, -ing, -ed) (Informal) drink quickly

down² n (pl -s) soft fine feathers ▷ **downiness** n
▷ **downy** adj (-nier, -niest)

downbeat adj (Informal) gloomy

downcast adj sad, dejected
downed v ▷ **down¹**

downfall n (pl -s) (cause of) a sudden loss of
position or reputation
downfalls n ▷ **downfall**

downgrade v (-grades, -grading, -graded)
reduce in importance or value
downgraded v ▷ **downgrade**
downgrades v ▷ **downgrade**
downgrading v ▷ **downgrade**

downhearted adj sad and discouraged
▷ **downheartedly** adv
downheartedly adv ▷ **downhearted**

downhill adj going or sloping down ▶ adv
towards the bottom of a hill
downier adj ▷ **down²**
downiest adj ▷ **down²**
downiness n ▷ **down²**
downing v ▷ **down¹**

download v (-s, -ing, -ed) transfer (data) from
the memory of one computer to that of
another, especially over the Internet ▶ n (pl -s)
file transferred in such a way
downloaded v ▷ **download**
downloading v ▷ **download**
downloads v, n ▷ **download**

downpour n (pl -s) heavy fall of rain
downpours n ▷ **downpour**

downright adj, adv extreme(ly)

downs pl n low grassy hills, esp. in S England
▶ v ▷ **down¹** ▶ n ▷ **down²**

downstairs adv to or on a lower floor ▶ n lower
or ground floor

downtrodden adj oppressed and lacking the
will to resist

downward adj, adv (descending) from a higher
to a lower level, condition, or position

downwards adv from a higher to a lower level,
condition, or position
downy adj ▷ **down²**
dowries n ▷ **dowry**

dowry n (pl -ries) property brought by a
woman to her husband at marriage

dowse [rhymes with **cows**] v (-ses, -sing, -sed)
search for underground water or minerals
using a divining rod
dowsed v ▷ **dowse**
dowses v ▷ **dowse**
dowsing v ▷ **dowse**
doxologies n ▷ **doxology**

doxology n (pl -gies) short hymn of praise
to God

doy n (**doys**). Doy is a dialect word for a
beloved person. Doy scores 7 points.

doyen [doy-en] n (pl -s) senior member of a
group, profession, or society ▷ **doyenne**
[doy-en] ▶ n fem
doyenne n ▷ **doyen**
doyennes n ▷ **doyen**
doyens n ▷ **doyen**

doze v (**dozes, dozing, dozed**) sleep lightly or
briefly ▶ n (pl -s) short sleep
dozed v ▷ **doze**

dozen adj, n (pl -s) twelve ▷ **dozenth** adj
dozens n ▷ **dozen**
dozenth adj ▷ **dozen**
dozes v, n ▷ **doze**
dozier adj ▷ **dozy**
doziest adj ▷ **dozy**
dozily adv ▷ **dozy**
doziness n ▷ **dozy**
dozing v ▷ **doze**

dozy adj (**dozier, doziest**) feeling sleepy
▷ **dozily** adv ▷ **doziness** adv

drab adj (**drabber, drabbest**) dull and dreary
▷ **drably** adv ▷ **drabness** n (pl -es)
drabber adj ▷ **drab**
drabbest adj ▷ **drab**
drably adv ▷ **drab**
drabness n ▷ **drab**
drabnesses n ▷ **drab**

drachm [dram] n (pl -s) (BRIT) one eighth of a
fluid ounce

drachma n (pl -mas, -mae) former monetary
unit of Greece
drachmae n ▷ **drachma**
drachmas n ▷ **drachma**
drachms n ▷ **drachm**

draconian adj severe, harsh

draft n (pl -s) plan, sketch, or drawing of
something (US & AUST) ▶ v (-s, -ing, -ed) draw
up an outline or plan of
drafted v ▷ **draft**
drafting v ▷ **draft**
drafts n, v ▷ **draft**

drag v (-s, -gging, -gged) pull with force, esp.
along the ground (foll. by **on** or **out**) ▶ n (pl -s)
person or thing that slows up progress
dragged v ▷ **drag**
dragging v ▷ **drag**

dragnet n (pl -s) net used to scour the bottom
of a pond or river to search for something
dragnets n ▷ **dragnet**

dragon n (pl -s) mythical fire-breathing
monster like a huge lizard
dragonflies n ▷ **dragonfly**

dragonfly n (pl -**flies**) brightly coloured insect

with a long slender body and two pairs of
wings
dragons n ▷ dragon
dragoon n (pl -s) heavily armed cavalryman ▶ v
(-s, -ing, -ed) coerce, force
dragooned v ▷ dragoon
dragooning v ▷ dragoon
dragoons n, v ▷ dragoon
drags v, n ▷ drag
drain n (pl -s) pipe or channel that carries off
water or sewage ▶ v (-s, -ing, -ed) draw off or
remove liquid from
drainage n (pl -s) system of drains
drainages n ▷ drainage
drained v ▷ drain
draining v ▷ drain
drains n, v ▷ drain
drake n (pl -s) male duck
drakes n ▷ drake
dram n (pl -s) small amount of a strong
alcoholic drink, esp. whisky
drama n (pl -s) serious play for theatre,
television, or radio
dramas n ▷ drama
dramatic adj of or like drama > **dramatically**
adv
dramatically adv ▷ dramatic
dramatist n (pl -s) person who writes plays
dramatists n ▷ dramatist
dramatization n ▷ dramatize
dramatizations n ▷ dramatize
dramatize v (-tizes, -tizing, -tized) rewrite (a
book) in the form of a play > **dramatization**
n (pl -s)
dramatized v ▷ dramatize
dramatizes v ▷ dramatize
dramatizing v ▷ dramatize
drams n ▷ dram
drank v ▷ drink
drape v (drapes, draping, draped) cover with
material, usu. in folds ▶ n (pl -s) (AUST, US &
CANADIAN) piece of cloth hung at a window or
opening as a screen
draped v ▷ drape
draper n (pl -s) (BRIT) person who sells fabrics
and sewing materials
draperies n ▷ drapery
drapers n ▷ draper
drapery n (pl -peries) fabric or clothing
arranged and draped
drapes v, n ▷ drape
draping v ▷ drape
drastic adj strong and severe > **drastically** adv
drastically adv ▷ drastic
draught n (pl -s) current of cold air, esp. in an

enclosed space ▶ pl game for two players
using a chessboard and twelve draughts
each ▶ adj (of an animal) used for pulling
heavy loads
draughtier adj ▷ draughty
draughtiest adj ▷ draughty
draughtiness n ▷ draughty
draughts n ▷ draught
draughtsman n (pl -men) person
employed to prepare detailed scale
drawings of machinery, buildings, etc.
> **draughtsmanship** n
draughtsmanship n ▷ draughtsman
draughtsmen n ▷ draughtsman
draughty adj (-tier, -tiest) exposed to draughts
of air > **draughtiness** n
draw v (draws, drawing, drew, drawn) sketch
(a figure, picture, etc.) with a pencil or pen ▶ n
(pl -s) raffle or lottery
drawback n (pl -s) disadvantage
drawbacks n ▷ drawback
drawbridge n (pl -s) bridge that may be raised
to prevent access or to enable vessels to pass
drawbridges n ▷ drawbridge
drawer n (pl -s) sliding box-shaped part of a
piece of furniture, used for storage ▶ pl (Old-
fashioned) undergarment worn on the lower
part of the body
drawers n ▷ drawer
drawing n (pl -s) picture or plan made by
means of lines on a surface ▶ v ▷ draw
drawl v (-s, -ing, -ed) speak slowly, with
long vowel sounds ▶ n (pl drawls) drawling
manner of speech
drawled v ▷ drawl
drawling v ▷ drawl
drawls v ▷ drawl
drawls n ▷ drawl
drawn v ▷ draw ▶ adj haggard, tired, or tense
in appearance
draws n, v ▷ draw
drawstring n (pl -s) cord run through a hem
around an opening, so that when it is pulled
tighter, the opening closes
drawstrings n ▷ drawstring
dray n (pl -s) low cart used for carrying heavy
loads
drays n ▷ dray
dread v (-s, -ing, -ed) anticipate with
apprehension or fear ▶ n (pl -s) great fear
dreaded v ▷ dread
dreadful adj very disagreeable or shocking
> **dreadfully** adv
dreadfully adv ▷ dreadful
dreading v ▷ dread

dreadlocks pl n hair worn in the Rastafarian style of tightly twisted strands
dreads v, n ▷ **dread**
dream n (pl -s) imagined series of events experienced in the mind while asleep (*Informal*) ▶ v (-s, -ing, -ed or -t) see imaginary pictures in the mind while asleep (*often foll. by of or about*) (*foll. by of*) ▶ adj ideal
> **dreamer** n (pl -s)
dreamed v ▷ **dream**
dreamer n ▷ **dream**
dreamers n ▷ **dream**
dreamier adj ▷ **dreamy**
dreamiest adj ▷ **dreamy**
dreamily adv ▷ **dreamy**
dreaminess n ▷ **dreamy**
dreaminesses n ▷ **dreamy**
dreaming v ▷ **dream**
dreams n, v ▷ **dream**
dreamt v ▷ **dream**
dreamy adj (-mier, -miest) vague or impractical > **dreamily** adv > **dreaminess** n (pl -es)
drearier adj ▷ **dreary**
dreariest adj ▷ **dreary**
drearily adv ▷ **dreary**
dreariness n ▷ **dreary**
dreary adj (drearier, dreariest) dull, boring > **drearily** adv > **dreariness** n
dredge¹ v (dredges, dredging, dredged) clear or search (a river bed or harbour) by removing silt or mud
dredge² v (dredges, dredging, dredged) sprinkle (food) with flour etc.
dredged v ▷ **dredge¹, ²**
dredger n (pl -s) boat fitted with machinery for dredging
dredgers n ▷ **dredger**
dredges v ▷ **dredge¹, ²**
dredging v ▷ **dredge¹, ²**
dregs pl n solid particles that settle at the bottom of some liquids
drench v (-es, -ing, -ed) make completely wet
drenched v ▷ **drench**
drenches v ▷ **drench**
drenching v ▷ **drench**
dress n (pl -es) one-piece garment for a woman or girl, consisting of a skirt and bodice and sometimes sleeves ▶ v (-es, -ing, -ed) put clothes on
dressage [dress-ahzh] n (pl -s) training of a horse to perform manoeuvres in response to the rider's body signals
dressages n ▷ **dressage**
dressed v ▷ **dress**

dresser¹ n (pl -s) piece of furniture with shelves and with cupboards, for storing or displaying dishes
dresser² n (pl -s) (THEATRE) person employed to assist actors with their costumes
dressers n ▷ **dresser¹, ²**
dresses n, v ▷ **dress**
dressier adj ▷ **dressy**
dressiest adj ▷ **dressy**
dressiness n ▷ **dressy**
dressinesses n ▷ **dressy**
dressing n (pl -s) sauce for salad ▶ v ▷ **dress**
dressings n ▷ **dressing**
dressmaker n (pl -s) person who makes women's clothes > **dressmaking** n
dressmakers n ▷ **dressmaker**
dressmaking n ▷ **dressmaker**
dressy adj (-ssier, -ssiest) (of clothes) elegant > **dressiness** n (pl -es)
drew v ▷ **draw**
drey n (pl -s) squirrel's nest
dreys n ▷ **drey**
dribble v (-les, -ling, -led) (allow to) flow in drops ▶ n (pl -s) small quantity of liquid falling in drops > **dribbler** n (pl -s)
dribbled v ▷ **dribble**
dribbler n ▷ **dribble**
dribblers n ▷ **dribble**
dribbles v, n ▷ **dribble**
dribbling v ▷ **dribble**
dried v ▷ **dry**
drier¹ adj ▷ **dry**
drier² n (pl -s) ▷ **dryer**
driers n ▷ **drier²**
dries v ▷ **dry**
driest adj ▷ **dry**
drift v (-s, -ing, -ed) be carried along by currents of air or water ▶ n (pl -s) something piled up by the wind or current, such as a snowdrift
drifted v ▷ **drift**
drifter n (pl -s) person who moves aimlessly from place to place or job to job
drifters n ▷ **drifter**
drifting v ▷ **drift**
drifts v, n ▷ **drift**
driftwood n (pl -s) wood floating on or washed ashore by the sea
driftwoods n ▷ **driftwood**
drill¹ n (pl -s) tool or machine for boring holes ▶ v (-s, -ing, -ed) bore a hole in (something) with or as if with a drill
drill² n (pl -s) machine for sowing seed in rows
drill³ n (pl -s) hard-wearing cotton cloth
drilled v ▷ **drill¹**

drilling v ▷ **drill¹**

drills n ▷ **drill¹, ², ³** ▶ v ▷ **drill¹**

drily adv ▷ **dry**

drink v (**drinks, drinking, drank, drunk**) swallow (a liquid) ▶ n (pl **-s**) (portion of) a liquid suitable for drinking > **drinkable** adj > **drinker** n (pl **-s**)

drinkable adj ▷ **drink**

drinker n ▷ **drink**

drinkers n ▷ **drink**

drinking v ▷ **drink**

drinks v, n ▷ **drink**

drip v (**drips, dripping, dripped**) (let) fall in drops ▶ n (pl **-s**) falling of drops of liquid

dripped v ▷ **drip**

dripping n (pl **-s**) fat that comes from meat while it is being roasted or fried ▶ v ▷ **drip**

drippings n ▷ **dripping**

drips v, n ▷ **drip**

drive v (**drives, driving, drove, driven**) guide the movement of (a vehicle) ▶ n (pl **-s**) journey by car, van, etc.; path for vehicles (also **driveway**) (pl **-s**)

drivel n (pl **-s**) foolish talk ▶ v (**-els, -elling, -elled**) speak foolishly

drivelled v ▷ **drivel**

drivelling v ▷ **drivel**

drivels v, n ▷ **drivel**

driven v ▷ **drive**

driver n (pl **-s**) person who drives a vehicle

drivers n ▷ **driver**

drives v, n ▷ **drive**

driveway n ▷ **drive**

driveways n ▷ **drive**

driving v ▷ **drive**

drizzle n (pl **-s**) very light rain ▶ v (**-zles, -zling, -zled**) rain lightly > **drizzly** adj

drizzled v ▷ **drizzle**

drizzles n, v ▷ **drizzle**

drizzling v ▷ **drizzle**

drizzly adj ▷ **drizzle**

droll adj (**-er, -est**) quaintly amusing > **drolly** adv > **drollery** n (pl **-ries**) > **drollness** n (pl **-es**)

droller adj ▷ **droll**

drolleries n ▷ **droll**

drollery n ▷ **droll**

drollest adj ▷ **droll**

drollness n ▷ **droll**

drollnesses n ▷ **droll**

drolly adv ▷ **droll**

dromedaries n ▷ **dromedary**

dromedary [drom-mid-er-ee] n (pl **-daries**) camel with a single hump

drone¹ n (pl **-s**) male bee

drone² v (**drones, droned, droning**) ▶ n (pl **-s**) (make) a monotonous low dull sound

droned v ▷ **drone²**

drones n ▷ **drone¹, ²** ▶ v ▷ **drone²**

drongo n (pl **-gos**) tropical songbird with a glossy black plumage, a forked tail, and a stout bill

drongos n ▷ **drongo**

droning v ▷ **drone²**

drool v (**-s, -ing, -ed**) (foll. by **over**) show excessive enthusiasm (for)

drooled v ▷ **drool**

drooling v ▷ **drool**

drools v ▷ **drool**

droop v (**-s, -ing, -ed**) hang downwards loosely > **droopy** adj (**-pier, -piest**)

drooped v ▷ **droop**

droopier adj ▷ **droop**

droopiest adj ▷ **droop**

drooping v ▷ **droop**

droops v ▷ **droop**

droopy adj ▷ **droop**

drop v (**-s, -pping, -pped**) (allow to) fall vertically ▶ n (pl **-s**) small quantity of liquid forming a round shape ▶ pl liquid medication applied in small drops > **droplet** n (pl **-s**)

droplet n ▷ **drop**

droplets n ▷ **drop**

dropout n (pl **-s**) person who rejects conventional society

dropouts n ▷ **dropout**

dropped v ▷ **drop**

dropping v ▷ **drop**

droppings pl n faeces of certain animals, such as rabbits or birds

drops v, n ▷ **drop**

dropsical adj ▷ **dropsy**

dropsies n ▷ **dropsy**

dropsy n (pl **-sies**) illness in which watery fluid collects in the body > **dropsical** adj

dross n (pl **-es**) scum formed on the surfaces of molten metals

drosses n ▷ **dross**

drought n (pl **-s**) prolonged shortage of rainfall

droughts n ▷ **drought**

drove¹ v ▷ **drive**

drove² n (pl **-s**) very large group, esp. of people

drover n (pl **-s**) person who drives sheep or cattle

drovers n ▷ **drover**

droves n ▷ **drove²**

drown v (**-s, -ing, -ed**) die or kill by immersion in liquid

drowned v ▷ **drown**

drowning v ▷ **drown**

drowns v ▷ **drown**

drowse v (-ses, -sing, -sed) be sleepy, dull, or sluggish ▷ **drowsy** adj (-sier, -siest) ▷ **drowsily** adv ▷ **drowsiness** n (pl -es)

drowsed v ▷ drowse

drowses v ▷ drowse

drowsier adj ▷ drowse

drowsiest adj ▷ drowse

drowsily adv ▷ drowse

drowsiness n ▷ drowse

drowsinesses n ▷ drowse

drowsing v ▷ drowse

drowsy adj ▷ drowse

drubbing n (pl -s) utter defeat in a contest etc.

drubbings n ▷ drubbing

drudge n (pl -s) person who works hard at uninteresting tasks ▷ **drudgery** n (pl -eries)

drudgeries n ▷ drudge

drudgery n ▷ drudge

drudges n ▷ drudge

drug n (pl -s) substance used in the treatment or prevention of disease ▶ v (drugs, drugging, drugged) give a drug to (a person or animal) to cause sleepiness or unconsciousness

drugged v ▷ drug

drugging v ▷ drug

drugs v, n ▷ drug

drugstore n (pl -s) (US) pharmacy where a wide range of goods are available

drugstores n ▷ drugstore

druid n (pl -s) member of an ancient order of Celtic priests ▷ **druidic, druidical** adj

druidic adj ▷ druid

druidical adj ▷ druid

druids adj ▷ druid

drum n (pl -s) percussion instrument sounded by striking a membrane stretched across the opening of a hollow cylinder ▶ v (drums, drumming, drummed) play (music) on a drum

drummed v ▷ drum

drummer n (pl -s) person who plays a drum or drums

drummers n ▷ drummer

drumming v ▷ drum

drums n, v ▷ drum

drumstick n (pl -s) stick used for playing a drum

drumsticks n ▷ drumstick

drunk v ▷ drink ▶ adj (-er, -est) intoxicated with alcohol to the extent of losing control over normal functions ▶ n (pl -s) person who is drunk or who frequently gets drunk

drunkard n (pl -s) person who frequently gets drunk

drunkards n ▷ drunkard

drunken adj drunk or frequently drunk ▷ **drunkenly** adv ▷ **drunkenness** n (pl -es)

drunkenly adv ▷ drunken

drunkenness n ▷ drunken

drunkennesses n ▷ drunken

drunker adj ▷ drunk

drunkest adj ▷ drunk

drunks n ▷ drunk

dry adj (drier, driest or dryer, dryest) lacking moisture ▶ v (dries, drying, dried) make or become dry ▷ **drily, dryly** adv ▷ **dryness** n (pl -es)

dryad n (pl -s) wood nymph

dryads n ▷ dryad

dryer, drier n (pl -s) apparatus for removing moisture

dryer adj ▷ dry

dryers n ▷ dryer

dryest adj ▷ dry

drying v ▷ dry

dryly adv ▷ dry

dryness n ▷ dry

drynesses n ▷ dry

> **dso** n (dsos). Dso is one of several spelling for a Tibetan animal bred from yaks and cattle. The other forms are **dzo, zho** and **zo**, and it's worth remembering all of them. Dso scores 4 points.

dual adj having two parts, functions, or aspects ▷ **duality** n (pl -ities) ▷ **dually** adv

dualities n ▷ dual

duality n ▷ dual

dually adv ▷ dual

dub[1] v (dubs, dubbing, dubbed) give (a person or place) a name or nickname

dub[2] v (dubs, dubbing, dubbed) provide (a film) with a new soundtrack, esp. in a different language

dubbed v ▷ dub[1, 2]

dubbin n (pl -s) (BRIT) thick grease applied to leather to soften and waterproof it

dubbing v ▷ dub[1, 2]

dubbins n ▷ dubbin

dubieties n ▷ dubious

dubiety n ▷ dubious

dubious [dew-bee-uss] adj feeling or causing doubt ▷ **dubiously** adv ▷ **dubiousness** n ▷ **dubiety** [dew-by-it-ee] n (pl -ities)

dubiously adv ▷ dubious

dubiousness n ▷ dubious

dubs v ▷ dub[1, 2]

ducal [duke-al] adj of a duke

ducat [duck-it] n (pl -s) former European gold or silver coin

ducats n ▷ ducat

duchess n (pl -es) woman who holds the rank of duke

duchesse n (pl -s) (NZ) dressing table with a mirror

duchesses n ▷ duchess, duchesse

duchies n ▷ duchy

duchy n (pl duchies) territory of a duke or duchess

duck¹ n (pl -s) water bird with short legs, webbed feet, and a broad blunt bill

duck² v (-s, -ing, -ed) move (the head or body) quickly downwards, to avoid being seen or to dodge a blow

ducked v ▷ duck²

ducking v ▷ duck²

duckling n (pl -s) baby duck

ducklings n ▷ duckling

ducks n ▷ duck¹, v ▷ duck²

duct n (pl -s) tube, pipe, or channel through which liquid or gas is conveyed

ductile adj (of a metal) able to be shaped into sheets or wires

ducts n ▷ duct

dud (Informal) n (pl -s) ineffectual person or thing ▸ adj bad or useless

dude n (pl -s) (US) (Informal) man

dudes n ▷ dude

dudgeon n (pl -s) anger, resentment

dudgeons n ▷ dudgeon

duds n ▷ dud

due adj expected or scheduled to be present or arrive ▸ n (pl -s) something that is owed or required ▸ pl charges for membership of a club or organization ▸ adv directly or exactly

duel n (pl -s) formal fight with deadly weapons between two people, to settle a quarrel ▸ v (-s, -lling, -lled) fight in a duel > duellist n (pl -s)

duelled v ▷ duel

duelling v ▷ duel

duellist n ▷ duel

duellists n ▷ duel

duels n, v ▷ duel

dues n ▷ due

duet n (pl -s) piece of music for two performers

duets n ▷ duet

duff adj (-er, -est) (CHIEFLY BRIT) broken or useless

duffel, duffle n (pl -s) heavy woollen cloth

duffels n ▷ duffel

duffer n (pl -s) (Informal) dull or incompetent person ▸ adj ▷ duff

duffers n ▷ duffer

duffest adj ▷ duff

duffle n ▷ duffel

duffles n ▷ duffel

dug¹ v ▷ dig

dug² n (pl -s) teat or udder

dugite [doo-gyte] n (pl -s) medium-sized Australian venomous snake

dugites n ▷ dugite

dugong n (pl -s) whalelike mammal of tropical waters

dugongs n ▷ dugong

dugout n (pl -s) (BRIT) (at a sports ground) covered bench where managers and substitutes sit

dugouts n ▷ dugout

dugs n ▷ dug²

duke n (pl -s) nobleman of the highest rank > dukedom n (pl -s)

dukedom n ▷ duke

dukedoms n ▷ duke

dukes n ▷ duke

dulcet [dull-sit] adj (of a sound) soothing or pleasant

dulcimer n (pl -s) tuned percussion instrument consisting of a set of strings stretched over a sounding board and struck with hammers

dulcimers n ▷ dulcimer

dull adj (-er, -est) not interesting ▸ v (-s, -ing, -ed) make or become dull > dullness n (pl -es) > dully adv

dullard n (pl -s) dull or stupid person

dullards n ▷ dullard

dulled v ▷ dull

duller adj ▷ dull

dullest adj ▷ dull

dulling v ▷ dull

dullness n ▷ dull

dullnesses n ▷ dull

dulls v ▷ dull

dully adv ▷ dull

duly adv in a proper manner

dumb adj (dumber, dumbest) lacking the power to speak > dumbly adv > dumbness n

dumbbell n (pl -s) short bar with a heavy ball or disc at each end, used for physical exercise

dumbbells n ▷ dumbbell

dumber adj ▷ dumb

dumbest adj ▷ dumb

dumbfounded adj speechless with astonishment

dumbly adv ▷ dumb

dumbness n ▷ dumb

dumdum n (pl -s) soft-nosed bullet that expands on impact and causes serious wounds

dumdums n ▷ dumdum

dummies n ▷ dummy

dummy n (pl **-mies**) figure representing the human form, used for displaying clothes etc. ▶ adj imitation, substitute

dump v (**-s, -ing, -ed**) drop or let fall in a careless manner ▶ n (pl **-s**) place where waste materials are left
  dumped v ▷ dump
  dumpier adj ▷ dumpy
  dumpiest adj ▷ dumpy
  dumpily adv ▷ dumpy
  dumpiness n ▷ dumpy
  dumping v ▷ dump

dumpling n (pl **-s**) small ball of dough cooked and served with stew
  dumplings n ▷ dumpling
  dumps v, n ▷ dump

dumpy adj (**dumpier, dumpiest**) short and plump > **dumpily** adv > **dumpiness** n

dun (**dunner, dunnest**) adj brownish-grey

dunce n (pl **-s**) person who is stupid or slow to learn
  dunces n ▷ dunce

dunderhead n (pl **-s**) slow-witted person
  dunderheads n ▷ dunderhead

dune n (pl **-s**) mound or ridge of drifted sand
  dunes n ▷ dune

dung n (pl **-s**) faeces from animals such as cattle

dungarees pl n trousers with a bib attached

dungeon n (pl **-s**) underground prison cell
  dungeons n ▷ dungeon
  dungs n ▷ dung

dunk v (**-s, -ing, -ed**) dip (a biscuit or bread) in a drink or soup before eating it
  dunked v ▷ dunk
  dunking v ▷ dunk
  dunks v ▷ dunk
  dunner adj ▷ dun
  dunnest adj ▷ dun
  dunnies n ▷ dunny

dunny n (pl **-nies**) (AUST & OLD-FASHIONED NZ) (Informal) toilet

duo n (pl **-s**) pair of performers
  duodena n ▷ duodenum
  duodenal adj ▷ duodenum

duodenum [dew-oh-**deen**-um] n (pl **-na, -nums**) first part of the small intestine, just below the stomach > **duodenal** adj
  duodenums n ▷ duodenum
  duos n ▷ duo

dupe v (**dupes, duping, duped**) deceive or cheat ▶ n (pl **-s**) person who is easily deceived
  duped v ▷ dupe
  dupes v, n ▷ dupe
  duping v ▷ dupe

duple adj (MUSIC) having two beats in a bar

duplex n (pl **-es**) (CHIEFLY US) apartment on two floors
  duplexes n ▷ duplex

duplicate adj copied exactly from an original ▶ n (pl **-s**) exact copy ▶ v (**-cates, -cating, -cated**) make an exact copy of > **duplication** n (pl **-s**) > **duplicator** n (pl **-s**)
  duplicated v ▷ duplicate
  duplicates n, v ▷ duplicate
  duplicating v ▷ duplicate
  duplication n ▷ duplicate
  duplications n ▷ duplicate
  duplicator n ▷ duplicate
  duplicators n ▷ duplicate
  duplicities n ▷ duplicity

duplicity n (pl **-ities**) deceitful behaviour
  durability n ▷ durable

durable adj long-lasting > **durability** n > **durably** adv

durables pl n goods that require infrequent replacement
  durably adv ▷ durable

duration n (pl **-s**) length of time that something lasts
  durations n ▷ duration

duress n compulsion by use of force or threats

during prep throughout or within the limit of (a period of time)

dusk n (pl **-s**) time just before nightfall, when it is almost dark
  duskier adj ▷ dusky
  duskiest adj ▷ dusky
  duskily adv ▷ dusky
  duskiness n ▷ dusky
  dusks n ▷ dusk

dusky adj (**duskier, duskiest**) dark in colour > **duskiness** n

dust n (pl **-s**) small dry particles of earth, sand, or dirt ▶ v (**-s, -ing, -ed**) remove dust from (furniture) by wiping

dustbin n (pl **-s**) large container for household rubbish
  dustbins n ▷ dustbin
  dusted v ▷ dust

duster n (pl **-s**) cloth used for dusting
  dusters n ▷ duster
  dustier adj ▷ dusty
  dustiest adj ▷ dusty
  dusting v ▷ dust

dustman n (pl **-men**) (BRIT) man whose job is to collect household rubbish
  dustmen n ▷ dustman

dustpan n (pl **-s**) short-handled shovel into which dust is swept from floors

dustpans n ▷ **dustpan**

dusts n, v ▷ **dust**

dusty adj (**dustier, dustiest**) covered with dust

dutiability n ▷ **dutiable**

dutiable adj (of goods) requiring payment of duty > **dutiability** n

duties n ▷ **duty**

dutiful adj doing what is expected > **dutifully** adv

dutifully adv ▷ **dutiful**

duty n (pl **-ties**) work or a task performed as part of one's job

duvet [**doo-vay**] n (pl **-s**) kind of quilt used in bed instead of a top sheet and blankets

duvets n ▷ **duvet**

> **dux** n (**duces**). A dux is the top pupil in a school. This is a handy word to have ready if someone else has played a word containing X. Dux scores 11 points.

dwang n (pl **-s**) (NZ & S AFR) short piece of wood inserted in a timber-framed wall

dwangs n ▷ **dwang**

dwarf n (pl **dwarfs, dwarves**) person who is smaller than average ▶ adj (of an animal or plant) much smaller than the usual size for the species ▶ v (**dwarfs, dwarfing** or **dwarfed**) cause (someone or something) to seem small by being much larger

dwarfed v ▷ **dwarf**

dwarfing v ▷ **dwarf**

dwarfs n, v ▷ **dwarf**

dwarves n ▷ **dwarf**

dwell v (**dwells, dwelling, dwelt** or **dwelled**) live, reside

dwelled v ▷ **dwell**

dweller n (pl **-s**) person who lives in a specified place

dwellers n ▷ **dweller**

dwelling n (pl **-s**) place of residence
▶ v ▷ **dwell**

dwellings n ▷ **dwelling**

dwells v ▷ **dwell**

dwelt v ▷ **dwell**

dwindle v (**-dles, -dling, -dled**) grow less in size, strength, or number

dwindled v ▷ **dwindle**

dwindles v ▷ **dwindle**

dwindling v ▷ **dwindle**

dye n (pl **-s**) colouring substance ▶ v (**dyes, dyeing, dyed**) colour (hair or fabric) by applying a dye > **dyer** n (pl **-s**)

dyed v ▷ **dye**

dyeing v ▷ **dye**

dyer n ▷ **dye**

dyers n ▷ **dye**

dyes n, v ▷ **dye**

dying v ▷ **die¹**

dyke n (pl **-s**) wall built to prevent flooding

dykes n ▷ **dyke**

dynamic adj full of energy, ambition, and new ideas > **dynamically** adv

dynamically adv ▷ **dynamic**

dynamics n branch of mechanics concerned with the forces that change or produce the motions of bodies ▶ pl forces that produce change in a system

dynamism n great energy and enthusiasm

dynamite n (pl **-s**) explosive made of nitroglycerine ▶ v (**-mites, -miting, -mited**) blow (something) up with dynamite

dynamited v ▷ **dynamite**

dynamites n, v ▷ **dynamite**

dynamiting v ▷ **dynamite**

dynamo n (pl **-s**) device for converting mechanical energy into electrical energy

dynamos n ▷ **dynamo**

dynastic adj ▷ **dynasty**

dynasties n ▷ **dynasty**

dynasty n (pl **-ties**) sequence of hereditary rulers > **dynastic** adj

dysenteries n ▷ **dysentery**

dysentery n (pl **-teries**) infection of the intestine causing severe diarrhoea

dysfunction n (pl **-s**) (MED) disturbance or abnormality in the function of an organ or part > **dysfunctional** adj
> **dysfunctionally** adv

dysfunctional adj ▷ **dysfunction**

dysfunctionally adv ▷ **dysfunction**

dysfunctions n ▷ **dysfunction**

dyslexia n (pl **-s**) disorder causing impaired ability to read > **dyslexic** adj

dyslexias n ▷ **dyslexia**

dyslexic adj ▷ **dyslexia**

dysmenorrhoea n (pl **-s**) painful menstruation

dysmenorrhoeas n ▷ **dysmenorrhoea**

dyspepsia n (pl **-s**) indigestion
> **dyspeptic** adj

dyspepsias n ▷ **dyspepsia**

dyspeptic adj ▷ **dyspepsia**

dystrophic adj ▷ **dystrophy**

dystrophies n ▷ **dystrophy**

dystrophy [**diss-trof-fee**] n (pl **-phies**) wasting disorder > **dystrophic** adj

dzho *n* (**dzhos**). A dzho is one of several ways of spelling the name of a Tibetan animal bred from yaks and cattle. This spelling is less useful than the others (**dso, dzo, zho** and **zo**) because it has four letters rather than two or three. It is, however, a very useful word to know when someone else has played zho, as you can use D to hook another word onto zho, or just to take advantage of the Z already on the board. Dzho scores 17 points.

dzo *n* (**dzos**). Dzo is one of several spelling for a Tibetan animal bred from yaks and cattle. The other forms are **dso, dzho, zho** and **zo,** and it's worth remembering all of them. Dzo scores 13 points.

Ee

E is the most common tile in the game and, while it is only worth one point, as the most frequent letter in English it is extremely useful. Many words contain two or more Es, so, unlike many tiles, it's good to have several Es on your rack. Keep in mind three-letter words formed by two Es either side of a consonant, like **eye**, **ewe** and **eve** (6 points each), and **eke** (7). E can also be handy for getting rid of double consonants: think of words like **egg** or **ebb** (each 5 points). E also combines well with K: as well as **eke**, we have **elk** and **eek** (both 7), and **ewk** (10). If you have an X on your rack, E offers you all kinds of options: just think of all the words that begin with ex-, like **exhaust** (17), which will give you a 50-point bonus if you use all of your tiles to form it. And don't forget **ex** itself, a nice little word that earns you 9 points.

ea n (**eas**). Ea is a dialect word for a river. This word won't earn you many points, but it does provide many opportunities to play longer words that form ea in the process. Ea scores 2 points.

each adj, pron every (one) taken separately

eager adj (**-er**, **-est**) showing or feeling great desire, keen > **eagerly** adv > **eagerness** n (pl **-es**)
  eagerer adj ▷ **eager**
  eagerest adj ▷ **eager**
  eagerly adv ▷ **eager**
  eagerness n ▷ **eager**
  eagernesses n ▷ **eager**

eagle n (pl **-s**) large bird of prey with keen eyesight
  eagles n ▷ **eagle**

eaglet n (pl **-s**) young eagle
  eaglets n ▷ **eaglet**

ear¹ n (pl **-s**) organ of hearing, esp. the external part of it

ear² n (pl **-s**) head of corn

earache n (pl **-s**) pain in the ear
  earaches n ▷ **earache**

earbash v (**-es**, **-ing**, **-ed**) (AUST & NZ) (Informal) talk incessantly > **earbashing** n (pl **-s**)
  earbashed v ▷ **earbash**
  earbashes n ▷ **earbash**
  earbashing v, n ▷ **earbash**
  earbashings n ▷ **earbash**

eardrum n (pl **-s**) thin piece of skin inside the ear which enables one to hear sounds
  eardrums n ▷ **eardrum**

earl n (pl **-s**) British nobleman ranking next below a marquess > **earldom** n (pl **-s**)
  earldom n ▷ **earl**
  earldoms n ▷ **earl**

earlier adj, adv ▷ **early**
earliest adj, adv ▷ **early**
earls n ▷ **earl**

early adj, adv (**-ier**, **-iest**) before the expected or usual time

earmark v (**-s**, **-ing**, **-ed**) set (something) aside for a specific purpose
  earmarked v ▷ **earmark**
  earmarking v ▷ **earmark**
  earmarks v ▷ **earmark**

earn v (**-s**, **-ing**, **-ed**) obtain by work or merit
  earned v ▷ **earn**

earnest¹ adj serious and sincere > **earnestly** adv

earnest² n (pl **-s**) part payment given in advance, esp. to confirm a contract
  earnests n ▷ **earnest²**
  earning v ▷ **earn**

earnings pl n money earned
  earns v ▷ **earn**

earphone n (pl **-s**) receiver for a radio etc., held to or put in the ear
  earphones n ▷ **earphone**

earring n (pl **-s**) ornament for the lobe of the ear
  earrings n ▷ **earring**
  ears n ▷ **ear¹, ²**

earshot n (pl **-s**) hearing range
  earshots n ▷ **earshot**

earth n (pl **-s**) land, the ground ▶ v (**-s**, **-ing**, **-ed**) connect (a circuit) to earth

earthed v ▷ **earth**

earthen adj made of baked clay or earth

earthenware n (pl **-s**) pottery made of baked clay

earthenwares n ▷ **earthenwares**

earthier adj ▷ **earthy**

earthiest adj ▷ **earthy**

earthing v ▷ **earth**

earthly adj conceivable or possible

earthquake n (pl **-s**) violent vibration of the earth's surface

earthquakes n ▷ **earthquake**

earths n, v ▷ **earth**

earthwork n (pl **-s**) fortification made of earth

earthworks n ▷ **earthwork**

earthworm n (pl **-s**) worm which burrows in the soil

earthworms n ▷ **earthworm**

earthy adj (**-thier, -thiest**) coarse or crude

earwig n (pl **-s**) small insect with a pincer-like tail

earwigs n ▷ **earwig**

ease n (pl **-ses**) freedom from difficulty, discomfort, or worry ▶ v (**-ses, -sing, -sed**) give bodily or mental ease to

eased v ▷ **ease**

easel n (pl **-s**) frame to support an artist's canvas or a blackboard

easels n ▷ **easel**

eases n, v ▷ **ease**

easier adj ▷ **easy**

easily adv ▷ **easy**

easiest adj ▷ **easy**

easiness n ▷ **easy**

easinesses n ▷ **easy**

easing v ▷ **ease**

east n (pl **-s**) (direction towards) the part of the horizon where the sun rises ▶ adj to or in the east ▶ adv in, to, or towards the east > **easterly** adj > **eastern** adj > **eastward** adj, adv > **eastwards** adv

easterly adj ▷ **east**

eastern adj ▷ **east**

easts n ▷ **east**

eastward adj, adv ▷ **east**

eastwards adv ▷ **east**

easy adj (**-ier, -iest**) not needing much work or effort > **easily** adv > **easiness** n (pl **-s**)

eat v (**eats, eating, ate, eaten**) take (food) into the mouth and swallow it

eatable adj fit or suitable for eating

eaten v ▷ **eat**

eating v ▷ **eat**

eats v ▷ **eat**

eaves pl n overhanging edges of a roof

eavesdrop v (**-s, -pping, -pped**) listen secretly to a private conversation > **eavesdropper** n (pl **-s**) > **eavesdropping** n (pl **-s**)

eavesdropped v ▷ **eavesdrop**

eavesdropper n ▷ **eavesdrop**

eavesdroppers n ▷ **eavesdrop**

eavesdropping v, n ▷ **eavesdrop**

eavesdroppings n ▷ **eavesdrop**

eavesdrops v ▷ **eavesdrop**

ebb v (**-s, -ing, -ed**) (of tide water) flow back ▶ n (pl **-s**) flowing back of the tide

ebbed v ▷ **ebb**

ebbing v ▷ **ebb**

ebbs v, n ▷ **ebb**

ebonies n ▷ **ebony**

ebony n (pl **-ies**) hard black wood ▶ adj deep black

ebullience n ▷ **ebullient**

ebulliences n ▷ **ebullient**

ebullient adj full of enthusiasm or excitement > **ebullience** n (pl **-s**)

eccentric adj odd or unconventional ▶ n (pl **-s**) eccentric person > **eccentrically** adv > **eccentricity** n (pl **-ies**)

eccentrically adv ▷ **eccentric**

eccentricities n ▷ **eccentric**

eccentricity n ▷ **eccentric**

eccentrics n ▷ **eccentric**

ecclesiastic n (pl **-s**) member of the clergy ▶ adj (also **ecclesiastical**) of the Christian Church or clergy

ecclesiastical adj ▷ **ecclesiastic**

ecclesiastics n ▷ **ecclesiastic**

> **ech** v (**echs, eching, eched**). Ech is an old word that Shakespeare uses, and means **eke**. It's a good one to have ready if you have C and H but no obvious place to play them. Ech scores 8 points.

echelon [esh-a-lon] n (pl **-s**) level of power or responsibility

echelons n ▷ **echelon**

echidna [ik-kid-na] n (pl **-nas, -nae**) [-nee] Australian spiny egg-laying mammal

echidnae n ▷ **echidna**

echidnas n ▷ **echidna**

echo n (pl **-es**) repetition of sounds by reflection of sound waves off a surface ▶ v (**-es, -ing, -ed**) repeat or be repeated as an echo

echoed v ▷ **echo**

echoes v, n ▷ **echo**

echoing v ▷ **echo**

éclair n (pl **-s**) finger-shaped pastry filled with

cream and covered with chocolate
éclairs n ▷ éclair
éclat [ake-lah] n brilliant success
eclectic adj selecting from various styles, ideas, or sources ▷ **eclecticism** n (pl -s)
  eclecticism n ▷ eclectic
  eclecticisms n ▷ eclectic
eclipse n (pl -es) temporary obscuring of one star or planet by another ▶ v (-ses, -sing, -sed) surpass or outclass
  eclipsed v ▷ eclipse
  eclipses v ▷ eclipse
  eclipsing v ▷ eclipse
ecliptic n (pl -s) apparent path of the sun
  ecliptics n ▷ ecliptic
ecological adj of ecology > **ecologically** adv
  ecologically adv ▷ ecological
  ecologist n ▷ ecology
  ecologists n ▷ ecology
ecology n study of the relationships between living things and their environment > **ecologist** n (pl -s)
economic adj of economics
economical adj not wasteful, thrifty > **economically** adv
  economically adv ▷ economical
economics n social science concerned with the production and consumption of goods and services
  economies n ▷ economy
economist n (pl -s) specialist in economics
  economists n ▷ economist
economize v (-izes, -izing, -ized) reduce expense or waste
  economized v ▷ economize
  economizes v ▷ economize
  economizing v ▷ economize
economy n (pl -ies) system of interrelationship of money, industry, and employment in a country
ecosystem n (pl -s) system involving interactions between a community and its environment
  ecosystems n ▷ ecosystem
ecru adj pale creamy-brown
  ecstasies n ▷ ecstasy
ecstasy n (pl -ies) state of intense delight > **ecstatic** adj > **ecstatically** adv
  ecstatic adj ▷ ecstasy
  ecstatically adv ▷ ecstasy
ectoplasm n (pl -s) (SPIRITUALISM) substance that supposedly is emitted from the body of a medium during a trance
  ectoplasms n ▷ ectoplasm
ecumenical adj of the Christian Church

throughout the world, esp. with regard to its unity
eczema [ek-sim-a] n (pl s) skin disease causing intense itching
  eczemas n ▷ eczema
  eddied v ▷ eddy
  eddies n, v ▷ eddy
eddy n (pl eddies) circular movement of air, water, etc. ▶ v (eddies, eddying, eddied) move with a circular motion
  eddying v ▷ eddy
edelweiss [ade-el-vice] n (pl -es) alpine plant with white flowers
  edelweisses n ▷ edelweiss
edge n (pl -s) border or line where something ends or begins ▶ v (edges, edging, edged) provide an edge or border for
  edged v ▷ edge
  edges n, v ▷ edge
edgeways adv with the edge forwards or uppermost
  edgier adj ▷ edgy
  edgiest adj ▷ edgy
  edging v ▷ edge ▶ n (pl -s) anything placed along an edge to finish it
  edgings n ▷ edging
edgy adj (edgier, edgiest) nervous or irritable
  edibilities n ▷ edible
  edibility n ▷ edible
edible adj fit to be eaten > **edibility** n (pl -ties)
edict [ee-dikt] n (pl -s) order issued by an authority
  edicts n ▷ edict
  edification n ▷ edify
  edifications n ▷ edify
edifice [ed-if-iss] n (pl -s) large building
  edifices n ▷ edifice
  edified v ▷ edify
  edifies v ▷ edify
edify [ed-if-fie] v (-fies, -fying, -fied) improve morally by instruction > **edification** n (pl -s)
  edifying v ▷ edify
edit v (-s, -ing, -ed) prepare (a book, film, etc.) for publication or broadcast
  edited v ▷ edit
  editing v ▷ edit
edition n (pl -s) number of copies of a new publication printed at one time
  editions n ▷ edition
editor n (pl -s) person who edits
editorial n (pl -s) newspaper article stating the opinion of the editor ▶ adj of editing or editors
  editorials n ▷ editorial
  editors n ▷ editor

edits v ▷ edit

educate v (-tes, -ting, -ted) teach > education n (pl -s) > educational adj > educationally adv

educated v ▷ educate

educates v ▷ educate

educating v ▷ educate

educational adj ▷ educate

educationalist n (pl -s) expert in the theory of education

educationalists n ▷ educationalist

educationally adv ▷ educate

educations n ▷ educate

educative adj educating

> ee n (een). Ee is a Scots word for eye. While this word won't earn you a big score on its own, it can be very useful when you're trying to form several words at once. Ee scores 2 points.
> eek interj. Eek is a noise that people make when they are startled or frightened. Eek scores 7 points.

eel n (pl -s) snakelike fish

eels n ▷ eel

eerie adj (-ier, -iest) uncannily frightening or disturbing > eerily adv

eerier adj ▷ eerie

eeriest adj ▷ eerie

eerily adv ▷ eerie

> ef n (efs). Ef is the letter F, and is a handy word to know when you want to play a longer word parallel to a word that's already on the board. Ef scores 5 points.

efface v (-ces, -cing, -ced) remove by rubbing > effacement n (pl -s)

effaced v ▷ efface

effacement n ▷ efface

effacements n ▷ efface

effaces v ▷ efface

effacing v ▷ efface

effect n (pl -s) change or result caused by someone or something ▶ pl personal belongings ▶ v (-s, -ing, -ed) cause to happen, accomplish

effected v ▷ effect

effecting v ▷ effect

effective adj producing a desired result > effectively adv

effectively adv ▷ effective

effects n, v ▷ effect

effectual adj producing the intended result > effectually adv

effectually adv ▷ effectual

effeminacies n ▷ effeminate

effeminacy n ▷ effeminate

effeminate adj (of a man) displaying

characteristics thought to be typical of a woman > effeminacy n (pl -ies)

effervescence n ▷ effervescent

effervescences n ▷ effervescent

effervescent adj (of a liquid) giving off bubbles of gas > effervescence n (pl -s)

effete [if-feet] adj powerless, feeble

efficacies n ▷ efficacious

efficacious adj producing the intended result > efficacy n (pl -ies)

efficacy n ▷ efficacious

efficiencies n ▷ efficient

efficiency n ▷ efficient

efficient adj functioning effectively with little waste of effort > efficiently adv > efficiency n (pl -ies)

efficiently adv ▷ efficient

effigies n ▷ effigy

effigy [ef-fij-ee] n (pl -ies) image or likeness of a person

efflorescence n (pl -s) flowering

efflorescences n ▷ efflorescence

effluent n (pl -s) liquid discharged as waste

effluents n ▷ effluent

effluvia n ▷ effluvium

effluvium n (pl -via) unpleasant smell, as of decaying matter or gaseous waste

effort n (pl -s) physical or mental exertion > effortless adj

effortless adj ▷ effort

efforts n ▷ effort

effronteries n ▷ effrontery

effrontery n (pl -ies) brazen impudence

effusion n (pl -s) unrestrained outburst

effusions n ▷ effusion

effusive adj openly emotional, demonstrative > effusively adv

effusively adv ▷ effusive

egalitarian adj upholding the equality of all people ▶ n (pl -s) person who holds egalitarian beliefs > egalitarianism n (pl -s)

egalitarianism n ▷ egalitarian

egalitarianisms n ▷ egalitarian

egalitarians n ▷ egalitarian

egg¹ n (pl -s) oval or round object laid by the females of birds and other creatures, containing a developing embryo

egg² v (-s, -ing, -ed) encourage or incite, esp. to do wrong

egged v ▷ egg²

egghead n (pl -s) (Informal) intellectual person

eggheads n ▷ egghead

egging v ▷ egg²

eggplant n (pl -s) (US, CANADIAN, AUST & NZ) aubergine

eggplants n ▷ eggplant

eggs n, v ▷ egg[1, 2]

ego n (pl -s) the conscious mind of an individual

egocentric adj self-centred

egoism, egotism n excessive concern for one's own interests > **egoist, egotist** n (pl -s) > **egoistic, egotistic** adj

egoist n ▷ egoism

egoistic adj ▷ egoism

egoists n ▷ egoism

egos n ▷ ego

egotist n ▷ egoism

egotistic adj ▷ egoism

egotists n ▷ egoism

egregious [ig-greej-uss] adj outstandingly bad

egress [ee-gress] n (pl -es) departure

egresses n ▷ egress

egret [ee-grit] n (pl -s) lesser white heron

egrets n ▷ egret

eider n (pl -s) Arctic duck

eiderdown n (pl -s) quilt (orig. stuffed with eider feathers)

eiderdowns n ▷ eiderdown

eiders n ▷ eider

eight adj, n (pl -s) one more than seven

eighteen adj, n (pl -s) eight and ten > **eighteenth** adj, n (pl -s)

eighteens n ▷ eighteen

eighteenth adj, n ▷ eighteen

eighteenths n ▷ eighteen

eighth adj, n (pl -s) (of) number eight in a series

eighths n ▷ eighth

eighties n ▷ eighty

eightieth n ▷ eighty

eightieths n ▷ eighty

eights n ▷ eight

eighty adj, n (pl -ies) eight times ten > **eightieth** adj, n (pl -s)

eisteddfod [ice-sted-fod] n (pl -s) Welsh festival with competitions in music and other performing arts

eisteddfods n ▷ eisteddfod

either adj, pron one or the other (of two) ▶ conj used preceding two or more possibilities joined by or ▶ adv likewise

ejaculate v (-tes, -ting, -ted) eject (semen) > **ejaculation** n (pl -s)

ejaculated v ▷ ejaculate

ejaculates v ▷ ejaculate

ejaculating v ▷ ejaculate

ejaculation n ▷ ejaculate

ejaculations n ▷ ejaculate

eject v (-s, -ing, -ed) force out, expel > **ejection** n (pl -s) > **ejector** n (pl -s)

ejected v ▷ eject

ejecting v ▷ eject

ejection n ▷ eject

ejections n ▷ eject

ejector n ▷ eject

ejectors n ▷ eject

ejects v ▷ eject

eke v (ekes, eking, eked) (usu. foll. by out) make (a living) with difficulty

eked v ▷ eke

ekes v ▷ eke

eking v ▷ eke

elaborate adj with a lot of fine detail ▶ v (-tes, -ting, -ted) expand upon > **elaboration** n (pl -s)

elaborated v ▷ elaborate

elaborates v ▷ elaborate

elaborating v ▷ elaborate

elaboration n ▷ elaborate

elaborations n ▷ elaborate

élan [ale-an] n (pl -s) style and vigour

eland [eel-and] n (pl -s) large antelope of southern Africa

elands n ▷ eland

élans n ▷ élan

elapse v (-ses, -sing, -sed) (of time) pass by

elapsed v ▷ elapse

elapses v ▷ elapse

elapsing v ▷ elapse

elastic adj resuming normal shape after distortion ▶ n (pl -s) tape or fabric containing interwoven strands of flexible rubber > **elasticity** n (pl -ies)

elasticities n ▷ elastic

elasticity n ▷ elastic

elastics n ▷ elastic

elate v (-tes, -ting, -ted) make extremely happy and excited > **elation** n (pl -s)

elated v ▷ elate

elates v ▷ elate

elating v ▷ elate

elation n ▷ elate

elations n ▷ elate

elbow n (pl -s) joint between the upper arm and the forearm ▶ v (-s, -ing, -ed) shove or strike with the elbow

elbowed v ▷ elbow

elbowing v ▷ elbow

elbows n, v ▷ elbow

elder[1] adj older ▶ n (pl -s) older person

elder[2] n (pl -s) small tree with white flowers and black berries

elderly adj (fairly) old

elders n ▷ elder[1, 2]

eldest adj oldest

eldritch adj (SCOT) weird, uncanny

elect v (-s, -ing, -ed) choose by voting ▶ adj appointed but not yet in office
elected v ▷ **elect**
electing v ▷ **elect**

election n (pl -s) choosing of representatives by voting

electioneering n (pl -s) active participation in a political campaign
electioneerings n ▷ **electioneering**
elections n ▷ **election**

elective adj chosen by election

elector n (pl -s) someone who has the right to vote in an election > **electoral** adj
electoral adj ▷ **elector**

electorate n (pl -s) people who have the right to vote
electorates n ▷ **electorate**
electors n ▷ **elector**

electric adj produced by, transmitting, or powered by electricity

electrical adj using or concerning electricity

electrician n (pl -s) person trained to install and repair electrical equipment
electricians n ▷ **electrician**
electricities n ▷ **electricity**

electricity n (pl -ies) form of energy associated with stationary or moving electrons or other charged particles

electrics pl n (BRIT) electric appliances
electrification n ▷ **electrify**
electrifications n ▷ **electrify**
electrified v ▷ **electrify**
electrifies v ▷ **electrify**

electrify v (-fies, -fying, -fied) adapt for operation by electric power > **electrification** n
electrifying v ▷ **electrify**

electrocute v (-tes, -ting, -ted) kill or injure by electricity > **electrocution** n (pl -s)
electrocuted v ▷ **electrocute**
electrocutes v ▷ **electrocute**
electrocuting v ▷ **electrocute**
electrocution n ▷ **electrocute**
electrocutions n ▷ **electrocute**

electrode n (pl -s) conductor through which an electric current enters or leaves a battery, vacuum tube, etc
electrodes n ▷ **electrode**

electrodynamics n branch of physics concerned with the interactions between electrical and mechanical forces
electrolyses n ▷ **electrolysis**

electrolysis [ill-lek-**troll**-iss-iss] n (pl -ses) conduction of electricity by an electrolyte,

esp. to induce chemical change

electrolyte n (pl -s) solution or molten substance that conducts electricity
> **electrolytic** adj
electrolytes n ▷ **electrolyte**
electrolytic adj ▷ **electrolyte**

electromagnet n (pl -s) magnet containing a coil of wire through which an electric current is passed

electromagnetic adj of or operated by an electomagnet
electromagnets n ▷ **electromagnet**

electron n (pl -s) elementary particle in all atoms that has a negative electrical charge

electronic adj (of a device) dependent on the action of electrons

electronics n technology concerned with the development of electronic devices and circuits
electrons n ▷ **electron**

electronvolt n (pl -s) unit of energy used in nuclear physics
electronvolts n ▷ **electronvolt**

electroplate v (-tes, -ting, -ted) coat with silver etc. by electrolysis
electroplated v ▷ **electroplate**
electroplates v ▷ **electroplate**
electroplating v ▷ **electroplate**
elects v ▷ **elect**

elegance n ▷ **elegant**
elegances n ▷ **elegant**

elegant adj pleasing or graceful in dress, style, or design > **elegance** n (pl -s)

elegiac adj mournful or plaintive
elegies n ▷ **elegy**

elegy [**el**-lij-ee] n (pl -ies) mournful poem, esp. a lament for the dead

element n (pl -s) component part ▶ pl basic principles of something

elemental adj of primitive natural forces or passions

elementary adj simple and straightforward
elements n ▷ **element**

elephant n (pl -s) huge four-footed thick-skinned animal with ivory tusks and a long trunk

elephantiasis [el-lee-fan-**tie**-a-siss] n disease with hardening of the skin and enlargement of the legs etc.

elephantine adj unwieldy, clumsy
elephants n ▷ **elephant**

elevate v (-ates, -ating, -ated) raise in rank or status
elevated v ▷ **elevate**
elevates v ▷ **elevate**

elevating v ▷ **elevate**

elevation n (pl -s) raising

elevator n (pl -s) (AUST, US & CANADIAN) lift for carrying people

elevators n ▷ **elevator**

eleven adj, n (pl -s) one more than ten

elevens n ▷ **eleven**

elevenses n (BRIT & S AFR) (Informal) mid-morning snack

eleventh adj, n (pl -s) (of) number eleven in a series

elevenths n ▷ **eleventh**

elf n (pl elves) (in folklore) small mischievous fairy

elfin adj small and delicate

elicit v (-s, -ing, -ed) bring about (a response or reaction)

elicited v ▷ **elicit**

eliciting v ▷ **elicit**

elicits v ▷ **elicit**

elide v (-des, -ding, -ded) omit (a vowel or syllable) from a spoken word > **elision** n (pl -s)

elided v ▷ **elide**

elides v ▷ **elide**

eliding v ▷ **elide**

eligibilities n ▷ **eligible**

eligibility n ▷ **eligible**

eligible adj meeting the requirements or qualifications needed > **eligibility** n (pl -ties)

eliminate v (-tes, -ting, -ted) get rid of > **elimination** n (pl -s)

eliminated v ▷ **eliminate**

eliminates v ▷ **eliminate**

eliminating v ▷ **eliminate**

elimination n ▷ **eliminate**

eliminations n ▷ **eliminate**

elision n ▷ **elide**

elisions n ▷ **elide**

elite [ill-eet] n (pl -s) most powerful, rich, or gifted members of a group

elites n ▷ **elite**

elitism n (pl -s) belief that society should be governed by a small group of superior people > **elitist** n, adj (pl -s)

elitisms n ▷ **elitism**

elitists n ▷ **elitist**

elixir [ill-ix-er] n (pl -s) imaginary liquid that can prolong life or turn base metals into gold

elixirs n ▷ **elixir**

elk n (pl -s) large deer of N Europe and Asia

elks n ▷ **elk**

ellipse n (pl -ses) oval shape

ellipses n ▷ **ellipse, ellipsis**

ellipsis n (pl -ses) omission of letters or words in a sentence

elliptical adj oval-shaped

elm n (pl -s) tree with serrated leaves

elms n ▷ **elm**

elocution n (pl -s) art of speaking clearly in public

elocutions n ▷ **elocution**

elongate [eel-long-gate] v (-tes, -ting, -ted) make or become longer > **elongation** n (pl -s)

elongated v ▷ **elongate**

elongates v ▷ **elongate**

elongating v ▷ **elongate**

elongation n ▷ **elongate**

elongations n ▷ **elongate**

elope v (-s, -ing, -ed) (of two people) run away secretly to get married > **elopement** n (pl -s)

eloped v ▷ **elope**

elopement n ▷ **elope**

elopements n ▷ **elope**

elopes v ▷ **elope**

eloping v ▷ **elope**

eloquence n (pl -s) fluent powerful use of language > **eloquent** adj > **eloquently** adv

eloquencies n ▷ **eloquence**

eloquent adj ▷ **eloquence**

eloquently adv ▷ **eloquence**

else adv in addition or more

elsewhere adv in or to another place

elucidate v (-tes, -ting, -ted) make (something difficult) clear > **elucidation** n (pl -s)

elucidated v ▷ **elucidate**

elucidates v ▷ **elucidate**

elucidating v ▷ **elucidate**

elucidation n ▷ **elucidate**

elucidations n ▷ **elucidate**

elude v (-s, -ing, -ed) escape from by cleverness or quickness

eluded v ▷ **elude**

eludes v ▷ **elude**

eluding v ▷ **elude**

elusive adj difficult to catch or remember

elver n (pl -s) young eel

elvers n ▷ **elver**

elves n ▷ **elf**

emaciated [im-mace-ee-ate-id] adj abnormally thin > **emaciation** n (pl -s)

emaciation n ▷ **emaciated**

emaciations n ▷ **emaciated**

emanate [em-a-nate] v (-tes, -ting, -ted) issue, proceed from a source > **emanation** n (pl -s)

emanated v ▷ **emanate**

emanates v ▷ **emanate**

emanating v ▷ **emanate**

emanation n ▷ **emanate**

emanations n ▷ **emanate**

emancipate v (-tes, -ting, -ted) free

from social, political, or legal restraints
> **emancipation** n (pl -**s**)
emancipated v ▷ emancipate
emancipates v ▷ emancipate
emancipating v ▷ emancipate
emancipation n ▷ emancipate
emancipations n ▷ emancipate
emasculate v (-**tes**, -**ting**, -**ted**) deprive of
power > **emasculation** n (pl -**s**)
emasculated v ▷ emasculate
emasculates v ▷ emasculate
emasculating v ▷ emasculate
emasculation n ▷ emasculate
emasculations n ▷ emasculate
embalm v (-**s**, -**ing**, -**ed**) preserve (a corpse)
from decay by the use of chemicals etc.
embalmed v ▷ embalm
embalming v ▷ embalm
embalms v ▷ embalm
embankment n (pl -**s**) man-made ridge that
carries a road or railway or holds back water
embankments n ▷ embankment
embargo n (pl -**oes**) order by a government
prohibiting trade with a country ▶ v (-**oes**,
-**oing**, -**oed**) put an embargo on
embargoed v ▷ embargo
embargoes n, v ▷ embargo
embargoing v ▷ embargo
embark v (-**s**, -**ing**, -**ed**) board a ship or aircraft
(foll. by **on**) > **embarkation** n (-**s**)
embarkation n ▷ embark
embarkations n ▷ embark
embarked v ▷ embark
embarking v ▷ embark
embarks v ▷ embark
embarrass v (-**es**, -**ing**, -**ed**) cause to feel self-
conscious or ashamed > **embarrassed** adj
> **embarrassing** adj > **embarrassment** n (pl -**s**)
embarrassed v, adj ▷ embarrass
embarrasses v ▷ embarrass
embarrassing v, adj ▷ embarrass
embarrassment n ▷ embarrass
embarrassments n ▷ embarrass
embassies n ▷ embassy
embassy n (pl -**ies**) offices or official residence
of an ambassador
embattled adj having a lot of difficulties
embed v (-**s**, -**dding**, -**dded**) fix firmly in
something solid
embedded adj (of a journalist) assigned
to accompany an active military unit ▶ v
▷ embed
embedding v ▷ embed
embeds v ▷ embed
embellish v (-**es**, -**ing**, -**ed**) decorate

> **embellishment** n (pl -**s**)
embellished v ▷ embellish
embellishes v ▷ embellish
embellishing v ▷ embellish
embellishment n ▷ embellish
embellishments n ▷ embellish
ember n (pl -**s**) glowing piece of wood or coal
in a dying fire
embers n ▷ ember
embezzle v (-**s**, -**ing**, -**ed**) steal money that has
been entrusted to one > **embezzlement** n (pl
-**s**) > **embezzler** n (pl -**s**)
embezzled v ▷ embezzle
embezzlement n ▷ embezzle
embezzlements n ▷ embezzle
embezzler n ▷ embezzle
embezzlers n ▷ embezzle
embezzles v ▷ embezzle
embezzling v ▷ embezzle
embittered adj feeling anger as a result of
misfortune
emblazon v (-**s**, -**ing**, -**ed**) decorate with bright
colours
emblazoned v ▷ emblazon
emblazoning v ▷ emblazon
emblazons v ▷ emblazon
emblem n (pl -**s**) object or design that
symbolizes a quality, type, or group
> **emblematic** adj
emblematic adj ▷ emblem
emblems n ▷ emblem
embodied v ▷ embody
embodies v ▷ embody
embodiment n ▷ embody
embodiments n ▷ embody
embody v (-**dies**, -**dying**, -**died**) be an example
or expression of > **embodiment** n (pl -**s**)
embodying v ▷ embody
embolden v (-**s**, -**ing**, -**ed**) encourage
(someone)
emboldened v ▷ embolden
emboldening v ▷ embolden
emboldens v ▷ embolden
embolism n (pl -**s**) blocking of a blood vessel by
a blood clot or air bubble
embolisms n ▷ embolism
embossed adj (of a design or pattern)
standing out from a surface
embrace v (-**ces**, -**cing**, -**ced**) clasp in the arms,
hug ▶ n (pl -**s**) act of embracing
embraced v ▷ embrace
embraces v, n ▷ embrace
embracing v ▷ embrace
embrasure n (pl -**s**) door or window having
splayed sides so that the opening is larger

on the inside
embrasures n ▷ **embrasure**
embrocation n (pl -s) lotion for rubbing into the skin to relieve pain
embrocations n ▷ **embrocation**
embroider v (-s, -ing, -ed) decorate with needlework > **embroidery** n (pl -ies)
embroidered v ▷ **embroider**
embroideries n ▷ **embroider**
embroidering v ▷ **embroider**
embroiders v ▷ **embroider**
embroidery n ▷ **embroider**
embroil v (-s, -ing, -ed) involve (a person) in problems
embroiled v ▷ **embroil**
embroiling v ▷ **embroil**
embroils v ▷ **embroil**
embryo [em-bree-oh] n (pl -s) unborn creature in the early stages of development > **embryology** n (pl -ies)
embryologies n ▷ **embryo**
embryology n ▷ **embryo**
embryonic adj at an early stage
embryos n ▷ **embryo**
emend v (-s, -ing, -ed) remove errors from > **emendation** n (pl emendations)
emendation n ▷ **emend**
emendations n ▷ **emend**
emended v ▷ **emend**
emending v ▷ **emend**
emends v ▷ **emend**
emerald n (pl -s) bright green precious stone ▶ adj bright green
emeralds n ▷ **emerald**
emerge v (-ges, -ging, -ged) come into view > **emergence** n (pl -s) > **emergent** adj
emerged v ▷ **emerge**
emergence n ▷ **emerge**
emergences n ▷ **emerge**
emergencies n ▷ **emergency**
emergency n (pl -ies) sudden unforeseen occurrence needing immediate action
emergent adj ▷ **emerge**
emerges v ▷ **emerge**
emerging v ▷ **emerge**
emeries n ▷ **emery**
emeritus [im-mer-rit-uss] adj retired, but retaining an honorary title
emery n (pl -ies) hard mineral used for smoothing and polishing
emetic [im-met-ik] n (pl -s) substance that causes vomiting ▶ adj causing vomiting
emetics n ▷ **emetic**
emigrant n ▷ **emigrate**
emigrants n ▷ **emigrate**

emigrate v (-tes, -ting, -ted) go and settle in another country > **emigrant** n (pl -s) > **emigration** n (pl -s)
emigrated v ▷ **emigrate**
emigrates v ▷ **emigrate**
emigrating v ▷ **emigrate**
emigration n ▷ **emigrate**
emigrations n ▷ **emigrate**
émigré [em-mig-gray] n (pl -s) someone who has left his native country for political reasons
émigrés n ▷ **émigré**
eminence n (pl -s) position of superiority or fame
eminences n ▷ **eminence**
eminent adj distinguished, well-known > **eminently** adv
eminently adv ▷ **eminent**
emir [em-meer] n (pl -s) Muslim ruler
emirate n (pl -s) country ruled by an emir
emirates n ▷ **emirate**
emirs n ▷ **emir**
emissaries n ▷ **emissary**
emissary n (pl -ies) agent sent on a mission by a government
emission n ▷ **emit**
emissions ▷ **emit**
emit v (-s, -tting, -tted) give out (heat, light, or a smell) > **emission** n (pl -s)
emits v ▷ **emit**
emitted v ▷ **emit**
emitting v ▷ **emit**
emollient adj softening, soothing ▶ n (pl -s) substance which softens or soothes the skin
emollients n ▷ **emollient**
emolument n (pl -s) (formal) fees or wages from employment
emoluments n ▷ **emolument**
emoticon [i-mote-i-kon] n (pl -s) (COMPUTERS) ▷ **smiley**
emoticons n ▷ **emoticon**
emotion n (pl -s) strong feeling
emotional adj readily affected by or appealing to the emotions > **emotionally** adv
emotionally adv ▷ **emotional**
emotions n ▷ **emotion**
emotive adj tending to arouse emotion
empathies n ▷ **empathy**
empathy n (pl -ies) ability to understand someone else's feelings as if they were one's own
emperor n (pl -s) ruler of an empire > **empress** n fem (pl -es)
emperors n ▷ **emperor**
emphases n ▷ **emphasis**

emphasis n (pl -ses) special importance or significance ▷ **emphasize** v (-s, -ing, -ed)
  emphasize v ▷ emphasis
  emphasized v ▷ emphasis
  emphasizes v ▷ emphasis
  emphasizing v ▷ emphasis
emphatic adj showing emphasis
  > **emphatically** adv
  emphatically adv ▷ emphatic
emphysema [em-fiss-**see**-ma] n (pl -s) condition in which the air sacs of the lungs are grossly enlarged, causing breathlessness
  emphysemas n ▷ emphysema
empire n (pl -s) group of territories under the rule of one state or person
  empires n ▷ empire
empirical adj relying on experiment or experience, not on theory > **empirically** adv
  empirically adv ▷ empirical
empiricism n (pl -s) doctrine that all knowledge derives from experience
  > **empiricist** n (pl -s)
  empiricisms n ▷ empiricism
  empiricist n ▷ empiricism
  empiricists n ▷ empiricism
emplacement n (pl -s) prepared position for a gun
  emplacements n ▷ emplacement
employ v (-s, -ing, -ed) hire (a person) ▶ n (pl -s) state of being employed > **employee** n (pl -s)
  employed v ▷ employ
  employee n ▷ employ
  employees n ▷ employ
employer n (pl -s) person or organization that employs someone
  employers n ▷ employer
  employing v ▷ employ
employment n (pl -s) state of being employed
  employments n ▷ employment
  employs v, n ▷ employ
  emporia n ▷ emporium
emporium n (pl -riums, -ria) (Old-fashioned) large general shop
  emporiums n ▷ emporia
empower v (-s, -ing, -ed) enable, authorize
  empowered v ▷ empower
  empowering v ▷ empower
  empowers v ▷ empower
  empress n ▷ emperor
  empresses n ▷ emperor
  emptied v ▷ empty
  emptier adj ▷ empty
empties pl n empty boxes, bottles, etc. ▶ v ▷ empty
  emptiest adj ▷ empty

  emptiness n ▷ empty
  emptinesses n ▷ empty
empty adj (-ier, -iest) containing nothing ▶ v (-ies, -ying, -ied) make or become empty
  > **emptiness** n (pl -es)
  emptying v ▷ empty
emu n (pl -s) large Australian flightless bird with long legs
emulate v (-tes, -ting, -ted) attempt to equal or surpass by imitating > **emulation** n (pl -s)
  emulated v ▷ emulate
  emulates v ▷ emulate
  emulating v ▷ emulate
  emulation n ▷ emulate
  emulations n ▷ emulate
  emulsified v ▷ emulsify
  emulsifier n ▷ emulsify
  emulsifiers n ▷ emulsify
  emulsifies v ▷ emulsify
emulsify v (-fies, -fying, -fied) (of two liquids) join together or join (two liquids) together
  > **emulsifier** n (pl -s)
  emulsifying v ▷ emulsify
emulsion n (pl -s) light-sensitive coating on photographic film ▶ v (-s, -ing, -ed) paint with emulsion paint
  emulsioned v ▷ emulsion
  emulsioning v ▷ emulsion
  emulsions n, v ▷ emulsion
  emus n ▷ emu
enable v (-les, -ling, -led) provide (a person) with the means, opportunity, or authority (to do something)
  enabled v ▷ enable
  enables v ▷ enable
  enabling v ▷ enable
enact v (-s, -ing, -ed) establish by law
  > **enactment** n (pl -s)
  enacted v ▷ enact
  enacting v ▷ enact
  enactment n ▷ enact
  enactments n ▷ enact
  enacts v ▷ enact
enamel n (pl -s) glasslike coating applied to metal etc. to preserve the surface ▶ v (-s, -lling, -lled) cover with enamel
  enamelled v ▷ enamel
  enamelling v ▷ enamel
  enamels n, v ▷ enamel
enamoured adj inspired with love
encamp v (-s, -ing, -ed) set up in a camp
  > **encampment** n (pl -s)
  encamped v ▷ encamp
  encamping v ▷ encamp
  encampment n ▷ encamp

encampments n ▷ encamp
encamps v ▷ encamp
encapsulate v (-tes, -ting, -ted) summarize
  encapsulated v ▷ encapsulate
  encapsulates v ▷ encapsulate
  encapsulating v ▷ encapsulate
encephalitis [en-sef-a-lite-iss] n (pl -es)
  inflammation of the brain
  encephalitises n ▷ encephalitis
enchant v (-s, -ing, -ed) delight and fascinate
  > **enchantment** n (pl -s) > **enchanter** n (pl -s)
  > **enchantress** n fem (pl -es)
  enchanted v ▷ enchant
  enchanter n ▷ enchant
  enchanters n ▷ enchant
  enchanting v ▷ enchant
  enchantment n ▷ enchant
  enchantments n ▷ enchant
  enchantress n ▷ enchant
  enchantresses n ▷ enchant
  enchants v ▷ enchant
encircle v (-s, -ling, -led) form a circle around
  > **encirclement** n (pl -s)
  encircled v ▷ encircle
  encirclement n ▷ encircle
  encirclements n ▷ encircle
  encircles v ▷ encircle
  encircling v ▷ encircle
enclave n (pl -s) part of a country entirely
  surrounded by foreign territory
  enclaves n ▷ enclave
enclose v (-s, -sing, -sed) surround completely
  > **enclosure** n (pl -s)
  enclosed v ▷ enclose
  encloses v ▷ enclose
  enclosing v ▷ enclose
  enclosure n ▷ enclose
  enclosures n ▷ enclose
  encomia n ▷ encomium
encomium n (pl -miums, -mia) formal
  expression of praise
  encomiums n ▷ encomiums
encompass v (-es, -ing, -ed) surround
  encompassed v ▷ encompass
  encompasses v ▷ encompass
  encompassing v ▷ encompass
encore interj again, once more ▶ n (pl -s) extra
  performance due to enthusiastic demand
  encores n ▷ encore
encounter v (-s, -ing, -ed) meet unexpectedly
  ▶ n (pl -s) unexpected meeting
  encountered v ▷ encounter
  encountering v ▷ encounter
  encounters v, n ▷ encounter
encourage v (-ges, -ging, -ged) inspire with

confidence > **encouragement** n (pl -s)
  encouraged v ▷ encourage
  encouragement n ▷ encourage
  encouragements n ▷ encourage
  encourages v ▷ encourage
  encouraging v ▷ encourage
encroach v (-es, -ing, -ed) intrude gradually
  on a person's rights or land > **encroachment**
  n (pl -s)
  encroached v ▷ encroach
  encroaches v ▷ encroach
  encroaching v ▷ encroach
  encroachment n ▷ encroach
  encroachments n ▷ encroach
encrust v (-s, -ing, -ed) cover with a layer of
  something
  encrusted v ▷ encrust
  encrusting v ▷ encrust
  encrusts v ▷ encrust
encumber v (-s, -ing, -ed) hinder or impede
  encumbered v ▷ encumber
  encumbering v ▷ encumber
  encumbers v ▷ encumber
encumbrance n (pl -s) something that
  impedes or is burdensome
  encumbrances n ▷ encumbrance
encyclical [en-sik-lik-kl] n (pl -s) letter sent by
  the Pope to all bishops
  encyclicals n ▷ encyclical
  encyclopaedia n ▷ encyclopedia
  encyclopaedias n ▷ encyclopedia
  encyclopaedic adj ▷ encyclopedia
encyclopedia, encyclopaedia n (pl -s) book
  or set of books containing facts about
  many subjects, usu. in alphabetical order
  > **encyclopedic, encyclopaedic** adj
  encyclopedias n ▷ encyclopedia
  encyclopedic adj ▷ encyclopedia
end n (pl -s) furthest point or part ▶ v (-s, -ing,
  -ed) bring or come to a finish > **ending** n (pl -s)
  > **endless** adj
endanger v (-s, -ing, -ed) put in danger
  endangered v ▷ endanger
  endangering v ▷ endanger
  endangers v ▷ endanger
endear v (-s, -ing, -ed) cause to be liked
  > **endearing** adj
  endeared v ▷ endear
  endearing v, adj ▷ endear
endearment n (pl -s) affectionate word or
  phrase
  endearments n ▷ endearment
  endears v ▷ endear
endeavour v (-s, -ing, -ed) try ▶ n (pl -s) effort
  endeavoured v ▷ endeavour

endeavouring v ▷ endeavour

endeavours v, n ▷ endeavour

ended v ▷ end

endemic adj present within a localized area or peculiar to a particular group of people

ending v, n ▷ end

endings n ▷ end

endive n (pl -s) curly-leaved plant used in salads

endives n ▷ endive

endless adj ▷ end

endocrine adj relating to the glands which secrete hormones directly into the bloodstream

endogenous [en-**dodge**-in-uss] adj originating from within

endorse v (-ses, -sing, -sed) give approval to > **endorsement** n (pl -s)

endorsed v ▷ endorse

endorsement n ▷ endorse

endorsements n ▷ endorse

endorses v ▷ endorse

endorsing v ▷ endorse

endow v (-s, -ing, -ed) provide permanent income for > **endowment** n (pl -s)

endowed v ▷ endow

endowing v ▷ endow

endowment v ▷ endow

endowments v ▷ endow

endows v ▷ endow

ends n, v ▷ end

endurable adj ▷ endure

endurance n (pl -s) act or power of enduring

endurances n ▷ endurance

endure v (-res, -ring, -red) bear (hardship) patiently > **endurable** adj

endured v ▷ endure

endures v ▷ endure

enduring v ▷ endure

endways adv having the end forwards or upwards

enema [en-**im-a**] n (pl -s) medicine injected into the rectum to empty the bowels

enemas n ▷ enema

enemies n ▷ enemy

enemy n (pl -ies) hostile person or nation, opponent

energetic adj ▷ energy

energetically adv ▷ energy

energies n ▷ energy

energize v (-izes, -izing, -ized) give vigour to

energized v ▷ energize

energizes v ▷ energize

energizing v ▷ energize

energy n (pl -ies) capacity for intense activity

> **energetic** adj > **energetically** adv

enervate v (-tes, -ting, -ted) deprive of strength or vitality > **enervation** n (pl -s)

enervated v ▷ enervate

enervates v ▷ enervate

enervating v ▷ enervate

enervation n ▷ enervate

enervations n ▷ enervate

enfeeble v (-les, -ling, -led) weaken

enfeebled v ▷ enfeeble

enfeebles v ▷ enfeeble

enfeebling v ▷ enfeeble

enfold v (-s, -ing, -ed) cover by wrapping something around

enfolded v ▷ enfold

enfolding v ▷ enfold

enfolds v ▷ enfold

enforce v (-ces, -cing, -ced) impose obedience (to a law etc.) > **enforceable** adj

> **enforcement** n (pl -s)

enforced v ▷ enforce

enforcement n ▷ enforce

enforcements n ▷ enforce

enforces v ▷ enforce

enforcing v ▷ enforce

enfranchise v (-ses, -sing, -sed) grant (a person) the right to vote > **enfranchisement** n (pl -s)

enfranchised v ▷ enfranchise

enfranchisement n ▷ enfranchise

enfranchisements n ▷ enfranchise

enfranchises v ▷ enfranchise

enfranchising v ▷ enfranchise

engage v (-ges, -ging, -ged) take part, participate > **engagement** n (pl -s)

engaged adj pledged to be married ▶ v ▷ engage

engagement n ▷ engage

engagements n ▷ engage

engages v ▷ engage

engaging adj charming ▶ v ▷ engage

engender v (-s, -ing, -ed) produce, cause to occur

engendered v ▷ engender

engendering v ▷ engender

engenders v ▷ engender

engine n (pl -s) any machine which converts energy into mechanical work

engineer n (pl -s) person trained in any branch of engineering ▶ v (-s, -ing, -ed) plan in a clever manner

engineered v ▷ engineer

engineering v ▷ engineer ▶ n (pl -s) profession of applying scientific principles to the design and construction of engines, cars, buildings, or machines

engineerings n ▷ engineering

engineers n, v ▷ engineer

engines n ▷ engine

English n (pl -es) official language of Britain, Ireland, Australia, New Zealand, South Africa, Canada, the US, and several other countries ▶ adj relating to England

Englishes n ▷ English

engrave v (-ves, -ving, -ved) carve (a design) onto a hard surface > **engraver** n (pl -s)

engraved v ▷ engrave

engraver n ▷ engrave

engravers n ▷ engrave

engraves v ▷ engrave

engraving v ▷ engrave ▶ n (pl -s) print made from an engraved plate

engravings n ▷ engraving

engross [en-groce] v (-es, -ing, -ed) occupy the attention of (a person) completely

engrossed v ▷ engross

engrosses v ▷ engross

engrossing v ▷ engross

engulf v (-s, -ing, -ed) cover or surround completely

engulfed v ▷ engulf

engulfing v ▷ engulf

engulfs v ▷ engulf

enhance v (-s, -ing, -ed) increase in quality, value, or attractiveness > **enhancement** n (pl -s)

enhanced v ▷ enhance

enhancement n ▷ enhance

enhancements n ▷ enhance

enhances v ▷ enhance

enhancing v ▷ enhance

enigma n (pl -s) puzzling thing or person > **enigmatic** adj > **enigmatically** adv

enigmas n ▷ enigma

enigmatic adj ▷ enigma

enigmatically adv ▷ enigma

enjoin v (-s, -ing, -ed) order (someone) to do something

enjoined v ▷ enjoin

enjoining v ▷ enjoin

enjoins v ▷ enjoin

enjoy v (-s, -ing, -ed) take joy in > **enjoyable** adj > **enjoyment** n (pl -s)

enjoyable adj ▷ enjoy

enjoyed v ▷ enjoy

enjoying v ▷ enjoy

enjoyment n ▷ enjoy

enjoyments n ▷ enjoy

enjoys v ▷ enjoy

enlarge v (-ges, -ging, -ged) make or grow

larger (foll. by **on**) > **enlargement** n (pl -s)

enlarged v ▷ enlarge

enlargement n ▷ enlarge

enlargements n ▷ enlarge

enlarges v ▷ enlarge

enlarging v ▷ enlarge

enlighten v (-s, -ing, -ed) give information to > **enlightenment** n (pl -s)

enlightened v ▷ enlighten

enlightening v ▷ enlighten

enlightenment n ▷ enlighten

enlightenments n ▷ enlighten

enlightens v ▷ enlighten

enlist v (-s, -ing, -ed) enter the armed forces > **enlistment** n (pl -s)

enlisted v ▷ enlist

enlisting v ▷ enlist

enlistment n ▷ enlist

enlistments n ▷ enlist

enlists v ▷ enlist

enliven v (-s, -ing, -ed) make lively or cheerful

enlivened v ▷ enliven

enlivening v ▷ enliven

enlivens v ▷ enliven

enmeshed adj deeply involved

enmities n ▷ enmity

enmity n (pl -ies) ill will, hatred

ennoble v (-s, -ing, -ed) make noble, elevate

ennobled v ▷ ennoble

ennobles v ▷ ennoble

ennobling v ▷ ennoble

ennui [on-nwee] n (pl -s) boredom, dissatisfaction

ennuis n ▷ ennui

enormities n ▷ enormity

enormity n (pl -ies) great wickedness

enormous adj very big, vast

enough adj as much or as many as necessary ▶ pron sufficient quantity ▶ adv sufficiently

enquire v (-res, -ring, -red) ▷ inquire > **enquiry** n (pl -ies)

enquired v ▷ enquire

enquires v ▷ enquire

enquiries n ▷ enquire

enquiring v ▷ enquire

enquiry n ▷ enquire

enraptured adj filled with delight and fascination

enrich v (-es, -ing, -ed) improve in quality

enriched v ▷ enrich

enriches v ▷ enrich

enriching v ▷ enrich

enrol v (-s, -lling, -lled) (cause to) become a member > **enrolment** n (pl -s)

enrolled v ▷ **enrol**

enrolling v ▷ **enrol**

enrolment n ▷ **enrol**

enrolments n ▷ **enrol**

enrols v ▷ **enrol**

ensconce v (**-ces, -cing, -ced**) settle firmly or comfortably

ensconced v ▷ **ensconce**

ensconces v ▷ **ensconce**

ensconcing v ▷ **ensconce**

ensemble [on-**som**-bl] n (pl **-s**) all the parts of something taken together

ensembles n ▷ **ensemble**

enshrine v (**-nes, -ning, -ned**) cherish or treasure

enshrined v ▷ **enshrine**

enshrines v ▷ **enshrine**

enshrining v ▷ **enshrine**

ensign n (pl **-s**) naval flag

ensigns n ▷ **ensign**

enslave v (**-ves, -ving, -ved**) make a slave of (someone) > **enslavement** n (pl **-s**)

enslaved v ▷ **enslave**

enslavement n ▷ **enslave**

enslavements n ▷ **enslave**

enslaves v ▷ **enslave**

enslaving v ▷ **enslave**

ensnare v (**-res, -ring, -red**) catch in or as if in a snare

ensnared v ▷ **ensnare**

ensnares v ▷ **ensnare**

ensnaring v ▷ **ensnare**

ensue v (**-sues, -suing, -sued**) come next, result

ensued v ▷ **ensue**

ensues v ▷ **ensue**

ensuing v ▷ **ensue**

ensure v (**-re, -ring, -red**) make certain or sure

ensured v ▷ **ensure**

ensures v ▷ **ensure**

ensuring v ▷ **ensure**

entail v (**-s, -ing, -ed**) bring about or impose inevitably

entailed v ▷ **entail**

entailing v ▷ **entail**

entails v ▷ **entail**

entangle v (**-les, -ling, -led**) catch or involve in or as if in a tangle > **entanglement** n (pl **-s**)

entangled v ▷ **entangle**

entanglement n ▷ **entangle**

entanglements n ▷ **entangle**

entangles v ▷ **entangle**

entangling v ▷ **entangle**

entente [on-**tont**] n (pl **-s**) friendly understanding between nations

ententes n ▷ **entente**

enter v (**-s, -ing, -ed**) come or go in

entered v ▷ **enter**

enteric [en-**ter**-ik] adj intestinal

entering v ▷ **enter**

enteritis [en-ter-**rite**-iss] n (pl **-es**) inflammation of the intestine, causing diarrhoea

enteritises n ▷ **enteritis**

enterprise n (pl **-s**) company or firm

enterprises n ▷ **enterprise**

enterprising adj full of boldness and initiative

enters v ▷ **enter**

entertain v (**-s, -ing, -ed**) amuse > **entertainer** n (pl **-s**)

entertained v ▷ **entertain**

entertainer n ▷ **entertain**

entertainers n ▷ **entertain**

entertaining v ▷ **entertain**

entertainment n ▷ **entertain**

entertainments n ▷ **entertain**

entertains v ▷ **entertain**

enthral [en-**thrawl**] v (**-s, -lling, -lled**) hold the attention of > **enthralling** adj

enthralled v ▷ **enthral**

enthralling v, adj ▷ **enthral**

enthrals v ▷ **enthral**

enthuse v (**-s, -ing, -ed**) (cause to) show enthusiasm

enthused v ▷ **enthuse**

enthuses v ▷ **enthuse**

enthusiasm n (pl **-s**) ardent interest, eagerness

enthusiasms n ▷ **enthusiasm**

enthusiast n (pl **-s**) ardent supporter of something > **enthusiastic** adj > **enthusiastically** adv

enthusiastic adj ▷ **enthusiast**

enthusiastically adv ▷ **enthusiast**

enthusiasts n ▷ **enthusiast**

enthusing v ▷ **enthuse**

entice v (**-ces, -cing, -ced**) attract by exciting hope or desire, tempt > **enticement** n (pl **-s**)

enticed v ▷ **entice**

enticement n ▷ **entice**

enticements n ▷ **entice**

entices v ▷ **entice**

enticing v ▷ **entice**

entire adj including every detail, part, or aspect of something > **entirely** adv > **entirety** n (pl **-ties**)

entirely adv ▷ **entire**

entireties n ▷ **entire**

entirety n ▷ **entire**

entities n ▷ **entity**

entitle v (**-les, -ling, -led**) give a right to > **entitlement** n (pl **-s**)

entitled v ▷ entitle
entitlement n ▷ entitle
entitlements n ▷ entitle
entitles v ▷ entitle
entitling v ▷ entitle
entity n (pl -ties) separate distinct thing
entomological adj ▷ entomology
entomologies n ▷ entomology
entomologist n ▷ entomology
entomologists n ▷ entomology
entomology n (pl -ies) study of insects
  > **entomological** adj > **entomologist** n (pl -s)
entourage [on-toor-ahzh] n (pl -s) group of
  people who assist an important person
  entourages n ▷ entourage
entrails pl n intestines
entrance¹ n (pl -s) way into a place
entrance² v (-s, -ing, -ed) delight
  entranced v ▷ entrance²
  entrances n ▷ entrance¹ ▶ v ▷ entrance²
  entrancing v ▷ entrance²
entrant n (pl -s) person who enters a
  university, contest, etc.
  entrants n ▷ entrant
entreat v (-s, -ing, -ed) ask earnestly
  entreated v ▷ entreat
  entreaties n ▷ entreaty
  entreating v ▷ entreat
  entreats v ▷ entreat
entreaty n (pl -ties) earnest request
entrée [on-tray] n (pl -s) dish served before a
  main course
  entrées n ▷ entrée
entrench v (-es, -ing, -ed) establish firmly
  > **entrenchment** n (pl -s)
  entrenched v ▷ entrench
  entrenches v ▷ entrench
  entrenching v ▷ entrench
  entrenchment n ▷ entrench
  entrenchments n ▷ entrench
entrepreneur n (pl -s) business person
  who attempts to make a profit by risk and
  initiative
  entrepreneurs n ▷ entrepreneur
  entries n ▷ entry
  entropies n ▷ entropy
entropy [en-trop-ee] n (pl -ies) lack of
  organization
entrust v (-s, -ing, -ed) put into the care or
  protection of
  entrusted v ▷ entrust
  entrusting v ▷ entrust
  entrusts v ▷ entrust
entry n (pl -ies) entrance
entwine v (-s, -ing, -ed) twist together or
  around
  entwined v ▷ entwine
  entwines v ▷ entwine
  entwining v ▷ entwine
enumerate v (-tes, -ting, -ted) name one by
  one > **enumeration** n (pl -s)
  enumerated v ▷ enumerate
  enumerates v ▷ enumerate
  enumerating v ▷ enumerate
  enumeration n ▷ enumerate
  enumerations n ▷ enumerate
  enunciation n ▷ enunciate
enunciate v (-tes, -ting, -ted) pronounce
  clearly > **enunciation** n (pl -s)
  enunciated v ▷ enunciate
  enunciates v ▷ enunciate
  enunciating v ▷ enunciate
  enunciation n ▷ enunciate
  enunciations n ▷ enunciate
envelop v (-s, -ing, -ed) wrap up, enclose
  > **envelopment** n (pl -s)
envelope n (pl -s) folded gummed paper cover
  for a letter
  enveloped v ▷ envelop
  envelopes n ▷ envelope
  enveloping v ▷ envelop
  envelopment n ▷ envelop
  envelopments n ▷ envelop
  envelops v ▷ envelop
enviable adj arousing envy, fortunate
  envied v ▷ envy
  envies n, v ▷ envy
envious adj full of envy
environment [en-vire-on-ment] n (pl -s)
  external conditions and surroundings
  in which people, animals, or plants live
  > **environmental** adj
  environmental adj ▷ environment
environmentalist n (pl -s) person concerned
  with the protection of the natural
  environment
  environmentalists n ▷ environmentalist
  environments n ▷ environment
environs pl n surrounding area, esp. of a town
envisage v (-ges, -ging, -ged) conceive of as a
  possibility
  envisaged v ▷ envisage
  envisages v ▷ envisage
  envisaging v ▷ envisage
envoy n (pl -s) messenger
  envoys n ▷ envoy
envy n (pl -ies) feeling of discontent aroused by
  another's good fortune ▶ v (-ies, -ying, -ied)
  grudge (another's good fortune, success, or
  qualities)

envying v ▷ envy

enzyme n (pl -s) any of a group of complex proteins that act as catalysts in specific biochemical reactions

enzymes n ▷ enzyme

eolithic adj of the early part of the Stone Age

epaulette n (pl -s) shoulder ornament on a uniform

epaulettes n ▷ epaulette

ephemeral adj short-lived

epic n (pl -s) long poem, book, or film about heroic events or actions ▶ adj very impressive or ambitious

epicentre n (pl -s) point on the earth's surface immediately above the origin of an earthquake

epicentres n ▷ epicentre

epics n ▷ epic

epicure n (pl -s) person who enjoys good food and drink

epicurean adj devoted to sensual pleasures, esp. food and drink ▶ n (pl -s) epicure

epicureans n ▷ epicurean

epicures n ▷ epicure

epidemic n (pl -s) widespread occurrence of a disease

epidemics n ▷ epidemic

epidermis n (pl -ses) outer layer of the skin

epidermises n ▷ epidermis

epidural [ep-pid-dure-al] adj, n (pl -s) (of) spinal anaesthetic injected to relieve pain during childbirth

epidurals n ▷ epidural

epiglottis n (pl -ses) thin flap that covers the opening of the larynx during swallowing

epiglottises n ▷ epiglottis

epigram n (pl -s) short witty remark or poem > epigrammatic adj

epigrammatic adj ▷ epigram

epigrams n ▷ epigram

epigraph n (pl -s) quotation at the start of a book

epigraphs n ▷ epigraph

epilepsies n ▷ epilepsy

epilepsy n (pl -ies) disorder of the nervous system causing loss of consciousness and sometimes convulsions

epileptic adj of or having epilepsy ▶ n (pl -s) person who has epilepsy

epileptics n ▷ epileptic

epilogue n (pl -s) short speech or poem at the end of a literary work, esp. a play

epilogues n ▷ epilogue

epiphanies n ▷ epiphany

epiphany n (pl -ies) a moment of great or sudden realization

episcopal [ip-**piss**-kop-al] adj of or governed by bishops

episcopalian adj advocating Church government by bishops ▶ n (pl -s) advocate of such Church government

episcopalians n ▷ episcopalian

episode n (pl -s) incident in a series of incidents

episodes n ▷ episode

episodic adj occurring at irregular intervals

epistemological adj ▷ epistemology

epistemologies n ▷ epistemology

epistemology [ip-iss-stem-**ol**-a-jee] n (pl -ies) study of the source, nature, and limitations of knowledge > **epistemological** adj

epistle n (pl -s) letter, esp. of an apostle > epistolary adj

epistles n ▷ epistle

epistolary adj ▷ epistle

epitaph n (pl -s) commemorative inscription on a tomb

epitaphs n ▷ epitaph

epithet n (pl -s) descriptive word or name

epithets n ▷ epithet

epitome [ip-pit-a-mee] n (pl -s) typical example

epitomes n ▷ epitome

epitomize v (-izes, -izing, -ized) be the epitome of

epitomized v ▷ epitomize

epitomizes v ▷ epitomize

epitomizing v ▷ epitomize

epoch [ee-pok] n (pl -s) period of notable events

epochs n ▷ epoch

eponymous [ip-pon-im-uss] adj after whom a book, play, etc. is named

equable [ek-wab-bl] adj even-tempered > equably adv

equably adv ▷ equable

equal adj identical in size, quantity, degree, etc. ▶ n (pl -s) person or thing equal to another ▶ v (-s, -lling, -lled) be equal to > **equally** adv

equalities n ▷ equality

equality n (pl -ies) state of being equal

equalization n ▷ equalize

equalizations n ▷ equalize

equalize v (-lizes, -lizing, -lized) make or become equal > **equalization** n (pl -s)

equalized v ▷ equalize

equalizes v ▷ equalize

equalizing v ▷ equalize

equalled v ▷ equal

equalling v ▷ equal

equally adv ▷ equal

equals n, v ▷ equal

equanimities n ▷ equanimity
equanimity n (pl -ies) calmness of mind
equate v (-tes, -ting, -ted) make or regard as equivalent
  equated v ▷ equate
  equates v ▷ equate
  equating v ▷ equate
equation n (pl -s) mathematical statement that two expressions are equal
  equations n ▷ equation
equator n (pl -s) imaginary circle round the earth, equidistant from the poles
  > **equatorial** adj
  equatorial adj ▷ equator
  equators n ▷ equator
  equerries n ▷ equerry
equerry [ek-kwer-ee] n (pl -ies) (BRIT) officer who acts as an attendant to a member of a royal family
equestrian adj of horses and riding
equidistant adj equally distant
equilateral adj having equal sides
  equilibria n ▷ equilibriums
equilibrium n (pl -ria) steadiness or stability
equine adj of or like a horse
  equinoctial adj ▷ equinox
equinox n (pl -es) time of year when day and night are of equal length > **equinoctial** adj
  equinoxes n ▷ equinox
equip v (-s, -pping, -pped) provide with supplies, components, etc.
equipment n (pl -s) set of tools or devices used for a particular purpose
  equipments n ▷ equipment
equipoise n (pl -es) perfect balance
  equipoises n ▷ equipoise
  equipped v ▷ equip
  equipping v ▷ equip
  equips v ▷ equips
equitable adj fair and reasonable > **equitably** adv
  equitably adv ▷ equitable
  equities n ▷ equity
equity n (pl -ties) fairness ▶ pl interest of ordinary shareholders in a company
  equivalence n ▷ equivalent
  equivalences n ▷ equivalent
equivalent adj equal in value ▶ n (pl -s) something that is equivalent > **equivalence** n (pl -s)
  equivalents n ▷ equivalent
equivocal adj ambiguous > **equivocally** adv
  equivocally adv ▷ equivocal
equivocate v (-tes, -ting, -ted) use vague or ambiguous language to mislead people

> **equivocation** n (pl -s)
  equivocated v ▷ equivocate
  equivocates v ▷ equivocate
  equivocating v ▷ equivocate
  equivocation n ▷ equivocate
  equivocations n ▷ equivocate
era n (pl -s) period of time considered as distinctive
eradicate v (-tes, -ting, -ted) destroy completely > **eradication** n (pl -s)
  eradicated v ▷ eradicate
  eradicates v ▷ eradicate
  eradicating v ▷ eradicate
  eradication n ▷ eradicate
  eradications n ▷ eradicate
  eras n ▷ era
erase v (-ses, -sing, -sed) rub out
  erased v ▷ erase
eraser n (pl -s) object for erasing something written
  erasers n ▷ eraser
  erases v ▷ erase
  erasing v ▷ erase
erasure n (pl -s) erasing
  erasures n ▷ erasure
ere prep, conj (Poetic) before
erect v (-s, -ing, -ed) build ▶ adj upright
  > **erection** n (pl -s)
  erected v ▷ erect
erectile adj capable of becoming erect from sexual excitement
  erecting v ▷ erect
  erection n ▷ erect
  erections n ▷ erect
  erects v ▷ erect
erg n (pl -s) unit of work or energy
  ergonomic adj ▷ ergonomics
ergonomics n (pl study of the relationship between workers and their environment
  > **ergonomic** adj
ergot n (pl -s) fungal disease of cereal
  ergots n ▷ ergot
  ergs n ▷ erg
ermine n (pl -s) stoat in northern regions
  ermines n ▷ ermine
erode v (-s, -ing, -ed) wear away > **erosion** n (pl -s)
  eroded v ▷ erode
  erodes v ▷ erode
  eroding v ▷ erode
erogenous [ir-roj-in-uss] adj sensitive to sexual stimulation
  erosion n ▷ erode
  erosions n ▷ erode
erotic adj relating to sexual pleasure or desire

> **eroticism** n (pl -s)

erotica n sexual literature or art
  eroticism n ▷ **erotic**
  eroticisms n ▷ **erotic**

err v (-s, -ing, -ed) make a mistake

errand n (pl -s) short trip to do something for someone
  errands n ▷ **errand**

errant adj behaving in a manner considered to be unacceptable
  errata n ▷ **erratum**

erratic adj irregular or unpredictable
  > **erratically** adv
  erratically adv ▷ **erratic**

erratum n (pl -ta) error in writing or printing
  erred v ▷ **err**
  erring v ▷ **err**

erroneous adj incorrect, mistaken

error n (pl -s) mistake, inaccuracy, or misjudgment
  errors n ▷ **error**
  errs v ▷ **err**

ersatz [air-zats] adj made in imitation

erstwhile adj former

erudite adj having great academic knowledge
  > **erudition** n (pl -s)
  erudition v ▷ **erudite**
  eruditions n ▷ **erudite**

erupt v (-s, -ing, -ed) eject (steam, water, or volcanic material) violently > **eruption** n (pl -s)
  erupted v ▷ **erupt**
  erupting v ▷ **erupt**
  eruption n ▷ **erupt**
  eruptions n ▷ **erupt**
  erupts v ▷ **erupt**

erysipelas [err-riss-**sip**-pel-ass] n (pl -es) acute skin infection causing purplish patches
  erysipelases n ▷ **erysipelas**

> **es** n (eses). Es is the letter S. This is a useful word when you want to play a high-scoring word that will touch words already on the board. Es scores 2 points.

escalate v (-tes, -ting, -ted) increase in extent or intensity > **escalation** n (pl -s)
  escalated v ▷ **escalate**
  escalates v ▷ **escalate**
  escalating v ▷ **escalate**
  escalation n ▷ **escalate**
  escalations n ▷ **escalate**

escalator n (pl -s) moving staircase
  escalators n ▷ **escalator**

escalope [ess-kal-lop] n (pl -s) thin slice of meat, esp. veal

escalopes n ▷ **escalope**

escapade n (pl -s) mischievous adventure
  escapades n ▷ **escapade**

escape v (-pes, -ping, -ped) get free (of) ▶ n (pl -s) act of escaping
  escaped v ▷ **escape**

escapee n (pl -s) person who has escaped
  escapees n ▷ **escapee**
  escapes v, n ▷ **escape**
  escaping v ▷ **escape**

escapism n (pl -s) taking refuge in fantasy to avoid unpleasant reality
  escapisms n ▷ **escapism**
  escapologies n ▷ **escapologist**

escapologist n (pl -s) entertainer who specializes in freeing himself from confinement > **escapology** n (pl -ies)
  escapologists n ▷ **escapologist**
  escapology n ▷ **escapologist**

escarpment n (pl -s) steep face of a ridge or mountain
  escarpments n ▷ **escarpment**

eschew [iss-**chew**] v (-s, -ing, -ed) abstain from, avoid
  eschewed v ▷ **eschew**
  eschewing v ▷ **eschew**
  eschews v ▷ **eschew**

escort n (pl -s) people or vehicles accompanying another person for protection or as an honour ▶ v (-s, -ing, -ed) act as an escort to
  escorted to ▷ **escort**
  escorting v ▷ **escort**
  escorts n, v ▷ **escort**

escudo [ess-**kyoo**-doe] n (pl -dos) former monetary unit of Portugal
  escudos n ▷ **escudo**

escutcheon n (pl -s) shield with a coat of arms
  escutcheons n ▷ **escutcheon**

esoteric [ee-so-**ter**-rik] adj understood by only a small number of people with special knowledge

espadrille [ess-pad-**drill**] n (pl -s) light canvas shoe with a braided cord sole
  espadrilles n ▷ **espadrille**

espalier [ess-**pal**-yer] n (pl -s) shrub or fruit tree trained to grow flat
  espaliers n ▷ **espalier**

esparto n (pl -s) grass of S Europe and N Africa used for making rope etc.
  espartos n ▷ **esparto**

especial adj (Formal) special

especially adv particularly
  espied v ▷ **espy**
  espies v ▷ **espy**

espionage [ess-pyon-ahzh] *n* (*pl* -s) spying
espionages *n* ▷ espionage
esplanade *n* (*pl* -s) wide open road used as a public promenade
esplanades *n* ▷ esplanade
espousal *n* ▷ espouse
espousals *n* ▷ espouse
espouse *v* (-ses, -sing, -sed) adopt or give support to (a cause etc.) > espousal *n* (*pl* -s)
espoused *v* ▷ espouse
espouses *v* ▷ espouse
espousing *v* ▷ espouse
espresso *n* (*pl* -s) strong coffee made by forcing steam or boiling water through ground coffee beans
espressos *n* ▷ espresso
esprit [ess-pree] *n* (*pl* -s) spirit, liveliness, or wit
esprits *n* ▷ esprit
espy *v* (-ies, -ying, -ied) catch sight of
espying *v* ▷ espy
esquire *n* (*pl* -s) courtesy title placed after a man's name
esquires *n* ▷ esquire
essay *n* (*pl* -s) short literary composition ▶ *v* (-s, -ing, -ed) attempt > essayist *n* (*pl* -s)
essayed *v* ▷ essay
essaying *v* ▷ essay
essayist *n* ▷ essay
essayists *n* ▷ essay
essays *n*, *v* ▷ essay
essence *n* (*pl* -s) most important feature of a thing which determines its identity
essences *n* ▷ essence
essential *adj* vitally important ▶ *n* (*pl* -s) something fundamental or indispensable > essentially *adv*
essentially *adv* ▷ essential
essentials *n* ▷ essential
establish *v* (-es, -ing, -ed) set up on a permanent basis
established *v* ▷ establish
establishes *v* ▷ establish
establishing *v* ▷ establish
establishment *n* (*pl* -s) act of establishing
establishments *n* ▷ establishment
estate *n* (*pl* -s) landed property
estates *n* ▷ estate
esteem *n* (*pl* -s) high regard ▶ *v* (-s, -ing, -ed) think highly of
esteemed *v* ▷ esteem
esteeming *v* ▷ esteem
esteems *n*, *v* ▷ esteem
ester *n* (*pl* -s) (CHEM) compound produced by the reaction between an acid and an alcohol
esters *n* ▷ ester

estimable *adj* worthy of respect
estimate *v* (-tes, -ting, -ted) calculate roughly ▶ *n* (*pl* -s) approximate calculation
estimated *v* ▷ estimate
estimates *v*, *n* ▷ estimate
estimating *v* ▷ estimate
estimation *n* (*pl* -s) considered opinion
estimations *n* ▷ estimation
estranged *adj* no longer living with one's spouse > estrangement *n* (*pl* -s)
estrangement *n* ▷ estranged
estrangements *n* ▷ estranged
estuaries *n* ▷ estuary
estuary *n* (*pl* -ies) mouth of a river
etch *v* (-es, -ing, -ed) wear away or cut the surface of (metal, glass, etc.) with acid > etching *n* (*pl* -s)
etched *v* ▷ etch
etches *v* ▷ etch
etching *v*, *n* ▷ etch
eternal *adj* without beginning or end > eternally *adv*
eternally *adv* ▷ eternal
eternities *n* ▷ eternity
eternity *n* (*pl* -ies) infinite time
ether *n* (*pl* -s) colourless sweet-smelling liquid used as an anaesthetic
ethereal [eth-eer-ee-al] *adj* extremely delicate
ethers *n* ▷ ether
ethic *n* (*pl* -s) moral principle > ethical *adj* > ethically *adv*
ethical *adj* ▷ ethic
ethically *adv* ▷ ethic
ethics *n* ▷ ethic
ethnic *adj* relating to a people or group that shares a culture, religion, or language
ethnological *adj* ▷ ethnology
ethnologies *n* ▷ ethnology
ethnologist *n* ▷ ethnology
ethnologists *n* ▷ ethnology
ethnology *n* (*pl* -ies) study of human races > ethnological *adj* > ethnologist *n* (*pl* -s)
ethos [eeth-oss] *n* (*pl* -es) distinctive spirit and attitudes of a people, culture, etc.
ethoses *n* ▷ ethos
ethyl [eeth-ile] *adj* of, consisting of, or containing the hydrocarbon group C_2H_5
ethylene *n* (*pl* -s) poisonous gas used as an anaesthetic and as fuel
ethylenes *n* ▷ ethylene
etiolate [ee-tee-oh-late] *v* (-tes, -ting, -ted) become pale and weak (BOTANY)
etiolated *v* ▷ etiolate
etiolates *v* ▷ etiolate
etiolating *v* ▷ etiolate

etiologies n ▷ etiology

etiology n (pl **-ies**) study of the causes of diseases

etiquette n (pl **-s**) conventional code of conduct

etiquettes n ▷ etiquette

étude [ay-tewd] n (pl **-s**) short musical composition for a solo instrument, esp. intended as a technical exercise

études n ▷ étude

etymological adj ▷ etymology

etymologies n ▷ etymology

etymology n (pl **-gies**) study of the sources and development of words > **etymological** adj

eucalypt n ▷ eucalyptus

eucalypts n ▷ eucalyptus

eucalyptus, eucalypt n (pl **-ses, -s**) tree, mainly grown in Australia, that provides timber, gum, and medicinal oil from the leaves

eucalyptuses n ▷ eucalyptus

eugenics [yew-jen-iks] n (pl study of methods of improving the human race

eulogies n ▷ eulogy

eulogistic adj ▷ euology

eulogize v (**-s, -ing, -ed**) praise (a person or thing) highly in speech or writing

eulogized v ▷ eulogize

eulogizes v ▷ eulogize

eulogizing v ▷ eulogize

eulogy n (pl **-ies**) speech or writing in praise of a person > **eulogistic** adj

eunuch n (pl **-s**) castrated man, esp. (formerly) a guard in a harem

eunuchs n ▷ eunuch

euphemism n (pl **-s**) inoffensive word or phrase substituted for one considered offensive or upsetting > **euphemistic** adj > **euphemistically** adv

euphemisms n ▷ euphemism

euphemistic ▷ euphemism

euphemistically ▷ euphemism

euphonies n ▷ euphony

euphonious adj pleasing to the ear

euphonium n (pl **-s**) brass musical instrument, tenor tuba

euphoniums n ▷ euphonium

euphony n (pl **-nies**) pleasing sound

euphoria n (pl **-s**) sense of elation > **euphoric** adj

euphorias n ▷ euphoria

euphoric adj ▷ euphoria

eureka [yew-reek-a] interj exclamation of triumph at finding something

euro n (pl **-s**) unit of the single currency of the

European Union

euros n ▷ euro

euthanasia n (pl **-s**) act of killing someone painlessly, esp. to relieve his or her suffering

euthanasias n ▷ euthanasia

evacuate v (**-tes, -ting, -ted**) send (someone) away from a place of danger > **evacuation** n (pl **-s**) > **evacuee** n (pl **-s**)

evacuated v ▷ evacuate

evacuates v ▷ evacuate

evacuating v ▷ evacuate

evacuation n ▷ evacuate

evacuations n ▷ evacuate

evacuee n ▷ evacuate

evacuees n ▷ evacuate

evade v (**-des, -ding, -ded**) get away from or avoid > **evasion** n (pl **-s**)

evaded v ▷ evade

evades v ▷ evade

evading v ▷ evade

evaluate v (**-tes, -ting, -ted**) find or judge the value of > **evaluation** n (pl **-s**)

evaluated v ▷ evaluate

evaluates v ▷ evaluate

evaluating v ▷ evaluate

evaluation n ▷ evaluate

evaluations n ▷ evaluate

evanescence n ▷ evanescent

evanescences n ▷ evanescent

evanescent adj quickly fading away > **evanescence** n (pl **-s**)

evangelical adj of or according to gospel teaching ▶ n (pl **-s**) member of an evangelical sect > **evangelicalism** n (pl **-s**)

evangelicalism n ▷ evangelical

evangelicalisms n ▷ evangelical

evangelicals n ▷ evangelical

evangelism n (pl **-s**) teaching and spreading of the Christian gospel

evangelisms n ▷ evangelism

evangelist n (pl **-s**) writer of one of the four gospels

evangelists n ▷ evangelist

evangelization n ▷ evangelize

evangelizations n ▷ evangelize

evangelize v (**-zes, -zing, -zed**) preach the gospel > **evangelization** n (pl **-s**)

evangelized v ▷ evangelize

evangelizes v ▷ evangelize

evangelizing v ▷ evangelize

evaporate v (**-tes, -ing, -ted**) change from a liquid or solid to a vapour > **evaporation** n (pl **-s**)

evaporated v ▷ evaporate

evaporates v ▷ evaporate

evaporating v ▷ **evaporate**
evaporation n ▷ **evaporate**
evaporations n ▷ **evaporate**
evasion n ▷ **evade**
evasions n ▷ **evade**
evasive adj not straightforward > **evasively** adv
evasively adv ▷ **evasive**
evasiveness n ▷ **evasive**
eve n (pl -s) evening or day before some special event
even (-er, -est) adj flat or smooth (foll. by **with**) ▶ adv equally ▶ v (-s, -ing, -ed) make even
evened v ▷ **even**
evener adj ▷ **even**
evenest adj ▷ **even**
evening n (pl -s) end of the day or early part of the night ▶ adj of or in the evening ▶ v ▷ **even**
evenings n ▷ **evening**
evens v ▷ **even**
evensong n (pl -s) evening prayer
evensongs n ▷ **evensong**
event n (pl -s) anything that takes place
eventful adj full of exciting incidents
eventing n (pl -s) (BRIT, AUST & NZ) riding competitions, usu. involving cross-country, jumping, and dressage
eventings n ▷ **eventing**
events n ▷ **event**
eventual adj ultimate
eventualities n ▷ **eventuality**
eventuality n (pl -ies) possible event
eventually adv at the end of a situation or process
ever adv at any time > **everlasting** adj
evergreen adj, n (pl -s) (tree or shrub) having leaves throughout the year
evergreens n ▷ **evergreen**
everlasting adj ▷ **ever**
evermore adv for all time to come
every adj each without exception
everybody pron every person
everyday adj usual or ordinary
everyone pron every person
everything pron all things
everywhere adv in all places
eves n ▷ **eve**
evict v (-s, -ing, -ed) legally expel (someone) from his or her home > **eviction** n (pl -s)
evicted v ▷ **evict**
evicting v ▷ **evict**
eviction n ▷ **evict**
evictions n ▷ **evict**
evicts v ▷ **evict**
evidence n (pl -s) ground for belief ▶ v (-ces,

-cing, -ced) demonstrate, prove
evidenced v ▷ **evidence**
evidences n, v ▷ **evidence**
evidencing v ▷ **evidence**
evident adj easily seen or understood > **evidently** adv
evidential adj of, serving as, or based on evidence
evidently adv ▷ **evident**
evil n (pl -s) wickedness ▶ adj (-ller, -llest) harmful > **evilly** adv
evildoer n (pl -s) wicked person
evildoers n ▷ **evildoer**
eviller adj ▷ **evil**
evillest adj ▷ **evil**
evilly adv ▷ **evil**
evils n ▷ **evil**
evince v (-s, -ing, -ed) make evident
evinced v ▷ **evince**
evinces v ▷ **evince**
evincing v ▷ **evince**
eviscerate v (-tes, -ting, -ted) disembowel > **evisceration** n (pl -s)
eviscerated v ▷ **eviscerate**
eviscerates v ▷ **eviscerate**
eviscerating v ▷ **eviscerate**
evisceration n ▷ **eviscerate**
eviscerations n ▷ **eviscerate**
evocation n ▷ **evoke**
evocations n ▷ **evoke**
evocative adj ▷ **evoke**
evoke v (-s, -ing, -ed) call or summon up (a memory, feeling, etc.) > **evocation** n (pl -s) > **evocative** adj
evoked v ▷ **evoke**
evokes v ▷ **evoke**
evoking v ▷ **evoke**
evolution n (pl -s) gradual change in the characteristics of living things over successive generations, esp. to a more complex form > **evolutionary** adj
evolutionary n ▷ **evolution**
evolutions n ▷ **evolution**
evolve v (-kes, -king, -ked) develop gradually
evolved v ▷ **evolve**
evolves v ▷ **evolve**
evolving v ▷ **evolve**
ewe n (pl -s) female sheep
ewer n (pl -s) large jug with a wide mouth
ewers n ▷ **ewer**
ewes n ▷ **ewe**

> **ewk** n (**ewks**). Ewk is a dialect word for **itch**. It's a handy little word and a good one to remember in case you end up with both K and W, as you're very likely

to be able to play it from an E already on the board. Ewk scores 10 points.

ex *n* (*pl* **-es**) (*Informal*) former wife or husband

exacerbate [ig-zass-er-bate] *v* (**-tes, -ting, -ted**) make (pain, emotion, or a situation) worse > **exacerbation** *n* (*pl* **-s**)
  exacerbated *v* ▷ exacerbate
  exacerbates *v* ▷ exacerbate
  exacerbating *v* ▷ exacerbate
  exacerbation *n* ▷ exacerbate
  exacerbations *n* ▷ exacerbate

exact *adj* (**-er, -est**) correct and complete in every detail ▶ *v* (**-s, -ing, -ed**) demand (payment or obedience) > **exactness** *n* (*pl* **-es**) > **exactitude** *n* (*pl* **-s**)
  exacted *v* ▷ exact
  exacter *adj* ▷ exact
  exactest *adj* ▷ exact

exacting *adj* making rigorous or excessive demands ▶ *v* ▷ exact
  exactitude *n* ▷ exact
  exactitudes *n* ▷ exact

exactly *adv* precisely, in every respect
  exactness *n* ▷ exact
  exactnesses *n* ▷ exact
  exacts *v* ▷ exact

exaggerate *v* (**-tes, -ting, -ted**) regard or represent as greater than is true > **exaggeratedly** *adv* > **exaggeration** *n* (*pl* **-s**)
  exaggerated *v* ▷ exaggerate
  exaggeratedly *adv* ▷ exaggerate
  exaggerates *v* ▷ exaggerate
  exaggerating *v* ▷ exaggerate
  exaggeration *n* ▷ exaggerate
  exaggerations *n* ▷ exaggerate

exalt *v* (**-s, -ing, -ed**) praise highly > **exalted** *adj* > **exaltation** *n* (*pl* **-s**)
  exaltation *n* ▷ exalt
  exaltations *n* ▷ exalt
  exalted *v*, *adj* ▷ exalt
  exalting *v* ▷ exalt
  exalts *v* ▷ exalt

exam *n* (*pl* **-s**) ▷ examination

examination *n* (*pl* **-s**) examining
  examinations *n* ▷ examination

examine *v* (**-nes, -ning, -ned**) look at closely > **examinee** *n* (*pl* **-s**) > **examiner** *n* (*pl* **-s**)
  examined *v* ▷ examine
  examinee *n* ▷ examine
  examinees *n* ▷ examine
  examiner *n* ▷ examine
  examiners *n* ▷ examine
  examines *v* ▷ examine
  examining *v* ▷ examine

example *n* (*pl* **-s**) specimen typical of its group

examples *n* ▷ example
exams *n* ▷ exam

exasperate *v* (**-tes, -ting, -ted**) cause great irritation to > **exasperation** *n* (*pl* **-s**)
  exasperated *v* ▷ exasperate
  exasperates *v* ▷ exasperate
  exasperating *v* ▷ exasperate
  exasperation *v* ▷ exasperate
  exasperations *v* ▷ exasperate

excavate *v* (**-tes, -ting, -ted**) unearth buried objects from (a piece of land) methodically to learn about the past > **excavation** *n* (*pl* **-s**)
  excavated *v* ▷ excavate
  excavates *v* ▷ excavate
  excavating *v* ▷ excavate
  excavation *n* ▷ excavate
  excavations *n* ▷ excavate

excavator *n* (*pl* **-s**) large machine used for digging
  excavators *n* ▷ excavator

exceed *v* (**-s, -ing, -ed**) be greater than
  exceeded *v* ▷ exceed
  exceeding *v* ▷ exceed

exceedingly *adv* very
  exceeds *v* ▷ exceed

excel *v* (**-s, -lling, -lled**) be superior to
  excelled *v* ▷ excel

excellence *n* ▷ excellent
  excellences *n* ▷ excellent

excellent *adj* exceptionally good > **excellence** *n* (*pl* **-s**)
  excelling *v* ▷ excel
  excels *v* ▷ excel

except *prep* (*sometimes foll. by* **for**) other than, not including ▶ *v* (**-s, -ing, -ed**) not include
  excepted *v* ▷ except

excepting *prep* except ▶ *v* ▷ except

exception *n* (*pl* **-s**) excepting

exceptional *adj* not ordinary
  exceptions *n* ▷ exception
  excepts *v* ▷ except

excerpt *n* (*pl* **-s**) passage taken from a book, speech, etc.
  excerpts *n* ▷ excerpt

excess *n* (*pl* **-es**) state or act of exceeding the permitted limits > **excessive** *adj* > **excessively** *adv*
  excesses *n* ▷ excess
  excessive *adj* ▷ excess
  excessively *adv* ▷ excess

exchange *v* (**-ges, -ging, -ged**) give or receive (something) in return for something else ▶ *n* (*pl* **-s**) act of exchanging > **exchangeable** *adj*
  exchangeable *adj* ▷ exchange
  exchanged *v* ▷ exchange

exchanges v, n ▷ exchange
exchanging v ▷ exchange
exchequer n (pl -s) (BRIT) government
department in charge of state money
exchequers n ▷ exchequer
excise v (-ses, -sing, -sed) cut out or away
> excision n (pl -s)
excised v ▷ excise
excises v ▷ excise
excising v ▷ excise
excision n ▷ excise
excisions n ▷ excise
excitabilities n ▷ excitable
excitability n ▷ excitable
excitable adj easily excited > excitability n
(pl -s)
excite v (-s, -ing, -ed) arouse to strong emotion
> excitement n (pl -s)
excited v ▷ excite
excitement n ▷ excite
excitements n ▷ excite
excites v ▷ excite
exciting v ▷ excite
exclaim v (-s, -ing, -ed) speak suddenly, cry out
> exclamation n ▷ exclamatory adj
exclaimed v ▷ exclaim
exclaiming v ▷ exclaim
exclaims v ▷ exclaim
exclamation n ▷ exclaim
exclamations n ▷ exclaim
exclamatory adj ▷ exclaim
exclude v (-s, -ing, -ed) keep out, leave out
> exclusion n (pl -s)
excluded v ▷ exclude
excludes v ▷ exclude
excluding v ▷ exclude
exclusion n ▷ exclude
exclusions n ▷ exclude
exclusive adj excluding everything else ▶ n
(pl -s) story reported in only one newspaper
> exclusively adv > exclusivity n (pl -ies)
> exclusiveness n (pl -es)
exclusively adv ▷ exclusive
exclusiveness n ▷ exclusive
exclusivenesses n ▷ exclusive
exclusives n ▷ exclusive
exclusivities n ▷ exclusive
exclusivity n ▷ exclusive
excommunicate v (-tes, -ting, -ted) exclude
from membership and the sacraments of the
Church > excommunication n (pl -s)
excommunicated v ▷ excommunicate
excommunicates v ▷ excommunicate
excommunicating v ▷ excommunicate
excommunication n ▷ excommunicate

excommunications n ▷ excommunicate
excoriate v (-tes, -ting, -ted) censure severely
> excoriation n (pl -s)
excoriated v ▷ excoriate
excoriates v ▷ excoriate
excoriating v ▷ excoriate
excoriation n ▷ excoriate
excoriations n ▷ excoriate
excrement n (pl -s) waste matter discharged
from the body
excrements n ▷ excrement
excrescence n (pl -s) lump or growth on the
surface of an animal or plant
excrescences n ▷ excrescence
excreta [ik-skree-ta] n excrement
excrete v (-tes, -ting, -ted) discharge (waste
matter) from the body > excretion n (pl -s)
> excretory adj
excreted v ▷ excrete
excretes v ▷ excrete
excreting v ▷ excrete
excretion n ▷ excrete
excretions n ▷ excrete
excretory adj ▷ excrete
excruciating adj agonizing > excruciatingly
adv
excruciatingly adv ▷ excruciating
exculpate v (-tes, -ting, -ted) free from blame
or guilt
exculpated v ▷ exculpate
exculpates v ▷ exculpate
exculpating v ▷ exculpate
excursion n (pl -s) short journey, esp. for
pleasure
excursions n ▷ excursion
excusable adj ▷ excuse
excuse n (pl -s) explanation offered to justify
(a fault etc.) ▶ v (-ses, -sing, -sed) put forward
a reason or justification for (a fault etc.)
> excusable adj
excused v ▷ excuse
excuses n, v ▷ excuse
excusing v ▷ excuse
execrable [eks-sik-rab-bl] adj of very poor
quality
execute v (-tes, -ting, -ted) put (a condemned
person) to death > execution n (pl -s)
> executioner n (pl -s)
executed v ▷ execute
executes v ▷ execute
executing v ▷ execute
execution n ▷ execute
executioner n ▷ execute
executioners n ▷ execute
executions n ▷ execute

executive n (pl -s) person or group in an administrative position ▶ adj having the function of carrying out plans, orders, laws, etc.
  executives n ▷ executive

executor n (pl -s) person appointed to perform the instructions of a will
  executors n ▷ executor
  executrices n ▷ executrix

executrix n (pl -ixes, -ices) woman appointed to perform the instructions of a will
  executrixes n ▷ executrix
  exegeses n ▷ exegesis

exegesis [eks-sij-**jee**-siss] n (pl -ses) [-seez] explanation of a text, esp. of the Bible

exemplar n (pl -s) person or thing to be copied, model
  exemplars n ▷ exemplar

exemplary adj being a good example
  exemplification n ▷ exemplify
  exemplifications n ▷ exemplify
  exemplified v ▷ exemplify
  exemplifies v ▷ exemplify

exemplify v (-ies, -fying, -ied) show an example of > **exemplification** n (pl -s)
  exemplifying v ▷ exemplify

exempt adj not subject to an obligation etc. ▶ v (-s, -ing, -ed) release from an obligation etc. > **exemption** n (pl -s)
  exempted v ▷ exempt
  exempting v ▷ exempt
  exemption n ▷ exempt
  exemptions n ▷ exempt
  exempts v ▷ exempt

> **exequy** n (**exequies**). An exequy is a funeral rite. This is a great word if you have the tiles for it, combining X and Q. Even better, if you have all the letters for the plural, exequies, and can play it, you'll score an extra 50 points for using all your tiles. Exequy scores 25 points.

exercise n (pl -s) activity to train the body or mind ▶ v (-ses, -sing, -sed) make use of
  exercised v ▷ exercise
  exercises n, v ▷ exercise
  exercising v ▷ exercise

exert v (-s, -ing, -ed) use (influence, authority, etc.) forcefully or effectively > **exertion** n (pl -s)
  exerted v ▷ exert
  exerting v ▷ exert
  exertion n ▷ exert
  exertions n ▷ exert
  exerts v ▷ exert
  exes n ▷ ex

exeunt [eks-**see**-unt] (LATIN) they go out: used as a stage direction

exhalation n ▷ exhale

exhalations n ▷ exhale

exhale v (-les, -ling, -led) breathe out
> **exhalation** n (pl -s)
  exhaled v ▷ exhale
  exhales v ▷ exhale
  exhaling v ▷ exhale

exhaust v (-s, -ing, -ed) tire out ▶ n (pl -s) gases ejected from an engine as waste products
  exhausted v ▷ exhaust
  exhausting v ▷ exhaust

exhaustion n (pl -s) extreme tiredness
  exhaustions n ▷ exhaustion

exhaustive adj comprehensive > **exhaustively** adv
  exhaustively adv ▷ exhaustive
  exhausts v, n ▷ exhaust

exhibit v (-s, -ing, -ed) display to the public ▶ n (pl -s) object exhibited to the public (LAW)
> **exhibitor** n (pl -s)
  exhibited v ▷ exhibit
  exhibiting v ▷ exhibit

exhibition n (pl -s) public display of art, skills, etc.

exhibitionism n (pl -s) compulsive desire to draw attention to oneself > **exhibitionist** n (pl -s)
  exhibitionisms n ▷ exhibitionism
  exhibitionist n ▷ exhibitionism
  exhibitionists n ▷ exhibitionism
  exhibitions n ▷ exhibition
  exhibitor n ▷ exhibit
  exhibitors n ▷ exhibit
  exhibits v, n ▷ exhibit

exhilarate v (-tes, -ting, -ted) make lively and cheerful > **exhilaration** n (pl -s)
  exhilarated v ▷ exhilarate
  exhilarates v ▷ exhilarate
  exhilarating v ▷ exhilarate
  exhilaration n ▷ exhilarate
  exhilarations n ▷ exhilarate

exhort v (-s, -ing, -ed) urge earnestly
> **exhortation** n (pl -s)
  exhortation n ▷ exhort
  exhortations n ▷ exhort
  exhorted v ▷ exhort
  exhorting v ▷ exhort
  exhorts v ▷ exhort
  exhumation n ▷ exhume
  exhumations n ▷ exhume

exhume [ig-**zyume**] v (-mes, -ming, -med) dig up (something buried, esp. a corpse)
> **exhumation** n (pl -s)

exhumed v ▷ exhume
exhumes v ▷ exhume
exhuming v ▷ exhume
exigencies n ▷ exigency
exigency n (pl -cies) urgent demand or need
> exigent adj
exigent adj ▷ exigency
exiguous adj scanty or meagre
exile n (pl -s) prolonged, usu. enforced, absence
from one's country ▶ v (-les, -ling, -led) expel
from one's country
exiled v ▷ exile
exiles n ▷ exile
exiles n, v ▷ exile
exiling v ▷ exile
exist v (-s, -ing, -ed) have being or reality
> existence n (pl -s) > existent adj
existed v ▷ exist
existence n ▷ exist
existences n ▷ exist
existent adj ▷ exist
existential adj of or relating to existence, esp.
human existence
existentialism n (pl -s) philosophical
movement stressing the personal experience
and responsibility of the individual, who
is seen as a free agent > existentialist adj,
n (pl -s)
existentialisms n ▷ existentialism
existentialist adj, n ▷ existentialism
existentialists n ▷ existentialism
existing v ▷ exist
exists v ▷ exist
exit n (pl -s) way out ▶ v (-s, -ing, -ed) go out
exited v ▷ exit
exiting v ▷ exit
exits n, v ▷ exit

> **exo** adj. Exo is an informal Australian
> way of saying excellent. This is a great
> little word as it allows you to combine
> X with two of the most common tiles
> in the game, E and O. Exo scores 10
> points.

exocrine adj relating to a gland, such as the
sweat gland, that secretes externally through
a duct
exodus [eks-so-duss] n (pl -es) departure of a
large number of people
exoduses n ▷ exodus
exonerate v (-tes, -ting, -ted) free from blame
or a criminal charge > exoneration n (pl -s)
exonerates v ▷ exonerate
exonerated v ▷ exonerate
exonerating v ▷ exonerate
exoneration v ▷ exonerate

exonerations v ▷ exonerate
exorbitant adj (of prices, demands, etc.)
excessive, immoderate > exorbitantly adv
exorbitantly adv ▷ exorbitant
exorcism n ▷ exorcize
exorcisms n ▷ exorcize
exorcist n ▷ exorcize
exorcists n ▷ exorcize
exorcize v (-zes, -zing, -zed) expel (evil spirits)
by prayers and religious rites > exorcism n (pl
-s) > exorcist n (pl -s)
exorcized v ▷ exorcize
exorcizes v ▷ exorcize
exorcizing v ▷ exorcize
exotic adj having a strange allure or beauty ▶ n
(pl -s) non-native plant > exotically adv
exotica pl n (collection of) exotic objects
exotically adv ▷ exotic
exotics n ▷ exotic
expand v (-s, -ing, -ed) make or become larger
(foll. by on) > expansion n (pl -s)
expanded v ▷ expand
expanding v ▷ expand
expands v ▷ expand
expanse n (pl -s) uninterrupted wide area
expanses n ▷ expanse
expansion n ▷ expand
expansions n ▷ expand
expansive adj wide or extensive
expat adj, n (pl -s) short for expatriate
expatiate [iks-pay-shee-ate] v (-tes, -ting, -ted)
(foll. by on) speak or write at great length (on)
expatiated v ▷ expatiate
expatiates v ▷ expatiate
expatiating v ▷ expatiate
expatriate [eks-pat-ree-it] adj living outside
one's native country ▶ n (pl -s) person
living outside his or her native country
> expatriation n (pl -s)
expatriates n ▷ expatriate
expatriation n ▷ expatriate
expatriations n ▷ expatriate
expats n ▷ expat
expect v (-s, -ing, -ed) regard as probable
expectancies n ▷ expectancy
expectancy n (pl -ies) something expected on
the basis of an average
expectant adj expecting or hopeful
> expectantly adv
expectantly adv ▷ expectant
expectation n (pl -s) act or state of expecting
expectations n ▷ expectation
expected v ▷ expect
expecting v ▷ expect
expectorant n (pl -s) medicine that helps

to bring up phlegm from the respiratory passages
expectorants n ▷ expectorant
expectorate v (-tes, -ting, -ted) spit out (phlegm etc.) > expectoration n (pl -s)
expectorated v ▷ expectorate
expectorates v ▷ expectorate
expectorating v ▷ expectorate
expectoration n ▷ expectorate
expectorations n ▷ expectorate
expects v ▷ expect
expediencies n ▷ expedient
expediency n ▷ expedient
expedient n (pl -s) something that achieves a particular purpose ▶ adj suitable to the circumstances, appropriate > expediency n (pl -ies)
expedients n ▷ expedient
expedite v (-s, -ing, -ed) hasten the progress of
expedited v ▷ expedite
expedites v ▷ expedite
expediting v ▷ expedite
expedition n (pl -s) organized journey, esp. for exploration
expeditionary adj relating to an expedition, esp. a military one
expeditions n ▷ expedition
expeditious adj done quickly and efficiently
expel v (-s, -lling, -lled) drive out with force > expulsion n (pl -s)
expelled v ▷ expel
expelling v ▷ expel
expels v ▷ expel
expend v (-s, -ing, -ed) spend, use up
expendable adj able to be sacrificed to achieve an objective
expended v ▷ expend
expending v ▷ expend
expenditure n (pl -s) something expended, esp. money
expenditures n ▷ expenditure
expends v ▷ expend
expense n (pl -s) cost ▶ pl charges, outlay incurred
expenses n ▷ expense
expensive adj high-priced
experience n (pl -s) direct personal participation ▶ v (-ces, -cing, -ced) participate in
experienced v ▷ experience ▶ adj skilful from extensive participation
experiences n, v ▷ experience
experiencing v ▷ experience
experiment n (pl experiments) test to provide evidence to prove or disprove a theory

▶ v (-s, -ing, -ed) carry out an experiment
> experimental adj > experimentally adv
> experimentation n (pl -s)
experimental adj ▷ experiment
experimentally adv ▷ experiment
experimentation n ▷ experiment
experimentations n ▷ experiment
experimented v ▷ experiment
experimenting v ▷ experiment
experiments n, v ▷ experiment
expert n (pl -s) person with extensive skill or knowledge in a particular field ▶ adj skilful or knowledgeable
expertise [eks-per-teez] n (pl -s) special skill or knowledge
expertises n ▷ expertise
experts n ▷ expert
expiate v (-tes, -ting, -ted) make amends for > expiation n (pl -s)
expiated v ▷ expiate
expiates v ▷ expiate
expiating v ▷ expiate
expiation n ▷ expiate
expiations n ▷ expiate
expiration n ▷ expire
expirations n ▷ expire
expire v (-res, -ring, -red) finish or run out (Lit) > expiration n (pl -s)
expired v ▷ expire
expires v ▷ expire
expiries n ▷ expiry
expiring v ▷ expire
expiry n (pl -ies) end, esp. of a contract period
explain v (-s, -ing, -ed) make clear and intelligible > explanation n (pl -s)
> explanatory adj
explained v ▷ explain
explaining v ▷ explain
explains v ▷ explain
explanation n ▷ explain
explanations n ▷ explain
explanatory adj ▷ explain
expletive n (pl -s) swearword
expletives n ▷ expletive
explicable adj able to be explained
explicate v (-tes, -ting, -ted) (Formal) explain > explication n (pl -s)
explicated v ▷ explicate
explicates v ▷ explicate
explicating v ▷ explicate
explication n ▷ explicate
explications n ▷ explicate
explicit adj precisely and clearly expressed > explicitly adv
explicitly adv ▷ explicit

explode v (-des, -ding, -ded) burst with great violence, blow up ► **explosion** n (pl -s)
  exploded v ▷ explode
  explodes v ▷ explode
  exploding v ▷ explode
exploit v (pl -s) take advantage of for one's own purposes ► n (pl -s) notable feat or deed > **exploitation** n (pl -s) > **exploiter** n (pl -s)
  exploitation n ▷ exploit
  exploitations n ▷ exploit
  exploited v ▷ exploit
  exploiter n ▷ exploit
  exploiters n ▷ exploit
  exploiting v ▷ exploit
  exploits v, n ▷ exploit
  exploration n ▷ explore
  explorations n ▷ explore
  exploratory adj ▷ explore
explore v (-res, -ring, -red) investigate > **exploration** n (pl -s) > **exploratory** adj > **explorer** n (pl -s)
  explored v ▷ explore
  explorer n ▷ explore
  explorers n ▷ explore
  explores v ▷ explore
  exploring v ▷ explore
  explosion n ▷ explode
  explosions n ▷ explode
explosive adj tending to explode ► n (pl -s) substance that causes explosions
  explosives n ▷ explosive
expo n (pl -s) (Informal) exposition, large public exhibition
exponent n (pl -s) person who advocates an idea, cause, etc.
exponential adj (Informal) very rapid > **exponentially** adv
  exponentially adv ▷ exponential
  exponents n ▷ exponent
export n (pl -s) selling or shipping of goods to a foreign country ► v (-s, -ing, -ed) sell or ship (goods) to a foreign country > **exporter** n (pl -s)
  exported v ▷ export
  exporter n ▷ export
  exporters n ▷ export
  exporting v ▷ export
  exports n, v ▷ export
  expos n ▷ expo
expose v (-ses, -sing, -sed) uncover or reveal > **exposure** n (pl -s) exposing
exposé [iks-pose-ay] n (pl -s) bringing of a crime, scandal, etc. to public notice
  exposed v ▷ expose
  exposes v ▷ expose

  exposés n ▷ exposé
  exposing v ▷ expose
  exposition n ▷ expound
  expositions n ▷ expound
expostulate v (-tes, -ting, -ted) (foll. by **with**) reason (with), esp. to dissuade
  expostulated v ▷ expostulate
  expostulates v ▷ expostulate
  expostulating v ▷ expostulate
  exposure n ▷ expose
  exposures n ▷ expose
expound v (-s, -ing, -ed) explain in detail > **exposition** n (pl -s) explanation
  expounded v ▷ expound
  expounding v ▷ expound
  expounds v ▷ expound
express v (-es, -ing, -ed) put into words ► adj explicitly stated ► n (pl -es) fast train or bus stopping at only a few stations ► adv by express delivery
  expressed v ▷ express
  expresses v, n ▷ express
  expressing v ▷ express
expression n (pl -s) expressing > **expressionless** adj > **expressive** adj
expressionism n (pl -s) early 20th-century artistic movement which sought to express emotions rather than represent the physical world > **expressionist** adj, n (pl -s)
  expressionisms n ▷ expressionism
  expressionist adj, n ▷ expressionism
  expressionists n ▷ expressionism
  expressionless adj ▷ expression
  expressions n ▷ expression
  expressive adj ▷ expression
expropriate v (-tes, -ting, -ted) deprive an owner of (property) > **expropriation** n (pl -s)
  expropriated v ▷ expropriate
  expropriates v ▷ expropriate
  expropriating v ▷ expropriate
  expropriation n ▷ expropriate
  expropriations n ▷ expropriate
  expulsion n ▷ expel
  expulsions n ▷ expel
expunge v (-ges, -ging, -ged) delete, erase, blot out
  expunged v ▷ expunge
  expunges v ▷ expunge
  expunging v ▷ expunge
expurgate v (-tes, -ting, -ted) remove objectionable parts from (a book etc.)
  expurgated v ▷ expurgate
  expurgates v ▷ expurgate
  expurgating v ▷ expurgate
exquisite adj of extreme beauty or delicacy

> **exquisitely** adv
exquisitely adv ▷ exquisite
extant adj still existing
extemporize v (-zes, -zing, -zed) speak, perform, or compose without preparation
extemporized v ▷ extemporize
extemporizes v ▷ extemporize
extemporizing v ▷ extemporize
extend v (-s, -ing, -ed) draw out or be drawn out, stretch (foll. by **to**) > **extendable** adj
extendable adj ▷ extend
extended v ▷ extend
extending v ▷ extend
extends v ▷ extend
extension n (pl -s) room or rooms added to an existing building
extensions n ▷ extension
extensive adj having a large extent, widespread
extensor n (pl -s) muscle that extends a part of the body
extensors n ▷ extensor
extent n (pl -s) range over which something extends, area
extents n ▷ extent
extenuate v (-tes, -ting, -ted) make (an offence or fault) less blameworthy
> **extenuation** n (pl -s)
extenuated v ▷ extenuate
extenuates v ▷ extenuate
extenuating v ▷ extenuate
extenuation n ▷ extenuate
extenuations n ▷ extenuate
exterior n (pl -s) part or surface on the outside ▶ adj of, on, or coming from the outside
exteriors n ▷ exterior
exterminate v (-tes, -ting, -ted) destroy (animals or people) completely
> **extermination** n (pl -s) > **exterminator** n (pl -s)
exterminated v ▷ exterminate
exterminates v ▷ exterminate
exterminating v ▷ exterminate
extermination n ▷ exterminate
exterminations n ▷ exterminate
exterminator n ▷ exterminate
exterminators n ▷ exterminate
external adj of, situated on, or coming from the outside > **externally** adv
externally adv ▷ external
extinct adj having died out > **extinction** n (pl -s)
extinction n ▷ extinct
extinctions n ▷ extinct
extinguish v (-es, -ing, -ed) put out (a fire or

light)
extinguished v ▷ extinguish
extinguisher n (pl -s) device for extinguishing a fire or light
extinguishers n ▷ extinguisher
extinguishes v ▷ extinguish
extinguishing v ▷ extinguish
extirpate v (-tes, -ting, -ted) destroy utterly
extirpated v ▷ extirpate
extirpates v ▷ extirpate
extirpating v ▷ extirpate
extol v (-s, -lling, -lled) praise highly
extolled v ▷ extol
extolling v ▷ extol
extols v ▷ extol
extort v (-s, -ing, -ed) get (something) by force or threats > **extortion** n (pl -s)
extorted v ▷ extort
extorting v ▷ extort
extortion n ▷ extort
extortionate adj (of prices) excessive
extortions n ▷ extort
extorts v ▷ extort
extra adj more than is usual, expected or needed ▶ n (pl -s) additional person or thing ▶ adv unusually or exceptionally
extract v (-s, -ing, -ed) pull out by force ▶ n (pl -s) something extracted, such as a passage from a book etc. > **extraction** n (pl -s) > **extractor** (pl -s) n
extracted v ▷ extract
extracting v ▷ extract
extraction n ▷ extract
extractions n ▷ extract
extractor n ▷ extract
extractors n ▷ extract
extracts n, v ▷ extract
extradite v (-tes, -ting, -ted) send (an accused person) back to his or her own country for trial > **extradition** n (pl -s)
extradited v ▷ extradite
extradites v ▷ extradite
extraditing v ▷ extradite
extradition n ▷ extradite
extraditions n ▷ extradite
extramural adj connected with but outside the normal courses of a university or college
extraneous [iks-train-ee-uss] adj irrelevant
extraordinarily adv ▷ extraordinary
extraordinary adj very unusual
> **extraordinarily** adv
extrapolate v (-tes, -ting, -ted) infer (something not known) from the known facts (MATHS) > **extrapolation** n (pl -s)
extrapolated v ▷ extrapolate

extrapolates v ▷ extrapolate
extrapolating v ▷ extrapolate
extrapolation n ▷ extrapolate
extrapolations n ▷ extrapolate
extras n ▷ extra
extrasensory adj beyond the normal range of the senses
extravagance n ▷ extravagant
extravagances n ▷ extravagant
extravagant adj spending money excessively > **extravagance** n (pl -s)
extravaganza n (pl -s) elaborate and lavish entertainment, display, etc.
extravaganzas n ▷ extravaganza
extreme adj of a high or the highest degree or intensity ▶ n (pl -s) either of the two limits of a scale or range > **extremely** adv
extremely adv ▷ extreme
extremes n ▷ extreme
extremist n (pl -s) person who favours immoderate methods ▶ adj holding extreme opinions
extremists n ▷ extremist
extremities n ▷ extremity
extremity n (pl -ies) farthest point
extricate v (-tes, -ting, -ted) free from complication or difficulty > **extrication** n (pl -s)
extricated v ▷ extricate
extricates v ▷ extricate
extricating v ▷ extricate
extrication n ▷ extricate
extrications n ▷ extricate
extrovert adj lively and outgoing ▶ n (pl -s) extrovert person
extroverts n ▷ extrovert
extrude v (-des, -ding, -ded) squeeze or force out > **extrusion** n (pl -s)
extruded v ▷ extrude
extrudes v ▷ extrude
extruding v ▷ extrude
extrusion n ▷ extrude
extrusions n ▷ extrude
exuberance n ▷ exuberant
exuberances n ▷ exuberant
exuberant adj high-spirited > **exuberance** n (pl -s)
exude v (-s, -ing, -ed) (of a liquid or smell) seep or flow out slowly and steadily

exuded v ▷ exude
exudes v ▷ exude
exuding v ▷ exude
exult v (-s, -ing, -ed) be joyful or jubilant > **exultation** n (pl -s) > **exultant** adj
exultant adj ▷ exult
exultation n ▷ exult
exultations n ▷ exult
exulted v ▷ exult
exulting v ▷ exult
exults v ▷ exult
eye n (pl -s) organ of sight ▶ v (-s, eyeing or eying, eyed) look at carefully or warily > **eyeless** adj
eyeball n (pl -s) ball-shaped part of the eye
eyeballs n ▷ eyeball
eyebrow n (pl -s) line of hair on the bony ridge above the eye
eyebrows n ▷ eyebrow
eyed v ▷ eye
eyeglass n (pl -es) lens for aiding defective vision
eyeglasses n ▷ eyeglass
eyeing v ▷ eye
eyelash n (pl -es) short hair that grows out from the eyelid
eyelashes n ▷ eyelash
eyeless adj ▷ eye
eyelet n (pl -s) small hole for a lace or cord to be passed through
eyelets n ▷ eyelet
eyelid n (pl -s) fold of skin that covers the eye when it is closed
eyelids n ▷ eyelid
eyeliner n (pl -s) cosmetic used to outline the eyes
eyeliners n ▷ eyeliner
eyes n, v ▷ eye
eyesight n (pl -s) ability to see
eyesights n ▷ eyesight
eyesore n (pl -s) ugly object
eyesores n ▷ eyesore
eyewitness n (pl -es) person who was present at an event and can describe what happened
eyewitnesses n ▷ eyewitness
eying v ▷ eye
eyrie n (pl -s) nest of an eagle
eyries n ▷ eyrie

Ff

F can be an awkward letter in Scrabble: there are only two two-letter words beginning with F, for example (**fa** and **fy**). But if you're aware of this, you won't waste time trying to think of other two-letter words. There are also quite a few words that combine F with X or Z, allowing high scores particularly if you can hit a bonus square with them. **Fax**, **fix** and **fox** are good examples (13 points each), and don't forgets **fez** (15). If you have a blank tile, you can use it for the second Z in **fuzz** (15) or **fuzzy** (19). **Fey**, **fly** and **fry** can also be useful (9 each).

fa n (**fas**). Fa is the musical note F. This word isn't going to win you a game on its own, but it's useful when you're trying to form several words at once. Fa scores 5 points.

fab adj Fab is a short form of **fabulous**. Fab scores 8 points.

fable n (pl **-s**) story with a moral

fabled adj made famous in legend

fables n ▷ **fable**

fabric n (pl **-s**) knitted or woven cloth

fabricate v (**-tes, -ting, -ted**) make up (a story or lie) > **fabrication** n (pl **-s**)

fabricated v ▷ **fabricate**

fabricates v ▷ **fabricate**

fabricating v ▷ **fabricate**

fabrication n ▷ **fabricate**

fabrications n ▷ **fabricate**

fabrics n ▷ **fabric**

fabulous adj (Informal) excellent > **fabulously** adv

fabulously adv ▷ **fabulous**

facade [fas-**sahd**] n (pl **-s**) front of a building

facades n ▷ **facade**

face n (pl **-s**) front of the head ▶ v (**-ces, -cing, -ced**) look or turn towards

faced v ▷ **face**

faceless adj impersonal, anonymous

faces n, v ▷ **face**

facet n (pl **-s**) aspect

facetious [fas-**see**-shuss] adj funny or trying to be funny, esp. at inappropriate times

facets n ▷ **facet**

facia n (pl **-ciae**) ▷ **fascia**

faciae n ▷ **fascia**

facial adj of the face ▶ n (pl **-s**) beauty treatment for the face

facials n ▷ **facial**

facile [fas-**sile**] adj (of a remark, argument, etc.) superficial and showing lack of real thought

facilitate v (**-tes, -ting, -ted**) make easy > **facilitation** n (pl **-s**)

facilitated v ▷ **facilitate**

facilitates v ▷ **facilitate**

facilitating v ▷ **facilitate**

facilitation n ▷ **facilitate**

facilitations n ▷ **facilitate**

facilities n ▷ **facility**

facility n (pl **-ties**) skill ▶ pl means or equipment for an activity

facing v ▷ **face**

facing n (pl **-s**) lining or covering for decoration or reinforcement ▶ pl contrasting collar and cuffs on a jacket

facings n ▷ **facing**

facsimile [fak-**sim**-ill-ee] n (pl **-s**) exact copy

facsimiles n ▷ **facsimile**

fact n (pl **-s**) event or thing known to have happened or existed > **factual** adj

faction n (pl **-s**) (dissenting) minority group within a larger body

factions n ▷ **faction**

factious adj of or producing factions

factitious adj artificial

factor n (pl **-s**) element contributing to a result

factorial n (pl **-s**) product of all the integers from one to a given number

factorials n ▷ **factorial**

factories n ▷ **factory**

factorize v (**-zes, -zing, -zed**) calculate the factors of (a number)

factorized v ▷ **factorize**

factorizes v ▷ **factorize**

factorizing v ▷ **factorize**

factors n ▷ factor

factory n (pl -ies) building where goods are manufactured

factotum n (pl -s) person employed to do all sorts of work

factotums n ▷ factotum

facts n ▷ fact

factual adj ▷ fact

faculties n ▷ faculty

faculty n (pl -ties) physical or mental ability

fad n (pl -s) short-lived fashion > **faddy** (**-ddier, -ddiest**), **faddish** adj

faddier adj ▷ fad

faddiest adj ▷ fad

faddish adj ▷ fad

faddy adj ▷ fad

fade v (**-des, -ding, -ded**) (cause to) lose brightness, colour, or strength

faded v ▷ fade

fades v ▷ fade

fading v ▷ fade

fads n ▷ fad

faecal adj ▷ faeces

faeces [fee-seez] pl n waste matter discharged from the anus > **faecal** [fee-kl] ▶ adj

fag[1] n (pl -s) (Informal) boring task (BRIT) ▶ v (**-gs, -gging, -gged**) (BRIT) do menial chores in a public school

fag[2] n (BRIT) (Slang) cigarette

fagged v ▷ fag[1]

fagging v ▷ fag[1]

faggot n (pl -s) (BRIT, AUST & NZ) ball of chopped liver, herbs, and bread

faggots n ▷ faggot

fags n, v ▷ fag[1, 2]

faïence [fie-ence] n (pl -s) tin-glazed earthenware

faïences n ▷ faïence

fail v (**-s, -ing, -ed**) be unsuccessful ▶ n (pl -s) instance of not passing an exam or test

failed v ▷ fail

failing n (pl -s) weak point ▶ prep in the absence of ▶ v ▷ fail

failings n ▷ failing

fails v, n ▷ fail

failure n (pl -s) act or instance of failing

failures n ▷ failure

fain adv (Obs) gladly

faint adj lacking clarity, brightness, or volume ▶ v (**-s, -ing, -ed**) lose consciousness temporarily ▶ n (pl -s) temporary loss of consciousness

fainted v ▷ faint

fainting v ▷ faint

faints v, n ▷ faint

fair[1] adj (**-er, -est**) unbiased and reasonable ▶ adv fairly > **fairness** n (pl -s)

fair[2] n (pl -s) travelling entertainment with sideshows, rides, and amusements

fairer adj ▷ fair[1]

fairest adj ▷ fair[1]

fairground n (pl -s) open space used for a fair

fairgrounds n ▷ fairground

fairies n ▷ fairy

fairly adv moderately

fairness n ▷ fair[1]

fairnesses n ▷ fair[1]

fairs n ▷ fair[1, 2]

fairway n (pl -s) (GOLF) smooth area between the tee and the green

fairways n ▷ fairway

fairy n (pl -ries) imaginary small creature with magic powers > **fairyland** n (pl -s)

fairyland n ▷ fairy

fairylands n ▷ fairy

faith n (pl -s) strong belief, esp. without proof

faithful adj loyal > **faithfully** adv

faithfully adv ▷ faithful

faithless adj disloyal or dishonest

faiths n ▷ faith

fake v (**-kes, -king, -ked**) cause something not genuine to appear real or more valuable by fraud ▶ n (pl -s) person, thing, or act that is not genuine ▶ adj not genuine

faked v ▷ fake

fakes v, n ▷ fake

faking v ▷ fake

fakir [fay-keer] n (pl -s) Muslim who spurns worldly possessions

fakirs n ▷ fakir

falcon n (pl -s) small bird of prey

falconer n ▷ falconry

falconers n ▷ falconry

falconries n ▷ falconry

falconry n (pl -ries) art of training falcons > **falconer** n (pl -s)

falcons n ▷ falcon

fall v (**-s, -ing, fell, fallen**) drop from a higher to a lower place through the force of gravity ▶ n (pl -s) falling

fallacies n ▷ fallacy

fallacious adj ▷ fallacy

fallacy n (pl -cies) false belief > **fallacious** adj

fallen v ▷ fall

fallibilities n ▷ fallible

fallibility n ▷ fallible

fallible adj (of a person) liable to make mistakes > **fallibility** n (pl -ties)

falling v ▷ fall

fallout n (pl -s) radioactive particles spread as

a result of a nuclear explosion
fallouts *n* ▷ **fallout**
fallow *adj* (of land) ploughed but left unseeded to regain fertility
falls *v, n* ▷ **fall**
false *adj* (-**r**, -**st**) not true or correct > **falsely** *adv* > **falseness** *n* (*pl* -**es**) > **falsity** *n* (*pl* -**ties**)
falsehood *n* (*pl* -**s**) quality of being untrue
falsehoods *n* ▷ **falsehood**
falsely *adv* ▷ **false**
falseness *n* ▷ **false**
falsenesses *n* ▷ **false**
falser *adj* ▷ **false**
falsest *adj* ▷ **false**
falsetto *n* (*pl* -**tos**) voice pitched higher than one's natural range
falsettos *n* ▷ **falsetto**
falsification *n* ▷ **falsify**
falsifications *n* ▷ **falsify**
falsified *v* ▷ **falsify**
falsifies *v* ▷ **falsify**
falsify *v* (-**fies**, -**fying**, -**fied**) alter fraudulently > **falsification** *n* (*pl* -**s**)
falsifying *v* ▷ **falsify**
falsities *n* ▷ **false**
falsity *v* ▷ **false**
falter *v* (-**s**, -**ing**, -**ed**) be hesitant, weak, or unsure
faltered *v* ▷ **falter**
faltering *v* ▷ **falter**
falters *v* ▷ **falter**
fame *n* (*pl* -**s**) state of being widely known or recognized
famed *adj* famous
famed *adj* ▷ **fame**
fames *n* ▷ **fame**
familial *adj* ▷ **family**
familiar *adj* well-known ▶ *n* (*pl* -**s**) demon supposed to attend a witch > **familiarly** *adv* > **familiarity** *n* (*pl* -**ties**)
familiarities *n* ▷ **familiarity**
familiarity *n* ▷ **familiarity**
familiarize (-**zes**, -**zing**, -**zed**) *v* acquaint fully with a particular subject > **familiarization** *n* (*pl* -**s**)
familiarization *n* ▷ **familiarize**
familiarizations *n* ▷ **familiarize**
familiarized *v* ▷ **familiarize**
familiarizes *v* ▷ **familiarize**
familiarizing *v* ▷ **familiarize**
familiarly *adv* ▷ **familiar**
familiars *n* ▷ **familiar**
families *n* ▷ **family**
family *n* (*pl* -**lies**) group of parents and their children ▶ *adj* suitable for parents and

children together > **familial** *adj*
famine *n* (*pl* -**s**) severe shortage of food
famines *n* ▷ **famine**
famished *adj* very hungry
famous *adj* very well-known
famously *adv* (*Informal*) excellently
fan[1] *n* (*pl* -**s**) hand-held or mechanical object used to create a current of air for ventilation or cooling ▶ *v* (-**s**, -**nning**, -**nned**) blow or cool with a fan
fan[2] *n* (*pl* -**s**) (*Informal*) devotee of a pop star, sport, or hobby
fanatic *n* (*pl* -**s**) person who is excessively enthusiastic about something > **fanatical** *adj* > **fanatically** *adv* > **fanaticism** *n* (*pl* -**s**)
fanatical *adj* ▷ **fanatic**
fanatically *adv* ▷ **fanatic**
fanaticism *n* ▷ **fanatic**
fanaticisms *n* ▷ **fanatic**
fanatics *n* ▷ **fanatic**
fanbase *n* (*pl* -**s**) body of admirers of a particular pop singer, sports team, etc
fanbases *n* ▷ **fanbase**
fancied *v* ▷ **fancy**
fancier *adj* ▷ **fancy**
fancies *n, v* ▷ **fancy**
fanciest *adj* ▷ **fancy**
fanciful *adj* not based on fact > **fancifully** *adv*
fancifully *adv* ▷ **fanciful**
fancy *adj* (-**cier**, -**ciest**) elaborate, not plain ▶ *n* (*pl* -**cies**) sudden irrational liking or desire ▶ *v* (-**cies**, -**cying**, -**cied**) (*Informal*) be sexually attracted to
fancy-free *adj* not in love
fancying *v* ▷ **fancy**
fandango *n* (*pl* -**os**) lively Spanish dance
fandangos *n* ▷ **fandango**
fanfare *n* (*pl* -**s**) short loud tune played on brass instruments
fanfares *n* ▷ **fanfare**
fang *n* (*pl* -**s**) snake's tooth which injects poison
fangs *n* ▷ **fang**
fanned *n* ▷ **fan**
fanning *n* ▷ **fan**
fans *n, v* ▷ **fan**
fantail *n* (*pl* -**s**) small New Zealand bird with a tail like a fan
fantails *n* ▷ **fantail**
fantasia *n* (*pl* -**s**) musical composition of an improvised nature
fantasias *n* ▷ **fantasia**
fantasies *n* ▷ **fantasy**
fantasize *v* (-**zes**, -**zing**, -**zed**) indulge in daydreams

fantasized v ▷ fantasize
fantasizes v ▷ fantasize
fantasizing v ▷ fantasize
fantastic adj (Informal) very good
> **fantastically** adv
fantastically adv ▷ fantastic
fantasy n (pl -sies) far-fetched notion
far adv (farther or further, farthest or furthest)
at, to, or from a great distance ▶ adj remote in
space or time
farad n (pl -s) unit of electrical capacitance
farads n ▷ farad
farce n (pl -s) boisterous comedy
farces n ▷ farce
farcical adj ludicrous > **farcically** adv
farcically adv ▷ farcical
fare n (pl -s) charge for a passenger's journey
▶ v (-res, -ring, -red) get on (as specified)
fared v ▷ fare
fares n, v ▷ fare
farewell interj goodbye ▶ n (pl -s) act of saying
goodbye and leaving ▶ v (-s, -ing, -ed) (NZ) say
goodbye
farewelled v ▷ farewell
farewelling v ▷ farewell
farewells n, v ▷ farewell
farinaceous adj containing starch or having a
starchy texture
faring v ▷ fare
farm n (pl -s) area of land for growing crops or
rearing livestock ▶ v (-s, -ing, -ed) cultivate
(land) > **farmhouse** n (pl -s) > **farmyard** n (pl -s)
farmed v ▷ farm
farmer n (pl -s) person who owns or runs a
farm
farmers n ▷ farmer
farmhouse n ▷ farm
farmhouses n ▷ farm
farming v ▷ farm
farms n, v ▷ farm
farmstead n (pl -s) farm and its buildings
farmsteads n ▷ farmstead
farmyard n ▷ farm
farmyards n ▷ farm
farrago [far-**rah**-go] n (pl -gos, -goes) jumbled
mixture of things
farragoes n ▷ farrago
farragos n ▷ farrago
farrier n (pl -s) person who shoes horses
farriers n ▷ farrier
farrow n (pl -s) litter of piglets ▶ v (-s, -ing, -ed)
(of a sow) give birth
farrowed v ▷ farrow
farrowing v ▷ farrow
farrows n, v ▷ farrow

farther, farthest adv, adj ▷ far
farthing n (pl -s) former British coin
equivalent to a quarter of a penny
farthings n ▷ farthing
fascia [**fay**-shya] n (pl -ciae, -cias) outer surface
of a dashboard
fasciae n ▷ fascia
fascias n ▷ fascia
fascinate v (-tes, -ting, -ted) attract
and interest strongly > **fascinating** adj
> **fascination** n (pl -s)
fascinated v ▷ fascinate
fascinates v ▷ fascinate
fascinating v, adj ▷ fascinate
fascination n ▷ fascinate
fascinations n ▷ fascinate
fascism [**fash**-iz-zum] n (pl -s) right-wing
totalitarian political system characterized
by state control and extreme nationalism
> **fascist** adj, n (pl -s)
fascisms n ▷ fascism
fascist n ▷ fascism
fascists n ▷ fascism
fashion n (pl -s) style in clothes, hairstyle, etc.,
popular at a particular time ▶ v (-s, -ing, -ed)
form or make into a particular shape
fashionable adj currently popular
> **fashionably** adv
fashionably adv ▷ fashionable
fashioned v ▷ fashion
fashioning v ▷ fashion
fashions n, v ▷ fashion
fast[1] adj (-er, -est) (capable of) acting or
moving quickly ▶ adv quickly
fast[2] v (-s, -ing, -ed) go without food, esp. for
religious reasons ▶ n (pl -s) period of fasting
fasted v ▷ fast[2]
fasten v (-s, -ing, -ed) make or become firmly
fixed or joined
fastened v ▷ fasten
fastener n (pl -s) device that fastens
fasteners n ▷ fastener
fastening v ▷ fasten ▶ n (pl -s) device that
fastens
fastenings n ▷ fastening
fastens v ▷ fasten
faster adj ▷ fast[1]
fastest adj ▷ fast[1]
fastidious adj very fussy about details
> **fastidiously** adv > **fastidiousness** n
fastidiously adv ▷ fastidious
fastidiousness n ▷ fastidious
fastidiousnesses n ▷ fastidious
fasting v ▷ fast[2]
fastness n (pl -es) fortress, safe place

fastnesses n ▷ fastness

fasts v, n ▷ fast²

fat adj (-er, -est) having excess flesh on the body ▶ n (pl -s) extra flesh on the body >fatness n (pl -es)

fatal adj causing death or ruin >**fatally** adv

fatalism n (pl -s) belief that all events are predetermined and people are powerless to change their destinies >**fatalist** n (pl -s) >**fatalistic** adj

fatalisms n ▷ fatalism

fatalist n ▷ fatalism

fatalistic adj ▷ fatalism

fatalists n ▷ fatalism

fatalities n ▷ fatality

fatality n (pl -ties) death caused by an accident or disaster

fatally adv ▷ fatal

fate n (pl -s) power supposed to predetermine events

fated adj destined

fateful adj having important, usu. disastrous, consequences

fates n ▷ fate

fathead n (pl -s) (Informal) stupid person >**fat-headed** adj

fatheaded adj ▷ fathead

fatheads n ▷ fathead

father n (pl -s) male parent ▶ v (-s, -ing, -ed) be the father of (offspring) >**fatherhood** n (pl -s) >**fatherless** adj >**fatherly** adj

fathered v ▷ father

fatherhood n ▷ father

fatherhoods n ▷ father

fathering v ▷ father

fatherland n one's native country

fatherlands n ▷ fatherland

fatherless adj ▷ father

fatherly adj ▷ father

fathers n, v ▷ father

fathom n (pl -s) unit of length, used in navigation, equal to six feet (1.83 metres) ▶ v (-s, -ing, -ed) understand >**fathomable** adj

fathomable adj ▷ fathom

fathomed v ▷ fathom

fathoming v ▷ fathom

fathomless adj too deep or difficult to fathom

fathoms n, v ▷ fathom

fatigue [fat-eeg] n (pl -s) extreme physical or mental tiredness ▶ v (-gues, -guing, -gued) tire out

fatigued v ▷ fatigue

fatigues v, n ▷ fatigue

fatiguing v ▷ fatigue

fatness n ▷ fat

fatnesses n ▷ fat

fats n ▷ fat

fatten v (-s, -ing, -ed) (cause to) become fat

fattened v ▷ fatten

fattening v ▷ fatten

fattens v ▷ fatten

fattier adj ▷ fatty

fattiest adj ▷ fatty

fatty adj (-ier, -iest) containing fat

fatuities n ▷ fatuous

fatuity n ▷ fatuous

fatuous adj foolish >**fatuously** adv >**fatuity** n (pl -s)

fatuously adv ▷ fatuous

faucet [faw-set] n (pl -s) (US) tap

faucets n ▷ faucet

fault n (pl -s) responsibility for something wrong ▶ v (-s, -ing, -ed) criticize or blame >**faulty** adj (-tier, -tiest) >**faultless** adj >**faultlessly** adv

faulted v ▷ fault

faultier adj ▷ fault

faultiest adj ▷ fault

faulting v ▷ fault

faultless adj ▷ fault

faultlessly adv ▷ fault

faults v ▷ fault

faulty n ▷ fault

faun n (pl -s) (in Roman legend) creature with a human face and torso and a goat's horns and legs

fauna n (pl -as, -ae) animals of a given place or time

faunae n ▷ fauna

faunas n ▷ fauna

fauns n ▷ faun

favour n (pl -s) approving attitude ▶ v (-s, -ing, -ed) prefer

favourable adj encouraging or advantageous >**favourably** adv

favourably adv ▷ favourable

favoured v ▷ favour

favouring v ▷ favour

favourite adj most liked ▶ n (pl -s) preferred person or thing

favourites n ▷ favourite

favouritism n (pl -s) practice of giving special treatment to a person or group

favouritisms n ▷ favouritism

favours n, v ▷ favour

> **faw** n (**faws**). A faw is a gypsy. This is a good word for taking advantage of a nearby bonus square. Faw scores 9 points.

fawn¹ n (pl -s) young deer ▶ adj light yellowish-brown

fawn² v (**-s, -ing, -ed**) (*foll. by* **on**) seek attention from (someone) by insincere flattery

fawned v ▷ fawn²

fawning v ▷ fawn²

fawns n, v ▷ fawn¹, ²

fax n (pl -**es**) electronic system for sending facsimiles of documents by telephone ▶ v (**-xes, -xing, -xed**) send (a document) by this system

faxed n ▷ fax

faxes n, v ▷ fax

faxing v ▷ fax

fay n (**fays**). A fay is a fairy. This is a fairly high-scoring short word that can be helpful in a tight game. Fay scores 9 points.

fealties n ▷ fealty

fealty n (pl -**ies**) (in feudal society) subordinate's loyalty to his ruler or lord

fear n (pl -**s**) distress or alarm caused by impending danger or pain ▶ v (**-s, -ing, -ed**) be afraid of (something or someone) > **fearless** adj > **fearlessly** adv

feared v ▷ fear

fearful adj feeling fear (*Informal*) > **fearfully** adv

fearfully adv ▷ fearful

fearing v ▷ fear

fearless n ▷ fear

fearlessly adv ▷ fear

fears n, v ▷ fear

fearsome adj terrifying

feasibilities n ▷ feasible

feasibility n ▷ feasible

feasible adj able to be done, possible > **feasibly** adv > **feasibility** n (pl -**s**)

feasibly adv ▷ feasible

feast n (pl -**s**) lavish meal ▶ v (**-s, -ing, -ed**) eat a feast

feasted v ▷ feast

feasting v ▷ feast

feasts n, v ▷ feast

feat n (pl -**s**) remarkable, skilful, or daring action

feather n (pl -**s**) one of the barbed shafts forming the plumage of birds ▶ v (**-s, -ing, -ed**) fit or cover with feathers > **feathered** adj > **feathery** adj (**-rier, -riest**)

feathered v, adj ▷ feather

featherier adj ▷ feather

featheriest adj ▷ feather

feathering v ▷ feather

feathers n, v ▷ feather

featherweight n (pl -**s**) boxer weighing up to

126lb (professional) or 57kg (amateur)

featherweights n ▷ featherweight

feathery adj ▷ feather

feats n ▷ feat

feature n (pl -**s**) part of the face, such as the eyes ▶ v (**-res, -ring, -red**) have as a feature or be a feature in > **featureless** adj

featured v ▷ feature

featureless adj ▷ feature

features n, v ▷ feature

featuring v ▷ feature

febrile [**fee**-brile] adj feverish

feckless adj ineffectual or irresponsible

fecund adj fertile > **fecundity** n (pl -**ties**)

fecundities n ▷ fecund

fecundity n ▷ fecund

fed v ▷ feed

federal adj of a system in which power is divided between one central government and several regional governments > **federalism** n (pl -**s**) > **federalist** n (pl -**s**)

federalism n ▷ federal

federalisms n ▷ federal

federalist n ▷ federal

federalists n ▷ federal

federate v (**-tes, -ting, -ted**) unite in a federation

federated v ▷ federate

federates v ▷ federate

federating v ▷ federate

federation n (pl -**s**) union of several states, provinces, etc.

federations n ▷ federation

fedora [fid-**or**-a] n (pl -**s**) man's soft hat with a brim

fedoras n ▷ fedora

fee n (pl -**s**) charge paid to be allowed to do something

feeble adj (**-r, -st**) lacking physical or mental power > **feebleness** n (pl -**es**) > **feebly** adv

feebleminded adj unable to think or understand effectively

feebleness n ▷ feeble

feeblenesses n ▷ feeble

feebler adj ▷ feeble

feeblest adj ▷ feeble

feebly adv ▷ feeble

feed v (**-s, -ing, fed**) give food to ▶ n (pl -**s**) act of feeding

feedback n (pl -**s**) information received in response to something done

feedbacks n ▷ feedback

feeder n (pl -**s**) road or railway line linking outlying areas to the main traffic network

feeders n ▷ feeder

feeding *v* ▷ **feed**

feeds *v*, *n* ▷ **feed**

feel *v* (**-s**, **-ing**, **felt**) have a physical or emotional sensation of ▶ *n* (*pl* **-s**) act of feeling

feeler *n* (*pl* **-s**) organ of touch in some animals

feelers *n* ▷ **feeler**

feeling *n* (*pl* **-s**) emotional reaction

feelings *n* ▷ **feeling** ▶ *v* ▷ **feel**

feels *v*, *n* ▷ **feel**

fees *n* ▷ **fee**

feet *n* ▷ **foot**

feign [fane] *v* (**-s**, **-ing**, **-ed**) pretend

feigned *v* ▷ **feign**

feigning *v* ▷ **feign**

feigns *v* ▷ **feign**

feint[1] [faint] *n* (*pl* **-s**) sham attack or blow meant to distract an opponent ▶ *v* (**-s**, **-ing**, **-ed**) make a feint

feint[2] [faint] *n* (*pl* **-s**) narrow lines on ruled paper

feinted *v* ▷ **feint**[1]

feinting *v* ▷ **feint**[1]

feints *n*, *v* ▷ **feint**[1, 2]

feldspar *n* (*pl* **-s**) hard mineral that is the main constituent of igneous rocks

feldspars *n* ▷ **feldspar**

felicitations *pl n* congratulations

felicities *n* ▷ **felicity**

felicitous *adj* ▷ **felicity**

felicity *n* (*pl* **-ties**) happiness > **felicitous** *adj*

feline *adj* of cats ▶ *n* (*pl* **-s**) member of the cat family

felines *n* ▷ **feline**

fell[1] *v* ▷ **fall**

fell[2] *v* (**-s**, **-ing**, **-ed**) cut down (a tree)

fell[3] *adj* (**-er**, **-est**) deadly

fell[4] *n* (*pl* **-s**) (SCOT & N ENGLISH) mountain, hill, or moor

felled *v* ▷ **fell**[2]

feller *adj* ▷ **fell**[3]

fellest *adj* ▷ **fell**[3]

felling *v* ▷ **fell**[2]

felloe *n* (*pl* **-oes**) (segment of) the rim of a wheel

felloes *n* ▷ **felloe**

fellow *n* (*pl* **-s**) man or boy ▶ *adj* in the same group or condition

fellows *n* ▷ **fellow**

fellowship *n* (*pl* **-s**) sharing of aims or interests

fellowships *n* ▷ **fellowship**

fells *v*, *n* ▷ **fell**[2, 4]

felon *n* (*pl* **-s**) (CRIMINAL LAW) (formerly) person guilty of a felony

felonies *n* ▷ **felony**

felonious *adj* ▷ **felony**

felons *n* ▷ **felon**

felony *n* (*pl* **-nies**) serious crime > **felonious** *adj*

felspar *n* (*pl* **-s**) ▷ **feldspar**

felspars *n* ▷ **felspar**

felt[1] *v* ▷ **feel**

felt[2] *n* (*pl* **-s**) matted fabric made by bonding fibres by pressure

felts *n* ▷ **felt**[2]

female *adj* of the sex which bears offspring ▶ *n* (*pl* **-s**) female person or animal

females *n* ▷ **female**

feminine *adj* having qualities traditionally regarded as suitable for, or typical of, women > **femininity** *n* (*pl* **-ties**)

femininities *n* ▷ **feminine**

femininity *n* ▷ **feminine**

feminism *n* (*pl* **-s**) advocacy of equal rights for women > **feminist** *adj*, *n* (*pl* **-s**)

feminisms *n* ▷ **feminism**

feminist *n* ▷ **feminism**

feminists *n* ▷ **feminism**

femoral *adj* of the thigh

femur [fee-mer] *n* (*pl* **-s**) thighbone

femurs *n* ▷ **femur**

fen *n* (*pl* **-s**) (BRIT) low-lying flat marshy land

fence *n* (*pl* **-s**) barrier of posts linked by wire or wood, enclosing an area ▶ *v* (**-ces**, **-cing**, **-ced**) enclose with or as if with a fence

fenced *v* ▷ **fence**

fencer *n* ▷ **fencing**

fencers *n* ▷ **fencing**

fences *n*, *v* ▷ **fence**

fencing *n* (*pl* **-s**) sport of fighting with swords ▶ *v* ▷ **fence** > **fencer** *n* (*pl* **-s**)

fencings *n* ▷ **fencing**

fend *v* (**-s**, **-ing**, **-ed**) provide (for oneself)

fended *v* ▷ **fend**

fender *n* (*pl* **-s**) low metal frame in front of a fireplace

fenders *n* ▷ **fender**

fending *v* ▷ **fend**

fends *v* ▷ **fend**

fennel *n* (*pl* **-s**) fragrant plant whose seeds, leaves, and root are used in cookery

fennels *n* ▷ **fennel**

fens *n* ▷ **fen**

fenugreek *n* (*pl* **-s**) Mediterranean plant grown for its heavily scented seeds

fenugreeks *n* ▷ **fenugreek**

feral *adj* wild

ferment *n* (*pl* **-s**) commotion, unrest ▶ *v* (**-s**, **-ing**, **-ed**) undergo or cause to undergo fermentation

fermentation *n* (*pl* **-s**) reaction in which

an organic molecule splits into simpler substances, esp. the conversion of sugar to alcohol

fermentations n ▷ fermentation

fermented n ▷ ferment

fermenting v ▷ ferment

ferments n, v ▷ ferment

fern n (pl -**s**) flowerless plant with fine fronds

ferns n ▷ fern

ferocious adj savagely fierce or cruel > **ferocity** n (pl -**ties**)

ferocities n ▷ ferocious

ferocity n ▷ ferocious

ferret n (pl -**s**) tamed polecat used to catch rabbits or rats ▶ v (-**s**, -**ing**, -**ed**) hunt with ferrets

ferreted v ▷ ferret

ferreting v ▷ ferret

ferrets n, v ▷ ferret

ferric, ferrous adj of or containing iron

ferried v ▷ ferry

ferries n, v ▷ ferry

ferrous adj ▷ ferric

ferry n (pl -**rries**) boat for transporting people and vehicles ▶ v (-**rries**, -**rrying**, -**rried**) carry by ferry > **ferryman** n (pl -**men**)

ferrying v ▷ ferry

ferryman n ▷ ferry

ferrymen n ▷ ferry

fertile adj capable of producing young, crops, or vegetation > **fertility** n (pl -**ties**)

fertilities n ▷ fertile

fertility n ▷ fertile

fertilization n ▷ fertilize

fertilizations n ▷ fertilize

fertilize v (-**zes**, -**zing**, -**zed**) provide (an animal or plant) with sperm or pollen to bring about fertilization > **fertilization** n (pl -**s**)

fertilized v ▷ fertilize

fertilizer n (pl -**s**) substance added to the soil to increase its productivity

fertilizers n ▷ fertilizer

fertilizes v ▷ fertilize

fertilizing v ▷ fertilize

fervent, fervid adj intensely passionate and sincere > **fervently** adv

fervently adv ▷ fervent

fervid adj ▷ fervent

fervour n (pl -**s**) intensity of feeling

fervours n ▷ fervour

fescue n (pl -**s**) pasture and lawn grass with stiff narrow leaves

fescues n ▷ fescue

fester v (-**s**, -**ing**, -**ed**) grow worse and increasingly hostile

festered v ▷ fester

festering v ▷ fester

festers v ▷ fester

festival n (pl -**s**) organized series of special events or performances

festivals n ▷ festival

festive adj of or like a celebration

festivities n ▷ festivity

festivity n (pl -**ties**) happy celebration ▶ pl celebrations

festoon v (-**s**, -**ing**, -**ed**) hang decorations in loops

festooned v ▷ festoon

festooning v ▷ festoon

festoons v ▷ festoon

feta n (pl -**as**) white salty Greek cheese

fetal adj ▷ fetus

fetas n ▷ feta

fetch v (-**es**, -**ing**, -**ed**) go after and bring back (Informal)

fetched v ▷ fetch

fetches v ▷ fetch

fetching v ▷ fetch ▶ adj attractive

fete [fate] n (pl -**s**) gala, bazaar, etc., usu. held outdoors ▶ v (-**tes**, -**ting**, -**ted**) honour or entertain regally

feted v ▷ fete

fetes n, v ▷ fete

fetid adj (-**er**, -**est**) stinking

fetider adj ▷ fetid

fetidest adj ▷ fetid

feting v ▷ fete

fetish n (pl -**es**) form of behaviour in which sexual pleasure is derived from looking at or handling an inanimate object > **fetishism** n (pl -**s**) > **fetishist** n (pl -**s**) n

fetishes n ▷ fetish

fetishism n ▷ fetish

fetishisms n ▷ fetish

fetishist n ▷ fetish

fetishists n ▷ fetish

fetlock n (pl -**s**) projection behind and above a horse's hoof

fetlocks n ▷ fetlock

fetter n (pl -**s**) chain or shackle for the foot ▶ pl restrictions ▶ v (-**s**, -**ing**, -**ed**) restrict

fettered v ▷ fetter

fettering v ▷ fetter

fetters n, v ▷ fetter

fettle n (pl -**s**) state of health or spirits

fettles n ▷ fettle

fetus [fee-tuss] n (pl -**tuses**) embryo of a mammal in the later stages of development > **fetal** adj

fetuses n ▷ fetus

feu n (pl **-s**) (in Scotland) right of use of land in return for a fixed annual payment

feud n (pl **-s**) long bitter hostility between two people or groups ▶ v (**-s, -ing, -ed**) carry on a feud

feudal adj of or like feudalism

feudalism n (pl **-s**) medieval system in which people held land from a lord, and in return worked and fought for him

feudalisms n ▷ feudalism

feuded v ▷ feud

feuding v ▷ feud

feuds n, v ▷ feud

feus n ▷ feu

fever n (pl **-s**) (illness causing) high body temperature > **fevered** adj

fevered adj ▷ fever

feverish adj suffering from fever > **feverishly** adv

feverishly adv ▷ feverish

fevers n ▷ fever

few adj (**-er, -est**) not many

fewer adj ▷ few

fewest adj ▷ few

fey adj (**-er, -est**) whimsically strange

feyer adj ▷ fey

feyest adj ▷ fey

fez n (pl **fezzes**) brimless tasselled cap, orig. from Turkey

fezzes n ▷ fez

fiancé [fee-on-say] n (pl **-cés**) man engaged to be married ▶ **fiancée** n fem (pl **-cées**)

fiancée n ▷ fiancé

fiancées n ▷ fiancé

fiancés n ▷ fiancé

fiasco n (pl **-cos, -coes**) ridiculous or humiliating failure

fiascoes n ▷ fiasco

fiascos n ▷ fiasco

fiat [fee-at] n (pl **-s**) arbitrary order

fiats n ▷ fiat

fib n (pl **-s**) trivial lie ▶ v (**-s, -bbing, -bbed**) tell a lie > **fibber** n (pl **-s**)

fibbed v ▷ fib

fibber n ▷ fib

fibbers n ▷ fib

fibbing v ▷ fib

fibre n (pl **-s**) thread that can be spun into yarn > **fibrous** adj

fibreglass n (pl **-es**) material made of fine glass fibres

fibreglasses n ▷ fibreglass

fibres n ▷ fibre

fibro n (pl **-ros**) (AUST) mixture of cement and asbestos fibre, used in sheets for building (also **fibrocement**)

fibroid [fibe-royd] n (pl **-s**) benign tumour composed of fibrous connective tissue

fibroids n ▷ fibroid

fibros n ▷ fibro

fibrosites n ▷ fibrositis

fibrositis [fibe-roh-site-iss] n (pl **-es**) inflammation of the tissues of muscle sheaths

fibrous adj ▷ fibre

fibs n, v ▷ fib

fibula n (pl **-lae, -las**) slender outer bone of the lower leg

fibulae n ▷ fibula

fibulas n ▷ fibula

fiche [feesh] n (pl **-s**) sheet of film for storing publications in miniaturized form

fiches n ▷ fiche

fickle adj changeable, inconstant > **fickleness** n (pl **-ess**)

fickleness n ▷ fickle

ficklenesses n ▷ fickle

fiction n (pl **-s**) literary works of the imagination, such as novels > **fictional** adj

fictional adj ▷ fiction

fictionalize v (**-zes, -zing, -zed**) turn into fiction

fictionalized v ▷ fictionalize

fictionalizes v ▷ fictionalize

fictionalizing v ▷ fictionalize

fictions n ▷ fiction

fictitious adj not genuine

fiddle n (pl **-s**) violin (Informal) ▶ v (**-les, -ling, -led**) play the violin

fiddled v ▷ fiddle

fiddles n, v ▷ fiddle

fiddlesticks interj expression of annoyance or disagreement

fiddlier adj ▷ fiddly

fiddliest adj ▷ fiddly

fiddling v ▷ fiddle ▶ adj trivial

fiddly adj (**-lier, -liest**) awkward to do or use

fidelities n ▷ fidelity

fidelity n (pl **-ies**) faithfulness

fidget v (**-s, -ing, -ed**) move about restlessly ▶ n (pl **-s**) person who fidgets ▶ pl restlessness > **fidgety** adj (**-tier, -tiest**)

fidgeted v ▷ fidget

fidgetier adj ▷ fidget

fidgetiest adj ▷ fidget

fidgeting v ▷ fidget

fidgets v, n ▷ fidget

fidgety adj ▷ fidget

fiduciaries n ▷ fiduciary

fiduciary [fid-yew-she-er-ee] (LAW) n (pl **-ies**)

person bound to act for someone else's benefit, as a trustee ▶ *adj* of a trust or trustee

fief [feef] *n* (*pl* -s) (HIST) land granted by a lord in return for war service
fiefs *n* ▷ fief

field *n* (*pl* -s) enclosed piece of agricultural land ▶ *v* (-s, -ing, -ed) (SPORT) catch and return (a ball)
fielded *v* ▷ field

fielder *n* (*pl* -s) (SPORT) player whose task is to field the ball
fielders *n* ▷ fielder

fieldfare *n* (*pl* -s) type of large Old World thrush
fieldfares *n* ▷ fieldfare

fielding *v* ▷ field

fields *n*, *v* ▷ field

fieldwork *n* (*pl* -s) investigation made in the field as opposed to the classroom or the laboratory
fieldworks *n* ▷ fieldwork

fiend [feend] *n* (*pl* -s) evil spirit (*Informal*) > **fiendish** *adj* > **fiendishly** *adv*
fiendish *adj* ▷ fiend
fiendishly *adv* ▷ fiend
fiends *n* ▷ fiend

fierce *adj* (-r, -st) wild or aggressive > **fiercely** *adv* > **fierceness** *n* (*pl* -es)
fiercely *adv* ▷ fierce
fierceness *n* ▷ fierce
fiercenesses *n* ▷ fierce
fiercer *adj* ▷ fierce
fiercest *adj* ▷ fierce
fierier *adj* ▷ fiery
fieriest *adj* ▷ fiery

fiery *adj* (-rier, -riest) consisting of or like fire

fiesta *n* (*pl* -s) religious festival, carnival
fiestas *n* ▷ fiesta

fife *n* (*pl* -s) small high-pitched flute
fifes *n* ▷ fife

fifteen *adj*, *n* (*pl* -s) five and ten > **fifteenth** *adj*, *n* (*pl* -s)
fifteens *n* ▷ fifteen
fifteenth *adj*, *n* ▷ fifteen
fifteenths *n* ▷ fifteenth

fifth *adj*, *n* (*pl* -s) (of) number five in a series
fifths *n* ▷ fifth
fifties *n* ▷ fifty
fiftieth *adj*, *n* ▷ fifty
fiftieths *n* ▷ fifty

fifty *adj*, *n* (*pl* -ties) five times ten > **fiftieth** *adj*, *n* (*pl* -s)

fig *n* (*pl* -s) soft pear-shaped fruit

fight *v* (-s, -ing, fought) struggle (against) in battle or physical combat ▶ *n* (*pl* -s) aggressive conflict between two (groups of) people

fighter *n* (*pl* -s) boxer
fighters *n* ▷ fighter
fighting *v* ▷ fight
fights *n*, *v* ▷ fight

figment *n* (*pl* -s) something imagined
figments *n* ▷ figment

figs *n* ▷ fig

figurative *adj* (of language) abstract, imaginative, or symbolic > **figuratively** *adv*
figuratively *adv* ▷ figurative

figure *n* (*pl* -s) numerical symbol (MATHS) ▶ *v* (-res, -ring, -red) consider, conclude
figured *v* ▷ figure

figurehead *n* (*pl* -s) nominal leader
figureheads *n* ▷ figurehead
figures *n*, *v* ▷ figure

figurine *n* (*pl* -s) statuette
figurines *n* ▷ figurine

figuring *v* ▷ figure

filament *n* (*pl* -s) fine wire in a light bulb that gives out light
filaments *n* ▷ filament

filbert *n* (*pl* -s) hazelnut
filberts *n* ▷ filbert

filch *v* (-es, -ing, -ed) steal (small amounts)
filched *v* ▷ filch
filches *v* ▷ filch
filching *v* ▷ filch

file¹ *n* (*pl* -s) box or folder used to keep documents in order ▶ *v* (-les, -ling, -led) place (a document) in a file

file² *n* (*pl* -s) tool with a roughened blade for smoothing or shaping ▶ *v* (-les, -ling, -led) shape or smooth with a file
filed *v* ▷ file¹, ²
files *n*, *v* ▷ file¹, ²

filial *adj* of or befitting a son or daughter

filibuster *n* (*pl* -s) obstruction of legislation by making long speeches ▶ *v* (-s, -ing, -ed) obstruct (legislation) with such delaying tactics
filibustered *v* ▷ filibuster
filibustering *v* ▷ filibuster
filibusters *n*, *v* ▷ filibuster

filigree *n* (*pl* -s) delicate ornamental work of gold or silver wire ▶ *adj* made of filigree
filigrees *n* ▷ filigree

filing *v* ▷ file¹, ²

filings *pl n* shavings removed by a file

fill *v* (-s, -ing, -ed) make or become full
filled *v* ▷ fill

filler *n* (*pl* -s) substance that fills a gap or increases bulk
fillers *n* ▷ filler

fillet *n* (*pl* -s) boneless piece of meat or fish ▶ *v*

filleted (**-s, -ing, -ed**) remove the bones from
filleted v ▷ fillet
filleting v ▷ fillet
fillets n, v ▷ fillet
fillies n ▷ filly
filling n (pl -s) substance that fills a gap or cavity, esp. in a tooth ▶ adj (of food) substantial and satisfying ▶ v ▷ fill
fillings n ▷ filling
fillip n (pl -s) something that adds stimulation or enjoyment
fillips n ▷ fillip
fills v ▷ fill
filly n (pl -lies) young female horse
film n (pl -s) sequence of images projected on a screen, creating the illusion of movement ▶ v (**-s, -ing, -ed**) photograph with a movie or video camera ▶ adj connected with films or the cinema
filmed v ▷ film
filmier adj ▷ filmy
filmiest adj ▷ filmy
filming v ▷ film
films n, v ▷ film
filmy adj (**-mier, -miest**) very thin, delicate
filter n (pl -s) material or device permitting fluid to pass but retaining solid particles ▶ v (**-s, -ing, -ed**) remove impurities from (a substance) with a filter
filtered v ▷ filter
filtering v ▷ filter
filters n, v ▷ filter
filth n (pl -s) disgusting dirt > **filthy** adj (**-thier, -thiest**) > **filthiness** n (pl -es)
filthier adj ▷ filth
filthiest adj ▷ filth
filthiness n ▷ filth
filthinesses n ▷ filth
filths n ▷ filth
filthy adj ▷ filth
filtrate n (pl -s) filtered gas or liquid ▶ v (**-tes, -ting, -ted**) remove impurities with a filter > **filtration** n (pl -s)
filtrated v ▷ filtrate
filtrates n, v ▷ filtrate
filtrating v ▷ filtrate
filtration n ▷ filtrate
filtrations n ▷ filtrate
fin n (pl -s) projection from a fish's body enabling it to balance and swim
finagle [fin-**nay**-gl] v (**-les, -ling, -led**) get or achieve by craftiness or trickery
finagled v ▷ finagle
finagles v ▷ finagle
finagling v ▷ finagle

final adj at the end ▶ n (pl -s) deciding contest between winners of previous rounds in a competition ▶ pl (BRIT G-S AFR) last examinations in an educational course > **finally** adv > **finality** n (pl -ties)
finale [fin-**nah**-lee] (pl -s) n concluding part of a dramatic performance or musical work
finales n ▷ finale
finalist n (pl -s) competitor in a final
finalists n ▷ finalist
finalities n ▷ final
finality n ▷ final
finalize v (**-zes, -zing, -zed**) put into final form
finalized v ▷ finalize
finalizes v ▷ finalize
finalizing v ▷ finalize
finally adv ▷ final
finals n ▷ final
finance v (**-ces, -cing, -ced**) provide or obtain funds for ▶ n (pl -s) management of money, loans, or credits ▶ pl money resources > **financial** adj > **financially** adv
financed v ▷ finance
finances v, n ▷ finance
financial adj ▷ finance
financially adv ▷ finance
financier n (pl -s) person involved in large-scale financial business
financiers n ▷ financier
financing v ▷ finance
finch n (pl -es) small songbird with a short strong beak
finches n ▷ finch
find v (**-s, -ing, found**) discover by chance ▶ n (pl -s) person or thing found, esp. when valuable > **finder** n (pl -s)
finder n ▷ find
finders n ▷ find
finding n (pl -s) conclusion from an investigation ▶ v ▷ find
findings n ▷ finding
finds v, n ▷ find
fine¹ adj (**-r, -st**) very good > **finely** adv > **fineness** n (pl -es)
fine² n (pl -s) payment imposed as a penalty ▶ v (**-nes, -ning, -ned**) impose a fine on
fined v ▷ fine²
finely adv ▷ fine¹
fineness n ▷ fine¹
finenesses n ▷ fine¹
finer adj ▷ fine¹
fineries n ▷ finery
finery n (pl -ries) showy clothing
fines n, v ▷ fine¹, ²
finesse [fin-**ness**] n (pl -s) delicate skill

finesses n ▷ finesse

finest adj ▷ fine¹

finger n (pl -s) one of the four long jointed parts of the hand ▶ v (-s, -ing, -ed) touch or handle with the fingers

fingerboard n part of a stringed instrument against which the strings are pressed

fingerboards n ▷ fingerboard

fingered v ▷ finger

fingering n technique of using the fingers in playing a musical instrument ▶ v ▷ finger

fingerprint n (pl -s) impression of the ridges on the tip of the finger ▶ v take the fingerprints of (someone)

fingerprints n ▷ fingerprint

fingers n, v ▷ finger

finickier adj ▷ finicky

finickiest adj ▷ finicky

finicky adj (-ckier, -ckiest) excessively particular, fussy

fining v ▷ fine

finish v (-es, -ing, -ed) bring to an end, stop ▶ n (pl -es) end, last part

finished v ▷ finish

finishes v, n ▷ finish

finishing v ▷ finish

finite adj having limits in space, time, or size

fins n ▷ fin

fiord n (pl -s) ▷ fjord

fiords n ▷ fiord

fir n (pl -s) pyramid-shaped tree with needle-like leaves and erect cones

fire n (pl -s) state of combustion producing heat, flames, and smoke ▶ v (-res, -ring, -red) operate (a weapon) so that a bullet or missile is released

firearm n (pl -s) rifle, pistol, or shotgun

firearms n ▷ firearm

firebrand n (pl -s) person who causes unrest

firebrands n ▷ firebrand

firebreak n strip of cleared land to stop the advance of a fire

firebreaks n ▷ firebreak

fired v ▷ fire

firedamp n (pl -s) explosive gas, composed mainly of methane, formed in mines

firedamps n ▷ firedamp

firefighter n (pl -s) member of a fire brigade

firefighters n ▷ firefighter

fireflies n ▷ firefly

firefly n (pl -flies) beetle that glows in the dark

fireguard n (pl -s) protective grating in front of a fire

fireguards n ▷ fireguard

fireplace n (pl -s) recess in a room for a fire

fireplaces n ▷ fireplace

fires n, v ▷ fire

firewall n (pl -s) (COMPUTERS) computer that prevents unauthorized access to a computer network from the Internet

firewalls n ▷ firewall

firework n (pl -s) device containing chemicals that is ignited to produce spectacular explosions and coloured sparks ▶ pl show of fireworks

fireworks n ▷ firework

firing v ▷ fire

firm¹ adj (-er, -est) not soft or yielding ▶ adv in an unyielding manner ▶ v (-s, -ing, -ed) make or become firm > **firmly** adv > **firmness** n (pl -es)

firm² n (pl -s) business company

firmament n (pl -s) (Lit) sky or the heavens

firmaments n ▷ firmament

firmed v ▷ firm¹

firmer adj ▷ firm¹

firmest adj ▷ firm¹

firming v ▷ firm¹

firmly adv ▷ firm¹

firmness n ▷ firm¹

firmnesses n ▷ firm¹

firms v, n ▷ firm¹,²

firs n ▷ fir

first adj earliest in time or order ▶ n (pl -s) person or thing coming before all others ▶ adv before anything else > **firstly** adv

firsthand adj, adv (obtained) directly from the original source

firstly adv ▷ first

firsts n ▷ first

firth n (pl -s) narrow inlet of the sea, esp. in Scotland

firths n ▷ firth

fiscal adj of government finances, esp. taxes

fish n (pl fish, fishes) cold-blooded vertebrate with gills, that lives in water ▶ v (-es, -ing, -ed) try to catch fish

fished v ▷ fish

fisheries n ▷ fishery

fisherman n (pl -men) person who catches fish for a living or for pleasure

fishermen n ▷ fisherman

fishery n (pl -ries) area of the sea used for fishing

fishes n, v ▷ fish

fishfinger n (pl -s) oblong piece of fish covered in breadcrumbs

fishfingers n ▷ fishfinger

fishier adj ▷ fishy

fishiest adj ▷ fishy

fishing v ▷ fish

fishmeal n (pl -s) dried ground fish used as animal feed or fertilizer

fishmeals n ▷ fishmeal

fishmonger n (pl -s) seller of fish

fishmongers n ▷ fishmonger

fishnet n (pl -s) open mesh fabric resembling netting

fishnets n ▷ fishnet

fishplate n (pl -s) metal plate holding rails together

fishplates n ▷ fishplate

fishwife n (pl -wives) coarse scolding woman

fishwives n ▷ fishwife

fishy adj (-shier, -shiest) of or like fish

fissile adj capable of undergoing nuclear fission

fission n (pl -s) splitting > fissionable adj

fissionable adj ▷ fission

fissions n ▷ fission

fissure [fish-er] n (pl -s) long narrow cleft or crack

fissures n ▷ fissure

fist n (pl -s) clenched hand

fisticuffs pl n fighting with the fists

fists n ▷ fist

fit¹ v (-s, -tting, -tted) be appropriate or suitable for ▶ adj appropriate ▶ n (-tter, -ttest) (pl -s) way in which something fits > fitness n (pl -es)

fit² n (pl -s) sudden attack or convulsion, such as an epileptic seizure

fitful adj occurring in irregular spells > fitfully adv

fitfully adv ▷ fitful

fitment n (pl -s) detachable part of the furnishings of a room

fitments n ▷ fitment

fitness n ▷ fit¹

fitnesses n ▷ fit¹

fits v, adj ▷ fit¹, ²

fitted v ▷ fit¹

fitter n (pl -s) person skilled in the installation and adjustment of machinery ▶ adj ▷ fit¹

fitters n ▷ fitter

fittest adj ▷ fit¹

fitting adj appropriate, suitable ▶ n (pl -s) accessory or part ▶ pl furnishings and accessories in a building ▶ v ▷ fit

fittings n ▷ fitting

five adj, n (pl -s) one more than four

fiver n (pl -s) (Informal) five-pound note

fivers n ▷ fiver

fives n ball game resembling squash but played with bats or the hands ▶ n ▷ five

fix v (-xes, -xing, -xed) make or become firm, stable, or secure ▶ n (pl -es) (Informal) difficult situation > fixed adj > fixedly adv steadily

fixated adj obsessed

fixation n (pl -s) obsessive interest in something

fixations n ▷ fixation

fixative n (pl -s) liquid used to preserve or hold things in place

fixatives n ▷ fixative

fixed v, adj ▷ fix

fixedly adv ▷ fix

fixer n (pl -s) solution used to make a photographic image permanent

fixers n ▷ fixer

fixes v, n ▷ fix

fixing v ▷ fix

fixture n (pl -s) permanently fitted piece of household equipment

fixtures n ▷ fixture

fizz v (-es, -ing, -ed) make a hissing or bubbling noise ▶ n (pl -es) hissing or bubbling noise > fizzy adj (-zzier, -zziest)

fizzed v ▷ fizz

fizzes v ▷ fizz

fizzier adj ▷ fizz

fizziest adj ▷ fizz

fizzing v ▷ fizz

fizzle v (-les, -ling, -led) make a weak hissing or bubbling sound

fizzled v ▷ fizzle

fizzles v ▷ fizzle

fizzling v ▷ fizzle

fizzy adj ▷ fizz

fjord [fee-ord] n (pl -s) long narrow inlet of the sea between cliffs, esp. in Norway

fjords n ▷ fjord

flab n (pl -s) (Informal) unsightly body fat

flabbergasted adj completely astonished

flabbier adj ▷ flabby

flabbiest adj ▷ flabby

flabby adj (-bbier, -bbiest) having flabby flesh

flabs n ▷ flab

flaccid [flas-sid] adj (-er, -est) soft and limp > flaccidity n (pl -ties)

flaccider adj ▷ flaccid

flaccidest adj ▷ flaccid

flaccidities n ▷ flaccid

flaccidity n ▷ flaccid

flag¹ n (pl -s) piece of cloth attached to a pole as an emblem or signal ▶ v (-s, -gging, -gged) mark with a flag or sticker

flag² v (-s, -gging, -gged) lose enthusiasm or vigour

flag³, flagstone (pl -s) n flat paving-stone

flagellant n (pl -s) person who whips himself or herself
flagellants n ▷ flagellant
flagellate [flaj-a-late] v (-tes, -ting, -ted) whip, esp. in religious penance or for sexual pleasure > **flagellation** n (pl -s)
flagellated v ▷ flagellate
flagellates v ▷ flagellate
flagellating v ▷ flagellate
flagellation n ▷ flagellate
flagellations n ▷ flagellate
flageolet [flaj-a-let] n (pl -s) small instrument like a recorder
flageolets n ▷ flageolet
flagged adj paved with flagstones ▶ v ▷ flag¹, ²
flagged v ▷ flag¹, ²
flagging v ▷ flag¹, ²
flagon n (pl -s) wide bottle for wine or cider
flagons n ▷ flagon
flagpole, flagstaff (pl -s) n pole for a flag
flagpoles n ▷ flagpole
flagrant [flayg-rant] adj openly outrageous > **flagrantly** adv
flagrantly adv ▷ flagrant
flags v, n ▷ flag¹, ², ³
flagship n (pl -s) admiral's ship
flagships n ▷ flagship
flagstaff n ▷ flagpole
flagstaffs n ▷ flagpole
flagstone n ▷ flag³
flagstones n ▷ flag³
flail v (-s, -ing, -ed) wave about wildly ▶ n (pl -s) tool formerly used for threshing grain by hand
flailed v ▷ flail
flailing v ▷ flail
flails v, n ▷ flail
flair n (pl -s) natural ability
flairs n ▷ flair
flak n (pl -s) anti-aircraft fire
flake¹ n (pl -s) small thin piece, esp. chipped off something ▶ v (-kes, -king, -ked) peel off in flakes > **flaky** adj (-kier, -kiest)
flake² n (pl -s) (in Australia) the commercial name for the meat of the gummy shark
flaked v ▷ flake¹, ²
flakes v, n ▷ flake¹, ²
flakier adj ▷ flaky
flakiest adj ▷ flaky
flaking v ▷ flake¹
flaks n ▷ flak
flaky adj ▷ flake¹
flambé [flahm-bay] v (-bés, -béing, -béed) cook or serve (food) in flaming brandy
flambéed v ▷ flambé

flambéing v ▷ flambé
flambés v ▷ flambé
flamboyances n ▷ flamboyant
flamboyant adj behaving in a very noticeable, extravagant way > **flamboyance** n (pl -s)
flamboyance n ▷ flamboyant
flame n (pl -s) luminous burning gas coming from burning material ▶ v (-mes, -ming, -med) burn brightly
flamed v ▷ flame
flamenco n (pl -cos) rhythmical Spanish dance accompanied by a guitar and vocalist
flamencos n ▷ flamenco
flames n, v ▷ flame
flaming v ▷ flame
flamingo n (pl -gos, -goes) large pink wading bird with a long neck and legs
flamingoes n ▷ flamingo
flamingos n ▷ flamingo
flammabilities n ▷ flammable
flammability n ▷ flammable
flammable adj easily set on fire > **flammability** n (pl -ties)
flan n (pl -s) open sweet or savoury tart
flange n (pl -s) projecting rim or collar
flanges n ▷ flange
flank n (pl -s) part of the side between the hips and ribs ▶ v (-s, -ing, -ed) be at or move along the side of
flanked v ▷ flank
flanking v ▷ flank
flanks n, v ▷ flank
flannel n (pl -s) (BRIT) small piece of cloth for washing the face ▶ pl trousers made of flannel ▶ v (-s, -nelling, -nelled) (Informal) talk evasively
flannelette n (pl -s) cotton imitation of flannel
flannelettes n ▷ flannelette
flannelled v ▷ flannel
flannelling v ▷ flannel
flannels n, v ▷ flannel
flans n ▷ flan
flap v (-s, -pping, -pped) move back and forwards or up and down ▶ n (pl -s) action or sound of flapping
flapjack n (pl -s) chewy biscuit made with oats
flapjacks n ▷ flapjack
flapped v ▷ flap
flapping v ▷ flap
flaps v, n ▷ flap
flare v (-res, -ring, -red) blaze with a sudden unsteady flame ▶ n (pl -s) sudden unsteady flame ▶ pl flared trousers
flared adj (of a skirt or trousers) becoming wider towards the hem ▶ v ▷ flare

flares v, n ▷ flare
flaring v ▷ flare
flash n (pl **-es**) sudden burst of light or flame ▶ v (**-es**, **-ing**, **-ed**) (cause to) burst into flame
flashback n (pl **-s**) scene in a book, play, or film, that shows earlier events
flashbacks n ▷ flashback
flashed v ▷ flash
flasher n (pl **-s**) (Slang) man who exposes himself indecently
flashers n ▷ flasher
flashes n, v ▷ flash
flashier adj ▷ flashy
flashiest adj ▷ flashy
flashing n (pl **-s**) watertight material used to cover joins in a roof ▶ v ▷ flash
flashings n ▷ flashing
flashlight n (pl **-s**) (US) torch
flashlights n ▷ flashlight
flashy adj (**-shier**, **-shiest**) vulgarly showy
flask n (pl **-s**) ▷ vacuum flask flat bottle for carrying alcoholic drink in the pocket
flasks n ▷ flask
flat¹ adj (**-tter**, **-ttest**) level and horizontal ▶ adv in or into a flat position ▶ n (pl **-s**) (MUSIC) symbol lowering the pitch of a note by a semitone > **flatly** adv > **flatness** n (pl **-es**) > **flatten** v (**-s**, **-ing**, **-ed**)
flat² n (pl **-s**) set of rooms for living in which are part of a larger building ▶ v (**-s**, **-tting**, **-tted**) (AUST & NZ) live in a flat
flatfish n (pl **-fish**, **-fishes**) sea fish, such as the sole, which has a flat body
flatfishes n ▷ flatfish
flatlet n (pl **-s**) (BRIT, AUST & S AFR) small flat
flatlets n ▷ flatlet
flatly adv ▷ flat¹
flatmate n (pl **-s**) person with whom one shares a flat
flatmates n ▷ flatmate
flatness n ▷ flat¹
flatnesses n ▷ flat¹
flat-pack adj (of furniture, etc.) supplied in pieces in a flat box for assembly by the buyer
flats n, v ▷ flat¹, ²
flatted v ▷ flat²
flatten v ▷ flat¹
flattened v ▷ flat¹
flattening v ▷ flat¹
flatter¹ v (**-s**, **-ing**, **-ed**) praise insincerely > **flatterer** n (pl **-s**) > **flattery** n (pl **-ries**)
flatter² adj ▷ flat¹
flattered v ▷ flatter¹
flatterer n ▷ flatter
flatterers n ▷ flatter

flatteries n ▷ flatter
flattering v ▷ flatter¹
flatters v ▷ flatter¹
flattery n ▷ flatter
flattest adj ▷ flat¹
flattie n (pl **-s**) (NZ & S AFR) (Informal) flat tyre
flatties n ▷ flattie
flatting v ▷ flat²
flatulence n ▷ flatulent
flatulences n ▷ flatulent
flatulent adj suffering from or caused by too much gas in the intestines > **flatulence** n (pl **-s**)
flaunt v (**-s**, **-ing**, **-ed**) display (oneself or one's possessions) arrogantly
flaunted v ▷ flaunt
flaunting v ▷ flaunt
flaunts v ▷ flaunt
flautist n (pl **-s**) flute player
flautists n ▷ flautist
flavour n (pl **-s**) distinctive taste ▶ v (**-s**, **-ing**, **-ed**) give flavour to > **flavourless** adj
flavoured v ▷ flavour
flavouring n (pl **-s**) substance used to flavour food ▶ v ▷ flavour
flavourings n ▷ flavouring
flavourless adj ▷ flavour
flavours n, v ▷ flavour
flaw n (pl **-s**) imperfection or blemish > **flawed** adj > **flawless** adj
flawed adj ▷ flaw
flawless adj ▷ flaw
flaws n ▷ flaw
flax n (pl **-es**) plant grown for its stem fibres and seeds
flaxen adj (of hair) pale yellow
flaxes n ▷ flax
flay v (**-s**, **-ing**, **-ed**) strip the skin off
flayed v ▷ flay
flaying v ▷ flay
flays v ▷ flay
flea n (pl **-s**) small wingless jumping bloodsucking insect
fleapit n (pl **-s**) (Informal) shabby cinema or theatre
fleapits n ▷ fleapit
fleas n ▷ flea
fleck n (pl **-s**) small mark, streak, or speck ▶ v (**-s**, **-ing**, **-ed**) speckle
flecked n ▷ fleck
flecking v ▷ fleck
flecks n, v ▷ fleck
fled v ▷ flee
fledged adj (of young birds) able to fly
fledgelings n ▷ fledgling

fledgling, fledgeling (pl -s) n young bird ▶ adj new or inexperienced
fledglings n ▷ **fledgling**
flee v (-lees, -leeing, fled) run away (from)
fleece n (pl -s) sheep's coat of wool ▶ v (-ces, -cing, -ced) defraud or overcharge
fleeced v ▷ **fleece**
fleeces n, v ▷ **fleece**
fleecier adj ▷ **fleecy**
fleeciest adj ▷ **fleecy**
fleecing v ▷ **fleece**
fleecy adj (-cier, -ciest) made of or like fleece
fleeing v ▷ **flee**
flees v ▷ **flee**
fleet[1] n (pl -s) number of warships organized as a unit
fleet[2] adj swift in movement
fleeting adj rapid and soon passing
> **fleetingly** adv
fleetingly adv ▷ **fleeting**
fleets n ▷ **fleet**[1, 2]
flesh n (pl -es) soft part of a human or animal body (Informal)
fleshes n ▷ **flesh**
fleshier adj ▷ **fleshy**
fleshiest adj ▷ **fleshy**
fleshly adj carnal
fleshy adj (-shier, -shiest) plump
flew v ▷ **fly**[1]
flex n (pl -xes) flexible insulated electric cable ▶ v (-xes, -xing, -xed) bend
flexed v ▷ **flex**
flexes n, v ▷ **flex**
flexibility n ▷ **flexible**
flexible adj easily bent > **flexibly** adv
> **flexibility** n (pl -ties)
flexibilities n ▷ **flexible**
flexibly adv ▷ **flexible**
flexing v ▷ **flex**
flexitime, flextime n (pl -s) system permitting variation in starting and finishing times of work
flexitimes n ▷ **flexitime**
flextimes n ▷ **flexitime**
flick v (-s, -ing, -ed) touch or move with the finger or hand in a quick movement ▶ n (pl -s) tap or quick stroke ▶ pl (Slang) the cinema
flicked v ▷ **flick**
flicker v (-s, -ing, -ed) shine unsteadily or intermittently ▶ n (pl -s) unsteady brief light
flickered v ▷ **flicker**
flickering v ▷ **flicker**
flickers v, n ▷ **flicker**
flicking v ▷ **flick**
flicks v, n ▷ **flick**

flier[1] adj ▷ **fly**[3]
flier[2] n ▷ **flyer**
fliers n ▷ **flyer**
flies v, n ▷ **fly**[1, 2]
fliest adj ▷ **fly**[3]
flight[1] n (pl -s) journey by air
flight[2] n (pl -s) act of running away
flightier adj ▷ **flighty**
flightiest adj ▷ **flighty**
flightless adj (of certain birds or insects) unable to fly
flights n ▷ **flight**[1, 2]
flighty adj (-tier, -tiest) frivolous and fickle
flimsier adj ▷ **flimsy**
flimsiest adj ▷ **flimsy**
flimsily adv ▷ **flimsy**
flimsiness n ▷ **flimsy**
flimsinesses n ▷ **flimsy**
flimsy adj (-sier, -siest) not strong or substantial > **flimsily** adv > **flimsiness** n (pl -es)
flinch v (-es, -ing, -ed) draw back or wince, as from pain
flinched v ▷ **flinch**
flinches v ▷ **flinch**
flinching v ▷ **flinch**
fling v (-s, -ing, flung) throw, send, or move forcefully or hurriedly ▶ n (pl -s) spell of self-indulgent enjoyment
flinging v ▷ **fling**
flings v, n ▷ **fling**
flint n (pl -s) hard grey stone
flintier adj ▷ **flinty**
flintiest adj ▷ **flinty**
flints n ▷ **flint**
flinty (-tier, -tiest) adj cruel
flip v (-s, -pping, -pped) throw (something small or light) carelessly ▶ adj (Informal) flippant
flippancies n ▷ **flippant**
flippancy n ▷ **flippant**
flippant adj treating serious things lightly
> **flippancy** n (pl -cies)
flipped v ▷ **flip**
flipper (pl -s) n limb of a sea animal adapted for swimming
flippers n ▷ **flipper**
flipping v ▷ **flip**
flips v ▷ **flip**
flirt v (-s, -ing, -ed) behave as if sexually attracted to someone ▶ n (pl -s) person who flirts > **flirtation** n (pl -s) > **flirtatious** adj
flirtation n ▷ **flirt**
flirtations n ▷ **flirt**
flirtatious adj ▷ **flirt**

flirted v ▷ **flirt**

flirting v ▷ **flirt**

flirts v, n ▷ **flirt**

flit v (-s, -tting, -tted) move lightly and rapidly ▶ n (pl -s) act of flitting

flits v, n ▷ **flit**

flitted v ▷ **flit**

flitting v ▷ **flit**

float v (-s, -ing, -ed) rest on the surface of a liquid ▶ n (pl -s) light object used to help someone or something float

floated v ▷ **float**

floating adj moving about, changing ▶ v ▷ **float**

floats v, n ▷ **float**

flock¹ n (pl -s) number of animals of one kind together ▶ v (-s, -ing, -ed) gather in a crowd

flock² n (pl -s) wool or cotton waste used as stuffing ▶ adj (of wallpaper) with a velvety raised pattern

flocked v ▷ **flock¹**

flocking v ▷ **flock¹**

flocks n, v ▷ **flock¹, ²**

floe n (pl -s) sheet of floating ice

floes n ▷ **floe**

flog v (-s, -gging, -gged) beat with a whip or stick ▷ **flogging** n (pl -s)

flogged v ▷ **flog**

flogging v, n ▷ **flog**

floggings n ▷ **flog**

flogs v ▷ **flog**

flood n (pl -s) overflow of water onto a normally dry area ▶ v (-s, -ing, -ed) cover or become covered with water

flooded v ▷ **flood**

floodgate n (pl -s) gate used to control the flow of water

floodgates n ▷ **floodgate**

flooding v ▷ **flood**

floodlight n (pl -s) lamp that casts a broad intense beam of light ▶ v (-lights, -lighting, -lit) illuminate by floodlight

floodlighting v ▷ **floodlight**

floodlights n, v ▷ **floodlight**

floodlit v ▷ **floodlight**

floods n, v ▷ **flood**

floor n (pl -s) lower surface of a room ▶ v (-s, -ing, -ed) knock down

floored adj covered with a floor ▶ v ▷ **floor**

flooring n (pl -s) material for floors ▶ v ▷ **floor**

floorings n ▷ **flooring**

floors n, v ▷ **floor**

floozies n ▷ **floozy**

floozy n (pl -zies) (Old-fashioned slang) disreputable woman

flop v (-s, -pping, -pped) bend, fall, or collapse loosely or carelessly ▶ n (pl -s) failure

flopped v ▷ **flop**

floppier adj ▷ **floppy**

floppies n ▷ **floppy**

floppiest adj ▷ **floppy**

flopping v ▷ **flop**

floppy adj (-ppier, -ppiest) hanging downwards, loose ▶ n (pl -ppies) (COMPUTERS) a flexible magnetic disk that stores information

flops v, n ▷ **flop**

flora n (pl -s) plants of a given place or time

floral adj consisting of or decorated with flowers

floras n ▷ **flora**

floret n (pl -s) small flower forming part of a composite flower head

florets n ▷ **floret**

floribunda n (pl -s) type of rose whose flowers grow in large clusters

floribundas n ▷ **floribunda**

florid adj (-er, -est) with a red or flushed complexion

florider adj ▷ **florid**

floridest adj ▷ **florid**

florin n (pl -s) former British and Australian coin

florins n ▷ **florin**

florist n (pl -s) seller of flowers

florists n ▷ **florist**

floss n (pl -es) fine silky fibres

flosses n ▷ **floss**

flotation n (pl -s) launching or financing of a business enterprise

flotations n ▷ **flotation**

flotilla n (pl -s) small fleet or fleet of small ships

flotillas n ▷ **flotilla**

flotsam n (pl -s) floating wreckage

flotsams n ▷ **flotsam**

flounce¹ v (-ces, -cing, -ced) go with emphatic movements ▶ n (pl -s) flouncing movement

flounce² n (pl -s) ornamental frill on a garment

flounced v ▷ **flounce**

flounces v, n ▷ **flounce¹, ²**

flouncing v ▷ **flounce**

flounder¹ v (-s, -ing, -ed) move with difficulty, as in mud

flounder² n (pl -s) edible flatfish

floundered v ▷ **flounder**

floundering v ▷ **flounder**

flounders v, n ▷ **flounder¹, ²**

flour n (pl -s) powder made by grinding grain, esp. wheat ▶ v (-s, -ing, -ed) sprinkle with flour ▷ **floury** adj (-rier, -riest)

floured v ▷ flour
flourier adj ▷ flour
flouriest adj ▷ flour
flouring v ▷ flour
flourish v (-es, -ing, -ed) be active, successful, or widespread ▶ n (pl -es) dramatic waving motion > **flourishing** adj
flourished v ▷ flourish
flourishes v, n ▷ flourish
flourishing n, adj ▷ flourish
flours n, v ▷ flour
floury adj ▷ flour
flout v (-s, -ing, -ed) deliberately disobey (a rule, law, etc.)
flouted v ▷ flout
flouting v ▷ flout
flouts v ▷ flout
flow v (-s, -ing, -ed) (of liquid) move in a stream ▶ n (pl -s) act, rate, or manner of flowing
flowed v ▷ flow
flower n (pl -s) part of a plant that produces seeds ▶ v (-s, -ing, -ed) produce flowers, bloom
flowerbed n (pl -s) piece of ground for growing flowers
flowerbeds n ▷ flowerbed
flowered adj decorated with a floral design ▶ v ▷ flower
flowerier adj ▷ flowery
floweriest adj ▷ flowery
flowering v ▷ flower
flowers n, v ▷ flower
flowery adj (-rier, -riest) decorated with a floral design
flowing v ▷ flow
flown v ▷ fly[1]
flows v, n ▷ flow
flu n (pl flus) ▷ influenza
fluctuate v (-tes, -ting, -ted) change frequently and erratically > **fluctuation** n (pl -s)
fluctuated v ▷ fluctuate
fluctuates v ▷ fluctuate
fluctuating v ▷ fluctuate
fluctuation n ▷ fluctuate
fluctuations n ▷ fluctuate
flue n (pl -s) passage or pipe for smoke or hot air
fluencies n ▷ fluent
fluency n ▷ fluent
fluent adj able to speak or write with ease > **fluently** adv ▷ fluency n (pl -cies)
fluently adv ▷ fluent
flues n ▷ flue
fluff n (pl -s) soft fibres ▶ v (-s, -ing, -ed) make

or become soft and puffy > **fluffy** adj (-ffier, -ffiest)
fluffed v ▷ fluff
fluffier adj ▷ fluff
fluffiest adj ▷ fluff
fluffing v ▷ fluff
fluffs n, v ▷ fluff
fluffy adj ▷ fluff
fluid n (pl -s) substance able to flow and change its shape; a liquid or a gas ▶ adj able to flow or change shape easily > **fluidity** n (pl -ies)
fluidities n ▷ fluid
fluidity n ▷ fluid
fluids n ▷ fluid
fluke[1] n (pl -s) accidental stroke of luck
fluke[2] (pl -s) n flat triangular point of an anchor
fluke[3] (pl -s) n parasitic worm
flukes n ▷ fluke[1, 2, 3]
flume n (pl -s) narrow sloping channel for water
flumes n ▷ flume
flummox v (-xes, -xing, -xed) puzzle or confuse
flummoxed v ▷ flummox
flummoxes v ▷ flummox
flummoxing v ▷ flummox
flung v ▷ fling
flunk v (flunks, flunking, flunked) (US, AUST, NZ & S AFR) (Informal) fail
flunked v ▷ flunk
flunkey n ▷ flunky
flunkeys n ▷ flunky
flunkies n ▷ flunky
flunking v ▷ flunk
flunks v ▷ flunk
flunky, flunkey n (pl -kies, -keys) servile person
fluoresce v (-ces, -cing, -ced) exhibit fluorescence
fluoresced v ▷ fluoresce
fluorescence n (pl -s) emission of light from a substance bombarded by particles, such as electrons, or by radiation
fluorescences n ▷ fluorescence
fluorescent adj of or resembling fluorescence
fluoresces v ▷ fluoresce
fluorescing v ▷ fluoresce
fluoridate v (-tes, -ting, -ted) add fluoride to (water) as protection against tooth decay > **fluoridation** n (pl -s)
fluoridated v ▷ fluoridate
fluoridates v ▷ fluoridate
fluoridating v ▷ fluoridate
fluoridation n ▷ fluoridate
fluoridations n ▷ fluoridate

fluoride n (pl -s) compound containing fluorine
fluorides n ▷ fluoride
fluorine n (pl -s) (CHEM) toxic yellow gas, most reactive of all the elements
fluorines n ▷ fluorine
flurried v ▷ flurry
flurries n, v ▷ flurry
flurry n (pl -rries) sudden commotion ▶ v (-rries, -rrying, -rried) confuse
flus n ▷ flu
flush[1] v (-es, -ing, -ed) blush or cause to blush ▶ n (pl -es) blush
flush[2] adj level with the surrounding surface
flush[3] v (-es, -ing, -ed) drive out of a hiding place
flush[4] n (pl -es) (in card games) hand all of one suit
flushed v ▷ flush[1, 3]
flushes v, n ▷ flush[1, 3, 4]
flushing v ▷ flush[1, 3]
fluster v (-s, -ing, -ed) make nervous or upset ▶ n (pl -s) nervous or upset state
flustered v ▷ fluster
flustering v ▷ fluster
flusters v, n ▷ fluster
flute n (pl -s) wind instrument consisting of a tube with sound holes and a mouth hole in the side
fluted adj having decorative grooves
flutes n ▷ flute
flutter v (-s, -ing, -ed) wave rapidly ▶ n (pl -s) flapping movement
fluttered v ▷ flutter
fluttering v ▷ flutter
flutters v, n ▷ flutter
fluvial adj of rivers
flux n (pl -es) constant change or instability
fluxes n ▷ flux
fly[1] v (flying, flew, flown) move through the air on wings or in an aircraft ▶ n (pl flies) (often pl (BRIT) fastening at the front of trousers ▶ pl space above a stage, used for storage
fly[2] n (pl flies) two-winged insect
fly[3] adj (flier, fliest) (Slang) sharp and cunning
flycatcher n (pl -s) small insect-eating songbird
flycatchers n ▷ flycatcher
flyer, flier n (pl -s) n small advertising leaflet
flyers n ▷ flyer
flying adj hurried and brief ▶ v ▷ fly
flyleaf n (pl -leaves) blank leaf at the beginning or end of a book
flyleaves n ▷ flyleaf
flyover n (pl -s) road passing over another by

a bridge
flyovers n ▷ flyover
flypaper n (pl -s) paper with a sticky poisonous coating, used to kill flies
flypapers n ▷ flypaper
flyweight n (pl -s) boxer weighing up to 112lb (professional) or 51kg (amateur)
flyweights n ▷ flyweight
flywheel (pl -s) n heavy wheel regulating the speed of a machine
flywheels n ▷ flywheel
foal n (pl -s) young of a horse or related animal ▶ v (-s, -ing, -ed) give birth to a foal
foaled v ▷ foal
foaling v ▷ foal
foals n, v ▷ foal
foam n (pl -s) mass of small bubbles on a liquid ▶ v (-s, -ing, -ed) produce foam > **foamy** adj (-ier, -iest)
foamed v ▷ foam
foamier adj ▷ foam
foamiest adj ▷ foam
foaming v ▷ foam
foams n, v ▷ foam
foamy adj ▷ foam
fob n (pl -s) short watch chain
fobs n ▷ fob
focal adj of or at a focus
foci n ▷ focus
fo'c's'le n (pl fo'c's'les) ▷ forecastle
fo'c's'les n ▷ fo'c's'le
focus n (pl -cuses, -ci) [-sye] point at which light or sound waves converge ▶ v (-cuses, -cusing, -cused or -cusses, -cussing, -cussed) bring or come into focus
focused v ▷ focus
focuses n, v ▷ focus
focusing v ▷ focus
focussed v ▷ focus
focussing v ▷ focus
fodder n (pl -s) feed for livestock
fodders n ▷ fodder
foe n (pl foes) enemy, opponent
foes n ▷ foe
foetid adj (-er, -est) ▷ fetid
foetider adj ▷ foetid
foetidest adj ▷ foetid
foetus n (pl -tuses) ▷ fetus
foetuses n ▷ foetus
fog n (pl -s) mass of condensed water vapour in the lower air, often greatly reducing visibility ▶ v (-s, fogging, fogged) cover with steam > **foggy** adj (-ggier, -ggiest)
fogey, fogy n (pl -geys, -gies) old-fashioned person

fogeys n ▷ fogey

fogged v ▷ fog

foggier adj ▷ fog

foggiest adj ▷ fog

fogging v ▷ fog

foggy adj ▷ fog

foghorn n (pl -s) large horn sounded to warn ships in fog

foghorns n ▷ foghorn

fogies n ▷ fogey

fogs n ▷ fog

fogy n ▷ fogey

foible n (pl -s) minor weakness or slight peculiarity

foibles n ▷ foible

foil¹ v (-s, -ing, -ed) ruin (someone's plan)

foil² n (pl -s) metal in a thin sheet, esp. for wrapping food

foil³ n (pl -s) light slender flexible sword tipped with a button

foiled v ▷ foil

foiling v ▷ foil

foils v, n ▷ foil¹, ², ³

foist v (-s, -ing, -ed) (foll. by on or upon) force or impose on

foisted v ▷ foist

foisting v ▷ foist

foists v ▷ foist

fold¹ v (-s, -ing, -ed) bend so that one part covers another ▶ n (pl -s) folded piece or part

fold² n (pl -s) (BRIT, AUST & S AFR) enclosure for sheep

folded v ▷ fold

folder n (pl -s) piece of folded cardboard for holding loose papers

folders n ▷ folder

folding v ▷ fold

folds v, n ▷ fold¹, ²

foliage n (pl -s) leaves

foliages n ▷ foliage

foliation n (pl -s) process of producing leaves

foliations n ▷ foliation

folio n (pl -lios) sheet of paper folded in half to make two leaves of a book

folios n ▷ folio

folk n (pl -s) people in general ▶ pl relatives

folklore n (pl -s) traditional beliefs and stories of a people

folklores n ▷ folklore

folks n ▷ folk

folksier adj ▷ folksy

folksiest adj ▷ folksy

folksy adj (-sier, -siest) simple and unpretentious

follicle n (pl -s) small cavity in the body, esp. one from which a hair grows

follicles n ▷ follicle

follies n ▷ folly

follow v (-s, -ing, -ed) go or come after

followed v ▷ follow

follower n (pl -s) disciple or supporter

followers n ▷ follower

following adj about to be mentioned ▶ n (pl -s) group of supporters ▶ prep as a result of ▶ v ▷ follow

followings n ▷ following

follows v ▷ follow

folly n (pl -llies) foolishness

foment [foam-ent] v (-s, -ing, -ed) encourage or stir up (trouble)

fomented v ▷ foment

fomenting v ▷ foment

foments v ▷ foment

fond adj (-er, -est) tender, loving > **fondly** adv > **fondness** n (pl -es)

fondant n (pl -s) (sweet made from) flavoured paste of sugar and water

fondants n ▷ fondant

fonder adj ▷ fond

fondest adj ▷ fond

fondle v (-les, -ling, -led) caress

fondled v ▷ fondle

fondles v ▷ fondle

fondling v ▷ fondle

fondly adv ▷ fond

fondness n ▷ fond

fondnesses n ▷ fond

fondue n (pl -dues) Swiss dish of a hot melted cheese sauce into which pieces of bread are dipped

fondues n ▷ fondue

font¹ n (pl -s) bowl in a church for baptismal water

font² (pl -s) n set of printing type of one style and size

fontanelle n (pl -s) soft membranous gap between the bones of a baby's skull

fontanelles n ▷ fontanelle

fonts n ▷ font¹, ²

food n (pl -dies) what one eats, solid nourishment

foodie n (pl -s) (Informal) gourmet

foodies n ▷ foodie

foods n ▷ food

foodstuff n (pl -s) substance used as food

foodstuffs n ▷ foodstuff

fool¹ n (pl -s) person lacking sense or judgment (HIST) ▶ v (-s, -ing, -ed) deceive (someone)

fool² (pl -s) n dessert of puréed fruit mixed with cream

fooled v ▷ fool
fooleries n ▷ foolery
foolery n (pl -ries) foolish behaviour
foolhardiness n ▷ foolhardy
foolhardinesses n ▷ foolhardy
foolhardy adj recklessly adventurous
> foolhardiness n (pl -es)
fooling v ▷ fool
foolish adj (-er, -est) unwise, silly, or absurd
> foolishly adv > foolishness n (pl -es)
foolisher adj ▷ foolish
foolishest adj ▷ foolish
foolishly adv ▷ foolish
foolishness n ▷ foolish
foolishnesses n ▷ foolish
foolproof adj unable to fail
fools n, v ▷ fool¹, ²
foolscap n (pl -s) size of paper, 34.3 × 43.2
centimetres
foolscaps n ▷ foolscap
foot n (pl feet) part of the leg below the ankle
footage n (pl -s) amount of film used
footages n ▷ footage
football n (pl -s) game played by two teams of
eleven players kicking a ball in an attempt to
score goals > footballer n (pl -s)
footballer n ▷ football
footballers n ▷ footballs
footballs n ▷ football
footbridge n (pl -s) bridge for pedestrians
footbridges n ▷ footbridge
footfall n (pl -s) sound of a footstep
footfalls n ▷ footfall
foothills pl n hills at the foot of a mountain
foothold n (pl -s) secure position from which
progress may be made
footholds n ▷ foothold
footing n (pl -s) basis or foundation
footings n ▷ footing
footlight n light at the front of a stage
footlights pl n ▷ footlight
footling adj (CHIEFLY BRIT) (Informal) trivial
footloose adj free from ties
footman n (pl -men) male servant in uniform
footmen n ▷ footman
footnote n note printed at the foot of a page
footnotes n ▷ footnote
footpath n (pl -s) narrow path for walkers only
footpaths n ▷ footpath
footplate n (pl -s) platform in the cab of a
locomotive for the driver
footplates n ▷ footplate
footprint n (pl -s) mark left by a foot
footprints n ▷ footprint
footsie n (pl -s) (Informal) flirtation involving
the touching together of feet
footsies n ▷ footsie
footstep n step in walking
footsteps n ▷ footstep
footstool n (pl -s) low stool used to rest the
feet on while sitting
footstools n ▷ footstool
footwear n (pl -s) anything worn to cover
the feet
footwears n ▷ footwear
footwork n (pl -s) skilful use of the feet, as in
sport or dancing
footworks n ▷ footwork
fop n (pl -s) man excessively concerned
with fashion > foppery n (pl -ies) > foppish
adj
fopperies n ▷ fop
foppery n ▷ fop
foppish n ▷ fop
fops n ▷ fop
for prep indicating a person intended to
benefit from or receive something, span of
time or distance, person or thing represented
by someone, etc. ▶ conj because
forage v (-ges, -ging, -ged) search about (for)
▶ n (pl -s) food for cattle or horses
foraged v ▷ forage
forages v, n ▷ forage
foraging v ▷ forage
foray n (pl -s) brief raid or attack
forays n ▷ foray
forbade v ▷ forbid
forbear v (-s, -ing, forbore, forborne) cease or
refrain (from doing something)
forbearance n (pl -s) tolerance, patience
forbearances n ▷ forbearance
forbearing v ▷ forbear
forbears v ▷ forbear
forbid v (-s, -dding, forbade, forbidden)
prohibit, refuse to allow > forbidden adj
forbidden v, adj ▷ forbid
forbidding adj severe, threatening ▶ v ▷ forbid
forbids v ▷ forbid
forbore v ▷ forbear
forborne v ▷ forbear
force n (pl -s) strength or power ▶ v (-ces, -cing,
-ced) compel, make (someone) do something
forced adj compulsory ▶ v ▷ force
forceful adj emphatic and confident
> forcefully adv
forceps pl n surgical pincers
forces n, v ▷ force
forcible adj involving physical force or violence
> forcibly adv
forcibly adv ▷ forcible

forcing v ▷ force

ford n (pl -s) shallow place where a river may be crossed ▶ v (-s, -ing, -ed) cross (a river) at a ford

forded v ▷ ford

fording v ▷ ford

fords n, v ▷ ford

fore adj in, at, or towards the front ▶ n (pl -s) front part

forearm¹ n (pl -s) arm from the wrist to the elbow

forearm² v (-s, -ing, -ed) prepare beforehand

forearmed v ▷ forearm²

forearming v ▷ forearm²

forearms n, v ▷ forearm¹, ²

forebear n (pl -s) ancestor

forebears n ▷ forebear

foreboding n (pl -s) feeling that something bad is about to happen

forebodings n ▷ foreboding

forecast v (-casts, -casting, -cast or -casted) predict (weather, events, etc.) ▶ n (pl -s) prediction

forecasted v ▷ forecast

forecasting v ▷ forecast

forecastle [foke-sl] n (pl -s) raised front part of a ship

forecastles n ▷ forecastle

forecasts v, n ▷ forecast

foreclose v (-ses, -sing, -sed) take possession of (property bought with borrowed money which has not been repaid) > **foreclosure** n (pl -s)

foreclosed v ▷ foreclose

forecloses v ▷ foreclose

foreclosing v ▷ foreclose

foreclosure n ▷ foreclose

foreclosures n ▷ foreclose

forecourt n (pl -s) courtyard or open space in front of a building

forecourts n ▷ forecourt

forefather n (pl -s) ancestor

forefathers n ▷ forefather

forefinger n (pl -s) finger next to the thumb

forefingers n ▷ forefinger

forefront n (pl -s) most active or prominent position

forefronts n ▷ forefront

foregather v (-s, -ing, -ed) meet together or assemble

foregathered v ▷ foregather

foregathering v ▷ foregather

foregathers v ▷ foregather

forego v (-goes, -going, -went, -gone) ▷ forgo

foregoes v ▷ forego

foregoing adj going before, preceding ▶ v ▷ forego

foregone v ▷ forego

foreground n (pl -s) part of a view, esp. in a picture, nearest the observer

foregrounds n ▷ foreground

forehand n (pl -s) (TENNIS ETC.) stroke played with the palm of the hand facing forward

forehands n ▷ forehand

forehead n (pl -s) part of the face above the eyebrows

foreheads n ▷ forehead

foreign adj not of, or in, one's own country > **foreigner** n (pl -s)

foreigner n ▷ foreign

foreigners n ▷ foreign

foreleg n (pl -s) either of the front legs of an animal

forelegs n ▷ foreleg

forelock n (pl -s) lock of hair over the forehead

forelocks n ▷ forelock

foreman n (pl -men) person in charge of a group of workers

foremast n (pl -s) mast nearest the bow of a ship

foremasts n ▷ foremast

foremen n ▷ foreman

foremost adj, adv first in time, place, or importance

forename n (pl -s) first name

forenames n ▷ forename

forenoon n (pl -s) (CHIEFLY US & CANADIAN) morning

forenoons n ▷ forenoon

forensic adj used in or connected with courts of law

foreplay n (pl -s) sexual stimulation before intercourse

foreplays n ▷ foreplay

forerunner n (pl -s) person or thing that goes before, precursor

forerunners n ▷ forerunner

fores n ▷ fore

foresail n (pl -s) main sail on the foremast of a ship

foresails n ▷ foresail

foresaw v ▷ foresee

foresee v (-sees, -seeing, -saw, -seen) see or know beforehand > **foreseeable** adj

foreseeable adj ▷ foresee

foreseeing v ▷ foresee

foreseen v ▷ foresee

foresees v ▷ foresee

foreshadow v (-s, -ing, -ed) show or indicate beforehand

foreshadowed v ▷ foreshadow

foreshadowing v ▷ foreshadow

foreshadows v ▷ foreshadow

foreshore n (pl **-s**) part of the shore between high- and low-tide marks

foreshores n ▷ foreshore

foreshorten v (**-s, -ing, -ed**) represent (an object) in a picture as shorter than it really is, in accordance with perspective

foreshortened v ▷ foreshorten

foreshortening v ▷ foreshorten

foreshortens v ▷ foreshorten

foresight n (pl **-s**) ability to anticipate and provide for future needs

foresights n ▷ foresight

foreskin n (pl **-s**) fold of skin covering the tip of the penis

foreskins n ▷ foreskin

forest n (pl **-s**) large area with a thick growth of trees > **forested** adj

forestall v (**-s, -ing, -ed**) prevent or guard against in advance

forestalled v ▷ forestall

forestalling v ▷ forestall

forestalls v ▷ forestall

forested adj ▷ forest

forester n (pl **-s**) person skilled in forestry

foresters n ▷ foresters

forestries n ▷ forestry

forestry n (pl **-ries**) science of planting and caring for trees

forests n ▷ forest

foretaste n (pl **-s**) early limited experience of something to come

foretastes n ▷ foretaste

foretell v (**-s, f-ing, -told**) tell or indicate beforehand

foretelling v ▷ foretell

foretells v ▷ foretell

forethought n (pl **-s**) thoughtful planning for future events

forethoughts n ▷ forethought

foretold v ▷ foretell

forever adv without end

forewarn v (**-s, -ing, -ed**) warn beforehand

forewarned v ▷ forewarn

forewarning v ▷ forewarn

forewarns v ▷ forewarn

forewent v ▷ forego

foreword n (pl **-s**) introduction to a book

forewords n ▷ foreword

forfeit [**for**-fit] n (pl **-s**) thing lost or given up as a penalty for a fault or mistake ▶ v (**-s, -ing, -ed**) lose as a forfeit ▶ adj lost as a forfeit > **forfeiture** n (pl **-s**)

forfeited v ▷ forfeit

forfeiting v ▷ forfeit

forfeits n, v ▷ forfeit

forfeiture n ▷ forfeit

forfeitures n ▷ forfeit

forgave v ▷ forgive

forge[1] n (pl **-s**) place where metal is worked, smithy ▶ v (**-ges, -ging, -ged**) make a fraudulent imitation of (something)

forge[2] v (**-ges, -ging, -ged**) advance steadily

forged n ▷ forge[1, 2]

forger n (pl **-s**) person who makes an illegal copy of something

forgeries n ▷ forgery

forgers n ▷ forgery

forgery n (pl **-ries**) illegal copy of something

forges v, n ▷ forge[1, 2]

forget v (**-s, -getting, -got, -gotten**) fail to remember

forgetful adj tending to forget > **forgetfulness** n (pl **-es**)

forgetfulness n ▷ forgetful

forgetfulnesses n ▷ forgetful

forgets v ▷ forget

forgetting v ▷ forget

forging v ▷ forge[1, 2]

forgive v (**-giving, -gave, -given**) cease to blame or hold resentment against, pardon > **forgiveness** n (pl **-es**)

forgiven v ▷ forgive

forgiveness n ▷ forgive

forgivenesses n ▷ forgive

forgiving v ▷ forgive

forgo v (**-goes, -going, -went, -gone**) do without or give up

forgoes v ▷ forgo

forgoing v ▷ forgo

forgone v ▷ forgo

forgot v ▷ forget

forgotten v ▷ forget

fork n (pl **-s**) tool for eating food, with prongs and a handle ▶ v (**-s, -ing, -ed**) pick up, dig, etc. with a fork > **forked** adj

forked v, adj ▷ fork

forking v ▷ fork

forks n, v ▷ fork

forlorn adj lonely and unhappy > **forlornly** adv

forlornly adv ▷ forlorn

form n (pl **-s**) shape or appearance ▶ v (**-s, -ing, -ed**) give a (particular) shape to or take a (particular) shape > **formless** adj

formal adj of or characterized by established conventions of ceremony and behaviour > **formally** adv

formaldehyde [for-**mal**-de-hide] n (pl **-s**)

colourless pungent gas used to make formalin

formaldehydes n ▷ formaldehyde

formalin n (pl -s) solution of formaldehyde in water, used as a disinfectant or a preservative for biological specimens

formalins n ▷ formalin

formalities n ▷ formality

formality n (pl -ties) requirement of custom or etiquette

formalize v (-zes, -zing, -zed) make official or formal

formalized v ▷ formalize

formalizes v ▷ formalize

formalizing v ▷ formalize

formally adv ▷ formal

format n (pl -s) style in which something is arranged ▶ v (-s, -matting, -matted) arrange in a format

formation n (pl -s) forming

formations n ▷ formation

formative adj of or relating to development

formats n, v ▷ format

formatted v ▷ format

formatting v ▷ format

formed v ▷ form

former adj of an earlier time, previous
> **formerly** adv

formerly adv ▷ former

formidable adj frightening because difficult to overcome or manage > **formidably** adv

formidably adv ▷ formidable

forming v ▷ form

formless adj ▷ form

forms n, v ▷ form

formula n (pl -las, -lae) group of numbers, letters, or symbols expressing a scientific or mathematical rule > **formulaic** adj

formulae n ▷ formula

formulaic adj ▷ formula

formulas n ▷ formula

formulate v (-tes, -ting, -ted) plan or describe precisely and clearly > **formulation** n (pl -s)

formulated v ▷ formulate

formulates v ▷ formulate

formulating v ▷ formulates

formulation n ▷ formulate

formulations n ▷ formulate

fornicate v (-tes, -ting, -ted) have sexual intercourse without being married
> **fornication** n (pl -s) > **fornicator** n (pl -s)

fornicated v ▷ fornicate

fornicates v ▷ fornicate

fornicating v ▷ fornicate

fornication n ▷ fornicate

fornications n ▷ fornicate

fornicator n ▷ fornicate

fornicators n ▷ fornicate

forsake v (-sakes, -saking, -sook, -saken) withdraw support or friendship from

forsaken v ▷ forsake

forsakes v ▷ forsake

forsaking v ▷ forsake

forsook v ▷ forsake

forsooth adv (Obs) indeed

forswear v (-s, -swearing, -swore, -sworn) renounce or reject

forswearing v ▷ forswear

forswears v ▷ forswear

forswore v ▷ forswear

forsworn v ▷ forswear

forsythia [for-syth-ee-a] n (pl -as) shrub with yellow flowers in spring

forsythias n ▷ forsythia

fort n (pl -s) fortified building or place

forte¹ [for-tay] n (pl -s) thing at which a person excels

forte² [for-tay] adv (MUSIC) loudly

fortes n ▷ forte

forth adv forwards, out, or away

forthcoming adj about to appear or happen

forthright adj direct and outspoken

forthwith adv at once

forties n ▷ forty

fortieth adj, n ▷ forty

fortieths n ▷ forty

fortifications n ▷ fortify

fortified v ▷ fortify

fortifies v ▷ fortify

fortify v (-fies, -fying, -fied) make (a place) defensible, as by building walls
> **fortification** n (pl -s)

fortification n ▷ fortify

fortifying v ▷ fortify

fortissimo adv (MUSIC) very loudly

fortitude n (pl -s) courage in adversity or pain

fortitudes n ▷ fortitude

fortnight n (pl -s) two weeks > **fortnightly** adv, adj

fortnightly adv, adj ▷ fortnight

fortnights n ▷ fortnight

fortress n (pl -es) large fort or fortified town

fortresses n ▷ fortress

forts n ▷ fort

fortuitous [for-tyew-it-uss] adj happening by (lucky) chance > **fortuitously** adv

fortuitously adv ▷ fortuitous

fortunate adj having good luck > **fortunately** adv

fortunately adv ▷ fortunate

fortune n (pl -s) luck, esp. when favourable ▶ pl person's destiny
  fortunes n ▷ fortune

forty adj, n (pl -ties) four times ten > **fortieth** adj, n (pl -s)

forum n (pl -ums) meeting or medium for open discussion or debate
  forums n ▷ forum

forward adj directed or moving ahead ▶ n (pl -s) attacking player in various team games, such as soccer or hockey ▶ adv forwards ▶ v (-s, -ing, -ed) send (a letter etc.) on to an ultimate destination
  forwarded v ▷ forward
  forwarding v ▷ forward

forwards adv towards or at a place further ahead in space or time ▶ n, v ▷ forward

fossick v (-s, -ing, -ed) (AUST & NZ) search, esp. for gold or precious stones
  fossicked v ▷ fossick
  fossicking v ▷ fossick
  fossicks v ▷ fossick

fossil n (pl -s) hardened remains of a prehistoric animal or plant preserved in rock

fossilize v (-zes, -zing, -zed) turn into a fossil
  fossilized v ▷ fossilize
  fossilizes v ▷ fossilize
  fossilizing v ▷ fossilize
  fossils n ▷ fossil

foster v (-s, -ing, -ed) promote the growth or development of ▶ adj of or involved in fostering a child
  fostered v ▷ foster
  fostering v ▷ foster
  fosters v ▷ foster
  fought v ▷ fight

foul adj (-er, -est) loathsome or offensive ▶ n (pl -s) (SPORT) violation of the rules ▶ v (-s, -ing, -ed) make dirty or polluted
  fouled v ▷ foul
  fouler adj ▷ foul
  foulest adj ▷ foul
  fouling v ▷ foul

foulmouthed adj habitually using foul language
  fouls n, v ▷ foul

found¹ v ▷ find

found² v (-s, -ing, -ed) establish or bring into being (foll. by on or upon) > **founder** n (pl -s)

found³ v (-s, -ing, -ed) cast (metal or glass) by melting and setting in a mould

foundation n (pl -s) basis or base
  foundations n ▷ foundation
  founded v ▷ found²,³
  founder¹ n ▷ found²

founder² v (-s, -ing, -ed) break down or fail
  foundered v ▷ founder
  foundering v ▷ founder
  founders¹ n ▷ found²
  founders² v ▷ founder
  founding v ▷ found²,³

foundling n (pl -s) (CHIEFLY BRIT) abandoned baby
  foundlings n ▷ foundling
  foundries n ▷ foundry

foundry n (pl -dries) place where metal is melted and cast
  founds v ▷ found²,³

fount¹ n (pl -s) (Lit) fountain

fount² (pl -s) n set of printing type of one style and size

fountain n (pl -s) jet of water

fountainhead n (pl -s) original source
  fountainheads n ▷ fountainhead
  fountains n ▷ fountain
  founts n ▷ fount¹,²

four adj, n (pl -s) one more than three
  fours n ▷ four

foursome n group of four people
  foursomes n (pl -s) ▷ foursome

fourteen adj, n (pl -s) four and ten > **fourteenth** adj, n (pl -s)
  fourteens n ▷ fourteen
  fourteenth adj, n ▷ fourteen
  fourteenths n ▷ fourteen

fourth adj, n (pl -s) (of) number four in a series ▶ n quarter
  fourths n ▷ fourth

fowl n (pl -s) domestic cock or hen
  fowls n ▷ fowl

fox n (pl -es) reddish-brown bushy-tailed animal of the dog family ▶ v (-s, -ing, -ed) (Informal) perplex or deceive
  foxed v ▷ fox
  foxes n, v ▷ fox

foxglove n (pl -s) tall plant with purple or white flowers
  foxgloves n ▷ foxglove

foxhole n (pl -s) (MIL) small pit dug for protection
  foxholes n ▷ foxhole

foxhound n (pl -s) dog bred for hunting foxes
  foxhounds n ▷ foxhound
  foxier adj ▷ foxy
  foxiest adj ▷ foxy
  foxing v ▷ fox

foxtrot n (pl -s) ballroom dance with slow and quick steps
  foxtrots n ▷ foxtrot

foxy adj (-xier, -xiest) of or like a fox, esp. in

craftiness

foy n (**foys**). Foy is an old dialect word meaning a farewell meal or gift. This unusual word can be useful when there is little space to form longer words. Foy scores 9 points.

foyer [foy-ay] n (pl -**s**) entrance hall in a theatre, cinema, or hotel
   foyers n ▷ foyer

fracas [frak-ah] n (pl -es) noisy quarrel
   fracases n ▷ fracas

fraction n (pl -**s**) numerical quantity that is not a whole number > **fractional** adj
   > **fractionally** adv
   fractional adj ▷ fraction
   fractionally adv ▷ fraction
   fractions n ▷ fraction

fractious adj easily upset and angered

fracture n (pl -**s**) breaking, esp. of a bone ▶ v (-res, -ring, -red) break
   fractured v ▷ fracture
   fractures n, v ▷ fracture
   fracturing v ▷ fracture

fragile adj easily broken or damaged > **fragility** n (pl -**lities**)
   fragilities n ▷ fragile
   fragility n ▷ fragile

fragment n (pl -**s**) piece broken off ▶ v (-**s**, -ing, -ed) break into pieces > **fragmentary** adj
   > **fragmentation** n (pl -**s**)
   fragmentary adj ▷ fragment
   fragmentation n ▷ fragment
   fragmentations n ▷ fragment
   fragmented v ▷ fragment
   fragmenting v ▷ fragment
   fragments n, v ▷ fragment

fragrance n (pl -**s**) pleasant smell
   fragrances n ▷ fragrance

fragrant adj sweet-smelling

frail adj (-**er**, -**est**) physically weak
   frailer adj ▷ frail
   frailest adj ▷ frail
   frailities n ▷ fraility

frailty n (pl -**ties**) physical or moral weakness

frame n (pl -**s**) structure giving shape or support ▶ v (-**mes**, -ming, -med) put together, construct
   framed v ▷ frame
   frames n, v ▷ frame

framework n (pl -**s**) supporting structure
   frameworks n ▷ framework
   framing v ▷ frame

franc n (pl -**s**) monetary unit of Switzerland, various African countries, and formerly of France and Belgium

franchise n (pl -**s**) right to vote
   franchises n ▷ franchise

francium n (pl -**s**) (CHEM) radioactive metallic element
   franciums n ▷ francium
   francs n ▷ franc

frangipani [fran-jee-**pah**-nee] n (pl -**nis**) Australian evergreen tree with large yellow fragrant flowers
   frangipanis n ▷ frangipani

frank adj (-**er**, -**est**) honest and straightforward in speech or attitude ▶ n (pl -**s**) official mark on a letter permitting delivery ▶ v (-**s**, -ing, -ed) put such a mark on (a letter) > **frankly** adv
   > **frankness** n (pl -**es**)
   franked v ▷ frank
   franker adj ▷ frank
   frankest adj ▷ frank

frankfurter n (pl -**s**) smoked sausage
   frankfurters n ▷ frankfurter

frankincense n (pl -**es**) aromatic gum resin burned as incense
   frankincenses n ▷ frankincense
   franking v ▷ frank
   frankly adv ▷ frank
   frankness n ▷ frank
   franknesses n ▷ frank
   franks n, v ▷ frank

frantic adj distracted with rage, grief, joy, etc.
   > **frantically** adv
   frantically adv ▷ frantic

fraternal adj of a brother, brotherly
   > **fraternally** adv

fraternity n (pl -**ties**) group of people with shared interests, aims, etc. (us)

fraternize v associate on friendly terms
   > **fraternization** n

fratricide n (pl -**s**) crime of killing one's brother
   fratricides n ▷ fratricide

frau [rhymes with how] n (pl **fraus, frauen**) married German woman

fraud n (pl -**s**) (criminal) deception, swindle
   > **fraudulent** adj > **fraudulence** n (pl -**s**)
   frauds n ▷ fraud
   fraudulence n ▷ fraud
   fraudulences n ▷ fraud
   fraudulent adj ▷ fraud
   frauen n ▷ frau

fraught [frawt] adj (-**er**, -**est**) tense or anxious
   fraughter adj ▷ fraught
   fraughtest adj ▷ fraught

fräulein [froy-line] n (pl -**leins**, -**lein**) unmarried German woman
   fräuleins n ▷ fräulein
   fraus n ▷ frau

fray¹ *n* (*pl* -s) (BRIT, AUST & NZ) noisy quarrel or conflict

fray² *v* (-s, -ing, -ed) make or become ragged at the edge
   frayed *v* ▷ fray²
   fraying *v* ▷ fray²
   frays *n*, *v* ▷ fray¹, ²

frazzle *n* (*pl* -s) (*Informal*) exhausted state
   frazzles *n* ▷ frazzle

freak *n* (*pl* -s) abnormal person or thing ▶ *adj* abnormal > **freakish** *adj*
   freakish *adj* ▷ freak
   freaks *n* ▷ freak

freckle *n* (*pl* -s) small brown spot on the skin

freckled *adj* marked with freckles
   freckles *n* ▷ freckle

free *adj* (freer, freest) able to act at will, not compelled or restrained ▶ *v* (frees, freeing, freed) release, liberate > **freely** *adv*
   freed *v* ▷ free

freedom *n* (*pl* -s) being free
   freedoms *n* ▷ freedom

freehand *adj* drawn without guiding instruments

freehold *n* (*pl* -s) tenure of land for life without restrictions > **freeholder** *n* (*pl* -s)
   freeholder *n* ▷ freehold
   freeholders *n* ▷ freehold
   freeholds *n* ▷ freehold
   freeing *v* ▷ free

freelance *adj*, *n* (*pl* -s) (of) a self-employed person doing specific pieces of work for various employers
   freelances *n* ▷ freelance

freeloader *n* (*pl* -s) (*Slang*) habitual scrounger
   freeloaders *n* ▷ freeloader
   freely *adv* ▷ free

freemason *n* (*pl* -s) member of a secret fraternity pledged to help each other
   freemasons *n* ▷ freemason
   freer *adj* ▷ free
   frees *v* ▷ free

freesia *n* (*pl* -s) plant with fragrant tubular flowers
   freesias *n* ▷ freesia
   freest *adj* ▷ free

freeway *n* (*pl* -s) (US & AUST) motorway
   freeways *n* ▷ freeway

freewheel *v* (-s, -ing, -ed) travel downhill on a bicycle without pedalling
   freewheeled *v* ▷ freewheel
   freewheeling *v* ▷ freewheel
   freewheels *v* ▷ freewheel

freeze *v* (-zes, -zing, froze, frozen) change from a liquid to a solid by the reduction of temperature, as water to ice ▶ *n* period of very cold weather

freezer *n* (*pl* -s) insulated cabinet for cold-storage of perishable foods
   freezers *n* ▷ freezer
   freezes *v* ▷ freeze

freezing *adj* (*Informal*) very cold ▶ *v* ▷ freeze

freight [frate] *n* (*pl* -s) commercial transport of goods ▶ *v* (-s, -ing, -ed) send by freight
   freighted *v* ▷ freight

freighter *n* (*pl* -s) ship or aircraft for transporting goods
   freighters *n* ▷ freighter
   freighting *v* ▷ freight
   freights *n*, *v* ▷ freight

frenetic [frin-net-ik] *adj* uncontrolled, excited > **frenetically** *adv*
   frenetically *adv* ▷ frenetic
   frenzied *adj* ▷ frenzy
   frenziedly *adv* ▷ frenzy
   frenzies *n* ▷ frenzy

frenzy *n* (*pl* -zies) violent mental derangement > **frenzied** *adj* > **frenziedly** *adv*
   frequencies *n* ▷ frequency

frequency *n* (*pl* -cies) rate of occurrence

frequent *adj* happening often ▶ *v* (-s, -ing, -ed) visit habitually > **frequently** *adv*
   frequented *v* ▷ frequent
   frequenting *v* ▷ frequent
   frequently *adv* ▷ frequent
   frequents *v* ▷ frequent

fresco *n* (*pl* -coes, -cos) watercolour painting done on wet plaster on a wall
   frescoes *n* ▷ fresco
   frescos *n* ▷ fresco

fresh *adj* (-er, -est) newly made, acquired, etc. > **freshly** *adv* > **freshness** *n* (*pl* -es)

freshen *v* (-s, -ing, -ed) make or become fresh or fresher
   freshened *v* ▷ freshen
   freshening *v* ▷ freshen
   freshens *v* ▷ freshen

fresher *n* (*pl* -s) first-year student ▶ *adj* ▷ fresh
   freshers *n* ▷ fresher
   freshest *adj* ▷ fresh
   freshly *adv* ▷ fresh

freshman *n* (*pl* -men) (BRIT & US) first-year student
   freshmen *n* ▷ freshman
   freshness *n* ▷ fresh
   freshnesses *n* ▷ fresh

fret¹ *v* (-s, -tting, -tted) be worried

fret² *n* (*pl* -s) small bar on the fingerboard of a guitar etc.

fretful *adj* irritable

frets n ▷ fret¹, ²

fretsaw n (pl -s) fine saw with a narrow blade, used for fretwork

fretsaws n ▷ fretsaw

fretted v ▷ fret¹

fretting v ▷ fret¹

fretwork n (pl -s) decorative carving in wood

fretworks n ▷ fretwork

friable adj easily crumbled

friar n (pl -s) member of a male Roman Catholic religious order

friaries n ▷ friary

friars n ▷ friar

friary n (pl -ries) house of friars

fricassee n (pl -s) stewed meat served in a thick white sauce

fricassees n ▷ fricassee

friction n (pl -s) resistance met with by a body moving over another > **frictional** adj

frictional adj ▷ friction

frictions n ▷ friction

fridge n (pl -s) apparatus in which food and drinks are kept cool

fridges n ▷ fridge

fried v ▷ fry¹

friend n (pl -s) person whom one knows well and likes ▷ **friendless** adj > **friendship** n (pl -s)

friendless adj ▷ friend

friendlier adj ▷ friendly

friendlies n ▷ friendly

friendliest adj ▷ friendly

friendliness n ▷ friendly

friendlinesses n ▷ friendly

friendly adj (-lier, -liest) showing or expressing liking ▶ n (pl -lies) (SPORT) match played for its own sake and not as part of a competition > **friendliness** n (pl -es)

friends n ▷ friend

friendship n ▷ friend

friendships n ▷ friend

fries v, n ▷ fry¹

Friesian [free-zhan] n (pl -s) breed of black-and-white dairy cattle

Friesians n ▷ Friesian

frieze [freeze] n (pl -s) ornamental band on a wall

friezes n ▷ frieze

frigate [frig-it] n (pl -s) medium-sized fast warship

frigates n ▷ frigate

fright n (pl -s) sudden fear or alarm

frighten v (-s, -ing, -ed) scare or terrify > **frightening** adj

frightened v ▷ frighten

frightened v ▷ frighten

frightening v, adj ▷ frighten

frightful adj horrifying (Informal) > **frightfully** adv

frightfully adv ▷ frightful

frights n ▷ fright

frigid [frij-id] adj (of a woman) sexually unresponsive > **frigidity** n (pl -ties)

frigidities n ▷ frigid

frigidity n ▷ frigid

frill n (pl -s) gathered strip of fabric attached at one edge ▶ pl superfluous decorations or details > **frilled** adj > **frilly** adj (-ier, -iest)

frilled adj ▷ frill

frillier adj ▷ frill

frilliest adj ▷ frill

frills n ▷ frill

frilly adj ▷ frill

fringe n (pl -es) hair cut short and hanging over the forehead ▶ v (-ges, -ging, -ged) decorate with a fringe ▶ adj (of theatre) unofficial or unconventional > **fringed** adj

fringed v, adj ▷ fringe

fringes n, v ▷ fringe

fringing v ▷ fringe

fripperies n ▷ frippery

frippery n (pl -ries) useless ornamentation

frisk v (-s, -ing, -ed) move or leap playfully

frisked v ▷ frisk

friskier adj ▷ frisky

friskiest adj ▷ frisky

frisking v ▷ frisk

frisks v ▷ frisk

frisky adj (-kier, -kiest) lively or high-spirited

frisson [frees-sonn] n (pl -s) shiver of fear or excitement

frissons n ▷ frisson

fritter n (pl -s) piece of food fried in batter

fritters n ▷ fritter

frivolities n ▷ frivolous

frivolity n ▷ frivolous

frivolous adj not serious or sensible > **frivolity** n (pl -ties)

frizz v (-es, -ing, -ed) form (hair) into stiff wiry curls > **frizzy** adj (-zzier, -zziest)

frizzed v ▷ frizz

frizzes v ▷ frizz

frizzier adj ▷ frizz

frizziest adj ▷ frizz

frizzing v ▷ frizz

frizzle v (-les, -ling, -led) cook or heat until crisp and shrivelled

frizzled v ▷ frizzle

frizzles v ▷ frizzle

frizzling v ▷ frizzle

frizzy adj ▷ frizz

frock *n* (*pl* -s) dress
  frocks *n* ▷ frock
frog *n* (*pl* -s) smooth-skinned tailless
  amphibian with long back legs used for
  jumping
frogman *n* (*pl* -men) swimmer with a rubber
  suit and breathing equipment for working
  underwater
  frogmen *n* ▷ frogman
  frogs *n* ▷ frog
frogspawn *n* (*pl* -s) jelly-like substance
  containing frog's eggs
  frogspawns *n* ▷ frogspawn
frolic *v* (-lics, -licking, -licked) run and play
  in a lively way ▶ *n* (*pl* -s) lively and merry
  behaviour
  frolicked *v* ▷ frolic
  frolicking *v* ▷ frolic
  frolics *v*, *n* ▷ frolic
frolicsome *adj* playful
from *prep* indicating the point of departure,
  source, distance, cause, change of state, etc.
frond *n* (*pl* -s) long leaf or leaflike part of a fern,
  palm, or seaweed
  fronds *n* ▷ frond
front *n* (*pl* -s) fore part ▶ *adj* of or at the front ▶ *v*
  (-s, -ing, -ed) face (onto) > frontal *adj*
frontage *n* (*pl* -s) facade of a building
  frontages *n* ▷ frontage
  frontal *adj* ▷ front
  fronted *v* ▷ front
frontier *n* (*pl* -s) area of a country bordering
  on another
  frontiers *n* ▷ frontier
  fronting *v* ▷ front
frontispiece *n* (*pl* -s) illustration facing the
  title page of a book
  frontispieces *n* ▷ frontispiece
frontrunner (*pl* -s) *n* (*Informal*) person regarded
  as most likely to win a race, election, etc.
  frontrunners *n* ▷ frontrunner
  fronts *n*, *v* ▷ front
frost *n* (*pl* -s) white frozen dew or mist ▶ *v* (-s,
  -ing, -ed) become covered with frost
frostbite *n* destruction of tissue, esp. of the
  fingers or ears, by cold (*pl* -s) > frostbitten *adj*
  frostbites *n* ▷ frostbite
  frostbitten *adj* ▷ frostbite
  frosted *v* ▷ frost ▶ *adj* (of glass) having a rough
  surface to make it opaque
  frostier *adj* ▷ frosty
  frostiest *adj* ▷ frosty
  frostily *adv* ▷ frosty
  frostiness *n* ▷ frosty
  frostinesses *n* ▷ frosty

frosting *v* ▷ frost ▶ *n* (*pl* -s) (CHIEFLY US) sugar
  icing
  frostings *n* ▷ frosting
  frosts *n*, *v* ▷ frost
frosty *adj* (-tier, -tiest) characterized or
  covered by frost > frostily *adv* > frostiness
  n (*pl* -es)
froth *n* (*pl* -s) mass of small bubbles ▶ *v* (-s, -ing,
  -ed) foam > frothy *adj* (-thier, -thiest)
  frothed *v* ▷ froth
  frothier *adj* ▷ froth
  frothiest *adj* ▷ froth
  frothing *v* ▷ froth
  froths *n*, *v* ▷ froth
  frothy *adj* ▷ froth
  frowiest *adj* ▷ frowzy
frown *v* (-s, -ing, -ed) wrinkle one's brows in
  worry, anger, or thought ▶ *n* (*pl* -s) frowning
  expression
  frowned *v* ▷ frown
  frowning *v* ▷ frown
  frowns *v*, *n* ▷ frown
  frowsier *adj* ▷ frowzy
  frowsiest *adj* ▷ frowzy
  frowstier *adj* ▷ frowsty
  frowstiest *adj* ▷ frowsty
frowsty *adj* (-ier, -iest) (BRIT) stale or musty
  frowzier *adj* ▷ frowzy
frowzy, frowsy *adj* (-zier, -ziest) dirty or
  unkempt
  froze *v* ▷ freeze
  frozen *v* ▷ freeze
frugal *adj* thrifty, sparing > frugally *adv*
  > frugality *n* (*pl* -ties)
  frugalities *n* ▷ frugal
  frugality *n* ▷ frugal
  frugally *adv* ▷ frugal
fruit *n* (*pl* -s) part of a plant containing seeds,
  esp. if edible ▶ *v* (-s, -ing, -ed) bear fruit
  fruited *v* ▷ fruit
fruiterer *n* (*pl* -s) person who sells fruit
  fruiterers *n* ▷ fruiterer
fruitful *adj* useful or productive > fruitfully *adv*
  fruitfully *adv* ▷ fruitful
  fruitier *adj* ▷ fruity
  fruitiest *adj* ▷ fruity
  fruiting *v* ▷ fruit
fruition [froo-ish-on] *n* (*pl* -s) fulfilment of
  something worked for or desired
  fruitions *n* ▷ fruition
fruitless *adj* useless or unproductive
  > fruitlessly *adv*
  fruitlessly *adv* ▷ fruitless
  fruits *n*, *v* ▷ fruit
fruity *adj* (-tier, -tiest) of or like fruit

frump n (pl -s) dowdy woman > **frumpy** adj (-pier, -piest)
frumpier adj > frump
frumpiest adj > frump
frumps n > frump
frumpy adj > frump
frustrate v (-tes, -ting, -ted) upset or anger > **frustrated** adj > **frustrating** adj > **frustration** n (pl -s)
frustrated v, adj > frustrate
frustrates v > frustrate
frustrating v, adj > frustrate
frustration n > frustrate
frustrations n > frustrate
fry[1] v (-ries, -rying, -ried) cook or be cooked in fat or oil ▶ n (pl fries) potato chip
fry[2] pl n young fishes
frying v > fry
fuchsia [fyew-sha] n (pl -s) ornamental shrub with hanging flowers
fuchsias n > fuchsia
fuddle v (-les, -ling, -led) cause to be intoxicated or confused > **fuddled** adj
fuddled v, adj > fuddle
fuddles v > fuddle
fuddling v > fuddle
fudge[1] n (pl -s) soft caramel-like sweet
fudge[2] v (-ges, -ging, -ged) avoid making a firm statement or decision
fudged v > fudge[2]
fudges n, v > fudge[1, 2]
fudging v > fudge[2]
fuel n (pl -s) substance burned or treated to produce heat or power ▶ v (-s, -lling, -lled) provide with fuel
fuelled v > fuel
fuelling v > fuel
fuels n, v > fuel
fug n (pl -s) hot stale atmosphere > **fuggy** adj (-ggier, -ggiest)
fuggier adj > fug
fuggiest adj > fug
fuggy adj > fug
fugitive [fyew-jit-iv] n (pl -s) person who flees, esp. from arrest or pursuit ▶ adj fleeing
fugitives n > fugitive
fugs n > fug
fugue [fyewg] n (pl -s) musical composition in which a theme is repeated in different parts
fugues n > fugue
fulcra n > fulcrum
fulcrum n (pl -crums, -cra) pivot about which a lever turns
fulcrums n > fulcrum
fulfil v (-s, -lling, -lled) bring about the

achievement of (a desire or promise) > **fulfilment** n (pl -s)
fulfilled n > fulfil
fulfilling v > fulfil
fulfilment n > fulfil
fulfilments n > fulfil
fulfils v > fulfil
full adj (-er, -est) containing as much or as many as possible ▶ adv completely > **fully** adv > **fullness** n (pl -es)
fuller adj > full
fullest adj > full
fullness n > full
fullnesses n > full
fully adv > full
fulmar n (pl -s) Arctic sea bird
fulmars n > fulmar
fulminate v (-tes, -ting, -ted) (foll. by **against**) criticize or denounce angrily
fulminated v > fulminate
fulminates v > fulminate
fulminating v > fulminate
fulsome adj distastefully excessive or insincere
fumble v (-les, -ling, -led) handle awkwardly ▶ n (pl -s) act of fumbling
fumbled v > fumble
fumbles n, v > fumble
fumbling v > fumble
fume v (-s, -ing, -ed) be very angry ▶ pl n pungent smoke or vapour
fumed v > fume
fumes v, n > fume
fumigate [fyew-mig-gate] v (-tes, -ting, -ted) disinfect with fumes > **fumigation** n (pl -s)
fumigated v > fumigate
fumigates v > fumigate
fumigating v > fumigate
fumigation n > fumigate
fumigations n > fuminate
fuming v > fume
fun n (pl -s) enjoyment or amusement
function n (pl -s) purpose something exists for ▶ v (-s, -ing, -ed) operate or work (foll. by **as**)
functional adj of or as a function > **functionally** adv
functionally adv > functional
functionaries n > functionary
functionary n (pl -ries) official
functioned v > function
functioning v > function
functions n, v > function
fund n (pl -s) stock of money for a special purpose ▶ pl money resources ▶ v (-s, -ing, -ed) provide money to > **funding** n (pl -s)

fundamental *adj* essential or primary ▶ *n* (*pl* -s) basic rule or fact > **fundamentally** *adv*

fundamentalism *n* (*pl* -s) literal or strict interpretation of a religion > **fundamentalist** *adj*, *n* (*pl* -s)

fundamentalisms *n* ▷ **fundamentalism**

fundamentalist *adj*, *n* ▷ **fundamentalism**

fundamentalists *n* ▷ **fundamentalism**

fundamentally *adv* ▷ **fundamental**

fundamentals *n* ▷ **fundamental**

funded *v* ▷ **fund**

fundi *n* (*pl* -dis) (s AFR) expert or boffin

funding *v*, *n* ▷ **fund**

fundings *n* ▷ **fund**

fundis *n* ▷ **fundi**

funds *n*, *v* ▷ **fund**

funeral *n* (*pl* -s) ceremony of burying or cremating a dead person

funerals *n* ▷ **funeral**

funerary *adj* of or for a funeral

funereal [fyew-**neer**-ee-al] *adj* gloomy or sombre

funfair *n* (*pl* -s) entertainment with machines to ride on and stalls

funfairs *n* ▷ **funfair**

fungal *adj* ▷ **fungus**

fungi *n* ▷ **fungus**

fungicide *n* (*pl* -s) substance that destroys fungi

fungicides *n* ▷ **fungicide**

fungous *adj* ▷ **fungus**

fungus *n* (*pl* -gi, -guses) plant without leaves, flowers, or roots, such as a mushroom or mould > **fungal**, **fungous** *adj*

funguses *n* ▷ **fungus**

funicular *n* (*pl* -s) cable railway on a mountainside or cliff

funiculars *n* ▷ **funicular**

funk[1] *n* (*pl* -s) style of dance music with a strong beat

funk[2] (*Informal*) *n* nervous or fearful state ▶ *v* (-s, -ing, -ed) avoid (doing something) through fear

funked *v* ▷ **funk**

funkier *adj* ▷ **funky**

funkiest *adj* ▷ **funky**

funking *v* ▷ **funk**

funks *n*, *v* ▷ **funk**[1, 2]

funky *adj* (-kier, -kiest) (of music) having a strong beat

funnel *n* (*pl* -s) cone-shaped tube for pouring liquids into a narrow opening ▶ *v* (-s, -lling, -lled) (cause to) move through or as if through a funnel

funnelled *v* ▷ **funnel**

funnelling *v* ▷ **funnel**

funnels *n*, *v* ▷ **funnel**

funnier *adj* ▷ **funny**

funniest *adj* ▷ **funny**

funnily *adv* ▷ **funny**

funny *adj* (-nnier, -nniest) comical, humorous > **funnily** *adv*

funs *n* ▷ **fun**

fur *n* (*pl* -s) soft hair of a mammal ▶ *v* (-s, -rring, -rred) cover or become covered with fur > **furry** (-rrier, -rriest) ▶ *adj*

furbish *v* (-es, -ing, -ed) smarten up

furbished *v* ▷ **furbish**

furbishes *v* ▷ **furbish**

furbishing *v* ▷ **furbish**

furies *n* ▷ **fury**

furious *adj* very angry > **furiously** *adv*

furiously *adv* ▷ **furious**

furl *v* (-s, -ing, -ed) roll up and fasten (a sail, umbrella, or flag)

furled *v* ▷ **furl**

furling *v* ▷ **furl**

furlong *n* (*pl* -s) unit of length equal to 220 yards (201.168 metres)

furlongs *n* ▷ **furlongs**

furlough [fur-loh] *n* (*pl* -s) leave of absence

furloughs *n* ▷ **furlough**

furls *v* ▷ **furl**

furnace *n* (*pl* -s) enclosed chamber containing a very hot fire

furnaces *n* ▷ **furnace**

furnish *v* (-es, -ing, -ed) provide (a house or room) with furniture

furnished *v* ▷ **furnish**

furnishes *v* ▷ **furnish**

furnishing *v* ▷ **furnish**

furnishings *pl n* furniture, carpets, and fittings

furniture *n* (*pl* -s) large movable articles such as chairs and wardrobes

furnitures *n* ▷ **furniture**

furore [fyew-**ror**-ee] *n* (*pl* -s) very excited or angry reaction

furores *n* ▷ **furore**

furred *v* ▷ **fur**

furrier *n* (*pl* -s) dealer in furs ▶ *adj* ▷ **fur**

furriers *n* ▷ **furrier**

furriest *adj* ▷ **fur**

furring *v* ▷ **fur**

furrow *n* (*pl* -s) trench made by a plough ▶ *v* (-s, -ing, -ed) make or become wrinkled

furrowed *v* ▷ **furrow**

furrowing *v* ▷ **furrow**

furrows *n*, *v* ▷ **furrow**

furry *adj* ▷ **fur**

furrying v ▷ **flurry**

furs n, v ▷ **fur**

further adv in addition ▶ adj additional ▶ v (**-s, -ing, -ed**) assist the progress of > **furtherance** n (pl **-s**)

furtherance n ▷ **further**

furtherances n ▷ **further**

furthered v ▷ **further**

furthering v ▷ **further**

furthermore adv besides

furthermost adj most distant

furthers v ▷ **further**

furthest adv to the greatest distance or extent ▶ adj most distant

furtive adj sly and secretive > **furtively** adv

furtively adv ▷ **furtive**

fury n (pl **-ries**) wild anger

furze n (pl **-s**) gorse

furzes n ▷ **furze**

fuse¹ n (pl **-s**) cord containing an explosive for detonating a bomb

fuse² n (pl **-s**) safety device for electric circuits, containing a wire that melts and breaks the connection when the circuit is overloaded ▶ v (**-ses, -sing, -sed**) (cause to) fail as a result of a blown fuse

fused v ▷ **fuse**

fuselage [fyew-zill-lahzh] n (pl **-s**) body of an aircraft

fuselages n ▷ **fuselage**

fuses v, n ▷ **fuse**

fusilier [fyew-zill-**leer**] n (pl **-s**) soldier of certain regiments

fusiliers n ▷ **fusilier**

fusillade [fyew-zill-**lade**] n (pl **-s**) continuous discharge of firearms

fusillades n ▷ **fusillade**

fusing v ▷ **fuse**

fusion n (pl **-s**) melting ▶ adj of a style of cooking that combines traditional Western techniques and ingredients with those used in Eastern cuisine

fusions n ▷ **fusion**

fuss n (pl **-es**) needless activity or worry ▶ v (**-es, -ing, -ed**) make a fuss

fussed v ▷ **fuss**

fusses n, v ▷ **fuss**

fussier adj ▷ **fussy**

fussiest adj ▷ **fussy**

fussily adv ▷ **fussy**

fussiness n ▷ **fussy**

fussinesses n ▷ **fussy**

fussing v ▷ **fuss**

fussy adj (**-ssier, -ssiest**) inclined to fuss > **fussily** adv > **fussiness** n (pl **-es**)

fustier adj ▷ **fusty**

fustiest adj ▷ **fusty**

fustiness n ▷ **fusty**

fustinesses n ▷ **fusty**

fusty adj (**-tier, -tiest**) stale-smelling > **fustiness** n (pl **-es**)

futile adj unsuccessful or useless > **futility** n (pl **-ties**)

futilities n ▷ **futile**

futility n ▷ **futile**

futon [**foo**-tonn] n (pl **-s**) Japanese-style bed

futons n ▷ **futon**

future n (pl **-s**) time to come ▶ adj yet to come or be

futures n ▷ **future**

futuristic adj of a design appearing to belong to some future time

fuzz¹ n (pl **-es**) mass of fine or curly hairs or fibres

fuzz² n (Slang) police

fuzzes n ▷ **fuzz¹**

fuzzier adj ▷ **fuzzy**

fuzziest adj ▷ **fuzzy**

fuzzily adv ▷ **fuzzy**

fuzziness n ▷ **fuzzy**

fuzzinesses n ▷ **fuzzy**

fuzzy adj (**-zzier, -zziest**) of, like, or covered with fuzz > **fuzzily** adv > **fuzziness** n (pl **-es**)

fy interj. Fy is an old word that people said when they were disgusted or dismayed. This very unusual word can be really useful when you're trying to form words in more than one direction. Fy scores 8 points.

Gg

Only three two-letter words begin with G (**gi**, **go** and **gu**). Knowing these will save you worrying about other possibilities. There are quite a few short words beginning with G that use Y, which can prove very useful. These include **gay**, **gey**, **goy** and **guy** (7 points each), as well as **gym** and **gyp** (9 points each).

gab n (pl -s) ▶ v (-s, -ing, -ed) (Informal) talk or chatter
  gababouts n ▷ gadabout
gabardine, gaberdine n (pl -s) strong twill cloth used esp. for raincoats
  gabardines n ▷ gabardine
  gabbed v ▷ gab
  gabbier adj ▷ gabby
  gabbiest adj ▷ gabby
  gabbing v ▷ gab
gabble v (-s, -ing, -ed) speak rapidly and indistinctly ▶ n (pl -s) rapid indistinct speech
  gabbled v ▷ gabble
  gabbles v, n ▷ gabble
  gabbling v ▷ gabble
gabby adj (-bbier, -bbiest) (Informal) talkative
gable n (pl -s) triangular upper part of a wall between sloping roofs > **gabled** adj
  gabled adj ▷ gable
  gables n ▷ gable
  gabs n, v ▷ gab
gad v (-s, -dding, -dded) go around in search of pleasure
gadabout n (pl -s) pleasure-seeker
  gadded v ▷ gad
  gadding v ▷ gad
  gadflies n ▷ gadfly
gadfly n (pl -flies) fly that bites cattle
gadget n (pl -s) small mechanical device or appliance
  gadgetries n ▷ gadgetry
gadgetry n (pl -ries) gadgets
  gadgets n ▷ gadget
  gads v ▷ gad
gaff n (pl -s) stick with an iron hook for landing large fish
gaffe n (pl -s) social blunder
gaffer n (pl -s) (BRIT) (Informal) foreman or boss

  gaffers n ▷ gaffer
  gaffes n ▷ gaffe
  gaffs n ▷ gaff
gag[1] v (-s, -gging, -gged) choke or retch ▶ n (pl -s) cloth etc. put into or tied across the mouth
gag[2] n (pl -s) (Informal) joke
gaga [gah-gah] adj (Slang) senile
  gagged v ▷ gag[1]
  gagging v ▷ gag[1]
gaggle n (pl -s) (Informal) disorderly crowd
  gaggles n ▷ gaggle
  gags v, n ▷ gag[1, 2]
  gaieties n ▷ gaiety
gaiety n (pl -ties) cheerfulness
gaily adv merrily
gain v (-s, -ing, -ed) acquire or obtain ▶ n (pl -s) profit or advantage
  gained v ▷ gain
gainful adj useful or profitable > **gainfully** adv
  gainfully adv ▷ gainful
  gaining v ▷ gain
  gains v, n ▷ gain
  gainsaid v ▷ gainsay
gainsay v (-s, -ing, -said) deny or contradict
  gainsaying v ▷ gainsay
  gainsays v ▷ gainsay
gait n (pl -s) manner of walking
gaiter n (pl -s) cloth or leather covering for the lower leg
  gaiters n ▷ gaiter
  gaits n ▷ gait
gala [gah-la] n (pl -s) festival
  galactic adj ▷ galaxy
  galas n ▷ gala
  galaxies n ▷ galaxy
galaxy n (pl -xies) system of stars > **galactic** adj
gale n (pl -s) strong wind
  gales n ▷ gale

gall¹ [gawl] *n* (*pl* -s) (*Informal*) impudence

gall² [gawl] *v* (-s, -ing, -ed) annoy

gall³ [gawl] *n* (*pl* -s) abnormal outgrowth on a tree or plant

gallant *adj* (-er, -est) brave and noble
> **gallantly** *adv*
　gallanter *adj* ▷ **gallant**
　gallantest *adj* ▷ **gallant**
　gallantly *adv* ▷ **gallant**
　gallantries *n* ▷ **gallantry**

gallantry *n* (*pl* -tries) showy, attentive treatment of women
　galled *v* ▷ **gall²**

galleon *n* (*pl* -s) large three-masted sailing ship of the 15th-17th centuries
　galleons *n* ▷ **galleon**
　galleries *n* ▷ **gallery**

gallery *n* (*pl* -ries) room or building for displaying works of art

galley *n* (*pl* -s) kitchen of a ship or aircraft
　galleys *n* ▷ **galley**
　galling *v* ▷ **gall²**

gallium *n* (*pl* -iums) (CHEM) soft grey metallic element used in semiconductors
　galliums *n* ▷ **gallium**

gallivant *v* (-s, -ing, -ed) go about in search of pleasure
　gallivanted *v* ▷ **gallivant**
　gallivanting *v* ▷ **gallivant**
　gallivants *v* ▷ **gallivant**

gallon *n* (*pl* -s) liquid measure of eight pints, equal to 4.55 litres
　gallons *n* ▷ **gallon**

gallop *n* (*pl* -s) horse's fastest pace ▶ *v* (-s, -ing, -ed) go or ride at a gallop
　galloped *v* ▷ **gallop**
　galloping *v* ▷ **gallop**
　gallops *n, v* ▷ **gallop**

gallows *n* (*pl* -ses) wooden structure used for hanging criminals
　gallowses *n* ▷ **gallows**
　galls *v, n* ▷ **gall¹, ², ³**

gallstone *n* (*pl* -s) hard mass formed in the gall bladder or its ducts
　gallstones *n* ▷ **gallstone**

galore *adv* in abundance

galoshes *pl n* (BRIT, AUST & NZ) waterproof overshoes

galumph *v* (-s, -ing, -ed) (BRIT, AUST & NZ) (*Informal*) leap or move about clumsily
　galumphed *v* ▷ **galumph**
　galumphing *v* ▷ **galumph**
　galumphs *v* ▷ **galumph**

galvanic *adj* of or producing an electric current generated by chemical means

galvanize *v* (-zes, -zing, -zed) stimulate into action
　galvanized *v* ▷ **galvanize**
　galvanizes *v* ▷ **galvanize**
　galvanizing *v* ▷ **galvanize**

gambit *n* (*pl* -s) opening line or move intended to secure an advantage (CHESS)
　gambits *n* ▷ **gambit**

gamble *v* (-les, -ling, -led) play games of chance to win money ▶ *n* (*pl* -s) risky undertaking ▶ **gambler** *n* (*pl* -s) > **gambling** *n* (*pl* -s)
　gambled *v* ▷ **gamble**
　gambler *n* ▷ **gamble**
　gamblers *n* ▷ **gamble**
　gambles *v, n* ▷ **gamble**
　gambling *v, n* ▷ **gamble**
　gamblings *n* ▷ **gamble**

gamboge [gam-**boje**] *n* (*pl* -s) gum resin used as a yellow pigment and purgative
　gamboges *n* ▷ **gamboge**

gambol *v* (-s, -bolling, -bolled) jump about playfully, frolic ▶ *n* (*pl* -s) frolic
　gambolled *v* ▷ **gambol**
　gambolling *v* ▷ **gambol**
　gambols *v, n* ▷ **gambol**

game¹ *n* (*pl* -s) amusement or pastime ▶ *v* (-mes, -ming, -med) gamble ▶ *adj* (-er, -est) brave > **gamely** *adv*

game² *adj* (-er, -est) (BRIT, AUST & NZ) lame, crippled
　gamed *v* ▷ **game¹**

gamekeeper *n* (*pl* -s) (BRIT, AUST & S AFR) person employed to breed game and prevent poaching
　gamekeepers *n* ▷ **gamekeeper**
　gamely *adv* ▷ **game¹**

gamer *n* person who plays computer games ▶ *adj* ▷ **game¹, ²**
　gamers *n* ▷ **gamer**
　games *n, v* ▷ **game¹**

gamesmanship *n* (-s) art of winning by cunning practices without actually cheating
　gamesmanships *n* ▷ **gamesmanship**
　gamest *adj* ▷ **game¹, ²**

gamete *n* (*pl* -s) (BIOL) reproductive cell
　gametes *n* ▷ **gamete**

gamine [gam-**een**] *n* (*pl* -s) slim boyish young woman
　gamines *n* ▷ **gamine**

gaming *n* gambling ▶ *v* ▷ **game¹**

gamma *n* (*pl* -s) third letter of the Greek alphabet
　gammas *n* ▷ **gamma**
　gammier *adj* ▷ **gammy**

gammiest adj ▷ gammy
gammon n (pl -s) cured or smoked ham
gammons n ▷ gammon
gammy adj (-mier, -miest) ▷ game²
gamut n (pl -s) whole range or scale (of music, emotions, etc.)
gamuts n ▷ gamut
gander n (pl -s) male goose
ganders n ▷ gander
gang n (pl -s) (criminal) group
gangland n (pl -s) criminal underworld
ganglands n ▷ gangland
gangling adj lanky and awkward
ganglion n (pl -s) group of nerve cells
ganglions n ▷ ganglion
gangplank n (pl -s) portable bridge for boarding or leaving a ship
gangplanks n ▷ gangplank
gangrene n (pl -s) decay of body tissue as a result of disease or injury > **gangrenous** adj
gangrenes n ▷ gangrene
gangs n ▷ gang
gangster n (pl -s) member of a criminal gang
gangsters n ▷ gangster
gangway n (pl -s) passage between rows of seats
gangways n ▷ gangway
gannet n (pl -s) large sea bird
gannets n ▷ gannet
gantries n ▷ gantry
gantry n (pl -ries) structure supporting something such as a crane or rocket
gaol [jayl] n (pl -s) ▷ jail
gaols n ▷ gaol
gap n (pl -s) break or opening > **gappy** adj (-pier, -piest)
gape v (-pes, -ping, -ped) stare in wonder > **gaping** adj
gaped v ▷ gape
gapes v ▷ gape
gaping v, adj ▷ gape
gappier adj ▷ gap
gappiest adj ▷ gap
gappy adj ▷ gap
gaps n ▷ gap
garage n (pl -s) building used to house cars ▶ v (-ges, -ging, -ged) put or keep a car in a garage
garaged v ▷ garage
garages n, v ▷ garage
garaging v ▷ garage
garb n (pl -s) clothes ▶ v (-s, -ing, -ed) clothe
garbage n (pl -s) rubbish
garbages n ▷ garbage
garbed v ▷ garb
garbing v ▷ garb

garbled adj (of a story etc.) jumbled and confused
garbs n, v ▷ garb
garden n (pl -s) piece of land for growing flowers, fruit, or vegetables ▶ pl ornamental park ▶ v (-s, -ing, -ed) cultivate a garden > **gardener** n (pl -s) > **gardening** n (pl -s)
gardened v ▷ garden
gardenia [gar-deen-ya] n (pl -s) large fragrant white waxy flower
gardenias n ▷ gardenia
gardening v ▷ garden
gardens n, v ▷ garden
garfish n (pl -fishes) freshwater fish with a long body and very long toothed jaws
garfishes n ▷ garfish
gargantuan adj huge
gargle v (-les, -ling, -led) wash the throat with (a liquid) by breathing out slowly through the liquid ▶ n (pl -s) liquid used for gargling
gargled v ▷ gargle
gargles v, n ▷ gargle
gargling v ▷ gargle
gargoyle n (pl -s) waterspout carved in the form of a grotesque face, esp. on a church
gargoyles n ▷ gargoyle
garish adj crudely bright or colourful > **garishly** adv > **garishness** n (pl -es)
garishly adv ▷ garish
garishness n ▷ garish
garishnesses n ▷ garish
garland n (pl -s) wreath of flowers worn or hung as a decoration ▶ v (-s, -ing, -ed) decorate with garlands
garlanded v ▷ garland
garlanding v ▷ garland
garlands n, v ▷ garland
garlic n (pl -s) pungent bulb of a plant of the onion family, used in cooking
garlics n ▷ garlic
garment n (pl -s) article of clothing ▶ pl clothes
garments n ▷ garment
garner v (-s, -ing, -ed) collect or store
garnered v ▷ garner
garnering v ▷ garner
garners v ▷ garner
garnet n (pl -s) red semiprecious stone
garnets n ▷ garnet
garnish v (-es, -ing, -ed) decorate (food) ▶ n (pl -es) decoration for food
garnished v ▷ garnish
garnishes v, n ▷ garnish
garnishing v ▷ garnish
garotte n ▷ garrotte
garotted v ▷ garrotte

garottes n, v ▷ garrotte
garotting v ▷ garrotte
garret n (pl -s) attic in a house
garrets n ▷ garret
garrison n (pl -s) troops stationed in a town or fort ▶ v (-s, -ing, -ed) station troops in
garrisoned v ▷ garrison
garrisoning v ▷ garrison
garrisons n, v ▷ garrison
garrotte, garotte n (pl -s) Spanish method of execution by strangling ▶ v (-tes, -ting, -ted) kill by this method
garrotted v ▷ garrotte
garrottes n, v ▷ garrotte
garrotting v ▷ garrotte
garrulous adj talkative
garter n (pl -s) band worn round the leg to hold up a sock or stocking
garters n ▷ garter
gas n (pl gases, gasses) airlike substance that is not liquid or solid ▶ v (gases, gasses, gassing, gassed) poison or render unconscious with gas
gasbag n (pl -s) (Informal) person who talks too much
gasbags n ▷ gasbag
gaseous adj of or like gas
gases n, v ▷ gas
gash v (-es, -ing, -ed) make a long deep cut in ▶ n (pl -es) long deep cut
gashed v ▷ gash
gashes v, n ▷ gash
gashing v ▷ gash
gasholder, gasometer [gas-**som**-it-er] (pl -s) n large tank for storing gas
gasholders n ▷ gasholder
gasket n (pl -s) piece of rubber etc. placed between the faces of a metal joint to act as a seal
gaskets n ▷ gasket
gasoline n (pl -s) (US) petrol
gasolines n ▷ gasoline
gasometers n ▷ gasholder
gasp v (-s, -ing, -ed) draw in breath sharply or with difficulty ▶ n (pl -s) convulsive intake of breath
gasped v ▷ gasp
gasping v ▷ gasp
gasps v, n ▷ gasp
gassed v ▷ gas
gasses n, v ▷ gas
gassier adj ▷ gassy
gassiest adj ▷ gassy
gassing v ▷ gas
gassy adj (-ssier, -ssiest) filled with gas

gastric adj of the stomach
gastritis n (pl -tes) inflammation of the stomach lining
gastritises n ▷ gastritis
gastroenteritis n inflammation of the stomach and intestines
gastronomies n ▷ gastronomy
gastronomy n (pl -mies) art of good eating > **gastronomic** adj
gastropod n (pl -s) mollusc, such as a snail, with a single flattened muscular foot
gastropods n ▷ gastropod
gate n (pl -s) movable barrier, usu. hinged, in a wall or fence
gâteau [gat-toe] n (pl -teaux) [-toes] rich elaborate cake
gâteaux n ▷ gâteau
gatecrash v (-es, -ing, -ed) enter (a party) uninvited
gatecrashed v ▷ gatecrash
gatecrashes v ▷ gatecrash
gatecrashing v ▷ gatecrash
gatehouse n (pl -s) building at or above a gateway
gatehouses n ▷ gatehouse
gates n ▷ gate
gateway n (pl -s) entrance with a gate
gateways n ▷ gateway
gather v (-s, -ing, -ed) assemble
gathered v ▷ gather
gathering n (pl -s) assembly ▶ v ▷ gather
gatherings n ▷ gathering
gathers pl n gathered folds in material ▶ v ▷ gather
gauche [gohsh] adj (-r, -st) socially awkward > **gaucheness** n (pl -es)
gaucheness n ▷ gauche
gauchenesses n ▷ gauche
gaucher adj ▷ gauche
gauchest adj ▷ gauche
gaucho [gow-choh] n (pl -hos) S American cowboy
gauchos n ▷ gaucho
gaudier adj ▷ gaudy
gaudiest adj ▷ gaudy
gaudily adv ▷ gaudy
gaudiness n ▷ gaudy
gaudinesses n ▷ gaudy
gaudy adj (-dier, -diest) vulgarly bright or colourful > **gaudily** adv > **gaudiness** n (pl -es)
gauge [gayj] v (-ges, -ging, -ged) estimate or judge ▶ n (pl -s) measuring instrument
gauged v ▷ gauge
gauges v, n ▷ gauge
gauging v ▷ gauge

gaunt adj (-er, -est) lean and haggard
> **gauntness** n (pl -es)
gaunter adj ▷ gaunt
gauntest adj ▷ gaunt

gauntlet n (pl -s) heavy glove with a long cuff
gauntlets n ▷ gauntlet
gauntness n ▷ gaunt
gauntnesses n ▷ gaunt

gauze n (pl -s) transparent loosely-woven fabric, often used for surgical dressings
> **gauzy** adj (-zier, -ziest)
gauzes n ▷ gauze
gauzier adj ▷ gauze
gauziest adj ▷ gauze
gauzy adj ▷ gauze

gave v ▷ give

gavel [gav-el] n (pl -s) small hammer banged on a table by a judge, auctioneer, or chairman to call for attention
gavels n ▷ gavel

gavotte n (pl -s) old formal dance
gavottes n ▷ gavotte

gawk v (-s, -ing, -ed) stare stupidly
gawked v ▷ gawk
gawkier adj ▷ gawky
gawkiest adj ▷ gawky
gawkiness n ▷ gawky
gawkinesses n ▷ gawky
gawking v ▷ gawk
gawks v ▷ gawk

gawky adj (-kier, -kiest) clumsy or awkward
> **gawkiness** n (pl -es)

gawp v (-s, -ing, -ed) (Slang) stare stupidly
gawped v ▷ gawp
gawping v ▷ gawp
gawps v ▷ gawp

gay adj (-er, -est) homosexual ▶ n (pl -s) homosexual
gayer adj ▷ gay
gayest adj ▷ gay

gayness n (pl -es) homosexuality
gaynesses n ▷ gayness
gays n ▷ gay

gaze v (-zes, -zing, -zed) look fixedly ▶ n (pl -s) fixed look

gazebo [gaz-zee-boh] n (pl -bos, -boes) summerhouse with a good view
gazeboes n ▷ gazebo
gazebos n ▷ gazebo
gazed v ▷ gaze

gazelle n (pl -s) small graceful antelope
gazelles n ▷ gazelle
gazes v, n ▷ gaze

gazette n (pl -s) official publication containing announcements

gazetteer n (part of) a book that lists and describes places
gazetteers n ▷ gazetteer
gazettes n ▷ gazette

gazillion n (pl -s) (Informal) extremely large, unspecified amount

gazillionaire n (Informal) enormously rich person
gazillionaires n ▷ gazillionaire
gazillions n ▷ gazillion

gazing v ▷ gaze

gazump v (-s, -ing, -ed) (BRIT & AUST) raise the price of a property after verbally agreeing it with (a prospective buyer)
gazumped v ▷ gazump
gazumping v ▷ gazump
gazumps v ▷ gazump

gear n (pl -s) set of toothed wheels connecting with another or with a rack to change the direction or speed of transmitted motion ▶ v (-s, -ing, -ed) prepare or organize for something

gearbox n (pl -es) case enclosing a set of gears in a motor vehicle
gearboxes n ▷ gearbox
geared v ▷ gear
gearing v ▷ gear
gears n, v ▷ gear

gecko n (pl -kos, -koes) small tropical lizard
geckoes n ▷ gecko
geckos n ▷ gecko

geebung [gee-bung] n (pl -s) Australian tree or shrub with an edible but tasteless fruit
geebungs n ▷ geebung

geek n (pl -s) (Informal) boring, unattractive person > **geeky** adj (-kier, -kiest)
geekier adj ▷ geek
geekiest adj ▷ geek
geeks n ▷ geek
geeky adj ▷ geek

geelbek n (pl -s) (S AFR) edible marine fish
geelbeks n ▷ geelbek
geese n ▷ goose

geezer n (pl -s) (BRIT, AUST & NZ) (Informal) man
geezers n ▷ geezer

geisha [gay-sha] n (pl -sha, -shas) (in Japan) professional female companion for men
geishas n ▷ geisha

gel [jell] n (pl -s) jelly-like substance, esp. one used to secure a hairstyle ▶ v (-s, gelling, gelled) form a gel

gelatine [jel-at-teen], **gelatin** n (pl -s) substance made by boiling animal bones
gelatines n ▷ gelatine

gelatinous [jel-at-in-uss] adj of or like jelly

geld v (**gelds, gelding, gelded**) castrate
gelded v ▷ **geld**
gelding n (pl -s) castrated horse ▶ v ▷ **geld**
geldings n ▷ **gelding**
gelds v ▷ **geld**
gelignite n (pl -s) type of dynamite used for
blasting
gelignites v ▷ **gelignite**
gelled v ▷ **gell**
gelling v ▷ **gell**
gels n, v ▷ **gel**
gem n (pl -s) precious stone or jewel
gemfish (pl -fishes) n Australian food fish with
a delicate flavour
gemfishes n ▷ **gemfish**
gems n ▷ **gem**
gen n (pl -s) (Informal) information
gendarme [zhohn-darm] n (pl -s) member of
the French police force
gendarmes n ▷ **gendarme**
gender n (pl -s) state of being male or female
genders n ▷ **gender**
gene [jean] n (pl -s) part of a cell which
determines inherited characteristics
genealogical adj ▷ **genealogy**
genealogies n ▷ **genealogy**
genealogist n ▷ **genealogy**
genealogists n ▷ **genealogy**
genealogy [jean-ee-al-a-gee] n (pl -gies) (study
of) the history and descent of a family or
families > **genealogical** adj > **genealogist**
n (pl -s)
genera [jen-er-a] ▷ **genus**
general adj common or widespread ▶ n (pl -s)
very senior army officer > **generally** adv
generalities n ▷ **generality**
generality n (pl -ties) general principle
generalization n ▷ **generalize**
generalizations n ▷ **generalize**
generalize v (-zes, -zing, -zed) draw general
conclusions > **generalization** n (pl -s)
generalized v ▷ **generalize**
generalizes v ▷ **generalize**
generalizing v ▷ **generalize**
generally adv ▷ **general**
generals n ▷ **general**
generate v (-tes, -ting, -ted) produce or bring
into being
generated v ▷ **generate**
generates v ▷ **generate**
generating v ▷ **generate**
generation n (pl -s) all the people born about
the same time
generations n ▷ **generation**
generative adj capable of producing

generator n (pl -s) machine for converting
mechanical energy into electrical energy
generators n ▷ **generator**
generic [jin-ner-ik] adj of a class, group, or
genus > **generically** adv
generically adv ▷ **generic**
generosities n ▷ **generous**
generosity n ▷ **generous**
generous adj free in giving > **generously** adv
> **generosity** n (pl -ties)
generously adv ▷ **generous**
genes n ▷ **gene**
geneses n ▷ **genesis**
genesis [jen-iss-iss] n (pl -ses) [-iss-eez]
beginning or origin
genetic [jin-net-tik] adj of genes or genetics
geneticist n ▷ **genetics**
geneticists n ▷ **genetics**
genetics n study of heredity and variation in
organisms > **geneticist** n (pl -s)
genial [jean-ee-al] adj cheerful and friendly
> **genially** adv > **geniality** n (pl -ties)
genialities n ▷ **genial**
geniality n ▷ **genial**
genially adv ▷ **genial**
genie [jean-ee] n (pl -s) (in fairy tales) servant
who appears by magic and grants wishes
genies n ▷ **genie**
genital adj of the sexual organs or
reproduction
genitalia n ▷ **genitals**
genitals, genitalia [jen-it-ail-ya] pl n external
sexual organs
genitive n (pl -s) grammatical case indicating
possession or association
genitives n ▷ **genitive**
genius [jean-yuss] n (pl -es) (person with)
exceptional ability in a particular field
geniuses n ▷ **genius**
genocide [jen-no-side] n (pl -s) murder of a race
of people
genocides n ▷ **genocide**
genre [zhohn-ra] n (pl -s) style of literary,
musical, or artistic work
genres n ▷ **genre**
gens n ▷ **gen**
gent n (pl -s) (BRIT, AUST & NZ) (Informal)
gentleman
genteel adj (-er, -est) affectedly proper and
polite > **genteelly** adv
genteeler adj ▷ **genteel**
genteelest adj ▷ **genteel**
genteelly adv ▷ **genteel**
gentian [jen-shun] n (pl -s) mountain plant
with deep blue flowers

gentians n ▷ gentian

gentile adj, n (pl -s) non-Jewish (person)
gentiles n ▷ gentile

gentle adj (-r, -st) mild or kindly > gentleness n
(pl -es) > gently adv

gentleman n (pl -men) polite well-bred man
> gentlemanly adj > gentlewoman n fem (pl
-women)

gentlemanly adj ▷ gentleman

gentlemen n ▷ gentleman

gentleness n ▷ gentle

gentlenesses n ▷ gentle

gentler adj ▷ gentle

gentlest adj ▷ gentle

gentlewoman n ▷ gentleman

gentlewomen n ▷ gentleman

gently adv ▷ gentle

gentries n ▷ gentry

gentries n ▷ gentry

gentrification n (pl -s) taking-over of a
traditionally working-class area by middle-
class incomers
> gentrify v (-fies, -fying, -fied)

gentrifications n ▷ gentrification

gentrified v ▷ gentrification

gentrifies v ▷ gentrification

gentrifying v ▷ gentrification

gentry n (pl -ies) people just below the nobility
in social rank

gents n men's public toilet ▶ n ▷ gent

genuflect v (-s, -ing, -ed) bend the knee
as a sign of reverence or deference
> genuflection, genuflexion n (pl -s)

genuflected v ▷ genuflect

genuflecting v ▷ genuflect

genuflection n ▷ genuflect

genuflections n ▷ genuflect

genuflects v ▷ genuflect

genuflexion n ▷ genuflect

genuflexions n ▷ genuflect

genuine adj not fake, authentic > genuinely
adv > genuineness n (-es)

genuinely adv ▷ genuine

genuineness n ▷ genuine

genuinenesses n ▷ genuine

genus [jean-uss] n (pl genera) group into which
a family of animals or plants is divided

geocentric adj having the earth as a centre

geographer n ▷ geography

geographers n ▷ geography

geographic adj ▷ geography

geographical adj ▷ geography

geographically adv ▷ geography

geographies n ▷ geography

geography n (pl -phies) study of the earth's

physical features, climate, population,
etc. > geographer n (pl -s) > geographical,
geographic adj > geographically adv

geological adj ▷ geology

geologically adv ▷ geology

geologies n ▷ geology

geologist n ▷ geology

geologists n ▷ geology

geology n (pl -gies) study of the earth's origin,
structure, and composition
> geological adj > geologically adv
> geologist n (pl -s)

geometric adj ▷ geometry

geometrical adj ▷ geometry

geometrically adv ▷ geometry

geometries n ▷ geometry

geometry n (pl -tries) branch of mathematics
dealing with points, lines, curves, and
surfaces > geometric, geometrical adj
> geometrically adv

geostationary adj (of a satellite) orbiting
so as to remain over the same point of the
earth's surface

geothermal adj of or using the heat in the
earth's interior

geranium n (pl -s) cultivated plant with red,
pink, or white flowers

geraniums n ▷ geranium

gerbil [jer-bill] n (pl -s) burrowing desert rodent
of Asia and Africa

gerbils n ▷ gerbil

geriatric adj, n (pl -s) old (person)

geriatrics n (pl branch of medicine dealing
with old age and its diseases
▶ n ▷ geriatric

germ n (pl -s) microbe, esp. one causing
disease

germane adj relevant to

germanium n (pl -s) (CHEM) brittle grey
element that is a semiconductor

germaniums n ▷ germanium

germinal adj of or in the earliest stage of
development

germinate v (-tes, -ting, -ted) (cause to)
sprout or begin to grow
> germination n (pl -s)

germinated v ▷ germinate

germinates v ▷ germinate

germinating v ▷ germinate

germination n ▷ germinate

germinations n ▷ germinate

germs n ▷ germ

gerrymandering n (pl -s) alteration of voting
constituencies in order to give an unfair
advantage to one party

gerrymanderings n ▷ gerrymandering

gerund [jer-rund] n (pl -s) noun formed from a verb

gerunds n ▷ gerund

gestation n (pl -s) (period of) carrying of young in the womb between conception and birth

gestations n ▷ gestation

gesticulate v (-tes, -ting, -ted) make expressive movements with the hands and arms > **gesticulation** n (pl -s)

gesticulated v ▷ gesticulate

gesticulates v ▷ gesticulate

gesticulating v ▷ gesticulate

gesticulation n ▷ gesticulate

gesticulations n ▷ gesticulate

gesture n (pl -s) movement to convey meaning ▶ v (-res, -ring, -red) gesticulate

gestured v ▷ gesture

gestures n, v ▷ gesture

gesturing v ▷ gesture

get v (-s, -tting, got) obtain or receive

getaway adj, n (pl -s) (used in) escape

getaways n ▷ getaway

gets v ▷ get

getting v ▷ get

> **gey** adv. Gey is a Scots word meaning **very**. If you have a G and a Y, it's highly likley that there will be an E you can use somewhere on the board. Gey scores 7 points.

geyser [geez-er] n (pl -s) spring that discharges steam and hot water (BRIT & S AFR)

geysers n ▷ geyser

ghastlier adj ▷ ghastly

ghastliest adj ▷ ghastly

ghastliness n ▷ ghastly

ghastlinesses n ▷ ghastly

ghastly adj (-lier, -liest) (Informal) unpleasant > **ghastliness** n (pl -es)

ghat n (pl -s) (in India) steps leading down to a river

ghats n ▷ ghat

ghee [gee] n (pl -s) (in Indian cookery) clarified butter

ghees n ▷ ghee

gherkin n (pl -s) small pickled cucumber

gherkins n ▷ gherkin

ghetto n (pl -ttos, -ttoes) slum area inhabited by a deprived minority

ghettoblaster n (Informal) large portable cassette recorder or CD player

ghettoblasters n ▷ ghettoblaster

ghettoes n ▷ ghetto

ghettos n ▷ ghetto

ghillie n (pl -s) ▷ gillie

ghillies n ▷ ghillie

ghost n (pl -s) disembodied spirit of a dead person ▶ v (-s, -ing, -ed) ghostwrite > **ghostly** adj (-ier, -iest)

ghosted v ▷ ghost

ghosting v ▷ ghost

ghostlier adj ▷ ghost

ghostliest adj ▷ ghost

ghostly adj ▷ ghost

ghosts n, v ▷ ghost

ghostwriter n (pl -s) writer of a book or article on behalf of another person who is credited as the author

ghostwriters n ▷ ghostwriter

ghoul [gool] n (pl -s) person with morbid interests > **ghoulish** adj

ghoulish adj ▷ ghoul

ghouls n ▷ ghoul

> **gi** n. A gi is a suit worn by judo or karate practitioners. Gi is one of only three two-letter words beginning with G, and so is worth knowing. Gi scores 3 points.

giant n (pl -s) mythical being of superhuman size ▶ adj huge

giants n ▷ giant

gibber[1] [jib-ber] v (-s, -ing, -ed) speak or utter rapidly and unintelligibly

gibber[2] [gib-ber] n (pl -s) (AUST) boulder

gibbered v ▷ gibber[1]

gibbering v ▷ gibber[1]

gibberish n rapid unintelligible talk

gibbers n, v ▷ gibber[1, 2]

gibbet [jib-bit] n (pl -s) gallows for displaying executed criminals

gibbets n ▷ gibbet

gibbon [gib-bon] n (pl -s) agile tree-dwelling ape of S Asia

gibbons n ▷ gibbon

gibbous adj (of the moon) more than half but less than fully illuminated

gibe [jibe] v, n (pl -s) ▷ jibe[1]

gibes n ▷ gibe

giblets [jib-lets] pl n gizzard, liver, heart, and neck of a fowl

gidday, g'day interj (AUST & NZ) expression of greeting

giddier adj ▷ giddy

giddiest adj ▷ giddy

giddily adv ▷ giddy

giddiness n ▷ giddy

giddinesses n ▷ giddy

giddy adj (-ddier, -ddiest) having or causing a feeling of dizziness > **giddily** adv > **giddiness**

n (pl -**es**)

gift n (pl -**s**) present ▶ v (-**s**, -**ing**, -**ed**) make a present of

gifted adj talented ▶ v ▷ **gift**

　gifting v ▷ **gift**

　gifts n, v ▷ **gift**

gig[1] n (pl -**s**) single performance by pop or jazz musicians ▶ v (-**s**, -**gging**, -**gged**) play a gig or gigs

gig[2] (pl -**s**) n light two-wheeled horse-drawn carriage

gigantic adj enormous

　gigged v ▷ **gig**[1]

　gigging v ▷ **gig**[1]

giggle v (-**les**, -**ling**, -**led**) laugh nervously or foolishly ▶ n (pl -**s**) such a laugh ▷ **giggly** adj (-**lier**, -**liest**)

　giggled v ▷ **giggle**

　giggles v, n ▷ **giggle**

　gigglier adj ▷ **giggle**

　giggliest adj ▷ **giggle**

　giggling v ▷ **giggle**

　giggly adj ▷ **giggle**

gigolo [jig-a-lo] n (pl -**los**) man paid by an older woman to be her escort or lover

　gigolos n ▷ **gigolo**

gigot n (pl -**s**) (CHIEFLY BRIT) leg of lamb or mutton

　gigots n ▷ **gigot**

　gigs n, v ▷ **gig**[1, 2]

gild v (-**s**, -**ing**, -**ed** or **gilt**) put a thin layer of gold on

　gilded v ▷ **gild**

　gilding v ▷ **gild**

　gilds v ▷ **gild**

gill [jill] n (pl -**s**) liquid measure of quarter of a pint, equal to 0.142 litres

gillie n (pl -**s**) (in Scotland) attendant for hunting or fishing

　gillies n ▷ **gillie**

gills [gillz] pl n breathing organs in fish and other water creatures ▶ n ▷ **gill**

gilt adj covered with a thin layer of gold ▶ n (pl -**s**) thin layer of gold used as decoration ▶ v ▷ **gild**

　gilts n ▷ **gilt**

gimbals pl n set of pivoted rings which allow nautical instruments to remain horizontal at sea

gimcrack [jim-krak] adj showy but cheap

gimlet [gim-let] n (pl -**s**) small tool with a screwlike tip for boring holes in wood

　gimlets n ▷ **gimlet**

gimmick n (pl -**s**) something designed to attract attention or publicity ▷ **gimmickry** n

(pl -**ries**) ▷ **gimmicky** adj (-**ier**, -**iest**)

　gimmickier adj ▷ **gimmick**

　gimmickiest adj ▷ **gimmick**

　gimmickries n ▷ **gimmick**

　gimmickry n ▷ **gimmick**

　gimmicks n ▷ **gimmick**

　gimmicky adj ▷ **gimmick**

gin[1] n (pl -**s**) spirit flavoured with juniper berries

gin[2] n (pl -**s**) wire noose used to trap small animals

gin[3] (pl -**s**) (AUST) (Offens) Aboriginal woman

ginger n (pl -**s**) root of a tropical plant, used as a spice ▷ **gingery** adj

gingerbread n (pl -**s**) moist cake flavoured with ginger

　gingerbreads n ▷ **gingerbread**

gingerly adv cautiously

　gingers n ▷ **ginger**

　gingery adj ▷ **ginger**

gingham n (pl -**s**) cotton cloth, usu. checked or striped

　ginghams n ▷ **gingham**

gingivitis [jin-jiv-vite-iss] n (pl -**tes**) inflammation of the gums

　gingivitises n ▷ **gingivitis**

ginkgo [gink-go] n (pl -**goes**) ornamental Chinese tree

　ginkgoes n ▷ **ginkgo**

　gins n ▷ **gin**[1, 2, 3]

ginseng [jin-seng] n (pl -**s**) (root of) a plant believed to have tonic and energy-giving properties

　ginsengs n ▷ **ginseng**

　gipsies n ▷ **gipsy**

gipsy n (pl -**sies**) ▷ **gypsy**

giraffe n (pl -**s**) African ruminant mammal with a spotted yellow skin and long neck and legs

　giraffes n ▷ **giraffe**

gird v (-**s**, **girding**, **girded** or **girt**) put a belt round

　girded v ▷ **gird**

girder n (pl -**s**) large metal beam

　girders n ▷ **girder**

　girding v ▷ **gird**

girdle[1] n (pl -**s**) woman's elastic corset ▶ v (-**les**, -**ling**, -**led**) surround or encircle

girdle[2] n (pl -**s**) (SCOT) griddle

　girdled v ▷ **girdle**[1]

　girdles v, n ▷ **girdle**[1, 2]

　girdling v ▷ **girdle**[1]

　girds v ▷ **gird**

girl n (pl -**s**) female child (Informal) ▷ **girlhood** n ▷ **girlish** adj

girlfriend n (pl -s) girl or woman with whom a person is romantically or sexually involved
girlfriends n ▷ girlfriend
girlhood n ▷ girl
girlhoods n ▷ girl
girlie, girly adj (Informal) featuring photographs of naked or scantily clad women
girlish adj ▷ girl
girls n ▷ girl
girly n ▷ girlie
giro [jire-oh] n (pl -os) (in some countries) system of transferring money within a post office or bank directly from one account to another
giros n ▷ giro
girt v ▷ gird
girth n (pl -s) measurement round something
girths n ▷ girth
gist [jist] n (pl -s) substance or main point of a matter
gists n ▷ gist
give v (-s, giving, gave, given) present (something) to another person ▶ n (pl -s) resilience or elasticity
giveaway n (pl -s) something that reveals hidden feelings or intentions ▶ adj very cheap or free
giveaways n ▷ giveaway
given v ▷ give
gives v, n ▷ give
giving v ▷ give
gizzard n (pl -s) part of a bird's stomach
gizzards n ▷ gizzard

> **gju** n (**gjus**). A gju (also spelt **gu**) is a kind of violin from Shetland. This unusual term is a great little word, especially when there's not much space on the board. Gju scores 11 points.

glacé [glass-say] adj preserved in a thick sugary syrup
glacial adj of ice or glaciers
glaciated adj covered with or affected by glaciers > **glaciation** n (pl -s)
glaciation n ▷ glaciated
glaciations n ▷ glaciated
glacier n (pl -s) slow-moving mass of ice formed by accumulated snow
glaciers n ▷ glacier
glad adj (-dder, -ddest) pleased and happy > **gladly** adv > **gladness** n (pl -es)
gladden v (-s, -ing, -ed) make glad
gladdened v ▷ gladden
gladdening v ▷ gladden

gladdens v ▷ gladden
gladder adj ▷ glad
gladdest adj ▷ glad
glade n (pl -s) open space in a forest
glades n ▷ glade
gladiator n (pl -s) (in ancient Rome) man trained to fight in arenas to provide entertainment
gladiators n ▷ gladiator
gladioli n ▷ gladiolus
gladiolus n (pl -lus, -li, -luses) garden plant with sword-shaped leaves
gladioluses n ▷ gladiolus
gladly adv ▷ glad
gladness n ▷ glad
gladnesses n ▷ glad
gladwrap ® (AUST, NZ & S AFR) n (pl -wraps) thin polythene material for wrapping food ▶ v (-wraps, -wrapping, -wrapped) wrap in gladwrap
gladwrapped v ▷ gladwrap
gladwrapping v ▷ gladwrap
gladwraps n, v ▷ gladwrap
glamorize v ▷ glamorous
glamorized v ▷ glamorous
glamorizes v ▷ glamorous
glamorizing v ▷ glamorous
glamorous adj alluring > **glamorize** v (-zes, -zing, -zed)
glamour n (pl -s) alluring charm or fascination
glamours n ▷ glamour
glance v (-ces, -cing, -ced) look rapidly or briefly ▶ n (pl -s) brief look
glanced v ▷ glance
glances v, n ▷ glance
glancing adj hitting at an oblique angle ▶ v ▷ glance
gland n (pl -s) organ that produces and secretes substances in the body > **glandular** adj
glands n ▷ gland
glandular adj ▷ gland
glare v (-res, -ring, -red) stare angrily ▶ n (pl -s) angry stare
glared v ▷ glare
glares v, n ▷ glare
glaring adj conspicuous ▶ v ▷ glare > **glaringly** adv
glaringly adv ▷ glaring
glass n (pl -es) hard brittle, usu. transparent substance consisting of metal silicates or similar compounds ▶ pl spectacles
glasses n ▷ glass
glasshouse n greenhouse
glasshouses n ▷ glasshouse

glassier adj ▷ glassy

glassiest adj ▷ glassy

glassy adj (-**sier**, -**siest**) like glass

glaucoma n (pl -**s**) eye disease

glaucomas n ▷ glaucoma

glaze v (-**zes**, -**zing**, -**zed**) fit or cover with glass ▶ n (pl -**s**) transparent coating

glazed v ▷ glaze

glazes v, n ▷ glaze

glazier (pl -**s**) n person who fits windows with glass

glaziers n ▷ glazier

glazing v ▷ glaze

gleam n (pl -**s**) small beam or glow of light ▶ v (-**s**, -**ing**, -**ed**) emit a gleam > **gleaming** adj

gleamed v ▷ gleam

gleaming v, adj ▷ gleam

gleams n, v ▷ gleam

glean v (-**s**, -**ing**, -**ed**) gather (facts etc.) bit by bit > **gleaner** n (pl -**s**)

gleaned v ▷ glean

gleaner n ▷ glean

gleaners n ▷ glean

gleaning v ▷ glean

gleans v ▷ glean

glee n (pl -**s**) triumph and delight > **gleeful** adj > **gleefully** adv

gleeful adj ▷ glee

gleefully adv ▷ glee

glees n ▷ glee

glen n (pl -**s**) deep narrow valley, esp. in Scotland

glens n ▷ glen

glib adj (-**bber**, -**bbest**) fluent but insincere or superficial > **glibly** adv > **glibness** n (pl -**es**)

glibber adj ▷ glib

glibbest adj ▷ glib

glibly adv ▷ glib

glibness n ▷ glib

glibnesses n ▷ glib

glide v (-**des**, -**ding**, -**ded**) move easily and smoothly ▶ n (pl -**s**) smooth easy movement

glided v ▷ glide

glider n (AUST) flying phalanger

gliders n ▷ glider

glides n ▷ glide

gliding n sport of flying gliders ▶ v ▷ glide

glimmer v (-**s**, -**ing**, -**ed**) shine faintly, flicker ▶ n (pl -**s**) faint gleam

glimmered v ▷ glimmer

glimmering v ▷ glimmer

glimmers v, n ▷ glimmer

glimpse n (pl -**s**) brief or incomplete view ▶ v (-**ses**, -**sing**, -**sed**) catch a glimpse of

glimpsed v ▷ glimpse

glimpses n, v ▷ glimpse

glimpsing v ▷ glimpse

glint v (-**s**, -**ing**, -**ed**) gleam brightly ▶ n (pl -**s**) bright gleam

glinted v ▷ glint

glinting v ▷ glint

glints v, n ▷ glint

glissando n (pl -**dos**) (MUSIC) slide between two notes in which all intermediate notes are played

glissandos n ▷ glissando

glisten v (-**s**, -**ing**, -**ed**) gleam by reflecting light

glistened v ▷ glisten

glistening v ▷ glisten

glistens v ▷ glisten

glitch n (pl -**es**) small problem that stops something from working properly

glitches n ▷ glitch

glitter v (-**s**, -**ing**, -**ed**) shine with bright flashes ▶ n (pl -**s**) sparkle or brilliance

glittered v ▷ glitter

glittering v ▷ glitter

glitters v, n ▷ glitter

gloaming n (pl -**s**) (SCOT) (poetic) twilight

gloamings n ▷ gloaming

gloat v (-**s**, -**ing**, -**ed**) regard one's own good fortune or the misfortune of others with smug or malicious pleasure

gloated v ▷ gloat

gloating v ▷ gloat

gloats v ▷ gloat

glob n (pl -**s**) rounded mass of thick fluid

global adj worldwide > **globally** adv

globalization n (pl -**s**) process by which a company, etc., expands to operate internationally

globalizations n ▷ globalization

globally adv ▷ global

globe n (pl **globes**) sphere with a map of the earth on it

globes n ▷ globe

globetrotter n habitual worldwide traveller > **globetrotting** adj, n (pl -**s**)

globetrotters n ▷ globetrotter

globetrotting n ▷ globetrotter

globetrottings n ▷ globetrotter

globs n ▷ glob

globular adj ▷ globule

globule n (pl -**s**) small round drop > **globular** adj

globules n ▷ globule

glockenspiel n (pl -**s**) percussion instrument consisting of small metal bars played with hammers

glockenspiels n ▷ glockenspiel

gloom n (pl **glooms**) melancholy or depression

> **gloomy** adj (**-mier, -miest**) > **gloomily** adv
gloomier adj ▷ **gloom**
gloomiest adj ▷ **gloom**
gloomily adv ▷ **gloom**
glooms n ▷ **gloom**
gloomy adj ▷ **gloom**
gloried v ▷ **glory**
glories n, v ▷ **glory**
glorification n ▷ **glorify**
glorifications n ▷ **glorify**
glorified v ▷ **glorify**
glorifies v ▷ **glorify**
glorify v (**-fies, -fying, -fied**) make (something) seem more worthy than it is > **glorification** n (pl **-s**)
glorifying v ▷ **glorify**
glorious adj brilliantly beautiful > **gloriously** adv
gloriously adv ▷ **glorious**
glory n (pl **-ries**) praise or honour ▶ v (**-ries, -rying, -ried**) (foll. by **in**) triumph or exalt
glorying v ▷ **glory**
gloss¹ n (pl **-es**) surface shine or lustre
gloss² n (pl **-es**) explanatory comment added to the text of a book ▶ v (**-es, -ing, -ed**) add glosses to
glossaries n ▷ **glossary**
glossary n (pl **-ries**) list of special or technical words with definitions
glossed v ▷ **gloss²**
glosses n, v ▷ **gloss¹, ²**
glossier adj ▷ **glossy**
glossiest adj ▷ **glossy**
glossily adv ▷ **glossy**
glossiness n ▷ **glossy**
glossinesses n ▷ **glossy**
glossing v ▷ **gloss²**
glossy adj (**-ssier, -ssiest**) smooth and shiny > **glossily** adv > **glossiness** n (pl **-es**)
glottal adj of the glottis
glottides n ▷ **glottis**
glottis n (pl **-tises, -tides**) vocal cords and the space between them
glottises n ▷ **glottis**
glove n (pl **-s**) covering for the hand with individual sheaths for each finger and the thumb
gloved adj covered by a glove or gloves
gloves n ▷ **glove**
glow v (**-s, -ing, -ed**) emit light and heat without flames ▶ n (pl **-s**) glowing light
glowed v ▷ **glow**
glower [rhymes with **power**] v (**-s, -ing, -ed**) ▶ n (pl **-s**) scowl
glowered v ▷ **glower**

glowering v ▷ **glower**
glowers v, n ▷ **glower**
glowing v ▷ **glow**
glows v, n ▷ **glow**
glowworm n (pl **-s**) insect giving out a green light
glowworms n ▷ **glowworm**
gloxinia n (pl **-s**) tropical plant with large bell-shaped flowers
gloxinias n ▷ **gloxinia**
glucose n (pl **-s**) kind of sugar found in fruit
glucoses n ▷ **glucose**
glue n (pl **glues**) natural or synthetic sticky substance used as an adhesive ▶ v (**glues, gluing** or **glueing, glued**) fasten with glue > **gluey** adj
glued v ▷ **glue**
glueing v ▷ **glue**
glues n, v ▷ **glue**
gluey adj ▷ **glue**
gluier adj ▷ **glue**
gluiest adj ▷ **glue**
gluing v ▷ **glue**
glum adj (**-mmer, -mmest**) sullen or gloomy > **glumly** adv
glumly adv ▷ **glum**
glummer adj ▷ **glum**
glummest adj ▷ **glum**
glut n (pl **-s**) excessive supply ▶ v (**-s, -tting, -tted**) oversupply
gluten [**gloo-ten**] n (pl **-s**) protein found in cereal grain
glutens n ▷ **gluten**
glutinous [**gloo-tin-uss**] adj sticky or gluey
gluts n, v ▷ **glut**
glutted v ▷ **glut**
glutting v ▷ **glut**
glutton n (pl **-s**) greedy person > **gluttonous** adj > **gluttony** n (pl **-nies**)
gluttonies n ▷ **glutton**
gluttonous adj ▷ **glutton**
gluttons n ▷ **glutton**
gluttony n ▷ **glutton**
glycerine, glycerin n (pl **-s**) colourless sweet liquid used widely in chemistry and industry
glycerines n ▷ **glycerine**
glycerins n ▷ **glycerine**
glycerol [**gliss-ser-ol**] n (pl **-s**) ▷ **glycerine**
glycerols n ▷ **glycerol**
gnarled adj rough, twisted, and knobbly
gnash v (**-es, -ing, -ed**) grind (the teeth) together in anger or pain
gnashed v ▷ **gnash**
gnashes v ▷ **gnash**
gnashing v ▷ **gnash**

gnat n (pl -s) small biting two-winged fly
gnats n ▷ gnat
gnaw v (-s, -ing, -ed or gnawn) bite or chew steadily
gnawed v ▷ gnaw
gnaws v ▷ gnaw
gneiss n (pl -es) coarse-grained metamorphic rock
gneisses n ▷ gneiss
gnome n (pl -s) imaginary creature like a little old man
gnomes n ▷ gnome
gnomic [no-mik] adj of pithy sayings
gnu [noo] n (pl -s) oxlike S African antelope
gnus n ▷ gnu
go v (going, went, gone) move to or from a place (pl goes) ▶ n attempt
goad v (-s, -ing, -ed) provoke (someone) to take some kind of action, usu. in anger ▶ n (pl -s) spur or provocation
goaded v ▷ goad
goading v ▷ goad
goads v, n ▷ goad
goal n (pl -s) (SPORT) posts through which the ball or puck has to be propelled to score
goalie n (pl -s) (Informal) goalkeeper
goalies n ▷ goalie
goalkeeper n (pl -s) player whose task is to stop shots entering the goal
goalkeepers n ▷ goalkeeper
goalpost (pl -s) n one of the two posts marking the limit of a goal
goalposts n ▷ goalpost
goals n ▷ goal
goanna n (pl -s) large Australian lizard
goannas n ▷ goanna
goat n (pl -s) sure-footed ruminant animal with horns
goatee n (pl -s) pointed tuftlike beard
goatees n ▷ goatee
goats n ▷ goat
gob n (pl -s) lump of a soft substance (BRIT, AUST & NZ)
gobbet n (pl -s) lump, esp. of food
gobbets n ▷ gobbet
gobble[1] v (-les, -ling, -led) eat hastily and greedily
gobble[2] n (pl -s) rapid gurgling cry of the male turkey ▶ v (-les, -ling, -led) make this noise
gobbled v ▷ gobble[1, 2]
gobbledegooks n ▷ gobbledegook
gobbledygooks n ▷ gobbledegook
gobbles v, n ▷ gobble[1, 2]

gobbledegook, gobbledygook n (pl -s) unintelligible (official) language or jargon
gobbling v ▷ gobble[1, 2]
gobies n ▷ goby
goblet n (pl -s) drinking cup without handles
goblets n ▷ goblet
goblin n (pl -s) (in folklore) small malevolent creature
goblins n ▷ goblin
gobs n ▷ gob
goby n (pl -by, -bies) small spiny-finned fish
god n (pl -s) spirit or being worshipped as having supernatural power
> **godlike** adj
godchild n (pl -s) child for whom a person stands as godparent
> **goddaughter** n (pl -s)
> **godson** n (pl -s)
goddaughter n ▷ godchild
goddaughters n ▷ godchild
goddess n fem (pl -es) female god
goddesses n ▷ goddess
godetia n (pl -s) plant with showy flowers
godetias n ▷ godetia
godfather n (pl -s) male godparent
> **godmother** n (pl -s)
godfathers n ▷ godfather
godforsaken adj desolate or dismal
godlier adj ▷ godly
godliest adj ▷ godly
godlike adj ▷ god
godliness n ▷ godly
godlinesses n ▷ godly
godly adj (-lier, -liest) devout or pious
> **godliness** n (pl -es)
godmother n ▷ godfather
godmothers n ▷ godfather
godparent n (pl -s) person who promises at a child's baptism to bring the child up as a Christian
godparents n ▷ godparent
gods n ▷ god
godsend n (pl -s) something unexpected but welcome
godsends n ▷ godsend
godson n ▷ godchild
godsons n ▷ godchild
gogga n (pl -s) (S AFR) (Informal) any small insect
goggas n ▷ gogga
goggle v (-les, -ling, -led) (of the eyes) bulge
goggled v ▷ goggle
goggles pl n protective spectacles ▶ v ▷ goggle
goggling v ▷ goggle
going n (pl -s) condition of the ground for

walking or riding over ▶ adj thriving ▶ v ▷ go
goings n ▷ going

goitre [goy-ter] n (pl -s) swelling of the thyroid gland in the neck
goitres n ▷ goitre

gold n (pl -s) yellow precious metal ▶ adj made of gold

goldcrest n (pl -s) small bird with a yellow crown
goldcrests n ▷ goldcrest

golden adj made of gold

goldfinch n (pl -es) kind of finch, the male of which has yellow-and-black wings
goldfinches n ▷ goldfinch

goldfish n (pl -es) orange fish kept in ponds or aquariums
goldfishes n ▷ goldfish

golds n ▷ gold

golf n (pl -s) outdoor game in which a ball is struck with clubs into a series of holes ▶ v (-s, -ing, -ed) play golf ▷ golfer n (pl -s)
golfed v ▷ golf
golfer n ▷ golf
golfers n ▷ golf
golfing v ▷ golf
golfs n, v ▷ golf

golliwog n (pl -s) soft black-faced doll
golliwogs n ▷ golliwog

gonad n (pl -s) organ producing reproductive cells, such as a testicle or ovary
gonads n ▷ gonad

gondola n (pl -s) long narrow boat used in Venice
gondolas n ▷ gondola

gondolier n (pl -s) person who propels a gondola
gondoliers n ▷ gondoliers

gone v ▷ go

goner n (pl -s) (Informal) person or thing beyond help or recovery
goners n ▷ goner

gong n (pl -s) rimmed metal disc that produces a note when struck
gongs n ▷ gong

gonorrhoea [gon-or-ree-a] n (pl -s) venereal disease with a discharge from the genitals
gonorrhoeas n ▷ gonorrhoea

good adj (better, best) giving pleasure ▶ n benefit ▶ pl merchandise > goodness n (pl -es)

goodbye interj, n (pl -s) expression used on parting
goodbyes n ▷ goodbye

goodly adj considerable
goodness n ▷ good

goodnesses n ▷ good

goodwill n (pl -s) kindly feeling
goodwills n ▷ goodwill

goody n (pl -dies) (Informal) hero in a book or film

gooey adj (gooier, gooiest) (Informal) sticky and soft

goof (Informal) n (pl -s) mistake ▶ v (-s, -ing, -ed) make a mistake
goofed v ▷ goof
goofing v ▷ goof
goofs n, v ▷ goof

googlies n ▷ googly

googly n (pl -lies) (CRICKET) ball that spins unexpectedly from off to leg on the bounce
gooier adj ▷ gooey
gooiest adj ▷ gooey

goon n (pl -s) (Informal) stupid person
goons n ▷ goon

goose n (pl geese) web-footed bird like a large duck
gooseberries n ▷ gooseberry

gooseberry n (pl -ries) edible yellowy-green berry

gopher [go-fer] n (pl -s) American burrowing rodent
gophers n ▷ gopher

gore¹ n (pl -s) blood from a wound

gore² v (-res, -ring, -red) pierce with horns
gored v ▷ gore²
gores n, v ▷ gore¹, ²

gorge n (pl -s) deep narrow valley ▶ v (-ges, -ging, -ged) eat greedily
gorged v ▷ gorge

gorgeous adj strikingly beautiful or attractive (Informal) > gorgeously adv
gorgeously adv ▷ gorgeous
gorges n, v ▷ gorge
gorging v ▷ gorge

gorgon n (pl -s) terrifying or repulsive woman
gorgons n ▷ gorgon
gorier adj ▷ gory
goriest adj ▷ gory

gorilla n (pl -s) largest of the apes, found in Africa
gorillas n ▷ gorilla
goring v ▷ gore²

gormless adj (Informal) stupid

gorse n (pl -s) prickly yellow-flowered shrub
gorses n ▷ gorse

gory adj (-rier, -riest) horrific or bloodthirsty
gos n ▷ go

goshawk n (pl -s) large hawk
goshawks n ▷ goshawk

gosling n (pl -s) young goose

goslings n ▷ gosling
gospel n (pl -s) any of the first four books of the New Testament
gospels n ▷ gospel
gossamer n (pl -s) very fine fabric
gossamers n ▷ gossamer
gossip n (pl -s) idle talk, esp. about other people ▶ v (-s, -ing, -ed) engage in gossip
> **gossipy** adj (-ier, -iest)
gossiped v ▷ gossip
gossipier adj ▷ gossip
gossipiest adj ▷ gossip
gossiping v ▷ gossip
gossips n, v ▷ gossip
gossipy adj ▷ gossip
got v ▷ get
gouache n (pl -s) (painting using) watercolours mixed with glue
gouaches n ▷ gouache
gouge [gowj] v (-ges, -ging, -ged) scoop or force out ▶ n (pl -s) hole or groove
gouged v ▷ gouge
gouges v, n ▷ gouge
gouging v ▷ gouge
goulash [goo-lash] n (pl -es) rich stew seasoned with paprika
goulashes n ▷ goulash
gourd [goord] n (pl -s) fleshy fruit of a climbing plant
gourds n ▷ gourd
gourmand [goor-mand] n (pl -s) person who is very keen on food and drink
gourmands n ▷ gourmand
gourmet [goor-may] n (pl -s) connoisseur of food and drink
gourmets n ▷ gourmet
gout [gowt] n (pl -s) disease causing inflammation of the joints
gouts n ▷ gout
govern v (-s, -ing, -ed) rule, direct, or control
> **governable** adj
governable adj ▷ govern
governance n (pl -s) governing
governances n ▷ governance
governed v ▷ govern
governess n (pl -es) woman teacher in a private household
governesses n ▷ governess
governing v ▷ govern
government n (pl -s) executive policy-making body of a state
> **governmental** adj
governmental adj ▷ government
governments n ▷ government
governor n (pl -s) official governing a province

or state
governors n ▷ governor
governs v ▷ govern
gown n (pl -s) woman's long formal dress
gowns n ▷ gown
goy n (pl -yim, -ys) (Slang) Jewish word for a non-Jew
goyim n ▷ goy
goys n ▷ goy

> **gox** n (goxes). Gox is a short word meaning gaseous oxygen. This unusual word can come in very useful, especially if you can use it to hit a bonus square. Gox scores 11 points.
> **goy** n (goyim) or (goys). Goy is a Yiddish word for someone who isn't Jewish. For a short word, this earns you a reasonable number of points, and the two plural forms can come in useful too. Goy scores 7 points.

grab v (-s, -bbing, -bbed) grasp suddenly, snatch ▶ n sudden snatch
grabbed v ▷ grab
grabbing v ▷ grab
grabs v ▷ grab
grace n (pl -s) beauty and elegance ▶ v (-ces, -cing, -ced) add grace to > **graceful** adj
> **gracefully** adv
> **graceless** adj
graced v ▷ grace
graceful adj ▷ grace
gracefully adv ▷ grace
graceless adj ▷ grace
graces n, v ▷ grace
gracing v ▷ grace
gracious adj kind and courteous > **graciously** adv
graciously adv ▷ gracious
gradation n (pl -s) (stage in) a series of degrees or steps
gradations n ▷ gradation
grade n (pl -s) place on a scale of quality, rank, or size ▶ v (-des, -ding, -ded) arrange in grades
graded v ▷ grade
grades n, v ▷ grade
gradient n (pl -s) (degree of) slope
gradients n ▷ gradient
grading v ▷ grade
gradual adj occurring, developing, or moving in small stages
> **gradually** adv
gradually adv ▷ gradual
graduate v (-tes, -ting, -ted) receive a degree or diploma ▶ n (pl -s) holder of a degree
> **graduation** n (pl -s)

graduated v ▷ graduate
graduates v, n ▷ graduate
graduating v ▷ graduate
graduation n ▷ graduate
graduations n ▷ graduate
graffiti [graf-fee-tee] pl n words or drawings scribbled or sprayed on walls etc.
graft¹ n (pl -s) surgical transplant of skin or tissue ▶ v (-s, -ing, -ed) transplant (living tissue) surgically
graft² (BRIT) (Informal) n hard work ▶ v work hard > **grafter** n (pl -s)
grafted v ▷ graft¹, ²
grafter n ▷ graft²
grafters n ▷ graft²
grafting v ▷ graft¹, ²
grafts n, v ▷ graft¹, ²
grain n (pl -s) seedlike fruit of a cereal plant > **grainy** adj (-ier, -iest)
grainier adj ▷ grain
grainiest adj ▷ grain
grains n ▷ grain
grainy adj ▷ grain
gram, gramme n (pl -s) metric unit of mass equal to one thousandth of a kilogram
grammar n (pl -s) branch of linguistics dealing with the form, function, and order of words > **grammarian** n (pl -s)
grammarian n ▷ grammar
grammarians n ▷ grammar
grammars n ▷ grammar
grammatical adj according to the rules of grammar > **grammatically** adv
grammatically adv ▷ grammatical
gramophone n (pl -s) old-fashioned type of record player
gramophones n ▷ gramophone
grampus n (pl -es) dolphin-like mammal
grampuses n ▷ grampus
grams n ▷ gram
gran n (pl -s) (BRIT, AUST & NZ) (Informal) grandmother
granaries n ▷ granary
granary n (pl -ries) storehouse for grain
grand adj large or impressive, imposing ▶ n (pl -s) (Slang) thousand pounds or dollars
grandchild n (pl -children) child of one's child
grandchildren n ▷ grandchild
granddaughter n (pl -s) female grandchild
granddaughters n ▷ granddaughter
grandee n (pl -s) person of high station
grandees n ▷ grandee
grandeur n (pl -s) magnificence
grandeurs n ▷ grandeur
grandfather n (pl -s) male grandparent

grandfathers n ▷ grandfather
grandiloquences n ▷ grandiloquent
grandiloquent adj using pompous language > **grandiloquence** n (pl -s)
grandiloquence n ▷ grandiloquent
grandiose adj imposing > **grandiosity** n (pl -ties)
grandiosities n ▷ grandiose
grandiosity n ▷ grandiose
grandmother n (pl -s) female grandparent
grandmothers n ▷ grandmother
grandparent n (pl -s) parent of one's parent
grandparents n ▷ grandparent
grands n ▷ grand
grandson n (pl -s) male grandchild
grandsons n ▷ grandson
grandstand n (pl -s) terraced block of seats giving the best view at a sports ground
grandstands n ▷ grandstand
grange n (pl -s) (BRIT) country house with farm buildings
granges n ▷ grange
granite [gran-nit] n (pl -s) very hard igneous rock often used in building
granites n ▷ granite
grannies n ▷ granny
granny, grannie n (pl -nies) (Informal) grandmother
grans n ▷ gran
grant v (-s, -ing, -ed) consent to fulfil (a request) ▶ n (pl -s) sum of money provided by a government for a specific purpose, such as education
granted v ▷ grant
granting v ▷ grant
grants v, n ▷ grant
granular adj of or like grains
granulated adj (of sugar) in the form of coarse grains
granule n (pl -s) small grain
granules n ▷ granule
grape n (pl -s) small juicy green or purple berry, eaten raw or used to produce wine, raisins, currants, or sultanas
grapefruit n (pl -s) large round yellow citrus fruit
grapefruits n ▷ grapefruit
grapes n ▷ grape
grapevine n (pl -s) grape-bearing vine
grapevines n ▷ grapevine
graph n (pl -s) drawing showing the relation of different numbers or quantities plotted against a set of axes
graphic adj vividly descriptive > **graphically** adv

graphically adv ▷ graphic

graphics pl n diagrams, graphs, etc., esp. as used on a television programme or computer screen

graphite n (pl -s) soft black form of carbon, used in pencil leads

graphites n ▷ graphite

graphologies n ▷ graphology

graphologist n ▷ graphology

graphologists n ▷ graphology

graphology n (pl -gies) study of handwriting > **graphologist** n (pl -s)

graphs n ▷ graph

grapnel n (pl -s) device with several hooks, used to grasp or secure things

grapnels n ▷ grapnel

grapple v (-les, -ling, -led) try to cope with (something difficult)

grappled v ▷ grapple

grapples v ▷ grapple

grappling v ▷ grapple

grasp v (-s, -ing, -ed) grip something firmly ▶ n (pl -s) grip or clasp

grasped v ▷ grasp

grasping adj greedy or avaricious ▶ v ▷ grasp

grasps v, n ▷ grasp

grass n (pl -es) common type of plant with jointed stems and long narrow leaves, including cereals and bamboo ▶ v (-es, -ing, -ed) cover with grass > **grassy** adj (-ssier, -ssiest)

grassed v ▷ grass

grasses n, v ▷ grass

grasshopper n (pl -s) jumping insect with long hind legs

grasshoppers n ▷ grasshopper

grassier adj ▷ grass

grassiest adj ▷ grass

grassing v ▷ grass

grassroots adj of the ordinary members of a group, rather than its leaders

grassy adj ▷ grass

grate¹ v (-tes, -ting, -ted) rub into small bits on a rough surface > **grater** n (pl -s)

grate² n (pl -s) framework of metal bars for holding fuel in a fireplace

grated v ▷ grate¹

grateful adj feeling or showing gratitude > **gratefully** adv

gratefully adv ▷ grateful

grater n ▷ grate¹

graters n ▷ grate¹

grates v, n ▷ grate¹, ²

gratification n ▷ gratify

gratifications n ▷ gratify

gratified v ▷ gratify

gratifies v ▷ gratify

gratify v (-fies, -fying, -fied) satisfy or please > **gratification** n (pl -s)

gratifying v ▷ gratify

grating n (pl -s) framework of metal bars covering an opening ▶ adj harsh or rasping ▶ v ▷ grate¹

gratings n ▷ grating

gratis adv, adj free, for nothing

gratitude n (pl -s) feeling of being thankful for a favour or gift

gratitudes n ▷ gratitude

gratuities n ▷ gratuity

gratuitous adj unjustified > **gratuitously** adv

gratuitously adv ▷ gratuitous

gratuity n (pl -ies) money given for services rendered, tip

grave¹ n (pl -s) hole for burying a corpse

grave² adj causing concern > **gravely** adv

grave³ [rhymes with **halve**] n (pl -s) accent (`) over a vowel to indicate a special pronunciation

gravel n (pl -s) mixture of small stones and coarse sand

gravelled adj covered with gravel

gravellier adj ▷ gravelly

gravelliest adj ▷ gravelly

gravelly adj (-llier, -lliest) covered with gravel

gravels n ▷ gravel

gravely adv ▷ grave²

graven adj carved or engraved

graves n ▷ grave¹, ³

gravestone n (pl -s) stone marking a grave

gravestones n ▷ gravestone

graveyard n (pl -s) cemetery

graveyards n ▷ graveyard

gravid [grav-id] adj (MED) pregnant

gravies n ▷ gravy

gravitate v (-tes, -ting, -ted) be influenced or drawn towards > **gravitation** n (pl -s) > **gravitational** adj

gravitated v ▷ gravitate

gravitates v ▷ gravitate

gravitating v ▷ gravitate

gravitation n ▷ gravitate

gravitational adj ▷ gravitate

gravitations n ▷ gravitate

gravities n ▷ gravity

gravity n (pl -ties) force of attraction of one object for another, esp. of objects to the earth

gravy n (pl -vies) juices from meat in cooking

grawing v ▷ gnaw

grawn v ▷ gnaw

gray adj (-er, -est) (CHIEFLY US) grey

grayer adj ▷ gray
grayest adj ▷ gray
grayling n (pl -s) fish of the salmon family
  graylings n ▷ grayling
graze[1] v (-zes, -zing, -zed) feed on grass
graze[2] v (-zes, -zing, -zed) scratch or scrape the skin ▶ n (pl -s) slight scratch or scrape
  grazed v ▷ graze[1, 2]
  grazes n, v ▷ graze[1, 2]
  grazing v ▷ graze[1, 2]
grease n (pl -s) soft melted animal fat ▶ v (-ses, -sing, -sed) apply grease to
  greased v ▷ grease
greasepaint n (pl -s) theatrical make-up
  greasepaints n ▷ greasepaint
  greases n, v ▷ grease
  greasier adj ▷ greasy
  greasiest adj ▷ greasy
  greasiness n ▷ greasy
  greasinesses n ▷ greasy
  greasing v ▷ grease
greasy adj (-sier, -siest) covered with or containing grease > **greasiness** n (pl -s)
great adj (-er, -est) large in size or number (Informal) > **greatly** adv > **greatness** n (pl -es)
greatcoat n (pl -s) heavy overcoat
  greatcoats n ▷ greatcoat
  greater adj ▷ great
  greatest adj ▷ great
  greatly adv ▷ great
  greatness n ▷ great
  greatnesses n ▷ great
greave n (pl -s) piece of armour for the shin
  greaves n ▷ greave
grebe n (pl -s) diving water bird
  grebes n ▷ grebe
greed n (pl -s) excessive desire for food, wealth, etc. > **greedy** adj (-dier, -diest) > **greedily** adv > **greediness** n (pl -es)
  greedier adj ▷ greed
  greediest adj ▷ greed
  greedily adv ▷ greed
  greediness n ▷ greed
  greedinesses n ▷ greed
  greeds n ▷ greed
  greedy adj ▷ greed
green adj (-er, -est) of a colour between blue and yellow ▶ n (pl -s) colour between blue and yellow ▶ pl green vegetables ▶ v (-s, -ing, -ed) make or become green > **greenness** n (pl -es) > **greenish, greeny** adj
  greened v ▷ green
  greener adj ▷ green
  greeneries n ▷ greenery
greenery n (pl -ries) vegetation

  greenest adj ▷ green
greenfinch n (pl -es) European finch with dull green plumage in the male
  greenfinches n ▷ greenfinch
  greenflies n ▷ greenfly
greenfly n (pl -flies) green aphid, a common garden pest
greengage n (pl -s) sweet green plum
  greengages n ▷ greengage
greengrocer n (pl -s) (BRIT) shopkeeper selling vegetables and fruit
  greengrocers n ▷ greengrocers
greenhorn n (pl -s) (CHIEFLY US) novice
  greenhorns n ▷ greenhorn
greenhouse n (pl -s) glass building for rearing plants
  greenhouses n ▷ greenhouse
  greening v ▷ green
  greenish adj ▷ green
  greenness n ▷ green
  greennesses n ▷ green
  greens n, v ▷ green
greenshank (pl -s) n large European sandpiper
  greenshanks n ▷ greenshanks
greenstone n (pl -s) (NZ) type of green jade used for Maori ornaments
  greenstones n ▷ greenstone
  greeny adj ▷ green
greet v (-s, -ing, -ed) meet with expressions of welcome > **greeting** n (pl -s)
  greeted v ▷ greet
  greeting v, n ▷ greet
  greetings n ▷ greet
  greets v ▷ greet
gregarious adj fond of company
gremlin n (pl -s) imaginary being blamed for mechanical malfunctions
  gremlins n ▷ gremlin
grenade n (pl -s) small bomb thrown by hand or fired from a rifle
  grenades n ▷ grenade
grenadier n (pl -s) soldier of a regiment formerly trained to throw grenades
  grenadiers n ▷ grenadier
grenadine [gren-a-deen] n (pl -s) syrup made from pomegranates
  grenadines n ▷ grenadine
grevillea n (pl -s) any of various Australian evergreen trees and shrubs
  grevilleas n ▷ grevillea
  grew v ▷ grow
grey adj (-er, -est) of a colour between black and white ▶ n (pl -s) grey colour
  greyer adj ▷ grey
  greyest adj ▷ grey

greyhound n (pl -s) swift slender dog used in racing
greyhounds n ▷ greyhound
greying adj (of hair) turning grey > **greyish** adj > **greyness** n (pl -es)
greyish adj ▷ grey
greyness n ▷ grey
greynesses n ▷ grey
greys n ▷ grey
grid n (pl -s) network of horizontal and vertical lines, bars, etc.
griddle n (pl -s) flat iron plate for cooking
griddles n ▷ griddle
gridiron n (pl -s) frame of metal bars for grilling food
gridirons n ▷ gridiron
gridlock n (pl -s) situation where traffic is not moving > **gridlocked** adj
gridlocked adj ▷ gridlock
gridlocks n ▷ gridlock
grids n ▷ grid
grief n (pl -s) deep sadness
griefs n ▷ grief
grievance (pl -s) n real or imaginary cause for complaint
grievances n ▷ grievances
grieve v (-ves, -ving, -ved) (cause to) feel grief
grieved v ▷ grieve
grieves v ▷ grieve
grieving adj ▷ grieve
grievous adj very severe or painful
griffin n (pl -s) mythical monster with an eagle's head and wings and a lion's body
griffins n ▷ griffin
grill n (pl -s) device on a cooker that radiates heat downwards ▶ v (-s, -ing, -ed) cook under a grill
grille, grill n (pl -s) grating over an opening
grilled v ▷ grill
grilles n ▷ grille
grilling n (pl -s) relentless questioning ▶ v ▷ grill
grillings n ▷ grilling
grills[1] n, v ▷ grill
grills[2] n ▷ grille
grilse [grillss] n (pl -s) salmon on its first return from the sea to fresh water
grilses n ▷ grilse
grim adj (-mmer, -mmest) stern > **grimly** adv > **grimness** n (pl -es)
grimace n (pl -s) ugly or distorted facial expression of pain, disgust, etc. ▶ v (-ces, -cing, -ced) make a grimace
grimaced v ▷ grimace
grimaces n, v ▷ grimace

grimacing v ▷ grimace
grime n (pl -s) ingrained dirt ▶ v (-mes, -ming, -med) make very dirty > **grimy** adj (-mier, -miest)
grimed v ▷ grime
grimes n, v ▷ grime
grimier adj ▷ grime
grimiest adj ▷ grime
griming v ▷ grime
grimly adv ▷ grim
grimmer adj ▷ grim
grimmest adj ▷ grim
grimness n ▷ grim
grimnesses n ▷ grim
grimy adj ▷ grime
grin v (-s, -nning, -nned) smile broadly, showing the teeth ▶ n (-s) broad smile
grind v (-s, -ing, ground) crush or rub to a powder ▶ n (-s) (Informal) hard work
grinding v ▷ grind
grinds v, n ▷ grind
grindstone n (pl -s) stone used for grinding
grindstones n ▷ grindstone
grinned v ▷ grin
grinning v ▷ grin
grins v, n ▷ grin
grip n (pl -s) firm hold or grasp (us) ▶ v (-s, -pping, -pped) grasp or hold tightly > **gripping** adj
gripe v (-pes, -ping, -ped) (Informal) complain persistently ▶ n (pl -s) (Informal) complaint
griped v ▷ gripe
gripes v, n ▷ gripe
griping v ▷ gripe
gripped v ▷ grip
gripping v, adj ▷ grip
grips n, v ▷ grip
grislier adj ▷ grisly
grisliest adj ▷ grisly
grisly adj (-lier, -liest) horrifying or ghastly
grist n (pl -s) grain for grinding
gristle n (pl -s) tough stringy animal tissue found in meat > **gristly** adj (-lier, -liest)
gristles n ▷ gristle
gristlier adj ▷ gristle
gristliest adj ▷ gristle
gristly adj ▷ gristle
grists n ▷ grist
grit n (pl -s) rough particles of sand ▶ v (-s, -tting, -tted) spread grit on (an icy road etc.) > **gritty** adj (-tier, -ttiest) > **grittiness** n (pl -es)
grits v ▷ grit
gritted v ▷ grit
grittier adj ▷ grit

grittiest adj ▷ grit
grittiness n ▷ grit
grittinesses n ▷ grit
gritting v ▷ grit
gritty adj ▷ grit
grizzle v (-les, -ling, -led) (BRIT, AUST & NZ) (Informal) whine or complain
grizzled adj grey-haired ▶ v ▷ grizzle
grizzles v ▷ grizzle
grizzlies n ▷ grizzly
grizzling v ▷ grizzle
grizzly n (pl -lies) large American bear
groan n (pl -s) deep sound of grief or pain ▶ v (-s, -ing, -ed) utter a groan
groaned v ▷ groan
groaning v ▷ groan
groans n, v ▷ groan
groat n (pl -s) (HIST) fourpenny piece
groats n ▷ groat
grocer n (pl -s) shopkeeper selling foodstuffs
groceries n ▷ grocery
grocers n ▷ grocer
grocery n (pl -ceries) business or premises of a grocer ▶ pl goods sold by a grocer
grog n (pl -s) (BRIT, AUST & NZ) spirit, usu. rum, and water
groggier adj ▷ groggy
groggiest adj ▷ groggy
groggy adj (-ggier, -ggiest) (Informal) faint, shaky, or dizzy
grogs n ▷ grog
groin n (pl -s) place where the legs join the abdomen
groins n ▷ groin
grommet n (pl -s) ring or eyelet
grommets n ▷ grommet
groom n (pl -s) person who looks after horses ▶ v (-s, -ing, -ed) make or keep one's clothes and appearance neat and tidy
groomed v ▷ groom
grooming v ▷ groom
grooms n, v ▷ groom
groove n (pl -s) long narrow channel in a surface
grooves n ▷ groove
grope v (-pes, -ping, -ped) feel about or search uncertainly > **groping** n (pl -s)
groped v ▷ grope
gropes v ▷ grope
groping v, n ▷ grope
gropings n ▷ grope
gross adj flagrant ▶ n (pl -es) twelve dozen ▶ v (-es, -ing, -ed) make as total revenue before deductions > **grossly** adv > **grossness** n (pl -es)
grossed v ▷ gross

grosses n, v ▷ gross
grossing v ▷ gross
grossly adv ▷ gross
grossness n ▷ gross
grossnesses n ▷ gross
grotesque [grow-**tesk**] adj (-quer, -quest) strangely distorted ▶ n (pl -s) grotesque person or thing > **grotesquely** adv
grotesquely adv ▷ grotesque
grotesquer adj ▷ grotesque
grotesques n ▷ grotesque
grotesquest adj ▷ grotesque
grottier adj ▷ grotty
grottiest adj ▷ grotty
grotto n (pl -ttoes, -ttos) small picturesque cave
grottoes n ▷ grotto
grottos n ▷ grotto
grotty adj (-ttier, -ttiest) (Informal) nasty or in bad condition
grouch (Informal) v (-es, -ing, -ed) grumble or complain ▶ n (pl -es) person who is always complaining > **grouchy** adj (-chier, -chiest)
grouched v ▷ grouch
grouches v, n ▷ grouch
grouchier adj ▷ grouch
grouchiest adj ▷ grouch
grouching v ▷ grouch
grouchy adj ▷ grouch
ground¹ n (pl -s) surface of the earth ▶ pl enclosed land round a house ▶ v (-s, -ing, -ed) base or establish
ground² v ▷ grind
grounded v ▷ ground¹
grounding n (pl -s) basic knowledge of a subject ▶ v ▷ ground¹
groundings n ▷ grounding
groundless adj without reason
groundnut n (pl -s) peanut
groundnuts n ▷ groundnut
grounds n, v ▷ ground¹
groundsheet n (pl -s) waterproof sheet put on the ground under a tent
groundsheets n ▷ groundsheet
groundsman n (pl -men) person employed to maintain a sports ground or park
groundsmen n ▷ groundsman
groundswell n (pl -s) rapidly developing general feeling or opinion
groundswells n ▷ groundswell
groundwork n (pl -s) preliminary work
groundworks n ▷ groundwork
group n (pl -s) number of people or things regarded as a unit ▶ v (-s, -ing, -ed) place or

form into a group
grouped v ▷ group
grouping v ▷ group
groups n, v ▷ group
grouse[1] n (pl -s) stocky game bird
grouse[2] v (-ses, -sing, -sed) grumble or
complain ▶ n (pl -s) complaint
groused v ▷ grouse[2]
grouses n, v ▷ grouse[1, 2]
grousing v ▷ grouse[2]
grout n (pl -s) thin mortar ▶ v (-s, -ing, -ed) fill
up with grout
grouted v ▷ grout
grouting v ▷ grout
grouts n, v ▷ grout
grove n (pl -s) small group of trees
grovel [grov-el] v (-s, -elling, -elled) behave
humbly in order to win a superior's favour
grovelled v ▷ grovel
grovelling v ▷ grovel
grovels v ▷ grovel
groves n ▷ grove
grow v (-s, growing, grew, grown) develop
physically
growing v ▷ grow
growl v (-s, -ing, -ed) make a low rumbling
sound ▶ n (pl -s) growling sound
growled v ▷ growl
growling v ▷ growl
growls v, n ▷ growl
grown v ▷ grow
grownup adj, n (pl -s) adult
grownups n ▷ grownup
grows v ▷ grow
growth n (pl -s) growing
growths n ▷ growth
groyne n (pl -s) wall built out from the shore to
control erosion
groynes n ▷ groyne
grub n (pl -s) legless insect larva ▶ v (-s, -bbing,
-bbed) search carefully for something by
digging or by moving things about
grubbed v ▷ grub
grubbier adj ▷ grubby
grubbiest adj ▷ grubby
grubbiness n ▷ grubby
grubbinesses n ▷ grubby
grubbing v ▷ grub
grubby adj (-bbier, -bbiest) dirty > grubbiness
n (pl -es)
grubs n, v ▷ grub
grudge v (-ges, -ging, -ged) be unwilling to
give or allow ▶ n (pl -s) resentment
grudged v ▷ grudge
grudges v, n ▷ grudge

grudging v ▷ grudge
gruel n (pl -s) thin porridge
gruelling adj exhausting or severe
gruels n ▷ gruel
gruesome adj (-er, -est) causing horror and
disgust
gruesomer adj ▷ gruesome
gruesomest adj ▷ gruesome
gruff adj (-er, -est) rough or surly in manner or
voice > gruffly adv > gruffness n (pl -es)
gruffer adj ▷ gruff
gruffest adj ▷ gruff
gruffly adv ▷ gruff
gruffness n ▷ gruff
gruffnesses n ▷ gruff
grumble v (-les, -ling, -led) complain ▶ n (pl -s)
complaint > grumbler n (pl -s) > grumbling
adj, n (pl -s)
grumbled v ▷ grumble
grumbler n ▷ grumble
grumblers n ▷ grumble
grumbles v, n ▷ grumble
grumbling v, n ▷ grumble
grumblings n ▷ grumble
grumpier adj ▷ grumpy
grumpiest adj ▷ grumpy
grumpily adv ▷ grumpy
grumpiness n ▷ grumpy
grumpinesses n ▷ grumpy
grumpy adj (-pier, -piest) bad-tempered
> grumpily adv > grumpiness n (pl -es)
grunge n (pl -s) style of rock music with a fuzzy
guitar sound
grunges n ▷ grunge
grunt v (-s, -ing, -ed) make a low short gruff
sound, like a pig ▶ n (pl -s) pig's sound
grunted v ▷ grunt
grunting v ▷ grunt
grunts v, n ▷ grunt
gryphon n (pl -s) ▷ griffin
gryphons n ▷ gryphon

> **gu** n (**gus**). A gu (also spelt **gju**) is a
> kind of violin from Shetland. This is
> one of only three two-letter words
> beginning with G, and so is a good one
> to remember. Gu scores 3 points.

guano [gwah-no] n (pl -nos) dried sea-bird
manure, used as fertilizer
guanos n ▷ guano
guarantee n (pl -s) formal assurance, esp. in
writing, that a product will meet certain
standards ▶ v (-s, -teeing, -teed) give a
guarantee
guaranteed v ▷ guarantee
guaranteeing v ▷ guarantee

guarantees n, v ▷ guarantee
guarantor n (pl -s) person who gives or is bound by a guarantee
  guarantors n ▷ guarantor
guard v (-s, -ing, -ed) watch over to protect or to prevent escape ▶ n (pl -s) person or group that guards ▶ (G-) pl regiment with ceremonial duties
guarded adj cautious or noncommittal ▶ v ▷ guard > **guardedly** adv
  guardedly adv ▷ guarded
guardian n (pl -s) keeper or protector > **guardianship** n (pl -s)
  guardians n ▷ guardian
  guardianship n ▷ guardian
  guardianships n ▷ guardian
  guarding v ▷ guard
  guards v, n ▷ guard
guardsman n (pl -s) member of the Guards
  guardsmen n ▷ guardsman
guava [gwah-va] n (pl -s) yellow-skinned tropical American fruit
  guavas n ▷ guava
gudgeon n (pl -s) small freshwater fish
  gudgeons n ▷ gudgeon
  guerillas n ▷ guerrilla
guerrilla, guerilla n (pl -s) member of an unofficial armed force fighting regular forces
  guerrillas n ▷ guerrilla
guess v (-es, -ing, -ed) estimate or draw a conclusion without proper knowledge ▶ n (pl -es) estimate or conclusion reached by guessing
  guessed v ▷ guess
  guesses v, n ▷ guess
  guessing v ▷ guess
guesswork n (pl -s) process or results of guessing
  guessworks n ▷ guesswork
guest n (pl -s) person entertained at another's house or at another's expense ▶ v (-s, -ing, -ed) appear as a visiting player or performer
  guested v ▷ guest
guesthouse n (pl -s) boarding house
  guesthouses n ▷ guesthouse
  guesting v ▷ guest
  guests n, v ▷ guest
guff n (pl -s) (BRIT, AUST & NZ) (Slang) nonsense
guffaw n (pl -s) crude noisy laugh ▶ v (-s, -ing, -ed) laugh in this way
  guffawed v ▷ guffaw
  guffawing v ▷ guffaw
  guffaws n, v ▷ guffaw
  guffs n ▷ guff
guidance n (pl -s) leadership, instruction, or advice
  guidances n ▷ guidance
guide n (pl -s) person who conducts tour expeditions ▶ v (-s, -ing, -ed) act as a guide for
  guided v ▷ guide
guideline n set principle for doing something
  guidelines n ▷ guideline
  guides n, v ▷ guide
  guiding v ▷ guide
guild n (pl -s) organization or club
guilder n (pl -s) former monetary unit of the Netherlands
  guilders n ▷ guilder
  guilds n ▷ guild
guile [gile] n (pl -s) cunning or deceit > **guileful** adj > **guileless** adj
  guileful adj ▷ guile
  guileless adj ▷ guile
  guiles n ▷ guile
guillemot [gil-lee-mot] n (pl -s) black-and-white diving sea bird of N hemisphere
  guillemots n ▷ guillemot
guillotine n (pl -s) machine for beheading people ▶ v (-s, -ing, -ed) behead by guillotine
  guillotined v ▷ guillotine
  guillotines n, v ▷ guillotine
  guillotining v ▷ guillotine
guilt n (pl -s) fact or state of having done wrong
  guiltier adj ▷ guilty
  guiltiest adj ▷ guilty
  guiltily adv ▷ guilty
  guiltless adj innocent
  guilts n ▷ guilt
guilty adj (-tier, -tiest) responsible for an offence or misdeed > **guiltily** adv
guinea n (pl -s) former British monetary unit worth 21 shillings (1.05 pounds)
  guineas n ▷ guinea
guise [rhymes with size] n (pl -s) false appearance
  guises n ▷ guise
guitar n (pl -s) stringed instrument with a flat back and a long neck, played by plucking or strumming > **guitarist** n
  guitarist n ▷ guitar
  guitarists n ▷ guitar
  guitars n ▷ guitar
gulch n (pl -es) (US) deep narrow valley
  gulches n ▷ gulch
gulf n (pl -s) large deep bay
  gulfs n ▷ gulf
gull n (pl -s) long-winged sea bird
gullet n (pl -s) muscular tube through which food passes from the mouth to the stomach
  gullets n ▷ gullet

gullibilities n ▷ gullible
gullibility n ▷ gullible
gullible adj easily tricked > **gullibility** n (pl -ties)
gullies n ▷ gully
gulls n ▷ gull
gully n (pl -llies) channel cut by running water
gulp v (-s, -ing, -ed) swallow hastily ▶ n (pl -s) gulping
gulped v ▷ gulp
gulping v ▷ gulp
gulps v, n ▷ gulp
gum¹ n (pl -s) firm flesh in which the teeth are set
gum² n (pl -s) sticky substance obtained from certain trees ▶ v (-s, -mming, -mmed) stick with gum
gumboot n (pl -s) (CHIEFLY BRIT) Wellington boot
gumboots n ▷ gumboot
gumdrop n (pl -s) hard jelly-like sweet
gumdrops n ▷ gumdrop
gummed v ▷ gum²
gummier adj ▷ gummy¹, ²
gummiest adj ▷ gummy¹, ²
gumming v ▷ gum²
gummy¹ adj (-mmier, -mmiest) toothless
gummy² adj (-mmier, -mmiest) sticky
gumption n (pl -s) (Informal) resourcefulness
gumptions n ▷ gumption
gums n ▷ gum¹, ²
gun n (pl -s) weapon with a metal tube from which missiles are fired by explosion ▶ v (-s, -nning, -nned) cause (an engine) to run at high speed
gunboat n (pl -s) small warship
gunboats n ▷ gunboat
gunge n (pl -s) (Informal) sticky unpleasant substance ▶ **gungy** adj (-gier, -giest)
gunges n ▷ gunge
gungier adj ▷ gung
gungiest adj ▷ gung
gungy adj ▷ gung
gunman n (pl -men) armed criminal
gunmen n ▷ gunman
gunmetal n (pl -s) alloy of copper, tin, and zinc ▶ adj dark grey
gunmetals n ▷ gunmetal
gunned v ▷ gun
gunnel n ▷ gunwale
gunnels n ▷ gunwale
gunner n (pl -s) artillery soldier
gunneries n ▷ gunnery
gunners n ▷ gunner
gunnery n (pl -ries) use or science of large guns
gunnies n ▷ gunny

gunning v ▷ gun
gunny n (pl -ies) strong coarse fabric used for sacks
gunpowder n (pl -s) explosive mixture of potassium nitrate, sulphur, and charcoal
gunpowders n ▷ gunpowder
gunrunner n ▷ gunrunning
gunrunners n ▷ gunrunning
gunrunning n (pl -s) smuggling of guns and ammunition ▶ **gunrunner** n (pl -s)
gunrunnings n ▷ gunrunning
guns n, v ▷ gun
gunshot n (pl -s) shot or range of a gun
gunshots n ▷ gunshot
gunwale, gunnel [gun-nel] n (pl -s) top of a ship's side
gunwales n ▷ gunwale
gunyah n (pl -s) (AUST) hut or shelter in the bush
gunyahs n ▷ gunyah
guppies n ▷ guppy
guppy n (pl -ppies) small colourful aquarium fish
gurgle v (-les, -ling, -led) ▶ n (pl -s) (make) a bubbling noise
gurgled v ▷ gurgle
gurgles v, n ▷ gurgle
gurgling v ▷ gurgle
guru n (pl -s) Hindu or Sikh religious teacher or leader
gurus n ▷ guru
gush v (-es, -ing, -ed) flow out suddenly and profusely ▶ n (pl -es) sudden copious flow
gushed v ▷ gush
gusher n (pl -s) spurting oil well
gushers n ▷ gusher
gushes v, n ▷ gush
gushing v ▷ gush
gusset n (pl -s) piece of material sewn into a garment to strengthen it
gussets n ▷ gusset
gust n (pl -s) sudden blast of wind ▶ v (-s, -ing, -ed) blow in gusts > **gusty** adj (-tier, -tiest)
gusted v ▷ gust
gustier adj ▷ gust
gustiest adj ▷ gust
gusting v ▷ gust
gusto n (pl -tos) enjoyment or zest
gustos n ▷ gusto
gusts n, v ▷ gust
gusty adj ▷ gust
gut n (pl -s) intestine (Informal) ▷ catgut ▶ pl internal organs ▶ v (-s, -tting, -tted) remove the guts from ▶ adj basic or instinctive
guts n ▷ gut
gutsier adj ▷ gutsy

gutsiest adj ▷ gutsy
gutsy adj (-sier, -siest) (Informal) courageous
gutted adj (BRIT, AUST & NZ) (Informal) disappointed and upset ▶ v ▷ gut
gutter n (pl -s) shallow channel for carrying away water from a roof or roadside ▶ v (-s, -ing, -ed) (of a candle) burn unsteadily, with wax running down the sides
guttered v ▷ gutter
guttering n material for gutters ▶ v ▷ gutter
gutters n, v ▷ gutter
guttersnipe n (pl -s) (BRIT) neglected slum child
guttersnipes n ▷ guttersnipe
gutting v ▷ gut
guttural adj (of a sound) produced at the back of the throat
guy¹ n (pl -s) (Informal) man or boy
guy² n (pl -s) rope or chain to steady or secure something
guys n ▷ guy¹, ²
guzzle v (-les, -ling, -led) eat or drink greedily
guzzled v ▷ guzzle
guzzles v ▷ guzzle
guzzling v ▷ guzzle
gybe [jibe] v (-bes, -bing, -bed) (of a fore-and-aft sail) swing suddenly from one side to the other
gybed v ▷ gybe
gybes v ▷ gybe
gybing v ▷ gybe
gym n (pl -s) gymnasium
gymkhana [jim-kah-na] n (pl -s) horse-riding competition
gymkhanas n ▷ gymkhana
gymnasium n (pl -s) large room with equipment for physical training
gymnasiums n ▷ gymnasium
gymnast n (pl -s) expert in gymnastics
gymnastic n ▷ gymnastics
gymnastics pl n exercises to develop strength and agility > **gymnastic** adj
gymnasts n ▷ gymnast

gyms n ▷ gym
gynaecological adj ▷ gynaecology
gynaecologies n ▷ gynaecology
gynaecologist n ▷ gynaecology
gynaecologists n ▷ gynaecology
gynaecology [guy-nee-kol-la-jee] n (pl -ies) branch of medicine dealing with diseases and conditions specific to women > **gynaecological** adj > **gynaecologist** n (pl -s)

> **gyp** n (gyps, gypping, gyped). Gyp is a slang word meaning to cheat or swindle. This word and its inflections can be very useful when dealing with a word ending in Y on the board. Gyp scores 9 points.

gypsies n ▷ gypsy
gypsophila n (pl -s) garden plant with small white flowers
gypsophilas n ▷ gypsophila
gypsum n (pl -s) chalklike mineral used to make plaster of Paris
gypsums n ▷ gypsum
gypsy n (pl -sies) member of a travelling people found throughout Europe
gyrate [jire-rate] v (-tes, -ting, -ted) rotate or spiral about a point or axis > **gyration** n (pl -s)
gyrated v ▷ gyrate
gyrates v ▷ gyrate
gyrating v ▷ gyrate
gyration n ▷ gyrate
gyrations n ▷ gyrate
gyratory adj ▷ gyrate
gyrocompass n (pl -es) compass using a gyroscope
gyrocompasses n ▷ gyrocompass
gyroscope [jire-oh-skohp] n (pl -s) disc rotating on an axis that can turn in any direction, so the disc maintains the same position regardless of the movement of the surrounding structure > **gyroscopic** adj
gyroscopes n ▷ gyroscope
gyroscopic adj ▷ gyroscope

Hh

H forms a two-letter word in front of every vowel except U (and you can make **uh** with U), making it a versatile tile when you want to form words in more than one direction. As H is worth 4 points on its own, you can earn some very high scores by doing this: even **ha**, **he**, **hi** and **ho** will give 5 points each. There are lots of good short words beginning with H, like **haw**, **hew**, **how**, **hay**, **hey** and **hoy** (9 each).

ha *interj*. Ha is a sound people make to express triumph or surprise. This gives a reasonable score for a two-letter word, and is a good one to form when making a longer word in another direction at the same time. Ha scores 5 points.

haberdasher *n* (*pl* -s) (BRIT, AUST & NZ) dealer in small articles used for sewing
> **haberdashery** *n* (*pl* -ries)
  haberdasheries *n* ▷ haberdasher
  haberdashers *n* ▷ haberdasher
  haberdashery *n* ▷ haberdasher

habit *n* (*pl* -s) established way of behaving

habitable *adj* fit to be lived in

habitat *n* (*pl* -s) natural home of an animal or plant

habitation *n* (*pl* -s) (occupation of) a dwelling place
  habitations *n* ▷ habitation
  habitats *n* ▷ habitat
  habits *n* ▷ habit

habitual *adj* done regularly and repeatedly
> **habitually** *adv*
  habitually *adv* ▷ habitual

habituate *v* (-tes, -ting, -ted) accustom
> **habituation** *n* (*pl* -s)
  habituated *v* ▷ habituate
  habituates *v* ▷ habituate
  habituating *v* ▷ habituate
  habituation *n* ▷ habituate
  habituations *n* ▷ habituate

habitué [hab-it-yew-ay] *n* (*pl* -s) frequent visitor to a place
  habitués *n* ▷ habitué

hacienda [hass-ee-end-a] *n* (*pl* -s) ranch or large estate in Latin America
  haciendas *n* ▷ hacienda

hack¹ *v* (-s, -ing, -ed) cut or chop violently (BRIT,

G NZ) (*Informal*)

hack² *n* (*pl* -s) (inferior) writer or journalist
  hacked *v* ▷ hack¹

hacker *n* (*pl* -s) (*Slang*) computer enthusiast, esp. one who breaks into the computer system of a company or government
  hackers *n* ▷ hacker
  hacking *v* ▷ hack¹

hackles *pl n* hairs on the neck and back of an animal

hackney *n* (*pl* -s) (BRIT) taxi

hackneyed *adj* (of a word or phrase) unoriginal and overused
  hackneys *n* ▷ hackney
  hacks *v* ▷ hack¹ ▶ *n* ▷ hack²

hacksaw *n* (*pl* -s) small saw for cutting metal
  hacksaws *n* ▷ hacksaw
  had *v* ▷ have

haddock *n* (*pl* -s) edible sea fish of N Atlantic
  haddocks *n* ▷ haddock
  hadj *n* (*pl* -es) ▷ hajj
  hadjes *n* ▷ hadj
  haematologies *n* ▷ haematology

haematology *n* (*pl* -gies) study of blood and its diseases

haemoglobin [hee-moh-globe-in] *n* (*pl* -s) protein found in red blood cells which carries oxygen
  haemoglobins *n* ▷ haemoglobin

haemophilia [hee-moh-fill-lee-a] *n* (*pl* -s) hereditary illness in which the blood does not clot > **haemophiliac** *n* (*pl* -s)
  haemophiliac *n* ▷ haemophilia
  haemophiliacs *n* ▷ haemophilia
  haemophilias *n* ▷ haemophilia

haemorrhage [hem-or-ij] *n* (*pl* -ges) heavy bleeding ▶ *v* (-ges, -ging, -ged) bleed heavily
  haemorrhaged *v* ▷ haemorrhage
  haemorrhages *n, v* ▷ haemorrhage

haemorrhaging v ▷ haemorrhage

haemorrhoids [hem-or-oydz] pl n swollen veins in the anus (also **piles**)

hafnium n (pl **-s**) (CHEM) metallic element found in zirconium ores

hafniums n ▷ hafnium

haft n (pl **-s**) handle of an axe, knife, or dagger

hafts n ▷ haft

hag n (pl **-s**) ugly old woman

haggard adj looking tired and ill

haggis n (pl **-es**) Scottish dish made from sheep's offal, oatmeal, suet, and seasonings, boiled in a bag made from the sheep's stomach

haggises n ▷ haggis

haggle v (**-les**, **-ling**, **-led**) bargain or wrangle over a price

haggled v ▷ haggle

haggles v ▷ haggle

haggling v ▷ haggle

hagiographies n ▷ hagiography

hagiography n (pl **-phies**) writing about the lives of the saints

hags n ▷ hag

hail[1] n (pl **-s**) (shower of) small pellets of ice ▶ v (**-s**, **-ing**, **-ed**) fall as or like hail > **hailstone** n (pl **-s**)

hail[2] v (**-s**, **-ing**, **-ed**) call out to, greet

hailed v ▷ hail[1,2]

hailing v ▷ hail[1,2]

hails v ▷ hail[1,2] ▶ n ▷ hail[1]

hailstone n ▷ hail[1]

hailstones n ▷ hail[1]

hair n (pl **hairs**) threadlike growth on the skin

hairclip n (pl **-s**) small bent metal hairpin

hairclips n ▷ hairclip

hairdo n (pl **-s**) (Informal) hairstyle

hairdos n ▷ hairdo

hairdresser n (pl **-s**) person who cuts and styles hair

hairdressers n ▷ hairdresser

hairgrip n (BRIT) (pl **-s**) ▷ hairclip

hairgrips n ▷ hairgrip

hairier adj ▷ hairy

hairiest adj ▷ hairy

hairiness n ▷ hairy

hairinesses n ▷ hairy

hairline n (pl **-s**) edge of hair at the top of the forehead ▶ adj very fine or narrow

hairlines n ▷ hairline

hairpin n (pl **-s**) U-shaped wire used to hold the hair in place

hairpins n ▷ hairpin

hairs n ▷ hair

hairsplitting n (pl **-s**) ▶ adj making petty

distinctions

hairsplittings n ▷ hairsplitting

hairstyle n (pl **-s**) cut and arrangement of a person's hair

hairstyles n ▷ hairstyle

hairy adj (**-rier**, **-riest**) covered with hair > **hairiness** n (pl **-es**)

> **haj** n. Haj is the same as **hajj**. This is a very useful word, especially when there isn't much space on the board. Remember that this spelling doesn't have a plural form. Haj scores 13 points.

hajj n (pl **-es**) pilgrimage a Muslim makes to Mecca

hajjes n ▷ hajj

haka n (pl **-s**) (NZ) ceremonial Maori dance with chanting

hakas n ▷ haka

hake n (pl **hakes**) edible sea fish of N hemisphere (AUST) ▷ barracouta

hakea [hah-kee-a] n (pl **-s**) Australian tree or shrub with hard woody fruit

hakeas n ▷ hakea

hakes n ▷ hake

halal n (pl **-s**) meat from animals slaughtered according to Muslim law

halals n ▷ halal

halberd n (pl **-s**) (HIST) spear with an axe blade

halberds n ▷ halberd

halcyon [hal-see-on] adj peaceful and happy

hale adj (**-ler**, **-lest**) healthy, robust

haler adj ▷ hale

halest adj ▷ hale

half n (pl **-lves**) either of two equal parts ▶ adj denoting one of two equal parts ▶ adv to the extent of half

halfhearted adj unenthusiastic

halflife n (pl **-ves**) time taken for half the atoms in radioactive material to decay

halflives n ▷ halflife

halfpennies n ▷ halfpenny

halfpenny [hayp-nee] n (pl **-nnies**) former British coin worth half an old penny

halftime n (pl **-s**) (SPORT) short rest period between two halves of a game

halftimes n ▷ halftime

halftone n (pl **-s**) illustration showing lights and shadows by means of very small dots

halftones n ▷ halftone

halfway adv, adj at or to half the distance

halfwit n (pl **-s**) foolish or stupid person

halfwits n ▷ halfwit

halibut n (pl **halibuts**) large edible flatfish of N Atlantic

halibuts n ▷ halibut

halitosis n (pl **-ises**) unpleasant-smelling breath
  halitosises n ▷ halitosis
hall n (pl **-s**) (also **hallway**) entrance passage
hallelujah [hal-ee-loo-ya] interj exclamation of praise to God
hallmark n (pl **-s**) typical feature ▸ v (**-s, -ing, -ed**) stamp with a hallmark
  hallmarked v ▷ hallmark
  hallmarking v ▷ hallmark
  hallmarks n, v ▷ hallmark
hallo interj ▷ hello
hallowed adj regarded as holy
Halloween, Hallowe'en n (pl **-s**) October 31, celebrated by children by dressing up as ghosts, witches, etc.
  Halloweens n ▷ Halloween
  halls n ▷ hall
hallucinate v (**-tes, -ting, -ted**) seem to see something that is not really there
  > **hallucination** n (pl **-s**) > **hallucinatory** adj
  hallucinated v ▷ hallucinate
  hallucinates v ▷ hallucinate
  hallucinating v ▷ hallucinate
  hallucination n ▷ hallucinate
  hallucinations n ▷ hallucinate
  hallucinatory adj ▷ hallucinate
hallucinogen n (pl **-s**) drug that causes hallucinations > **hallucinogenic** adj
  hallucinogenic adj ▷ hallucinogen
  hallucinogens n ▷ hallucinogen
halo [hay-loh] n (pl **-loes, -los**) ring of light round the head of a sacred figure
  haloes n ▷ halo
halogen [hal-oh-jen] n (pl **-s**) (CHEM) any of a group of nonmetallic elements including chlorine and iodine
  halogens n ▷ halogen
  halos n ▷ halo
halt v (**-s, -ing, -ed**) come or bring to a stop ▸ n (pl **-s**) temporary stop
  halted v ▷ halt
halter n (pl **-s**) strap round a horse's head with a rope to lead it with
halterneck n (pl **-s**) woman's top or dress with a strap fastened at the back of the neck
  halternecks n ▷ halterneck
  halters n ▷ halter
halting adj hesitant, uncertain ▸ v ▷ halt
  halts v, n ▷ halt
halve v (**-ves, -ving, -ved**) divide in half
  halved v ▷ halve
  halves v ▷ halve ▸ n ▷ half
  halving v ▷ halve
halyard n (pl **-s**) rope for raising a ship's sail or flag
  halyards n ▷ halyard
ham[1] n (pl **-s**) smoked or salted meat from a pig's thigh
ham[2] (Informal) n (pl **-s**) amateur radio operator ▸ v (**-s, -mming, -mmed**) overact
hamburger n (pl **-s**) minced beef shaped into a flat disc, cooked and usu. served in a bread roll
  hamburgers n ▷ hamburger
hamlet n (pl **-s**) small village
  hamlets n ▷ hamlet
  hammed v ▷ ham[2]
hammer n (pl **-s**) tool with a heavy metal head and a wooden handle, used to drive in nails etc. ▸ v (**-s, -ing, -ed**) hit (as if) with a hammer
  hammered v ▷ hammer
hammerhead n (pl **-s**) shark with a wide flattened head
  hammerheads n ▷ hammerhead
  hammering v ▷ hammer
  hammers n, v ▷ hammer
  hamming v ▷ ham[2]
hammock n (pl **-s**) hanging bed made of canvas or net
  hammocks n ▷ hammock
hamper[1] v (**-s, -ing, -ed**) make it difficult for (someone or something) to move or progress
hamper[2] n (pl **-s**) large basket with a lid
  hampered v ▷ hamper[1]
  hampering v ▷ hamper[1]
  hampers v, n ▷ hamper[1, 2]
  hams n, v ▷ ham[1, 2]
hamster n (pl **-s**) small rodent with a short tail and cheek pouches
  hamsters n ▷ hamster
hamstring n (pl **-s**) tendon at the back of the knee ▸ v (**-s, -ing, -rung**) make it difficult for (someone) to take any action
  hamstringing v ▷ hamstring
  hamstrings n, v ▷ hamstring
  hamstrung v ▷ hamstring
hand n (pl **-s**) part of the body at the end of the arm, consisting of a palm, four fingers, and a thumb ▸ v (**-s, -ing, -ed**) pass, give
handbag n (pl **-s**) woman's small bag for carrying personal articles in
  handbags n ▷ handbag
handbill n (pl **-s**) small printed notice
  handbills n ▷ handbill
handbook n (pl **-s**) small reference or instruction book
  handbooks n ▷ handbook
handcuff n (pl **-s**) one of a linked pair of metal rings designed to be locked round a

prisoner's wrists by the police ▶ v (-s, -ing, -ed) put handcuffs on
handcuffed v ▷ handcuff
handcuffing v ▷ handcuff
handcuffs n, v ▷ handcuff
handed v ▷ hand
handful n (pl -s) amount that can be held in the hand
handfuls n ▷ handful
handheld adj (of a film camera) held rather than mounted, as in close-up action shots ▶ n (pl -s) computer that can be held in the hand
handhelds n ▷ handheld
handicap n (pl -s) physical or mental disability ▶ v (-s, -pping, -pped) make it difficult for (someone) to do something
handicapped v ▷ handicap
handicapping v ▷ handicap
handicaps n, v ▷ handicap
handicraft n (pl -s) objects made by hand
handicrafts n ▷ handicraft
handier adj ▷ handy
handiest adj ▷ handy
handily adv ▷ handy
handing v ▷ hand
handiwork n (pl -s) result of someone's work or activity
handiworks n ▷ handiwork
handkerchief n (pl -s) small square of fabric used to wipe the nose
handkerchiefs n ▷ handkerchief
handle n (pl -s) part of an object that is held so that it can be used ▶ v (-les, -ling, -led) hold, feel, or move with the hands
handlebars pl n curved metal bar used to steer a cycle
handled v ▷ handle
handler n (pl -s) person who controls an animal
handlers n ▷ handler
handles n, v ▷ handle
handling v ▷ handle
handout n (pl -s) clothing, food, or money given to a needy person
handouts n ▷ handout
hands n, v ▷ hand
handsome adj (esp. of a man) good-looking
handstand n (pl -s) act of supporting the body on the hands in an upside-down position
handstands n ▷ handstand
handwriting n (pl -s) (style of) writing by hand
handwritings n ▷ handwriting
handy adj (-dier, -diest) convenient, useful > **handily** adv
handyman n (pl -men) man who is good at

making or repairing things
handymen n ▷ handyman
hang v (-s, -ing, hung or hanged) attach or be attached at the top with the lower part free
hangar n (pl -s) large shed for storing aircraft
hangars n ▷ hangar
hangdog adj guilty, ashamed
hanged v ▷ hang
hanger n (pl -s) curved piece of wood, wire, or plastic, with a hook, for hanging up clothes (also **coat hanger**)
hangers n ▷ hanger
hangi n (pl -gi, -gis) (NZ) Maori oven consisting of a hole in the ground filled with hot stones
hanging v ▷ hang
hangis n ▷ hangi
hangman n (pl -men) man who executes people by hanging
hangmen n ▷ hangman
hangover n (pl -s) headache and nausea as a result of drinking too much alcohol
hangovers n ▷ hangover
hangs v ▷ hang
hangup n (pl -s) (Informal) emotional or psychological problem
hangups n ▷ hangup
hank n (pl -s) coil, esp. of yarn
hanker v (-s, -ing, -ed) (foll. by after or for) desire intensely
hankered v ▷ hanker
hankering v ▷ hanker
hankers v ▷ hanker
hankie n ▷ hanky
hankies n ▷ hanky
hanks n ▷ hank
hanky, hankie n (pl hankies) (Informal) handkerchief
haphazard adj not organized or planned > **haphazardly** adv
haphazardly adv ▷ haphazard
hapless adj unlucky
happen v (-s, -ing, -ed) take place, occur
happened v ▷ happen
happening n (pl -s) event, occurrence ▶ v ▷ happen
happenings n ▷ happening
happens v ▷ happen
happier adj ▷ happy
happiest adj ▷ happy
happily adv ▷ happy
happiness n ▷ happy
happinesses n ▷ happiness
happy adj (-ppier, -ppiest) feeling or causing joy > **happily** adv > **happiness** n (pl -es)
harangue v (-gues, -guing, -gued) address

angrily or forcefully ▶ n (pl **-gues**) angry or forceful speech
  harangued v ▷ harangue
  harangues v, n ▷ harangue
  haranguing v ▷ harangue
harass v (**-es, -ing, -ssed**) annoy or trouble constantly > **harassed** adj > **harassment** n (pl **-s**)
  harassed v, adj ▷ harass
  harasses v ▷ harass
  harassing v ▷ harass
  harassment n ▷ harass
  harassments n ▷ harassment
harbinger [har-binj-a] n (pl **-s**) someone or something that announces the approach of something
  harbingers n ▷ harbinger
harbour n (pl **-s**) sheltered port ▶ v (**-s, -ing, -ed**) maintain secretly in the mind
  harboured v ▷ harbour
  harbouring v ▷ harbour
  harbours n, v ▷ harbour
hard adj firm, solid, or rigid ▶ adv with great energy or effort > **harden** v (**-s, -ing, -ed**) > **hardness** n (pl **-es**)
hardboard n (pl ▷ **-s**) thin stiff board made of compressed sawdust and wood chips
  hardboards n ▷ hardboard
  harden v ▷ hard
  hardened v ▷ hard
  hardening v ▷ hard
  hardens v ▷ hard
hardfill n (pl **-s**) (NZ & S AFR) stone waste material used for landscaping
  hardfills n ▷ hardfill
hardheaded adj shrewd, practical
hardhearted adj unsympathetic, uncaring
  hardier adj ▷ hardy
  hardiest adj ▷ hardy
  hardiness n ▷ hardy
  hardinesses n ▷ hardy
hardly adv scarcely or not at all
  hardness n ▷ hard
  hardnesses n ▷ hard
hardship n (pl **-s**) suffering
  hardships n ▷ hardship
hardware n (pl **-s**) metal tools or implements
  hardwares n ▷ hardware
hardwood n (pl **-s**) wood of a broadleaved tree such as oak or ash
  hardwoods n ▷ hardwood
hardy adj (**-dier, -diest**) able to stand difficult conditions > **hardiness** n (pl **-es**)
hare n (pl **-s**) animal like a large rabbit, with longer ears and legs ▶ v (**-res, -ring, -red**) (usu.

foll. by **off**) run (away) quickly
harebell n (pl **-s**) blue bell-shaped flower
  harebells n ▷ harebell
harebrained adj foolish or impractical
  hared v ▷ hare
harelip n (pl **-s**) slight split in the upper lip
  harelips n ▷ harelip
harem n (pl **-s**) (apartments of) a Muslim man's wives and concubines
  harems n ▷ harem
  hares v, n ▷ hare
  haring v ▷ hare
hark v (**-s, -ing, -ed**) (Old-fashioned) listen
  harked v ▷ hark
  harking v ▷ hark
  harks v ▷ hark
harlequin n (pl **-s**) stock comic character with a diamond-patterned costume and mask ▶ adj in many colours
  harlequins n ▷ harlequin
harlot n (pl **-s**) (Lit) prostitute
  harlots n ▷ harlot
harm v (**-s, -ing, -ed**) injure physically, mentally, or morally ▶ n (pl **-s**) physical, mental, or moral injury > **harmful** adj > **harmless** adj
  harmed v ▷ harm
  harmful adj ▷ harm
  harming v ▷ harm
  harmless adj ▷ harm
harmonic adj of harmony
harmonica n (pl **-s**) small wind instrument played by sucking and blowing
  harmonicas n ▷ harmonica
  harmonics n science of musical sounds
  harmonies n ▷ harmony
  harmonious adj ▷ harmony
  harmoniously adv ▷ harmony
harmonium n (pl **-s**) keyboard instrument like a small organ
  harmoniums n ▷ harmonium
  harmonization v ▷ harmonize
  harmonizations v ▷ harmonize
harmonize v (**-zes, -zing, -zed**) blend well together > **harmonization** n (pl **-s**)
  harmonized v ▷ harmonize
  harmonizes v ▷ harmonize
  harmonizing v ▷ harmonize
harmony n (pl **-nies**) peaceful agreement and cooperation > **harmonious** adj > **harmoniously** adv
  harms v, n ▷ harm
harness n (pl **-es**) arrangement of straps for attaching a horse to a cart or plough ▶ v (**-es, -ing, -ed**) put a harness on

harnessed v ▷ harness

harnesses n, v ▷ harness

harnessing v ▷ harness

harp n (pl -s) large triangular stringed instrument played with the fingers > **harpist** n (pl -s)

harpies n ▷ harpy

harpist n ▷ harp

harpists n ▷ harp

harpoon n (pl -s) barbed spear attached to a rope used for hunting whales ▸ v (-s, -ing, -ed) spear with a harpoon

harpooned v ▷ harpoon

harpooning v ▷ harpoon

harpoons n, v ▷ harpoon

harps n ▷ harp

harpsichord n (pl -s) stringed keyboard instrument

harpsichords n ▷ harpsichord

harpy n (pl -pies) nasty or bad-tempered woman

harridan n (pl -s) nagging or vicious woman

harridans n ▷ harridan

harried v ▷ harry

harrier n (pl -s) cross-country runner

harriers n ▷ harrier

harries v ▷ harry

harrow n (pl -s) implement used to break up lumps of soil ▸ v (-s, -ing, -ed) draw a harrow over

harrowed v ▷ harrow

harrowing adj very distressing ▸ v ▷ harrow

harrows n, v ▷ harrow

harry v (-rries, -rrying, -rried) keep asking (someone) to do something, pester

harrying v ▷ harry

harsh adj severe and difficult to cope with > **harshly** adv > **harshness** n (pl -es)

harshly adv ▷ harsh

harshness n ▷ harsh

harshnesses n ▷ harsh

hart n (pl -s) adult male deer

harts n ▷ hart

harvest n (pl -s) (season for) the gathering of crops ▸ v (-s, -ing, -ed) gather (a ripened crop) > **harvester** n (pl -s)

harvested v ▷ harvest

harvester n ▷ harvest

harvesters n ▷ harvest

harvesting v ▷ harvest

harvests n, v ▷ harvest

has v ▷ have

hash[1] n (pl -es) dish of diced cooked meat and vegetables reheated

hash[2] n (pl -es) (Informal) hashish

hashes n ▷ hash[1, 2]

hashish [hash-eesh] n (pl -es) drug made from the cannabis plant, smoked for its intoxicating effects

hashishes n ▷ hashish

hasp n (pl -s) clasp that fits over a staple and is secured by a bolt or padlock, used as a fastening

hasps n ▷ hasp

hassle (Informal) n (pl -s) trouble, bother ▸ v (-les, -ling, -led) bother or annoy

hassled v ▷ hassle

hassles n, v ▷ hassle

hassling v ▷ hassle

hassock n (pl -s) cushion for kneeling on in church

hassocks n ▷ hassock

haste n (pl -s) (excessive) quickness

hasten v (-s, -ing, -ed) (cause to) hurry

hastened v ▷ hasten

hastening v ▷ hasten

hastens n ▷ hasten

hastes n ▷ haste

hastier adj ▷ hasty

hastiest adj ▷ hasty

hastily adv ▷ hasty

hasty adj (-tier, -tiest) (too) quick > **hastily** adv

hat n (pl -s) covering for the head, often with a brim, usu. worn to give protection from the weather

hatch[1] v (-es, -ing, -ed) (cause to) emerge from an egg

hatch[2] n (pl -es) hinged door covering an opening in a floor or wall

hatchback n (pl -s) car with a lifting door at the back

hatchbacks n ▷ hatchback

hatched v ▷ hatch[1]

hatches v ▷ hatch[1] ▸ n ▷ hatch[2]

hatchet n (pl -s) small axe

hatchets n ▷ hatchet

hatching v ▷ hatch[1]

hatchway n (pl -s) opening in the deck of a ship

hatchways n ▷ hatchway

hate v (-tes, -ting, -ted) dislike intensely ▸ n (pl -s) intense dislike > **hater** n (pl -s)

hated v ▷ hate

hateful adj causing or deserving hate

hater n ▷ hate

haters n ▷ hate

hates v, n ▷ hate

hating v ▷ hate

hatred n (pl -s) intense dislike

hatreds n ▷ hatred

hats *n* ▷ hat
haughtier *adj* ▷ haughty
haughtiest *adj* ▷ haughty
haughtily *adv* ▷ haughty
haughtiness *n* ▷ haughty
haughtinesses *n* ▷ haughty
haughty *adj* (-tier, -tiest) proud, arrogant > haughtily *adv* > haughtiness *n* (*pl* -es)
haul *v* (-s, -ing, -ed) pull or drag with effort ▶ *n* (*pl* -s) amount gained by effort or theft
haulage *n* (*pl* -s) (charge for) transporting goods
haulages *n* ▷ haulage
hauled *v* ▷ haul
haulier *n* (*pl* -s) firm or person that transports goods by road
hauliers *n* ▷ haulier
hauling *v* ▷ haul
hauls *v*, *n* ▷ haul
haunch *n* (*pl* -es) human hip or fleshy hindquarter of an animal
haunches *n* ▷ haunch
haunt *v* (-s, -ing, -ed) visit in the form of a ghost ▶ *n* (*pl* -s) place visited frequently
haunted *adj* frequented by ghosts ▶ *v* ▷ haunt
haunting *adj* memorably beautiful or sad ▶ *v* ▷ haunt
haunts *v*, *n* ▷ haunt
hauteur [oat-ur] *n* (*pl* -s) haughtiness
hauteurs *n* ▷ hauteur
have *v* (has, having, had) possess, hold
haven *n* (*pl* -s) place of safety
havens *n* ▷ haven
haversack *n* (*pl* -s) canvas bag carried on the back or shoulder
haversacks *n* ▷ haversack
having *v* ▷ have
havoc *n* (*pl* -s) disorder and confusion
havocs *n* ▷ havoc
haw *n* (*pl* -s) hawthorn berry
hawk[1] *n* (*pl* -s) bird of prey with a short hooked bill and very good eyesight > hawkish, hawklike *adj*
hawk[2] *v* (-s, -ing, -ed) offer (goods) for sale in the street or door-to-door > hawker *n* (*pl* -s)
hawk[3] *v* (-s, -ing, -ed) cough noisily
hawked *v* ▷ hawk[2, 3]
hawker *n* ▷ hawk[2]
hawkers *n* ▷ hawk[2]
hawk-eyed *adj* having very good eyesight
hawking *v* ▷ hawk[2, 3]
hawkish *adj* ▷ hawk[1]
hawks *n* ▷ hawk[1] ▶ *v* ▷ hawk[2, 3]
hawklike *adj* ▷ hawk[1]
haws *n* ▷ haw

hawser *n* (*pl* -s) large rope used on a ship
hawsers *n* ▷ hawser
hawthorn *n* (*pl* -s) thorny shrub or tree
hawthorns *n* ▷ hawthorn
hay *n* (*pl* hays) grass cut and dried as fodder
hays *n* ▷ hay
haystack *n* (*pl* -s) large pile of stored hay
haystacks *n* ▷ haystack
haywire *adj* (*Informal*) not functioning properly
hazard *n* (*pl* -s) something that could be dangerous ▶ *v* (-s, -ing, -ed) put in danger > hazardous *adj*
hazarded *v* ▷ hazard
hazarding *v* ▷ hazard
hazardous *adj* ▷ hazard
hazards *n*, *v* ▷ hazard
haze *n* (*pl* -s) mist, often caused by heat
hazel *n* (*pl* -s) small tree producing edible nuts ▶ *adj* (of eyes) greenish-brown > hazelnut *n* (*pl* -s)
hazelnut *n* ▷ hazel
hazelnuts *n* ▷ hazel
hazels *n* ▷ hazel
hazes *n* ▷ haze
hazier *adj* ▷ hazy
haziest *adj* ▷ hazy
hazy *adj* (-zier, -ziest) not clear, misty
he *pron* refers to: male person or animal ▶ *n* (*pl* -s) male person or animal
head *n* (*pl* -s) upper or front part of the body, containing the sense organs and the brain ▶ *adj* chief, principal ▶ *v* (-s, -ing, -ed) be at the top or front of
headache *n* (*pl* -s) continuous pain in the head
headaches *n* ▷ headache
headboard *n* (*pl* -s) vertical board at the top end of a bed
headboards *n* ▷ headboard
headdress *n* (*pl* -s) decorative head covering
headdresses *n* ▷ headdress
headed *v* ▷ head
header *n* (*pl* -s) striking a ball with the head
headers *n* ▷ header
headhunt *v* (-s, -ing, -ed) (of a company) approach and offer a job to (a person working for a rival company) > headhunter *n* (*pl* -s)
headhunted *v* ▷ headhunt
headhunter *n* ▷ headhunt
headhunters *n* ▷ headhunt
headhunting *v* ▷ headhunt
headhunts *v* ▷ headhunt
headier *adj* ▷ heady
headiest *adj* ▷ heady
heading *n* (*pl* -s) title written or printed at the top of a page ▶ *v* ▷ head

headings n ▷ heading

headland n (pl -s) area of land jutting out into the sea

headlands n ▷ headland

headlight n (pl -s) powerful light on the front of a vehicle

headlights n ▷ headlight

headline n (pl -s) title at the top of a newspaper article, esp. on the front page

headlines n ▷ headline ▶ pl n main points of a news broadcast

headlong adv, adj with the head first

headphones pl n two small loudspeakers held against the ears

headquarters pl n centre from which operations are directed

heads adv (Informal) with the side of a coin which has a portrait of a head on it uppermost ▶ n, v ▷ head

headstone n (pl -s) memorial stone on a grave

headstones n ▷ headstone

headstrong adj self-willed, obstinate

headway n (pl -s) progress

headways n ▷ headway

headwind n (pl -s) wind blowing against the course of an aircraft or ship

headwinds n ▷ headwind

heady adj (-dier, -diest) intoxicating or exciting

heal v (-s, -ing, -ed) make or become well > healer n (pl -s)

healed v ▷ heal

healer n ▷ heal

healers n ▷ heal

healing v ▷ heal

heals v ▷ heal

health n (pl -s) normal (good) condition of someone's body

healthier adj ▷ healthy

healthiest adj ▷ healthy

healthily adv ▷ healthy

healths n ▷ health

healthy adj (-thier, -thiest) having good health > healthily adv

heap n (pl -s) pile of things one on top of another ▶ v (-s, -ing, -ed) gather into a pile

heaped v ▷ heap

heaping v ▷ heap

heaps n, v ▷ heap

hear v (-s, -ing, heard) perceive (a sound) by ear > hearer n (pl -s)

heard v ▷ hear

hearer n ▷ hear

hearers n ▷ hear

hearing n (pl -s) ability to hear ▶ v ▷ hear

hearings n ▷ hearing

hears v ▷ hear

hearsay n (pl -s) gossip, rumour

hearsays n ▷ hearsay

hearse n (pl -s) funeral car used to carry a coffin

hearses n ▷ hearse

heart n (pl -s) organ that pumps blood round the body

heartache n (pl -s) intense anguish

heartaches n ▷ heartache

heartbeat n (pl -s) one complete pulsation of the heart

heartbeats n ▷ heartbeat

heartbreak n (pl -s) intense grief

heartbreaks n ▷ heartbreak

heartburn n (pl -s) burning sensation in the chest caused by indigestion

heartburns n ▷ heartburn

hearten v (-s, -ing, -ed) encourage, make cheerful

heartened v ▷ hearten

heartening v ▷ hearten

heartens v ▷ hearten

heartfelt adj felt sincerely or strongly

hearth n (pl -s) floor of a fireplace

hearths n ▷ hearth

heartier adj ▷ hearty

heartiest adj ▷ hearty

heartily adv ▷ hearty

heartless adj cruel, unkind

heartrending adj causing great sorrow

hearts n ▷ heart

heartthrob n (pl -s) (Slang) very attractive man, esp. a film or pop star

heartthrobs n ▷ heartthrob

hearty adj (-tier, -tiest) substantial, nourishing > heartily adv

heat v (-s, -ing, -ed) make or become hot ▶ n (pl -s) state of being hot > heater n (pl -s)

heated v ▷ heat ▶ adj angry and excited > heatedly adv

heatedly adv ▷ heated

heater n ▷ heat

heaters n ▷ heat

heath n (pl -s) (BRIT) area of open uncultivated land

heathen adj, n (pl -s) (of) a person who does not believe in an established religion

heathens n ▷ heathen

heather n (pl -s) low-growing plant with small purple, pinkish, or white flowers, growing on heaths and mountains

heathers n ▷ heather

heaths n ▷ heath

heating v ▷ heat

heats v, n ▷ heat

heave v (-ves, -ving, -ved) lift with effort ▶ n (pl -s) heaving

heaved v ▷ heave

heaven n (pl -s) place believed to be the home of God, where good people go when they die

heavenly adj of or like heaven

heavens n ▷ heaven

heaves v, n ▷ heave

heavier adj ▷ heavy

heaviest adj ▷ heavy

heavily adv ▷ heavy

heaviness n ▷ heavy

heavinesses n ▷ heavy

heaving v ▷ heave

heavy adj (-vier, -viest) of great weight > heavily adv > heaviness n (pl -es)

heavyweight n (pl -s) boxer weighing over 175lb (professional) or 81kg (amateur)

heavyweights n ▷ heavyweight

heckle v (-les, -ling, -led) interrupt (a public speaker) with comments, questions, or taunts > heckler n (pl -s)

heckled v ▷ heckle

heckler n ▷ heckle

hecklers n ▷ heckle

heckles v ▷ heckle

heckling v ▷ heckle

hectare n (pl -s) one hundred ares or 10 000 square metres (2.471 acres)

hectares n ▷ hectare

hectic adj rushed or busy

hector v (-s, -ing, -ed) bully

hectored v ▷ hector

hectoring v ▷ hector

hectors v ▷ hector

hedge n (pl -s) row of bushes forming a barrier or boundary ▶ v (-ges, -ging, -ged) be evasive or noncommittal

hedged v ▷ hedge

hedgehog n (pl -s) small mammal with a protective covering of spines

hedgehogs n ▷ hedgehog

hedgerow n (pl -s) bushes forming a hedge

hedgerows n ▷ hedgerow

hedges n, v ▷ hedge

hedging v ▷ hedge

hedonism n (pl -s) doctrine that pleasure is the most important thing in life > hedonist n (pl -s) > hedonistic adj

hedonisms n ▷ hedonism

hedonist n ▷ hedonism

hedonistic n ▷ hedonism

hedonists n ▷ hedonism

heed n (pl -s) careful attention ▶ v (-s, -ing, -ed)

pay careful attention to

heeded v ▷ heed

heeding v ▷ heed

heedless adj taking no notice of

heeds v, n ▷ heed

heel¹ n (pl -s) back part of the foot ▶ v (-s, -ing, -ed) repair the heel of (a shoe)

heel² v (-s, -ing, -ed) (foll. by over) lean to one side

heeled v ▷ heel¹, ²

heeler n (pl -s) (AUST & NZ) dog that herds cattle by biting at their heels

heelers n ▷ heeler

heeling v ▷ heel¹, ²

heels n ▷ heel¹ ▶ v ▷ heel¹, ²

heftier adj ▷ hefty

heftiest adj ▷ hefty

hefty adj (-tier, -tiest) large, heavy, or strong

hegemonies n ▷ hegemony

hegemony [hig-em-on-ee] n (pl -nies) political domination

hegira n (pl -s) Mohammed's flight from Mecca to Medina in 622 AD

hegiras n ▷ hegira

heifer [hef-fer] n (pl -s) young cow

heifers n ▷ heifer

height n (pl -s) distance from base to top

heighten v (-s, -ing, -ed) make or become higher or more intense

heightened v ▷ heighten

heightening v ▷ heighten

heightens v ▷ heighten

heights n ▷ height

heinous adj evil and shocking

heir n (pl -s) person entitled to inherit property or rank > heiress n fem (pl -es)

heiresses n ▷ heiress

heirloom n (pl -s) object that has belonged to a family for generations

heirlooms n ▷ heirloom

heirs n ▷ heir

held v ▷ hold¹

helical adj spiral

helices n ▷ helix

helicopter n (pl -s) aircraft lifted and propelled by rotating overhead blades

helicopters n ▷ helicopter

heliotrope n (pl -s) plant with purple flowers ▶ adj light purple

heliotropes n ▷ heliotrope

heliport n (pl -s) airport for helicopters

heliports n ▷ heliport

helium [heel-ee-um] n (pl -s) (CHEM) very light colourless odourless gas

heliums n ▷ helium

helix [heel-iks] n (pl -ices, -ixes) spiral
helixes n ▷ helix
hell n (pl -s) place believed to be where wicked people go when they die ▷ hellish adj
hellbent adj (foll. by **on**) intent
hellish adj ▷ hell
hello interj expression of greeting or surprise
hells n ▷ hell
helm n (pl -s) tiller or wheel for steering a ship
helmet n (pl -s) hard hat worn for protection
helmets n ▷ helmet
helms n ▷ helm
help v (-s, -ing, -ed) make something easier, better, or quicker for (someone) ▶ n (pl -s) assistance or support ▷ **helper** n (pl -s) ▷ **helpful** adj
helped v ▷ help
helper n ▷ help
helpers n ▷ help
helpful adj ▷ help
helping n (pl -s) single portion of food ▶ v ▷ help
helpings n ▷ helping
helpless adj weak or incapable ▷ **helplessly** adv
helplessly adv ▷ helpless
helpline n (pl -s) telephone line set aside for callers to contact an organization for help with a problem
helplines n ▷ helpline
helpmate n (pl -s) companion and helper, esp. a husband or wife
helpmates n ▷ helpmate
helps v, n ▷ help
hem n (pl -s) bottom edge of a garment, folded under and stitched down ▶ v (-s, -mming, -mmed) provide with a hem
hemisphere n (pl -s) half of a sphere, esp. the earth ▷ **hemispherical** adj
hemispheres n ▷ hemisphere
hemline n (pl -s) level to which the hem of a skirt hangs
hemlines n ▷ hemline
hemlock n (pl -s) poison made from a plant with spotted stems and small white flowers
hemlocks n ▷ hemlock
hemmed v ▷ hem
hemming v ▷ hem
hemp n (pl -s) (also **cannabis**) Asian plant with tough fibres
hemps n ▷ hemp
hems n, v ▷ hem
hen n (pl -s) female domestic fowl
hence conj for this reason ▶ adv from this time
henceforth adv from now on
henchman n (pl -men) person employed by

someone powerful to carry out orders
henchmen n ▷ henchman
henna n (pl -s) reddish dye made from a shrub or tree ▶ v (-s, -ing, -ed) dye (the hair) with henna
hennaed v ▷ henna
hennaing v ▷ henna
hennas n, v ▷ henna
henpecked adj (of a man) dominated by his wife
henries n ▷ henry
henry n (pl -ries, -rys) unit of electrical inductance
henrys n ▷ henry
hens n ▷ hen
hepatitis n (pl -es) inflammation of the liver
hepatitises n ▷ hepatitis
heptagon n (pl -s) geometric figure with seven sides
heptagons n ▷ heptagon
heptathlon n (pl -s) athletic contest for women, involving seven events
heptathlons n ▷ heptathlon
her pron refers to a female person or animal or anything personified as feminine when the object of a sentence or clause ▶ adj belonging to her
herald n (pl -s) person who announces important news ▶ v (-s, -ing, -ed) signal the approach of
heralded v ▷ herald
heraldic adj ▷ heraldry
heralding v ▷ herald
heraldries n ▷ heraldry
heraldry n (pl -ries) study of coats of arms and family trees ▷ **heraldic** adj
heralds n, v ▷ herald
herb n (pl -s) plant used for flavouring in cookery, and in medicine ▷ **herbal** adj
herbaceous adj (of a plant) soft-stemmed
herbal adj ▷ herb
herbalist n (pl -s) person who grows or specializes in the use of medicinal herbs
herbalists n ▷ herbalist
herbicide n (pl -s) chemical used to destroy plants, esp. weeds
herbicides n ▷ herbicide
herbivore n (pl -s) animal that eats only plants ▷ **herbivorous** [her-biv-or-uss] ▶ adj
herbivores n ▷ herbivore
herbivorous adj ▷ herbivore
herbs n ▷ herb
herculean [her-kew-lee-an] adj requiring great strength or effort
herd n (pl -s) group of animals feeding and

living together ▶ v (-s, -ing, -ed) collect into a herd

herded v ▷ herd

herding v ▷ herd

herds n, v ▷ herd

herdsman n (pl -men) man who looks after a herd of animals

herdsmen n ▷ herd

here adv in, at, or to this place or point

hereabouts adv near here

hereafter adv after this point or time

hereby adv by means of or as a result of this

hereditary adj passed on genetically from one generation to another

heredities n ▷ heredity

heredity [hir-red-it-ee] n (pl -ties) passing on of characteristics from one generation to another

herein adv in this place, matter, or document

heresies n ▷ heresy

heresy [herr-iss-ee] n (pl -sies) opinion contrary to accepted opinion or belief

heretic [herr-it-ik] n (pl -s) person who holds unorthodox opinions > **heretical** [hir-ret-ik-al] ▶ adj

heretical n ▷ heretic

heretics n ▷ heretic

herewith adv with this

heritage n (pl -s) something inherited

heritages n ▷ heritage

hermaphrodite [her-maf-roe-dite] n (pl -s) animal, plant, or person with both male and female reproductive organs

hermaphrodites n ▷ hermaphrodite

hermetic adj sealed so as to be airtight > **hermetically** adv

hermetically adv ▷ hermetic

hermit n (pl -s) person living in solitude, esp. for religious reasons

hermitage n (pl -s) home of a hermit

hermitages n ▷ hermitage

hermits n ▷ hermit

hernia n (pl -s) protrusion of an organ or part through the lining of the surrounding body cavity

hernias n ▷ hernia

hero n (pl -es) principal character in a film, book, etc. > **heroine** n fem (pl -s) > **heroism** [herr-oh-izz-um] n (pl -s)

heroes n ▷ hero

heroic adj courageous > **heroically** adv

heroically adv ▷ heroic

heroics pl n extravagant behaviour

heroin n (pl -s) highly addictive drug derived from morphine

heroine n ▷ hero

heroines n ▷ hero

heroins n ▷ heroin

heroism n ▷ hero

heroisms n ▷ hero

heron n (pl -s) long-legged wading bird

herons n ▷ heron

herpes [her-peez] n (pl -es) any of several inflammatory skin diseases, including shingles and cold sores

herpeses n ▷ herpes

herring n (pl -s) important food fish of northern seas

herringbone n (pl -s) pattern of zigzag lines

herringbones n ▷ herringbone

herrings n ▷ herring

hertz n (pl -es) (PHYSICS) unit of frequency

hertzes n ▷ hertz

hes n ▷ he

hesitancies n ▷ hesitant

hesitancy n ▷ hesitant

hesitant adj undecided or wavering > **hesitantly** adv > **hesitancy** n (pl -cies)

hesitantly adv ▷ hesitant

hesitate v (-tes, -ting, -ted) be slow or uncertain in doing something > **hesitation** n (pl -s)

hesitated v ▷ hesitate

hesitates v ▷ hesitate

hesitating v ▷ hesitate

hesitation n ▷ hesitate

hesitations n ▷ hesitate

hessian n (pl -s) coarse jute fabric

hessians n ▷ hessian

heterodox adj differing from accepted doctrines or beliefs > **heterodoxy** n (pl -xies)

heterodoxies n ▷ heterodox

heterodoxy n ▷ heterodox

heterogeneities n ▷ heterogeneous

heterogeneity n ▷ heterogeneous

heterogeneous [het-er-oh-jean-ee-uss] adj composed of diverse elements > **heterogeneity** n (pl -ties)

heterosexual n (pl -s) person sexually attracted to members of the opposite sex ▶ adj > **heterosexuality** n (pl -ties)

heterosexualities n ▷ heterosexual

heterosexuality n ▷ heterosexual

heterosexuals n ▷ heterosexual

heuristic [hew-rist-ik] adj involving learning by investigation

hew v (-s, -ing, -ed or hewn) cut with an axe

hewed v ▷ hew

hewing v ▷ hew

hewn v ▷ hew

hews v ▷ hew

hex n hexes. A hex is a curse or spell. This is a really useful word to remember when you have an X, as there is likely to be an E or H on the board already.

hexagon n (pl -s) geometrical figure with six sides ▷ **hexagonal** adj

hexagonal adj ▷ **hexagon**

hexagons n ▷ **hexagon**

hey interj expression of surprise or for catching attention

heyday n (pl -s) time of greatest success, prime

heydays n ▷ **heyday**

hi interj. Hi is an informal word for **hello**. This everyday word is worth keeping in mind when you want to form a word adjacent to a parallel word below or above. Hi scores 5 points.

hiatus [hie-ay-tuss] n (pl -tuses, -tus) pause or interruption in continuity

hiatuses n ▷ **hiatus**

hibernate v (-tes, -ting, -ted) (of an animal) pass the winter as if in a deep sleep > **hibernation** n (pl -s)

hibernated v ▷ **hibernate**

hibernates v ▷ **hibernate**

hibernating v ▷ **hibernate**

hibernation n ▷ **hibernate**

hibernations n ▷ **hibernate**

hibiscus n (pl -cuses) tropical plant with large brightly coloured flowers

hibiscuses n ▷ **hibiscus**

hiccough n, v ▷ **hiccup**

hiccoughed v ▷ **hiccup**

hiccoughing v ▷ **hiccup**

hiccoughs n, v ▷ **hiccup**

hiccup, hiccough n (pl -s) spasm of the breathing organs with a sharp coughlike sound (Informal) ▶ v (-s, -pping, -pped) make a hiccup

hiccupped v ▷ **hiccup**

hiccupping v ▷ **hiccup**

hiccups n, v ▷ **hiccup**

hick n (pl -s) (US, AUST & NZ) (Informal) unsophisticated country person

hickories n ▷ **hickory**

hickory n (pl -ries) N American nut-bearing tree

hicks n ▷ **hick**

hid v ▷ **hide¹**

hidden v ▷ **hide¹**

hide¹ v (-des, -ding, hid, hidden) put (oneself or an object) somewhere difficult to see or find ▶ n (pl -s) place of concealment, esp. for a bird-watcher

hide² n (pl -s) skin of an animal

hidebound adj unwilling to accept new ideas

hideous [hid-ee-uss] adj ugly, revolting > **hideously** adv

hideously adv ▷ **hideous**

hideout n (pl -s) place to hide in

hideouts n ▷ **hideout**

hides v ▷ **hide¹** ▶ n ▷ **hide¹, ²**

hiding n (pl -s) (Slang) severe beating ▶ v ▷ **hide¹**

hidings n ▷ **hiding**

hierarchical adj ▷ **hierarchy**

hierarchies n ▷ **hierarchy**

hierarchy [hire-ark-ee] n (pl -chies) system of people or things arranged in a graded order > **hierarchical** adj

hieroglyphic [hire-oh-gliff-ik] adj of a form of writing using picture symbols, as used in ancient Egypt ▶ n (pl -s) symbol that is difficult to decipher (also **hieroglyph**)

hieroglyphics n ▷ **hieroglyphic**

high adj (-er, -est) of a great height ▶ adv at or to a high level > **highly** adv

highbrow adj, n (pl -s) intellectual and serious (person)

highbrows n ▷ **highbrow**

higher adj ▷ **high**

highest adj ▷ **high**

highlands pl n area of high ground

highlight n (pl -s) outstanding part or feature ▶ v (-s, -ing, -ed) give emphasis to

highlighted v ▷ **highlight**

highlighting v ▷ **highlight**

highlights n, v ▷ **highlight**

highly adv ▷ **high**

highway n (pl -s) (US, AUST & NZ) main road

highwayman n (pl -men) (formerly) robber, usu. on horseback, who robbed travellers at gunpoint

highwaymen n ▷ **highwayman**

highways n ▷ **highway**

hijack v (-s, -ing, -ed) seize control of (an aircraft or other vehicle) while travelling > **hijacker** n (pl -s)

hijacked v ▷ **hijack**

hijacker n ▷ **hijack**

hijackers n ▷ **hijack**

hijacking v ▷ **hijack**

hijacks v ▷ **hijack**

hike n (pl -s) long walk in the country, esp. for pleasure ▶ v (-kes, -king, -ked) go for a long walk > **hiker** n (pl -s)

hiked v ▷ **hike**

hiker n ▷ **hike**

hikers n ▷ **hike**

hikes n, v ▷ hike

hiking v ▷ hike

hilarious adj very funny > **hilariously** adv
> **hilarity** n (pl -ties)

hilariously adv ▷ hilarious

hilarities n ▷ hilarious

hilarity n ▷ hilarious

hill n (pl -s) raised part of the earth's surface,
less high than a mountain > **hilly** adj (-lier,
-liest)

hillbillies n ▷ hillbilly

hillbilly n (pl -lies) (US) unsophisticated
country person

hillier adj ▷ hill

hilliest adj ▷ hill

hillock n (pl -s) small hill

hillocks n ▷ hillock

hills n ▷ hill

hilly adj ▷ hill

hilt n (pl -s) handle of a sword or knife

hilts n ▷ hilt

him pron refers to a male person or animal
when the object of a sentence or clause

hind[1] adj (-er, -most) situated at the back

hind[2] n (pl -s) female deer

hinder adj ▷ hind[1] ▶ v (-s, -ing, -ed) get in the
way of ▶ **hindrance** n (pl -s)

hindered v ▷ hinder

hindering v ▷ hinder

hinders v ▷ hinder

hindmost adj ▷ hind[1]

hindrance n ▷ hinder

hindrances n ▷ hinder

hinds n ▷ hind[2]

hinge n (pl -s) device for holding together two
parts so that one can swing freely ▶ v (-ges,
-ging, -ged) (foll. by on) depend (on)

hinged v ▷ hinge

hinges n, v ▷ hinge

hinging v ▷ hinge

hint n (pl -s) indirect suggestion ▶ v (-s, -ing,
-ed) suggest indirectly

hinted v ▷ hint

hinterland n (pl -s) land lying behind a coast or
near a city, esp. a port

hinterlands n ▷ hinterland

hinting v ▷ hint

hints n, v ▷ hint

hip[1] n (pl -s) either side of the body between
the pelvis and the thigh

hip[2] n (pl -s) rosehip

hippie adj, n (pl -s) ▷ hippy

hippies n ▷ hippie

hippo n (pl -ppos) (Informal) hippopotamus

hippodrome n (pl -s) music hall, variety
theatre, or circus

hippodromes n ▷ hippodrome

hippopotami n ▷ hippopotamus

hippopotamus n (pl -muses, -mi) large African
mammal with thick wrinkled skin, living
near rivers

hippopotamuses n ▷ hippopotamus

hippos n ▷ hippo

hippy adj, n (pl -ppies) (esp. in the 1960s) (of)
a person whose behaviour and dress imply a
rejection of conventional values

hips n ▷ hip[1, 2]

hire v (-res, -ring, -red) pay to have temporary
use of ▶ n (pl -s) hiring

hired v ▷ hire

hireling n (pl -s) person who works only for
wages

hirelings n ▷ hireling

hires v, n ▷ hire

hiring v ▷ hire

hirsute [her-suit] adj hairy

his pron, adj (something) belonging to him

hiss n (pl -es) sound like that of a long s (as an
expression of contempt) ▶ v (-es, -ing, -ed)
utter a hiss

hissed v ▷ hiss

hisses n, v ▷ hiss

hissing v ▷ hiss

histamine [hiss-ta-meen] n (pl -s) substance
released by the body tissues in allergic
reactions

histamines n ▷ histamine

histogram n (pl -s) statistical graph in which
the frequency of values is represented by
vertical bars of varying heights and widths

histograms n ▷ histogram

histologies n ▷ histology

histology n (pl -gies) study of the tissues of an
animal or plant

historian n (pl -s) writer of history

historians n ▷ historian

historic adj famous or significant in history

historical adj occurring in the past
> **historically** adv

historically adv ▷ historical

histories n ▷ history

history n (pl -ries) (record or account of) past
events and developments

histrionic adj excessively dramatic

histrionics pl n excessively dramatic
behaviour

hit v (-s, -tting, hit) strike, touch forcefully ▶ n
(pl -s) hitting ▶ adj sometimes successful and
sometimes not

hitch n (pl -es) minor problem ▶ v (-es, -ing, -ed)

(*Informal*) obtain (a lift) by hitchhiking
hitched v ▷ hitch
hitches n, v ▷ hitch
hitchhike v (**-kes, -king, -ked**) travel by obtaining free lifts ▷ **hitchhiker** n (pl **-s**)
hitchhiked n ▷ hitchhike
hitchhiker n ▷ hitchhike
hitchhikers n ▷ hitchhike
hitchhikes n ▷ hitchhike
hitchhiking n ▷ hitchhike
hitching v ▷ hitch
hither adv (*Old-fashioned*) to or towards this place
hitherto adv until this time
hits n, v ▷ hit
hitting v ▷ hit
hive n (pl **-s**) ▷ beehive
hives n ▷ hive

> **hm** or **hmm** interj. This is a noise that
> people make when they are thinking
> or considering something. Both forms
> of this word are useful because neither
> contains a vowel, which is great if
> you have no vowels on your rack. Hm
> scores 5 points, while hmm scores 8.
> **ho** interj. Ho is a noise people make
> when they laugh. This little word is
> useful when you want to go in two
> directions at once. It's also worth
> remembering that ho is oh backwards:
> if you can't use one, you might be able
> to use the other. Ho scores 5 points.

hoard n (pl **-s**) store hidden away for future use ▶ v (**-s, -ing, -ed**) save or store ▷ **hoarder** n (pl **-s**)
hoarded v ▷ hoard
hoarder n ▷ hoard
hoarders n ▷ hoard
hoarding n (pl **-s**) large board for displaying advertisements ▶ v ▷ hoard
hoardings n ▷ hoarding
hoards n, v ▷ hoard
hoarfrost n (pl **-s**) white ground frost
hoarfrosts n ▷ hoarfrost
hoarier adj ▷ hoary
hoariest adj ▷ hoary
hoarse adj (**-ser, -sest**) (of a voice) rough and unclear ▷ **hoarsely** adv ▷ **hoarseness** n (pl **-es**)
hoarsely adv ▷ hoarse
hoarseness n ▷ hoarse
hoarsenesses n ▷ hoarse
hoarsest adj ▷ hoarse
hoarsest adj ▷ hoarse
hoary adj (**-rier, -riest**) grey or white(-haired)
hoax n (pl **-es**) deception or trick ▶ v (**-es, -ing,**

-ed) deceive or play a trick upon ▷ **hoaxer** n
hoaxed v ▷ hoax
hoaxer n ▷ hoax
hoaxers n ▷ hoax
hoaxes n, v ▷ hoax
hoaxing v ▷ hoax
hob n (pl **-s**) (BRIT) flat top part of a cooker, or a separate flat surface, containing gas or electric rings for cooking on
hobbies n ▷ hobby
hobble v (**-les, -ling, -led**) walk lamely
hobbled v ▷ hobble
hobbles v ▷ hobble
hobbling v ▷ hobble
hobby n (pl **-bbies**) activity pursued in one's spare time
hobbyhorse n (pl **-s**) favourite topic
hobbyhorses n ▷ hobbyhorse
hobgoblin n (pl **-s**) mischievous goblin
hobgoblins n ▷ hobgoblin
hobnob v (**-s, -nobbing, -nobbed**) (foll. by **with**) be on friendly terms (with)
hobnobbed v ▷ hobnob
hobnobbing v ▷ hobnob
hobnobs v ▷ hobnob
hobo n (pl **-s**) (US, AUST & NZ) tramp or vagrant
hobos n ▷ hobo
hobs n ▷ hob
hock[1] n (pl **-s**) joint in the back leg of an animal such as a horse that corresponds to the human ankle
hock[2] n (pl **-s**) white German wine
hock[3] v (**-s, -ing, -ed**) (*Informal*) pawn
hocked v ▷ hock
hockey n (pl **-s**) team game played on a field with a ball and curved sticks
hockeys n ▷ hockey
hocking v ▷ hock
hocks n ▷ hock[1, 2] ▶ v ▷ hock[3]
hod n (pl **-s**) open wooden box attached to a pole, for carrying bricks or mortar
hods n ▷ hod
hoe n (pl **-s**) long-handled tool used for loosening soil or weeding ▶ v (**-oes, -oeing, -oed**) scrape or weed with a hoe
hoed v ▷ hoe
hoeing v ▷ hoe
hoes n, v ▷ hoe
hog n (pl **-s**) castrated male pig (*Informal*) ▶ v (**-s, -gging, -gged**) (*Informal*) take more than one's share of
hogged v ▷ hog
hogging v ▷ hog
hogmanay n (pl **-s**) (in Scotland) New Year's Eve

hogmanays n ▷ hogmanay
hogs n, v ▷ hog
hogshead n (pl -s) large cask
  hogsheads n ▷ hogshead
hogwash n (pl -es) (Informal) nonsense
  hogwashes n ▷ hogwash
hoick v (-s, -ing, -ed) raise abruptly and sharply
  hoicked v ▷ hoick
  hoicking v ▷ hoick
  hoicks v ▷ hoick
hoist v (-s, -ing, -ed) raise or lift up ▶ n (pl -s)
  device for lifting things
  hoisted v ▷ hoist
  hoisting v ▷ hoist
  hoists v, n ▷ hoist
hold[1] v (-s, -ing, held) keep or support in or
  with the hands or arms ▶ n (pl -s) act or way of
  holding ▶ **holder** n (pl -s)
hold[2] n (pl -s) cargo compartment in a ship
  or aircraft
holdall n (pl -s) large strong travelling bag
  holdalls n ▷ holdall
  holder n ▷ hold[1]
  holders n ▷ hold[1]
holding n (pl -s) property, such as land or
  stocks and shares ▶ v ▷ hold[1]
  holds n ▷ hold[1, 2], v ▷ hold[1]
holdup n (pl -s) armed robbery
  holdups n ▷ holdup
hole n (pl -s) area hollowed out in a solid ▶ v
  (-les, -ling, -led) make holes in
  holed v ▷ hole
  holes n, v ▷ hole
holiday n (pl -s) time spent away from home
  for rest or recreation
  holidays n ▷ holiday
  holier adj ▷ holy
  holiest adj ▷ holy
holiness n (pl -es) state of being holy
  holinesses n ▷ holiness
  holing v ▷ hole
  holisms n ▷ holism
holistic adj considering the complete person,
  physically and mentally, in the treatment of
  an illness > **holism** n (pl -s)
  hollies n ▷ holly
  holloganism n ▷ hooligan
hollow adj having a hole or space inside ▶ n
  (pl -s) cavity or space ▶ v (-s, -ing, -ed) form a
  hollow in
  hollowed v ▷ hollow
  hollowing v ▷ hollow
  hollows n, v ▷ hollow
holly n (pl -llies) evergreen tree with prickly
  leaves and red berries

hollyhock n (pl -s) tall garden plant with spikes
  of colourful flowers
  hollyhocks n ▷ hollyhock
holocaust n (pl -s) destruction or loss of life on
  a massive scale
  holocausts n ▷ holocaust
hologram n (pl -s) three-dimensional
  photographic image
  holograms n ▷ hologram
holograph n (pl -s) document handwritten by
  the author
  holographs n ▷ holograph
holster n (pl -s) leather case for a pistol, hung
  from a belt
  holsters n ▷ holster
holy adj (-lier, -liest) of God or a god
homage n (pl -s) show of respect or honour
  towards someone or something
  homages n ▷ homage
home n (pl -s) place where one lives ▶ adj of
  one's home, birthplace, or native country
  (SPORT) ▶ adv to or at home ▶ v (-mes, -ming,
  -med) (foll. by in or in on) direct towards
  (a point or target) > **homeward** adj, adv
  > **homewards** adv
  homed v ▷ home
homeland n (pl -s) country from which a
  person's ancestors came
  homelands n ▷ homeland
homeless adj having nowhere to live
  ▶ pl n people who have nowhere to live
  > **homelessness** n (pl -es)
  homelessness n ▷ homeless
  homelessnesses n ▷ homeless
  homelier adj ▷ homely
  homeliest adj ▷ homely
homely adj (-lier, -liest) simple, ordinary, and
  comfortable
homemade adj made at home or on the
  premises
homeopath n (pl -s) person who practises
  homeopathy > **homeopathic** adj
  homeopathic adj ▷ homeopath
  homeopathies n ▷ homeopathy
  homeopaths n ▷ homeopath
homeopathy [home-ee-op-ath-ee] n (pl -thies)
  treatment of disease by small doses of a drug
  that produces symptoms of the disease in
  healthy people
  homes n, v ▷ home
homesick adj sad because missing one's home
  and family > **homesickness** n (pl -es)
  homesickness n ▷ homesick
  homesicknesses n ▷ homesick
homeward adj, adv ▷ home

homewards adv ▷ **home**
homework n (pl **-s**) school work done at home
homeworks n ▷ **homework**
homicidal adj ▷ **homicide**
homicide n (pl **-s**) killing of a human being > **homicidal** adj
homicides n ▷ **homicide**
homilies n ▷ **homily**
homily n (pl **-lies**) speech telling people how they should behave
homing v ▷ **home**
hominid n (pl **-s**) man or any extinct forerunner of man
hominids n ▷ **hominid**
homogeneities n ▷ **homogeneous**
homogeneity n ▷ **homogeneous**
homogeneous [home-oh-**jean**-ee-uss] adj formed of similar parts > **homogeneity** n (pl **-ties**)
homogenize v (**-zes**, **-zing**, **-zed**) break up fat globules in (milk or cream) to distribute them evenly
homogenized v ▷ **homogenize**
homogenizes v ▷ **homogenize**
homogenizing v ▷ **homogenize**
homograph n (pl **-s**) word spelt the same as another, but with a different meaning
homographs n ▷ **homograph**
homologous [hom-**ol**-log-uss] adj having a related or similar position or structure
homonym n (pl **-s**) word spelt or pronounced the same as another, but with a different meaning
homonyms n ▷ **homonym**
homophobia n (pl **-s**) hatred or fear of homosexuals > **homophobic** adj
homophobias n ▷ **homophobia**
homophobic adj ▷ **homophobia**
homophone n (pl **-s**) word pronounced the same as another, but with a different meaning or spelling
homophones n ▷ **homophone**
homosexual n (pl **-s**) ▶ adj (person) sexually attracted to members of the same sex > **homosexuality** n (pl **-ties**)
homosexualities n ▷ **homosexual**
homosexuality n ▷ **homosexual**
homosexuals n ▷ **homosexual**
hone v (**-nes**, **-ning**, **-ned**) sharpen
honed v ▷ **hone**
hones v ▷ **hone**
honest adj (**-er**, **-est**) truthful and moral > **honestly** adv
honester adj ▷ **honest**
honestest adj ▷ **honest**

honesties n ▷ **honesty**
honestly adv ▷ **honest**
honesty n (pl **-ties**) quality of being honest
honey n (pl **-s**) sweet edible sticky substance made by bees from nectar
honeycomb n (pl **-s**) waxy structure of six-sided cells in which honey is stored by bees in a beehive
honeycombs n ▷ **honeycomb**
honeymoon n (pl **-s**) holiday taken by a newly married couple
honeymoons n ▷ **honeymoon**
honeys n ▷ **honey**
honeysuckle n (pl **-s**) climbing shrub with sweet-smelling flowers
honeysuckles n ▷ **honeysuckle**
hongi [hong-jee] n (pl **-s**) (NZ) Maori greeting in which people touch noses
hongis n ▷ **hongi**
honing v ▷ **hone**
honk n (pl **-s**) sound made by a car horn ▶ v (**-s**, **-ing**, **-ed**) (cause to) make this sound
honked v ▷ **honk**
honking v ▷ **honk**
honks n, v ▷ **honk**
honorary adj held or given only as an honour
honorific adj showing respect
honour n (pl **-s**) sense of honesty and fairness ▶ v (**-s**, **-ing**, **-ed**) give praise and attention to
honourable adj worthy of respect or esteem > **honourably** adv
honourably adv ▷ **honourable**
honoured v ▷ **honour**
honouring v ▷ **honour**
honours n, v ▷ **honour** ▶ pl n university degree of a higher standard than an ordinary degree
hood[1] n (pl **-s**) head covering, often attached to a coat or jacket
hood[2] n (pl **-s**) (CHIEFLY US) (Slang) hoodlum
hooded adj (of a garment) having a hood
hoodlum n (pl **-s**) (Slang) violent criminal, gangster
hoodlums n ▷ **hoodlum**
hoodoo n (pl **-s**) (cause of) bad luck
hoodoos n ▷ **hoodoo**
hoods n ▷ **hood**[1, 2]
hoodwink v (**-s**, **-ing**, **-ed**) trick, deceive
hoodwinked v ▷ **hoodwink**
hoodwinking v ▷ **hoodwink**
hoodwinks v ▷ **hoodwink**
hoof n (pl **hooves**, **hoofs**) horny covering of the foot of a horse, deer, etc.
hoofs n ▷ **hoof**
hook n (pl **-s**) curved piece of metal, plastic, etc., used to hang, hold, or pull something

▶ v (-s, -ing, -ed) fasten or catch (as if) with a hook

hookah n (pl -s) oriental pipe in which smoke is drawn through water and a long tube
  hookahs n ▷ hookah

hooked adj bent like a hook ▶ v ▷ hook

hooker n (pl -s) (CHIEFLY US) (Slang) prostitute
  hookers n ▷ hooher
  hooking v ▷ hook
  hooks n, v ▷ hook

hookup n (pl -s) linking of radio or television stations
  hookups n ▷ hookup

hookworm n (pl -s) blood-sucking worm with hooked mouthparts
  hookworms n ▷ hookworm

hooligan n (pl -s) rowdy young person
  > **hooliganism** n (pl -s)
  hooliganisms n ▷ hooligan
  hooligans n ▷ hooligan

hoon n (pl -s) (AUST & NZ) (Slang) loutish youth who drives irresponsibly
  hoons n ▷ hoon

hoop n (pl -s) rigid circular band, used esp. as a child's toy or for animals to jump through in the circus

hoopla n (pl -s) fairground game in which hoops are thrown over objects in an attempt to win them
  hooplas n ▷ hoopla
  hoops n ▷ hoop

hooray interj ▷ hurrah

hoot n (pl -s) sound of a car horn ▶ v (-s, -ing, -ed) sound (a car horn)
  hooted v ▷ hoot

hooter n (pl -s) device that hoots
  hooters n ▷ hooter
  hooting v ▷ hoot
  hoots n, v ▷ hoot

hoover n ® (pl -s) vacuum cleaner ▶ v (-s, -ing, -ed) clean with a vacuum cleaner
  hoovered v ▷ hoover
  hoovering v ▷ hoover
  hoovers n, v ▷ hoover
  hooves n ▷ hoof

hop¹ n (-s, -pping, -pped) jump on one foot ▶ n (pl -s) instance of hopping

hop² n (pl -s) (often pl) climbing plant, the dried flowers of which are used to make beer

hope v (-pes, -ping, -ped) want (something) to happen or be true ▶ n (pl -s) expectation of something desired > **hopeless** adj
  hoped v ▷ hope

hopeful adj having, expressing, or inspiring hope ▶ n (pl -s) person considered to be on the brink of success

hopefully adv in a hopeful manner
  hopefully adj ▷ hopeful
  hopefuls n ▷ hopeful

hopeless adj ▷ hope

hopes v, n ▷ hope

hoping v ▷ hope

hopped v ▷ hop¹

hopper n (pl -s) container for storing substances such as grain or sand
  hoppers n ▷ hopper

hopping v ▷ hop¹

hops n ▷ hop¹, ² ▶ v ▷ hop¹

hopscotch n (pl -es) children's game of hopping in a pattern drawn on the ground
  hopscotches n ▷ hopscotch

horde n (pl -s) large crowd
  hordes n ▷ horde ▶ pl n limits of scope, interest, or knowledge

horizon n (pl -s) apparent line that divides the earth and the sky
  horizons n ▷ horizon ▶ pl n limits of scope, interest, or knowledge

horizontal adj parallel to the horizon, level, flat > **horizontally** adv
  horizontally adv ▷ horizontal

hormonal adj ▷ hormone

hormone n (pl -s) substance secreted by certain glands which stimulates certain organs of the body > **hormonal** adj
  hormones n ▷ hormone

horn n (pl -s) one of a pair of bony growths sticking out of the heads of cattle, sheep, etc. > **horned** adj

hornbeam n (pl -s) tree with smooth grey bark
  hornbeams n ▷ hornbeam

hornbill n (pl -s) bird with a bony growth on its large beak
  hornbills n ▷ hornbill

hornblende n (pl -s) mineral containing aluminium, calcium, sodium, magnesium, and iron
  hornblendes n ▷ hornblende
  horned adj ▷ horn

hornet n (pl -s) large wasp with a severe sting
  hornets n ▷ hornet

hornpipe n (pl -s) (music for) a solo dance, traditionally performed by sailors
  hornpipes n ▷ hornpipe
  horns n ▷ horn

horny adj (-nier, -niest) of or like horn

horoscope n (pl -s) prediction of a person's future based on the positions of the planets, sun, and moon at his or her birth
  horoscopes n ▷ horoscope

horrendous adj very unpleasant and shocking

horrible adj disagreeable, unpleasant
> **horribly** adv
  horribly adv ▷ horrible
horrid adj disagreeable, unpleasant
horrific adj causing horror
  horrified v ▷ horrify
  horrifies v ▷ horrify
horrify v (-fies, -fying, -fied) cause to feel horror or shock
  horrifying v ▷ horrify
horror n (pl -s) (thing or person causing) terror or hatred
  horrors n ▷ horror
horse n (pl -s) large animal with hooves, a mane, and a tail, used for riding and pulling carts etc.
  horseflies n ▷ horsefly
  horsefly n (pl -flies) large bloodsucking fly
  horsehair n (pl -s) hair from the tail or mane of a horse
  horsehairs n ▷ horsehair
  horseman n (pl -men) person riding a horse
  horsemen n ▷ horseman
  horseplay n (pl -s) rough or rowdy play
  horseplays n ▷ horseplay
horsepower n (pl -s) unit of power (equivalent to 745.7 watts), used to measure the power of an engine
  horsepowers n ▷ horsepower
horseradish n (pl -es) strong-tasting root of a plant, usu. made into a sauce
  horseradishes n ▷ horseradish
  horses n ▷ horse
horseshoe n (pl -s) protective U-shaped piece of iron nailed to a horse's hoof, regarded as a symbol of good luck
  horseshoes n ▷ horseshoe
horsewoman n (pl -men) woman riding a horse
  horsewomen n ▷ horsewoman
horsey, horsy adj (-sier, -siest) very keen on horses
  horsier adj ▷ horsey
  horsiest adj ▷ horsey
  horsy adj ▷ horsey
  horticultural adj ▷ horticulture
  horticulturalist n ▷ horticulture
  horticulturalists n ▷ horticulture
horticulture n (pl -s) art or science of cultivating gardens > **horticultural** adj
> **horticulturalist, horticulturist** n (pl -s)
  horticultures n ▷ horticulture
  horticulturist n ▷ horticulture
  horticulturists n ▷ horticulture
hosanna interj exclamation of praise to God

hose¹ n (pl -s) flexible pipe for conveying liquid
  ▶ v (-ses, -sing, -sed) water with a hose
hose² n (pl -s) stockings, socks, and tights
  hosed v ▷ hose¹
  hoses n, v ▷ hose¹, ² ▶ v ▷ hose¹
  hosieries n ▷ hosiery
hosiery n (pl -ries) stockings, socks, and tights collectively
  hosing v ▷ hose¹
hospice [hoss-piss] n (pl -s) nursing home for the terminally ill
  hospices n ▷ hospice
hospitable adj welcoming to strangers or guests
hospital n (pl -s) place where people who are ill are looked after and treated
  hospitalities n ▷ hospitality
  hospitalities n ▷ hospitality
hospitality n (pl -ties) kindness in welcoming strangers or guests
  hospitalization n ▷ hospitalize
  hospitalizations n ▷ hospitalize
hospitalize v (-izes, -izing, -ized) send or admit to hospital ▶ **hospitalization** n (pl -s)
  hospitalized v ▷ hospitalize
  hospitalizes v ▷ hospitalize
  hospitalizing v ▷ hospitalize
  hospitals n ▷ hospital
host¹ n (pl -s) man who entertains guests, esp. in his own home ▶ v (-s, -ing, -ed) be the host of
host² n (pl -s) large number
hostage n (pl -s) person who is illegally held prisoner until certain demands are met by other people
  hostages n ▷ hostage
  hosted v ▷ host¹
hostel n (pl -s) building providing accommodation at a low cost for a specific group of people such as students, travellers, homeless people, etc.
  hostelries n ▷ hostelry
hostelry n (pl -ries) (Old-fashioned or facetious) inn, pub
  hostels n ▷ hostel
hostess n (pl -es) woman who entertains guests, esp. in her own home
  hostesses n ▷ hostess
hostile adj unfriendly
  hostilities n ▷ hostility ▶ pl n acts of warfare
hostility n (pl -ties) unfriendly and aggressive feelings or behaviour
  hosting v ▷ host¹
  hosts n ▷ host¹, ² ▶ v ▷ host¹
hot adj (-tter, -ttest) having a high

temperature in trouble ▷ **hotly** adv

hotbed n (pl -s) any place encouraging a particular activity
hotbeds n ▷ **hotbed**

hotchpotch n (pl -es) jumbled mixture
hotchpotches n ▷ **hotchpotch**

hotel n (pl -s) commercial establishment providing lodging and meals

hotelier n (pl -s) owner or manager of a hotel
hoteliers n ▷ **hotelier**
hotels n ▷ **hotel**

hotfoot adv (Informal) quickly and eagerly

hotheaded adj rash, having a hot temper

hothouse n (pl -s) greenhouse
hothouses n ▷ **hothouse**

hotline n (pl -s) direct telephone link for emergency use
hotlines n ▷ **hotline**
hotly adv ▷ **hot**

hotplate n (pl -s) heated metal surface on an electric cooker
hotplates n ▷ **hotplate**
hotter adj ▷ **hot**
hottest adj ▷ **hot**

hound n (pl -s) hunting dog ▶ v (-s, -ing, -ed) pursue relentlessly
hounded v ▷ **hound**
hounding v ▷ **hound**
hounds n, v ▷ **hound**

hour n (pl -s) twenty-fourth part of a day, sixty minutes

hourglass n (pl -es) device with two glass compartments, containing a quantity of sand that takes an hour to trickle from the top section to the bottom one
hourglasses n ▷ **hourglass**

houri n (pl -s) (ISLAM) any of the nymphs of paradise
houris n ▷ **houri**

hourly adj, adv (happening) every hour

hours pl n period regularly appointed for work or business ▶ n ▷ **hour**

house n (pl -s) building used as a home ▶ v (-ses, -sing, -sed) give accommodation to
houseboat n (pl -s) stationary boat used as a home
houseboats n ▷ **houseboat**

housebreaker n (pl -s) burglar
housebreakers n ▷ **housebreaker**

housecoat n (pl -s) woman's long loose coat-shaped garment for wearing at home
housecoats n ▷ **housecoat**
housed v ▷ **house**

household n (pl -s) all the people living in a house

householder n (pl -s) person who owns or rents a house
householders n ▷ **householder**
households n ▷ **household**

housekeeper n (pl -s) person employed to run someone else's household
housekeepers n ▷ **housekeeper**

housekeeping n (pl -s) (money for) running a household
housekeepings n ▷ **housekeeping**

housemaid n (pl -s) female servant employed to do housework
housemaids n ▷ **housemaid**
houses n, v ▷ **house**

housewarming n (pl -s) party to celebrate moving into a new home
housewarmings n ▷ **housewarming**

housewife n (pl -wives) woman who runs her own household and does not have a job
housewives n ▷ **housewife**

housework n (pl -s) work of running a home, such as cleaning, cooking, and shopping
houseworks n ▷ **housework**

housing n (pl -s) (providing of) houses ▶ v ▷ **house**
housings n ▷ **housing**

hovea n (pl -s) Australian plant with purple flowers
hoveas n ▷ **hovea**

hovel n (pl -s) small dirty house or hut
hovels n ▷ **hovel**

hover v (-s, -ing, -red) (of a bird etc.) remain suspended in one place in the air

hovercraft n (pl -s) vehicle which can travel over both land and sea on a cushion of air
hovercrafts n ▷ **hovercraft**
hovered v ▷ **hover**
hovering v ▷ **hover**
hovers v ▷ **hover**

how adv in what way, by what means

howdah n (pl -s) canopied seat on an elephant's back
howdahs n ▷ **howdah**

however adv nevertheless

howitzer n (pl -s) large gun firing shells at a steep angle
howitzers n ▷ **howitzer**

howl n (pl -s) loud wailing cry ▶ v (-s, -ing, -ed) utter a howl
howled v ▷ **howl**

howler n (pl -s) (Informal) stupid mistake
howlers n ▷ **howler**
howling v ▷ **howl**
howls n, v ▷ **howl**

hoyden n (pl -s) (Old-fashioned) wild or

boisterous girl

hoydens n ▷ hoyden

hox v (**hoxes, hoxing, hoxed**). This is a word found in Shakespeare's plays, and means to cut a horse's hamstring. This unusual word is a handy one to remember if you draw an X. Hox scores 12 points.

hub n (pl -s) centre of a wheel, through which the axle passes

hubbies n ▷ hubby

hubbub n (pl -s) confused noise of many voices

hubbubs n ▷ hubbub

hubby n (pl -bbies) (*Informal*) husband

hubris [hew-briss] n (pl -es) (*Formal*) pride, arrogance

hubrises ▷ hubris

hubs n ▷ hub

huckster n (pl -s) person using aggressive methods of selling

hucksters n ▷ huckster

huddle v (-les, -ling, -led) hunch (oneself) through cold or fear ▶ n (pl -s) small group

huddled v ▷ huddle

huddles n, v ▷ huddle

huddling v ▷ huddle

hue n (pl -s) colour, shade

hues n ▷ hue

huff n (pl -s) passing mood of anger or resentment ▶ v (-s, -ing, -ed) blow or puff heavily > **huffy** adj (-ffier, -ffiest) > **huffily** adv

huffed v ▷ huff

huffier adj ▷ huff

huffiest adj ▷ huff

huffily adv ▷ huff

huffing v ▷ huff

huffs n, v ▷ huff

huffy adj ▷ huff

hug v (-s, -gging, -gged) clasp tightly in the arms, usu. with affection ▶ n (pl -s) tight or fond embrace

huge adj (-r, -st) very big > **hugely** adv

huger adj ▷ huge

hugest adj ▷ huge

hugged v ▷ hug

hugging v ▷ hug

hugs n, v ▷ hug

huh interj exclamation of derision, bewilderment, or inquiry

hui [hoo-ee] n (pl huies) (NZ) meeting of Maori people

huies n ▷ hui

hula n (pl -s) swaying Hawaiian dance

hulas n ▷ hula

hulk n (pl -s) body of an abandoned ship

hulking adj bulky, unwieldy

hulks n ▷ hulk

hull n (pl -s) main body of a boat ▶ v (-s, -ing, -ed) remove the hulls from

hullabaloo n (pl -loos) loud confused noise or clamour

hullabaloos n ▷ hullabaloo

hulled v ▷ hull

hulling v ▷ hull

hulls n, v ▷ hull

hum v (-s, -mming, -mmed) make a low continuous vibrating sound ▶ n (pl -s) humming sound

human adj of or typical of people ▶ n (pl -s) human being

humane adj (-r, -st) kind or merciful > **humanely** adv

humanely adv ▷ humane

humaner adj ▷ humane

humanest adj ▷ humane

humanism n (pl -s) belief in human effort rather than religion > **humanist** n (pl -s)

humanisms n ▷ humanism

humanist n ▷ humanism

humanists n ▷ humanism

humanitarian adj, n (pl -s) (person) having the interests of humankind at heart

humanitarians n ▷ humanitarian

humanities n ▷ humanity ▶ pl n study of literature, philosophy, and the arts

humanity n (pl -ties) human race

humanize v (-zes, -zing, -zed) make human or humane

humanized v ▷ humanize

humanizes v ▷ humanize

humanizing v ▷ humanize

humankind n (pl -s) human race

humankinds n ▷ humankind

humanly adv by human powers or means

humans n ▷ human

humble adj (-r, -st) conscious of one's failings ▶ v (-les, -ling, -led) cause to feel humble, humiliate > **humbly** adv

humbled v ▷ humble

humbler adj ▷ humble

humbles v ▷ humble

humblest adj ▷ humble

humbling v ▷ humble

humbly adv ▷ humble

humbug n (pl -s) (BRIT) hard striped peppermint sweet

humbugs n ▷ humbug

humdinger n (pl -s) (*Slang*) excellent person or thing

humdingers n ▷ humdinger

humdrum *adj* ordinary, dull
  humeri *n* ▷ humerus
humerus [hew-mer-uss] *n* (*pl* -**meri**) [-mer-rye] bone from the shoulder to the elbow
humid *adj* (-**er**, -**est**) damp and hot > **humidity** *n* (*pl* -**ties**) > **humidify** *v* (-**fies**, -**fying**, -**fied**)
  humider *adj* ▷ humid
  humidest *adj* ▷ humid
  humidified *v* ▷ humidify
humidifier *n* (*pl* -**s**) device for increasing the amount of water vapour in the air in a room
  humidifiers *n* ▷ humidifier
  humidifies *v* ▷ humidify
  humidifying *v* ▷ humidify
  humidities *n* ▷ humid
  humidity *n* ▷ humid
humiliate *v* (-**tes**, -**ting**, -**ted**) lower the dignity or hurt the pride of > **humiliating** *adj* > **humiliation** *n* (*pl* -**s**)
  humiliated *v* ▷ humiliate
  humiliates *v* ▷ humiliate
  humiliating *v, adj* ▷ humiliate
  humiliation *n* ▷ humiliate
  humiliations *n* ▷ humiliate
  humilities *n* ▷ humility
humility *n* (*pl* humilities) quality of being humble
  hummed *v* ▷ hum
  humming *v* ▷ hum
hummingbird *n* (*pl* -**s**) very small American bird whose powerful wings make a humming noise as they vibrate
  hummingbirds *n* ▷ hummingbird
hummock *n* (*pl* -**s**) very small hill
  hummocks *n* ▷ hummock
humorist *n* (*pl* -**s**) writer or entertainer who uses humour in his or her work
  humorists *n* ▷ humorist
  humorous *adj* ▷ humour
  humorously *adj* ▷ humour
humour *n* (*pl* -**s**) ability to say or perceive things that are amusing ▶ *v* (-**s**, -**ing**, -**ed**) be kind and indulgent to > **humorous** *adj* > **humorously** *adv*
  humoured *v* ▷ humour
  humouring *v* ▷ humour
  humours *n, v* ▷ humour
hump *n* (*pl* -**s**) raised piece of ground ▶ *v* (-**s**, -**ing**, -**ed**) (*Slang*) carry or heave
  humped *v* ▷ hump
  humping *v* ▷ hump
  humps *n, v* ▷ hump
  hums *v, n* ▷ hum
humus [hew-muss] *n* (*pl* -**es**) decomposing vegetable and animal mould in the soil

  humuses *n* ▷ humus
hunch *n* (*pl* -**es**) feeling or suspicion not based on facts ▶ *v* (-**es**, -**ing**, -**ed**) draw (one's shoulders) up or together
hunchback *n* (*pl* -**s**) (*Offens*) person with an abnormal curvature of the spine
  hunchbacks *n* ▷ hunchback
  hunched *v* ▷ hunch
  hunches *n, v* ▷ hunch
  hunching *v* ▷ hunch
hundred *adj* ten times ten ▶ *n* (*pl* -**s**) (*often pl*) large but unspecified number > **hundredth** *adj, n* (*pl* -**s**)
  hundreds *n* ▷ hundred
  hundredth *n* ▷ hundred
  hundredths *n* ▷ hundred
hundredweight *n* (*pl* -**s**) (BRIT) unit of weight of 112 pounds (50.8 kilograms)
  hundredweights *n* ▷ hundredweight
hung *v* ▷ hang ▶ *adj* (of a parliament or jury) with no side having a clear majority
hunger *n* (*pl* -**s**) discomfort or weakness from lack of food ▶ *v* (-**s**, -**ing**, -**ed**) (*foll. by* for) want very much
  hungered *v* ▷ hunger
  hungering *v* ▷ hunger
  hungers *n, v* ▷ hunger
  hungrier *adj* ▷ hungry
  hungriest *adj* ▷ hungry
  hungrily *adv* ▷ hungry
hungry *adj* (-**rier**, -**riest**) desiring food (*foll. by* for) > **hungrily** *adv*
hunk *n* (*pl* -**s**) large piece
  hunks *n* ▷ hunk
hunt *v* (-**s**, -**ing**, -**ed**) seek out and kill (wild animals) for food or sport ▶ *n* (*pl* -**s**) hunting
huntaway *n* (*pl* -**s**) (NZ) sheepdog trained to drive sheep by barking
  huntaways *n* ▷ huntaway
  hunted *v* ▷ hunt
hunter *n* (*pl* -**s**) person or animal that hunts wild animals for food or sport
  hunters *n* ▷ hunter
  hunting *v* ▷ hunt
  hunts *v, n* ▷ hunt
huntsman *n* (*pl* -**men**) man who hunts wild animals, esp. foxes
  huntsmen *n* ▷ huntsman
hurdle *n* (*pl* -**s**) (SPORT) light barrier for jumping over in some races ▶ *v* (-**les**, -**ling**, -**led**) jump over (something) > **hurdler** *n* (*pl* -**s**)
  hurdled *v* ▷ hurdle
  hurdler *n* ▷ hurdle
  hurdlers *n* ▷ hurdle
hurdles *n, v* ▷ hurdle ▶ *pl n* race involving

hurdles
hurdling v ▷ **hurdle**
hurl v (**-s, -ing, -ed**) throw or utter forcefully
hurled v ▷ **hurl**
hurley n ▷ **hurling**
hurleys n ▷ **hurling**
hurling, hurley n (pl **-s**) Irish game like hockey
▶ v ▷ **hurl**
hurlings n ▷ **hurling**
hurls v ▷ **hurl**
hurrah, hurray interj exclamation of joy or
applause
hurricane n (pl **-s**) very strong, often
destructive, wind or storm
hurricanes n ▷ **hurricane**
hurried v ▷ **hurry**
hurriedly adv ▷ **hurry**
hurries v, n ▷ **hurry**
hurry v (**-ries, -rying, -ried**) (cause to) move or
act very quickly ▶ n (pl **-ries**) doing something
quickly or the need to do something quickly
> **hurriedly** adv
hurrying v ▷ **hurry**
hurt v (**-s, -ing, hurt**) cause physical or
mental pain to ▶ n (pl **-s**) physical or mental
pain
hurtful adj unkind
hurting v ▷ **hurt**
hurtle v (**-les, -ling, -led**) move quickly or
violently
hurtled v ▷ **hurtle**
hurtles v ▷ **hurtle**
hurtling v ▷ **hurtle**
hurts v, n ▷ **hurt**
husband n (pl **-s**) woman's partner in marriage
▶ v (**-s, -ing, -ed**) use economically
husbanded v ▷ **husband**
husbanding v ▷ **husband**
husbandries n ▷ **husbandry**
husbandry n (pl **-ries**) farming
husbands n, v ▷ **husband**
hush v (**-es, -ing, -ed**) make or be silent ▶ n (pl
-es) stillness or silence
hushed v ▷ **hush**
hushes v, n ▷ **hush**
hushing v ▷ **hush**
husk n (pl **-s**) outer covering of certain seeds
and fruits ▶ v (**-s, -ing, -ed**) remove the husk
from
husked v ▷ **husk**
huskier adj ▷ **husky**[1]
huskies n ▷ **husky**[2]
huskiest adj ▷ **husky**[1]
huskily adv ▷ **husky**[1]
husking v ▷ **husk**

husks n, v ▷ **husk**
husky[1] adj (**-kier, -kiest**) slightly hoarse
> **huskily** adv
husky[2] n (pl **-kies**) Arctic sledge dog with thick
hair and a curled tail
hussar [hoo-**zar**] n (pl **-s**) (HIST) lightly armed
cavalry soldier
hussars n ▷ **hussar**
hussies n ▷ **hussy**
hussy n (pl **-sies**) immodest or promiscuous
woman
hustings pl n political campaigns and
speeches before an election
hustle v (**-les, -ling, -led**) push about, jostle ▶ n
(pl **-les**) lively activity or bustle
hustled v ▷ **hustle**
hustles v, n ▷ **hustle**
hustling v ▷ **hustle**
hut n (pl **-s**) small house, shelter, or shed
hutch n (pl **-es**) cage for pet rabbits etc.
hutches n ▷ **hutch**
huts n ▷ **hut**
hyacinth n (pl **-s**) sweet-smelling spring flower
that grows from a bulb
hyacinths n ▷ **hyacinth**
hyaena n (pl **-s**) ▷ **hyena**
hyaenas n ▷ **hyaena**
hybrid n (pl **-s**) offspring of two plants or
animals of different species ▶ adj of mixed
origin
hybrids n ▷ **hybrid**
hydra n (pl **-s**) mythical many-headed water
serpent
hydrangea n (pl **-s**) ornamental shrub with
clusters of pink, blue, or white flowers
hydrangeas n ▷ **hydrangea**
hydrant n (pl **-s**) outlet from a water main with
a nozzle for a hose
hydrants n ▷ **hydrant**
hydras n ▷ **hydra**
hydrate n (pl **-tes**) chemical compound of
water with another substance
hydrates n ▷ **hydrate**
hydraulic adj operated by pressure forced
through a pipe by a liquid such as water or oil
hydraulically adv ▷ **hydraulics**
hydraulics n study of the mechanical
properties of fluids as they apply to practical
engineering > **hydraulically** adv
hydro[1] n (pl **-s**) hotel offering facilities for
hydropathy
hydro[2] adj ▷ **hydroelectric**
hydrocarbon n (pl **-s**) compound of hydrogen
and carbon
hydrocarbons n ▷ **hydrocarbon**

hydroelectric *adj* of the generation of electricity by water pressure

hydrofoil *n* (*pl* **-s**) fast light boat with its hull raised out of the water on one or more pairs of fins
hydrofoils *n* ▷ **hydrofoil**

hydrogen *n* (*pl* **-s**) (CHEM) light flammable colourless gas that combines with oxygen to form water
hydrogens *n* ▷ **hydrogen**
hydrolyses *n* ▷ **hydrolysis**

hydrolysis [hie-drol-iss-iss] *n* (*pl* **-yses**) decomposition of a chemical compound reacting with water

hydrometer [hie-drom-it-er] *n* (*pl* **-s**) instrument for measuring the density of a liquid
hydrometers *n* ▷ **hydrometer**
hydropathies *n* ▷ **hydropathy**

hydropathy *n* (*pl* **-thies**) method of treating disease by the use of large quantities of water both internally and externally

hydrophobia *n* (*pl* **-s**) rabies
hydrophobias *n* ▷ **hydrophobia**

hydroplane *n* (*pl* **-s**) light motorboat that skims the water
hydroplanes *n* ▷ **hydroplane**

hydroponics *n* method of growing plants in water rather than soil
hydros *n* ▷ **hydro¹**
hydrotherapies *n* ▷ **hydrotherapy**

hydrotherapy *n* (*pl* **-pies**) (MED) treatment of certain diseases by exercise in water

hyena *n* (*pl* **-s**) scavenging doglike mammal of Africa and S Asia
hyenas *n* ▷ **hyena**

hygiene *n* (*pl* **-s**) principles and practice of health and cleanliness > **hygienic** *adj*
> **hygienically** *adv*
hygienic *adj* ▷ **hygiene**
hygienically *adj* ▷ **hygiene**

hymen *n* (*pl* **-s**) membrane partly covering the opening of a girl's vagina, which breaks before puberty or at the first occurrence of sexual intercourse
hymens *n* ▷ **hymen**

hymn *n* (*pl* **-s**) Christian song of praise sung to God or a saint

hymnal *n* (*pl* **-s**) book of hymns (*also* **hymn book**)
hymnals *n* ▷ **hymnal**
hymns *n* ▷ **hymn**

hype *n* (*pl* **-s**) intensive or exaggerated publicity or sales promotion ▶ *v* (**-pes, -ping, -ped**) promote (a product) using intensive or exaggerated publicity
hyped *v* ▷ **hype**

hyper *adj* (*Informal*) overactive or overexcited

hyperbola [hie-per-bol-a] *n* (*pl* **-s**) (GEOM) curve produced when a cone is cut by a plane at a steeper angle to its base than its side
hyperbolas *n* ▷ **hyperbola**

hyperbole [hie-per-bol-ee] *n* (*pl* **-s**) deliberate exaggeration for effect
> **hyperbolic** *adj*
hyperboles *n* ▷ **hyperbole**
hyperbolic *adj* ▷ **hyperbole**

hyperlink (COMPUTERS) *n* (*pl* **-s**) link from a hypertext file that gives users instant access to related material in another file ▶ *v* (**-s, -ing, -ed**) link (files) in this way
hyperlinked *v* ▷ **hyperlink**
hyperlinking *v* ▷ **hyperlink**
hyperlinks *v, n* ▷ **hyperlink**

hypermarket *n* (*pl* **-s**) huge self-service store
hypermarkets *n* ▷ **hypermarket**

hypersensitive *adj* extremely sensitive to certain drugs, extremes of temperature, etc.

hypersonic *adj* having a speed of at least five times the speed of sound

hypertension *n* (*pl* **-s**) very high blood pressure
hypertensions *n* ▷ **hypertension**
hypertensions *n* ▷ **hypertension**

hypertext *n* (*pl* **-s**) computer software and hardware that allows users to store and view text and move between related items easily
hypertexts *n* ▷ **hypertext**
hypes *n, v* ▷ **hype**

hyphen *n* (*pl* **-s**) punctuation mark (-) indicating that two words or syllables are connected

hyphenated *adj* (of two words or syllables) having a hyphen between them
> **hyphenation** *n* (*pl* **-s**)
hyphenation *n* ▷ **hyphenated**
hyphenations *n* ▷ **hyphenated**
hyphens *n* ▷ **hyphen**
hyping *v* ▷ **hype**
hypnoses *n* ▷ **hypnosis**

hypnosis *n* (*pl* **-noses**) artificially induced state of relaxation in which the mind is more than usually receptive to suggestion

hypnotic *adj* of or (as if) producing hypnosis

hypnotism *n* (*pl* **-s**) inducing hypnosis in someone > **hypnotist** *n* (*pl* **-s**) > **hypnotize** *v* (**-tizes, -tizing, -tized**)
hypnotisms *n* ▷ **hypnotism**
hypnotist *n* ▷ **hypnotism**
hypnotists *n* ▷ **hypnotism**
hypnotize *v* ▷ **hypnotism**

hypnotized v ▷ hypnotism
hypnotizes v ▷ hypnotism
hypnotizing v ▷ hypnotism
hypoallergenic adj (of cosmetics) not likely to cause an allergic reaction
hypochondria n (pl -s) undue preoccupation with one's health > **hypochondriac** n (pl -s)
hypochondriac n ▷ hypochondria
hypochondriacs n ▷ hypochondria
hypochondrias n ▷ hypochondria
hypocrisies n ▷ hypocrisy
hypocrisy [hip-ok-rass-ee] n (pl -sies) (instance of) pretence of having standards or beliefs that are contrary to one's real character or actual behaviour
hypocrite [hip-oh-krit] n (pl -s) person who pretends to be what he or she is not > **hypocritical** adj > **hypocritically** adv
hypocrites n ▷ hypocrite
hypocritical adj ▷ hypocrite
hypocritically adv ▷ hypocrite
hypodermic adj, n (pl -s) (denoting) a syringe or needle used to inject a drug beneath the skin
hypodermics n ▷ hypodermic
hypotension n (pl -s) very low blood pressure
hypotenuse [hie-pot-a-news] n (pl -s) side of a right-angled triangle opposite the right angle
hypotenuses n ▷ hypotenuse
hypothermia n (pl -s) condition in which a person's body temperature is dangerously low as a result of prolonged exposure to severe cold
hypothermias n ▷ hypothermia
hypotheses n ▷ hypothesis
hypothesis [hie-poth-iss-iss] n (pl -ses) [-seez] suggested but unproved explanation of something
hypothetical adj based on assumption rather than fact or reality > **hypothetically** adv
hypothetically adj ▷ hypothetical
hyraces n ▷ hyrax
hyrax n (pl -raxes or -races) type of hoofed rodent-like animal of Africa and Asia
hyraxes n ▷ hyrax
hysterectomies n ▷ hysterectomy
hysterectomy n (pl -mies) surgical removal of the womb
hysteria n (pl -s) state of uncontrolled excitement, anger, or panic > **hysterical** adj > **hysterically** adv
hysterias n ▷ hysteria
hysterical adj ▷ hysteria
hysterically adj ▷ hysteria
hysterics pl n attack of hysteria

I i

The letter I can prove a difficult tile to use effectively in Scrabble. It's one of the most common tiles in the game, so you often end up with two or more on your rack, but it can be hard to get rid of. Where I does come in very useful, though, is in the number of everyday short words that can be formed from it, which are very helpful when you need to form short words in addition to the main word that you want to play. These words include **in, is, it** (2 points each), **id** (3) and **if** (5). Other handy words are **icy** (8), **ivy** (9) and **imp** (7). Don't forget the three-letter words that use K: **ilk, ink** and **irk** (7 each).

ibex [ibe-eks] *n* (*pl* **-es**) wild goat of N with large backward-curving horns
 ibexes *n* ▷ **ibex**
ibis [ibe-iss] *n* (*pl* **-es**) large wading bird with long legs
 ibises *n* ▷ **ibis**
ice *n* (*pl* **-s**) frozen water ▶ *v* (**-ces, -cing, -ced**) (*foll. by* **up** *or* **over**) become covered with ice
iceberg *n* (*pl* **-s**) large floating mass of ice
 icebergs *n* ▷ **iceberg**
icebox *n* (*pl* **-es**) (us) refrigerator
 iceboxes *n* ▷ **icebox**
icecap *n* (*pl* **-s**) mass of ice permanently covering an area
 icecaps *n* ▷ **icecap**
iced *adj* covered with icing ▶ *v* ▷ **ice**
 ices *v*, *n* ▷ **ice**

> **ich** *pron.* Ich is an old dialect form of I. This is a useful little word that is worth remembering because of its unusual combination of letters and relatively high score. Ich scores 8 points.

 ichthyologies *n* ▷ **ichthyology**
ichthyology [ik-thi-**ol**-a-jee] *n* (*pl* **-gies**) scientific study of fish
icicle *n* (*pl* **-s**) tapering spike of ice hanging where water has dripped
 icicles *n* ▷ **icicle**
 icier *adj* ▷ **icy**
 iciest *adj* ▷ **icy**
 icily *adv* ▷ **icy**
 iciness *n* ▷ **icy**
 icinesses *n* ▷ **icy**
icing *v* ▷ **ice** ▶ *n* (*pl* **-s**) mixture of sugar and water etc., used to cover and decorate cakes
 icings *n* ▷ **icing**

> **ick** *interj.* Ick is something that people say when they encounter something unpleasant or disgusting. Ick is a good word to remember because, in addition to being useful when there's little space, it's one of the highest-scoring three-letter word beginning with I. Ick scores 9 points.

icon *n* (*pl* **-s**) picture of Christ or another religious figure, regarded as holy in the Orthodox Church
iconoclast *n* (*pl* **-s**) person who attacks established ideas or principles > **iconoclastic** *adj*
 iconoclastic *adj* ▷ **iconoclast**
 iconoclasts *n* ▷ **iconoclast**
 icons *n* ▷ **icon**
icy *adj* (**-cier, -ciest**) very cold > **icily** *adv*
 > **iciness** *n* (*pl* **-es**)
id *n* (*pl* **-s**) (PSYCHOANALYSIS) the mind's instinctive unconscious energies

> **ide** *n* (**ides**). An ide is a kind of fish. This combination of letters is a good one to keep in mind because it is both a suffix that can be added to words already on the board and a word in its own right. Ide scores 4 points.

idea *n* (*pl* **-s**) plan or thought formed in the mind
ideal *adj* most suitable ▶ *n* (*pl* **-s**) conception of something that is perfect > **idealist** *n* (*pl* **-s**) > **idealistic** *adj* > **ideally** *adv*
idealism *n* (*pl* **-s**) tendency to seek perfection in everything
 idealisms *n* ▷ **idealism**
 idealist *n* ▷ **ideal**
 idealistic *adj* ▷ **ideal**
 idealists *n* ▷ **ideal**

idealization *n* ▷ idealize
idealizations *n* ▷ idealize
idealize *v* (-izes, -izing, -ized) regard or portray as perfect or nearly perfect ▷ **idealization** *n* (*pl* -s)
idealized *n* ▷ idealize
idealizes *n* ▷ idealize
idealizing *n* ▷ idealize
ideally *adv* ▷ ideal
ideals *n* ▷ ideal
ideas *n* ▷ idea
idem *pron, adj* (LATIN) the same: used to refer to an article, chapter, or book already quoted
identical *adj* exactly the same ▷ **identically** *adv*
identically *adv* ▷ identical
identifiable *adj* ▷ identify
identification *n* ▷ identify
identifications *n* ▷ identify
identified *v* ▷ identify
identifies *v* ▷ identify
identify *v* (-fies, -fying, -fied) prove or recognize as being a certain person or thing ▷ **identifiable** *adj* ▷ **identification** *n* (*pl* -s)
identifying *v* ▷ identify
identities *n* ▷ identity
identity *n* (*pl* -ties) state of being a specified person or thing
ideological *adj* ▷ ideology
ideologies *n* ▷ ideology
ideologist *n* ▷ ideology
ideologists *n* ▷ ideology
ideology *n* (*pl* -gies) body of ideas and beliefs of a group, nation, etc. ▷ **ideological** *adj* ▷ **ideologist** *n* (*pl* -s)
idiocies *n* ▷ idiocy
idiocy *n* (*pl* -cies) utter stupidity
idiom *n* (*pl* -s) group of words which when used together have a different meaning from the words individually ▷ **idiomatic** *adj* ▷ **idiomatically** *adv*
idiomatic *adj* ▷ idiom
idiomatically *adv* ▷ idiom
idioms *n* ▷ idiom
idiosyncrasies *n* ▷ idiosyncrasy
idiosyncrasy *n* (*pl* -sies) personal peculiarity of mind, habit, or behaviour
idiot *n* (*pl* -s) foolish or stupid person ▷ **idiotic** *adj* ▷ **idiotically** *adv*
idiotic *adj* ▷ idiot
idiotically *adv* ▷ idiot
idiots *n* ▷ idiot
idle *adj* not doing anything ▶ *v* (-les, -ling, -led) (*usu. foll. by away*) spend (time) doing very little ▷ **idleness** *n* (*pl* -s) ▷ **idler** *n* (*pl* -s) ▷ **idly** *adv*

idled *v* ▷ idle
idleness *n* ▷ idle
idlenesses *n* ▷ idle
idler *n* ▷ idle
idlers *n* ▷ idle
idles *v* ▷ idle
idling *v* ▷ idle
idly *adj* ▷ idle
idol *n* (*pl* -s) object of excessive devotion
idolatries *n* ▷ idolatry
idolatrous *adj* ▷ idolatry
idolatry *n* (*pl* -ries) worship of idols ▷ **idolatrous** *adj*
idolize *v* (-izes, -izing, -ized) love or admire excessively
idolized *v* ▷ idolize
idolizes *v* ▷ idolize
idolizing *v* ▷ idolize
idols *n* ▷ idol
ids *n* ▷ id
idyll [id-ill] *n* (*pl* -s) scene or time of great peace and happiness ▷ **idyllic** *adj* ▷ **idyllically** *adv*
idyllic *adj* ▷ idyll
idyllically *adj* ▷ idyll
idylls *n* ▷ idyll
if *conj* on the condition or supposition that ▶ *n* (*pl* -s) uncertainty or doubt

> **iff** *conj*. Iff is a word used in logic to mean if and only if. This word is worth remembering: not only can it come in handy when there isn't much space on the board, but it's also one of the highest-scoring three-letter word beginning with I. Iff scores 9 points.

iffy *adj* (*Informal*) doubtful, uncertain
ifs *n* ▷ if
igloo *n* (*pl* -loos) dome-shaped Inuit house made of snow and ice
igloos *n* ▷ igloo
igneous [ig-nee-uss] *adj* (of rock) formed as molten rock cools and hardens
ignite *v* (-tes, -ting, -ted) catch fire or set fire to
ignited *v* ▷ ignite
ignites *v* ▷ ignite
igniting *v* ▷ ignite
ignition *n* (*pl* -s) system that ignites the fuel-and-air mixture to start an engine
ignitions *n* ▷ ignition
ignoble *adj* dishonourable
ignominies *n* ▷ ignominy
ignominious *adj* ▷ ignominy
ignominiously *adj* ▷ ignominy
ignominy [ig-nom-in-ee] *n* (*pl* -nies) humiliating disgrace ▷ **ignominious** *adj* ▷ **ignominiously** *adv*

ignoramus n (pl **-muses**) ignorant person
  ignoramuses n ▷ ignoramus
ignorance n ▷ ignorant
  ignorances n ▷ ignorance
ignorant adj lacking knowledge > **ignorance** n (pl **-s**)
ignore v (**-res, -ring, -red**) refuse to notice, disregard deliberately
  ignored v ▷ ignore
  ignores v ▷ ignore
  ignoring v ▷ ignore
iguana n (pl **-s**) large tropical American lizard
  iguanas n ▷ iguana
ileum n (pl **-s**) lowest part of the small intestine
  ileums n ▷ ileum
ilk n (pl **-s**) type
  ilks n ▷ ilk
ill adj not in good health ▶ n (pl **-s**) evil, harm ▶ adv badly > **illness** n (pl **-s**)
illegal adj against the law > **illegally** adv > **illegality** n (pl **-ties**)
  illegalities n ▷ illegal
  illegality n ▷ illegal
  illegally adv ▷ illegal
illegible adj unable to be read or deciphered
  illegitimacies n ▷ illegitimate
  illegitimacy n ▷ illegitimate
illegitimate adj born of parents not married to each other > **illegitimacy** n (pl **-s**)
illicit adj illegal
  illiteracies n ▷ illiterate
  illiteracy n ▷ illiterate
illiterate n (pl **-s**) ▶ adj (person) unable to read or write > **illiteracy** n (pl **-s**)
  illiterates n ▷ illiterate
  illness n ▷ ill
  illnesses n ▷ ill
illogical adj unreasonable > **illogicality** n (pl **-lities**)
  illogicalities adj ▷ illogical
  illogicality adj ▷ illogical
  ills n ▷ ill
illuminate v (**-tes, -ting, -ted**) light up > **illumination** n (pl **-s**) > **illuminating** adj
  illuminated v ▷ illuminate
  illuminates v ▷ illuminate
illuminating adj, v ▷ illuminate
  illumination n ▷ illuminate
  illuminations n ▷ illuminate
illusion n (pl **-s**) deceptive appearance or belief
illusionist n (pl **-s**) conjuror
  illusionists n ▷ illusionist
  illusions n ▷ illusion
illusory adj seeming to be true, but actually false

illustrate v (**-tes, -ting, -ted**) explain by use of examples > **illustrative** adj > **illustrator** n (pl **-s**)
  illustrated v ▷ illustrate
  illustrates v ▷ illustrate
  illustrating v ▷ illustrate
illustration n (pl **-s**) picture or diagram
  illustrations n ▷ illustrate
  illustrative adj ▷ illustrate
  illustrator n ▷ illustrate
  illustrators n ▷ illustrate
illustrious adj famous and distinguished
image n (pl **-s**) mental picture of someone or something
  imageries n ▷ imagery
imagery n (pl **-ries**) images collectively, esp. in the arts
  images n ▷ image
  imaginable adj ▷ imagine
imaginary adj existing only in the imagination
imagination n (pl **-s**) ability to make mental images of things that may not exist in real life
  imaginations n ▷ imagination
imaginative adj having or showing a lot of creative mental ability > **imaginatively** adv
  imaginatively adv ▷ imaginative
imagine v (**-nes, -ning, -ned**) form a mental image of > **imaginable** adj
  imagined v ▷ imagine
  imagines v ▷ imagine ▶ n ▷ imago
  imagining v ▷ imagine
imago [im-may-go] n (pl **-goes, -gines**) [im-maj-in-ees] sexually mature adult insect
  imagoes n ▷ imago
imam n (pl **-s**) leader of prayers in a mosque
  imams n ▷ imam
imbalance n (pl **-s**) lack of balance or proportion
  imbalances n ▷ imbalance
imbecile [imb-ess-eel] n (pl **-s**) stupid person ▶ adj (also **imbecilic**) stupid or senseless > **imbecility** n (pl **-ties**)
  imbeciles n ▷ imbecile
  imbecilic adj ▷ imbecile
  imbecilities n ▷ imbecile
  imbecility n ▷ imbecile
imbibe v (**-bes, -bing, -bed**) drink (alcoholic drinks)
  imbibed v ▷ imbibe
  imbibes v ▷ imbibe
  imbibing v ▷ imbibe
imbroglio [imb-role-ee-oh] n (pl **-ios**) confusing and complicated situation

imbroglios n ▷ imbroglio

imbue v (-ues, -uing, -ued) (usu. foll. by **with**) fill or inspire with (ideals or principles)

imbued v ▷ imbue

imbues v ▷ imbue

imbuing v ▷ imbue

imitate v (-tes, -ting, -ted) take as a model > imitative adj > imitator n (pl -s)

imitated v ▷ imitate

imitates v ▷ imitate

imitating v ▷ imitate

imitation n (pl -s) copy of an original

imitations n ▷ imitation

imitative adj ▷ imitate

imitator n ▷ imitate

imitators n ▷ imitate

immaculate adj completely clean or tidy > immaculately adv

immaculately adv ▷ immaculate

immanence n ▷ immanent

immanences n ▷ immanent

immanent adj present within and throughout something > immanence n (pl -s)

immaterial adj not important, not relevant

immature adj not fully developed > immaturity n (pl -ties)

immaturities n ▷ immature

immaturity n ▷ immature

immediacies n ▷ immediate

immediacy n ▷ immediate

immediate adj occurring at once > immediately adv > immediacy n (pl -cies)

immediately adv ▷ immediate

immemorial adj longer than anyone can remember

immense adj extremely large > immensity n (pl -ties)

immensely adv to a very great degree

immensities n ▷ immense

immensity n ▷ immense

immerse v (-ses, -sing, -sed) involve deeply, engross > immersion n (pl -s)

immersed v ▷ immerse

immerses v ▷ immerse

immersing v ▷ immerse

immersion n ▷ immerse

immersions n ▷ immerse

immigrant n ▷ immigration

immigrants n ▷ immigration

immigration n (pl -s) coming to a foreign country in order to settle there > immigrant n (pl -s)

immigrations n ▷ immigration

imminence n ▷ imminent

imminences n ▷ imminent

imminent adj about to happen > imminently adv > imminence n (pl -s)

imminently adv ▷ imminent

immobile adj not moving > immobility n (pl -ties)

immobilities adj ▷ immobile

immobility n ▷ immobile

immobilize v (-izes, -izing, -ized) make unable to move or work

immobilized v ▷ immobilize

immobilizes v ▷ immobilize

immobilizing v ▷ immobilize

immoderate adj excessive or unreasonable

immolate v (-tes, -ting, -ted) kill as a sacrifice > immolation n (pl -s)

immolated v ▷ immolate

immolates v ▷ immolate

immolating v ▷ immolate

immolation n ▷ immolate

immolations n ▷ immolate

immoral adj morally wrong, corrupt > immorality n (pl -ties)

immoralities n ▷ immoral

immorality n ▷ immoral

immortal adj living forever ▶ n (pl -s) person whose fame will last for all time > immortality n (pl -s) > immortalize v (-lizes, -lizing, -lized)

immortalities n ▷ immortal

immortality n ▷ immortal

immortalized v ▷ immortal

immortalizes v ▷ immortal

immortalizing v ▷ immortal

immortals n ▷ immortal

immune adj protected against a specific disease

immunities n ▷ immunity

immunity n (pl -ties) ability to resist disease

immunization n ▷ immunize

immunizations n ▷ immunize

immunize v (-izes, -izing, -ized) make immune to a disease > immunization n (pl -s)

immunized v ▷ immunize

immunizes v ▷ immunize

immunizing v ▷ immunize

immunodeficiencies n ▷ immunodeficiency

immunodeficiency n (pl -cies) deficiency in or breakdown of a person's ability to fight diseases

immunological adj ▷ immunology

immunologies n ▷ immunology

immunologist n ▷ immunology

immunologists n ▷ immunology

immunology n (pl -gies) branch of medicine concerned with the study of immunity

> immunological *adj* > immunologist *n* (*pl* -s)

immutabilities *n* > immutable

immutability *n* > immutable

immutable [im-mute-a-bl] *adj* unchangeable > immutability *n* (*pl* -ties)

imp *n* (*pl* -s) (in folklore) mischievous small creature with magical powers

impact *n* (*pl* -s) strong effect ▶ *v* (-s, -ing, -ed) press firmly into something

impacted *v* > impact

impacting *v* > impact

impacts *n*, *v* > impact

impair *v* (-s, -ing, -ed) weaken or damage > impairment *n* (*pl* -s)

impaired *v* > impair

impairing *v* > impair

impairment *n* > impair

impairments *n* > impair

impairs *v* > impair

impala [imp-ah-la] *n* (*pl* -s) southern African antelope

impalas *n* > impala

impale *v* (-les, -ling, -led) pierce with a sharp object

impaled *v* > impale

impales *v* > impale

impaling *v* > impale

impalpable *adj* difficult to define or understand

impart *v* (-s, -ing, -ed) communicate (information)

imparted *v* > impart

impartial *adj* not favouring one side or the other > impartially *adv* > impartiality *n* (*pl* -ties)

impartialities *n* > impartial

impartiality *n* > impartial

impartially *adv* > impartial

imparting *v* > impart

imparts *v* > impart

impassable *adj* (of a road etc.) impossible to travel through or over

impasse [am-pass] *n* (*pl* -s) situation in which progress is impossible

impasses *n* > impasse

impassioned *adj* full of emotion

impassive *adj* showing no emotion, calm

impatience *n* > impatient

impatiences *n* > impatient

impatient *adj* irritable at any delay or difficulty > impatiently *adv* > impatience *n* (*pl* -s)

impatiently *adv* > impatient

impeach *v* (-es, -ing, -ed) charge with a serious crime against the state > impeachment *n*

(*pl* -s)

impeached *v* > impeach

impeaches *v* > impeach

impeaching *v* > impeach

impeachment *n* > impeach

impeachments *n* > impeach

impeccable *adj* without fault, excellent > impeccably *adv*

impeccably *adv* > impeccable

impecunious *adj* penniless, poor

impedance [imp-eed-anss] *n* (*pl* -s) (ELECTRICITY) measure of the opposition to the flow of an alternating current

impedances *n* > impedance

impede *v* (-des, -ding, -ded) hinder in action or progress

impeded *v* > impede

impedes *v* > impede

impediment *n* (*pl* -s) something that makes action, speech, or progress difficult

impedimenta *pl n* objects impeding progress, esp. baggage or equipment

impediments *n* > impediment

impeding *v* > impede

impel *v* (-s, -lling, -lled) push or force (someone) to do something

impelled *v* > impel

impelling *v* > impel

impels *v* > impel

impending *adj* (esp. of something bad) about to happen

impenetrable *adj* impossible to get through

imperative *adj* extremely urgent, vital ▶ *n* (*pl* -s) (GRAMMAR) imperative mood

imperatives *n* > imperative

imperceptible *adj* too slight or gradual to be noticed > imperceptibly *adv*

imperceptibly *adv* > imperceptible

imperfect *adj* having faults or mistakes ▶ *n* (*pl* -s) (GRAMMAR) imperfect tense > imperfection *n* (*pl* -s)

imperfection *n* > imperfect

imperfections *n* > imperfect

imperfects *n* > imperfect

imperial *adj* of or like an empire or emperor

imperialism *n* (*pl* -s) rule by one country over many others > imperialist *adj*, *n* (*pl* -s)

imperialisms *n* > imperialism

imperialist *adj*, *n* > imperial

imperialists *n* > imperialist

imperil *v* (-s, -lling, -lled) put in danger

imperilled *v* > imperil

imperilling *v* > imperil

imperils *v* > imperil

imperious *adj* proud and domineering

impersonal *adj* not relating to any particular person, objective > **impersonality** *n* (*pl* -**ties**)
impersonalities *n* ▷ **impersonal**
impersonality *n* ▷ **impersonal**
impersonate *v* (-**tes**, -**ting**, -**ted**) pretend to be (another person) > **impersonation** *n* (*pl* -**s**) > **impersonator** *n* (*pl* -**s**)
impersonated *v* ▷ **impersonate**
impersonates *v* ▷ **impersonate**
impersonating *v* ▷ **impersonate**
impersonation *n* ▷ **impersonate**
impersonations *n* ▷ **impersonate**
impersonator *n* ▷ **impersonate**
impersonators *n* ▷ **impersonate**
impertinence *n* ▷ **impertinent**
impertinences *n* ▷ **impertinent**
impertinent *adj* disrespectful or rude > **impertinently** *adv* > **impertinence** *n* (*pl* -**s**)
impertinently *adv* ▷ **impertinent**
imperturbable *adj* calm, not excitable
impervious *adj* (*foll. by* **to**) not letting (water etc.) through
impetigo [imp-it-**tie**-go] *n* (*pl* -**s**) contagious skin disease
impetigos *n* ▷ **impetigo**
impetuosities *n* ▷ **impetuous**
impetuosity *n* ▷ **impetuous**
impetuous *adj* done or acting without thought, rash > **impetuously** *adv* > **impetuosity** *n* (*pl* -**ties**)
impetuously *adv* ▷ **impetuous**
impetus [imp-it-uss] *n* (*pl* -**es**) incentive, impulse
impetuses *n* ▷ **impetus**
impinge *v* (-**ges**, -**ging**, -**ged**) (*foll. by* **on**) affect or restrict
impinged *v* ▷ **impinge**
impinges *v* ▷ **impinge**
impinging *v* ▷ **impinge**
impious [imp-ee-uss] *adj* showing a lack of respect or reverence
impish *adj* mischievous
implacabilities *n* ▷ **implacable**
implacability *n* ▷ **implacable**
implacable *adj* not prepared to be appeased, unyielding > **implacably** *adv* > **implacability** *n* (*pl* -**ties**)
implacably *adv* ▷ **implacably**
implant *n* (MED) something put into someone's body, usu. by surgical operation ▶ *v* (-**s**, -**ing**, -**ed**) put (something) into someone's body, usu. by surgical operation > **implantation** *n* (*pl* -**s**)
implantation *n* ▷ **implant**
implantations *n* ▷ **implant**

implanted *v* ▷ **implant**
implanting *v* ▷ **implant**
implants *n*, *v* ▷ **implant**
implement *v* (-**s**, -**ing**, -**ed**) carry out (instructions etc.) ▶ *n* (*pl* -**s**) tool, instrument > **implementation** *n* (*pl* -**s**)
implementation *n* ▷ **implement**
implementations *n* ▷ **implement**
implemented *v* ▷ **implement**
implementing *v* ▷ **implement**
implements *v*, *n* ▷ **implement**
implicate *v* (-**tes**, -**ting**, -**ted**) show to be involved, esp. in a crime
implicated *v* ▷ **implicate**
implicates *v* ▷ **implicate**
implicating *v* ▷ **implicate**
implication *n* (*pl* -**s**) something implied
implications *n* ▷ **implication**
implicit *adj* expressed indirectly > **implicitly** *adv*
implicitly *adv* ▷ **implicit**
implied *v* ▷ **imply**
implies *v* ▷ **imply**
implore *v* (-**res**, -**ring**, -**red**) beg earnestly
implored *v* ▷ **implore**
implores *v* ▷ **implore**
imploring *v* ▷ **implore**
imply *v* (-**lies**, -**lying**, -**lied**) indicate by hinting, suggest
implying *v* ▷ **imply**
impolitic *adj* unwise or inadvisable
imponderable *n* (*pl* -**s**) ▶ *adj* (something) impossible to assess
imponderables *n* ▷ **imponderable**
import *v* (-**s**, -**ing**, -**ed**) bring in (goods) from another country ▶ *n* (*pl* -**s**) something imported > **importation** *n* (*pl* -**s**) > **importer** *n* (*pl* -**s**)
importance *n* ▷ **important**
importances *n* ▷ **important**
important *adj* of great significance or value > **importance** *n* (*pl* -**s**)
importation *n* ▷ **import**
importations *n* ▷ **import**
imported *v* ▷ **import**
importer *n* ▷ **import**
importers *n* ▷ **import**
importing *v* ▷ **import**
imports *v*, *n* ▷ **import**
importunate *adj* persistent or demanding
importune *v* (-**nes**, -**ning**, -**ned**) harass with persistent requests > **importunity** *n* (*pl* -**ties**)
importuned *v* ▷ **importune**
importunes *v* ▷ **importune**
importuning *v* ▷ **importune**

importunities n ▷ importune
importunity n ▷ importune
impose v (-ses, -sing, -sed) force the acceptance of
imposed v ▷ impose
imposes v ▷ impose
imposing adj grand, impressive ▶ v ▷ impose
imposition n (pl -s) unreasonable demand
impositions n ▷ imposition
impossibilities n ▷ impossible
impossibility n ▷ impossible
impossible adj not able to be done or to happen > **impossibly** adv > **impossibility** n (pl -ties)
impossibly adv ▷ impossible
imposter, impostor n (pl -s) person who cheats or swindles by pretending to be someone else
imposters n ▷ imposter
impostor n ▷ imposter
impostors n ▷ imposter
impotence n ▷ impotent
impotences n ▷ impotent
impotent [imp-a-tent] adj powerless > **impotence** n (pl -s) > **impotently** adv
impotently adv ▷ impotent
impound v (-s, -ing, -ed) take legal possession of, confiscate
impounded v ▷ impound
impounding v ▷ impound
impounds v ▷ impound
impoverish v (-es, -ing, -ed) make poor or weak > **impoverishment** n (pl -s)
impoverished v ▷ impoverish
impoverishes v ▷ impoverish
impoverishing v ▷ impoverish
impoverishment n ▷ impoverish
impoverishments n ▷ impoverish
impracticable adj incapable of being put into practice
impractical adj not sensible
imprecation n (pl -s) curse
imprecations n ▷ imprecation
impregnabilities n ▷ impregnable
impregnability n ▷ impregnable
impregnable adj impossible to break into > **impregnability** n (pl -ties)
impregnate v (-tes, -ting, -ted) saturate, spread all through > **impregnation** n (pl -s)
impregnated v ▷ impregnate
impregnates v ▷ impregnate
impregnating v ▷ impregnate
impregnation n ▷ impregnate
impregnations n ▷ impregnate
impresario n (pl -s) person who runs theatre

performances, concerts, etc.
impresarios n ▷ impresario
impress v (-es, -ing, -ed) affect strongly, usu. favourably
impressed v ▷ impress
impresses v ▷ impress
impressing v ▷ impress
impression n (pl -s) effect, esp. a strong or favourable one
impressionable adj easily impressed or influenced
impressionism n (pl -s) art style that gives a general effect or mood rather than form or structure > **impressionist** n (pl -s) > **impressionistic** adj
impressionisms n ▷ impressionism
impressionist n ▷ impressionism
impressionistic adj ▷ impressionism
impressionists n ▷ impressionism
impressions n ▷ impression
impressive adj making a strong impression, esp. through size, importance, or quality
imprimatur [imp-rim-**ah**-ter] n (pl -s) official approval to print a book
imprimaturs n ▷ imprimatur
imprint n (pl -s) mark made by printing or stamping ▶ v (-s, -ing, -ed) produce (a mark) by printing or stamping
imprinted v ▷ imprint
imprinting v ▷ imprint
imprints n, v ▷ imprint
imprison v (-s, -ing, -ed) put in prison > **imprisonment** n (pl -s)
imprisoned v ▷ imprison
imprisoning v ▷ imprison
imprisonment n ▷ imprison
imprisonments n ▷ imprisonment
imprisons v ▷ imprison
improbabilities n ▷ improbable
improbability n ▷ improbable
improbable adj not likely to be true or to happen > **improbability** n (pl -ties)
impromptu adj without planning or preparation
improper adj indecent
improprieties n ▷ impropriety
impropriety [imp-roe-**pry**-a-tee] n (pl -ties) unsuitable or slightly improper behaviour
improve v (-ves, -ving, -ved) make or become better > **improvement** n (pl -s)
improved v ▷ improve
improvement n ▷ improvement
improvements n ▷ improvement
improves v ▷ improve
improvidence n ▷ improvident

improvidences n ▷ improvident
improvident adj not planning for future needs
> **improvidence** n (pl -s)
improving v ▷ improve
improvisation n ▷ improvise
improvisations n ▷ improvise
improvise v (-ises, -sing, -sed) make use of whatever materials are available
> **improvisation** n (pl -s)
improvised v ▷ improvise
improvises v ▷ improvise
improvising v ▷ improvise
imps n ▷ imp
impudence n ▷ impudent
impudences n ▷ impudent
impudent adj cheeky, disrespectful
> **impudently** adv > **impudence** n (pl -s)
impudently adv ▷ impudent
impugn [imp-yoon] v (-s, -ing, -ed) challenge the truth or validity of
impugned v ▷ impugn
impugning v ▷ impugn
impugns v ▷ impugn
impulse n (pl -s) sudden urge to do something
> **impulsive** adj acting or done without careful consideration > **impulsively** adv
impulses n ▷ impulse
impulsive adj ▷ impulse
impulsively adv ▷ impulse
impunities n ▷ impunity
impunity [imp-yoon-it-ee] n (pl -ties) without punishment
impure adj having dirty or unwanted substances mixed in > **impurity** n (pl -ties)
impurities n ▷ impure
impurity n ▷ impure
imputation n ▷ impute
imputations n ▷ impute
impute v (-tes, -ting, -ted) attribute responsibility to > **imputation** n (pl -s)
imputed v ▷ impute
imputes v ▷ impute
imputing v ▷ impute
in prep indicating position inside, state or situation, etc. ▶ adv indicating position inside, entry into, etc. ▶ adj fashionable
inabilities n ▷ inability
inability n (pl -ties) lack of means or skill to do something
inaccuracies n ▷ inaccurate
inaccuracy n ▷ inaccurate
inaccurate adj not correct > **inaccuracy** n (pl -cies)
inadequacies n ▷ inadequate
inadequacy n ▷ inadequate

inadequate adj not enough > **inadequacy** n (pl -cies)
inadvertent adj unintentional
> **inadvertently** adv
inadvertently adv ▷ inadvertent
inalienable adj not able to be taken away
inane adj senseless, silly > **inanity** n (pl -ties)
inanimate adj not living
inanities n ▷ inane
inanity n ▷ inane
inappropriate adj not suitable
inarticulate adj unable to express oneself clearly or well
inaugural adj ▷ inaugurate
inaugurate v (-tes, -ting, -ted) open or begin the use of, esp. with ceremony > **inaugural** adj > **inauguration** n (pl -s)
inaugurated v ▷ inaugurate
inaugurates v ▷ inaugurate
inaugurating v ▷ inaugurate
inauguration n ▷ inaugurate
inaugurations n ▷ inaugurate
inauspicious adj unlucky, likely to have an unfavourable outcome
inboard adj (of a boat's engine) inside the hull
inborn adj existing from birth, natural
inbred adj produced as a result of inbreeding
inbreeding n (pl -s) breeding of animals or people that are closely related
inbreedings n ▷ inbreeding
inbuilt adj present from the start
incalculable adj too great to be estimated
incandescence n ▷ incandescent
incandescences n ▷ incandescent
incandescent adj glowing with heat
> **incandescence** n (pl -s)
incantation n (pl -s) ritual chanting of magic words or sounds
incantations n ▷ incantation
incapable adj (foll. by of) unable (to do something)
incapacitate v (-tates, -tating, -tated) deprive of strength or ability > **incapacity** n (pl -ties)
incapacitated v ▷ incapacitate
incapacitates v ▷ incapacitate
incapacitating v ▷ incapacitate
incapacities n ▷ incapacitate
incapacity n ▷ incapacitate
incarcerate v (-tes, -ting, -ted) imprison
> **incarceration** n (pl -s)
incarcerated v ▷ incarcerate
incarcerates v ▷ incarcerate
incarcerating v ▷ incarcerate
incarceration n ▷ incarcerate
incarcerations n ▷ incarcerate

incarnate *adj* in human form ▷ **incarnation** *n (pl -s)*
  incarnation *n* ▷ **incarnate**
  incarnations *n* ▷ **incarnate**
  incendiaries *n* ▷ **incendiary**
incendiary [in-send-ya-ree] *adj* (of a bomb, attack, etc.) designed to cause fires ▶ *n (pl -ries)* bomb designed to cause fires
incense¹ *v (-ses, -sing, -sed)* make very angry
incense² *n (pl incenses)* substance that gives off a sweet perfume when burned
  incensed *v* ▷ **incense¹**
  incenses *v* ▷ **incense¹** ▶ *n* ▷ **incense²**
  incensing *v* ▷ **incense¹**
incentive *n (pl -s)* something that encourages effort or action
  incentives *n* ▷ **incentive**
inception *n (pl -s)* beginning
  inceptions *n* ▷ **inception**
incessant *adj* never stopping > **incessantly** *adv*
  incessantly *adv* ▷ **incessant**
incest *n (pl -s)* sexual intercourse between two people too closely related to marry > **incestuous** *adj*
  incests *n* ▷ **incest**
  incestuous *adj* ▷ **incest**
inch *n (pl -es)* unit of length equal to one twelfth of a foot or 2.54 centimetres ▶ *v (-ches, -ching, -ched)* move slowly and gradually
  inched *v* ▷ **inch**
  inches *v, n* ▷ **inch**
  inching *v* ▷ **inch**
inchoate [in-koe-ate] *adj* just begun and not yet properly developed
incidence *n (pl -s)* extent or frequency of occurrence
  incidences *n* ▷ **incidence**
incident *n (pl -s)* something that happens
incidental *adj* occurring in connection with or resulting from something more important > **incidentally** *adv*
  incidentally *adv* ▷ **incidental**
  incidents *n* ▷ **incident**
incinerate *v (-tes, -ting, -ted)* burn to ashes > **incineration** *n (pl -s)*
  incinerated *v* ▷ **incinerate**
  incinerates *v* ▷ **incinerate**
  incinerating *v* ▷ **incinerate**
  incineration *n* ▷ **incinerate**
  incinerations *n* ▷ **incineration**
incinerator *n (pl -s)* furnace for burning rubbish
  incinerators *n* ▷ **incinerator**
incipient *adj* just starting to appear or happen

incise *v (-ses, -sing, -sed)* cut into with a sharp tool > **incision** *n (pl -s)*
  incised *v* ▷ **incise**
  incises *v* ▷ **incise**
  incising *v* ▷ **incise**
  incision *n* ▷ **incise**
  incisions *n* ▷ **incise**
incisive *adj* direct and forceful
incisor *n (pl -s)* front tooth, used for biting into food
  incisors *n* ▷ **incisor**
incite *v (-tes, -ting, -ted)* stir up, provoke > **incitement** *n (pl -s)*
  incited *v* ▷ **incite**
  incitement *n* ▷ **incite**
  incitements *n* ▷ **incite**
  incites *v* ▷ **incite**
  inciting *v* ▷ **incite**
  incivilities *n* ▷ **incivility**
incivility *n (pl -ties)* rudeness or a rude remark
inclement *adj* (of weather) stormy or severe
inclination *n (pl -s)* liking, tendency, or preference
  inclinations *n* ▷ **inclination**
incline *v (-nes, -ning, -ned)* lean, slope ▶ *n (pl -s)* slope
  inclined *v* ▷ **incline**
  inclines *v, n* ▷ **incline**
  inclining *v* ▷ **incline**
include *v (-des, -ding, -ded)* have as part of the whole > **inclusion** *n (pl -s)*
  included *v* ▷ **include**
  includes *v* ▷ **include**
  including *v* ▷ **include**
  inclusion *n* ▷ **include**
  inclusions *n* ▷ **include**
inclusive *adj* including everything (specified) > **inclusively** *adv*
  inclusively *adv* ▷ **inclusive**
incognito [in-kog-nee-toe] *adj, adv* having adopted a false identity ▶ *n (pl -tos)* false identity
  incognitos *n* ▷ **incognito**
  incoherence *n* ▷ **incoherent**
  incoherences *n* ▷ **incoherent**
incoherent *adj* unclear and impossible to understand > **incoherence** *n (pl -s)* > **incoherently** *adv*
  incoherently *adv* ▷ **incoherent**
income *n (pl -s)* amount of money earned from work, investments, etc.
  incomes *n* ▷ **income**
incoming *adj* coming in
incommode *v (-des, -ding, -ded)* cause inconvenience to

incommoded v ▷ **incommode**
incommodes v ▷ **incommode**
incommoding v ▷ **incommode**
incommunicado adj, adv deprived of communication with other people
incomparable adj beyond comparison, unequalled > **incomparably** adv
incomparably adv ▷ **incomparable**
incompatibilities n ▷ **incompatible**
incompatibility n ▷ **incompatible**
incompatible adj inconsistent or conflicting > **incompatibility** n (pl -**ties**)
incompetence n ▷ **incompetent**
incompetences n ▷ **incompetent**
incompetent adj not having the necessary ability or skill to do something > **incompetence** n (pl -**s**)
inconceivable adj extremely unlikely, unimaginable
inconclusive adj not giving a final decision or result
incongruities n ▷ **incongruous**
incongruity n ▷ **incongruous**
incongruous adj inappropriate or out of place > **incongruously** adv > **incongruity** n (pl -**ties**)
incongruously adv ▷ **incongruous**
inconsequential adj unimportant, insignificant
inconsiderable adj fairly large
inconstant adj liable to change one's loyalties or opinions
incontinence n ▷ **incontinent**
incontinences n ▷ **incontinent**
incontinent adj unable to control one's bladder or bowels > **incontinence** n (pl -**s**)
incontrovertible adj impossible to deny or disprove
inconvenience n (pl -**s**) trouble or difficulty ▶ v (-**ces**, -**ncing**, -**nced**) cause trouble or difficulty to > **inconvenient** adj
inconvenienced v ▷ **inconvenience**
inconveniences n, v ▷ **inconvenience**
inconveniencing v ▷ **inconvenience**
inconvenient adj ▷ **inconvenience**
incorporate v (-**tes**, -**ting**, -**ted**) include or be included as part of a larger unit
incorporated v ▷ **incorporate**
incorporates v ▷ **incorporate**
incorporating v ▷ **incorporate**
incorporeal adj without material form
incorrigible adj beyond correction or reform
incorruptible adj too honest to be bribed or corrupted
increase v (-**ses**, -**sing**, -**sed**) make or become greater in size, number, etc. ▶ n (pl -**s**) rise in

number, size, etc. > **increasingly** adv
increased v ▷ **increase**
increases v, n ▷ **increase**
increasing v ▷ **increase**
increasingly adv ▷ **increase**
incredible adj hard to believe or imagine > **incredibly** adv
incredibly adv ▷ **incredible**
incredulities n ▷ **incredulous**
incredulity n ▷ **incredulous**
incredulous adj not willing to believe something > **incredulity** n (pl -**ties**)
increment n (pl -**s**) increase in money or value, esp. a regular salary increase > **incremental** adj
incremental adj ▷ **increment**
increments n ▷ **increment**
incriminate v (-**tes**, -**ting**, -**ted**) make (someone) seem guilty of a crime > **incriminating** adj
incriminated v ▷ **incriminate**
incriminates v ▷ **incriminate**
incriminating v, adj ▷ **incriminate**
incubate [in-cube-ate] v (-**tes**, -**ting**, -**ted**) (of a bird) hatch (eggs) by sitting on them > **incubation** n (pl -**s**)
incubated v ▷ **incubate**
incubates v ▷ **incubate**
incubating v ▷ **incubate**
incubation n ▷ **incubate**
incubations n ▷ **incubate**
incubator n (pl -**s**) heated enclosed apparatus for rearing premature babies
incubators n ▷ **incubator**
incubi n ▷ **incubus**
incubus [in-cube-uss] n (pl -**bi**, -**buses**) (in folklore) demon believed to have sex with sleeping women
incubuses n ▷ **incubus**
inculcate v (-**tes**, -**ting**, -**ted**) fix in someone's mind by constant repetition > **inculcation** n (pl -**s**)
inculcated v ▷ **inculcate**
inculcates v ▷ **inculcate**
inculcating v ▷ **inculcate**
inculcation n ▷ **inculcate**
inculcations n ▷ **inculcate**
incumbencies n ▷ **incumbent**
incumbency n ▷ **incumbent**
incumbent n (pl -**s**) person holding a particular office or position ▶ adj it is the duty of > **incumbency** n (pl -**cies**)
incumbents n ▷ **incumbent**
incur v (-**s**, -**rring**, -**rred**) cause (something unpleasant) to happen

incurable adj not able to be cured > **incurably** adv

incurably adv ▷ **incurable**

incurious adj showing no curiosity or interest

incurred v ▷ **incur**

incurring v ▷ **incur**

incurs v ▷ **incur**

incursion n (pl -s) sudden brief invasion

incursions n ▷ **incursion**

indebted adj owing gratitude for help or favours > **indebtedness** n (pl -es)

indebtedness n ▷ **indebted**

indebtednesses n ▷ **indebted**

indecencies n ▷ **indecent**

indecency n ▷ **indecent**

indecent adj morally or sexually offensive > **indecently** adv > **indecency** n (pl -cies)

indecently adv ▷ **indecent**

indecipherable adj impossible to read

indeed adv really, certainly ▸ interj expression of indignation or surprise

indefatigable adj never getting tired > **indefatigably** adv

indefatigably adv ▷ **indefatigable**

indefensible adj unable to be justified

indefinite adj without exact limits > **indefinitely** adv

indefinitely adv ▷ **indefinite**

indelible adj impossible to erase or remove > **indelibly** adv

indelibly adv ▷ **indelible**

indelicate adj offensive or embarrassing

indemnified v ▷ **indemnify**

indemnifies v ▷ **indemnify**

indemnify v (-fies, -fying, -fied) secure against loss, damage, or liability

indemnifying v ▷ **indemnify**

indemnities v ▷ **indemnify**

indemnity n (pl -ties) insurance against loss or damage

indent v (-s, -ing, -ed) start (a line of writing) further from the margin than the other lines

indentation n (pl -s) dent in a surface or edge

indentations n ▷ **indentation**

indented v ▷ **indent**

indenting v ▷ **indent**

indents v ▷ **indent**

indenture n (pl -s) contract, esp. one binding an apprentice to his or her employer

indentures n ▷ **indenture**

independence n ▷ **independent**

independences n ▷ **independent**

independent adj free from the control or influence of others ▸ n (pl -s) politician who does not represent any political party

> **independently** adv > **independence** n (pl -s)

independently adsv ▷ **independent**

independents n ▷ **independent**

indescribable adj too intense or extreme for words > **indescribably** adv

indescribably adv ▷ **indescribable**

indeterminacies n ▷ **indeterminate**

indeterminacy n ▷ **indeterminate**

indeterminate adj uncertain in extent, amount, or nature > **indeterminacy** n (pl -cies)

index n (pl -dices) [in-diss-eez] alphabetical list of names or subjects dealt with in a book ▸ v (-dexes, -dexing, -dexed) provide (a book) with an index

indexed v ▷ **index**

indexes v ▷ **index**

indexing v ▷ **index**

indicate v (-tes, -ting, -ted) be a sign or symptom of > **indication** n (pl -s)

indicated v ▷ **indicate**

indicates v ▷ **indicate**

indicating v ▷ **indicate**

indication n ▷ **indicate**

indications n ▷ **indicate**

indicative adj (foll. by of) suggesting ▸ n (pl -s) (GRAMMAR) indicative mood

indicatives n ▷ **indicative**

indicator n (pl -s) something acting as a sign or indication

indicators n ▷ **indicator**

indices n ▷ **index**

indict [in-dite] v (-s, -ing, -ed) formally charge with a crime > **indictable** adj > **indictment** n (pl -s)

indictable adj ▷ **indict**

indicted v ▷ **indict**

indicting v ▷ **indict**

indictment n ▷ **indict**

indictments n ▷ **indict**

indicts v ▷ **indict**

indie adj (Informal) (of rock music) released by an independent record company

indifference n ▷ **indifferent**

indifferences n ▷ **indifferent**

indifferent adj showing no interest or concern > **indifference** n (pl -s) > **indifferently** adv

indifferently adv ▷ **indifferent**

indigence n ▷ **indigent**

indigences n ▷ **indigent**

indigenous [in-**dij**-in-uss] adj born in or natural to a country

indigent adj extremely poor > **indigence** n (pl -s)

indigestible adj ▷ **indigestion**

indigestion n (pl -s) (discomfort or pain

caused by) difficulty in digesting food
> **indigestible** adj

indigestions n ▷ indigestion

indignant adj feeling or showing indignation
> **indignantly** adv

indignantly adv ▷ indignant

indignation n (pl -s) anger at something
unfair or wrong

indignations n ▷ indignation

indignities n ▷ indignity

indignity n (pl -ties) embarrassing or
humiliating treatment

indigo adj deep violet-blue ▶ n (pl -s) dye of
this colour

indigos n ▷ indigo

indirect adj done or caused by someone or
something else

indiscreet adj incautious or tactless
in revealing secrets > **indiscreetly** adv
> **indiscretion** n (pl -s)

indiscreetly adv ▷ indiscreet

indiscretion n ▷ indiscreet

indiscretions n ▷ indiscreet

indiscriminate adj showing lack of careful
thought

indispensable adj absolutely essential

indisposed adj unwell, ill > **indisposition** n
(pl -s)

indisposition n ▷ indisposed

indispositions n ▷ indisposed

indisputable adj beyond doubt > **indisputably**
adv

indisputably adv ▷ indisputable

indissoluble adj permanent

indium n (pl -s) (CHEM) soft silvery-white
metallic element

indiums n ▷ indium

individual adj characteristic of or meant for a
single person or thing ▶ n (pl -s) single person
or thing > **individually** adv > **individuality**
n (pl -ties)

individualism n (pl -s) principle of living one's
life in one's own way > **individualist** n (pl -s)
> **individualistic** adj

individualisms n ▷ individualism

individualist n ▷ individualism

individualistic adj ▷ individualism

individualists n ▷ individualism

individualities n ▷ individual

individuality n ▷ individual

individually adv ▷ individual

individuals n ▷ individual

indoctrinate v (-tes, -ting, -ted) teach
(someone) to accept a doctrine or belief
uncritically > **indoctrination** n (pl -s)

indoctrinated v ▷ indoctrinate

indoctrinates v ▷ indoctrinate

indoctrinating v ▷ indoctrinate

indoctrination n ▷ indoctrinate

indoctrinations n ▷ indoctrinate

indolence n ▷ indolent

indolences n ▷ indolent

indolent adj lazy > **indolence** n (pl -s)

indomitable adj too strong to be defeated or
discouraged > **indomitably** adv

indomitably adv ▷ indomitable

indoor adj inside a building > **indoors** adv

indoors adv ▷ indoor

indubitable adj beyond doubt, certain
> **indubitably** adv

indubitably adv ▷ indubitable

induce v (-ces, -cing, -ced) persuade or
influence

induced v ▷ induce

inducement n (pl -s) something used to
persuade someone to do something

inducements n ▷ inducement

induces v ▷ induce

inducing v ▷ induce

induct v (-s, -ing, -ed) formally install
(someone, esp. a clergyman) in office

inductance n (pl -s) property of an electric
circuit creating voltage by a change of
current

inductances n ▷ inductance

inducted v ▷ induct

inducting v ▷ induct

induction n (pl -s) reasoning process by
which general conclusions are drawn from
particular instances > **inductive** adj

inductions n ▷ induction

inductive adj ▷ induction

inducts v ▷ induct

indulge v (-ges, -ging, -ged) allow oneself
pleasure > **indulgent** adj > **indulgently** adv

indulged v ▷ indulge

indulgence n (pl -s) something allowed
because it gives pleasure

indulgences n ▷ indulgence

indulgent adj ▷ indulge

indulgently adj ▷ indulge

indulges v ▷ indulge

indulging v ▷ indulge

industrial adj of, used in, or employed in
industry

industrialization n ▷ industrialize

industrializations n ▷ industrialize

industrialize v (-izes, -izing, -ized) develop
large-scale industry in (a country or region)
> **industrialization** n (pl -s)

industrialized v ▷ industrialize
industrializes v ▷ industrialize
industrializing v ▷ industrialize
industries n ▷ industry
industrious adj ▷ industry
industry n (pl -tries) manufacture of goods
> industrious adj hard-working
inebriate n (pl -s) ▸ adj (person who is)
habitually drunk
inebriated adj drunk > inebriation n (pl -s)
inebriates n ▷ inebriate
inebriation n ▷ inebriated
inebriations n ▷ inebriated
inedible adj not fit to be eaten
ineffable adj too great for words > ineffably
adv
ineffably adv ▷ ineffable
ineffectual adj having very little effect
ineligible adj not qualified for or entitled to
something
ineluctable adj impossible to avoid
inept adj clumsy, lacking skill > ineptitude
n (pl -s)
ineptitude n ▷ inept
ineptitudes n ▷ inept
inequitable adj unfair
ineradicable adj impossible to remove
inert adj without the power of motion or
resistance > inertness n (pl -es)
inertia n (pl -s) feeling of unwillingness to do
anything
inertias n ▷ inertia
inertness n ▷ inert
inertnesses n ▷ inert
inescapable adj unavoidable
inestimable adj too great to be estimated
> inestimably adv
inestimably adv ▷ inestimable
inevitabilities n ▷ inevitable
inevitability n ▷ inevitable
inevitable adj unavoidable, sure to happen
> inevitably adv > inevitability n (pl -ties)
inevitably adv ▷ inevitable
inexorable adj unable to be prevented from
continuing or progressing > inexorably adv
inexorably adv ▷ inexorable
inexpert adj lacking skill
inexplicable adj impossible to explain
> inexplicably adv
inexplicably adv ▷ inexplicable
inextricable adj impossible to escape from
infallibilities adv ▷ infallible
infallibility adv ▷ infallible
infallible adj never wrong > infallibly adv
> infallibility n (pl -ties)

infallibly adv ▷ infallible
infamies n ▷ infamous
infamous [in-fam-uss] adj well-known for
something bad > infamously adv > infamy
n (pl -mies)
infamously adv ▷ infamous
infamy n ▷ infamous
infancies n ▷ infancy
infancy n (pl -cies) early childhood
infant n (pl -s) very young child
infanticide n (pl -s) murder of an infant
infanticides n ▷ infanticide
infantile adj childish
infantries n ▷ infantry
infantry n (pl -ries) soldiers who fight on foot
infants n ▷ infant
infatuated adj feeling intense unreasoning
passion
infatuation n (pl -s) intense unreasoning
passion
infatuations n ▷ infatuation
infect v (-s, -ing, -ed) affect with a disease
> infection n (pl -s)
infected v ▷ infect
infecting v ▷ infect
infection n ▷ infect
infections n ▷ infect
infectious adj (of a disease) spreading without
actual contact
infects v ▷ infect
infer v (-s, -rring, -rred) work out from
evidence > inference n (pl -s)
inference n ▷ infer
inferences n ▷ infer
inferior adj lower in quality, position, or status
▸ n (pl -s) person of lower position or status
> inferiority n (pl -ties)
inferiorities n ▷ inferior
inferiority n ▷ inferior
inferiors n ▷ inferior
infernal adj of hell (Informal) > infernally adv
infernally adv ▷ infernal
inferno n (pl -s) intense raging fire
infernos n ▷ inferno
inferred v ▷ infer
inferring v ▷ infer
infers v ▷ infer
infertile adj unable to produce offspring
> infertility n (pl -ties)
infertilities n ▷ infertile
infertility n ▷ infertile
infest v (-s, -ing, -ed) inhabit or overrun in
unpleasantly large numbers > infestation
n (pl -s)
infestation n ▷ infest

infestations n ▷ infest
infested v ▷ infest
infesting v ▷ infest
infests v ▷ infest
infidel n (pl -s) person with no religion
infidelities n ▷ infidelity
infidelity n (pl -ties) (act of) sexual
unfaithfulness to one's husband, wife, or lover
infidels n ▷ infidel
infighting n (pl -s) quarrelling within a group
infightings n ▷ infighting
infiltrate v (-tes, -ting, -ted) enter gradually
and secretly > infiltration n (pl -s) > infiltrator
n (pl -s)
infiltrated v ▷ infiltrate
infiltrates v ▷ infiltrate
infiltrating v ▷ infiltrate
infiltration n ▷ infiltrate
infiltrations n ▷ infiltrate
infiltrator n ▷ infiltrate
infiltrators n ▷ infiltrate
infinite [in-fin-it] adj without any limit or end
> infinitely adv
infinitely adv ▷ infinite
infinitesimal adj extremely small
infinities n ▷ infinity
infinitive n (pl -s) (GRAMMAR) form of a verb not
showing tense, person, or number
infinitives n ▷ infinitive
infinity n (pl -ties) endless space, time, or
number
infirm adj physically or mentally weak
> infirmity n (pl -ties)
infirmaries n ▷ infirmary
infirmary n (pl -ries) hospital
infirmities n ▷ infirm
infirmity n ▷ infirm
inflame v (-mes, -ming, -med) make angry
or excited
inflamed adj (of part of the body) red, swollen,
and painful because of infection ▶ v ▷ inflame
> inflammation n (pl -s)
inflames v ▷ inflame
inflaming v ▷ inflame
inflammable adj easily set on fire
inflammation n ▷ inflamed
inflammations n ▷ inflamed
inflammatory adj likely to provoke anger
inflatable adj able to be inflated ▶ n (pl -s)
plastic or rubber object which can be inflated
inflatables n ▷ inflatable
inflate v (-tes, -ting, -ted) expand by filling
with air or gas
inflated v ▷ inflate
inflates v ▷ inflate

inflating v ▷ inflate
inflation n (pl -s) inflating > inflationary adj
inflationary adj ▷ inflationary
inflations n ▷ inflation
inflection, inflexion n (pl -s) change in the
pitch of the voice
inflections n ▷ inflection
inflexibilities n ▷ inflexible
inflexibility n ▷ inflexible
inflexible adj unwilling to be persuaded,
obstinate > inflexibly adv > inflexibility n
(pl -ties)
inflexibly n ▷ inflexibly
inflexion n ▷ inflection
inflexions n ▷ inflection
inflict v (-s, -ing, -ed) impose (something
unpleasant) on > infliction n (pl -s)
inflicted v ▷ inflict
inflicting v ▷ inflict
infliction n ▷ inflict
inflictions n ▷ inflict
inflicts v ▷ inflict
inflorescence n (pl -s) (BOTANY) arrangement of
flowers on a stem
inflorescences n ▷ inflorescence
influence n (pl -s) effect of one person or thing
on another ▶ v (-ces, -cing, -ced) have an
effect on > influential adj
influenced v ▷ influence
influences n, v ▷ influence
influencing v ▷ influence
influential adj ▷ influence
influenza n (pl -s) contagious viral disease
causing headaches, muscle pains, and fever
influenzas n ▷ influenza
influx n (pl -es) arrival or entry of many people
or things
influxes n ▷ influx
info n (pl -s) (Informal) information
inform v (-s, -ing, -ed) tell
informal adj relaxed and friendly > informally
adv > informality n (pl -s)
informalities n ▷ informal
informality n ▷ informal
informally adv ▷ informal
informant n (pl -s) person who gives
information
informants n ▷ informant
information n (pl -s) knowledge or facts
informations n ▷ information
informative adj giving useful information
informed v ▷ inform
informer n (pl -s) person who informs the
police
informers n ▷ informer

informing v ▷ inform
informs v ▷ inform
infos n ▷ info
infrared adj of or using rays below the red end of the visible spectrum
infrastructure n (pl -s) basic facilities, services, and equipment needed for a country or organization to function properly
infrastructures n ▷ infrastructure
infringe v (-ges, -ging, -ged) break (a law or agreement) > **infringement** n (pl -s)
infringed v ▷ infringe
infringement n ▷ infringe
infringements n ▷ infringe
infringes v ▷ infringe
infringing v ▷ infringe
infuriate v (-tes, -ting, -ted) make very angry
infuriated v ▷ infuriate
infuriates v ▷ infuriate
infuriating v ▷ infuriate
infuse v (-ses, -sing, -sed) fill (with an emotion or quality) > **infusion** n (pl -s) infusing
infused v ▷ infuse
infuses v ▷ infuse
infusing v ▷ infuse
infusion n ▷ infuse
infusions n ▷ infuse
ingenious [in-jean-ee-uss] adj showing cleverness and originality > **ingeniously** adv > **ingenuity** [in-jen-new-it-ee] n (pl -ties)
ingeniously adv ▷ ingenious
ingénue [an-jay-new] n (pl -s) naive young woman, esp. as a role played by an actress
ingénues n ▷ ingénue
ingenuities n ▷ ingenious
ingenuity n ▷ ingenious
ingenuous [in-jen-new-uss] adj unsophisticated and trusting > **ingenuously** adv
ingenuously adv ▷ ingenuous
ingest v (-s, -ing, -ed) take (food or liquid) into the body > **ingestion** n (pl -s)
ingested v ▷ ingest
ingesting v ▷ ingest
ingestion n ▷ ingest
ingestions n ▷ ingest
ingests v ▷ ingest
inglorious adj dishonourable, shameful
ingot n (pl -s) oblong block of cast metal
ingots n ▷ ingot
ingrained adj firmly fixed
ingratiate v (-iates, -iating, -iated) try to make (oneself) popular with someone > **ingratiating** adj > **ingratiatingly** adv
ingratiated v ▷ ingratiate
ingratiates v ▷ ingratiate

ingratiating v, adj ▷ ingratiate
ingratiatingly adv ▷ ingratiatingly
ingredient n (pl -s) component of a mixture or compound
ingredients n ▷ ingredient
ingress n (pl -es) act or right of entering
ingresses n ▷ ingress
ingrowing adj (of a toenail) growing abnormally into the flesh
inhabit v (-s, -ing, -ed) live in > **inhabitable** adj > **inhabitant** n (pl -s)
inhabitable adj ▷ inhabitable
inhabitant n ▷ inhabit
inhabitants n ▷ inhabit
inhabited v ▷ inhabit
inhabiting v ▷ inhabit
inhabits v ▷ inhabit
inhalant n (pl -s) medical preparation inhaled to help breathing problems
inhalants n ▷ inhalant
inhalations n ▷ inhalation
inhale v (-les, -ling, -led) breathe in (air, smoke, etc.) > **inhalation** n (pl -s)
inhaled v ▷ inhale
inhaler n (pl -s) container for an inhalant
inhalers n ▷ inhaler
inhales v ▷ inhale
inhaling v ▷ inhale
inherent adj existing as an inseparable part > **inherently** adv
inherently adv ▷ inherent
inherit v (-s, -ing, -ed) receive (money etc.) from someone who has died > **inheritance** n (pl -s) > **inheritor** n (pl -s)
inheritance n ▷ inherit
inheritances n ▷ inherit
inherited v ▷ inherit
inheriting v ▷ inherit
inheritor n ▷ inherit
inheritors n ▷ inherit
inherits v ▷ inherit
inhibit v (-s, -ing, -ed) restrain (an impulse or desire) > **inhibited** adj
inhibited v, adj ▷ inhibit
inhibiting v ▷ inhibit
inhibition n (pl -s) feeling of fear or embarrassment that stops one from behaving naturally
inhibitions n ▷ inhibition
inhibits v ▷ inhibit
inhospitable adj not welcoming, unfriendly
inhuman adj cruel or brutal
inhumane adj cruel or brutal > **inhumanity** n (pl -ties)
inhumanities n ▷ inhumane

inhumanity n ▷ inhumane
inimical adj unfavourable or hostile
inimitable adj impossible to imitate, unique
iniquities n ▷ iniquity
iniquitous adj ▷ iniquity
iniquity n (pl -ties) injustice or wickedness
> **iniquitous** adj
initial adj first, at the beginning ▶ n (pl -s) first
letter, esp. of a person's name ▶ v (-s, -lling,
-lled) sign with one's initials > **initially** adv
initialled v ▷ initial
initialling v ▷ initial
initially adv ▷ initial
initials n, v ▷ initial
initiate v (-tes, -ting, -ted) begin or set
going ▶ n (pl -s) recently initiated person
> **initiation** n (pl -s) > **initiator** n (pl -s)
initiated v ▷ initiate
initiates v, n ▷ initiate
initiating v ▷ initiate
initiation n ▷ initiate
initiations n ▷ initiate
initiative n (pl -ves) first step, commencing
move
initiatives n ▷ initiative
initiator n ▷ initiation
initiators n ▷ initiation
inject v (-s, -ing, -ed) put (a fluid) into the body
with a syringe > **injection** n (pl -s)
injected v ▷ inject
injecting v ▷ inject
injection n ▷ inject
injections n ▷ inject
injects v ▷ inject
injudicious adj showing poor judgment,
unwise
injunction n (pl -s) court order not to do
something
injunctions n ▷ injunction
injure v (-res, -ring, -red) hurt physically or
mentally > **injury** n (pl -ries) > **injurious** adj
injured v ▷ injure
injures v ▷ injure
injuries n ▷ injure
injuring v ▷ injure
injurious adj ▷ injure
injury n ▷ injure
injustice n (pl -s) unfairness
injustices n ▷ injustice
ink n (pl -s) coloured liquid used for writing or
printing ▶ v (-s, -ing, -ed) (foll. by in) mark in
ink (something already marked in pencil)
inked v ▷ ink
inking v ▷ ink
inkling n (pl -s) slight idea or suspicion

inklings n ▷ inkling
inks v, n ▷ ink
inky adj dark or black
inlaid adj set in another material so that the
surface is smooth
inland adj, adv in or towards the interior of a
country, away from the sea
inlay n (pl -s) inlaid substance or pattern
inlays n ▷ inlay
inlet n (pl -s) narrow strip of water extending
from the sea into the land
inlets n ▷ inlet
inmate n (pl -s) person living in an institution
such as a prison
inmates n ▷ inmate
inmost adj innermost
inn n (pl -s) pub or small hotel, esp. in the
country > **innkeeper** n (pl -s)
innards pl n (Informal) internal organs
innate adj being part of someone's nature,
inborn
inner adj happening or located inside
innermost adj furthest inside
innings n (SPORT) player's or side's turn of
batting
innkeeper n ▷ inn
innkeepers n ▷ inn
innocence n ▷ innocent
innocences n ▷ innocent
innocent adj not guilty of a crime ▶ n (pl -s)
innocent person, esp. a child > **innocently** adv
> **innocence** n (pl -s)
innocently adv ▷ innocent
innocents n ▷ innocent
innocuous adj not harmful > **innocuously** adv
innocuously adv ▷ innocuous
innovated v ▷ innovation
innovates v ▷ innovation
innovating v ▷ innovation
innovation n (pl -s) new idea or method
> **innovate** v (-tes, -ting, -ted) > **innovative**
adj > **innovator** n (pl -s)
innovations n ▷ innovation
innovative adj ▷ innovation
innovator n ▷ innovation
innovators n ▷ innovation
inns n ▷ inn
innuendo n (pl -does) (remark making) an
indirect reference to something rude or
unpleasant
innuendoes n ▷ innuendo
innumerable adj too many to be counted
innumeracies n ▷ innumerate
innumeracy n ▷ innumerate
innumerate adj having no understanding

of mathematics or science > **innumeracy** n
(pl **-cies**)

inoculate v (**-tes, -ting, -ted**) protect
against disease by injecting with a vaccine
> **inoculation** n (pl **-s**)
  inoculated v ▷ inoculate
  inoculates v ▷ inoculate
  inoculating v ▷ inoculate
  inoculation n ▷ inoculate
  inoculations n ▷ inoculate
inoperable adj (of a tumour or cancer) unable
to be surgically removed
inopportune adj badly timed, unsuitable
inordinate adj excessive
inorganic adj not having the characteristics of
living organisms
inpatient n (pl **-s**) patient who stays in a
hospital for treatment
  inpatients n ▷ inpatient
input n (pl **-s**) resources put into a project etc.
  ▶ v (**-s, -tting, -put**) enter (data) in a computer
  inputs v, n ▷ input
  inputting v, n ▷ input
inquest n (pl **-s**) official inquiry into a sudden
death
  inquests n ▷ inquest
inquire v (**-res, -ring, -red**) seek information or
ask (about) > **inquirer** n (pl **-s**)
  inquired v ▷ inquire
  inquirer n ▷ inquire
  inquirers n ▷ inquire
  inquires v ▷ inquire
  inquiries n ▷ inquiry
  inquiring v ▷ inquire
inquiry n (pl **-ries**) question
inquisition n (pl **-s**) thorough investigation
  > **inquisitor** n (pl **-s**) > **inquisitorial** adj
  inquisitions n ▷ inquisition
inquisitive adj excessively curious about
other people's affairs > **inquisitively** adv
  inquisitively adv ▷ inquisitive
  inquisitor n ▷ inquisition
  inquisitorial adj ▷ inquisition
  inquisitors n ▷ inquisition
inquorate adj without enough people present
to make a quorum
inroads pl n start affecting or reducing
insalubrious adj unpleasant, unhealthy, or
sordid
insane adj mentally ill > **insanely** adv
  > **insanity** n (pl **-ties**)
  insanely adv ▷ insane
insanitary adj dirty or unhealthy
  insanities n ▷ insane
  insanity n ▷ insane

insatiable [in-**saysh**-a-bl] adj unable to be
satisfied
inscribe v (**-bes, -bing, -bed**) write or carve
words on
  inscribed v ▷ inscribe
  inscribes v ▷ inscribe
  inscribing v ▷ inscribe
inscription n (pl **-s**) words inscribed
  inscriptions n ▷ inscription
inscrutable adj mysterious, enigmatic
  > **inscrutably** adv
  inscrutably adv ▷ inscrutable
insect n (pl **-s**) small animal with six legs and
usu. wings, such as an ant or fly
insecticide n (pl **-s**) substance for killing
insects
  insecticides n ▷ insecticide
insectivorous adj insect-eating
  insects n ▷ insect
insecure adj anxious, not confident
  inseminated v ▷ insemination
  inseminates v ▷ insemination
  inseminating v ▷ insemination
insemination n (pl **-s**) putting semen into a
woman's or female animal's body to try to
make her pregnant > **inseminate** v (**-tes,
-ting, -ted**)
  inseminations n ▷ insemination
insensate adj without sensation, unconscious
insensible adj unconscious, without feeling
insensitive adj unaware of or ignoring other
people's feelings > **insensitivity** n (pl **-ties**)
  insensitivities n ▷ insensitive
  insensitivity n ▷ insensitive
inseparable adj (of two people) spending
most of the time together
insert v (**-s, -ing, -ed**) put inside or include ▶ n
(pl **-s**) something inserted > **insertion** n (pl **-s**)
  inserted v ▷ insert
  inserting v ▷ insert
  insertion n ▷ insert
  insertions n ▷ insert
  inserts v, n ▷ insert
inset n (pl **-s**) small picture inserted within a
larger one
  insets n ▷ inset
inshore adj close to the shore ▶ adj, adv
towards the shore
inside prep in or to the interior of ▶ adj on or
of the inside ▶ adv on, in, or to the inside,
indoors ▶ n (pl **-s**) inner side, surface, or part
insider n (pl **-s**) member of a group who has
privileged knowledge about it
  insiders n ▷ insider
  insides n ▷ inside ▶ pl n (Informal) stomach

and bowels

insidious adj subtle or unseen but dangerous > **insidiously** adv
  insidiously adv ▷ insidious
insight n (pl -s) deep understanding
  insights n ▷ insight
insignia n (pl -s) badge or emblem of honour or office
  insignias n ▷ insignia
  insignificance n ▷ insignificant
  insignificances n ▷ insignificant
insignificant adj not important > **insignificance** n (pl -s)
insincere adj showing false feelings, not genuine > **insincerely** adv > **insincerity** n (pl -ties)
  insincerely adv ▷ insincerely
  insincerities n ▷ insincere
  insincerity n ▷ insincere
insinuate v (-tes, -ting, -ted) suggest indirectly > **insinuation** n (pl -s)
  insinuated v ▷ insinuate
  insinuates v ▷ insinuate
  insinuating v ▷ insinuate
  insinuation n ▷ insinuate
  insinuations n ▷ insinuate
insipid adj lacking interest, spirit, or flavour
insist v (-s, -ing, -ed) demand or state firmly > **insistent** adj making persistent demands > **insistently** adv > **insistence** n (pl -s)
  insisted v ▷ insist
  insistence n ▷ insist
  insistences n ▷ insist
  insistent adj ▷ insist
  insistently adv ▷ insist
  insisting v ▷ insist
  insists v ▷ insist
insole n (pl -s) inner sole of a shoe or boot
  insolence n ▷ insolent
  insolences n ▷ insolent
insolent adj rude and disrespectful > **insolence** n (pl -s) > **insolently** adv
  insolently adv ▷ insolent
  insoles n ▷ insole
insoluble adj incapable of being solved
  insolvencies n ▷ insolvent
  insolvency n ▷ insolvent
insolvent adj unable to pay one's debts > **insolvency** n (pl -cies)
insomnia n (pl -s) inability to sleep > **insomniac** n (pl -s)
  insomniac n ▷ insomnia
  insomniacs n ▷ insomnia
  insomnias n ▷ insomnia
  insouciance n ▷ insouciant

  insouciances n ▷ insouciant
insouciant adj carefree and unconcerned > **insouciance** n (pl -s)
inspect v (-s, -ing, -ed) check closely or officially > **inspection** n (pl -s)
  inspected v ▷ inspect
  inspecting v ▷ inspect
  inspection n ▷ inspect
  inspections n ▷ inspect
inspector n (pl -s) person who inspects
  inspectors n ▷ inspector
  inspects v ▷ inspect
inspiration n (pl -s) creative influence or stimulus > **inspirational** adj
  inspirational adj ▷ inspiration
  inspirations n ▷ inspiration
inspire v (-res, -ring, -red) fill with enthusiasm, stimulate
  inspired v ▷ inspire
  inspires v ▷ inspire
  inspiring v ▷ inspire
  instabilities n ▷ instability
instability n (pl -ties) lack of steadiness or reliability
install v (-lls, -lling, -lled) put in and prepare (equipment) for use
installation n (pl -s) installing
  installations n ▷ installation
  installed v ▷ install
  installing v ▷ install
  installs v ▷ install
instalment n (pl -s) any of the portions of a thing presented or a debt paid in successive parts
  instalments n ▷ instalment
instance n (pl -s) particular example ▸ v (-ces, -cing, -ced) mention as an example
  instanced v ▷ instance
  instances n, v ▷ instance
  instancing v ▷ instance
instant n (pl -s) very brief time ▸ adj happening at once > **instantly** adv
instantaneous adj happening at once > **instantaneously** adv
  instantaneously adv ▷ instantaneous
  instantly adv ▷ instant
  instants n ▷ instant
instead adv as a replacement or substitute
instep n (pl -s) part of the foot forming the arch between the ankle and toes
  insteps n ▷ instep
instigate v (-tes, -ting, -ted) cause to happen > **instigation** n (pl -s) > **instigator** n (pl -s)
  instigated v ▷ instigate
  instigates v ▷ instigate

instigating v ▷ instigate
instigation n ▷ instigate
instigations n ▷ instigate
instigator n ▷ instigate
instigators n ▷ instigate
instil v (-s, -lling, -lled) introduce (an idea etc.) gradually into someone's mind
instilled v ▷ instil
instilling v ▷ instil
instils v ▷ instil
instinct n (pl -s) inborn tendency to behave in a certain way > instinctive adj > instinctively adv
instinctive adj ▷ instinct
instinctively adv ▷ instinct
instincts n ▷ instinct
institute n (pl -s) organization set up for a specific purpose, esp. research or teaching ▶ v (-tutes, -tuting, -tuted) start or establish
instituted v ▷ institute
institutes n, v ▷ institute
instituting v ▷ institute
institution n (pl -s) large important organization such as a university or bank > institutional adj > institutionalize v (-izes, -izing, -ized)
institutional adj ▷ institution
institutionalize v ▷ institution
institutionalized v ▷ institution
institutionalizes v ▷ institution
institutionalizing n ▷ institution
institutions n ▷ institution
instruct v (-s, -ing, -ed) order to do something > instructor n (pl -s)
instructed v ▷ instruct
instructing v ▷ instruct
instruction n (pl -s) order to do something
instructions n ▷ instruction ▶ pl n information on how to do or use something
instructive adj informative or helpful
instructor n ▷ instruct
instructors n ▷ instruct
instructs v ▷ instruct
instrument n (pl -s) tool used for particular work
instrumental adj (foll. by in) having an important function (in)
instrumentalist n (pl -s) player of a musical instrument
instrumentalists n ▷ instrumentalist
instrumentation n (pl -s) set of instruments in a car etc.
instrumentations n ▷ instrumentation
instruments n ▷ instrument
insubordinate adj not submissive to

authority > insubordination n (pl -s)
insubordination n ▷ insubordinate
insubordinations n ▷ insubordinate
insufferable adj unbearable
insular adj not open to new ideas, narrow-minded > insularity n (pl -ties)
insularities n ▷ insular
insularity n ▷ insular
insulate v (-tes, -ting, -ted) prevent or reduce the transfer of electricity, heat, or sound by surrounding or lining with a nonconducting material > insulation n (pl -s) > insulator n (pl -s)
insulated v ▷ insulate
insulates v ▷ insulate
insulating v ▷ insulate
insulation n ▷ insulate
insulations n ▷ insulate
insulator n ▷ insulate
insulators n ▷ insulate
insulin n (pl -s) hormone produced in the pancreas that controls the amount of sugar in the blood
insulins n ▷ insulin
insult v (-s, -ing, -ed) behave rudely to, offend ▶ n (pl -s) insulting remark or action > insulting adj
insulted v ▷ insult
insulting v, adj ▷ insult
insults v, n ▷ insult
insuperable adj impossible to overcome
insupportable adj impossible to tolerate
insurance n (pl -ces) agreement by which one makes regular payments to a company who pay an agreed sum if damage, loss, or death occurs
insurances n ▷ insurance
insure v (-res, -ring, -red) protect by insurance
insured v ▷ insure
insures v ▷ insure
insurgent n (pl -s) ▶ adj (person) in revolt against an established authority
insurgents n ▷ insurgent
insuring v ▷ insure
insurrection n (pl -s) rebellion
insurrections n ▷ insurrection
intact adj not changed or damaged in any way
intaglio [in-tah-lee-oh] n (pl -s) (gem carved with) an engraved design
intaglios n ▷ intaglio
intake n (pl -kes) amount or number taken in
intakes n ▷ intake
integer n (pl -s) positive or negative whole number or zero
integers n ▷ integer

integral *adj* being an essential part of a whole ▶ *n* (*pl* -s) (MATHS) sum of a large number of very small quantities
  integrals *n* ▷ **integral**
integrate *v* (-tes, -ting, -ted) combine into a whole > **integration** *n* (*pl* -s)
  integrated *v* ▷ **integrate**
  integrates *v* ▷ **integrate**
  integrating *v* ▷ **integrate**
  integration *n* ▷ **integrate**
  integrations *n* ▷ **integrate**
  integrities *n* ▷ **integrity**
integrity *n* (*pl* -ties) quality of having high moral principles
intellect *n* (*pl* -s) power of thinking and reasoning
  intellects *n* ▷ **intellect**
intellectual *adj* of or appealing to the intellect ▶ *n* (*pl* -s) intellectual person > **intellectually** *adv*
  intellectually *adv* ▷ **intellectual**
  intellectuals *n* ▷ **intellectual**
intelligence *n* (*pl* -s) quality of being intelligent
  intelligences *n* ▷ **intelligence**
intelligent *adj* able to understand, learn, and think things out quickly > **intelligently** *adv*
  intelligently *adv* ▷ **intelligent**
intelligentsia *n* (*pl* -s) intellectual or cultured people in a society
  intelligentsias *n* ▷ **intelligentsia**
  intelligibilities *n* ▷ **intelligibile**
  intelligibility *n* ▷ **intelligibile**
intelligible *adj* able to be understood > **intelligibility** *n* (*pl* -ties)
  intemperance *n* ▷ **intemperate**
  intemperances *n* ▷ **intemperate**
intemperate *adj* unrestrained, uncontrolled > **intemperance** *n* (*pl* -s)
intend *v* (-s, -ing, -ed) propose or plan (to do something)
  intended *v* ▷ **intend**
  intending *v* ▷ **intend**
  intends *v* ▷ **intend**
intense *adj* of great strength or degree > **intensity** *n* (*pl* -ties)
  intensification *n* ▷ **intensify**
  intensifications *n* ▷ **intensify**
  intensified *v* ▷ **intensify**
  intensifies *v* ▷ **intensify**
intensify *v* (-fies, -fying, -fied) make or become more intense > **intensification** *n* (*pl* -s)
  intensifying *v* ▷ **intensify**
  intensities *n* ▷ **intense**
  intensity *n* ▷ **intense**

intensive *adj* using or needing concentrated effort or resources > **intensively** *adv*
  intensively *adv* ▷ **intensive**
intent *n* (*pl* -s) intention ▶ *adj* paying close attention > **intently** *adv* > **intentness** *n* (*pl* -s)
intention *n* (*pl* -s) something intended
intentional *adj* planned in advance, deliberate > **intentionally** *adv*
  intentionally *adv* ▷ **intentional**
  intentions *n* ▷ **intention**
  intently *adv* ▷ **intent**
  intentness *n* ▷ **intent**
  intentnesses *n* ▷ **intent**
  intents *n* ▷ **intent**
inter [in-ter] *v* (-s, -rring, -rred) bury (a corpse) > **interment** *n* (*pl* -s)
interact *v* (-s, -ing, -ed) act on or in close relation with each other > **interaction** *n* (*pl* -s) > **interactive** *adj*
  interacted *v* ▷ **interact**
  interacting *v* ▷ **interact**
  interaction *n* ▷ **interact**
  interactions *n* ▷ **interact**
  interactive *adj* ▷ **interact**
  interacts *v* ▷ **interact**
  interbred *v* ▷ **interbreed**
interbreed *v* (-s, -ing, -bred) breed within a related group
  interbreeding *v* ▷ **interbreed**
  interbreeds *v* ▷ **interbreed**
intercede *v* (-des, -ding, -ded) try to end a dispute between two people or groups > **intercession** *n* (*pl* -s)
  interceded *v* ▷ **intercede**
  intercedes *v* ▷ **intercede**
  interceding *v* ▷ **intercede**
intercept *v* (-s, -ing, -ed) seize or stop in transit > **interception** *n* (*pl* -s)
  intercepted *v* ▷ **intercept**
  intercepting *v* ▷ **intercept**
  interception *n* ▷ **intercept**
  interceptions *n* ▷ **intercept**
  intercepts *v* ▷ **intercept**
  intercession *n* ▷ **intercede**
  intercessions *n* ▷ **intercede**
interchange *v* (-ges, -ging, -ged) (cause to) exchange places ▶ *n* (*pl* -ges) motorway junction > **interchangeable** *adj*
  interchangeable *adj* ▷ **interchange**
  interchanged *v* ▷ **interchange**
  interchanges *v, n* ▷ **interchange**
  interchanging *v* ▷ **interchange**
intercom *n* (*pl* -s) internal communication system with loudspeakers
  intercoms *n* ▷ **intercom**

intercontinental adj travelling between or linking continents

intercourse n (pl -s) sexual intercourse

intercourses n ▷ intercourse

interdict n ▷ interdiction

interdiction, interdict n (pl -s) formal order forbidding something

interdictions n ▷ interdiction

interdicts n ▷ interdiction

interdisciplinary adj involving more than one branch of learning

interest n (pl -s) desire to know or hear more about something ▶ v (-s, -ing, -ed) arouse the interest of > **interesting** adj > **interestingly** adv

interested adj feeling or showing interest ▶ v ▷ interest

interesting v, adj ▷ interest

interestingly adv ▷ interest

interests n, v ▷ interest

interface n (pl -s) area where two things interact or link

interfaces n ▷ interface

interfere v (-res, -ring, -red) try to influence other people's affairs where one is not involved or wanted > **interfering** adj > **interference** n (pl -s) interfering

interfered v ▷ interfere

interference n ▷ interfere

interferences n ▷ interfere

interferes v ▷ interfere

interfering v, adj ▷ interfere

interferon n (pl -s) protein that stops the development of an invading virus

interferons n ▷ interferon

interim adj temporary or provisional

interior n (pl -s) inside ▶ adj inside, inner

interiors n ▷ interior

interject v (-s, -ing, -ed) make (a remark) suddenly or as an interruption > **interjection** n (pl -s)

interjected v ▷ interject

interjecting v ▷ interject

interjection n ▷ interject

interjections n ▷ interject

interjects v ▷ interject

interlace v (-ces, -cing, -ced) join together as if by weaving

interlaced v ▷ interlace

interlaces v ▷ interlace

interlacing v ▷ interlace

interlink v (-s, -ing, -ed) connect together

interlinked v ▷ interlink

interlinking v ▷ interlink

interlinks v ▷ interlink

interlock v (-s, -ing, -ed) join firmly together

interlocked v ▷ interlock

interlocking v ▷ interlock

interlocks v ▷ interlock

interlocutor [in-ter-**lok**-yew-ter] n (pl -s) person who takes part in a conversation

interlocutors n ▷ interlocutor

interloper [in-ter-**lope**-er] n (pl -s) person in a place or situation where he or she has no right to be

interlopers n ▷ interloper

interlude n (pl -s) short rest or break in an activity or event

interludes n ▷ interlude

intermarriage n ▷ intermarry

intermarriages n ▷ intermarry

intermarried v ▷ intermarry

intermarries v ▷ intermarry

intermarry v (-rries, -rrying, -rried) (of families, races, or religions) become linked by marriage > **intermarriage** n (pl -s)

intermarrying v ▷ intermarry

intermediaries n ▷ intermediary

intermediary n (pl -ries) person trying to create agreement between others

intermediate adj coming between two points or extremes

interment n ▷ inter

interments n ▷ inter

intermezzo [in-ter-**met**-so] n (pl -s) short piece of music, esp. one performed between the acts of an opera

intermezzos n ▷ intermezzo

interminable adj seemingly endless because boring > **interminably** adv

interminably adv ▷ interminable

intermingle v (-les, -ling, -led) mix together

intermingled v ▷ intermingle

intermingles v ▷ intermingle

intermingling v ▷ intermingle

intermission n (pl -s) interval between parts of a play, film, etc.

intermissions n ▷ intermission

intermittent adj occurring at intervals > **intermittently** adv

intermittently adv ▷ intermittent

intern v (-s, -ing, -ed) imprison, esp. during a war ▶ n (pl -s) trainee doctor in a hospital > **internment** n (pl -s)

internal adj of or on the inside > **internally** adv

internally adv ▷ internal

international adj of or involving two or more countries ▶ n (pl -s) game or match between teams of different countries > **internationally** adv

internationally adv ▷ international
internationals n ▷ international
internecine adj mutually destructive
interned v ▷ intern
internee n (pl -s) person who is interned
internees n ▷ internee
interning v ▷ intern
internment n ▷ intern
internments n ▷ intern
interns v, n ▷ intern
interplanetary adj of or linking planets
interplay n (pl -s) action and reaction of two
    things upon each other
interplays n ▷ interplay
interpolate [in-ter-pole-ate] v (-tes, -ting,
    -ted) insert (a comment or passage) into (a
    conversation or text) > **interpolation** n (pl -s)
interpolated v ▷ interpolate
interpolates v ▷ interpolate
interpolating v ▷ interpolate
interpolation n ▷ interpolate
interpolations n ▷ interpolate
interpose v (-ses, -sing, -sed) insert between
    or among things
interposed v ▷ interpose
interposes v ▷ interpose
interposing v ▷ interpose
interpret v (-s, -ing, -ed) explain the meaning
    of > **interpretation** n (pl -s)
interpretation n ▷ interpret
interpretations n ▷ interpret
interpreted v ▷ interpret
interpreter n (pl -s) person who translates
    orally from one language into another
interpreters n ▷ interpreter
interpreting v ▷ interpret
interprets v ▷ interpret
interred v ▷ inter
interregna n ▷ interregnum
interregnum n (pl -nums, -na) interval
    between reigns
interregnums n ▷ interregnum
interring v ▷ inter
interrogate v (-tes, -ting, -ted) question
    closely > **interrogation** n (pl -s)
interrogated v ▷ interrogate
interrogates v ▷ interrogate
interrogating v ▷ interrogate
interrogation n ▷ interrogate
interrogations n ▷ interrogate
interrogative adj questioning ▶ n (pl -s) word
    used in asking a question, such as how or why
    > **interrogator** n (pl -s)
interrogatives n ▷ interrogative
interrogator n ▷ interrogative

interrogators n ▷ interrogative
interrupt v (-s, -ing, -ed) break into (a
    conversation etc.) > **interruption** n (pl -s)
interrupted v ▷ interrupt
interrupting v ▷ interrupt
interruption n ▷ interrupt
interruptions n ▷ interrupt
interrupts v ▷ interrupt
inters v ▷ inter
intersect v (-s, -ing, -ed) (of roads) meet and
    cross > **intersection** n (pl -s)
intersected v ▷ intersect
intersecting v ▷ intersect
intersection n ▷ intersect
intersections n ▷ intersect
intersects v ▷ intersect
interspersed adj scattered (among, between,
    or on)
interstellar adj between or among stars
interstice [in-ter-stiss] n (pl -ces) small crack or
    gap between things
interstices n ▷ interstice
intertwine v (-nes, -ning, -ned) twist together
intertwined v ▷ intertwine
intertwines v ▷ intertwine
intertwining v ▷ intertwine
interval n (pl -s) time between two particular
    moments or events
intervals n ▷ interval
intervene v (-nes, -ning, -ned) involve oneself
    in a situation, esp. to prevent conflict
    > **intervention** n (pl -s)
intervened v ▷ intervene
intervenes v ▷ intervene
intervening v ▷ intervene
intervention n ▷ intervene
interventions n ▷ intervene
interview n (pl -s) formal discussion, esp.
    between a job-seeker and an employer ▶ v
    (-s, -ing, -ed) conduct an interview with
    > **interviewee** n (pl -s) > **interviewer** n (pl -s)
interviewed v ▷ interview
interviewee n ▷ interview
interviewees n ▷ interview
interviewer n ▷ interview
interviewers n ▷ interview
interviewing v ▷ interview
interviews n, v ▷ interview
interweave v (-ves, -ving, -wove, -woven)
    weave together
interweaves v ▷ interweave
interweaving v ▷ interweave
interwove v ▷ interweave
interwoven v ▷ interweave
intestacies n ▷ intestate

intestacy *n* ▷ intestate

intestate *adj* not having made a will
> intestacy *n* (*pl* -cies)

intestinal *adj* ▷ intestine

intestinally *adv* ▷ intestine

intestine *n* (*pl* -s) (*often pl* lower part of the alimentary canal between the stomach and the anus > intestinal *adj* > intestinally *adv*

intestines *n* ▷ intestine

intimacies *n* ▷ intimate¹

intimacy *n* ▷ intimate¹

intimate¹ *adj* having a close personal relationship ▶ *n* (*pl* -s) close friend
> intimately *adv* > intimacy *n* (*pl* -cies)

intimate² *v* (-tes, -ting, -ted) hint at or suggest
> intimation *n* (*pl* -s)

intimated *v* ▷ intimate²

intimately *adv* ▷ intimate¹

intimates *n* ▷ intimate¹ ▶ *v* ▷ intimate²

intimating *v* ▷ intimate²

intimation *n* ▷ intimate²

intimations *n* ▷ intimate²

intimidate *v* (-tes, -ting, -ted) subdue or influence by fear > intimidating *adj*
> intimidation *n* (*pl* -s)

intimidated *v* ▷ intimidate

intimidates *v* ▷ intimidate

intimidating *v*, *adj* ▷ intimidate

intimidation *n* ▷ intimidate

intimidations *n* ▷ intimidate

into *prep* indicating motion towards the centre, result of a change, division, etc.

intolerable *adj* more than can be endured
> intolerably *adv*

intolerably *adv* ▷ intolerable

intolerance *n* ▷ intolerant

intolerances *n* ▷ intolerant

intolerant *adj* refusing to accept practices and beliefs different from one's own
> intolerance *n* (*pl* -s)

intonation *n* (*pl* -s) sound pattern produced by variations in the voice

intonations *n* ▷ intonation

intone *v* (-nes, -ning, -ned) speak or recite in an unvarying tone of voice

intoned *v* ▷ intone

intones *v* ▷ intone

intoning *v* ▷ intone

intoxicant *n* (*pl* -s) intoxicating drink

intoxicants *n* ▷ intoxicant

intoxicate *v* (-tes, -ting, -ted) make drunk

intoxicated *v* ▷ intoxicate

intoxicates *v* ▷ intoxicate

intoxicating *v* ▷ intoxicate

intoxication *n* (*pl* -s) state of being drunk

intoxications *n* ▷ intoxication

intractable *adj* (of a person) difficult to control

intranet *n* (*pl* -s) (COMPUTERS) internal network that makes use of Internet technology

intranets *n* ▷ intranet

intransigence *n* ▷ intransigent

intransigences *n* ▷ intransigent

intransigent *adj* refusing to change one's attitude > intransigence *n* (*pl* -s)

intransitive *adj* (of a verb) not taking a direct object

intrauterine *adj* within the womb

intravenous [in-tra-vee-nuss] *adj* into a vein
> intravenously *adv*

intravenously *adv* ▷ intravenous

intrepid *adj* fearless, bold > intrepidity *n* (*pl* -ties)

intrepidities *n* ▷ intrepid

intrepidity *n* ▷ intrepid

intricacies *n* ▷ intricate

intricacy *n* ▷ intricate

intricate *adj* involved or complicated
> intricately *adv* > intricacy *n* (*pl* -cies)

intricately *adv* ▷ intricate

intrigue *v* (-gues, -guing, -gued) make interested or curious ▶ *n* (*pl* -gues) secret plotting > intriguing *adj*

intrigued *v* ▷ intrigue

intrigues *v*, *n* ▷ intrigue

intriguing *v*, *adj* ▷ intrigue

intrinsic *adj* essential to the basic nature of something > intrinsically *adv*

intrinsically *adv* ▷ intrinsic

introduce *v* (-ces, -cing, -ced) present (someone) by name (to another person)

introduced *v* ▷ introduce

introduces *v* ▷ introduce

introducing *v* ▷ introduce

introduction *n* (*pl* -s) presentation of one person to another > introductory *adj*

introductions *n* ▷ introduction

introductory *adj* ▷ introduction

introspection *n* (*pl* -s) examination of one's own thoughts and feelings > introspective *adj*

introspections *n* ▷ introspection

introspective *adj* ▷ introspection

introversion *n* ▷ introvert

introversions *n* ▷ introvert

introvert *n* (*pl* -s) person concerned more with his or her thoughts and feelings than with the outside world > introverted *adj*
> introversion *n* (*pl* -s)

introverted *adj* ▷ introvert

introverts *n* ▷ introvert

intrude *v* (-des, -ding, -ded) come in or join

in without being invited > **intrusion** n (pl **-s**)
> **intrusive** adj

intruded v ⊳ **intrude**

intruder n (pl **-s**) person who enters a place
without permission

intruders n ⊳ **intruder**

intrudes v ⊳ **intrude**

intruding v ⊳ **intrude**

intrusion n ⊳ **intrude**

intrusions n ⊳ **intrude**

intrusive adj ⊳ **intrude**

intuition n (pl **-s**) instinctive knowledge
or insight without conscious reasoning
> **intuitive** adj > **intuitively** adv

intuitions n ⊳ **intuition**

intuitive adj ⊳ **intuition**

intuitively adv ⊳ **intuition**

inundate v (**-tes, -ting, -ted**) flood
> **inundation** n (pl **-s**)

inundated v ⊳ **inundate**

inundates v ⊳ **inundate**

inundating v ⊳ **inundate**

inundation n ⊳ **inundate**

inundations n ⊳ **inundate**

inured adj accustomed, esp. to hardship or
danger

invade v (**-des, -ding, -ded**) enter (a country) by
military force > **invader** n (pl **-s**)

invaded v ⊳ **invade**

invader n ⊳ **invade**

invaders n ⊳ **invade**

invades v ⊳ **invade**

invading v ⊳ **invade**

invalid¹ adj, n (pl **-s**) disabled or chronically ill
(person) ▶ v (**-s, -ing, -ed**) (often foll. by **out**)
dismiss from active service because of illness
or injury > **invalidity** n (pl **-ties**)

invalid² adj having no legal force

invalidate v (**-tes, -ting, -ted**) make or show
to be invalid

invalidated v ⊳ **invalidate**

invalidates v ⊳ **invalidate**

invalidating v ⊳ **invalidate**

invalided v ⊳ **invalid¹**

invaliding v ⊳ **invalid¹**

invalidities n ⊳ **invalid¹**

invalidity n ⊳ **invalid¹**

invalids n, v ⊳ **invalid¹**

invaluable adj of very great value or worth

invasion n (pl **-s**) invading

invasions n ⊳ **invasion**

invective n (pl **-s**) abusive speech or writing

invectives n ⊳ **invective**

inveigh [in-**vay**] v (**-s, -ing, -ed**) (foll. by **against**)
criticize strongly

inveighed v ⊳ **inveigh**

inveighing v ⊳ **inveigh**

inveighs v ⊳ **inveigh**

inveigle v (**-les, -ling, -led**) coax by cunning
or trickery

inveigled v ⊳ **inveigle**

inveigles v ⊳ **inveigle**

inveigling v ⊳ **inveigle**

invent v (**-s, -ing, -ed**) think up or create
(something new)

invented v ⊳ **invent**

inventing v ⊳ **invent**

invention n (pl **-s**) something invented

inventive adj creative and resourceful
> **inventiveness** n (pl **-s**) > **inventor** n (pl **-s**)

inventiveness n ⊳ **inventive**

inventivenesses n ⊳ **inventive**

inventor n ⊳ **inventive**

inventories v ⊳ **inventory**

inventors n ⊳ **inventive**

inventory n (pl **-ries**) detailed list of goods or
furnishings

invents v ⊳ **invent**

inverse adj reversed in effect, sequence,
direction, etc. > **inversely** adv

inversely adv ⊳ **inverse**

inversion n ⊳ **invert**

inversions n ⊳ **invert**

invert v (**-s, -ing, -ed**) turn upside down or
inside out > **inversion** n (pl **-s**)

invertebrate n (pl **-s**) animal with no
backbone

invertebrates n ⊳ **invertebrate**

inverted v ⊳ **invert**

inverting v ⊳ **invert**

inverts v ⊳ **invert**

invest v (**-s, -ing, -ed**) spend (money, time, etc.)
on something with the expectation of profit

invested v ⊳ **invest**

investigate v (**-tes, -ting, -ted**) inquire
into, examine > **investigation** n (pl **-s**)
> **investigative** adj > **investigator** n (pl **-s**)

investigated v ⊳ **investigate**

investigates v ⊳ **investigate**

investigating v ⊳ **investigate**

investigation n ⊳ **investigate**

investigations n ⊳ **investigate**

investigative adj ⊳ **investigate**

investigator n ⊳ **investigate**

investigators n ⊳ **investigate**

investing v ⊳ **invest**

investiture n (pl **-s**) formal installation of a
person in an office or rank

investitures n ⊳ **investiture**

investment n (pl **-s**) money invested

> **investor** n (pl -s)
investments n ▷ investment
investor n ▷ investment
investors n ▷ investment
invests v ▷ invest
inveterate adj firmly established in a habit or condition
invidious adj likely to cause resentment
invigilate v (-tes, -ting, -ted) supervise people sitting an examination > **invigilator** n (pl -s)
invigilated v ▷ invigilate
invigilates v ▷ invigilate
invigilating v ▷ invigilate
invigilation n ▷ invigilate
invigilations n ▷ invigilate
invigilator n ▷ invigilate
invigilators n ▷ invigilate
invigorate v (-tes, -ting, -ted) give energy to, refresh
invigorated v ▷ invigorate
invigorates v ▷ invigorate
invigorating v ▷ invigorate
invincibilities n ▷ invincibile
invincibility n ▷ invincibile
invincible adj impossible to defeat
> **invincibility** n (pl -ties)
inviolable adj unable to be broken or violated
inviolate adj unharmed, unaffected
invisibilities n ▷ invisible
invisibility adv ▷ invisible
invisible adj not able to be seen > **invisibly** adv
> **invisibility** n (pl -ties)
invisibly adv ▷ invisible
invitation n ▷ invite
invitations n ▷ invite
invite v (-tes, -ting, -ted) request the company of ▷ n (pl -s) (Informal) invitation > **invitation** n (pl -s)
invited v ▷ invite
invites v, n ▷ invite
inviting adj tempting, attractive ▶ v ▷ invite
invocation n ▷ invoke
invocations n ▷ invoke
invoice v (-ces, -cing, -ced) ▶ n (pl -s) (present with) a bill for goods or services supplied
invoiced v ▷ invoice
invoices n, v ▷ invoice
invoicing v ▷ invoice
invoke v (-kes, -king, -ked) put (a law or penalty) into operation > **invocation** n (pl -s)
invoked v ▷ invoke
invokes v ▷ invoke
invoking v ▷ invoke
involuntarily adv ▷ involuntary
involuntary adj not done consciously, unintentional > **involuntarily** adv
involve v (-lves, -lving, -lved) include as a necessary part > **involved** adj complicated
> **involvement** n (pl -s)
involved v, adj ▷ involve
involvement n ▷ involve
involvements n ▷ involve
involves v ▷ involve
involving v ▷ involve
invulnerable adj not able to be wounded or harmed
inward adj directed towards the middle ▶ adv (also **inwards**) towards the inside or middle
> **inwardly** adv
inwardly adv ▷ inward
inwards adv ▷ inward

> **io** n (ios). An io a cry of joy or grief. While io doesn't earn many points, it's useful when you want to form words in more than one direction: I and O are two of the most common tiles in the game, so there's a good chance that you'll be able to use io when forming a word in another direction. Io scores 2 points.

iodine n (pl -s) (CHEM) bluish-black element used in medicine and photography
iodines n ▷ iodine
iodize v (-izes, -izing, -ized) treat with iodine
iodized n ▷ iodize
iodizes n ▷ iodize
iodizing n ▷ iodize
ion n (pl -s) electrically charged atom > **ionic** adj
ionic adj ▷ ion
ionization n ▷ ionize
ionizations n ▷ ionize
ionize v (-izes, -izing, -ized) change into ions
> **ionization** n (pl -s)
ionized v ▷ ionize
ionizes v ▷ ionize
ionizing v ▷ ionize
ionosphere n (pl -s) region of ionized air in the upper atmosphere that reflects radio waves
ionospheres n ▷ ionosphere
ions n ▷ ion
iota n (pl -s) very small amount
iotas n ▷ iota
irascibilities n ▷ irascible
irascibility n ▷ irascible
irascible adj easily angered > **irascibility** n (pl -ties)
irate adj very angry
ire n (pl -s) (Lit) anger
ires n ▷ ire
iridescence n ▷ iridescent

iridescences n ▷ iridescent
iridescent adj having shimmering changing colours like a rainbow > **iridescence** n (pl -s)
iridium n (pl -s) (CHEM) very hard corrosion-resistant metal
iridiums n ▷ iridium
iris n (pl -ses) coloured circular membrane of the eye containing the pupil
irises n ▷ iris
irk v (-s, -ing, -ed) irritate, annoy
irked v ▷ irk
irking v ▷ irk
irks v ▷ irk
irksome adj irritating, annoying
iron n (pl -s) strong silvery-white metallic element, widely used for structural and engineering purposes ▶ adj made of iron ▶ v (-s, -ing, -ed) smooth (clothes or fabric) with an iron
ironbark n (pl -s) Australian eucalyptus with hard rough bark
ironbarks n ▷ ironbark
ironed v ▷ iron
ironic, ironical adj using irony > **ironically** adv
ironical adj ▷ ironic
ironically adv ▷ ironic
ironies n ▷ irony
ironing n (pl -s) clothes to be ironed ▶ v ▷ iron
ironings n ▷ ironing
ironmonger n (pl -s) shopkeeper or shop dealing in hardware > **ironmongery** n (pl -ries)
ironmongeries n ▷ ironmonger
ironmongers n ▷ ironmonger
ironmongery n ▷ ironmonger
irons n, v ▷ iron ▶ pl n chains, restraints
ironstone n (pl -s) rock consisting mainly of iron ore
ironstones n ▷ ironstone
irony n (pl -nies) mildly sarcastic use of words to imply the opposite of what is said
irradiate v (-tes, -ting, -ted) subject to or treat with radiation > **irradiation** n (pl -s)
irradiated v ▷ irradiate
irradiates v ▷ irradiate
irradiating v ▷ irradiate
irradiation n ▷ irradiate
irradiations n ▷ irradiate
irrational adj not based on or not using logical reasoning
irredeemable adj not able to be reformed or corrected
irreducible adj impossible to put in a simpler form
irrefutable adj impossible to deny or disprove

irregular adj not regular or even > **irregularly** adv > **irregularity** n (pl -ties)
irregularities n ▷ irregular
irregularity n ▷ irregular
irregularly adv ▷ irregular
irrelevance n ▷ irrelevant
irrelevances n ▷ irrelevant
irrelevant adj not connected with the matter in hand > **irrelevantly** adv > **irrelevance** n (pl -s)
irrelevantly adv ▷ irrelevant
irreparable adj not able to be repaired or put right > **irreparably** adv
irreparably adv ▷ irreparable
irreplaceable adj impossible to replace
irreproachable adj blameless, faultless
irresistible adj too attractive or strong to resist > **irresistibly** adv
irresistibly adv ▷ irresistible
irresponsibilities n ▷ irresponsible
irresponsibility n ▷ irresponsible
irresponsible adj not showing or not done with due care for the consequences of one's actions or attitudes > **irresponsibility** n (pl -ties)
irreverence n ▷ irreverent
irreverences n ▷ irreverent
irreverent adj not showing due respect > **irreverence** n (pl -s)
irreversible adj not able to be reversed or put right again > **irreversibly** adv
irreversibly adv ▷ irreversible
irrevocable adj not possible to change or undo > **irrevocably** adv
irrevocably adv ▷ irrevocable
irrigate v (-tes, -ting, -ted) supply (land) with water by artificial channels or pipes > **irrigation** n (pl -s)
irrigated v ▷ irrigate
irrigates v ▷ irrigate
irrigating v ▷ irrigate
irrigation n ▷ irrigate
irrigations n ▷ irrigate
irritable adj easily annoyed > **irritably** adv
irritably adv ▷ irritable
irritant n (pl -s) ▶ adj (person or thing) causing irritation
irritants n ▷ irritant
irritate v (-tes, -ting, -ted) annoy, anger > **irritation** n (pl -s)
irritated v ▷ irritate
irritates v ▷ irritate
irritating v ▷ irritate
irritation n ▷ irritate
irritations n ▷ irritate

is *v* ▷ **be**

> **ish** *n* (**ishes**). An ish is a word for an issue in Scots law. If you have I, S and H on your rack, remember that as well as adding **ish** to the end of many words, you can also play those letters as a word in its own right. Ish scores 6 points.

isinglass [ize-ing-glass] *n* (*pl* -**es**) kind of gelatine obtained from some freshwater fish
isinglasses *n* ▷ **isinglass**
island *n* (*pl* -**s**) piece of land surrounded by water
islander *n* (*pl* -**s**) person who lives on an island
islanders *n* ▷ **islander**
islands *n* ▷ **island**
isle *n* (*pl* -**s**) (*Poetic*) island
isles *n* ▷ **isle**
islet *n* small island
islets *n* ▷ **islet**

> **ism** *n* (**isms**). An ism is an informal word for a belief or doctrine. While **ism** can be added to the ends of many words as a suffix, it's worth remembering as a word in its own right. Ism scores 5 points.

isobar [ice-oh-bar] *n* (*pl* -**s**) line on a map connecting places of equal atmospheric pressure
isobars *n* ▷ **isobar**
isolate *v* (-**tes**, -**ting**, -**ted**) place apart or alone
> **isolation** *n* (*pl* -**s**)
isolated *v* ▷ **isolate**
isolates *v* ▷ **isolate**
isolating *v* ▷ **isolate**
isolation *n* ▷ **isolate**
isolationism *n* (*pl* -**s**) policy of not participating in international affairs
> **isolationist** *n* (*pl* -**s**) *adj*
isolationisms *n* ▷ **isolationism**
isolationist *n, adj* ▷ **isolationism**
isolationists *n* ▷ **isolationsim**
isolations *n* ▷ **isolation**
isomer [ice-oh-mer] *n* (*pl* -**s**) substance whose molecules contain the same atoms as another but in a different arrangement
isomers *n* ▷ **isomer**
isometric *adj* relating to muscular contraction without shortening of the muscle
isometrics *pl n* isometric exercises
isotherm [ice-oh-therm] *n* (*pl* -**s**) line on a map connecting points of equal temperature
isotherms *n* ▷ **isotherm**
isotope [ice-oh-tope] *n* (*pl* -**s**) one of two or more atoms with the same number of protons in the nucleus but a different number of neutrons
isotopes *n* ▷ **isotope**
issue *n* (*pl* -**s**) topic of interest or discussion ▶ *v* (-**ssues**, -**ssuing**, -**ssued**) make (a statement etc.) publicly
issued *v* ▷ **issue**
issues *n, v* ▷ **issue**
issuing *v* ▷ **issue**
isthmus [iss-muss] *n* (*pl* -**muses**) narrow strip of land connecting two areas of land
isthmuses *n* ▷ **isthmus**
it *pron* refers to a nonhuman, animal, plant, or inanimate object ▶ *its adj, pron* belonging to it
italic *adj* (of printing type) sloping to the right
italicize *v* (-**izes**, -**izing**, -**ized**) put in italics
italicized *v* ▷ **italicize**
italicizes *v* ▷ **italicize**
italicizing *v* ▷ **italicize**
italics *pl n* this type, used for emphasis
itch *n* (*pl* -**es**) skin irritation causing a desire to scratch ▶ *v* (-**es**, -**ing**, -**ed**) have an itch
> **itchy** *adj*
itched *v* ▷ **itch**
itches *n, v* ▷ **itch**
itching *v* ▷ **itch**
itchy *adj* ▷ **itch**
item *n* (*pl* -**s**) single thing in a list or collection
> **itemize** *v* (-**izes**, -**izing**, -**ized**) make a list of
itemized *n* ▷ **item**
itemizes *n* ▷ **item**
itemizing *n* ▷ **item**
items *n* ▷ **item**
iterate *v* (-**tes**, -**ting**, -**ted**) repeat > **iteration** *n* (*pl* -**s**)
iterated *v* ▷ **iterate**
iterates *v* ▷ **iterate**
iterating *v* ▷ **iterate**
iteration *n* ▷ **iterate**
iterations *n* ▷ **iterate**
itinerant *adj* travelling from place to place
itineraries *n* ▷ **itinerary**
itinerary *n* (*pl* -**aries**) detailed plan of a journey
itself *pron* ▷ **it**
ivies *n* ▷ **ivy**
ivories *n* ▷ **ivory**
ivory *n* (*pl* -**ries**) hard white bony substance forming the tusks of elephants ▶ *adj* yellowish-white
ivy *n* (*pl* -**vies**) evergreen climbing plant
iwi [ee-wee] *n* (*pl* -**s**) (NZ) Maori tribe
iwis *n* ▷ **iwi**

Jj

J is one of the best tiles to have in Scrabble, as it is worth 8 points on its own. J also forms a number of words with X and Z, allowing you to earn some huge scores if you get the right tiles to go with it. Even better, some of these words are seven letters in length, so the right combination of tiles will give you a 50-point bonus if you are lucky enough to have it on your rack. On the other hand, J isn't the easiest tile to use when forming words in different directions. There's only one two-letter word that begins with J **jo**. If you remember this, however, you won't waste time trying to think of others. As J has such a high value, look out for double- and triple-letter squares when playing it. There are plenty of good three-letter words starting with J: **jab** (12 points), **jam** (12), **jar** (10), **jaw** (13), **jay** (13), **jet** (10), **jib** (12), **jig** (11), **job** (12), **jog** (11), **jot** (10), **joy** (13), **jug** (11) and **jut** (10). In addition to these, there are other fantastic words beginning with J. **Jazz** (19) is very useful – you'll need a blank tile for the second Z, but if you can form it, you may also be able to play **jazzes** (21) or **jazzy** (23). **Jinx** (18) is also handy, and don't forget **jukebox** (27), which can be formed from **box** or **ox** if someone has played those.

jab v (-s, -bbing, -bbed) poke sharply ▶ n (pl -s)
   jabbed v ▷ jab
jabber v (-s, -ing, -ed) talk rapidly or incoherently
   jabbered v ▷ jabber
   jabbering v ▷ jabber
   jabbers v ▷ jabber
   jabbing v ▷ jab
jabiru n (pl -s) large white-and-black Australian stork
   jabirus n ▷ jabiru
   jabs v, n ▷ jab
jacaranda n (pl -s) tropical tree with sweet-smelling wood
   jacarandas n ▷ jacaranda
jack n (pl -s) device for raising a motor vehicle or other heavy object
   jacks n ▷ jack
jackal n (pl -s) doglike wild animal of Africa and Asia
   jackals n ▷ jackal
jackaroo, jackeroo n (pl -roos) (AUST) trainee on a sheep station
   jackaroos n ▷ jackaroo
jackass n (pl -es) fool
   jackasses n ▷ jackass
jackboot n (pl -s) high military boot

jackboots n ▷ jackboot
jackdaw n (pl -s) black-and-grey Eurasian bird of the crow family
   jackdaws n ▷ jackdaw
   jackeroo n ▷ jackaroo
   jackeroos n ▷ jackaroo
jacket n (pl -s) short coat
   jackets n ▷ jacket
jackknife v (-s, -fing, -fed) (of an articulated truck) go out of control so that the trailer swings round at a sharp angle to the cab ▶ n (pl -knives) large clasp knife
   jackknifed v ▷ jackknife
   jackknifes v ▷ jackknife
   jackknifing v ▷ jackknife
   jackknives n ▷ jackknife
jackpot n (pl -s) largest prize that may be won in a game
   jackpots n ▷ jackpot
jacuzzi [jak-oo-zee] n ® (pl -s) circular bath with a device that swirls the water
   jacuzzis n ▷ jacuzzi
jade n (pl -s) ornamental semiprecious stone, usu. dark green ▶ adj bluish-green
jaded adj tired and unenthusiastic
   jades n ▷ jade
jagged [jag-gid] adj having an uneven edge

with sharp points

jaguar n (pl -s) large S American spotted cat
  jaguars n ▷ jaguar

jail n (pl -s) prison ▶ v (-s, -ing, -ed) send to prison > **jailer** n (pl -s)

jailbird n (pl -s) (Informal) person who has often been in prison
  jailbirds n ▷ jailbird
  jailed v ▷ jail
  jailer n ▷ jail
  jailers n ▷ jail
  jailing v ▷ jail
  jails n, v ▷ jail
  jalopies n ▷ jalopy

jalopy [jal-**lop**-ee] n (pl -**pies**) (Informal) old car

jam¹ v (-s, -ming, -mmed) pack tightly into a place ▶ n (pl -s) hold-up of traffic

jam² n (pl -s) food made from fruit boiled with sugar

jamb n (pl -s) side post of a door or window frame

jamboree n (pl -s) large gathering or celebration
  jamborees n ▷ jamboree
  jambs n ▷ jamb
  jammed v ▷ jam¹
  jamming v ▷ jam¹
  jams v ▷ jam¹ ▶ n ▷ jam¹, ²

jandal n (pl -s) (Nz) sandal with a strap between the toes
  jandals n ▷ jandal

jangle v (-les, -ling, -led) (cause to) make a harsh ringing noise
  jangled v ▷ jangle
  jangles v ▷ jangle
  jangling v ▷ jangle

janitor n (pl -s) caretaker of a school or other building
  janitors n ▷ janitor

> **janizar** or **janizary** n (**janizars**, **janizaries**). A janizar was an elite soldier in the armies of the Ottoman Empire. This is a very useful word, and will earn you a 50-point bonus if you are able to use all your letters in playing it. Also, if janizar is already on the board, you have an opportunity to earn a good score by adding an S, Y or IES. Janizar scores 23 points.

japan n (pl -s) very hard varnish, usu. black ▶ v (-s, -nning, -nned) cover with this varnish
  japanned v ▷ japan
  japanning v ▷ japan
  japans n, v ▷ japan

jape n (pl -s) (Old-fashioned) joke or prank

japes n ▷ jape

japonica n (pl -s) shrub with red flowers
  japonicas n ▷ japonica

jar¹ n (pl -s) wide-mouthed container, usu. round and made of glass

jar² v (-s, -rring, -rred) have a disturbing or unpleasant effect ▶ n (pl -s) jolt or shock

jargon n (pl -s) specialized technical language of a particular subject
  jargons n ▷ jargon

jarrah n (pl -s) Australian eucalypt yielding valuable timber
  jarrahs n ▷ jarrah
  jarred v ▷ jar²
  jarring v ▷ jar²
  jars v ▷ jar² ▶ n ▷ jar¹, ²

jasmine n (pl -s) shrub with sweet-smelling yellow or white flowers
  jasmines n ▷ jasmine

jasper n (pl -s) red, yellow, dark green, or brown variety of quartz
  jaspers n ▷ jasper

jaundice n (pl -s) disease marked by yellowness of the skin

jaundiced adj (of an attitude or opinion) bitter or cynical
  jaundices n ▷ jaundice

jaunt n (pl -s) short journey for pleasure
  jauntier adj ▷ jaunty
  jauntiest adj ▷ jaunty
  jauntily adv ▷ jaunty
  jaunts n ▷ jaunt

jaunty adj (-tier, -tiest) sprightly and cheerful
  > **jauntily** adv

javelin n (pl -s) light spear thrown in sports competitions
  javelins n ▷ javelin

jaw n (pl -s) one of the bones in which the teeth are set ▶ v (-s, -ing, -ed) (Slang) talk lengthily

> **jawbox** n (**jawboxes**). Jawbox is a Scots word for a sink. Watch out for opportunities to form this if someone else has played either jaw or box, and if jawbox itself is on the board, you can earn 27 points just by making it plural with es. Jawbox scores 25 points.

  jawed v ▷ jaw
  jawing v ▷ jaw
  jaws n, v ▷ jaw ▶ n mouth

jay n (pl -s) bird with a pinkish body and blue-and-black wings
  jays n ▷ jay

jaywalker n (pl -s) person who crosses the road in a careless or dangerous manner
  > **jaywalking** n (pl -s)

jaywalkers n ▷ jaywalker
jaywalking n ▷ jaywalker
jaywalkings n ▷ jaywalker

jazy n (jazies). Jazy is an old word for a wig. This is a marvellous word, combining J and Z. If you get this combination and have either an A or a Y, look for the missing letter on the board, as it's highly likely to be there. Jazy scores 23 points.

jazz n (pl -es) kind of music with an exciting rhythm, usu. involving improvisation
jazzes n ▷ jazz
jazzier adj ▷ jazzy
jazziest adj ▷ jazzy
jazzy adj (-zier, -ziest) flashy or showy
jealous adj fearful of losing a partner or possession to a rival > jealously adv
> jealousy n (pl -sies)
jealousies n ▷ jealous
jealously adv ▷ jealous
jealousy n ▷ jealous
jeans pl n casual denim trousers
jeer v (-s, -ing, -ed) scoff or deride ▶ n (pl -s) cry of derision
jeered v ▷ jeer
jeering v ▷ jeer
jeers v, n ▷ jeer
jejune adj simple or naive
jell v (-s, -ing, -ed) form into a jelly-like substance
jelled v ▷ jell
jellied adj prepared in a jelly
jelling v ▷ jell
jells v ▷ jell
jellies n ▷ jelly
jelly n (pl -llies) soft food made of liquid set with gelatine
jellyfish n (pl jellyfish) small jelly-like sea animal
jemmies n ▷ jemmy
jemmy n (pl -mmies) short steel crowbar used by burglars
jennies n ▷ jenny
jenny n (pl -nnies) female ass or wren
jeopardies n ▷ jeopardy
jeopardize v (-izes, -izing, -ized) place in danger
jeopardized n ▷ jeopardy
jeopardizes n ▷ jeopardy
jeopardizing n ▷ jeopardy
jeopardy n (pl -dies) danger
jerboa n (pl -s) small mouselike rodent with long hind legs
jerboas n ▷ jerboa

jerk v (-s, -ing, -ed) move or throw abruptly ▶ n (pl -s) sharp or abruptly stopped movement
jerked v ▷ jerk
jerkily adv ▷ jerky
jerkin n (pl -s) sleeveless jacket
jerkiness n ▷ jerky
jerkinesses n ▷ jerky
jerking v ▷ jerk
jerkins n ▷ jerkin
jerks v, n ▷ jerk
jerky adj sudden or abrupt > jerkily adv
> jerkiness n (pl -s)

jerque v (jerques, jerquing, jerqued), n (jerquer, jerquers, jerquing, jerquings). Jerque means to search a ship for smuggled goods. If you have all the tiles for jerques, jerquer or jerqued, you'll get a 50-point bonus for using all your letters, which will give you a fantastic score. Jerque scores 22 points.

jersey n (pl -s) knitted jumper
jerseys n ▷ jersey
jest n (pl -s) ▶ v (-s, -ing, -ed) joke
jested v ▷ jest
jester n (pl -s) (HIST) professional clown at court
jesters n ▷ jester
jesting v ▷ jest
jests n, v ▷ jest
jet¹ n (pl -s) aircraft driven by jet propulsion ▶ v (-s, jetting, jetted) fly by jet aircraft
jet² n (pl -s) hard black mineral
jetboat n (pl -s) motorboat propelled by a jet of water
jetboats n ▷ jetboat
jets n ▷ jet¹, ² ▶ v ▷ jet¹
jetsam n (pl -s) goods thrown overboard to lighten a ship
jetsams n ▷ jetsam
jetted v ▷ jet¹
jetties n ▷ jetty
jetting v ▷ jet¹
jettison v (-s, -ing, -ed) abandon
jettisoned v ▷ jettison
jettisoning v ▷ jettison
jettisons v ▷ jettison
jetty n (pl -ties) small pier

jeu n (jeux). Jeu is the French word for game or play. The plural form, jeux, is a great little word, using both J and X particularly if you can play it on a double- or triple-word square. Jeux scores 18 points.

jewel n (pl -s) precious stone
jeweller n (pl -s) dealer in jewels
jewelleries n ▷ jewellery

jewellers n ▷ **jeweller**

jewellery n (pl **-s**) objects decorated with precious stones

jewels n ▷ **jewel**

jewfish n (pl **jewfish**) (AUST) freshwater catfish

> **jezail** n (**jezails**). A jezail is a kind of heavy Afghan musket. This word is potentially a very high scorer, as its plural uses seven tiles. If you can play all of these at once, you'll earn the 50-point bonus for a total of 73 points! Jezail scores 22 points.

jib¹ n (pl **-s**) triangular sail set in front of a mast

jib² v (**-s, -bbing, -bbed**) (of a horse, person, etc.) stop and refuse to go on

jib³ n (pl **-s**) projecting arm of a crane or derrick

jibbed v ▷ **jib²**

jibbing v ▷ **jib²**

jibe¹ n (pl **-s**) ▷ v (**-jibes, -jibing, -jibed**) taunt or jeer

jibed v ▷ **jibe¹**

jibes n, v ▷ **jibe¹**

jibing v ▷ **jibe¹**

jibs n ▷ **jib¹,³** ▷ v ▷ **jib²**

jiffies n ▷ **jiffy**

jiffy n (pl **-ffies**) (Informal) very short period of time

jig n (pl **-s**) type of lively dance ▷ v (**-s, -gging, -gged**) make jerky up-and-down movements

jigged v ▷ **jig**

jigging v ▷ **jig**

jiggle v (**-ggles, -ggling, -ggled**) move up and down with short jerky movements

jiggled v ▷ **jiggle**

jiggles v ▷ **jiggle**

jiggling v ▷ **jiggle**

jigs n, v ▷ **jig**

jigsaw n (pl **-s**) (also **jigsaw puzzle**) picture cut into interlocking pieces, which the user tries to fit together again

jigsaws n ▷ **jigsaw**

jihad n (pl **-s**) Islamic holy war against unbelievers

jihads n ▷ **jihad**

jilt v (**-s, -ing, -ed**) leave or reject (one's lover)

jilted v ▷ **jilt**

jilting v ▷ **jilt**

jilts v ▷ **jilt**

jingle n (pl **-s**) catchy verse or song used in a radio or television advert ▷ v (**-les, -ling, -led**) (cause to) make a gentle ringing sound

jingled v ▷ **jingle**

jingles n, v ▷ **jingle**

jingling v ▷ **jingle**

jingoism n (pl **-s**) aggressive nationalism

> **jingoistic** adj

jingoisms n ▷ **jingoism**

jingoistic adj ▷ **jingoism**

jinks pl n boisterous merrymaking

jinn n ▷ **jinni**

jinni n (pl **jinn**) spirit in Muslim mythology

jinx n (pl **-es**) person or thing bringing bad luck ▶ v (**-xes, -xing, -xed**) be or put a jinx on

jinxed v ▷ **jinx**

jinxes n, v ▷ **jinx**

jinxing v ▷ **jinx**

jitters pl n worried nervousness

jittery adj nervous

jive n (pl **-s**) lively dance of the 1940s and '50s ▶ v (**-ves, -ving, -ved**) dance the jive

jived v ▷ **jive**

jives n, v ▷ **jive**

jiving v ▷ **jive**

> **jiz** n (**jizes**). Jiz is an old word for a wig. This is a very useful word for when you find yourself with J and Z but nothing else that looks promising: there will almost certainly be an I on the board around which you can form jiz. Jiz scores 19 points.

> **jizz** n (**jizzes**). A jizz is the combination of characteristics used to identify a bird or plant species. A blank tile is required to form jizz because it contains two Zs. If **jiz** is already on the board, a blank or a blank and ES will earn you 19 or 21 points. Jizz scores 19 points.

> **jo** n (**joes**). Jo is a Scots word for a sweetheart. This is the only two-letter word that starts with J, and is worth remembering for that reason. It's also a good word to form when playing in more than one direction at once. Jo scores 9 points.

job n (pl **-s**) occupation or paid employment

jobbing adj doing individual jobs for payment

jobless adj, pl n unemployed (people)

jobs n ▷ **job**

jockey n (pl **-s**) (professional) rider of racehorses ▶ v (**-ys, -ying, -yed**) manoeuvre to obtain an advantage

jockeyed v ▷ **jockey**

jockeying v ▷ **jockey**

jockeys n, v ▷ **jockey**

jockstrap n (pl **-s**) belt with a pouch to support the genitals, worn by male athletes

jockstraps n ▷ **jockstrap**

jocose [joke-**kohss**] adj playful or humorous

jocular adj fond of joking ▷ **jocularity** n (pl

-ties) > **jocularly** adv
jocularities n ▷ jocular
jocularity n ▷ jocular
jocularly adv ▷ jocular
jocund [jok-kund] adj (Lit) merry or cheerful
jodhpurs pl n riding trousers, loose-fitting above the knee but tight below
joey n (pl -**ys**) (AUST) young kangaroo
joeys n ▷ joey
jog v (-**s**, -**gging**, -**gged**) run at a gentle pace, esp. for exercise ▶ n (pl -**s**) slow run > **jogger** n (pl -**s**) > **jogging** n (pl -**s**)
jogged v ▷ jog
jogger n ▷ jog
joggers n ▷ jog
jogging n, v ▷ jog
joggings n ▷ jog
joggle v (-**les**, -**ling**, -**led**) shake or move jerkily
joggled v ▷ joggle
joggles v ▷ joggle
joggling v ▷ joggle
jogs n, v ▷ jog
join v (-**s**, -**ing**, -**ed**) become a member (of) ▶ n (pl -**s**) place where two things are joined
joined v ▷ join
joiner n (pl -**s**) maker of finished woodwork
joineries n ▷ joinery
joiners n ▷ joiner
joinery n (pl -**ries**) joiner's work
joining v ▷ join
joins n, v ▷ join
joint adj shared by two or more ▶ n (pl -**s**) place where bones meet but can move ▶ v (-**s**, -**ing**, -**ed**) divide meat into joints > **jointed** adj > **jointly** adv
jointed v, adj ▷ joint
jointing v ▷ joint
jointly adv ▷ joint
joints n, v ▷ joint
joist n (pl -**s**) horizontal beam that helps support a floor or ceiling
joists n ▷ joist
jojoba [hoe-hoe-ba] n (pl -**s**) shrub of SW North America whose seeds yield oil used in cosmetics
jojobas n ▷ jojoba
joke n (pl -**s**) thing said or done to cause laughter ▶ v (-**kes**, -**king**, -**ked**) make jokes > **jokey** adj > **jokingly** adv
joked v ▷ joke
joker n (pl -**s**) person who jokes
jokers n ▷ joker
jokes n, v ▷ joke
jokey adj ▷ joke
joking v ▷ joke

jokingly adv ▷ joke
jollied v ▷ jolly
jollier adj ▷ jolly
jollies v ▷ jolly
jolliest adj ▷ jolly
jollities n ▷ jolly
jollity n ▷ jolly
jolly adj (-**lier**, -**liest**) (of a person) happy and cheerful ▶ v (-**lies**, -**lying**, -**lied**) try to keep (someone) cheerful by flattery or coaxing > **jollity** n (pl -**ties**)
jollification n (pl -**s**) merrymaking
jollifications n ▷ jolly
jollying v ▷ jolly
jolt n (pl -**s**) unpleasant surprise or shock ▶ v (-**s**, -**ing**, -**ed**) surprise or shock
jolted v ▷ jolt
jolting v ▷ jolt
jolts n, v ▷ jolt
jonquil n (pl -**s**) fragrant narcissus
jonquils n ▷ jonquil
josh v (-**es**, -**ing**, -**ed**) (CHIEFLY US) (Slang) tease
joshed v ▷ josh
joshes v ▷ josh
joshing v ▷ josh
jostle v (-**les**, -**ling**, -**led**) knock or push against
jostled v ▷ jostle
jostles v ▷ jostle
jostling v ▷ jostle
jot v (-**s**, -**tting**, -**tted**) write briefly ▶ n (pl -**s**) very small amount
jotted v ▷ jot
jotting v ▷ jot
jotter n (pl -**s**) notebook
jotters n ▷ jotter
jottings pl n notes jotted down
jots v, n ▷ jot
joule [jool] n (pl -**s**) (PHYSICS) unit of work or energy
joules n ▷ joule
journal n (pl -**s**) daily newspaper or magazine
journalese n (pl -**s**) superficial style of writing, found in some newspapers
journaleses n ▷ journalese
journalism n (pl -**s**) writing in or editing of newspapers and magazines > **journalist** n (pl -**s**) > **journalistic** adj
journalisms n ▷ journalism
journalist n ▷ journalism
journalistic adj ▷ journalism
journalists n ▷ journalism
journals n ▷ journal
journey n (pl -**s**) act or process of travelling from one place to another ▶ v (-**s**, -**ing**, -**ed**) travel

journeyed v ▷ journey

journeying v ▷ journey

journeyman n (pl -men) qualified craftsman employed by another

journeymen n ▷ journeyman

journeys n, v ▷ journey

joust (HIST) n (pl -s) combat with lances between two mounted knights ▶ v (-s, -ing, -ed) fight on horseback using lances

jousted v ▷ joust

jousting v ▷ joust

jousts n, v ▷ joust

jovial adj happy and cheerful > jovially adv > joviality n (pl -ties)

jovialities n ▷ jovial

joviality n ▷ jovial

jovially adv ▷ jovial

jowl¹ n (pl -s) lower jaw

jowl² n (pl -s) fatty flesh hanging from the lower jaw

jowls n ▷ jowl¹, ² ▶ pl n cheeks

joy n (pl -s) feeling of great delight or pleasure > joyful adj > joyless adj

joyful adj ▷ joy

joyless adj ▷ joy

joyous adj extremely happy and enthusiastic

joyride n ▷ joyriding

joyrider n ▷ joyriding

joyriders n ▷ joyriding

joyrides n ▷ joyriding

joyriding n (pl -s) driving for pleasure, esp. in a stolen car > joyride n (pl -s) > joyrider n (pl -s)

joyridings n ▷ joyriding

joystick n (pl -s) control device for an aircraft or computer

joysticks n ▷ joystick

joys n ▷ joy

jubilant adj feeling or expressing great joy > jubilantly adv > jubilation n (pl -s)

jubilantly adv ▷ jubilant

jubilation n ▷ jubilant

jubilations n ▷ jubilant

jubilee n (pl -s) special anniversary, esp. 25th (silver jubilee) or 50th (golden jubilee)

jubilees n ▷ jubilee

judder v (-s, -ing, -ed) vibrate violently ▶ n (pl -s) violent vibration

juddered v ▷ judder

juddering v ▷ judder

judders v, n ▷ judder

judge n (pl -s) public official who tries cases and passes sentence in a court of law ▶ v (-dges, -dging, -dged) act as a judge

judged v ▷ judge

judgement n ▷ judgment

judgements n ▷ judgment

judgemental adj ▷ judgment

judges n, v ▷ judge

judging v ▷ judge

judgment, judgement n (pl -s) opinion reached after careful thought > judgmental, judgemental adj

judgmental adj ▷ judgment

judgments n ▷ judgment

judicial adj of or by a court or judge > judicially adv

judicially adv ▷ judicial

judiciary n (pl -ries) system of courts and judges

judiciaries n ▷ judiciary

judicious adj well-judged and sensible > judiciously adv

judiciously adv ▷ judicious

judo n sport in which two opponents try to throw each other to the ground

jug n (pl -s) container for liquids, with a handle and small spout

juggernaut n (pl -s) (BRIT) large heavy truck

juggernauts n ▷ juggernaut

juggle v (-les, -ling, -led) throw and catch (several objects) so that most are in the air at the same time > juggler n (pl -s)

juggled v ▷ juggle

juggler n ▷ juggle

jugglers n ▷ juggle

juggles v ▷ juggle

juggling v ▷ juggle

jugs n ▷ jug

jugular n (pl -s) one of three large veins of the neck that return blood from the head to the heart

jugulars n ▷ jugular

juice n (pl -s) liquid part of vegetables, fruit, or meat

juices n ▷ juice

juicier adj ▷ juicy

juiciest adj ▷ juicy

juicy adj (-cier, -ciest) full of juice

jujitsu n (pl -s) Japanese art of wrestling and self-defence

jujitsus n ▷ jujitsu

juju n (pl -s) W African magic charm or fetish

jujus n ▷ juju

jukebox n (pl -es) coin-operated machine on which records, CDs, or videos can be played

jukeboxes n ▷ jukebox

julep n (pl -s) sweet alcoholic drink

juleps n ▷ julep

jumble n (pl -s) confused heap or state ▶ v (-les, -ling, -led) mix in a disordered way

jumbled v ▷ jumble

jumbles n, v ▷ jumble

jumbling v ▷ jumble

jumbo adj (Informal) very large ▶ n (pl -s) (also **jumbo jet**) large jet airliner

jumbos n ▷ jumbo

jumbuck n (pl -s) (AUST) (Old-fashioned slang) sheep

jumbucks n ▷ jumbuck

jump v (-s, -ing, -ed) leap or spring into the air using the leg muscles ▶ n (pl -s) act of jumping

jumped v ▷ jump

jumper n (pl -s) sweater or pullover

jumpers n ▷ jumper

jumpier adj ▷ jumpy

jumpiest adj ▷ jumpy

jumping v ▷ jump

jumps v, n ▷ jump

jumpy adj (-pier, -piest) nervous

junction n (pl -s) place where routes, railway lines, or roads meet

junctions n ▷ junction

juncture n (pl -s) point in time, esp. a critical one

junctures n ▷ juncture

jungle n (pl -s) tropical forest of dense tangled vegetation

jungles n ▷ jungle

junior adj of lower standing ▶ n (pl -s) junior person

juniors n ▷ junior

juniper n (pl -s) evergreen shrub with purple berries

junipers n ▷ juniper

junk¹ n (pl -s) discarded or useless objects

junk² n (pl -s) flat-bottomed Chinese sailing boat

junket n (pl -s) excursion by public officials paid for from public funds

junkets n ▷ junket

junkie, junky n (pl -kies) (Slang) drug addict

junkies n ▷ junkie

junks n ▷ junk¹, ²

junky n ▷ junkie

junta n (pl -s) group of military officers holding power in a country, esp. after a coup

juntas n ▷ junta

juridical adj of law or the administration of justice

juries n ▷ jury

jurisdiction n (pl -s) right or power to administer justice and apply laws

jurisdictions n ▷ jurisdiction

jurisprudence n (pl -s) science or philosophy of law

jurisprudences n ▷ jurisprudence

jurist n (pl -s) expert in law

jurists n ▷ jurist

juror n (pl -s) member of a jury

jurors n ▷ juror

jury n (pl -ries) group of people sworn to deliver a verdict in a court of law

just adv very recently ▶ adj fair or impartial in action or judgment > **justly** adv > **justness** n (pl -s)

justice n (pl -s) quality of being just

justices n ▷ justice

justifiable adj ▷ justify

justifiably adv ▷ justify

justification n ▷ justify

justifications n ▷ justify

justified v ▷ justify

justifies v ▷ justify

justify v (-fies, -fying, -fied) prove right or reasonable > **justifiable** adj > **justifiably** adv > **justification** n (pl -s)

justifying v ▷ justify

justly adv ▷ just

justness n ▷ just

justnesses n ▷ just

jut v (-s, -tting, -tted) project or stick out

jute n (pl -s) plant fibre, used for rope, canvas, etc.

jutes n ▷ jute

juts v ▷ jut

jutted v ▷ jut

jutting v ▷ jut

juvenilia pl n works produced in an author's youth

juvenile adj young ▶ n (pl -s) young person or child

juveniles n ▷ juvenile

juxtapose v (-ses, -sing, -sed) put side by side > **juxtaposition** n (pl -s)

juxtaposed v ▷ juxtapose

juxtaposes v ▷ juxtapose

juxtaposing v ▷ juxtapose

juxtaposition n ▷ juxtapose

juxtapositions n ▷ juxtapose

> **jynx** n (**jynxes**). A jynx is a kind of woodpecker. This unusual word is unique in combining J, Y and Z without using any vowels. Jynx scores 21 points.

Kk

Worth 5 points, K is a valuable tile to have in your rack. However, it's not the most useful tile for the short words that you need when forming words in different directions at the same time. There are only three two-letter words beginning with K: **ka, ko** and **ky**. Remembering these will stop you wasting time trying to think of others. There aren't very many three-letter words either, but remember **kak** (11 points), **keg** (8), **ken** (7), **key** (10), **kid** (8), **kin** (7), **kip** (9) and **kit** (7).

ka n (kas). A ka is a supernatural being in ancient Egyptian mythology. This is worth remembering as, along with **ko** and **ky,** it's one of only three two-letter words starting with K. Ka scores 6 points.

kaftan n (pl -s) long loose Eastern garment
  kaftans n ▷ kaftan
kaiser [kize-er] n (pl -s) (HIST) German or Austro-Hungarian emperor
  kaisers n ▷ kaiser
kak n (s AFR) (Slang) faeces
kalashnikov n (pl -s) Russian-made automatic rifle
  kalashnikovs n ▷ kalashnikov
kale n (pl -s) cabbage with crinkled leaves
  kales n ▷ kale
kaleidoscope n (pl -s) tube-shaped toy containing loose coloured pieces reflected by mirrors so that intricate patterns form when the tube is twisted > **kaleidoscopic** adj
  kaleidoscopes n ▷ kaleidoscope
  kaleidoscopic adj ▷ kaleidoscope
kamikaze [kam-mee-**kah**-zee] n (pl -s) (in World War II) Japanese pilot who performed a suicide mission ▶ adj (of an action) undertaken in the knowledge that it will kill or injure the person performing it
  kamikazes n ▷ kamikaze
kangaroo n (pl -s) Australian marsupial which moves by jumping with its powerful hind legs
  kangaroos n ▷ kangaroo
kaolin n (pl -s) fine white clay used to make porcelain and in some medicines
  kaolins n ▷ kaolin
kapok n (pl -s) fluffy fibre from a tropical tree, used to stuff cushions etc.

kapoks n ▷ kapok
kaput [kap-**poot**] adj (Informal) ruined or broken
karaoke n (pl -s) form of entertainment in which people sing over a prerecorded backing tape
  karaokes n ▷ karaoke
karate n (pl -s) Japanese system of unarmed combat using blows with the feet, hands, elbows, and legs
  karates n ▷ karate
karma n (pl -s) (BUDDHISM, HINDUISM) person's actions affecting his or her fate in the next reincarnation
  karmas n ▷ karma
karri n (pl -s) Australian eucalypt
  karris n ▷ karri
katipo n (pl -s) small poisonous New Zealand spider
  katipos n ▷ katipo
kayak n (pl -s) Inuit canoe made of sealskins stretched over a frame
  kayaks n ▷ kayak
kebab n (pl -s) dish of small pieces of meat grilled on skewers
  kebabs n ▷ kebab
kedgeree n (pl -s) dish of fish with rice and eggs
  kedgerees n ▷ kedgeree
keel n (pl -s) main lengthways timber or steel support along the base of a ship
  keels n ▷ keel
keen[1] adj (-er, -est) eager or enthusiastic
  > **keenly** adv > **keenness** n
keen[2] v (-s, -ing, -ed) wail over the dead
  keened v ▷ keen[2]
  keener adj ▷ keen[1]
  keenest adj ▷ keen[1]
  keening v ▷ keen[2]

keenly *adv* ▷ keen[1]

keenness *n* ▷ keen[1]

keens *v* ▷ keen[2]

keep *v* (-s, -ing, kept) have or retain possession of ▶ *n* (-s) cost of food and everyday expenses

keeper *n* (-s) person who looks after animals in a zoo ▶ *n* ▷ keeper

keeping *v* ▷ keep ▶ *n* (-s) care or charge ▶ *n* ▷ keeping ▶ *v* ▷ keep ▶ *n* ▷ keep > keepsake *n* (-s) gift treasured for the sake of the giver

keepsakes *n* ▷ keepsake

keg *n* (pl -s) small metal beer barrel

kegs *n* ▷ keg

kelp *n* (pl -s) large brown seaweed

kelpie *n* (pl -s) Australian sheepdog with a smooth coat and upright ears

kelpies *n* ▷ kelpie

kelps *n* ▷ kelp

kelvin *n* (pl -s) SI unit of temperature

kelvins *n* ▷ kelvin

ken *v* (-s, -nning, -nned or kent) (SCOT) know

kenning *v* ▷ ken

kenned *v* ▷ ken

kendo *n* (pl -s) Japanese sport of fencing using wooden staves

kendos *n* ▷ kendo

kennel *n* (pl -s) hutlike shelter for a dog

kennels *n* ▷ kennel

kens *v* ▷ ken

kent *v* ▷ ken

kept *v* ▷ keep

keratin *n* (pl -s) fibrous protein found in the hair and nails

keratins *n* ▷ keratin

kerb *n* (pl -s) edging to a footpath

kerbs *n* ▷ kerb

kerchief *n* (pl -s) piece of cloth worn over the head or round the neck

kerchiefs *n* ▷ kerchief

kerfuffle *n* (pl -s) (*Informal*) commotion or disorder

kerfuffles *n* ▷ kerfuffle

kernel *n* (pl -s) seed of a nut, cereal, or fruit stone

kernels *n* ▷ kernel

kerosene *n* (pl -s) (US, CANADIAN, AUST & NZ) liquid mixture distilled from petroleum and used as a fuel or solvent

kerosenes *n* ▷ kerosene

kestrel *n* (pl -s) type of small falcon

kestrels *n* ▷ kestrel

ketch *n* (pl -es) two-masted sailing ship

ketches *n* ▷ ketch

ketchup *n* (pl -s) thick cold sauce, usu. made of tomatoes

ketchups *n* ▷ ketchup

kettle *n* (pl -s) container with a spout and handle used for boiling water

kettledrum *n* (pl -s) large bowl-shaped metal drum

kettledrums *n* ▷ kettledrum

kettles *n* ▷ kettle

key *n* (pl -s) device for operating a lock by moving a bolt ▶ *adj* of great importance ▶ *v* (-s, -ing, -ed) enter (text) using a keyboard

keyboard *n* (pl -s) set of keys on a piano, computer, etc. ▶ *v* (-s, -ing, -ed) enter (text) using a keyboard

keyboarded *v* ▷ keyboard

keyboarding *v* ▷ keyboard

keyboards *n, v* ▷ keyboard

keyed *v* ▷ key

keyhole *n* (pl -s) opening for inserting a key into a lock

keyholes *n* ▷ keyhole

keying *v* ▷ key

keynote *n* (pl -s) dominant idea of a speech etc.

keynotes *n* ▷ keynote

keys *n, v* ▷ key

keystone *n* (pl -s) most important part of a process, organization, etc.

keystones *n* ▷ keystone

> **kex** *n* (**kexes**). A kex is a hollow-stemmed plant. This is a great three-letter word, combining K with X. If you have these letters on your rack, you can be confident that there will be, or will soon be, an E on the board, around which you can form kex. Kex scores 14 points.

khaki *adj* dull yellowish-brown ▶ *n* (pl -s) hard-wearing fabric of this colour used for military uniforms

khakis *n* ▷ khaki

> **khi** *n* (**khis**). Khi is a letter of the Greek alphabet, also spelt **chi**. This is one of the higher-scoring three-letter words starting with K, and so is worth remembering. Khi scores 10 points.

kibbutz *n* (pl -im) communal farm or factory in Israel

kibbutzim *n* ▷ kibbutz

kick *v* (-s, -ing, -ed) drive, push, or strike with the foot ▶ *n* (pl **kicks**) thrust or blow with the foot

kickback (*Informal*) *n* (pl -s) money paid illegally for favours done

kickbacks *n* ▷ kickback

kicked *v* ▷ kick

kicking n, v ▷ **kick**

kicks n, v ▷ **kick**

kid¹ n (pl **-s**) (*Informal*) child

kid² v (**-s, -dding, -dded**) (*Informal*) tease or deceive (someone)

kidded v ▷ **kid**²

kidding v ▷ **kid**²

kidnap v (**-s, -pping, -pped**) seize and hold (a person) to ransom > **kidnapper** n (pl **-s**)

kidnapped n ▷ **kidnap**

kidnapper n ▷ **kidnap**

kidnappers n ▷ **kidnap**

kidnapping n ▷ **kidnap**

kidnaps n ▷ **kidnap**

kidney n (pl **kidneys**) either of the pair of organs that filter waste products from the blood to produce urine

kidneys n ▷ **kidney**

kids n ▷ **kid**¹ ▶ v ▷ **kid**²

kill v (**-s, -ing, -ed**) cause the death of (*Informal*) ▶ n (pl **-s**) act of killing > **killer** n (pl **killers**)

killed v ▷ **kill**

killer n ▷ **kill**

killers n ▷ **kill**

killing (*Informal*) adj very tiring ▶ n (pl **-s**) sudden financial success ▶ v ▷ **kill**

killings n ▷ **killing**

killjoy n (pl **-s**) person who spoils others' pleasure

killjoys n ▷ **killjoy**

kills v, n ▷ **kill**

kiln n (pl **-s**) oven for baking, drying, or processing pottery, bricks, etc.

kilns n ▷ **kiln**

kilobyte n (pl **-s**) (COMPUTERS) 1024 units of information

kilobytes n ▷ **kilobyte**

kilogram, kilogramme n (pl **-s**) one thousand grams

kilogrammes n ▷ **kilogram**

kilograms n ▷ **kilogram**

kilohertz n (pl **-es**) one thousand hertz

kilohertzes n ▷ **kilohertz**

kilometre n (pl **-s**) one thousand metres

kilometres n ▷ **kilometre**

kilowatt n (pl **-s**) (ELECTRICITY) one thousand watts

kilowatts n ▷ **kilowatt**

kilt n (pl **-s**) knee-length pleated tartan skirt worn orig. by Scottish Highlanders > **kilted** adj

kilted n ▷ **kilt**

kilts n ▷ **kilt**

kimono n (pl **-s**) loose wide-sleeved Japanese robe, fastened with a sash

kimonos n ▷ **kimono**

kin, kinsfolk n person's relatives collectively > **kinship** (pl **-s**) ▶ n

kind¹ adj (**-er, -est**) considerate, friendly, and helpful > **kindness** n (pl **-es**) > **kindliness** n (pl **-es**) > **kind-hearted** adj

kind² n (pl **-s**) class or group with common characteristics

kinder adj ▷ **kind**¹

kindergarten n (pl **-s**) class or school for children under six years old

kindergartens n ▷ **kindergarten**

kindest adj ▷ **kind**¹

kindhearted adj ▷ **kind**¹

kindies n ▷ **kindy**

kindliness n (pl **-es**) ▷ **kind**¹

kindlinesses n ▷ **kind**¹

kindle v (**-les, -ling, -led**) set (a fire) alight

kindled v ▷ **kindle**

kindles v ▷ **kindle**

kindling n (pl **-s**) dry wood or straw for starting fires ▶ v ▷ **kindle**

kindly adj having a warm-hearted nature ▶ adv in a considerate way

kindness n (pl **-es**) ▷ **kind**¹

kindnesses n ▷ **kind**¹

kinds n ▷ **kind**²

kindred adj having similar qualities ▶ n (pl **-s**) ▷ **kin**

kindy, kindie n (pl **-dies**) (AUST & NZ) (*Informal*) kindergarten

kinetic [kin-**net**-ik] adj relating to or caused by motion

king n (pl **kings**) male ruler of a monarchy > **kingship** n (pl **-s**)

kingdom n (pl **-s**) state ruled by a king or queen

kingdoms n ▷ **kingdom**

kings n ▷ **king**

kingship n (pl **-s**) ▷ **king**

kingships n ▷ **king**

kingfisher n (pl **-s**) small bird, often with a bright-coloured plumage, that dives for fish

kingfishers n ▷ **kingfisher**

kingpin n (pl **-s**) most important person in an organization

kingpins n ▷ **kingpin**

kink n (pl **-s**) twist or bend in rope, wire, hair, etc.

kinks n ▷ **kink**

kinky adj (*Slang*) given to unusual sexual practices

kinships n ▷ **kinship**

kiosk n (pl **-s**) small booth selling drinks, cigarettes, newspapers, etc.

kiosks n ▷ **kiosk**

kip (*Informal*) *n* (*pl* -s) sleep ▶ *v* (-s, -pping, -pped) sleep
  kipped *v* ▷ kip

kipper *n* (*pl* -s) cleaned, salted, and smoked herring
  kippers *n* ▷ kipper
  kipping *v* ▷ kip
  kips *v* ▷ kip

kirk *n* (*pl* -s) (SCOT) church
  kirks *n* ▷ kirk

kismet *n* (*pl* -s) fate or destiny
  kismets *n* ▷ kismet

kiss *v* (-es, -ing, -ed) touch with the lips in affection or greeting ▶ *n* (*pl* -es) touch with the lips

kissagram *n* (*pl* -s) greetings service in which a messenger kisses the person celebrating
  kissagrams *n* ▷ kissagram
  kissed *v* ▷ kiss

kisser *n* (*pl* -s) (*Slang*) mouth or face
  kissers *n* ▷ kisser
  kisses *v*, *n* ▷ kiss
  kissing *v* ▷ kiss

kist *n* (*pl* -s) (S AFR) large wooden chest
  kists *n* ▷ kist

kit *n* (*pl* -s) outfit or equipment for a specific purpose

kitbag *n* (*pl* -s) bag for a soldier's or traveller's belongings
  kitbags *n* ▷ kitbag
  kits *n* ▷ kit

kitset *n* (*pl* -s) (NZ) unassembled pieces for constructing a piece of furniture

kitchen *n* (*pl* -s) room used for cooking

kitchenette *n* (*pl* -s) small kitchen
  kitchenettes *n* ▷ kitchetenette
  kitchens *n* ▷ kitchen
  kitches *n* ▷ kitch

kite *n* (*pl* -s) light frame covered with a thin material flown on a string in the wind
  kites *n* ▷ kite

kith *n* (*pl* -s) friends and relatives
  kiths *n* ▷ kith

kitsch *n* (*pl* -es) art or literature with popular sentimental appeal

kitten *n* (*pl* -s) young cat

kittenish *adj* lively and flirtatious
  kittens *n* ▷ kitten
  kitties *n* ▷ kitty

kittiwake *n* (*pl* -s) type of seagull
  kittiwakes *n* ▷ kittiwake

kitty *n* (*pl* -ties) communal fund

kiwi *n* (*pl* -s) New Zealand flightless bird with a long beak and no tail
  kiwis *n* ▷ kiwi

klaxon *n* (*pl* -s) loud horn used on emergency vehicles as a warning signal
  klaxons *n* ▷ klaxon

kleptomania *n* (*pl* -s) compulsive tendency to steal > **kleptomaniac** *n* (*pl* -s)

kleptomaniac *n* (*pl* -s) ▷ kleptomania
  kleptomaniacs *n* ▷ kleptomania

kloof *n* (*pl* kloofs) (S AFR) mountain pass or gorge
  kloofs *n* ▷ kloof

knack *n* (*pl* knacks) skilful way of doing something
  knacks *n* ▷ knack

knacker *n* (*pl* -s) (BRIT) buyer of old horses for killing

knackered *adj* (*Slang*) extremely tired
  knackers *n* ▷ knacker

knapsack *n* (*pl* -s) soldier's or traveller's bag worn strapped on the back
  knapsacks *n* ▷ knapsack

knave *n* (*pl* -s) jack at cards (*Obs*)
  knaves *n* ▷ knave

knead *v* (-s, -ing, -ed) work (dough) into a smooth mixture with the hands
  kneaded *v* ▷ knead
  kneading *v* ▷ knead
  kneads *v* ▷ knead

knee *n* (*pl* knees) joint between thigh and lower leg ▶ *v* (-s, -ing, -d) strike or push with the knee

kneecap *n* (*pl* kneecaps) bone in front of the knee ▶ *v* (-pping, -pped) shoot in the kneecap
  kneed *v* ▷ knee
  kneeing *v* ▷ knee

kneejerk *adj* (of a reply or reaction) automatic and predictable

kneel *v* (-s, -ing, -ed *or* knelt) fall or rest on one's knees
  kneeled, knelt *v* ▷ kneel
  kneeling *v* ▷ kneel
  kneels *v* ▷ kneel
  knees *n*, *v* ▷ knee

knell *n* (*pl* -s) sound of a bell, esp. at a funeral or death
  knells *n* ▷ knell
  knelt *v* ▷ kneel
  knew *v* ▷ know

knickerbockers *pl n* loose-fitting short trousers gathered in at the knee

knickers *pl n* woman's or girl's undergarment covering the lower trunk and having legs or legholes

knife *n* (*pl* knives) cutting tool or weapon consisting of a sharp-edged blade with a handle ▶ *v* (-s, -ing, -ed) cut or stab with a

knife
knifed v ▷ knife
knifes v ▷ knife
knifing v ▷ knife
knight n (pl -s) man who has been given a knighthood ▶ v (-s, -ing, -ed) award a knighthood to > **knightly** adj > **knighthood** n (pl -s) honorary title given to a man by the British sovereign
knighted v ▷ knight
knighthoods n ▷ knighthood
knighting v ▷ knight
knights n, v ▷ knight
knit v (-s, -tting, -tted or knit) make (a garment) by interlocking a series of loops in wool or other yarn > **knitting** n (pl -s)
knits v ▷ knit
knitted v ▷ knit
knitting v ▷ knit
knittings n ▷ knit
knitwear n (pl -s) knitted clothes, such as sweaters
knitwears n ▷ knitwear
knives n ▷ knife
knob n (pl -s) rounded projection, such as a switch on a radio
knobblier adj ▷ knobbly
knobbliest adj ▷ knobbly
knobbly adj (-lier, -liest) covered with small bumps
knobkerrie n (pl -s) (S AFR) club with a rounded end
knobkerries n ▷ knobkerrie
knobs n ▷ knob
knock v (-s, -ing, -ed) give a blow or push to ▶ n (pl -s) blow or rap
knockabout adj (of comedy) boisterous
knockdown adj (of a price) very low
knocked v ▷ knock
knocker n (pl -s) metal fitting for knocking on a door
knockers n ▷ knocker
knocking v ▷ knock
knockout n (pl -s) blow that renders an opponent unconscious
knockouts n ▷ knockout
knocks v, n ▷ knock
knoll n (pl -s) small rounded hill
knolls n ▷ knoll
knot n (pl -s) fastening made by looping and pulling tight strands of string, cord, or rope ▶ v (-s, -tting, -tted) tie with or into a knot
knots n ▷ knot
knotted v ▷ knot

knotting n ▷ knot
knotty adj full of knots
know v (-s, -ing, knew, known) be or feel certain of the truth of (information etc.) > **knowable** adj
knowing v ▷ know ▶ adj suggesting secret knowledge
knowingly adv deliberately
knowhow n (pl -s) (Informal) ingenuity, aptitude, or skill
knowhows n ▷ know-how
knowledgable n ▷ knowledgeable
knowledge n (pl -s) facts or experiences known by a person
knowledgeable, knowledgable adj intelligent or well-informed
knowledges n ▷ knowledge
known v ▷ know
knows v ▷ know
knuckle n (pl -s) bone at the finger joint
knuckles n ▷ knuckle

> **ko** n (kos). A ko is a Maori digging-stick. This is worth remembering as, along with ka and ky, it's one of only three two-letter words starting with K. Ko scores 6 points.

koala n (pl -s) tree-dwelling Australian marsupial with dense grey fur
koalas n ▷ koala
kohl n (pl -s) cosmetic powder used to darken the edges of the eyelids
kohls n ▷ kohls
kookaburra n (pl -s) large Australian kingfisher with a cackling cry
kookaburras n ▷ kookaburra
koori n (pl -s) Australian Aborigine
kooris n ▷ koori
kopje, koppie n (pl -s) (S AFR) small hill
kopjes n ▷ kopje
kosher [koh-sher] adj conforming to Jewish religious law, esp. (of food) to Jewish dietary law ▶ n (pl -s) kosher food
koshers n ▷ kosher
kowhai n (pl -s) New Zealand tree with clusters of yellow flowers
kowhais n ▷ kowhai

> **kow** n (kows). A kow is a Scots word for a bunch of twigs. Kow is relatively high-scoring for a three-letter word, and so can be a good one to form when playing in more than one direction. Kow scores 10 points.

kowtow v (-s, -ing, -ed) be servile (towards)
kowtowed v ▷ kowtow

kowtowing v ▷ **kowtow**
kowtows v ▷ **kowtow**
kraal n (pl -s) S African village surrounded by a strong fence
kraals n ▷ **kraal**
krill n small shrimplike sea creature(s)
krypton n (pl -s) (CHEM) colourless gas present in the atmosphere and used in fluorescent lights
kryptons n ▷ **krypton**
kudos n (pl -es) fame or credit
kudoses n ▷ **kudos**
kugel [koog-el] n (pl -s) (S AFR) rich, fashion-conscious, materialistic young woman
kugels n ▷ **kugel**
kumara n (pl -s) (NZ) tropical root vegetable with yellow flesh
kumaras n ▷ **kumara**

kumquat [kumm-kwott] n (pl -s) citrus fruit resembling a tiny orange
kumquats n ▷ **kumquat**
kurrajong n (pl -s) Australian tree or shrub with tough fibrous bark
kurrajongs n ▷ **kurrajong**

> **ky** or **kye** n. Ky is a Scots word for **cows.** If you are playing a longer word beginning with K, you may be able to use ky to tag onto a word on the board that ends in Y. Ky scores 9 points.
>
> **kyu** n (**kyus**). A kyu is a beginner's grade in judo. The unusual combination of letters makes this a useful word to have when you have an unpromising set of letters on your rack. Kyu scores 10 points.

L l

L can be a difficult letter to use well, especially when you need to play short words. Just three two-letter words begin with L: **la**, **li** and **lo**. Knowing this will save you valuable time in a game, especially when you are trying to fit words into a crowded board. There aren't a great number of three-letter words either, but don't forget common words like **lab** (5 points), **law** (6), **lay** (6), **low** (6) and **lye** (6). Try to remember the three-letter words that combine L with X: **lax**, **lex**, **lox** and **lux** (10 points each). These are particularly useful towards the end of a game if you have an X but little opportunity to play it.

la n (**las**). In music, la is the sixth note of a major scale. La is also spelt **lah**. La scores 2 points.

label n (pl **-s**) piece of card or other material fixed to an object to show its ownership, destination, etc. ▶ v (**-s, -lling, -lled**) give a label to
labels n ▷ **label**

labia pl n (sing **-bium**) four liplike folds of skin forming part of the female genitals

labial [lay-bee-al] adj of the lips
labium n ▷ **labia**

labor n (pl **-s**) (US & AUST) ▷ **labour**

laboratories n ▷ **laboratory**

laboratory n (pl **-ies**) building or room designed for scientific research or for the teaching of practical science

laborious adj involving great prolonged effort > **laboriously** adv
laboriously adv ▷ **laborious**
labors n ▷ **labor**

labour, (US & AUST) **labor** n (pl **-s**) physical work or exertion ▶ v (**-s, -ing, -ed**) work hard

laboured adj uttered or done with difficulty ▶ v ▷ **labour**

labourer n (pl **-s**) person who labours, esp. someone doing manual work for wages
labourers n ▷ **labourer**
labouring v ▷ **labour**
labours n, v ▷ **labour**

labrador n (pl **-s**) large retriever dog with a usu. gold or black coat
labradors n ▷ **labrador**

laburnum n (pl **-s**) ornamental tree with yellow hanging flowers
laburnums n ▷ **laburnum**

labyrinth [lab-er-inth] n (pl **-s**) complicated network of passages > **labyrinthine** adj
labyrinthine adj ▷ **labyrinth**
labyrinths n ▷ **labyrinth**

lace n (pl **-s**) delicate decorative fabric made from threads woven into an open weblike pattern ▶ v (**-ces, -cing, -ced**) fasten with laces
laced v ▷ **lace**
laces n, v ▷ **lace**
lacing v ▷ **lace**

lacerate [lass-er-rate] v (**-tes, -ting, -ted**) tear (flesh) > **laceration** n (pl **-s**)
lacerated v ▷ **lacerate**
lacerates v ▷ **lacerate**
lacerating v ▷ **lacerate**
lacerations v ▷ **lacerate**

lachrymose adj tearful

lack n (pl **-s**) shortage or absence of something needed or wanted ▶ v (**-s, -ing, -ed**) need or be short of (something)
lacked v ▷ **lack**

lackadaisical adj lazy and careless in a dreamy way
lacked v ▷ **lack**

lackey n (pl **-s**) servile follower
lackeys n ▷ **lackey**
lacking v ▷ **lack**

lacklustre adj lacking brilliance or vitality

laconic adj using only a few words, terse > **laconically** adv
laconically adv ▷ **laconic**

lacquer n (pl **-s**) hard varnish for wood or metal
lacquers n ▷ **lacquer**

lacrimal adj of tears or the glands which produce them

lacrosse n (pl **-s**) sport in which teams catch

and throw a ball using long sticks with a pouched net at the end, in an attempt to score goals

lacks n, v ▷ **lack**

lactation n (pl **-s**) secretion of milk by female mammals to feed young

lactations n ▷ **lactation**

lactic adj of or derived from milk

lactose n (pl **-s**) white crystalline sugar found in milk

lactoses n ▷ **lactose**

lacuna [lak-**kew**-na] n (pl **-e**) gap or missing part, esp. in a document or series

lacy adj fine, like lace

lad n (pl **-s**) boy or young man

lads n ▷ **lad**

ladder n (pl **-s**) frame of two poles connected by horizontal steps used for climbing ▶ v (**-s, -ing, -ed**) have or cause to have such a line of undone stitches

laddered v ▷ **ladder**

laddering v ▷ **ladder**

ladders n, v ▷ **ladder**

laden adj loaded

ladle n (pl **-s**) spoon with a long handle and a large bowl, used for serving soup etc. ▶ v (**-les, -ling, -led**) serve out

ladled v ▷ **ladle**

ladles n, v ▷ **ladle**

ladling v ▷ **ladle**

lady n (pl **-dies**) woman regarded as having characteristics of good breeding or high rank

ladybird n (pl **-s**) small red beetle with black spots

ladybirds n ▷ **ladybird**

ladykiller n (pl **-s**) (Informal) man who is or thinks he is irresistible to women

ladykillers n ▷ **ladykiller**

ladylike adj polite and dignified

lag[1] v (**-s, -gging, -gged**) go too slowly, fall behind ▶ n (pl **-s**) delay between events

lag[2] v (**-s, -gging, -gged**) wrap (a boiler, pipes, etc.) with insulating material

lag[3] n (pl **-s**) (BRIT, AUST & NZ) (Slang) convict

laggard n (pl **-s**) person who lags behind

laggards n ▷ **laggard**

lagging n (pl **-s**) insulating material ▶ v ▷ **lag**[1,2]

laggings n ▷ **lagging**

lager n (pl **-s**) light-bodied beer

lagers n ▷ **lager**

lagoon n (pl **-s**) body of water cut off from the open sea by coral reefs or sand bars

lagoons n ▷ **lagoon**

lags n ▷ **lag**[1,3]

laid v ▷ **lay**[1]

lain v ▷ **lie**[2]

lair n (pl **-s**) resting place of an animal

lairs n ▷ **lair**

laird n (pl **-s**) Scottish landowner

lairds n ▷ **laird**

laity [**lay**-it-ee] n (pl **-ties**) people who are not members of the clergy

laities n ▷ **laity**

lake[1] n (pl **-s**) expanse of water entirely surrounded by land ▷ **lakeside** n (pl **-s**)

lake[2] n (pl **-s**) red pigment

lakes n ▷ **lake**[1,2]

lakesides n ▷ **lake**[1]

lama n (pl **-s**) Buddhist priest in Tibet or Mongolia

lamas n ▷ **lama**

lamb n (pl **-s**) young sheep ▶ v (**-s, -ing, -ed**) (of sheep) give birth to a lamb or lambs ▷ **lambskin** n (pl **-s**) ▷ **lambswool** n (pl **-s**)

lambast, lambaste v (**-s, -ing, -ed**) beat or thrash

lambasted v ▷ **lambast**

lambasting v ▷ **lambast**

lambasts v ▷ **lambast**

lambed v ▷ **lamb**

lambent adj (Lit) (of a flame) flickering softly

lambing v ▷ **lamb**

lambs n, v ▷ **lamb**

lambskin n ▷ **lamb**

lambswool n ▷ **lamb**

lame adj (**-er, -est**) having an injured or disabled leg or foot ▶ v (**-mes, -ming, -med**) make lame ▷ **lamely** adv ▷ **lameness** n (pl **-s**)

lamé [**lah**-may] n (pl **-s**) ▶ adj (fabric) interwoven with gold or silver thread

lamed v ▷ **lame**

lamely adv ▷ **lame**

lamenesses n ▷ **lame**

lament v (**-s, -ing, -ed**) feel or express sorrow (for) ▶ n (pl **-s**) passionate expression of grief ▷ **lamentation** n (pl **-s**)

lamentable adj very disappointing

lamentations v ▷ **lament**

lamented adj grieved for ▶ v ▷ **lament**

lamenting v ▷ **lament**

laments v, n ▷ **lament**

lamer adj ▷ **lame**

lames v ▷ **lame**

lamés n ▷ **lamé**

lamest adj ▷ **lame**

laminate v (**-tes, -ting, -ted**) make (a sheet of material) by sticking together thin sheets ▶ n (pl **-s**) laminated sheet ▷ **laminated** adj

laminated v, adj ▷ **laminate**

laminates v, n ▷ **laminate**

laminating v ▷ laminate
laming v ▷ lame
lamington n (pl -s) (AUST & NZ) sponge cake coated with a sweet coating
  lamingtons n ▷ lamington
lamp n (pl -s) device which produces light from electricity, oil, or gas > **lampshade** (pl -s) ▶ n
lamppost n (pl -s) post supporting a lamp in the street
  lampposts n ▷ lamppost
  lamps n ▷ lamp
lampoon n (pl -s) humorous satire ridiculing someone ▶ v (-s, -ing, -ed) satirize or ridicule
  lampooned v ▷ lampoon
  lampooning v ▷ lampoon
  lampoons n, v ▷ lampoon
lamprey n (pl -s) eel-like fish with a round sucking mouth
  lampreys n ▷ lamprey
  lampshades n ▷ lamp
lance n (pl -s) long spear used by a mounted soldier ▶ v (-ces, -cing, -ced) pierce (a boil or abscess) with a lancet
  lanced v ▷ lance
lancer n (pl -s) formerly, cavalry soldier armed with a lance
  lancers n ▷ lancer
  lances n, v ▷ lance
  lancing v ▷ lance
lancet n (pl -s) pointed two-edged surgical knife
  lancets n ▷ lancet
land n (pl -s) solid part of the earth's surface ▶ v (-s, -ing, -ed) come or bring to earth after a flight, jump, or fall > **landless** adj
landau [lan-daw] n (pl -s) four-wheeled carriage with two folding hoods
  landaus n ▷ landau
landed adj possessing or consisting of lands ▶ v ▷ land
landfall n (pl -s) ship's first landing after a voyage
  landfalls n ▷ landfall
landing n (pl -s) floor area at the top of a flight of stairs ▶ v ▷ land
  landings n ▷ landing
landlocked adj completely surrounded by land
  lands n, v ▷ land
landlady n (pl -dies) woman who rents out land, houses, etc.
  landladies n ▷ landlady
  landless n ▷ land
landlord n (pl -s) man who rents out land, houses, etc.
  landlords n ▷ landlord

landlubber n (pl -s) person who is not experienced at sea
  landlubbers n ▷ landlubber
landmark n (pl -s) prominent object in or feature of a landscape
  landmarks n ▷ landmark
landscape n (pl -s) extensive piece of inland scenery seen from one place ▶ v (-pes, -ping, -ped) improve natural features of (a piece of land)
  landscaped v ▷ landscape
  landscapes n, v ▷ landscape
  landscaping v ▷ landscape
landslide (also **landslip**) n (pl -s) falling of soil, rock, etc. down the side of a mountain
  landslides n ▷ landslide
  landslip n ▷ landslide
  landslips n ▷ landslide ▶ adj nearest to or facing the land ▶ adv (also **landwards**) towards land
  landwards adv ▷ landward
lane n (pl -s) narrow road
  lanes n ▷ lane
language n (pl -s) system of sounds, symbols, etc. for communicating thought
  languages n ▷ language
languid adj lacking energy or enthusiasm > **languidly** adv
  languidly adv ▷ languid
languish v (-es, -ing, -ed) suffer neglect or hardship
  languished v ▷ languish
  languishes v ▷ languish
  languishing v ▷ languish
languor [lang-ger] n (pl -s) state of dreamy relaxation > **languorous** adj
  languorous n ▷ languor
  languors n ▷ languor
lank adj (-er, -est) (of hair) straight and limp
  lanker adj ▷ lank
  lankest adj ▷ lank
  lankier adj ▷ lanky
  lankiest adj ▷ lanky
lanky adj (-kier, -kiest) ungracefully tall and thin
lanolin n (pl -s) grease from sheep's wool used in ointments etc.
  lanolins n ▷ lanolin
lantana [lan-tay-na] n (pl -s) shrub with orange or yellow flowers, considered a weed in Australia
  lantanas n ▷ lantana
lantern n (pl -s) light in a transparent protective case
  lanterns n ▷ lantern

lanthanum n (pl -s) (CHEM) silvery-white metallic element
lanthanums n ▷ lanthanum
lanyard n (pl -s) cord worn round the neck to hold a knife or whistle
lanyards n ▷ lanyard
lap¹ n (pl -s) part between the waist and knees of a person when sitting
lap² n (pl -s) single circuit of a racecourse or track ▶ v (-s, -pping, -pped) overtake an opponent so as to be one or more circuits ahead
lap³ v (-s, -pping, -pped) (of waves) beat softly against (a shore etc.)
lapel [lap-**pel**] n (pl -s) part of the front of a coat or jacket folded back towards the shoulders
lapels n ▷ lapel
lapidary adj of or relating to stones
lapped v ▷ lap², ³
lapping v ▷ lap², ³
laps n ▷ lap¹, ² ▶ v ▷ lap², ³
lapse n (pl -s) temporary drop in a standard, esp. through forgetfulness or carelessness ▶ v (-ses, -sing, -sed) drop in standard > **lapsed** adj
lapsed v ▷ lapse
lapses n, v ▷ lapse
lapsing v ▷ lapse
laptop adj (of a computer) small enough to fit on a user's lap ▶ n (pl -s) computer small enough to fit on a user's lap
laptops n ▷ laptop
lapwing n (pl -s) plover with a tuft of feathers on the head
lapwings n ▷ lapwing
larboard adj, n (pl -s) (Old-fashioned) port (side of a ship)
larboards n ▷ larboard
larcenies n ▷ larceny
larceny n (pl -nies) (LAW) theft
larch n (pl -es) deciduous coniferous tree
larches n ▷ larch
lard n (pl -s) soft white fat obtained from a pig ▶ v (-s, -ing, -ed) insert strips of bacon in (meat) before cooking
larded v ▷ lard
larder n (pl -s) storeroom for food
larders n ▷ larder
larding v ▷ lard
lards n, v ▷ lard
large adj (-r, -st) great in size, number, or extent > **largely** adv > **largish** adj
largely adv ▷ large
larger adj ▷ large
largess n (pl -es) ▷ largesse
largesse, largess [lar-**jess**] n (pl -(es)) generous

giving, esp. of money
largesses n ▷ largesse
largest adj ▷ large
largish adj ▷ large
largo n (pl -s) ▶ adv (MUSIC) (piece to be played) in a slow and dignified manner
largos n ▷ largo
lariat n (pl -s) lasso
lariats n ▷ lariat
lark¹ n (pl -s) small brown songbird, skylark
lark² n (pl -s) (Informal) harmless piece of mischief or fun
larks n ▷ lark¹, ²
larkspur n (pl -s) plant with spikes of blue, pink, or white flowers with spurs
larkspurs n ▷ larkspur
larrikin n (pl -s) (AUST & NZ) (Old-fashioned slang) mischievous or unruly person
larrikins n ▷ larrikin
larva n (pl -e) insect in an immature stage, often resembling a worm > **larval** adj
larval adj ▷ larva
larynges n ▷ larynx
laryngeal adj ▷ larynx
laryngitis n (pl -ses) inflammation of the larynx
laryngitises n ▷ laryngitis
larynx n (pl -nges) part of the throat containing the vocal cords > **laryngeal** adj
lasagne, lasagna [laz-**zan**-ya] n (pl -s) pasta in wide flat sheets
lasagnas n ▷ lasagne
lasagnes n ▷ lasagne
lascivious [lass-**iv**-ee-uss] adj showing or producing sexual desire > **lasciviously** adv
lasciviously adv ▷ lascivious
laser [**lay**-zer] n (pl -s) device that produces a very narrow intense beam of light, used for cutting very hard materials and in surgery etc.
lasers n ▷ laser
lash¹ n (pl -es) eyelash ▶ v (-es, -ing, -ed) hit with a whip
lash² v (-es, -ing, -ed) fasten or bind tightly with cord etc.
lashed v ▷ lash¹, ²
lashes n ▷ lash¹ ▶ v ▷ lash¹, ²
lashing v ▷ lash¹, ²
lashings pl n (Old-fashioned) large amounts
lass, lassie n (pl -es, -s) (SCOT & N ENGLISH) girl
lasses n ▷ lass
lassies n ▷ lass
lassitude n (pl -s) physical or mental weariness
lassitudes n ▷ lassitude
lasso [lass-**oo**] n (pl -s, -es) rope with a noose for

catching cattle and horses ▶ v (-s, -ing, -ed) catch with a lasso

lassoed v ▷ lasso
lassoes n ▷ lasso
lassoing v ▷ lasso
lassos n, v ▷ lasso

last¹ adj, adv coming at the end or after all others ▶ adj only remaining ▶ n (pl -s) last person or thing ▷ **lastly** adv

last² v (-s, -ing, -ed) continue ▷ **lasting** adj

last³ n (pl -s) model of a foot on which shoes and boots are made or repaired

lasted v ▷ last²
lasting v, adj ▷ last²
lastly adv ▷ last¹
lasts n ▷ last¹,³ ▶ v ▷ last²

latch n (pl -es) fastening for a door with a bar and lever ▶ v (-es, -ing, -ed) fasten with a latch

latched v ▷ latch
latches n, v ▷ latch
latching v ▷ latch

late adj (-r, -st) after the normal or expected time ▶ adv after the normal or expected time ▷ **lateness** n (pl -es)

lately adv in recent times

latencies n ▷ latent
lateness n ▷ late
latenesses n ▷ late

latent adj hidden and not yet developed ▷ **latency** n (pl -cies)

later adj ▷ late

lateral [lat-ter-al] adj of or relating to the side or sides ▷ **laterally** adv

latest adj ▷ late

latex n (pl -es) milky fluid found in some plants, esp. the rubber tree, used in making rubber

latexes n ▷ latex

lath n (pl -s) thin strip of wood used to support plaster, tiles, etc.

laths n ▷ lath

lathe n (pl -s) machine for turning wood or metal while it is being shaped

lathes n ▷ lathe

lather n (pl -s) froth of soap and water ▶ v (-s, -ing, -ed) make frothy

lathered v ▷ lather
lathering v ▷ lather
lathers n, v ▷ lather

lathery adj (-rier, -riest) frothy

latherier adj ▷ lathery
latheriest adj ▷ lathery

latitude n (pl -s) angular distance measured in degrees N or S of the equator

latitudes n ▷ latitude

latrine n (pl -s) toilet in a barracks or camp

latrines n ▷ latrine

latter adj second of two ▷ **latterly** adv

latter-day adj modern

latterly adv ▷ latter

lattice [lat-iss] n (pl -s) framework of intersecting strips of wood, metal, etc. ▷ **latticed** adj

latticed adj ▷ lattice
lattices n ▷ lattice

laud v (-s, -ing, -ed) praise or glorify ▷ **laudably** adv

laudable adj praiseworthy

laudably adv ▷ laudable

laudanum [lawd-a-num] n (pl -s) opium-based sedative

laudanums n ▷ laudanum

laudatory adj praising or glorifying

lauded v ▷ laud
lauding v ▷ laud
lauds v ▷ laud

laugh v (-s, -ing, -ed) make inarticulate sounds with the voice expressing amusement, merriment, or scorn ▶ n (pl -s) act or instance of laughing

laughable adj ▷ laugh
laughed v ▷ laugh
laughing v ▷ laugh
laughs v, n ▷ laugh

laughter n (pl -s) sound or action of laughing

laughters n ▷ laughter

launch¹ v (-es, -ing, -ed) put (a ship or boat) into the water, esp. for the first time ▶ n (pl -es) launching ▷ **launcher** n (pl -s)

launch² n (pl -s) open motorboat

launched v ▷ launch¹
launcher n ▷ launch¹
launchers n ▷ launch¹
launches v ▷ launch¹ ▶ n ▷ launch¹,²
launches n ▷ launch¹
launching v ▷ launch¹

launder v (-s, -ing, -ed) wash and iron (clothes and linen)

launderette n ® (pl -s) shop with coin-operated washing and drying machines

laundered v ▷ launder
launderettes n ▷ launderette
laundering v ▷ launder
launders v ▷ launder

laundry n (pl -ries) clothes etc. for washing or which have recently been washed

laundries n ▷ laundry

laureate [lor-ee-at] adj (of a poet) appointed to the court of Britain

laurel n (pl -s) glossy-leaved shrub, bay tree ▶ pl wreath of laurel, an emblem of victory or merit laurels n ▷ laurel

lava n (pl -e) molten rock thrown out by volcanoes, which hardens as it cools

lavae n ▷ lava

lavatory n (pl -ries) toilet

lavatories n ▷ lavatory

lavender n (pl -s) shrub with fragrant flowers ▶ adj bluish-purple

lavenders n ▷ lavender

lavish adj great in quantity or richness ▶ v (-es, -ing, -ed) give or spend generously > lavishly adv

lavished v ▷ lavish

lavishes v ▷ lavish

lavishing v ▷ lavish

lavishly adv ▷ lavish

law n (pl -s) rule binding on a community > lawfully adv > lawlessness n (pl -es) > law-breaker n (pl -s)

lawful adj allowed by law

lawfully adv ▷ law

lawless adj breaking the law, esp. in a violent way

lawlessness n ▷ law

lawlessnesses n ▷ law

lawn¹ n (pl -s) area of tended and mown grass

lawn² n (pl -s) fine linen or cotton fabric

lawns n ▷ lawn¹,²

laws n ▷ law

lawsuit n (pl -s) court case brought by one person or group against another

lawsuits n ▷ lawsuit

lawyer n (pl -s) professionally qualified legal expert

lawyers n ▷ lawyer

lax adj not strict > laxity n (pl -ties)

laxative n (pl -s) ▶ adj (medicine) inducing the emptying of the bowels

laxatives n ▷ laxative

laxities n ▷ lax

laxity n ▷ lax

lay¹ v (-s, -ing, laid) cause to lie

lay² v ▷ lie²

lay³ adj of or involving people who are not clergymen

lay⁴ n (pl -s) short narrative poem designed to be sung

layabout n (pl -s) lazy person

layabouts n ▷ layabout

layer n (pl -s) single thickness of some substance, as a cover or coating on a surface ▶ v (-s, -ing, -ed) form a layer > layered adj

layered v, adj ▷ layer

layering v ▷ layer

layers n, v ▷ layer

layette n (pl -s) clothes for a newborn baby

layettes n ▷ layette

laying v ▷ lay¹

layman n (pl -men) person who is not a member of the clergy

laymen n ▷ layman

layout n (pl -s) arrangement, esp. of matter for printing or of a building

layouts n ▷ layout

lays v ▷ lay¹ ▶ v ▷ lay⁴

laze v (-s, -ing, -ed) be idle or lazy ▶ n (pl -s) time spent lazing

lazed v ▷ laze

lazes v, n ▷ laze

lazily adv ▷ lazy

laziness adv ▷ lazy

lazinesses adv ▷ lazy

lazing v ▷ laze

lazy adj (-zier, -ziest) not inclined to work or exert oneself > lazily adv > laziness n (pl -s)

lea n (pl -s) (Poetic) meadow

leas n ▷ lea

leach v (-es, -ing, -ed) remove or be removed from a substance by a liquid passing through it

leached v ▷ leach

leaches v ▷ leach

leaching v ▷ leach

lead¹ v (-s, -ing, led) guide or conduct ▶ n (pl -s) first or most prominent place ▶ adj acting as a leader or lead

lead² n (pl -s) soft heavy grey metal

leaded adj (of windows) made from many small panes of glass held together by lead strips

leaden adj heavy or sluggish

leader n (pl -s) person who leads > leadership n (pl -s)

leaders n ▷ leader

leaderships n ▷ leader

leading adj principal

leads n ▷ lead¹,² ▶ v ▷ lead¹

leaf n (pl leaves) flat usu. green blade attached to the stem of a plant > leafy (-fier, -fiest) ▶ adj > leafless adj

leafier adj ▷ leaf

leafiest adj ▷ leaf

leafless adj ▷ leaf

leaflet n (pl -s) sheet of printed matter for distribution

leaflets n ▷ leaflet

leafy adj ▷ leaf

league¹ n (pl -s) association promoting the interests of its members

league² n (Obs) measure of distance, about

three miles
leagues n ▷ **league¹,²**

leak n (pl **-s**) hole or defect that allows the escape or entrance of liquid, gas, radiation, etc. ▶ v (**-s, -ing, -ed**) let liquid etc. in or out > **leaky** (**-kier, -kiest**) ▶ adj
leakage n (pl **-s**) act or instance of leaking
leakages n ▷ **leakage**
leaked v ▷ **leak**
leakier adj ▷ **leak**
leakiest adj ▷ **leak**
leaking v ▷ **leak**
leaks n, v ▷ **leak**
leaky adj (**-kier, -kiest**) ▷ **leak**

lean¹ v (**-ing, -ed** or **leant**) rest against
lean² adj (**-er, -est**) thin but healthy-looking ▶ n (pl **-s**) lean part of meat ▶ **leanness** n (pl **-es**)
leaner adj ▷ **lean**
leanest adj ▷ **lean**
leaning n (pl **-s**) tendency ▶ v ▷ **lean¹**
leanings n ▷ **leaning**
leanness n ▷ **lean²**
leannesses n ▷ **lean²**
leans v, n ▷ **lean¹**
leant n ▷ **lean¹**

leap v (**-s, -ing, leapt** or **-ed**) make a sudden powerful jump ▶ n (pl **-s**) sudden powerful jump
leaped v ▷ **leap**
leapfrog n (pl **-s**) game in which a player vaults over another bending down
leapfrogs n ▷ **leapfrog**
leaping v ▷ **leap**
leaps v, n ▷ **leap**
leapt v ▷ **leap**

learn v (**-s, -ing, -ed** or **learnt**) gain skill or knowledge by study, practice, or teaching > **learner** n (pl **-s**)
learned adj erudite, deeply read
learner n ▷ **learn**
learners n ▷ **learn**
learning n (pl **-s**) knowledge got by study ▶ v ▷ **learn**
learnings n ▷ **learning**

lease n (pl **-s**) contract by which land or property is rented for a stated time by the owner to a tenant ▶ v (**-ses, -sing, -sed**) let or rent by lease > **leaseholder** n (pl **-s**)
leasehold n, adj (land or property) held on lease
leaseholder n ▷ **lease**
leaseholders n ▷ **lease**
leaseholds n ▷ **leasehold**
leased v ▷ **lease**
leases n, v ▷ **lease**

leash n (pl **-es**) lead for a dog
leashes n ▷ **leash**
leasing v ▷ **lease**

least adj ▷ **little** smallest ▶ n smallest one ▶ adv in the smallest degree
leather n (pl **-s**) material made from specially treated animal skins ▶ adj made of leather ▶ v (**-s, -ing, -ed**) beat or thrash
leathered v ▷ **leather**
leatherier adj ▷ **leathery**
leatheriest adj ▷ **leathery**
leathering v ▷ **leather**
leathers n, v ▷ **leather**
leathery adj (**-rier, -riest**) like leather, tough

leave¹ v (**-s, -ing, left**) go away from
leave² n (pl **-s**) permission to be absent from work or duty
leaven [lev-ven] n substance that causes dough to rise ▶ v (**-s, -ing, -ed**) raise with leaven
leavens v ▷ **leaven**
leavening v ▷ **leaven**
leavened v ▷ **leaven**
leaves v ▷ **leave**
leaving v ▷ **leave**

lecher n (pl **-s**) man who has or shows excessive sexual desire > **lechery** n (pl **-ries**)
lecheries n ▷ **lechery**
lecherous [letch-er-uss] adj (of a man) having or showing excessive sexual desire
lechers n ▷ **lecher**
lectern n (pl **-s**) sloping reading desk, esp. in a church
lecterns n ▷ **lectern**
lecture n (pl **-s**) informative talk to an audience on a subject ▶ v (**-s, -ing, -ed**) give a talk
lectured v ▷ **lecture**
lecturer n (pl **-s**) person who lectures, esp. in a university or college
lecturers n ▷ **lecturer**
lectures n, v ▷ **lecture**
lectureship n (pl **-s**) appointment as a lecturer
lectureships n ▷ **lectureship**
lecturing v ▷ **lecture**
ledge n (pl **-s**) narrow shelf sticking out from a wall
ledger n (pl **-s**) book of debit and credit accounts of a firm
ledgers n ▷ **ledger**
ledges n ▷ **ledge**
lee n (pl **-s**) sheltered part or side ▶ adv towards this side
leech n (pl **-es**) species of bloodsucking worm
leeches n ▷ **leech**
leek n (pl **-s**) vegetable of the onion family with

a long bulb and thick stem
leeks n ▷ **leek**

leer v (**-s, -ing, -ed**) look or grin at in a sneering or suggestive manner ▶ n (pl **-s**) sneering or suggestive look or grin
leered v ▷ **leer**
leerier adj ▷ **leery**
leeriest adj ▷ **leery**
leering v ▷ **leer**
leers v, n ▷ **leer**

leery adj (Informal) (**-rier, -riest**) suspicious or wary (of)

lees pl n sediment of wine ▶ n ▷ **lee**

leeward adj, n (pl **-s**) (on) the lee side
leewards n ▷ **leeward**

leeway n (pl **-s**) room for free movement within limits
leeways n ▷ **leeway**

left¹ adj of the side that faces west when the front faces north ▶ adv on or towards the left ▶ n (pl **-s**) left hand or part

left² v ▷ **leave¹**

leftist n (pl **-s**) ▶ adj (person) of the political left
leftists n ▷ **leftist**

leftover n (pl **-s**) unused portion of food or material
leftovers n ▷ **leftover**
lefts n ▷ **left¹**

leg n (pl **-s**) one of the limbs on which a person or animal walks, runs, or stands
legacies n ▷ **legacy**

legacy n (pl **-cies**) thing left in a will

legal adj established or permitted by law > **legally** adv > **legality** n (pl **-ties**) > **legalization** n (pl **-s**)
legalities n ▷ **legal**
legality n ▷ **legal**
legalization n ▷ **legal**
legalizations n ▷ **legal**

legalize v (**-zes, -zing, -zed**) make legal
legalized adv ▷ **legalize**
legalizes adv ▷ **legalize**
legalizing adv ▷ **legalize**
legally adv ▷ **legal**

legate n (pl **-s**) messenger or representative, esp. from the Pope

legatee n (pl **-s**) recipient of a legacy
legatees n ▷ **legatee**
legates n ▷ **legate**

legation n (pl **-s**) diplomatic minister and his staff
legations n ▷ **legation**

legato [leg-ah-toe] n (pl **-s**), adv (MUSIC) (piece to be played) smoothly
legatos n ▷ **legato**

legend n (pl **-s**) traditional story or myth

legendary adj famous
legends n ▷ **legend**

legerdemain [lej-er-de-main] n (pl **-s**) sleight of hand
legerdemains n ▷ **legerdemain**
leggier adj ▷ **leggy**
leggiest adj ▷ **leggy**

leggings pl n covering of leather or other material for the legs

leggy adj (**-gier, -giest**) having long legs
legibilities n ▷ **legible**
legibility n ▷ **legible**

legible adj easily read > **legibility** n (pl **-ties**) > **legibly** adv
legibly adv ▷ **legible**

legion n (pl **-s**) large military force > **legionary** adj, n (pl **-ries**)
legionaries n ▷ **legion**
legionary adj, n ▷ **legion**

legionnaire n (pl **-s**) member of a legion
legionnaires n ▷ **legionnaire**
legions n ▷ **legion**

legislate v (**-tes, -ting, -ted**) make laws > **legislative** adj
legislated v ▷ **legislate**
legislates v ▷ **legislate**
legislating v ▷ **legislate**

legislation n (pl **-s**) legislating
legislations n ▷ **legislation**
legislative v ▷ **legislate**

legislator n (pl **-s**) maker of laws
legislators n ▷ **legislator**

legislature n (pl **-s**) body of people that makes, amends, or repeals laws
legislatures n ▷ **legislature**
legitimacies n ▷ **legitimate**
legitimacy n ▷ **legitimate**

legitimate adj authorized by or in accordance with law ▶ v (**-tes, -ting, -ted**) make legitimate > **legitimacy** n (pl **-cies**) > **legitimately** adv
legitimated v ▷ **legitimate**
legitimately adv ▷ **legitimate**
legitimates v ▷ **legitimate**
legitimating v ▷ **legitimate**

legitimize v (**-zes, -zing, -zed**) make legitimate, legalize > **legitimization** n (pl **-s**)
legitimization n ▷ **legitimize**
legitimizations n ▷ **legitimize**
legitimized v ▷ **legitimize**
legitimizes v ▷ **legitimize**
legitimizing v ▷ **legitimize**

legless adj without legs
legs n ▷ **leg**

leguaan [leg-oo-ahn] n (pl -s) large S African lizard

leguaans n ▷ **leguaan**

legume n (pl -s) pod of a plant of the pea or bean family ▶ pl peas or beans

legumes n ▷ **legume**

leguminous adj (of plants) pod-bearing

lei n (pl -s) (in Hawaii) garland of flowers

leis n ▷ **lei**

leisure n (pl -s) time for relaxation or hobbies

leisured adj with plenty of spare time

leisurely adj deliberate, unhurried ▶ adv slowly

leisures n ▷ **leisure**

leitmotif [lite-mote-eef] n (pl -s) (MUSIC) recurring theme associated with a person, situation, or thought

leitmotifs n ▷ **leitmotif**

lekker adj (S AFR) (Slang) attractive or nice

lemming n (pl -s) rodent of arctic regions, reputed to run into the sea and drown during mass migrations

lemmings n ▷ **lemming**

lemon n (pl -s) yellow oval fruit that grows on trees ▶ adj pale-yellow

lemonade n (pl -s) lemon-flavoured soft drink, often fizzy

lemonades n ▷ **lemonade**

lemons n ▷ **lemon**

lemur n (pl -s) nocturnal animal like a small monkey, found in Madagascar

lemurs n ▷ **lemur**

lend v (-s, -ing, lent) give the temporary use of > **lender** n (pl -s)

lending v ▷ **lend**

lender n ▷ **lend**

lenders n ▷ **lend**

lends v ▷ **lend**

length n (pl -s) extent or measurement from end to end > **lengthily** adv > **lengthways, lengthwise** adj, adv

lengthen v (-s, -ing, -ed) make or become longer

lengthened v ▷ **lengthen**

lengthening v ▷ **lengthen**

lengthens v ▷ **lengthen**

lengthier adj ▷ **length**

lengthiest adj ▷ **length**

lengthily adv ▷ **length**

lengths n ▷ **length**

lengthways adj, adv ▷ **length**

lengthwise adj, adv ▷ **lengthen**

lengthy adj (-thier, -thiest) very long or tiresome

leniencies n ▷ **lenient**

leniency n ▷ **lenient**

lenient [lee-nee-ent] adj tolerant, not strict or severe > **leniency** n (pl -cies) > **leniently** adv

leniently adv ▷ **lenient**

lens n (pl -es) piece of glass or similar material with one or both sides curved, used to bring together or spread light rays in cameras, spectacles, telescopes, etc.

lenses n ▷ **lens**

lent v ▷ **lend**

lentil n (pl -s) edible seed of a leguminous Asian plant

lentils n ▷ **lentil**

lento n (pl -tos), adv (MUSIC) (piece to be played) slowly

lentos n ▷ **lento**

Lents n ▷ **Lent**

leonine adj like a lion

leopard n (pl -s) large spotted carnivorous animal of the cat family

leopards n ▷ **leopard**

leotard n (pl -s) tight-fitting garment covering the upper body, worn for dancing or exercise

leotards n ▷ **leotard**

leper n (pl -s) person suffering from leprosy

lepers n ▷ **leper**

lepidoptera pl n order of insects with four wings covered with fine gossamer scales, as moths and butterflies

lepidopterist n (pl -s) person who studies or collects butterflies or moths

lepidopterists n ▷ **lepidopterist**

leprechaun n (pl -s) mischievous elf of Irish folklore

leprechauns n ▷ **leprechaun**

leprosy n (pl -sies) disease attacking the nerves and skin, resulting in loss of feeling in the affected parts > **leprous** adj

leprosies n ▷ **leprosy**

leprous adj ▷ **leprosy**

lesbian n (pl -s) homosexual woman ▶ adj of homosexual women > **lesbianism** n (pl -s)

lesbians n ▷ **lesbian**

lesbianisms n ▷ **lesbian**

lesion n (pl -s) structural change in an organ of the body caused by illness or injury

lesions n ▷ **lesion**

less adj smaller in extent, degree, or duration ▷ **little** ▶ pron smaller part or quantity ▶ adv to a smaller extent or degree ▶ prep after deducting, minus

lessee n (pl -s) person to whom a lease is granted

lessees n ▷ **lessee**

lessen v (-s, -ing, -ed) make or become smaller or not as much

lessened v ▷ lessen

lessening v ▷ lessen

lessens v ▷ lessen

lesser adj not as great in quantity, size, or worth

lesson n (pl -s) single period of instruction in a subject

lessons n ▷ lesson

lest conj so as to prevent any possibility that

let¹ v (-s, -tting, let) allow, enable, or cause

let² n (pl -s) (TENNIS) minor infringement or obstruction of the ball requiring a replay of the point

letdown n (pl -s) disappointment

letdowns n ▷ letdown

lets v ▷ let¹ ▶ n ▷ let²

lethal adj deadly

lethargic adj ▷ lethargy

lethargically adv ▷ lethargy

lethargies n ▷ lethargy

lethargy n (pl -gies) sluggishness or dullness > lethargic adj > lethargically adv

letter n (pl -s) written message, usu. sent by post ▶ pl literary knowledge or ability > lettering n (pl -s)

lettered adj learned

letterhead n (pl -s) printed heading on stationery giving the sender's name and address

letterheads n ▷ letterhead

lettering n ▷ letter

letterings n ▷ letter

letters n ▷ letter

letting v ▷ let¹

lettuce n (pl -s) plant with large green leaves used in salads

lettuces n ▷ lettuce

leucocyte [loo-koh-site] n (pl -s) white blood cell

leucocytes n ▷ leucocyte

leukaemia [loo-kee-mee-a] n (pl -s) disease caused by uncontrolled overproduction of white blood cells

leukaemias n ▷ leukaemia

levee n (pl -s) (US) natural or artificial river embankment

levees n ▷ levee

level adj (-llest, -ller) horizontal ▶ v (-s, -lling, -lled, -ller) make even or horizontal ▶ n (pl -s) horizontal line or surface

levelled v ▷ level

leveller v ▷ level

levellest adj ▷ level

levelling v ▷ level

levels v, n ▷ level

lever n (pl -s) handle used to operate machinery ▶ v (-s, -ing, -ed) prise or move with a lever

leverage n (pl -s) action or power of a lever

leverages n ▷ leverage

levered v ▷ lever

levering v ▷ lever

levers n, v ▷ lever

leveret [lev-ver-it] n (pl -s) young hare

leverets n ▷ leveret

leviathan [lev-vie-ath-an] n (pl -s) sea monster

leviathans n ▷ leviathan

levitate v (-tes, -ting, -ted) rise or cause to rise into the air

levitated v ▷ levitate

levitates v ▷ levitate

levitating v ▷ levitate

levitation n (pl -s) raising of a solid body into the air supernaturally

levitations n ▷ levitation

levities n ▷ levity

levity n (pl -ties) inclination to make a joke of serious matters

levy [lev-vee] v (-vies, -ing, -vied) impose and collect (a tax) ▶ n (pl -vies) imposition or collection of taxes

levied v ▷ levy

levies v, n ▷ levy

levying v ▷ levy

lewd adj (-er, -est) lustful or indecent > lewdly adv > lewdness n (pl -es)

lewder adj ▷ lewd

lewdest adj ▷ lewd

lewdly adv ▷ lewd

lewdness n ▷ lewd

lewdnesses n ▷ lewd

> **lex** n (**leges**). A lex is a system or body of laws. This is a really handy word when you have L and X, as there is likely to be an E available on the board. Lex scores 10 points.

lexical adj relating to the vocabulary of a language

lexicographer n (pl -s) writer of dictionaries

lexicographers n ▷ lexicographer

lexicography n ▷ lexicon

lexicographies n ▷ lexicon

lexicon n (pl -s) dictionary > lexicography n (pl -phies)

lexicons n ▷ lexicon

> **li** n (**lis**). The li is a Chinese unit of length. This low-scoring word is worth knowing for when you want to form words in more than one direction at the same time. Li scores 2 points.

liability n (pl -ties) hindrance or disadvantage

liable adj legally obliged or responsible

liaise v (**-ses, -sing, -sed**) establish and maintain communication (with)
  liaised v ▷ liaise
  liaises v ▷ liaise
  liaising v ▷ liaise

liaison n (pl **-s**) communication and contact between groups
  liaisons n ▷ liaison

liana n (pl **-s**) climbing plant in tropical forests
  lianas n ▷ liana

liar n (pl **-s**) person who tells lies
  liars n ▷ liar

libation [lie-**bay**-shun] n (pl **-s**) drink poured as an offering to the gods
  libations n ▷ libation

libel n (pl **-s**) published statement falsely damaging a person's reputation ▶ v (**-s, -lling, -lled**) falsely damage the reputation of (someone) > **libellous** adj
  libelled v ▷ libel
  libelling v ▷ libel
  libellous adj ▷ libel
  libels n, v ▷ libel

liberal adj having social and political views that favour progress and reform ▶ n (pl **-s**) person who has liberal ideas or opinions > **liberally** adv > **liberalization** n (pl **-s**)

liberalism n (pl **-s**) belief in democratic reforms and individual freedom
  liberalisms n ▷ liberalism
  liberalities n ▷ liberality

liberality n (pl **-ties**) generosity
  liberalization n ▷ liberal
  liberalizations n ▷ liberal

liberalize v (**-zes, -zing, -zed**) make (laws, a country, etc.) less restrictive
  liberalized v ▷ liberalize
  liberalizes v ▷ liberalize
  liberalizing v ▷ liberalize
  liberally adv ▷ liberal
  liberals n ▷ liberal

liberate v (**-tes, -ting, -ted**) set free > **liberation** n (pl **-s**) > **liberator** n (pl **-s**)
  liberated v ▷ liberate
  liberates v ▷ liberate
  liberating v ▷ liberate
  liberation n ▷ liberate
  liberations n ▷ liberate
  liberator n ▷ liberate
  liberators n ▷ liberate

libertarian n (pl **-s**) believer in freedom of thought and action ▶ adj having such a belief
  libertarians n ▷ libertarian

libertine [**lib**-er-teen] n (pl **-s**) morally dissolute person

  libertines n ▷ libertine
  liberties n ▷ liberty

liberty n (pl **-ties**) freedom

libidinous adj lustful

libido [lib-**ee**-doe] n (pl **-s**) psychic energy
  libidos n ▷ libido

librarian n (pl **-s**) keeper of or worker in a library > **librarianship** n (pl **-s**)
  librarians n ▷ librarian
  librarianship n ▷ librarian
  librarianships n ▷ librarian
  libraries n ▷ library

library n (pl **-ries**) room or building where books are kept
  libretti n ▷ libretto
  librettist n ▷ libretto
  librettists n ▷ libretto

libretto n (pl **-ttos, -tti**) words of an opera > **librettist** n (pl **-s**)
  librettos n ▷ libretto

lice n ▷ louse

licence n (pl **-s**) document giving official permission to do something
  licences n ▷ licence

license v (**-ses, -sing, -sed**) grant a licence to > **licensed** adj
  licensed v, adj ▷ license

licensee n (pl **-s**) holder of a licence, esp. to sell alcohol
  licensees n ▷ licensee
  licenses v ▷ license
  licensing v ▷ license

licentiate n (pl **-s**) person licensed as competent to practise a profession
  licentiates n ▷ licentiate

licentious adj sexually unrestrained or promiscuous

lichen n (pl **-s**) small flowerless plant forming a crust on rocks, trees, etc.
  lichens n ▷ lichen

licit adj lawful, permitted

lick v (**-s, -ing, -ed**) pass the tongue over ▶ n (pl **-s**) licking
  licked v ▷ lick
  licking v ▷ lick
  licks v, n ▷ lick

licorice n (pl **-s**) ▷ liquorice
  licorices n ▷ licorice

lid n (pl **-s**) movable cover
  lids n ▷ lid

lido [**lee**-doe] n (pl **-s**) open-air centre for swimming and water sports
  lidos n ▷ lido

lie¹ v (**-s, lying, lied**) make a deliberately false

statement ▶ n (pl -s) deliberate falsehood

lie² v (-s, lying, lay, lain) place oneself or be in a horizontal position ▶ n (pl -s) way something lies

lied¹ v ▷ **lie¹**

lied² [leed] n (pl lieder) (MUSIC) setting for voice and piano of a romantic poem

liege [leej] adj bound to give or receive feudal service ▶ n (pl -s) lord

lieges n ▷ **liege**

lien n (pl -s) (LAW) right to hold another's property until a debt is paid

liens n ▷ **lien**

lies v, n ▷ **lie¹,²**

lieutenant [lef-ten-ant] n (pl -s) junior officer in the army or navy

lieutenants n ▷ **lieutenant**

life n (pl lives) state of living beings, characterized by growth, reproduction, and response to stimuli > **lifelike** adj

lifeboat n (pl -s) boat used for rescuing people at sea

lifeboats adj ▷ **lifeboat**

lifeless adj dead

lifelike adj ▷ **life**

lifeline n (pl -s) means of contact or support

lifelines n ▷ **lifeline**

lifelong adj lasting all of a person's life

lifestyle n (pl -s) particular attitudes, habits, etc.

lifestyles n ▷ **lifestyle**

lifetime n (pl -s) length of time a person is alive

lifetimes n ▷ **lifetime**

lift v (lifts, lifting, lifted) move upwards in position, status, volume, etc. ▶ n (pl lifts) cage raised and lowered in a vertical shaft to transport people or goods

liftoff n moment a rocket leaves the ground

lifts v ▷ **lift**

lifting v ▷ **lift**

lifted v ▷ **lift**

lifts n ▷ **lift**

ligament n (pl -s) band of tissue joining bones

ligaments n ▷ **ligament**

ligature n (pl -s) link, bond, or tie

ligatures n ▷ **ligature**

light¹ n (pl -s) electromagnetic radiation by which things are visible ▶ pl traffic lights ▶ adj bright ▶ v (-s, -ing, lit) ignite

light² adj (-er, -est) not heavy, weighing relatively little ▶ adv with little equipment or luggage ▶ v (-s, -ing, -ed, lit) (esp. of birds) settle after flight > **lightly** adv > **lightness** n (pl -s)

lighted v ▷ **light²**

lighten¹ v (-s, -ing, -ed) make less dark

lighten² v (-s, -ing, -ed) make less heavy or burdensome

lightened v ▷ **lighten¹,²**

lightening v ▷ **lighten¹,²**

lightens v ▷ **lighten¹,²**

lighter adj ▷ **light²**

lightest adj ▷ **light²**

lighthouse n (pl -s) tower with a light to guide ships

lighthouses n ▷ **lighthouse**

lighting n (pl -s) apparatus for and use of artificial light in theatres, films, etc. ▶ v ▷ **light¹,²**

lightings n ▷ **lighting**

lighter¹ n (pl -s) device for lighting cigarettes etc.

lighter² n (pl -s) flat-bottomed boat for unloading ships

lighters n ▷ **lighter¹,²**

lightly adv ▷ **light²**

lightness n ▷ **light²**

lightnesses n ▷ **light²**

lightning n (pl -s) visible discharge of electricity in the atmosphere ▶ adj fast and sudden

lightnings n ▷ **lightning**

lights pl n lungs of animals as animal food ▶ n ▷ **light¹** ▶ v ▷ **light¹,²**

lightweight n (pl -s) ▶ adj (person) of little importance

lightweights n ▷ **lightweight**

ligneous adj of or like wood

lignite [lig-nite] n (pl -s) woody textured rock used as fuel

lignites n ▷ **lignite**

like¹ prep, conj adj, pron indicating similarity, comparison, etc.

like² v (-s, -ing, -ed) find enjoyable > **likeable, likable** adj > **liking** n fondness

liked v ▷ **like**

liken v (-s, -ing, -ed) compare

likelier adj ▷ **likely**

likeliest adj ▷ **likely**

likelihood n (pl -s) probability

likelihoods n ▷ **likelihood**

likely adj (-lier, -liest) tending or inclined ▶ adv probably

likened v ▷ **liken**

likeness n resemblance

likening v ▷ **liken**

likens v ▷ **liken**

likes v ▷ **like**

likewise adv similarly

liking v ▷ **like**

lilac n (pl -s) shrub with pale mauve or white flowers ▸ adj light-purple
  lilacs n ▷ lilac
lilt n (pl -s) pleasing musical quality in speaking > **lilting** adj
  lilting adj ▷ lilt
  lilts n ▷ lilt
lily n (pl -lies) plant which grows from a bulb and has large, often white, flowers
limb n (pl -s) arm, leg, or wing
  limbs n ▷ limb
limber adj pliant or supple
limbo n (pl -s) West Indian dance in which dancers lean backwards to pass under a bar
  limbos n ▷ limbo
lime¹ n (pl -s) calcium compound used as a fertilizer or in making cement
lime² n (pl -s) small green citrus fruit
lime³ n (pl -s) deciduous tree with heart-shaped leaves and fragrant flowers
limelight n (pl -s) glare of publicity
  limelights n ▷ lime
limerick [lim-mer-ik] n (pl -s) humorous verse of five lines
  limericks n ▷ limerick
  limes n ▷ lime¹,²,³
limestone n (pl -s) sedimentary rock used in building
  limestones n ▷ limestone
limey n (pl -s) (US) (Slang) British person
  limeys n ▷ limey
limit n (pl -s) ultimate extent, degree, or amount of something ▸ v (-s, -ing, -ed) restrict or confine > **limitation** n (pl -s) > **limitless** adj
  limitation n ▷ limit
  limitations n ▷ limit
  limited v ▷ limit
  limiting v ▷ limit
  limitless v ▷ limit
  limits n, v ▷ limit
limousine n (pl -s) large luxurious car
  limousines n ▷ limousine
limp¹ v (-s, -ing, -ed) walk with an uneven step ▸ n (pl -s) limping walk
limp² (-er, -est) adj without firmness or stiffness > **limply** adv
  limped v ▷ limp¹
  limper adj ▷ limp²
  limpest adj ▷ limp²
  limping v ▷ limp¹
  limply adv ▷ limp²
  limps v, n ▷ limp¹
limpet n (pl -s) shellfish which sticks tightly to rocks

  limpets n ▷ limpet
limpid adj clear or transparent > **limpidity** n (pl -ties)
  limpidities n ▷ limpid
  limpidity n ▷ limpid
linchpin, lynchpin n (pl -s) pin to hold a wheel on its axle
  linchpins n ▷ linchpin
linctus n (pl -es) syrupy cough medicine
  linctuses n ▷ linctus
linden n (pl -s) ⊳ lime³
  lindens n ▷ linden
line¹ n (pl -s) long narrow mark ▸ pl words of a theatrical part ▸ v (-s, -ing, -ed) mark with lines
line² v (-s, -ning, -ned) give a lining to
  lined v ▷ line¹,²
  lines n, v ▷ line¹,²
  lining v ▷ line¹,²
lineage [lin-ee-ij] n (pl -s) descent from an ancestor
  lineages n ▷ lineage
lineament n (pl -s) facial feature
  lineaments n ▷ lineament
linear [lin-ee-er] adj of or in lines
linen n (pl -s) cloth or thread made from flax
  linens n ▷ linen
liner¹ n (pl -s) large passenger ship or aircraft
liner² n something used as a lining
  liners n ▷ liner¹,²
linesman n (pl -men) (in some sports) an official who helps the referee or umpire
  linesmen n ▷ linesman
ling¹ n slender food fish
ling² n (pl lings) heather
linger v (-s, -ing, -ed) delay or prolong departure
  lingered v ▷ linger
lingerie [lan-zher-ee] n (pl -s) women's underwear or nightwear
  lingeries n ▷ lingerie
  lingering v ▷ linger
  lingers v ▷ linger
lingo n (pl -s) (Informal) foreign or unfamiliar language or jargon
  lingos n ▷ lingo
  lings n ▷ ling²
lingual adj of the tongue
linguist n (pl -s) person skilled in foreign languages
linguistic adj of languages
linguistics n (pl -s) scientific study of language
  linguists n ▷ linguist
liniment n (pl -s) medicated liquid rubbed on the skin to relieve pain or stiffness

liniments *n* ▷ liniment

lining *n* (*pl* -s) layer of cloth attached to the inside of a garment etc.

linings *n* ▷ lining

link *n* (*pl* -s) any of the rings forming a chain ▸ *v* (-s, -ing, -ed) connect with or as if with links
> **linkage** *n* (*pl* -s)

linkage *n* ▷ link

linkages *n* ▷ link

linked *v* ▷ link

linking *v* ▷ link

links *pl n* golf course, esp. one by the sea

links *n*, *v* ▷ link

linnet *n* (*pl* -s) songbird of the finch family

linnets *n* ▷ linnet

linoleum *n* (*pl* -s) floor covering of hessian or jute with a smooth decorative coating of powdered cork

linoleums *n* ▷ linoleum

linseed *n* (*pl* -s) seed of the flax plant

linseeds *n* ▷ linseed

lint *n* (*pl* -s) soft material for dressing a wound

lintel *n* (*pl* -s) horizontal beam at the top of a door or window

lintels *n* ▷ lintel

lints *n* ▷ lint

lion *n* (*pl* -s) large animal of the cat family, the male of which has a shaggy mane > **lioness** *n fem*

lioness *n* ▷ lion

lions *n* ▷ lion

lip *n* (*pl* -s) either of the fleshy edges of the mouth

lips *n* ▷ lip

lipstick *n* (*pl* -s) cosmetic in stick form, for colouring the lips

liquefy *v* (-fies, -fying, -fied) make or become liquid > **liquefaction** *n* (*pl* -s)

liquefaction *n* ▷ liquefy

liquefactions *n* ▷ liquefy

liquefied *v* ▷ liquefy

liquefies *v* ▷ liquefy

liquefying *v* ▷ liquefy

liqueur [lik-cure] *n* (*pl* -s) flavoured and sweetened alcoholic spirit

liqueurs *n* ▷ liqueur

liquid *n* (*pl* -s) substance in a physical state which can change shape but not size ▸ *adj* of or being a liquid

liquidate *v* (-tes, -ting, -ted) pay (a debt)
> **liquidation** *n* (*pl* -s)

liquidated *v* ▷ liquidate

liquidates *v* ▷ liquidate

liquidating *v* ▷ liquidate

liquidation *n* ▷ liquidate

liquidations *n* ▷ liquidate

liquidities *n* ▷ liquidity

liquidator *n* (*pl* -s) official appointed to liquidate a business

liquidators *n* ▷ liquidator

liquidity *n* (*pl* -ties) state of being able to meet financial obligations ▸ *v* (-zes, -zing, -zed) make or become liquid

liquidized *v* ▷ liquidize

liquidizer *n* (*pl* -s) kitchen appliance that liquidizes food

liquidizers *v* ▷ liquidizer

liquidizes *v* ▷ liquidize

liquidizing *v* ▷ liquidize

liquids *n* ▷ liquid

liquor *n* (*pl* -s) alcoholic drink, esp. spirits

liquors *n* ▷ liquor

liquorice [lik-ker-iss] *n* (*pl* -s) black substance used in medicine and as a sweet

liquorices *n* ▷ liquorice

lira *n* (*pl* -re, -ras) monetary unit of Turkey and formerly of Italy

liras *n* ▷ lira

lire *n* ▷ lira

lisle [rhymes with **mile**] *n* (*pl* -s) strong fine cotton thread or fabric

lisles *n* ▷ lisle

lisp *n* (*pl* -s) speech defect in which s and z are pronounced *th* ▸ *v* (-s, -ing, -ed) speak or utter with a lisp

lisped *v* ▷ lisp

lisping *v* ▷ lisp

lisps *n*, *v* ▷ lisp

lissom, lissome *adj* supple, agile

lissome *adj* ▷ lissom

list[1] *n* (*pl* -s) item-by-item record of names or things, usu. written one below another ▸ *v* (-s, -ing, -ed) make a list of

list[2] *v* (-s, -ing, -ed) (of a ship) lean to one side ▸ *n* (*pl* -s) leaning to one side

listed *v* ▷ list[1,2]

listing *v* ▷ list[1,2]

lists *n*, *v* ▷ list[1,2]

listen *v* (-s, -ing, -ed) concentrate on hearing something > **listener** *n* (*pl* -s)

listened *v* ▷ listen

listener *n* ▷ listen

listeners *n* ▷ listen

listening *v* ▷ listen

listens *v* ▷ listen

listeriosis *n* (*pl* -ses) dangerous form of food poisoning

listerioses *n* ▷ listeriosis

listless *adj* lacking interest or energy
> **listlessly** *adv*

listlessly adv ▷ listless
lit v ▷ light[1,2]
litanies n ▷ litany
litany n (pl -nies) prayer with responses from the congregation
literacies n ▷ literacy
literacy n (pl -cies) ability to read and write
literal adj according to the explicit meaning of a word or text, not figurative > **literally** adv
literally adv ▷ literal
literary adj of or knowledgeable about literature
literate adj able to read and write
literati pl n literary people
literature n (pl -s) written works such as novels, plays, and poetry
literatures n ▷ literature
lithe adj (-ther, -thest) flexible or supple, pliant
lither adj ▷ lithe
lithest adj ▷ lithe
lithium n (pl -s) (CHEM) chemical element, the lightest known metal
lithograph n (pl -s) print made by lithography
lithographer n ▷ lithography
lithographers n ▷ lithography
lithographic adj ▷ lithography
lithographied v ▷ lithography
lithographies n, v ▷ lithography
lithographs n ▷ lithograph
lithography [lith-og-ra-fee] n (pl -phies) method of printing from a metal or stone surface in which the printing areas are made receptive to ink ▶ v (-phies, -ying, -phied) reproduce by lithography > **lithographer** n (pl -s) > **lithographic** adj
lithographying v ▷ lithography
litigant n (pl -s) person involved in a lawsuit
litigants n ▷ litigant
litigate v (-tes, -ting, -ted) bring or contest a law suit
litigated v ▷ litigate
litigates v ▷ litigate
litigating v ▷ litigate
litigation n (pl -s) legal action
litigations n ▷ litigation
litigious [lit-ij-uss] adj frequently going to law
litmus n (pl -es) blue dye turned red by acids and restored to blue by alkalis
litmuses n ▷ litmus
litotes [lie-toe-teez] n ironical understatement used for effect
litre n (pl -s) unit of liquid measure equal to 1000 cubic centimetres or 1.76 pints
litres n ▷ litre
litter n (pl -s) untidy rubbish dropped in public

places ▶ v (-s, -ing, -ed) strew with litter
littered v ▷ litter
littering v ▷ litter
litters n, v ▷ litter
little adj small or smaller than average ▶ adv not a lot ▶ n small amount, extent, or duration
littoral adj of or by the seashore ▶ n (pl -s) coastal district
littorals n ▷ littoral
liturgical n ▷ liturgy
liturgies n ▷ liturgy
liturgy n (pl -gies) prescribed form of public worship > **liturgical** adj
live[1] v (-s, -ing, -ed) be alive
live[2] adj living, alive ▶ adv in the form of a live performance > **liveliness** n (pl -es)
lived v ▷ live[1]
liveliness n ▷ live[2]
livelinesses n ▷ live[2]
lively adj full of life or vigour
livelihood n (pl livelihoods) occupation or employment
livelihoods n ▷ livelihood
lively adj full of life or vigour
liver[1] n (pl -s) organ secreting bile
liver[2] n (pl -s) person who lives in a specified way
liveried adj ▷ livery
liverish adj having a disorder of the liver
livers n ▷ liver[1,2]
livery n (pl -ries) distinctive dress, esp. of a servant or servants > **liveried** adj
lives v ▷ live[1] ▶ n ▷ life
livestock n (pl -s) farm animals
livestocks n ▷ livestock
livid adj (Informal) (-er, -est) angry or furious
livider adj ▷ livid
lividest adj ▷ livid
living adj possessing life, not dead or inanimate ▶ n (pl -s) condition of being alive ▶ v ▷ live
livings n ▷ live
lizard n (pl -s) four-footed reptile with a long body and tail
lizards n ▷ lizard
llama n (pl -s) woolly animal of the camel family used as a beast of burden in S America
llamas n ▷ llama

> **lo** interj. Lo is a command that means look! Along with **la** and **li**, lo is one of just three two-letter words that begin with L. Lo scores 2 points.

loach n (pl -es) carplike freshwater fish
loaches n ▷ loach

load n (pl -s) burden or weight ▶ pl (Informal) lots ▶ v (-s, -ing, -ed) put a load on or into

loaded adj (of a question) containing a hidden trap or implication

loaded v, adj ▷ load

loads n, v ▷ load

loading v ▷ load

loaf n (pl loaves) shaped mass of baked bread

loaf² v (-s, -ing, -ed) idle, loiter > **loafer** n (pl -s)

loafed v ▷ loaf²

loafer n ▷ loaf²

loafers n ▷ loaf²

loafing v ▷ loaf²

loafs v ▷ loaf²

loam n (pl -s) fertile soil

loams n ▷ loam

loan n (pl -s) money lent at interest ▶ v (-s, -ing, -ed) lend

loaned v ▷ loan

loaning v ▷ loan

loans n, v ▷ loan

loath, loth [rhymes with both] adj unwilling or reluctant (to)

loathe v (-s, -thing, -thed) hate, be disgusted by > **loathing** n (pl -s) **loathsome** adj

loathed v ▷ loathe

loathes v ▷ loathe

loathing v, n ▷ loathe

loathings n ▷ loathe

loathsome adj ▷ loathe

loaves n ▷ loaf¹

lob (SPORT) n (pl -s) ball struck or thrown in a high arc ▶ v (-s, -bbing, -bbed) strike or throw (a ball) in a high arc

lobbed v ▷ lob

lobbied v ▷ lobby

lobbies n, v ▷ lobby

lobbing v ▷ lob

lobby n (pl -bies) corridor into which rooms open ▶ v (-bies, -ing, -bied) try to influence (legislators) in the formulation of policy > **lobbyist** n

lobbying v ▷ lobby

lobe n (pl -s) rounded projection > **lobed** adj

lobed n ▷ lobe

lobelia n (pl -s) garden plant with blue, red, or white flowers

lobelias n ▷ lobelia

lobes n ▷ lobe

lobola [law-bawl-a] n (pl -s) (S AFR) (in African custom) price paid by a bridegroom's family to his bride's family

lobolas n ▷ lobola

lobotomy n (pl -mies) surgical incision into a lobe of the brain to treat mental disorders

lobotomies n ▷ lobotomy

lobs n, v ▷ lob

lobster n (pl -s) shellfish with a long tail and claws, which turns red when boiled

lobsters n ▷ lobster

local adj of or existing in a particular place ▶ n (pl -s) person belonging to a particular district > **locally** adv

locale [loh-kahl] n (pl -s) scene of an event

localities n ▷ locality

locality n (pl -ties) neighbourhood or area

localize v (-zes, -zing, -zed) restrict to a particular place

localized v ▷ localize

localizes v ▷ localize

localizing v ▷ localize

locally adv ▷ local

locals n ▷ local

locate v (-s, -ing, -ed) discover the whereabouts of

located v ▷ locate

locates v ▷ locate

locating v ▷ locate

location n (pl -s) site or position

locations n ▷ location

loch n (pl -s) (SCOT) lake

lochs n ▷ loch

loci n ▷ locus

lock¹ n (pl -s) appliance for fastening a door, case, etc. ▶ v (-s, -ing, -ed) fasten or become fastened securely

lock² n (pl -s) strand of hair

locked v ▷ lock¹

locker n (pl -s) small cupboard with a lock

lockers n ▷ locker

locket n (pl -s) small hinged pendant for a portrait etc.

lockets n ▷ locket

locking v ▷ lock¹

lockjaw n (pl -s) tetanus

lockjaws n ▷ lockjaw

locomotion n (pl -s) action or power of moving

locomotions n ▷ locomotion

locomotive n (pl -s) self-propelled engine for pulling trains ▶ adj of locomotion

locomotives n ▷ locomotive

lockout n (pl -s) closing of a workplace by an employer to force workers to accept terms

lockouts n ▷ lockout

locks n ▷ lock¹,² v ▷ lock¹

locksmith n (pl -s) person who makes and mends locks

locksmiths n ▷ locksmith

lockup n (pl -s) prison

lockups n ▷ lockup

locum n (pl -s) temporary stand-in for a doctor or clergyman
  locums n ▷ locum
locus [loh-kuss] n (pl -ci) [loh-sigh] area or place where something happens
locust n (pl -s) destructive African insect that flies in swarms and eats crops
  locusts n ▷ locust
lode n (pl -s) vein of ore
  lodes n ▷ lode
lodestar n (pl -s) star used in navigation or astronomy as a point of reference
  lodestars n ▷ lodestar
lodestone n (pl -s) magnetic iron ore
  lodestones n ▷ lodestone
lodge n (pl -s) (CHIEFLY BRIT) gatekeeper's house ▶ v (-dges, -dging, -dged) live in another's house at a fixed charge > **lodger** n (pl -s)
  lodged v ▷ lodge
  lodger n ▷ lodge
  lodgers n ▷ lodge
  lodges n, v ▷ lodge
lodging n (pl -s) temporary residence ▶ pl rented room or rooms in another person's house ▶ v ▷ lodge
  lodgings n ▷ lodging
loft n (pl -s) space between the top storey and roof of a building ▶ v (-s, -ing, -ed) (SPORT) strike, throw, or kick (a ball) high into the air
  lofted v ▷ loft
  loftier adj ▷ lofty
  loftiest adj ▷ lofty
loftily adv haughtily
  lofting v ▷ loft
  lofts n, v ▷ loft
lofty adj (-tier, -tiest) of great height
log¹ n (pl -s) portion of a felled tree stripped of branches ▶ v (-s, -gging, -gged) saw logs from a tree
  log² n ▷ logarithm
loganberry n (pl -rries) purplish-red fruit, similar to a raspberry
  loganberries n ▷ loganberry
logarithm n (pl -s) one of a series of arithmetical functions used to make certain calculations easier
  logarithms n ▷ logarithm
logbook n (pl -s) book recording the details about a car or ship's journeys
  logbooks n ▷ logbook
  logged v ▷ log¹
loggerheads pl n quarrelling, disputing
loggia [loj-ya] n (pl -s) covered gallery at the side of a building
  loggias n ▷ loggia

logging n (pl -s) work of cutting and transporting logs ▶ v ▷ log¹
  loggings n ▷ logging
logic n (pl -s) philosophy of reasoning > **logically** adv > **logician** n (pl -s)
logical adj of logic
  logically adv ▷ logic
  logician n ▷ logic
  logicians n ▷ logic
  logics n ▷ logic
logistical adj ▷ logistics
logistics n detailed planning and organization of a large, esp. military, operation > **logistical, logistic** adj
logo [loh-go] n (pl -s) emblem used by a company or other organization
  logos n ▷ logo
  logs n ▷ log¹
loin n (pl -s) part of the body between the ribs and the hips
loincloth n (pl -s) piece of cloth covering the loins only
  loincloths n ▷ loincloth
  loins n ▷ loin
loiter v (-s, -ing, -ed) stand or wait aimlessly or idly
  loitered v ▷ loiter
  loitering v ▷ loiter
  loiters v ▷ loiter
loll v (-s, -ing, -ed) lounge lazily
  lolled v ▷ loll
  lollies n ▷ lolly
  lolling v ▷ loll
lollipop n (pl -s) boiled sweet on a small wooden stick
  lollipops n ▷ lollipop
  lolls v ▷ loll
lolly n (pl -llies) (Informal) lollipop or ice lolly
lone adj solitary > **lonesome** adj lonely
  loneliness n ▷ lonely
  lonelinesses n ▷ lonely
lonely adj sad because alone > **loneliness** n (pl -s)
loner n (pl -s) (Informal) person who prefers to be alone
  loners n ▷ -s
lonesome adj ▷ lone
long¹ adj (-er, -est) having length, esp. great length, in space or time ▶ adv for an extensive period
long² v (-s, -ing, -ed) have a strong desire (for)
  longed v ▷ long²
  longer adj ▷ long¹
  longest adj ▷ long¹
  longevities n ▷ longevity

longevity [lon-jev-it-ee] n (pl -ties) long life
longhand n (pl -s) ordinary writing, not shorthand or typing
  longhands n ▷ longhand
longing n (pl -s) yearning ▶ v ▷ long²
  > **longingly** adv
  longingly adv ▷ longing
  longings n ▷ longing
longitude n (pl -s) distance east or west from a standard meridian
  longitudes n ▷ longitude
longitudinal adj of length or longitude
longs v ▷ long²
longshoreman n (pl -men) (US) docker
  longshoremen n ▷ longshoreman
loo n (pl -s) (Informal) toilet
  loos n ▷ loo
loofah n (pl -s) sponge made from the dried pod of a gourd
  loofahs n ▷ loofah
look v (-s, -ing, -ed) direct the eyes or attention (towards) ▶ n (pl -s) instance of looking
lookalike n (pl -s) person who is the double of another
  lookalikes n ▷ lookalike
  looked v ▷ look
  looking v ▷ look
lookout n (pl -s) guard
  lookouts n ▷ lookout
  looks v, n ▷ look
loom¹ n (pl -s) machine for weaving cloth
loom² v (-s, -ing, -ed) appear dimly
  loomed v ▷ loom²
  looming v ▷ loom²
  looms n ▷ loom¹ ▶ v loom²
  loonies n ▷ loony
loony (Slang) adj (-nier, -niest) foolish or insane ▶ n (pl -nies) foolish or insane person
loop n (pl -s) rounded shape made by a curved line or rope crossing itself ▶ v (-s, -ing, -ed) form or fasten with a loop
  looped v ▷ loop
loophole n (pl -s) means of evading a rule without breaking it
  loopholes n ▷ loophole
  looping v ▷ loop
  loops n, v ▷ loop
loose adj (-r, -est) not tight, fastened, fixed, or tense ▶ adv in a loose manner ▶ v (-s, -ing, -sing, -sed) free > **loosely** adv > **looseness** n (pl -s)
  loosed v ▷ loose
  loosely adv ▷ loose
loosen v (-s, -ing, -ed) make loose
  loosened v ▷ loosen
  looseness n ▷ loose

  loosenesses n ▷ loose
  loosening v ▷ loosen
  loosens v ▷ loosen
  looser adj ▷ loose
  looses v ▷ loose
  loosest adj ▷ loose
  loosing v ▷ loose
loot n, v (-s, -ing, -ed) plunder ▶ n (pl -s) (Informal) money > **looter** n (pl -s) > **looting** n (pl -s)
  looted v ▷ loot
  looter n ▷ loot
  looters n ▷ loot
  looting v, n ▷ loot
  lootings n ▷ loot
  loots v, n ▷ loot
lop v (-s, -pping, -pped) cut away twigs and branches
lope v (-s, -ing, -ed) run with long easy strides
  loped v ▷ lope
  lopes v ▷ lope
  loping v ▷ lope
lopsided adj greater in height, weight, or size on one side
loquacious adj talkative > **loquacity** n (pl -ties)
  loquacities n ▷ loquacity
lord n (pl -s) person with power over others, such as a monarch or master
  lordlier adj ▷ lordly
  lordliest adj ▷ lordly
lordly adj (-lier, -liest) imperious, proud
  lords n ▷ lord
lore n (pl -s) body of traditions on a subject
  lores n ▷ lore
lorgnette [lor-nyet] n (pl -s) pair of spectacles mounted on a long handle
  lorgnettes n ▷ lorgnette
  lorries n ▷ lorry
lorikeet n (pl -s) small brightly coloured Australian parrot
  lorikeets n ▷ lorikeet
lorry n (pl -rries) (BRIT & S AFR) large vehicle for transporting loads by road
lose v (-s, -ing, -sing, lost) come to be without, esp. by accident or carelessness
loser n (pl -s) person or thing that loses
  losers n ▷ loser
  loses v ▷ lose
  losing v ▷ lose
loss n (pl -es) losing
  losses n ▷ loss
  lost v ▷ lose ▶ adj unable to find one's way
lot pron great number ▶ n (pl -s) collection of people or things
  lots n ▷ lot

loth *adj* ▷ **loath**

lotion *n* (*pl* -s) medical or cosmetic liquid for use on the skin

lotions *n* ▷ **lotion**

lottery *n* (*pl* -ries) method of raising money by selling tickets that win prizes by chance

lotto *n* (*pl* -s) game of chance like bingo

lottos *n* ▷ **lotto**

lotus *n* (*pl* -es) legendary plant whose fruit induces forgetfulness

lotuses *n* ▷ **lotus**

loud *adj* (-er, -est) relatively great in volume > **loudly** *adv* > **loudness** *n* (*pl* -es)

louder *adj* ▷ **loud**

loudest *adj* ▷ **loud**

loudly *adv* ▷ **loud**

loudness *n* ▷ **loud**

loudnesses *n* ▷ **loud**

loudspeaker *n* (*pl* -s) instrument for converting electrical signals into sound

loudspeakers *n* ▷ **loudspeaker**

lough *n* (*pl* -s) (IRISH) loch

loughs *n* ▷ **lough**

lounge *n* (*pl* -s) living room in a private house ▶ *v* (-s, -ging, -ged) sit, lie, or stand in a relaxed manner

lounged *v* ▷ **lounge**

lounges *n, v* ▷ **lounge**

lounging *v* ▷ **lounge**

lour *v* (-s, -ing, -ed) ▷ **lower²**

loured *v* ▷ **lour**

louring *v* ▷ **lour**

lours *v* ▷ **lour**

louse *n* (*pl* lice, louses) wingless parasitic insect

louses *n* ▷ **louse**

lousier *adj* ▷ **lousy**

lousiest *adj* ▷ **lousy**

lousy *adj* (-sier, -siest) (Slang) mean or unpleasant

lout *n* (*pl* -s) crude, oafish, or aggressive person > **loutish** *adj*

loutish *adj* ▷ **lout**

louts *n* ▷ **lout**

louvre [loo-ver] *n* (*pl* -s) one of a set of parallel slats slanted to admit air but not rain > **louvred** *adj*

louvred *adj* ▷ **louvre**

louvres *n* ▷ **louvre**

love *v* (-s, -ving, -ved) have a great affection for ▶ *n* (*pl* -s) great affection > **lovable, loveable** *adj* > **loveless** *adj* > **lovemaking** *n* (*pl* -s)

lovable *adj* ▷ **love**

loveable *adj* ▷ **love**

lovebird *n* (*pl* -s) small parrot

lovebirds *n* ▷ **lovebird**

loved *v* ▷ **love**

loveless *adj* ▷ **love**

lovelier *adj* ▷ **lovely**

loveliest *adj* ▷ **lovely**

lovelorn *adj* miserable because of unhappiness in love

lovely *adj* (-lier, -liest) very attractive

lovemaking *n* ▷ **love**

lovemakings *n* ▷ **love**

lover *n* (*pl* -s) person having a sexual relationship outside marriage

lovers *n* ▷ **lover**

loves *v, n* ▷ **love**

loving *adj* affectionate, tender ▶ *v* ▷ **love** > **lovingly** *adv*

lovingly *adv* ▷ **loving**

low¹ *adj* not tall, high, or elevated ▶ *adv* in or to a low position, level, or degree ▶ *n* (*pl* -s) low position, level, or degree > **lowland** *n* (*pl* -s)

low² *n* (*pl* -s) cry of cattle, moo ▶ *v* (-s, -ing, -ed) moo

lowbrow *n* (*pl* -s) ▶ *adj* (person) with nonintellectual tastes and interests

lowbrows *n* ▷ **lowbrow**

lowdown *n* (*pl* -s) (Informal) inside information

lowdowns *n* ▷ **lowdown**

lowed *v* ▷ **low²**

lower¹ *adj* (-est) below one or more other things ▶ *v* (-s, -ing, -ed) cause or allow to move down

lower², lour *v* (of the sky or weather) look gloomy or threatening

lowered *v* ▷ **lower¹·²**

lowering *v* ▷ **lower¹·²**

lowers *v* ▷ **lower¹·²**

lowest *adj* ▷ **lower**

lowing *v* ▷ **low²**

lowland *n* (*pl* -s) low-lying country

lowlands *n* ▷ **lowland**

lowlier *adj* ▷ **lowly**

lowliest *adj* ▷ **lowly**

lowliness *n* ▷ **lowly**

lowlinesses *n* ▷ **lowly**

lowly *adj* (-lier, -liest) modest, humble > **lowliness** *n* (*pl* -s)

lows *n* ▷ **low¹·²** ▶ *v* ▷ **low²**

> **lox** *n* (loxes). Lox is a kind of smoked salmon. This is a good word if you get have an X and L in the late stages of the game: there's likely to be a usable O on the board already. Lox scores 10 points.

loyal *adj* (-ler, -lest) faithful to one's friends, country, or government > **loyally** *adv* > **loyalty** *n* (*pl* -ties) > **loyalist** *n* (*pl* -s)

loyalist n ▷ loyal
loyalists n ▷ loyal
loyaller adj ▷ loyal
loyallest adj ▷ loyal
loyally adv ▷ loyal
loyalties n ▷ loyal
loyalty n ▷ loyal
lozenge n (pl -s) medicated tablet held in the mouth until it dissolves
lozenges n ▷ lozenge
lubricate [loo-brik-ate] v (-tes, -ting, -ted) oil or grease to lessen friction > **lubrication** n (pl -s)
lubricant n (pl -s) lubricating substance, such as oil
lubricants n ▷ lubricant
lubricated v ▷ lubricate
lubricates v ▷ lubricate
lubricating v ▷ lubricate
lubrication n ▷ lubricate
lubrications n ▷ lubricate
lubricious adj (Lit) lewd
lucerne n (pl -s) fodder plant like clover, alfalfa
lucernes n ▷ lucerne
lucid adj clear and easily understood > **lucidly** adv > **lucidity** n (pl -ties)
lucidities n ▷ lucid
lucidity n ▷ lucid
lucidly adv ▷ lucid
luck n (pl -s) fortune, good or bad
luckily adv fortunately
luckless adj having bad luck
lucrative adj very profitable
lucre [loo-ker] n (pl -s) (Facetious) money
lucks n having bad luck
lucky adj having or bringing good luck
luderick n (pl -s) Australian fish, usu. black or dark brown in colour
ludericks n ▷ luderick
ludicrous adj absurd or ridiculous > **ludicrously** adv
ludicrously adv ▷ ludicrous
ludo n (pl -s) game played with dice and counters on a board
lug[1] v (-s, -gging, -gged) carry or drag with great effort
lug[2] n (pl -s) projection serving as a handle
luggage n (pl -s) traveller's cases, bags, etc.
luggages n projection serving as a handle ▷ luggage
lugs v ▷ lug[1] ▶ n ▷ lug[2]
lugubrious adj mournful, gloomy > **lugubriously** adv
lugubriously adv ▷ lugubrious
lugworm n (pl -s) large worm used as bait
lugworms n ▷ lugworm

lukewarm adj moderately warm, tepid
lull v (-s, -ing, -ed) soothe (someone) by soft sounds or motions ▶ n (pl -s) brief time of quiet in a storm etc.
lullabies n ▷ lullaby
lullaby n (pl -bies) quiet song to send a child to sleep
lulled v ▷ lull
lulling v ▷ lull
lulls v, n ▷ lull
lumbago [lum-bay-go] n (pl -s) pain in the lower back
lumbagos n ▷ lumbago
lumbar adj relating to the lower back
lumber[1] n (pl -s) (BRIT) unwanted disused household articles ▶ v (-s, -ing, -ed) (Informal) burden with something unpleasant
lumber[2] v move heavily and awkwardly > **lumbering** adj
lumbered v ▷ lumber[1,2]
lumbering v ▷ lumber[1,2] ▶ adj ▷ lumber[2]
lumberjack n (pl -s) (US) man who fells trees and prepares logs for transport
lumberjacks n ▷ lumberjack
lumbers n[1] ▶ v ▷ lumber[1,2]
luminary n (pl -s) famous person
luminescence n (pl -s) emission of light at low temperatures by any process other than burning
luminescences n ▷ luminescence
luminescent adj ▷ luminous
luminosities n ▷ luminous
luminosity n ▷ luminous
luminous adj reflecting or giving off light > **luminosity** n (pl -s) > **luminescent** adj
lump[1] n (pl -s) shapeless piece or mass ▶ v (-s, -ing, -ed) consider as a single group > **lumpy** adj (-pier, -piest)
lump[2] v (Informal) tolerate or put up with it
lumped v ▷ lump[1,2]
lumpier adj ▷ lump[1]
lumpiest adj ▷ lump[1]
lumping v ▷ lump[1,2]
lumps n, v ▷ lump[1,2]
lumpy adj ▷ lump[1]
lunar adj relating to the moon
lunacies n ▷ lunacy
lunatic adj foolish and irresponsible ▶ n (pl -s) foolish or annoying person > **lunacy** n (pl -cies)
lunatics n ▷ lunatic
lunch n (pl lunches) meal taken in the middle of the day ▶ v (-es, -ing, -ed) eat lunch
lunched v ▷ lunch
luncheon n (pl -s) formal lunch

luncheons n ▷ luncheon
lunches n, v ▷ lunch
lunching v ▷ lunch
lung n (pl **-s**) organ that allows an animal or bird to breathe air: humans have two lungs in the chest
lungfish n freshwater bony fish with an air-breathing lung of South America and Australia
lungs n ▷ lung
lunge n (pl **-s**) sudden forward motion ▶ v (**-s, -ging, -ged**) move with or make a lunge
lunged v ▷ lunge
lunges n, v ▷ lunge
lunging v ▷ lunge
lupin n (pl **-s**) garden plant with tall spikes of flowers
lupins n ▷ lupin
lupine adj like a wolf
lurch v (**-es, -ing, -ed**) tilt or lean suddenly to one side ▶ n (pl **-es**) lurching movement
lurched v ▷ lurch
lurcher n (pl **-s**) crossbred dog trained to hunt silently
lurchers n ▷ lurcher
lurches v, n ▷ lurch
lurching v ▷ lurch
lure v (**-s, -red, -ring**) tempt or attract by the promise of reward ▶ n (pl **-s**) person or thing that lures
lured v ▷ lure
lures v, n ▷ lure
luring v ▷ lure
lurid adj (**-er, -est**) vivid in shocking detail, sensational > **luridly** adv
lurider adj ▷ lurid
luridest adj ▷ lurid
luridly adv ▷ lurid
luring v ▷ lure
lurk v (**-s, -ing, -ed**) lie hidden or move stealthily, esp. for sinister purposes
lurked v ▷ lurk
lurking v ▷ lurk
lurks v ▷ lurk
luscious [lush-uss] adj extremely pleasurable to taste or smell
lush[1] adj (**-er, -est**) (of grass etc.) growing thickly and healthily
lush[2] n (pl **-es**) (Slang) alcoholic
lusher adj ▷ lush[1]
lushes n ▷ lush[2]
lushest adj ▷ lush[1]
lust n (pl **-s**) strong sexual desire ▶ v (**-s, -ing, -ed**) have passionate desire (for) > **lustful** adj > **lusty** adj vigorous, healthy > **lustily** adv

lusted v ▷ lust
lustful adj ▷ lust
lustier adj ▷ lusty
lustiest adj ▷ lusty
lustily adv ▷ lust
lusting v ▷ lust
lustre n (pl **-s**) gloss, sheen
lustres n ▷ lustre
lustrous adj shining, luminous
lusts n, v ▷ lust
lusty adj (**-tier, -tiest**) vigorous, healthy
lute n (pl **-s**) ancient guitar-like musical instrument with a body shaped like a half pear
lutes n ▷ lute

> **lux** n (lux). A lux is a unit of illumination. This is a great word to know when you have an X but little opportunity to play it. Lux scores 10 points.

luxuriant adj rich and abundant > **luxuriance** n (pl **-ces**) > **luxuriantly** adv
luxuriance n ▷ luxuriant
luxuriances n ▷ luxuriant
luxuriantly adv ▷ luxuriant
luxuriate v (**-tes, -ting, -ted**) take self-indulgent pleasure (in)
luxuriated v ▷ luxuriate
luxuriates v ▷ luxuriate
luxuriating v ▷ luxuriate
luxurious adj full of luxury, sumptuous > **luxuriously** adv
luxuriously adv ▷ luxurious
luxury n (pl **-ries**) enjoyment of rich, very comfortable living ▶ adj of or providing luxury

> **luz** n (**luzzes**). In traditional Jewish writings, the luz was a bone that was supposed to be indestructible. This very unusual word is very useful, especially if you have a Z at the end of a game when there is little opportunity to use it in a longer word. Luz scores 12 points.

lychee [lie-chee] n (pl **-s**) Chinese fruit with a whitish juicy pulp
lychees n ▷ lychee
lye n (pl **-s**) caustic solution obtained by leaching wood ash
lyes n ▷ lye
lying v ▷ lie[1,2]
lymph n (pl **-s**) colourless bodily fluid consisting mainly of white blood cells > **lymphatic** adj
lymphatic adj ▷ lymph
lymphocyte n (pl **-s**) type of white blood cell
lymphocytes n ▷ lymphocyte

lymphs *n* ▷ lymph
lynch *v* (**-es, -ing, -ed**) put to death without a trial
  lynched *v* ▷ lynch
  lynches *v* ▷ lynch
  lynching *v* ▷ lynch
  lynchpin *n* ▷ lynchpin
  lynchpins *n* ▷ lynchpin
lynx *n* (*pl* **-es**) animal of the cat family with tufted ears and a short tail
  lynxes *n* ▷ lynx

lyre *n* (*pl* **-s**) ancient musical instrument like a U-shaped harp
  lyres *n* ▷ lyre
lyric *adj* (of poetry) expressing personal emotion in songlike style ▶ *n* (*pl* **-s**) short poem in a songlike style > **lyrical** *adj* lyric
  lyrical *n* ▷ lyric
lyricist *n* (*pl* **-s**) person who writes the words of songs or musicals
  lyricists *n* ▷ lyricist
  lyrics *n* ▷ lyric

Mm

M is a very useful letter when you need to form short words as it starts a two-letter word with every vowel, as well as with Y and with another M. Remembering this allows you to use M effectively when you're forming a word parallel to, and in contact with, a word that is already on the board. M also combines well with X and Z, so there is a lot of potential for high-scoring words. Keep **max**, **mix** and **mux** (12 points each) in mind, as well as **miz** and **muz** (14 each). It's also worth remembering the three-letter words ending in W: **maw**, **mew** and **mow** (8 points each).

ma n (pl **-s**) (Informal) mother
  mas n ▷ **ma**
mac n (pl **-s**) (BRIT) (Informal) mackintosh
  macs n ▷ **mac**
macabre [mak-**kahb**-ra] adj strange and horrible, gruesome
macadam n (pl **-s**) road surface of pressed layers of small broken stones
  macadams n ▷ **macadam**
macadamia n (pl **-s**) Australian tree with edible nuts
  macadamias n ▷ **macadamia**
macaroni n (pl **-s**) pasta in short tube shapes
  macaronis n ▷ **macaroni**
macaroon n (pl **-s**) small biscuit or cake made with ground almonds
  macaroons n ▷ **macaroon**
macaw n (pl **-s**) large tropical American parrot
  macaws n ▷ **macaw**
mace¹ n (pl **-s**) ceremonial staff of office
mace² n (pl **-s**) spice made from the dried husk of the nutmeg
  maces n ▷ **mace**¹,²
macerate [**mass**-er-ate] v (**-tes**, **-ting**, **-ted**) soften by soaking > **maceration** n (pl **-s**)
  macerated v ▷ **macerate**
  macerates v ▷ **macerate**
  macerating v ▷ **macerate**
  maceration n ▷ **macerate**
  macerations n ▷ **macerate**
machete [mash-**ett**-ee] n (pl **-s**) broad heavy knife used for cutting or as a weapon
  machetes n ▷ **machete**
machinations [mak-in-**nay**-shunz] pl n cunning plots and ploys
machine n (pl **-s**) apparatus, usu. powered by electricity, designed to perform a particular task ▶ v (**-nes**, **-ning**, **-ned**) make or produce by machine
  machined v ▷ **machine**
machinegun v (**-s**, **-nning**, **-nned**) fire at with such a gun
  machinegunned v ▷ **machinegun**
  machinegunning v ▷ **machinegun**
  machineguns v ▷ **machinegun**
  machineries n ▷ **machinery**
machinery n (pl **-ries**) machines or machine parts collectively
  machines n, v ▷ **machine**
  machining v ▷ **machine**
machinist n (pl **-s**) person who operates a machine
  machinists n ▷ **machinist**
machismo [mak-**izz**-moh] n (pl **-s**) exaggerated or strong masculinity
  machismos n ▷ **machismo**
macho [**match**-oh] adj strongly or exaggeratedly masculine
mackerel n edible sea fish
mackintosh n (pl **-es**) waterproof raincoat of rubberized cloth
  mackintoshes n ▷ **mackintosh**
macramé [mak-**rah**-mee] n (pl **-s**) ornamental work of knotted cord
  macramés n ▷ **macramé**
macrobiotics n dietary system advocating whole grains and vegetables grown without chemical additives > **macrobiotic** adj
  macrobiotic adj ▷ **macrobiotics**
macrocosm n (pl **-s**) the universe
  macrocosms n ▷ **macrocosm**
mad adj (**madder**, **maddest**) mentally deranged, insane > **madly** adv > **madness** n (pl **-es**) > **madman** n (pl **-men**) > **madwoman**

n (*pl* -**women**)

madam *n* (*pl* **madams**) polite form of address to a woman
madams *n* ▷ **madam**

madame [mad-**dam**] *n* (*pl* **mesdames**) [may-dam] French title equivalent to *Mrs*

madcap *adj* foolish or reckless

madden *v* (-**s**, -**ed**, -**ing**) infuriate or irritate
> **maddening** *adj*
maddened *v* ▷ **madden**
maddening *v* ▷ **madden** ▶ *adj* ▷ **madden**
maddens *v* ▷ **madden**

madder *n* (*pl* -**s**) climbing plant ▶ *adj* ▷ **mad**
maddest *adj* ▷ **mad**
made *v* ▷ **make**

madeira [mad-**deer**-a] *n* (*pl* -**s**) fortified white wine
madeiras *n* ▷ **madeira**

mademoiselle [mad-mwah-**zel**, maid-mwah-**zel**] *n* (*pl* -**s**) French title equivalent to *Miss*
mademoiselles *n* ▷ **mademoiselle**

madonna *n* (*pl* -**s**) the Virgin Mary
madly *adv* ▷ **mad**
madman *n* ▷ **mad**
madmen *n* ▷ **mad**
madness *n* ▷ **mad**
madnesses *n* ▷ **madness**
madonnas *n* ▷ **madonna**

madrigal *n* (*pl* -**s**) 16th–17th-century part song for unaccompanied voices
madrigals *n* ▷ **madrigal**
madwoman *n* ▷ **mad**
madwomen *n* ▷ **mad**

maelstrom [**male**-strom] *n* (*pl* -**s**) great whirlpool
maelstroms *n* ▷ **maelstrom**
maestri *n* ▷ **maestro**

maestro [my-**stroh**] *n* (*pl* -**tri**, -**tros**) outstanding musician or conductor
maestros *n* ▷ **maestro**

mafia *n* (*pl* -**s**) international secret criminal organization
mafias *n* ▷ **mafia**
mafiosi *n* ▷ **mafioso**

mafioso *n* (*pl* -**sos**, -**si**) member of the Mafia
mafiosos *n* ▷ **mafioso**

magazine *n* (*pl* -**s**) periodical publication with articles by different writers
magazines *n* ▷ **magazine**

magenta [maj-**jen**-ta] *adj* deep purplish-red

maggot *n* (*pl* -**s**) larva of an insect > **maggoty** *adj*
maggots *n* ▷ **maggot**
maggoty *adj* ▷ **maggot**

magi [**maje**-eye] *pl n* wise men from the East who came to worship the infant Jesus

magic *n* (*pl* -**s**) supposed art of invoking supernatural powers to influence events ▶ *adj* (also **magical**) of, using, or like magic
> **magically** *adv*
magical *adj* ▷ **magic**
magically *adv* ▷ **magic**

magician *n* (*pl* -**s**) conjuror
magicians *n* ▷ **magician**
magics *n* ▷ **magic**

magisterial *adj* commanding or authoritative

magistrate *n* (*pl* -**s**) public officer administering the law
magistrates *n* ▷ **magistrate**

magma *n* (*pl* -**s**) molten rock inside the earth's crust
magmas *n* ▷ **magma**

magnanimous *adj* noble and generous
> **magnanimously** *adv* > **magnanimity** *n* (*pl* -**ties**)
magnanimities *n* ▷ **magnanimous**
magnanimity *n* ▷ **magnanimous**
magnanimously *n* ▷ **magnanimous**

magnate *n* (*pl* -**s**) influential or wealthy person, esp. in industry
magnates *n* ▷ **magnate**

magnesia *n* (*pl* -**s**) white tasteless substance used as an antacid and a laxative; magnesium oxide
magnesias *n* ▷ **magnesia**

magnesium *n* (*pl* -**s**) (CHEM) silvery-white metallic element
magnesiums *n* ▷ **magnesium**

magnet *n* (*pl* -**s**) piece of iron or steel capable of attracting iron and pointing north when suspended

magnetic *adj* having the properties of a magnet > **magnetically** *adv*
magnetically *adv* ▷ **magnetic**

magnetism *n* (*pl* -**s**) magnetic property
magnetisms *n* ▷ **magnetism**

magnetize *v* (-**zes**, -**zed**, -**zing**) make into a magnet
magnetized *v* ▷ **magnetize**
magnetizes *v* ▷ **magnetize**
magnetizing *v* ▷ **magnetize**
magnets *n* ▷ **magnet**

magneto [mag-**nee**-toe] *n* (*pl* -**s**) apparatus for ignition in an internal-combustion engine

magnificent *adj* splendid or impressive
> **magnificently** *adv* > **magnificence** *n* (*pl* -**s**)
magnificence *n* ▷ **magnificent**
magnificences *n* ▷ **magnificent**
magnificently *adv* ▷ **magnificent**

magnify *v* (-**fies**, -**ing**, -**fied**) increase in apparent size, as with a lens > **magnification** n (pl -s)

magnification n ▷ magnify

magnifications n ▷ magnify

magnified v ▷ magnify

magnifies v ▷ magnify

magnifying v ▷ magnify

magnitude n (pl -s) relative importance or size

magnitudes n ▷ magnitude

magnolia n (pl -s) shrub or tree with showy white or pink flowers

magnolias n ▷ magnolia

magnum n (pl s) large wine bottle holding about 1.5 litres

magnums n ▷ magnum

magpie n (pl -s) black-and-white bird

magpies n ▷ magpie

maharajah n (pl -s) former title of some Indian princes > **maharani** n fem (pl -s)

maharajahs n ▷ maharajah

maharani n ▷ maharajah

maharanis n ▷ maharajah

mahogany n (pl -nies) hard reddish-brown wood of several tropical trees

mahoganies n ▷ mahogany

mahout [ma-howt] n (pl s) (in India and the East Indies) elephant driver or keeper

mahouts n ▷ mahout

maid (also **maidservant**) n (pl -s) female servant

maiden n (pl -s) (Lit) young unmarried woman ▶ adj unmarried

maidenhair n (pl -s) fern with delicate fronds

maidenhairs n ▷ maidenhair

maidenhead n (pl -s) virginity

maidenheads n ▷ maidenhead

maidenly adj modest

maidens n ▷ maiden

maids n ▷ maid

maidservant n ▷ maid

maidservants n ▷ maid

mail¹ n (pl -s) letters and packages transported and delivered by the post office ▶ v (-s, -ing, -ed) send by mail

mail² n (pl -s) flexible armour of interlaced rings or links

mailbox n (pl -es) (US, CANADIAN & AUST) box into which letters and parcels are delivered

mailboxes n ▷ mailbox

mailed v ▷ mail¹

mailing v ▷ mail¹

mails n ▷ mail¹,² ▶ v ▷ mail²

mailshot n (pl -s) (BRIT) posting of advertising material to many selected people at once

mailshots n ▷ mailshot

maim v (-s, -ing, -ed) cripple or mutilate

maimed v ▷ maim

maiming v ▷ maim

maims v ▷ maim

main adj chief or principal ▶ n (pl -s) principal pipe or line carrying water, gas, or electricity

mainframe n (pl -s) (COMPUTERS) (denoting) a high-speed general-purpose computer

mainframes n ▷ mainframe

mainland n (pl -s) stretch of land which forms the main part of a country

mainlands n ▷ mainland

mainly adv for the most part, chiefly

mainmast n (pl -s) chief mast of a ship

mainmasts n ▷ mainmast

mains n ▷ main

mainsail n (pl -s) largest sail on a mainmast

mainsails n ▷ mainsail

mainspring n (pl -s) chief cause or motive

mainsprings n ▷ mainspring

mainstay n (pl -s) chief support

mainstays n ▷ mainstay

mainstream adj (of) a prevailing cultural trend

maintain v (-s, -ing, -ed) continue or keep in existence

maintained v ▷ maintain

maintaining v ▷ maintain

maintains v ▷ maintain

maintenance n (pl -s) maintaining

maintenances n ▷ maintenance

maisonette n (pl -s) (BRIT) flat with more than one floor

maisonettes n ▷ maisonette

maize n (pl -s) type of corn with spikes of yellow grains

maizes n ▷ maize

majesty n (pl -ties) stateliness or grandeur > **majestic** adj > **majestically** adv

majestic adj ▷ majesty

majestically adv ▷ majesty

majesties n ▷ majesty

major adj greater in number, quality, or extent ▶ n (pl -s) middle-ranking army officer ▶ v (-s, -ing, -ed) (foll. by **in**) (US, CANADIAN, S AFR, AUST & NZ) do one's principal study in (a particular subject)

majordomo n (pl -s) chief steward of a great household

majordomos n ▷ majordomo

majored v ▷ major

majoring v ▷ major

majorities n ▷ majority

majority n (pl -ties) greater number

majors n, v ▷ **major**

make v (-**kes**, -**king**, **made**) create, construct, or establish ▶ n (pl -**s**) brand, type, or style

maker n (pl -**s**) ▷ **makeweight** n (pl -**s**) something unimportant added to make up a lack

maker n ▷ **make**

makers n ▷ **make**

makes n, v ▷ **make**

makeshift adj serving as a temporary substitute

makeup n (pl -**s**) cosmetics

makeups n ▷ **makeup**

making v ▷ **make** ▶ n (pl -**s**) creation or production

makings n ▷ **making**

malachite [mal-a-kite] n (pl -**s**) green mineral

malachites n ▷ **malachite**

maladjusted adj (PSYCHOL) unable to meet the demands of society > **maladjustment** n (pl -**s**)

maladjustment n ▷ **maladjusted**

maladjustments n ▷ **maladjusted**

maladministration n (pl -**s**) inefficient or dishonest administration

maladministrations n ▷ **maladministration**

maladroit adj clumsy or awkward

malady n (pl -**dies**) disease or illness

maladies n ▷ **malady**

malaise [mal-**laze**] n (pl -**s**) vague feeling of unease, illness, or depression

malaises n ▷ **malaise**

malapropism n (pl -**s**) comical misuse of a word by confusion with one which sounds similar, e.g. *I am not under the affluence of alcohol*

malapropisms n ▷ **malapropism**

malaria n (pl -**s**) infectious disease caused by the bite of some mosquitoes > **malarial** adj

malarias n ▷ **malaria**

malarial adj ▷ **malaria**

malcontent n (pl -**s**) discontented person

malcontents n ▷ **malcontent**

male adj of the sex which can fertilize female reproductive cells ▶ n (pl **males**) male person or animal

males n ▷ **male**

malediction [mal-lid-**dik**-shun] n (pl -**s**) curse

maledictions n ▷ **malediction**

malefactor [**mal**-if-act-or] n (pl -**s**) criminal or wrongdoer

malefactors n ▷ **malefactor**

malevolent [mal-**lev**-a-lent] adj wishing evil to others > **malevolently** adv > **malevolence** n (pl -**s**)

malevolence n ▷ **malevolent**

malevolences n ▷ **malevolent**

malevolently adv ▷ **malevolent**

malfeasance [mal-**fee**-zanss] n (pl -**s**) misconduct, esp. by a public official

malfeasances n ▷ **malfeasance**

malformed adj misshapen or deformed > **malformation** n (pl -**s**)

malformation n ▷ **malformed**

malformations n ▷ **malformed**

malfunction v (-**s**, -**ing**, -**ed**) function imperfectly or fail to function ▶ n (pl -**s**) defective functioning or failure to function

malfunctioned v ▷ **malfunction**

malfunctioning v ▷ **malfunction**

malfunctions v, n ▷ **malfunction**

malice [**mal**-iss] n (pl -**s**) desire to cause harm to others > **malicious** adj > **maliciously** adv

malices n ▷ **malice**

malicious adj ▷ **malice**

maliciously adj ▷ **malice**

malign [mal-**line**] v (-**s**, -**ing**, -**ed**) slander or defame ▶ adj evil in influence or effect > **malignity** n (pl -**nities**) evil disposition

malignancies n ▷ **malignant**

malignancy n ▷ **malignant**

malignant [mal-**lig**-nant] adj seeking to harm others > **malignancy** n (pl -**cies**)

maligned v ▷ **malign**

maligning v ▷ **malign**

malignities n ▷ **malign**

malignity n ▷ **malign**

maligns v ▷ **malign**

malinger v (-**s**, -**ing**, -**ed**) feign illness to avoid work > **malingerer** n (pl -**s**)

malingered v ▷ **malinger**

malingerer n ▷ **malinger**

malingering v ▷ **malinger**

malingerers n ▷ **malinger**

malingers v ▷ **malinger**

mall [**mawl**] n (pl -**s**) street or shopping area closed to vehicles

mallard n wild duck

malleable [**mal**-lee-a-bl] adj capable of being hammered or pressed into shape > **malleability** n (pl -**ties**)

malleability n ▷ **malleable**

malleabilities n ▷ **malleable**

mallee n (pl -**s**) (AUST) low-growing eucalypt in dry regions

mallees n ▷ **mallee**

mallet n (pl -**s**) (wooden) hammer

mallets n ▷ **mallet**

mallow n (pl -**s**) plant with pink or purple flowers

mallows n ▷ **mallow**

malls *n* ▷ mall

malnutrition *n* (*pl* -s) inadequate nutrition
malnutritions *n* ▷ malnutrition

malodorous [mal-**lode**-or-uss] *adj* bad-smelling

malpractice *n* (*pl* -s) immoral, illegal, or
unethical professional conduct
malpractices *n* ▷ malpractice

malt *n* (*pl* -s) grain, such as barley, prepared for
use in making beer or whisky
malts *n* ▷ malt

maltreat *v* (-s, -ing, -ed) treat badly
> maltreatment *n* (*pl* -s)
maltreated *v* ▷ maltreat
maltreating *v* ▷ maltreat
maltreatment *n* ▷ maltreat
maltreatments *n* ▷ maltreat
maltreats *v* ▷ maltreat

mama *n* (*pl* -s) (*Old-fashioned*) mother
mamas *n* ▷ mama

mamba *n* (*pl* -s) deadly S African snake
mambas *n* ▷ mamba
mamma *n* (*pl* -s) ▷ mama
mammas *n* ▷ mamma

mammal *n* (*pl* -s) animal of the type that
suckles its young > mammalian *adj*
mammalian *adj* ▷ mammal
mammals *n* ▷ mammal

mammary *adj* of the breasts or milk-
producing glands

mammon *n* (*pl* -s) wealth regarded as a source
of evil
mammons *n* ▷ mammon

mammoth *n* (*pl* -s) extinct elephant-like
mammal ▶ *adj* colossal
mammoths *n* ▷ mammoth

man *n* (*pl* men) adult male ▶ *v* (-s, -nning,
-nned) supply with sufficient people for
operation or defence > manhood *n* (*pl* -s)

mana *n* (*pl* -s) (NZ) authority, influence

manacle [**man**-a-kl] *n* (*pl* -s) handcuff or fetter
▶ *v* (-les, -ling, -led) handcuff or fetter
manacled *v* ▷ manacle
manacling *v* ▷ manacle
manacles *n*, *v* ▷ manacle

manage *v* (-ges, -ging, -ged) succeed in doing
> manageable *adj* > management *n* (*pl* -s)
managers collectively
manageable *adj* ▷ manage
managed *v* ▷ manage
managing *v* ▷ manage
management *n* ▷ manage
managements *n* ▷ manage
manages *v* ▷ manage

manager *n* (*pl* -s) person in charge of a
business, institution, actor, sports team, etc.

> managerial *adj*

manageress *n* (*pl* -es) woman in charge of a
business, institution, actor, sports team, etc.
manageresses *n* ▷ manager
managerial *adj* ▷ manager
managers *n* ▷ manager

manas *n* ▷ mana

manatee *n* (*pl* -s) large tropical plant-eating
aquatic mammal
manatees *n* ▷ manatee

mandarin *n* (*pl* -s) high-ranking government
official
mandarins *n* ▷ mandarin

mandate *n* (*pl* -s) official or authoritative
command ▶ *v* (-tes, -ting, -ted) give authority
to
mandated *v* ▷ mandate
mandates *n*, *v* ▷ mandate
mandating *v* ▷ mandate

mandatory *adj* compulsory

mandible *n* (*pl* -s) lower jawbone or jawlike
part
mandibles *n* ▷ mandible

mandolin *n* (*pl* s) musical instrument with
four pairs of strings
mandolins *n* ▷ mandolin

mandrake *n* (*pl* -s) plant with a forked root,
formerly used as a narcotic
mandrakes *n* ▷ mandrake

mandrel *n* (*pl* -s) shaft on which work is held
in a lathe
mandrels *n* ▷ mandrel

mandrill *n* (*pl* -s) large blue-faced baboon
mandrills *n* ▷ mandrill

mane *n* (*pl* -s) long hair on the neck of a horse,
lion, etc.
manes *n* ▷ mane

manful *adj* determined and brave > manfully
adv
manfully *adv* ▷ manful

manganese *n* (*pl* -s) (CHEM) brittle greyish-
white metallic element
manganeses *n* ▷ manganese

mange *n* (*pl* -s) skin disease of domestic
animals
manges *n* ▷ mange

mangelwurzel *n* (*pl* -s) variety of beet used as
cattle food
mangelwurzels *n* ▷ mangelwurzel

manger *n* (*pl* -s) eating trough in a stable or
barn
mangers *n* ▷ manger

mangetout [**mawnzh**-too] *n* (*pl* -s) variety of
pea with an edible pod
mangetouts *n* ▷ mangetout

mangier adj ▷ mangy
mangiest adj ▷ mangy
mangle[1] v (-les, -ling, -led) destroy by crushing and twisting
mangle[2] n (pl -s) machine with rollers for squeezing water from washed clothes ▶ v (-les, -ling, -led) put through a mangle
mangled v ▷ mangle[1,2]
mangling v ▷ mangle[1,2]
mangles v ▷ mangle[1,2] ▶ n ▷ mangle[2]
mango n (pl -goes, -gos) tropical fruit with sweet juicy yellow flesh
mangoes n ▷ mango
mangos n ▷ mango
mangrove n (pl -s) tropical tree with exposed roots, which grows beside water
mangroves n ▷ mangrove
mangy adj (-gier, -giest) having mange
manhandle v (-les, -ling, -led) treat roughly
manhandled v ▷ manhandle
manhandling v ▷ manhandle
manhandles v ▷ manhandle
manhole n (pl -s) hole with a cover, through which a person can enter a drain or sewer
manholes n ▷ manhole
manhood n ▷ man
manhoods n ▷ man
mania n (pl -s) extreme enthusiasm > **maniacal** [man-**eye**-a-kl] ▶ adj
maniac n (pl -s) mad person
maniacal adj ▷ mania
maniacs n ▷ mania
manias n ▷ mania
manic adj affected by mania
manicure n (pl -s) cosmetic care of the fingernails and hands ▶ v (-res, -ring, -red) care for (the fingernails and hands) in this way > **manicurist** n (pl -s)
manicured v ▷ manicure
manicures n, v ▷ manicure
manicuring v ▷ manicure
manicurist n ▷ manicure
manicurists n ▷ manicure
manifest adj easily noticed, obvious ▶ v (-s, -ing, -ed) show plainly ▶ n (pl -s) list of cargo or passengers for customs > **manifestation** n (pl -s)
manifestation n ▷ manifest
manifestations n ▷ manifest
manifested v ▷ manifest
manifesting v, n ▷ manifest
manifesto n (pl -tos, -toes) declaration of policy as issued by a political party
manifestoes n ▷ manifesto
manifestos n ▷ manifesto

manifests v ▷ manifest
manifold adj numerous and varied ▶ n (pl -s) pipe with several outlets, esp. in an internal-combustion engine
manifolds n ▷ manifold
manikin n (pl -s) little man or dwarf
manikins n ▷ manikin
manila, manilla n (pl -s) strong brown paper used for envelopes
manilas n ▷ manila
manillas n ▷ manila
manipulate v (-tes, -ting, -ted) handle skilfully > **manipulation** n (pl -s) > **manipulative** adj > **manipulator** n (pl -s)
manipulated v ▷ manipulate
manipulates v ▷ manipulate
manipulating v ▷ manipulate
manipulation n ▷ manipulate
manipulations n ▷ manipulate
manipulative adj ▷ manipulate
manipulator n ▷ manipulate
manipulators n ▷ manipulate
mankind n (pl -s) human beings collectively
mankinds n ▷ mankind
manlier adj ▷ manly
manliest adj ▷ manly
manliness n ▷ manly
manlinesses n ▷ manly
manly adj (-lier, -liest) (possessing qualities) appropriate to a man > **manliness** n (pl -s)
manna n (pl -s) (BIBLE) miraculous food which sustained the Israelites in the wilderness
mannas n ▷ manna
manned v ▷ man
mannequin n (pl -s) woman who models clothes at a fashion show
mannequins n ▷ mannequin
manner n (pl -s) way a thing happens or is done > **mannered** adj affected
mannered adj ▷ manner
mannerism n (pl -s) person's distinctive habit or trait
mannerisms n ▷ manner
manners n ▷ manner
mannikin n (pl -s) ▷ manikin
mannikins n ▷ mannikin
manning v ▷ man
mannish adj (of a woman) like a man
manoeuvre [man-**noo**-ver] n (pl -s) skilful movement military or naval exercises ▶ v (-res, -ring, -red) manipulate or contrive skilfully or cunningly > **manoeuvrable** adj
manoeuvred v ▷ manoeuvre
manoeuvres n, v ▷ manoeuvre
manoeuvring v ▷ manoeuvre

manor n (pl -s) (BRIT) large country house and its lands > **manorial** adj

manorial adj ▷ **manor**

manors n ▷ **manor**

manpower n (pl -s) available number of workers

manpowers n ▷ **manpower**

manqué [mong-kay] adj would-be

mans v ▷ **man**

manse n (pl -s) house provided for a minister in some religious denominations

manses n ▷ **manse**

manservant n (pl **menservants**) male servant, esp. a valet

mansion n (pl -s) large house

mansions n ▷ **mansion**

manslaughter n (pl -s) unlawful but unintentional killing of a person

manslaughters n ▷ **manslaughter**

mantel n (pl -s) structure round a fireplace

mantelpiece n (pl -es) shelf above a fireplace

mantelpieces n ▷ **mantelpiece**

mantels n ▷ **mantel**

mantilla n (pl -s) (in Spain) a lace scarf covering a woman's head and shoulders

mantillas n ▷ **mantilla**

mantis n (pl -ses, -tes) carnivorous insect like a grasshopper

mantes n ▷ **mantis**

mantises n ▷ **mantis**

mantle n (pl -s) loose cloak

mantles n ▷ **mantle**

mantra n (pl -s) (HINDUISM, BUDDHISM) any sacred word or syllable used as an object of concentration

mantras n ▷ **mantra**

manual adj of or done with the hands ▶ n (pl -s) handbook > **manually** adv

manually adv ▷ **manual**

manuals n ▷ **manual**

manufacture v (-res, -ring, -red) process or make (goods) on a large scale using machinery ▶ n (pl -s) process of manufacturing goods

manufactured v ▷ **manufacture**

manufacturer n (pl -s) company that manufactures goods

manufacturers n ▷ **manufacturer**

manufactures v, n ▷ **manufacture**

manufacturing v ▷ **manufacture**

manure n (pl -s) animal excrement used as a fertilizer

manures n ▷ **manure**

manuscript n (pl -s) book or document, orig. one written by hand

manuscripts n ▷ **manuscript**

many adj (**more, most**) numerous ▶ n large number

map n (pl -s) representation of the earth's surface or some part of it, showing geographical features ▶ v (-s, -pping, -pped) make a map of

maple n (pl -s) tree with broad leaves, a variety of which (**sugar maple**) yields sugar

maples n ▷ **maple**

mapped v ▷ **map**

mapping v ▷ **map**

maps n, v ▷ **map**

mar v (-s, -rring, -rred) spoil or impair

marabou n (pl -s) large black-and-white African stork

marabous n ▷ **marabou**

maraca [mar-rak-a] n (pl -s) shaken percussion instrument made from a gourd containing dried seeds etc.

maracas n ▷ **maraca**

marae n (pl -s) (NZ) enclosed space in front of a Maori meeting house

maraes n ▷ **marae**

marathon n (pl -s) long-distance race of 26 miles 385 yards (42.195 kilometres)

marathons n ▷ **marathon**

marauder n ▷ **marauding**

marauders n ▷ **marauder**

marauding adj wandering or raiding in search of plunder > **marauder** n (pl -s)

marble n (pl -s) kind of limestone with a mottled appearance, which can be highly polished > **marbled** adj having a mottled appearance like marble

marbled n ▷ **marble**

marbles n ▷ **marble**

march[1] v (-es, -ing, -ed) walk with a military step ▶ n (pl -es) action of marching > **marcher** n (pl -s)

march[2] n (pl -s) border or frontier

marched v ▷ **march**[1]

marches v ▷ **march**[1] ▶ n ▷ **march**[1,2]

marching v ▷ **march**[1]

marchioness [marsh-on-ness] n (pl -es) woman holding the rank of marquis

marchionesses n ▷ **marchioness**

mare n (pl -s) female horse or zebra

mares n ▷ **mare**

margarine n (pl -s) butter substitute made from animal or vegetable fats

margarines n ▷ **margarine**

marge n (pl -s) (Informal) margarine

marges n ▷ **marge**

margin n (pl -s) edge or border > **marginal** adj

insignificant, unimportant ▷ **marginally** *adv*
marginal *adj* ▷ **margin**
marginalize *v* (**-zes, -zing, -zed**) make or treat as insignificant
marginalized *v* ▷ **marginalize**
marginalizes *v* ▷ **marginalize**
marginalizing *v* ▷ **marginalize**
margins *n* ▷ **margin**
marguerite *n* (*pl* **-s**) large daisy
marguerites *n* ▷ **marguerite**
marigold *n* (*pl* **-s**) plant with yellow or orange flowers
marigolds *n* ▷ **marigold**
marijuana [mar-ree-**wah**-na] *n* (*pl* **-s**) dried flowers and leaves of the cannabis plant, used as a drug, esp. in cigarettes
marijuanas *n* ▷ **marijuana**
marina *n* (*pl* **-s**) harbour for yachts and other pleasure boats
marinas *n* ▷ **marina**
marinade *n* (*pl* **-s**) seasoned liquid in which fish or meat is soaked before cooking ▶ *v* (**-des, -ding, -ded**) ▷ **marinate**
marinaded *v* ▷ **marinade**
marinades *n, v* ▷ **marinade**
marinading *v* ▷ **marinade**
marinate *v* (**-tes, -ting, -ted**) soak in marinade
marinated *v* ▷ **marinate**
marinates *v* ▷ **marinate**
marinating *v* ▷ **marinate**
marine *adj* of the sea or shipping ▶ *n* (*pl* **-s**) (esp. in Britain and the US) soldier trained for land and sea combat
mariner *n* (*pl* **-s**) sailor
mariners *n* ▷ **mariner**
marines *n* ▷ **marine**
marionette *n* (*pl* **-s**) puppet worked with strings
marionettes *n* ▷ **marionette**
marital *adj* relating to marriage
maritime *adj* relating to shipping
marjoram *n* (*pl* **-s**) aromatic herb used for seasoning food and in salads
marjorams *n* ▷ **marjoram**
mark[1] *n* (*pl* **-s**) line, dot, scar, etc. visible on a surface ▶ *v* (**-s, -ing, -ed**) make a mark on ▷ **marked** *adj* noticeable ▷ **markedly** *adv* ▷ **marker** *n* (*pl* **-s**)
mark[2] *n* ▷ **Deutschmark**
marked *v, adj* ▷ **mark**[1]
markedly *adv* ▷ **mark**[1]
marker *n* ▷ **mark**[1]
markers *n* ▷ **mark**
marking *v* ▷ **mark**[1]
marks *n* ▷ **mark**[1,2] ▶ *v* ▷ **mark**[1]

market *n* (*pl* **-s**) assembly or place for buying and selling ▶ *v* (**-s, -ing, -ed**) offer or produce for sale ▷ **marketable** *adj*
marketable *adj* ▷ **market**
marketing *n* (*pl* **-s**) part of a business that controls the way that goods or services are sold
marketings *n* ▷ **marketing**
marketplace *n* (*pl* **-s**) market
marketplaces *n* ▷ **marketplace**
markets *n, v* ▷ **market**
marksman *n* (*pl* **-men**) person skilled at shooting ▷ **marksmanship** *n* (*pl* **-s**)
marksmanship *n* ▷ **marksman**
marksmanships *n* ▷ **marksman**
marksmen *n* ▷ **marksman**
marl *n* (*pl* **-s**) soil formed of clay and lime, used as fertilizer
marls *n* ▷ **marl**
marlin *n* large food and game fish of warm and tropical seas, with a very long upper jaw
marlinespike, marlinspike *n* (*pl* **-s**) pointed hook used to separate strands of rope
marlinespikes *n* ▷ **marlinespike**
marlinspikes *n* ▷ **marlinespike**
marmalade *n* (*pl* **-s**) jam made from citrus fruits
marmalades *n* ▷ **marmalade**
marmoreal *adj* of or like marble
marmoset *n* (*pl* **-s**) small bushy-tailed monkey
marmosets *n* ▷ **marmoset**
marmot *n* (*pl* **-s**) burrowing rodent
marmots *n* ▷ **marmot**
maroon[1] *adj* reddish-purple
maroon[2] *v* (**-s, -ing, -ed**) abandon ashore, esp. on an island
marooned *v* ▷ **maroon**
marooning *v* ▷ **maroon**
maroons *v* ▷ **maroon**
marquee *n* (*pl* **-s**) large tent used for a party or exhibition
marquees *n* ▷ **marquee**
marquess [mar-kwiss] *n* (*pl* **-es**) (BRIT) nobleman of the rank below a duke
marquesses *n* ▷ **marquess**
marquetry *n* (*pl* **-ries**) ornamental inlaid work of wood
marquetries *n* ▷ **marquetry**
marquis *n* (*pl* **-es**) (in some European countries) nobleman of the rank above a count
marquises *n* ▷ **marquis**
marred *v* ▷ **mar**
marriage *n* (*pl* **-s**) state of being married ▷ **marriageable** *adj*

marriageable adj ▷ marriage
marriages n ▷ marriage
married v ▷ marry
marries v ▷ marry
marring v ▷ mar
marrow n (pl -s) fatty substance inside bones
marrows n ▷ marrow
marry v (-ries, -ing, -ried) take as a husband
  or wife
marrying v ▷ marry
mars v ▷ mar
marsala [mar-sah-la] n (pl -s) dark sweet wine
marsh n (pl -es) low-lying wet land > **marshy**
  adj (-shier, -shiest)
marshal n (pl -s) officer of the highest rank ▶ v
  (-s, -shalling, -shalled) arrange in order
marshalled v ▷ marshal
marshalling v ▷ marshal
marshals n, v ▷ marshal
marshes n ▷ marsh
marshier adj ▷ marsh
marshiest adj ▷ marsh
marshmallow n (pl -s) spongy pink or white
  sweet
marshmallows n ▷ marshmallow
marshy n ▷ marsh
marsupial [mar-soop-ee-al] n (pl -s) animal
  that carries its young in a pouch, such as a
  kangaroo
marsupials n ▷ marsupial
mart n (pl -s) market
marts n ▷ mart
marten n (pl -s) weasel-like animal
martens n ▷ marten
martial adj of war, warlike
martian [marsh-an] adj of Mars ▶ n (pl -s)
  supposed inhabitant of Mars
martians n ▷ martian
martin n (pl -s) bird with a slightly forked tail
martins n ▷ martin
martinet n (pl -s) person who maintains strict
  discipline
martinets n ▷ martinet
martini n (pl -s) cocktail of vermouth and gin
martinis n ▷ martini
martyr n (pl -s) person who dies or suffers
  for his or her beliefs ▶ v (-s, -ing, -ed) make a
  martyr of > **martyrdom** n (pl -s)
martyrdom n ▷ martyr
martyrdoms n ▷ martyr
martyred v ▷ martyr
martyring v ▷ martyr
martyrs n, v ▷ martyr
marvel v (-s, -velling, -velled) be filled with
  wonder ▶ n wonderful thing

marvelled v ▷ marvel
marvelling v ▷ marvel
marvellous adj amazing
marvels v ▷ marvel
marzipan n (pl -s) paste of ground almonds,
  sugar, and egg whites
marzipans n ▷ marzipan
mascara n (pl -s) cosmetic for darkening the
  eyelashes
mascaras n ▷ mascara
mascot n (pl -s) person, animal, or thing
  supposed to bring good luck
mascots n ▷ mascot
masculine adj relating to males > **masculinity**
  n (pl -ties)
masculinities n ▷ masculine
masculinity n ▷ masculine
mash n (pl -es) (Informal) mashed potatoes ▶ v
  (-es, -ing, -ed) crush into a soft mass
mashed v ▷ mash
mashes n, v ▷ mash
mashing v ▷ mash
mask n (pl -s) covering for the face, as a
  disguise or protection ▶ v (-s, -ing, -ed) cover
  with a mask
masked v ▷ mask
masking v ▷ mask
masks n, v ▷ mask
masochism [mass-oh-kiz-zum] n (pl -s)
  condition in which (sexual) pleasure
  is obtained from feeling pain or from
  being humiliated > **masochist** n (pl -s)
  > **masochistic** adj
masochist n ▷ masochism
masochistic n ▷ masochism
masochists n ▷ masochism
mason n (pl -s) person who works with stone
masonic adj of Freemasonry
masonry n (pl -ries) stonework
masonries n (pl -ries) stonework
masons n ▷ mason
masque [mask] n (pl -s) (HIST) 16th–17th-century
  form of dramatic entertainment
masques n ▷ masque
masquerade [mask-er-aid] n (pl -s) deceptive
  show or pretence ▶ v (-des, -ding, -ded)
  pretend to be someone or something else
masqueraded v ▷ masquerade
masquerades n, v ▷ masquerade
masquerading v ▷ masquerade
mass n (pl -es) coherent body of matter ▶ adj
  large-scale ▶ v (-es, -ing, -ed) form into a mass
massacre [mass-a-ker] n (pl -s) indiscriminate
  killing of large numbers of people ▶ v (-res,
  -ring, -red) kill in large numbers

massacred v ▷ massacre

massacres n, v ▷ massacre

massacring v ▷ massacre

massage [mass-ahzh] n (pl -s) rubbing and kneading of parts of the body to reduce pain or stiffness ▶ v (-ges, -ging, -ged) give a massage to

massaged v ▷ massage

massages n, v ▷ massage

massaging v ▷ massage

massed v ▷ mass

masses n, v ▷ mass

masseur, fem **masseuse** n (pl -s) person who gives massages

masseurs n ▷ masseur

masseuse n ▷ masseuses

massing v ▷ mass

massive adj large and heavy

massif [mass-seef] n (pl -s) connected group of mountains

massifs n ▷ massif

mast¹ n (pl -s) tall pole for supporting something, esp. a ship's sails

mast² n (pl -s) fruit of the beech, oak, etc., used as pig fodder

masts n ▷ mast¹,²

mastectomies n ▷ mastectomy

mastectomy [mass-tek-tom-ee] n (pl -mies) surgical removal of a breast

master n (pl -s) person in control, such as an employer or an owner of slaves or animals ▶ adj overall or controlling ▶ v (-s, -ing, -ed) acquire knowledge of or skill in

mastered v ▷ master

masterful adj domineering

masteries n ▷ mastery

mastering v ▷ master

masterly adj showing great skill

mastermind v plan and direct (a complex task) n person who plans and directs a complex task

masterpiece n outstanding work of art

masters n, v ▷ master

mastery n (pl -ries) expertise

mastic n (pl -s) gum obtained from certain trees

mastics n ▷ mastic

masticate v (-tes, -ting, -ted) chew > **mastication** n (pl -s)

masticated v ▷ masticate

masticates v ▷ masticate

masticating v ▷ masticate

mastication n ▷ masticate

mastications n ▷ masticate

mastiff n (pl -s) large dog

mastiffs n ▷ mastiff

mastitis n (pl -tises) inflammation of a breast or udder

mastitises n ▷ mastitis

mastodon n (pl -s) extinct elephant-like mammal

mastodons n ▷ mastodon

mastoid n (pl -s) projection of the bone behind the ear

mastoids n ▷ mastoid

masturbate v (-tes, -ting, -ted) fondle the genitals (of) > **masturbation** n (pl -s)

masturbated v ▷ masturbate

masturbates v ▷ masturbate

masturbating v ▷ masturbate

masturbation n ▷ masturbate

masturbations n ▷ masturbate

mat n (pl -s) piece of fabric used as a floor covering or to protect a surface ▶ v (-s, -tting, -tted) tangle or become tangled into a dense mass

matador n (pl -s) man who kills the bull in bullfights

matadors n ▷ matador

match¹ n (pl -es) contest in a game or sport ▶ v (-es, -ing, -ed) be exactly like, equal to, or in harmony with

match² n small stick with a tip which ignites when scraped on a rough surface > **matchbox** n (pl -es)

matchbox n ▷ match²

matchboxes n ▷ match²

matched v ▷ match¹

matches v ▷ match¹ ▶ n ▷ match¹,²

matching v ▷ match¹

matchless adj unequalled

matchmaker n (pl -s) person who schemes to bring about a marriage > **matchmaking** n (pl -s) adj

matchmakers n ▷ matchmaker

matchmaking n ▷ matchmaker

matchmakings n ▷ matchmaker

matchstick n (pl -s) wooden part of a match ▶ adj (of drawn figures) thin and straight

matchsticks n ▷ matchstick

matchwood n (pl -s) small splinters

matchwoods n ▷ matchwood

mate¹ n (pl -s) (Informal) friend ▶ v (-tes, -ting, -ted) pair (animals) or (of animals) be paired for reproduction

mate² n (pl -s) checkmate ▶ v (-tes, -ting, -ted) (CHESS) checkmate

mated v ▷ mate¹,²

mates n, v ▷ mate¹,²

mating v ▷ mate¹,²

material n (pl **-s**) substance of which a thing is made ▸ adj of matter or substance > **materialist** adj, n > **materialistic** adj
materialism n (pl **-s**) excessive interest in or desire for money and possessions
 materialisms n ▷ **materialism**
 materialist adj, n (pl **-s**) ▷ **material**
 materialistic adj ▷ **material**
 materialists n ▷ **material**
materialize v (**-zes, -zing, -zed**) actually happen > **materialization** n (pl **-s**)
 materialization n ▷ **materialize**
 materializations n ▷ **materialize**
 materialized v ▷ **materialize**
 materializes v ▷ **materialize**
 materializing v ▷ **materialize**
materially adv considerably
 materials n ▷ **material**
maternal adj of a mother ▸ adj of or for pregnant women
 maternities n ▷ **maternity**
maternity n (pl **-ties**) motherhood
matey adj (**-tier, -tiest**) (BRIT) (Informal) friendly or intimate
mathematics n science of number, quantity, shape, and space > **mathematical** adj > **mathematically** adv > **mathematician** n (pl **-s**)
 mathematical adj ▷ **mathematics**
 mathematically adv ▷ **mathematics**
 mathematician n ▷ **mathematics**
 mathematicians n ▷ **mathematics**
maths n (Informal) mathematics
 matier adj ▷ **matey**
 matiest adj ▷ **matey**
matilda n (pl **-s**) (AUST HIST) swagman's bundle of belongings
 matildas n ▷ **matilda**
matinée [mat-in-nay] n (pl **-s**) afternoon performance in a theatre or cinema
 matinées n ▷ **matinée**
matins pl n early morning service in various Christian Churches
matriarch [mate-ree-ark] n (pl **-s**) female head of a tribe or family > **matriarchal** adj
 matriarchal n ▷ **matriarch**
 matriarchies n ▷ **matriarch**
 matriarchs n ▷ **matriarch**
matriarchy n (pl **-chies**) society governed by a female, in which descent is traced through the female line
 matrices n ▷ **matrix**
matricide n (pl **-s**) crime of killing one's mother
 matricides n ▷ **matricide**
matriculate v (**-tes, -ting, -ted**) enrol or

be enrolled in a college or university
 > **matriculation** n (pl **-s**)
 matriculated v ▷ **matriculate**
 matriculates v ▷ **matriculate**
 matriculating v ▷ **matriculate**
 matriculation n ▷ **matriculate**
 matriculations n ▷ **matriculate**
 matrimonial adj ▷ **matrimony**
 matrimonies n ▷ **matrimony**
matrimony n (pl **-nies**) marriage
 > **matrimonial**
matrix [**may-trix**] n (pl **-trices**) substance or situation in which something originates, takes form, or is enclosed
matron n (pl **-s**) staid or dignified married woman > **matronly** adj
 matrons n ▷ **matron**
 mats n, v ▷ **mat**
matt adj dull, not shiny
 matted v ▷ **mat**
matter n (pl **-s**) substance of which something is made ▸ v (**-s, -ing, -ed**) be of importance
 mattered v ▷ **matter**
 mattering v ▷ **matter**
 matters n, v ▷ **matter**
 matting v ▷ **mat**
mattock n (pl **-s**) large pick with one of its blade ends flattened for loosening soil
 mattocks n ▷ **mattock**
mattress n (pl **-es**) large stuffed flat case, often with springs, used on or as a bed
 mattresses n ▷ **mattress**
mature adj fully developed or grown-up ▸ v (**-res, -ring, -red**) make or become mature
 > **maturation** n (pl **-s**)
 maturation n ▷ **mature**
 maturations n ▷ **mature**
 matured v ▷ **mature**
 matures v ▷ **mature**
 maturing v ▷ **mature**
 maturities n ▷ **maturity**
maturity n (pl **-ties**) state of being mature
maudlin adj foolishly or tearfully sentimental
maul v (**-s, -ing, -ed**) handle roughly
 mauled v ▷ **maul**
 mauling v ▷ **maul**
 mauls v ▷ **maul**
maunder v (**-s, -ing, -ed**) talk or act aimlessly or idly
 maundered v ▷ **maunder**
 maundering v ▷ **maunder**
 maunders v ▷ **maunder**
mausoleum [maw-so-**lee**-um] n (pl **-s**) stately tomb
 mausoleums n ▷ **mausoleum**

mauve adj (-r, -est) pale purple
   mauver adj ▷ mauve
   mauvest adj ▷ mauve
maverick n (pl -s) ▶ adj independent and unorthodox (person)
   mavericks n ▷ maverick
maw n (pl -s) animal's mouth, throat, or stomach
   maws n ▷ maw
mawkish adj foolishly sentimental

> **max** n (**maxes**). Max is a short form of **maximum**. This is a useful word, particularly if you find yourself with an X toward the end of the game, with limited opportunity to play it. Max scores 12 points.

maxim n (pl -s) general truth or principle
   maxima n ▷ maximum
   maximal adj ▷ maxim
   maxims n ▷ maxim
maximum adj, n (pl -s, -ma) greatest possible (amount or number) > **maximal** adj
maximize v (-zes, -zing, -zed) increase to a maximum
   maximized v ▷ maximize
   maximizes v ▷ maximize
   maximizing v ▷ maximize
   maximums n ▷ maximum
may¹ v (past tense **might**) used as an auxiliary to express possibility, permission, opportunity, etc.
   may² n (pl -s) ▷ hawthorn
   mays n ▷ may²
maybe adv perhaps, possibly
mayday n (pl -s) international radio distress signal
   maydays n ▷ mayday
   mayflies n ▷ mayfly
mayfly n (pl -lies) short-lived aquatic insect
mayhem n (pl -s) violent destruction or confusion
   mayhems n ▷ mayhem
mayonnaise n (pl -s) creamy sauce of egg yolks, oil, and vinegar
   mayonnaises n ▷ mayonnaise
mayor n (pl -s) head of a municipality
   mayoralties n ▷ mayoralty
mayoralty n (pl -ies) (term of) office of a mayor
mayoress n (pl -es) mayor's wife
   mayoresses n ▷ mayoress
   mayors n ▷ mayor
maypole n (pl -s) pole set up for dancing round on the first day of May to celebrate spring
   maypoles n ▷ maypole
maze n (pl -s) complex network of paths or

lines designed to puzzle
   mazes n ▷ maze
mazurka n (pl -s) lively Polish dance
   mazurkas n ▷ mazurka
me pron ▷ I
mead n (pl -s) alcoholic drink made from honey
   meads n ▷ mead
meadow n (pl -s) piece of grassland
   meadows n ▷ meadow
meadowsweet n (pl -s) plant with dense heads of small fragrant flowers
   meadowseets n ▷ meadowsweet
meagre adj scanty or insufficient
meal¹ n (pl -s) occasion when food is served and eaten
meal² n (pl -s) grain ground to powder > **mealy -lier, -liest**) ▶ adj
mealie n (pl -s) (S AFR) maize
   mealier adj ▷ meal²
   mealies n ▷ mealie
   mealiest adj ▷ meal²
   meals n ▷ meal¹,²
   mealy adj ▷ meal²
mealymouthed adj not outspoken enough
mean¹ v (-s, -ing, meant) intend to convey or express > **meaningful** adj > **meaningless** adj
mean² adj (-er, -est) miserly, ungenerous, or petty > **meanly** adv > **meanness** n (pl -es)
mean³ n (pl -s) middle point between two extremes ▶ pl method by which something is done ▶ adj intermediate in size or quantity
   meaner adj ▷ mean²
   meanest adj ▷ mean²
meaning n (pl -s) sense, significance
   meaningful adj ▷ mean¹
   meaningless adj ▷ mean¹
   meanings n ▷ meaning
   meanly adv ▷ mean²
   meanness n ▷ mean²
   meannesses n ▷ mean²
   means v ▷ mean¹ ▶ n ▷ mean³
meander [mee-and-er] v (-s, -ing, -ed) follow a winding course ▶ n (pl -s) winding course
   meandered v ▷ meander
   meandering v ▷ meander
   meanders v, n ▷ meander
meantime n (pl -s) intervening period ▶ adv meanwhile
   meantimes n ▷ meantime
meanwhile adv during the intervening period
measles n infectious disease producing red spots
measly adj (Informal) meagre
measure n (pl -s) size or quantity ▶ v (-res, -ring, -red) determine the size or quantity of

> **measurable** adj
measurable adj ▷ **measure**
measured adj slow and steady ▶ v ▷ **measure**
measurement n (pl -s) measuring
measures n, v ▷ **measure**
measuring v ▷ **measure**
meat n (pl -s) animal flesh as food
meatier adj ▷ **meaty**
meatiest adj ▷ **meaty**
meats n ▷ **meat**
meaty adj (-tier, -tiest) (tasting) of or like meat
mechanic n (pl -s) person skilled in repairing
or operating machinery
mechanical adj of or done by machines
> **mechanically** adv
mechanically adv ▷ **mechanical**
mechanics n scientific study of motion and
force ▷ **mechanic**
mechanism n (pl -s) way a machine works
mechanisms n ▷ **mechanism**
mechanization n ▷ **mechanize**
mechanizations n ▷ **mechanism**
mechanize v (-zes, -zing, -zed) equip with
machinery > **mechanization** n (pl -s)
mechanized v ▷ **mechanize**
mechanizes v ▷ **mechanize**
mechanizing v ▷ **mechanize**
medal n (pl -s) piece of metal with an
inscription etc., given as a reward or
memento
medallion n (pl -s) disc-shaped ornament
worn on a chain round the neck
medallions n ▷ **medallion**
medallist n (pl -s) winner of a medal
medallists n ▷ **medallist**
medals n ▷ **medal**
meddle v (-les, -ling, -led) interfere annoyingly
> **meddler** n (pl -s) > **meddlesome** adj
meddled v ▷ **meddle**
meddler n ▷ **meddle**
meddlers n ▷ **meddle**
meddles v ▷ **meddle**
meddlesome adj ▷ **meddle**
meddling v ▷ **meddle**
media n (pl -iae) ▷ **medium** the mass media
collectively
mediae n ▷ **media**
mediaeval adj ▷ **medieval**
medial adj of or in the middle
median adj, n (pl -s) middle (point or line)
medians n ▷ **median**
mediate v (-tes, -ting, -ted) intervene
in a dispute to bring about agreement
> **mediation** n (pl -s) > **mediator** n (pl -s)
mediated v ▷ **mediate**

mediates v ▷ **mediate**
mediating v ▷ **mediate**
mediation n ▷ **mediate**
mediations n ▷ **mediate**
mediator n ▷ **mediate**
mediators n ▷ **mediate**
medic n (pl -s) (Informal) doctor or medical
student
medics n ▷ **medic**
medical adj of the science of medicine
▶ n (pl -s) (Informal) medical examination
> **medically** adv
medically adv ▷ **medical**
medicals n ▷ **medical**
medicate v (-tes, -ting, -ted) treat with a
medicinal substance
medicated v ▷ **medicate**
medicates v ▷ **medicate**
medicating v ▷ **medicine**
medication n (pl -s) (treatment with) a
medicinal substance
medications n ▷ **medication**
medicine n (pl -s) substance used to treat
disease
medicinal [med-**diss**-in-al] adj having
therapeutic properties
medicines n ▷ **medicine**
medieval [med-ee-**eve**-al] adj of the Middle
Ages
mediocre [mee-dee-**oak**-er] adj average in
quality > **mediocrity** [mee-dee-**ok**-rit-ee] ▶ n
(pl -**ties**)
mediocrities n ▷ **mediocre**
mediocrity n ▷ **mediocre**
meditate v (-tes, -ting, -ted) reflect deeply,
esp. on spiritual matters > **meditation** n
(pl -s) > **meditative** adj > **meditatively** adv
> **meditator** n (pl -s)
meditated v ▷ **meditate**
meditates v ▷ **meditate**
meditating v ▷ **meditate**
meditation n ▷ **meditate**
meditations n ▷ **meditate**
meditative adj ▷ **meditate**
meditatively adv ▷ **meditate**
meditator n ▷ **meditate**
meditators n ▷ **meditate**
medium adj midway between extremes,
average ▶ n (pl -**dia**, -**diums**) middle state,
degree, or condition
mediums n ▷ **medium**
medlar n (pl -s) apple-like fruit of a small tree,
eaten when it begins to decay
medlars n ▷ **medlar**
medley n (pl -s) miscellaneous mixture

medleys n ▷ medley

medulla [mid-**dull**-la] n (pl **-las, -lae**) marrow, pith, or inner tissue

medullae n ▷ medulla

medullas n ▷ medulla

meek adj (**-er, -est**) submissive or humble > **meekly** adv > **meekness** n (pl **-es**)

meeker adj ▷ meek

meekest adj ▷ meek

meekly adv ▷ meek

meekness n ▷ meek

meeknesses n ▷ meek

meerkat n (pl **-s**) S African mongoose

meerkats n ▷ meerkat

meerschaum [**meer**-shum] n (pl **-s**) white substance like clay

meerschaums n ▷ meerschaum

meet[1] v (**-s, meeting, met**) come together (with) ▶ n (pl **-s**) meeting, esp. a sports meeting

meet[2] adj (**-er, -est**) (Obs) fit or suitable

meeter adj ▷ meet[2]

meetest adj ▷ meet[2]

meeting n (pl **-s**) coming together ▶ v ▷ meet[1]

meets v, n ▷ meek[1]

megabyte n (pl **-s**) (COMPUTERS) 2^{20} or 1 048 576 bytes

megabytes n ▷ megabyte

megahertz n one million hertz

megalith n (pl **-s**) great stone, esp. as part of a prehistoric monument > **megalithic** adj

megalithic adj ▷ megalith

megaliths n ▷ megalith

megalomania n (pl **-s**) craving for or mental delusions of power > **megalomaniac** adj, n (pl **-s**)

megalomaniac n ▷ megalomania

megalomaniacs n ▷ megalomania

megalomanias n ▷ megalomania

megaphone n (pl **-s**) cone-shaped instrument used to amplify the voice

megaphones n ▷ megaphone

megapode n (pl **-s**) bird of Australia, New Guinea, and adjacent islands

megapodes n ▷ megapode

megaton n (pl **-s**) explosive power equal to that of one million tons of TNT

megatons n ▷ megaton

melaleuca [mel-a-**loo**-ka] n (pl **-s**) Australian shrub or tree with a white trunk and black branches

melaleucas n ▷ melaleuca

melancholia [mel-an-**kole**-lee-a] n (pl **-s**) state of depression

melancholias n ▷ melancholia

melancholic adj ▷ melancholy

melancholies n ▷ melancholy

melancholy [**mel**-an-kol-lee] n (pl **-lies**) sadness or gloom ▶ adj sad or gloomy > **melancholic** adj, n (pl **-s**)

melange [may-**lahnzh**] n (pl **-s**) mixture

melanges n ▷ melange

melanin n (pl **-s**) dark pigment found in the hair, skin, and eyes of humans and animals

melanins n ▷ melanin

mêlée [**mel**-lay] n (pl **-s**) noisy confused fight or crowd

mêlées n ▷ mêlée

mellifluous [mel-**lif**-flew-uss] adj (of sound) smooth and sweet

mellow adj soft, not harsh ▶ v (**-s, -ing, -ed**) make or become mellow

mellowed v ▷ mellow

mellowing v ▷ mellow

mellows v ▷ mellow

melodic [mel-**lod**-ik] adj of melody

melodious [mel-**lode**-ee-uss] adj pleasing to the ear

melodrama n (pl **-s**) play full of extravagant action and emotion > **melodramatic** adj

melodramas n ▷ melodrama

melodramatic adj ▷ melodrama

melody n (pl **-dies**) series of musical notes which make a tune

melon n (pl **-s**) large round juicy fruit with a hard rind

melons n ▷ melon

melt v (**-s, -ing, -ed**) (cause to) become liquid by heat

meltdown n (pl **-s**) (in a nuclear reactor) melting of the fuel rods, with the possible release of radiation

meltdowns n ▷ meltdown

melted v ▷ melt

melting v ▷ melt

melts v ▷ melt

member n (pl **-s**) individual making up a body or society > **membership** n (pl **-s**)

members n ▷ member

membership n ▷ member

memberships n ▷ member

membrane n (pl **-s**) thin flexible tissue in a plant or animal body > **membranous** adj

membranes n ▷ membrane

membranous adj ▷ membrane

memento n (pl **-tos, -toes**) thing serving to remind, souvenir

mementoes n ▷ memento

mementos n ▷ memento

memo n (pl **-s**) ▷ memorandum

memos n ▷ memo

memoir [mem-wahr] n (pl -s) biography or historical account based on personal knowledge ▶ pl collection of these

memoirs n ▷ memoir

memorable adj worth remembering, noteworthy > **memorably** adv

memorably adv ▷ memorable

memoranda n ▷ memorandum

memorandum n (pl -dums, -da) written record or communication within a business

memorandums n ▷ memorandum

memorial n (pl -s) something serving to commemorate a person or thing ▶ adj serving as a memorial

memorials n ▷ memorandum

memorize v (-zes, -zing, -zed) commit to memory

memorized v ▷ memorize

memorizes v ▷ memorize

memorizing v ▷ memorize

memory n (pl -ries) ability to remember

men n ▷ man

menace n (pl -s) threat ▶ v (-ces, -cing, -ced) threaten, endanger > **menacing** adj

menaced v ▷ menace

menaces n, v ▷ menace

menacing v, adj ▷ menace

ménage [may-nahzh] n (pl -s) household

ménages n ▷ ménage

menagerie [min-naj-er-ee] n (pl -s) collection of wild animals for exhibition

menageries n ▷ menagerie

mend v (-s, -ing, -ed) repair or patch ▶ n (pl -s) mended area

mendacious adj ▷ mendacity

mendacities n ▷ mendacity

mendacity n (pl -ties) (tendency to) untruthfulness > **mendacious** adj

mended v ▷ mend

mendicant adj begging ▶ n (pl -s) beggar

mendicants n ▷ mendicant

mending v ▷ mend

mends v, n ▷ mend

menhir [men-hear] n (pl -s) single upright prehistoric stone

menhirs n ▷ menhir

menial [mean-eel-al] adj involving boring work of low status ▶ n (pl -s) person with a menial job

menials n ▷ menial

meningitis [men-in-jite-iss] n (pl -es) inflammation of the membranes of the brain

meningitises n ▷ meningitis

meniscus n (pl -ci) curved surface of a liquid

menisci n ▷ meniscus

menopausal adj ▷ menopause

menopause n (pl -s) time when a woman's menstrual cycle ceases > **menopausal** adj

menopauses n ▷ menopause

menservants n ▷ manservant

menstruation n (pl -s) approximately monthly discharge of blood and cellular debris from the womb of a nonpregnant woman > **menstruate** v (-tes, -ting, -ted) > **menstrual** adj

menstrual adj ▷ menstruation

menstruated v ▷ menstruation

menstruates v ▷ menstruation

menstruating v ▷ menstruation

menstruations n ▷ menstruation

mensuration n (pl -s) measuring, esp. in geometry

mensurations n ▷ mensuration

mental adj of, in, or done by the mind > **mentally** adv

mentalities n ▷ mentality

mentality n (pl -ties) way of thinking

mentally adv ▷ mental

menthol n (pl -s) organic compound found in peppermint, used medicinally

menthols n ▷ menthol

mention v (-s, -ing, -ed) refer to briefly ▶ n (pl -s) brief reference to a person or thing

mentioned v ▷ mention

mentioning v ▷ mention

mentions v, n ▷ mention

mentor n (pl -s) adviser or guide

mentors n ▷ mentor

menu n (pl -s) list of dishes to be served, or from which to order

menus n ▷ menu

mercantile adj of trade or traders

mercenaries n ▷ mercenary

mercenary adj influenced by greed ▶ n (pl -ries) hired soldier

merchandises n ▷ merchandise

merchandise (pl -s) commodities

merchant n (pl -s) person engaged in trade, wholesale trader

merchantman n (pl -men) trading ship

merchantmen n ▷ merchantman

merchants n ▷ merchant

merciful adj compassionate

merciless adj ▷ mercy

mercurial adj lively, changeable

mercuries n ▷ mercury

mercury n (pl -ries) (CHEM) silvery liquid metal

mercy n (pl -cies) compassionate treatment of an offender or enemy who is in one's power

> **merciless** adj

mere[1] adj (**-r**, **-st**) nothing more than > **merely**
adv

mere[2] n (pl **-s**) (BRIT) (Obs) lake

merely adv ▷ **mere**[1]

merer adj ▷ **mere**[1]

meres n ▷ **mere**[2]

merest adj ▷ **mere**[1]

meretricious adj superficially or garishly
attractive but of no real value

merganser [mer-gan-ser] n (pl **-s**) large crested
diving duck

mergansers n ▷ **merganser**

merge v (**-ges**, **-ging**, **-ged**) combine or blend

merged v ▷ **merge**

merger n (pl **-s**) combination of business firms
into one

merges v ▷ **merge**

merging v ▷ **merge**

mergers n ▷ **merger**

meridian n (pl **-s**) imaginary circle of the earth
passing through both poles

meridians n ▷ **meridian**

meringue [mer-rang] n (pl **-s**) baked mixture of
egg whites and sugar

meringues n ▷ **meringue**

merino n (pl **-s**) breed of sheep with fine soft
wool

merinos n ▷ **merino**

merit n (pl **-s**) excellence or worth ▶ pl
admirable qualities ▶ v (**-s**, **-ing**, **-ed**) deserve

merited v ▷ **merit**

meriting v ▷ **merit**

meritocracies n ▷ **meritocracy**

meritocracy [mer-it-tok-rass-ee] n (pl **-s**) rule by
people of superior talent or intellect

meritorious adj deserving praise

merits n, v ▷ **merit**

merlin n (pl **-s**) small falcon

merlins n ▷ **merlin**

mermaid n (pl **-s**) imaginary sea creature with
the upper part of a woman and the lower
part of a fish

mermaids n ▷ **mermaid**

merrier adj ▷ **merry**

merriest adj ▷ **merry**

merrily adv ▷ **merry**

merriment n ▷ **merry**

merriments n ▷ **merry**

merry adj (**-rier**, **-riest**) cheerful or jolly
> **merrily** adv > **merriment** n (pl **-s**)

merrymaking n (pl **-s**) noisy, cheerful
celebrations or fun

merrymakings n ▷ **merrymaking**

mesdames n ▷ **madame**

mesdemoiselles n ▷ **mademoiselle**

mesh n (pl **-es**) network or net ▶ v (**-es**, **-ing**, **-ed**)
(of gear teeth) engage

meshed v ▷ **mesh**

meshes n, v ▷ **mesh**

meshing v ▷ **mesh**

mesmerize v (**-zes**, **-zing**, **-zed**) hold
spellbound

mesmerized v ▷ **mesmerize**

mesmerizes v ▷ **mesmerize**

mesmerizing v ▷ **mesmerize**

meson [mee-zon] n (pl **-s**) elementary atomic
particle

mesons n ▷ **meson**

mess n (pl **-es**) untidy or dirty confusion ▶ v
(**-es**, **-ing**, **-ed**) muddle or dirty

message n (pl **-s**) communication sent

messages n ▷ **message**

messaging n (pl **-s**) sending and receiving of
textual communications by mobile phone

messagings n ▷ **message**

messed v ▷ **mess**

messeigneurs n ▷ **monseigneur**

messenger n (pl **-s**) bearer of a message

messengers n ▷ **messenger**

messes n, v ▷ **mess**

messiah n (pl **-s**) promised deliverer
> **messianic** adj

messiahs n ▷ **messiah**

messianic adj ▷ **messiah**

messier adj ▷ **messy**

messiest adj ▷ **messy**

messieurs n ▷ **monsieur**

messily adv ▷ **messy**

messing v ▷ **mess**

messy adj (**-ssier**, **-ssiest**) dirty, confused, or
untidy > **messily** adv

met v ▷ **meet**[1]

metabolic adj ▷ **metabolism**

metabolism [met-tab-oh-liz-zum] n (pl
-s) chemical processes of a living body
> **metabolic** adj

metabolisms n ▷ **metabolism**

metabolize v (**-zes**, **-zing**, **-zed**) produce or be
produced by metabolism

metabolized v ▷ **metabolize**

metabolizes v ▷ **metabolize**

metabolizing v ▷ **metabolize**

metal n (pl **-s**) chemical element, such as iron
or copper, that is malleable and capable of
conducting heat and electricity > **metallic** adj

metallic adj ▷ **metal**

metallurgical adj ▷ **metallurgy**

metallurgist n ▷ **metallurgy**

metallurgists n ▷ **metallurgy**

metallurgy n (pl -gies) scientific study of the structure, properties, extraction, and refining of metals > **metallurgical** adj > **metallurgist** n (pl -s)
metals n ▷ metal
metamorphic adj (of rocks) changed in texture or structure by heat and pressure
metamorphose v (-ses, -sing, -sed) transform
metamorphosed v ▷ metamorphose
metamorphoses n, v ▷ metamorphosis
metamorphosing v ▷ metamorphose
metamorphosis [met-a-more-foss-is] n (pl -ses) [-foss-eez] change of form or character
metaphor n (pl -s) figure of speech in which a term is applied to something it does not literally denote in order to imply a resemblance > **metaphorical** adj > **metaphorically** adv
metaphorically adv ▷ metaphor
metaphors n ▷ metaphor
metaphysical adj ▷ metaphysics
metaphysics n branch of philosophy concerned with being and knowing > **metaphysical** adj
mete v (-tes, -ting, -ted) (usu. with out) deal out as punishment
meted v ▷ mete
meteor n (pl -s) small fast-moving heavenly body, visible as a streak of incandescence if it enters the earth's atmosphere
meteoric [meet-ee-or-rik] adj of a meteor
meteorite n (pl -s) meteor that has fallen to earth
meteorites n ▷ meteorite
meteorological adj ▷ meteorology
meteorologies n ▷ meteorology
meteorologist n ▷ meteorology
meteorologists n ▷ meteorology
meteorology n (pl -gies) study of the earth's atmosphere, esp. for weather forecasting > **meteorological** adj > **meteorologist** n (pl -s)
meteors n ▷ meteor
meter n (pl -s) instrument for measuring and recording something, such as the consumption of gas or electricity ▶ v (-s, -ing, -ed) measure by meter
meters n, v ▷ meter
metes v ▷ mete
meting v ▷ mete
methane n (pl -s) colourless inflammable gas
methanes n ▷ methane
methanol n (pl -s) colourless poisonous liquid used as a solvent and fuel (also **methyl alcohol**)
methanols n ▷ methanol

methinks v (past tense **methought**) (Obs) it seems to me
method n (pl -s) way or manner
methodical adj orderly > **methodically** adv
methodically adv ▷ methodical
methodism n ▷ methodist
methodisms n ▷ methodist
methodist n (pl -s) member of any of the Protestant churches originated by John Wesley and his followers ▶ adj of methodists or their Church > **methodism** n (pl -s)
methodists n ▷ methodist
methodologies n ▷ methodology
methodology n (pl -gies) particular method or procedure
methods n ▷ method
meths n (Informal) methylated spirits
methyl n (pl -s) (compound containing) a saturated hydrocarbon group of atoms
methyls n ▷ methyl
meticulous adj very careful about details > **meticulously** adv
meticulously adv ▷ meticulous
métier [met-ee-ay] n (pl -s) profession or trade
métiers n ▷ métier
metonymies n ▷ metonymy
metonymy [mit-on-im-ee] n (pl -mies) figure of speech in which one thing is replaced by another associated with it, such as 'the Crown' for 'the queen'
metre n (pl -s) basic unit of length equal to about 1.094 yards (100 centimetres)
metres n ▷ metre
metric adj of the decimal system of weights and measures based on the metre
metrical adj of measurement
metrication n (pl -s) conversion to the metric system
metrications n ▷ metrication
metronome n (pl -s) instrument which marks musical time by means of a ticking pendulum
metronomes n ▷ metronome
metropolis [mit-trop-oh-liss] n (pl -es) chief city of a country or region
metropolises n ▷ metropolis
metropolitan adj of a metropolis
metrosexual adj, n (pl -s) (of) a heterosexual man who is preoccupied with his appearance
metrosexuals n ▷ metrosexual
mettle n (pl -s) courage or spirit
mettles n ▷ mettle
mew n (pl -s) cry of a cat ▶ v (-s, -ing, -ed) utter this cry
mewed v ▷ mew
mewing v ▷ mew

mews n, v ▷ **mew**

mezquit n (**mezquit**). A mezquit is a small spiny tree or shrub. With its combination of Q and Z, mezquit is a very high-scoring word. As it contains seven letters, mezquit can earn you a bonus of 50 points if you manage to use all the letters on your rack to form it. Mezquit scores 28 points.

mezzanine [mez-zan-een] n (pl -s) intermediate storey, esp. between the ground and first floor

mezzanines n ▷ **mezzanine**

mezzotint [met-so-tint] n (pl -s) method of engraving by scraping the roughened surface of a metal plate

mezzotints n ▷ **mezzotint**

mi n (**mis**). Mi is the third degree of a major scale in music. This isn't a high-scoring word, but can be very helpful when you want to form words in more than one direction. Mi scores 4 points.

miaow [mee-ow] n (pl -s) ▶ v (-s, -ing, -wed) ▷ **mew**

miaowed v ▷ **miaow**

miaowing v ▷ **miaow**

miaows v, n ▷ **miaow**

miasma [mee-azz-ma] n (pl -mata) unwholesome or foreboding atmosphere

miasmata n ▷ **miasma**

mica [my-ka] n (pl -s) glasslike mineral used as an electrical insulator

micas n ▷ **mica**

mice n ▷ **mouse**

microbe n (pl -s) minute organism, esp. one causing disease ▶ **microbial** adj

microbes n ▷ **microbe**

microbial adj ▷ **microbe**

microchip n (pl -s) small wafer of silicon containing electronic circuits

microchips n ▷ **microchip**

microcomputer n (pl -s) computer with a central processing unit contained in one or more silicon chips

microcomputers n ▷ **microcomputer**

microcosm n (pl -s) miniature representation of something

microcosms n ▷ **microcosm**

microfiche [my-kroh-feesh] n (pl -s) microfilm in sheet form

microfiches n ▷ **microfiche**

microfilm n (pl -s) miniaturized recording of books or documents on a roll of film

microfilms n ▷ **microfilm**

microlight n (pl -s) very small light private aircraft with large wings

microlights n ▷ **microlight**

micrometer [my-krom-it-er] n (pl -s) instrument for measuring very small distances or angles

micrometers n ▷ **micrometer**

micron [my-kron] n (pl -s) one millionth of a metre

microns n ▷ **micron**

microorganism n (pl -ms) organism of microscopic size

microorganisms n ▷ **microorganism**

microphone n (pl -s) instrument for amplifying or transmitting sounds

microphones n ▷ **microphone**

microprocessor n (pl -s) integrated circuit acting as the central processing unit in a small computer

microprocessors n ▷ **microprocessor**

microscope n (pl -s) instrument with lens(es) which produces a magnified image of a very small object ▶ **microscopic** adj too small to be seen except with a microscope ▶ **microscopically** adv

microscopes n ▷ **microscope**

microscopic adj ▷ **microscope**

microscopically adv ▷ **microscope**

microscopies n ▷ **microscopy**

microscopy n (pl -pies) use of a microscope

microsurgeries n ▷ **microsurgery**

microsurgery n (pl -ries) intricate surgery using a special microscope and miniature precision instruments

microwave n (pl -s) electromagnetic wave with a wavelength of a few centimetres, used in radar and cooking ▶ v (-ves, -ving, -ved) cook in a microwave oven

microwaved v ▷ **microwave**

microwaves n, v ▷ **microwave**

microwaving v ▷ **microwave**

mid adj intermediate, middle

midday n (pl -s) noon

middays n ▷ **midday**

midden n (pl -s) (BRIT & AUST) dunghill or rubbish heap

middens n ▷ **midden**

middle adj equidistant from two extremes ▶ n (pl -s) middle point or part

middleman n (pl -men) trader who buys from the producer and sells to the consumer

middlemen n ▷ **middleman**

middles n ▷ **middle**

middleweight n (pl -s) boxer weighing up to 160lb (professional) or 75kg (amateur)

middleweights n ▷ **middleweight**

middling adj mediocre

midge n (pl -s) small mosquito-like insect
  midges n ▷ midge

midget n (pl -s) very small person or thing
  midgets n ▷ midget

midland n (pl -s) (BRIT, AUST & US) middle part
  of a country
  midlands n ▷ midland

midnight n (pl -s) twelve o'clock at night
  midnights n ▷ midnight

midriff n (pl -s) middle part of the body
  midriffs n ▷ midriff

midshipman n (pl -men) naval officer of the
  lowest commissioned rank
  midshipmen n ▷ midshipman

midsummer n (pl -s) middle of summer
  midsummers n ▷ midsummer

midway adj, adv halfway

midwife n (pl -wives) trained person who
  assists at childbirth > **midwifery** n (pl -ries)
  midwiferies n ▷ midwife
  midwifery n ▷ midwife
  midwives n ▷ midwife

midwinter n (pl -s) middle or depth of winter
  midwinters n ▷ midwinter

mien [mean] n (pl -s) (Lit) person's bearing,
  demeanour, or appearance
  miens n ▷ mien

miffed adj (Informal) offended or upset

might¹ ▷ may

might² n (pl -s) power or strength
  mightier adj ▷ mighty
  mightiest adj ▷ mighty
  mightily adv ▷ mighty

mighty adj (-tier, -tiest) powerful ▶ adv (US &
  AUST) (Informal) very > **mightily** adv

migraine [mee-grain] n (pl -s) severe headache,
  often with nausea and visual disturbances
  migraines n ▷ migraine

migrant n (pl -s) person or animal that moves
  from one place to another ▶ adj moving from
  one place to another
  migrants n ▷ migrant

migrate v (-tes, -ting, -ted) move from one
  place to settle in another > **migration** n (pl -s)
  migrated v ▷ migrate
  migrates v ▷ migrate
  migrating v ▷ migrate
  migration n ▷ migrate
  migrations n ▷ migrate

migratory adj (of an animal) migrating every
  year

mike n (pl -s) (Informal) microphone
  mikes n ▷ mike

milch adj (CHIEFLY BRIT) (of a cow) giving milk

mild adj (-er, -est) not strongly flavoured
  > **mildly** adv > **mildness** n (pl -es)
  milder adj ▷ mild
  mildest adj ▷ mild

mildew n (pl -s) destructive fungus on plants
  or things exposed to damp > **mildewed** adj
  mildewed adj ▷ mildew
  mildews n ▷ mildew
  mildly adv ▷ mild
  mildness n ▷ mild
  mildnesses n ▷ mild

mile n (pl -s) unit of length equal to 1760 yards
  or 1.609 kilometres

mileage n (pl -s) distance travelled in miles
  mileages n ▷ mileage

mileometer n (pl -s) (BRIT) device that records
  the number of miles a vehicle has travelled
  mileometers n ▷ mileometer
  miles n ▷ mile

milestone n (pl -s) significant event
  milestones n ▷ milestone

milieu [meal-yer] n (pl milieux, milieus) [meal-
  yerz] environment or surroundings
  milieus n ▷ milieu
  milieux n ▷ milieu

militancies n ▷ militant
  militancy n ▷ militant

militant adj aggressive or vigorous in support
  of a cause > **militancy** n (pl -cies)
  militants n ▷ militant
  militaries n ▷ military

militarism n (pl -s) belief in the use of military
  force and methods
  militarisms n ▷ militarism
  militarist n ▷ military
  militarists n ▷ military
  militarized adj ▷ military

military adj of or for soldiers, armies, or war
  ▶ n (pl -ries) armed services > **militarist** n (pl
  -s) > **militarized** adj

militate v (-tes, -ting, -ted) (usu. with against
  or for) have a strong influence or effect
  militated v ▷ militate
  militates v ▷ militate
  militating v ▷ militate

militia [mill-ish-a] n (pl -s) military force of
  trained citizens for use in emergency only
  militias n ▷ militia

milk n (pl -s) white fluid produced by female
  mammals to feed their young ▶ v (-s, -ing, -ed)
  draw milk from > **milky** adj (-kier, -kiest)
  milked v ▷ milk
  milkier adj ▷ milk
  milkiest adj ▷ milk
  milking v ▷ milk

milkmaid n (pl -s) (esp. in former times) woman who milks cows
  milkmaids n ▷ milkmaid
milkman n (pl -men) (BRIT, AUST & NZ) man who delivers milk to people's houses
  milkmen n ▷ milkman
  milks n, v ▷ milk
milkshake n (pl -s) frothy flavoured cold milk drink
  milkshakes n ▷ milkshake
milksop n (pl -s) feeble man
  milksops n ▷ milk
  milky adj ▷ milk
mill n (pl -s) factory ▶ v (-s, -ing, -ed) grind, press, or process in or as if in a mill
  milled v ▷ mill
millennium n (pl -nnia, -nniums) period of a thousand years
  millennia n ▷ mill
  millenniums n ▷ mill
miller n (pl -s) person who works in a mill
  millers n ▷ miller
millet n (pl -s) type of cereal grass
  millets n ▷ millet
millibar n (pl -s) unit of atmospheric pressure
  millibars n ▷ millibar
millimetre n (pl -s) thousandth part of a metre
  millimetres n ▷ millimetre
milliner n (pl -s) maker or seller of women's hats > **millinery** n (pl -ries)
  millineries n ▷ milliner
  milliners n ▷ milliner
  millinery n ▷ milliner
  milling v ▷ mill
million n (pl -s) one thousand thousands
  > **millionth** adj, n (pl -s)
millionaire n (pl -s) person who owns at least a million pounds, dollars, etc.
  millionaires n ▷ millionaire
  millions n ▷ million
  millionths n ▷ million
millipede n (pl -s) small animal with a jointed body and many pairs of legs
  millipedes n ▷ millipede
  mills n, v ▷ mill
millstone n (pl -s) flat circular stone for grinding corn
  millstones n ▷ millstone
millwheel n (pl -s) waterwheel that drives a mill
  millwheels n ▷ millwheel
milometer n (pl -s) (BRIT) ▷ mileometer
  milometers n ▷ milometer
milt n (pl -s) sperm of fish
  milts n ▷ milt

mime n (pl -s) acting without the use of words
  ▶ v (-mes, -ming, -med) act in mime
  mimed v ▷ mime
  mimes n, v ▷ mime
  miming v ▷ mime
mimic v (-ics, -icking, -icked) imitate (a person or manner), esp. for satirical effect ▶ n (pl -s) person or animal that is good at mimicking
  > **mimicry** n (pl -ries)
  mimicked v ▷ mimic
  mimicking v ▷ mimic
  mimicry n ▷ mimic
  mimics n, v ▷ mimic
  mina n ▷ myna
  minas n ▷ myna
minaret n (pl -s) tall slender tower of a mosque
  minarets n ▷ minaret
mince v (-ces, -cing, -ced) cut or grind into very small pieces ▶ n (pl -s) minced meat
  minced v ▷ mince
mincemeat n (pl -s) sweet mixture of dried fruit and spices
  mincemeats n ▷ mincemeat
mincer n (pl -s) machine for mincing meat
  mincers n ▷ mince
  minces v, n ▷ mince
  mincing adj affected in manner ▶ v ▷ mince
mind n (pl -s) thinking faculties ▶ v (-s, -ing, -ed) take offence at
  minded adj having an inclination as specified ▶ v ▷ mind
minder n (pl -s) (Informal) aide or bodyguard
  minders n ▷ minder
  mindful adj heedful
  minding v ▷ mind
  mindless adj stupid
  minds n, v ▷ mind
  mine¹ pron belonging to me
mine² n (pl -s) deep hole for digging out coal, ores, etc. ▶ v (-nes, -ning, -ned) dig for minerals
  mined v ▷ mine
minefield n (pl -s) area of land or water containing mines
  minefields n ▷ minefield
miner n (pl -s) person who works in a mine
mineral n (pl -s) naturally occurring inorganic substance, such as metal ▶ adj of, containing, or like minerals
  mineralogies n ▷ mineralogy
mineralogy [min-er-**al**-a-jee] n (pl -gies) study of minerals
  minerals n ▷ mineral
  miners n ▷ miner
  mines n, v ▷ mine

minestrone [min-ness-**strone**-ee] *n* (*pl* -**s**) soup containing vegetables and pasta
minestrones *n* ▷ minestrone
minesweeper *n* (*pl* -**s**) ship for clearing away mines
minesweepers *n* ▷ minesweeper
mining *v* ▷ mine
minger *n* (*pl* -**s**) (BRIT) (*Informal*) unattractive person
mingers *n* ▷ minger
mingier *adj* ▷ mingy
mingiest *adj* ▷ mingy
minging *adj* (BRIT) (*Informal*) unattractive or unpleasant
mingle *v* (-**les**, -**ling**, -**led**) mix or blend
mingled *v* ▷ mingle
mingles *v* ▷ mingle
mingling *v* ▷ mingle
mingy *adj* (-**gier**, -**giest**) (*Informal*) miserly
mini *n* (*pl* -**s**) ▶ *adj* (-**ier**, -**iest**) (something) small or miniature
minier *adj* ▷ mini
miniest *adj* ▷ mini
minis *n* ▷ mini
miniature *n* (*pl* -**s**) small portrait, model, or copy ▶ *adj* small-scale ▷ **miniaturist** *n* (*pl* -**s**)
miniatures *n* ▷ miniature
miniaturist *n* ▷ miniature
miniaturists *n* ▷ miniature
miniaturize *v* (-**zes**, -**zing**, -**zed**) make to a very small scale
miniaturized *v* ▷ miniaturize
miniaturizes *v* ▷ miniaturize
miniaturizing *v* ▷ miniaturize
minibar *n* (*pl* -**s**) selection of drinks and confectionery provided in a hotel room
minibus *n* (*pl* -**es**) small bus
minibuses *n* ▷ minibus
minicab *n* (*pl* -**s**) (BRIT) ordinary car used as a taxi
minicabs *n* ▷ minicab
minicomputer *n* (*pl* -**s**) computer smaller than a mainframe but more powerful than a microcomputer
minicomputers *n* ▷ minicomputer
minidisc *n* (*pl* -**s**) small recordable compact disc
minidiscs *n* ▷ minidisc
minim *n* (*pl* -**s**) (MUSIC) note half the length of a semibreve
minima *n* ▷ minimum
minimal *adj* minimum
minimize *v* (-**zes**, -**zing**, -**zed**) reduce to a minimum
minimized *v* ▷ minimize

minimizes *v* ▷ minimize
minimizing *v* ▷ minimize
minims *n* ▷ minim
minimum *adj*, *n* (*pl* -**mums**, -**ma**) least possible (amount or number)
minimums *n* ▷ minimum
minion *n* (*pl* -**s**) servile assistant
minions *n* ▷ minion
miniseries *n* (*pl* -**ries**) TV programme shown in several parts, often on consecutive days
miniseries *n* ▷ miniseries
minister *n* (*pl* -**s**) head of a government department ▶ *v* (-**s**, -**ing**, -**ed**) (*foll. by* **to**) attend to the needs of ▷ **ministerial** *adj*
ministered *v* ▷ minister
ministerial *adj* ▷ minister
ministering *v* ▷ minister
ministers *n*, *v* ▷ minister
ministration *n* (*pl* -**s**) giving of help
ministrations *n* ▷ ministration
ministries *n* ▷ ministry
ministry *n* (*pl* -**tries**) profession or duties of a clergyman
mink *n* stoatlike animal
minnow *n* (*pl* -**s**) small freshwater fish
minnows *n* ▷ minnow
minor *adj* lesser ▶ *n* (*pl* -**s**) person regarded legally as a child
minorities *n* ▷ minority
minority *n* (*pl* -**ties**) lesser number
minors *n* ▷ minor
minster *n* (*pl* -**s**) (BRIT) cathedral or large church
minsters *n* ▷ minster
minstrel *n* (*pl* -**s**) medieval singer or musician
minstrels *n* ▷ minstrel
mint¹ *n* (*pl* -**s**) plant with aromatic leaves used for seasoning and flavouring
mint² *n* place where money is coined ▶ *v* (-**s**, -**ing**, -**ed**) make (coins)
minted *v* ▷ mint²
minting *v* ▷ mint²
mints *n* ▷ mint¹,² ▶ *v* ▷²
minuet [min-new-**wet**] *n* (*pl* -**s**) stately dance
minuets *n* ▷ minuet
minus *prep*, *adj* indicating subtraction ▶ *adj* less than zero ▶ *n* (*pl* -**es**) sign (-) denoting subtraction or a number less than zero
minuses *n* ▷ minus
minuscule [min-niss-**skyool**] *adj* very small
minute¹ [**min**-it] *n* (*pl* -**s**) 60th part of an hour or degree ▶ *pl* record of the proceedings of a meeting ▶ *v* (-**tes**, -**ting**, -**ted**) record in the minutes
minute² [my-**newt**] *adj* (-**r**, -**st**) very small ▷ **minutely** *adv*

minuted v ▷ minute¹
minutely adv ▷ minute²
minuter adj ▷ minute²
minutes n, v ▷ minute¹
minutest adj ▷ minute²
minutiae [my-**new**-shee-eye] pl n trifling or precise details
minuting v ▷ minute¹
minx n (pl -es) bold or flirtatious girl
minxes n ▷ minx
miracle n (pl -s) wonderful supernatural event > **miraculous** adj > **miraculously** adv
miracles n ▷ miracle
miraculous adj ▷ miracle
miraculously adv ▷ miracle
mirage [mir-**rahzh**] n (pl -s) optical illusion, esp. one caused by hot air
mirages n ▷ mirage
mire n (pl -s) swampy ground
mires n ▷ mire
mirror n (pl -s) coated glass surface for reflecting images ► v (-s, -ing, -ed) reflect in or as if in a mirror
mirrored v ▷ mirror
mirroring v ▷ mirror
mirrors n, v ▷ mirror
mirth n (pl -s) laughter, merriment, or gaiety > **mirthful** adj > **mirthless** adj
mirthful adv ▷ mirth
mirthless adj ▷ mirth
mirths n ▷ mirth
misadventure n (pl -s) unlucky chance
misadventures n ▷ misadventure
misanthrope [**miz**-zan-thrope] n (pl -s) person who dislikes people in general > **misanthropic** [miz-zan-**throp**-ik] ► adj > **misanthropy** [miz-**zan**-throp-ee] ► n (pl -pies)
misanthropes n ▷ misanthrope
misanthropies n ▷ misanthrope
misanthropic adj ▷ misanthrope
misanthropy n ▷ misanthrope
misapprehend v (-s, -ing, -ed) misunderstand > **misapprehension** n (pl -s)
misapprehended v ▷ misapprehend
misapprehending v ▷ misapprehend
misapprehends v ▷ misapprehend
misapprehension n ▷ misapprehend
misapprehensions n ▷ misapprehend
misappropriate v (-tes, -ting, -ted) take and use (money) dishonestly > **misappropriation** n (pl -s)
misappropriated v ▷ misappropriate
misappropriates v ▷ misappropriate
misappropriating v ▷ misappropriate
misappropriation n ▷ misappropriate

misappropriations n ▷ misappropriate
miscarriage n (pl -s) spontaneous premature expulsion of a fetus from the womb
miscarriages n ▷ miscarriage
miscarried v ▷ miscarry
miscarries v ▷ miscarry
miscarry v (-ries, -rying, -ried) have a miscarriage
miscarrying v ▷ miscarry
miscast v (-s, -ing, -cast) cast (a role or actor) in (a play or film) inappropriately
miscasting v ▷ miscast
miscasts v ▷ miscast
miscegenation [miss-ij-in-**nay**-shun] n (pl -s) interbreeding of races
miscegenations n ▷ miscegenation
miscellaneous [miss-sell-**lane**-ee-uss] adj mixed or assorted
miscellanies n ▷ miscellany
miscellany [miss-**sell**-a-nee] n (pl -nies) mixed assortment
mischance n (pl -es) unlucky event
mischances n ▷ mischance
mischief n (pl -s) annoying but not malicious behaviour
mischiefs n ▷ mischief
mischievous adj full of mischief > **mischievously** adv
mischievously adv ▷ mischievous
miscible [**miss**-sib-bl] adj able to be mixed
misconception n (pl -s) wrong idea or belief
misconceptions n ▷ misconception
misconduct n (pl -s) immoral or unethical behaviour
misconducts n ▷ misconduct
miscreant [**miss**-kree-ant] n (pl -s) wrongdoer
miscreants n ▷ miscreant
misdeed n (pl -s) wrongful act
misdeeds n ▷ misdeed
misdemeanour n (pl -s) minor wrongdoing
misdemeanours n ▷ misdemeanour
miser n (pl -s) person who hoards money and hates spending it > **miserly** adj
miserable adj very unhappy, wretched
miseries adj ▷ misery
miserly adj ▷ miser
misers n ▷ miser
misery n (pl -ries) great unhappiness
misfire v (-res, -ring, -red) (of a firearm or engine) fail to fire correctly
misfired v ▷ misfire
misfires n ▷ misfire
misfiring v ▷ misfire
misfit n (pl -s) person not suited to his or her social environment

misfits n ▷ misfit
misfortune n (pl -s) (piece of) bad luck
  misfortunes n ▷ misfortune
misgiving n (pl -s) feeling of fear or doubt
  misgivings n ▷ misgiving
misguided adj mistaken or unwise
mishandle v (-les, -ling, -led) handle badly or inefficiently
  mishandled v ▷ mishandle
  mishandles v ▷ mishandle
  mishandling v ▷ mishandle
mishap n (pl -s) minor accident
  mishaps n ▷ mishap
misinform v (-s, -ing, -ed) give incorrect information to ▷ **misinformation** n (pl -s)
  misinformation n ▷ misinform
  misinformations n ▷ misinform
  misinformed v ▷ misinform
  misinforming v ▷ misinform
  misinforms v ▷ misinform
misjudge v (-ges, -ging, -ged) judge wrongly or unfairly ▷ **misjudgment, misjudgement** n (pl -s)
  misjudged v ▷ misjudge
  misjudgement n ▷ misjudge
  misjudges v ▷ misjudge
  misjudging v ▷ misjudge
  misjudgment n ▷ misjudge
mislaid v ▷ mislay
mislay v (-s, -ing, -laid) lose (something) temporarily
  mislaying v ▷ mislay
  mislays v ▷ mislay
mislead v (-s, -ing, -led) give false or confusing information to ▷ **misleading** adj
  misleading v, adj ▷ mislead
  misleads v ▷ mislead
  misled v ▷ mislead
mismanage v (-ges, -ging, -ged) organize or run (something) badly ▷ **mismanagement** n (pl -s)
  mismanaged v ▷ mismanage
  mismanagement n ▷ mismanage
  mismanagements n ▷ mismanage
  mismanages v ▷ mismanage
  mismanaging v ▷ mismanage
misnomer [miss-no-mer] n (pl -s) incorrect or unsuitable name
  misnomers n ▷ misnomer
misogyny [miss-oj-in-ee] n (pl -nies) hatred of women ▷ **misogynist** n (pl -s)
  misogynies n ▷ misogyny
  misogynist n ▷ misogyny
  misogynists n ▷ misogyny
misplace v (-ces, -cing, -ced) mislay

misplaced v ▷ misplace
misplaces v ▷ misplace
misplacing v ▷ misplace
misprint n (pl -s) printing error
  misprints n ▷ misprint
misrepresent v (-s, -ing, -ed) represent wrongly or inaccurately
  misrepresented v ▷ misrepresent
  misrepresenting v ▷ misrepresent
  misrepresents v ▷ misrepresent
miss v (-es, -ing, -ed) fail to notice, hear, hit, reach, find, or catch ▶ n (pl -es) fact or instance of missing
  missed v ▷ miss
  misses v, n ▷ miss
missing adj lost or absent ▶ v ▷ miss
missal n (pl -s) book containing the prayers and rites of the Mass
  missals n ▷ missal
misshapen adj badly shaped, deformed
missile n (pl -s) object or weapon thrown, shot, or launched at a target
  missiles n ▷ missile
mission n (pl -s) specific task or duty
  missionaries n ▷ mission
missionary n (pl -ries) person sent abroad to do religious and social work
  missions n ▷ mission
missive n (pl -s) letter
  missives n ▷ missive
misspent adj wasted or misused
mist n (pl -s) thin fog
  mists n ▷ mist
mistake n (pl -s) error or blunder ▶ v (-takes, -taking, -took, -taken) misunderstand
  mistaken v ▷ mistake
  mistakes n, v ▷ mistake
  mistaking v ▷ mistake
mister n (pl -s) an informal form of address for a man
  misters n ▷ mister
  mistier adj ▷ misty
  mistiest adj ▷ misty
mistletoe n (pl -s) evergreen plant with white berries growing as a parasite on trees
  mistletoes n ▷ mistletoe
  mistook v ▷ mistake
mistral n (pl -s) strong dry northerly wind of S France
  mistrals n ▷ mistral
mistress n (pl -es) woman who has a continuing sexual relationship with a married man
  mistresses n ▷ mistress
mistrial n (pl -s) (LAW) trial made void because

of some error

mistrials n ▷ mistrial

mistrust v (-s, -ing, -ed) have doubts or suspicions about ▶ n (pl -s) lack of trust > **mistrustful** adj

mistrusted v ▷ mistrust

mistrustful adj ▷ mistrust

mistrusting v ▷ mistrust

mistrusts v, n ▷ mistrust

misty adj full of mist

misunderstand v (-stands, -standing, -stood) fail to understand properly > **misunderstanding** n (pl -s)

misunderstanding v, n ▷ misunderstand

misunderstandings n ▷ misunderstand

misunderstands v ▷ misunderstand

misunderstood v ▷ misunderstand

misuse n (pl -s) incorrect, improper, or careless use ▶ v (-ses, -sing, -sed) use wrongly

misused v ▷ misuse

misuses n, v ▷ misuse

misusing v ▷ misuse

mite n (pl -s) very small spider-like animal

mites n ▷ mite

mitigate v (-tes, -ting, -ted) make less severe > **mitigation** n (pl -s)

mitigated v ▷ mitigate

mitigating v ▷ mitigate

mitigates v ▷ mitigate

mitigation n ▷ mitigate

mitigations n ▷ mitigate

mitre [my-ter] n (pl -s) bishop's pointed headdress ▶ v (-res, -ring, -red) join with a mitre joint

mitred v ▷ mitre

mitres n, v ▷ mitre

mitring v ▷ mitre

mitt n (pl -s) baseball catcher's glove

mitts n ▷ mitt

mitten n (pl -s) glove with one section for the thumb and one for the four fingers together

mittens n ▷ mitten

mix v (-es, -ing, -ed) combine or blend into one mass ▶ n (pl -es) mixture > **mixed** adj > **mixup** n (pl -s) > **mixer** n (pl -s)

mixed v, adj ▷ mix

mixer n ▷ mix

mixers n ▷ mix

mixes v, n ▷ mix

mixing v ▷ mix

mixture n (pl -s) something mixed

mixtures n ▷ mixture

mixup n ▷ mix

mixups n ▷ mix

▓▓ **miz** n (mizzes). Miz is an informal short

form of **misery.** This is a useful word, giving a high score for three letters. Remember that you'll need a blank tile for the second Z if you want to form the plural. Miz scores 14 points.

mizzenmast n (pl -s) (on a vessel with three or more masts) third mast from the bow

mizzenmasts n ▷ mizzenmast

▓▓ **mm** interj. Mm is a sound that people make to express satisfaction. This two-letter word with no vowels can be very handy when forming several words at once. Mm scores 6 points.

mnemonic [nim-on-ik] n (pl -s) ▶ adj (something, such as a rhyme) intended to help the memory

mnemonics n ▷ mnemonic

▓▓ **mo** n (mos). Mo is an informal short form of **moment.** This word can come in handy when you are trying to play words in more than one direction at once. Mo scores 5 points.

moa n (pl -s) large extinct flightless New Zealand bird

moas n ▷ moa

moan n (pl -s) low cry of pain ▶ v (-s, -ing, -ed) make or utter with a moan

moaned v ▷ moan

moaning v ▷ moan

moans n, v ▷ moan

moat n (pl -s) deep wide ditch, esp. round a castle

moats n ▷ moat

mob n (pl -s) disorderly crowd ▶ v (-s, -bbing, -bbed) surround in a mob to acclaim or attack

mobbed v ▷ mob

mobbing v ▷ mob

mobs n, v ▷ mob

mobile adj able to move ▶ n (pl -s) hanging structure designed to move in air currents > **mobility** n (pl -ties)

mobiles n ▷ mobile

mobilities n ▷ mobile

mobility n ▷ mobile

mobilization n ▷ mobilize

mobilizations n ▷ mobilize

mobilize v (-zes, -zing, -zed) (of the armed services) prepare for active service > **mobilization** n (pl -s)

mobilized v ▷ mobilize

mobilizes v ▷ mobilize

mobilizing v ▷ mobilize

moccasin n (pl -s) soft leather shoe

moccasins n ▷ moccasin

mocha [mock-a] n (pl -s) kind of strong dark

coffee

mochas n ▷ mocha

mock v (-s, -ing, -ed) make fun of ▶ adj sham or imitation

mocked v ▷ mock

mockeries n ▷ mockery

mockery n (pl -ries) derision

mocking v ▷ mock

mockingbird n (pl -s) N American bird which imitates other birds' songs

mockingbirds n ▷ mockingbird

mocks pl n (Informal) (in England and Wales) practice exams taken before public exams ▶ v ▷ mock

mock-up n (pl -s) full-scale model for test or study

mock-ups n ▷ mock-up

mode n (pl -s) method or manner

modes n ▷ mode

model n (pl -s) (miniature) representation ▶ v (-s, -elling, -elled) make a model of

modelled n ▷ model

modelling n ▷ model

models n ▷ model

modem [mode-em] n (pl -s) device for connecting two computers by a telephone line

modems n ▷ modem

moderate adj not extreme ▶ n (pl -s) person of moderate views ▶ v (-tes, -ting, -ted) make or become less violent or extreme > **moderately** adv > **moderation** (pl -s) n

moderated v ▷ moderate

moderately adv ▷ moderate

moderates n, v ▷ moderate

moderating v ▷ moderate

moderation n ▷ moderate

moderations n ▷ moderate

moderator n (pl -s) (Presbyterian Church) minister appointed to preside over a Church court, general assembly, etc.

moderators n ▷ moderate

modern adj (-er, -est) of present or recent times > **modernity** n (pl -ties)

moderner adj ▷ modern

modernest adj ▷ modern

modernism n (pl -s) (support of) modern tendencies, thoughts, or styles > **modernist** adj, n (pl -s)

modernisms n ▷ modern

modernisms n ▷ modern

modernist n ▷ modern

modernists n ▷ modern

modernities n ▷ modern

modernity n ▷ modern

modernization n ▷ modernize

modernizations n ▷ modernize

modernize v (-izes, -izing, -ized) bring up to date > **modernization** n (pl -s)

modest adj (-er, -est) not vain or boastful > **modestly** adv > **modesty** n (pl -s)

modester adj ▷ modest

modestest adj ▷ modest

modesties n ▷ modest

modestly adv ▷ modest

modesty n ▷ modest

modicum n (pl -s) small quantity

modicums n ▷ modicum

modify v (-fies, -fying, -fied) change slightly > **modification** n (pl -s)

modified v ▷ modify

modifier n (pl -s) word that qualifies the sense of another

modifiers n ▷ modifier

modish [mode-ish] adj in fashion

modulate v (-tes, -ting, -ted) vary in tone > **modulation** n (pl -s) > **modulator** n (pl -s)

modulated v ▷ modulate

modulates v ▷ modulate

modulating v ▷ modulate

modulation n ▷ modulate

modulations n ▷ modulate

module n (pl -s) self-contained unit, section, or component with a specific function

modules n ▷ module

mogul [moh-gl] n (pl -s) important or powerful person

moguls n ▷ mogul

mohair n (pl -s) fine hair of the Angora goat

mohairs n ▷ mohair

mohican n (pl -s) punk hairstyle with shaved sides and a stiff central strip of hair, often brightly coloured

mohicans n ▷ mohican

moieties n ▷ moieties

moiety [moy-it-ee] n (pl -ties) half

moist adj (-er, -est) slightly wet

moisten v (-s, -ing, -ed) make or become moist

moistened v ▷ moisten

moistening v ▷ moisten

moistens v ▷ moisten

moister adj ▷ moist

moistest adj ▷ moist

moisture n (pl -s) liquid diffused as vapour or condensed in drops

moistures n ▷ moisture

moisturize v (-zes, -zing, -zed) add moisture to (the skin etc.)

moisturized v ▷ moisten

moisturizes v ▷ moisten

moisturizing v ▷ **moisten**

molar n (pl -s) large back tooth used for grinding

molars n ▷ **molar**

molasses n dark syrup, a by-product of sugar refining

mole¹ n (pl -s) small dark raised spot on the skin

mole² n (pl -s) small burrowing mammal

mole³ n (pl -s) unit of amount of substance

mole⁴ n (pl -s) breakwater

molecule [mol-lik-kyool] n (pl -s) simplest freely existing chemical unit, composed of two or more atoms > **molecular** [mol-lek-yew-lar] ▶ adj

molecular adj ▷ **molecule**

molecules n ▷ **molecule**

moles n ▷ **mole¹,²,³,⁴**

molest v (-s, -ing, -ed) interfere with sexually > **molester** n (pl -s) > **molestation** n (pl -s)

molested v ▷ **molest**

molester n ▷ **molest**

molesters n ▷ **molest**

molesting v ▷ **molest**

molests v ▷ **molest**

moll n (pl -s) (Slang) gangster's female accomplice

mollified v ▷ **mollify**

mollifies v ▷ **mollify**

mollify v (-fies, -fying, -fied) pacify or soothe

mollifying v ▷ **mollify**

molls n ▷ **moll**

mollusc n (pl -s) soft-bodied, usu. hard-shelled, animal, such as a snail or oyster

molluscs n ▷ **mollusc**

mollycoddle v (-les, -ling, -led) pamper

mollycoddled v ▷ **mollycoddle**

mollycoddles v ▷ **mollycoddle**

mollycoddling v ▷ **mollycoddle**

molten adj liquefied or melted

molybdenum [mol-**lib**-din-um] n (pl -s) (CHEM) hard silvery-white metallic element

molybdenums n ▷ **molybdenum**

moment n (pl -s) short space of time

momenta n ▷ **momentum**

momentarily adv ▷ **momentary**

momentary adj lasting only a moment > **momentarily** adv

momentous [moh-**men**-tuss] adj of great significance

moments n ▷ **moment**

momentum n (pl -ta) impetus of a moving body

monarch n (pl -s) sovereign ruler of a state > **monarchical** adj

monarchical adj ▷ **monarch**

monarchies n ▷ **monarchy**

monarchist n (pl -s) supporter of monarchy

monarchists n ▷ **monarchist**

monarchs n ▷ **monarch**

monarchy n (pl -chies) government by or a state ruled by a sovereign

monasteries n ▷ **monastery**

monastery n (pl -ries) residence of a community of monks > **monasticism** n (pl -s)

monastic adj of monks, nuns, or monasteries

monasticism n ▷ **monastery**

monasticisms n ▷ **monastery**

monetarism n (pl -s) theory that inflation is caused by an increase in the money supply > **monetarist** n (pl -s) adj

monetarisms n ▷ **monetarism**

monetarist n, adj ▷ **monetarism**

monetarists n ▷ **monetarism**

monetary adj of money or currency

money n (pl -s) medium of exchange, coins or banknotes > **moneyed, monied** adj rich

moneyed adj ▷ **money**

moneys n ▷ **money**

mongoose n (pl -s) stoatlike mammal of Asia and Africa that kills snakes

mongooses n ▷ **money**

mongrel n (pl -s) animal, esp. a dog, of mixed breed ▶ adj of mixed breed or origin

mongrels n ▷ **mongrel**

monied adj ▷ **money**

monitor n (pl -s) person or device that checks, controls, warns, or keeps a record of something ▶ v (-s, -ing, -ed) watch and check on

monitored v ▷ **monitor**

monitoring v ▷ **monitor**

monitors n, v ▷ **monitor**

monk n (pl -s) member of an all-male religious community bound by vows > **monkish** adj

monkey n (pl -s) long-tailed primate ▶ v (-s, -ing, -ed) (usu. foll. by about or around) meddle or fool

monkeyed v ▷ **monkey**

monkeying v ▷ **monkey**

monkeys n, v ▷ **monkey**

monkish adj ▷ **monk**

monks n ▷ **monk**

monochrome adj (PHOTOG) black-and-white

monocle n (pl -s) eyeglass for one eye only

monocles n ▷ **monocle**

monograms n ▷ **monogamy**

monogamy n (pl -mies) custom of being married to one person at a time

monogram n (pl -s) design of combined

letters, esp. a person's initials
monograms n ▷ monogram
monograph n (pl -s) book or paper on a single
subject
monographs n ▷ monograph
monolith n (pl -s) large upright block of stone
> **monolithic** adj
monolithic n ▷ monolith
monoliths n ▷ monolith
monologue n (pl -s) long speech by one person
monologues n ▷ monologue
monomania n (pl -s) obsession with one thing
> **monomaniac** n, adj
monomaniac adj ▷ monomania
monomanias n ▷ monomania
monoplane n (pl -s) aeroplane with one pair
of wings
monoplanes n ▷ monoplane
monopolies n ▷ monopoly
monopolize v (-zes, -zing, -zed) have or take
exclusive possession of
monopolized v ▷ monopoly
monopolizes v ▷ monopoly
monopolizing v ▷ monopoly
monopoly n (pl -lies) exclusive possession of
or right to do something
monorail n (pl -s) single-rail railway
monorails n ▷ monorail
monotheism n (pl -s) belief in only one God
> **monotheistic** adj
monotheisms n ▷ monorail
monotheistic adj ▷ monotheism
monotone n (pl -s) unvaried pitch in speech or
sound > **monotony** n (pl -s)
monotones n ▷ monotone
monotonies n ▷ monotone
monotonous adj tedious due to lack of variety
> **monotonously** adv
monotonously adv ▷ monotous
monseigneur [mon-sen-**nyur**] n (pl
messeigneurs) [may-sen-**nyur**] title of French
prelates
monsieur [muss-**syur**] n (pl messieurs) [may-
syur] French title of address equivalent to
sir or Mr
monsignor n (pl -s) (RC CHURCH) title attached
to certain offices
monsignors n ▷ monsignor
monsoon n (pl -s) seasonal wind of SE Asia
monsoons n ▷ monsoon
monster n (pl -s) imaginary, usu. frightening,
beast ▸ adj huge
monsters n ▷ monster
monstrance n (pl -ces) (RC CHURCH) container
in which the consecrated Host is exposed for
adoration
monstrances n ▷ monstrance
monstrocities n ▷ monstrosity
monstrosity n (pl -ties) large ugly thing
monstrous adj unnatural or ugly
> **monstrously** adv
monstrously adv ▷ monstrous
montage [mon-**tahzh**] n (pl -s) (making of) a
picture composed from pieces of others
montages n ▷ montage
month n (pl -s) one of the twelve divisions of
the calendar year
monthlies n ▷ month
monthly adj happening or payable once
a month ▸ adv once a month ▸ n (pl -lies)
monthly magazine
months n ▷ month
monument n (pl -s) something, esp. a building
or statue, that commemorates something
monumental adj large, impressive, or lasting
> **monumentally** adv
monumentally adv ▷ monumental
monuments n ▷ monument
moo n (pl -s) long deep cry of a cow ▸ v (-s, -ing,
-ed) make this noise
mooed v ▷ moo
mooing v ▷ moo
moos n, v ▷ moo
mooch v (-es, -ing, -ed) (Slang) loiter about
aimlessly
mooched v ▷ mooch
mooches v ▷ mooch
mooching v ▷ mooch
mood¹ n (pl -s) temporary (gloomy) state of
mind
mood² n (GRAMMAR) form of a verb indicating
whether it expresses a fact, wish,
supposition, or command
moodier adj ▷ moody
moodiest adj ▷ moody
moodily adv ▷ moody
moods n ▷ mood¹,²
moody adj (-dier, -iest) sullen or gloomy
> **moodily** adv
moon n (pl -s) natural satellite of the earth ▸ v
(-s, -ing, -ed) (foll. by about or around) be idle
in a listless or dreamy way
mooned v ▷ moon
mooning v ▷ moon
moonlight n (pl -s) light from the moon ▸ v (-s,
-ing, -ed) (Informal) work at a secondary job,
esp. illegally
moonlighted v ▷ moonlight
moonlighting v ▷ moonlight
moonlights n, v ▷ moonlight

moons n, v ▷ moon

moonshine n (pl -s) (US & CANADIAN) illicitly distilled whisky

moonshines n ▷ moonshine

moonstone n (pl -s) translucent semiprecious stone

moonstones n ▷ moonstone

moonstruck adj slightly mad or odd

moor¹ n (pl -s) (BRIT) tract of open uncultivated ground covered with grass and heather

moor² v (-s, -ing, -ed) secure (a ship) with ropes etc. ▷ **mooring** n (pl -s)

moored v ▷ moor²

moorhen n (pl -s) small black water bird

moorhens n ▷ moorhen

mooring v, n ▷ moor²

moors n ▷ moor¹ ▶ v ▷ moor²

moose n large N American deer

moot adj (-er, -est) debatable ▶ v (-s, -ing, -ed) bring up for discussion

mooted v ▷ moot

mooter adj ▷ moot

mootest adj ▷ moot

mooting v ▷ moot

moots v ▷ moot

mop n (pl -s) long stick with twists of cotton or a sponge on the end, used for cleaning ▶ v (-s, -pping, -pped) clean or soak up with or as if with a mop

mope v (-pes, -ping, -ped) be gloomy and apathetic

moped n (pl -s) light motorized cycle ▶ v ▷ mope

mopeds v ▷ mope

mopes v ▷ mope

moping v ▷ mope

mopoke n (pl -s) small spotted owl of Australia and New Zealand

mopokes n ▷ mopoke

mopped v ▷ mop

mopping v ▷ mop

mops n, v ▷ mop

moraine n (pl -s) accumulated mass of debris deposited by a glacier

moraines n ▷ moraine

moral adj concerned with right and wrong conduct ▶ n (pl -s) lesson to be obtained from a story or event ▷ **morally** adv

morale [mor-**rahl**] n (pl -s) degree of confidence or hope of a person or group

morales n ▷ morale

moralist n (pl -s) person with a strong sense of right and wrong

moralists n ▷ moralist

moralities n ▷ morality

morality n (pl -ties) good moral conduct

moralize v (-zes, -zing, -zed) make moral pronouncements

moralized v ▷ moralize

moralizes v ▷ moralize

moralizing v ▷ moralize

morally adv ▷ moral

morals n ▷ moral

morass n (pl -es) marsh

morasses n ▷ morass

moratoria n ▷ moratorium

moratorium n (pl -ria, -riums) legally authorized ban or delay

moratoriums n ▷ moratorium

moray n (pl -s) large voracious eel

morays n ▷ moray

morbid adj unduly interested in death or unpleasant events

mordant adj sarcastic or scathing ▶ n (pl -s) substance used to fix dyes

mordants n ▷ mordant

more adj greater in amount or degree ▷ **much, many** ▶ adv to a greater extent ▶ pron greater or additional amount or number

moreover adv in addition to what has already been said

mores [**more**-rayz] pl n customs and conventions embodying the fundamental values of a community

morgue n (pl -s) mortuary

morgues n ▷ morgue

moribund adj without force or vitality

morn n (pl morns) (Poetic) morning

morns n ▷ morn

morning n (pl -s) part of the day before noon

mornings n ▷ morning

morocco n (pl -s) goatskin leather

moroccos n ▷ morocco

moron n (pl -s) (Informal) foolish or stupid person ▷ **moronic** adj

moronic adj ▷ moron

morons n ▷ moron

morose [mor-**rohss**] adj (-r, -st) sullen or moody

moroser adj ▷ morose

morosest adj ▷ morose

morphia n ▷ morphine

morphines n ▷ morphine

morphine, morphia n (pl -s) drug extracted from opium, used as an anaesthetic and sedative

morphological adj ▷ morphology

morphologies n ▷ morphology

morphology n (pl -gies) science of forms and structures of organisms or words ▷ **morphological** adj

morrow *n* (*pl* -**s**) (*Poetic*) next day
  morrows *n* ▷ morrow
morse *n* (*pl* -**s**) clasp or fastening
morsel *n* (*pl* -**s**) small piece, esp. of food
  morsels *n* ▷ morsel
  morses *n* ▷ morse
mortal *adj* subject to death ▶ *n* (*pl* -**s**) human being > **mortally** *adv*
  mortalities *n* ▷ mortal
mortality *n* (*pl* -**ties**) state of being mortal
  mortally *adj* ▷ mortal
  mortals *n* ▷ mortal
mortar *n* (*pl* -**s**) small cannon with a short range
mortarboard *n* (*pl* -**s**) black square academic cap
  mortarboards *n* ▷ mortarboard
  mortars *n* ▷ mortar
mortgage *n* (*pl* -**s**) conditional pledging of property, esp. a house, as security for the repayment of a loan ▶ *v* (-**ges**, -**ging**, -**ged**) pledge (property) as security thus
  mortgaged *v* ▷ mortgage
mortgagee *n* (*pl* -**s**) creditor in a mortgage
  mortgagees *n* ▷ mortgagee
  mortgages *n, v* ▷ mortgage
  mortgaging *v* ▷ mortgage
mortgagor *n* (*pl* -**s**) debtor in a mortgage
  mortgagors *n* ▷ mortgagor
mortice, mortise [more-tiss] *n* (*pl* -**s**) hole in a piece of wood or stone shaped to receive a matching projection on another piece
  mortices *n* ▷ mortice
  mortification *n* ▷ mortify
  mortifications *n* ▷ mortify
  mortified *v* ▷ mortify
  mortifies *v* ▷ mortify
mortify *v* (-**fies**, -**fying**, -**fied**) humiliate > **mortification** *n* (*pl* -**s**)
  mortifying *v* ▷ mortify
  mortise *n* ▷ mortice
  mortises *n* ▷ mortice
  mortuaries *n* ▷ mortuary
mortuary *n* (*pl* -**aries**) building where corpses are kept before burial or cremation
mosaic [mow-zay-ik] *n* (*pl* -**s**) design or decoration using small pieces of coloured stone or glass
  mosaics *n* ▷ mosaic
mosque *n* (*pl* -**s**) Muslim temple
  mosques *n* ▷ mosque
mosquito *n* (*pl* -**toes**, -**tos**) blood-sucking flying insect
  mosquitoes *n* ▷ mosquito
  mosquitos *n* ▷ mosquito

moss *n* (*pl* -**es**) small flowerless plant growing in masses on moist surfaces > **mossy** *adj* (-**ssier**, -**ssiest**)
  mosses *n* ▷ moss
  mossier *adj* ▷ moss
  mossiest *adj* ▷ moss
  mossy *adj* (-**ssier**, -**ssiest**) ▷ moss
most *n* greatest number or degree ▶ *adj* greatest in number or degree ▷ **much, many** ▶ *adv* in the greatest degree
mostly *adv* for the most part, generally
motel *n* (*pl* -**s**) roadside hotel for motorists
  motels *n* ▷ motel
motet *n* (*pl* -**s**) short sacred choral song
  motets *n* ▷ motet
moth *n* (*pl* -**s**) nocturnal insect like a butterfly
mothball *n* (*pl* -**s**) small ball of camphor or naphthalene used to repel moths from stored clothes ▶ *v* (-**balled**, -**balling**, -**ed**) store (something operational) for future use
  mothballed *v* ▷ moth
  mothballing *v* ▷ moth
  mothballs *n, v* ▷ moth
  moths *n* ▷ moth
mother *n* (*pl* -**s**) female parent ▶ *adj* native or inborn ▶ *v* (-**s**, -**ing**, -**ed**) look after as a mother > **motherhood** *n* (*pl* -**s**) > **motherly** *adj* > **motherless** *adj*
  mothered *v* ▷ mother
  motherhood *n* ▷ mother
  motherhoods *n* ▷ mother
  mothering *v* ▷ mother
  motherless *adj* ▷ mother
  motherly *adj* ▷ mother
  mothers *n, v* ▷ mother
  mothers-in-law *n* ▷ mother-in-law
motif [moh-teef] *n* (*pl* -**s**) (recurring) theme or design
  motifs *n* ▷ motif
motion *n* (*pl* -**s**) process, action, or way of moving ▶ *v* (-**s**, -**ing**, -**ed**) direct (someone) by gesture
  motioned *v* ▷ motion
  motioning *v* ▷ motion
motionless *adj* not moving
  motions *n, v* ▷ motion
motivate *v* (-**tes**, -**ting**, -**ted**) give incentive to > **motivation** *n* (*pl* -**s**)
  motivated *v* ▷ motivate
  motivates *v* ▷ motivate
  motivating *v* ▷ motivate
  motivation *n* ▷ motivate
  motivations *n* ▷ motivate
motive *n* (*pl* -**s**) reason for a course of action ▶ *adj* causing motion

motives n ▷ motive

motley adj miscellaneous

motocross n (pl -es) motorcycle race over a rough course
> motocrosses n ▷ motocross

motor n (pl -s) engine, esp. of a vehicle ▶ v (-s, -ing, -ed) travel by car > motorized adj equipped with a motor or motor transport
> motorbike n (pl -s) > motorboat n (pl -s)
> motorcar n (pl -s) > motorcycle n (pl -s)
> motorcyclist n (pl -s)

motorbike n ▷ motor

motorbikes n ▷ motor

motorboat n ▷ motor

motorboats n ▷ motor

motorcar n ▷ motor

motorcars n ▷ motor

motorcycle n ▷ motor

motorcycles n ▷ motor

motorcyclist n ▷ motor

motorcyclists n ▷ motor

motored v ▷ motor

motoring v ▷ motor

motorist n (pl -s) driver of a car

motorists n ▷ motorist

motorized adj ▷ motor

motors n, v ▷ motor

motorway n (pl -s) main road for fast-moving traffic
> motorways n ▷ motorway

mottled adj marked with blotches

motto n (pl -ttoes, -ttos) saying expressing an ideal or rule of conduct
> mottoes n ▷ motto
> mottos n ▷ motto

mould¹ n (pl -s) hollow container in which metal etc. is cast ▶ v (-s, -ing, -ed) shape

mould² n (pl -s) fungal growth caused by dampness

mould³ n (pl -s) loose soil

moulded v ▷ mould¹

moulder v (-s, -ing, -ed) decay into dust

mouldered v ▷ moulder

mouldering v ▷ moulder

moulders v ▷ moulder

mouldier adj ▷ mouldy

mouldiest adj ▷ mouldy

moulding n (pl -s) moulded ornamental edging ▶ v ▷ mould¹
> moulds n ▷ mould¹,²,³ ▶ v ▷ mould¹

mouldy adj (-dier, -diest) stale or musty; dull or boring

moult v (-s, -ing, -ed) shed feathers, hair, or skin to make way for new growth ▶ n (pl -s) process of moulting

moulted v ▷ moult

moulting v ▷ moult

moults v, n ▷ moult

mound n (pl -s) heap, esp. of earth or stones

mounds n ▷ mound

mount v (-s, -ing, -ed) climb or ascend ▶ n (pl -s) backing or support on which something is fixed

mountain n (pl -s) hill of great size
> mountainous adj full of mountains
n (pl -s) person who climbs mountains
> mountaineering n (pl -s)

mountaineer n ▷ mountaineer

mountaineerings n ▷ mountaineer

mountaineers n ▷ mountaineer

mountains n ▷ mountain

mountebank n (pl -s) charlatan or fake

mountebanks n ▷ mountebank

mounted v ▷ mount

mounting v ▷ mount

mounts v, n ▷ mount

mourn v (-s, -ing, -ed) feel or express sorrow for (a dead person or lost thing)

mourned v ▷ mourn

mourner n (pl mourners) person attending a funeral

mourners n ▷ mourner

mournful adj (-ler, -lest) sad or dismal
> mournfully adv

mournfuller adj ▷ mournful

mournfullest adj ▷ mournful

mournfully adv ▷ mournful

mourning n (pl -s) grieving ▶ v ▷ mourn

mournings n ▷ mourning

mourns v ▷ mourn

mouse n (pl mice) small long-tailed rodent

mouser n (pl -s) cat used to catch mice

mousers n ▷ mouser

mousse n (pl -s) dish of flavoured cream whipped and set

mousses n ▷ mousse

moustache n (pl -s) hair on the upper lip

moustaches n ▷ moustache

mousy adj like a mouse, esp. in hair colour

mouth n (pl -s) opening in the head for eating and issuing sounds ▶ v (-s, -ing, -ed) form (words) with the lips without sound

mouthed v ▷ mouth

mouthful n (pl -s) amount of food or drink put into the mouth at any one time when eating or drinking

mouthfuls n ▷ mouthful

mouthing v ▷ mouth

mouthpiece n (pl -s) part of a telephone into which a person speaks mouthpieces n ▷ mouthpiece

mouths n, v ▷ mouth

move v (-ves, -ving, -ved) change in place or position ▶ n (pl -s) moving > movable, moveable adj

movement n (pl -s) action or process of moving

movements n ▷ movement

moved v ▷ move

moves v, n ▷ move

movie n (pl -s) (Informal) cinema film

movies n ▷ movie

moving v ▷ move

mow v (-s, -ing, -ed or mown) cut (grass or crops)

mowed v ▷ mow

mower n (pl -s) machine for cutting grass

mowers n ▷ mower

mowing v ▷ mow

mown v ▷ mow

mows v ▷ mow

> moz n (mozes). Moz is an old Australian slang word for a jinx or hex. This is an unusual word that is worth remembering as it can be very useful if you have a Z but little chance to play it on a crowded board. Moz scores 14 points.

mozzarella [mot-sa-rel-la] n (pl -s) moist white cheese originally made in Italy from buffalo milk

mozzarellas n ▷ mozzarella

> mu n (mus). Mu is the 12th letter in the Greek alphabet. This is a useful word to remember: it won't score you many points on its own, but it can be very helpful on a crowded board when you need to form words in different directions. Mu scores 4 points.

much adj (more, most) large amount or degree of ▶ n large amount or degree ▶ adv (more, most) to a great degree

mucilage [mew-sill-ij] n (pl -s) gum or glue

mucilages n ▷ mucilage

muck n (pl -s) dirt, filth > mucky adj

mucks n ▷ mucks

mucky adj ▷ mucks

mucus [mew-kuss] n (pl -s) slimy secretion of the mucous membranes

mucuses n ▷ mucus

mud n (pl -s) wet soft earth > muddy adj

muddier adj ▷ mud

muddiest adj ▷ mud

muddy adj (-ddier, -ddiest) ▷ mud

mudguard n (pl -s) cover over a wheel to prevent mud or water being thrown up by it

mudguards n ▷ mudguard

muds n ▷ mud

muddle v (-les, -ling, -led) (often foll. by up) confuse ▶ n (pl -s) state of confusion

muddled v ▷ muddle

muddles v, n ▷ muddle

muddling v ▷ muddle

muesli [mewz-lee] n (pl -s) mixture of grain, nuts, and dried fruit, eaten with milk

mueslis n ▷ muesli

muezzin [moo-ezz-in] n (pl -s) official who summons Muslims to prayer

muezzins n ▷ muezzin

muff¹ n (pl -s) tube-shaped covering to keep the hands warm

muff² v (-s, -ing, -ed) bungle (an action)

muffed v ▷ muff

muffin n (pl -s) light round flat yeast cake

muffing v ▷ muff

muffins n ▷ muffin

muffs n ▷ muff¹ ▶ v ▷ muff²

muffle v (-les, -ling, -led) wrap up for warmth or to deaden sound

muffled v ▷ muffle

muffler n (pl -s) (BRIT) scarf

mufflers n ▷ muffle

muffles v ▷ muffle

muffling v ▷ muffle

mufti n (pl -s) civilian clothes worn by a person who usually wears a uniform

muftis n ▷ mufti

mug¹ n (pl -s) large drinking cup

mug² n (pl -s) (Slang) face ▶ v (-s, -gging, -gged) (Informal) attack in order to rob > mugger n (pl -s)

mug³ v (-s, -gging, -gged) (foll. by up) (Informal) study hard

mugged v ▷ mug²,³

mugger v ▷ mug²

muggers v ▷ mug²

muggier adj ▷ muggy

muggiest adj ▷ muggy

mugging v ▷ mug²,³

muggins n (Informal) stupid or gullible person

muggy adj (-ggier, -ggiest) (of weather) damp and stifling

mugs n ▷ mug¹,²

mulatto [mew-lat-toe] n (pl -tos, -toes) child of one Black and one White parent

mulattoes adj ▷ mulatto

mulattos adj ▷ mulatto

mulberries n ▷ mulberry

mulberry n (pl -rries) tree whose leaves are used to feed silkworms

mulch n (pl -es) mixture of wet straw, leaves, etc., used to protect the roots of plants ▸ v (-es, -ing, -ed) cover (land) with mulch
mulched v ▷ mulch
mulches n, v ▷ mulch
mulching v ▷ mulch
mule[1] n (pl -s) offspring of a horse and a donkey > **mulish** adj obstinate
mule[2] n backless shoe or slipper
mules n ▷ mule[1,2]
mulga n (pl -s) Australian acacia shrub growing in desert regions
mulgas n ▷ mulga
mulish adj ▷ mule[1]
mull v (-s, -ing, -ed) think (over) or ponder > **mulled** adj (of wine or ale) flavoured with sugar and spices and served hot
mullah n (pl -s) Muslim scholar, teacher, or religious leader
mullahs n ▷ mullah
mulled v, adj ▷ mull
mullet[1] n (pl -s) edible sea fish
mullet[2] n (pl -s) haircut in which the hair is short at the top and sides and long at the back
mullets n ▷ mullet[1,2]
mulling v ▷ mull
mulls v ▷ mull
mulligatawnies n ▷ mulligatawny
mulligatawny n (pl -nies) soup made with curry powder
mullion n (pl -s) vertical dividing bar in a window > **mullioned** adj
mullioned adj ▷ mullion
mullions n ▷ mullion
mulloway n (pl -s) large Australian sea fish, valued for sport and food
mulloways n ▷ mulloway
multifarious [mull-tee-**fare**-ee-uss] adj having many various parts
multiple adj having many parts ▸ n (pl -s) quantity which contains another an exact number of times
multiples n ▷ multiple
multiplex n (pl -es) purpose-built complex containing several cinemas and usu. restaurants and bars ▸ adj having many elements, complex
multiplexes n ▷ multiplex
multiplicities n ▷ multiplicity
multiplicity n (pl -ties) large number or great variety
multiply v (-lies, -lying, -lied) (cause to) increase in number, quantity, or degree > **multiplication** n (pl -s)

multiplicand n (pl -s) (MATHS) number to be multiplied
multiplicands n ▷ multiplicand
multiplication n ▷ multiply
multiplications n ▷ multiply
multiplied v ▷ multiply
multiplies v ▷ multiply
multiplying v ▷ multiply
multipurpose adj having many uses
multitude n (pl -s) great number
multitudes n ▷ multitude
multitudinous adj very numerous
mum n (pl -s) (Informal) mother
mums n ▷ mum
mumble v (-les, -ling, -led) speak indistinctly, mutter
mumbled v ▷ mumble
mumbles v ▷ mumble
mumbling v ▷ mumble
mummer n (pl -s) actor in a traditional English folk play or mime
mummers n ▷ mummer
mummies n ▷ mummer
mummified adj (of a body) preserved as a mummy
mummy[1] n (pl -mmies) body embalmed and wrapped for burial in ancient Egypt
mummy[2] n (pl -mmies) ▷ mother
mumps n infectious disease with swelling in the glands of the neck
munch v (-es, -ing, -ed) chew noisily and steadily
munched v ▷ munch
munches v ▷ munch
munching v ▷ munch
mundane adj everyday
municipal adj relating to a city or town
municipalities n ▷ municipality
municipality n (pl -ties) city or town with local self-government
munificence n ▷ munificent
munificences n ▷ munificent
munificent [mew-**niff**-fiss-sent] adj very generous > **munificence** n (pl -s)
muniments pl n title deeds or similar documents
munitions pl n military stores
munted adj (NZ) (Slang) destroyed or ruined
mural n (pl -s) painting on a wall
murals n ▷ mural
murder n (pl -s) unlawful intentional killing of a human being ▸ v (-s, -ing, -ed) kill in this way > **murderer, murderess** n (pl -s) > **murderous** adj
murdered v ▷ murder

murderer n ▷ murder
murderers n ▷ murder
murderess n ▷ murder
murderesses n ▷ murder
murdering v ▷ murder
murderous adj ▷ murder
murders v, n ▷ murder
murk n (pl -s) thick darkness
murkier adj ▷ murky
murkiest adj ▷ murky
murks n ▷ murk
murky adj (-kier, -kiest) dark or gloomy
murmur v (-s, -ing, -ed) speak or say in a quiet
  indistinct way ▶ n (pl -s) continuous low
  indistinct sound
murmured v ▷ murmur
murmuring v ▷ murmur
murmurs v, n ▷ murmur
muscle n (pl -s) tissue in the body which
  produces movement by contracting
muscles n ▷ muscle
muscular adj with well-developed muscles
muse v (-ses, -sing, -sed) ponder quietly
mused v ▷ muse
musing v ▷ muse
muses v ▷ muse
museum n (pl -s) building where natural,
  artistic, historical, or scientific objects are
  exhibited and preserved
museums n ▷ museum
mush n (pl -es) soft pulpy mass > **mushy** adj
  (-shier, -shiest)
mushes n ▷ mush
mushier adj ▷ mush
mushiest adj ▷ mush
mushroom n (pl -s) edible fungus with a stem
  and cap ▶ v (-s, -ing, -ed) grow rapidly
mushroomed v ▷ mushroom
mushrooming v ▷ mushroom
mushrooms n, v ▷ mushroom
mushy (-shier, -shiest) adj ▷ mush
music n (pl -s) art form using a melodious
  and harmonious combination of notes ▶ n
  (pl -s) play or film with songs and dancing
  > **musician** n (pl -s)
musical adj of or like music > **musically** adv
musically adv ▷ musical
musician n ▷ music
musicians n ▷ music
musicologies n ▷ musicology
musicologist n ▷ musicology
musicologists n ▷ musicology
musicology n (pl -gies) scientific study of
  music > **musicologist** n (pl -s)
musics n ▷ music

musk n (pl -s) scent obtained from a gland
  of the musk deer or produced synthetically
  > **musky** adj (-kier, -kiest)
musket n (pl -s) (HIST) long-barrelled gun
  > **musketeer** n (pl -s)
musketeer n ▷ musket
musketeers n ▷ musket
musketries n ▷ musketry
musketry n (pl -ries) (use of) muskets
muskets n ▷ musket
muskier adj ▷ musk
muskiest adj ▷ musk
muskrat n (pl -s) N American beaver-like
  rodent
muskrats n ▷ muskrat
musks n ▷ musk
musky adj (-kier, -kiest) ▷ musk
muslin n (pl -s) fine cotton fabric
muslins n ▷ muslin
mussel n (pl -s) edible shellfish with a dark
  hinged shell
mussels n ▷ mussel
must¹ v used as an auxiliary to express
  obligation, certainty, or resolution ▶ n (pl -s)
  essential or necessary thing
must² n (pl -s) newly pressed grape juice
musts n ▷ must¹,²
mustang n (pl -s) wild horse of SW USA
mustangs n ▷ mustang
mustard n (pl -s) paste made from the
  powdered seeds of a plant, used as a
  condiment
mustards n ▷ mustard
muster v (-s, -ing, -ed) assemble ▶ n (pl -s)
  assembly of military personnel
mustered v ▷ muster
mustering v ▷ muster
musters v, n ▷ muster
mustier adj ▷ musty
mustiest adj ▷ musty
mustiness n ▷ musty
mustinesses n ▷ musty
musty adj (mustier, mustiest) smelling
  mouldy and stale > **mustiness** n (pl -es)
mutabilities n ▷ mutable
mutability n ▷ mutable
mutable [mew-tab-bl] adj liable to change
  > **mutability** n (pl -ties)
mutant n (pl -s) mutated animal, plant, etc.
mutants n ▷ mutant
mutate v (-tes, -ting, -ted) (cause to) undergo
  mutation
mutated v ▷ mutate
mutates v ▷ mutate
mutating v ▷ mutate

mutation *n* (*pl* -s) (genetic) change
mutations *n* ▷ mutation
mute *adj* (-r, -st) silent ▶ *n* (*pl* -s) person who is
unable to speak > mutely *adv*
muted *adj* (of sound or colour) softened
mutely *adv* ▷ mute
muter *adj* ▷ mute
mutes *n* ▷ mute
mutest *adj* ▷ mute
muti [moo-ti] *n* (*pl* -s) (S AFR) (Informal) medicine,
esp. herbal medicine
mutis *n* ▷ muti
mutilate [mew-till-ate] *v* (-tes, -ting, -ted)
deprive of a limb or other part > mutilation
n (*pl* -s)
mutilated *v* ▷ mutilate
mutilates *v* ▷ mutilate
mutilating *v* ▷ mutilate
mutilation *n* ▷ mutilate
mutilations *n* ▷ mutilate
mutineer *n* ▷ mutiny
mutineers *n* ▷ mutiny
mutinied *v* ▷ mutiny
mutinies *v* ▷ mutiny
mutinous *n* ▷ mutiny
mutiny [mew-tin-ee] *n* (*pl* -nies) rebellion
against authority, esp. by soldiers or sailors
▶ *v* (-nies, -nying, -nied) commit mutiny
> mutineer *n* (*pl* -s) > mutinous *adj*
mutinying *v* ▷ mutiny
mutt *n* (*pl* -s) (Slang) mongrel dog
mutts *n* ▷ mutt
mutter *v* (-s, -ing, -ed) utter or speak
indistinctly ▶ *n* (*pl* -s) muttered sound or
grumble
muttered *v* ▷ mutter
muttering *v* ▷ mutter
mutters *v, n* ▷ mutter
mutton *n* (*pl* -s) flesh of sheep, used as food
muttons *n* ▷ mutton
mutual [mew-chew-al] *adj* felt or expressed
by each of two people about the other
> mutually *adv*
mutually *adv* ▷ mutual

mux *v* (muxes, muxing, muxed). Mux
is an old American word meaning
to make a mess of something. This
word is very useful not only because
it contains an X, but because its verb
forms can enable you to clear your rack
of unpromising letters. Mux scores
12 points.

muzjik *n* (muzjiks). A muzjik is a
Russian peasant. This is a great high-
scoring word, combining Z, J and K. If

you can play the plural using all of your
tiles, you'll get a bonus of 50 points.
Muzjik scores 28 points.

muzzle *n* (*pl* -s) animal's mouth and nose ▶ *v*
(-les, -ling, -led) prevent from being heard
or noticed
muzzled *v* ▷ muzzle
muzzles *n, v* ▷ muzzle
muzzling *v* ▷ muzzle
muzzy *adj* (-zzier, -zziest) confused or muddled
my *adj* belonging to me
myall *n* (*pl* -s) Australian acacia with hard
scented wood
myalls *n* ▷ myall
mycology *n* (*pl* -gies) study of fungi
mycologies *n* ▷ mycology
myna, mynah, mina *n* (*pl* -s) Asian bird which
can mimic human speech
mynah *n* ▷ myna
mynahs *n* ▷ myna
mynas *n* ▷ myna
myopia [my-oh-pee-a] *n* (*pl* -s) short-
sightedness > myopic [my-op-ik] ▶ *adj*
myopias *n* ▷ myopia
myopic *adj* ▷ myopia
myriad [mir-ree-ad] *adj* innumerable ▶ *n* (*pl* -s)
large indefinite number
myriads *n* ▷ myriad
myrrh [mur] *n* (*pl* -s) aromatic gum used in
perfume, incense, and medicine
myrrhs *n* ▷ myrrh
myrtle [mur-tl] *n* (*pl* -s) flowering evergreen
shrub
myrtles *n* ▷ myrtle
myself *pron* ▷ I
mysteries *n* ▷ mystery
mysterious *adj* ▷ mystery
mysteriously *adv* ▷ mystery
mystery *n* (*pl* -ries) strange or inexplicable
event or phenomenon > mysterious *adj*
> mysteriously *adv*
mystic *n* (*pl* -s) person who seeks spiritual
knowledge ▶ *adj* mystical > mysticism *n* (*pl* -s)
mystical *adj* having a spiritual or religious
significance beyond human understanding
mysticism *n* ▷ mystic
mysticisms *n* ▷ mystic
mystics *n* ▷ mystic
mystification *v* ▷ mystify
mystifications *v* ▷ mystify
mystified *v* ▷ mystify
mystifies *v* ▷ mystify
mystify *v* (-fies, -fying, -fied) bewilder or
puzzle > mystification *n* (*pl* -s)
mystifying *v* ▷ mystify

mystique [miss-**steek**] *n* (*pl* -**s**) aura of mystery or power
mystiques *n* ▷ **mystique**
myth *n* (*pl* -**s**) tale with supernatural characters, usu. of how the world and mankind began > **mythical, mythic** *adj*
mythic *adj* ▷ **myth**
mythical *adj* ▷ **myth**

mythological *adj* ▷ **mythology**
mythologies *n* ▷ **mythology**
mythology *n* (*pl* -**gies**) myths collectively
  > **mythological** *adj*
myths *n* ▷ **myth**
myxomatoses *n* ▷ **myxomatosis**
myxomatosis [mix-a-mat-**oh**-siss] *n* (*pl* -**ses**) contagious fatal viral disease of rabbits

N n

Along with R and T, N is one of the most common consonants in Scrabble. As you'll often have it on your rack, it's well worth learning what N can do in different situations. N is useful when you need short words, as it begins two-letter words with every vowel except I, and with Y as well. There are plenty of three-letter words starting with N, but there aren't many high-scoring ones. Remember words like **nab** (5 points), **nag** (4), **nap** (5), **nay** (6), **new** (6), **nib** (5), **nob** (5), **nod** (4) and **now** (6).

na *interj*. Na is a Scots word for **no** or **not**. This word can be very convenient when you need to form words in different directions. Na scores 2 points.

naan *n* (*pl* -s) ▷ **nan bread**
  naans *n* ▷ **naan**
naartjie [nahr-chee] *n* (*pl* -s) (S AFR) tangerine
  naartjies *n* ▷ **naartjie**
nab *v* (-s, -bbing, -bbed) (*Informal*) arrest (someone)
  nabbed *v* ▷ **nab**
  nabbing *v* ▷ **nab**
  nabs *v* ▷ **nab**
nadir *n* (*pl* -s) point in the sky opposite the zenith
  nadirs *n* ▷ **nadir**
  naevi *n* ▷ **naevus**
naevus [nee-vuss] *n* (*pl* -vi) birthmark or mole
naff *adj* (-er, -est) (BRIT) (*Slang*) lacking quality or taste
  naffer *adj* ▷ **naff**
  naffest *adj* ▷ **naff**
nag¹ *v* (-s, -gging, -gged) scold or find fault constantly ▶ *n* (*pl* -s) person who nags
  > **nagging** *adj*, *n* (*pl* -s)
nag² *n* (*pl* -s) (*Informal*) old horse
  nagged *v* ▷ **nag**¹
nagging *v*, *adj n* ▷ **nag**¹
  naggings *n* ▷ **nag**¹
  nags *v* ▷ **nag**¹ ▶ *n* ▷ **nag**¹,²
naiad [nye-ad] *n* (*pl* -s) (GREEK MYTH) nymph living in a lake or river
  naiads *n* ▷ **naiad**
nail *n* (*pl* -s) pointed piece of metal with a head, hit with a hammer to join two objects together ▶ *v* (-s, -ing, -ed) attach (something) with nails

nailed *v* ▷ **nail**
nailing *v* ▷ **nail**
nails *n*, *v* ▷ **nail**
naive [nye-eev] *adj* (-r, -st) innocent and gullible > **naively** *adv* > **naivety** [nye-eev-tee] *n* (*pl* -ties), **naïveté** (*pl* -s)
  naively *adv* ▷ **naive**
  naiver *adj* ▷ **naive**
  naivest *adj* ▷ **naive**
  naïveté *n* ▷ **naive**
  naïvetés *n* ▷ **naive**
  naiveties *n* ▷ **naive**
  naivety *n* ▷ **naive**
naked *adj* (-er, -est) without clothes > **nakedness** *n* (*pl* -es)
  nakeder *adj* ▷ **naked**
  nakedest *adj* ▷ **naked**
  nakedness *n* ▷ **naked**
  nakednesses *n* ▷ **naked**
name *n* (*pl* -s) word by which a person or thing is known ▶ *v* (-mes, -ming, -med) give a name to
  named *v* ▷ **name**
nameless *adj* without a name
namely *adv* that is to say
  names *n*, *v* ▷ **name**
namesake *n* (*pl* -s) person with the same name as another
  namesakes *n* ▷ **namely**
  naming *v* ▷ **name**
  nannies *n* ▷ **nanny**
nanny *n* (*pl* -nnies) woman whose job is looking after young children
nap¹ *n* (*pl* -s) short sleep ▶ *v* (-s, -pping, -pped) have a short sleep
nap² *n* (*pl* -s) raised fibres of velvet or similar cloth

nap³ n (pl **-s**) card game similar to whist
napalm n (pl **-s**) highly inflammable jellied
 petrol, used in bombs
 napalms n ▷ napalm
nape n (pl **-s**) back of the neck
 napes n ▷ nape
naphtha n (pl **-s**) liquid mixture distilled from
 coal tar or petroleum, used as a solvent and
 in petrol
naphthalene n (pl **-s**) white crystalline
 product distilled from coal tar or petroleum,
 used in disinfectants, mothballs, and
 explosives
 naphthalenes n ▷ naphthalene
 naphthas n ▷ naphtha
napkin n (pl **-s**) piece of cloth or paper for
 wiping the mouth or protecting the clothes
 while eating
 napkins n ▷ napkin
 napped v ▷ nap¹
 nappies n ▷ nappy
 napping v ▷ nap¹
nappy n (pl **-ppies**) piece of absorbent material
 fastened round a baby's lower torso to absorb
 urine and faeces
 naps n ▷ nap¹ ▶ v ▷ nap¹
narcissism n (pl **-s**) exceptional interest in or
 admiration for oneself > **narcissistic** adj
 narcissisms n ▷ narcissism
 narcissistic adj ▷ narcissism
 narcissi n ▷ narcissus
narcissus n (pl **-cissi**) yellow, orange, or white
 flower related to the daffodil
 narcoses n ▷ narcosis
narcosis n (pl **-ses**) effect of a narcotic
narcotic n (pl **-s**) ▶ adj (of) a drug, such as
 morphine or opium, which produces
 numbness and drowsiness, used medicinally
 but addictive
 narcotics n ▷ narcotic
nark (Slang) v (**-s, -ing, -ed**) annoy ▶ n (pl **-s**)
 informer or spy
 narked v ▷ nark
 narkier adj ▷ narky
 narkiest adj ▷ narky
 narking v ▷ nark
 narks v, n ▷ nark
narky adj (Slang) (**-kier, -kiest**) irritable or
 complaining
narrate v (**-tes, -ting, -ted**) tell (a story)
 > **narration** n (pl **-s**) > **narrator** n (pl **-s**)
 narrated v ▷ narrate
 narrates v ▷ narrate
 narrating v ▷ narrate
 narration n ▷ narrate

 narrations n ▷ narrate
narrative n (pl **-s**) account, story
 narratives n ▷ narrative
 narrator n ▷ narrate
 narrators n ▷ narrate
narrow adj (**-er, -est**) small in breadth in
 comparison to length ▶ v (**-s, -ing, -ed**)
 make or become narrow > **narrowly** adv
 > **narrowness** n (pl **-es**)
 narrowed v ▷ narrow
 narrower adj ▷ narrow
 narrowest adj ▷ narrow
 narrowing v ▷ narrow
 narrowly adv ▷ narrow
 narrowness n ▷ narrow
 narrownesses n ▷ narrow
 narrows v ▷ narrow ▶ pl n narrow part of a
 strait, river, or current
narwhal n (pl **-s**) arctic whale with a long
 spiral tusk
 narwhals n ▷ narwhal
nasal adj of the nose > **nasally** adv
 nasally adv ▷ nasal
nascent adj starting to grow or develop
 nastier adj ▷ nasty
 nastiest adj ▷ nasty
 nastily adv ▷ nasty
 nastiness n ▷ nasty
 nastinesses n ▷ nasty
nasturtium n (pl **-s**) plant with yellow, red, or
 orange trumpet-shaped flowers
 nasturtiums n ▷ nasturtium
nasty adj (**-tier, -tiest**) unpleasant > **nastily** adv
 > **nastiness** n (pl **-es**)
natal adj of or relating to birth
nation n (pl **nations**) people of one or more
 cultures or races organized as a single state
 nations n ▷ nation
national adj characteristic of a particular
 nation ▶ n (pl **-s**) citizen of a nation
 > **nationally** adv
nationalism n (pl **-s**) policy of national
 independence > **nationalist** n (pl **-s**) adj
 nationalisms n ▷ nationalism
 nationalist n ▷ nationalism
 nationalists n ▷ nationalism
 nationalities n ▷ nationality
nationality n (pl **-ties**) fact of being a citizen of
 a particular nation
 nationalization n ▷ nationalize
 nationalizations n ▷ nationalize
nationalize v (**-izes, -izing, -ized**) put (an
 industry or a company) under state control
 > **nationalization** n (pl **-s**)
 nationalized v ▷ nationalize

nationalizes v ▷ nationalize

nationalizing v ▷ nationalize

nationally adv ▷ national

nationals n ▷ national

native adj relating to a place where a person was born ▸ n (pl -s) person born in a specified place

natives n ▷ native

nativities n ▷ nativity

nativity n (pl -ties) birth or origin

natter (Informal) v (-s, -ing, -ed) talk idly or chatter ▸ n (pl -s) long idle chat

nattered v ▷ natter

nattering v ▷ natter

natters v, n ▷ natter

nattier adj ▷ natty

nattiest adj ▷ natty

natty adj (-tier, -ttiest) (Informal) smart and spruce

natural adj normal or to be expected ▸ n (pl -s) person with an inborn talent or skill

naturalism n (pl -s) movement in art and literature advocating detailed realism > naturalistic adj

naturalisms n ▷ naturalism

naturalist n (pl -s) student of natural history

naturalistic n ▷ naturalism

naturalists n ▷ naturalist

naturalization n ▷ naturalize

naturalizations n ▷ naturalize

naturalize v (-izes, -izing, -ized) give citizenship to (a person born in another country) > naturalization n (pl -s)

naturalized v ▷ naturalize

naturalizes v ▷ naturalize

naturalizing v ▷ naturalize

naturally adv of course

naturals n ▷ natural

nature n (pl -s) whole system of the existence, forces, and events of the physical world that are not controlled by human beings

natures n ▷ nature

naturism n (pl -s) nudism > naturist n (pl -s)

naturisms n ▷ naturism

naturist n ▷ naturism

naturists n ▷ naturism

naught n (pl -s) (Lit) nothing

naughtier adj ▷ naughty

naughtiest adj ▷ naughty

naughtily adv ▷ naughty

naughtiness n ▷ naughty

naughtinesses n ▷ naughty

naughts n ▷ naught

naughty adj (-tier, -tiest) disobedient or mischievous > naughtily adv > naughtiness

n (pl -es)

nausea [naw-zee-a] n (pl -s) feeling of being about to vomit

nauseas n ▷ nausea

nauseate v (-tes, -ting, -ted) make (someone) feel sick

nauseated v ▷ nauseate

nauseates v ▷ nauseate

nauseating v ▷ nauseate

nauseous adj as if about to vomit

nautical adj of the sea or ships

nautili n ▷ nautilus

nautilus n (pl -luses, -li) shellfish with many tentacles

nautiluses n ▷ nautilus

naval adj ▷ navy

nave n (pl -s) long central part of a church

navel n (pl -s) hollow in the middle of the abdomen where the umbilical cord was attached

navels n ▷ navel

naves n ▷ nave

navies n ▷ navy

navigable adj wide, deep, or safe enough to be sailed through

navigate v (-tes, -ting, -ted) direct or plot the path or position of a ship, aircraft, or car > navigation n (pl -s) > navigator n (pl -s)

navigated v ▷ navigate

navigates v ▷ navigate

navigating v ▷ navigate

navigation n ▷ navigate

navigations n ▷ navigate

navigator n ▷ navigate

navigators n ▷ navigate

navvies n ▷ navvy

navvy n (pl -vvies) (BRIT) labourer employed on a road or a building site

navy n (pl -vies) branch of a country's armed services comprising warships with their crews and organization

nay interj (Obs) no

> **ne** adv. Ne is an old word meaning **not**. This handy little word can be very helpful when you are trying to form several words at once. Ne scores 2 points.

neanderthal [nee-ann-der-tahl] adj of a type of primitive man that lived in Europe before 12 000 BC

near prep, adv adj (-er, -est) indicating a place or time not far away ▸ adj almost being the thing specified ▸ v (-s, -ing, -ed) draw close (to) > nearness n (pl -es)

nearby adj not far away

neared v ▷ near
nearer adj ▷ near
nearest adj ▷ near
nearing v ▷ near
nearly adv almost
nearness n ▷ near
nearnesses n ▷ near
nears v ▷ near
nearside n (pl -s) side of a vehicle that is nearer the kerb
nearsides n ▷ nearside
neat adj (-er, -est) tidy and clean > **neatly** adv > **neatness** n (pl -es)
neater adj ▷ neat
neatest adj ▷ neat
neatly adv ▷ neat
neatness n ▷ neat
neatnesses n ▷ neat
nebula n (pl -lae) (ASTRONOMY) hazy cloud of particles and gases > **nebulous** adj vague and unclear
nebulae n ▷ nebula
nebulous adj ▷ nebula
necessarily adv ▷ necessary
necessary adj needed to obtain the desired result > **necessarily** adv
necessitate v (-tes, -ting, -ted) compel or require
necessitated v ▷ necessitate
necessitates v ▷ necessitate
necessitating v ▷ necessitate
necessities n ▷ necessity
necessity n (pl -ties) circumstances that inevitably require a certain result
neck n (pl -s) part of the body joining the head to the shoulders ▶ v (-s, -ing, -ed) (Slang) kiss and cuddle
necked v ▷ neck
neckerchief n (pl -s) piece of cloth worn tied round the neck
neckerchiefs n ▷ neckerchief
necking v ▷ neck
necklace n (pl -s) decorative piece of jewellery worn around the neck
necklaces n ▷ necklace
necks n, v ▷ neck
necromancies n ▷ necromancy
necromancy n (pl -cies) communication with the dead
necropolis [neck-rop-pol-liss] n (pl -ses) cemetery
necropolises n ▷ necropolis
nectar n (pl -s) sweet liquid collected from flowers by bees
nectars n ▷ nectar

nectarine n (pl -s) smooth-skinned peach
nectarines n ▷ nectarine
née [nay] prep indicating the maiden name of a married woman
need v (-s, -ing, -ed) require or be in want of ▶ n (pl -s) condition of lacking something
needed v ▷ need
needful adj necessary or required
needier adj ▷ needy
neediest adj ▷ needy
needing v ▷ need
needle n (pl -s) thin pointed piece of metal with an eye through which thread is passed for sewing ▶ v (-les, -ling, -led) (Informal) goad or provoke
needled v ▷ needle
needles n, v ▷ needle
needless adj unnecessary
needlework n (pl -s) sewing and embroidery
needleworks n ▷ needlework
needling v ▷ needle
needs v, n ▷ need ▶ adv (preceded or foll. by **must**) necessarily
needy adj (-dier, -diest) poor, in need of financial support
nefarious [nif-fair-ee-uss] adj wicked
negate v (-tes, -ting, -ted) invalidate > **negation** n (pl -s)
negated v ▷ negate
negates v ▷ negate
negating v ▷ negate
negation n ▷ negate
negations n ▷ negate
negative adj expressing a denial or refusal ▶ n (pl -s) negative word or statement
negatives n ▷ negative
neglect v (-s, -ing, -ed) take no care of ▶ n (pl -s) neglecting or being neglected > **neglectful** adj
neglected v ▷ neglect
neglectful adj ▷ neglect
neglecting v ▷ neglect
neglects v, n ▷ neglect
negligee [neg-lee-zhay] n (pl -s) woman's lightweight usu. lace-trimmed dressing gown
negligees n ▷ negligee
negligence n (pl -s) neglect or carelessness > **negligent** adj > **negligently** adv
negligences n ▷ negligence
negligent adj ▷ negligence
negligently adv ▷ negligence
negligible adj so small or unimportant as to be not worth considering
negotiable adj ▷ negotiate

negotiate v (**-tes, -ting, -ted**) discuss in order to reach (an agreement) > **negotiation** n (pl **-s**) > **negotiator** n (pl **-s**) > **negotiable** adj
  negotiated v ▷ negotiate
  negotiates v ▷ negotiate
  negotiating v ▷ negotiate
  negotiation n ▷ negotiate
  negotiations n ▷ negotiate
  negotiator n ▷ negotiate
  negotiators n ▷ negotiate
neigh n (pl **-s**) loud high-pitched sound made by a horse ▶ v (**-s, -ing, -ed**) make this sound
  neighed v ▷ neigh
  neighing v ▷ neigh
  neighs n, v ▷ neigh
neighbour n (pl **-s**) person who lives or is situated near another
  neighbourhood n (pl **-s**) district
  neighbourhoods n ▷ neighbourhood
  neighbouring adj situated nearby
  neighbourly adj kind, friendly, and helpful
  neighbours n ▷ neighbour
neither adj, pron not one nor the other ▶ conj not
  nemeses n ▷ nemesis
nemesis [nem-miss-iss] n (pl **-ses**) retribution or vengeance
neo- combining form new, recent, or a modern form of
neolith n (pl **-s**) stone implement from the Neolithic age
  neoliths n ▷ neolith
neologism [nee-ol-a-jiz-zum] n (pl **-s**) newly-coined word or an established word used in a new sense
  neologisms n ▷ neologism
neon n (pl **-s**) (CHEM) colourless odourless gaseous element used in illuminated signs and lights
  neons n ▷ neon
neophyte n (pl **-s**) beginner or novice
  neophytes n ▷ neophyte
nephew n (pl **-s**) son of one's sister or brother
  nephews n ▷ nephew
nephritis [nif-frite-tiss] n (pl **-tises**) inflammation of a kidney
  nephritises n ▷ nephritis
nepotism [nep-a-tiz-zum] n (pl **-s**) favouritism in business shown to relatives and friends
  nepotisms n ▷ nepotism
nerd n (pl **-s**) (Slang) boring person obsessed with a particular subject
  nerds n ▷ nerd
nerve n (pl **-s**) cordlike bundle of fibres that conducts impulses between the brain and other parts of the body
nerveless adj numb, without feeling
nerves n ▷ nerve ▶ pl n anxiety or tension
nervier adj ▷ nervy
nerviest adj ▷ nervy
nervous adj apprehensive or worried > **nervously** adv > **nervousness** n (pl **-es**)
  nervously adv ▷ nervous
  nervousness n ▷ nervous
  nervousnesses n ▷ nervous
nervy adj (**-vier, -viest**) excitable or nervous
nest n (pl **-s**) place or structure in which birds or certain animals lay eggs or give birth to young ▶ v (**-s, -ing, -ed**) make or inhabit a nest
  nested v ▷ nest
  nesting v ▷ nest
  nests v, n ▷ nest
nestle v (**-les, -ling, -led**) snuggle
  nestled v ▷ nestle
  nestles v ▷ nestle
nestling n (pl **-s**) bird too young to leave the nest ▶ v ▷ nestle
  nestlings n ▷ nestling
net[1] n (pl **-s**) fabric of meshes of string, thread, or wire with many openings ▶ v (**-s, -tting, -tted**) catch (a fish or animal) in a net
net[2], **nett** adj left after all deductions ▶ v (**-s, -tting, -tted**) yield or earn as a clear profit
netball n (pl **-s**) team game in which a ball has to be thrown through a net hanging from a ring at the top of a pole
  netballs n ▷ netball
nether adj lower
  nets v ▷ net[1, 2]
  nets n ▷ net[1]
  nett adj ▷ net[2]
  netted v ▷ net[1, 2]
  netting v ▷ net[1, 2] ▶ n (pl **-s**) material made of net
  nettings n ▷ netting
nettle n (pl **-s**) plant with stinging hairs on the leaves
  nettled adj irritated or annoyed
  nettles n ▷ nettle
network n (pl **-s**) system of intersecting lines, roads, etc.
  networks n ▷ network
neural adj of a nerve or the nervous system
neuralgia n (pl **-s**) severe pain along a nerve
  neuralgias n ▷ neuralgia
neuritis [nyoor-rite-tiss] n (pl **-tises**) inflammation of a nerve or nerves
  neuritises n ▷ neuritis
  neurologies n ▷ neurology
  neurologist n ▷ neurology

neurologists n ▷ neurology
neurology n (pl -gies) scientific study of the nervous system > **neurologist** n (pl -s)
neuroses n ▷ neurosis
neurosis n (pl -ses) mental disorder producing hysteria, anxiety, depression, or obsessive behaviour
neurotic adj emotionally unstable ▶ n (pl -s) neurotic person
neurotics n ▷ neurotic
neuter adj belonging to a particular class of grammatical inflections in some languages ▶ v (-s, -ing, -ed) castrate (an animal)
neutered v ▷ neuter
neutering v ▷ neuter
neuters v ▷ neuter
neutral adj taking neither side in a war or dispute ▶ n (pl -s) neutral person or nation > **neutrality** n (pl -ties)
neutralities n ▷ neutral
neutrality n ▷ neutral
neutralize v (-izes, -izing, -ized) make ineffective or neutral
neutralized v ▷ neutralize
neutralizes v ▷ neutralize
neutralizing v ▷ neutralize
neutrals n ▷ neutral
neutrino [new-tree-no] n (pl -nos) elementary particle with no mass or electrical charge
neutrinos n ▷ neutrino
neutron n (pl -s) electrically neutral elementary particle of about the same mass as a proton
neutrons n ▷ neutron
never adv at no time
nevertheless adv in spite of that
new adj (-er, -est) not existing before (foll. by to) ▶ adv recently
newbie (Informal) n (pl -s) person new to a job, club, etc
newbies n ▷ newbie
newborn adj recently or just born
newcomer n (pl -s) recent arrival or participant
newcomers n ▷ newcomer
newel n (pl -s) post at the top or bottom of a flight of stairs that supports the handrail
newels n ▷ newel
newer adj ▷ new
newest adj ▷ new
newfangled adj objectionably or unnecessarily modern
newlyweds pl n recently married couple
newness n (pl -es) novelty
newnesses n ▷ newness

news n important or interesting new happenings
newsagent n (pl -s) (BRIT) shopkeeper who sells newspapers and magazines
newsagents n ▷ newsagent
newscaster n ▷ newsreader
newscasters n ▷ newsreader
newsflash n (pl -es) brief important news item, which interrupts a radio or television programme
newsflashes n ▷ newsflash
newsier adj ▷ newsy
newsiest adj ▷ newsy
newsletter n (pl -s) bulletin issued periodically to members of a group
newsletters n ▷ newsletter
newspaper n (pl -s) weekly or daily publication containing news
newspapers n ▷ newspaper
newsprint n (pl -s) inexpensive paper used for newspapers
newsprints n ▷ newsprint
newsreader, newscaster n (pl -s) person who reads the news on the television or radio
newsreaders n ▷ newsreader
newsreel n (pl -s) short film giving news
newsreels n ▷ newsreel
newsroom n (pl -s) room where news is received and prepared for publication or broadcasting
newsrooms n ▷ newsroom
newsworthy adj sufficiently interesting to be reported as news
newsy adj (-sier, -siest) full of news
newt n (pl -s) small amphibious creature with a long slender body and tail
newton n (pl -s) unit of force
newtons n ▷ newton
newts n ▷ newt
next adj, adv immediately following
nexus n (pl nexus) connection or link
nib n (pl -s) writing point of a pen
nibble v (-les, -ling, -led) take little bites (of) ▶ n (pl -les) little bite
nibbled v ▷ nibble
nibbles v, n ▷ nibble
nibbling v ▷ nibble
nibs n (pl ▷ nib
nibses n ▷ nibs
nice adj (-r, -st) pleasant > **nicely** adv > **niceness** n (pl -es)
nicely adv ▷ nice
niceness n ▷ nice
nicenesses n ▷ nice
nicer adj ▷ nice

nicest adj ▷ nice
niceties n ▷ nicety
nicety n (pl -ties) subtle point
niche [neesh] n (pl -s) hollow area in a wall
   niches n ▷ niche
nick v (-s, -ing, -ed) make a small cut in ▶ n (pl -s) small cut
   nicked v ▷ nick
nickel n (pl -s) (CHEM) silvery-white metal often used in alloys
nickelodeon n (pl -s) (US) early type of jukebox
   nickelodeons n ▷ nickelodeon
   nickels n ▷ nickel
   nicking v ▷ nick
nickname n (pl -s) familiar name given to a person or place ▶ v (-mes, -ming, -med) call by a nickname
   nicknamed v ▷ nickname
   nicknames n, v ▷ nickname
   nicknaming v ▷ nickname
   nicks v, n ▷ nick
nicotine n (pl -s) poisonous substance found in tobacco
   nicotines n ▷ nicotine
niece n (pl -s) daughter of one's sister or brother
   nieces n ▷ niece
   niftier adj ▷ nifty
   niftiest adj ▷ nifty
nifty adj (-tier, -tiest) (Informal) neat or smart
   niggard n ▷ niggardly
niggardly adj stingy > **niggard** n (pl -s) stingy person
   niggards n ▷ niggardly
niggle v (-les, -ling, -led) worry slightly ▶ n (pl -s) small worry or doubt
   niggled v ▷ niggle
   niggles v, n ▷ niggle
   niggling v ▷ niggle
nigh adv, prep (Lit) near
night n (pl -s) time of darkness between sunset and sunrise
nightcap n (pl -s) drink taken just before bedtime
   nightcaps n ▷ nightcap
nightclub n (pl -s) establishment for dancing, music, etc., open late at night
   nightclubs n ▷ nightclub
nightdress n (pl -es) woman's loose dress worn in bed
   nightdresses n ▷ nightdress
nightfall n (pl -s) approach of darkness
   nightfalls n ▷ nightfall
nightie n (pl -s) (Informal) nightdress
   nighties n ▷ nightie

nightingale n (pl -s) small bird with a musical song usu. heard at night
   nightingales n ▷ nightingale
nightjar n (pl -s) nocturnal bird with a harsh cry
   nightjars n ▷ nightjar
nightlife n (pl -s) entertainment and social activities available at night in a town or city
   nightlifes n ▷ nightlife
nightly adj, adv (happening) each night
nightmare n (pl -s) very bad dream
   nightmares n ▷ nightmare
   nights n ▷ night
nightshade n (pl -s) plant with bell-shaped flowers which are often poisonous
   nightshades n ▷ nightshade
nightshirt n (pl -s) long loose shirt worn in bed
   nightshirts n ▷ nightshirt
nihilism [nye-ill-liz-zum] n (pl -s) rejection of all established authority and institutions > **nihilist** n (pl -s) > **nihilistic** adj
   nihilisms n ▷ nihilism
   nihilist n ▷ nihilism
   nihilistic adj ▷ nihilism
   nihilists n ▷ nihilism
nil n (pl -s) nothing, zero
   nils n ▷ nil
   nimbi n ▷ nimbus
nimble adj (-r, -st) agile and quick > **nimbly** adv
   nimbler adj ▷ nimble
   nimblest adj ▷ nimble
   nimbly adv ▷ nimble
nimbus n (pl -bi, -buses) dark grey rain cloud
   nimbuses n ▷ nimbus
nincompoop n (pl -s) (Informal) stupid person
   nincompoops n ▷ nincompoop
nine adj, n (pl -s) one more than eight
ninepins n game of skittles
   nines n ▷ nine
nineteen adj, n (pl -s) ten and nine > **nineteenth** adj, n (pl -s)
   nineteens n ▷ nineteen
   nineteenth adj, n ▷ nineteen
   nineteenths n ▷ nineteen
   nineties n ▷ ninety
   ninetieth adj, n ▷ ninety
   ninetieths n ▷ ninety
ninety adj, n (pl -ties) ten times nine > **ninetieth** adj, n (pl -s)
ninth adj, n (pl -s) (of) number nine in a series
   ninths n ▷ ninth
niobium n (pl -s) (CHEM) white superconductive metallic element
   niobiums n ▷ niobium
nip¹ v (-s, -pping, -pped) (Informal) hurry ▶ n (pl

-s) pinch or light bite

nip² n (pl **nips**) small alcoholic drink

nipped v ▷ **nip¹**

nipper n (pl -s) (BRIT, AUST & NZ) (Informal) small child

nippers n ▷ **nipper**

nippier adj ▷ **nippy**

nippiest adj ▷ **nippy**

nipping v ▷ **nip¹**

nipple n (pl -s) projection in the centre of a breast

nipples n ▷ **nipple**

nippy adj (Informal) (-**pier**, -**piest**) frosty or chilly

nips v ▷ **nip¹** ▶ n ▷ **nip¹,²**

nirvana [near-vah-na] n (pl -s) (BUDDHISM) (HINDUISM) absolute spiritual enlightenment and bliss

nirvanas n ▷ **nirvana**

nit n (pl -s) egg or larva of a louse (Informal) ▷ **nitwit**

nitrate n (pl -s) compound of nitric acid, used as a fertilizer

nitrates n ▷ **nitrate**

nitric, nitrous, nitrogenous adj of or containing nitrogen

nitrogen [nite-roj-jen] n (pl -s) (CHEM) colourless odourless gas that forms four fifths of the air

nitrogenous n ▷ **nitric**

nitrogens n ▷ **nitrogen**

nitroglycerin n ▷ **nitroglycerine**

nitroglycerine, nitroglycerin n (pl -s) explosive liquid

nitroglycerines n ▷ **nitroglycerine**

nitroglycerins n ▷ **nitroglycerine**

nitrous adj ▷ **nitric**

nits n ▷ **nit**

nitwit n (pl -s) (Informal) stupid person

nitwits n ▷ **nitwit**

> **nix** n (**nixes**). A nix is a water sprite in Germanic mythology. This is a handy little word, combining X with two of the most common tiles in the game. If you have an X on your rack, look out for opportunities on the board to play this as there's most likely an N or I available. Nix scores 10 points.

no interj expresses denial, disagreement, or refusal ▶ adj not any, not a ▶ adv not at all ▶ n (pl **noes, nos**) answer or vote of 'no'

nob n (pl -s) (CHIEFLY BRIT) (Slang) person of wealth or social distinction

nobs n ▷ **nob**

nobble v (-**les**, -**ling**, -**led**) (BRIT) (Slang) attract the attention of (someone) in order to talk to him or her

nobbled v ▷ **nobble**

nobbles v ▷ **nobble**

nobbling v ▷ **nobble**

nobelium n (pl -s) (CHEM) artificially-produced radioactive element

nobeliums n ▷ **nobelium**

nobilities n ▷ **nobility**

nobility n (pl -**ties**) quality of being noble > **nobleman, noblewoman** n (pl -**men**)

noble adj (-**r**, -**st**) showing or having high moral qualities ▶ n (pl -s) member of the nobility > **nobly** adv

nobleman n ▷ **nobility**

noblemen n ▷ **nobility**

nobler adj ▷ **noble**

nobles n ▷ **noble**

noblest adj ▷ **noble**

noblewoman n ▷ **nobility**

noblewomen n ▷ **nobility**

nobly adv ▷ **noble**

nobodies n ▷ **nobody**

nobody pron no person ▶ n (pl -**dies**) person of no importance

nocturnal adj of the night

nocturne n (pl -s) short dreamy piece of music

nocturnes n ▷ **nocturne**

nod v (-s, -**dding**, -**dded**) lower and raise (one's head) briefly in agreement or greeting ▶ n (pl -s) act of nodding

nodded v ▷ **nod**

nodding v ▷ **nod**

noddle n (pl s) (CHIEFLY BRIT) (Informal) the head

noddles n ▷ **noddle**

node n (pl -s) point on a plant stem from which leaves grow

nodes n ▷ **node**

nods v, n ▷ **nod**

nodule n (pl -s) small knot or lump

nodules n ▷ **nodule**

noel n (pl -s) Christmas carol

noels n ▷ **noel**

noes n ▷ **no**

noggin n (pl -s) (Informal) head

noggins n ▷ **noggin**

noise n (pl -s) sound, usu. a loud or disturbing one > **noiseless** adj

noiseless adj ▷ **noise**

noises n ▷ **noise**

noisier adj ▷ **noisy**

noisiest adj ▷ **noisy**

noisily adv ▷ **noisy**

noisy adj (-**sier**, -**siest**) making a lot of noise > **noisily** adv

noisome adj (of smells) offensive

nomad n (pl -s) member of a tribe with no fixed

dwelling place, wanderer ▷ **nomadic** adj
nomadic adj ▷ **nomad**
nomads n ▷ **nomad**
nomenclature n (pl -s) system of names used in a particular subject
nomenclatures n ▷ **nomenclature**
nominal adj in name only ▷ **nominally** adv
nominally adv ▷ **nominal**
nominate v (-tes, -ting, -ted) suggest as a candidate ▷ **nomination** n (pl -s)
nominated v ▷ **nominate**
nominates v ▷ **nominate**
nominating v ▷ **nominate**
nomination n ▷ **nominate**
nominations n ▷ **nominate**
nominative n (pl -s) form of a noun indicating the subject of a verb
nominatives n ▷ **nominative**
nominee n (pl -s) candidate
nominees n ▷ **nominee**
non- prefix indicating: negation
nonagenarian n (pl -s) person aged between ninety and ninety-nine
nonagenarians n ▷ **nonagenarian**
nonaggression n (pl -s) policy of not attacking other countries
nonaggressions n ▷ **nonaggression**
nonagon n (pl -s) geometric figure with nine sides
nonagons n ▷ **nonagon**
nonalcoholic adj containing no alcohol
nonaligned adj (of a country) not part of a major alliance or power bloc
nonce n (pl -s) for the present
nonces n ▷ **nonce**
nonchalance n ▷ **nonchalant**
nonchalances n ▷ **nonchalant**
nonchalant adj casually unconcerned or indifferent ▷ **nonchalantly** adv ▷ **nonchalance** n (pl -s)
nonchalantly adv ▷ **nonchalant**
noncombatant n (pl -s) member of the armed forces whose duties do not include fighting
noncombatants n ▷ **noncombatant**
noncommittal adj not committing oneself to any particular opinion
nonconductor n (pl -s) substance that is a poor conductor of heat, electricity, or sound
nonconductors n ▷ **nonconductor**
nonconformist n (pl -s) person who does not conform to generally accepted patterns of behaviour or thought (N-) ▷ adj (of behaviour or ideas) not conforming to accepted patterns ▷ **nonconformity** n (pl -ties)
nonconformists n ▷ **nonconformist**

nonconformities n ▷ **nonconformist**
nonconformity n ▷ **nonconformist**
noncontributory adj (BRIT) denoting a pension scheme for employees, the premiums of which are paid entirely by the employer
nondescript adj lacking outstanding features
none pron not any
nonentities n ▷ **nonentity**
nonentity [non-enn-tit-tee] n (pl -ties) insignificant person or thing
nonetheless adv despite that, however
nonevent n (pl -s) disappointing or insignificant occurrence
nonevents n ▷ **nonevent**
nonflammable adj not easily set on fire
nonintervention n (pl refusal to intervene in the affairs of others
nonpareil [non-par-rail] n (pl -s) person or thing that is unsurpassed
nonpareils n ▷ **nonpareil**
nonpayment n (pl -s) failure to pay money owed
nonpayments n ▷ **nonpayment**
nonplussed adj perplexed
nonsense n (pl -s) something that has or makes no sense ▷ **nonsensical** adj
nonsenses n ▷ **nonsense**
nonsensical adj ▷ **nonsense**
nonstandard adj denoting language that is not regarded as correct by educated native speakers
nonstarter n (pl -s) person or idea that has little chance of success
nonstarters n ▷ **nonstarter**
nonstick adj coated with a substance that food will not stick to when cooked
nonstop adj, adv without a stop
nontoxic adj not poisonous
noodles pl n long thin strips of pasta
nook n (pl -s) sheltered place
nooks n ▷ **nook**
noon n (pl -s) twelve o'clock midday
noonday adj happening at noon
noons n ▷ **noon**
noose n (pl -s) loop in the end of a rope, tied with a slipknot
nooses n ▷ **noose**
nor conj and not
norm n (pl -s) standard that is regarded as normal
normal adj usual, regular, or typical ▷ **normally** adv ▷ **normality** n (pl -ties) ▷ **normalize** v (-izes, -izing, -ized)
normalities n ▷ **normal**

normality n ▷ **normal**
normalized v ▷ **normal**
normalizes v ▷ **normal**
normalizing v ▷ **normal**
normally adv ▷ **normal**
norms n ▷ **norm**
north n (pl -s) direction towards the North Pole, opposite south ▶ adj to or in the north ▶ adv in, to, or towards the north > **northerly** adj > **northern** adj > **northward** adj, adv > **northwards** adv
northerly adj ▷ **north**
northern adj ▷ **north**
northerner n (pl -s) person from the north of a country or area
northerners n ▷ **northerner**
norths n ▷ **north**
northward adj, adv ▷ **north**
northwards adv ▷ **north**
nos n ▷ **no**
nose n (pl -s) organ of smell, used also in breathing ▶ v (-ses, -sing, -sed) move forward slowly and carefully
nosed v ▷ **nose**
nosegay n (pl -s) small bunch of flowers
nosegays n ▷ **nosegay**
noses n, v ▷ **nose**
nosey, nosy adj (Informal) (-sier, -siest) prying or inquisitive > **nosiness** n (pl -es)
nosier adj ▷ **nosey**
nosiest adj ▷ **nosey**
nosiness n ▷ **nosey**
nosinesses n ▷ **nosey**
nosing v ▷ **nose**
nosh n (pl -es) (BRIT, AUST & NZ) (Slang) food ▶ v (-shes, -shing, -shed) eat
noshed v ▷ **nosh**
noshes n, v ▷ **nosh**
noshing v ▷ **nosh**
nostalgia n (pl -s) sentimental longing for the past > **nostalgic** adj
nostalgias n ▷ **nostalgia**
nostalgic adj ▷ **nostalgia**
nostril n (pl -s) one of the two openings at the end of the nose
nostrils n ▷ **nostril**
nostrum n (pl -s) quack medicine
nostrums n ▷ **nostrum**
nosy adj (-sier, -siest) ▷ **nosey**
not adv expressing negation, refusal, or denial
notable adj worthy of being noted, remarkable ▶ n (pl -s) person of distinction > **notably** adv
notabilities n ▷ **notability**
notability n (pl -ties)

notables n ▷ **notable**
notably adv ▷ **notable**
notaries n ▷ **notary**
notary n (pl -ries) person authorized to witness the signing of legal documents
notation n (pl -s) representation of numbers or quantities in a system by a series of symbols
notations n ▷ **notation**
notch n (pl -es) V-shaped cut ▶ v (-ches, -ching, -ched) make a notch in (foll. by **up**)
notched v ▷ **notch**
notches n, v ▷ **notch**
notching v ▷ **notch**
note n (pl -s) short letter ▶ v (-tes, -ting, -ted) notice, pay attention to
notebook n (pl -s) book for writing in
notebooks n ▷ **notebook**
noted v ▷ **note** ▶ adj well-known
notes n, v ▷ **note**
noteworthy adj worth noting, remarkable
nothing pron not anything ▶ adv not at all
nothingness n (pl -es) nonexistence
nothingnesses n ▷ **nothingness**
notice n (pl -s) observation or attention ▶ v (-ces, -cing, -ced) observe, become aware of
noticeable adj easily seen or detected, appreciable
noticed v ▷ **notice**
notices n, v ▷ **notice**
noticing v ▷ **notice**
notifiable adj having to be reported to the authorities
notification n ▷ **notify**
notifications n ▷ **notify**
notified v ▷ **notify**
notifies v ▷ **notify**
notify v (-fies, -fying, -fied) inform > **notification** n (pl -s)
notifying v ▷ **notify**
noting v ▷ **note**
notion n (pl -s) idea or opinion
notional adj speculative, imaginary, or unreal
notions n ▷ **notion**
notorieties n ▷ **notorious**
notoriety n ▷ **notorious**
notorious adj well known for something bad > **notoriously** adv > **notoriety** n (pl -ties)
notoriously adv ▷ **notorious**
notwithstanding prep in spite of
nougat n (pl -s) chewy sweet containing nuts and fruit
nougats n ▷ **nougat**
nought n (pl -s) figure o
noughties pl n (Informal) decade from 2000 to 2009

noughts *n* ▷ **nought**

noun *n* (*pl* -s) word that refers to a person, place, or thing

nouns *n* ▷ **noun**

nourish *v* (-shes, -shing, -shed) feed
> **nourishment** *n* (*pl* -s)

nourished *v* ▷ **nourish**

nourishes *v* ▷ **nourish**

nourishing *adj* providing the food necessary for life and growth ▶ *v* ▷ **nourish**

nourishment *n* ▷ **nourish**

nourishments *n* ▷ **nourish**

nova *n* (*pl* -vae, -vas) star that suddenly becomes brighter and then gradually decreases to its original brightness

novae *n* ▷ **nova**

novas *n* ▷ **nova**

novel[1] *n* (*pl* -s) long fictitious story in book form

novel[2] *adj* fresh, new, or original > **novelist** *n* (*pl* -s) writer of novels

novelists *n* ▷ **novelist**

novella *n* (*pl* -s, -llae) short novel

novellae *n* ▷ **novella**

novellas *n* ▷ **novella**

novels *n* ▷ **novel**[1]

novelties *n* ▷ **novelty**

novelty *n* (*pl* -ties) newness

novena [no-vee-na] *n* (*pl* -s) (RC CHURCH) set of prayers or services on nine consecutive days

novenas *n* ▷ **novena**

novice *n* (*pl* -s) beginner

novices *n* ▷ **novice**

now *adv* at or for the present time ▶ *conj* seeing that, since

nowadays *adv* in these times

nowhere *adv* not anywhere

> **nox** *n* (**noxes**). In chemistry, nox is short for nitrogen oxide. This is an unusual word which can come in useful in the later stages of the game when there isn't much space left, or when you have an X but can't form a longer word with it. Nox scores 10 points.

noxious *adj* poisonous or harmful

nozzle *n* (*pl* -s) projecting spout through which fluid is discharged

nozzles *n* ▷ **nozzle**

> **nth** *adv*. In mathematics, nth represents an unspecified ordinal number. Nth is a good word to remember for awkward situations on the board, as it's one of very few three-letter words that doesn't contain a vowel. Nth scores 6 points.

> **nu** *n* nus. Nu is the 13th letter in the Greek alphabet. This word is worth remembering, as it can be really useful when you want to form short words in the process of playing a longer one. Nu scores 2 points.

nuance [new-ahnss] *n* (*pl* -s) subtle difference in colour, meaning, or tone

nuances *n* ▷ **nuance**

nub *n* (*pl* -s) point or gist (of a story etc.)

nubs *n* ▷ **nub**

nubile [new-bile] *adj* (of a young woman) sexually attractive

nuclear *adj* of nuclear weapons or energy

nuclei *n* ▷ **nucleus**

nucleus *n* (*pl* -clei) centre, esp. of an atom or cell

nude *adj* (-r, -st) naked ▶ *n* (*pl* -s) naked figure in painting, sculpture, or photography > **nudity** *n* (*pl* -ties)

nuder *adj* ▷ **nude**

nudes *n* ▷ **nude**

nudest *adj* ▷ **nude**

nudge *v* (-dges, -dging, -dged) push gently, esp. with the elbow ▶ *n* (*pl* -s) gentle push or touch

nudged *v* ▷ **nudge**

nudges *v*, *n* ▷ **nudge**

nudging *v* ▷ **nudge**

nudism *n* (*pl* -s) practice of not wearing clothes > **nudist** *n* (*pl* -s)

nudisms *n* ▷ **nudism**

nudist *n* ▷ **nudism**

nudists *n* ▷ **nudism**

nudities *n* ▷ **nude**

nudity *n* ▷ **nude**

nugatory [new-gat-tree] *adj* of little value

nugget *n* (*pl* -s) small lump of gold in its natural state ▶ *v* (-s, -tting, -tted) (NZ & S AFR) polish footwear

nuggets *n*, *v* ▷ **nugget**

nuggetted *v* ▷ **nugget**

nuggetting *v* ▷ **nugget**

nuisance *n* (*pl* -s) something or someone that causes annoyance or bother

nuisances *n* ▷ **nuisance**

nuke (*Slang*) *v* (-kes, -king, -ked) attack with nuclear weapons ▶ *n* (*pl* -s) nuclear weapon

nuked *v* ▷ **nuke**

nukes *v*, *n* ▷ **nuke**

nuking *v* ▷ **nuke**

null *adj* not legally valid > **nullity** *n* (*pl* -s)

nullified *v* ▷ **nullify**

nullifies *v* ▷ **nullify**

nullify v (**-fies, -fying, -fied**) make ineffective
　nullifying v ▷ nullify
　nullities n ▷ null
　nullity n ▷ null
numb adj (**-er, -est**) without feeling, as through cold, shock, or fear ▶ v (**-s, -ing, -ed**) make numb > **numbly** adv > **numbness** n (pl **-es**)
numbat n (pl **-s**) small Australian marsupial with a long snout and tongue
　numbats n ▷ numbat
　numbed v ▷ numb
　number¹ adj ▷ numb
number² n (pl **-s**) sum or quantity ▶ v (**-s, -ing, -ed**) count
　numbered v ▷ number
　numbering v ▷ number
numberless adj too many to be counted
numberplate n (pl **-s**) plate on a car showing the registration number
　numberplates n ▷ numberplate
　numbers n, v ▷ number
　numbest adj ▷ numb
　numbing v ▷ numb
　numbly adv ▷ numb
　numbness n ▷ numb
　numbnesses n ▷ numb
　numbs v ▷ numb
numbskull n (pl **-s**) stupid person
　numbskulls n ▷ numbskull
　numeracies n ▷ numerate
　numeracy n ▷ numerate
numeral n (pl **-s**) word or symbol used to express a sum or quantity
　numerals n ▷ numeral
numerate adj able to do basic arithmetic > **numeracy** n (pl **-cies**)
numeration n (pl **-s**) act or process of numbering or counting
　numerations n ▷ numeration
numerator n (pl **-s**) (MATHS) number above the line in a fraction
　numerators n ▷ numerator
numerical adj measured or expressed in numbers > **numerically** adv
　numerically adv ▷ numerical
numerous adj existing or happening in large numbers
numismatist n (pl **-s**) coin collector
　numismatists n ▷ numismatist
numskull n (pl **-s**) ▷ numbskull
　numskulls n ▷ numbskull
nun n (pl **-s**) female member of a religious order
nuncio n (pl **-s**) (RC CHURCH) pope's ambassador
　nuncios n ▷ nuncio

　nunneries n ▷ nunnery
nunnery n (pl **-ries**) convent
　nuns n ▷ nun
nuptial adj relating to marriage
nuptials pl n wedding
nurse n (pl **-s**) person employed to look after sick people, usu. in a hospital ▶ v (**-ses, -sing, -sed**) look after (a sick person)
　nursed v ▷ nurse
　nurseries n ▷ nursery
nursery n (pl **-ries**) room where children sleep or play
nurseryman n (pl **-men**) person who raises plants for sale
　nurserymen n ▷ nurseryman
　nurses n, v ▷ nurse
　nursing v ▷ nurse
nurture n (pl **-s**) act or process of promoting the development of a child or young plant ▶ v (**-res, -ring, -red**) promote or encourage the development of
　nurtured v ▷ nurture
　nurtures n, v ▷ nurture
　nurturing v ▷ nurture
nut n (pl **-s**) fruit consisting of a hard shell and a kernel
nutcracker n (pl **-s**) device for cracking the shells of nuts
　nutcrackers n ▷ nutcracker
nuthatch n (pl **-es**) small songbird
　nuthatches n ▷ nuthatch
nutmeg n (pl **-s**) spice made from the seed of a tropical tree
　nutmeg n ▷ nutmeg
nutria n (pl **-s**) fur of the coypu
　nutrias n ▷ nutria
nutrient n (pl **-s**) substance that provides nourishment
　nutrients n ▷ nutrient
nutriment n (pl **-s**) food or nourishment required by all living things to grow and stay healthy
　nutriments n ▷ nutriment
nutrition n (pl **-s**) process of taking in and absorbing nutrients > **nutritional** adj
　nutritional adj ▷ nutrition
　nutritions n ▷ nutrition
nutritious, nutritive adj nourishing
　nutritive adj ▷ nutritious
　nuts n ▷ nut
nutter n (pl **-s**) (BRIT) (Slang) insane person
　nutters n ▷ nutter
　nuttier adj ▷ nutty
　nuttiest adj ▷ nutty
nutty adj (**-ttier, -ttiest**) containing or

resembling nuts

nuzzle v (**-les, -ling, -led**) push or rub gently with the nose or snout

nuzzled v ▷ nuzzle

nuzzles v ▷ nuzzle

nuzzling v ▷ nuzzle

ny *adj, adv.* Ny is an old spelling of **nigh.** This word can be useful when you're forming one word adjacent to another, and so need to form two-letter words where the two words meet. Ny is also unusual in that it doesn't contain a vowel. Ny scores 5 points.

nylon *n* (*pl* **-s**) synthetic material used for clothing etc.

nylons *n* ▷ nylon ▶ *pl n* stockings made of nylon

nymph *n* (*pl* **-s**) mythical spirit of nature, represented as a beautiful young woman

nymphs *n* ▷ nymph

nymphet *n* (*pl* **-s**) sexually precocious young girl

nymphets *n* ▷ nymphet

Oo

With eight Os in the bag, you're likely to have at least one on your rack during a game. There are plenty of good two-letter words starting with O. It's worth knowing that O will form a two-letter word in front of every other vowel except A, as well as in front of Y. O also combines well with X, with **ox** (9 points) as the obvious starting point, and several words that refer to **oxygen** (17), including **oxo** (10) and **oxy** (13). Don't forget the short everyday words that begin with O. While **on** and **or** (2 each) won't earn you many points, they can be very helpful when you are trying to score in more than one direction at a time. **Of** and **oh** (5 each) can also prove very useful.

oaf n (pl -s) stupid or clumsy person ▷ **oafish** adj
  oafish adj ▷ oaf
  oafs n ▷ oaf

oak n (pl -s) deciduous forest tree ▷ **oaken** adj
  oaken adj ▷ oak
  oaks n ▷ oak

oakum n (pl -s) fibre obtained by unravelling old rope
  oakums n ▷ oakum

oar n (pl -s) pole with a broad blade, used for rowing a boat
  oars n ▷ oar

oasis n (pl -ses) fertile area in a desert
  oases n ▷ oasis

oast n (pl -s) (CHIEFLY BRIT) oven for drying hops
  oasts n ▷ oast

oat n (pl -s) hard cereal grown as food ▶ pl grain of this cereal

oath n (pl -s) solemn promise, esp. to be truthful in court
  oaths n ▷ oath

oatmeal adj pale brownish-cream
  oats n ▷ oat

obbligato [ob-lig-gah-toe] n (pl -os) (MUSIC) essential part or accompaniment
  obbligatos n ▷ obbligato
  obduracies n ▷ obdurate
  obduracy n ▷ obdurate

obdurate adj hardhearted or stubborn ▷ **obduracy** n (pl -cies)
  obedience n ▷ obedient
  obediences n ▷ obedient

obedient adj obeying or willing to obey ▷ **obedience** n (pl -s) ▷ **obediently** adv
  obediently adv ▷ obedient

obeisance [oh-bay-sanss] n (pl -s) attitude of respect
  obeisances n ▷ obeisance

obelisk [ob-bill-isk] n (pl -s) four-sided stone column tapering to a pyramid at the top
  obelisks n ▷ obelisk

obese [oh-beess] adj (-r, -st) very fat ▷ **obesity** n (pl -ties)
  obeser adj ▷ obese
  obesest adj ▷ obese
  obesities n ▷ obese
  obesity n ▷ obese

obey v (-s, -ing, -ed) carry out instructions or orders
  obeyed v ▷ obey
  obeying v ▷ obey
  obeys v ▷ obey

obfuscate v (-tes, -ting, -ted) make (something) confusing
  obfuscated v ▷ obfuscate
  obfuscates v ▷ obfuscate
  obfuscating v ▷ obfuscate
  obituaries n ▷ obituary
  obituarist n ▷ obituary
  obituarists n ▷ obituary

obituary n (pl -ies) announcement of someone's death, esp. in a newspaper ▷ **obituarist** n (pl -s)

object¹ n (pl -s) physical thing

object² v (-s, -ing, -ed) express disapproval ▷ **objection** n (pl -s) ▷ **objector** n (pl -s)
  objected v ▷ object²
  objecting v ▷ object²
  objection n ▷ object²

objectionable adj unpleasant
  objections n ▷ object²

objective n (pl -s) aim or purpose ▶ adj not

biased > **objectively** adv > **objectivity** n (pl -ties)

objectively adv ▷ objective
objectives n ▷ objective
objectivities n ▷ objective
objectivity n ▷ objective
objector n ▷ object²
objectors n ▷ object²
objects n, v ▷ object¹, ²
oblation n (pl -s) religious offering
oblations n ▷ oblation
obligated adj obliged to do something
obligation n (pl -s) duty
obligations n ▷ obligation
obligatory adj required by a rule or law
oblige v (-ges, -ging, -ged) compel (someone) morally or by law to do something
obliged v ▷ oblige
obliges v ▷ oblige
obliging adj ready to help other people ▶ v ▷ oblige > **obligingly** adv
obligingly adv ▷ oblige
oblique [oh-bleak] adj (-r, -st) slanting ▶ n (pl -s) the symbol (/) > **obliquely** adv
obliquely adv ▷ oblique
obliquer adj ▷ oblique
obliques n ▷ oblique
obliquest adj ▷ oblique
obliterate v (-tes, -ting, -ted) wipe out, destroy > **obliteration** n (pl -s)
obliterated v ▷ obliterate
obliterates v ▷ obliterate
obliterating v ▷ obliterate
obliteration n ▷ obliterate
obliterations n ▷ obliterate
oblivion n (pl -s) state of being forgotten
oblivions n ▷ oblivion
oblivious adj unaware
oblong adj having two long sides, two short sides, and four right angles ▶ n (pl -s) oblong figure
oblongs n ▷ oblong
obloquies n ▷ obloquy
obloquy [ob-lock-wee] n (pl -quies) verbal abuse
obnoxious adj offensive
oboe n (pl -s) double-reeded woodwind instrument > **oboist** n (pl -s)
oboes n ▷ oboe
oboist n ▷ oboe
oboists n ▷ oboe
obscene adj (-r, -st) portraying sex offensively > **obscenity** n (pl -ies)
obscener adj ▷ obscene
obscenest adj ▷ obscene
obscenities n ▷ obscene

obscenity n ▷ obscene
obscure adj (-r, -st) not well known ▶ v (-res, -ring, -red) make (something) obscure > **obscurity** n (pl -ties)
obscured v ▷ obscure
obscurer adj ▷ obscure
obscures v ▷ obscure
obscurest adj ▷ obscure
obscuring v ▷ obscure
obscurities n ▷ obscure
obscurity n ▷ obscure
obsequies [ob-sick-weez] pl n funeral rites
obsequious [ob-seek-wee-uss] adj overattentive in order to gain favour > **obsequiousness** n
obsequiousness n ▷ obsequious
observe v (-ves, -ving, -ved) see or notice > **observable** adj
observable adj ▷ observe
observance n (pl -s) observing of a custom
observances n ▷ observance
observant adj quick to notice things
observation n (pl -s) action or habit of observing
observations n ▷ observation
observatories n ▷ observatory
observatory n (pl -ries) building equipped for studying the weather and the stars
observed v ▷ observe
observer n (pl -s) person who observes, esp. one who watches someone or something carefully
observers n ▷ observer
observes v ▷ observe
observing v ▷ observe
obsess v (-es, -ing, -ed) preoccupy (someone) compulsively > **obsessed** adj > **obsessive** adj > **obsession** n (pl -s)
obsessed v, adj ▷ obsess
obsesses v ▷ obsess
obsessing v ▷ obsess
obsession n ▷ obsess
obsessions n ▷ obsess
obsessive adj ▷ obsess
obsidian n (pl -s) dark glassy volcanic rock
obsidians n ▷ obsidian
obsolescence n ▷ obsolescent
obsolescences n ▷ obsolescent
obsolescent adj becoming obsolete > **obsolescence** n (pl -s)
obsolete adj no longer in use
obstacle n (pl -s) something that makes progress difficult
obstacles n ▷ obstacle
obstetric adj ▷ obstetrics

obstetrician *n* ▷ obstetrics
obstetricians *n* ▷ obstetrics
obstetrics *n* branch of medicine concerned with pregnancy and childbirth > **obstetric** *adj*
> **obstetrician** *n* (*pl* **-s**)
obstinacy *n* ▷ obstinate
obstinacies *n* ▷ obstinate
obstinate *adj* stubborn > **obstinately** *adv*
> **obstinacy** *n* (*pl* **-cies**)
obstinately *adv* ▷ obstinate
obstreperous *adj* unruly, noisy
obstruct *v* (**-s, -ing, -ed**) block with an obstacle
> **obstruction** *n* (*pl* **-s**) > **obstructive** *adj*
obstructed *v* ▷ obstruct
obstructing *v* ▷ obstruct
obstruction *n* ▷ obstruct
obstructions *n* ▷ obstruct
obstructive *adj* ▷ obstruct
obstructs *v* ▷ obstruct
obtain *v* (**-s, -ing, -ed**) acquire intentionally
> **obtainable** *adj*
obtainable *adj* ▷ obtain
obtained *v* ▷ obtain
obtaining *v* ▷ obtain
obtains *v* ▷ obtain
obtrude *v* (**-des, -ding, -ded**) push oneself or one's ideas on others
obtruded *v* ▷ obtrude
obtrudes *v* ▷ obtrude
obtruding *v* ▷ obtrude
obtuse *adj* (**-r, -st**) mentally slow > **obtuseness** *n* (*pl* **-es**)
obtuseness *n* ▷ obtuse
obtusenesses *n* ▷ obtuse
obtuser *adj* ▷ obtuse
obtusest *adj* ▷ obtuse
obtrusive *adj* unpleasantly noticeable
> **obtrusively** *adv*
obtrusively *adv* ▷ obtrusive
obverse *n* (*pl* **-s**) opposite way of looking at an idea
obverses *n* ▷ obverse
obviate *v* (**-tes, -ting, -ted**) make unnecessary
obviated *v* ▷ obviate
obviates *v* ▷ obviate
obviating *v* ▷ obviate
obvious *adj* easy to see or understand, evident
> **obviously** *adv*
obviously *adv* ▷ obvious
ocarina *n* (*pl* **-s**) small oval wind instrument
ocarinas *n* ▷ ocarina
occasion *n* (*pl* **-s**) time at which a particular thing happens ▶ *v* (**-s, -ing, -ed**) cause
occasional *adj* happening sometimes
> **occasionally** *adv*

occasionally *adv* ▷ occasional
occasioned *v* ▷ occasion
occasioning *v* ▷ occasion
occasions *n, v* ▷ occasion
occident *n* (*pl* occidents) (*Lit*) west
> **occidental** *adj*
occidental *adj* ▷ occident
occidents *n* ▷ occident
occiput [ox-sip-put] *n* (*pl* **-s**) back of the head
occiputs *n* ▷ occiput
occlude *v* (**-des, -ding, -ded**) obstruct
> **occlusion** *n* (*pl* **-s**)
occluded *v* ▷ occlude
occludes *v* ▷ occlude
occluding *v* ▷ occlude
occlusion *n* ▷ occlude
occlusions *n* ▷ occlude
occult *adj* relating to the supernatural
occupancies *n* ▷ occupancy
occupancy *n* (*pl* **-cies**) (length of) a person's stay in a specified place
occupant *n* (*pl* **-s**) person occupying a specified place
occupants *n* ▷ occupant
occupation *n* (*pl* **-s**) profession > **occupational** *adj*
occupational *adj* ▷ occupation
occupations *n* ▷ occupation
occupied *v* ▷ occupy
occupier *n* ▷ occupy
occupiers *n* ▷ occupy
occupies *v* ▷ occupy
occupy *v* (**-pies, -pying, -pied**) live or work in (a building) > **occupier** *n* (*pl* **-s**)
occur *v* (**-s, -rring, -rred**) happen
occurrence *n* (*pl* **-s**) something that occurs
occurrences *n* ▷ occurrence
occurred *v* ▷ occur
occurring *v* ▷ occur
occurs *v* ▷ occur
ocean *n* (*pl* **-s**) vast area of sea between continents > **oceanic** *adj*
oceanic *adj* ▷ ocean
oceanographies *n* ▷ oceanography
oceanography *n* (*pl* **-phies**) scientific study of the oceans
oceans *n* ▷ ocean
ocelot [oss-ill-lot] *n* (*pl* **-s**) American wild cat with a spotted coat
ocelots *n* ▷ ocelot
oche [ok-kee] *n* (*pl* **-s**) (DARTS) mark on the floor behind which a player must stand
oches *n* ▷ oche
ochre [oak-er] *adj, n* (*pl* **-s**) brownish-yellow (earth)

ochres n ▷ ochre

octagon n (pl -s) geometric figure with eight sides ▷ **octagonal** adj

octagonal adj ▷ octagon

octagons n ▷ octagon

octahedra n ▷ octahedron

octahedron [ok-ta-heed-ron] n (pl -drons, -dra) three-dimensional geometric figure with eight faces

octahedrons n ▷ octahedra

octane n (pl -s) hydrocarbon found in petrol

octanes n ▷ octane

octave n (pl -s) (MUSIC) (interval between the first and) eighth note of a scale

octaves n ▷ octave

octet n (pl -s) group of eight performers

octets n ▷ octet

octogenarian n (pl -s) person aged between eighty and eighty-nine

octogenarians n ▷ octogenarian

octopus n (pl -es) sea creature with a soft body and eight tentacles

octopuses n ▷ octopus

ocular adj relating to the eyes or sight

odd (-er, -est) adj unusual

odder adj ▷ odd

oddest adj ▷ odd

oddities n ▷ oddity

oddity n (pl -ties) odd person or thing

oddments pl n things left over

oddness n (pl -es) quality of being odd

oddnesses n ▷ oddness

odds pl n (ratio showing) the probability of something happening

ode n (pl -s) lyric poem, usu. addressed to a particular subject

odes n ▷ ode

odious adj offensive

odium [oh-dee-um] n (pl -s) widespread dislike

odiums n ▷ odium

odorous adj ▷ odour

odour n (pl -s) particular smell ▷ **odorous** adj ▷ **odourless** adj

odourless adj ▷ odour

odours n ▷ odour

odyssey [odd-iss-ee] n (pl -s) long eventful journey

odysseys n ▷ odyssey

oe n (oes). Oe is a Scots word for a grandchild. This is a good word to remember, as it combines two of the most common letters in the game without using any consonants. Oe scores 2 points.

oedema [id-deem-a] n (pl -mata) (MED)

abnormal swelling

oedemata n ▷ oedema

oesophagi n ▷ oesophagus

oesophagus [ee-soff-a-guss] n (pl -gi) passage between the mouth and stomach

oestrogen [ee-stra-jen] n (pl -s) female hormone that controls the reproductive cycle

oestrogens n ▷ oestrogen

of prep belonging to

off prep away from ▶ adv away ▶ adj not operating ▶ n (pl -s) (CRICKET) side of the field to which the batsman's feet point

offal n (pl -s) edible organs of an animal, such as liver or kidneys

offals n ▷ offal

offcut n (pl -s) piece remaining after the required parts have been cut out

offcuts n ▷ offcut

offend v (-s, -ing, -ed) hurt the feelings of, insult

offence n (pl -s) (cause of) hurt feelings or annoyance

offences n ▷ offence

offended v ▷ offend

offender n (pl -s) person who commits a crime

offenders n ▷ offender

offending v ▷ offend

offends v ▷ offend

offensive adj disagreeable ▶ n (pl -s) position or action of attack

offensives n ▷ offensive

offer v (-s, -ing, -ed) present (something) for acceptance or rejection ▶ n (pl -s) instance of offering something

offering n (pl -s) thing offered

offered v ▷ offer

offering v ▷ offer

offerings n ▷ offering

offers v, n ▷ offer

offertories n ▷ offertory

offertory n (-ries) (CHRISTIANITY) offering of the bread and wine for Communion

offhand adj casual, curt ▶ adv without preparation

office n (pl -s) room or building where people work at desks

officer n (pl -s) person in authority in the armed services

officers n ▷ officer

offices n ▷ office

official adj of a position of authority ▶ n (pl -s) person who holds a position of authority ▷ **officially** adv

officialdom n (pl -s) officials collectively

officialdoms n ▷ officialdom

officially adv ▷ official

officials n ▷ official

officiate v (-tes, -ting, -ted) act in an official role

officiated v ▷ officiate

officiates v ▷ officiate

officiating v ▷ officiate

officious adj interfering unnecessarily

offing n (pl -s) area of the sea visible from the shore

offings n ▷ offing

offs n ▷ off

offset v (-sets, -setting, -set) cancel out, compensate for

offsets v ▷ offset

offsetting v ▷ offset

offshoot n (pl -s) something developed from something else

offshoots n ▷ offshoot

offside adj, adv (SPORT) (positioned) illegally ahead of the ball

offspring n (pl -s) child

offsprings n ▷ offspring

oft adv (Poetic) often

often adv frequently, much of the time

ogle v (-les, -ling, -led) stare at (someone) lustfully

ogled v ▷ ogle

ogles v ▷ ogle

ogling v ▷ ogle

ogre n (pl -s) giant that eats human flesh

ogres n ▷ ogre

oh interj exclamation of surprise, pain, etc.

ohm n (pl -s) unit of electrical resistance

ohms n ▷ ohm

> **oi** interj. Oi is something people shout to attract attention. This is a good word to remember, as it combines two of the most common letters in the game without using any consonants. Oi scores 2 points.

oil n (pl -s) viscous liquid, insoluble in water and usu. flammable ▷ **petroleum** ▶ pl oil-based paints used in art ▶ v (-s, -ing, -ed) lubricate (a machine) with oil > **oily** adj (-lier, -liest)

oiled v ▷ oil

oilfield n (-s) area containing oil reserves

oilfields n ▷ oilfield

oilier adj ▷ oil

oiliest adj ▷ oil

oiling v ▷ oil

oils n, v ▷ oil

oilskin n (pl -s) (garment made from) waterproof material

oilskins n ▷ oilskin

oily adj ▷ oil

ointment n (pl -s) greasy substance used for healing skin or as a cosmetic

ointments n ▷ ointment

okapi [ok-kah-pee] n (pl -s) African animal related to the giraffe but with a shorter neck

okapis n ▷ okapi

okra n (pl -s) tropical plant with edible green pods

okras n ▷ okra

okay (Informal) interj expression of approval ▶ v (-s, -ing, -ed) approve (something) ▶ n (pl -s) approval

okayed v ▷ okay

okaying v ▷ okay

okays v, n ▷ okay

old adj (-er, -est) having lived or existed for a long time

olden adj old

older adj ▷ old

oldest adj ▷ old

oldie n (pl -s) (Informal) old but popular song or film

oldies n ▷ oldie

oleaginous [ol-lee-aj-in-uss] adj oily, producing oil

oleander [ol-lee-ann-der] n (pl -s) Mediterranean flowering evergreen shrub

oleanders n ▷ oleander

olfactory adj relating to the sense of smell

oligarchic adj ▷ oligarchy

oligarchical adj ▷ oligarchy

oligarchies n ▷ oligarchy

oligarchy [ol-lee-gark-ee] n (pl -ies) government by a small group of people > **oligarchic, oligarchical** adj

olive n (pl -s) small green or black fruit used as food or pressed for its oil ▶ adj greyish-green

olives n ▷ olive

ombudsman n (pl -men) official who investigates complaints against government organizations

ombudsmen n ▷ ombudsman

omelette n (pl -s) dish of eggs beaten and fried

omelettes n ▷ omelette

omen n (pl pl -s) happening or object thought to foretell success or misfortune

omens n ▷ omen

ominous adj worrying, seeming to foretell misfortune

omit v (-s, -tting, -tted) leave out > **omission** n (pl -s)

omission n ▷ omit

omissions n ▷ omit

omits v ▷ omit
omitted v ▷ omit
omitting v ▷ omit
omnibus n (pl -es) several books or TV or radio programmes made into one
omnibuses n ▷ omnibus
omnipotence n ▷ omnipotent
omnipotences n ▷ omnipotent
omnipotent adj having unlimited power
> omnipotence n (pl -s)
omnipresence n ▷ omnipresent
omnipresences n ▷ omnipresent
omnipresent adj present everywhere
> omnipresence n (pl -s)
omniscience n ▷ omniscient
omnisciences n ▷ omniscient
omniscient [om-niss-ee-ent] adj knowing everything > omniscience n (pl -s)
omnivore n (pl -s) omnivorous animal
omnivores n ▷ omnivore
omnivorous [om-niv-vor-uss] adj eating food obtained from both animals and plants
on prep indicating position above, attachment, closeness, etc. ▶ adv in operation ▶ adj operating ▶ n (pl -s) (CRICKET) side of the field on which the batsman stands
once adv on one occasion ▶ conj as soon as
oncogene [on-koh-jean] n (pl -s) gene that can cause cancer when abnormally activated
oncogenes n ▷ oncogene
oncoming adj approaching from the front
one adj single, lone ▶ n (pl -s) number or figure 1 ▶ pron any person
oneness n (pl -es) unity
onenesses n ▷ oneness
onerous [own-er-uss] adj (of a task) difficult to carry out
ones n ▷ one
oneself pron ▷ one
ongoing adj in progress, continuing
onion n (pl -s) strongly flavoured edible bulb
onions n ▷ onion
online adj (of a computer) directly controlled by a central processor
onlooker n (pl -s) person who watches without taking part
onlookers n ▷ onlooker
only adj alone of its kind ▶ adv exclusively ▶ conj but
onomatopoeia [on-a-mat-a-pee-a] n (pl -s) use of a word which imitates the sound it represents, such as hiss > onomatopoeic adj
onomatopoeias n ▷ onomatopoeia
onomatopoeic adj ▷ onomatopoeia
onset n (pl -s) beginning

onsets n ▷ onset
onslaught n (pl -s) violent attack
onslaughts n ▷ onslaught
onto prep to a position on
ontological adj ▷ ontology
ontologies n ▷ ontology
ontology n (pl -gies) branch of philosophy concerned with existence > ontological adj
onus [own-uss] n (pl -es) responsibility or burden
onuses n ▷ onus
onward adj directed or moving forward ▶ adv (also onwards) ahead, forward
onwards see ▷ onward
onyx n (pl -es) type of quartz with coloured layers
onyxes n ▷ onyx

oo n (oos). Oo is a Scots word for wool. This is a good word to remember, as it combines two of the most common letters in the game without using any consonants. Oo scores two points.

oodles pl n (Informal) great quantities
ooze¹ v (-zes, -zing, -zed) flow slowly ▶ n (pl -s) sluggish flow > oozy adj (-zier, -ziest)
ooze² n (-s) soft mud at the bottom of a lake or river
oozed v ▷ ooze
oozes v, n ▷ ooze¹, ²
oozier adj ▷ ooze¹
ooziest adj ▷ ooze¹
oozing v ▷ ooze¹
oozy adj ▷ ooze¹
opacities n ▷ opaque
opacity n ▷ opaque
opal n (pl -s) iridescent precious stone
opalescent adj iridescent like an opal
opals n ▷ opal
opaque adj (-r, -st) not able to be seen through, not transparent > opacity n (-ties)
opaquer adj ▷ opaque
opaquest adj ▷ opaque
open adj (-er, -est) not closed ▶ v (-s, -ing, -ed) (cause to) become open ▶ n (pl -s) (SPORT) competition which all may enter
opened v ▷ open
opener n instrument for opening containers
openest adj ▷ open
opening n (pl -s) opportunity ▶ adj first ▶ v ▷ open
openings n ▷ opening
openly adv without concealment
opens v, n ▷ open
opera¹ n (pl -s) drama in which the text is sung to an orchestral accompaniment > operatic

adj

opera² *n* ▷ **opus**

operas *n* ▷ **opera**

operate *v* (**-tes, -ting, -ted**) (cause to) work > **operator** *n* (*pl* **-s**)

operated *v* ▷ **operate**

operates *v* ▷ **operate**

operatic *adj* ▷ **opera¹**

operating *v* ▷ **operate**

operation *n* (*pl* **-s**) method or procedure of working

operational *adj* in working order

operations *n* ▷ **operation**

operative *adj* working ▶ *n* (*pl* **-s**) worker with a special skill

operatives *n* ▷ **operative**

operator *n* ▷ **operate**

operators *n* ▷ **operate**

operetta *n* (*pl* **-s**) light-hearted comic opera

operettas *n* ▷ **operetta**

ophthalmic *adj* relating to the eye

ophthalmologies *n* ▷ **ophthalmology**

ophthalmologist *n* ▷ **ophthalmology**

ophthalmologists *n* ▷ **ophthalmology**

ophthalmology *n* (*pl* **-gies**) study of the eye and its diseases > **ophthalmologist** *n* (*pl* **-s**)

opiate *n* (*pl* **-s**) narcotic drug containing opium

opiates *n* ▷ **opiate**

opine *v* (**-nes, -ning, -ned**) (*Old-fashioned*) express an opinion

opined *v* ▷ **opine**

opines *v* ▷ **opine**

opining *v* ▷ **opine**

opinion *n* (*pl* **-s**) personal belief or judgment

opinionated *adj* having strong opinions

opinions *n* ▷ **opinion**

opium *n* (*pl* **-s**) addictive narcotic drug made from poppy seeds

opiums *n* ▷ **opium**

opossum *n* (*pl* **-s**) small marsupial of America or Australasia

opossums *n* ▷ **opossum**

opponent *n* (*pl* **-s**) person one is working against in a contest, battle, or argument

opponents *n* ▷ **opponent**

opportune *adj* happening at a suitable time

opportunism *n* ▷ **opportunist**

opportunisms , ▷ **opportunist**

opportunist *n* (*pl* **-s**) ▶ *adj* (person) doing whatever is advantageous without regard for principles > **opportunism** *n* (*pl* **-s**)

opportunists *n* ▷ **opportunist**

opportunities *n* ▷ **opportunity**

opportunity *n* (*pl* **-ties**) favourable time or condition

oppose *v* (**-ses, -sing, -sed**) work against

opposed *v* ▷ **oppose**

opposes *v* ▷ **oppose**

opposing *v* ▷ **oppose**

opposition *n* (*pl* **-s**) obstruction or hostility

oppositions *n* ▷ **opposition**

opposite *adj* situated on the other side ▶ *n* (*pl* **-s**) person or thing that is opposite ▶ *prep* facing ▶ *adv* on the other side

opposites *n* ▷ **opposite**

oppress *v* (**-es, -ing, -ed**) control by cruelty or force > **oppression** *n* (*pl* **-s**) > **oppressor** *n* (*pl* **-s**)

oppressed *v* ▷ **oppress**

oppresses *v* ▷ **oppress**

oppressing *v* ▷ **oppress**

oppression *n* ▷ **oppress**

oppressions *n* ▷ **oppress**

oppressive *adj* tyrannical > **oppressively** *adv*

oppressively *adv* ▷ **oppressive**

oppressor *n* ▷ **oppress**

oppressors *n* ▷ **oppress**

opprobrium [op-probe-ree-um] *n* (*pl* **-s**) state of being criticized severely for wrong one has done

opprobriums *n* ▷ **opprobrium**

opt *v* (**-s, -ing, -ed**) show a preference, choose

opted *v* ▷ **opt**

opting *v* ▷ **opt**

opts *v* ▷ **opt**

optic *adj* relating to the eyes or sight > **optical** *adj*

optical *adj* ▷ **optic**

optics *n* science of sight and light

optician *n* (*pl* **-s**) (*also* **ophthalmic optician**) person qualified to prescribe glasses (*also* **dispensing optician**)

opticians *n* ▷ **optician**

optimism *n* (*pl* **-s**) tendency to take the most hopeful view > **optimist** *n* (*pl* **-s**) > **optimistic** *adj* > **optimistically** *adv*

optimisms *n* ▷ **optimism**

optimist *n* ▷ **optimism**

optimistic *adj* ▷ **optimism**

optimistically *adv* ▷ **optimism**

optimists *n* ▷ **optimism**

optima *n* ▷ **optimum**

optimal *adj* ▷ **optimum**

optimize *v* (**-zes, -zing, -zed**) make the most of

optimized *v* ▷ **optimize**

optimizes *v* ▷ **optimize**

optimizing *v* ▷ **optimize**

optimum *n* (*pl* **-ma, -mums**) best possible conditions ▶ *adj* most favourable > **optimal** *adj*

optimums n ▷ optimum

option n (pl -s) choice

optional adj possible but not compulsory

options n ▷ option

optometries n ▷ optometry

optometrist n (pl -s) person qualified to prescribe glasses > **optometry** n (-ries)

optometrists n ▷ optometrist

optometry n ▷ optometrist

opulence n ▷ opulent

opulences n ▷ opulent

opulent [op-pew-lent] adj having or indicating wealth > **opulence** n (-s)

opulent-yellow

opus n (pl **opuses, opera**) artistic creation, esp. a musical work

opuses n ▷ opus

or conj used to join alternatives

oracle n (pl -s) shrine of an ancient god > **oracular** adj

oracles n ▷ oracle

oracular adj ▷ oracle

oral adj spoken ▸ n (pl -s) spoken examination > **orally** adv

orally adv ▷ oral

orals n ▷ oral

orange n (pl -s) reddish-yellow citrus fruit ▸ adj reddish-yellow

orangeade n (BRIT) orange-flavoured, usu. fizzy drink

orangeades n ▷ orangeade

orangeries n ▷ orangery

orangery n (pl -ries) greenhouse for growing orange trees

oranges n ▷ orange

oration n (pl -s) formal speech

orations n ▷ oration

orator [or-rat-tor] n (pl -s) skilful public speaker

oratorical adj ▷ oratory

oratories n ▷ oratory¹, ²

oratorio [or-rat-tor-ee-oh] n (pl -s) musical composition for choir and orchestra, usu. with a religious theme

oratorios n ▷ oratorio

orators n ▷ orator

oratory¹ [or-rat-tree] n (pl -ries) art of making speeches > **oratorical** adj

oratory² n (pl -ries) small private chapel

orb n (pl -s) ceremonial decorated sphere with a cross on top, carried by a monarch

orbs n ▷ orb

orbit n (pl -s) curved path of a planet, satellite, or spacecraft around another body ▸ v (-s, -ing, -ed) move in an orbit around > **orbital** adj

orbital adj ▷ orbit

orbited v ▷ orbit

orbiting v ▷ orbit

orbits n, v ▷ orbit

orchard n (pl -s) area where fruit trees are grown

orchards n ▷ orchard

orchestra n (pl -s) large group of musicians, esp. playing a variety of instruments (also **orchestra pit**) > **orchestral** adj

orchestral adj ▷ orchestra

orchestras n ▷ orchestra

orchestrate v (-tes, -ting, -ted) arrange (music) for orchestra > **orchestration** n (pl -s)

orchestrated v ▷ orchestrate

orchestrates v ▷ orchestrate

orchestrating v ▷ orchestrate

orchestration n ▷ orchestrate

orchestrations n ▷ orchestrate

orchid n (pl -s) plant with flowers that have unusual lip-shaped petals

orchids n ▷ orchid

ordain v (-s, -ing, -ed) make (someone) a member of the clergy

ordained v ▷ ordain

ordaining v ▷ ordain

ordains v ▷ ordain

ordeal n (pl -s) painful or difficult experience

ordeals n ▷ ordeal

order n (pl -s) instruction to be carried out ▸ v (-s, -ing, -ed) give an instruction to

orderlies n ▷ orderly

orderliness n ▷ orderly

orderlinesses n ▷ orderly

orderly adj well-organized ▸ n (pl -lies) male hospital attendant > **orderliness** n (pl -es)

ordered v ▷ order

ordering v ▷ order

orders n, v ▷ order

ordinance n (pl -s) official rule or order

ordinances n ▷ ordinance

ordinarily adv ▷ ordinary

ordinary adj usual or normal > **ordinarily** adv

ordination n (pl -s) act of making someone a member of the clergy

ordinations n ▷ ordination

ordnance n (pl -s) weapons and military supplies

ordnances n ▷ ordnance

ordure n (pl -s) excrement

ordures n ▷ ordure

ore n (pl -s) (rock containing) a mineral which yields metal

ores n ▷ ore

oregano [or-rig-gah-no] n (pl -nos) sweet-smelling herb used in cooking

oreganos n ▷ oregano

organ n (pl -s) part of an animal or plant that has a particular function, such as the heart or lungs

organdie n (pl -s) fine cotton fabric

  organdies n ▷ organdie

organic adj of or produced from animals or plants (CHEM) > **organically** adv

  organically adv ▷ organic

organism n (-s) any living animal or plant

  organisms n ▷ organism

organist n (pl -s) organ player

  organists n ▷ organist

organization n (pl -s) group of people working together > **organizational** adj

  organizational adj ▷ organization

  organizations n ▷ organization

organize v (-zes, -zing, -zed) make arrangements for > **organizer** n (pl -s)

  organized v ▷ organize

  organizer n ▷ organize

  organizers n ▷ organize

  organizes v ▷ organize

  organizing v ▷ organize

  organs n ▷ organ

orgasm n (pl -s) most intense point of sexual pleasure > **orgasmic** adj

  orgasmic adj ▷ orgasm

  orgasms n ▷ orgasm

  orgiastic adj ▷ orgy

  orgies n ▷ orgy

orgy n (pl -gies) party involving promiscuous sexual activity > **orgiastic** adj

orient¹, **orientate** v (-s, -ing, -ed) position (oneself) according to one's surroundings > **orientation** n (pl -s)

orient² n (pl -s) (Lit) east > **oriental** adj

  oriental adj ▷ orient²

  orientate v ▷ orient

  orientated v ▷ orient

  orientates v ▷ orient

  orientating v ▷ orient

  orientation n ▷ orient

  orientations n ▷ orient

  oriented v ▷ orient

orienteering n (pl -s) sport in which competitors hike over a course using a compass and map

  orienteerings n ▷ orienteering

  orienting v ▷ orient

  orients v ▷ orient

  Orients n ▷ Orient

Orientalist n (pl -s) specialist in the languages and history of the Far East

  Orientalists n ▷ Orientalist

orifice [or-rif-fiss] n (pl -s) opening or hole

  orifices n ▷ orifice

origami [or-rig-gah-mee] n (pl -mis) Japanese decorative art of paper folding

  origamis n ▷ origami

origin n (pl -s) point from which something develops

original adj first or earliest ▶ n (pl -s) first version, from which others are copied > **originality** n (pl -ies) > **originally** adv

  originalities n ▷ original

  originality n ▷ original

  originally adv ▷ original

  originals n ▷ original

originate v (-tes, -ting, -ted) come or bring into existence > **origination** n (pl -s) > **originator** n (pl -s)

  originated v ▷ originate

  originates v ▷ originate

  originating v ▷ originate

  origination n ▷ origination

  originations n ▷ origination

  originator n ▷ originate

  originator n ▷ originate

  origins n ▷ origin

oriole n (pl -s) tropical or American songbird

  orioles n ▷ oriole

ormolu n (pl -lus) gold-coloured alloy used for decoration

  ormulus n ▷ ormulu

ornament n (pl -s) decorative object ▶ v (-s, -ing, -ed) decorate > **ornamental** adj > **ornamentation** n (pl -s)

  ornamental adj ▷ ornament

  ornamentation n ▷ ornament

  ornamentations n ▷ ornament

  ornamented v ▷ ornament

  ornamenting v ▷ ornament

  ornaments n, v ▷ ornament

ornate adj highly decorated, elaborate

  ornithological adj ▷ ornithology

  ornithologies n ▷ ornithology

  ornithologist n ▷ ornithology

  ornithologists n ▷ ornithology

ornithology n (pl -gies) study of birds > **ornithological** adj > **ornithologist** n (pl -s)

orphan n (pl -s) child whose parents are dead

orphanage n (pl -s) children's home for orphans

  orphanages n ▷ orphanage

orphaned adj having no living parents

  orphans n ▷ orphan

  orreries n ▷ orrery

orrery n (pl -ries) mechanical model of the solar system

orris n (pl -es) kind of iris (also **orris root**)

orrises *n* ▷ orris

orthodontics *n* (*pl* branch of dentistry concerned with correcting irregular teeth > **orthodontist** *n* (*pl* -**s**)
  orthodontist *n* ▷ orthodontics
  orthodontists *n* ▷ orhtodontics

orthodox *adj* conforming to established views > **orthodoxy** *n* (*pl* -**ies**)
  orthodoxies *n* ▷ orthodox
  orthodoxy *n* ▷ orthodox

orthography *n* (*pl* -**phies**) correct spelling
  orthographies *n* ▷ orthography

orthopaedic *adj* ▷ orthopaedics

orthopaedics *n* (*pl* branch of medicine concerned with disorders of the bones or joints > **orthopaedic** *adj*

oryx *n* (*pl* -**es**) large African antelope
  oryxes *n* ▷ oryx

> **os** *n* (**ossa**). Os is a technical word for bone. This word won't score many points on its own, but will allow you to connect a word beginning with O to one ending in S (e.g. most plurals). Os scores 2 points.

oscillate [oss-ill-late] *v* (-**tes**, -**ting**, -**ted**) swing back and forth > **oscillation** *n* (*pl* -**s**) > **oscillator** *n* (*pl* -**s**)
  oscillated *v* ▷ oscillate
  oscillates *v* ▷ oscillate
  oscillating *v* ▷ oscillate
  oscillation *n* ▷ oscillate
  oscillation *n* ▷ oscillate
  oscillations *n* ▷ oscillate
  oscillator *n* ▷ oscillate
  oscillators *n* ▷ oscillate

oscilloscope [oss-sill-oh-scope] *n* (*pl* -**s**) instrument that shows the shape of a wave on a cathode-ray tube
  oscilloscopes *n* ▷ oscilloscope

osier [oh-zee-er] *n* (*pl* -**s**) willow tree
  osiers *n* ▷ osier

osmium *n* (*pl* -**s**) (CHEM) heaviest known metallic element
  osmiums *n* ▷ osmium

osmosis *n* (*pl* -**ses**) movement of a liquid through a membrane from a lower to a higher concentration > **osmotic** *adj*
  osmoses *n* ▷ osmosis
  osmotic *adj* ▷ osmosis

osprey *n* (*pl* -**s**) large fish-eating bird of prey
  ospreys *n* ▷ osprey

ossification *n* ▷ ossify
  ossifications *n* ▷ ossify
  ossified *v* ▷ ossify
  ossifies *v* ▷ ossify

ossify *v* (-**fies**, -**fying**, -**fied**) (cause to) become bone, harden > **ossification** *n* (*pl* -**s**)
  ossifying *v* ▷ ossify

ostensible *adj* apparent, seeming > **ostensibly** *adv*
  ostensibly *adv* ▷ ostensible

ostentation *n* (*pl* -**s**) pretentious display > **ostentatious** *adj* > **ostentatiously** *adv*
  ostentations *n* ▷ ostentation
  ostentatious *adj* ▷ ostentation
  ostentatiously *adv* ▷ ostentation

osteopath *n* ▷ osteopathy
  osteopathies *n* ▷ osteopathy
  osteopaths *n* ▷ osteopathy

osteopathy *n* (*pl* -**thies**) medical treatment involving manipulation of the joints > **osteopath** *n* (*pl* -**s**)

osteoporosis *n* (*pl* -**ses**) brittleness of the bones, caused by lack of calcium
  osteoporoses *n* ▷ osteoporosis

ostracism *n* ▷ ostracize
  ostracisms *n* ▷ ostracize

ostracize *v* (-**zes**, -**zing**, -**zed**) exclude (a person) from a group > **ostracism** *n* (*pl* -**s**)
  ostracized *v* ▷ ostracize
  ostracizes *v* ▷ ostracize
  ostracizing *v* ▷ ostracize

ostrich *n* (*pl* -**es**) large African bird that runs fast but cannot fly
  ostriches *n* ▷ ostrich

other *adj* remaining in a group of which one or some have been specified ► *n* (*pl* -**s**) other person or thing
  others *n* ▷ other

otherwise *conj* or else, if not ► *adv* differently, in another way

otherworldly *adj* concerned with spiritual rather than practical matters

otiose [oh-tee-oze] *adj* not useful

otter *n* (*pl* -**s**) small brown freshwater mammal that eats fish
  otters *n* ▷ otter

ottoman *n* (*pl* -**mans**) storage chest with a padded lid for use as a seat
  ottomans *n* ▷ ottoman

> **ou** *n* (**ous**). Ou is a South African slang word for a man. This word doesn't score many points, but is very useful when you are trying to form words in more than one direction. Ou scores 2 points.

oubliette [oo-blee-ett] *n* (*pl* -**s**) dungeon entered only by a trapdoor
  oubliettes *n* ▷ oubliette

ouch *interj* exclamation of sudden pain

ought v used to express: obligation

ounce n (pl -s) unit of weight equal to one sixteenth of a pound (28.4 grams)
ounces n ▷ ounce

our adj belonging to us

ours pron thing(s) belonging to us
ourselves pron ▷ we, us

ousel n (pl -s) ▷ dipper
ousels n ▷ ousel

oust v (-s, -ing, -ed) force (someone) out, expel
ousted v ▷ oust
ousting v ▷ oust
ousts v ▷ oust

out adv, adj denoting movement or distance away from, a state of being used up or extinguished, public availability, etc. ▶ v (-s, -ing, -ed) (Informal) name (a public figure) as being homosexual

outback n (pl -s) remote bush country of Australia
outbacks n ▷ outback

outbid v (-bids, -bidding, -bid, -bidden) offer a higher price than
outbid v ▷ outbid
outbidden v ▷ outbid
outbidding v ▷ outbid
outbids v ▷ outbid

outbreak n (pl -s) sudden occurrence (of something unpleasant)
outbreaks n ▷ outbreak

outburst n (pl -s) sudden expression of emotion
outbursts n ▷ outburst

outcast n (pl -s) person rejected by a particular group
outcasts n ▷ outcast

outclass v (-es, -ing, -ed) surpass in quality
outclassed v ▷ outclass
outclasses v ▷ outclass
outclassing v ▷ outclass

outcome n (pl -s) result
outcomes n ▷ outcome

outcries n ▷ outcry

outcrop n (pl -s) part of a rock formation that sticks out of the earth
outcrops n ▷ outcrop

outcry n (pl -ries) vehement or widespread protest

outdo v (-does, -doing, -did, -done) surpass in performance
outdid v ▷ outdo
outdoes v ▷ outdo
outdoing v ▷ outdo
outdone v ▷ outdo
outdoor adj ▷ outdoors

outdoors adv in(to) the open air ▶ n (pl the open air > outdoor adj
outed v ▷ out

outer adj on the outside

outermost adj furthest out

outface v (-ces, -cing, -ced) subdue or disconcert (someone) by staring
outfaced v ▷ outface
outfaces v ▷ outface
outfacing v ▷ outface

outfield n (pl -s) (CRICKET) area far from the pitch
outfields n ▷ outfield

outfit n (pl -s) matching set of clothes
outfits n ▷ outfit

outfitter n (pl -s) supplier of men's clothes
outfitters n ▷ outfitter

outflank v (-s, -ing, -ed) get round the side of (an enemy army)
outflanked v ▷ outflank
outflanking v ▷ outflank
outflanks v ▷ outflank

outgoing adj leaving

outgoings pl n expenses

outgrow v (-grows, -growing, -grew, -grown) become too large or too old for
outgrew v ▷ outgrow
outgrowing v ▷ outgrow
outgrown v ▷ outgrow
outgrows v ▷ outgrow

outgrowth n natural development
outgrowths n ▷ outgrowth

outhouse n (pl -s) building near a main building
outhouses n ▷ outhouse

outing n (pl -s) leisure trip ▶ v ▷ out
outings n ▷ outing

> **outjinx** v (outjinxes, outjinxing, outjinxed). Outjinx means to outmanoeuvre. If someone else plays **jinx**, you can outjinx them by adding O, U and T! If you can form the whole word using all of your letters, you'll get a 50-point bonus. Outjinx scores 21 points.

outlandish adj extremely unconventional

outlaw n (pl -s) (HIST) criminal deprived of legal protection, bandit ▶ v (-s, -ing, -ed) make illegal (HIST)
outlawed v ▷ outlaw
outlawing v ▷ outlaw
outlaws n, v ▷ outlaw

outlay n (pl -s) expenditure
outlays n ▷ outlay

outlet n (pl -s) means of expressing emotion
outlets n ▷ outlet

outline n (pl -s) short general explanation ▸ v (-nes, -ning, -ned) summarize
  outlined v ▷ outline
  outlines n, v ▷ outline
  outlining v ▷ outline
outlook n (pl -s) attitude
  outlooks n ▷ outlook
outlying adj distant from the main area
outmanoeuvre v (-res, -ring, -red) get an advantage over
  outmanoeuvred v ▷ outmanoeuvre
  outmanoeuvres v ▷ outmanoeuvre
  outmanoeuvring v ▷ outmanoeuvre
outmoded adj no longer fashionable or accepted
outnumber v (-s, -ing, -ed) exceed in number
  outnumbered v ▷ outnumber
  outnumbering v ▷ outnumber
  outnumbers v ▷ outnumber
outpatient n (pl -s) patient who does not stay in hospital overnight
  outpatients n ▷ outpatient
outpost n (pl -s) outlying settlement
  outposts n ▷ outpost
outpouring n (pl -s) passionate outburst
  outpourings n ▷ outpouring
output n (pl -s) amount produced ▸ v (-puts, -putting, -putted) (COMPUTERS) produce (data) at the end of a process
  outputted v ▷ output
  outputting v ▷ output
  outputs n, v ▷ output
outrage n (pl -s) great moral indignation ▸ v (-s, -ing, -ed) offend morally
  outraged v ▷ outrage
outrageous adj shocking > **outrageously** adv
  outrageously adv ▷ outrageous
  outrages n, v ▷ outrage
  outraging v ▷ outrage
outré [oo-tray] adj shockingly eccentric
outrider n (pl -s) motorcyclist acting as an escort
  outriders n ▷ outrider
outrigger n (pl -s) stabilizing frame projecting from a boat
  outriggers n ▷ outrigger
outright adj, adv absolute(ly)
outrun v (-runs, -running, -ran, -run) run faster than
  outran v ▷ outrun
  outrun v ▷ outrun
  outrunning v ▷ outrun
  outruns v ▷ outrun
  outs v ▷ out
outset n (pl -s) beginning

outsets n ▷ outset
outshine v (-shines, -shining, -shone) surpass (someone) in excellence
  outshines v ▷ outshine
  outshining v ▷ outshine
  outshone v ▷ outshine
outside prep, adj adv indicating movement to or position on the exterior ▸ adj unlikely ▸ n (pl -s) external area or surface
outsider n (pl -s) person outside a specific group
  outsiders n ▷ outsider
  outsides n ▷ outside
outsize, outsized adj larger than normal
  outsized adj ▷ outsize
outskirts pl n outer areas, esp. of a town
outsmart v (-s, -ing, -ed) (Informal) outwit
  outsmarted v ▷ outsmart
  outsmarting v ▷ outsmart
  outsmarts v ▷ outsmart
outspan v (-s, -nning, -nned) (S AFR) relax
  outspanned v ▷ outspan
  outspanning v ▷ outspan
  outspans v ▷ outspan
outspoken adj tending to say what one thinks
outstanding adj excellent
outstrip v (-s, -pping, -pped) surpass
  outstripped v ▷ outstrip
  outstripping v ▷ outstrip
  outstrips v ▷ outstrip
outtake n (pl -s) unreleased take from a recording session, film, or TV programme
  outtakes n ▷ outtake
outward adj apparent ▸ adv (also **outwards**) away from somewhere > **outwardly** adv
  outwardly adv ▷ outward
outweigh v (-s, -ing, -ed) be more important, significant, or influential than
  outweighed v ▷ outweigh
  outweighing v ▷ outweigh
  outweighs v ▷ outweigh
outwit v (-s, -tting, -tted) get the better of (someone) by cunning
  outwits v ▷ outwit
  outwitted v ▷ outwit
  outwitting v ▷ outwit
ouzel [ooze-el] n (pl -s) ▷ dipper
  ouzels n ▷ ouzel
  ova n ▷ ovum
oval adj egg-shaped ▸ n (pl -s) anything that is oval in shape
  ovals n ▷ oval
  ovarian adj ▷ ovary
  ovaries n ▷ ovary
ovary n (pl -ries) female egg-producing organ

> **ovarian** *adj*

ovation *n* (*pl* -s) enthusiastic round of applause

ovations *n* ▷ ovation

oven *n* (*pl* -s) heated compartment or container for cooking or for drying or firing ceramics

ovens *n* ▷ oven

over *prep, adv* indicating position on the top of, movement to the other side of, amount greater than, etc. ▶ *adj* finished ▶ *n* (*pl* -s) (CRICKET) series of six balls bowled from one end

overall *adj, adv* in total ▶ *n* (*pl* -s) coat-shaped protective garment ▶ *pl* protective garment consisting of trousers with a jacket or bib and braces attached

overalls *n* ▷ overall

overarm *adj, adv* (thrown) with the arm above the shoulder

overawe *v* (-wes, -wing, -wed) affect (someone) with an overpowering sense of awe

overawed *v* ▷ overawe

overawes *v* ▷ overawe

overawing *v* ▷ overawe

overbalance *v* (-ces, -cing, -ced) lose balance

overbalanced *v* ▷ overbalance

overbalances *v* ▷ overbalance

overbalancing *v* ▷ overbalance

overbearing *adj* unpleasantly forceful

overblown *adj* excessive

overboard *adv* from a boat into the water

overcame *v* ▷ overcome

overcast *adj* (of the sky) covered by clouds

overcoat *n* (*pl* -s) heavy coat

overcoats *n* ▷ overcoat

overcome *v* (-comes, -coming, -came, -come) gain control over after an effort

overcomes *v* ▷ overcome

overcoming *v* ▷ overcome

overcrowded *adj* containing more people or things than is desirable

overdid *v* ▷ overdo

overdo *v* (-does, -doing, -did, -done) do to excess

overdoes *v* ▷ overdo

overdoing *v* ▷ overdo

overdone *v* ▷ overdo

overdose *n* (*pl* -s) excessive dose of a drug ▶ *v* (-ses, -sing, -sed) take an overdose

overdosed *n* ▷ overdose

overdoses *n, v* ▷ overdose

overdosing *v* ▷ overdose

overdraft *n* (*pl* -s) overdrawing

overdrafts *n* ▷ overdraft

overdraw *v* (-draws, -drawing, -drew, -drawn) withdraw more money than is in (one's bank account)

overdrawing *v* ▷ overdraw

overdrawn *v* ▷ overdraw

overdraws *v* ▷ overdraw

overdrew *v* ▷ overdraw

overdrawn *adj* having overdrawn one's account

overdrive *n* (*pl* -s) very high gear in a motor vehicle

overdrives *n* ▷ overdrive

overdue *adj* still due after the time allowed

overgrown *adj* thickly covered with plants and weeds

overhaul *v* (-s, -ing, -ed) examine and repair ▶ *n* (*pl* -s) examination and repair

overhauled *v* ▷ overhaul

overhauling *v* ▷ overhaul

overhauls *v, n* ▷ overhaul

overhead *adv, adj* above one's head

overheads *pl n* general cost of maintaining a business

overhear *v* (-hears, -hearing, -heard) hear (a speaker or remark) unintentionally or without the speaker's knowledge

overheard *v* ▷ overhear

overhearing *v* ▷ overhear

overhears *v* ▷ overhear

overjoyed *adj* extremely pleased

overkill *n* (*pl* -s) treatment that is greater than required

overkills *n* ▷ overkill

overland *adj, adv* by land

overlap *v* (-s, -pping, -pped) share part of the same space or period of time (as) ▶ *n* (*pl* -s) area overlapping

overlapped *v* ▷ overlap

overlapping *v* ▷ overlap

overlaps *v, n* ▷ overlap

overleaf *adv* on the back of the current page

overlook *v* (-s, -ing, -ed) fail to notice

overlooked *v* ▷ overlook

overlooking *v* ▷ overlook

overlooks *v* ▷ overlook

overly *adv* excessively

overnight *adj, adv* (taking place) during one night

overpower *v* (-s, -ing, -ed) subdue or overcome (someone)

overpowered *v* ▷ overpower

overpowering *v* ▷ overpower

overpowers *v* ▷ overpower

overran *v* ▷ overrun

overreach v (**-es, -ing, -ed**) fail by trying to be too clever
  overreached v ▷ overreach
  overreaches v ▷ overreach
  overreaching v ▷ overreach

override v (**-rides, -riding, -rode, -ridden**) overrule
  overridden v ▷ override
  overrides v ▷ override
  overriding v ▷ override
  overrode v ▷ override

overrule v (**-les, -ling, -led**) reverse the decision of (a person with less power)
  overruled v ▷ overrule
  overrules v ▷ overrule
  overruling v ▷ overrule

overrun v (**-runs, -running, -ran, -run**) spread over (a place) rapidly
  overrunning v ▷ overrun
  overruns v ▷ overrun
  overs n ▷ over
  oversaw v ▷ oversee

overseas adv, adj to, of, or from a distant country

oversee v (**-sees, -seeing, -saw, -seen**) watch over from a position of authority > **overseer** n (**-s**)
  overseeing v ▷ oversee
  overseen v ▷ oversee
  overseer n ▷ oversee
  overseers n ▷ oversee
  oversees v ▷ oversee

overshadow v (**-s, -ing, -ed**) reduce the significance of (a person or thing) by comparison
  overshadowed v ▷ overshadow
  overshadowing v ▷ overshadow
  overshadows v ▷ overshadow

oversight n (pl **-s**) mistake caused by not noticing something
  oversights n ▷ oversight

overspill n (pl **-s**) (BRIT) rehousing of people from crowded cities in smaller towns
  overspills n ▷ overspill

overstay v (**-s, -ing, -ed**) stay longer than one's host or hostess would like
  overstayed v ▷ overstay

overstayer n (**-s**) (NZ) person who remains in New Zealand after their permit has expired
  overstayers n ▷ overstayer
  overstaying v ▷ overstay
  overstays v ▷ overstay

overt adj open, not hidden > **overtly** adv
  overtly adv ▷ overt

overtake v (**-takes, -taking, -took, -taken**) move past (a vehicle or person) travelling in the same direction
  overtaken v ▷ overtake
  overtakes v ▷ overtake
  overtaking v ▷ overtake
  overtook v ▷ overtake
  overthrew v ▷ overthrow

overthrow v (**-throws, -throwing, -threw, -thrown**) defeat and replace ▶ n (pl **-s**) downfall, destruction
  overthrowing v ▷ overthrow
  overthrown v ▷ overthrow
  overthrows v, n ▷ overthrow

overtime n, adv (pl **-s**) (paid work done) in addition to one's normal working hours
  overtimes n ▷ overtime

overtone n (pl **-s**) additional meaning
  overtones n ▷ overtone

overture n (pl **-s**) (MUSIC) orchestral introduction ▶ pl opening moves in a new relationship
  overtures n ▷ overture

overturn v (**-s, -ing, -ed**) turn upside down
  overturned v ▷ overturn
  overturning v ▷ overturn
  overturns v ▷ overturn

overweight adj weighing more than is healthy

overwhelm v (**-s, -ing, -ed**) overpower, esp. emotionally > **overwhelming** adj > **overwhelmingly** adv
  overwhelmed v ▷ overwhelm
  overwhelming v, adj ▷ overwhelm
  overwhelmingly adv ▷ overwhelm
  overwhelms v ▷ overwhelm

overwrought adj nervous and agitated

ovoid [oh-void] adj egg-shaped

ovulate [ov-yew-late] v (**-tes, -ting, -ted**) produce or release an egg cell from an ovary > **ovulation** n (**-s**)
  ovulated v ▷ ovulate
  ovulates v ▷ ovulate
  ovulating v ▷ ovulate
  ovulation n ▷ ovulate
  ovulations n ▷ ovulate

ovum [oh-vum] n (pl **ova**) unfertilized egg cell

owe v (**owes, owing, owed**) be obliged to pay (a sum of money) to (a person)
  owed v ▷ owe
  owes v ▷ owe
  owing v ▷ owe

owl n (pl **-s**) night bird of prey > **owlish** adj
  owlish adj ▷ owl
  owls n ▷ owl

own adj used to emphasize possession

▶ v (-s, -ing, -ed) possess ▷ **owner** n (pl -s)
> **ownership** n (pl -s)
owned v ▷ own
owner n ▷ own
owners n ▷ own
ownership n ▷ own
ownerships n ▷ own
owning v ▷ own
owns v ▷ own
ox n (pl **oxen**) castrated bull
oxen n ▷ ox
oxide n (pl -s) compound of oxygen and one other element
oxides n ▷ oxide
oxidize v (-zes, -zing, -zed) combine chemically with oxygen, as in burning or rusting
oxidized v ▷ oxidize
oxidizes v ▷ oxidize
oxidizing v ▷ oxidize
oxygen n (pl -s) (CHEM) gaseous element

essential to life and combustion
oxygenate v (-tes, -ting, -ted) add oxygen to
oxygenated v ▷ oxygenate
oxygenates v ▷ oxygenate
oxygenating v ▷ oxygenate
oxygens n ▷ oxygen
oxymora n ▷ oxymoron
oxymoron [ox-see-more-on] n (pl -**mora**, -**morons**) figure of speech that combines two apparently contradictory ideas
oxymorons n ▷ oxymoron
oyez interj (HIST) shouted three times by a public crier, listen
oyster n (pl -s) edible shellfish
oystercatcher n (pl -s) wading bird with black-and-white feathers
oystercatchers n ▷ oystercatcher
oysters n ▷ oyster
ozone n (pl -s) strong-smelling form of oxygen
ozones n ▷ ozone

Pp

P forms a two-letter word in front of every vowel except U, which makes it very useful for joining a new word to one already on the board. It also forms several three-letter words with X: **pax, pix, pox** (12 points each) and **pyx** (15). You should also remember one of the strangest words in Scrabble – **pH** (7), which is valid because it doesn't start with a capital letter. When you have the letter P on your rack, look for an H on the board, as they may allow you to play a word beginning or ending in PH, adding to your options.

pa n (pl **-s**) (NZ) (formerly) a fortified Maori settlement

pace n (pl **-s**) single step in walking ▶ v (**-ces, -cing, -ced**) walk up and down, esp. in anxiety
  paced v ▷ pace

pacemaker n (pl **-s**) electronic device surgically implanted in a person with heart disease to regulate the heartbeat
  pacemakers n ▷ pacemaker
  paces n, v ▷ pace

pachyderm [pak-ee-durm] n (pl **-s**) thick-skinned animal such as an elephant
  pachyderms n ▷ pachyderm
  pacification n ▷ pacify
  pacifications n ▷ pacify
  pacified v ▷ pacify
  pacifies v ▷ pacify
  pacifism n ▷ pacifist
  pacifisms n ▷ pacifist

pacifist n (pl **-s**) person who refuses on principle to take part in war > **pacifism** n (pl **-s**)
  pacifists n ▷ pacifist

pacify v (**-fies, -fying, -fied**) soothe, calm > **pacification** n (pl **-s**)
  pacifying v ▷ pacify
  pacing v ▷ pace

pack v (**-s, -ing, -ed**) put (clothes etc.) together in a suitcase or bag ▶ n (pl **-s**) bag carried on a person's or animal's back
  packed v ▷ pack
  packing v ▷ pack
  packs v, n ▷ pack

package n (pl **-s**) small parcel ▶ v (**-ges, -ging, -ged**) put into a package > **packaging** n (pl **-s**)
  packaged v ▷ package

packages n, v ▷ package
  packaging v, n ▷ package
  packagings n ▷ package

packet n (pl **-s**) small container (and contents)
  packets n ▷ packet

packhorse n (pl **-s**) horse used for carrying goods
  packhorses n ▷ packhorse

pact n (pl **-s**) formal agreement
  pacts n ▷ pact

pad n (pl **-s**) piece of soft material used for protection, support, absorption of liquid, etc. ▶ v (**padding, padded**) protect or fill with soft material
  padded v ▷ pad
  paddies n ▷ paddy

padding n (pl **-s**) soft material used to pad something ▶ v ▷ pad
  paddings n ▷ padding

paddle[1] n (pl **-s**) short oar with a broad blade at one or each end ▶ v (**-les, -ling, -led**) move (a canoe etc.) with a paddle

paddle[2] v (**-les, -ling, -led**) walk barefoot in shallow water
  paddled v ▷ paddle[1, 2]
  paddles n, v ▷ paddle[1, 2]
  paddling v ▷ paddle[1, 2]

paddock n (pl **-s**) small field or enclosure for horses
  paddocks n ▷ paddock

paddy n (pl **-ies**) (BRIT) (Informal) fit of temper
  paddymelons n ▷ pademelon

pademelon, paddymelon [pad-ee-mel-an] n (pl **-s**) small Australian wallaby
  pademelons n ▷ pademelon

padlock n (pl **-s**) detachable lock with a hinged

hoop fastened over a ring on the object to be secured

padlocks n ▷ padlock

padre [pah-dray] n (pl -s) chaplain to the armed forces

padres n ▷ padre

pads v, n ▷ pad

paean [pee-an] n (pl -s) song of triumph or thanksgiving

paeans n ▷ paean

paediatrics n branch of medicine concerned with diseases of children > paediatrician n

paella [pie-ell-a] n (pl -s) Spanish dish of rice, chicken, shellfish, and vegetables

paellas n ▷ paella

pagan n (pl -s) ▶ adj (person) not belonging to one of the world's main religions

pagans n ▷ pagan

page¹ n (pl -s) (one side of) a sheet of paper forming a book etc.

page² n (also pageboy) small boy who attends a bride at her wedding ▶ v (-ges, -ging, -ged) summon (someone) by bleeper or loudspeaker, in order to pass on a message

pageant n (pl -s) parade or display of people in costume, usu. illustrating a scene from history > pageantry n (pl -ries)

pageantries n ▷ pageant

pageantry n ▷ pageant

pageants n ▷ pageant

paged v ▷ page²

pages n, v ▷ page¹, ²

pagination n (pl -s) numbering of the pages of a book etc.

paginations n ▷ pagination

paging v ▷ page²

pagoda n (pl -s) pyramid-shaped Asian temple or tower

pagodas n ▷ pagoda

paid v ▷ pay

pail n (pl -s) (contents of) a bucket

pails n ▷ pail

pain n (pl -s) physical or mental suffering ▶ pl trouble, effort ▶ painful adj ▶ painfully adv > painless adj > painlessly adv

painful adj ▷ pain

painfully adv ▷ pain

painkiller n (pl -s) drug that relieves pain

painkillers n ▷ painkiller

painless adj ▷ pain

painlessly adv ▷ pain

pains n ▷ pain

painstaking adj extremely thorough and careful

paint n (pl -s) coloured substance, spread on a surface with a brush or roller ▶ v (-s, -ing, -ed) colour or coat with paint > painter n (pl -s) > painting n (pl -s)

painted v ▷ paint

painter¹ n ▷ paint

painter² n (pl -s) rope at the front of a boat, for tying it up

painters n ▷ paint painter²

painting v, n ▷ paint

paintings n ▷ paint

paints n, v ▷ paint

pair n (pl -s) set of two things matched for use together ▶ v (-s, -ing, -ed) group or be grouped in twos

paired v ▷ pair

pairing v ▷ pair

pairs n, v ▷ pair

pakeha [pah-kee-ha] n (pl -s) (NZ) New Zealander who is not of Maori descent

pakehas n ▷ pakeha

pal n (pl -s) (Informal) (Old-fashioned in NZ) friend

pals n ▷ pal

palace n (pl -s) residence of a king, bishop, etc.

palaces n ▷ palace

palaeographies n ▷ palaeography

palaeography [pal-ee-og-ra-fee] n (pl -ies) study of ancient manuscripts

palaeolithic [pal-ee-oh-lith-ik] adj of the Old Stone Age

palaeontologies n ▷ palaeontology

palaeontology [pal-ee-on-tol-a-jee] n (pl -ies) study of past geological periods and fossils

palagi [pa-lang-gee] n (pl -s) (NZ) Samoan name for a pakeha

palagis n ▷ palagi

palatable adj pleasant to taste

palate n (pl -s) roof of the mouth

palates n ▷ palate

palatial adj like a palace, magnificent

palaver [pal-lah-ver] n (pl -s) time-wasting fuss

palavers n ▷ palaver

pale¹ adj (-er, -est) light, whitish ▶ v (-les, -ling, -led) become pale

pale² n (pl -s) wooden or metal post used in fences

paled v ▷ pale

paler adj ▷ pale¹

pales v ▷ pale¹, ²

palest adj ▷ pale¹

paling v ▷ pale

palette n (pl -s) artist's flat board for mixing colours on

palettes n ▷ palette

palindrome n (pl -s) word or phrase that reads the same backwards as forwards

palindromes n ▷ palindrome

paling n (pl -s) wooden or metal post used in fences

palings n ▷ paling

palisade n (pl -s) fence made of wooden posts driven into the ground

palisades n ▷ palisade

pall¹ n (pl -s) cloth spread over a coffin

pall² v (-s, -ing, -ed) become boring

pallbearer n (pl -s) person who helps to carry the coffin at a funeral

pallbearers n ▷ pallbearer

palled v ▷ pall²

palling v ▷ pall²

palls n ▷ pall¹ ▶ v ▷ pall²

palladium n (pl -s) (CHEM) silvery-white element of the platinum metal group

palladiums n ▷ palladium

pallet¹ n (pl -s) portable platform for storing and moving goods

pallet² n straw-filled mattress or bed

pallets n ▷ pallet¹, ²

palliate v (-tes, -ting, -ted) lessen the severity of (something) without curing it

palliated v ▷ palliate

palliates v ▷ palliate

palliating v ▷ palliate

palliative adj giving temporary or partial relief ▶ n (pl -s) something, for example a drug, that palliates

palliatives n ▷ palliative

pallid adj pale, esp. because ill or weak > **pallor** n (pl -s)

pallider adj ▷ pallid

pallidest adj ▷ pallid

pallier adj ▷ pally

palliest adj ▷ pally

pallor n ▷ pallid

pallors n ▷ pallid

pally adj (-lier, -lliest) (Informal) on friendly terms

palm¹ n (pl -s) inner surface of the hand

palm² n (pl -s) tropical tree with long pointed leaves growing out of the top of a straight trunk

palmist n ▷ palmistry

palmistries n ▷ palmistry

palmistry n (pl -ries) fortune-telling from lines on the palm of the hand > **palmist** n (pl -s)

palmists n ▷ palmistry

palms n ▷ palm¹, ²

palmtop adj (of a computer) small enough to be held in the hand ▶ n (pl -s) computer small enough to be held in the hand

palmtops n ▷ palmtop

palomino n (pl -s) gold-coloured horse with a white mane and tail

palominos n ▷ palomino

palpable adj obvious > **palpably** adv

palpably adv ▷ palpable

palpate v (-tes, -ting, -ted) (MED) examine (an area of the body) by touching

palpated v ▷ palpate

palpates v ▷ palpate

palpating v ▷ palpate

palpitate v (-tes, -ting, -ted) (of the heart) beat rapidly > **palpitation** n (pl -s)

palpitated v ▷ palpitate

palpitates v ▷ palpitate

palpitating v ▷ palpitate

palpitation n ▷ palpitate

palpitations v ▷ palpitate

palsied adj affected with palsy

palsies n ▷ palsy

palsy [pawl-zee] n (pl -sies) paralysis

paltrier adj ▷ paltry

paltriest adj ▷ paltry

paltry adj (-rier, -riest) insignificant

pampas pl n vast grassy plains in S America

pamper v (-s, -ing, -ed) treat (someone) with great indulgence, spoil

pampered v ▷ pamper

pampering v ▷ pamper

pampers v ▷ pamper

pamphlet n (pl -s) thin paper-covered booklet

pamphleteer n (pl -s) writer of pamphlets

pamphleteers n ▷ pamphleteer

pamphlets n ▷ pamphlet

pan¹ n (pl -s) wide long-handled metal container used in cooking ▶ v (-s, -nning, -nned) sift gravel from (a river) in a pan to search for gold (Informal)

pan² v (-s, -nning, -nned) (of a film camera) be moved slowly so as to cover a whole scene or follow a moving object

panacea [pan-a-see-a] n (pl -s) remedy for all diseases or problems

panaceas n ▷ panacea

panache [pan-ash] n (pl -s) confident elegant style

panaches n ▷ panache

panatella n (pl -s) long slender cigar

panatellas n ▷ panatella

pancake n (pl -s) thin flat circle of fried batter

pancakes n ▷ pancake

panchromatic adj (PHOTOG) sensitive to light of all colours

pancreas [pang-kree-ass] n (pl -es) large gland behind the stomach that produces insulin and helps digestion > **pancreatic** adj

pancreases n ▷ pancreas
pancreatic adj ▷ pancreas
panda n (pl -s) large black-and-white bearlike mammal from China
pandas n ▷ panda
pandemic adj (of a disease) occurring over a wide area
pandemonium n (pl -s) wild confusion, uproar
pandemoniums n ▷ pandemonium
pander¹ v (-s, -ing, -ed) (foll. by to) indulge (a person his or her desires)
pander² n (pl -s) (Old-fashioned) person who procures a sexual partner for someone
pandered v ▷ pander
pandering v ▷ pander
panders v, n ▷ pander¹, ²
pane n (pl -s) sheet of glass in a window or door
panes n ▷ pane
panegyric [pan-ee-jire-ik] n (pl -s) formal speech or piece of writing in praise of someone or something
panegyrics n ▷ panegyric
panel n (pl -s) flat distinct section of a larger surface, for example in a door ▶ v (-s, -lling, -lled) cover or decorate with panels
panelled v ▷ panel
panelling n (pl -s) panels collectively, esp. on a wall ▶ v ▷ panel
panellings n ▷ panelling
panellist n (pl -s) member of a panel
panellists n ▷ panellist
panels n ▷ panel
pang n (pl -s) sudden sharp feeling of pain or sadness
pangs n ▷ pang
pangolin n (pl -s) animal of tropical countries with a scaly body and a long snout for eating ants and termites (also **scaly anteater**)
pangolins n ▷ pangolin
panic n (pl -s) sudden overwhelming fear, often affecting a whole group of people ▶ v (-s, -cking, -cked) feel or cause to feel panic ▷ **panicky** adj (-ier, -iest)
panicked v ▷ panic
panickier adj ▷ panic
panickiest adj ▷ panic
panicking v ▷ panic
panicky adj ▷ panic
panics n, v ▷ panic
panic-stricken adj ▷ panic
pannier n (pl -s) bag fixed on the back of a cycle
panniers n ▷ pannier
panoplies n ▷ panoply
panoply n (pl -ies) magnificent array
panorama n (pl -s) wide unbroken view of a scene ▷ **panoramic** adj

panoramas n ▷ panorama
panoramic adj ▷ panorama
pansies n ▷ pansy
pansy n (pl -sies) small garden flower with velvety purple, yellow, or white petals
pant v (-s, -ing, -ed) breathe quickly and noisily during or after exertion
pantaloons pl n baggy trousers gathered at the ankles
pantechnicon n (pl -s) large van for furniture removals
pantechnicons n ▷ pantechnicon
panted v ▷ pant
pantheism n (pl -s) belief that God is present in everything ▷ **pantheist** n (pl -s) ▷ **pantheistic** adj
pantheisms n ▷ pantheism
pantheist n ▷ pantheism
pantheistic adj ▷ pantheism
pantheists n ▷ pantheism
pantheon n (pl -s) (in ancient Greece and Rome) temple built to honour all the gods
pantheons n ▷ pantheon
panther n (pl -s) leopard, esp. a black one
panthers n ▷ panther
panties pl n women's underpants
pantile n (pl -s) roofing tile with an S-shaped cross section
pantiles n ▷ pantile
panting v ▷ pant
pantomime n (pl -s) play based on a fairy tale, performed at Christmas time
pantomimes n ▷ pantomime
pantries n ▷ pantry
pantry n (pl -ries) small room or cupboard for storing food
pants v ▷ pant
pants pl n undergarment for the lower part of the body
pap n (pl -s) soft food for babies or invalids
papacies n ▷ papacy
paps n ▷ pap
papacy [pay-pa-see] n (pl -cies) position or term of office of a pope
papal adj of the pope
paparazzi n ▷ paparazzo
paparazzo [pap-a-rat-so] n (pl -razzi) photographer specializing in candid photographs of famous people
papaya [pa-pie-ya] n (pl -s) large sweet West Indian fruit
papayas n ▷ papaya
paper n (pl -s) material made in sheets from wood pulp or other fibres ▶ pl personal

documents ▸ v (-s, -ing, -ed) cover (walls) with wallpaper

paperback n (pl -s) book with covers made of flexible card

paperbacks n ▷ paperback

papering v ▷ paper

papered v ▷ paper

papers n, v ▷ paper

paperweight n (pl -s) heavy decorative object placed on top of loose papers

paperweights n ▷ paperweight

paperwork n (pl -s) clerical work, such as writing reports and letters

paperworks n ▷ paperwork

papoose n (pl -s) Native American child

papooses n ▷ papoose

paprika n (pl -s) mild powdered seasoning made from red peppers

paprikas n ▷ paprika

papyri n ▷ papyrus

papyrus [pap-ire-uss] n (pl -ri, -ruses) tall water plant

papyruses n ▷ papyrus

par n (pl -s) usual or average condition

parable n (pl -s) story that illustrates a religious teaching

parables n ▷ parable

parabola [par-ab-bol-a] n (pl -s) regular curve resembling the course of an object thrown forward and up ▸ **parabolic** adj

parabolas n ▷ parabola

parabolic adj ▷ parabola

paracetamol n (pl -s) mild pain-relieving drug

paracetamols n ▷ paracetamol

parachute n (pl -s) large fabric canopy that slows the descent of a person or object from an aircraft ▸ v (-tes, -ting, -ted) land or drop by parachute ▸ **parachutist** n (pl -s)

parachuted n, v ▷ parachute

parachutes v ▷ parachute

parachuting v ▷ parachute

parachutist n ▷ parachute

parachutists n ▷ parachute

parade n (pl -s) procession or march ▸ v (-des, -ding, -ded) display or flaunt

paraded v ▷ parade

parades n, v ▷ parade

parading v ▷ parade

paradigm [par-a-dime] n (pl -s) example or model

paradigms n ▷ paradigm

paradise n (pl -s) heaven

paradises n ▷ paradise

paradox n (pl -xes) statement that seems self-contradictory but may be true ▸ **paradoxical**

adj ▸ **paradoxically** adv

paradoxes n ▷ paradox

paradoxical adj ▷ paradox

paradoxically adv ▷ paradox

paraffin n (pl -s) (BRIT & S AFR) liquid mixture distilled from petroleum and used as a fuel or solvent

paraffins n ▷ paraffin

paragliding n (pl -s) cross-country gliding wearing a parachute shaped like wings

paraglidings n ▷ paragliding

paragon n (pl -s) model of perfection

paragons n ▷ paragon

paragraph n (pl -s) section of a piece of writing starting on a new line

paragraphs n ▷ paragraph

parakeet n (pl -s) small long-tailed parrot

parakeets n ▷ parakeet

parallax n (pl -es) apparent change in an object's position due to a change in the observer's position

parallaxes n ▷ parallax

parallel adj separated by an equal distance at every point ▸ n (pl -s) line separated from another by an equal distance at every point ▸ v (-s, -ing, -ed) correspond to

paralleled v ▷ parallel

paralleling v ▷ parallel

parallels n, v ▷ parallel

parallelogram n (pl -s) four-sided geometric figure with opposite sides parallel

parallelograms n ▷ parallelogram

paralyse v (-ses, -sing, -sed) affect with paralysis

paralysed v ▷ paralyse

paralyses v ▷ paralyse ▸ n ▷ paralysis

paralysing ▷ paralyse

paralysis n (pl -ses) inability to move or feel, because of damage to the nervous system

paralytic n (pl -s) ▸ adj (person) affected with paralysis

paralytics n ▷ paralytic

paramedic n (pl -s) person working in support of the medical profession > **paramedical** adj

paramedical n ▷ paramedic

paramedics n ▷ paramedic

parameter [par-am-it-er] n (pl -s) limiting factor, boundary

parameters n ▷ parameter

paramilitary adj organized on military lines

paramount adj of the greatest importance

paramour n (pl -s) (Old-fashioned) lover, esp. of a person married to someone else

paramours n ▷ paramour

paranoia n (pl -s) mental illness causing

delusions of grandeur or persecution
(*Informal*) > **paranoid, paranoiac** *adj, n* (*pl* **-s**)

paranoiac *adj, n* ▷ paranoia

paranoiacs *n* ▷ paranoia

paranoias *n* ▷ paranoia

paranoid *adj, n* ▷ paranoia

paranoids *n* ▷ paranoia

paranormal *adj* beyond scientific explanation

parapet *n* (*pl* **-s**) low wall or railing along the edge of a balcony or roof

parapets *n* ▷ parapet

paraphernalia *n* (*pl* **-s**) personal belongings or bits of equipment

paraphernalias *n* ▷ paraphernalia

paraphrase *v* (**-ses, -sing, -sed**) put (a statement or text) into other words

paraphrased *v* ▷ paraphrase

paraphrases *v* ▷ paraphrase

paraphrasing *v* ▷ paraphrase

paraplegia [par-a-**pleej**-ya] *n* (*pl* **-s**) paralysis of the lower half of the body > **paraplegic** *adj, n* (*pl* **-s**)

paraplegias *n* ▷ paraplegia

paraplegic *adj, n* ▷ paraplegia

paraplegics *n* ▷ paraplegia

parapsychologies *n* ▷ parapsychology

parapsychology *n* (*pl* **-gies**) study of mental phenomena such as telepathy

parasite *n* (*pl* **-s**) animal or plant living in or on another > **parasitic** *adj*

parasites *n* ▷ parasite

parasitic *adj* ▷ parasite

parasol *n* (*pl* **-s**) umbrella-like sunshade

parasols *n* ▷ parasol

paratrooper *n* (*pl* **-s**) soldier trained to be dropped by parachute into a battle area > **paratroops** *pl n*

paratroopers *n* ▷ paratrooper

paratroops *n* ▷ paratrooper

parboil *v* (**-s, -ing, -ed**) boil until partly cooked

parboiled *v* ▷ parboil

parboiling *v* ▷ parboil

parboils *v* ▷ parboil

parcel *n* (*pl* **-s**) something wrapped up, package ▶ *v* (**-s, -lling, -lled**) (*often foll. by* **up**) wrap up

parcelled *v* ▷ parcel

parcelling *v* ▷ parcel

parcels *n, v* ▷ parcel

parch *v* (**-es, -ing, -ed**) make very hot and dry

parched *v* ▷ parch

parches *v* ▷ parch

parching *v* ▷ parch

parchment *n* (*pl* **-s**) thick smooth writing material made from animal skin

parchments *n* ▷ parchment

pardon *v* (**-s, -ing, -ed**) forgive, excuse ▶ *n* (*pl* **-s**) forgiveness > **pardonable** *adj*

pardonable *adj* ▷ pardon

pardoned *v* ▷ pardon

pardoning *v* ▷ pardon

pardons *v, n* ▷ pardon

pare *v* (**-res, -ring, -red**) cut off the skin or top layer of (*often foll. by* **down**)

pared *v* ▷ pare

pares *v* ▷ pare

paring *v* ▷ pare ▶ *n* (*pl* **-s**) piece pared off

parings *n* ▷ pareing

parent *n* (*pl* **-s**) father or mother > **parental** *adj* > **parenthood** *n* (*pl* **-s**)

parentage *n* (*pl* **-s**) ancestry or family

parentages *n* ▷ parentage

parental *adj* ▷ parent

parenthood *n* ▷ parent

parenthoods *n* ▷ parent

parenting *n* (*pl* **-s**) activity of bringing up children

parentings *n* ▷ parenting

parents *n* ▷ parent

parenthesis [par-en-**thiss**-iss] *n* (*pl* **-ses**) word or sentence inserted into a passage, marked off by brackets or dashes ▶ *pl* round brackets, ( ) > **parenthetical** *adj*

parentheses *n* ▷ parenthesis

parenthetical *adj* ▷ parenthesis

pariah [par-**rye**-a] *n* (*pl* **-s**) social outcast

pariahs *n* ▷ pariah

parietal [par-**rye**-it-al] *adj* of the walls of a body cavity such as the skull

parish *n* (*pl* **-es**) area that has its own church and a priest or pastor

parishes *n* ▷ parish

parishioner *n* (*pl* **-s**) inhabitant of a parish

parishioners *n* ▷ parishioner

parities *n* ▷ parity

parity *n* (*pl* **-ties**) equality or equivalence

park *n* (*pl* **-s**) area of open land for recreational use by the public ▶ *v* (**-s, -ing, -ed**) stop and leave (a vehicle) temporarily

parked *v* ▷ park

parking *v* ▷ park

parks *n, v* ▷ park

parka *n* (*pl* **-s**) large waterproof jacket with a hood

parkas *n* ▷ parka

parkier *adj* ▷ parky

parkiest *adj* ▷ parky

parky *adj* (**-kier, -kiest**) (BRIT) (*Informal*) (of the weather) chilly

parlance *n* (*pl* **-s**) particular way of speaking,

idiom
parlances n ▷ parlance
parley n (pl -s) meeting between leaders or representatives of opposing forces to discuss terms ▶ v (-s, -ing, -ed) have a parley
parleyed v ▷ parley
parleying v ▷ parley
parleys n, v ▷ parley
parliament n (pl -s) law-making assembly of a country > **parliamentary** adj
parliamentary adj ▷ parliament
parliaments n ▷ parliament
parlour n (pl -s) (Old-fashioned) living room for receiving visitors
parlours n ▷ parlour
parlous adj (Old-fashioned) dire
parochial adj narrow in outlook > **parochialism** n (pl -s)
parochialism n ▷ parochial
parochialisms n ▷ parochial
parodied v ▷ parody
parodies n, v ▷ parody
parody n (pl -dies) exaggerated and amusing imitation of someone else's style ▶ v (-ies, -ying, -ied) make a parody of
parodying v ▷ parody
parole n (pl -s) early freeing of a prisoner on condition that he or she behaves well ▶ v (-les, -ling, -led) put on parole
paroled v ▷ parole
paroles n, v ▷ parole
paroling v ▷ parole
paroxysm n (pl -s) uncontrollable outburst of rage, delight, etc.
paroxysms n ▷ paroxysm
parquet [par-kay] n (pl -s) floor covering made of wooden blocks arranged in a geometric pattern > **parquetry** n (pl -ies)
parquetries n ▷ parquet
parquetry n ▷ parquet
parquets n ▷ parquet
parricide n (pl -s) crime of killing either of one's parents
parricides n ▷ parricide
parried v ▷ parry
parries v ▷ parry
parrot n (pl -s) tropical bird with a short hooked beak and an ability to imitate human speech ▶ v (-s, -ing, -ed) repeat (someone else's words) without thinking
parroted v ▷ parrot
parroting v ▷ parrot
parrots n, v ▷ parrot
parry v (-rries, -rrying, -rried) ward off (an attack)

parrying v ▷ parry
pars n ▷ par
parse [parz] v (-ses, -sing, -sed) analyse (a sentence) in terms of grammar
parsed v ▷ parse
parses v ▷ parse
parsing v ▷ parse
parsimonies n ▷ parsimony
parsimonious adj ▷ parsimony
parsimony n (pl -nies) extreme caution in spending money > **parsimonious** adj
parsley n (pl -s) herb used for seasoning and decorating food
parsleys n ▷ parsley
parsnip n (pl -s) long tapering cream-coloured root vegetable
parsnips n ▷ parsnip
parson n (pl -s) Anglican parish priest
parsons n ▷ parson
parsonage n (pl -s) parson's house
parsonages n ▷ parsonage
part n (pl -s) one of the pieces that make up a whole ▶ v (-s, -ing, -ed) divide or separate
partake v (-takes, -taking, -took, -taken) (foll. by **of**) take (food or drink)
partaken v ▷ partake
partakes v ▷ partake
partaking v ▷ partake
partial adj not complete > **partiality** n (pl -ties) > **partially** adv
partialities n ▷ partial
partiality n ▷ partial
partially adv ▷ partial
parted v ▷ part
participate v (-tes, -ting, -ted) become actively involved > **participant** n (pl -s) > **participation** n (pl -s)
participant n ▷ participate
participants n ▷ participate
participated v ▷ participate
participates v ▷ participate
participating v ▷ participate
participation n ▷ participation
participations n ▷ participation
participle n (pl -s) form of a verb used in compound tenses or as an adjective
participles n ▷ participle
particle n (pl -s) extremely small piece or amount
particles n ▷ particle
particular adj relating to one person or thing, not general ▶ n (pl -s) item of information, detail > **particularly** adv
particularize v (-zes, -zing, -zed) give details about

particularized v ▷ particularize
particularizes v ▷ particularize
particularizing v ▷ particularize
particularly adv ▷ particular
particulars n ▷ particular
parties n ▷ party
parting n (pl -s) occasion when one person leaves another ▶ v ▷ part
partings n ▷ parting
partisan n (pl -s) strong supporter of a party or group ▶ adj prejudiced or one-sided
partisans n ▷ partisan
partition n (pl -s) screen or thin wall that divides a room ▶ v (-s, -ing, -ed) divide with a partition
partitioned v ▷ partition
partitioning v ▷ partition
partitions n, v ▷ partition
partly adv not completely
partner n (pl -s) either member of a couple in a relationship or activity ▶ v (-s, -ing, -ed) be the partner of
partnered v ▷ partner
partnering v ▷ partner
partners n, v ▷ partner
partnership n (pl -s) joint business venture between two or more people
partnerships n ▷ partnership
partook v ▷ partake
partridge n (pl -s) game bird of the grouse family
partridges n ▷ partridge
parts n, v ▷ part
parturition n (pl -s) act of giving birth
party n (pl -ties) social gathering for pleasure
parvenu [par-ven-new] n (pl -s) person newly risen to a position of power or wealth
parvenus n ▷ parvenu
pas n ▷ pa
pascal n (pl -s) unit of pressure
pascals n ▷ pascal
paspalum [pass-pale-um] n (pl -s) (AUST & NZ) type of grass with wide leaves
paspalums n ▷ paspalum
pass v (-es, -ing, -ed) go by, past, or through (SPORT) ▶ n (pl -es) successful result in a test or examination
passable adj (just) acceptable
passage n (pl -s) channel or opening providing a way through
passages n ▷ passage
passageway n (pl -s) passage or corridor
passageways n ▷ passageway
passbook n (pl -s) book issued by a bank or building society for keeping a record of deposits and withdrawals
passbooks n ▷ passbook
passé [pas-say] adj out-of-date
passed v ▷ pass
passenger n (pl -s) person travelling in a vehicle driven by someone else
passengers n ▷ passenger
passes v, n ▷ pass
passim adv (LATIN) everywhere, throughout
passing adj brief or transitory ▶ v ▷ pass
passion n (pl -s) intense sexual love
> **passionate** adj
passionate adj ▷ passion
passionflower n (pl -s) tropical American plant
passionflowers n ▷ passionflower
passions n ▷ passion
passive adj not playing an active part
> **passivity** n (pl -ties)
passivities n ▷ passive
passivity n ▷ passive
passport n (pl -s) official document of nationality granting permission to travel abroad
passports n ▷ passport
password n (pl -s) secret word or phrase that ensures admission
passwords n ▷ password
past adj of the time before the present ▶ n (pl -s) period of time before the present ▶ adv by, along ▶ prep beyond
pasta n (pl -s) type of food, such as spaghetti, that is made in different shapes from flour and water
pastas n ▷ pasta
paste n (pl -s) moist soft mixture, such as toothpaste ▶ v (-tes, -ting, -ted) fasten with paste
pasteboard n (pl -s) stiff thick paper
pasteboards n ▷ pasteboard
pasted v ▷ paste
pastel n (pl -s) coloured chalk crayon for drawing ▶ adj pale and delicate in colour
pastels n ▷ pastel
pastes n, v ▷ paste
pasteurize v (-zes, -zing, -zed) sterilize by heating > **pasteurization** n (pl -s)
pasteurization n ▷ pasteurize
pasteurizations n ▷ pasteurize
pasteurized v ▷ pasteurize
pasteurizes v ▷ pasteurize
pasteurizing v ▷ pasteurize
pastiche [pass-teesh] n (pl -s) work of art that mixes styles or copies the style of another artist
pastiches n ▷ pastiche

pastier adj ▷ pasty¹
pasties n ▷ pasty²
pastiest adj ▷ pasty¹
pastille n (pl -s) small fruit-flavoured and sometimes medicated sweet
pastilles n ▷ pastille
pastime n (pl -s) activity that makes time pass pleasantly
pastimes n ▷ pastime
pasting n (pl -s) (Informal) heavy defeat ▶ v ▷ paste
pastings n ▷ pasting
pastor n (pl -s) member of the clergy in charge of a congregation
pastoral adj of or depicting country life
pastors n ▷ pastor
pastrami n (pl -s) highly seasoned smoked beef
pastramis n ▷ pastrami
pastries n ▷ pastry
pastry n (pl -ries) baking dough made of flour, fat, and water
pasts n ▷ past
pasture n (pl -s) grassy land for farm animals to graze on
pastures n ▷ pasture
pasty¹ [pay-stee] adj (-tier, -tiest) (of a complexion) pale and unhealthy
pasty² [pass-tee] n (pl -ties) round of pastry folded over a savoury filling
pat¹ v (-s, -tting, -tted) tap lightly ▶ n (pl -s) gentle tap or stroke
pat² adj quick, ready, or glib
patch n (pl -es) piece of material sewn on a garment ▶ v (-es, -ing, -ed) mend with a patch
patched v ▷ patch
patches n, v ▷ patch
patchier adj ▷ patchy
patchiest adj ▷ patchy
patching v ▷ patch
patchwork n (pl -s) needlework made of pieces of different materials sewn together
patchworks n ▷ patchwork
patchy adj (-hier, -hiest) of uneven quality or intensity
pate n (pl -s) (Old-fashioned) head
pates n ▷ pate
pâté [pat-ay] n (pl -s) spread of finely minced liver etc.
pâtés n ▷ pâté
patella n (pl -ae) kneecap
patellae n ▷ patella
patent n (pl -s) document giving the exclusive right to make or sell an invention ▶ adj open to public inspection ▶ v (-s, -ing, -ed) obtain

a patent for
patented v ▷ patent
patenting v ▷ patent
patently adv obviously
patents n, v ▷ patent
paternal adj fatherly
paternities n ▷ paternity
paternity n (pl -ties) fact or state of being a father
paternalism n (pl -s) authority exercised in a way that limits individual responsibility > **paternalistic** adj
paternalisms n ▷ paternalism
paternalistic adj ▷ paternalism
path n (pl -s) surfaced walk or track
pathname n (pl -s) (COMPUTERS) file name listing the sequence of directories leading to a particular file or directory
pathnames n ▷ pathname
paths n ▷ path
pathetic adj causing feelings of pity or sadness > **pathetically** adv
pathetically adv ▷ pathetic
pathogen n (pl -s) thing that causes disease > **pathogenic** adj
pathogenic adj ▷ pathogen
pathogens n ▷ pathogen
pathologies n ▷ pathology
pathology n (pl -gies) scientific study of diseases > **pathologist** n (pl -s)
pathological adj of pathology
pathologist n ▷ pathology
pathologists n ▷ pathology
pathos n (pl -es) power of arousing pity or sadness
pathoses n ▷ pathos
patience n (pl -s) quality of being patient
patiences n ▷ patience
patient adj enduring difficulties or delays calmly ▶ n (pl -s) person receiving medical treatment
patients n ▷ patient
patina n (pl -s) fine layer on a surface
patinas n ▷ patina
patio n (pl -os) paved area adjoining a house
patios n ▷ patio
patois [pat-wah] n (pl patois) [pat-wahz] regional dialect, esp. of French
patriarch n (pl -s) male head of a family or tribe > **patriarchal** adj
patriarchal adj ▷ patriarch
patriarchies n ▷ patriarchy
patriarchs n ▷ patriarch
patriarchy n (pl -hies) society in which men have most of the power

patrician n (pl -s) member of the nobility ▶ adj of noble birth
patricians n ▷ patrician
patricide n (pl -s) crime of killing one's father
patricides n ▷ patricide
patrimonies n ▷ patrimony
patrimony n (pl -nies) property inherited from ancestors
patriot n (pl -s) person who loves his or her country and supports its interests > **patriotic** adj > **patriotism** n (pl -s)
patriotic adj ▷ patriot
patriotism n ▷ patriot
patriotisms n ▷ patriot
patriots n ▷ patriot
patrol n (pl -s) regular circuit by a guard ▶ v (-s, -lling, -lled) go round on guard, or reconnoitring
patrolled v ▷ patrol
patrolling v ▷ patrol
patrols n, v ▷ patrol
patron n (pl -s) person who gives financial support to charities, artists, etc.
patronage n (pl -s) support given by a patron
patronages n ▷ patronage
patronize v (-zes, -zing, -zed) treat in a condescending way
patronized v ▷ patronize
patronizes v ▷ patronize
patronizing v ▷ patronize
patrons n ▷ patron
patronymic n (pl -s) name derived from one's father or a male ancestor
patronymics n ▷ patronymic
pats v, n ▷ pat¹
patted v ▷ pat¹
patter¹ v (-s, -ing, -ed) make repeated soft tapping sounds ▶ n (pl -s) quick succession of taps
patter² n (pl -s) glib rapid speech
pattered v ▷ patter¹
pattering v ▷ patter¹
patters v, n ▷ patter¹, ²
pattern n (pl -s) arrangement of repeated parts or decorative designs
patterned adj decorated with a pattern
patterns n ▷ pattern
patties n ▷ patty
patting v ▷ pat¹
patty n (pl -tties) small flattened cake of minced food
paucities n ▷ paucity
paucity n (pl -ties) scarcity
paunch n (pl -es) protruding belly
paunches n ▷ paunch

pauper n (pl -s) very poor person
paupers n ▷ pauper
pause v (-ses, -sing, -sed) stop for a time ▶ n (pl -s) stop or rest in speech or action
paused v ▷ pause
pauses v, n ▷ pause
pausing v ▷ pause
pave v (-ves, -ving, -ved) form (a surface) with stone or brick
paved v ▷ pave
pavement n (pl -s) paved path for pedestrians
pavements n ▷ pavement
paves v ▷ pave
paving v ▷ pave
pavilion n (pl -s) building on a playing field etc.
pavilions n ▷ pavilion
paw n (pl -s) animal's foot with claws and pads ▶ v (-s, -ing, -ed) scrape with the paw or hoof
pawed v ▷ paw
pawing v ▷ paw
paws n, v ▷ paw
pawn¹ v (-s, -ing, -ed) deposit (an article) as security for money borrowed
pawn² n (pl -s) chessman of the lowest value
pawnbroker n (pl -s) lender of money on goods deposited
pawnbrokers n ▷ pawnbroker
pawned v ▷ pawn¹
pawning v ▷ pawn¹
pawns v, n ▷ pawn¹, ²
pay v (-s, -ing, paid) give money etc. in return for goods or services ▶ n (pl -s) wages or salary
payable adj due to be paid
payee n (pl -s) person to whom money is paid or due
payees n ▷ payee
paying v ▷ pay
payload n (pl -s) passengers or cargo of an aircraft
payloads n ▷ payload
payment n (pl -s) act of paying
payments n ▷ payment
payola n (pl -s) (CHIEFLY US) (Informal) bribe to get special treatment, esp. to promote a commercial product
pays v, n ▷ pay
payolas n ▷ payola

> **pax** n (paxes). A pax is a period of peace, especially when there is one dominant nation. If you have a P and an X on your rack, there is likely to be an A available on the board. Pax gives a decent score for a three-letter word, so watch out for chances to play it on a bonus square. Pax scores 12 points.

pe n (**pes**). Pe is the 17th letter in the Hebrew alphabet. This is a very handy word because it allows you to connect words beginning with P to those ending in E, or vice versa and E is the most common tile in the game. Pe scores 4 points.

pea n (pl -**s**) climbing plant with seeds growing in pods
  peas n ▷ pea

peace n (pl -**s**) calm, quietness ▷ **peaceful** adj ▷ **peacefully** adv

peaceable adj inclined towards peace ▷ **peaceably** adv
  peaceably adv ▷ peaceable
  peaceful adj ▷ peace
  peacefully adv ▷ peace
  peaces n ▷ peace

peach n (pl -**es**) soft juicy fruit with a stone and a downy skin ▶ adj pinkish-orange
  peaches n ▷ peach

peacock n (pl -**s**) large male bird with a brilliantly coloured fanlike tail ▷ **peahen** n fem (pl -**s**)
  peacocks n ▷ peacock
  peahen n ▷ peacock
  peahens n ▷ peacock

peak n (pl -**s**) pointed top, esp. of a mountain ▶ v (-**s**, -**ing**, -**ed**) form or reach a peak ▶ adj of or at the point of greatest demand ▷ **peaked** adj
  peaked adj, v ▷ peak
  peakier adj ▷ peaky
  peakiest adj ▷ peaky
  peaking v ▷ peak
  peaks n, v ▷ peak

peaky adj (-**kier**, -**kiest**) pale and sickly

peal n (pl -**s**) long loud echoing sound, esp. of bells or thunder ▶ v (-**s**, -**ing**, -**ed**) sound with a peal or peals
  pealed v ▷ peal
  pealing v ▷ peal
  peals n, v ▷ peal

peanut n (pl -**s**) pea-shaped nut that ripens underground ▶ pl (Informal) trifling amount of money
  peanuts n ▷ peanut

pear n (pl -**s**) sweet juicy fruit with a narrow top and rounded base
  pears n ▷ pear

pearl n (pl -**s**) hard round shiny object found inside some oyster shells and used as a jewel ▷ **pearly** adj (-**lier**, -**liest**)
  pearlier adj ▷ pearl
  pearliest adj ▷ peral

pearls n ▷ pearl
pearly adj ▷ pearl

peasant n (pl -**s**) person working on the land, esp. in poorer countries or in the past
  peasantries n ▷ peasantry

peasantry n (pl -**ries**) peasants collectively
  peasants n ▷ peasant

peat n (pl -**s**) decayed vegetable material found in bogs, used as fertilizer or fuel
  peats n ▷ peat

pebble n (pl -**s**) small roundish stone ▷ **pebbly** adj (-**lier**, -**liest**)
  pebbles n ▷ pebble
  pebblier adj ▷ pebble
  pebbliest adj ▷ pebble
  pebbly adj ▷ pebble

pecan [pee-kan] n (pl -**s**) edible nut of a N American tree
  pecans n ▷ pecan

peccadillo n (pl -**lloes**, -**llos**) trivial misdeed
  peccadilloes n ▷ peccadillo
  peccadillos n ▷ peccadillo

peck v (-**s**, -**ing**, -**ed**) strike or pick up with the beak ▶ n (pl -**s**) pecking movement
  pecked v ▷ peck
  pecking v ▷ peck

peckish adj (Informal) slightly hungry
  pecks v, n ▷ peck

pecs pl n (Informal) pectoral muscles

pectin n (pl -**s**) substance in fruit that makes jam set
  pectins n ▷ pectin

pectoral adj of the chest or thorax ▶ n (pl -**s**) pectoral muscle or fin
  pectorals n ▷ pectoral

peculiar adj strange
  peculiarities n ▷ peculiarity

peculiarity n (pl -**ties**) oddity, eccentricity

pecuniary adj relating to, or consisting of, money

pedagogue n (pl -**s**) schoolteacher, esp. a pedantic one
  pedagogues n ▷ pedagogue

pedal n (pl -**s**) foot-operated lever used to control a vehicle or machine, or to modify the tone of a musical instrument ▶ v (-**s**, -**lling**, -**lled**) propel (a bicycle) by using its pedals
  pedalled v ▷ pedal
  pedalling v ▷ pedal
  pedals n ▷ pedal

pedant n (pl -**s**) person who is excessively concerned with details and rules, esp. in academic work ▷ **pedantic** adj ▷ **pedantry** n (pl -**ries**)
  pedantic adj ▷ pedant

pedantries n ▷ pedant

pedantry n ▷ pedant

pedants n ▷ pedant

peddle v (-les, -ling, -led) sell (goods) from door to door

peddled v ▷ peddle

peddles v ▷ peddle

peddling v ▷ peddle

peddler n (pl -s) person who sells illegal drugs

peddlers n ▷ peddler

pedestal n (pl -s) base supporting a column, statue, etc.

pedestals n ▷ pedestal

pedestrian n (pl -s) person who walks ▶ adj dull, uninspiring

pedestrians n ▷ pedestrian

pedicure n (pl -s) medical or cosmetic treatment of the feet

pedicures n ▷ pedicure

pedigree n (pl -s) register of ancestors, esp. of a purebred animal

pedigrees n ▷ pedigree

pediment n (pl -s) triangular part over a door etc.

pediments n ▷ pediment

pedlar n (pl -s) person who sells goods from door to door

pedlars n ▷ pedlar

pee (Informal) v (-s, -ing, peed) urinate ▶ n (-s) act of urinating

peed v ▷ pee

peeing v ▷ pee

pees v, n ▷ pee

peek v, n (pl -s) peep or glance

peeks n ▷ peek

peel v (-s, -ing, -ed) remove the skin or rind of (a vegetable or fruit) ▶ n (pl -s) rind or skin > **peelings** pl n

peeled v ▷ peel

peeling v ▷ peel

peelings n ▷ peel

peels v, n ▷ peel

peep[1] v (-s, -ing, -ed) look slyly or quickly ▶ n (pl -s) peeping look

peep[2] v (-s, -ing, -ed) make a small shrill noise ▶ n (-s) small shrill noise

peeped v ▷ peep[1, 2]

peeping v ▷ peep[1, 2]

peeps v, n ▷ peep[1, 2]

peer[1] n (pl -s), fem **peeress** (pl -es) (in Britain) member of the nobility

peer[2] v (-s, -ing, -ed) look closely and intently

peerage n (BRIT) whole body of peers

peerages n ▷ peerage

peered v ▷ peer[2]

peeress n ▷ peer

peeresses n ▷ peer

peering v ▷ peer[2]

peerless adj unequalled, unsurpassed

peers n, v ▷ peer[1, 2]

peers v ▷ peer

peering v ▷ peer

peered v ▷ peer

peeved adj (Informal) annoyed

peevish adj fretful or irritable > **peevishly** adv

peevishly adv ▷ peevish

peewee n (pl -s) black-and-white Australian bird

peewees n ▷ peewee

peewit n (pl -s) ▷ lapwing

peewits n ▷ peewit

peg n (pl -s) pin or clip for joining, fastening, marking, etc. ▶ v (-s, -gging, -gged) fasten with pegs

pegged v ▷ peg

pegging v ▷ peg

pegs n, v ▷ peg

peignoir [pay-nwahr] n (pl -s) woman's light dressing gown

peignoirs n ▷ peignoir

pejorative [pij-jor-a-tiv] adj (of words etc.) with an insulting or critical meaning

pelargonium n (pl -s) plant with red, white, purple, or pink flowers

pelargoniums n ▷ pelargonium

pelican n (pl -s) large water bird with a pouch beneath its bill for storing fish

pelicans n ▷ pelican

pellagra n (pl -s) disease caused by lack of vitamin B

pellagras n ▷ pellagra

pellet n (pl -s) small ball of something

pellets n ▷ pellet

pellucid adj very clear

pelmet n (pl -s) ornamental drapery or board, concealing a curtain rail

pelmets n ▷ pelmet

pelt[1] v (-s, -ing, -ed) throw missiles at

pelt[2] n (pl -s) skin of a fur-bearing animal

pelted v ▷ pelt[1]

pelting v ▷ pelt[1]

pelts v, n ▷ pelt[1, 2]

pelvic adj ▷ pelvis

pelvis n (pl -es) framework of bones at the base of the spine, to which the hips are attached > **pelvic** adj

pelvises n ▷ pelvis

pen[1] n (pl -s) instrument for writing in ink ▶ v (-s, -nning, -nned) write or compose

pen[2] n small enclosure for domestic animals

▶ v (-s, -nning, -nned) put or keep in a pen

pen³ n (pl -s) female swan

penal [pee-nal] adj of or used in punishment

penalize (-zes, -zing, -zed) v impose a penalty on

  penalized v ▷ penalize

  penalizes v ▷ penalize

  penalizing v ▷ penalize

  penalties n ▷ penalty

penalty n (pl -ties) punishment for a crime or offence

penance n (pl (pl -s) voluntary self-punishment to make amends for wrongdoing

  penances n ▷ penance

pence n (BRIT) ▷ penny

penchant [pon-shon] n (pl -s) inclination or liking

  penchants n ▷ penchant

pencil n (pl -s) thin cylindrical instrument containing graphite, for writing or drawing ▶ v (-s, -lling, -lled) draw, write, or mark with a pencil

  pencilled v ▷ pencil

  pencilling v ▷ pencil

  pencils n, v ▷ pencil

pendant n (pl -s) ornament worn on a chain round the neck

  pendants n ▷ pendant

pendent adj hanging

pending prep while waiting for ▶ adj not yet decided or settled

pendulous adj hanging, swinging

pendulum n (pl -s) suspended weight swinging to and fro, esp. as a regulator for a clock

  pendulums n ▷ pendulum

penetrate v (-tes, -ting, -ted) find or force a way into or through > **penetration** n (pl -s)

penetrable adj capable of being penetrated

  penetrated v ▷ penetrate

  penetrates v ▷ penetrate

penetrating adj (of a sound) loud and unpleasant ▶ v ▷ penetrate

  penetration n ▷ penetrate

  penetrations n ▷ penetrate

penguin n (pl -s) flightless black-and-white sea bird of the southern hemisphere

  penguins n ▷ penguin

penicillin n (pl -s) antibiotic drug effective against a wide range of diseases and infections

  penicillins n ▷ penicillin

peninsula n (pl -s) strip of land nearly surrounded by water > **peninsular** adj

  penisular adj ▷ penisula

  peninsulas n ▷ peninsula

penis n (pl -es) organ of copulation and urination in male mammals

  penises n ▷ penis

  penitence n ▷ penitent

  penitences n ▷ penitent

penitent adj feeling sorry for having done wrong ▶ n (pl -s) someone who is penitent > **penitence** n (pl -s)

  penitentiaries n ▷ penitentiary

penitentiary n (pl -ries) (us) prison ▶ adj (also **penitential**) relating to penance

  penitents n ▷ penitent

penknife n (pl -knives) small knife with blade(s) that fold into the handle

  penknives n ▷ penknife

pennant n (pl -s) long narrow flag

  pennants n ▷ pennant

  penned v ▷ pen¹,²

  pennies n ▷ penny

penniless adj very poor

  penning v ▷ pen¹,²

penny n (pl **pence, pennies**) British bronze coin worth one hundredth of a pound

  pens n ▷ pen¹,²,³

pension¹ n (pl -s) regular payment to people above a certain age, retired employees, widows, etc. > **pensionable** adj

pension² [pon-syon] n (pl -s) boarding house in Europe

  pensionable adj ▷ pension

pensioner n (pl -s) person receiving a pension

  pensioners n ▷ pension

  pensions n ▷ pension¹,²

pensive adj deeply thoughtful, often with a tinge of sadness

pentagon n (pl -s) geometric figure with five sides > **pentagonal** adj

  pentagonal adj ▷ pentagon

  pentagons n ▷ pentagon

pentameter [pen-tam-it-er] n (pl -s) line of poetry with five metrical feet

  pentameters n ▷ pentameter

penthouse n (pl -s) flat built on the roof or top floor of a building

  penthouses n ▷ penthouse

penultimate adj second last

penumbra n (pl -brae, -bras) (in an eclipse) the partially shadowed region which surrounds the full shadow

  penumbrae n ▷ penumbra

  penumbras n ▷ penumbra

  penuries n ▷ penury

  penurious adj ▷ penury

penury n (pl -ries) extreme poverty

> penurious adj
peonies n ▷ peony
peony n (pl -nies) garden plant with showy red, pink, or white flowers
people pl n persons generally ▶ n (pl -s) race or nation ▶ v (-les, -ling, -led) provide with inhabitants
peopled v ▷ people
peoples n, v ▷ people
peopling v ▷ people
pep n (pl -s) (Informal) high spirits, energy, or enthusiasm
pepper n (pl -s) sharp hot condiment made from the fruit of an East Indian climbing plant ▶ v (-s, -ing, -ed) season with pepper
peppercorn n dried berry of the pepper plant
peppercorns n ▷ peppercorn
peppered v ▷ pepper
pepperier adj ▷ peppery
pepperiest adj ▷ peppery
peppering v ▷ pepper
peppermint n (pl -s) plant that yields an oil with a strong sharp flavour
peppermints n ▷ peppermint
peppers n, v ▷ pepper
peppery adj (-rier, -riest) tasting of pepper
peps n ▷ pep
peptic adj relating to digestion or the digestive juices
per prep for each
perambulate v (-tes, -ting, -ted) (Old-fashioned) walk through or about (a place)
> perambulation n (pl -s)
perambulated v ▷ perambulate
perambulates v ▷ perambulate
perambulating v ▷ perambulate
perambulation n ▷ perambulate
perambulations n ▷ perambulate
perambulator n (pl -s) pram
perambulators n ▷ perambulator
perceive v (-ves, -ving, -ved) become aware of (something) through the senses
perceived v ▷ perceive
perceives v ▷ perceive
perceiving v ▷ perceive
perceptible adj discernible, recognizable
perception n (pl -s) act of perceiving
> perceptive adj
perceptions n ▷ perception
perceptive adj ▷ perception
perch¹ n (pl -es) resting place for a bird ▶ v (-es, -ing, -ed) alight, rest, or place on or as if on a perch
perch² n (pl -es) any of various edible fishes
perchance adv (Old-fashioned) perhaps

perches n, v ▷ perch¹, ²
perching v ▷ perch¹, ²
perched v ▷ perch¹, ²
percipient adj quick to notice things, observant
percolate v (-tes, -ting, -ted) pass or filter through small holes > percolation n
percolated v ▷ percolate
percolates v ▷ percolate
percolating v ▷ percolate
percolation n ▷ percolate
percolations n ▷ percolate
percolator n (pl -s) coffeepot in which boiling water is forced through a tube and filters down through coffee
percolators n ▷ percolator
percussion n (pl -s) striking of one thing against another
percussions n ▷ percussion
perdition n (pl -s) (CHRISTIANITY) spiritual ruin
perditions n ▷ perdition
peregrination n (pl -s) (Obs) travels, roaming
peregrinations n ▷ peregrination
peremptory adj authoritative, imperious
perennial adj lasting through many years ▶ n (pl -s) plant lasting more than two years
> perennially adv
perennially adv ▷ perennial
perennials n ▷ perennial
perfect adj (-er, -est) having all the essential elements ▶ n (pl -s) (GRAMMAR) perfect tense ▶ v (-s, -ing, -ed) improve > perfectly adv
perfected n ▷ perfect
perfecter adj ▷ perfect
perfectest adj ▷ perfect
perfecting v ▷ perfect
perfection n (pl -s) state of being perfect
perfectionist n (pl -s) person who demands the highest standards of excellence
> perfectionism n (pl -s)
perfectionism n ▷ perfectionist
perfectionisms n ▷ perfectionist
perfectionists n ▷ perfectionist
perfections n ▷ perfection
perfectly adv ▷ perfect
perfects n, v ▷ perfect
perfidious adj (Lit) treacherous, disloyal
> perfidy n (pl -ies)
perfidies n ▷ perfidious
perfidy n ▷ perfidious
perforate v (-es, -ing, -ed) make holes in
> perforation n (pl -s)
perforated v ▷ perforate
perforates v ▷ perforate
perforating v ▷ perforate

perforation n ▷ perforate

perforations n ▷ perforate

perforce adv of necessity

perform v (-s, -ing, -ed) carry out (an action)
> performance n (pl -s) > performer n (pl -s)

performance n ▷ perform

performances n ▷ perform

performed v ▷ perform

performer n ▷ perform

performers n ▷ perform

performing v ▷ perform

performs v ▷ perform

perfume n (pl -s) liquid cosmetic worn for
its pleasant smell ▶ v (-es, -ing, -ed) give a
pleasant smell to

perfumed v ▷ perfume

perfumeries n ▷ perfumery

perfumery n (pl -ries) perfumes in general

perfumes n, v ▷ perfume

perfuming v ▷ perfume

perfunctorily adv ▷ perfunctory

perfunctory adj done only as a matter of
routine, superficial > perfunctorily adv

pergola n (pl -s) arch or framework of trellis
supporting climbing plants

pergolas n ▷ pergola

perhaps adv possibly, maybe

pericardia n ▷ pericardum

pericardium n (pl -dia) membrane enclosing
the heart

perihelia n ▷ perihelion

perihelion n (pl -lia) point in the orbit of a
planet or comet that is nearest to the sun

peril n (pl -s) great danger > perilous adj
> perilously adv

perilous adj ▷ peril

perilously adv ▷ peril

perils n ▷ peril

perimeter [per-**rim**-it-er] n (pl -s) (length of) the
outer edge of an area

perimeters n ▷ perimeter

perinatal adj of or in the weeks shortly before
or after birth

period n (pl -s) particular portion of time (us)
▶ adj (of furniture, dress, a play, etc.) dating
from or in the style of an earlier time

periodic adj recurring at intervals

periodical n (pl -s) magazine issued at regular
intervals ▶ adj periodic

periodicals n ▷ periodical

periods n ▷ period

peripatetic [per-rip-a-**tet**-ik] adj travelling
about from place to place

peripheral [per-**if**-er-al] adj unimportant, not
central

peripheries n ▷ periphery

periphery [per-**if**-er-ee] n (pl -ries) boundary
or edge

periscope n (pl -s) instrument used, esp. in
submarines, to give a view of objects on a
different level

periscopes n ▷ periscope

perish v (-es, -ing, -ed) be destroyed or die

perishable adj liable to rot quickly

perished v ▷ perish

perishes v ▷ perish

perishing adj (Informal) very cold ▶ v ▷ perish

peritonea n ▷ peritoneum

peritoneum [per-rit-toe-**nee**-um] n (pl -nea,
-neums) membrane lining the internal
surface of the abdomen

peritoneums n ▷ peritoneum

peritonitis [per-rit-tone-**ite**-iss] n (pl -tises)
inflammation of the peritoneum

peritonitises n ▷ peritonitis

periwinkle¹ n (pl -s) small edible shellfish,
the winkle

periwinkle² n (pl -s) plant with trailing stems
and blue flowers

periwinkles n ▷ periwinkle¹, ²

perjuries n ▷ perjury

perjury n (pl -ies) act or crime of lying while
under oath in a court

perk n (pl -s) (Informal) incidental benefit
gained from a job, such as a company car

perkier adj ▷ perk

perkiest adj ▷ perk

perks n ▷ perk

perky adj (-kier, -kiest) lively or cheerful

perlemoen n (pl -s) (S AFR) edible sea creature
with a shell lined with mother of pearl

perlemoens n ▷ perlemoen

perm n (pl -s) long-lasting curly hairstyle
produced by treating the hair with chemicals
▶ v (-s, -ing, -ed) give (hair) a perm

permafrost n (pl -s) permanently frozen
ground

permafrosts n ▷ permafrost

permanence n ▷ permanent

permanences n ▷ permanent

permanent adj lasting forever > permanence
n (pl -s) > permanently adv

permanently adv ▷ permanent

permeate v (-tes, -ting, -ted) pervade or pass
through the whole of (something)

permeable adj able to be permeated, esp.
by liquid

permeated v ▷ permeate

permeates v ▷ permeate

permeating v ▷ permeate

permed v ▷ perm

perming v ▷ perm

permissible adj ▷ permit

permission n (pl -s) authorization to do something

permissions n ▷ permission

permissive adj (excessively) tolerant, esp. in sexual matters

permit v (-s, -tting, -tted) give permission, allow ► n (pl -s) document giving permission to do something > **permissible** adj

permits v, n ▷ permit

permitted v ▷ permit

permitting v ▷ permit

perms n, v ▷ perm

permutation n (pl -s) any of the ways a number of things can be arranged or combined

permutations n ▷ permutation

pernicious adj wicked

pernickety adj (Informal) (excessively) fussy about details

peroration n (pl -s) concluding part of a speech, usu. summing up the main points

perorations n ▷ peroration

peroxide n (pl -s) hydrogen peroxide used as a hair bleach

peroxides n ▷ peroxide

perpendicular adj at right angles to a line or surface ► n (pl -s) line or plane at right angles to another

perpendiculars n ▷ perpendicular

perpetrate v (-tes, -ting, -ted) commit or be responsible for (a wrongdoing) > **perpetration** n (pl -s) > **perpetrator** n (pl -s)

perpetrated v ▷ perpetrate

perpetrates v ▷ perpetrate

perpetrating v ▷ perpetrate

perpetration n ▷ perpetrate

perpetrations n ▷ perpetrate

perpetrator n ▷ perpetrate

perpetrators n ▷ perpetrate

perpetual adj lasting forever > **perpetually** adv

perpetually adv ▷ perpetual

perpetuate v (-tes, -ting, -ted) cause to continue or be remembered > **perpetuation** n (pl -s)

perpetuated v ▷ perpetuate

perpetuates v ▷ perpetuate

perpetuating v ▷ perpetuate

perpetuation n ▷

perpetuations n ▷

perplex v (-es, -ing, -ed) puzzle, bewilder > **perplexity** n (pl -ties)

perplexed v ▷ perplex

perplexes v ▷ perplex

perplexing v ▷ perplex

perplexities n ▷ perplex

perplexity n ▷ perplex

perquisite n (pl -s) (Formal) ▷ perk

perquisites n ▷ perquisite

perries n ▷ perry

perry n (pl -rries) alcoholic drink made from fermented pears

persecute v (-tes, -ting, -ted) treat cruelly because of race, religion, etc. > **persecution** n (pl -s) > **persecutor** n (pl -s)

persecuted v ▷ persecute

persecutes v ▷ persecute

persecuting v ▷ persecute

persecution n ▷ persecute

persecutions n ▷ persecute

persecutor n ▷ persecute

persecutors n ▷ persecute

persevere v (-res, -ring, -red) keep making an effort despite difficulties > **perseverance** n (pl -s)

perseverance n ▷ persevere

perseverances n ▷ persevere

persevered v ▷ persevere

perseveres v ▷ persevere

persevering v ▷ persevere

persimmon n (pl -s) sweet red tropical fruit

persimmons n ▷ persimmon

persist v (-s, -ing, -ed) continue to be or happen, last > **persistent** adj > **persistently** adv > **persistence** n (pl -s)

persisted v ▷ persist

persistence adj ▷ persist

persistences adj ▷ persist

persistent adj ▷ persist

persistently v ▷ persist

persisting v ▷ persist

persists v ▷ persist

person n (pl -s) human being

persons n ▷ person

persona [per-soh-na] n (pl -nae) [-nee] someone's personality as presented to others

personable adj pleasant in appearance and personality

personae n ▷ persona

personage n (pl -s) important person

personages n ▷ personage

personal adj individual or private

personalities n ▷ personality

personality n (pl -ties) person's distinctive characteristics

personally adv directly, not by delegation to others

personification n ▷ personify

personifications n ▷ personify
personified v ▷ personify
personifies v ▷ personify
personify v (-fies, -fying, -fied) give human characteristics to > **personification** n (pl -s)
personifying v ▷ personify
personnel n (pl -s) people employed in an organization
personnels n ▷ personnel
perspective n (pl -s) view of the relative importance of situations or facts
perspectives n ▷ perspective
perspicacious adj having quick mental insight > **perspicacity** n (pl -ties)
perspicacities n ▷ perspicacious
perspicacity n ▷ perspicacious
perspiration n ▷ perspire
perspirations n ▷ perspire
perspire v (-res, -ring, -red) sweat
> **perspiration** n (pl -s)
perspired v ▷ perspire
perspires v ▷ perspire
perspiring v ▷ perspire
persuade v (-des, -ding, -ded) make (someone) do something by argument, charm, etc.
> **persuasive** adj
persuasion n (pl -s) act of persuading
persuasions n ▷ persuasion
persuasive adj ▷ persuade
persuaded v ▷ persuade
persuades v ▷ persuade
persuading v ▷ persuade
pert adj (-er, -est) saucy and cheeky
pertain v (-s, -ing, -ed) belong or be relevant (to)
pertained v ▷ pertain
pertaining v ▷ pertain
pertains v ▷ pertain
perter adj ▷ pert
pertest adj ▷ pert
pertinacious adj (Formal) very persistent and determined > **pertinacity** n (pl -ties)
pertinacities n ▷ pertinacious
pertinacity n ▷ pertinacious
pertinence n ▷ pertinent
pertinences n ▷ pertinent
pertinent adj relevant > **pertinence** n (pl -s)
perturb v (-s, -ing, -ed) disturb greatly
> **perturbation** n (pl -s)
perturbation n ▷ perturb
perturbation n ▷ perturb
perturbed v ▷ perturb
perturbing v ▷ perturb
perturbs v ▷ perturb
perusal n ▷ peruse

perusals n ▷ peruse
peruse v (-ses, -sing, -sed) read in a careful or leisurely manner > **perusal** n (pl -s)
perused v ▷ peruse
peruses v ▷ peruse
perusing v ▷ peruse
pervade v (-des, -ding, -ded) spread right through (something) > **pervasive** adj
pervaded v ▷ pervade
pervades v ▷ pervade
pervading v ▷ pervade
pervasive adj ▷ pervade
perverse adj (-r, -st) deliberately doing something different from what is thought normal or proper > **perversely** adv
> **perversity** n (pl -ties)
perversely n ▷ perverse
perverser adj ▷ perverse
perversest adj ▷ perverse
perversion n (pl -s) sexual act or desire considered abnormal
perversions n ▷ perversion
perversities n ▷ perverse
perversity n ▷ perverse
pervert v (-s, -ing, -ed) use or alter for a wrong purpose ▶ n (pl -s) person who practises sexual perversion
perverted v ▷ pervert
perverting v ▷ pervert
perverts v, n ▷ pervert
pervious adj able to be penetrated, permeable
peseta [pa-say-ta] n (pl -s) former monetary unit of Spain
pesetas n ▷ peseta
pessaries n ▷ pessary
pessary n (pl -ries) appliance worn in the vagina, either to prevent conception or to support the womb
pessimism n (pl -s) tendency to expect the worst in all things > **pessimist** n (pl -s)
> **pessimistic** adj > **pessimistically** adv
pessimisms n ▷ pessimism
pessimist n ▷ pessimism
pessimistic adj ▷ pessimism
pessimistically adv ▷ pessimism
pessimists n ▷ pessimism
pest n (pl -s) annoying person
pesticide n (pl -s) chemical for killing insect pests
pesticides n ▷ pesticide
pester v (-s, -ing, -ed) annoy or nag continually
pestered v ▷ pester
pestering v ▷ pester
pesters v ▷ pester
pestilence n (pl -s) deadly epidemic disease

pestilences n ▷ pestilence
pestilent adj annoying, troublesome
  > **pestilential** adj
pestilential adj ▷ pestilent
pestle n (pl -s) club-shaped implement for grinding things to powder in a mortar
pestles n ▷ pestle
pests n ▷ pest
pet n (pl -s) animal kept for pleasure and companionship ▶ adj particularly cherished
  ▶ v (-s, -tting, -tted) treat as a pet
petal n (pl -s) one of the brightly coloured outer parts of a flower > **petalled** adj
petalled adj ▷ petal
petals n ▷ petal
petard n (pl -s) being the victim of one's own schemes
petards n ▷ petard
petite adj (of a woman) small and dainty
petition n (pl -s) formal request, esp. one signed by many people and presented to parliament ▶ v (-s, -ing, -ed) present a petition to > **petitioner** n (pl -s)
petitioned v ▷ petition
petitioner n ▷ petition
petitioners n ▷ petition
petitioning v ▷ petition
petitions n, v ▷ petition
petrel n (pl -s) sea bird with a hooked bill and tubular nostrils
petrels n ▷ petrel
petrification n ▷ petrify
petrifications n ▷ petrify
petrified v ▷ petrify
petrifies v ▷ petrify
petrify v (-fies, -fying, -fied) frighten severely
  > **petrification** n (pl -s)
petrochemical n (pl -s) substance, such as acetone, obtained from petroleum
petrochemicals n ▷ petrochemical
petrol n (pl -s) flammable liquid obtained from petroleum, used as fuel in internal-combustion engines
petroleum n (pl -s) thick dark oil found underground
petroleums n ▷ petroleums
petrols n ▷ petrol
pets n, v ▷ pet
petted v ▷ pet
petticoat n (pl -s) woman's skirt-shaped undergarment
petticoats n ▷ petticoat
pettier adj ▷ petty
pettiest adj ▷ petty
pettifogging adj excessively concerned with unimportant detail
pettiness n ▷ petty
pettinesses n ▷ petty
petting v ▷ pet
petty adj (-ttier, -ttiest) unimportant, trivial
  > **pettiness** n (pl -es)
petulance n ▷ petulant
petulances n ▷ petulant
petulant adj childishly irritable or peevish
  > **petulance** n (pl -s) > **petulantly** adv
petulantly adv ▷ petulant
petunia n (pl -s) garden plant with funnel-shaped flowers
petunias n ▷ petunia
pew n (pl -s) fixed benchlike seat in a church
pews n ▷ pew
pewter n (pl -s) greyish metal made of tin and lead
pewters n ▷ pewter
phalanger n (pl -s) long-tailed Australian tree-dwelling marsupial
phalangers n ▷ phalanger
phalanx n (pl -es) closely grouped mass of people
phalanxes n ▷ phalanx
phalli n ▷ phallus
phallic adj ▷ phallus
phallus n (pl -lluses, -lli) penis, esp. as a symbol of reproductive power in primitive rites
  > **phallic** adj
phalluses n ▷ phallus
phantasm n (pl -s) unreal vision, illusion
  > **phantasmal** adj
phantasmal adj ▷ phantasm
phantasms n ▷ phantasm
phantasmagoria n (pl -s) shifting medley of dreamlike figures
phantasmagorias n ▷ phantasmagoria
phantom n (pl -s) ghost
phantoms n ▷ phantom
pharmaceutical adj of pharmacy
pharmacies n ▷ pharmacy
pharmacist n (pl -s) person qualified to prepare and sell drugs and medicines
pharmacists n ▷ pharmacist
pharmacological adj ▷ pharmacology
pharmacologies n ▷ pharmacology
pharmacologist n ▷ pharmacology
pharmacologists n ▷ pharmacology
pharmacology n (pl -gies) study of drugs
  > **pharmacological** adj > **pharmacologist** n (pl -s)
pharmacopoeia [far-ma-koh-**pee**-a] n (pl -s) book with a list of and directions for the use of drugs

pharmacopeias n ▷ pharmacopeia
pharmacy n (pl -cies) preparation and dispensing of drugs and medicines
pharynges n ▷ pharynx
pharyngitis [far-rin-jite-iss] n (pl -tes) inflammation of the pharynx
pharyngitises n ▷ pharynx
pharynx [far-rinks] n (pl -nges, -nxes) cavity forming the back part of the mouth
pharynxes ▷ pharynx
phase n (pl -s) any distinct or characteristic stage in a development or chain of events ▶ v (-ses, -sing, -sed) arrange or carry out in stages or to coincide with something else
phased v ▷ phase
phases n, v ▷ phase
phasing v ▷ phase
pheasant n (pl -s) game bird with bright plumage
pheasants n ▷ pheasant
phenobarbitone n (pl -s) drug inducing sleep or relaxation
phenobarbitones n ▷ phenobarbitone
phenol n (pl -s) chemical used in disinfectants and antiseptics
phenols n ▷ phenol
phenomena n ▷ phenomenon
phenomenal adj extraordinary, outstanding > **phenomenally** adv
phenomenally adv ▷ phenomenal
phenomenon n (pl -mena) anything appearing or observed
phial n (pl -s) small bottle for medicine etc.
phials n ▷ phial
philadelphus n (pl -es) shrub with sweet-scented flowers
philadelphuses n ▷ philadelphus
philanderer n (pl -s) man who flirts or has many casual love affairs > **philandering** adj, n (pl -s)
philanderers n ▷ philanderer
philandering n ▷ philanderer
philanderings n ▷ philanderer
philanthropic adj ▷ philanthropy
philanthropies n ▷ philanthropy
philanthropist n ▷ philanthropy
philanthropists n ▷ philanthropy
philanthropy n (pl -pies) practice of helping people less well-off than oneself > **philanthropic** adj > **philanthropist** n (pl -s)
philatelies n ▷ philately
philatelist n ▷ philately
philatelists n ▷ philately
philately [fill-lat-a-lee] n (pl -lies) stamp collecting > **philatelist** n (pl -s)

philharmonic adj (in names of orchestras etc.) music-loving
philistine adj, n (pl -s) boorishly uncultivated (person) > **philistinism** n (pl -s)
philistines n ▷ philistine
philistinism n ▷ philistine
philistinisms n ▷ philistine
philological adj ▷ philology
philologies n ▷ philology
philologist n ▷ philology
philologists n ▷ philology
philology n (pl -gies) science of the structure and development of languages > **philological** adj > **philologist** n (pl -s)
philosopher n (pl -s) person who studies philosophy
philosophers n ▷ philosopher
philosophize v (-zes, -zing, -zed) discuss in a philosophical manner
philosophized v ▷ philosophize
philosophizes v ▷ philosophize
philosophizing v ▷ philosophize
philosophic adj ▷ philosophy
philosophical adj ▷ philosophy
philosophically adv ▷ philosophy
philosophies n ▷ philosophy
philosophy n (pl -phies) study of the meaning of life, knowledge, thought, etc. > **philosophical, philosophic** adj of philosophy > **philosophically** adv
philtre n (pl -s) magic drink supposed to arouse love in the person who drinks it
philtres n ▷ philtre
phlebitis [fleb-bite-iss] n (pl -es) inflammation of a vein
phlebitises n ▷ phlebitis
phlegm [flem] n (pl -s) thick yellowish substance formed in the nose and throat during a cold
phlegmatic [fleg-mat-ik] adj not easily excited, unemotional > **phlegmatically** adv
phlegmatically adv ▷ phlegmatic
phlegms n ▷ phlegm
phlox n (pl phlox, -xes) flowering garden plant
phloxes n ▷ phlox
phobia n (pl -s) intense and unreasoning fear or dislike
phobias n ▷ phobia
phoenix n (pl -es) legendary bird said to set fire to itself and rise anew from its ashes
phoenixes n ▷ phoenix
phone n, v (-nes, -ning, -ned) (Informal) telephone
phonecard n (pl -s) card used to operate certain public telephones

phonecards *n* ▷ phonecard

phoned *v* ▷ phone

phones *v* ▷ phone

phonetic *adj* of speech sounds > phonetically *adv*

phonetically *adv* ▷ phonetic

phonetics *n* science of speech sounds

phoney, phony (*Informal*) *adj* (-nier, -niest) not genuine ▸ *n* (*pl* -neys, -nies) phoney person or thing

phoneys *n* ▷ phoney

phonier *adj* ▷ phoney

phonies *n* ▷ phoney

phoniest *adj* ▷ phoney

phoning *v* ▷ phone

phonograph *n* (*pl* -s) (US) (*old-fashioned*) record player

phonographs *n* ▷ phonograph

phony *adj* ▷ phoney

phosphorescence *n* (*pl* -s) faint glow in the dark > phosphorescent *adj*

phosphorescences *n* ▷ phosphorescence

phosphorescent *adj* ▷ phosphorescence

phosphate *n* (*pl* -s) compound of phosphorus

phosphates *n* ▷ phosphate

phosphorus *n* (*pl* -es) (CHEM) toxic flammable nonmetallic element which appears luminous in the dark

phosphoruses *n* ▷ phosphorus

photo *n* (*pl* -s) ▷ photograph

photocopied *v* ▷ photocopy

photocopier *n* ▷ photocopy

photocopiers *n* ▷ photocopy

photocopies *n*, *v* ▷ photocopy

photocopy *n* (*pl* -pies) photographic reproduction ▸ *v* (-pies, -pying, -pied) make a photocopy of > photocopier *n* (*pl* -s)

photocopying *v* ▷ photocopy

photoelectric *adj* using or worked by electricity produced by the action of light

photogenic *adj* always looking attractive in photographs

photograph *n* (*pl* -s) picture made by the chemical action of light on sensitive film ▸ *v* (-s, -ing, -ed) take a photograph of > photographic *adj*

photographed *v* ▷ photograph

photographer *n* (*pl* -s) person who takes photographs, esp. professionally

photographers *n* ▷ photographer

photographic *adj* ▷ photograph

photographing *v* ▷ photograph

photographs *n*, *v* ▷ photograph

photographies *n* ▷ photography

photography *n* (*pl* -s) art of taking photographs

photos *n* ▷ photo

photostat *n* (*pl* -s) copy made by photocopying machine

photostats *n* ▷ photostat

photosyntheses *n* ▷ photosynthesis

photosynthesis *n* (*pl* -ses) process by which a green plant uses sunlight to build up carbohydrate reserves

phrase *n* (*pl* -s) group of words forming a unit of meaning, esp. within a sentence ▸ *v* (-ses, -sing, -sed) express in words

phrased *v* ▷ phrase

phrases *n*, *v* ▷ phrase

phrasing *v* ▷ phrase

phraseologies *n* ▷ phraseology

phraseology *n* (*pl* -gies) way in which words are used

physical *adj* of the body, as contrasted with the mind or spirit > physically *adv*

physically *adv* ▷ physical

physician *n* (*pl* -s) doctor of medicine

physicians *n* ▷ physician

physics *n* science of the properties of matter and energy

physicist *n* (*pl* -s) person skilled in or studying physics

physicists *n* ▷ physicist

physiognomies *n* ▷ physiognomy

physiognomy [fiz-ee-on-om-ee] *n* (*pl* -mies) face

physiological *adj* ▷ physiology

physiologies *n* ▷ physiology

physiologist *n* ▷ physiology

physiologists *n* ▷ physiology

physiology *n* (*pl* -gies) science of the normal function of living things > physiological *adj* > physiologist *n* (*pl* -s)

physiotherapies *n* ▷ physiotherapy

physiotherapist *n* ▷ physiotherapy

physiotherapists *n* ▷ physiotherapy

physiotherapy *n* (*pl* -pies) treatment of disease or injury by physical means such as massage, rather than by drugs > physiotherapist *n* (*pl* -s)

physique *n* (*pl* -s) person's bodily build and muscular development

physiques *n* ▷ physique

pi *n* (*pl* -s) (MATHS) ratio of the circumference of a circle to its diameter

pis *n* ▷ pi

pianissimo *adv* (MUSIC) very quietly

piano¹ *n* (*pl* -os) musical instrument with strings which are struck by hammers worked by a keyboard (*also* pianoforte) (*pl* -s) > pianist n (pl -s)

pianist n ▷ piano¹

pianists n ▷ piano¹

piano² adv (MUSIC) quietly

pianoforte n ▷ piano¹

pianofortes n ▷ piano¹

pianos n ▷ piano¹

piazza n (pl -s) square or marketplace, esp. in Italy

piazzas n ▷ piazza

pic n (pl -s, pix) (Informal) photograph or illustration

picador n (pl -s) mounted bullfighter with a lance

picadors n ▷ picador

picaresque adj denoting a type of fiction in which the hero, a rogue, has a series of adventures

piccalilli n (pl -s) pickle of vegetables in mustard sauce

piccalillis n ▷ piccalilli

piccolo n (pl -os) small flute

piccolos n ▷ piccolo

pick¹ v (-s, -ing, -ed) choose ▶ n (pl -s) choice

pick² n (pl -s) tool with a curved iron crossbar and wooden shaft, for breaking up hard ground or rocks

pickaxe n (pl -s) large pick

pickaxes n ▷ pickaxe

picked v ▷ pick¹

picket n (pl -s) person or group standing outside a workplace to deter would-be workers during a strike ▶ v (-s, -ing, -ed) form a picket outside (a workplace)

picketed v ▷ picket

picketing v ▷ picket

pickets n, v ▷ picket

picking v ▷ pick¹

pickings pl n money easily acquired

pickle n (pl -s) food preserved in vinegar or salt water ▶ v (-les, -ling, -led) preserve in vinegar or salt water

pickled adj (of food) preserved ▶ n ▷ pickle

pickles n, v ▷ pickle

pickling v ▷ pickle

pickpocket n (pl -s) thief who steals from someone's pocket

pickpockets n ▷ pickpocket

picks n, v ▷ pick¹, ²

picnic n (pl -s) informal meal out of doors ▶ v (-s, -cking, -cked) have a picnic

picnicked v ▷ picnic

picnicking v ▷ picnic

picnics n, v ▷ picnic

pics n ▷ pic

pictorial adj of or in painting or pictures

picture n (pl -s) drawing or painting ▶ pl cinema ▶ v (-res, -ring, -red) visualize, imagine

pictured v ▷ picture

pictures n, v ▷ picture

picturesque adj (of a place or view) pleasant to look at

picturing v ▷ picture

piddle v (-les, -ling, -led) (Informal) urinate

piddled v ▷ piddle

piddles v ▷ piddle

piddling v ▷ piddle

pidgin n (pl -s) language, not a mother tongue, made up of elements of two or more other languages

pidgins n ▷ pidgin

pie n (pl -s) dish of meat, fruit, etc. baked in pastry

pies n ▷ pie

piebald adj, n (pl -s) (horse) with irregular black-and-white markings

piebalds n ▷ piebald

piece n (pl -s) separate bit or part

pieces n ▷ piece

piecemeal adv bit by bit

piecework n (pl -s) work paid for according to the quantity produced

pieceworks n ▷ piecework

pied adj having markings of two or more colours

pier n (pl -s) platform on stilts sticking out into the sea

piers n ▷ pier

pierce v (-ces, -cing, -ced) make a hole in or through with a sharp instrument

pierced v ▷ pierce

pierces v ▷ pierce

piercing adj (of a sound) shrill and high-pitched ▶ v ▷ pierce

pierrot [pier-roe] n (pl -s) pantomime clown with a whitened face

pierrots n ▷ pierrot

pieties n ▷ piety

piety n (pl -ties) deep devotion to God and religion

piffle n (pl -s) (Informal) nonsense

piffles n ▷ piffle

pig n (pl -s) animal kept and killed for pork, ham, and bacon

pigeon¹ n (pl -s) bird with a heavy body and short legs, sometimes trained to carry messages

pigeon² n (Informal) concern or responsibility

pigeonhole n (-s) compartment for papers in a desk etc. ▶ v (-les, -ling, -led) classify
  pigeonholed v ▷ pigeonhole
  pigeonholing v ▷ pigeonhole
pigeonholes n, v ▷ pigeonhole
pigeons n ▷ pigeon[1,2]
piggeries n ▷ piggery
piggery n (pl -ries) place for keeping and breeding pigs
  piggier adj ▷ piggy
  piggiest adj ▷ piggy
piggish, piggy (-ggier, -ggiest) adj (Informal) dirty
  piggy adj ▷ piggish
piggyback n (pl -s) ride on someone's shoulders ▶ adv carried on someone's shoulders
  piggybacks n ▷ piggyback
pigment n (pl -s) colouring matter, paint or dye > **pigmentation** n (pl -s)
  pigmentation n ▷ pigment
  pigmentations n ▷ pigment
  pigments n ▷ pigment
  pigmies n ▷ pygmy
pigmy n (pl -mies) ▷ pygmy
  pigs n ▷ pig
pigtail n (pl -s) plait of hair hanging from the back or either side of the head
  pigtails n ▷ pigtail
pike[1] n (pl -s) large predatory freshwater fish
pike[2] n (pl -s) (HIST) long-handled spear
  pikes n ▷ pike[1,2]
pikelet n (pl -s) (AUST & NZ) small thick pancake
  pikelets n ▷ pikelet
piker n (pl -s) (AUST & NZ) (Slang) shirker
  pikers n ▷ piker
pilaster n (pl -s) square column, usu. set in a wall
  pilasters n ▷ pilaster
pilau, pilaf, pilaff n (pl -s) Middle Eastern dish of meat, fish, or poultry boiled with rice, spices, etc.
  pilaffs n ▷ pilaff
  pilafs n ▷ pilaf
pilchard n (pl -s) small edible sea fish of the herring family
  pilchards n ▷ pilchard
pile[1] n (pl -s) number of things lying on top of each other ▶ v (-les, -ling, -led) collect into a pile
pile[2] n (pl -s) beam driven into the ground, esp. as a foundation for building
pile[3] n (pl -s) fibres of a carpet or a fabric, esp. velvet, that stand up from the weave
  piled v ▷ pile[1]

piling v ▷ pile[1]
piles pl n swollen veins in the rectum, haemorrhoids ▶ v, n ▷ pile[1,2,3]
pilfer v (-s, -ing, -ed) steal in small quantities
  pilfered v ▷ pilfer
  pilfering v ▷ pilfer
  pilfers v ▷ pilfer
pilgrim n (pl -s) person who journeys to a holy place > **pilgrimage** n (pl -s)
  pilgrimage n ▷ pilgrim
  pilgrimages n ▷ pilgrim
  pilgrims n ▷ pilgrim
pill n (pl -s) small ball of medicine swallowed whole
  pills n ▷ pill
pillage v (-ges, -ging, -ged) steal property by violence in war ▶ n (pl -s) violent seizure of goods, esp. in war
  pillaged v ▷ pillage
  pillages v, n ▷ pillage
  pillaging v ▷ pillage
pillar n (pl -s) upright post, usu. supporting a roof
  pillars n ▷ pillar
pillion n (pl -s) seat for a passenger behind the rider of a motorcycle
  pillions n ▷ pillion
  pilloried v ▷ pillory
  pillories n, v ▷ pillory
pillory n (pl -ries) (HIST) frame with holes for the head and hands in which an offender was locked and exposed to public abuse ▶ v (-ies, -ying, -ied) ridicule publicly
pillow n (pl -s) stuffed cloth bag for supporting the head in bed ▶ v (-s, -ing, -ed) rest as if on a pillow
pillowcase, pillowslip n (pl -s) removable cover for a pillow
  pillowcases n ▷ pillowcase
  pillowed v ▷ pillow
  pillowing v ▷ pillow
  pillows n, v ▷ pillow
  pillowslip n ▷ pillowcase
  pillowslips n ▷ pillowcase
pilot n (pl -s) person qualified to fly an aircraft or spacecraft ▶ adj experimental and preliminary ▶ v (-s, -ing, -ed) act as the pilot of
  piloted v ▷ pilot
  piloting v ▷ pilot
  pilots n, v ▷ pilot
pimento n (pl -tos) mild-tasting red pepper
  pimentos n ▷ pimento
pimp n (pl -s) man who gets customers for a prostitute in return for a share of his or her earnings ▶ v (-s, -ing, -ed) act as a pimp

pimped v ▷ pimp

pimpernel n (pl -s) wild plant with small star-shaped flowers

    pimpernels n ▷ pimpernel

    pimping v ▷ pimp

pimple n (pl -s) small pus-filled spot on the skin > **pimply** adj (-lier, -liest)

    pimples n ▷ pimple

    pimplier v ▷ pimple

    pimpliest v ▷ pimple

    pimply v ▷ pimple

    pimps n, v ▷ pimp

pin n (pl -s) short thin piece of stiff wire with a point and head, for fastening things ▶ v (-s, **pinning, pinned**) fasten with a pin

pinafore n (pl -s) apron

    pinafores n ▷ pinafore

pinball n (pl -s) electrically operated table game in which a small ball is shot through various hazards

    pinballs n ▷ pinball

pincers pl n tool consisting of two hinged arms, for gripping

pinch v (-es, -ing, -ed) squeeze between finger and thumb ▶ n (pl -s) act of pinching

pinchbeck n (pl -s) alloy of zinc and copper, used as imitation gold

    pinchbecks n ▷ pinchbeck

    pinched v ▷ pinch

    pinches v, n ▷ pinch

    pinching v ▷ pinch

    pinned v ▷ pin

    pinning v ▷ pin

    pins n, v ▷ pin

pine[1] n (pl -s) evergreen coniferous tree

pine[2] v (-nes, -ning, -ned) (foll. by **for**) feel great longing (for)

pineapple n (pl -s) large tropical fruit with juicy yellow flesh and a hard skin

    pineapples n ▷ pineapple

    pined v ▷ pine[2]

    pines n, v ▷ pine[1, 2]

ping v (-s, -ing, -ed) ▶ n (pl -s) (make) a short high-pitched sound

    pinged v ▷ ping

    pinging v ▷ ping

    pings v, n ▷ ping

    pining v ▷ pine[2]

pinion[1] n (pl -s) bird's wing ▶ v (-s, -ing, -ed) immobilize (someone) by tying or holding his or her arms

pinion[2] n (pl -s) small cogwheel

    pinioned v ▷ pinion

    pinioning v ▷ pinion

    pinions n, v ▷ pinion[1, 2]

pink n (pl -s) pale reddish colour ▶ adj (-er, -est) of the colour pink ▶ v (-s, -ing, -ed) (of an engine) make a metallic noise because not working properly, knock

    pinked v ▷ pink

    pinker adj ▷ pink

    pinkest adj ▷ pink

    pinking v ▷ pink

    pinks n, v ▷ pink

pinnacle n (pl -s) highest point of fame or success

    pinnacles n ▷ pinnacle

pinotage [pin-no-tajj] n (pl -s) blended red wine of S Africa

    pinotages n ▷ pinotage

pinpoint v (-s, -ing, -ed) locate or identify exactly

    pinpointed v ▷ pinpoint

    pinpointing v ▷ pinpoint

    pinpoints v ▷ pinpoint

pinstripe n (pl -s) very narrow stripe in fabric

    pinstripes n ▷ pinstripe

pint n (pl -s) liquid measure, 1/8 gallon (.568 litre)

    pints n ▷ pint

pioneer n (pl -s) explorer or early settler of a new country ▶ v (-s, -ing, -ed) be the pioneer or leader of

    pioneered v ▷ pioneer

    pioneering v ▷ pioneer

    pioneers n, v ▷ pioneer

pious adj deeply religious, devout

pip[1] n (pl -s) small seed in a fruit

pip[2] n high-pitched sound used as a time signal on radio (Informal)

    pips n ▷ pip[1, 2]

pipe n (pl -s) tube for conveying liquid or gas ▶ pl bagpipes ▶ v (-pes, -ping, -ped) play on a pipe

    piped v ▷ pipe

piper n (pl -s) player on a pipe or bagpipes

    pipers n ▷ piper

piping n (pl -s) system of pipes ▶ v ▷ pipe

    pipings n ▷ piping

pipeline n (pl -s) long pipe for transporting oil, water, etc.

    pipelines n ▷ pipeline

    pipes n, v ▷ pipe

pipette n (pl -s) slender glass tube used to transfer or measure fluids

    pipettes n ▷ pipette

pipi n (pl -s) (AUST) mollusc often used as bait

pipit n (pl -s) small brownish songbird

    pipits n ▷ pipit

pippin n (pl -s) type of eating apple

pippins n ▷ pippin
pips n ▷ pip[1, 2]
piquancies n ▷ piquant
piquancy n ▷ piquant
piquant [pee-kant] adj having a pleasant spicy taste > piquancy n (pl -cies)
pique [peek] n (pl -s) feeling of hurt pride, baffled curiosity, or resentment ▶ v (-ques, -quing, -qued) hurt the pride of
piqué [pee-kay] n (pl -s) stiff ribbed cotton fabric
piqued v ▷ pique
piques n, v ▷ pique
piqués n ▷ piqué
piquing v ▷ pique
piquet [pik-ket] n (pl -s) card game for two
piquets n ▷ piquet
piracies n ▷ pirate
piracy n ▷ pirate
piranha n (pl -s) small fierce freshwater fish of tropical America
piranhas n ▷ piranha
pirate n (pl -s -s) sea robber ▶ v (-tes, -ting, -ted) sell or reproduce (artistic work etc.) illegally > piracy n (pl -cies) > piratical adj
pirated v ▷ pirate
pirates n, v ▷ pirate
piratical adj ▷ pirate
pirating v ▷ pirate
pirouette n, n (pl -s) (make) a spinning turn balanced on the toes of one foot
pirouettes n ▷ pirouette
pistachio n (pl -s) edible nut of a Mediterranean tree
pistachios n ▷ pistachio
piste [peest] n (pl -s) ski slope
pistes n ▷ piste
pistil n (pl -s) seed-bearing part of a flower
pistils n ▷ pistil
pistol n (pl -s) short-barrelled handgun
pistols n ▷ pistol
piston n (pl -s) cylindrical part in an engine that slides to and fro in a cylinder
pistons n ▷ piston
pit n (pl -s) deep hole in the ground ▷ orchestra pit ▶ v (-s, -tting, -tteds) mark with small dents or scars
pitch[1] v (-es, -ing, -ed) throw, hurl ▶ n (pl -es) area marked out for playing sport
pitch[2] n dark sticky substance obtained from tar
pitched v ▷ pitch[1]
pitches v, n ▷ pitch[1]
pitching v ▷ pitch[1]
pitchblende n (pl -s) mineral composed largely

of uranium oxide, yielding radium
pitchblendes n ▷ pitchblende
pitcher n (pl -s) large jug with a narrow neck
pitchers n ▷ pitcher
pitchfork n (pl -s) large long-handled fork for lifting hay ▶ v (-s, -ing, -ed) thrust abruptly or violently
pitchforked v ▷ pitchfork
pitchforking v ▷ pitchfork
pitchforks n, v ▷ pitchfork
piteous, pitiable adj arousing pity
pitfall n (pl -s) hidden difficulty or danger
pitfalls n ▷ pitfall
pith n (pl -s) soft white lining of the rind of oranges etc.
pithier adj ▷ pithy
pithiest adj ▷ pithy
piths n ▷ pith
pithy adj (-thier, -thiest) short and full of meaning
pitiable adj ▷ piteous
pitied v ▷ pity
pities n, v ▷ pity
pitiful adj arousing pity > pitifully adv
pitifully adv ▷ pitiful
pitiless adj feeling no pity or mercy > pitilessly adv
pitilessly adv ▷ pitiless
piton [peet-on] n (pl -s) metal spike used in climbing to secure a rope
pitons n ▷ piton
pits n, v ▷ pit
pittance n (pl -s) very small amount of money
pittances n ▷ pittance
pitted v ▷ pit
pitting v ▷ pit
pituitaries n ▷ pituitary
pituitary n (pl -ies) gland at the base of the brain, that helps to control growth
pity n (pl -ties) sympathy or sorrow for others' suffering ▶ v (-ies, -ying, -ied) feel pity for
pitying v ▷ pity
pivot n (pl -s) central shaft on which something turns ▶ v (-s, -ing, -ed) provide with or turn on a pivot
pivotal adj of crucial importance
pivoted v ▷ pivot
pivoting v ▷ pivot
pivots n, v ▷ pivot
pix n (Informal) ▷ pic
pixie n (pl -s) (in folklore) fairy
pixies n ▷ pixie
pizza n (pl -s) flat disc of dough covered with a wide variety of savoury toppings and baked
pizzas n ▷ pizza

pizzazz n (pl -es) (Informal) attractive combination of energy and style
pizzazzes n ▷ pizzazz

pizzicato [pit-see-**kah**-toe] adj (MUSIC) played by plucking the string of a violin etc. with the finger

placard n (pl -s) notice that is carried or displayed in public
placards n ▷ placard

placate v (-tes, -ting, -ted) make (someone) stop feeling angry or upset > **placatory** adj
placated v ▷ placate
placates v ▷ placate
placating v ▷ placate
placatory adj ▷ placate

place n (pl -s) particular part of an area or space ▶ v (-ces, -cing, -ced) put in a particular place
placed v ▷ place
places n, v ▷ place

placebo [plas-**see**-bo] n (pl -bos, -boes) sugar pill etc. given to an unsuspecting patient instead of an active drug
placeboes n ▷ placebo
placebos n ▷ placebo

placenta [plass-**ent**-a] n (pl -tas, -tae) organ formed in the womb during pregnancy, providing nutrients for the fetus > **placental** adj
placentae n ▷ placenta
placental adj ▷ placenta
placentas n ▷ placenta

placid adj (-er, -est) not easily excited or upset, calm > **placidity** n (pl -ties)
placider adj ▷ placid
placidest adj ▷ placid
placidities n ▷ placid
placidity n ▷ placid
placing v ▷ place

plagiarize [**play**-jer-ize] v (-zes, -zing, -zed) steal ideas, passages, etc. from (someone else's work) and present them as one's own > **plagiarism** n (pl -s)
plagiarism n ▷ plagiarize
plagiarisms n ▷ plagiarize
plagiarized v ▷ plagiarize
plagiarizes v ▷ plagiarize
plagiarizing v ▷ plagiarize

plague n (pl -s) fast-spreading fatal disease ▶ v (-gues, -guing, -gued) trouble or annoy continually
plagued v ▷ plague
plagues n, v ▷ plague
plaguing v ▷ plague

plaice n (pl plaice) edible European flatfish

plaid n (pl -s) long piece of tartan cloth worn as part of Highland dress
plaids n ▷ plaid

plain (-er, -est) adj easy to see or understand ▶ n (pl -s) large stretch of level country > **plainly** adv > **plainness** n (pl -es)
plainer adj ▷ plain
plainest adj ▷ plain
plainly adj ▷ plain
plainness n ▷ plain
plainnesses n ▷ plain
plains n ▷ plain

plainsong n (pl -s) unaccompanied singing, esp. in a medieval church
plainsongs n ▷ plainsong

plaintiff n (pl -s) person who sues in a court of law
plaintiffs n ▷ plaintiff

plaintive adj sad, mournful > **plaintively** adv
plaintively adv ▷ plaintive

plait [platt] n (pl -s) intertwined length of hair ▶ v (-s, -ing, -ed) intertwine separate strands in a pattern
plaited v ▷ plait
plaiting v ▷ plait
plaits n, v ▷ plait

plan n (pl -s) way thought out to do or achieve something ▶ v (-s, -nning, -nned) arrange beforehand > **planner** n (pl -s)

plane¹ n (pl -s) aeroplane ▶ adj perfectly flat or level ▶ v (-nes, -ning, -ned) glide or skim

plane² n (pl -s) tool for smoothing wood ▶ v (-nes, -ning, -ned) smooth (wood) with a plane

plane³ n (pl -s) tree with broad leaves
planed v ▷ plane¹, ²
planes n, v ▷ plane¹, ², ³

planet n (pl -s) large body in space that revolves round the sun or another star > **planetary** adj
planetaria n ▷ planetarium

planetarium n (pl -iums, -ia) building where the movements of the stars, planets, etc. are shown by projecting lights on the inside of a dome
planetariums n ▷ planetarium
planetary adj ▷ planet
planets n ▷ planet

plangent adj (of sounds) mournful and resounding
planing v ▷ plane¹, ²

plank n (pl -s) long flat piece of sawn timber
planks n ▷ plank

plankton n (pl -s) minute animals and plants floating in the surface water of a sea or lake

planktons n ▷ plankton
planned v ▷ plan
planner n ▷ plan
planners n ▷ plan
planning v ▷ plan
plans n, v ▷ plan
plant n (pl -s) living organism that grows in the ground and has no power to move ▶ v (-s, -ing, -ed) put in the ground to grow
plantain¹ n (pl -s) low-growing wild plant with broad leaves
plantain² n (-s) tropical fruit like a green banana
plantains n ▷ plantain¹, ²
plantation n (pl -s) estate for the cultivation of tea, tobacco, etc.
plantations n ▷ plantation
planted v ▷ plant
planter n (pl -s) owner of a plantation
planters n ▷ planter
planting v ▷ plant
plants n, v ▷ plant
plaque n (pl -s) inscribed commemorative stone or metal plate
plaques n ▷ plaque
plasma n (pl -s) clear liquid part of blood
plasmas n ▷ plasma
plaster n (pl -s) mixture of lime, sand, etc. for coating walls ▶ v (-s, -ing, -ed) cover with plaster
plastered adj (Slang) drunk ▶ v ▷ plaster
plastering v ▷ plaster
plasters n, v ▷ plaster
plastic n (pl -s) synthetic material that can be moulded when soft but sets in a hard long-lasting shape ▶ adj made of plastic
plasticities n ▷ plasticity
plasticity n (pl -ties) ability to be moulded
plastics n ▷ plastic
plate n (pl -s) shallow dish for holding food ▶ v (-tes, -ting, -ted) cover with a thin coating of gold, silver, or other metal ▷ **plateful** n (pl -s)
plateau n (pl -teaus, -teaux) area of level high land
plateaus n ▷ plateau
plateaux n ▷ plateau
plated v ▷ plate
plateful n ▷ plate
platefuls n ▷ plate
platen n (pl -s) roller of a typewriter, against which the paper is held
platens n ▷ platen
plates n, v ▷ plate
platform n (pl -s) raised floor
platforms n ▷ platform

plating v ▷ plate
platinum n (pl -s) (CHEM) valuable silvery-white metal
platinums n ▷ platinum
platitude n (pl -s) remark that is true but not interesting or original ▷ **platitudinous** adj
platitudes n ▷ platitude
platitudinous adj ▷ platitude
platonic adj (of a relationship) friendly or affectionate but not sexual
platoon n (pl -s) smaller unit within a company of soldiers
platoons n ▷ platoon
platteland n (pl -s) (S AFR) rural district
plattelands n ▷ plattelands
platter n (pl -s) large dish
platters n ▷ platter
platypus n (pl -es) Australian egg-laying amphibious mammal, with dense fur, webbed feet, and a ducklike bill (also **duck-billed platypus**)
platypuses n ▷ platypus
plaudits pl n expressions of approval
plausible adj apparently true or reasonable ▷ **plausibly** adv ▷ **plausibility** n (pl -ties)
plausibilities n ▷ plausible
plausibility n ▷ plausible
plausibly adj ▷ plausible
play v (-s, -ing, -ed) occupy oneself in (a game or recreation) ▶ n (pl -s) story performed on stage or broadcast
playboy n (pl -s) rich man who lives only for pleasure
playboys n ▷ playboy
playcentre n (pl -s) (NZ & S AFR) centre for preschool children run by parents
playcentres n ▷ playcentre
played v ▷ play
player n (pl -s) person who plays a game or sport
players n ▷ player
playful adj lively
playgroup n (pl -s) regular meeting of very young children for supervised play
playgroups n ▷ playgroup
playhouse n theatre
playhouses n ▷ playhouse
playing v ▷ play
plays v, n ▷ play
playschool n (pl -s) nursery group for young children
playschools n ▷ playschool
plaything n toy
playthings n ▷ plaything
playwright n author of plays

playwrights n ▷ **playwright**

plaza n (pl -s) open space or square

 plazas n ▷ **plaza**

plea n (pl -s) serious or urgent request, entreaty

 pleas n ▷ **plea**

plead v (-s, -ing, -ed) ask urgently or with deep feeling (LAW)

 pleaded v ▷ **plead**

 pleading v ▷ **plead**

 pleads v ▷ **plead**

pleasant adj (-er, -est) pleasing, enjoyable > **pleasantly** adv

 pleasanter adj ▷ **pleasant**

 pleasantest adj ▷ **pleasant**

 pleasantly adv ▷ **pleasant**

 pleasantries n ▷ **pleasantry**

pleasantry n (pl -ries) polite or joking remark

please v (-ses, -sing, -sed) give pleasure or satisfaction to ▶ adv polite word of request > **pleased** adj > **pleasing** adj

 pleased v, adj ▷ **please**

 pleasing v, adj ▷ **please**

 pleases v ▷ **please**

pleasurable adj giving pleasure > **pleasurably** adv

 pleasurably adv ▷ **pleasurable**

pleasure n (pl -s) feeling of happiness and satisfaction

 pleasures n ▷ **pleasure**

pleat n (pl -s) fold made by doubling material back on itself ▶ v (-s, -ing, -ed) arrange (material) in pleats

 pleated v ▷ **pleat**

 pleating v ▷ **pleat**

 pleats n, v ▷ **pleat**

plebeian [pleb-ee-an] adj of the lower social classes ▶ n (pl -s) (also **pleb**) member of the lower social classes

 plebeians n ▷ **plebeian**

plebiscite [pleb-iss-ite] n (pl -s) decision by direct voting of the people of a country

 plebiscites n ▷ **plebiscite**

 plectra n ▷ **plectrum**

plectrum n (pl -rums, -ra) small implement for plucking the strings of a guitar etc.

 plectrums n ▷ **plectrum**

pledge n (pl -s) solemn promise ▶ v (-ges, -ging, -ged) promise solemnly

 pledged v ▷ **pledge**

 pledges n, v ▷ **pledge**

 pledging v ▷ **pledge**

plenary adj (of a meeting) attended by all members

plenipotentiary adj having full powers

 ▶ n diplomat or representative having full powers

plenitude n (pl -s) completeness, abundance

 plenitudes n ▷ **plenitude**

plenteous adj plentiful

 plenties n ▷ **plenty**

plenty n (pl -ties) large amount or number

plentiful adj existing in large amounts or numbers > **plentifully** adv

 plentifully adv ▷ **plentiful**

pleonasm n (pl -s) use of more words than necessary

 pleonasms n ▷ **pleonasm**

plethora n (pl -s) excess

 plethoras n ▷ **plethora**

 pleurisies n ▷ **pleurisy**

pleurisy n (pl -sies) inflammation of the membrane covering the lungs

 pliabilities n ▷ **pliable**

 pliability n ▷ **pliable**

pliable adj easily bent > **pliability** n (pl -ties)

 pliancies n ▷ **pliant**

 pliancy n ▷ **pliant**

pliant adj pliable > **pliancy** n (pl -cies)

 plied v ▷ **ply**

 plies v, n ▷ **ply**

pliers pl n tool with hinged arms and jaws for gripping

plight[1] n (pl -s) difficult or dangerous situation

plight[2] v (-s, -ing, -ed) pledge

 plighted v ▷ **plight**[2]

 plighting v ▷ **plight**[2]

 plights n, v ▷ **plight**[1, 2]

plimsolls pl n (BRIT) rubber-soled canvas shoes

plinth n (pl -s) slab forming the base of a statue, column, etc.

 plinths n ▷ **plinth**

plod v (-s, -dding, -dded) walk with slow heavy steps > **plodder** n (pl -s)

 plodded v ▷ **plod**

 plodder n ▷ **plod**

 plodders n ▷ **plod**

 plodding v ▷ **plod**

 plods v ▷ **plod**

plonk[1] v (-s, -ing, -ed) put (something) down heavily and carelessly

plonk[2] n (pl -s) (Informal) cheap inferior wine

 plonked v ▷ **plonk**[1]

 plonking v ▷ **plonk**[1]

 plonks v, n ▷ **plonk**[1, 2]

plop n (pl -s) sound of an object falling into water without a splash ▶ v (-s, -pping, -pped) make this sound

 plopped v ▷ **plop**

 plopping v ▷ **plop**

plops *n*, *v* ▷ **plop**

plot¹ *n* (*pl* **-s**) secret plan to do something illegal or wrong ▶ *v* (**-s**, **-tting**, **-tted**) plan secretly, conspire

plot² *n* (**-s**) small piece of land

plotted *v* ▷ **plot¹**

plotting *v* ▷ **plot¹**

plots *n*, *v* ▷ **plot¹, ²**

plough *n* (*pl* **-s**) agricultural tool for turning over soil ▶ *v* (**-s**, **-ing**, **-ed**) turn over (earth) with a plough > **ploughman** *n* (*pl* **-men**)

ploughed *v* ▷ **plough**

ploughing *v* ▷ **plough**

ploughman *n* ▷ **plough**

ploughmen *n* ▷ **plough**

ploughs *n*, *v* ▷ **plough**

ploughshare *n* (*pl* **-s**) blade of a plough

ploughshares *n* ▷ **ploughshare**

plover *n* (*pl* **-s**) shore bird with a straight bill and long pointed wings

plovers *n* ▷ **plover**

ploy *n* (*pl* **-s**) manoeuvre designed to gain an advantage

ploys *n* ▷ **ploy**

pluck *v* (**-s**, **-ing**, **-ed**) pull or pick off ▶ *n* (*pl* **-s**) courage

plucked *v* ▷ **pluck**

pluckier *adj* ▷ **plucky**

pluckiest *adj* ▷ **plucky**

pluckily *adj* ▷ **plucky**

plucking *v* ▷ **pluck**

plucks *v*, *n* ▷ **pluck**

plucky *adj* (**-kier**, **-kiest**) brave > **pluckily** *adv*

plug *n* (*pl* **-s**) thing fitting into and filling a hole ▶ *v* (**-s**, **-gging**, **-gged**) block or seal (a hole or gap) with a plug

plugged *v* ▷ **plug**

plugging *v* ▷ **plug**

plugs *n*, *v* ▷ **plug**

plum *n* (*pl* **-s**) oval usu. dark red fruit with a stone in the middle ▶ *adj* dark purplish-red

plumage *n* (*pl* **-s**) bird's feathers

plumages *n* ▷ **plumage**

plumb *v* (**-s**, **-ing**, **-ed**) understand (something obscure) ▶ *adv* exactly

plumbed *v* ▷ **plumb**

plumber *n* (*pl* **-s**) person who fits and repairs pipes and fixtures for water and drainage systems

plumbers *n* ▷ **plumber**

plumbing *n* pipes and fixtures used in water and drainage systems ▶ *v* ▷ **plumb**

plumbs *v* ▷ **plumb**

plume *n* (*pl* **-s**) feather, esp. one worn as an ornament

plumes *n* ▷ **plume**

plummet *v* (**-s**, **-ing**, **-ed**) plunge downward

plummeted *v* ▷ **plummet**

plummeting *v* ▷ **plummet**

plummets *v* ▷ **plummet**

plump¹ *adj* (**-er**, **-est**) moderately or attractively fat > **plumpness** *n* (*pl* **-es**)

plump² *v* (**-s**, **-ing**, **-ed**) sit or fall heavily and suddenly

plumper *adj* ▷ **plump¹**

plumpest *adj* ▷ **plump¹**

plumped *v* ▷ **plump²**

plumping *v* ▷ **plump²**

plumpness *n* ▷ **plump**

plumpnesses *n* ▷ **plump**

plumps *v* ▷ **plump²**

plums *n* ▷ **plum**

plunder *v* (**-s**, **-ing**, **-ed**) take by force, esp. in time of war ▶ *n* (*pl* **-s**) things plundered, spoils

plundered *v* ▷ **plunder**

plundering *v* ▷ **plunder**

plunders *v*, *n* ▷ **plunder**

plunge *v* (**-ges**, **-ging**, **-ged**) put or throw forcibly or suddenly (into) ▶ *n* (*pl* **-s**) plunging, dive

plunged *v* ▷ **plunge**

plunger *n* (*pl* **-s**) rubber suction cup used to clear blocked pipes

plungers *n* ▷ **plunger**

plunges *v*, *n* ▷ **plunge**

plunging *v* ▷ **plunge**

pluperfect *adj*, *n* (*pl* **-s**) (GRAMMAR) (tense) expressing an action completed before a past time, e.g. *had gone* in *his wife had gone already*

pluperfects *n* ▷ **pluperfect**

plural *adj* of or consisting of more than one ▶ *n* (*pl* **-s**) word indicating more than one

plurals *n* ▷ **plural**

pluralism *n* (*pl* **-s**) existence and toleration of a variety of peoples, opinions, etc. in a society > **pluralist** *n* (*pl* **-s**) > **pluralistic** *adj*

pluralisms *n* ▷ **pluralism**

pluralist *n* ▷ **pluralism**

pluralists *n* ▷ **pluralism**

pluralistic *adj* ▷ **pluralism**

plus *prep*, *adj* indicating addition ▶ *adj* more than zero ▶ *n* (*pl* **-es**) sign (+) denoting addition

pluses *n* ▷ **plus**

plush *n* (*pl* **-es**) fabric with long velvety pile ▶ *adj* (**-er**, **-est**) (*also* **plushy**) (**-ier**, **-iest**) luxurious

plusher *adj* ▷ **plush**

plushest *adj* ▷ **plush**

plushes *n* ▷ **plush**

plushier adj ▷ plush

plushiest adj ▷ plush

plutocrat n (pl **-s**) person who is powerful because of being very rich ▷ **plutocratic** adj

plutocratic adj ▷ plutocrat

plutocrats n ▷ plutocrat

plutonium n (pl **-s**) (CHEM) radioactive metallic element used esp. in nuclear reactors and weapons

plutoniums n ▷ plutonium

ply[1] v (**-ies, -ying, -ied**) work at (a job or trade)

ply[2] n (pl **-ies**) thickness of wool, fabric, etc.

plying v ▷ ply[1]

plywood n (pl **-s**) board made of thin layers of wood glued together

plywoods n ▷ plywood

pneumatic adj worked by or inflated with wind or air

pneumonia n (pl **-s**) inflammation of the lungs

pneumonias n ▷ pneumonia

> **po** n (pos). A po is an informal word for a chamber pot. This is a good word to have ready in case you see an opportunity to play a good word beginning with P next to a word ending in O, or vice versa. Po scores 4 points.

poach[1] v (**-es, -ing, -ed**) catch (animals) illegally on someone else's land

poach[2] v (**-es, -ing, -ed**) simmer (food) gently in liquid

poached v ▷ poach

poacher n (pl **-s**) person who catches animals illegally on someone else's land

poachers n ▷ poacher

poaches v ▷ poach

poaching v ▷ poach

pocket n (pl **-s**) small bag sewn into clothing for carrying things ▶ v (**-s, -ing, -ed**) put into one's pocket ▶ adj small

pocketed v ▷ pocket

pocketing v ▷ pocket

pockets n, v ▷ pocket

pockmarked adj (of the skin) marked with hollow scars where diseased spots have been

pod n (pl **-s**) long narrow seed case of peas, beans, etc.

podgier adj ▷ podgy

podgiest adj ▷ podgy

pods n ▷ pod

podgy adj (**-gier, -giest**) short and fat

podia n ▷ podium

podium n (pl **-diums, -dia**) small raised platform for a conductor or speaker

podiums n ▷ podium

poem n (pl **-s**) imaginative piece of writing in rhythmic lines

poems n ▷ poem

poep n (pl **-s**) (S AFR) (Slang) emission of gas from the anus

poeps n ▷ poep

poesies n ▷ poesy

poesy n (pl **-sies**) (Obs) poetry

poet n (pl **-s**) writer of poems

poetic, poetical adj of or like poetry > **poetically** adv

poetical adj ▷ poetic

poetically adv ▷ poetic

poetries n ▷ poetry

poetry n (pl **-ries**) poems

poets n ▷ poet

pogrom n (pl **-s**) organized persecution and massacre

pogroms n ▷ pogrom

poignancies n ▷ poignant

poignancy n ▷ poignant

poignant adj sharply painful to the feelings > **poignancy** n (pl **-cies**)

poinsettia n (pl **-s**) Central American shrub widely grown for its clusters of scarlet leaves, which resemble petals

poinsettias n ▷ poinsettia

point n (pl **-s**) main idea in a discussion, argument, etc. ▶ v (**-s, -ing, -ed**) show the direction or position of something or draw attention to it by extending a finger or other pointed object towards it

pointed adj having a sharp end ▶ adj ▷ point > **pointedly** adv

pointedly adv ▷ pointed

pointer n (pl **-s**) helpful hint

pointers n ▷ pointer

pointing v ▷ point

pointless adj meaningless, irrelevant

points n, v ▷ point

poise n (pl **-s**) calm dignified manner

poised adj absolutely ready

poises n ▷ poise

poison n (pl **-s**) substance that kills or injures when swallowed or absorbed ▶ v (**-s, -ing, -ed**) give poison to > **poisoner** n (pl **-s**) > **poisonous** adj

poisoned v ▷ poison

poisoner n ▷ poison

poisoners n ▷ poison

poisoning v ▷ poison

poisonous adj ▷ poison

poisons n, v ▷ poison

poke v (**-kes, -king, -ked**) jab or prod with one's finger, a stick, etc. ▶ n (pl **-s**) poking

poked v ▷ poke
poker¹ n (pl -s) metal rod for stirring a fire
poker² n (pl -s) card game in which players bet on the hands dealt
pokers n ▷ poker¹, ²
pokier adj ▷ poky
pokiest adj ▷ poky
poking v ▷ poke
pokes v, n ▷ poke
poky adj (-kier, -kiest) small and cramped
polar adj of or near either of the earth's poles
polarize v (-zes, -zing, -zed) form or cause to form into groups with directly opposite views ▷ **polarization** n (pl -s)
polarization n ▷ polarize
polarizations n ▷ polarize
polarized v ▷ polarize
polarizes v ▷ polarize
polarizing v ▷ polarize
polder n (pl -s) land reclaimed from the sea, esp. in the Netherlands
polders n ▷ polder
pole¹ n (pl -s) long rounded piece of wood etc.
pole² n (pl -s) point furthest north or south on the earth's axis of rotation
poleaxe v (-xes, -xing, -xed) hit or stun with a heavy blow
poleaxed v ▷ poleaxe
poleaxes v ▷ poleaxe
poleaxing v ▷ poleaxe
polecat n (pl -s) small animal of the weasel family
polecats n ▷ polecat
polemic [pol-em-ik] n (pl -s) fierce attack on or defence of a particular opinion, belief, etc. ▷ **polemical** adj
polemical adj ▷ polemic
polemics n ▷ polemic
poles n ▷ pole¹, ²
police n organized force in a state which keeps law and order ▷ v (-ces, -cing, -ced) control or watch over with police or a similar body
policed v ▷ police
policeman, policewoman n (pl -men, -women) member of a police force
policemen n ▷ policeman
polices v ▷ police
policewomen n ▷ policeman
policies n ▷ policy¹, ²
policing v ▷ police
policy¹ n (pl -cies) plan of action adopted by a person, group, or state
policy² n (pl -cies) document containing an insurance contract
polio n (pl -s) disease affecting the spinal

cord, which often causes paralysis (also **poliomyelitis**)
polios n ▷ polio
polish v (-es, -ing, -ed) make smooth and shiny by polishing ▷ n (pl -es) substance used for polishing
polished adj accomplished ▶ v ▷ polish
polishing v ▷ polish
polishes v, n ▷ polish
polite adj showing consideration for others in one's manners, speech, etc. ▷ **politely** adv ▷ **politeness** n (pl -es)
politely adv ▷ polite
politeness n ▷ polite
politenesses n ▷ politeness
politic adj wise and likely to prove advantageous
political adj of the state, government, or public administration ▷ **politically** adv
politically adv ▷ political
politician n (pl -s) person actively engaged in politics, esp. a member of parliament
politicians n ▷ politician
politics n winning and using of power to govern society
polka n (pl -s) lively 19th-century dance
polkas n ▷ polka
poll n (pl -s) (also **opinion poll**) questioning of a random sample of people to find out general opinion ▶ v (-s, -ing, -ed) receive (votes)
pollarded adj (of a tree) growing very bushy because its top branches have been cut short
polled v ▷ poll
pollen n (pl -s) fine dust produced by flowers to fertilize other flowers
pollens ▷
pollinate v (-tes, -ting, -ted) fertilize with pollen
pollinated v ▷ pollinate
pollinates v ▷ pollinate
pollinating v ▷ pollinate
polling v ▷ poll
polls n, v ▷ poll
pollster n (pl -s) person who conducts opinion polls
pollsters n ▷ pollster
pollute v (-tes, -ting, -ted) contaminate with something poisonous or harmful ▷ **pollution** n (pl -s)
pollutant n (pl -s) something that pollutes
pollutants n ▷ pollutant
polluted v ▷ pollute
pollutes v ▷ pollute
polluting v ▷ pollute
pollution n ▷ pollute

pollutions n ▷ pollute

polo n (pl -s) game like hockey played by teams of players on horseback

polonaise n (pl -s) stately dance
   polonaises n ▷ polonaise

polonium n (pl -s) (CHEM) radioactive element that occurs in trace amounts in uranium ores
   poloniums n ▷ polonium
   polos n ▷ polo

poltergeist n (pl -s) spirit believed to move furniture and throw objects around
   poltergeists n ▷ poltergeist

poltroon n (pl -s) (Obs) utter coward
   poltroons n ▷ poltroon
   polyandries n ▷ polyandry

polyandry n (pl -ries) practice of having more than one husband at the same time

polyanthus n (pl -es) garden primrose
   polyanthuses n ▷ polyanthus

polychromatic adj many-coloured

polyester n (pl -s) synthetic material used to make plastics and textile fibres
   polyesters n ▷ polyester
   polygamies n ▷ polygamy
   polygamist n ▷ polygamy
   polygamists n ▷ polygamy
   polygamous adj ▷ polygamy

polygamy [pol-ig-a-mee] n (pl -mies) practice of having more than one husband or wife at the same time > **polygamous** adj > **polygamist** n (pl -s)

polyglot adj, n (pl -s) (person) able to speak or write several languages
   polyglots n ▷ polyglot

polygon n (pl -s) geometrical figure with three or more angles and sides > **polygonal** adj
   polygonal adj ▷ polygon
   polygons n ▷ polygon
   polyhedra n ▷ polyhedron

polyhedron n (pl -rons, -ra) solid figure with four or more sides
   polyhedrons n ▷ polyhedron

polymer n (pl -s) chemical compound with large molecules made of simple molecules of the same kind

polymerize v (-zes, -zing, -zed) form into polymers > **polymerization** n (pl -s)
   polymerization n ▷ polymerize
   polymerizations n ▷ polymerize
   polymerized v ▷ polymerize
   polymerizes v ▷ polymerize
   polymerizing v ▷ polymerize
   polymers n ▷ polymer

polyp n (pl -s) small simple sea creature with a hollow cylindrical body

polyps n ▷ polyp

polyphonic adj (MUSIC) consisting of several melodies played simultaneously

polystyrene n (pl -s) synthetic material used esp. as white rigid foam for packing and insulation
   polystyrenes n ▷ polystyrene

polytechnic n (pl -s) (in New Zealand and formerly in Britain) college offering courses in many subjects at and below degree level
   polytechnics n ▷ polytechnic

polytheism n (pl -s) belief in many gods > **polytheistic** adj
   polytheisms n ▷ polytheism
   polytheistic n ▷ polytheism

polythene n (pl -s) light plastic used for bags etc.
   polythenes n ▷ polythene

polyunsaturated adj of a group of fats that do not form cholesterol in the blood

polyurethane n (pl -s) synthetic material used esp. in paints
   polyurethanes n ▷ polyurethane

pom n (pl -s) (AUST & NZ) (Slang) person from England (also **pommy**) (pl -mmies)

pomander n (pl -s) (container for) a mixture of sweet-smelling petals, herbs, etc.
   pomanders n ▷ pomander

pomegranate n (pl -s) round tropical fruit with a thick rind containing many seeds in a red pulp
   pomegranates n ▷ pomegranate

pommel n (pl -s) raised part on the front of a saddle
   pommels n ▷ pommel
   pommies n ▷ pom
   pommy n ▷ pom
   poms n ▷ pom

pomp n (pl -s) stately display or ceremony
   pomps n ▷ pomp

pompom n (pl -s) decorative ball of tufted wool, silk, etc.
   pompoms n ▷ pompom
   pomposities n ▷ pompous
   pomposity n ▷ pompous

pompous adj foolishly serious and grand, self-important > **pompously** adv > **pomposity** n (pl -ties)
   pompously adv ▷ pompous

poncho n (pl -os) loose circular cloak with a hole for the head
   ponchos n ▷ poncho

pond n (pl -s) small area of still water
   ponds n ▷ pond

ponder v (-s, -ing, -ed) think thoroughly or

pondered v ▷ ponder

pondering v ▷ ponder

ponderous adj serious and dull > **ponderously** adv

ponderously adv ▷ ponderous

ponders v ▷ ponder

pong v, n (pl -s) (Informal) (give off) a strong unpleasant smell

pongs n ▷ pong

ponies n ▷ pony

pontiff n (pl -s) the Pope

pontiffs n ▷ pontiff

pontificate v (-tes, -ting, -ted) state one's opinions as if they were the only possible correct ones ▶ n (pl -s) period of office of a Pope

pontificated v ▷ pontificate

pontificates v, n ▷ pontificate

pontificating v ▷ pontificate

pontoon[1] n (pl -s) floating platform supporting a temporary bridge

pontoon[2] n (pl -s) gambling card game

pontoons n ▷ pontoon[1, 2]

pony n (pl -nies) small horse

ponytail n (pl -s) long hair tied in one bunch at the back of the head

ponytails n ▷ ponytail

poodle n (pl -s) dog with curly hair often clipped fancifully

poodles n ▷ poodle

pool[1] n (pl -s) small body of still water

pool[2] n (pl -s) shared fund or group of workers or resources ▶ pl (BRIT) ▷ **football pools** ▶ v (-s, -ing, -ed) put in a common fund

pooled v ▷ pool[2]

pooling v ▷ pool[2]

pools n, v ▷ pool[1, 2]

poop n (pl -s) raised part at the back of a sailing ship

poops n ▷ poop

poor adj having little money and few possessions

poorlier adj ▷ poorly

poorliest adj ▷ poorly

poorly adv in a poor manner ▶ adj (-lier, -liest) not in good health

pop[1] v (-s, -pping, -pped) make or cause to make a small explosive sound (Informal) ▶ n small explosive sound (BRIT)

pop[2] n (pl -s) music of general appeal, esp. to young people

pop[3] n (pl -s) (Informal) father

popcorn n (pl -s) grains of maize heated until they puff up and burst

popcorns n ▷ popcorn

pope n (pl -s) head of the Roman Catholic Church

popes n ▷ pope

poplar n (pl -s) tall slender tree

poplars n ▷ poplar

poplin n (pl -s) ribbed cotton material

poplins n ▷ poplin

poppadom n (pl -s) thin round crisp Indian bread

poppadoms n ▷ poppadom

popped v ▷ pop[1]

poppies n ▷ poppy

popping v ▷ pop[1]

poppy n (pl -ppies) plant with a large red flower

pops n ▷ pop

populace n (pl -s) the ordinary people

populaces n ▷ populace

popular adj widely liked and admired > **popularly** adv > **popularity** n (pl -ties)

popularize v (-zes, -zing, -zed) make popular

popularized v ▷ popularize

popularizes v ▷ popularize

popularizing v ▷ popularize

popularities n ▷ popular

popularity n ▷ popular

popularly adv ▷ popular

populate v (-tes, -ting, -ted) live in, inhabit

populated v ▷ populate

populates v ▷ populate

populating v ▷ populate

population n (pl -s) all the people who live in a particular place

populations n ▷ population

populous adj densely populated

porbeagle n (pl -s) kind of shark

porbeagles n ▷ porbeagle

porcelain n (pl -s) fine china

porcelains n ▷ porcelain

porch n (pl -es) covered approach to the entrance of a building

porches n ▷ porch

porcine adj of or like a pig

porcupine n (pl -s) animal covered with long pointed quills

porcupines n ▷ porcupine

pore n (pl -s) tiny opening in the skin or in the surface of a plant

pores n ▷ pore

pork n (pl -s) pig meat

porker n (pl -s) pig raised for food

porkers n ▷ porker

porks n ▷ pork

porn, porno adj, n (pl -s) (Informal)
▷ **pornography, pornographic**

pornographies n ▷ pornography
pornography n (pl -**hies**) writing, films, or pictures designed to be sexually exciting > **pornographic** adj
pornographer n (pl -**s**) producer of pornography
pornographers n ▷ pornographer
pornographic n ▷ pornography
pornos n ▷ porn
porns n ▷ porn
porosities n ▷ porous
porosity n ▷ porous
porous adj allowing liquid to pass through gradually > **porosity** n (pl -**ties**)
porphyries n ▷ porphyry
porphyry [por-fir-ee] n (pl -**ries**) reddish rock with large crystals in it
porpoise n (pl -**s**) fishlike sea mammal
porpoises n ▷ porpoise
porridge n (pl -**s**) breakfast food made of oatmeal cooked in water or milk
porridges n ▷ porridge
port¹ n (pl -**s**) (town with) a harbour
port² n (pl -**s**) left side of a ship or aircraft when facing the front of it
port³ n (pl -**s**) strong sweet wine, usu. red
port⁴ n (pl -**s**) opening in the side of a ship
portabilities n ▷ portable
portability n ▷ portable
portable adj easily carried > **portability** n (pl -**ties**)
portal n (pl -**s**) large imposing doorway or gate
portals n ▷ portal
portcullis n (pl -**es**) grating suspended above a castle gateway, that can be lowered to block the entrance
portcullises n ▷ portcullis
portend v (-**s**, -**ing**, -**ed**) be a sign of
portended v ▷ portend
portending v ▷ portend
portends v ▷ portend
portent n (pl -**s**) sign of a future event
portentous adj of great or ominous significance
portents n ▷ portent
porter¹ n (pl -**s**) man who carries luggage
porter² n (pl -**s**) doorman or gatekeeper of a building
porters n ▷ porter¹, ²
portfolio n (pl -**s**) (flat case for carrying) examples of an artist's work
portfolios n ▷ portfolio
porthole n (pl -**s**) small round window in a ship or aircraft
portholes n ▷ porthole

portico n (pl -**coes**, -**cos**) porch or covered walkway with columns supporting the roof
porticoes n ▷ portico
porticos n ▷ portico
portion n (pl -**s**) part or share
portions n ▷ portion
portlier adj ▷ portly
portliest adj ▷ portly
portly adj (-**lier**, -**liest**) rather fat
portmanteau n (pl -**eaus**, -**eaux**) (Old-fashioned) large suitcase that opens into two compartments ▶ adj combining aspects of different things
portmanteaus n ▷ portmanteau
portmanteaux n ▷ portmanteau
portrait n (pl -**s**) picture of a person
portraits n ▷ portrait
portray v (-**s**, -**ing**, -**ed**) describe or represent by artistic means, as in writing or film > **portrayal** n (pl -**s**)
portrayal n ▷ portray
portrayals n ▷ portray
portrayed v ▷ portray
portraying v ▷ portray
portrays v ▷ portray
ports n ▷ port¹, ², ³, ⁴
pose v (-**ses**, -**sing**, -**sed**) place in or take up a particular position to be photographed or drawn ▶ n (pl -**s**) position while posing
posed v ▷ pose
poser n (pl -**s**) puzzling question
posers n ▷ poser
poses v, n ▷ pose
poseur n (pl -**s**) person who behaves in an affected way to impress others
poseurs n ▷ poseur
posies n ▷ posy
posing v ▷ pose
posh adj (Informal) smart, luxurious
posit [pozz-it] v (-**s**, -**ing**, -**ed**) lay down as a basis for argument
posited v ▷ posit
positing v ▷ posit
position n (pl -**s**) place ▶ v (-**s**, -**ing**, -**ed**) place
positioned v ▷ position
positioning v ▷ position
positions n, v ▷ position
posits v ▷ posit
positive adj feeling no doubts, certain (MATHS) > **positively** adv
positively adv ▷ positive
positron n (pl -**s**) (PHYSICS) particle with same mass as electron but positive charge
positrons n ▷ positron
posse [poss-ee] n (pl -**s**) (US) group of men

organized to maintain law and order
posses n ▷ posse
possess v (-es, -ing, -ed) have as one's property
> **possessor** n (pl -s)
possessed v ▷ possess
possesses v ▷ possess
possessing v ▷ possess
possession n (pl -s) state of possessing,
ownership ▶ pl things a person possesses
possessions n ▷ possession
possessive adj wanting all the attention or
love of another person > **possessiveness** n
possessiveness n ▷ possessive
possessor n ▷ possess
possessors n ▷ possess
possibilities n ▷ possibility
possibility n ▷ possible
possible adj able to exist, happen, or be done
▶ n (pl -s) person or thing that might be
suitable or chosen > **possibility** n (pl -ties)
possibles n ▷ possible
possibly adv perhaps, not necessarily
possum n (pl -s) ▷ opossum (AUST & NZ)
▷ **phalanger**
possums n ▷ possum
post¹ n (pl -s) official system of delivering
letters and parcels ▶ v (-s, -ing, -ed) send by
post > **postal** adj
post² n (pl -s) length of wood, concrete, etc.
fixed upright to support or mark something
▶ v (-s, -ing, -ed) put up (a notice) in a public
place
post³ n (pl -s) job ▶ v (-s, -ing, -ed) send (a
person) to a new place to work
postage n charge for sending a letter or parcel
by post
postages n ▷ postage
postal adj ▷ post¹
postbag n (pl -s) postman's bag
postbags n ▷ postbag
postcard n (pl -s) card for sending a message
by post without an envelope
postcards n ▷ postcard
postcode n system of letters and numbers
used to aid the sorting of mail
postcodes n ▷ postcode
postdate v (-tes, -ting, -ted) write a date on (a
cheque) that is later than the actual date
postdated v ▷ postdate
postdates v ▷ postdate
postdating v ▷ postdate
posted v ▷ post¹, ², ³
poster n (pl -s) large picture or notice stuck
on a wall
posterior n (pl -s) buttocks ▶ adj behind, at

the back of
posteriors n ▷ posterior
posterities n ▷ posterity
posterity n (pl -ties) future generations,
descendants
postern n (pl -s) small back door or gate
posterns n ▷ postern
posters n ▷ poster
postgraduate n (pl -s) person with a degree
who is studying for a more advanced
qualification
postgraduates n ▷ postgraduate
posthaste adv with great speed
posthumous [poss-tume-uss] adj occurring
after one's death > **posthumously** adv
posthumously adv ▷ posthumous
postie n (pl -s) (SCOT, AUST & NZ) (Informal)
postman
posties n ▷ postie
postilion, postillion n (pl -s) (HIST) person
riding one of a pair of horses drawing a
carriage
postilions n ▷ postilion
postillion n ▷ postilion
postillions n ▷ postilion
posting v ▷ post¹, ², ³
postman, postwoman n (pl -men, -women)
person who collects and delivers post
postmark n (pl -s) official mark stamped on
letters showing place and date of posting
postmarks n ▷ postmark
postmen n ▷ postman
postmaster, postmistress n (pl -s, -es) (in
some countries) official in charge of a post
office
postmasters n ▷ postmaster
postmistress n ▷ postmaster
postmistresses n ▷ postmaster
postmortem ▶ n (pl -s) medical examination
of a body to establish the cause of death
postmortems n ▷ postmortem
postnatal adj occurring after childbirth
postpone v (-nes, -ning, -ned) put off to a later
time > **postponement** n (pl -s)
postponed v ▷ postpone
postponement n ▷ postpone
postponements n ▷ postpone
postpones v ▷ postpone
postponing v ▷ postpone
posts n, v ▷ post¹, ², ³
postscript n (pl -s) passage added at the end
of a letter
postscripts n ▷ postscript
postulant n (pl -s) candidate for admission to
a religious order

postulants n ▷ postulant

postulate v (-tes, -ting, -ted) assume to be true as the basis of an argument or theory

postulated v ▷ postulate

postulates v ▷ postulate

postulating v ▷ postulate

posture n (pl -s) position or way in which someone stands, walks, etc. ▶ v (-res, -ring, -red) behave in an exaggerated way to get attention

postured v ▷ posture

postures n, v ▷ posture

posturing v ▷ posture

postwomen n ▷ postman

posy n (pl -sies) small bunch of flowers

pot[1] n (pl -s) round deep container ▶ pl (Informal) large amount ▶ v (-s, -tting, -tted) plant in a pot

pot[2] n (Slang) cannabis

potted adj grown in a pot ▶ v ▷ pot[1]

potting v ▷ pot[1]

pots n ▷ pot[1]

potable [pote-a-bl] adj drinkable

potash n (pl -es) white powdery substance obtained from ashes and used as fertilizer

potashes n ▷ potash

potassium n (pl -s) (CHEM) silvery metallic element

potassiums n ▷ potassium

potato ▶ n (pl -oes) roundish starchy vegetable that grows underground

potatoes n ▷ potato

poteen n (in Ireland) illegally made alcoholic drink

poteens n ▷ poteen

potencies n ▷ potent

potency n ▷ potent

potent adj having great power or influence > **potency** n (pl -cies)

potentate n (pl -s) ruler or monarch

potentates n ▷ potentate

potential adj possible but not yet actual ▶ n (pl -s) ability or talent not yet fully used > **potentially** adv > **potentiality** n (pl -ties)

potentialities n ▷ potential

potentiality n ▷ potential

potentially adv ▷ potential

potentials n ▷ potential

pothole n (pl -s) hole in the surface of a road

potholer n ▷ potholing

potholers n ▷ potholing

potholes n ▷ pothole

potholing n (pl -s) sport of exploring underground caves > **potholer** n (pl -s)

potholings n ▷ potholing

potion n (pl -s) dose of medicine or poison

potions n ▷ potion

potoroo n (pl -s) Australian leaping rodent

potoroos n ▷ potoroo

potpourri [po-poor-ee] n (pl -s) fragrant mixture of dried flower petals

potpourris n ▷ potpourri

pottage n (pl -s) (Old-fashioned) thick soup or stew

pottages n ▷ pottage

potter[1] n (pl -s) person who makes pottery

potter[2] v (-s, -ing, -ed) be busy in a pleasant but aimless way

pottered v ▷ potter[2]

potteries n ▷ pottery

pottering v ▷ potter[2]

potters n, v ▷ potter[1, 2]

pottery n (pl -ries) articles made from baked clay

pottier adj ▷ potty

potties n ▷ potty[2]

pottiest adj ▷ potty

potty[1] adj (-tier, -tiest) (Informal) crazy or silly

potty[2] n (pl -ties) bowl used by a small child as a toilet

pouch n (pl -es) small bag

pouches n ▷ pouch

pouf, pouffe [poof] n (pl -s) large solid cushion used as a seat

pouffe n ▷ pouf

pouffes n ▷ pouf

poufs n ▷ pouf

poulterer n (pl -s) (BRIT) person who sells poultry

poulterers n ▷ poulterer

poultice [pole-tiss] n (pl -s) moist dressing, often heated, applied to inflamed skin

poultices n ▷ poultice

poultries n ▷ poultry

poultry n (pl -ries) domestic fowls

pounce v (-ces, -cing, -ced) spring upon suddenly to attack or capture ▶ n (pl -s) pouncing

pounced v ▷ pounce

pouncing v ▷ pounce

pounces v, n ▷ pounce

pound[1] n (pl -s) monetary unit of Britain and some other countries

pound[2] v (-s, -ing, -ed) hit heavily and repeatedly

pound[3] n (pl -s) enclosure for stray animals or officially removed vehicles

pounded v ▷ pound[2]

pounding v ▷ pound[2]

pounds n, v ▷ pound[1, 3]

pour v (-s, -ing, -ed) flow or cause to flow out in a stream
poured v ▷ pour
pouring v ▷ pour
pours v ▷ pour
pout v (-s, -ing, -ed) thrust out one's lips, look sulky ▶ n (pl -s) pouting look
pouted v ▷ pout
pouting v ▷ pout
pouts v, n ▷ pout
poverties n ▷ poverty
poverty n (pl -ties) state of being without enough food or money
powder n (pl -s) substance in the form of tiny loose particles ▶ v (-s, -ing, -ed) apply powder to > powdery adj (-rier, -riest)
powdered adj, v ▷ powder
powderier adj ▷ powder
powderiest adj ▷ powder
powdering v ▷ powder
powders n, v ▷ powder
power n (pl -s) ability to do or act ▶ powerful adj > powerless adj
powered adj having or operated by mechanical or electrical power
powerful adj ▷ power
powerless adj ▷ power
powers n ▷ power
powwow n (pl -s) (Informal) talk or conference
powwows n ▷ powwow
pox n (pl -es) disease in which skin pustules form
poxes n ▷ pox

> poz adj. Poz is an old-fashioned short form of positive. This is a good word for a crowded board towards the end of the game, especially if you can form another word in the process, or form it on a bonus square. Poz scores 24 points.

practicabilities n ▷ practicable
practicability n ▷ practicable
practicable adj capable of being done successfully > practicability n (pl -ties)
practical adj involving experience or actual use rather than theory ▶ n (pl -s) examination in which something has to be made or done > practically adv
practically adv ▷ practical
practicals n ▷ practical
practice n (pl -s) something done regularly or habitually
practices n ▷ practice
practise v (-ses, -sing, -sed) do repeatedly so as to gain skill

practised v ▷ practise
practises v ▷ practise
practising v ▷ practise
practitioner n (pl -s) person who practises a profession
practitioners n ▷ practitioner
pragmatic adj concerned with practical consequences rather than theory
> pragmatism n (pl -s) > pragmatist n (pl -s)
pragmatism n ▷ pragmatic
pragmatisms n ▷ pragmatic
pragmatist n ▷ pragmatic
pragmatists n ▷ pragmatic
prairie n (pl -s) large treeless area of grassland, esp. in N America and Canada
prairies n ▷ prairie
praise v (-ses, -sing, -sed) express approval or admiration of (someone or something) ▶ n (pl -s) something said or written to show approval or admiration > praiseworthy adj
praised v ▷ praise
praises v, n ▷ praise
praiseworthy adj ▷ praise
praising v ▷ praise
praline [prah-leen] n (pl -s) sweet made of nuts and caramelized sugar
pralines n ▷ praline
pram n (pl -s) four-wheeled carriage for a baby, pushed by hand
prams n ▷ pram
prance v (-ces, -cing, -ced) walk with exaggerated bouncing steps
pranced v ▷ prance
prances v ▷ prance
prancing v ▷ prance
prang v, n (pl -s) (Slang) (have) a crash in a car or aircraft
prangs n ▷ prang
prank n (pl -s) mischievous trick
pranks n ▷ prank
prat n (pl -s) (BRIT, AUST & NZ) (Informal) stupid person
prats n ▷ prat
prattle v (-les, -ling, -led) chatter in a childish or foolish way ▶ n (pl -s) childish or foolish talk
prattled v ▷ prattle
prattles v, n ▷ prattle
prattling v ▷ prattle
prawn n (pl -s) edible shellfish like a large shrimp
prawns n ▷ prawn
praxis n (pl praxises) practice as opposed to theory
praxises n ▷ praxis
pray v (-s, -ing, -ed) say prayers

prayed v ▷ pray

prayer n (pl -s) thanks or appeal addressed to one's God

prayers n ▷ prayer

praying v ▷ pray

prays v ▷ pray

preach v (-es, -ing, -ed) give a talk on a religious theme as part of a church service

preached v ▷ preach

preaches v ▷ preach

preaching v ▷ preach

preacher n (pl -s) person who preaches, esp. in church

preachers n ▷ preacher

preamble n (pl -s) introductory part to something said or written

preambles n ▷ preamble

prearranged adj arranged beforehand

prebendaries n ▷ prebendary

prebendary n (pl -ries) clergyman who is a member of the chapter of a cathedral

precarious adj insecure, unsafe, likely to fall or collapse > **precariously** adv

precariously adv ▷ precarious

precaution n (pl -s) action taken in advance to prevent something bad happening > **precautionary** adj

precautionary adj ▷ precaution

precautions n ▷ precaution

precede v (-des, -ding, -ded) go or be before

preceded v ▷ precede

precedence [press-ee-denss] n (pl -s) formal order of rank or position

precedences n ▷ precedence

precedent n (pl -s) previous case or occurrence regarded as an example to be followed

precedents n ▷ precedent

precedes v ▷ precede

preceding v ▷ precede

precentor n (pl -s) person who leads the singing in a church

precentors n ▷ precentor

precept n (pl -s) rule of behaviour > **preceptive** adj

preceptive adj ▷ precept

precepts n ▷ precept

precinct n (pl -s) (BRIT, AUST & S AFR) area in a town closed to traffic ▶ pl surrounding region

precincts n ▷ precinct

precious adj of great value and importance

precipice n (pl -s) very steep face of cliff or rockface

precipices n ▷ precipice

precipitate v (-tes, -ting, -ted) cause to happen suddenly ▶ adj done rashly or hastily

▶ n (pl -s) (CHEM) substance precipitated from a solution > **precipitately** adv > **precipitation** n (pl -s) precipitating

precipitated v, n ▷ precipitate

precipitately adv ▷ precipitate

precipitates v, n ▷ precipitate

precipitating v ▷ precipitate

precipitation n ▷ precipitate

precipitations n ▷ precipitate

precipitous adj sheer

précis [pray-see] n (pl précis) short written summary of a longer piece ▶ v (-ses, -sing, -sed) make a précis of

precise adj (-r, -st) exact, accurate in every detail > **precisely** adv > **precision** n (pl -s)

précised v ▷ précis

précises v ▷ précis

precisely adv ▷ precise

preciser adj ▷ precise

precisest adj ▷ precise

précising v ▷ précis

precision n ▷ precise

precisions n ▷ precise

preclude v (-des, -ding, -ded) make impossible to happen

precluded v ▷ preclude

precludes v ▷ preclude

precluding v ▷ preclude

precocious adj having developed or matured early or too soon > **precocity** n (pl -ties)

precocities n ▷ precocious

precocity n ▷ precocious

precognition n (pl -s) alleged ability to foretell the future

precognitions n ▷ precognition

preconceived adj (of an idea) formed without real experience or reliable information > **preconception** n (pl -s)

preconception n ▷ preconceived

preconceptions n ▷ preconcieve

precondition n (pl -s) something that must happen or exist before something else can

preconditions n ▷ precondition

precursor n (pl -s) something that precedes and is a signal of something else, forerunner

precursors n ▷ precursor

predate v (-tes, -ting, -ted) occur at an earlier date than

predated v ▷ predate

predates v ▷ predate

predating v ▷ predate

predator n (pl -s) predatory animal

predators n ▷ predators

predatory [pred-a-tree] adj habitually hunting and killing other animals for food

predecease v (-ses, -sing, -sed) die before (someone else)
predeceased v ▷ predecease
predeceases v ▷ predecease
predeceasing v ▷ predecease
predecessor n (pl -s) person who precedes another in an office or position
predecessors n ▷ predecessor
predestination n (pl -s) (THEOLOGY) belief that future events have already been decided by God or fate ▷ predestined adj
predestinations n ▷ predestine
predestined adj ▷ predestination
predetermined adj decided in advance
predicament n (pl -s) embarrassing or difficult situation
predicaments n ▷ predicament
predicate n (pl -tes) (GRAMMAR) part of a sentence in which something is said about the subject, e.g. went home in I went home ▶ v (-tes, -ting, -ted) declare or assert
predicated v ▷ predicate
predicates n, v ▷ predicate
predicating v ▷ predicate
predict v (-s, -ing, -ed) tell about in advance, prophesy ▷ predictable adj ▷ prediction n (pl -s)
predictable adj ▷ predict
predicted v ▷ predict
predicting v ▷ predict
prediction n ▷ predict
predictions n ▷ predict
predictive adj relating to or able to make predictions
predicts v ▷ predict
predilection n (pl -s) (Formal) preference or liking
predilections n ▷ predilection
predispose v (-ses, -sing, -sed) influence (someone) in favour of something ▷ predisposition n (pl -s)
predisposed v ▷ predispose
predisposes v ▷ predispose
predisposing v ▷ predispose
predisposition n ▷ predispose
predispositions n ▷ predispose
predominate v (-tes, -ting, -ted) be the main or controlling element ▷ predominance n (pl -s) ▷ predominant adj ▷ predominantly adv
predominance n ▷ predominance
predominances n ▷ predominance
predominant n ▷ predominate
predominantly adv ▷ predominate
predominated v ▷ predominate
predominates v ▷ predominate

predominating v ▷ predominate
preen v (-s, -ing, -ed) (of a bird) clean or trim (feathers) with the beak
preened v ▷ preen
preening v ▷ preen
preens v ▷ preen
prefab n (pl -s) prefabricated house
prefabricated adj (of a building) manufactured in shaped sections for rapid assembly on site
prefabs n ▷ prefab
preface [pref-iss] n (pl -s) introduction to a book ▶ v (-ces, -cing, -ced) serve as an introduction to (a book, speech, etc.) ▷ prefatory adj
prefaced v ▷ preface
prefaces n, v ▷ preface
prefacing v ▷ preface
prefatory adj ▷ preface
prefect n (pl -s) senior pupil in a school, with limited power over others
prefects n ▷ prefect
prefecture n (pl -s) office or area of authority of a prefect
prefectures n ▷ prefecture
prefer v (-s, -rring, -rred) like better ▷ preference n (pl -s)
preferable adj more desirable ▷ preferably adv
preferably adv ▷ preferable
preference n ▷ prefer
preferences n ▷ prefer
preferential adj showing preference
preferment n (pl -s) promotion or advancement
preferments n ▷ preferment
preferred v ▷ prefer
preferring v ▷ prefer
prefers v ▷ prefer
prefigure v (-res, -ring, -red) represent or suggest in advance
prefigured v ▷ prefigure
prefigures v ▷ prefigure
prefiguring v ▷ prefigure
prefix n (pl -es) letter or group of letters put at the beginning of a word to make a new word, such as un- in unhappy ▶ v (-es, -ing, -ed) put as an introduction or prefix (to)
prefixed v ▷ prefix
prefixes n, v ▷ prefix
prefixing v ▷ prefix
pregnacies n ▷ pregnant
pregnancy n ▷ pregnant
pregnant adj carrying a fetus in the womb ▷ pregnancy n (pl -cies)
prehensile adj capable of grasping

prehistoric adj of the period before written history begins > **prehistoric** n (pl -**ries**)
prehistories n > **prehistoric**
prehistory n > **prehistoric**

prejudice n (pl -**s**) unreasonable or unfair dislike or preference ▶ v (-**ces**, -**cing**, -**ced**) cause (someone) to have a prejudice > **prejudicial** adj disadvantageous, harmful
prejudiced v > **prejudice**
prejudicial adj > **prejudice**
prejudicing v > **prejudice**
prejudices n, v > **prejudice**

prelate [**prel**-it] n (pl -**s**) bishop or other churchman of high rank
prelates n > **prelate**
preliminaries n > **preliminary**

preliminary adj happening before and in preparation, introductory ▶ n (pl -**ries**) preliminary remark, contest, etc.

prelude n (pl -**s**) introductory movement in music
preludes n > **prelude**

premarital adj occurring before marriage

premature adj happening or done before the normal or expected time > **prematurely** adv
prematurely adv > **premature**

premeditated adj planned in advance
> **premeditation** n (pl -**s**)
premeditation n > **premeditated**
premeditations n > **premeditated**

premenstrual adj occurring or experienced before a menstrual period

premier n (pl -**s**) prime minister ▶ adj chief, leading > **premiership** n (pl -**s**)

première n (pl -**s**) first performance of a play, film, etc.
premières n > **première**
premiers n > **premier**
premiership n > **premier**
premierships n > **premier**

premise, premiss n (pl -**s**, -**es**) statement assumed to be true and used as the basis of reasoning
premises n > **premise**

premises pl n house or other building and its land
premisses n > **premise**

premium n (pl -**s**) additional sum of money, as on a wage or charge
premiums n > **premium**

premonition n (pl -**s**) feeling that something unpleasant is going to happen; foreboding
> **premonitory** adj
premonitions n > **premonition**
premonitory adj > **premonition**

prenatal adj before birth, during pregnancy
preoccupied v > **preoccupy**
preoccupies v > **preoccupy**

preoccupy v (-**pied**, -**pying**, -**pied**) fill the thoughts or attention of (someone) to the exclusion of other things > **preoccupation** n (pl -**s**)
preoccupation n > **preoccupy**
preoccupations n > **preoccupy**
preoccupying v > **preoccupy**

preordained adj decreed or determined in advance

prep. preparatory

prepacked adj sold already wrapped

prepaid adj paid for in advance

prepare v (-**res**, -**ring**, -**red**) make or get ready

preparation n (pl -**s**)
preparations n > **preparation**

preparatory [prip-**par**-a-tree] adj preparing for

prepared adj willing ▶ v > **prepare**
prepares v > **prepare**
preparing v > **prepare**

preponderance n (pl -**s**) greater force, amount, or influence > **preponderant** adj
preponderances adj > **preponderance**
preponderant adj > **preponderance**

preposition n (pl -**s**) word used before a noun or pronoun to show its relationship with other words, such as by in go by bus
> **prepositional** adj
prepositional n > **preposition**
prepositions n > **preposition**

prepossessing adj making a favourable impression, attractive

preposterous adj utterly absurd

prepuce [**pree**-pyewss] n (pl -**s**) retractable fold of skin covering the tip of the penis, foreskin
prepuces n > **prepuce**

prerecorded adj recorded in advance to be played or broadcast later

prerequisite adj, n (pl -**s**) (something) required before something else is possible
prerequisites n > **prerequisite**

prerogative n (pl -**s**) special power or privilege
prerogatives n > **prerogative**

presage [**press**-ij] v (-**ges**, -**ging**, -**ged**) be a sign or warning of
presaged v > **presage**
presages v > **presage**
presaging v > **presage**
presbyteries n > **presbytery**

presbytery n (pl -**ies**) (PRESBYTERIAN CHURCH) local church court

prescience [**press**-ee-enss] n (pl -**s**) knowledge of events before they happen > **prescient** adj

presciences n ▷ prescience

prescient adj ▷ prescience

prescribe v (-bes, -bing, -bed) recommend the use of (a medicine)

prescribed v ▷ prescribe

prescribes v ▷ prescribe

prescribing v ▷ prescribe

prescription n written instructions from a doctor for the making up and use of a medicine

prescriptions n ▷ prescription

prescriptive adj laying down rules

presence n (pl -s) fact of being in a specified place

presences n ▷ presence

present[1] adj being in a specified place ▶ n (pl -s) present time or tense

present[2] n something given to bring pleasure to another person ▶ v (-s, -ing, -ed) introduce formally or publicly > **presentation** n (pl -s)

presentable adj attractive, neat, fit for people to see

presented n ▷ present[2]

presenter n (pl -s) person introducing a TV or radio show

presenters n ▷ presenter

presentiment [priz-zen-tim-ent] n (pl -s) sense of something unpleasant about to happen

presentiments n ▷ presentiment

presenting v ▷ present[2]

presently adv soon (US & SCOT)

presents n, v ▷ present[1, 2]

preserve v (-ves, -ving, -ved) keep from being damaged, changed, or ended ▶ n (pl -s) area of interest restricted to a particular person or group > **preservation** n (pl -s)

preservation n ▷ preserve

preservations n ▷ preserve

preservative n (pl -s) chemical that prevents decay

preservatives n ▷ preservative

preserved v ▷ preserve

preserves v, n ▷ preserve

preserving v ▷ preserve

preshrunk adj (of fabric or a garment) having been shrunk during manufacture so that further shrinkage will not occur when washed

preside v (-des, -ding, -ded) be in charge, esp. of a meeting

presided v ▷ preside

presidencies n ▷ president

presidency n ▷ president

president n (pl -s) head of state in many countries > **presidential** adj > **presidency** n

(pl -cies)

presidential n ▷ president

presidents n ▷ president

presides v ▷ preside

presiding v ▷ preside

press v (-es, -ing, -ed) apply force or weight to ▶ n (pl -es) printing machine

pressed v ▷ press

presses v, n ▷ press

pressing adj urgent ▶ v ▷ press

presses n ▷ press

pressure n (pl -s) force produced by pressing

pressures n ▷ pressure

prestidigitation n (pl -s) skilful quickness with the hands, conjuring

prestidigitations n ▷ prestidigitation

prestige n (pl -s) high status or respect resulting from success or achievements > **prestigious** adj

prestiges n ▷ prestige

prestigious adj ▷ prestige

presumed v ▷ presume

presto adv (MUSIC) very quickly

prestressed adj (of concrete) containing stretched steel wires to strengthen it

presume v (-mes, -ing, -med) suppose to be the case

presumably adv one supposes (that)

presumed v ▷ presume

presumes v ▷ presume

presuming v ▷ presume

presumption (pl -s) n bold insolent behaviour

presumption n ▷ presumption

presumptive adj assumed to be true or valid until the contrary is proved

presumptuous adj doing things one has no right to do

presuppose v (-ses, -sing, -sed) need as a previous condition in order to be true > **presupposition** n (pl -s)

presupposed v ▷ presuppose

presupposes v ▷ presuppose

presupposing v ▷ presuppose

presupposition n ▷ presuppose

presuppositions v ▷ presuppose

pretence n (pl -s) behaviour intended to deceive, pretending

pretences n ▷ pretence

pretend v (-s, -ing, -ed) claim or give the appearance of (something untrue) to deceive or in play

pretended v ▷ pretend

pretender n (pl -s) person who makes a false or disputed claim to a position of power

pretenders n ▷ pretender

pretending v ▷ pretend
pretends v ▷ pretend
pretension n ▷ pretentious
pretensions n ▷ pretentious
pretentious adj making (unjustified) claims to special merit or importance > **pretension** n (pl -s)
preternatural adj beyond what is natural, supernatural
pretext n (pl -s) false reason given to hide the real one
pretexts n ▷ pretext
prettier adj ▷ pretty
prettiest adj ▷ pretty
prettily adv ▷ pretty
prettiness n ▷ pretty
prettinesses n ▷ pretty
pretty adj (-ttier, -ttiest) pleasing to look at ▶ adv fairly, moderately > **prettily** adv > **prettiness** n (pl -es)
pretzel n (pl -s) brittle salted biscuit
pretzels n ▷ pretzel
prevail v (-s, -ing, -ed) gain mastery
prevailed v ▷ prevail
prevailing adj widespread ▶ v ▷ prevail
prevails v ▷ prevail
prevalence n ▷ prevalent
prevalences n ▷ prevalent
prevalent adj widespread, common > **prevalence** n (pl -s)
prevaricate v (-tes, -ting, -ted) avoid giving a direct or truthful answer > **prevarication** n (pl -s)
prevaricated v ▷ prevaricate
prevaricates v ▷ prevaricate
prevaricating v ▷ prevaricate
prevarication n ▷ prevaricate
prevarications n ▷ prevaricate
prevent v (-s, -ing, -ed) keep from happening or doing > **preventable** adj > **prevention** n (pl -s) > **preventive** adj, n (pl -s)
preventable adj ▷ prevent
prevented v ▷ prevent
preventing v ▷ prevent
prevention n ▷ prevent
preventions n ▷ prevent
preventive adj, n ▷ prevent
preventives n ▷ prevent
prevents v ▷ prevent
preview n (pl -s) advance showing of a film or exhibition before it is shown to the public
previews n ▷ preview
previous adj coming or happening before > **previously** adv
previously adv ▷ previous

prey n (pl -s) animal hunted and killed for food by another animal
preys n ▷ prey
price n (pl -s) amount of money for which a thing is bought or sold ▶ v (-ces, -cing, -ced) fix or ask the price of
priced v ▷ price
priceless adj very valuable
prices n, v ▷ price
pricier adj ▷ pricey
priciest adj ▷ pricey
pricing v ▷ price
pricey adj (-cier, -ciest) (Informal) expensive
prick v (-s, -ing, -ed) pierce lightly with a sharp point ▶ n (pl -s) sudden sharp pain caused by pricking
pricked v ▷ prick
pricking v ▷ prick
prickle n (pl -s) thorn or spike on a plant ▶ v (-les, -ling, -led) have a tingling or pricking sensation > **prickly** adj (-lier, -liest)
prickled v ▷ prickle
prickles n, v ▷ prickle
pricklier adj ▷ prickle
prickliest adj ▷ prickle
prickling v ▷ prickle
prickly adj ▷ prickle
pricks v, n ▷ prick
pride n (pl -s) feeling of pleasure and satisfaction when one has done well
prides n ▷ pride
pried v ▷ pry
pries v ▷ pry
priest n (pl -s) (in the Christian church) a person who can administer the sacraments and preach > **priestess** n fem (pl -es) > **priesthood** n (pl -s) > **priestly** adj (-lier, -liest)
priestess n ▷ priest
priestesses n ▷ priest
priesthood n ▷ priest
priesthoods n ▷ priest
priestlier adj ▷ priest
priestliest adj ▷ priest
priestly adj ▷ priest
priests n ▷ priest
prig n (pl -s) self-righteous person who acts as if superior to others > **priggish** adj > **priggishness** n (pl -s)
priggish adj ▷ prig
priggishness n ▷ prig
prigishnesses n ▷ prig
prigs n ▷ prig
prim adj (-mmer, -mmest) formal, proper, and rather prudish > **primly** adv
primacies n ▷ primacy

primacy n (pl -**ies**) state of being first in rank, grade, etc.

primaeval adj ▷ **primeval**

primal adj of basic causes or origins

primarily adv ▷ **primary**

primary adj chief, most important > **primarily** adv

primate[1] n (pl -**s**) member of an order of mammals including monkeys and humans

primate[2] n (pl -**s**) archbishop

primates n ▷ **primate**[1, 2]

prime adj main, most important ▶ n (pl -**s**) time when someone is at his or her best or most vigorous ▶ v (-**mes**, -**ming**, -**med**) give (someone) information in advance to prepare them for something

primed v ▷ **prime**

primer n (pl -**s**) special paint applied to bare wood etc. before the main paint

primers n ▷ **primer**

primes n, v ▷ **prime**

priming v ▷ **prime**

primeval [prime-**ee**-val] adj of the earliest age of the world

primitive adj of an early simple stage of development

primly adv ▷ **prim**

primmer adj ▷ **prim**

primmest adj ▷ **prim**

primogeniture n (pl -**s**) system under which the eldest son inherits all his parents' property

primogenitures n ▷ **primogeniture**

primordial adj existing at or from the beginning

primrose n (pl -**s**) pale yellow spring flower

primroses n ▷ **primrose**

primula n (pl -**s**) type of primrose with brightly coloured flowers

primulas n ▷ **primula**

prince n (pl -**s**) male member of a royal family, esp. the son of the king or queen

princelier adj ▷ **princely**

princeliest adj ▷ **princely**

princely adj (-**lier**, -**liest**) of or like a prince

princess n (pl -**es**) female member of a royal family, esp. the daughter of the king or queen

princes n ▷ **prince**

princesses n ▷ **princess**

principal adj main, most important ▶ n (pl -**s**) head of a school or college > **principally** adv

principalities n ▷ **principality**

principality n (pl -**ties**) territory ruled by a prince

principally adv ▷ **principal**

principals n ▷ **principal**

principle n (pl -**s**) moral rule guiding behaviour

principles n ▷ **principle**

print v (-**s**, -**ing**, -**ed**) reproduce (a newspaper, book, etc.) in large quantities by mechanical or electronic means ▶ n (pl -**s**) printed words etc. > **printing** n (pl -**s**)

printed v ▷ **print**

printer n (pl -**s**) person or company engaged in printing

printers n ▷ **printer**

printing n, v ▷ **print**

printings n ▷ **print**

prints v ▷ **print**

printing v ▷ **print**

printed v ▷ **print**

prints n ▷ **print**

prior[1] adj earlier

prior[2] n (pl -**s**) head monk in a priory

prioress n (pl -**es**) deputy head nun in a convent

prioresses n ▷ **prioress**

priories n ▷ **priory**

priors n ▷ **prior**[2]

priory n (pl -**ries**) place where certain orders of monks or nuns live

priors n ▷ **prior**

priorities n ▷ **priority**

priority n (pl -**ties**) most important thing that must be dealt with first

prise v (-**ses**, -**sing**, -**sed**) force open by levering

prised v ▷ **prise**

prises v ▷ **prise**

prising v ▷ **prise**

prism n (pl -**s**) transparent block usu. with triangular ends and rectangular sides, used to disperse light into a spectrum or refract it in optical instruments

prismatic adj of or shaped like a prism

prisms n ▷ **prism**

prison n (pl -**s**) building where criminals and accused people are held

prisons n ▷ **prison**

prisoner n (pl -**s**) person held captive

prisoners n ▷ **prisoner**

prissier adj ▷ **prissy**

prissiest adj ▷ **prissy**

prissily adv ▷ **prissy**

prissy adj (-**ssier**, -**ssiest**) prim, correct, and easily shocked > **prissily** adv

pristine adj clean, new, and unused

privacies n ▷ **privacy**

privacy n ▷ **private**

private adj for the use of one person or group only ▶ n (pl -**s**) soldier of the lowest rank

> privately adv ▷ privacy n (pl -cies)
privately adv ▷ private
privates n ▷ private
privateer n (pl -s) (HIST) privately owned armed vessel authorized by the government to take part in a war
privateers n ▷ privateer
privation n (pl -s) loss or lack of the necessities of life
privations n ▷ privation
privatization n ▷ privatize
privatizations n ▷ privatize
privatize v (-zes, -zing, -zed) sell (a publicly owned company) to individuals or a private company > privatization n (pl -s)
privatized v ▷ privatize
privatizes v ▷ privatize
privatizing v ▷ privatize
privet n (pl -s) bushy evergreen shrub used for hedges
privets n ▷ privet
privier adj ▷ privy
privies n ▷ privy
priviest adj ▷ privy
privilege n (pl -s) advantage or favour that only some people have
privileged adj enjoying a special right or immunity
privileges n ▷ privilege
privy adj (-vier, -viest) sharing knowledge of something secret ▶ n (pl -ies) (Obs) toilet, esp. an outside one
prize¹ n (pl -s) reward given for success in a competition etc. ▶ adj winning or likely to win a prize
prize² v (-zes, -zing, -zed) value highly
prize³ v ▷ prise
prized v ▷ prize
prizefighter n (pl -s) boxer who fights for money
prizefighters n ▷ prizefighter
prizes n, v ▷ prize¹,²
prizing v ▷ prize²
pro¹ adv, prep in favour of
pro² n (pl -s) (Informal) professional
probabilities n ▷ probable
probability n ▷ probable
probable adj likely to happen or be true
> probability n (pl -ties)
probably adv in all likelihood
probate n (pl -s) process of proving the validity of a will
probates n ▷ probate
probation n (pl -s) system of dealing with law-breakers, esp. juvenile ones, by placing them under supervision
probationer n (pl -s) person on probation
probationers n ▷ probationer
probations n ▷ probation
probe v (-bes, -bing, -bed) search into or examine closely ▶ n (pl -s) surgical instrument used to examine a wound, cavity, etc.
probed v ▷ probe
probes v, n ▷ probe
probing v ▷ probe
probiotic adj, n (pl -s) (of) a bacterium that protects the body from harmful bacteria
probiotics n ▷ probiotic
probities n ▷ probity
probity n (pl -ties) honesty, integrity
problem n (pl -s) something difficult to deal with or solve > problematic, problematical adj
problematic adj ▷ problem
problematical adj ▷ problem
problems n ▷ problem
proboscis [pro-boss-iss] n (pl -scises) long trunk or snout
proboscises n ▷ proboscis
procedural adj ▷ procedure
procedure n (pl -s) way of doing something, esp. the correct or usual one > procedural adj
procedures n ▷ procedure
proceed v (-s, -ing, -ed) start or continue doing
proceeded v ▷ proceed
proceeds pl n money obtained from an event or activity ▶ v ▷ proceed
proceeding v ▷ proceed
proceedings pl n organized or related series of events
process n (pl -es) series of actions or changes ▶ v (-es, -ing, -ed) handle or prepare by a special method of manufacture > processor n (pl -s)
processed adj (of food) treated to prevent it decaying ▶ v ▷ process
processes n, v ▷ process
processing v ▷ process
procession n (pl -s) line of people or vehicles moving forward together in order
processions n ▷ procession
processor n ▷ process
processors n ▷ process
proclaim v (-s, -ing, -ed) declare publicly
> proclamation n (pl -s)
proclaimed v ▷ proclaim
proclaiming v ▷ proclaim
proclaims v ▷ proclaim
proclamation n ▷ proclaim
proclamations n ▷ proclaim

proclivities n ▷ proclivity
proclivity n (pl -ties) inclination, tendency
procrastinate v (-tes, -ting, -ted) put off taking action, delay ▷ **procrastination** n (pl -s)
procrastinated v ▷ procrastinate
procrastinates v ▷ procrastinate
procrastinating v ▷ procrastinate
procrastination n ▷ procrastinate
procrastinations n ▷ procrastinate
procreate v (-tes, -ting, -ted) (Formal) produce offspring > **procreation** n (pl -s)
procreated v ▷ procreate
procreates v ▷ procreate
procreating v ▷ procreate
procreation n ▷ procreate
procreations n ▷ procreate
procure v (-res, -ring, -red) get, provide > **procurement** n (pl -s)
procured v ▷ procure
procurement n ▷ procure
procurements n ▷ procure
procurer, procuress n (pl -s, -es) person who obtains people to act as prostitutes
procurers n ▷ procurer
procures v ▷ procure
procuress n ▷ procurer
procuresses n ▷ procurer
procuring v ▷ procure
prod v (-s, -dding, -dded) poke with something pointed ▶ n (pl -s) prodding
prodded v ▷ prod
prodding v ▷ prod
prodigal adj recklessly extravagant, wasteful > **prodigality** n (pl -s)
prodigalities n ▷ prodigal
prodigality n ▷ prodigal
prodigies n ▷ prodigy
prodigious adj very large, immense > **prodigiously** adv
prodigiously adv ▷ prodigious
prodigy n (pl -gies) person with some marvellous talent
prods v, n ▷ prod
produce v (-ces, -cing, -ced) bring into existence ▶ n (pl -s) food grown for sale
produced v ▷ produce
producer n (pl -s) person with control over the making of a film, record, etc.
producers n ▷ producer
produces v, n ▷ produce
producing v ▷ produce
product n (pl -s) something produced
production n (pl -s) producing
productions n ▷ production
productive adj producing large quantities

> **productivity** n (pl -ies)
productivities n ▷ productive
productivity n ▷ productive
products n ▷ product
profane adj showing disrespect for religion or holy things ▶ v (-nes, -ning, -ned) treat (something sacred) irreverently, desecrate
profanation n (pl -s) act of profaning
profanations n ▷ profanation
profaned v ▷ profane
profanes v ▷ profane
profaning v ▷ profane
profanities n ▷ profanity
profanity n (pl -ties) profane talk or behaviour, blasphemy
profess v (-es, -ing, -ed) state or claim (something as true), sometimes falsely > **professed** adj supposed
professed v, adj ▷ profess
professes v ▷ profess
professing v ▷ profess
profession n (pl -s) type of work, such as being a doctor, that needs special training
professional adj working in a profession ▶ n person who works in a profession > **professionally** adv > **professionalism** n (pl -s)
professionally adv ▷ professional
professionalism n ▷ professional
professionalisms n ▷ professional
professions n ▷ profession
professor n (pl -s) teacher of the highest rank in a university > **professorial** adj > **professorship** n (pl -s)
professorial adj ▷ professor
professors n ▷ professor
professorship n ▷ professor
professorships n ▷ professor
proffer v (-s, -ing, -ed) offer
proffered v ▷ proffer
proffering v ▷ proffer
proffers v ▷ proffer
proficiencies n ▷ proficient
proficiency n ▷ proficient
proficient adj skilled, expert > **proficiency** n (pl -cies)
profile n (pl -s) outline, esp. of the face, as seen from the side
profiles n ▷ profile
profit n (pl -s) money gained ▶ v (-s, -ing, -ed) gain or benefit
profitable adj making profit > **profitably** adv > **profitability** n (pl -ties)
profitabilities n ▷ profitable
profitability n ▷ profitable

profitably adv ▷ profitable
profited v ▷ profit
profiteer n (pl -s) person who makes excessive profits at the expense of the public > **profiteering** n (pl -s)
profiteering n ▷ profiteer
profiteerings n ▷ profiteer
profiteers n ▷ profiteer
profiting v ▷ profit
profits n, v ▷ profit
profligacies n ▷ profligate
profligacy n ▷ profligate
profligate adj recklessly extravagant ▶ n (pl -s) profligate person > **profligacy** n (pl -cies)
profligates n ▷ profligate
profound adj (-er, -est) showing or needing great knowledge > **profundity** n (pl -ties)
profounder adj ▷ profound
profoundest adj ▷ profound
profundities n ▷ profound
profundity n ▷ profound
profuse adj plentiful > **profusion** n (pl -s)
profusion n ▷ profuse
profusions n ▷ profuse
progenies n ▷ progeny
progeny [proj-in-ee] n (pl -nies) children
progenitor [pro-jen-it-er] n (pl -s) ancestor
progenitors n ▷ progenitor
progesterone n (pl -s) hormone which prepares the womb for pregnancy and prevents further ovulation
progesterones n ▷ progesterone
prognoses n ▷ prognosis
prognosis n (pl -noses) doctor's forecast about the progress of an illness
prognostication n (pl -s) forecast or prediction
prognostications n ▷ prognostication
program n (pl -s) sequence of coded instructions for a computer ▶ v (-s, -mming, --mmed) arrange (data) so that it can be processed by a computer > **programmer** n (pl -s) > **programmable** adj
programmable adj ▷ program
programmed v ▷ program
programmer n ▷ program
programmers n ▷ program
programming v ▷ program
programs n, v ▷ program
programme n (pl -s) planned series of events
programmes n ▷ programme
progress n (pl -es) improvement, development ▶ v (-es, -ing, -ed) become more advanced or skilful > **progression** n (pl -s)
progressed v ▷ progress

progresses v ▷ progress
progressing v ▷ progress
progression n ▷ progress
progressions n ▷ progress
progressive adj favouring political or social reform > **progressively** adv
progressively adv ▷ progressive
prohibit v (-s, -ing, -ed) forbid or prevent from happening
prohibited v ▷ prohibit
prohibiting v ▷ prohibit
prohibition n (pl -s) act of forbidding
prohibitions n ▷ prohibition
prohibitive adj (of prices) too high to be affordable > **prohibitively** adv
prohibitively adv ▷ prohibitive
prohibits v ▷ prohibit
project n (pl projects) planned scheme to do or examine something over a period ▶ v (-s, -ing, -ed) make a forecast based on known data > **projection** n (pl -s)
projected v ▷ project
projectile n (pl -s) object thrown as a weapon or fired from a gun
projectiles n ▷ projectile
projecting v ▷ project
projection n ▷ project
projectionist n (pl -s) person who operates a projector
projectionists n ▷ projectionist
projections n ▷ project
projector n (pl -s) apparatus for projecting photographic images, films, or slides on a screen
projectors n ▷ projector
projects n, v ▷ project
prolapse n (pl -s) slipping down of an internal organ of the body from its normal position
prolapses n ▷ prolapse
prole adj, n (pl -s) (CHIEFLY BRIT) (Slang) proletarian
proles n ▷ prole
proletariat [pro-lit-air-ee-at] n (pl -s) working class > **proletarian** adj, n (pl -s)
proletarian adj ▷ proletariat
proletarians n ▷ proletariat
proletariats n ▷ proletariat
proliferate v (-tes, -ting, -ted) grow or reproduce rapidly > **proliferation** n (pl -s)
proliferated v ▷ proliferate
proliferates v ▷ proliferate
proliferating v ▷ proliferate
proliferation n ▷ proliferate
proliferations n ▷ proliferate
prolific adj very productive > **prolifically** adv

prolifically *adv* ▷ prolific

prolix *adj* (of speech or a piece of writing) overlong and boring

prologue *n* (*pl* -s) introduction to a play or book

prologues *n* ▷ prologue

prolong *v* (-s, -ing, -ed) make (something) last longer > prolongation *n* (*pl* -s)

prolongation *n* ▷ prolong

prolongations *n* ▷ prolong

prolonged *v* ▷ prolong

prolonging *v* ▷ prolong

prolongs *v* ▷ prolong

prom *n* (*pl* -s) ▷ promenade

promenade *n* (*pl* -s) (CHIEFLY BRIT) paved walkway along the seafront at a holiday resort ▶ *v* (-des, -ding, -ded) ▶ *n* (Old-fashioned) (take) a leisurely walk

promenaded *v* ▷ promenade

promenades *n, v* ▷ promenade

promenading *v* ▷ promenade

prominence *n* ▷ prominent

prominences *n* ▷ prominent

prominent *adj* very noticeable > prominently *adv* > prominence *n* (*pl* -s)

prominently *adv* ▷ prominent

promiscuities *n* ▷ promiscuous

promiscuity *n* ▷ promiscuous

promiscuous *adj* having many casual sexual relationships > promiscuity *n* (*pl* -ties)

promise *v* (-ses, -sing, -sed) say that one will definitely do or not do something ▶ *n* (*pl* -s) undertaking to do or not to do something

promised *v* ▷ promise

promises *v* ▷ promise

promising *adj* likely to succeed or turn out well ▶ *v* ▷ promise

promo *n* (*pl* -os) (Informal) short film to promote a product

promontories *n* ▷ promontory

promontory *n* (*pl* -ries) point of high land jutting out into the sea

promos *n* ▷ promo

promote *v* (-tes, -ting, -ted) help to make (something) happen or increase > promotion *n* (*pl* -s) > promotional *adj*

promoted *v* ▷ promote

promoter *n* (*pl* -s) person who organizes or finances an event etc.

promoters *n* ▷ promoter

promotes *v* ▷ promote

promoting *v* ▷ promote

promotion *n* ▷ promote

promotional *adj* ▷ promote

promotions *n* ▷ promote

prompt *v* (-s, -ing, -ed) cause (an action) ▶ *adj* done without delay ▶ *adv* exactly > promptness *n* (*pl* -es)

prompted *v* ▷ prompt

prompter, prompt *n* (*pl* -s) person offstage who prompts actors

prompter *n* ▷ prompter

prompting *v* ▷ prompt

promptly *adv* immediately, without delay

promptness *n* ▷ prompt

promptnesses *n* ▷ prompt

prompts *v, n* ▷ prompt

proms *n* ▷ prom

promulgate *v* (-tes, -ting, -ted) put (a law etc.) into effect by announcing it officially > promulgation *n* (*pl* -s)

promulgated *v* ▷ promulgate

promulgates *v* ▷ promulgate

promulgating *v* ▷ promulgate

promulgation *n* ▷ promulgate

promulgations *n* ▷ promulgate

prone *adj* (-r, -st) (foll. by to) likely to do or be affected by (something)

proner *adj* ▷ prone

pronest *adj* ▷ prone

prong *n* (*pl* -s) one spike of a fork or similar instrument > pronged *adj*

pronged *adj* ▷ prong

prongs *n* ▷ prong

pronoun *n* (*pl* -s) word, such as *she* or *it*, used to replace a noun

pronouns *n* ▷ pronoun

pronounce *v* (-ces, -cing, -ced) form the sounds of (words or letters), esp. clearly or in a particular way > pronounceable *adj*

pronounceable *adj* ▷ pronounce

pronounced *adj* very noticeable ▶ *v* ▷ pronounce

pronounces *v* ▷ pronounce

pronouncement *n* (*pl* -s) formal announcement

pronouncements *n* ▷ pronouncement

pronouncing *v* ▷ pronounce

pronunciation *n* (*pl* -s) way in which a word or language is pronounced

pronunciations *n* ▷ pronunciation

pronto *adv* (Informal) at once

proof *n* (*pl* -s) evidence that shows that something is true or has happened ▶ *adj* able to withstand

proofread *v* (-s, -ing, -read) read and correct (printer's proofs) > proofreader *n* (*pl* -s)

proofreader *n* ▷ proofread

proofreaders *n* ▷ proofread

proofreading *v* ▷ proofread

proofreads v ▷ proofread

proofs n ▷ proof

prop[1] v (-s, -pping, -pped) support (something) so that it stays upright or in place ▶ n (pl -s) pole, beam, etc. used as a support

prop[2] n (pl -s) movable object used on the set of a film or play

prop[3] n (pl -s) (Informal) propeller

propaganda n (pl -s) (organized promotion of) information to assist or damage the cause of a government or movement > **propagandist** n (pl -s)

propagandas n ▷ propaganda

propagandist n ▷ propaganda

propagandists n ▷ propaganda

propagate v (-tes, -ting, -ted) spread (information and ideas) > **propagation** n (pl -s)

propagated v ▷ propagate

propagates v ▷ propagate

propagating v ▷ propagate

propagation n ▷ propagate

propagations n ▷ propagate

propane n (pl -s) flammable gas found in petroleum and used as a fuel

propanes n ▷ propane

propel v (-s, -lling, -lled) cause to move forward

propellant n (pl -s) something that provides or causes propulsion

propellants n ▷ propellant

propelled v ▷ propel

propeller n (pl -s) revolving shaft with blades for driving a ship or aircraft

propellers n ▷ propeller

propelling v ▷ propel

propels v ▷ propel

propped v ▷ prop[1]

propping v ▷ prop[1]

props v, n ▷ prop[1, 2, 3]

propulsion n (pl -s) method by which something is propelled

propulsions n ▷ propulsion

propensities n ▷ propensity

propensity n (pl -ies) natural tendency

proper adj (-er, -est) real or genuine > **properly** adv

properer adj ▷ proper

properest adj ▷ proper

properly adv ▷ proper

properties n ▷ property

property n (pl -ties) something owned

prophecies n ▷ prophecy

prophecy n (pl -cies) prediction

prophesied v ▷ prophesy

prophesies v ▷ prophesy

prophesy v (-sies, -sying, -sied) foretell

prophesying v ▷ prophesy

prophet n (pl -s) person supposedly chosen by God to spread His word > **prophetic** adj > **prophetically** adv

prophetic adj ▷ prophet

prophetically adv ▷ prophet

prophets n ▷ prophet

prophylactic n (pl -s) ▶ adj (drug) used to prevent disease

prophylactics n ▷ prophylactic

propitiate v (-tes, -ting, -ted) appease, win the favour of > **propitiation** n

propitiated v ▷ propitiate

propitiates v ▷ propitiate

propitiating v ▷ propitiate

propitiation n ▷ propitiate

propitiations n ▷ propitiate

propitious adj favourable or auspicious

proponent n (pl -s) person who argues in favour of something

proponents n ▷ proponent

proportion n (pl -s) relative size or extent ▶ pl dimensions or size ▶ v (-s, -ing, -ed) adjust in relative amount or size

proportional, proportionate adj being in proportion > **proportionally, proportionately** adv

proportionally adv ▷ proportional

proportionate adj ▷ proportional

proportionately adv ▷ proportional

proportioned v ▷ proportion

proportioning v ▷ proportion

proportions n, v ▷ proportion

propose v (-ses, -sing, -sed) put forward for consideration > **proposal** n (pl -s)

proposal n ▷ propose

proposals n ▷ propose

proposed v ▷ propose

proposes v ▷ propose

proposing v ▷ propose

proposition n (pl -s) offer ▶ v (-s, -ing, -ed) (Informal) ask (someone) to have sexual intercourse

propositioned v ▷ proposition

propositioning v ▷ proposition

propositions n, v ▷ proposition

propound v (-s, -ing, -ed) put forward for consideration

propounded v ▷ propound

propounding v ▷ propound

propounds v ▷ propound

proprietor n (pl -s) owner of a business establishment > **proprietress** n fem (pl -es)

proprietary adj made and distributed under

a trade name

proprieties n ▷ propriety
proprietors n ▷ proprietor
proprietress n ▷ proprietor
proprietresses n ▷ proprietor
propriety n (pl **-ties**) correct conduct
propulsion n ▷ propel
prorogue v (**-gues, -guing, -gued**) suspend (parliament) without dissolving it
    > **prorogation** n (pl **-s**)
prorogation n ▷ prorogue
prorogations n ▷ prorogue
prorogued v ▷ prorogue
prorogues v ▷ prorogue
proroguing v ▷ prorogue
pros n ▷ pro
prosaic [pro-**zay**-ik] adj lacking imagination, dull > **prosaically** adv
prosaically adv ▷ prosaic
proscenia n ▷ proscenium
proscenium n (pl **-nia, -niums**) arch in a theatre separating the stage from the auditorium
prosceniums n ▷ proscenium
proscribe v (**-bes, -bing, -bed**) prohibit, outlaw > **proscription** n (pl **-s**) > **proscriptive** adj
proscribed v ▷ proscribe
proscribes v ▷ proscribe
proscribing v ▷ proscribe
proscription n ▷ proscribe
proscriptions n ▷ proscribe
proscriptive adj ▷ proscribe
prose n (pl **-s**) ordinary speech or writing in contrast to poetry
proses n ▷ prose
prosecute v (**-tes, -ting, -ted**) bring a criminal charge against > **prosecution** n (pl **-s**)
    > **prosecutor** n (pl **-s**)
prosecuted v ▷ prosecute
prosecutes v ▷ prosecute
prosecuting v ▷ prosecute
prosecution n ▷ prosecute
prosecutions n ▷ prosecute
prosecutor n ▷ prosecute
prosecutors n ▷ prosecute
proselyte [pross-ill-ite] n (pl **-s**) recent convert
proselytes n ▷ proselyte
proselytize [pross-ill-it-ize] v (**-zes, -zing, -zed**) attempt to convert
proselytized v ▷ proselytize
proselytized v ▷ proselytize
proselytizing v ▷ proselytize
prospect n (pl **-s**) something anticipated (Old-fashioned) ▶ pl probability of future success ▶ v (**-s, -ing, -ed**) explore, esp. for gold

> **prospector** n (pl **-s**)
prospected v ▷ prospect
prospecting v ▷ prospect
prospective adj future
prospector n ▷ prospect
prospectors n ▷ prospect
prospects n, v ▷ prospect
prospectus n (pl **-es**) booklet giving details of a university, company, etc.
prospectuses n ▷ prospectus
prosper v (**-s, -ing, -ed**) be successful
    > **prosperous** adj
prospered v ▷ prosper
prospering v ▷ prosper
prosperities n ▷ prosperity
prosperity n success and wealth
prosperous adj ▷ prosper
prospers v ▷ prosper
prostate n (pl **-s**) gland in male mammals that surrounds the neck of the bladder
prostates n ▷ prostate
prostheses n ▷ prosthesis
prosthesis [pross-**theess**-iss] n (pl **-ses**) [-seez] artificial body part, such as a limb or breast
    > **prosthetic** adj
prosthetic adj ▷ prosthesis
prostitute n (pl **-s**) person who offers sexual intercourse in return for payment ▶ v (**-tes, -ting, -ted**) make a prostitute of
    > **prostitution** n (pl **-s**)
prostituted v ▷ prostitute
prostitutes n, v ▷ prostitute
prostituting v ▷ prostitute
prostitution n ▷ prostitute
prostitutions n ▷ prostitute
prostrate adj lying face downwards ▶ v (**-tes, -ting, -ted**) lie face downwards > **prostration** n (pl **-s**)
prostrated v ▷ prostrate
prostrates v ▷ prostrate
prostrating v ▷ prostrate
prostration n ▷ prostrate
prostrations n ▷ prostrate
protagonist n (pl **-s**) supporter of a cause
protagonists n ▷ protagonist
protea [pro-**tee**-a] n (pl **-s**) African shrub with showy flowers
protean [pro-**tee**-an] adj constantly changing
proteas n ▷ protea
protect v (**-s, -ing, -ed**) defend from trouble, harm, or loss > **protection** n (pl **-s**)
protected v ▷ protect
protecting v ▷ protect
protection n ▷ protect
protectionism n policy of protecting

industries by taxing competing imports
> **protectionist** n (pl -s) adj

protectionisms n ▷ protectionism

protectionist n ▷ protectionism

protectionists n ▷ protectionism

protections n ▷ protect

protective adj giving protection

protector n (pl -s) person or thing that
protects

protectorate n (pl -s) territory largely
controlled by a stronger state

protectorates n ▷ protectorate

protectors n ▷ protector

protects v ▷ protect

protégé, fem **protégée** [pro-ti-zhay] n (pl
-s) person who is protected and helped by
another

protégés n ▷ protégé

protein n (pl -s) any of a group of complex
organic compounds that are essential for life

proteins n ▷ protein

protest n (pl -s) declaration or demonstration
of objection ▶ v (-s, -ing, -ed) object, disagree

protestant n (pl -s) one who protests

protestants n ▷ protestant

protestation n (pl -s) strong declaration

protestations n ▷ protestation

protested v ▷ protest

protesting v ▷ protest

protests n, v ▷ protest

protocol n (pl -s) rules of behaviour for formal
occasions

protocols n ▷ protocol

proton n (pl -s) positively charged particle in
the nucleus of an atom

protons n ▷ proton

protoplasm n (pl -s) substance forming the
living contents of a cell

protoplasms n ▷ protoplasm

prototype n (pl -s) original or model to be
copied or developed

prototypes n ▷ prototype

protozoa n ▷ protozoan

protozoan [pro-toe-zoe-an] n (pl -zoa)
microscopic one-celled creature

protracted adj lengthened or extended

protractor n (pl -s) instrument for measuring
angles

protractors n ▷ protractor

protrude v (-des, -ding, -ded) stick out, project
> **protrusion** n (pl -s)

protruded v ▷ protrude

protrudes v ▷ protrude

protruding v ▷ protrude

protrusion n ▷ protrude

protrusions n ▷ protrude

protuberance n ▷ protuberant

protuberances n ▷ protuberant

protuberant adj swelling out, bulging
> **protuberance** n (pl -s)

proud adj (-er, -est) feeling pleasure and
satisfaction > **proudly** adv

prouder adj ▷ proud

proudest adj ▷ proud

proudly adv ▷ proud

prove v (-ves, -ving, -ved or -ven) establish the
validity of

proved v ▷ prove

proven adj known from experience to work
▶ v ▷ prove

provenance [prov-in-anss] n (pl -s) place of
origin

provenances n ▷ provenance

provender n (pl -s) (Old-fashioned) fodder

provenders n ▷ provender

proverb n (pl -s) short saying that expresses a
truth or gives a warning > **proverbial** adj

proverbial adj ▷ proverb

proverbs n ▷ proverb

proves v ▷ prove

provide v (-des, -ding, -ded) make available
> **provider** n (pl -s)

provided v ▷ provide

providence n (pl -s) God or nature seen as a
protective force that arranges people's lives

providences n ▷ providence

provident adj thrifty

providential adj lucky

provider n ▷ provide

providers n ▷ provide

provides v ▷ provide

providing v ▷ provide

province n (pl -s) area governed as a unit of
a country or empire ▶ pl parts of a country
outside the capital

provincial adj of a province or the provinces
▶ n (pl -s) unsophisticated person

provincialism n (pl -s) narrow-mindedness
and lack of sophistication

provincialisms n ▷ provincialism

provincials n ▷ provincial

provinces n ▷ province

proving v ▷ prove

provision n (pl -s) act of supplying something
▶ pl food ▶ v (-s, -ing, -ed) supply with food

provisional adj temporary or conditional
> **provisionally** adv

provisionally adv ▷ provisional

provisioned v ▷ provision

provisioning v ▷ provision

provisions *n*, *v* ▷ **provision**
proviso [pro-**vize**-oh] *n* (*pl* **-sos, -soes**)
   condition, stipulation
provisoes *n* ▷ **proviso**
provisos *n* ▷ **proviso**
provocation *n* ▷ **provoke**
provocations *n* ▷ **provoke**
provocative *adj* ▷ **provoke**
provoke *v* (**-kes, -king, -ked**) deliberately anger
   > **provocation** *n* (*pl* **-s**) > **provocative** *adj*
provoked *v* ▷ **provoke**
provokes *v* ▷ **provoke**
provoking *v* ▷ **provoke**
provost *n* (*pl* **-s**) head of certain university
   colleges in Britain
provosts *n* ▷ **provost**
prow *n* (*pl* **-s**) bow of a vessel
prows *n* ▷ **prow**
prowess *n* (*pl* **-es**) superior skill or ability
prowesses *n* ▷ **prowess**
prowl *v* (**-s, -ing, -ed**) move stealthily around a
   place as if in search of prey or plunder ▶ *n* (*pl*
   -s) prowling
prowled *v* ▷ **prowl**
prowler *n* (*pl* **-s**) person who moves stealthily
   around a place as if in search of prey or
   plunder
prowlers *n* ▷ **prowler**
prowling *v* ▷ **prowl**
prowls *v*, *n* ▷ **prowl**
proxies *n* ▷ **proxy**
proximate *n* ▷ **proximity**
proximities *n* ▷ **proximity**
proximity *n* (*pl* **-ties**) nearness in space or time
   > **proximate** *adj*
proxy *n* (*pl* **-xies**) person authorized to act on
   behalf of someone else
prude *n* (*pl* **-s**) person who is excessively
   modest, prim, or proper > **prudish** *adj*
   > **prudery** *n* (*pl* **-ries**)
prudence *n* ▷ **prudent**
prudences *n* ▷ **prudent**
prudent *adj* cautious, discreet, and sensible
   > **prudence** *n* (*pl* **-s**)
prudential *adj* (*Old-fashioned*) prudent
prudes *n* ▷ **prude**
pruderies *n* ▷ **prude**
prudery *n* ▷ **prude**
prudish *adj* ▷ **prude**
prune[1] *n* (*pl* **-s**) dried plum
prune[2] *v* (**-nes, -ning, -ned**) cut off dead parts
   or excessive branches from (a tree or plant)
pruned *v* ▷ **prune**
prunes *n*, *v* ▷ **prune**[1, 2]
pruning *v* ▷ **prune**

prurience *n* ▷ **prurient**
pruriences *n* ▷ **prurient**
prurient *adj* excessively interested in sexual
   matters > **prurience** *n* (*pl* **-s**)
pry *v* (**prys, prying, pried**) make an
   impertinent or uninvited inquiry into a
   private matter
prying *v* ▷ **pry**
psalm *n* (*pl* **-s**) sacred song
psalmist *n* (*pl* **-s**) writer of psalms
psalmists *n* ▷ **psalmist**
psalms *n* ▷ **psalm**
psalter *n* (*pl* **-s**) book containing (a version of)
   psalms from the Bible
psalteries *n* ▷ **psalter**
psaltery *n* (*pl* **-ries**) ancient instrument played
   by plucking strings
psalters *n* ▷ **psalter**
psephologies *n* ▷ **psephology**
psephology [sef-**fol**-a-jee] *n* (*pl* **-gies**) statistical
   study of elections
pseud *n* (*pl* **-s**) (*Informal*) pretentious person
pseuds *n* ▷ **pseud**
pseudonym *n* (*pl* **-s**) fictitious name adopted
   esp. by an author > **pseudonymous** *adj*
pseudonymous *adj* ▷ **pseudonym**
pseudonyms *n* ▷ **pseudonym**

> **psi** *n* (**psis**). Psi is the 23rd letter of
> the Greek alphabet. This word can
> be useful if you have a difficult rack,
> especially if you can form another
> word at the same time. Psi scores 5
> points.

psittacosis *n* (*pl* **-ses**) disease of parrots that
   can be transmitted to humans
psittacoses *n* ▷ **psittacosis**

> **pst** *interj*. Pst is a sound people make
> when they want to draw someone's
> attention to something without
> making too much noise. This is a useful
> word to remember because it doesn't
> use any vowels, and so can be useful if
> you have no vowels on your rack. Pst
> scores 5 points.

psyche [**sye**-kee] *n* (*pl* **-s**) human mind or soul
psychedelic *adj* denoting a drug that causes
   hallucinations
psyche *n* ▷ **psyche**
psychiatric *adj* ▷ **psychiatry**
psychiatries *n* ▷ **psychiatry**
psychiatrist *n* ▷ **psychiatry**
psychiatrists *n* ▷ **psychiatry**
psychiatry *n* (*pl* **-ries**) branch of medicine
   concerned with mental disorders
   > **psychiatric** *adj* > **psychiatrist** *n*

psychic adj (also **psychical**) having mental powers which cannot be explained by natural laws ► n (pl -s) person with psychic powers
  psychics n ▷ **psychic**
psycho n (pl -s) (Informal) psychopath
  psychoanalyse v ▷ **psychoanalysis**
  psychoanalysed v ▷ **psychoanalysis**
psychoanalyses n, v ▷ **psychoanalysis**
  psychoanalysing v ▷ **psychoanalysis**
psychoanalysis n (pl -ses) method of treating mental and emotional disorders by discussion and analysis of one's thoughts and feelings > **psychoanalyse** v (-ses, -sing, -sed) > **psychoanalyst** n (pl -s)
  psychoanalyst n ▷ **psychoanalysis**
  psychoanalysts n ▷ **psychoanalysis**
psychological adj of or affecting the mind
> **psychologically** adv
  psychologically adv ▷ **psychological**
  psychologies n ▷ **psychology**
  psychologist n ▷ **psychology**
  psychologists n ▷ **psychology**
psychology n (pl -gies) study of human and animal behaviour > **psychologist** n (pl -s)
psychopath n (pl -s) person afflicted with a personality disorder causing him or her to commit antisocial or violent acts
> **psychopathic** adj
  psychopathic adj ▷ **psychopath**
  psychopaths n ▷ **psychopath**
  psychos n ▷ **psycho**
  psychoses n ▷ **psychosis**
psychosis n (pl -ses) severe mental disorder in which the sufferer's contact with reality becomes distorted > **psychotic** adj
psychosomatic adj (of a physical disorder) thought to have psychological causes
  psychotherapeutic adj ▷ **psychotherapy**
  psychotherapies n ▷ **psychotherapy**
  psychotherapist n ▷ **psychotherapy**
  psychotherapists n ▷ **psychotherapy**
psychotherapy n (pl -pies) treatment of nervous disorders by psychological methods
> **psychotherapeutic** adj > **psychotherapist** n
  psychotic adj ▷ **psychosis**
ptarmigan [tar-mig-an] n (pl -s) bird of the grouse family which turns white in winter
  ptarmigans n ▷ **ptarmigan**
pterodactyl [terr-roe-dak-til] n (pl -s) extinct flying reptile with batlike wings
  pterodactyls n ▷ **pterodactyl**
ptomaine [toe-main] n (pl -s) any of a group of poisonous alkaloids found in decaying matter
  ptomaines n ▷ **ptomaine**

pub n (pl -s) building with a bar licensed to sell alcoholic drinks
  pubertal adj ▷ **puberty**
  puberties n ▷ **puberty**
puberty n (pl -ties) beginning of sexual maturity > **pubertal** adj
pubic adj of the lower abdomen
public adj of or concerning the people as a whole ► n (pl -s) the community, people in general > **publicly** adv
publican n (pl -s) (BRIT, AUST & NZ) person who owns or runs a pub
  publicans n ▷ **publican**
  publication n ▷ **publish**
  publications n ▷ **publish**
publicist n (pl -s) person, esp. a press agent or journalist, who publicizes something
  publicists n ▷ **publicist**
  publicities n ▷ **publicity**
publicity n (pl -ties) process or information used to arouse public attention
publicize v (-zes, -zing, -zed) bring to public attention
  publicized v ▷ **publicize**
  publicizes v ▷ **publicize**
  publicizing v ▷ **publicize**
  publicly adv ▷ **public**
  publics n ▷ **public**
publish v (-es, -ing, -ed) produce and issue (printed matter) for sale > **publication** n (pl -s)
> **publisher** n (pl -s)
  published v ▷ **publish**
  publisher n ▷ **publish**
  publishers n ▷ **publish**
  publishes v ▷ **publish**
  publishing v ▷ **publish**
  pubs n ▷ **pub**
puce adj (pucer, pucest) purplish-brown
  pucer adj ▷ **puce**
  pucest adj ▷ **puce**
puck[1] n (pl -s) small rubber disc used in ice hockey
puck[2] n (pl -s) mischievous or evil spirit
> **puckish** adj
pucker v (-s, -ing, -ed) gather into wrinkles ► n (pl -s) wrinkle or crease
  puckered v ▷ **pucker**
  puckering v ▷ **pucker**
  puckers v, n ▷ **pucker**
  puckish adj ▷ **puck**[2]
  pucks n ▷ **puck**[1, 2]
pudding n (pl -s) dessert, esp. a cooked one served hot
  puddings n ▷ **pudding**
puddle n (pl -s) small pool of water, esp. of rain

puddles n ▷ **puddle**

puerile adj silly and childish

puerperal [pew-er-per-al] adj concerning the period following childbirth

puff n (pl -s) (sound of) a short blast of breath, wind, etc. ▶ v (-s, -ing, -ed) blow or breathe in short quick draughts ▷ **puffy** adj (-ffier, -ffiest)

puffball n (pl -s) ball-shaped fungus

puffballs n ▷ **puffball**

puffed v ▷ **puff**

puffier adj ▷ **puff**

puffiest adj ▷ **puff**

puffin n (pl -s) black-and-white sea bird with a brightly-coloured beak

puffins n ▷ **puffin**

puffing v ▷ **puff**

puffs n, v ▷ **puff**

puffy adj ▷ **puff**

pug n (pl -s) small snub-nosed dog

pugs n ▷ **pug**

pugilist [pew-jil-ist] n (pl -s) boxer ▷ **pugilism** n (pl -s) ▷ **pugilistic** adj

pugilism n ▷ **pugilist**

pugilisms n ▷ **pugilist**

pugilistic adj ▷ **pugilist**

pugilists n ▷ **pugilist**

pugnacious adj ready and eager to fight ▷ **pugnacity** n (pl -ties)

pugnacities n ▷ **pugnacious**

pugnacity n ▷ **pugnacious**

puissance [pwee-sonce] n (pl -s) showjumping competition that tests a horse's ability to jump large obstacles

puissances n ▷ **puissance**

puke (Slang) v (-kes, -king, -ked) vomit ▶ n (pl -s) act of vomiting

puked v ▷ **puke**

pukes v, n ▷ **puke**

puking v ▷ **puke**

pulchritude n (pl -s) (Lit) beauty

pulchritudes n ▷ **pulchritude**

pull v (-s, -ing, -ed) exert force on (an object) to move it towards the source of the force ▶ n (pl -s) act of pulling

pulled v ▷ **pull**

pullet n (pl -s) young hen

pullets n ▷ **pullet**

pulley n (pl -s) wheel with a grooved rim in which a belt, chain, or rope runs in order to lift weights by a downward pull

pulleys n ▷ **pulley**

pulling v ▷ **pull**

pullover n (pl -s) sweater that is pulled on over the head

pullovers n ▷ **pullover**

pulls v, n ▷ **pull**

pulmonary adj of the lungs

pulp n (pl -s) soft wet substance made from crushed or beaten matter ▶ v (-s, -ing, -ed) reduce to pulp

pulped v ▷ **pulp**

pulping v ▷ **pulp**

pulpit n (pl -s) raised platform for a preacher

pulpits n ▷ **pulpit**

pulps n, v ▷ **pulp**

pulsar n (pl -s) small dense star which emits regular bursts of radio waves

pulsars n ▷ **pulsar**

pulsate v ▷ **pulse¹**

pulsated v ▷ **pulse¹**

pulsates v ▷ **pulse¹**

pulsating v ▷ **pulse¹**

pulsation n ▷ **pulse¹**

pulsations n ▷ **pulse¹**

pulse¹ n (pl -s) regular beating of blood through the arteries at each heartbeat ▷ **pulsate** v (-s, -ing, -ed) throb, quiver ▷ **pulsation** n (pl -s)

pulse² n (pl -s) edible seed of a pod-bearing plant such as a bean or pea

pulses n ▷ **pulse¹, ²**

pulverize v (-zes, -zing, -zed) reduce to fine pieces

pulverized v ▷ **pulverize**

pulverizes v ▷ **pulverize**

pulverizing v ▷ **pulverize**

puma n (pl -s) large American wild cat with a greyish-brown coat

pumas n ▷ **puma**

pumice [pumm-iss] n (pl -s) light porous stone used for scouring

pumices n ▷ **pumice**

pummel v (-s, -lling, -lled) strike repeatedly with or as if with the fists

pummelled v ▷ **pummel**

pummelling v ▷ **pummel**

pummels v ▷ **pummel**

pump¹ n (pl -s) machine used to force a liquid or gas to move in a particular direction ▶ v (-s, -ing, -ed) raise or drive with a pump

pump² n (pl -s) light flat-soled shoe

pumped v ▷ **pump**

pumping v ▷ **pump**

pumpkin n (pl -s) large round fruit with an orange rind, soft flesh, and many seeds

pumpkins n ▷ **pumpkin**

pumps n, v ▷ **pump¹, ²**

pun n (pl -s) use of words to exploit double meanings for humorous effect ▶ v (-s, -nning, -nned) make puns

punch[1] v (-es, -ing, -ed) strike at with a clenched fist ▶ n (pl -es) blow with a clenched fist (*Informal*)

punch[2] n (pl -es) tool or machine for shaping, piercing, or engraving ▶ v (-es, -ing, -ed) pierce, cut, stamp, shape, or drive with a punch

punch[3] n (pl -es) drink made from a mixture of wine, spirits, fruit, sugar, and spices

punched v ▷ punch[1, 2]

punches v, n ▷ punch

punchier adj ▷ punchy

punchiest adj ▷ punchy

punching v ▷ punch[1, 2]

punchy adj (-chier, -chiest) forceful

punctilious adj paying great attention to correctness in etiquette

punctual adj arriving or taking place at the correct time > **punctuality** n (pl -ties) > **punctually** adv

punctualities n ▷ punctual

punctuality n ▷ punctual

punctually adv ▷ punctual

punctuate v (-tes, -ting, -ted) put punctuation marks in

punctuated v ▷ punctuate

punctuates v ▷ punctuate

punctuating v ▷ punctuate

punctuation n (pl -s) (use of) marks such as commas, colons, etc. in writing, to assist in making the sense clear

punctuations n ▷ punctuation

puncture n (pl -s) small hole made by a sharp object, esp. in a tyre ▶ v (-res, -ring, -red) pierce a hole in

punctured v ▷ puncture

punctures n, v ▷ puncture

puncturing v ▷ puncture

pundit n (pl -s) expert who speaks publicly on a subject

pundits n ▷ pundit

pungencies n ▷ pungent

pungency n ▷ pungent

pungent adj having a strong sharp bitter flavour > **pungency** n (pl -cies)

punier adj ▷ puny

puniest adj ▷ puny

punish v (-es, -ing, -ed) cause (someone) to suffer or undergo a penalty for some wrongdoing > **punishment** n (pl -s)

punished v ▷ punish

punishes v ▷ punish

punishing adj harsh or difficult ▶ v ▷ punish

punishment n ▷ punish

punishments n ▷ punish

punitive [pew-nit-tiv] adj relating to punishment

punk n (pl -s) anti-Establishment youth movement and style of rock music of the late 1970s

punks n ▷ punk

punned v ▷ pun

punnet n (pl -s) small basket for fruit

punnets n ▷ punnet

punning v ▷ pun

puns n, v ▷ pun

punt[1] n (pl -s) open flat-bottomed boat propelled by a pole ▶ v (-s, -ing, -ed) travel in a punt

punt[2] (SPORT) n (pl -s) kick of a ball before it touches the ground when dropped from the hands ▶ v (-s, -ing, -ed) kick (a ball) in this way

punt[3] n (pl -s) former monetary unit of the Irish Republic

punted v ▷ punt

punter n (pl -s) person who bets

punters n ▷ punter

punting v ▷ punt

punts n, v ▷ punt[1, 2, 3]

puny adj (-nier, -niest) small and feeble

pup n (pl -s) young of certain animals, such as dogs and seals

pupa n (pl -pae, -pas) insect at the stage of development between a larva and an adult

pupae n ▷ pupa

pupas n ▷ pupa

pupil[1] n (pl -s) person who is taught by a teacher

pupil[2] n (pl -s) round dark opening in the centre of the eye

pupils n ▷ pupil[1, 2]

puppet n (pl -s) small doll or figure moved by strings or by the operator's hand > **puppeteer** n (pl -s)

puppeteer n ▷ puppet

puppeteers n ▷ puppet

puppets n ▷ puppet

puppies n ▷ puppy

puppy n (pl -ppies) young dog

pups n ▷ pup

purchase v (-ses, -sing, -sed) obtain by payment ▶ n (pl -s) thing that is bought > **purchaser** n (pl -s)

purchased v ▷ purchase

purchaser n ▷ purchase

purchasers n ▷ purchase

purchases v, n ▷ purchase

purchasing v ▷ purchase

purdah n (pl -s) Muslim and Hindu custom of keeping women in seclusion, with clothing that conceals them completely when they go out

purdahs n ▷ purdah

pure adj (-r, -st) unmixed, untainted > **purely** adv > **purity** n (pl -**ies**)

purely adv ▷ pure

purée [pure-ray] n (pl -s) pulp of cooked food ▸ v (-s, -réeing, -réed) make into a purée

puréed v ▷ purée

puréeing v ▷ purée

purées n, v ▷ purée

purer adj ▷ pure

purest adj ▷ pure

purgatorial adj ▷ purgatory

purgatories n ▷ purgatory

purgatory n (pl -**ries**) place or state of temporary suffering > **purgatorial** adj

purge v (-**ges**, -**ging**, -**ged**) rid (a thing or place) of (unwanted things or people) ▸ n (pl -s) purging

purgative n, adj (medicine) designed to cause defecation

purgatives n ▷ purgative

purged v ▷ purge

purges v, n ▷ purge

purging v ▷ purge

purification n ▷ purify

purifications n ▷ purify

purified v ▷ purify

purifies v ▷ purify

purify v (-**fies**, -**fying**, -**fied**) make or become pure > **purification** n (pl -s)

purifying v ▷ purify

purist n (pl -s) person concerned with strict obedience to the traditions of a subject

purists n ▷ purist

puritan n (pl -s) person with strict moral and religious principles > **puritanical** adj > **puritanism** n (pl -s)

puritanical adj ▷ puritan

puritanism n ▷ puritan

puritanisms n ▷ puritan

puritans n ▷ puritan

purities n ▷ pure

purity n ▷ pure

purl n (pl -s) stitch made by knitting a plain stitch backwards ▸ v (-s, -ing, -ed) knit in purl

purled v ▷ purl

purlieus [per-lyooz] pl n (Lit) outskirts

purling v ▷ purl

purloin v (-s, -ing, -ed) steal

purloined v ▷ purloin

purloining v ▷ purloin

purloins v ▷ purloin

purls n, v ▷ purl

purple adj, n (pl -s) (of) a colour between red and blue

purples n ▷ purple

purport v (-s, -ing, -ed) claim (to be or do something) ▸ n (pl -s) apparent meaning, significance

purported v ▷ purport

purporting v ▷ purport

purports v, n ▷ purport

purpose n (pl -s) reason for which something is done or exists

purposely adv intentionally

purposes n ▷ purpose

purr v (-s, -ing, -ed) (of cats) make low vibrant sound, usu. when pleased ▸ n (pl -s) this sound

purred v ▷ purr

purring v ▷ purr

purrs v, n ▷ purr

purse n (pl -s) small bag for money (US & NZ) ▸ v (-ses, -sing, -sed) draw (one's lips) together into a small round shape

pursed v ▷ purse

purser n (pl -s) ship's officer who keeps the accounts

pursers n ▷ purser

purses n, v ▷ purse

pursing v ▷ purse

pursue v (-sues, -suing, -sued) chase > **pursuer** n (pl -s)

pursued v ▷ pursue

pursuer n ▷ pursue

pursuers n ▷ pursue

pursues v ▷ pursue

pursuing v ▷ pursue

pursuit n (pl -s) pursuing

pursuits n ▷ pursuit

purview n (pl -s) scope or range of activity or outlook

purviews n ▷ purview

pus n (pl -es) yellowish matter produced by infected tissue

puses n ▷ pus

push v (-es, -ing, -ed) move or try to move by steady force (Informal) ▸ n (pl -es) act of pushing

purulent [pure-yoo-lent] adj of or containing pus

purvey v (-s, -ing, -ed) supply (provisions) > **purveyor** n (pl -s)

purveyed v ▷ purvey

purveying v ▷ purvey

purveyor n ▷ purvey

purveyors n ▷ purvey

purveys v ▷ purvey

pushed v ▷ push
pusher n (pl -s) person who sells illegal drugs
pushers n ▷ pusher
pushes v, n ▷ push
pushier adj ▷ pushy
pushiest adj ▷ pushy
pushing v ▷ push
pushy adj (-shier, -shiest) too assertive or ambitious
pushchair n (pl -s) (BRIT) folding chair on wheels for a baby
pushchairs n ▷ pushchair
pusillanimous adj timid and cowardly > **pusillanimity** n (pl -ies)
pusillanimities n ▷ pusillanimous
pusillanimity n ▷ pusillanimous
puss, pussy n (pl -es, -ies) (Informal) cat
pusses n ▷ puss
pussies n ▷ puss
pussyfoot v (-s, -ing, -ed) (Informal) behave too cautiously
pussyfooted v ▷ pussyfoot
pussyfooting v ▷ pussyfoot
pussyfoots v ▷ pussyfoot
pustule n (pl -s) pimple containing pus
pustules n ▷ pustule
put v (puts, putting, put) cause to be (in a position, state, or place) ▶ n (pl -s) throw in putting the shot
putative adj reputed, supposed
putrefied v ▷ putrify
putrefies v ▷ putrify
putrefy v (-fies, -fying, -fied) rot and produce an offensive smell > **putrefaction** n (pl -s)
putrefaction n ▷ putrefy
putrefactions n ▷ putrefy
putrefying v ▷ putrefy
putrescent adj rotting
putrid adj rotten and foul-smelling
puts v, n ▷ put
putsch n (pl -es) sudden violent attempt to remove a government from power
putsches n ▷ putsch
putt (GOLF) n (pl -s) stroke on the putting green to roll the ball into or near the hole ▶ v (-s, -ing, -ed) strike (the ball) in this way
putted n, v ▷ putt
putter n (pl -s) golf club for putting
putters n ▷ putter

putties n ▷ putty
putting v ▷ put putt
putts v, n ▷ putt
putty n (pl -ies) adhesive used to fix glass into frames and fill cracks in woodwork
puzzle v (-les, -ling, -led) perplex and confuse or be perplexed or confused ▶ n (pl -s) problem that cannot be easily solved > **puzzlement** n (pl -s) > **puzzling** adj
puzzled v ▷ puzzle
puzzlement n ▷ puzzle
puzzlements n ▷ puzzle
puzzles v, n ▷ puzzle
puzzling v, adj ▷ puzzle
pygmies n ▷ pygmy
pygmy n (pl -ies) something that is a very small example of its type ▶ adj (p-) very small
pyjamas pl n loose-fitting trousers and top worn in bed
pylon n (pl -s) steel tower-like structure supporting electrical cables
pylons n ▷ pylon
pyramid n (pl -s) solid figure with a flat base and triangular sides sloping upwards to a point > **pyramidal** adj
pyramidal adj ▷ pyramid
pyramids n ▷ pyramid
pyre n (pl -s) pile of wood for burning a corpse on
pyres n ▷ pyre
pyromania n (pl -s) uncontrollable urge to set things on fire > **pyromaniac** n (pl -s)
pyromanias n ▷ pyromania
pyromaniac n ▷ pyromania
pyromaniacs n ▷ pyromania
pyrotechnics n art of making fireworks > **pyrotechnic** adj
pyrotechnic adj ▷ pyrotechnics
python n (pl -s) large nonpoisonous snake that crushes its prey
pythons n ▷ python

> **pyx** n (**pyxes**). A **pyx** is a container used for testing the weight of coins. This word can also be spelt **pix**. It's a great word to know as it earns a good score and doesn't use any vowels very helpful if you have a difficult rack. Pyx scores 15 points.

Qq

With a value of 10 points, Q is one of the best tiles to have on your rack. It can, however, be a difficult letter to use, especially if you don't have a U to play it with. It's therefore a good idea to remember the short words beginning with Q that don't need a U. This is easy, as there's only one two-letter word starting with Q: **qi** (11 points). There are three three-letter words, only one of which needs a U: **qua** (12). The other two are **qat** and **qis** (12 each). If you do have a U, remember **quiz** (22), which is a very useful word. If you have a blank tile for the second Z, you may be able to form its plural or verb inflections: **quizzes** (24), **quizzed** (25) and **quizzing** (26). This is especially worth remembering in case someone else plays quiz. Don't forget **quartz** (24) either.

qat n (**qats**). Qat is a shrub that grows in Africa and Arabia. This is a great word as it combines Q with two of the most common letters in the game, and thus is very handy if there isn't a U on your rack or the board. Qat scores 12 points.

qi n (**qis**). In Chinese medicine, qi is vital energy believed to circulate in the body. This is an exceptionally useful word, as it's the only two-letter word containing Q, and doesn't contain a U. The plural is one of only three three-letter words that begin with Q. As I is one of the more common letters on the board, it's highly likely that you will be able to play qi if you have a Q. Qi scores 11 points.

qua prep. Qua means in the capacity of. This is the only three-letter word beginning with Q that needs a U, and is useful when you have a U, or there is a U on the board, but don't have any promising tiles to go with it. Qua scores 12 points.

quack[1] v (**-s, -ing, -ed**) (of a duck) utter a harsh guttural sound ▶ n (pl **-s**) sound made by a duck

quack[2] n (pl **-s**) unqualified person who claims medical knowledge
quacked v ▷ **quack**[1]
quacking v ▷ **quack**[1]
quacks v ▷ **quack**[1] ▶ n ▷ **quack**[1, 2]

quad n (pl **-s**) ▷ **quadrangle** ▶ adj
  ▷ **quadraphonic**
quadrangle n (pl **-s**) (also **quad**) rectangular courtyard with buildings on all four sides
  > **quadrangular** adj
quadrangles n ▷ **quadrangle**
quadrangular adj ▷ **quadrangle**
quadrant n (pl **-s**) quarter of a circle
quadrants n ▷ **quadrant**
quadraphonic adj (also **quad**) using four independent channels to reproduce or record sound
quadratic (MATHS) n (pl **-s**) equation in which the variable is raised to the power of two, but nowhere raised to a higher power ▶ adj of the second power
quadratics n ▷ **quadratic**
quadrennial adj occurring every four years
quadrilateral adj having four sides ▶ n (pl **-s**) polygon with four sides
quadrilaterals n ▷ **quadrilateral**
quadrille n (pl **-s**) square dance for four couples
quadrilles n ▷ **quadrille**
quadriplegia n (pl **-s**) paralysis of all four limbs
quadriplegias n ▷ **quadriplegia**
quadruped [kwod-roo-ped] n (pl **-s**) any animal with four legs
quadrupeds n ▷ **quadruped**
quadruple v (**-les, -ling, -led**) multiply by four ▶ adj four times as much or as many
quadrupled v ▷ **quadruple**
quadruples v ▷ **quadruple**
quadruplet n (pl **-s**) one of four offspring born

at one birth
quadruplets n ▷ quadruplet
quadrupling v ▷ quadruple
quads n ▷ quad
quaff [kwoff] v (-s, -ing, -ed) drink heartily or in one draught
quaffed v ▷ quaff
quaffing v ▷ quaff
quaffs v ▷ quaff
quagmire [kwog-mire] n (pl -s) soft wet area of land
quagmires n ▷ quagmire
quail[1] n (pl -s) small game bird of the partridge family
quail[2] v (-s, -ing, -ed) shrink back with fear
quailed v ▷ quail
quailing v ▷ quail
quails n ▷ quail[1] ▶ v ▷ quail[2]
quaint adj (-er, -est) attractively unusual, esp. in an old-fashioned style ▷ **quaintly** adv
quainter adj ▷ quaint
quaintest adj ▷ quaint
quaintly adv ▷ quaint
quake v (-kes, -king, -ked) shake or tremble with or as if with fear ▶ n (pl -s) (Informal) earthquake
quaked v, n ▷ quake
quakes v ▷ quake
quaking v ▷ quake
qualification n (pl -s) official record of achievement in a course or examination
qualifications n ▷ qualification
qualified v, adj ▷ qualify
qualifies v ▷ qualify
qualify v (-fies, -fying, -fied) provide or be provided with the abilities necessary for a task, office, or duty ▷ **qualified** adj
qualifying v ▷ qualify
qualitative adj of or relating to quality
qualities n ▷ quality
quality n (pl -ties) degree or standard of excellence ▶ adj excellent or superior
qualm [kwahm] n (pl -s) pang of conscience
qualms n ▷ qualm
quandaries n ▷ quandary
quandary n (pl -ries) difficult situation or dilemma
quandong [kwon-dong] n (pl -s) small Australian tree with edible fruit and nuts used in preserves
quandongs n ▷ quandong
quango n (pl -s) (CHIEFLY BRIT) quasi-autonomous nongovernmental organization: any partly independent official body set up by a government

quangos n ▷ quango
quanta n ▷ quantum
quantifiable adj ▷ quantify
quantification n ▷ quantify
quantifications n ▷ quantify
quantified v ▷ quantify
quantifies v ▷ quantify
quantify v (-fies, -fying, -fied) discover or express the quantity of ▷ **quantifiable** adj ▷ **quantification** n (pl -s)
quantifying v ▷ quantify
quantitative adj of or relating to quantity
quantities n ▷ quantity
quantity n (pl -ties) specified or definite amount or number
quantum n (pl -ta) desired or required amount, esp. a very small one
quarantine n (pl -s) period of isolation of people or animals to prevent the spread of disease ▶ v (-nes, -ning, -ned) isolate in or as if in quarantine
quarantined v ▷ quarantine
quarantines n, v ▷ quarantine
quarantining v ▷ quarantine
quark n (pl -s) (PHYSICS) subatomic particle thought to be the fundamental unit of matter
quarks n ▷ quark
quarrel n (pl -s) angry disagreement ▶ v (-s, -lling, -lled) have a disagreement or dispute ▷ **quarrelsome** adj
quarrelled v ▷ quarrel
quarrelling v ▷ quarrel
quarrels n, v ▷ quarrel
quarrelsome adj ▷ quarrel
quarried v ▷ quarry
quarries n ▷ quarry[1, 2] ▶ v ▷ quarry[1]
quarry[1] n (pl -rries) place where stone is dug from the surface of the earth ▶ v (-rries, -rrying, -rried) extract (stone) from a quarry
quarry[2] n (pl -rries) person or animal that is being hunted
quart n (pl -s) unit of liquid measure equal to two pints (1.136 litres)
quarter n (pl -s) one of four equal parts of something ▶ v (-s, -ing, -ed) divide into four equal parts
quarterdeck n (pl -s) (NAUT) rear part of the upper deck of a ship
quarterdecks n ▷ quarterdeck
quartered v ▷ quarter
quarterfinal n (pl -s) round before the semifinal in a competition
quarterfinals n ▷ quarterfinal
quartering v ▷ quarter

quarterlies n ▷ quarterly

quarterly adj occurring, due, or issued at intervals of three months ▶ n (pl -**lies**) magazine issued every three months ▶ adv once every three months

quartermaster n (pl -**s**) military officer responsible for accommodation, food, and equipment

quartermasters n ▷ quartermaster

quarters n, v ▷ quarter

quartet n (pl -**s**) group of four performers

quartets n ▷ quartet

quarto n (pl -**s**) book size in which the sheets are folded into four leaves

quarto n ▷ quarto

quarts n ▷ quart

quartz n (pl -**es**) hard glossy mineral

quartzes n ▷ quartz

quasar [kway-zar] n (pl -**s**) extremely distant starlike object that emits powerful radio waves

quasars n ▷ quasar

quash v (-**shes**, -**shing**, -**shed**) annul or make void

quashed v ▷ quash

quashes v ▷ quash

quashing v ▷ quash

quatrain n (pl -**s**) stanza or poem of four lines

quatrains n ▷ quatrain

quaver v (-**s**, -**ing**, -**ed**) (of a voice) quiver or tremble ▶ n (pl -**s**) (MUSIC) note half the length of a crotchet

quavered v ▷ quaver

quavering v ▷ quaver

quavers v, n ▷ quaver

quay [kee] n (pl -**s**) wharf built parallel to the shore

quays n ▷ quay

queasier adj ▷ queasy

queasiest adj ▷ queasy

queasiness n ▷ queasy

queasinesses n ▷ queasy

queasy adj (-**sier**, -**siest**) having the feeling that one is about to vomit > **queasiness** n (pl -**es**)

queen n (pl -**s**) female sovereign who is the official ruler or head of state > **queenly** adj

queenly adj ▷ queen

queens n ▷ queen

queer adj (-**er**, -**est**) not normal or usual

queerer adj ▷ queer

queerest adj ▷ queer

quell v (-**s**, -**ing**, -**ed**) suppress

quelled v ▷ quell

quelling v ▷ quell

quells v ▷ quell

quench v (-**es**, -**ing**, -**ed**) satisfy (one's thirst)

quenched v ▷ quench

quenches v ▷ quench

quenching v ▷ quench

queried v ▷ query

queries n, v ▷ query

quern n (pl -**s**) stone hand mill for grinding corn

querns n ▷ quern

querulous [kwer-yoo-luss] adj complaining or whining > **querulously** adv

querulously adv ▷ querulous

query n (pl -**ries**) question, esp. one raising doubt ▶ v (-**ries**, -**rying**, -**ried**) express uncertainty, doubt, or an objection concerning (something)

querying v ▷ query

quest n (pl -**s**) long and difficult search ▶ v (-**s**, -**ing**, -**ed**) (foll. by **for** or **after**) go in search of

quested v ▷ quest

questing v ▷ quest

question n (pl -**s**) form of words addressed to a person in order to obtain an answer ▶ v (-**s**, -**ing**, -**ed**) put a question or questions to (a person)

questionable adj of disputable value or authority > **questionably** adv

questionably adv ▷ questionable

questioned v ▷ question

questioning v ▷ question

questionnaire n (pl -**s**) set of questions on a form, used to collect information from people

questionnaires n ▷ questionnaire

questions n, v ▷ question

quests n, v ▷ quest

> **quetzal** or **quezal** n (**quetzals**, **quezales**, **quetzales**, **quezals**). The quetzal is a crested bird of Central and South America. This is a great word if you can get the tiles for it, so it's well worth remembering both spellings and the three plural forms. If you can use all your letters to play quetzal or quezals, you'll earn a bonus of 50 points. Quetzal scores 25 points.

queue n (pl -**s**) line of people or vehicles waiting for something ▶ v (**queues**, **queuing** or **queueing**, **queued**) (often foll. by **up**) form or remain in a line while waiting

queued v ▷ queue

queueing v ▷ queue

queues n, v ▷ queue

queuing v ▷ queue

quibble v (-**les**, -**ling**, -**led**) make trivial

objections ► *n* (*pl* -s) trivial objection

quibbled *v* ▷ quibble

quibbles *v, n* ▷ quibble

quibbling *v* ▷ quibble

quiche [keesh] *n* (*pl* -s) savoury flan with an egg custard filling to which vegetables etc. are added

quiches *n* ▷ quiche

quick *adj* (-er, -est) speedy, fast ► *n* (*pl* -s) area of sensitive flesh under a nail ► *adv* (Informal) in a rapid manner > **quickly** *adv*

quicken *v* (-s, -ing, -ed) make or become faster

quickened *v* ▷ quicken

quickening *v* ▷ quicken

quickens *v* ▷ quicken

quicker *adj* ▷ quick

quickest *adj* ▷ quick

quicklime *n* (*pl* -s) white solid used in the manufacture of glass and steel

quicklimes *n* ▷ quicklime

quickly *adv* ▷ quick

quicks *n* ▷ quick

quicksand *n* (*pl* -s) deep mass of loose wet sand that sucks anything on top of it into it

quicksands *n* ▷ quicksand

quicksilver *n* (*pl* -s) mercury

quicksilvers *n* ▷ quicksilver

quickstep *n* (*pl* -s) fast modern ballroom dance

quicksteps *n* ▷ quickstep

quid *n* (*pl* quid, -s) (BRIT) (Slang) pound (sterling)

quids *n* ▷ quid

quiescence *n* ▷ quiescent

quiescences *n* ▷ quiescent

quiescent [kwee-ess-ent] *adj* quiet, inactive, or dormant > **quiescence** *n* (*pl* -s)

quiet *adj* (-er, -est) with little noise ► *n* (*pl* -s) quietness ► *v* (-s, -ing, -ed) make or become quiet > **quietly** *adv* > **quietness** *n* (*pl* -es)

quieted *v* ▷ quiet

quieten *v* (-s, -ing, -ed) (often foll. by **down**) make or become quiet

quieter *adj* ▷ quiet

quietest *adj* ▷ quiet

quieting *v* ▷ quiet

quietism *n* (*pl* -s) passivity and calmness of mind towards external events

quietisms *n* ▷ quietism

quietly *adv* ▷ quiet

quietness *n* ▷ quiet

quietnesses *n* ▷ quiet

quiets *v, n* ▷ quiet

quietude *n* (-s) quietness, peace, or tranquillity

quietudes *n* ▷ quietude

quiff *n* (*pl* -s) tuft of hair brushed up above the forehead

quiffs *n* ▷ quiff

quill *n* (*pl* -s) pen made from the feather of a bird's wing or tail

quills *n* ▷ quill

quilt *n* (*pl* -s) padded covering for a bed

quilted *adj* consisting of two layers of fabric with a layer of soft material between them

quilts *n* ▷ quilt

quince *n* (*pl* -s) acid-tasting pear-shaped fruit

quinces *n* ▷ quince

quinine *n* (*pl* -s) bitter drug used as a tonic and formerly to treat malaria

quinines *n* ▷ quinine

quinquennial *adj* occurring every five years

quins *n* ▷ quin

quinsies *n* ▷ quinsy

quinsy *n* (*pl* -sies) inflammation of the throat or tonsils

quintessence *n* (*pl* -s) most perfect representation of a quality or state > **quintessential** *adj*

quintessences *n* ▷ quintessence

quintessential *adj* ▷ quintessence

quintet *n* (*pl* -s) group of five performers

quintets *n* ▷ quintet

quintuplet *n* (*pl* -s) one of five offspring born at one birth

quintuplets *n* ▷ quintuplet

quinze (quinzes). Quinze is a card game. This is a high-scoring word, and if you can use all of your tiles to form the plural, you'll get a 50-points bonus. Quinze scores 24 points.

quip *n* (*pl* -s) witty saying ► *v* (-s, -pping, -pped) make a quip

quipped *v* ▷ quip

quipping *v* ▷ quip

quips *n, v* ▷ quip

quire *n* (*pl* -s) set of 24 or 25 sheets of paper

quires *n* ▷ quire

quirk *n* (*pl* -s) peculiarity of character > **quirky** *adj* (-kier, -kiest)

quirks *n* ▷ quirk

quirky *adj* ▷ quirk

quisling *n* (*pl* -s) traitor who aids an occupying enemy force

quislings *n* ▷ quisling

quit *v* (quits, quitting, quit) stop (doing something)

quite *adv* somewhat ► *interj* expression of agreement

quits *adj* (Informal) on an equal footing ► *v* ▷ quit

quitter *n* (*pl* -s) person who lacks perseverance

quitters n ▷ quitter
quitting v ▷ quit
quiver¹ v (-s, -ing, -ed) shake with a tremulous movement ▶ n (pl -s) shaking or trembling
quiver² n (pl -s) case for arrows
quivered v ▷ quiver¹
quivering v ▷ quiver¹
quivers v ▷ quiver¹ ▶ n ▷ quiver¹, ²

> **quixote** n (**quixotes**). A quixote is an impractically idealistic person. This is a high-scoring word; if you have all the letters to play it, and can place them on the board, you'll score a 50-point bonus for using all of your tiles. Quixote scores 23 points.

quixotic [kwik-sot-ik] adj romantic and unrealistic > **quixotically** adv
quixotically adv ▷ quixotic
quiz n (pl -**zzes**) entertainment in which the knowledge of the players is tested by a series of questions ▶ v (-**zzes, -zzing, -zzed**) investigate by close questioning
quizzed v ▷ quiz
quizzes n, v ▷ quiz
quizzical adj questioning and mocking > **quizzically** adv
quizzically adv ▷ quizzical
quizzing v ▷ quiz
quod n (pl -**s**) (BRIT) (Slang) jail
quods n ▷ quod
quoit n (pl -**s**) large ring used in the game of

quoits ▶ pl game in which quoits are tossed at a stake in the ground in attempts to encircle it
quoits n ▷ quoit
quokka n (pl -**s**) small Australian wallaby
quokkas n ▷ quokka
quorum n (pl -**s**) minimum number of people required to be present at a meeting before any transactions can take place
quorums n ▷ quorum
quota n (pl -**s**) share that is due from, due to, or allocated to a group or person
quotable adj ▷ quote
quotas n ▷ quota
quotation n (pl -**s**) written or spoken passage repeated exactly in a later work, speech, or conversation
quotations n ▷ quotation
quote v (-**tes, -ting, -ted**) repeat (words) exactly from (an earlier work, speech, or conversation) ▶ n (pl -**s**) (Informal) quotation > **quotable** adj
quoted v ▷ quote
quotes v, n ▷ quote
quoth v (Obs) said
quotidian adj daily
quotient n (pl -**s**) result of the division of one number or quantity by another
quotients n ▷ quotient
quoting v ▷ quote

Rr

R is one of the most common consonants in Scrabble, along with N and T. Despite this, however, there is only one two-letter word beginning with R: **re** (2 points). This is worth remembering, as you won't need to waste time trying to think of others. There are some good three-letter words with R, however, some of which are quite unusual: **raj**, **rax**, **rex** (10 each) and **rez** and **riz** (12 each). Also, don't forget common words like **raw**, **ray** and **row** (6 each).

rabbi [rab-bye] *n* (*pl* **-s**) Jewish spiritual leader
> **rabbinical** *adj*
rabbinical *adj* ▷ rabbi
rabbis *n* ▷ rabbi
rabbit *n* (*pl* **-s**) small burrowing mammal with long ears
rabbits *n* ▷ rabbit
rabble *n* (*pl* **-s**) disorderly crowd of noisy people
rabbles *n* ▷ rabble
rabid *adj* (**-er**, **-est**) fanatical > **rabidly** *adv*
rabider *adj* ▷ rabid
rabidest *adj* ▷ rabid
rabidly *adv* ▷ rabid
rabies [ray-beez] *n* usu. fatal viral disease transmitted by dogs and certain other animals
raccoon *n* (*pl* **-s**) small N American mammal with a long striped tail
raccoons *n* ▷ raccoon
race[1] *n* (*pl* **-s**) contest of speed ▶ *pl* meeting for horse racing ▶ *v* (**-ces**, **-cing**, **-ced**) compete with in a race > **racer** *n* (*pl* **-s**) > **racecourse** *n* (*pl* **-s**) > **racehorse** *n* (*pl* **-s**) > **racetrack** *n* (*pl* **-s**)
race[2] *n* (*pl* **-s**) group of people of common ancestry with distinguishing physical features, such as skin colour > **racial** *adj*
raced *n*, *v* ▷ race[1]
racecourse *n* ▷ race[1]
racecourses *n* ▷ race[1]
raced *n*, *v* ▷ race[1]
racehorse *n* ▷ race[1]
racehorses *n* ▷ race[1]
raceme [rass-eem] *n* (*pl* **-s**) cluster of flowers along a central stem, as in the foxglove
racemes *n* ▷ raceme
racer *n* ▷ race[1]
racers *n* ▷ race[1]
races *n* ▷ race[1, 2] ▶ *v* ▷ race[1]

racetrack *n* ▷ race[1]
racetracks *n* ▷ race[1]
racial *adj* ▷ race[2]
racialism *n* ▷ racism
racialisms *adj*, *n* ▷ racism
racialist *n* ▷ racism
racialists *n* ▷ racism
racier *adj* ▷ racy
raciest *adj* ▷ racy
racing *v* ▷ race[1]
racism, racialism *n* (*pl* **-s**) hostile attitude or behaviour to members of other races, based on a belief in the innate superiority of one's own race > **racist, racialist** *adj*, *n* (*pl* **-s**)
racisms *n* ▷ racism
racist *n* ▷ racism
racists *n* ▷ racism
rack *n* (*pl* **-s**) framework for holding particular articles, such as coats or luggage (HIST) ▶ *v* (**-s**, **-ing**, **-ed**) cause great suffering to
racked *v* ▷ rack
racket[1] *n* (*pl* **-s**) noisy disturbance
racket[2], **racquet** *n* (**-s**) bat with strings stretched in an oval frame, used in tennis etc.
racketeer *n* (*pl* **-s**) person making illegal profits
racketeers *n* ▷ racketeer
rackets *n* ball game played in a paved walled court ▶ *n* ▷ racket[1, 2]
racking *v* ▷ rack
racks *n*, *v* ▷ rack
raconteur [rak-on-tur] *n* (*pl* **-s**) skilled storyteller
raconteurs *n* ▷ raconteur
racquet *n* ▷ racket[2]
racquets *n* ▷ racket[2]
racy *adj* (**-cier**, **-ciest**) slightly shocking
radar *n* (*pl* **-s**) device for tracking distant objects by bouncing high-frequency radio

pulses off them

radars n ▷ **radar**

radial adj spreading out from a common central point

radiance n ▷ **radiant**

radiances n ▷ **radiant**

radiant adj looking happy > **radiance** n (**-s**)

radiate v (**-tes, -ting, -ted**) spread out from a centre

radiated v ▷ **radiate**

radiates v ▷ **radiate**

radiating v ▷ **radiate**

radiation n (pl **-s**) transmission of energy from one body to another

radiations n ▷ **radiation**

radiator n (**-s**) (BRIT) arrangement of pipes containing hot water or steam to heat a room

radiators n ▷ **radiator**

radical adj fundamental ▶ n (pl **-s**) person advocating fundamental (political) change > **radically** adv ▷ **radical** n (**-s**)

radicalism n ▷ **radical**

radicalisms n ▷ **radical**

radically adv ▷ **radical**

radicals n ▷ **radical**

radicle n (pl **-s**) small or developing root

radicles n ▷ **radicle**

radii n ▷ **radius**

radio n (**-s**) use of electromagnetic waves for broadcasting, communication, etc. ▶ v (**-s, -ing, -ed**) transmit (a message) by radio

radioactive adj emitting radiation as a result of nuclear decay > **radioactivity** n (pl **-ies**)

radioactivities n ▷ **radioactive**

radioactivity n ▷ **radioactive**

radioed v ▷ **radio**

radiographer n ▷ **radiography**

radiographers n ▷ **radiography**

radiographies n ▷ **radiography**

radiography [ray-dee-og-ra-fee] n (pl **-phies**) production of an image on a film or plate by radiation > **radiographer** n (pl **-s**)

radioing v ▷ **radio**

radiologies n ▷ **radiology**

radiologist n ▷ **radiology**

radiologists n ▷ **radiology**

radiology [ray-dee-ol-a-jee] n (pl **-gies**) science of using x-rays in medicine > **radiologist** n (pl **-s**)

radios n, v ▷ **radio**

radiotherapies n ▷ **radiotherapy**

radiotherapist n ▷ **radiotherapy**

radiotherapists n ▷ **radiotherapy**

radiotherapy n (pl **-pies**) treatment of disease,

esp. cancer, by radiation > **radiotherapist** n (pl **-s**)

radish n (pl **-es**) small hot-flavoured root vegetable eaten raw in salads

radishes n ▷ **radish**

radium n (pl **-s**) (CHEM) radioactive metallic element

radiums n ▷ **radium**

radius n (pl **radii, radiuses**) (length of) a straight line from the centre to the circumference of a circle

radiuses n ▷ **radius**

radon [ray-don] n (pl **-s**) (CHEM) radioactive gaseous element

radons n ▷ **radon**

raffia n (pl **-s**) prepared palm fibre for weaving mats etc.

raffias n ▷ **raffia**

raffish adj slightly disreputable

raffle n (pl **-s**) lottery with goods as prizes ▶ v (**-les, -ling, -led**) offer as a prize in a raffle

raffled v ▷ **raffle**

raffles n, v ▷ **raffle**

raffling v ▷ **raffle**

raft n (pl **-s**) floating platform of logs, planks, etc.

rafter n (pl **-s**) one of the main beams of a roof

rafters n ▷ **rafter**

rafts n ▷ **raft**

rag[1] n (pl **-s**) fragment of cloth ▶ pl tattered clothing

rag[2] (BRIT) v (**-s, -gging, -gged**) tease ▶ adj, n (pl **-s**) (of) events organized by students to raise money for charities

rage n (pl **-s**) violent anger or passion ▶ v (**-ges, -ging, -ged**) speak or act with fury

raged v ▷ **rage**

rages n, v ▷ **rage**

ragamuffin n (pl **-s**) ragged dirty child

ragamuffins n ▷ **ragamuffin**

ragged [rag-gid] adj dressed in shabby or torn clothes ▶ v ▷ **rag**[2]

ragging v ▷ **rag**[2]

raging v ▷ **rage**

raglan adj (of a sleeve) joined to a garment by diagonal seams from the neck to the underarm

ragout [rag-goo] n (pl **-s**) richly seasoned stew of meat and vegetables

ragouts n ▷ **ragout**

rags n, v ▷ **rag**[1, 2]

ragtime n (pl **-s**) style of jazz piano music

ragtimes n ▷ **ragtime**

raid n (pl **-s**) sudden surprise attack or search ▶ v (**-s, -ing, -ed**) make a raid on > **raider** n

(pl -s)
raided v ▷ raid
raider n ▷ raid
raiders n ▷ raid
raiding v ▷ raid
raids n, v ▷ raid
rail¹ n (pl -s) horizontal bar, esp. as part of a fence or track
rail² v (-s, -ing, -ed) (foll. by at or against) complain bitterly or loudly
rail³ n (pl -s) small marsh bird
railed v ▷ rail²
railing n (pl -s) fence made of rails supported by posts ▶ v ▷ rail²
railings n ▷ railing
railleries n ▷ raillery
raillery n (pl -ies) teasing or joking
rails n ▷ rail¹, ², ³ ▶ v ▷ rail²
railway n (pl -s) track of iron rails on which trains run
railways n ▷ railway
raiment n (pl -s) (Obs) clothing
raiments n ▷ raiment
rain n (pl -s) water falling in drops from the clouds ▶ v (-s, -ing, -ed) fall or pour down as rain > **rainy** adj (-nier, -niest)
rainbow n (pl -s) arch of colours in the sky
rainbows n ▷ rainbow
raincoat n (pl -s) water-resistant overcoat
raincoats n ▷ raincoat
rained v ▷ rain
rainier adj ▷ rainy
rainiest adj ▷ rainy
rainfall n (pl -s) amount of rain
rainfalls n ▷ rainfall
rainforest n (pl -s) dense forest in tropical and temperate areas
rainforests n ▷ rainforest
raining v ▷ rain
rains n, v ▷ rain
rainy adj ▷ rain
raise v (-ses, -sing, -sed) lift up
raised v ▷ raise
raises v ▷ raise
raisin n (pl -s) dried grape
raising v ▷ raise
raisins n ▷ raisin

raj n (rajes). Raj is an Indian word for government. This word can be very useful when there isn't much space on the board. If you can't play raj, remember that it's just **jar** backwards you might be able to fit that in somewhere. Raj scores 10 points.

raja, rajah n (pl -s) (HIST) Indian prince or ruler

rajah n ▷ raja
rajahs n ▷ raja
rajas n ▷ raja
rake¹ n (pl -s) tool with a long handle and a crosspiece with teeth, used for smoothing earth or gathering leaves, hay, etc. ▶ v (-kes, -king, -ked) gather or smooth with a rake
rake² n (pl -s) dissolute or immoral man
raked v ▷ rake¹
rakes n, v ▷ rake¹, ² ▶ v ▷ rake¹
raking v ▷ rake¹
rakish adj dashing or jaunty
rallied v ▷ rally
rallies n, v ▷ rally
rally n (pl -ies) large gathering of people for a meeting ▶ v (-ies, -ying, -ied) bring or come together after dispersal or for a common cause
rallying v ▷ rally
ram n (pl -s) male sheep ▶ v (-s, -mming, -mmed) strike against with force
ramble v (-les, -ling, -led) walk without a definite route ▶ n (pl -s) walk, esp. in the country
rambled v ▷ ramble
rambler n (pl -s) person who rambles
ramblers n ▷ rambler
rambles v, n ▷ ramble
rambling v ▷ ramble
ramekin [ram-ik-in] n (pl -s) small ovenproof dish for a single serving of food
ramekins n ▷ ramekin
ramifications pl n consequences resulting from an action
rammed v ▷ ram
ramming v ▷ ram
ramp n (pl -s) slope joining two level surfaces
rampage v (-ges, -ging, -ged) dash about violently
rampaged v ▷ rampage
rampages v ▷ rampage
rampaging v ▷ rampage
rampant adj growing or spreading uncontrollably
rampart n (pl -s) mound or wall for defence
ramparts n ▷ rampart
ramps n ▷ ramp
rams n, v ▷ ram
ramshackle adj tumbledown, rickety, or makeshift
ran v ▷ run
ranch n (pl -es) large cattle farm in the American West > **rancher** n (pl -s)
rancher n ▷ ranch
ranchers n ▷ ranch

ranches n ▷ ranch
rancid adj (of butter, bacon, etc.) stale and having an offensive smell > **rancidity** n (pl -ies)
  rancidities n ▷ rancidity
  rancidity n ▷ rancid
  rancorous adj ▷ rancour
rancour n (pl -s) deep bitter hate > **rancorous** adj
  rancours n ▷ rancour
rand n (pl -s) monetary unit of S Africa
  randier adj ▷ randy
  randiest adj ▷ randy
random adj made or done by chance or without plan
  rands n ▷ rand
randy adj (-ier, -iest) (Informal) sexually aroused
  rang v ▷ ring[1]
range n (pl -s) limits of effectiveness or variation ▶ v (-ges, -ging, -ged) vary between one point and another
  ranged v ▷ range
ranger n (pl -s) official in charge of a nature reserve etc.
  rangers n ▷ ranger
rangefinder n (pl -s) instrument for finding how far away an object is
  rangefinders n ▷ rangefinder
  ranges n, v ▷ range
  rangier adj ▷ rangy
  rangiest adj ▷ rangy
  ranging v ▷ range
rangy [rain-jee] adj (-ier, -iest) having long slender limbs
rank[1] n (pl -s) relative place or position ▶ v (-s, -ing, -ed) have a specific rank or position
rank[2] adj complete or absolute
  ranked v ▷ rank
  ranking v ▷ rank
rankle v (-les, -ling, -led) continue to cause resentment or bitterness
  rankled v ▷ rankle
  rankles v ▷ rankle
  rankling v ▷ rankle
  ranks n, v ▷ rank[1]
ransack v (-s, -ing, -ed) search thoroughly
  ransacked v ▷ ransack
  ransacking v ▷ ransack
  ransacks v ▷ ransack
ransom n (pl -s) money demanded in return for the release of someone who has been kidnapped
  ransoms n ▷ ransom
rant v (-s, -ing, -ed) talk in a loud and excited way > **ranter** n (pl -s)

  ranted v ▷ rant
  ranter n ▷ rant
  ranters n ▷ rant
  ranting v ▷ rant
  rants v ▷ rant
rap v (-s, -pping, -pped) hit with a sharp quick blow ▶ n (pl -s) quick sharp blow > **rapper** n (pl -s)
rapacious adj greedy or grasping > **rapacity** n (pl -ies)
  rapacities n ▷ rapacious
  rapacity n ▷ rapacious
rape[1] v (-pes, -ping, -ped) force to submit to sexual intercourse ▶ n (pl -s) act of raping > **rapist** n (pl -s)
rape[2] n (pl -s) plant with oil-yielding seeds, also used as fodder
  raped v ▷ rape[1]
  rapes v ▷ rape[1] ▶ n ▷ rape[1,2]
rapid adj (-er, -est) quick, swift > **rapidly** adv > **rapidity** n (pl -ies)
  rapider adj ▷ rapid
  rapidest adj ▷ rapid
  rapidities n ▷ rapid
  rapidity n ▷ rapid
  rapidly adv ▷ rapid
rapids pl n part of a river with a fast turbulent current
rapier [ray-pyer] n (pl -s) fine-bladed sword
  rapiers n ▷ rapier
  raping v ▷ rape[1]
  rapist n ▷ rape[1]
  rapists n ▷ rape[1]
  rapped v ▷ rap
  rapper n ▷ rap
  rappers n ▷ rap
  rapping v ▷ rap
rapport [rap-pore] n (pl -s) harmony or agreement
  rapports n ▷ rapport
rapprochement [rap-prosh-mong] n (pl -s) re-establishment of friendly relations, esp. between nations
  rapprochements n ▷ rapprochement
  raps v, n ▷ rap
rapt adj engrossed or spellbound
rapture n (pl -s) ecstasy > **rapturous** adj
  raptures n ▷ rapture
  rapturous adj ▷ rapture
rare[1] adj (-r, -st) uncommon > **rarity** n (pl -ies)
rare[2] adj (-r, -st) (of meat) lightly cooked
rarebit n (pl -s) dish of melted cheese on toast
  rarebits n ▷ rarebit
rarefied [rare-if-ide] adj highly specialized, exalted

rarely adv seldom
　rarer adj ▷ rare[1,2]
　rarest adj ▷ rare[1,2]
raring adj enthusiastic, willing, or ready to
　rarities n ▷ rare[1]
　rarity n ▷ rare[1]
rascal n (pl -s) rogue ▷ **rascally** adj (-ier, -iest)
　rascalliest adj ▷ rascal
　rascally adj ▷ rascal
　rascals n ▷ rascal
rash[1] adj (-er, -est) hasty, reckless, or
　incautious ▷ **rashly** adv
rash[2] n (pl -es) eruption of spots or patches
　on the skin
rasher n (pl -s) thin slice of bacon ▷ adj ▷ rash[1]
　rashers n ▷ rasher
　rashes n ▷ rash[2]
　rashest adj ▷ rash[1]
　rashly adv ▷ rash[1]
rasp n (pl -s) harsh grating noise ▷ v (-s, -ing,
　-ed) speak in a grating voice
　raspberries n ▷ raspberry
raspberry n (pl -ies) red juicy edible berry
　(Informal)
　rasped v ▷ rasp
　rasping v ▷ rasp
　rasps n, v ▷ rasp
rat n (pl -s) small rodent (Informal) ▷ v (-s, -tting,
　-tted) (Informal) inform (on)
ratafia [rat-a-fee-a] n (pl -s) liqueur made from
　fruit
　ratafias n ▷ ratafia
ratatouille [rat-a-twee] n (pl -s) vegetable
　casserole of tomatoes, aubergines, etc.
　ratatouilles n ▷ ratatouille
ratchet n (pl -s) set of teeth on a bar or wheel
　allowing motion in one direction only
　ratchets n ▷ ratchet
rate n (pl -s) degree of speed or progress ▷ pl
　local tax on business ▷ v (-tes, -ting, -ted)
　consider or value ▷ **ratepayer** n (pl -s)
rateable adj able to be rated
　rated v ▷ rate
　ratepayer n ▷ rate
　ratepayers n ▷ rate
　rates n, v ▷ rate
rather adv to some extent
　ratification n ▷ ratify
　ratifications n ▷ ratify
　ratified v ▷ ratify
　ratifies v ▷ ratify
ratify v (-ies, -ying, -ied) give formal approval
　to ▷ **ratification** n (pl -s)
　ratifiying v ▷ ratify
rating n (pl -s) valuation or assessment ▷ pl

size of the audience for a TV programme ▷ v
▷ **rate**
　ratings n ▷ rating
ratio n (pl -s) relationship between two
　numbers or amounts expressed as a
　proportion
ration n (pl -s) fixed allowance of food etc. ▷ v
　(-s, -ing, -ed) limit to a certain amount per
　person
rational adj reasonable, sensible ▷ **rationally**
　adv ▷ **rationality** n (pl -ies)
rationale [rash-a-nahl] n (pl -s) reason for an
　action or decision
　rationales n ▷ rationale
rationalism n (pl -s) philosophy that regards
　reason as the only basis for beliefs or actions
　▷ **rationalist** n (pl -s)
　rationalisms n ▷ rationalism
　rationalist n ▷ rationalism
　rationalists n ▷ rationalism
　rationalities n ▷ rational
　rationality n ▷ rational
rationalize v (-zes, -zing, -zed) justify by
　plausible reasoning ▷ **rationalization** n (pl -s)
　rationalization n ▷ rationalize
　rationalizations n ▷ rationalize
　rationalized v ▷ rationalize
　rationalizes v ▷ rationalize
　rationalizing v ▷ rationalize
　rationally adv ▷ rational
　rationed v ▷ ration
　rationing v ▷ ration
　rations n, v ▷ ration
　ratios n ▷ ratio
　rats n ▷ rat
rattan n (pl -s) climbing palm with jointed
　stems used for canes
　rattans n ▷ rattan
　ratted v ▷ rat
　rattier adj ▷ ratty
　rattiest adj ▷ ratty
　ratting v ▷ rat
rattle v (-les, -ling, -led) give out a succession
　of short sharp sounds ▷ n (pl -s) short sharp
　sound
　rattled v ▷ rattle
rattlesnake n (pl -s) poisonous snake with
　loose horny segments on the tail that make a
　rattling sound
　rattlesnakes n ▷ rattlesnake
　rattles v, n ▷ rattle
　rattling v ▷ rattle
ratty adj (-ier, -iest) (BRIT & NZ) (Informal) bad-
　tempered, irritable
raucous adj hoarse or harsh

raunchier adj ▷ **raunchy**

raunchiest adj ▷ **raunchy**

raunchy adj (-chier, -chiest) (Slang) earthy, sexy

ravage v (-ges, -ging, -ged) cause extensive damage to

ravaged v ▷ **ravage**

ravages pl n damaging effects ▶ v ▷ **ravage**

ravaging v ▷ **ravage**

rave v (-ves, -ving, -ved) talk wildly or with enthusiasm ▶ n (pl -s) (Slang) large-scale party with electronic dance music

raved v ▷ **rave**

ravel v (-s, -lling, -lled) tangle or become entangled

ravelled v ▷ **ravel**

ravelling v ▷ **ravel**

ravels v ▷ **ravel**

raven n (pl -s) black bird like a large crow ▶ adj (of hair) shiny black

ravens n ▷ **raven**

ravenous adj very hungry

raves v, n ▷ **rave**

ravine [rav-veen] n (pl -s) narrow steep-sided valley worn by a stream

ravines n ▷ **ravine**

raving adj delirious ▶ v ▷ **rave**

ravioli pl n small squares of pasta with a savoury filling

ravish v (-es, -ing, -ed) enrapture

ravished v ▷ **ravish**

ravishes v ▷ **ravish**

ravishing adj, v ▷ **ravish**

raw adj (-er, -est) uncooked

rawer adj ▷ **raw**

rawest adj ▷ **raw**

rawhide n (pl -s) untanned hide

rawhides n ▷ **rawhide**

> **rax** v (**raxes, raxing, raxed**). Rax is a Scots word that means to stretch or extend. This is a good word to have ready when you have an X on your rack, as there is probably an A or R on the board already. The verb forms can also help you to get a better score. Rax scores 10 points.

ray¹ n (pl -s) single line or narrow beam of light

ray² n (pl -s) large sea fish with a flat body and a whiplike tail

rays n ▷ **ray¹,²**

rayon n (pl -s) (fabric made of) a synthetic fibre

rayons n ▷ **rayon**

raze v (-zes, -zing, -zed) destroy (buildings or a town) completely

razed v ▷ **raze**

razes v ▷ **raze**

razing v ▷ **raze**

razor n (pl -s) sharp instrument for shaving

razorbill n (pl -s) sea bird of the North Atlantic with a stout sideways flattened bill

razorbills n ▷ **razorbill**

razors n ▷ **razor**

> **re** n (**res**). Re is a musical note. This is the only two-letter word beginning with R, and so is a good one to remember. Re is very useful as it allows you to connect a word beginning with R to one ending in E, or vice versa and R and E are two of the most common tiles in the game. Re scores 2 points.

reach v (-es, -ing, -ed) arrive at ▶ n (pl -es) distance that one can reach; stretch of a river > **reachable** adj

reachable adj ▷ **reach**

reached v ▷ **reach**

reaches v, n ▷ **reach**

reaching v ▷ **reach**

react v (-s, -ing, -ed) act in response (to) (foll. by **against**)

reactance n (pl -s) (ELECTRICITY) resistance to the flow of an alternating current caused by the inductance or capacitance of the circuit

reactances n ▷ **reactance**

reacted v ▷ **react**

reacting v ▷ **react**

reaction n (pl -s) physical or emotional response to a stimulus

reactionaries n ▷ **reactionary**

reactionary n, adj (pl -ies) (person) opposed to change, esp. in politics

reactionary n ▷ **reaction**

reactions n ▷ **reaction**

reactive adj chemically active

reactor n (pl -s) apparatus in which a nuclear reaction is maintained and controlled to produce nuclear energy

reactors n ▷ **reactor**

reacts v ▷ **react**

read v (-s, -ing, **read**) look at and understand or take in (written or printed matter) ▶ n matter suitable for reading > **reading** n (pl -s)

readable adj enjoyable to read

reader n (pl -s) person who reads

readers n ▷ **reader**

readership n (pl -s) readers of a publication collectively

readerships n ▷ **readership**

readier adj ▷ **ready**

readiest adj ▷ **ready**

readily adv ▷ **ready**

readiness n ▷ **ready**

readinesses n ▷ ready
reading n, v ▷ read
readings n ▷ read
readjust v (-s, -ing, -ed) adapt to a new situation ▷ **readjustment** n (pl -s)
readjusted v ▷ readjust
readjusting v ▷ readjust
readjustment n ▷ readjust
readjustments n ▷ readjust
readjusts v ▷ readjust
reads v ▷ read
ready adj (-dier, -diest) prepared for use or action ▷ **readily** adv ▷ **readiness** n (pl -es)
reagent [ree-age-ent] n (pl -s) chemical substance that reacts with another, used to detect the presence of the other
reagents n ▷ reagent
real adj (-er, -est) existing in fact
realism n ▷ realistic
realisms n ▷ realistic
realist n ▷ realistic
realistically adv ▷ realistic
realists n ▷ realistic
realistic adj seeing and accepting things as they really are, practical ▷ **realistically** adv ▷ **realism** n (pl -s) ▷ **realist** n (pl -s)
realities n ▷ reality
reality n (pl -ies) state of things as they are
realize v (-zes, -zing, -zed) become aware or grasp the significance of ▷ **realization** n (pl -s)
realization n ▷ realize
realizations n ▷ realize
realized v ▷ realize
realizes v ▷ realize
realizing v ▷ realize
really adv very ▶ interj exclamation of dismay, doubt, or surprise
realm n (pl -s) kingdom
realms n ▷ realm
ream n (pl -s) twenty quires of paper, generally 500 sheets ▶ pl (Informal) large quantity (of written matter)
reams n ▷ ream
reap v (-s, -ing, -ed) cut and gather (a harvest) ▷ **reaper** n (pl -s)
reaped v ▷ reap
reaper n ▷ reap
reapers n ▷ reap
reaping v ▷ reap
reappear v (-s, -ing, -ed) appear again ▷ **reappearance** n (pl -s)
reappearance n ▷ reappear
reappearances n ▷ reappear
reappeared v ▷ reappear
reappearing v ▷ reappear

reappears v ▷ reappear
reaps v ▷ reap
rear[1] n (pl -s) back part ▷ **rearmost** adj
rear[2] v (-s, -ing, -ed) care for and educate (children)
reared v ▷ rear
rearguard n (pl -s) troops protecting the rear of an army
rearguards n ▷ rearguard
rearing v ▷ rear
rearmost adj ▷ rear[1]
rearrange v (-ges, -ging, -ged) organize differently, alter ▷ **rearrangement** n (pl -s)
rearranged v ▷ rearrange
rearrangement n ▷ rearrange
rearrangements n ▷ rearrange
rearranges v ▷ rearrange
rearranging v ▷ rearrange
rears n ▷ rear[1] ▶ v ▷ rear[2]
reason n (pl -s) cause or motive ▶ v (-s, -ing, -ed) think logically in forming conclusions
reasonable adj sensible ▷ **reasonably** adv
reasoned v ▷ reason
reasoning v ▷ reason
reasons n, v ▷ reason
reassess v (-es, -ing, -ed) reconsider the value or importance of
reassessed v ▷ reassess
reassesses v ▷ reassess
reassessing v ▷ reassess
reassure v (-res, -ring, -red) restore confidence to ▷ **reassurance** n (pl -s)
reassurance n ▷ reassure
reassurances n ▷ reassure
reassured v ▷ reassure
reassures v ▷ reassure
reassuring v ▷ reassure
rebate n (pl -s) discount or refund
rebates n ▷ rebate
rebel v (-s, -lling, -lled) revolt against the ruling power ▶ n (pl -s) person who rebels ▷ **rebellious** adj
rebelled v ▷ rebel
rebelling v ▷ rebel
rebellion n (pl -s) organized open resistance to authority
rebellions n ▷ rebellion
rebellious adj ▷ rebel
rebels v, n ▷ rebel
rebore, reboring n (pl -s) boring of a cylinder to restore its true shape
rebores n ▷ rebore
reboring n ▷ rebore
reborings n ▷ rebore
rebound v (-s, -ing, -ed) spring back

rebounded v ▷ **rebound**

rebounding v ▷ **rebound**

rebounds v ▷ **rebound**

rebuff v (-s, -ing, -ed) reject or snub ▶ n (pl -s) blunt refusal, snub

rebuffed v ▷ **rebuff**

rebuffing v ▷ **rebuff**

rebuffs v, n ▷ **rebuff**

rebuke v (-kes, -king, -ked) scold sternly ▶ n (pl -s) stern scolding

rebuked v ▷ **rebuke**

rebukes v, n ▷ **rebuke**

rebuking v ▷ **rebuke**

rebus n (pl -es) puzzle consisting of pictures and symbols representing words or syllables

rebuses n ▷ **rebus**

rebut v (-s, -tting, -tted) prove that (a claim) is untrue > **rebuttal** n (pl -s)

rebuts v ▷ **rebut**

rebuttal n ▷ **rebut**

rebuttals n ▷ **rebut**

rebutted v ▷ **rebut**

rebutting v ▷ **rebut**

recalcitrant adj wilfully disobedient > **recalcitrance** n (pl -s)

recalcitrance n ▷ **recalcitrant**

recalcitrances n ▷ **recalcitrant**

recall v (-s, -ing, -ed) recollect or remember ▶ n (pl (pl -s) ability to remember

recalled v ▷ **recall**

recalling v ▷ **recall**

recalls v, n ▷ **recall**

recant v (-s, -ing, -ed) withdraw (a statement or belief) publicly > **recantation** n (pl -s)

recantation n ▷ **recant**

recantations n ▷ **recant**

recanted v ▷ **recant**

recanting v ▷ **recant**

recants v ▷ **recant**

recap (Informal) v (-s, -pping, -pped) recapitulate ▶ n (pl -s) recapitulation

recapitulate v (-tes, -ting, -ted) state again briefly, repeat > **recapitulation** n (pl -s)

recapitulated v ▷ **recapitulate**

recapitulates v ▷ **recapitulate**

recapitulating v ▷ **recapitulate**

recapitulation n ▷ **recapitulate**

recapitulations n ▷ **recapitulate**

recapped v ▷ **recap**

recapping v ▷ **recap**

recaps v, n ▷ **recap**

recapture v (-res, -ring, -red) experience again

recaptured v ▷ **recapture**

recaptures v ▷ **recapture**

recapturing v ▷ **recapture**

recce (CHIEFLY BRIT) (Slang) v (-s, -ceing, -ced or -ceed) reconnoitre ▶ n (pl -s) reconnaissance

recced v ▷ **recce**

recceed v ▷ **recce**

recceing v ▷ **recce**

recces v, n ▷ **recce**

recede v (-des, -ding, -ded) move to a more distant place

receded v ▷ **recede**

recedes v ▷ **recede**

receding v ▷ **recede**

receipt n (pl -s) written acknowledgment of money or goods received

receipts n ▷ **receipt**

receive v (-ves, -ving, -ved) take, accept, or get

received adj generally accepted ▶ v ▷ **receive**

receiver n (pl -s) part of telephone that is held to the ear

receivers n ▷ **receiver**

receivership n (pl -s) state of being administered by a receiver

receiverships n ▷ **receivership**

receives v ▷ **receive**

receiving v ▷ **receive**

recent adj (-er, -est) having happened lately > **recently** adv

recenter adj ▷ **recent**

recentest adj ▷ **recent**

recently adv ▷ **recent**

receptacle n (pl -s) object used to contain something

receptacles n ▷ **receptacle**

reception n (pl -s) area for receiving guests, clients, etc.

receptionist n (pl -s) person who receives guests, clients, etc.

receptionists n ▷ **receptionist**

receptions n ▷ **reception**

receptive adj willing to accept new ideas, suggestions, etc. > **receptivity** n (pl -ies)

receptivities n ▷ **receptive**

receptivity n ▷ **receptive**

recess n (pl -es) niche or alcove

recessed adj hidden or placed in a recess

recesses n ▷ **recess**

recession n (pl -s) period of economic difficulty when little is being bought or sold

recessions n ▷ **recession**

recessive adj receding

recherché [rish-air-shay] adj refined or elegant

recidivism n (pl -s) habitual relapse into crime > **recidivist** n (pl -s)

recidivisms n ▷ **recidivism**

recidivist n ▷ **recidivism**

recidivists n ▷ **recidivism**

recipe n (pl -s) directions for cooking a dish
  recipes n ▷ **recipe**
recipient n (pl -s) person who receives
  something
  recipients n ▷ **recipient**
reciprocal [ris-**sip**-pro-kl] adj mutual
  > **reciprocally** adv
  reciprocally adv ▷ **reciprocal**
reciprocate v (-tes, -ting, -ted) give or feel in
  return > **reciprocation** n (pl -s) > **reciprocity**
  n (pl -s)
  reciprocated v ▷ **reciprocate**
  reciprocates v ▷ **reciprocate**
  reciprocating v ▷ **reciprocate**
  reciprocation n ▷ **reciprocate**
  reciprocations n ▷ **reciprocate**
  reciprocities n ▷ **reciprocate**
  reciprocity n ▷ **reciprocate**
recital n (pl -s) musical performance by a
  soloist or soloists
  recitals n ▷ **recital**
recitation n (pl -s) recital, usu. from memory,
  of poetry or prose
  recitations n ▷ **recitation**
recitative [ress-it-a-**teev**] n (pl -s) speechlike
  style of singing, used esp. for narrative
  passages in opera
  recitatives n ▷ **recitative**
recite v (-tes, -ting, -ted) repeat (a poem etc.)
  aloud to an audience
  recited v ▷ **recite**
  recites v ▷ **recite**
  reciting v ▷ **recite**
reckless adj heedless of danger > **recklessly**
  adv > **recklessness** n (pl -s)
  recklessly adv ▷ **reckless**
  recklessness n ▷ **reckless**
  recklessnesses n ▷ **reckless**
reckon v (-s, -ing, -ed) consider or think
  > **reckoning** n (pl -s)
  reckoned v ▷ **reckon**
  reckoning v, n ▷ **reckon**
  reckonings n ▷ **reckon**
  reckons v ▷ **reckon**
reclaim v (-s, -ing, -ed) regain possession of
  > **reclamation** n (pl -s)
  reclaimed v ▷ **reclaim**
  reclaiming v ▷ **reclaim**
  reclaims v ▷ **reclaim**
  reclamation n ▷ **reclaim**
  reclamations n ▷ **reclaim**
recline v (-nes, -ning, -ned) rest in a leaning
  position > **reclining** adj
  reclined v ▷ **recline**
  reclines v ▷ **recline**

reclining v, adj ▷ **recline**
recluse n (pl -s) person who avoids other
  people > **reclusive** adj
  recluses n ▷ **recluse**
  reclusive adj ▷ **recluse**
recognition n ▷ **recognize**
  recognitions n ▷ **recognize**
  recognizable adj ▷ **recognize**
recognizance [rik-**og**-nizz-anss] n (pl -s)
  undertaking before a court to observe some
  condition
  recognizances n ▷ **recognizance**
recognize v (-zes, -zing, -zed) identify
  as (a person or thing) already known
  > **recognition** n (pl -s) > **recognizable** adj
  recognized v ▷ **recognize**
  recognizes v ▷ **recognize**
  recognizing v ▷ **recognize**
recoil v (-s, -ing, -ed) jerk or spring back ▶ n (pl
  -s) backward jerk
  recoiled v ▷ **recoil**
  recoiling v ▷ **recoil**
  recoils v, n ▷ **recoil**
recollect v (-s, -ing, -ed) call back to mind,
  remember > **recollection** n (pl -s)
  recollected v ▷ **recollect**
  recollecting v ▷ **recollect**
  recollection n ▷ **recollect**
  recollections n ▷ **recollect**
  recollects v ▷ **recollect**
recommend v (-s, -ing, -ed) advise or counsel
  > **recommendation** n (pl -s)
  recommendation n ▷ **recommend**
  recommendations n ▷ **recommend**
  recommended v ▷ **recommend**
  recommending v ▷ **recommend**
  recommends v ▷ **recommend**
recompense v (-ses, -sing, -sed) pay or reward
  ▶ n (pl -s) compensation
  recompensed v ▷ **recompense**
  recompenses v, n ▷ **recompense**
  recompensing v ▷ **recompense**
reconcile v (-les, -ling, -led) harmonize
  (conflicting beliefs etc.) > **reconciliation**
  n (pl -s)
  reconciled v ▷ **reconcile**
  reconciles v ▷ **reconcile**
  reconciliation n ▷ **reconcile**
  reconciliations n ▷ **reconcile**
  reconciling v ▷ **reconcile**
recondite adj difficult to understand
recondition v (-s, -ing, -ed) restore to good
  condition or working order
  reconditioned v ▷ **recondition**
  reconditioning v ▷ **recondition**

reconditions v ▷ recondition
reconnaissance [rik-kon-iss-anss] n (pl -s) survey for military or engineering purposes
reconnaissances n ▷ reconnaissance
reconnoitre [rek-a-noy-ter] v (-res, -ring, -red) make a reconnaissance of
reconnoitred v ▷ reconnoitre
reconnoitres v ▷ reconnoitre
reconnoitring v ▷ reconnoitre
reconsider v (-s, -ing, -ed) think about again, consider changing
reconsidered v ▷ reconsider
reconsidering v ▷ reconsider
reconsiders v ▷ reconsider
reconstitute v (-tes, -ting, -ted) reorganize > **reconstitution** n (pl -s)
reconstituted v ▷ reconstitute
reconstitutes v ▷ reconstitute
reconstituting v ▷ reconstitute
reconstitution n ▷ reconstitute
reconstitutions n ▷ reconstitute
reconstruct v (-s, -ing, -ed) rebuild > **reconstruction** n (pl -s)
reconstructed v ▷ reconstruct
reconstructing v ▷ reconstruct
reconstruction n ▷ reconstruct
reconstructions n ▷ reconstruct
reconstructs v ▷ reconstruct
record n (pl -s) [rek-ord] document or other thing that preserves information ▶ v (-s, -ing, -ed) [rik-kord] put in writing > **recording** n (pl -s)
recorded v ▷ record
recorder n (pl -s) person or machine that records, esp. a video, cassette, or tape recorder
recorders n ▷ recorder
recording n ▷ record
records n, v ▷ record
recount v (-s, -ing, -ed) tell in detail
recounted v ▷ recount
recounting v ▷ recount
recounts v ▷ recount
recoup [rik-koop] v (-s, -ing, -ed) regain or make good (a loss)
recouped v ▷ recoup
recouping v ▷ recoup
recoups v ▷ recoup
recourse n (pl -s) source of help
recourses n ▷ recourse
recover v (-s, -ing, -ed) become healthy again > **recovery** n (pl -ies) > **recoverable** adj
recoverable adj ▷ recover
recovered v ▷ recover
recoveries n ▷ recover

recovering v ▷ recover
recovers v ▷ recover
recovery v ▷ recover
recreation n (pl -s) agreeable or refreshing occupation, relaxation, or amusement > **recreational** adj
recreational adj ▷ recreation
recreations n ▷ recreation
recrimination n (pl -s) mutual blame > **recriminatory** adj
recriminations n ▷ recrimination
recriminatory adj ▷ recrimination
recruit v (-s, -ing, -ed) enlist (new soldiers, members, etc.) ▶ n (pl -s) newly enlisted soldier > **recruitment** n (pl -s)
recruited v ▷ recruit
recruiting v ▷ recruit
recruitment n ▷ recruit
recruitments n ▷ recruit
recruits v, n ▷ recruit
recta n ▷ rectum
rectangle n (pl -s) oblong four-sided figure with four right angles > **rectangular** adj
rectangles n ▷ rectangle
rectangular adj ▷ rectangle
rectification n ▷ rectify
rectifications n ▷ rectify
rectified v ▷ rectify
rectifier n ▷ rectify
rectifiers n ▷ rectify
rectifies v ▷ rectify
rectify v (-ies, -ying, -ied) put right, correct (CHEM) (ELECTRICITY) > **rectification** n (pl -s)
rectifying v ▷ rectify
rectilinear adj in a straight line
rectitude n (pl -s) moral correctness
rectitudes n ▷ rectitude
recto n (pl -os) right-hand page of a book
rector n (pl -s) clergyman in charge of a parish
rectories n ▷ rectory
rectors n ▷ rector
rectory n (pl -s) rector's house
rectos n ▷ recto
rectum n (pl -tums, -ta) final section of the large intestine
rectums n ▷ rectum
recumbent adj lying down
recuperate v (-tes, -ting, -ted) recover from illness > **recuperation** n (pl -s) > **recuperative** adj
recuperated v ▷ recuperate
recuperates v ▷ recuperate
recuperating v ▷ recuperate
recuperation n ▷ recuperate
recuperations n ▷ recuperate

recuperative *adj* ▷ **recuperate**
recur *v* (**-s, -rring, -rred**) happen again
> **recurrence** *n* (*pl* **-s**) repetition > **recurrent**
adj
recurred *v* ▷ **recur**
recurrence *n* ▷ **recur**
recurrences *n* ▷ **recur**
recurrent *adj* ▷ **recur**
recurring *v* ▷ **recur**
recurs *v* ▷ **recur**
recycle *v* (**-les, -ling, -led**) reprocess (used
materials) for further use > **recyclable** *adj*
recyclable *adj* ▷ **recycle**
recycled *v* ▷ **recycle**
recycles *v* ▷ **recycle**
recycling *v* ▷ **recycle**
red *adj* (**-dder, -ddest**) of a colour varying from
crimson to orange and seen in blood, fire, etc.
▶ *n* (*pl* **-s**) red colour > **reddish** *adj* > **redness**
n (*pl* **-es**)
redbrick *adj* (of a university in Britain)
founded in the late 19th or early 20th century
redcoat *n* (*pl* **-s**) (HIST) British soldier
redcoats *n* ▷ **redcoat**
redcurrant *n* (*pl* **-s**) small round edible red
berry
redcurrants *n* ▷ **redcurrant**
redden *v* (**-s, -ing, -ed**) make or become red
reddened *v* ▷ **redden**
reddening *v* ▷ **redden**
reddens *v* ▷ **redden**
redder *adj* ▷ **red**
reddest *adj* ▷ **red**
reddish *adj* ▷ **red**
redeem *v* (**-s, -ing, -ed**) make up for
> **redeemable** *adj* > **redemption** *n* (*pl* **-s**)
> **redemptive** *adj*
redeemable *adj* ▷ **reddem**
redeemed *v* ▷ **redeem**
redeeming *v* ▷ **redeem**
redeems *v* ▷ **redeem**
redemption *adj* ▷ **reddem**
redemptions *adj* ▷ **reddem**
redemptive *adj* ▷ **reddem**
redeploy *v* (**-s, -ing, -ed**) assign to a new
position or task > **redeployment** *n* (*pl* **-s**)
redeployed *v* ▷ **redeploy**
redeploying *v* ▷ **redeploy**
redeployment *n* ▷ **redeploy**
redeployment *n* ▷ **redeploy**
redeploys *v* ▷ **redeploy**
redevelop *v* (**-s, -ing, -ed**) rebuild or renovate
(an area or building) > **redevelopment** *n* (*pl* **-s**)
redeveloped *v* ▷ **redevelop**
redeveloping *v* ▷ **redevelop**

redevelopment *n* ▷ **redevelop**
redevelopments *n* ▷ **redevelop**
redevelops *v* ▷ **redevelop**
redness *n* ▷ **red**
redolent *adj* reminiscent (of)
redouble *v* (**-les, -ling, -led**) increase, multiply,
or intensify
redoubled *v* ▷ **redouble**
redoubles *v* ▷ **redouble**
redoubling *v* ▷ **redouble**
redoubt *n* (*pl* **-s**) small fort defending a hilltop
or pass
redoubtable *adj* formidable
redoubts *n* ▷ **redoubt**
redound *v* (**-s, -ing, -ed**) cause advantage or
disadvantage (to)
redounded *v* ▷ **redound**
redounding *v* ▷ **redound**
redounds *v* ▷ **redound**
redox *n* (*pl* **-es**) chemical reaction in which
one substance is reduced and the other is
oxidized
redoxes *n* ▷ **redox**
redress *v* (**-es, -ing, -ed**) make amends for ▶ *n*
(*pl* **-es**) compensation or amends
redressed *v* ▷ **redress**
redresses *v, n* ▷ **redress**
redressing *v* ▷ **redress**
reds *n* ▷ **red**
reduce *v* (**-ces, -cing, -ced**) bring down, lower
> **reducible** *adj* > **reduction** *n* (*pl* **-s**)
reduced *v* ▷ **reduce**
reduces *v* ▷ **reduce**
reducible *adj* ▷ **reduce**
reducing *v* ▷ **reduce**
reduction *n* ▷ **reduce**
reductions *n* ▷ **reduce**
redundancies *n* ▷ **redundant**
redundancy *n* ▷ **redundant**
redundant *adj* (of a worker) no longer needed
> **redundancy** *n* (*pl* **-s**)
reed *n* (*pl* **-s**) tall grass that grows in swamps
and shallow water
reedier *adj* ▷ **reedy**
reediest *n* ▷ **reedy**
reeds *n* ▷ **reed**
reedy (**-dier, -diest**) *adj* harsh and thin in tone
reef *n* (*pl* **-s**) ridge of rock or coral near the
surface of the sea
reef^2 *n* (*pl* **-s**) part of a sail which can be rolled
up to reduce its area ▶ *v* (**-s, -ing, -ed**) take
in a reef of
reefed *v* ▷ **reef**^{2}
reefer *n* (*pl* **-s**) short thick jacket worn esp.
by sailors

reefers n ▷ reefer
reefing v ▷ reef²
reefs n ▷ reef¹, ² ▶ v ▷ reef²
reek v (-s, -ing, -ed) smell strongly ▶ n (pl -s) strong unpleasant smell
reeked v ▷ reek
reeking v ▷ reek
reeks v, n ▷ reek
reel¹ n (pl -s) cylindrical object on which film, tape, thread, or wire is wound
reel² v (-s, -ing, -ed) stagger, sway, or whirl
reel³ n (pl -s) lively Scottish dance
reeled v ▷ reel²
reeling v ▷ reel²
reels n ▷ reel¹, ³ ▶ v ▷ reel²
ref n (pl -s) (*Informal*) referee in sport
refectories n ▷ refectory
refectory n (pl -ies) room for meals in a college etc.
refer v (-s, -rring, -rred) (foll. by *to*) allude (to) > **referral** n (pl -s)
referee n (pl -s) umpire in sports, esp. soccer or boxing ▶ v (-s, -ing, -eed) act as referee of
refereed v ▷ referee
refereeing v ▷ referee
referees n, v ▷ referee
reference n (pl -s) act of referring
references n ▷ reference
referenda n ▷ referendum
referendum n (pl -dums, -da) direct vote of the electorate on an important question
referendums n ▷ referendum
referral n ▷ refer
referrals n ▷ refer
referred v ▷ refer
referring v ▷ refer
refers v ▷ refer
refill v (-s, -ing, -ed) fill again ▶ n (pl -s) second or subsequent filling
refilled v ▷ refill
refilling v ▷ refill
refills v, n ▷ refill
refine v (-nes, -ning, -ned) purify
refined adj cultured or polite ▶ v ▷ refine
refinement n (pl -s) improvement or elaboration
refinements n ▷ refinement
refineries n ▷ refinery
refinery n (pl -ies) place where sugar, oil, etc. is refined
refines v ▷ refine
refining v ▷ refine
reflate v ▷ reflation
reflated v ▷ reflation
reflates v ▷ reflation

reflating v ▷ reflation
reflation n (pl -s) increase in the supply of money and credit designed to encourage economic activity > **reflate** v (-tes, -ting, -ted) > **reflationary** adj
reflationary adj ▷ reflation
reflations n ▷ reflation
reflect v (-s, -ing, -ed) throw back, esp. rays of light, heat, etc.
reflected v ▷ reflect
reflecting v ▷ reflect
reflection n (pl -s) act of reflecting
reflections n ▷ reflect
reflective adj quiet, contemplative
reflector n (pl -s) polished surface for reflecting light etc.
reflectors n ▷ reflector
reflects v ▷ reflect
reflex n (pl -es) involuntary response to a stimulus or situation ▶ adj (of a muscular action) involuntary
reflexes n ▷ reflex
reflexive adj (GRAMMAR) denoting a verb whose subject is the same as its object
reflexologies n ▷ reflexology
reflexology n (pl -ies) foot massage as a therapy in alternative medicine
reform n (pl -s) improvement ▶ v (-s, -ing, -ed) improve > **reformer** n (pl -s)
reformation n (pl -s) act or instance of something being reformed
reformations n ▷ reformation
reformatories n ▷ reformatory
reformatory n (pl -s) (formerly) institution for reforming young offenders
reformed v ▷ reform
reformer n ▷ reform
reformers n ▷ reform
reforming v ▷ reform
reforms n, v ▷ reform
refract v (-s, -ing, -ed) change the course of (light etc.) passing from one medium to another > **refraction** n (pl -s) > **refractive** adj > **refractor** n (pl -s)
refracted v ▷ refract
refracting v ▷ refract
refraction n ▷ refract
refractions n ▷ refract
refractive adj ▷ refract
refractor n ▷ refract
refractors n ▷ refract
refractory adj unmanageable or rebellious
refracts v ▷ refract
refrain¹ v (-s, -ing, -ed) keep oneself from doing
refrain² n (pl -s) frequently repeated part of

a song
refrained v ▷ refrain¹
refraining v ▷ refrain¹
refrains n ▷ refrain¹, ² ▶ v ▷ refrain²
refresh v (-es, -ing, -ed) revive or reinvigorate,
as through food, drink, or rest > **refresher**
n (pl -s)
refreshed v ▷ refresh
refresher n ▷ refresh
refreshers n ▷ refresh
refreshes v ▷ refresh
refreshing adj having a reviving effect ▶ v
▷ refresh
refreshment n (pl -s) something that
refreshes, esp. food or drink
refreshments n ▷ refreshment
refrigerate v (-tes, -ting, -ted) cool or freeze in
order to preserve > **refrigeration** n (pl -s)
refrigerated v ▷ refrigerate
refrigerates v ▷ refrigerate
refrigerating v ▷ refrigerate
refrigeration n ▷ refrigerate
refrigerations n ▷ refrigerate
refrigerator n (pl -s) > **fridge**
refrigerators n ▷ refrigerator
refs n ▷ ref
refuge n (pl -s) (source of) shelter or protection
refugee n (pl -s) person who seeks refuge, esp.
in a foreign country
refugees n ▷ refugee
refuges n ▷ refuge
refulgent adj shining, radiant
refund v (-s, -ing, -ed) pay back ▶ n (pl -s) return
of money
refunded v ▷ refund
refunding v ▷ refund
refunds v, n ▷ refund
refurbish v (-es, -ing, -ed) renovate and
brighten up
refurbished v ▷ refurbish
refurbishes v ▷ refurbish
refurbishing v ▷ refurbish
refusal n (pl -s) denial of anything demanded
or offered
refusals n ▷ refusal
refuse¹ v (-ses, -sing, -sed) decline, deny, or
reject
refuse² n (pl -s) rubbish or useless matter
refused v ▷ refuse¹
refuses v ▷ refuse¹ ▶ n ▷ refuse²
refusing v ▷ refuse¹
refute v (-tes, -ting, -ted) disprove > **refutation**
n (pl -s)
refutation n ▷ refute
refutations n ▷ refute

refuted v ▷ refute
refutes v ▷ refute
refuting v ▷ refute
regain v (-s, -ing, -ed) get back or recover
regained v ▷ regain
regaining v ▷ regain
regains v ▷ regain
regal adj of or like a king or queen > **regally** adv
regalia pl n ceremonial emblems of royalty or
high office
regale v (-les, -ling, -led) entertain (someone)
with stories etc.
regaled v ▷ regale
regales v ▷ regale
regaling v ▷ regale
regally adv ▷ regal
regard v (-s, -ing, -ed) consider ▶ n (pl -s)
respect or esteem ▶ pl expression of goodwill
regarded v ▷ regard
regarding in respect of, concerning v ▷ regard
regardless adj heedless ▶ adv in spite of
everything
regards v, n ▷ regard
regatta n (pl -s) meeting for yacht or boat races
regattas n ▷ regatta
regenerate v (-tes, -ting, -ted) (cause to)
undergo spiritual, moral, or physical renewal
> **regeneration** n (pl -s) > **regenerative** adj
regenerated v ▷ regenerate
regenerates v ▷ regenerate
regenerating v ▷ regenerate
regeneration n ▷ regenerate
regenerations n ▷ regenerate
regenerative adj ▷ regenerate
regencies n ▷ regency
regency n (pl -ies) status or period of office of
a regent
regent n (pl -s) ruler of a kingdom during the
absence, childhood, or illness of its monarch
▶ adj ruling as a regent
regents n ▷ regent
reggae n (pl -s) style of Jamaican popular
music with a strong beat
reggaes n ▷ reggae
regicide n (pl -s) killing of a king
regicides n ▷ regicide
regime [ray-zheem] n (pl -s) system of
government
regimen n (pl -s) prescribed system of diet etc.
regimens n ▷ regimen
regiment n (pl -s) organized body of troops
as a unit of the army > **regimental** adj
> **regimentation** n (pl -s)
regimental adj ▷ regiment
regimentation n ▷ regiment

regimentations n ▷ regiment
regimented adj very strictly controlled
regiments n ▷ regiment
regimes n ▷ regime
region n (pl -s) administrative division of a country > **regional** adj
regional adj ▷ region
regions n ▷ region
register n (pl -s) (book containing) an official list or record of things ▶ v (-s, -ing, -ed) enter in a register or set down in writing > **registration** n (pl -s)
registered v ▷ register
registering v ▷ register
registers n, v ▷ register
registrar n (pl -s) keeper of official records
registrars n ▷ registrar
registration n ▷ register
registrations n ▷ registers
regress v (-es, -ing, -ed) revert to a former worse condition
regressed v ▷ regress
regresses v ▷ regress
regressing v ▷ regress
regression n (pl -s) act of regressing (PSYCHOL) > **regressive** adj
regressions n ▷ regression
regressive adj ▷ regression
regret v (-s, -tting, -tted) feel sorry about ▶ n (pl -s) feeling of repentance, guilt, or sorrow > **regretful** adj > **regrettable** adj
regretful adj ▷ regret
regrets v ▷ regret
regrettable adj ▷ regret
regretted v ▷ regret
regretting v ▷ regret
regular adj normal, customary, or usual ▶ n (pl -s) regular soldier > **regularity** n (pl -s) > **regularize** v (-zes, -zing, -zed) > **regularly** adv
regularities n ▷ regular
regularity n ▷ regular
regularize v ▷ regular
regularized v ▷ regular
regularizes v ▷ regular
regularizing v ▷ regular
regularly adv ▷ regular
regulars n ▷ regular
regulate v (-tes, -ting, -ted) control, esp. by rules
regulated v ▷ regulate
regulates v ▷ regulate
regulating v ▷ regulate
regulation n (pl -s) rule
regulations n ▷ regulation

regulator n (pl -s) device that automatically controls pressure, temperature, etc.
regulators n ▷ regulator
regurgitate v (-tes, -ting, -ted) vomit > **regurgitation** n (pl -s)
regurgitated v ▷ regurgitate
regurgitates v ▷ regurgitate
regurgitating v ▷ regurgitate
regurgitation n ▷ regurgitate
regurgitations n ▷ regurgitate
rehabilitate v (-tes, -ting, -ted) help (a person) to readjust to society after illness, imprisonment, etc. > **rehabilitation** n (pl -s)
rehabilitated v ▷ rehabilitate
rehabilitates v ▷ rehabilitate
rehabilitating v ▷ rehabilitate
rehabilitation n ▷ rehabilitate
rehabilitations n ▷ rehabilitate
rehash v (-es, -ing, -ed) rework or reuse ▶ n (pl -es) old ideas presented in a new form
rehashed v ▷ rehash
rehashes v, n ▷ rehash
rehashing v ▷ rehash
rehearse v (-ses, -sing, -sed) practise (a play, concert, etc.) > **rehearsal** n (pl -s)
rehearsal n ▷ rehearse
rehearsals n ▷ rehearse
rehearsed v ▷ rehearse
rehearses v ▷ rehearse
rehearsing v ▷ rehearse
rehouse v (-ses, -sing, -sed) provide with a new (and better) home
rehoused v ▷ rehouse
rehouses v ▷ rehouse
rehousing v ▷ rehouse
reign n (pl -s) period of a sovereign's rule ▶ v (-s, -ing, -ed) rule (a country)
reigned v ▷ reign
reigning v ▷ reign
reigns n, v ▷ reign
reimburse v (-ses, -sing, -sed) refund, pay back > **reimbursement** n (pl -s)
reimbursed v ▷ reimburse
reimbursement n ▷ reimburse
reimbursements n ▷ reimburse
reimburses v ▷ reimburse
reimbursing v ▷ reimburse
rein v (-s, -ing, -ed) check or manage with reins
reincarnation n (pl -s) rebirth of a soul in successive bodies > **reincarnate** v (-tes, -ting, -ted)
reincarnate v ▷ reincarnation
reincarnated v ▷ reincarnation
reincarnates v ▷ reincarnation
reincarnating v ▷ reincarnation

reincarnations *n* ▷ reincarnation

reindeer *n* (*pl* **-deer, -deers**) deer of arctic regions with large branched antlers

reindeers *n* ▷ reindeer

reined *v* ▷ rein

reining *v* ▷ rein

reinforce *v* (**-ces, -cing, -ced**) strengthen with new support, material, or force ▷ **reinforcement** *n* (*pl* **-s**)

reinforced *v* ▷ reinforce

reinforcement *n* ▷ reinforce

reinforcements *n* ▷ reinforce

reinforces *v* ▷ reinforce

reinforcing *v* ▷ reinforce

reins *pl n* narrow straps attached to a bit to guide a horse ▶ *v* ▷ rein

reinstate *v* (**-tes, -ting, -ted**) restore to a former position ▷ **reinstatement** *n* (*pl* **-s**)

reinstated *v* ▷ reinstate

reinstatement *n* ▷ reinstate

reinstatements *n* ▷ reinstate

reinstates *v* ▷ reinstate

reinstating *v* ▷ reinstate

reiterate *v* (**-tes, -ting, -ted**) repeat again and again ▷ **reiteration** *n* (*pl* **-s**)

reiterated *v* ▷ reiterate

reiterates *v* ▷ reiterate

reiterating *v* ▷ reiterate

reiteration *n* ▷ reiterate

reiterations *n* ▷ reiterate

reject *v* (**-s, -ing, -ed**) refuse to accept or believe ▶ *n* (*pl* **-s**) person or thing rejected as not up to standard ▷ **rejection** *n* (*pl* **-s**)

rejected *v* ▷ reject

rejecting *v* ▷ reject

rejection *n* ▷ reject

rejections *n* ▷ reject

rejects *v*, *n* ▷ reject

rejig *v* (**-s, -gging, -gged**) re-equip (a factory or plant)

rejigged *v* ▷ rejig

rejigging *v* ▷ rejig

rejigs *v* ▷ rejig

rejoice *v* (**-ces, -cing, -ced**) feel or express great happiness

rejoiced *v* ▷ rejoice

rejoices *v* ▷ rejoice

rejoicing *v* ▷ rejoice

rejoin¹ *v* (**-s, -ing, -ed**) join again

rejoin² *v* (**-s, -ing, -ed**) reply

rejoinder (*pl* **-s**) *n* answer, retort

rejoinders *n* ▷ rejoinder

rejoined *v* ▷ rejoin¹,²

rejoining *v* ▷ rejoin¹,²

rejoins *v* ▷ rejoin¹,²

rejuvenate *v* (**-tes, -ting, -ted**) restore youth or vitality to ▷ **rejuvenation** *n* (*pl* **-s**)

rejuvenated *v* ▷ rejuvenate

rejuvenates *v* ▷ rejuvenate

rejuvenating *v* ▷ rejuvenate

rejuvenation *n* ▷ rejuvenate

rejuvenations *n* ▷ rejuvenate

relapse *v* (**-ses, -sing, -sed**) fall back into bad habits, illness, etc. ▶ *n* (*pl* **-s**) return of bad habits, illness, etc.

relapsed *v* ▷ relapse

relapses *v*, *n* ▷ relapse

relapsing *v* ▷ relapse

relate *v* (**-tes, -ting, -ted**) establish a relation between ▷ **related** *adj*

related *adj*, *v* ▷ relate

relates *v* ▷ relate

relating *v* ▷ relate

relation *n* (*pl* **-s**) connection between things ▶ *pl* social or political dealings

relations *n* ▷ relation

relationship *n* (*pl* **-s**) dealings and feelings between people or countries

relationships *n* ▷ relationship

relative *adj* dependent on relation to something else, not absolute ▶ *n* (*pl* **-s**) person connected by blood or marriage ▷ **relatively** *adv*

relatively *adv* ▷ relative

relatives *n* ▷ relative

relativities *n* ▷ relativity

relativity *n* (*pl* **-ies**) subject of two theories of Albert Einstein, dealing with relationships of space, time, and motion, and acceleration and gravity

relax *v* (**-es, -ing, -ed**) make or become looser, less tense, or less rigid ▷ **relaxing** *adj* ▷ **relaxation** *n* (*pl* **-s**)

relaxation *n* ▷ relax

relaxations *n* ▷ relax

relaxed *v* ▷ relax

relaxes *v* ▷ relax

relaxing *v*, *adj* ▷ relax

relay *n* (*pl* **-s**) fresh set of people or animals relieving others ▶ *v* (**-s, -ing, -ed**) pass on (a message)

relayed *v* ▷ relay

relaying *v* ▷ relay

relays *n*, *v* ▷ relay

release *v* (**-ses, -sing, -sed**) set free ▶ *n* (*pl* **-s**) setting free

released *v* ▷ release

releases *v*, *n* ▷ release

releasing *v* ▷ release

relegate *v* (**-tes, -ting, -ted**) put in a less

important position > **relegation** n (pl -s)

relegated v ▷ relegate

relegates v ▷ relegate

relegating v ▷ relegate

relegation n ▷ relegate

relegations n ▷ relegate

relent v (-s, -ing, -ed) give up a harsh intention, become less severe

relented v ▷ relent

relenting v ▷ relent

relentless adj unremitting

relents v ▷ relent

relevance n ▷ relevant

relevances n ▷ relevant

relevant adj to do with the matter in hand

> **relevance** n (pl -s)

reliabilities n ▷ reliable

reliability n ▷ reliable

reliable adj able to be trusted, dependable

> **reliably** adv > **reliability** n (pl -ies)

reliably adv ▷ reliable

reliance n (pl -s) dependence, confidence, or trust > **reliant** adj

reliances n ▷ reliance

reliant adj ▷ reliance

relic n (pl -s) something that has survived from the past ▶ pl remains or traces

relics n ▷ relic

relict n (pl -s) (Obs) widow

relicts n ▷ relict

relied v ▷ rely

relief n (pl -s) gladness at the end or removal of pain, distress, etc.

reliefs n ▷ relief

relies v ▷ rely

relieve v (-ves, -ving, -ved) bring relief to

relieved v ▷ relieve

relieves v ▷ relieve

relieving v ▷ relieve

religion n (pl -s) system of belief in and worship of a supernatural power or god

religious adj of religion > **religiously** adv

religiously adv ▷ religious

religions n ▷ religion

relinquish v (-es, -ing, -ed) give up or abandon

relinquished v ▷ relinquish

relinquishes v ▷ relinquish

relinquishing v ▷ relinquish

reliquaries n ▷ reliquary

reliquary n (pl -ies) case or shrine for holy relics

relish v (-es, -ing, -ed) enjoy, like very much ▶ n (pl -es) liking or enjoyment

relished v ▷ relish

relishes v, n ▷ relish

relishing v ▷ relish

relocate v (-tes, -ting, -ted) move to a new place to live or work > **relocation** n (pl -s)

relocated v ▷ relocate

relocates v ▷ relocate

relocating v ▷ relocate

relocation n ▷ relocate

relocations n ▷ relocate

reluctance n ▷ reluctant

reluctances n ▷ reluctant

reluctant adj unwilling or disinclined

> **reluctantly** adv > **reluctance** n (pl -s)

reluctantly adv ▷ reluctant

rely v (-ies, -ying, -ied) depend (on)

relying v ▷ rely

remain v (-s, -ing, -ed) continue

remainder n (pl -s) part which is left ▶ v (-s, -ing, -ed) offer (copies of a poorly selling book) at reduced prices

remaindered v ▷ remainders

remaindering v ▷ remainders

remainders n, v ▷ remainders

remained v ▷ remain

remaining v ▷ remain

remains pl n relics, esp. of ancient buildings

▶ v ▷ remain

remand v (-s, -ing, -ed) send back into custody or put on bail before trial

remanded v ▷ remand

remanding v ▷ remand

remands v ▷ remand

remark v (-s, -ing, -ed) make a casual comment (on) ▶ n (pl -s) observation or comment

remarkable adj worthy of note or attention

> **remarkably** adv

remarkably adv ▷ remarkable

remarked v ▷ remark

remarking v ▷ remark

remarks v, n ▷ remark

remedial adj intended to correct a specific disability, handicap, etc.

remedied v ▷ remedy

remedies n, v ▷ remedy

remedy n (pl -ies) means of curing pain or disease ▶ v (-ies, -ying, -ied) put right

remedying v ▷ remedy

remember v (-s, -ing, -ed) retain in or recall to one's memory

remembered v ▷ remember

remembering v ▷ remember

remembers v ▷ remember

remembrance n (pl -s) memory

remembrances n ▷ remembrance

remind v (-s, -ing, -ed) cause to remember

reminded v ▷ remind

reminder n (pl -s) something that recalls the

past
reminders n ▷ reminder
reminding v ▷ remind
reminds v ▷ remind
reminisce v (-ces, -cing, -ced) talk or write of past times, experiences, etc.
reminisced v ▷ reminisce
reminiscence n (pl -s) remembering ▶ pl memoirs
reminiscences n ▷ reminiscence
reminiscent adj reminding or suggestive (of)
reminisces v ▷ reminisce
reminiscing v ▷ reminisce
remiss adj negligent or careless
remission n (pl -s) reduction in the length of a prison term
remissions n ▷ remission
remit v (-s, -tting, -tted) send (money) for goods, services, etc., esp. by post ▶ n (pl -s) [ree-mitt] area of competence or authority
remits v, n ▷ remit
remittance n (pl -s) money sent as payment
remittances n ▷ remittance
remitted v ▷ remit
remitting v ▷ remit
remnant n (pl -s) small piece, esp. of fabric, left over
remnants n ▷ remnant
remonstrance n ▷ remonstrate
remonstrances n ▷ remonstrate
remonstrate v (-tes, -ting, -ted) argue in protest > **remonstrance** n (pl -s)
remonstrated v ▷ remonstrate
remonstrates v ▷ remonstrate
remonstrating v ▷ remonstrate
remorse n (pl -s) feeling of sorrow and regret for something one did > **remorseful** adj
remorseful adj ▷ remorse
remorseless adj pitiless > **remorselessly** adv
remorselessly adv ▷ remorseless
remorses n ▷ remorse
remote adj (-er, -est) far away, distant > **remotely** adv
remoter adj ▷ remote
remotest adj ▷ remote
remotely adv ▷ remote
remould v (-s, -ing, -ed) (BRIT) renovate (a worn tyre) ▶ n (pl -s) (BRIT) renovated tyre
remoulded v ▷ remould
remoulding v ▷ remould
remoulds v, n ▷ remould
remove v (-ves, -ving, -ved) take away or off ▶ n (pl -s) degree of difference > **removable** adj
removable adj ▷ remove
removal n (pl -s) removing, esp. changing

residence
removals n ▷ removal
removed v ▷ remove
removes v, n ▷ remove
removing v ▷ remove
remunerate v (-tes, -ting, -ted) reward or pay > **remunerative** adj
remunerated v ▷ remunerate
remunerates v ▷ remunerate
remunerating v ▷ remunerate
remuneration n (pl -s) reward or payment
remunerations n ▷ remuneration
remunerative adj ▷ remuneration
renaissance n (pl -s) revival or rebirth
renaissances n ▷ renaissance
renal [ree-nal] adj of the kidneys
renascent adj becoming active or vigorous again
rend v (-s, -ing, rent) tear or wrench apart
render v (-s, -ing, -ed) cause to become
rendered v ▷ render
rendering v ▷ render
renders v ▷ render
rendezvous [ron-day-voo] n (pl -vous) appointment ▶ v (-vous, -vousing, -voused) meet as arranged
rendezvoused v ▷ rendezvous
rendezvousing v ▷ rendezvous
rending v ▷ rend
rendition n (pl -s) performance
renditions n ▷ rendition
rends v ▷ rend
renegade n (pl -s) person who deserts a cause
renegades n ▷ renegade
renege [rin-nayg] v (-ges, -ging, -ged) go back (on a promise etc.)
reneged v ▷ renege
reneges v ▷ renege
reneging v ▷ renege
renew v (-s, -ing, -ed) begin again > **renewable** adj ▷ renewal n (pl -s)
renewable adj ▷ renew
renewal n ▷ renew
renewals n ▷ renew
renewed v ▷ renew
renewing v ▷ renew
renews v ▷ renew
rennet n (pl -s) substance for curdling milk to make cheese
rennets n ▷ rennet
renounce v (-ces, -cing, -ced) give up (a belief, habit, etc.) voluntarily > **renunciation** n (pl -s)
renounced v ▷ renounce
renounces v ▷ renounce
renouncing v ▷ renounce

renovate v (-tes, -ting, -ted) restore to good condition ▷ **renovation** n (pl -s)
renovated v ▷ renovate
renovates v ▷ renovate
renovating v ▷ renovate
renovation n ▷ renovate
renovations n ▷ renovate
renown n (pl -s) widespread good reputation
renowned adj famous
renowns n ▷ renown
rent¹ v (-s, -ing, -ed) give or have use of in return for regular payments ▶ n (pl -s) regular payment for use of land, a building, machine, etc.
rent² n (pl -s) tear or fissure ▶ v ▷ rend
rental n (pl -s) sum payable as rent
rentals n ▷ rental
rented v ▷ rent¹
renting v ▷ rent¹
rents v ▷ rent¹ ▶ n ▷ rent²
renunciation n ▷ renounce
renunciations n ▷ renounce
reorganize v (-zes, -zing, -zed) organize in a new and more efficient way ▷ **reorganization** n (pl -s)
reorganization n ▷ reorganize
reorganizations n ▷ reorganize
reorganized v ▷ reorganize
reorganizes v ▷ reorganize
reorganizing v ▷ reorganize
rep¹ n (pl -s) repertory company
rep² n (pl -s) ▷ representative
repair¹ v (-s, -ing, -ed) restore to good condition, mend ▶ n (pl -s) act of repairing
repair² v (-s, -ing, -ed) go (to)
repaired v ▷ repair¹, ²
repairing v ▷ repair¹, ²
repairs v ▷ repair¹, ² ▶ n ▷ repair¹
reparation n (pl -s) something done or given as compensation
reparations n ▷ reparation
repartee n (pl -s) interchange of witty retorts
repartees n ▷ repartee
repast n (pl -s) meal
repasts n ▷ repast
repatriate v (-tes, -ting, -ted) send (someone) back to his or her own country ▷ **repatriation** n (pl -s)
repatriated v ▷ repatriate
repatriates v ▷ repatriate
repatriating v ▷ repatriate
repatriation n ▷ repatriate
repatriations n ▷ repatriate
repay v (-s, -ing, -paid) pay back, refund ▷ **repayable** adj ▷ **repayment** n (pl -s)

repayable adj ▷ repay
repaying v ▷ repay
repayment n ▷ repay
repayments n ▷ repay
repays v ▷ repay
repeal v (-s, -ing, -ed) cancel (a law) officially ▶ n (pl -s) act of repealing
repealed v ▷ repeal
repealing v ▷ repeal
repeals v, n ▷ repeal
repeat v (-s, -ing, -ed) say or do again ▶ n (pl -s) act or instance of repeating ▷ **repeatedly** adv
repeated v ▷ repeat
repeatedly adv ▷ repeat
repeater n (pl -s) firearm that may be discharged many times without reloading
repeaters n ▷ repeater
repeating v ▷ repeat
repeats v, n ▷ repeat
repel v (-s, -lling, -lled) be disgusting to
repelled v ▷ repel
repellent adj distasteful ▶ n (pl -s) something that repels, esp. a chemical to repel insects
repellents n ▷ repellent
repelling v ▷ repel
repels v ▷ repel
repent v (-s, -ing, -ed) feel regret for (a deed or omission) ▷ **repentance** n (pl -s) ▷ **repentant** adj
repentance n ▷ repent
repentances n ▷ repent
repentant adj ▷ repent
repented v ▷ repent
repenting v ▷ repent
repents v ▷ repent
repercussions pl n indirect effects, often unpleasant
repertoire n (pl -s) stock of plays, songs, etc. that a player or company can give
repertoires n ▷ repertoire
repertories n ▷ repertory
repertory n (pl -ies) repertoire
repetition n (pl -s) act of repeating
repetitions n ▷ repetition
repetitious adj ▷ repetitive
repetitive, repetitious adj full of repetition
rephrase v (-ses, -sing, -sed) express in different words
rephrased v ▷ rephrase
rephrases v ▷ rephrase
rephrasing v ▷ rephrase
repine v (-nes, -ning, -ned) fret or complain
repined v ▷ repine
repines v ▷ repine
repining v ▷ repine

replace v (-ces, -cing, -ced) substitute for
> **replacement** n (pl -s)
replaced v ▷ replace
replacement n ▷ replace
replacements n ▷ replace
replaces v ▷ replace
replacing v ▷ replace
replay n (pl -s) immediate reshowing on TV of an incident in sport, esp. in slow motion ▶ v (-s, -ing, -ed) play (a match, recording, etc.) again
replayed v ▷ replay
replaying v ▷ replay
replays n, v ▷ replay
replenish v (-es, -ing, -ed) fill up again, resupply > **replenishment** n (pl -s)
replenished v ▷ replenish
replenishes v ▷ replenish
replenishing v ▷ replenish
replenishment n ▷ replenish
replenishments n ▷ replenish
replete adj filled or gorged
replica n (pl -s) exact copy
replicas n ▷ replica
replicate v (-s, -ing, -ed) make or be a copy of
replicated v ▷ replicate
replicates v ▷ replicate
replicating v ▷ replicate
replied v ▷ reply
replies v, n ▷ reply
reply v (-ies, -ying, -ied) answer or respond ▶ n (pl -ies) answer or response
replying v ▷ reply
report v (-s, -ing, -ed) give an account of ▶ n (pl -s) account or statement
reported v ▷ report
reportedly adv according to rumour
reporter n (pl -s) person who gathers news for a newspaper, TV, etc.
reporters n ▷ reporter
reporting v ▷ report
reports v, n ▷ report
repose n (pl -s) peace ▶ v (-ses, -sing, -sed) lie or lay at rest
reposed v ▷ repose
reposes n, v ▷ repose
reposing v ▷ repose
repositories n ▷ repository
repository n (pl -ies) place where valuables are deposited for safekeeping, store
repossess v (-es, -ing, -ed) (of a lender) take back property from a customer who is behind with payments > **repossession** n (pl -s)
repossessed v ▷ repossess
repossesses v ▷ repossess

repossessing v ▷ repossess
repossession n ▷ repossess
repossessions n ▷ repossess
reprehensible adj open to criticism, unworthy
represent v (-s, -ing, -ed) act as a delegate or substitute for > **representation** n (pl -s)
representation n ▷ represent
representations n ▷ represent
representative n (pl -s) person chosen to stand for a group ▶ adj typical
representatives n ▷ representative
represented v ▷ represent
representing v ▷ represent
represents v ▷ represent
repress v (-es, -ing, -ed) keep (feelings) in check > **repression** n (pl -s) > **repressive** adj
repressed v ▷ repress
represses v ▷ repress
repressing v ▷ repress
repression n ▷ repress
repressions n ▷ repress
repressive adj ▷ repress
reprieve v (-ves, -ving, -ved) postpone the execution of (a condemned person) ▶ n (pl -s) (document granting) postponement or cancellation of a punishment
reprieved v ▷ reprieve
reprieves v, n ▷ reprieve
reprieving v ▷ reprieve
reprimand v (-s, -ing, -ed) blame (someone) officially for a fault ▶ n (pl -s) official blame
reprimanded v ▷ reprimand
reprimanding v ▷ reprimand
reprimands v, n ▷ reprimand
reprint v (-s, -ing, -ed) print further copies of (a book) ▶ n (pl -s) reprinted copy
reprinted v ▷ reprint
reprinting v ▷ reprint
reprints v, n ▷ reprint
reprisal n (pl -s) retaliation
reprisals n ▷ reprisal
reproach n, v (-es, -ing, -ed) blame, rebuke > **reproachful** adj > **reproachfully** adv
reproached v ▷ reproach
reproaches v ▷ reproach
reproachful adj ▷ reproach
reproachfully adv ▷ reproach
reproaching v ▷ reproach
reprobate adj, n (pl -s) depraved or disreputable (person)
reprobates n ▷ reprobate
reproduce v (-ces, -cing, -ced) produce a copy of > **reproducible** adj
reproduced v ▷ reproduce

reproduces v ▷ reproduce

reproducible adj ▷ reproduce

reproducing v ▷ reproduce

reproduction n (pl -s) process of reproducing > reproductive adj

reproductions n ▷ reproduction

reproductive adj ▷ reproduction

reproof n (pl -s) severe blaming of someone for a fault

reproofs n ▷ reproof

reprove v (-ves, -ving, -ved) speak severely to (someone) about a fault

reproved v ▷ reprove

reproves v ▷ reprove

reproving v ▷ reprove

reps n ▷ rep¹, ²

reptile n (pl -s) cold-blooded egg-laying vertebrate with horny scales or plates, such as a snake or tortoise > reptilian adj

reptiles n ▷ reptile

reptilian adj ▷ reptile

republic n (pl -s) form of government in which the people or their elected representatives possess the supreme power

republican n (pl -s) supporter or advocate of a republic > republicanism n (pl -s)

republicans n ▷ republican

republicanism n ▷ republican

republicanisms n ▷ republican

republics n ▷ republic

repudiate [rip-pew-dee-ate] v (-tes, -ting, -ted) reject the authority or validity of > repudiation n (pl -s)

repudiated v ▷ repudiate

repudiates v ▷ repudiate

repudiating v ▷ repudiate

repudiation n ▷ repudiate

repudiations n ▷ repudiate

repugnance n ▷ repugnant

repugnances n ▷ repugnant

repugnant adj offensive or distasteful > repugnance n (pl -s)

repulse v (-ses, -sing, -sed) be disgusting to ▶ n (pl -s) driving back

repulsed v ▷ repulse

repulsing v ▷ repulse

repulses v, n ▷ repulse

repulsion n (pl -s) distaste or aversion

repulsions n ▷ repulsion

repulsive adj loathsome, disgusting

reputable adj of good reputation, respectable

reputation n (pl -s) estimation in which a person is held

reputations n ▷ reputation

repute n (pl -s) reputation

reputed adj supposed > reputedly adv

reputedly adv ▷ reputed

reputes n ▷ repute

request v (-s, -ing, -ed) ask ▶ n (pl -s) asking

requested v ▷ request

requesting v ▷ request

requests v, n ▷ request

requiem [rek-wee-em] n (pl -s) Mass for the dead

requiems n ▷ requiem

require v (-res, -ring, -red) want or need

required v ▷ require

requirement n (pl -s) essential condition

requirements n ▷ requirement

requires v ▷ require

requiring v ▷ require

requisite [rek-wizz-it] adj necessary, essential ▶ n (pl -s) essential thing

requisites n ▷ requisite

requisition v (-s, -ing, -ed) demand (supplies) ▶ n (pl -s) formal demand, such as for materials or supplies

requisitioned v ▷ requisition

requisitioning v ▷ requisition

requisitions v, n ▷ requisition

requite v (-tes, -ting, -ted) return to someone (the same treatment or feeling as received)

requited v ▷ requite

requites v ▷ requite

requiting v ▷ requite

reredos [rear-doss] n (pl -es) ornamental screen behind an altar

reredoses n ▷ reredos

resat v ▷ resit

rescind v (-s, -ing, -ed) annul or repeal

rescinded v ▷ rescind

rescinding v ▷ rescind

rescinds v ▷ rescind

rescue v (-cues, -cuing, -cued) deliver from danger or trouble, save ▶ n (pl -s) rescuing > rescuer n (pl -s)

rescued v ▷ rescue

rescuer n ▷ rescue

rescuers n ▷ rescue

rescues v, n ▷ rescue

rescuing v ▷ rescue

research n (pl -es) systematic investigation to discover facts or collect information ▶ v (-es, -ing, -ed) carry out investigations > researcher n (pl -s)

researched v ▷ research

researcher n ▷ research

researchers n ▷ research

researches n, v ▷ research

researching v ▷ research

resemblance n ▷ resemble
resemblances n ▷ resemble
resemble v (-les, -ling, -led) be or look like
> resemblance n (pl -s)
resembled v ▷ resemble
resembles v ▷ resemble
resembling v ▷ resemble
resent v (-s, -ing, -ed) feel bitter about
> resentful adj > resentment n (pl -s)
resented v ▷ resent
resentful adj ▷ resent
resenting v ▷ resent
resentment n ▷ resent
resentments n ▷ resent
resents v ▷ resent
reservation n (pl -s) doubt
reservations n ▷ reservation
reserve v (-ves, -ving, -ved) set aside, keep for
future use ▶ n (pl -s) something, esp. money
or troops, kept for emergencies (SPORT)
reserved adj not showing one's feelings,
lacking friendliness ▶ v ▷ reserve
reserves v, n ▷ reserve
reserving v ▷ reserve
reservist n (pl -s) member of a military reserve
reservists n ▷ reservist
reservoir n (pl -s) natural or artificial lake
storing water for community supplies
reservoirs n ▷ reservoir
reshuffle n (pl -s) reorganization ▶ v (-s, -ing,
-ed) reorganize
reshuffled n ▷ reshuffle
reshuffles n, v ▷ reshuffle
reshuffling v ▷ reshuffle
reside v (-des, -ding, -ded) dwell permanently
resided v ▷ reside
residence n (pl -s) home or house
residences n ▷ residence
resident n (pl -s) person who lives in a place
▶ adj living in a place
residential adj (of part of a town) consisting
mainly of houses
residents n ▷ resident
resides v ▷ reside
residing v ▷ reside
residue n (pl -s) what is left, remainder
> residual adj
residual adj ▷ residue
residues n ▷ residue
resign v (-s, -ing, -ed) give up office, a job, etc.
resignation n (pl -s) resigning
resignations n ▷ resignation
resigned adj content to endure ▶ v ▷ resign
resigning v ▷ resign
resigns v ▷ resign

resilience n ▷ resilient
resiliences n ▷ resilient
resilient adj (of a person) recovering quickly
from a shock etc. > resilience n (pl -s)
resin [rezz-in] n (pl -s) sticky substance from
plants, esp. pines > resinous adj
resinous adj ▷ resin
resins n ▷ resin
resist v (-s, -ing, -ed) withstand or oppose
> resistant adj > resistible adj
resistance n (pl -s) act of resisting
resistances n ▷ resistance
resistant adj ▷ resist
resisted v ▷ resist
resistible adj ▷ resist
resisting v ▷ resist
resistor n (pl -s) component of an electrical
circuit producing resistance
resistors n ▷ resistor
resists v ▷ resist
resit v (-s, -tting, -sat) take (an exam) again ▶ n
(pl -s) exam that has to be taken again
resitting v ▷ resit
resits v, n ▷ resit
resolute adj firm in purpose > resolutely adv
resolutely adv ▷ resolute
resolution n (pl -s) firmness of conduct or
character
resolutions n ▷ resolution
resolve v (-ves, -ving, -ved) decide with an
effort of will
resolved adj determined ▶ v ▷ resolve
resolves v ▷ resolve
resolving v ▷ resolve
resonance n (pl -s) echoing, esp. with a deep
sound > resonant adj > resonate v (-tes,
-ting, -ted)
resonances n ▷ resonance
resonant adj ▷ resonance
resonate v ▷ resonance
resonated v ▷ resonance
resonates v ▷ resonance
resonating v ▷ resonance
resort v (-s, -ing, -ed) have recourse (to) for
help etc. ▶ n (pl -s) place for holidays
resorted v ▷ resort
resorting v ▷ resort
resorts v, n ▷ resort
resound [riz-zownd] v (-s, -ing, -ed) echo or ring
with sound
resounded v ▷ resound
resounding adj echoing ▶ v ▷ resound
resounds v ▷ resound
resource n (pl -s) thing resorted to for
support ▶ pl sources of economic wealth

> **resourceful** *adj* > **resourcefulness** *n*
resourceful *adj* ▷ **resource**
resourcefulness *n* ▷ **resource**
resources *n* ▷ **resource**
respect *n* (*pl* -s) consideration ▶ *v* (-s, -ing, -ed) treat with esteem > **respecter** *n* (*pl* -s) > **respectful** *adj*
respectable *adj* worthy of respect
> **respectably** *adv* > **respectability** *n* (*pl* -ies)
respectabilities *n* ▷ **respectable**
respectability *n* ▷ **respectable**
respectably *adv* ▷ **respectable**
respected *v* ▷ **respect**
respecter *n* ▷ **respect**
respecters *n* ▷ **respect**
respectful *adj* ▷ **respect**
respecting *prep* concerning ▶ *v* ▷ **respect**
respective *adj* relating separately to each of those in question > **respectively** *adv*
respectively *adv* ▷ **respective**
respects *n*, *v* ▷ **respect**
respiration [ress-per-ray-shun] *n* (*pl* -s) breathing > **respiratory** *adj*
respirations *n* ▷ **respiration**
respirator *n* apparatus worn over the mouth and breathed through as protection against dust, poison gas, etc., or to provide artificial respiration
respirators *n* ▷ **respirator**
respiratory *adj* ▷ **respiration**
respire *v* (-res, -ring, -red) breathe
respired *v* ▷ **respire**
respires *v* ▷ **respire**
respiring *v* ▷ **respire**
respite *n* (*pl* -s) pause, interval of rest
respites *n* ▷ **respite**
resplendence *n* ▷ **resplendent**
resplendences *n* ▷ **resplendent**
resplendent *adj* brilliant or splendid
> **resplendence** *n* (*pl* -s)
respond *v* (-s, -ing, -ed) answer
responded *v* ▷ **respond**
respondent *n* (*pl* -s) (LAW) defendant
respondents *n* ▷ **respondent**
responding *v* ▷ **respond**
responds *v* ▷ **respond**
response *n* (*pl* -s) answer
responses *n* ▷ **response**
responsibilities *n* ▷ **responsibility**
responsibility *n* (*pl* -ies) state of being responsible
responsible *adj* having control and authority
> **responsibly** *adv*
responsibly *adv* ▷ **responsible**
responsive *adj* readily reacting to some

influence > **responsiveness** *n*
responsiveness *n* ▷ **responsive**
rest[1] *n* (*pl* -s) freedom from exertion etc. ▶ *v* (-s, -ing, -ed) take a rest > **restful** *adj* > **restless** *adj*
rest[2] *n* what is left ▶ *v* (-s, -ing, -ed) remain, continue to be
restaurant *n* (*pl* -s) commercial establishment serving meals
restaurants *n* ▷ **restaurant**
restaurateur [rest-er-a-tur] *n* (*pl* -s) person who owns or runs a restaurant
restaurateurs *n* ▷ **restaurateur**
rested *v* ▷ **rest**[1, 2]
restful (-ler, -lest) *adj* ▷ **rest**[1]
restfuller *adj* ▷ **restful**
restfullest *adj* ▷ **restful**
resting *v* ▷ **rest**[1, 2]
restitution *n* (*pl* -s) giving back
restitutions *n* ▷ **restitution**
restive *adj* restless or impatient
restless *adj* ▷ **rest**[1]
restore *v* (-res, -ring, -red) return (a building, painting, etc.) to its original condition
> **restoration** *n* (*pl* -s) > **restorer** *n* (*pl* -s)
restoration *n* ▷ **restore**
restorations *n* ▷ **restore**
restorative *adj* restoring ▶ *n* (*pl* -s) food or medicine to strengthen etc.
restoratives *n* ▷ **restorative**
restored *v* ▷ **restore**
restorer *n* ▷ **restore**
restorers *n* ▷ **restore**
restores *v* ▷ **restore**
restoring *v* ▷ **restore**
restrain *v* (-s, -ing, -ed) hold (someone) back from action
restrained *adj* not displaying emotion ▶ *v*
▷ **restrain**
restraining *v* ▷ **restrain**
restrains *v* ▷ **restrain**
restraint *n* (*pl* -s) control, esp. self-control
restraints *n* ▷ **restraint**
restrict *v* (-s, -ing, -ed) confine to certain limits > **restriction** *n* (*pl* -s) > **restrictive** *adj*
restricted *v* ▷ **restrict**
restricting *v* ▷ **restrict**
restriction *n* ▷ **restrict**
restrictions *n* ▷ **restrict**
restrictive *adj* ▷ **restrict**
restricts *v* ▷ **restrict**
restructure *v* (-res, -ring, -red) organize in a different way
restructured *v* ▷ **restructure**
restructures *v* ▷ **restructure**
restructuring *v* ▷ **restructure**

rests n, v ▷ rest[1,2]

result n (pl -s) outcome or consequence ▶ v (-s, -ing, -ed) (foll. by **from**) be the outcome or consequence (of) ▷ **resultant** adj
resultant adj ▷ result
resulted v ▷ result
resulting v ▷ result
results n, v ▷ result

resume v (-mes, -ming, -med) begin again ▷ **resumption** n (pl -s)

résumé [rezz-yew-may] n (pl -s) summary
resumed v ▷ resume
resumes v ▷ resume
résumés n ▷ résumé
resuming v ▷ resume
resumption n ▷ resume
resumptions n ▷ resume

resurgence n (pl -s) rising again to vigour ▷ **resurgent** adj
resurgences n ▷ resurgence
resurgent adj ▷ resurgence

resurrect v (-s, -ing, -ed) restore to life
resurrected v ▷ resurrect
resurrecting v ▷ resurrect

resurrection n (pl -s) rising again (esp. from the dead)
resurrections n ▷ resurrection
resurrects v ▷ resurrect

resuscitate [ris-suss-it-tate] v (-tes, -ting, -ted) restore to consciousness ▷ **resuscitation** n (pl -s)
resuscitated v ▷ resuscitate
resuscitates v ▷ resuscitate
resuscitating v ▷ resuscitate
resuscitation n ▷ resuscitate
resuscitations n ▷ resuscitate

retail n (pl -s) selling of goods individually or in small amounts to the public ▶ adv by retail ▶ v (-s, -ing, -ed) sell or be sold retail
retailed v ▷ retail

retailer n (pl -s) person or company that sells goods to the public
retailers n ▷ retailer
retailing v ▷ retail
retails n, v ▷ retail

retain v (-s, -ing, -ed) keep in one's possession
retained v ▷ retain

retainer n (pl -s) fee to retain someone's services
retainers n ▷ retainer
retaining v ▷ retain
retains v ▷ retain

retaliate v (-tes, -ting, -ted) repay an injury or wrong in kind ▷ **retaliation** n (pl -s) ▷ **retaliatory** adj

retaliated v ▷ retaliate
retaliates v ▷ retaliate
retaliating v ▷ retaliate
retaliation n ▷ retaliate
retaliations n ▷ retaliate
retaliatory adj ▷ retaliate

retard v (-s, -ing, -ed) delay or slow (progress or development) ▷ **retardation** n (pl -s)
retardation n ▷ retard
retardations n ▷ retard

retarded adj underdeveloped, esp. mentally ▶ v ▷ retard
retarding v ▷ retard
retards v ▷ retard

retch v (-es, -ing, -ed) try to vomit
retched v ▷ retch
retches v ▷ retch
retching v ▷ retch

rethink v (-s, -ing, -thought) consider again, esp. with a view to changing one's tactics
rethinks v ▷ rethink
rethinking v ▷ rethink
rethought v ▷ rethink

reticence n ▷ reticent
reticences n ▷ reticent

reticent adj uncommunicative, reserved ▷ **reticence** n (pl -s)

retina n (pl -nas, -nae) light-sensitive membrane at the back of the eye
retinae n ▷ retina
retinas n ▷ retina

retinue n (pl -s) band of attendants
retinues n ▷ retinue

retire v (-res, -ring, -red) (cause to) give up office or work, esp. through age ▷ **retirement** n (pl -s)

retired adj having retired from work etc. ▶ v ▷ retire
retirement n ▷ retire
retirements n ▷ retire
retires v ▷ retire

retiring adj shy ▶ v ▷ retire

retort[1] v (-s, -ing, -ed) reply quickly, wittily, or angrily ▶ n (pl -s) quick, witty, or angry reply

retort[2] n (pl -s) glass container with a bent neck used for distilling
retorted v ▷ retort[1]
retorting v ▷ retort[1]
retorts v ▷ retort[1] ▶ n ▷ retort[1,2]

retouch v (-es, -ing, -ed) restore or improve by new touches, esp. of paint
retouched v ▷ retouch
retouches v ▷ retouch
retouching v ▷ retouch

retrace v (-ces, -cing, -ced) go back over (a

route etc.) again
retraced v ▷ retrace
retraces v ▷ retrace
retracing v ▷ retrace
retract v (**-s, -ing, -ed**) withdraw (a statement etc.) > **retraction** n (pl -s)
retractable, retractile adj able to be retracted
retracted v ▷ retract
retractile adj ▷ retractable
retracting v ▷ retract
retracts v ▷ retract
retraction n ▷ retract
retractions n ▷ retract
retread v (**-s, -ing, -ed**) ▶ n (pl -s) ▷ remould
retreaded v ▷ retread
retreading v ▷ retread
retreads v, n ▷ retread
retreat v (**-s, -ing, -ed**) move back from a position, withdraw ▶ n (pl -s) act of or military signal for retiring or withdrawal
retreated v ▷ retreat
retreating v ▷ retreat
retreats v, n ▷ retreat
retrench v (**-es, -ing, -ed**) reduce expenditure, cut back > **retrenchment** n (pl -s)
retrenched v ▷ retrench
retrenches v ▷ retrench
retrenching v ▷ retrench
retrenchment n ▷ retrench
retrenchments n ▷ retrench
retrial n (pl -s) second trial of a case or defendant in a court of law
retrials n ▷ retrial
retribution n (pl -s) punishment or vengeance for evil deeds > **retributive** adj
retributions n ▷ retribution
retributive adj ▷ retributions
retrieve v (**-ves, -ving, -ved**) fetch back again > **retrievable** adj > **retrieval** n (pl -s)
retrievable adj ▷ retrieve
retrieval n ▷ retrieve
retrievals n ▷ retrieve
retrieved v ▷ retrieve
retriever n (pl -s) dog trained to retrieve shot game
retrievers n ▷ retrieve
retrieves v ▷ retrieve
retrieving v ▷ retrieve
retroactive adj effective from a date in the past
retrograde adj tending towards an earlier worse condition
retrogressive adj going back to an earlier worse condition > **retrogression** n (pl -s)
retrogression n ▷ retrogressive

retrogressions n ▷ retrogressive
retrorocket n (pl -s) small rocket engine used to slow a spacecraft
retrorockets n ▷ retrorocket
retrospective adj looking back in time ▶ n (pl -s) exhibition of an artist's life's work
retrospectives n ▷ retrospective
retroussé [rit-troo-say] adj (of a nose) turned upwards
retsina n (pl -s) Greek wine flavoured with resin
retsinas n ▷ retsina
return v (**-s, -ing, -ed**) go or come back ▶ n (pl -s) returning > **returnable** adj
returnable adj ▷ return
returned v ▷ return
returning v ▷ return
returns v, n ▷ return
reunion n (pl -s) meeting of people who have been apart
reunions n ▷ reunion
reunite v (**-tes, -ting, -ted**) bring or come together again after a separation
reunited v ▷ reunite
reunites v ▷ reunite
reuniting v ▷ reunite
reuse v (**-ses, -sing, -sed**) use again > **reusable** adj
reusable adj ▷ reuse
reused v ▷ reuse
reuses v ▷ reuse
reusing v ▷ reuse
rev (Informal) n (pl -s) revolution (of an engine) ▶ v (**-s, -vving, -vved**) (foll. by **up**) increase the speed of revolution of (an engine)
revalue v (**-ues, -uing, -ued**) adjust the exchange value of (a currency) upwards > **revaluation** n (pl -s)
revaluation n ▷ revalue
revaluations n ▷ revalue
revalued v ▷ revalue
revalues v ▷ revalue
revaluing v ▷ revalue
revamp v (**-s, -ing, -ed**) renovate or restore
revamped v ▷ revamp
revamping v ▷ revamp
revamps v ▷ revamp
reveal v (**-s, -ing, -ed**) make known > **revelation** n (pl -s)
revealed v ▷ reveal
revealing v ▷ reveal
reveals v ▷ reveal
reveille [riv-val-ee] n (pl -s) morning bugle call to waken soldiers
reveilles n ▷ reveille

revel v (-s, -lling, -lled) take pleasure (in)
> **reveller** n (pl -s)
   revelation n ▷ **revel**
   revelations n ▷ **revel**
   revelled v ▷ **revel**
   reveller n ▷ **revel**
   revellers n ▷ **revel**
   revelling v ▷ **revel**
   revelries n ▷ **revelry**
revelry n (pl -s) festivity
revels pl n merrymaking ▶ v ▷ **revel**
revenge n (pl -s) retaliation for wrong done
▶ v (-ges, -ging, -ged) make retaliation for
> **revengeful** adj
   revenged v ▷ **revenge**
   revengeful adj ▷ **revenge**
   revenges n, v ▷ **revenge**
   revenging v ▷ **revenge**
revenue n (pl -s) income, esp. of a state
   revenues n ▷ **revenue**
reverberate v (-tes, -ting, -ted) echo or
resound > **reverberation** n (pl -s)
   reverberated v ▷ **reverberate**
   reverberates v ▷ **reverberate**
   reverberating v ▷ **reverberate**
   reverberation n ▷ **reverberate**
   reverberations n ▷ **reverberate**
revere v (-s, -ing, -ed) be in awe of and respect
greatly
   revered v ▷ **revere**
reverence n (pl -s) awe mingled with respect
and esteem
   reverences n ▷ **reverence**
reverent adj showing reverence > **reverently**
adv
reverential adj marked by reverence
   reverently adv ▷ **reverent**
   reveres v ▷ **revere**
   revering v ▷ **revere**
reverie n (pl -s) absent-minded daydream
   reveries n ▷ **reverie**
revers [riv-veer] n (pl -s) turned back part of a
garment, such as the lapel
reverse v (-ses, -sing, -sed) turn upside down
or the other way round ▶ n (pl -s) opposite
▶ adj opposite or contrary > **reversal** n (pl -s)
> **reversible** adj
   reversal n ▷ **reverse**
   reversals n ▷ **reverse**
   reversed v ▷ **reverse**
   reverses v, n ▷ **reverse**
   reversible adj ▷ **reverse**
   reversing v ▷ **reverse**
   reversion n ▷ **revert**
   reversions n ▷ **revert**

revert v (-s, -ing, -ed) return to a former state
> **reversion** n (pl -s)
   reverted v ▷ **revert**
   reverting v ▷ **revert**
   reverts v ▷ **revert**
review n (pl -s) critical assessment of a book,
concert, etc. ▶ v (-s, -ing, -ed) hold or write
a review of
   reviewed v ▷ **review**
reviewer n (pl -s) writer of reviews
   reviewers n ▷ **reviewer**
   reviewing v ▷ **review**
   reviews n, v ▷ **review**
revile v (-les, -ling, -led) be abusively scornful
of
   reviled v ▷ **revile**
   reviles v ▷ **revile**
   reviling v ▷ **revile**
revise v (-ses, -sing, -sed) change or alter
> **revision** n (pl -s)
   revised v ▷ **revise**
   revises v ▷ **revise**
   revising v ▷ **revise**
   revision n ▷ **revise**
   revisions n ▷ **revise**
revival n (pl -s) reviving or renewal
> **revivalism** n (pl -s) > **revivalist** n (pl -s)
   revivalism n ▷ **revival**
   revivalisms n ▷ **revival**
   revivalist n ▷ **revival**
   revivalists n ▷ **revival**
   revivals n ▷ **revival**
revive v (-ves, -ving, -ved) bring or come back
to life, vigour, use, etc.
   revived v ▷ **revive**
   revives v ▷ **revive**
   reviving v ▷ **revive**
   revocation n ▷ **revoke**
   revocations n ▷ **revoke**
revoke v (-kes, -king, -ked) cancel (a will,
agreement, etc.) > **revocation** n (pl -s)
   revoked v ▷ **revoke**
   revokes v ▷ **revoke**
   revoking v ▷ **revoke**
revolt n (pl -s) uprising against authority ▶ v
(-s, -ing, -ed) rise in rebellion
   revolted v ▷ **revolt**
revolting adj disgusting, horrible ▶ v ▷ **revolt**
   revolts n, v ▷ **revolt**
revolution n (pl -s) overthrow of a government
by the governed
   revolutionaries n ▷ **revolutionary**
revolutionary adj advocating or engaged in
revolution ▶ n (pl -ies) person advocating or
engaged in revolution

revolutionize v (-zes, -zing, -zed) change considerably
revolutionized v ▷ revolutionize
revolutionizes v ▷ revolutionize
revolutionizing v ▷ revolutionize
revolutions n ▷ revolution
revolve v (-ves, -ving, -ved) turn round, rotate
revolved v ▷ revolve
revolver n (pl -s) repeating pistol
revolvers n ▷ revolver
revolves v ▷ revolve
revolving v ▷ revolve
revs n, v ▷ rev
revue n (pl -s) theatrical entertainment with topical sketches and songs
revues n ▷ revue
revulsion n (pl -s) strong disgust
revulsions n ▷ revulsion
revved v ▷ rev
revving v ▷ rev
reward n (pl -s) something given in return for a service ▶ v (-s, -ing, -ed) pay or give something to (someone) for a service, information, etc.
rewarded v ▷ reward
rewarding v ▷ reward
rewards n, v ▷ reward
rewind v (-s, -ing, -wound) run (a tape or film) back to an earlier point in order to replay
rewinding v ▷ rewind
rewinds v ▷ rewind
rewire v (-res, -ring, -red) provide (a house, engine, etc.) with new wiring
rewired v ▷ rewire
rewires v ▷ rewire
rewiring v ▷ rewire
rewound v ▷ rewind
rewrite v (-tes, -ting, -wrote, -written) write again in a different way ▶ n (pl -s) something rewritten
rewrites v, n ▷ rewrite
rewriting v ▷ rewrite
rewritten v ▷ rewrite
rewrote v ▷ rewrite

> **rex** n (rexes). Rex is a Latin word for king. This is a very useful word, as it combines X with two of the most common letters on the board, making it one to look for when you get an X. Rex scores 10 points.

> **rez** n (rezes). Rez is a short informal word for reservation. Combining Z with two of the most common tiles on the board, this is one of the first words to think about when you draw a Z and

don't have the letters for a longer word. Rez scores 12 points.

rhapsodic adj ▷ rhapsody
rhapsodies n ▷ rhapsody
rhapsodize v (-zes, -zing, -zed) speak or write with extravagant enthusiasm
rhapsodized v ▷ rhapsodize
rhapsodizes v ▷ rhapsodize
rhapsodizing v ▷ rhapsodize
rhapsody n (pl -ies) freely structured emotional piece of music > **rhapsodic** adj
rhea [ree-a] n (pl -s) S American three-toed ostrich
rheas n ▷ rhea
rhenium n (pl -s) (CHEM) silvery-white metallic element with a high melting point
rheniums n ▷ rhenium
rheostat n (pl -s) instrument for varying the resistance of an electrical circuit
rheostats n ▷ rheostat
rhesus [ree-suss] n (pl -es) small long-tailed monkey of S Asia
rhesuses n ▷ rhesus
rhetoric n (pl -s) art of effective speaking or writing
rhetorical adj (of a question) not requiring an answer > **rhetorically** adv
rhetorically adv ▷ rhetorical
rhetorics n ▷ rhetoric
rheumatic n, adj (pl -s) (person) affected by rheumatism
rheumatics n ▷ rheumatic
rheumatism n (pl -s) painful inflammation of joints or muscles
rheumatisms n ▷ rheumatism
rheumatoid adj of or like rheumatism
rhinestone n (pl -s) imitation diamond
rhinestones n ▷ rhinestone
rhino n (pl -s) rhinoceros
rhinoceros n (pl -oses, -os) large thick-skinned animal with one or two horns on its nose
rhinoceroses n ▷ rhinoceros
rhinos n ▷ rhino
rhizome n (pl -s) thick underground stem producing new plants
rhizomes n ▷ rhizome

> **rho** n (rhos). Rho is the 17th letter of the Greek alphabet. It's useful to remember words that start with RH, as there are quite a few that can come in useful. If you or someone else plays rho, remember that it could be expanded to **rhodium, rhombus** or **rhomboid**. Rho scores 6 points.

rhodium n (pl -s) (CHEM) hard metallic element

rhodiums n ▷ rhodium
rhododendron n (pl -s) evergreen flowering shrub
    rhododendrons n ▷ rhododendron
    rhombi n ▷ rhombus
rhomboid n (pl -s) parallelogram with adjacent sides of unequal length
    rhomboids n ▷ rhomboid
rhombus n (pl -buses, -bi) parallelogram with sides of equal length but no right angles, diamond-shaped figure
    rhombuses n ▷ rhombus
rhubarb n (pl -s) garden plant of which the fleshy stalks are cooked as fruit
    rhubarbs n ▷ rhubarb

> **rhy** n (**rhys**) Rhy is an alternative spelling of rye. This is a useful word as it doesn't contain a vowel, and so can be helpful when you have a poor combination of tiles on your rack. Rhy scores 9 points.

rhyme n (pl -s) sameness of the final sounds at the ends of lines of verse, or in words ▶ v (-mes, -ming, -med) make a rhyme
    rhymed v ▷ rhyme
    rhymes n, v ▷ rhyme
    rhyming v ▷ rhyme
rhythm n (pl -s) any regular movement or beat > **rhythmic, rhythmical** adj > **rhythmically** adv
    rhythmic adj ▷ rhythm
    rhythmical adj ▷ rhythm
    rhythmically adv ▷ rhythm
    rhythms n ▷ rhythm
rib[1] n (pl -s) one of the curved bones forming the framework of the upper part of the body ▶ v (-s, -bbing, -bbed) provide or mark with ribs > **ribbed** adj > **ribbing** n (pl -s)
rib[2] v (-s, -bbing, -bbed) (Informal) tease or ridicule > **ribbing** n (pl -s)
ribald adj humorously or mockingly rude or obscene > **ribaldry** n (pl -s)
    ribaldries n ▷ ribald
    ribaldry n ▷ ribald
    ribbed v, adj ▷ rib[1, 2]
    ribbing v, n ▷ rib[1, 2]
    ribbings n ▷ rib[1, 2]
ribbon n (pl -s) narrow band of fabric used for trimming, tying, etc.
    ribbons n ▷ ribbon
ribcage n (pl -s) bony structure of ribs enclosing the lungs
    ribcages n ▷ ribcage
riboflavin [rye-boe-**flay**-vin] n (pl -s) form of vitamin B

riboflavins n ▷ riboflavin
ribs n, v ▷ rib[1, 2]
rice n (pl -s) cereal plant grown on wet ground in warm countries
    rices n ▷ rice
rich adj (-er, -est) owning a lot of money or property, wealthy > **richness** n (pl -es)
    richer adj ▷ rich
riches pl n wealth
    richest adj ▷ rich
richly adv elaborately
    richness n ▷ rich
    richnesses n ▷ rich
rick[1] n (pl -s) stack of hay etc.
rick[2] v, n (-s, -ing, -ed) sprain or wrench
    ricked v ▷ rick[2]
    ricketier adj ▷ rickety
    ricketiest adj ▷ rickety
rickets n disease of children marked by softening of the bones, bow legs, etc., caused by vitamin D deficiency
rickety adj (-tier, -tiest) shaky or unstable
    ricking v ▷ rick[1]
    ricks n ▷ rick[1] ▶ v ▷ rick[2]
rickshaw n (pl -s) light two-wheeled man-drawn Asian vehicle
    rickshaws n ▷ rickshaw
ricochet [rik-osh-ay] v (-s, -ing, -ed) (of a bullet) rebound from a solid surface ▶ n (pl -s) such a rebound
    ricocheted v ▷ ricochet
    ricocheting v ▷ ricochet
    ricochets v, n ▷ ricochet
rid v (-s, -dding, rid) clear or relieve (of)
ridden v ▷ ride ▶ adj afflicted or affected by the thing specified
    ridding v ▷ rid
riddle[1] n (pl -s) question made puzzling to test one's ingenuity
riddle[2] v (-les, -ling, -led) pierce with many holes ▶ n (pl -s) coarse sieve for gravel etc.
    riddled v ▷ riddle[2]
    riddles n ▷ riddle[1, 2] ▶ v ▷ riddle[2]
    riddling v ▷ riddle[2]
ride v (-des, -ding, rode, ridden) sit on and control or propel (a horse, bicycle, etc.) ▶ n (pl -s) journey on a horse etc., or in a vehicle
rider n (pl -s) person who rides
    riders n ▷ rider
    rides v, n ▷ ride
ridge n (pl -s) long narrow hill > **ridged** adj
    ridged adj ▷ ridge
    ridges n ▷ ridge
ridicule n (pl -s) treatment of a person or thing as ridiculous ▶ v (-les, -ling, -led) laugh at,

make fun of
ridiculed v ▷ ridicule
ridicules n, v ▷ ridicule
ridiculing v ▷ ridicule
ridiculous adj deserving to be laughed at, absurd
riding¹ v ▷ ride
riding² n (pl -s) (in Canada) parliamentary constituency
ridings n ▷ riding
rids v ▷ rid
riesling n (pl -s) type of white wine
rieslings n ▷ riesling
rife adj (-r, -st) widespread or common
rifer adj ▷ rife
rifest adj ▷ rife
riff n (pl -s) (JAZZ, ROCK) short repeated melodic figure
riffle v (-les, -ling, -led) flick through (pages etc.) quickly
riffled v ▷ riffle
riffles v ▷ riffle
riffling v ▷ riffle
riffraff n (pl -s) rabble, disreputable people
riffraffs n ▷ riffraff
riffs n ▷ riff
rifle¹ n (pl -s) firearm with a long barrel
rifle² v (-les, -ling, -led) search and rob
rifled v ▷ rifle²
rifles n ▷ rifle¹ ▶ v ▷ rifle²
rifling v ▷ rifle²
rift n (pl -s) break in friendly relations
rifts n ▷ rift
rig v (-s, -gging, -gged) arrange in a dishonest way ▶ n (pl -s) apparatus for drilling for oil and gas
rigged v ▷ rig
rigging n ship's spars and ropes ▶ v ▷ rig
right adj (-er, -est) just ▶ adv properly ▶ n (pl -s) claim, title, etc. allowed or due ▶ v (-s, -ing, -ed) bring or come back to a normal or correct state > **rightly** adv > **rightful** adj > **rightfully** adv
righted v ▷ right
righteous [rye-chuss] adj upright, godly, or virtuous > **righteousness** n (pl -s)
righteousness n ▷ righteous
righteousnesses n ▷ righteous
righter adj ▷ right
rightest adj ▷ right
rightful adj ▷ right
rightfully adv ▷ right
righting v ▷ right
rightist n (pl -s) ▶ adj (person) on the political right

rightists n ▷ rightist
rightly adv ▷ right
rights n, v ▷ right
rigid adj (-er, -est) inflexible or strict > **rigidly** adv > **rigidity** n (pl -s)
rigider adj ▷ rigid
rigidest adj ▷ rigid
rigidities n ▷ rigid
rigidity n ▷ rigid
rigidly n ▷ rigid
rigmarole n (pl -s) long complicated procedure
rigmaroles n ▷ rigmarole
rigorous adj harsh, severe, or stern
rigour n (pl -s) harshness, severity, or strictness
rigours n ▷ rigour
rigs v, n ▷ rig
rile v (-les, -ling, -led) anger or annoy
riled v ▷ rile
riles v ▷ rile
riling v ▷ rile
rill n (pl -s) small stream
rills n ▷ rill
rim n (pl -s) edge or border > **rimmed** adj
rime n (pl -s) (Lit) hoarfrost
rimes n ▷ rime
rimmed adj ▷ rim
rims n ▷ rim
rimu n (pl -s) (NZ) New Zealand tree whose wood is used for building and furniture
rimus n ▷ rimu
rind n (pl -s) tough outer coating of fruits, cheese, or bacon
rinds n ▷ rind
ring¹ v (-s, -ing, rang, rung) give out a clear resonant sound, as a bell ▶ n (pl -s) ringing
ring² n (pl -s) circle of gold etc., esp. for a finger ▶ v (-s, -ing, -ed) put a ring round
ringed v ▷ ring²
ringer n (pl -s) (BRIT, AUST & NZ) (Slang) person or thing apparently identical to another
ringers n ▷ ringer
ringing v ▷ ring¹,²
ringleader n (pl -s) instigator of a mutiny, riot, etc.
ringleaders n ▷ ringleader
ringlet n (pl -s) curly lock of hair
ringlets n ▷ ringlet
rings n, v ▷ ring¹,²
ringside n (pl -s) row of seats nearest a boxing or circus ring
ringsides n ▷ ringside
ringtail n (pl -s) (AUST) possum with a curling tail used to grip branches while climbing
ringtails n ▷ ringtail

ringtone n (pl -s) tune played by a mobile phone when it receives a call
　ringtones n ▷ ringtone

ringworm n (pl -s) fungal skin disease in circular patches
　ringworms n ▷ ringworm

rink n (pl -s) sheet of ice for skating or curling
　rinks n ▷ rink

rinse v (-ses, -sing, -sed) remove soap from (washed clothes, hair, etc.) by applying clean water ▶ n (pl -s) rinsing
　rinsed v ▷ rinse
　rinses v, n ▷ rinse
　rinsing v ▷ rinse

riot n (pl -s) disorderly unruly disturbance ▶ v (-s, -ing, -ed) take part in a riot
　rioted v ▷ riot
　rioting v ▷ riot

riotous adj unrestrained
　riots n, v ▷ riot

rip v (-s, -pping, -pped) tear violently (*Informal*) ▶ n (pl -s) split or tear

riparian [rip-pair-ee-an] adj of or on the banks of a river

ripcord n (pl -s) cord pulled to open a parachute
　ripcords n ▷ ripcord

ripe adj (-er, -est) ready to be reaped, eaten, etc.

ripen v (-s, -ing, -ed) grow ripe
　ripened v ▷ ripen
　ripening v ▷ ripen
　ripens v ▷ ripen
　riper adj ▷ ripe
　ripest adj ▷ ripe

riposte [rip-posst] n (pl -s) verbal retort ▶ v (-tes, -ting, -ted) make a riposte
　riposted v ▷ riposte
　ripostes n, v ▷ riposte
　riposting v ▷ riposte
　ripped v ▷ rip
　ripping v ▷ rip

ripple n (pl -s) slight wave or ruffling of a surface ▶ v (-les, -ling, -led) flow or form into little waves (on)
　rippled v ▷ ripple
　ripples n, v ▷ ripple
　rippling v ▷ ripple
　rips v, n ▷ rip

rise v (-ses, -sing, rose, risen) get up from a lying, sitting, or kneeling position ▶ n (pl -s) rising
　risen v ▷ rise

riser n (pl -s) person who rises, esp. from bed
　risers n ▷ riser
　rises v, n ▷ rise

rising n (pl -s) revolt ▶ adj increasing in rank or maturity ▶ v ▷ rise
　risings n ▷ rising

risible [riz-zib-bl] adj causing laughter, ridiculous

risk n (pl -s) chance of disaster or loss ▶ v (-s, -ing, -ed) act in spite of the possibility of (injury or loss)
　risked v ▷ risk
　riskier adj ▷ risky
　riskiest adj ▷ risky
　risking v ▷ risk
　risks n, v ▷ risk

risky adj (-kier, -kiest) full of risk, dangerous

risotto n (pl -s) dish of rice cooked in stock with vegetables, meat, etc.
　risottos n ▷ risotto

risqué [risk-ay] adj bordering on indecency

rissole n (pl -s) cake of minced meat, coated with breadcrumbs and fried
　rissoles n ▷ rissole

rite n (pl -s) formal practice or custom, esp. religious
　rites n ▷ rite

ritual n (pl -s) prescribed order of rites ▶ adj concerning rites > **ritually** adv

ritualistic adj like a ritual
　ritually adv ▷ ritual
　rituals n ▷ ritual
　ritzier adj ▷ ritzy
　ritziest adj ▷ ritzy

ritzy adj (-zier, -ziest) (*Slang*) luxurious or elegant

rival n (pl -s) person or thing that competes with or equals another for favour, success, etc. ▶ adj in the position of a rival ▶ v (-s, -lling, -lled) (try to) equal
　rivalled v ▷ rival
　rivalling v ▷ rival
　rivalries n ▷ rivalry

rivalry n (pl -s) keen competition
　rivals v, n ▷ rival

riven adj split apart

river n (pl -s) large natural stream of water
　rivers n ▷ river

rivet [riv-vit] n (pl -s) bolt for fastening metal plates, the end being put through holes and then beaten flat ▶ v (-s, -ing, -ed) fasten with rivets
　riveted v ▷ rivet

riveting adj very interesting and exciting ▶ v ▷ rivet
　rivets n, v ▷ rivet

rivulet n (pl -s) small stream
　rivulets n ▷ rivulet

riz v. Riz is the past tense of rise in some US dialects. This unusual word can be very useful if you get a Z in the later stages of the game, as you will probably be able to find either I or R on the board already. Riz scores 12 points.

roach n (pl -es) Eurasian freshwater fish
  roaches n ▷ roach
road n (pl -s) way prepared for passengers, vehicles, etc.
roadblock n (pl -s) barricade across a road to stop traffic for inspection etc.
  roadblocks n ▷ roadblock
roadhouse n (pl -s) (BRIT, AUST & S AFR) pub or restaurant on a country road
  roadhouses n ▷ roadhouse
roadie n (pl -s) (BRIT, AUST & NZ) (Informal) person who transports and sets up equipment for a band
  roadies n ▷ roadie
  roads v, n ▷ road
roadside n (pl -s) ▶ adj by the road
  roadsides n ▷ roadside
roadway n (pl -s) the part of a road used by vehicles
  roadways n ▷ roadway
roadworks pl n repairs to a road, esp. blocking part of the road
roadworthy adj (of a vehicle) mechanically sound
roam v (-s, -ing, -ed) wander about
  roamed v ▷ roam
  roaming v ▷ roam
  roams v ▷ roam
roan adj (of a horse) having a brown or black coat sprinkled with white hairs ▶ n (pl -s) roan horse
  roans n ▷ roan
roar v (-s, -ing, -ed) make or utter a loud deep hoarse sound like that of a lion ▶ n (pl -s) such a sound
  roared v ▷ roar
  roaring v ▷ roar
  roars v, n ▷ roar
roast v (-s, -ing, -ed) cook by dry heat, as in an oven ▶ n (pl -s) roasted joint of meat ▶ adj roasted
  roasted v ▷ roast
roasting (Informal) adj extremely hot ▶ n (pl -s) severe criticism or scolding ▶ v ▷ roast
  roastings n ▷ roasting
  roasts v, n ▷ roast
rob v (-s, -bbing, -bbed) steal from > **robber** n (pl -s) > **robbery** n (pl -ies)
  robbed v ▷ rob

robber n ▷ rob
robberies n ▷ rob
robbers n ▷ rob
robbery n ▷ rob
robbing v ▷ rob
robe n (pl -s) long loose outer garment ▶ v (-bes, -bing, -bed) put a robe on
  robed v ▷ robe
  robes v, n ▷ robe
robin n (pl -s) small brown bird with a red breast
  robing v ▷ robe
  robins n ▷ robin
robot n (pl -s) automated machine, esp. one performing functions in a human manner > **robotic** adj
  robotic adj ▷ robot
robotics n science of designing and using robots
  robots n ▷ robot
  robs v ▷ rob
robust adj (-er, -est) very strong and healthy > **robustly** adv > **robustness** n (pl -s)
  robuster adj ▷ robust
  robustest adj ▷ robust
  robustly adv ▷ robust
  robustness n ▷ robust
  robustnesses n ▷ robust
roc n (pl -s) monstrous bird of Arabian mythology
rock¹ n (pl -s) hard mineral substance that makes up part of the earth's crust, stone
rock² v (-s, -ing, -ed) (cause to) sway to and fro ▶ n style of pop music with a heavy beat
  rocked v ▷ rock²
rocker n (pl -s) rocking chair
  rockeries n ▷ rockery
  rockers n ▷ rocker
rockery n (pl -ies) mound of stones in a garden for rock plants
rocket n (pl -s) self-propelling device powered by the burning of explosive contents (used as a firework, weapon, etc.) ▶ v (-s, -ing, -ed) move fast, esp. upwards, like a rocket
  rocketed v ▷ rocket
  rocketing v ▷ rocket
  rockets n, v ▷ rocket
  rockier adj ▷ rocky¹, rocky²
  rockiest adj ▷ rocky¹, rocky²
  rocking v ▷ rock²
  rocks n ▷ rock¹ ▶ v ▷ rock²
rocky¹ adj (-ier, -iest) having many rocks
rocky² adj (-ier, -iest) shaky or unstable
rococo [rok-koe-koe] adj (of furniture, architecture, etc.) having much elaborate

decoration in an early 18th-century style

rocs n ▷ **roc**

rod n (pl **-s**) slender straight bar, stick

rode v ▷ **ride**

rodent n (pl **-s**) animal with teeth specialized for gnawing, such as a rat, mouse, or squirrel

rodents n ▷ **rodent**

rodeo n (pl **-s**) display of skill by cowboys, such as bareback riding

rodeos n ▷ **rodeo**

rods n ▷ **rod**

roe[1] n (pl **-s**) mass of eggs in a fish, sometimes eaten as food

roe[2] n (pl **-s**) small species of deer

roentgen [ront-gan] n (pl **-s**) unit measuring a radiation dose

roentgens n ▷ **roentgen**

roes n ▷ **roe**[1, 2]

rogue n (pl **-s**) dishonest or unprincipled person ▶ adj (of a wild beast) having a savage temper and living apart from the herd > **roguish** adj

rogues n ▷ **rogue**

roguish adj ▷ **rogue**

rogee n ▷ **rogee**

> **rok** n (**roks**). Rok is an alternative spelling of **roc**. This uncommon word can be helpful if you have a K without the tiles needed for a longer word. Rok scores 7 points.

role n (pl **-s**) task or function

roles n ▷ **role**

roll v (**-s**, **-ing**, **-ed**) move by turning over and over ▶ n (pl **-s**) act of rolling over or from side to side

rolled v ▷ **roll**

roller n (pl **-s**) rotating cylinder used for smoothing or supporting a thing to be moved, spreading paint, etc.

rollers n ▷ **roller**

rollicking adj boisterously carefree

rolling v ▷ **roll**

rolls v, n ▷ **roll**

roman n roman type or print

romance n (pl **-s**) love affair

romances n ▷ **romance**

romantic adj of or dealing with love ▶ n (pl **-s**) romantic person or artist > **romantically** adv > **romanticism** n (pl **-s**)

romantically adv ▷ **romantic**

romanticism n ▷ **romantic**

romanticisms n ▷ **romantic**

romanticize v (**-zes**, **-zing**, **-zed**) describe or regard in an idealized and unrealistic way

romanticized v ▷ **romanticize**

romanticizes v ▷ **romanticize**

romanticizing v ▷ **romanticize**

romantics n ▷ **romantic**

romp v (**-s**, **-ing**, **-ed**) play wildly and joyfully ▶ n (pl **-s**) boisterous activity

romped v ▷ **romp**

rompers pl n child's overalls

romping v ▷ **romp**

romps v, n ▷ **romp**

rondo n (pl **-s**) piece of music with a leading theme continually returned to

rondos n ▷ **rondo**

roo n (pl **-s**) (AUST) (Informal) kangaroo

rood n (pl **-s**) (CHRISTIANITY) the Cross

roods n ▷ **rood**

roof n (pl **-s**) outside upper covering of a building, car, etc. ▶ v put a roof on

roofs n ▷ **roofs**

rooibos [roy-boss] n (pl **-es**) (S AFR) tea prepared from the dried leaves of an African plant

rooiboses n ▷ **rooibos**

rook[1] n (pl **-s**) Eurasian bird of the crow family

rook[2] n (pl **-s**) chess piece shaped like a castle

rookeries n ▷ **rookery**

rookery n (pl **-ies**) colony of rooks, penguins, or seals

rookie n (pl **-s**) (Informal) new recruit

rookies n ▷ **rookie**

rooks n ▷ **rook**

room n (pl **-s**) enclosed area in a building ▶ pl lodgings

roomier adj ▷ **roomy**

roomiest adj ▷ **roomy**

rooms n ▷ **room**

roomy adj (**-ier**, **-iest**) spacious

roos n ▷ **roo**

roost[1] n (pl **-s**) perch for fowls ▶ v (**-s**, **-ing**, **-ed**) perch

roosted v ▷ **roost**

rooster n (pl **-s**) domestic cock

roosters n ▷ **rooster**

roosting v ▷ **roost**

roosts v, n ▷ **roost**

root[1] n (pl **-s**) part of a plant that grows down into the earth obtaining nourishment ▶ pl person's sense of belonging ▶ v (**-s**, **-ing**, **-ed**) establish a root and start to grow

root[2] v (**-s**, **-ing**, **-ed**) dig or burrow

rooted v ▷ **root**[1, 2]

rooting v ▷ **root**[1, 2]

rootless adj having no sense of belonging

roots n ▷ root[1] ► v ▷ root[1, 2]

rope n (pl -s) thick cord

ropes n ▷ rope

ropey, ropy adj (-pier, -piest) (BRIT) (Informal) inferior or inadequate

ropier adj ▷ ropy

ropiest adj ▷ ropy

ropy adj ▷ ropey

rorqual n (pl -s) toothless whale with a dorsal fin

rorquals n ▷ rorqual

rort (AUST) (Informal) n (pl -s) dishonest scheme ► v (-s, -ing, -ed) take unfair advantage of something

rorted v ▷ rort

rorting v ▷ rort

rorts n, v ▷ rort

rosaries n ▷ rosary

rosary n (pl -ies) series of prayers

rose[1] n (pl -s) shrub or climbing plant with prickly stems and fragrant flowers ► adj pink

rose[2] v ▷ rise

roseate [roe-zee-ate] adj rose-coloured

rosehip n (pl -s) berry-like fruit of a rose plant

rosehips n ▷ rosehip

rosella n (pl -s) type of Australian parrot

rosellas n ▷ rosella

rosemaries n ▷ rosemary

rosemary n (pl -ies) fragrant flowering shrub

roses n ▷ rose[1]

rosette n (pl -s) rose-shaped ornament, esp. a circular bunch of ribbons

rosettes n ▷ rosette

rosewood n (pl -s) fragrant wood used to make furniture

rosewoods n ▷ rosewood

rosier adj ▷ rosy

rosiest adj ▷ rosy

rosin [rozz-in] n (pl -s) resin used for treating the bows of violins etc.

rosins n ▷ rosin

roster n (pl -s) list of people and their turns of duty

rosters n ▷ roster

rostra n ▷ rostrum

rostrum n (pl -trums, -tra) platform or stage

rostrums n ▷ rostrum

rosy adj (-sier, -siest) pink-coloured

rot v (-s, -tting, -tted) decompose or decay ► n (pl -s) decay (Informal)

rota n (pl -s) list of people who take it in turn to do a particular task

rotas n ▷ rota

rotary adj revolving

rotate v (-tes, -ting, -ted) (cause to) move

round a centre or on a pivot ► **rotation** n (pl -s)

rotated v ▷ rotate

rotates v ▷ rotate

rotating v ▷ rotate

rotation n ▷ rotate

rotations n ▷ rotate

rote n (pl -s) mechanical repetition

rotes n ▷ rote

rotisserie n (pl -s) rotating spit for cooking meat

rotisseries n ▷ rotisserie

rotor n (pl -s) revolving portion of a dynamo, motor, or turbine

rotors n ▷ rotor

rots v, n ▷ rot

rotted v ▷ rot

rotten adj (-er, -est) decaying (Informal)

rottener adj ▷ rotten

rottenest adj ▷ rotten

rotter n (pl -s) (CHIEFLY BRIT) (Slang) despicable person

rotters n ▷ rotter

rotting v ▷ rot

rotund [roe-tund] adj round and plump > **rotundity** n (pl -ies)

rotunda n (pl -s) circular building or room, esp. with a dome

rotundas n ▷ rotunda

rotundities n ▷ rotund

rotundity n ▷ rotund

rouble [roo-bl] n (pl -s) monetary unit of Russia, Belarus, and Tajikistan

roubles n ▷ rouble

roué [roo-ay] n (pl -s) man given to immoral living

roués n ▷ roué

rouge n (pl -s) red cosmetic used to colour the cheeks

rouges n ▷ rouge

rough adj (-er, -est) uneven or irregular ► v (-s, -ing, -ed) make rough ► n (pl -s) rough state or area > **roughen** v (-s, -ing, -ed) > **roughly** adv > **roughness** n (pl -s)

roughage n (pl -s) indigestible constituents of food which aid digestion

roughages n ▷ roughage

roughcast n (pl -s) mixture of plaster and small stones for outside walls ► v (-s, -ing, -cast) coat with this

roughcasting v ▷ roughcast

roughcasts n, v ▷ roughcast

roughed v ▷ rough

roughen v ▷ rough

roughened v ▷ rough

roughening v ▷ rough

roughens v ▷ rough
rougher adj ▷ rough
roughest adj ▷ rough
roughhouse n (pl -s) (CHIEFLY US) (Slang) fight
roughhouses n ▷ roughhouse
roughing v ▷ roughhouse
roughly adv ▷ rough
roughness n ▷ rough
roughnesses n ▷ rough
roughs v, n ▷ rough
roughshod adv with total disregard
roulette n (pl -s) gambling game played with a revolving wheel and a ball
roulettes n ▷ roulette
round adj (-er, -est) spherical, cylindrical, circular, or curved ▶ adv, prep indicating an encircling movement, presence on all sides, etc. ▶ v (-s, -ing, -ed) move round ▶ n (pl -s) customary course, as of a milkman
roundabout n (pl -s) road junction at which traffic passes round a central island ▶ adj not straightforward
roundabouts n ▷ roundabout
rounded v ▷ round
roundel n (pl -s) small disc
roundelay n (pl -s) simple song with a refrain
roundelays n ▷ roundelay
roundels n ▷ roundel
rounder adj ▷ round
roundest adj ▷ round
rounders n bat-and-ball team game
rounding v ▷ round
roundly adv thoroughly
rounds v, n ▷ round
rouse¹ [rhymes with **cows**] v (-ses, -sing, -sed) wake up
rouse² [rhymes with **mouse**] v (-ses, -sing, -sed) (foll. by **on**) (AUST) scold or rebuke
rouseabout n (pl -s) (AUST & NZ) labourer in a shearing shed
rouseabouts n ▷ rouseabout
roused v ▷ rouse¹, ²
rouses v ▷ rouse¹, ²
rousing v ▷ rouse¹, ²
roustabout n (pl -s) labourer on an oil rig
roustabouts n ▷ roustabout
rout n (pl -s) overwhelming defeat ▶ v (-s, -ing, -ed) defeat and put to flight
route n (pl -s) roads taken to reach a destination
routed v ▷ rout
routes n ▷ route
routine n (pl -s) usual or regular method of procedure ▶ adj ordinary or regular
routines n ▷ routine

routing v ▷ rout
routs n, v ▷ rout
roux [roo] n (pl roux) fat and flour cooked together as a basis for sauces
rove v (-ves, -ving, -ved) wander
roved v ▷ rove
rover n (pl -s) wanderer, traveller
rovers n ▷ rover
roves v ▷ rove
roving v ▷ rove
row¹ [rhymes with **go**] n (pl -s) straight line of people or things
row² [rhymes with **go**] v (-s, -ing, -ed) propel (a boat) by oars ▶ n (-s) spell of rowing
row³ [rhymes with **now**] (Informal) n (-s) dispute ▶ v (-s, -ing, -ed) quarrel noisily
rowan n (pl -s) tree producing bright red berries, mountain ash
rowans n ▷ rowan
rowdier adj ▷ rowdy
rowdiest adj ▷ rowdy
rowdies n ▷ rowdy
rowdy adj (-dier, -diest) disorderly, noisy, and rough ▶ n (pl -ies) person like this
rowed v ▷ row², ³
rowel [rhymes with **towel**] n (pl -s) small spiked wheel on a spur
rowels n ▷ rowel
rowing v ▷ row², ³
rowlock [rol-luk] n (pl -s) device on a boat that holds an oar in place
rowlocks n ▷ rowlock
rows n ▷ row¹, ², ³ ▶ v ▷ row², ³
royal adj (-ler, -lest) of, befitting, or supported by a king or queen ▶ n (pl -s) (Informal) member of a royal family > **royally** adv
royalist n (pl -s) supporter of monarchy
royalists n ▷ royalist
royaller adj ▷ royal
royallest adj ▷ royal
royally adv ▷ royal
royals n ▷ royal
royalties n ▷ royalty
royalty n (pl -ies) royal people
rub v (-s, -bbing, -bbed) apply pressure and friction to (something) with a circular or backwards-and-forwards movement ▶ n (-s) act of rubbing
rubato adv, n (pl -s) (MUSIC) (with) expressive flexibility of tempo
rubatos n ▷ rubato
rubbed v ▷ rub
rubber¹ n (pl -s) strong waterproof elastic material, orig. made from the dried sap of a tropical tree, now usu. synthetic ▶ adj made

of or producing rubber > **rubbery** adj (**-rier, -riest**)

rubber² n (pl **-s**) match consisting of three games of bridge, whist, etc.

  rubberier adj ▷ **rubber¹**

  rubberiest adj ▷ **rubber¹**

rubberneck v (**-s, -ing, -ed**) stare with unthinking curiosity

  rubbernecked v ▷ **rubberneck**

  rubbernecking v ▷ **rubberneck**

  rubbernecks v ▷ **rubberneck**

  rubbers n ▷ **rubber¹, ²**

  rubbery adj ▷ **rubber¹**

  rubbing v ▷ **rub**

rubbish n (pl **-es**) waste matter > **rubbishy** adj

  rubbishes n ▷ **rubbish**

  rubbishy adj ▷ **rubbish**

rubble n (pl **-s**) fragments of broken stone, brick, etc.

  rubbles n ▷ **rubble**

rubella n (pl **-s**) ▷ German measles

  rubellas n ▷ **rubella**

rubicund adj ruddy

rubidium n (pl **-s**) (CHEM) soft highly reactive radioactive element

  rubidiums n ▷ **rubidium**

  rubies n ▷ **ruby**

rubric n (pl **-s**) heading or explanation inserted in a text

  rubrics n ▷ **rubric**

  rubs v, n ▷ **rub**

ruby n (pl **-ies**) red precious gemstone ▶ adj deep red

ruck¹ n (pl **-s**) rough crowd of common people

ruck² n, v (**-s, -ing, -ed**) wrinkle or crease

  rucked v ▷ **ruck²**

  rucking v ▷ **ruck²**

  rucks v, n ▷ **ruck¹, ²** ▶ v ▷ **ruck²**

rucksack n (pl **-s**) (BRIT, AUST & S AFR) large pack carried on the back

  rucksacks n ▷ **rucksack**

ructions pl n (Informal) noisy uproar

rudder n (pl **-s**) vertical hinged piece at the stern of a boat or at the rear of an aircraft, for steering

  rudders n ▷ **rudder**

  ruddier adj ▷ **ruddy**

  ruddiest adj ▷ **ruddy**

ruddy adj (**-dier, -diest**) of a fresh healthy red colour

rude adj (**-r, -st**) impolite or insulting > **rudely** adv > **rudeness** n (pl **-s**)

  rudely adv ▷ **rude**

  rudeness n ▷ **rude**

  rudenesses n ▷ **rude**

  ruder adj ▷ **rude**

  rudest adj ▷ **rude**

rudimentary adj basic, elementary

rudiments pl n simplest and most basic stages of a subject

rue¹ v (**rues, ruing, rued**) feel regret for

rue² n (pl **-s**) plant with evergreen bitter leaves

rueful adj regretful or sorry > **ruefully** adv

  ruefully adv ▷ **rueful**

  rued v ▷ **rue¹**

  rues v ▷ **rue¹** ▶ n ▷ **rue²**

ruff n (pl **-s**) starched and frilled collar

ruffian n (pl **-s**) violent lawless person

  ruffians n ▷ **ruffian**

ruffle v (**-les, -ling, -led**) disturb the calm of ▶ n (pl **-s**) frill or pleat

  ruffled v ▷ **ruffle**

  ruffles v, n ▷ **ruffle**

  ruffling v ▷ **ruffle**

  ruffs n ▷ **ruff**

rug n (pl **-s**) small carpet

  rugbies n ▷ **rugby**

rugby n (pl **-ies**) form of football played with an oval ball which may be handled by the players

rugged [rug-gid] adj rocky or steep

rugger n (pl **-s**) (CHIEFLY BRIT) (Informal) rugby

  ruggers n ▷ **rugger**

  rugs n ▷ **rug**

ruin v (**-s, -ing, -ed**) destroy or spoil completely ▶ n (pl **-s**) destruction or decay

ruination n (pl **-s**) act of ruining

  ruinations n ▷ **ruination**

  ruined v ▷ **ruin**

  ruing v ▷ **rue¹**

  ruining v ▷ **ruin**

ruinous adj causing ruin > **ruinously** adv

  ruinously adv ▷ **ruinous**

  ruins v, n ▷ **ruin**

rule n (pl **-s**) statement of what is allowed, for example in a game or procedure ▶ v (**-les, -ling, -led**) govern

  ruled v ▷ **rule**

ruler n (pl **-s**) person who governs

  rulers n ▷ **ruler**

  rules n, v ▷ **rule**

ruling n (pl **-s**) formal decision ▶ v ▷ **rule**

  rulings n ▷ **ruling**

rum n (pl **-s**) alcoholic drink distilled from sugar cane

rumba n (pl **-s**) lively ballroom dance of Cuban origin

  rumbas n ▷ **rumba**

rumble v (**-les, -ling, -led**) make a low continuous noise (BRIT) (Informal) ▶ n (pl **-s**) deep resonant sound

rumbled v ▷ rumble
rumbles v, n ▷ rumble
rumbling v ▷ rumble
rumbustious adj boisterous or unruly
ruminate v (-tes, -ting, -ted) chew the cud
ruminant adj, n (pl -s) cud-chewing (animal, such as a cow, sheep, or deer)
ruminants n ▷ ruminant
ruminated v ▷ ruminate
ruminates v ▷ ruminate
ruminating v ▷ ruminate
rumination n (pl -s) quiet meditation and reflection > **ruminative** adj
ruminations n ▷ rumination
ruminative adj ▷ rumination
rummage v (-ges, -ging, -ged) search untidily and at length ▶ n (pl -s) untidy search through a collection of things
rummaged v ▷ rummage
rummages v, n ▷ rummage
rummaging v ▷ rummage
rummies n ▷ rummy
rummy n (pl -ies) card game in which players try to collect sets or sequences
rumour n (pl -s) unproved statement
rumoured adj suggested by rumour
rumours n ▷ rumour
rump n (pl -s) buttocks
rumple v (-les, -ling, -led) make untidy, crumpled, or dishevelled
rumpled v ▷ rumple
rumples v ▷ rumple
rumpling v ▷ rumple
rumps n ▷ rump
rumpus n (pl -es) noisy commotion
rumpuses n ▷ rumpus
rums n ▷ rum
run v (runs, running, ran, run) move with a more rapid gait than walking ▶ n (pl -s) act or spell of running
rune n (pl -s) any character of the earliest Germanic alphabet > **runic** adj
runes n ▷ rune
rung[1] n (pl -s) crossbar on a ladder
rung[2] v ▷ ring[1]
rungs n ▷ rung[1]
runic adj ▷ rune
runnel n (pl -s) small brook
runnels n ▷ runnel
runner n (pl -s) competitor in a race
runners n ▷ runner
runnier adj ▷ runny
runniest adj ▷ runny
running adj continuous ▶ n (pl -s) act of moving or flowing quickly ▶ v ▷ run

runnings n ▷ running
runny adj (-nier, -niest) tending to flow
runs v, n ▷ run
runt n (pl -s) smallest animal in a litter
runts n ▷ runt
runway n (pl -s) hard level roadway where aircraft take off and land
runways n ▷ runway
rupee n (pl -s) monetary unit of India and Pakistan
rupees n ▷ rupee
rupture n (pl -s) breaking, breach ▶ v (-res, -ring, -red) break, burst, or sever
ruptured v ▷ rupture
ruptures n, v ▷ rupture
rupturing v ▷ rupture
rural adj in or of the countryside
ruse [rooz] n (pl -s) stratagem or trick
ruses n ▷ ruse
rush[1] v (-es, -ing, -ed) move or do very quickly ▶ n (pl -es) sudden quick or violent movement ▶ pl first unedited prints of a scene for a film ▶ adj done with speed, hasty
rush[2] n (pl -es) marsh plant with a slender pithy stem
rushed v ▷ rush[1]
rushes v, n ▷ rush[1, 2]
rushier adj ▷ rushy
rushiest adj ▷ rushy
rushing v ▷ rush[1]
rushy adj (-shier, -shiest) full of rushes
rusk n (pl -s) hard brown crisp biscuit, used esp. for feeding babies
rusks n ▷ rusk
russet adj reddish-brown ▶ n (pl -s) apple with rough reddish-brown skin
russets n ▷ russet
rust n (pl -s) reddish-brown coating formed on iron etc. that has been exposed to moisture ▶ adj reddish-brown ▶ v (-s, -ing, -ed) become coated with rust
rusted v ▷ rust
rustic adj of or resembling country people ▶ n (pl -s) person from the country
rustics n ▷ rustic
rustier adj ▷ rusty
rustiest adj ▷ rusty
rusting v ▷ rust
rustle[1] v, n (pl -s) (make) a low whispering sound
rustle[2] v (-les, -ling, -led) (US) steal (cattle)
rustled v ▷ rustle
rustler n (pl -s) (US) cattle thief
rustlers n ▷ rustler
rustles n, v ▷ rustle

rustling v ▷ **rustle**
rusts n, v ▷ **rust**
rusty adj (**-tier, -tiest**) coated with rust
rut[1] n (pl **-s**) furrow made by wheels
rut[2] n recurrent period of sexual excitability in male deer ▶ v (**-s, -tting, -tted**) be in a period of sexual excitability
ruthenium n (pl **-s**) (CHEM) rare hard brittle white element
rutheniums n ▷ **ruthenium**
ruthless adj pitiless, merciless > **ruthlessly** adv

> **ruthlessness** n (pl **-es**)
ruthlessly adv ▷ **ruthless**
ruthlessness n ▷ **ruthless**
ruthlessnesses n ▷ **ruthless**
ruts n ▷ **rut**[1, 2] ▶ v ▷ **rut**[2]
rutted v ▷ **rut**[2]
rutting v ▷ **rut**[2]
rye n (pl **-s**) kind of grain used for fodder and bread
ryes n ▷ **rye**

Ss

S begins only four two-letter words, **sh** (5 points), **si**, **so** and **st** (2 each). These are easy to remember, and it's worth noting that two of them, **sh** and **st**, don't use any vowels. Interestingly, there are quite a few three-letter words beginning with S that don't contain vowels, some of which give good scores. These are **shh** (9), **shy** (9), **sky** (10), **sly** (6), **sny** (6), **spy** (8), **sty** (6), **swy** (9) and **syn** (9). S also forms a number of three-letter words with X. These are easy to remember as they use every vowel except U: **sax**, **sex**, **six** and **sox** (10 each). Apart from the two- and three-letter words, don't forget **squeeze** (25), which uses the two highest-scoring tiles in the game.

sabbath n (pl -s) day of worship and rest: Saturday for Jews, Sunday for Christians
  sabbaths n ▷ sabbath
sabbatical adj, n (pl -s) (denoting) leave for study
  sabbaticals n ▷ sabbatical
sable n (pl -s) dark fur from a small weasel-like Arctic animal ▶ adj black
  sables n ▷ sable
sabot [sab-oh] n (pl -s) wooden shoe traditionally worn by peasants in France
sabotage n (pl -s) intentional damage done to machinery, systems, etc. ▶ v (-ges, -ging, -ged) damage intentionally
  sabotaged v ▷ sabotage
  sabotages n, v ▷ sabotage
  sabotaging v ▷ sabotage
saboteur n (pl -s) person who commits sabotage
  saboteurs n ▷ saboteur
  sabots n ▷ sabot
sabre n (pl -s) curved cavalry sword
  sabres n ▷ sabre
sac n (pl -s) pouchlike structure in an animal or plant
saccharin n (pl -s) artificial sweetener > **saccharine** adj excessively sweet
  saccharine adj ▷ saccharin
  saccharins n ▷ saccharin
sacerdotal adj of priests
sachet n (pl -s) small envelope or bag containing a single portion
  sachets n ▷ sachet
sack¹ n (pl -s) large bag made of coarse material ▶ v (-s, -ing, -ed) (Informal) dismiss

sack² n (pl -s) plundering of a captured town ▶ v (-s, -ing, -ed) plunder (a captured town)
sackcloth n (pl -s) coarse fabric used for sacks, formerly worn as a penance
  sackcloths n ▷ sackcloth
  sacked v ▷ sack¹,²
  sacking v ▷ sack¹,²
  sacks v, n ▷ sack¹,²
  sacra n ▷ sacrum
sacrament n (pl -s) ceremony of the Christian Church, esp. Communion > **sacramental** adj
  sacramental adj ▷ sacrament
  sacraments n ▷ sacrament
sacred adj holy
sacrifice n (pl -s) giving something up ▶ v (-es, -ing, -ced) offer as a sacrifice > **sacrificial** adj
  sacrificed v ▷ sacrifice
  sacrifices n, v ▷ sacrifice
  sacrificial adj ▷ sacrifice
  sacrificing v ▷ sacrifice
sacrilege n (pl -s) misuse or desecration of something sacred > **sacrilegious** adj
  sacrileges n ▷ sacrilege
  sacrilegious adj ▷ sacrilege
sacristan n (pl -s) person in charge of the contents of a church
  sacristans n ▷ sacristan
  sacristies n ▷ sacristy
sacristy n (pl -ties) room in a church where sacred objects are kept
sacrosanct adj regarded as sacred, inviolable
sacrum [say-krum] n (pl -cra) wedge-shaped bone at the base of the spine
  sacs n ▷ sac
sad adj (-dder, -ddest) sorrowful, unhappy

> sadly adv > sadness n (pl -es)
sadden v (-s, -ing, -ed) make sad
　saddened v ▷ sadden
　saddening v ▷ sadden
　saddens v ▷ sadden
　sadder adj ▷ sad
　saddest adj ▷ sad
saddle n (pl -les) rider's seat on a horse or
　bicycle ▶ v (-les, -ling, -led) put a saddle on
　(a horse)
　saddled v ▷ saddle
saddler n (pl -s) maker or seller of saddles
　saddlers n ▷ saddler
　saddles n, v ▷ saddle
　saddling v ▷ saddle
saddo n (pl -s, -es) (BRIT) (Informal) socially
　inadequate or pathetic person
　saddoes n ▷ saddo
　saddos n ▷ saddo
sadism [say-dizz-um] n (pl -s) gaining of
　(sexual) pleasure from inflicting pain > sadist
　n (pl -s) > sadistic adj > sadistically adv
　sadisms n ▷ sadism
　sadist n ▷ sadism
　sadistic adj ▷ sadism
　sadistically adv ▷ sadism
　sadists n ▷ sadism
　sadly adv ▷ sad
　sadness n ▷ sad
　sadnesses n ▷ sad
sadomasochism n (pl -s) combination of
　sadism and masochism > sadomasochist
　n (pl -s)
　sadomasochisms n ▷ sadomasochism
　sadomasochist n ▷ sadomasochism
　sadomasochists n ▷ sadomasochism
safari n (pl -s) expedition to hunt or observe
　wild animals, esp. in Africa
　safaris n ▷ safari
safe adj (-r, -st) secure, protected ▶ n (pl -s)
　strong lockable container > safely adv
safeguard v (-s, -ing, -ed) protect ▶ n (pl -s)
　protection
　safeguarded v ▷ safeguard
　safeguarding v ▷ safeguard
　safeguards v, n ▷ safeguard
safekeeping n (pl -s) protection
　safekeepings n ▷ safekeeping
　safely adv ▷ safe
　safer adj ▷ safe
　safes n ▷ safe
　safest adj ▷ safe
　safeties n ▷ safety
safety n (pl -ties) state of being safe
saffron n (pl -s) orange-coloured flavouring

obtained from a crocus ▶ adj orange
　saffrons n ▷ saffron
sag v (sags, sagging, sagged) sink in the
　middle ▶ n (pl -s) droop
saga [sah-ga] n (pl -s) legend of Norse heroes
sagacious adj wise > sagacity n (pl -ties)
　sagacities n ▷ sagacious
　sagacity n ▷ sagacious
　sagas n ▷ saga
sage¹ n (pl -s) very wise man ▶ adj (-r, -st) (Lit)
　wise > sagely adv
sage² n (pl -s) aromatic herb with grey-green
　leaves
　sagely adv ▷ sage¹
　sager adj ▷ sage¹
　sages n ▷ sage¹, ²
　sagest adj ▷ sage¹
　sagged v ▷ sag
　sagging v ▷ sag
sago n (pl -s) starchy cereal from the powdered
　pith of the sago palm tree
　sagos n ▷ sago
　sags v, n ▷ sag
　said v ▷ say
sail n (pl -s) sheet of fabric stretched to catch
　the wind for propelling a sailing boat ▶ v (-s,
　-ing, -ed) travel by water
sailboard n (pl -s) board with a mast and single
　sail, used for windsurfing
　sailboards n ▷ sailboard
　sailed v ▷ sail
　sailing v ▷ sail
sailor n (pl -s) member of a ship's crew
　sailors n ▷ sailor
　sails n, v ▷ sail
saint n (pl -s) (CHRISTIANITY) person venerated
　after death as specially holy > saintly adj
　> saintliness n (pl -es)
　saintliness n ▷ saint
　saintlinesses n ▷ saint
　saintly adj ▷ saint
　saints n ▷ saint
sake¹ n (pl -s) benefit
sake², saki [sah-kee] n (pl -s) Japanese alcoholic
　drink made from fermented rice
　sakes n ▷ sake¹, ²
　saki n ▷ sake²
　sakis n ▷ sake²
salaam [sal-ahm] n (pl -s) low bow of greeting
　among Muslims
　salaams n ▷ salaam
salacious adj excessively concerned with sex
salad n (pl -s) dish of raw vegetables, eaten as a
　meal or part of a meal
　salads n ▷ salad

salamander n (pl -s) amphibian which looks like a lizard
salamanders n ▷ salamander
salami n (pl -s) highly spiced sausage
salamis n ▷ salami
salaried adj ▷ salary
salaries n ▷ salary
salary n (pl -ries) fixed regular payment, usu. monthly, to an employee > **salaried** adj
sale n (pl -s) exchange of goods for money > **saleable** adj fit or likely to be sold
saleable adj ▷ sale
sales n ▷ sale
salesman, saleswoman (pl -men, -women) > **salesperson** (pl -people) n person who sells goods
salesmanship n (pl -s) skill in selling
salesmanships n ▷ salesmanship
salesmen n ▷ salesman
salespeople n ▷ salesman
salesperson n ▷ salesman
saleswoman n ▷ salesman
saleswomen n ▷ salesman
salient [say-lee-ent] adj prominent, noticeable ▶ n (pl -s) (MIL) projecting part of a front line
salients n ▷ salient
saline [say-line] adj containing salt > **salinity** n (pl -ties)
salinities n ▷ saline
salinity n ▷ saline
saliva n (pl -s) liquid that forms in the mouth, spittle > **salivary** adj
salivary adj ▷ saliva
salivas n ▷ saliva
salivate v (-tes, -ting, -ted) produce saliva
salivated v ▷ salivate
salivates v ▷ salivate
salivating v ▷ salivate
sallee n (pl -s) (AUST) SE Australian eucalyptus with a pale grey bark
sallees n ▷ sallee
sallied v ▷ sally
sallies n, v ▷ sally
sallow adj (-er, -est) of an unhealthy pale or yellowish colour
sallower adj ▷ sallow
sallowest adj ▷ sallow
sally n (pl -lies) witty remark ▶ v (-lies, -lying, -lied) (foll. by forth) rush out
sallying v ▷ sally
salmon n (pl -s) large fish with orange-pink flesh valued as food ▶ adj orange-pink
salmonella n (pl -lae) bacterium causing food poisoning
salmonellae n ▷ salmonella

salmons n ▷ salmon
salon n (pl -s) commercial premises of a hairdresser, beautician, etc.
salons n ▷ salon
saloon n (pl -s) two-door or four-door car with body closed off from rear luggage area
saloons n ▷ saloon
salt n (pl -s) white crystalline substance used to season food ▶ v (-s, -ing, -ed) season or preserve with salt > **salty** adj (-tier, -tiest)
saltbush n (pl -es) shrub that grows in alkaline desert regions
saltbushes n ▷ saltbush
salted v ▷ salt
saltier adj ▷ salt
saltiest adj ▷ salt
salting v ▷ salt
saltire n (pl -s) (HERALDRY) diagonal cross on a shield
saltires n ▷ saltire
saltpetre n (pl -s) compound used in gunpowder and as a preservative
saltpetres n ▷ saltpetre
salts n, v ▷ salt
salty adj ▷ salt
salubrious adj favourable to health
saluki n (pl -s) tall hound with a silky coat
salukis n ▷ saluki
salutary adj producing a beneficial result
salutation n (pl -s) greeting by words or actions
salutations n ▷ salutation
salute n (pl -s) motion of the arm as a formal military sign of respect ▶ v (-tes, -ting, -ted) greet with a salute
saluted v ▷ salute
salutes n, v ▷ salute
saluting v ▷ salute
salvage n (pl -s) saving of a ship or other property from destruction ▶ v (-ges, -ging, -ged) save from destruction or waste
salvaged v ▷ salvage
salvages n, v ▷ salvage
salvaging v ▷ salvage
salvation n (pl -s) fact or state of being saved from harm or the consequences of sin
salvations n ▷ salvation
salve n (pl -s) healing or soothing ointment ▶ v (-ves, -ving, -ved) soothe or appease
salved v ▷ salve
salver n (pl -s) (silver) tray on which something is presented
salvers n ▷ salver
salves n, v ▷ salve
salvia n (pl -s) plant with blue or red flowers

salvias n ▷ salvia

salving v ▷ salve

salvo n (pl -s, -es) simultaneous discharge of guns etc.

salvoes n ▷ salvo

salvos n ▷ salvo

samaritan n (pl -s) person who helps people in distress

samaritans n ▷ samaritan

samba n (pl -s) lively Brazilian dance

sambas n ▷ samba

same adj identical, not different, unchanged > **sameness** n (pl -es)

sameness n ▷ same

samenesses n ▷ same

samovar n (pl -s) Russian tea urn

samovars n ▷ samovar

sampan n (pl -s) small boat with oars used in China

sampans n ▷ sampan

samphire n (pl -s) plant found on rocks by the seashore

samphires n ▷ samphire

sample n (pl -s) part taken as representative of a whole ▶ v (-les, -ling, -led) take and test a sample of > **sampling** n (pl -s)

sampled v ▷ sample

sampler n (pl -s) piece of embroidery showing the embroiderer's skill

samplers n ▷ sampler

samples v, n ▷ sample

sampling v, n ▷ sample

samplings n ▷ sample

samurai n (pl -rai) member of an ancient Japanese warrior caste

sanatoria n ▷ sanatorium

sanatorium n (pl -riums, -ria) institution for invalids or convalescents

sanatoriums n ▷ sanatorium

sancta n ▷ sanctum

sanctified v ▷ sanctify

sanctifies v ▷ sanctify

sanctify v (-fies, -fying, -fied) make holy

sanctifying v ▷ sanctify

sanctimonious adj pretending to be religious and virtuous

sanction n (pl -s) permission, authorization ▶ v (-s, -ing, -ed) allow, authorize

sanctioned v ▷ sanction

sanctioning v ▷ sanction

sanctions n, v ▷ sanction

sanctities n ▷ sanctity

sanctity n (pl -ties) sacredness, inviolability

sanctuaries n ▷ sanctuary

sanctuary n (pl -ries) holy place

sanctum n (pl -tums, -ta) sacred place

sanctums n ▷ sanctum

sand n (pl -s) substance consisting of small grains of rock, esp. on a beach or in a desert ▶ v (-s, -ing, -ed) smooth with sandpaper

sandal n (pl -s) light shoe consisting of a sole attached by straps

sandals n ▷ sandal

sandalwood n (pl -s) sweet-scented wood

sandalwoods n ▷ sandalwood

sandbag n (pl -s) bag filled with sand, used as protection against gunfire or flood water

sandbags n ▷ sandbag

sandblast v (-s, -ing, -ed) ▶ n (pl -s) (clean with) a jet of sand blown from a nozzle under pressure

sandblasted v ▷ sandblast

sandblasting v ▷ sandblast

sandblasts v, n ▷ sandblast

sanded v ▷ sand

sander n (pl -s) power tool for smoothing surfaces

sanders n ▷ sander

sandier adj ▷ sandy

sandiest adj ▷ sandy

sanding v ▷ sand

sandpaper n (pl -s) paper coated with sand for smoothing a surface

sandpapers n ▷ sandpaper

sandpiper n (pl -s) shore bird with a long bill and slender legs

sandpipers n ▷ sandpiper

sands n, v ▷ sand ▶ pl n stretches of sand forming a beach or desert

sandstone n (pl -s) rock composed of sand

sandstones n ▷ sandstone

sandstorm n (pl -s) desert wind that whips up clouds of sand

sandstorms n ▷ sandstorm

sandwich n (pl -es) two slices of bread with a layer of food between ▶ v (-es, -ing, -ed) insert between two other things

sandwiched v ▷ sandwich

sandwiches n, v ▷ sandwich

sandwiching v ▷ sandwich

sandy adj (-dier, -diest) covered with sand

sane adj (-r, -st) of sound mind > **sanity** n (pl -ties)

saner adj ▷ sane

sanest adj ▷ sane

sang v ▷ sing

sangoma n (pl -s) (s AFR) witch doctor or herbalist

sangomas n ▷ sangoma

sanguinary adj accompanied by bloodshed

sanguine adj cheerful, optimistic

sanitary adj promoting health by getting rid of dirt and germs

sanitation n (pl -s) sanitary measures, esp. drainage or sewerage

  sanitations n ▷ sanitation

  sanities n ▷ sane

  sanity n ▷ sane

  sank v ▷ sink

sap[1] n (pl -s) moisture that circulates in plants

sap[2] v (saps, sapping, sapped) undermine

sapient [say-pee-ent] adj (Lit) wise, shrewd

sapling n (pl -s) young tree

  saplings n ▷ sapling

  sapped v ▷ sap[2]

sapper n (pl -s) soldier in an engineering unit

  sappers n ▷ sapper

sapphire n (pl -s) blue precious stone ▶ adj deep blue

  sapphires n ▷ sapphire

  sapping v ▷ sap[2]

  saps ▷ sap[1] ▶ v ▷ sap[2]

  saraband n ▷ sarabande

saraband, sarabande n (pl -s) slow stately Spanish dance

  sarabandes n ▷ sarabande

  sarabands n ▷ sarabande

sarcasm n (pl -s) (use of) bitter or wounding ironic language > **sarcastic** adj > **sarcastically** adv

  sarcasms n ▷ sarcasm

  sarcastic adj ▷ sarcasm

  sarcastically adv ▷ sarcasm

  sarcophagi n ▷ sarcophagus

sarcophagus n (pl -gi, -guses) stone coffin

  sarcophaguses n ▷ sarcophagus

sardine n (pl -s) small fish of the herring family, usu. preserved tightly packed in tins

  sardines n ▷ sardine

sardonic adj mocking or scornful > **sardonically** adv

  sardonically adv ▷ sardonic

  saree n ▷ sari

  sarees n ▷ sari

  sargasso n ▷ sargassum

  sargassos n ▷ sargassum

sargassum, sargasso n (pl -s) type of floating seaweed

  sargassums n ▷ sargassum

sari, saree n (pl -s) long piece of cloth draped around the body and over one shoulder, worn by Hindu women

  saris n ▷ sari

sarmie n (pl -s) (s AFR) (Slang) sandwich

  sarmies n ▷ sarmie

sarong n (pl -s) long piece of cloth tucked around the waist or under the armpits, worn esp. in Malaysia

  sarongs n ▷ sarong

sarsaparilla n (pl -s) soft drink, orig. made from the root of a tropical American plant

  sarsaparillas n ▷ sarsaparilla

sartorial adj of men's clothes or tailoring

sash[1] n (pl -es) decorative strip of cloth worn round the waist or over one shoulder

sash[2] n (pl -es) wooden frame containing the panes of a window

  sashes n ▷ sash[1,2]

sassafras n (pl -rases) American tree with aromatic bark used medicinally

  sassafrases n ▷ sassafras

  sat v ▷ sit

satanic adj of Satan

satanism n (pl -s) worship of Satan

  satanisms n ▷ satanism

satay, saté [sat-ay] n (pl -s) Indonesian and Malaysian dish consisting of pieces of chicken, pork, etc., grilled on skewers and served with peanut sauce

  satays n ▷ satay

satchel n (pl -s) bag, usu. with a shoulder strap, for carrying books

  satchels n ▷ satchel

sate v (-tes, -ting, -ted) satisfy (a desire or appetite) fully

  sated v ▷ sate

satellite n (pl -s) man-made device orbiting in space ▶ adj of or used in the transmission of television signals from a satellite to the home

  satellites n ▷ satellite

  sates v ▷ sate

satiate [say-she-ate] v (-tes, -ting, -ted) provide with more than enough, so as to disgust

  satiated v ▷ satiate

  satiates v ▷ satiate

  satiating v ▷ satiate

  satieties n ▷ satiety

satiety [sat-**tie**-a-tee] n (pl -ties) feeling of having had too much

satin n (pl -s) silky fabric with a glossy surface on one side

  sating v ▷ sate

  satins n ▷ satin

satinwood n (pl -s) tropical tree yielding hard wood

  satinwoods n ▷ satinwood

satiny adj of or like satin

satire n (pl -s) use of ridicule to expose vice or folly > **satirical** adj > **satirist** n (pl -s)

satires n ▷ satire
satirical adj ▷ satire
satirist n ▷ satire
satirists n ▷ satire
satirize v (-zes, -zing, -zed) ridicule by means of satire
satirized v ▷ satirize
satirizes v ▷ satirize
satirizing v ▷ satirize
satisfaction n ▷ satisfy
satisfactions n ▷ satisfy
satisfactory adj ▷ satisfy
satisfied v ▷ satisfy
satisfies v ▷ satisfy
satisfy v (-fies, -fying, -fied) please, content > **satisfaction** n (pl -s) > **satisfactory** adj
satisfying v ▷ satisfy
satnav n (pl -s) (MOTORING) (Informal) satellite navigation
satnavs n ▷ satnav
satsuma n (pl -s) kind of small orange
satsumas n ▷ satsuma
saturate v (-tes, -ting, -ted) soak thoroughly > **saturation** n (pl -s)
saturated v ▷ saturate
saturates v ▷ saturate
saturating v ▷ saturate
saturation n ▷ saturate
saturations n ▷ saturate
saturnalia n (pl -s) wild party or orgy
saturnalias n ▷ saturnalia
saturnine adj gloomy in temperament or appearance
satyr n (pl -s) woodland god, part man, part goat
satyrs n ▷ satyr
sauce n (pl -s) liquid added to food to enhance flavour
saucepan n (pl -s) cooking pot with a long handle
saucepans n ▷ saucepan
saucer n (pl -s) small round dish put under a cup
saucers n ▷ saucer
sauces n ▷ sauce
saucier adj ▷ saucy
sauciest adj ▷ saucy
saucily adv ▷ saucy
saucy adj (-cier, -ciest) impudent > **saucily** adv
sauerkraut n (pl -s) shredded cabbage fermented in brine
sauerkrauts n ▷ sauerkraut
sauna n (pl -s) Finnish-style steam bath
saunas n ▷ sauna
saunter v (-s, -ing, -ed) walk in a leisurely

manner, stroll ▶ n (pl -s) leisurely walk
sauntered v ▷ saunter
sauntering v ▷ saunter
saunters v, n ▷ saunter
sausage n (pl -s) minced meat in an edible tube-shaped skin
sausages n ▷ sausage
sauté [so-tay] v (-tés, -téing or -teeing, -téed) fry quickly in a little fat
sautéed v ▷ sauté
sautéeing v ▷ sauté
sautéing v ▷ sauté
sautés v ▷ sauté
savage adj (-r, -st) wild, untamed ▶ n (pl -s) uncivilized person ▶ v (-ges, -ging, -ged) attack ferociously > **savagely** adv > **savagery** n (pl -ries)
savaged v ▷ savage
savagely adv ▷ savage
savager adj ▷ savage
savageries n ▷ savage
savagery n ▷ savage
savages n, v ▷ savage
savagest adj ▷ savage
savaging v ▷ savage
savanna n ▷ savannah
savannah, savanna n (pl -s) extensive open grassy plain in Africa
savannahs n ▷ savannah
savannas n ▷ savanna
save v (-ves, -ving, -ved) rescue or preserve from harm, protect ▶ n (pl -s) (SPORT) act of preventing a goal > **saver** n (pl -s)
saved v ▷ save
saveloy n (pl -s) (BRIT, AUST & NZ) spicy smoked sausage
saveloys n ▷ saveloy
saver n ▷ save
savers n ▷ save
saves v, n ▷ save
saving v ▷ save ▶ n (pl -s) economy
savings n pl money put by for future use
saviour n (pl -s) person who rescues another
saviours n ▷ saviour
savories n ▷ savory
savory n (pl -ries) aromatic herb used in cooking
savour v (-s, -ing, -ed) enjoy, relish (foll. by of) ▶ n (pl -s) characteristic taste or odour
savoured v ▷ savour
savourier adj ▷ savoury
savouries n ▷ savoury
savouriest adj ▷ savoury

savouring v ▷ savour
savours v, n ▷ savour
savoury adj (-rier, -riest) salty or spicy ▶ n (pl -ries) savoury dish served before or after a meal
savoy n (pl -s) variety of cabbage
savoys n ▷ savoy
savvied v ▷ savvy
savvies v, n ▷ savvy
savvy (Slang) v (-vies, -vying, -vied) understand ▶ n (pl -vies) understanding, intelligence
savvying v ▷ savvy
saw[1] n (pl -s) cutting tool with a toothed metal blade ▶ v (-s, -ing, -ed, -ed or sawn) cut with a saw
saw[2] ▷ see[1]
saw[3] n (pl -s) wise saying, proverb
sawdust n (pl -s) fine wood fragments made in sawing
sawdusts n ▷ sawdust
sawed v ▷ saw[1]
sawfish n (pl -es) fish with a long toothed snout
sawfishes n ▷ sawfish
sawing v ▷ saw[1]
sawmill n (pl -s) mill where timber is sawn into planks
sawmills n ▷ sawmill
sawn v ▷ saw[1]
saws n (pl -s)[1, 3] ▶ v ▷ saw[1]
sawyer n (pl -s) person who saws timber for a living
sawyers n ▷ sawyer
sax n (pl -es) (Informal) ▷ saxophone
saxes n ▷ sax
saxifrage n (pl -s) alpine rock plant with small flowers
saxifrages n ▷ saxifrage
saxophone n (pl -s) brass wind instrument with keys and a curved body > **saxophonist** n (pl -s)
saxophones n ▷ saxophone
saxophonist n ▷ saxophone
saxophonists n ▷ saxophone
say v (-s, -ing, said) speak or utter ▶ n (pl -s) right or chance to speak
saying n (pl -s) maxim, proverb ▶ v ▷ say
sayings n ▷ saying
says v, n ▷ say

> **saz** (sazes). A saz is a Turkish musical instrument. This is a very useful word, and one to remember for when you get a Z in the later stages of the game, with little space left on the board. Saz scores 12 points.

scab n (pl -s) crust formed over a wound
scabbard n (pl -s) sheath for a sword or dagger
scabbards n ▷ scabbard
scabbier adj ▷ scabby
scabbiest adj ▷ scabby
scabby adj (-bbier, -bbiest) covered with scabs
scabies [skay-beez] n itchy skin disease
scabrous [skay-bruss] adj rough and scaly
scabs n ▷ scab
scaffold n (pl -s) temporary platform for workmen
scaffolding n (pl -s) (materials for building) scaffolds
scaffoldings n ▷ scaffolding
scaffolds n ▷ scaffold
scalar n (pl -s) ▶ adj (variable quantity) having magnitude but no direction
scalars n ▷ scalar
scald v (-s, -ing, -ed) burn with hot liquid or steam ▶ n (pl -s) injury by scalding
scalded v ▷ scald
scalding v ▷ scald
scalds v, n ▷ scald
scale[1] n (pl -s) one of the thin overlapping plates covering fishes and reptiles ▶ v (-les, -ling, -led) remove scales from > **scaly** adj (-lier, -liest)
scale[2] n (pl -s) (often pl) weighing instrument
scale[3] n (pl -s) graduated table or sequence of marks at regular intervals, used as a reference in making measurements ▶ v (-les, -ling, -led) climb
scaled v ▷ scale[1, 3]
scalene adj (of a triangle) with three unequal sides
scales n ▷ scale[1, 2, 3] ▶ v ▷ scale[1, 3]
scalier adj ▷ scale[1]
scaliest adj ▷ scale[1]
scaling v ▷ scale[1, 3]
scallop n (pl -s) edible shellfish with two fan-shaped shells
scalloped adj decorated with small curves along the edge
scallops n ▷ scallop
scallywag n (pl -s) (Informal) scamp, rascal
scallywags n ▷ scallywag
scalp n (pl -s) skin and hair on top of the head ▶ v (-s, -ing, -ed) cut off the scalp of
scalped v ▷ scalp
scalpel n (pl -s) small surgical knife
scalpels n ▷ scalpel
scalping v ▷ scalp
scalps n, v ▷ scalp
scaly adj ▷ scale[1]
scam n (pl -s) (Informal) dishonest scheme

scamp n (pl -s) mischievous child

scamper v (-s, -ing, -ed) run about hurriedly or in play ▶ n (pl -s) scampering
  scampered v ▷ scamper
  scampering v ▷ scamper
  scampers v, n ▷ scamper

scampi pl n large prawns
  scamps n ▷ scamp
  scams n ▷ scam

scan v (-s, -nning, -nned) scrutinize carefully ▶ n (pl -s) scanning

scandal n (pl -s) disgraceful action or event
  > scandalous adj

scandalize v (-zes, -zing, -zed) shock by scandal
  scandalized v ▷ scandalize
  scandalizes v ▷ scandalize
  scandalizing v ▷ scandalize
  scandalous adj ▷ scandal
  scandals n ▷ scandal

scandium n (pl -s) (CHEM) rare silvery-white metallic element
  scandiums n ▷ scandium
  scanned v ▷ scan

scanner n (pl -s) electronic device used for scanning
  scanners n ▷ scanner
  scanning v ▷ scan
  scans v, n ▷ scan

scansion n (pl -s) metrical scanning of verse
  scansions n ▷ scansion

scant adj (-er, -est) barely sufficient, meagre
  scanter adj ▷ scant
  scantest adj ▷ scant
  scantier adj ▷ scanty
  scantiest adj ▷ scanty
  scantily n ▷ scanty

scanty adj (-tier, -tiest) barely sufficient or not sufficient > **scantily** adv

scapegoat n (pl -s) person made to bear the blame for others
  scapegoats n ▷ scapegoat

scapula n (pl -lae, -las) shoulder blade
  > scapular adj
  scapulae n ▷ scapula
  scapular adj ▷ scapula
  scapulas n ▷ scapula

scar n (pl -s) mark left by a healed wound ▶ v (-s, -rring, -rred) mark or become marked with a scar

scarab n (pl -s) sacred beetle of ancient Egypt
  scarabs n ▷ scarab

scarce adj (-r, -st) insufficient to meet demand
  > **scarcity** n (pl -ties)

scarcely adv hardly at all

scarcer adj ▷ scarce
scarcest adj ▷ scarce
scarcities n ▷ scarce
scarcity n ▷ scarce

scare v (-res, -ring, -red) frighten or be frightened ▶ n (pl -s) fright, sudden panic

scarecrow n (pl -s) figure dressed in old clothes, set up to scare birds away from crops
  scarecrows n ▷ scarecrow
  scared v ▷ scare

scaremonger n (pl -s) person who spreads alarming rumours
  scaremongers n ▷ scaremonger
  scares v, n ▷ scare

scarf[1] n (pl scarves, -s) piece of material worn round the neck, head, or shoulders

scarf[2] n (pl -s) joint between two pieces of timber made by notching the ends and fastening them together ▶ v (-s, -ing, -ed) join in this way
  scarfed v ▷ scarf[2]
  scarfing v ▷ scarf[2]
  scarfs n ▷ scarf[1, 2] ▶ v ▷ scarf[2]
  scarier adj ▷ scary
  scariest adj ▷ scary
  scarification n ▷ scarify
  scarifications n ▷ scarify
  scarified v ▷ scarify
  scarifies v ▷ scarify

scarify v (-fies, -fying, -fied) scratch or cut slightly all over > **scarification** n (pl -s)
  scarifying v ▷ scarify
  scaring v ▷ scare

scarlatina n (pl -s) scarlet fever
  scarlatinas n ▷ scarlatina

scarlet adj, n (pl -s) brilliant red
  scarlets n ▷ scarlet

scarp n (pl -s) steep slope

scarper v (-s, -ing, -ed) (BRIT) (Slang) run away
  scarpered v ▷ scarper
  scarpering v ▷ scarper
  scarpers v ▷ scarper
  scarps n ▷ scarp
  scarred v ▷ scar
  scarring v ▷ scar
  scars n, v ▷ scar
  scarves n ▷ scarf[1]

scary adj (-rier, -riest) (Informal) frightening

scat[1] v (-s, -tting, -tted) (Informal) go away

scat[2] n (pl -s) jazz singing using improvised vocal sounds instead of words

scathing adj harshly critical

scatological adj preoccupied with obscenity, esp. with references to excrement
  > **scatology** n (pl -gies)

scatologies n ▷ scatology
scatology n ▷ scatological
scats n ▷ scat² ▶ v ▷ scat¹
scatted v ▷ scat¹
scatter v (-s, -ing, -ed) throw about in various directions
scatterbrain n (pl -s) empty-headed person
scatterbrains n ▷ scatterbrain
scattered v ▷ scatter
scattering v ▷ scatter
scatters v ▷ scatter
scattier adj ▷ scatty
scattiest adj ▷ scatty
scatting v ▷ scat¹
scatty adj (-tier, -tiest) (*Informal*) empty-headed
scavenge v (-ges, -ging, -ged) search for (anything usable) among discarded material
scavenged v ▷ scavenge
scavenger n (pl -s) person who scavenges
scavengers n ▷ scavenger
scavenges v ▷ scavenge
scavenging v ▷ scavenge
scenario n (pl -rios) summary of the plot of a play or film
scenarios n ▷ scenario
scene n (pl -s) place of action of a real or imaginary event
sceneries n ▷ scenery
scenery n (pl -ries) natural features of a landscape
scenes n ▷ scene
scenic adj picturesque
scent n (pl -s) pleasant smell ▶ v (-s, -ing, -ed) detect by smell
scented v ▷ scent
scenting v ▷ scent
scents n, v ▷ scent
sceptic [skep-tik] n (pl -s) person who habitually doubts generally accepted beliefs > **sceptical** adj > **sceptically** adv > **scepticism** n (pl -s)
sceptical adj ▷ sceptic
sceptically adv ▷ sceptic
scepticism n ▷ sceptic
scepticisms n ▷ sceptic
sceptics n ▷ sceptic
sceptre n (pl -s) ornamental rod symbolizing royal power
sceptres n ▷ sceptre
schedule n (pl -s) plan of procedure for a project ▶ v (-les, -ling, -led) plan to occur at a certain time
scheduled v ▷ schedule
schedules n, v ▷ schedule

scheduling v ▷ schedule
schema n (pl -mata) overall plan or diagram
schematic adj presented as a plan or diagram
scheme n (pl -s) systematic plan ▶ v (-mes, -ming, -med) plan in an underhand manner > **scheming** adj, n (pl -s)
schemed v ▷ scheme
schemes n, v ▷ scheme
scheming v, adj n ▷ scheme
schemings n ▷ scheme
scherzi n ▷ scherzo
scherzo [skairt-so] n (pl -zos, -zi) brisk lively piece of music
scherzos n ▷ scherzo
schism [skizz-um] n (pl -s) (group resulting from) division in an organization > **schismatic** adj, n (pl -s)
schismatic adj, n ▷ schism
schismatics n ▷ schism
schisms n ▷ schism
schist [shist] n (pl -s) crystalline rock which splits into layers
schists n ▷ schist
schizoid adj abnormally introverted ▶ n (pl -s) schizoid person
schizoids n ▷ schizoid
schizophrenia n (pl -s) mental disorder involving deterioration of or confusion about the personality > **schizophrenic** adj, n (pl -s)
schizophrenias n ▷ schizophrenia
schizophrenic adj, n ▷ schizophrenia
schizophrenics n ▷ schizophrenia
schmaltz n (pl -es) excessive sentimentality > **schmaltzy** adj (-zier, -ziest)
schmaltzes n ▷ schmaltz
schmaltzier adj ▷ schmaltz
schmaltziest adj ▷ schmaltz
schmaltzy adj ▷ schmaltz
schnapps n (pl -es) strong alcoholic spirit
schnapses n ▷ schnapps
schnitzel n (pl -s) thin slice of meat, esp. veal
schnitzels n ▷ schnitzel
scholar n (pl -s) learned person
scholarly adj learned
scholars n ▷ scholar
scholarship n (pl -s) learning
scholarships n ▷ scholarship
scholastic adj of schools or scholars
school¹ n (pl -s) place where children are taught or instruction is given in a subject ▶ v (-s, -ing, -ed) educate or train
school² n (pl -s) shoal of fish, whales, etc.
schooled v ▷ school¹
schoolie n (pl -s) (AUST) schoolteacher or high-school student

schoolies n ▷ schoolie
schooling v ▷ school[1]
schools n ▷ school[1, 2] ▶ v ▷ school[1]
schooner n (pl -s) sailing ship rigged fore-and-aft
schooners n ▷ schooner
sciatic adj of the hip
sciatica n (pl -s) severe pain in the large nerve in the back of the leg
sciaticas n ▷ sciatica
science n (pl -s) systematic study and knowledge of natural or physical phenomena
sciences n ▷ science
scientific adj of science > scientifically adv
scientifically adv ▷ scientific
scientist n (pl -s) person who studies or practises a science
scientists n ▷ scientist
scimitar n (pl -s) curved oriental sword
scimitars n ▷ scimitar
scintillate v (-tes, -ting, -ted) give off sparks
scintillated v ▷ scintillate
scintillates v ▷ scintillate
scintillating adj very lively and amusing ▶ v ▷ scintillate
scion [sy-on] n (pl -s) descendant or heir
scions n ▷ scion
scissors pl n cutting instrument with two crossed pivoted blades
scleroses n ▷ sclerosis
sclerosis n (pl -ses) abnormal hardening of body tissues
scoff[1] v (-s, -ing, -ed) express derision
scoff[2] v (-s, -ing, -ed) (Informal) eat rapidly
scoffed v ▷ scoff[1, 2]
scoffing v ▷ scoff[1, 2]
scoffs v ▷ scoff[1, 2]
scold v (-s, -ing, -ed) find fault with, reprimand ▶ n (pl -s) person who scolds > scolding n (pl -s)
scolded v ▷ scold
scolding v, n ▷ scold
scoldings n ▷ scold
scolds v, n ▷ scold
sconce n (pl -s) bracket on a wall for holding candles or lights
sconces n ▷ sconce
scone n (pl -s) small plain cake baked in an oven or on a griddle
scones n ▷ scone
scoop n (pl -s) shovel-like tool for ladling or hollowing out ▶ v (-s, -ing, -ed) take up or hollow out with or as if with a scoop
scooped v ▷ scoop
scooping v ▷ scoop
scoops n, v ▷ scoop

scoot v (-s, -ing, -ed) (Slang) leave or move quickly
scooted v ▷ scoot
scooter n (pl -s) child's vehicle propelled by pushing on the ground with one foot
scooters n ▷ scooter
scooting v ▷ scoot
scoots v ▷ scoot
scope n (pl -s) opportunity for using abilities
scopes n ▷ scope
scorch v (-es, -ing, -ed) burn on the surface ▶ n (pl -es) slight burn
scorched v ▷ scorch
scorcher n (pl -s) (Informal) very hot day
scorchers n ▷ scorcher
scorches v, n ▷ scorch
scorching v ▷ scorch
score n (pl -s) points gained in a game or competition ▶ v (-res, -ring, -red) gain (points) in a game
scored v ▷ score
scores n, v ▷ score ▶ pl n lots
scoring v ▷ score
scorn n (pl -s) open contempt ▶ v (-s, -ing, -ed) despise > scornful adj > scornfully adv
scorned v ▷ scorn
scornful adj ▷ scorn
scornfully adv ▷ scorn
scorning v ▷ scorn
scorns n, v ▷ scorn
scorpion n (pl -s) small lobster-shaped animal with a sting at the end of a jointed tail
scorpions n ▷ scorpion
scotch v (-es, -ing, -ed) put an end to
scotched v ▷ scotch
scotches v ▷ scotch
scotching v ▷ scotch
scoundrel n (pl -s) (Old-fashioned) cheat or deceiver
scoundrels n ▷ scoundrel
scour[1] v (-s, -ing, -ed) clean or polish by rubbing with something rough
scour[2] v (-s, -ing, -ed) search thoroughly and energetically
scoured v ▷ scour[1, 2]
scourer n (pl -s) small rough nylon pad used for cleaning pots and pans
scourers n ▷ scourer
scourge n (pl -s) person or thing causing severe suffering ▶ v (-ges, -ging, -ged) cause severe suffering to
scourged v ▷ scourge
scourges n, v ▷ scourge
scourging v ▷ scourge
scouring v ▷ scour[1, 2]

scours v ▷ scour[1, 2]

scout n (pl -s) person sent out to reconnoitre
▶ v (-s, -ing, -ed) act as a scout
  scouted v ▷ scout
  scouting v ▷ scout
  scouts n, v ▷ scout

scowl v (-s, -ing, -ed) ▶ n (pl -s) (have) an angry
or sullen expression
  scowled v ▷ scowl
  scowling v ▷ scowl
  scowls v, n ▷ scowl

scrabble v (-les, -ling, -led) scrape at with the
hands, feet, or claws
  scrabbled v ▷ scrabble
  scrabbles v ▷ scrabble
  scrabbling v ▷ scrabble

scrag n (pl -s) thin end of a neck of mutton
  scraggier adj ▷ scraggy
  scraggiest adj ▷ scraggy

scraggy adj (-ggier, -ggiest) thin, bony
  scrags n ▷ scrag

scram v (-s, -mming, -mmed) (Informal) go
away quickly

scramble v (-les, -ling, -led) climb or crawl
hastily or awkwardly ▶ n (pl -les) scrambling
  scrambled v ▷ scramble

scrambler n (pl -s) electronic device that
makes transmitted speech unintelligible
  scramblers n ▷ scrambler
  scrambles v, n ▷ scramble
  scrambling v ▷ scramble
  scrammed v ▷ scram
  scramming v ▷ scram
  scrams v ▷ scram

scrap[1] n (pl -s) small piece ▶ v (-s, -pping, -pped)
discard as useless

scrap[2] n (pl -s) ▶ v (-s, -pping, -pped) (Informal)
fight or quarrel

scrapbook n (pl -s) book with blank pages in
which newspaper cuttings or pictures are
stuck
  scrapbooks n ▷ scrapbook

scrape v (-pes, -ping, -ped) rub with
something rough or sharp ▶ n (pl -s) act or
sound of scraping > **scraper** n (pl -s)
  scraped v ▷ scrape
  scraper n ▷ scrape
  scrapers n ▷ scrape
  scrapes v, n ▷ scrape
  scraping v ▷ scrape
  scrapped v ▷ scrap[1, 2]
  scrappier adj ▷ scrappy
  scrappiest adj ▷ scrappy
  scrapping v ▷ scrap[1, 2]

scrappy adj (-ppier, -ppiest) fragmentary,
disjointed

scraps v ▷ scrap[1, 2] ▶ n ▷ scrap[1, 2] ▶ pl n leftover
food

scratch v (-es, -ing, -ed) mark or cut with
claws, nails, or anything rough or sharp
▶ n (pl -es) wound, mark, or sound made by
scratching ▶ adj put together at short notice
> **scratchy** adj (-chier, -chiest)

scratchcard n (pl -s) ticket that reveals
whether or not the holder has won a prize
when the surface is removed by scratching
  scratchcards n ▷ scratchcard
  scratched v ▷ scratch
  scratches v, n ▷ scratch
  scratchier adj ▷ scratch
  scratchiest adj ▷ scratch
  scratching v ▷ scratch
  scratchy adj ▷ scratch

scrawl v (-s, -ing, -ed) write carelessly or
hastily ▶ n (pl -s) scribbled writing
  scrawled v ▷ scrawl
  scrawling v ▷ scrawl
  scrawls v, n ▷ scrawl
  scrawnier adj ▷ scrawny
  scrawniest adj ▷ scrawny

scrawny adj (-nier, -niest) thin and bony

scream v (-s, -ing, -ed) utter a piercing cry, esp.
of fear or pain ▶ n (pl -s) shrill piercing cry
  screamed v ▷ scream
  screaming v ▷ scream
  screams v, n ▷ scream

scree n (pl -s) slope of loose shifting stones

screech v (-es, -ing, -ed) ▶ n (pl -es) (utter) a
shrill cry
  screeched v ▷ screech
  screeches v, n ▷ screech
  screeching v ▷ screech

screed n (pl -s) long tedious piece of writing
  screeds n ▷ screed

screen n (pl -s) surface of a television set, VDU,
etc., on which an image is formed ▶ v (-s,
-ing, -ed) shelter or conceal with or as if with
a screen
  screened v ▷ screen
  screening v ▷ screen
  screens n, v ▷ screen
  screes n ▷ scree

screw n (pl -s) metal pin with a spiral ridge
along its length, twisted into materials to
fasten them together ▶ v (-s, -ing, -ed) turn
(a screw)

screwdriver n (pl -s) tool for turning screws
  screwdrivers n ▷ screwdriver
  screwed v ▷ screw
  screwier adj ▷ screwy

screwiest adj ▷ screwy
screwing v ▷ screw
screws n, v ▷ screw
screwy adj (-wier, -wiest) (Informal) crazy or eccentric
scribble v (-les, -ling, -led) write hastily or illegibly ▶ n (pl -s) something scribbled
scribbled v ▷ scribble
scribbles v, n ▷ scribble
scribbling v ▷ scribble
scribe n (pl -s) person who copied manuscripts before the invention of printing
scribes n ▷ scribe
scrimmage n (pl -s) rough or disorderly struggle
scrimmages n ▷ scrimmage
scrimp v (-s, -ing, -ed) be very economical
scrimped v ▷ scrimp
scrimping v ▷ scrimp
scrimps v ▷ scrimp
scrip n (pl -s) certificate representing a claim to stocks or shares
scrips n ▷ scrip
script n (pl -s) text of a film, play, or TV programme
scripts n ▷ script
scriptural adj ▷ scripture
scripture n (pl -s) sacred writings of a religion > **scriptural** adj
scriptures n ▷ scripture
scrofula n (pl -s) tuberculosis of the lymphatic glands > **scrofulous** adj
scrofulas n ▷ scrofula
scrofulous adj ▷ scrofula
scroggin n (pl -s) (NZ) mixture of nuts and dried fruits
scroggins n ▷ scroggin
scroll n (pl -s) roll of parchment or paper ▶ v (-s, -ing, -ed) move (text) up or down on a VDU screen
scrolled v ▷ scroll
scrolling v ▷ scroll
scrolls n, v ▷ scroll
scrota n ▷ scrotum
scrotum n (pl -ta, -tums) pouch of skin containing the testicles
scrotums n ▷ scrotum
scrounge v (-ges, -ging, -ged) (Informal) get by cadging or begging > **scrounger** n (pl -s)
scrounged v ▷ scrounge
scrounger n ▷ scrounge
scroungers n ▷ scrounge
scrounges v ▷ scrounge
scrounging v ▷ scrounge
scrub¹ v (-s, -bbing, -bbed) clean by rubbing,

often with a hard brush and water ▶ n (pl -s) scrubbing
scrub² n (pl -s) stunted trees
scrubbed v ▷ scrub¹
scrubbier adj ▷ scrubby
scrubbiest adj ▷ scrubby
scrubbing v ▷ scrub¹
scrubby adj (-bbier, -bbiest) covered with scrub
scrubs v ▷ scrub¹ ▶ n ▷ scrub¹,²
scruff¹ n (pl -s) nape (of the neck)
scruff² n (pl -s) (Informal) untidy person
scruffier adj ▷ scruffy
scruffiest adj ▷ scruffy
scruffs n ▷ scruff¹,²
scruffy adj (-fier, -ffiest) unkempt or shabby
scrum, scrummage n (pl -s) (RUGBY) restarting of play in which opposing packs of forwards push against each other to gain possession of the ball
scrummage n ▷ scrum
scrummages n ▷ scrum
scrumptious adj (Informal) delicious
scrums n ▷ scrum
scrunch v (-es, -ing, -ed) crumple or crunch or be crumpled or crunched ▶ n (pl -es) act or sound of scrunching
scrunched v ▷ scrunch
scrunches v, n ▷ scrunch
scrunching v ▷ scrunch
scruple n (pl -s) doubt produced by one's conscience or morals ▶ v (-les, -ling, -led) have doubts on moral grounds
scrupled v ▷ scruple
scruples n, v ▷ scruple
scrupling v ▷ scruple
scrupulous adj very conscientious > **scrupulously** adv
scrupulously adv ▷ scrupulous
scrutinies n ▷ scrutiny
scrutinize v (-zes, -zing, -zed) examine closely
scrutinized v ▷ scrutinize
scrutinizes v ▷ scrutinize
scrutinizing v ▷ scrutinize
scrutiny n (pl -nies) close examination
scud v (-s, -dding, -dded) move along swiftly
scudded v ▷ scud
scudding v ▷ scud
scuds v ▷ scud
scuff v (-s, -ing, -ed) drag (the feet) while walking ▶ n (pl -s) mark caused by scuffing
scuffed v ▷ scuff
scuffing v ▷ scuff
scuffle v (-les, -ling, -led) fight in a disorderly manner ▶ n (pl -s) disorderly struggle

scuffled v ▷ scuffle

scuffles v, n ▷ scuffle

scuffling v ▷ scuffle

scuffs v, n ▷ scuff

scull n (pl -s) small oar ▶ v (-s, -ing, -ed) row (a boat) using sculls

sculled v ▷ scull

sculleries n ▷ scullery

scullery n (pl -ries) small room where washing-up and other kitchen work is done

sculling v ▷ scull

sculls n, v ▷ scull

sculptor n ▷ sculpture

sculptors n ▷ sculpture

sculptress n ▷ sculpture

sculptresses n ▷ sculpture

sculptural adj ▷ sculpture

sculpture n (pl -s) art of making figures or designs in wood, stone, etc. ▶ v (-res, -ring, -red) (also sculpt) represent in sculpture > sculptor, sculptress n (pl -s, -es) > sculptural adj

sculptured v ▷ sculpture

sculptures n, v ▷ sculpture

sculpturing v ▷ sculpture

scum n (pl -s) impure or waste matter on the surface of a liquid > scummy adj (-mmier, -mmiest)

scummier adj ▷ scum

scummiest adj ▷ scum

scummy adj ▷ scum

scums n ▷ scum

scungier adj ▷ scungy

scungiest adj ▷ scungy

scungy adj (-ier, -iest) (AUST & NZ) (Informal) sordid or dirty

scupper v (-s, -ing, -ed) (Informal) defeat or ruin

scuppered v ▷ scupper

scuppering v ▷ scupper

scuppers v ▷ scupper

scurf n (pl -s) flaky skin on the scalp

scurfs n ▷ scurf

scurried v ▷ scurry

scurries v, n ▷ scurry

scurrilous adj untrue and defamatory

scurry v (-ries, -rying, -ried) move hastily ▶ n (pl -ries) act or sound of scurrying

scurrying v ▷ scurry

scurvies n ▷ scurvy

scurvy n (pl -vies) disease caused by lack of vitamin C

scut n (pl -s) short tail of the hare, rabbit, or deer

scuts n ▷ scut

scuttle¹ n (pl -s) fireside container for coal

scuttle² v (-les, -ling, -led) run with short quick steps ▶ n (pl -s) hurried run

scuttle³ v (-les, -ling, -ed) make a hole in (a ship) to sink it

scuttled v ▷ scuttle²,³

scuttles n ▷ scuttle¹,² ▶ v ▷ scuttle²,³

scuttling v ▷ scuttle²,³

scythe n (pl -s) long-handled tool with a curved blade for cutting grass ▶ v (-thes, -thing, -thed) cut with a scythe

scythed v ▷ scythe

scythes n, v ▷ scythe

scything v ▷ scythe

sea n (pl -s) mass of salt water covering three quarters of the earth's surface

seaboard n (pl -s) coast

seaboards n ▷ seaboard

seafaring adj working or travelling by sea

seafood n (pl -s) edible saltwater fish or shellfish

seafoods n ▷ seafood

seagull n (pl -s) gull

seagulls n ▷ seagull

seal¹ n (pl -s) piece of wax, lead, etc. with a special design impressed upon it, attached to a letter or document as a mark of authentication ▶ v (-s, -ing, -ed) close with or as if with a seal

seal² n (pl -s) amphibious mammal with flippers as limbs > sealskin n (pl -s)

sealant n (pl -s) any substance used for sealing

sealants n ▷ sealant

sealed v ▷ seal¹

sealing v ▷ seal¹

seals n ▷ seal¹,² ▶ v ▷ seal¹

sealskin n ▷ seal²

sealskins n ▷ seal²

seaman n (pl -men) sailor

seamed v ▷ seam

seamen n ▷ seaman

seamier adj ▷ seamy

seamiest adj ▷ seamy

seaming v ▷ seam

seamless adj ▷ seam

seams n, v ▷ seam

seam n (pl -s) line where two edges are joined, as by stitching ▶ v (-s, -ing, -ed) mark with furrows or wrinkles > seamless adj

seamstress n (pl -es) woman who sews, esp. professionally

seamstresses n ▷ seamstress

seamy adj (-mier, -miest) sordid

seance [say-anss] n (pl -s) meeting at which spiritualists attempt to communicate with the dead

seances n ▷ seance

seaplane n (pl -s) aircraft designed to take off from and land on water

seaplanes n ▷ seaplane

sear v (-s, -ing, -ed) scorch, burn the surface of

search v (-es, -ing, -ed) examine closely in order to find something ▶ n (pl -es) searching

searched v ▷ search

searches v, n ▷ search

searching adj keen or thorough ▶ v ▷ search

searchlight n (pl -s) powerful light with a beam that can be shone in any direction

searchlights n ▷ searchlight

seared v ▷ sear

searing adj (of pain) very sharp ▶ v ▷ sear

sears v ▷ sear

seas n ▷ sea

seasick adj suffering from nausea caused by the motion of a ship > **seasickness** n (pl -es)

seasickness n ▷ seasick

seasicknesses n ▷ seasick

seaside n (pl -s) area, esp. a holiday resort, on the coast

seasides n ▷ seaside

season n (pl -s) one of four divisions of the year, each of which has characteristic weather conditions ▶ v (-s, -ing, -ed) flavour with salt, herbs, etc.

seasonable adj appropriate for the season

seasonal adj depending on or varying with the seasons

seasoned adj experienced ▶ v ▷ season

seasoning n (pl -s) salt, herbs, etc. added to food to enhance flavour

seasonings n ▷ seasoning

seasons n, v ▷ season

seat n (pl -s) thing designed or used for sitting on ▶ v (-s, -ing, -ed) cause to sit

seated v ▷ seat

seating v ▷ seat

seats n, v ▷ seat

seaweed n (pl -s) plant growing in the sea

seaweeds n ▷ seaweed

seaworthy adj (of a ship) in fit condition for a sea voyage

sebaceous adj of, like, or secreting fat or oil

secateurs pl n small pruning shears

secede v (-des, -ding, -ded) withdraw formally from a political alliance or federation > **secession** n (pl -s)

seceded v ▷ secede

secedes v ▷ secede

seceding v ▷ secede

secession n ▷ secede

secessions n ▷ secede

seclude v (-des, -ding, -ded) keep (a person) from contact with others

secluded adj private, sheltered ▶ v ▷ seclude > **seclusion** n (pl -s)

secludes v ▷ seclude

secluding v ▷ seclude

seclusion n ▷ secluded

seclusions n ▷ secluded

second¹ adj coming directly after the first ▶ n (pl -s) person or thing coming second ▶ v (-s, -ing, -ed) express formal support for (a motion proposed in a meeting) > **secondly** adv

second² n (pl -s) sixtieth part of a minute of an angle or time

second³ [si-kond] v (-s, -ing, -ed) transfer (a person) temporarily to another job > **secondment** n (pl -s)

secondary adj of less importance

seconded v ▷ second¹, ³

secondhand adj bought after use by another

seconding v ▷ second¹, ³

secondly adv ▷ second¹

secondment n ▷ second³

secondments n ▷ second³

seconds v ▷ second¹, ³, ³ ▶ n ▷ second¹, ² ▶ pl n inferior goods

secrecies n ▷ secret

secrecy n ▷ secret

secret adj kept from the knowledge of others ▶ n (pl -s) something kept secret > **secretly** adv > **secrecy** n (pl -cies)

secretarial adj ▷ secretary

secretariat n (pl -s) administrative office or staff of a legislative body

secretariats n ▷ secretariat

secretaries n ▷ secretary

secretary n (pl -ries) person who deals with correspondence and general clerical work > **secretarial** adj

secrete¹ v (-tes, -ting, -ted) (of an organ, gland, etc.) produce and release (a substance) > **secretion** n (pl -s) > **secretory** [sek-reet-or-ee] adj

secrete² v (-tes, -ting, -ted) hide or conceal

secreted v ▷ secrete¹, ²

secretes v ▷ secrete¹, ²

secreting v ▷ secrete¹, ²

secretion n ▷ secrete¹

secretions n ▷ secrete¹

secretive adj inclined to keep things secret > **secretiveness** n (pl -es)

secretiveness n ▷ secretive

secretivenesses n ▷ secretive

secretly adv ▷ secret

secretory *adj* ▷ secrete¹

secrets *n* ▷ secret

sect *n* (*pl* -s) subdivision of a religious or political group, esp. one with extreme beliefs

sectarian *adj* of a sect

section *n* (*pl* -s) part cut off ▶ *v* (-s, -ing, -ed) cut or divide into sections > sectional *adj*

sectional *adj* ▷ section

sectioned *v* ▷ section

sectioning *v* ▷ section

sections *n*, *v* ▷ section

sector *n* (*pl* -s) part or subdivision

sectors *n* ▷ sector

sects *n* ▷ sect

secular *adj* worldly, as opposed to sacred

secure *adj* (-r, -st) free from danger ▶ *v* (-res, -ring, -red) obtain > securely *adv*

secured *v* ▷ secure

securely *adv* ▷ secure

securer *adj* ▷ secure

secures *v* ▷ secure

securest *adj* ▷ secure

securing *v* ▷ secure

securities *n* ▷ security

security *n* (*pl* -ties) precautions against theft, espionage, or other danger

sedan *n* (*pl* -s) (US, AUST & NZ) two-door or four-door car with the body closed off from the rear luggage area

sedans *n* ▷ sedan

sedate¹ *adj* (-r, -st) calm and dignified > sedately *adv*

sedate² *v* (-tes, -ting, -ted) give a sedative drug to > sedation *n* (*pl* -s)

sedated *v* ▷ sedate²

sedately *adv* ▷ sedate¹

sedater *adj* ▷ sedate¹

sedates *v* ▷ sedate²

sedatest *adj* ▷ sedate¹

sedating *v* ▷ sedate²

sedation *n* ▷ sedate²

sedations *n* ▷ sedate²

sedative *adj* having a soothing or calming effect ▶ *n* (*pl* -s) sedative drug

sedatives *n* ▷ sedative

sedentary *adj* done sitting down, involving little exercise

sedge *n* (*pl* -s) coarse grasslike plant growing on wet ground

sedges *n* ▷ sedge

sediment *n* (*pl* -s) matter which settles to the bottom of a liquid > sedimentary *adj*

sedimentary *adj* ▷ sediment

sediments *n* ▷ sediment

sedition *n* (*pl* -s) speech or action encouraging rebellion against the government > seditious *adj*

seditions *n* ▷ sedition

seditious *adj* ▷ sedition

seduce *v* (-ces, -cing, -ced) persuade into sexual intercourse > seducer, seductress *n* (*pl* -s, -es) > seduction *n* (*pl* -s) > seductive *adj*

seduced *v* ▷ seduce

seducer *n* ▷ seduce

seducers *n* ▷ seduce

seduces *v* ▷ seduce

seducing *v* ▷ seduce

seduction *n* ▷ seduce

seductions *n* ▷ seduce

seductive *adj* ▷ seduce

seductress *n* ▷ seduce

seductresses *n* ▷ seduce

sedulous *adj* diligent or persevering > sedulously *adv*

sedulously *adv* ▷ sedulous

see¹ *v* (-s, -ing, saw, seen) perceive with the eyes or mind

see² *n* (*pl* -s) diocese of a bishop

seed *n* (*pl* -s) mature fertilized grain of a plant ▶ *v* (-s, -ing, -ed) sow with seed

seeded *v* ▷ seed

seedier *adj* ▷ seedy

seediest *adj* ▷ seedy

seeding *v* ▷ seed

seedling *n* (*pl* -s) young plant raised from a seed

seedlings *n* ▷ seedling

seeds *n*, *v* ▷ seed

seedy *adj* (-dier, -diest) shabby

seeing *conj* in view of the fact that ▶ *v* ▷ see¹

seek *v* (-s, -ing, sought) try to find or obtain

seeking *v* ▷ seek

seeks *v* ▷ seek

seem *v* (-s, -ing, -ed) appear to be

seemed *v* ▷ seem

seeming *adj* apparent but not real > seemingly *adv*, *v* ▷ seem

seemingly *adv* ▷ seeming

seemlier *adj* ▷ seemly

seemliest *adj* ▷ seemly

seemly *adj* (-lier, -liest) proper or fitting

seems *v* ▷ seem

seen *v* ▷ see¹

seep *v* (-s, -ing, -ed) trickle through slowly, ooze > seepage *n* (*pl* -s)

seepage *n* ▷ seep

seepages *n* ▷ seep

seeped *v* ▷ seep

seeping *v* ▷ seep

seeps *v* ▷ seep

seer n (pl -s) prophet
  seers n ▷ seer
seersucker n (pl -s) light cotton fabric with a slightly crinkled surface
  seersuckers n ▷ seersucker
  sees b ▷ see² ▶ v ▷ see¹
seesaw n (pl -s) plank balanced in the middle so that two people seated on either end ride up and down alternately ▶ v (-s, -ing, -ed) move up and down
  seesawed v ▷ seesaw
  seesawing v ▷ seesaw
  seesaws n, v ▷ seesaw
seethe v (-thes, -thing, -thed) be very agitated
  seethed v ▷ seethe
  seethes v ▷ seethe
  seething v ▷ seethe
segment n (pl -s) one of several sections into which something may be divided ▶ v (-s, -ing, -ed) divide into segments > **segmentation** n (pl -s)
  segmentation n ▷ segment
  segmentations n ▷ segment
  segmented v ▷ segment
  segmenting v ▷ segment
  segments n, v ▷ segment
segregate v (-tes, -ting, -ted) set apart > **segregation** n (pl -s)
  segregated v ▷ segregate
  segregates v ▷ segregate
  segregating v ▷ segregate
  segregation n ▷ segregate
  segregations n ▷ segregate
seine [sane] n (pl -s) large fishing net that hangs vertically from floats
  seines n ▷ seine
seismic adj relating to earthquakes
seismograph, seismometer n (pl -s) instrument that records the strength of earthquakes
  seismographs n ▷ seismograph
  seismological adj ▷ seismology
  seismologies n ▷ seismology
  seismologist n ▷ seismology
  seismologists n ▷ seismology
seismology n (pl -gies) study of earthquakes > **seismological** adj > **seismologist** n (pl -s)
  seismometer n ▷ seismograph
  seismometers n ▷ seismograph
seize v (-zes, -zing, -zed) take hold of forcibly or quickly (usu. foll. by up)
  seized v ▷ seize
  seizes v ▷ seize
  seizing v ▷ seize
seizure n (pl -s) sudden violent attack of an illness
  seizures n ▷ seizure
seldom adv not often, rarely
select v (-s, -ing, -ed) pick out or choose ▶ adj chosen in preference to others > **selector** n (pl -s)
  selected v ▷ select
  selecting v ▷ select
selection n (pl -s) selecting
  selections n ▷ selection
selective adj chosen or choosing carefully > **selectively** adv > **selectivity** n (pl -ties)
  selectively adv ▷ selective
  selectivities n ▷ selective
  selectivity n ▷ selective
  selector n ▷ select
  selectors n ▷ select
  selects v ▷ select
selenium n (pl -s) (CHEM) nonmetallic element with photoelectric properties
  seleniums n ▷ selenium
self n (pl selves) distinct individuality or identity of a person or thing
selfish adj caring too much about oneself and not enough about others > **selfishly** adv > **selfishness** n (pl -es)
  selfishly adv ▷ selfish
  selfishness n ▷ selfish
  selfishnesses n ▷ selfish
selfless adj unselfish
selfsame adj the very same
sell v (-s, -ing, sold) exchange (something) for money (foll. by **for**) ▶ n (pl -s) manner of selling > **seller** n (pl -s)
  seller n ▷ sell
  sellers n ▷ sell
  selling v ▷ sell
sellotape n (pl -s)® type of adhesive tape ▶ v (-pes, -ping, -ped) stick with sellotape
  sellotaped v ▷ sellotape
  sellotapes n, v ▷ sellotape
  sellotaping v ▷ sellotape
sellout n (pl -s) performance of a show etc. for which all the tickets are sold
  sellouts n ▷ sellout
  sells v, n ▷ sell
selvage, selvedge n (pl -s) edge of cloth, woven so as to prevent unravelling
  selvages n ▷ selvage
  selvedge n ▷ selvage
  selvedges n ▷ selvage
  selves n ▷ self
semantic adj relating to the meaning of words
semantics n study of linguistic meaning
semaphore n (pl -s) system of signalling by

holding two flags in different positions to represent letters of the alphabet

semaphores n ▷ **semaphore**

semblance n (pl -s) outward or superficial appearance

semblances n ▷ **semblance**

semen n (pl -s) sperm-carrying fluid produced by male animals

semens n ▷ **semen**

semester n (pl -s) either of two divisions of the academic year

semesters n ▷ **semester**

semi n (pl -s) (BRIT & S AFR) (Informal) semidetached house

semibreve n (pl -s) musical note four beats long

semibreves n ▷ **semibreve**

semicolon n (pl -s) the punctuation mark (;)

semicolons n ▷ **semicolon**

semiconductor n (pl -s) substance with an electrical conductivity that increases with temperature

semiconductors n ▷ **semiconductor**

semidetached adj (of a house) joined to another one on one side

semifinal n (pl -s) match or round before the final > **semifinalist** n (pl -s)

semifinalist n ▷ **semifinal**

semifinalists n ▷ **semifinal**

semifinals n ▷ **semifinal**

seminal adj original and influential

seminar n (pl -s) meeting of a group of students for discussion

seminaries n ▷ **seminary**

seminars n ▷ **seminar**

seminary n (pl -ries) college for priests

semiprecious adj (of gemstones) having less value than precious stones

semiquaver n (pl -s) musical note half the length of a quaver

semiquavers n ▷ **semiquaver**

semis n ▷ **semi**

semitone n (pl -s) smallest interval between two notes in Western music

semitones n ▷ **semitone**

semitrailer n (pl -s) (AUST) large truck in two separate sections joined by a pivoted bar

semitrailers n ▷ **semitrailer**

semolina n (pl -s) hard grains of wheat left after the milling of flour, used to make puddings and pasta

semolinas n ▷ **semolina**

senate n (pl -s) upper house of some parliaments; governing body of some universities

senates n ▷ **senate**

senator n (pl -s) member of a senate > **senatorial** adj

senatorial adj ▷ **senator**

senators n ▷ **senator**

send v (-s, -ing, sent) cause (a person or thing) to go to or be taken or transmitted to a place

sending v ▷ **send**

sendoff n (pl -s) demonstration of good wishes at a person's departure

sendoffs n ▷ **sendoff**

sends v ▷ **send**

sendup n (pl -s) (Informal) imitation

sendups n ▷ **sendup**

senile adj mentally or physically weak because of old age > **senility** n (pl -ties)

senilities n ▷ **senile**

senility n ▷ **senile**

senior adj superior in rank or standing ▶ n (pl -s) senior person > **seniority** n (pl -ties)

seniorities n ▷ **senior**

seniority n ▷ **senior**

seniors n ▷ **senior**

senna n (pl -s) tropical plant

sennas n ▷ **senna**

señor [sen-nyor] n (pl -ores) Spanish term of address equivalent to sir or Mr

señora [sen-nyor-a] n (pl -s) Spanish term of address equivalent to madam or Mrs

señoras n ▷ **señora**

señorita [sen-nyor-ee-ta] n (pl -s) Spanish term of address equivalent to madam or Miss

señoritas n ▷ **señorita**

señors n ▷ **señor**

sensation n (pl -s) ability to feel things physically

sensational adj causing intense shock, anger, or excitement

sensationalism n (pl -s) deliberate use of sensational language or subject matter > **sensationalist** adj, n (pl -s)

sensationalisms n ▷ **sensationalism**

sensationalist adj, n ▷ **sensationalism**

sensationalists n ▷ **sensationalism**

sensations n ▷ **sensation**

sense n (pl -s) any of the faculties of perception or feeling (sight, hearing, touch, taste, or smell ▶ v (-ses, -sing, -sed) perceive > **senseless** adj

sensed v ▷ **sense**

senseless adj ▷ **sense**

senses n, v ▷ **sense**

sensibilities n ▷ **sensibility**

sensibility n (pl -ties) ability to experience deep feelings

sensible adj (**-r, -st**) having or showing good sense > **sensibly** adv
sensibler adj ▷ **sensible**
sensiblest adj ▷ **sensible**
sensibly adv ▷ **sensible**
sensing v ▷ **sense**
sensitive adj easily hurt or offended > **sensitively** adv > **sensitivity** n (pl **-s**)
sensitively adv > **sensitive**
sensitivities n ▷ **sensitive**
sensitivity n ▷ **sensitive**
sensitize v (**-zes, -zing, -zed**) make sensitive
sensitized v ▷ **sensitize**
sensitizes v ▷ **sensitize**
sensitizing v ▷ **sensitize**
sensor n (pl **-s**) device that detects or measures the presence of something, such as radiation
sensors n ▷ **sensor**
sensory adj of the senses or sensation
sensual adj giving pleasure to the body and senses rather than the mind > **sensually** adv > **sensuality** n (pl **-ties**) > **sensualist** n (pl **-s**)
sensualist n ▷ **sensual**
sensualists n ▷ **sensual**
sensuality n ▷ **sensual**
sensually adj ▷ **sensual**
sensuous adj pleasing to the senses > **sensuously** adv
sensuously adv ▷ **sensuous**
sent v ▷ **send**
sentence n (pl **-s**) sequence of words capable of standing alone as a statement, question, or command ▶ v (**-ces, -cing, -ced**) pass sentence on (a convicted person)
sentenced v ▷ **sentence**
sentences n, v ▷ **sentence**
sentencing n, v ▷ **sentence**
sententious adj trying to sound wise
sentience n ▷ **sentient**
sentiences n ▷ **sentient**
sentient [sen-tee-ent] adj capable of feeling > **sentience** n (pl **-s**)
sentiment n (pl **-s**) thought, opinion, or attitude
sentimental adj excessively romantic or nostalgic > **sentimentalism** n (pl **-s**) > **sentimentality** n (pl **-ties**)
sentimentalism n ▷ **sentimental**
sentimentalisms n ▷ **sentimental**
sentimentalities n ▷ **sentimentality**
sentimentality n ▷ **sentimental**
sentimentalize v (**-zes, -zing, -zed**) make sentimental
sentimentalized v ▷ **sentimentalize**

sentimentalizes v ▷ **sentimentalize**
sentiments n ▷ **sentiment**
sentinel n (pl **-s**) sentry
sentinels n ▷ **sentinel**
sentries n ▷ **sentry**
sentry n (pl **-tries**) soldier on watch
sepal n (pl **-s**) leaflike division of the calyx of a flower
sepals n ▷ **sepal**
separable adj ▷ **separate**
separate v (**-tes, -ting, -ted**) act as a barrier between ▶ adj not the same, different > **separable** adj > **separately** adv
separated v ▷ **separate**
separately adv ▷ **separate**
separates v ▷ **separate**
separating v ▷ **separate**
separation n (pl **-s**) separating or being separated
separations n ▷ **separation**
separatism n ▷ **separatist**
separatisms n ▷ **separatist**
separatist n (pl **-s**) person who advocates the separation of a group from an organization or country > **separatism** n (pl **-s**)
separatists n ▷ **separatist**
sepia adj, n (pl **-s**) reddish-brown (pigment)
sepias n ▷ **sepia**
sepses n ▷ **sepsis**
sepsis n (pl **-ses**) poisoning caused by pus-forming bacteria
septet n (pl **-s**) group of seven performers
septets n ▷ **septet**
septic adj (of a wound) infected
septicaemia [sep-tis-see-mee-a] n (pl **-s**) infection of the blood
septicaemias n ▷ **septicaemia**
septuagenarian n (pl **-s**) person aged between seventy and seventy-nine
septuagenarians n ▷ **septuagenarian**
sepulchral [sip-pulk-ral] adj gloomy
sepulchre [sep-pull-ker] n (pl **-s**) tomb or burial vault
sepulchres n ▷ **sepulchre**
sequel n (pl **-s**) novel, play, or film that continues the story of an earlier one
sequels n ▷ **sequel**
sequence n (pl **-s**) arrangement of two or more things in successive order > **sequential** adj
sequences n ▷ **sequence**
sequential adj ▷ **sequence**
sequester v (**-s, -ing, -ed**) seclude
sequestered v ▷ **sequester**
sequestering v ▷ **sequester**
sequesters v ▷ **sequester**

sequestrate v (-tes, -ting, -ted) confiscate (property) until its owner's debts are paid or a court order is complied with > **sequestration** n (pl -s)
  sequestrated v ▷ sequestrate
  sequestrates v ▷ sequestrate
  sequestrating v ▷ sequestrate
  sequestration n ▷ sequestrate
  sequestrations n ▷ sequestrate

sequin n (pl -s) small ornamental metal disc on a garment > **sequined** adj
  sequined adj ▷ sequin
  sequins n ▷ sequin

sequoia n (pl -s) giant Californian coniferous tree
  sequoias n ▷ sequoia

seraglio [sir-ah-lee-oh] n (pl -s) harem of a Muslim palace
  seraglios n ▷ seraglio

seraph n (pl -s, -aphim) member of the highest order of angels > **seraphic** adj
  seraphic adj ▷ seraph
  seraphim n ▷ seraph
  seraphs n ▷ seraph

serenade n (pl -s) music played or sung to a woman by a lover ▶ v (-des, -ding, -ded) sing or play a serenade to (someone)
  serenaded v ▷ serenade
  serenades n, v ▷ serenade
  serenading v ▷ serenade
  serendipities n ▷ serendipity

serendipity n (pl -ties) gift of making fortunate discoveries by accident

serene adj (-r, -st) calm, peaceful > **serenely** adv > **serenity** n (pl -ties)
  serenely adv ▷ serene
  serener adj ▷ serene
  serenest adj ▷ serene
  serenities n ▷ serene
  serenity n ▷ serene

serf n (pl -s) medieval farm labourer who could not leave the land he worked on > **serfdom** n (pl -s)
  serfdom n ▷ serf
  serfdoms n ▷ serf
  serfs n ▷ serf

serge n (pl -s) strong woollen fabric

sergeant n (pl -s) noncommissioned officer in the army
  sergeants n ▷ sergeant
  serges n ▷ serge

serial n (pl -s) story or play produced in successive instalments ▶ adj of or forming a series

serialize v (-zes, -zing, -zed) publish or present as a serial
  serialized v ▷ serialize
  serializes v ▷ serialize
  serializing v ▷ serialize
  serials n ▷ serial

series n (pl series) group or succession of related things, usu. arranged in order

serious adj giving cause for concern > **seriously** adv > **seriousness** n (pl -es)
  seriously adv ▷ serious
  seriousness n ▷ serious
  seriousnesses n ▷ serious

sermon n (pl -s) speech on a religious or moral subject by a clergyman in a church service

sermonize v (-zes, -zing, -zed) make a long moralizing speech
  sermonized v ▷ sermonize
  sermonizes v ▷ sermonize
  sermonizing v ▷ sermonize
  sermons n ▷ sermon

serpent n (pl -s) (Lit) snake

serpentine adj twisting like a snake
  serpents n ▷ serpent

serrated adj having a notched or sawlike edge

serried adj in close formation

serum [seer-um] n (pl -s) watery fluid left after blood has clotted
  serums n ▷ serum

servant n (pl -s) person employed to do household work for another
  servants n ▷ servant

serve v (-s, -ing, -ed) work for (a person, community, or cause) ▶ n (pl -s) (TENNIS ETC.) act of serving the ball
  served v ▷ serve

server n (pl -s) player who serves in racket games
  servers n ▷ server
  serves n, v ▷ serve

service n (pl -s) system that provides something needed by the public ▶ v (-ces, -cing, -ced) overhaul (a machine or vehicle)

serviceable adj useful or helpful
  serviced v ▷ service

serviceman, servicewoman n (pl -men, -women) member of the armed forces
  servicemen n ▷ serviceman
  services n, v ▷ service ▶ pl n armed forces
  servicewoman n ▷ serviceman
  servicewomen n ▷ serviceman
  servicing v ▷ service

serviette n (pl -s) table napkin
  serviettes n ▷ serviette

servile adj too eager to obey people, fawning > **servility** n (pl -s)

servilities n ▷ servile
servility n ▷ servile
serving v ▷ serve
servitude n (pl -s) bondage or slavery
　servitudes n ▷ servitude
sesame [sess-am-ee] n (pl -s) plant cultivated for its seeds and oil, which are used in cooking
　sesames n ▷ sesame
session n (pl -s) period spent in an activity
　sessions n ▷ session
set¹ v (-s, -tting, set) put in a specified position or state ▶ n (pl -s) scenery used in a play or film ▶ adj fixed or established beforehand
set² n (pl -s) number of things or people grouped or belonging together
setback n (pl -s) anything that delays progress
　setbacks n ▷ setback
　sets v ▷ set¹ ▶ n ▷ set²
sett, set n (p -s) badger's burrow
settee n (pl -s) couch
　settees n ▷ settee
setter n (pl -s) long-haired gun dog
　setters n ▷ setter
setting n (pl -s) background or surroundings ▶ v ▷ set
　settings n ▷ setting
settle¹ v (-les, -ling, -led) arrange or put in order
settle² n (pl -s) long wooden bench with high back and arms
　settled v ▷ settle¹
settlement n (pl -s) act of settling
　settlements n ▷ settlement
settler n (pl -s) colonist
　settlers n ▷ settler
　settles v ▷ settle¹ ▶ n ▷ settle²
　settling v ▷ settle¹
　setts n ▷ sett
setup n (pl -s) way in which anything is organized or arranged
　setups n ▷ setup
seven adj, n (pl -s) one more than six
　sevens n ▷ seven
seventeen adj, n (pl -s) ten and seven
　> **seventeenth** adj, n (pl -s)
　seventeens n ▷ seventeen
　seventeenth n ▷ seventeen
　seventeenths n ▷ seventeen
seventh adj, n (pl -s) (of) number seven in a series
　sevenths n ▷ seventh
　seventies n ▷ seventy
　seventieth n ▷ seventy
　seventieths n ▷ seventy

seventy adj, n (pl -ties) ten times seven
　> **seventieth** adj, n (pl -s)
sever v (-s, -ing, -ed) cut through or off
　> **severance** n (pl -s)
several adj some, a few
severally adv separately
　severance n ▷ sever
　severances n ▷ sever
severe adj (-r, -st) strict or harsh > **severely** adv
　> **severity** n (pl -ties)
　severed v ▷ sever
　severely adv ▷ severe
　severer adj ▷ severe
　severest adj ▷ severe
　severing v ▷ sever
　severities n ▷ severe
　severity n ▷ severe
　severs v ▷ sever
sew v (-s, -ing, -ed, sewn or -ed) join with thread repeatedly passed through with a needle
sewage n (pl -s) waste matter or excrement carried away in sewers
　sewages n ▷ sewage
　sewed v ▷ sew
sewer n (pl -s) drain to remove waste water and sewage > **sewerage** n (pl -s) system of sewers
　sewerage n ▷ sewer
　sewerages n ▷ sewer
　sewers n ▷ sewer
　sewing v ▷ sew
　sewn v ▷ sew
　sews v ▷ sew
sex n (pl -es) state of being male or female ▶ v (-es, -ing, -ed) find out the sex of > **sexual** adj > **sexually** adv > **sexuality** n (pl -ties)
sexagenarian n (pl -s) person aged between sixty and sixty-nine
　sexagenarians n ▷ sexagenarian
　sexed v ▷ sex
　sexes n, v ▷ sex
　sexier adj ▷ sexy
　sexiest adj ▷ sexy
　sexing v ▷ sex
sexism n (pl -s) discrimination on the basis of a person's sex > **sexist** adj, n (pl -s)
　sexisms n ▷ sexism
　sexist n ▷ sexism
　sexists n ▷ sexism
sextant n (pl -s) navigator's instrument for measuring angles, as between the sun and horizon, to calculate one's position
　sextants n ▷ sextant
sextet n (pl -s) group of six performers

sextets n ▷ sextet
sexton n (pl -s) official in charge of a church and churchyard
sextons n ▷ sexton
sexual adj ▷ sex
sexualities n ▷ sex
sexuality n ▷ sex
sexually adv ▷ sex
sexy adj (-xier, -xiest) sexually exciting or attractive

> **sez** v. Sez is an short informal form of **says**. This word can be very useful when there isn't much space on the board, as it gives a good score. Sez scores 12 points.
>
> **sh** interj. Sh is a sound people make to request silence or quiet. This is one of two two-letter words beginning with S that do not contain a vowel. It's useful when you want to connect a word beginning with H to one ending in S or vice versa. Sh scores 5 points.

shabbier adj ▷ shabby
shabbiest adj ▷ shabby
shabbily adv ▷ shabby
shabbiness n ▷ shabby
shabbinesses n ▷ shabby
shabby adj (-bier, -biest) worn or dilapidated in appearance > **shabbily** adv > **shabbiness** n (pl -es)
shack n (pl -s) rough hut
shackle n (pl -s) one of a pair of metal rings joined by a chain, for securing a person's wrists or ankles ▶ v (-les, -ling, -led) fasten with shackles
shackled v ▷ shackle
shackles n, v ▷ shackle
shackling v ▷ shackle
shacks n ▷ shack
shad n (pl -s) herring-like fish
shade n (pl -s) relative darkness ▶ v (-des, -ding, -ded) screen from light ▶ **shady** adj (-dier, -diest) situated in or giving shade
shaded v ▷ shade
shades n, v ▷ shade ▶ pl n (Slang) sunglasses
shadier adj ▷ shade
shadiest adj ▷ shade
shading v ▷ shade
shadow n (pl -s) dark shape cast on a surface when something stands between a light and the surface ▶ v (-s, -ing, -ed) cast a shadow over > **shadowy** adj (-wier, -wiest)
shadowboxing n (pl -s) boxing against an imaginary opponent for practice
shadowboxings n ▷ shadowboxing

shadowed v ▷ shadow
shadowier adj ▷ shadow
shadowiest adj ▷ shadow
shadowing v ▷ shadow
shadows n, v ▷ shadow
shadowy adj ▷ shadow
shads n ▷ shad
shady adj ▷ shade
shaft n (pl -s) long narrow straight handle of a tool or weapon
shafts n ▷ shaft
shag[1] n (pl -s) coarse shredded tobacco ▶ adj (of a carpet) having a long pile
shag[2] n (pl -s) kind of cormorant
shaggier adj ▷ shaggy
shaggiest adj ▷ shaggy
shaggy adj (-ggier, -ggiest) covered with rough hair or wool
shagreen n (pl -s) sharkskin
shagreens n ▷ shagreen
shags n ▷ shag[1, 2]
shah n (pl -s) formerly, ruler of Iran
shahs n ▷ shah
shake v (-kes, -king, shook, -en) move quickly up and down or back and forth ▶ n (pl -s) shaking (Informal)
shaken v ▷ shake
shakes v, n ▷ shake
shakier adj ▷ shaky
shakiest adj ▷ shaky
shakily adv ▷ shaky
shaking v ▷ shake
shaky adj (-kier, -kiest) unsteady > **shakily** adv
shale n (pl -s) flaky sedimentary rock
shales n ▷ shale
shall v (past tense **should**) used as an auxiliary to make the future tense or to indicate intention, obligation, or inevitability
shallot n (pl -s) kind of small onion
shallots n ▷ shallot
shallow adj (-er, -est) not deep > **shallowness** n (pl -es)
shallower adj ▷ shallow
shallowest adj ▷ shallow
shallowness n ▷ shallow
shallownesses n ▷ shallow
shallows pl n area of shallow water
sham n (pl -s) thing or person that is not genuine ▶ adj not genuine ▶ v (-s, -mming, -mmed) fake, feign
shamble v (-les, -ling, -led) walk in a shuffling awkward way
shambled v ▷ shamble
shambles n (pl disorderly event or place ▶ v ▷ shamble

shambling *v* ▷ shamble

shame *n* (*pl* -s) painful emotion caused by awareness of having done something dishonourable or foolish ▶ *v* (-mes, -ming, -med) cause to feel shame ▶ *interj* (S AFR) (*Informal*) exclamation of sympathy or endearment

shamed *v* ▷ shame

shamefaced *adj* looking ashamed

shameful *adj* causing or deserving shame > shamefully *adv*

shamefully *adv* ▷ shameful

shameless *adj* with no sense of shame

shames *n*, *v* ▷ shame

shaming *v* ▷ shame

shammed *v* ▷ sham

shammies *n* ▷ shammy

shamming *v* ▷ sham

shammy *n* (*pl* -mies) (*Informal*) piece of chamois leather

shampoo *n* (*pl* -s) liquid soap for washing hair, carpets, or upholstery ▶ *v* (-s, -ing, -ed) wash with shampoo

shampooed *v* ▷ shampoo

shampooing *v* ▷ shampoo

shampoos *n*, *v* ▷ shampoo

shamrock *n* (*pl* -s) clover leaf, esp. as the Irish emblem

shamrocks *n* ▷ shamrock

shams *n*, *v* ▷ sham

shandies *n* ▷ shandy

shandy *n* (*pl* -dies) drink made of beer and lemonade

shanghai *v* (-hais, -haiing, -haied) force or trick (someone) into doing something ▶ *n* (*pl* -s) (AUST & NZ) catapult

shanghaied *v* ▷ shanghai

shanghaiing *v* ▷ shanghai

shanghais *v*, *n* ▷ shanghai

shank *n* (*pl* -s) lower leg

shanks *n* ▷ shank

shanties *n* ▷ shanty¹, ²

shantung *n* (*pl* -s) soft Chinese silk with a knobbly surface

shantungs *n* ▷ shantung

shanty¹ *n* (*pl* -ties) shack or crude dwelling

shanty² *n* (*pl* -ties) sailor's traditional song

shantytown *n* (*pl* -s) slum consisting of shanties

shantytowns *n* ▷ shantytown

shape *n* (*pl* -s) outward form of an object ▶ *v* (-pes, -ping, -ped) form or mould > shapeless *adj*

shaped *v* ▷ shape

shapeless *adj* ▷ shape

shapelier *adj* ▷ shapely

shapeliest *adj* ▷ shapely

shapely *adj* (-lier, -liest) having an attractive shape

shapes *n*, *v* ▷ shape

shaping *v* ▷ shape

shard *n* (*pl* -s) broken piece of pottery or glass

shards *n* ▷ shard

share¹ *n* (*pl* -s) part of something that belongs to or is contributed by a person ▶ *v* (-res, -ring, -red) give or take a share of (something) > shareholder *n* (*pl* -s)

share² *n* (*pl* -s) blade of a plough

shared *v* ▷ share¹

shareholder *n* ▷ share¹

shareholders *n* ▷ share¹

sharemilker *n* (*pl* -s) (NZ) person who works on a dairy farm belonging to someone else

sharemilkers *n* ▷ sharemilker

shares *v* ▷ share¹ ▶ *n* ▷ share¹, ²

sharing *v* ▷ share¹

shark *n* (*pl* -s) large usu. predatory sea fish

sharks *n* ▷ shark

sharkskin *n* (*pl* -s) stiff glossy fabric

sharkskins *n* ▷ sharkskin

sharp *adj* having a keen cutting edge or fine point ▶ *adv* promptly ▶ *n* (MUSIC) symbol raising a note one semitone above natural pitch > sharply *adv* > sharpness *n* (*pl* -es)

sharpen *v* (-s, -ing, -ed) make or become sharp or sharper > sharpener *n* (*pl* -s)

sharpened *v* ▷ sharpen

sharpener *n* ▷ sharpen

sharpeners *n* ▷ sharpen

sharpening *v* ▷ sharpen

sharpens *v* ▷ sharpen

sharply *adv* ▷ sharp

sharpness *n* ▷ sharp

sharpnesses *n* ▷ sharp

sharps *n* ▷ sharp

sharpshooter *n* (*pl* -s) marksman

sharpshooters *n* ▷ sharpshooter

shatter *v* (-s, -ing, -ed) break into pieces

shattered *adj* (*Informal*) completely exhausted ▶ *v* ▷ shatter

shattering *v* ▷ shatter

shatters *v* ▷ shatter

shave *v* (-ves, -ving, -ved, -ved or shaven) remove (hair) from (the face, head, or body) with a razor or shaver ▶ *n* (*pl* -s) shaving

shaved *v* ▷ shave

shaven *v* ▷ shave

shaver *n* (*pl* -s) electric razor

shavers *n* ▷ shaver

shaves *v*, *n* ▷ shave

shaving v ▷ **shave**

shavings pl n parings

shawl n (pl -s) piece of cloth worn over a woman's head or shoulders or wrapped around a baby

shawls n ▷ **shawl**

she pron refers to: female person or animal previously mentioned

sheaf n (pl **sheaves**) bundle of papers

shear v (-s, -ing, -ed, -ed or **shorn**) clip hair or wool from > **shearer** n (pl -s)

sheared v ▷ **shear**

shearer n ▷ **shear**

shearers n ▷ **shear**

shearing v ▷ **shear**

shears pl n large scissors or a cutting tool shaped like these ► v ▷ **shear**

shearwater n (pl -s) medium-sized sea bird

shearwaters n ▷ **shearwater**

sheath n (pl -s) close-fitting cover, esp. for a knife or sword

sheathe v (-thes, -thing, -thed) put into a sheath

sheathed v ▷ **sheathe**

sheathes v ▷ **sheathe**

sheathing v ▷ **sheathe**

sheaths n ▷ **sheath**

sheaves n ▷ **sheaf**

shebeen n (pl -s) (SCOT, IRISH & S AFR) place where alcohol is sold illegally

shebeens n ▷ **shebeen**

shed[1] n (pl -s) building used for storage or shelter or as a workshop

shed[2] v (-s, -dding, **shed**) pour forth (tears)

shedding v ▷ **shed**[2]

sheds n ▷ **shed**[1] ► v ▷ **shed**[2]

sheen n (pl -s) glistening brightness on the surface of something

sheens n ▷ **sheen**

sheep n (pl **sheep**) ruminant animal bred for wool and meat

sheepdog n (pl -s) dog used for herding sheep

sheepdogs n ▷ **sheepdog**

sheepish adj embarrassed because of feeling foolish > **sheepishly** adv

sheepishly adv ▷ **sheepish**

sheepskin n (pl -s) skin of a sheep with the fleece still on, used for clothing or rugs

sheepskins n ▷ **sheepskin**

sheer[1] adj (-er, -est) absolute, complete

sheer[2] v (-s, -ing, -ed) change course suddenly

sheered v ▷ **sheer**[2]

sheerer adj ▷ **sheer**[1]

sheerest adj ▷ **sheer**[1]

sheering v ▷ **sheer**[2]

sheers v ▷ **sheer**[2]

sheet[1] n (pl -s) large piece of cloth used as an inner bed cover

sheet[2] n (pl -s) rope for controlling the position of a sail

sheets n ▷ **sheet**[1, 2]

sheikdom n ▷ **sheikh**

sheikdoms n ▷ **sheikh**

sheikh, sheik [shake] n (pl -s) Arab chief > **sheikhdom, sheikdom** n (pl -s)

sheikhdoms n ▷ **sheikhdom**

sheikhs n ▷ **sheikh**

sheiks n ▷ **sheikh**

sheila n (pl -s) (AUST & NZ) (Slang) girl or woman

sheilas n ▷ **sheila**

shekel n (pl -s) monetary unit of Israel

shekels n ▷ **shekel** ► pl n (Informal) money

shelf n (pl **-ves**) board fixed horizontally for holding things

shell n (pl -s) hard outer covering of an egg, nut, or certain animals ► v (-s, -lling, -lled) take the shell from

shellac n (pl -s) resin used in varnishes ► v (-cs, -cking, -cked) coat with shellac

shellacked v ▷ **shellac**

shellacking v ▷ **shellac**

shellacs n, v ▷ **shellac**

shelled v ▷ **shell**

shellfish n (pl -s) sea-living animal, esp. one that can be eaten, with a shell

shellfishes n ▷ **shellfish**

shelling v ▷ **shell**

shells n, v ▷ **shell**

shelter n (pl -s) structure providing protection from danger or the weather ► v (-s, -ing, -ed) give shelter to

sheltered v ▷ **shelter**

sheltering v ▷ **shelter**

shelters n, v ▷ **shelter**

shelve[1] v (-ves, -ving, -ved) put aside or postpone

shelve[2] v (-ves, -ving, -ved) slope

shelved v ▷ **shelve**[1, 2]

shelves v ▷ **shelve**[1, 2] ► n ▷ **shelf**

shelving n (pl -s) (material for) shelves ► v ▷ **shelve**[1, 2]

shenanigans pl n (Informal) mischief or nonsense

shepherd n (pl -s) person who tends sheep ► v (-s, -ing, -ed) guide or watch over (people) > **shepherdess** n fem (pl -s)

shepherded v ▷ **shepherd**

shepherdess n ▷ **shepherd**

shepherdesses n ▷ **shepherd**

shepherding v ▷ **shepherd**

shepherds n, v ▷ **shepherd**

sherbet n (pl **-s**) (BRIT, AUST & NZ) fruit-flavoured fizzy powder

sherbets n ▷ **sherbet**

sheriff n (pl **-s**) (in the US) chief law enforcement officer of a county

sheriffs n ▷ **sheriff**

sherries n ▷ **sherry**

sherry n (pl **-ries**) pale or dark brown fortified wine

> **shh** interj. Shh is a sound people make to request silence or quiet. As it doesn't contain a vowel, shh can help you to clear an unpromising rack. Shh scores 9 points.

shibboleth n (pl **-s**) slogan or principle, usu. considered outworn, characteristic of a particular group

shibboleths n ▷ **shibboleth**

shied v ▷ **shy**[1, 2]

shield n (pl **-s**) piece of armour carried on the arm to protect the body from blows or missiles ▶ v (**-s, -ing, -ed**) protect

shielded v ▷ **shield**

shielding v ▷ **shield**

shields n, v ▷ **shield**

shies v ▷ **shy**[1, 2] ▶ n ▷ **shy**[2]

shift v (**-s, -ing, -ed**) move ▶ n (pl **-s**) shifting

shifted v ▷ **shift**

shiftier adj ▷ **shifty**

shiftiest adj ▷ **shifty**

shiftiness n ▷ **shifty**

shiftinesses n ▷ **shifty**

shifting v ▷ **shift**

shiftless adj lacking in ambition or initiative

shifts v, n ▷ **shift**

shifty adj (**-tier, -tiest**) evasive or untrustworthy ▶ **shiftiness** n (pl **-es**)

shillelagh [shil-lay-lee] n (pl **-s**) (in Ireland) a cudgel

shillelaghs n ▷ **shillelagh**

shilling n (pl **-s**) former British coin, replaced by the 5p piece

shillings n ▷ **shilling**

shillyshallied v ▷ **shillyshally**

shillyshallies v ▷ **shillyshally**

shillyshally v (**-lies, -lying, -lied**) (Informal) be indecisive

shillyshallying v ▷ **shillyshally**

shimmer v (**-s, -ing, -ed**) ▶ n (pl **-s**) (shine with) a faint unsteady light

shimmered v ▷ **shimmer**

shimmering v ▷ **shimmer**

shimmers v, n ▷ **shimmer**

shin n (pl **-s**) front of the lower leg ▶ v (**-s,**

-nning, -nned) climb by using the hands or arms and legs

shinbone n (pl **-s**) tibia

shinbones n ▷ **shinbone**

shindig n (pl **-s**) (Informal) noisy party

shindigs n ▷ **shindig**

shine v (**-s, -ing, shone**) give out or reflect light ▶ n (pl **-s**) brightness or lustre ▷ **shiny** adj (**-nier, -niest**)

shiner n (pl **-s**) (Informal) black eye

shiners n ▷ **shiner**

shines v, n ▷ **shine**

shingle[1] n (pl **-s**) wooden roof tile ▶ v (**-les, -ling, -led**) cover (a roof) with shingles

shingle[2] n (pl **-s**) coarse gravel found on beaches

shingled v ▷ **shingle**[1]

shingles n disease causing a rash of small blisters along a nerve ▷ **shingle**[1, 2] ▶ v ▷ **shingle**[1]

shingling v ▷ **shingle**[1]

shinier adj ▷ **shine**

shiniest adj ▷ **shine**

shining v ▷ **shine**

shinned v ▷ **shin**

shinning v ▷ **shin**

shins n, v ▷ **shin**

shinties n ▷ **shinty**

shinty n (pl **-ties**) game like hockey

shiny adj ▷ **shine**

ship n (pl **-s**) large seagoing vessel ▶ v (**-s, -pping, -pped**) send or transport by carrier, esp. a ship

shipment n (pl **-s**) act of shipping cargo

shipments n ▷ **shipment**

shipped v ▷ **ship**

shipping n (pl **-s**) freight transport business ▶ v ▷ **ship**

shippings n ▷ **shipping**

ships n, v ▷ **ship**

shipshape adj orderly or neat

shipwreck n (pl **-s**) destruction of a ship through storm or collision ▶ v (**-s, -ing, -ed**) cause to undergo shipwreck

shipwrecked v ▷ **shipwreck**

shipwrecking v ▷ **shipwreck**

shipwrecks n, v ▷ **shipwreck**

shipyard n (pl **-s**) place where ships are built

shipyards n ▷ **shipyard**

shire n (pl **-s**) (BRIT) county

shires n ▷ **shire**

shirk v (**-s, -ing, -ed**) avoid (duty or work) ▷ **shirker** n (pl **-s**)

shirked v ▷ **shirk**

shirker n ▷ **shirk**

shirkers n ▷ shirk

shirking v ▷ shirk

shirks v ▷ shirk

shirt n (pl -s) garment for the upper part of the body

shirtier adj ▷ shirty

shirtiest adj ▷ shirty

shirts n ▷ shirt

shirty adj (-tier, -tiest) (CHIEFLY BRIT) (Slang) bad-tempered or annoyed

shiver[1] v (-s, -ing, -ed) tremble, as from cold or fear ▶ n (pl -s) shivering

shiver[2] v (-s, -ing, -ed) splinter into pieces

shivered v ▷ shiver[1, 2]

shivering v ▷ shiver[1, 2]

shivers v ▷ shiver[1, 2] ▶ n ▷ shiver[1]

shoal[1] n (pl -s) large number of fish swimming together

shoal[2] n (pl -s) stretch of shallow water

shoals n ▷ shoal[1, 2]

shock[1] v (-s, -ing, -ed) horrify, disgust, or astonish ▶ n (pl -s) sudden violent emotional disturbance ▷ **shocker** n (pl -s)

shock[2] n (pl -s) bushy mass (of hair)

shocked v ▷ shock[1]

shocker n ▷ shock[1]

shockers n ▷ shock[1]

shocking adj causing horror, disgust, or astonishment ▶ v ▷ shock[1]

shocks v ▷ shock[1] ▶ n ▷ shock[1, 2]

shod v ▷ shoe

shoddier adj ▷ shoddy

shoddiest adj ▷ shoddy

shoddy adj (-dier, -diest) made or done badly

shoe n (pl -s) outer covering for the foot, ending below the ankle ▶ v (shoes, shoeing, shod) fit with a shoe or shoes

shoehorn n (pl -s) smooth curved implement inserted at the heel of a shoe to ease the foot into it

shoehorns n ▷ shoehorn

shoeing v ▷ shoe

shoes n, v ▷ shoe

shoestring n (pl -s) (foll. by on a) using a very small amount of money

shoestrings n ▷ shoestring

shone v ▷ shine

shonkier adj ▷ shonky

shonkiest adj ▷ shonky

shonky adj (-kier, -kiest) (AUST & NZ) (Informal) unreliable or unsound

shoo interj go away! ▶ v (-s, -ing, -ed) drive away as by saying 'shoo'

shooed v ▷ shoo

shooing v ▷ shoo

shook v ▷ shake

shoos v ▷ shoo

shoot v (-s, -ing, shot) hit, wound, or kill with a missile fired from a weapon ▶ n (pl -s) new branch or sprout of a plant

shooting v ▷ shoot

shoots v, n ▷ shoot

shop n (pl -s) place for sale of goods and services ▶ v (-s, -pping, -pped) visit a shop or shops to buy goods

shoplifter n (pl -s) person who steals from a shop

shoplifters n ▷ shoplifter

shopped v ▷ shop

shopping v ▷ shop

shops n, v ▷ shop

shopsoiled adj soiled or faded from being displayed in a shop

shore[1] n (pl -s) edge of a sea or lake

shore[2] v (-res, -ring, -red) (foll. by up) prop or support

shored v ▷ shore[2]

shores n ▷ shore[1] ▶ v ▷ shore[2]

shoring v ▷ shore[2]

shorn v ▷ shear

short adj (-er, -est) not long ▶ adv abruptly ▶ n (pl -s) drink of spirits

shortage n (pl -s) deficiency

shortages n ▷ shortage

shortbread, shortcake n (pl -s) crumbly biscuit made with butter

shortbreads n ▷ shortbread

shortcake n ▷ shortbread

shortcakes n ▷ shortbread

shortchange v (-ges, -ging, -ed) give (someone) less than the correct amount of change

shortchanged v ▷ shortchange

shortchanges v ▷ shortchange

shortchanging v ▷ shortchange

shortcoming n (pl -s) failing or defect

shortcomings n ▷ shortcoming

shorten v (-s, -ing, -ed) make or become shorter

shortened v ▷ shorten

shortening v ▷ shorten

shortens v ▷ shorten

shorter adj ▷ short

shortest adj ▷ short

shortfall n (pl -s) deficit

shortfalls n ▷ shortfall

shorthand n (pl -s) system of rapid writing using symbols to represent words

shorthanded adj not having enough workers

shorthands n ▷ shorthand

shortlist v (-s, -ing, -ed) put on a short list
shortlisted v ▷ shortlist
shortlisting v ▷ shortlist
shortlists v ▷ shortlist
shortly adv soon
shorts n ▷ short ▸ pl n short trousers
shortsighted adj unable to see distant things clearly
shot n (pl -s) shooting ▸ v ▷ shoot
shotgun n (pl -s) gun for firing a charge of shot at short range
shotguns n ▷ shotgun
shots n ▷ shot
should v ▷ shall
shoulder n (pl -s) part of the body to which an arm, foreleg, or wing is attached ▸ v (-s, -ing, -ed) bear (a burden or responsibility)
shouldered v ▷ shoulder
shouldering v ▷ shoulder
shoulders n, v ▷ shoulder
shout n (pl -s) loud cry (Informal) ▸ v (-s, -ing, -ed) cry out loudly
shouted v ▷ shout
shouting v ▷ shout
shouts n, v ▷ shout
shove v (-ves, -ving, -ved) push roughly ▸ n (pl -s) rough push
shoved v ▷ shove
shovel n (pl -s) tool for lifting or moving loose material ▸ v (-s, -lling, -lled) lift or move with a shovel
shovelled v ▷ shovel
shovelling v ▷ shovel
shovels n, v ▷ shovel
shoves n ▷ shove
shoving v ▷ shove
show v (-s, -ing, -ed, shown or showed) make, be, or become noticeable or visible ▸ n (pl -s) public exhibition
showcase n (pl -s) situation in which something is displayed to best advantage
showcases n ▷ showcase
showdown n (pl -s) confrontation that settles a dispute
showdowns n ▷ showdown
showed v ▷ show
shower n (pl -s) kind of bath in which a person stands while being sprayed with water ▸ v (-s, -ing, -ed) wash in a shower > **showery** adj (-rier, -riest)
showered v ▷ shower
showerier adj ▷ shower
showeriest adj ▷ shower
showering v ▷ shower
showers n, v ▷ shower

showery adj ▷ shower
showier adj ▷ showy
showiest adj ▷ showy
showily adv ▷ showy
showing v ▷ show
showjumping n (pl -s) competitive sport of riding horses to demonstrate skill in jumping
showjumpings n ▷ showjumping
showman n (pl -men) man skilled at presenting anything spectacularly > **showmanship** n (pl -s)
showmanship n ▷ showman
showmanships n ▷ showman
showmen n ▷ showman
shown v ▷ show
showoff n (pl -s) (Informal) person who shows off
showoffs n ▷ showoff
showpiece n (pl -s) excellent specimen shown for display or as an example
showpieces n ▷ showpiece
showroom n (pl -s) room in which goods for sale are on display
showrooms n ▷ showroom
shows v, n ▷ show
showy adj (-wier, -wiest) gaudy > **showily** adv
shrank v ▷ shrink
shrapnel n (pl -s) artillery shell filled with pellets which scatter on explosion
shrapnels n ▷ shrapnel
shred n (pl -s) long narrow strip torn from something ▸ v (-s, -dding, -dded or shred) tear to shreds
shredded v ▷ shred
shredding v ▷ shred
shreds n, v ▷ shred
shrew n (pl -s) small mouselike animal > **shrewish** adj
shrewd adj (-er, -est) clever and perceptive > **shrewdly** adv > **shrewdness** n (pl -es)
shrewder adj ▷ shrewd
shrewdest adj ▷ shrewd
shrewdly adv ▷ shrewd
shrewdness n ▷ shrewd
shrewdnesses n ▷ shrewd
shrewish adj ▷ shrew
shrews n ▷ shrew
shriek n (pl -s) shrill cry ▸ v (-s, -ing, -ed) utter (with) a shriek
shrieked v ▷ shriek
shrieking v ▷ shriek
shrieks n, v ▷ shriek
shrike n (pl -s) songbird with a heavy hooked bill
shrikes n ▷ shrike

shrill *adj* (**-er, -est**) (of a sound) sharp and high-pitched > **shrillness** *n* (*pl* **-es**) > **shrilly** *adv*
  shriller *adj* ▷ **shrill**
  shrillest *adj* ▷ **shrill**
  shrillness *n* ▷ **shrill**
  shrillnesses *n* ▷ **shrill**
  shrilly *adv* ▷ **shrill**
shrimp *n* (*pl* **-s**) small edible shellfish (*Informal*)
shrimping *n* (*pl* **-s**) fishing for shrimps
  shrimpings *n* ▷ **shrimping**
  shrimps *n* ▷ **shrimp**
shrine *n* (*pl* **-s**) place of worship associated with a sacred person or object
  shrines *n* ▷ **shrine**
shrink *v* (**-s, -ing, shrank** or **shrunk** or **shrunken**) become or make smaller ▶ *n* (*pl* **-s**) (*Slang*) psychiatrist
shrinkage *n* (*pl* **-s**) decrease in size, value, or weight
  shrinkages *n* ▷ **shrinkage**
  shrinking *v* ▷ **shrink**
  shrinks *v, n* ▷ **shrink**
shrivel *v* (**-s, -lling, -lled**) shrink and wither
  shrivelled *v* ▷ **shrivel**
  shrivelling *v* ▷ **shrivel**
  shrivels *v* ▷ **shrivel**
shroud *n* (*pl* **-s**) piece of cloth used to wrap a dead body ▶ *v* (**-s, -ing, -ed**) conceal
  shrouded *v* ▷ **shroud**
  shrouding *v* ▷ **shroud**
  shrouds *n, v* ▷ **shroud**
shrub *n* (*pl* **-s**) woody plant smaller than a tree
  shrubberies *n* ▷ **shrubbery**
shrubbery *n* (*pl* **-ries**) area planted with shrubs
  shrubs *n* ▷ **shrub**
shrug *v* (**-s, -gging, -gged**) raise and then drop (the shoulders) as a sign of indifference, ignorance, or doubt ▶ *n* (*pl* **-s**) shrugging
  shrugged *v* ▷ **shrug**
  shrugging *v* ▷ **shrug**
  shrugs *v, n* ▷ **shrug**
  shrunk *v* ▷ **shrink**
  shrunken *v* ▷ **shrink**
shudder *v* (**-s, -ing, -ed**) shake or tremble violently, esp. with horror ▶ *n* (*pl* **-s**) shaking or trembling
  shuddered *v* ▷ **shudder**
  shuddering *v* ▷ **shudder**
  shudders *v, n* ▷ **shudder**
shuffle *v* (**-s, -ling, -led**) walk without lifting the feet ▶ *n* (*pl* **-s**) shuffling
  shuffled *v* ▷ **shuffle**
  shuffles *v, n* ▷ **shuffle**
  shuffling *v* ▷ **shuffle**
shun *v* (**-s, -nning, -nned**) avoid

  shunned *v* ▷ **shun**
  shunning *v* ▷ **shun**
  shuns *v* ▷ **shun**
shunt *v* (**-s, -ing, -ed**) move (objects or people) to a different position
  shunted *v* ▷ **shunt**
  shunting *v* ▷ **shunt**
  shunts *v* ▷ **shunt**
shush *interj* be quiet!
shut *v* (**-s, -tting, shut**) bring together or fold, close
shutdown *n* (*pl* **-s**) closing
  shutdowns *n* ▷ **shutdown**
  shuts *v* ▷ **shut**
shutter *n* (*pl* **-s**) hinged doorlike cover for closing off a window
  shutters *n* ▷ **shutter**
  shutting *v* ▷ **shut**
shuttle *n* (*pl* **-s**) vehicle going to and fro over a short distance ▶ *v* (**-les, -ling, -led**) travel by or as if by shuttle
shuttlecock *n* (*pl* **-s**) small light cone with feathers stuck in one end, struck to and fro in badminton
  shuttlecocks *n* ▷ **shuttlecock**
  shuttled *v* ▷ **shuttle**
  shuttles *n, v* ▷ **shuttle**
  shuttling *v* ▷ **shuttle**
shy¹ *adj* (**-er, -est**) not at ease in company (foll. by **of**) ▶ *v* (**shies, shying, shied**) start back in fear (foll. by **away from**) > **shyly** *adv* > **shyness** *n* (*pl* **-es**)
shy² *v* (**shies, shying, shied**) throw ▶ *n* (*pl* **shies**) throw
  shyer *adj* ▷ **shy¹**
  shyest *adj* ▷ **shy¹**
  shying *v* ▷ **shy¹, ²**
  shyly *adv* ▷ **shy¹**
  shyness *n* ▷ **shy¹**
  shynesses *n* ▷ **shy¹**

> **si** *n* (**sis**). Si means the same as **te**, a musical note This is an unusual word which can be helpful when you want to form words in more than one direction Si scores 2 points

sibilant *adj* hissing ▶ *n* (*pl* **-s**) consonant pronounced with a hissing sound
  sibilants *n* ▷ **sibilant**
sibling *n* (*pl* **-s**) brother or sister
  siblings *n* ▷ **sibling**
sibyl *n* (*pl* **-s**) (in ancient Greece and Rome) prophetess
  sibyls *n* ▷ **sibyl**
sic (*LATIN*) thus: used to indicate that an odd spelling or reading is in fact accurate

sick adj (**-er, -est**) vomiting or likely to vomit > **sickness** n (pl **-es**)

sicken v (**-s, -zing, -ed**) make nauseated or disgusted

sickened v ▷ sicken

sickening v ▷ sicken

sickens v ▷ sicken

sicker adj ▷ sick

sickest adj ▷ sick

sickle n (pl **-s**) tool with a curved blade for cutting grass or grain

sickles n ▷ sickle

sicklier adj ▷ sickly

sickliest adj ▷ sickly

sickly adj (**-lier, -liest**) unhealthy, weak

sickness n ▷ sick

sicknesses n ▷ sick

side n (pl **-s**) line or surface that borders anything ▶ adj at or on the side

sideboard n (pl **-s**) piece of furniture for holding plates, cutlery, etc. in a dining room

sideboards n ▷ sideboard ▶ pl n ▷ sideburns

sideburns, sideboards pl n man's side whiskers

sidekick n (pl **-s**) (Informal) close friend or associate

sidekicks n ▷ sidekick

sidelight n (pl **-s**) either of two small lights on the front of a vehicle

sidelights n ▷ sidelight

sideline n (pl **-s**) subsidiary interest or source of income

sidelines n ▷ sideline

sidelong adj sideways ▶ adv obliquely

sidereal [side-eer-ee-al] adj of or determined with reference to the stars

sides n ▷ side

sidesaddle n (pl **-s**) saddle designed to allow a woman rider to sit with both legs on the same side of the horse

sidesaddles n ▷ sidesaddle

sidestep v (**-s, -pping, -pped**) dodge (an issue)

sidestepped v ▷ sidestep

sidestepping v ▷ sidestep

sidesteps v ▷ sidestep

sidetrack v (**-s, -ing, -ed**) divert from the main topic

sidetracked v ▷ sidetrack

sidetracking v ▷ sidetrack

sidetracks v ▷ sidetrack

sidewalk n (pl **-s**) (US) paved path for pedestrians, at the side of a road

sidewalks n ▷ sidewalk

sideways adv to or from the side

siding n (pl **-s**) short stretch of railway track

on which trains or wagons are shunted from the main line

sidings n ▷ siding

sidle v (**-les, -ling, -led**) walk in a furtive manner

sidled v ▷ sidle

sidles v ▷ sidle

sidling v ▷ sidle

siege n (pl **-s**) surrounding and blockading of a place

sieges n ▷ siege

sienna n (pl **-s**) reddish- or yellowish-brown pigment made from natural earth

siennas n ▷ sienna

sierra n (pl **-s**) range of mountains in Spain or America with jagged peaks

sierras n ▷ sierra

siesta n (pl **-s**) afternoon nap, taken in hot countries

siestas n ▷ siesta

sieve [siv] n (pl **-s**) utensil with mesh through which a substance is sifted or strained ▶ v (**-ves, -ving, -ved**) sift or strain through a sieve

sieved v ▷ sieve

sieves n, v ▷ sieve

sieving v ▷ sieve

sift v (**-s, -ing, -ed**) remove the coarser particles from a substance with a sieve

sifted v ▷ sift

sifting v ▷ sift

sifts v ▷ sift

sigh n (pl **-s**) long audible breath expressing sadness, tiredness, relief, or longing ▶ v (**-s, -ing, -ed**) utter a sigh

sighed v ▷ sigh

sighing v ▷ sigh

sighs n, v ▷ sigh

sight n (pl **-s**) ability to see ▶ v (**-s, -ing, -ed**) catch sight of

sighted v ▷ sight

sighting v ▷ sight

sightless adj blind

sights n, v ▷ sight

sightseeing n (pl **-s**) visiting places of interest > **sightseer** n (pl **-s**)

sightseeings n ▷ sightseeing

sightseer n ▷ sightseeing

sightseers n ▷ sightseeing

sign n (pl **-s**) indication of something not immediately or outwardly observable ▶ v (**-s, -ing, -ed**) write (one's name) on (a document or letter) to show its authenticity or one's agreement

signal n (pl **-s**) sign or gesture to convey information ▶ adj (Formal) very important

▶ v (-s, -lling, -lled) convey (information) by signal > **signally** adv
signalled v ▷ signal
signalling v ▷ signal
signally adv ▷ signal
signalman n (pl -men) railwayman in charge of signals and points
signalmen n ▷ signalman
signals n, v ▷ signal
signatories n ▷ signatory
signatory n (pl -ries) one of the parties who sign a document
signature n (pl -s) person's name written by himself or herself in signing something
signatures n ▷ signature
signed v ▷ sign
signet n (pl -s) small seal used to authenticate documents
signets n ▷ signet
significance n ▷ significant
significances n ▷ significant
significant adj important > **significantly** adv > **significance** n (pl -s)
significantly adv ▷ significant
signification n ▷ signify
significations n ▷ signify
signified v ▷ signify
signifies v ▷ signify
signify v (-fies, -fying, -fied) indicate or suggest > **signification** n (pl -s)
signifying v ▷ signify
signing n (pl -s) system of communication by gestures, as used by deaf people ▶ v ▷ sign
signings n ▷ signing
signor [see-**nyor**] n (pl -s) Italian term of address equivalent to sir or Mr
signora [see-**nyor**-a] n (pl -s) Italian term of address equivalent to madam or Mrs
signoras n ▷ signora
signorina [see-nyor-**ee**-na] n (pl -s) Italian term of address equivalent to madam or Miss
signorinas n ▷ signorina
signors n ▷ signor
signpost n (pl -s) post bearing a sign that shows the way
signposts n ▷ signpost
signs n, v ▷ sign
silage [**sile**-ij] n (pl -s) fodder crop harvested while green and partially fermented in a silo or plastic bags
silages n ▷ silage
silence n (pl -s) absence of noise or speech ▶ v (-ces, -cing, -ced) make silent > **silent** adj > **silently** adv
silenced v ▷ silence

silencer n (pl -s) device to reduce the noise of an engine exhaust or gun
silencers n ▷ silencer
silences n, v ▷ silence
silencing v ▷ silence
silent adj ▷ silencet
silently adv ▷ silence
silhouette n (pl -s) outline of a dark shape seen against a light background ▶ v (-s, -ing, -ed) show in silhouette
silhouetted v ▷ silhouette
silhouettes n, v ▷ silhouette
silhouetting v ▷ silhouette
silica n (pl -s) hard glossy mineral found as quartz and in sandstone
silicas n ▷ silica
silicon n (pl -s) (CHEM) brittle nonmetallic element widely used in chemistry and industry
silicone n (pl -s) tough synthetic substance made from silicon and used in lubricants, paints, and resins
silicones n ▷ silicone
silicons n ▷ silicon
silicoses n ▷ silicosis
silicosis n (pl -ses) lung disease caused by inhaling silica dust
silk n (pl -s) fibre made by the larva of a certain moth
silken adj ▷ silky
silkier adj ▷ silky
silkiest adj ▷ silky
silks n ▷ silk
silky (-ier, -iest), **silken** adj of or like silk
sill n (pl -s) ledge at the bottom of a window or door
sillier adj ▷ silly
silliest adj ▷ silly
silliness n ▷ silly
sillinesses n ▷ silly
sills n ▷ sill
silly adj (-lier, -liest) foolish > **silliness** n (pl -es)
silo n (pl -los) pit or airtight tower for storing silage or grains
silos n ▷ silo
silt n (pl -s) mud deposited by moving water ▶ v (-s, -ing, -ed) (foll. by up) fill or be choked with silt
silted v ▷ silt
silting v ▷ silt
silts n, v ▷ silt
silvan adj ▷ sylvan
silver n (pl -s) white precious metal ▶ adj made of or of the colour of silver
silverbeet n (pl -s) (AUST & NZ) leafy green

vegetable with white stalks
silverbeets n ▷ silverbeet
silverfish n (pl -es) small wingless silver-coloured insect
silverfishes n ▷ silverfish
silvers n ▷ silver
silverside n (pl -s) cut of beef from below the rump and above the leg
silversides ▷ silverside
sim n (pl -s) computer game that simulates an activity such as flying or playing a sport
simian adj, n (pl -s) (of or like) a monkey or ape
simians n ▷ simian
similar adj alike but not identical > **similarity** n (pl -s) > **similarly** adv
similarities n ▷ similar
similarity n ▷ similar
similarly adv ▷ similar
simile [sim-ill-ee] n (pl -s) figure of speech comparing one thing to another, using 'as' or 'like'
similes n ▷ simile
similitude n (pl -s) similarity, likeness
similitudes n ▷ similitude
simmer v (-s, -ing, -ed) cook gently at just below boiling point
simmered v ▷ simmer
simmering v ▷ simmer
simmers v ▷ simmer
simper v (-s, -ing, -ed) smile in a silly or affected way ▶ n (pl -s) simpering smile
simpered v ▷ simper
simpering v ▷ simper
simpers v, n ▷ simper
simple adj (-r, -st) easy to understand or do > **simply** adv > **simplicity** n (pl -ties)
simpler adj ▷ simple
simplest adj ▷ simple
simpleton n (pl -s) foolish or half-witted person
simpletons n ▷ simpleton
simplicities n ▷ simple
simplicity n ▷ simple
simplification n ▷ simplify
simplifications n ▷ simplify
simplified v ▷ simplify
simplifies v ▷ simplify
simplify v (-fies, -fying, -fied) make less complicated > **simplification** n (pl -s)
simplifying v ▷ simplify
simplistic adj too simple or naive
simply adv ▷ simpl
sims n ▷ sim
simulate v (-tes, -ting, -ted) make a pretence of > **simulation** n (pl -s) > **simulator** n (pl -s)

simulated v ▷ simulate
simulates v ▷ simulate
simulating v ▷ simulate
simulation n ▷ simulate
simulations n ▷ simulate
simulator n ▷ simulate
simulators n ▷ simulate
simultaneous adj occurring at the same time > **simultaneously** adv
simultaneously adv ▷ simultaneous
sin[1] n (pl -s) breaking of a religious or moral law ▶ v (-s, -nning, -nned) commit a sin > **sinner** n (pl -s)
sin[2] (MATHS) sine
since prep during the period of time after ▶ conj from the time when ▶ adv from that time
sincere adj (-r, -st) without pretence or deceit > **sincerely** adv > **sincerity** n (pl -ties)
sincerely adv ▷ sincere
sincerer adj ▷ sincere
sincerest adj ▷ sincere
sincerities n ▷ sincere
sincerity n ▷ sincere
sine n (pl -s) (in trigonometry) ratio of the length of the opposite side to that of the hypotenuse in a right-angled triangle
sinecure [sin-ee-cure] n (pl -s) paid job with minimal duties
sinecures n ▷ sinecure
sines n ▷ sine
sinew n (pl -s) tough fibrous tissue joining muscle to bone > **sinewy** adj (-wier, -wiest)
sinewier adj ▷ sinew
sinewiest adj ▷ sinew
sinews n ▷ sinew
sinewy adj ▷ sinew
sinful adj guilty of sin > **sinfully** adv
sinfully adv ▷ sinful
sing v (-s, -ing, sang, sung) make musical sounds with the voice
singe v (-ges, -geing, -ged) burn the surface of ▶ n (pl -s) superficial burn
singed v ▷ singe
singeing v ▷ singe
singer n (pl -s) person who sings, esp. professionally
singers n ▷ singer
singes v, n ▷ singe
singing v ▷ sing
single adj one only ▶ n (pl -s) single thing ▶ v (-les, -ling, -led) (foll. by out) pick out from others > **singly** adv
singled v ▷ single
singles n, v ▷ single ▶ pl n game between two players

singlet n (pl -s) sleeveless vest
  singlets n ▷ singlet
  singling v ▷ single
  singly adv ▷ single
  sings v ▷ sing

singsong n (pl -s) informal singing session
  ▶ adj (of the voice) repeatedly rising and
  falling in pitch
  singsongs n ▷ singsong

singular adj (of a word or form) denoting one
  person or thing ▶ n (pl -s) singular form of a
  word > **singularity** n (pl -ties) > **singularly** adv
  singularities n ▷ singular
  singularity n ▷ singular
  singularly adv ▷ singular
  singulars n ▷ singular

sinister adj threatening or suggesting evil
  or harm

sink v (-s, -ing, sank, sunk or sunken) submerge
  (in liquid) ▶ n (pl -s) fixed basin with a water
  supply and drainage pipe

sinker n (pl -s) weight for a fishing line
  sinkers n ▷ sinker
  sinking v ▷ sink
  sinks v, n ▷ sink
  sinned v ▷ sin¹
  sinner n ▷ sin¹
  sinners n ▷ sin¹
  sinning v ▷ sin¹
  sins n, v ▷ sin¹

sinuous adj curving > **sinuously** adv
  sinuously adv ▷ sinuous

sinus [sine-uss] n (pl -nuses) hollow space in
  a bone, esp. an air passage opening into
  the nose
  sinuses n ▷ sinus

sip v (-s, -pping, -pped) drink in small
  mouthfuls ▶ n (pl -s) amount sipped

siphon n (pl -s) bent tube which uses air
  pressure to draw liquid from a container ▶ v
  (-s, -ing, -ed) draw off thus
  siphoned v ▷ siphon
  siphoning v ▷ siphon
  siphons n, v ▷ siphon
  sipped v ▷ sip
  sipping v ▷ sip
  sips v, n ▷ sip

sir n (pl -s) polite term of address for a man

sire n (pl -s) male parent of a horse or other
  domestic animal ▶ v (-res, -ring, -red) father
  sired v ▷ sire

siren n (pl -s) device making a loud wailing
  noise as a warning
  sirens n ▷ siren
  sires n, v ▷ sire

siring v ▷ sire

sirloin n (pl -s) prime cut of loin of beef
  sirloins n ▷ sirloin

sirocco n (pl -s) hot wind blowing from N Africa
  into S Europe
  siroccos n ▷ sirocco
  sirs n ▷ sir

sis interj (s AFR) (Informal) exclamation of disgust

sisal [size-al] n (pl -s) (fibre of) plant used in
  making ropes
  sisals n ▷ sisal

siskin n (pl -s) yellow-and-black finch
  siskins n ▷ siskin
  sissier adj ▷ sissy
  sissies n ▷ sissy
  sissiest adj ▷ sissy

sissy adj (-ssier, -ssiest) ▶ n (pl -ssies) weak or
  cowardly (person)

sister n (pl -s) girl or woman with the same
  parents as another person ▶ adj closely
  related, similar > **sisterly** adj

sisterhood n (pl -s) state of being a sister
  sisterhoods n ▷ sisterhood
  sisterly adj ▷ sister
  sisters n ▷ sister

sit v (-s, -tting, sat) rest one's body upright on
  the buttocks

sitar n (pl -s) Indian stringed musical
  instrument
  sitars n ▷ sitar

sitcom n (pl -s) (Informal) situation comedy
  sitcoms n ▷ sitcom

site n (pl -s) place where something is, was, or
  is intended to be located > **website** ▶ v (-tes,
  -ting, -ted) provide with a site
  sited v ▷ site
  sites n, v ▷ site
  siting v ▷ site
  sits v ▷ sit
  sitting v ▷ sit

situate v (-tes, -ting, -ted) place
  situated v ▷ situate
  situates v ▷ situate
  situating v ▷ situate

situation n (pl -s) state of affairs
  situations n ▷ situation

six adj, n (pl -es) one more than five
  sixes n ▷ six

sixteen adj, n (pl -s) six and ten > **sixteenth**
  adj, n (pl -s)
  sixteens n ▷ sixteen
  sixteenth n ▷ sixteen
  sixteenths n ▷ sixteen

sixth adj, n (pl -s) (of) number six in a series
  sixths n ▷ sixth

sixties n ▷ **sixty**
sixtieth n ▷ **sixty**
sixtieths n ▷ **sixty**
sixty adj, n (pl **-s**) six times ten > **sixtieth** adj, n (pl **-s**)
sizable adj ▷ **sizeable**
size¹ n (pl **-s**) dimensions, bigness ▶ v (**-zes, -zing, -zed**) arrange according to size
size² n (pl **-s**) gluey substance used as a protective coating
sizeable, sizable adj quite large
sized v ▷ **size¹**
sizes n ▷ **size¹, ²** ▶ v ▷ **size¹**
sizing v ▷ **size¹**
sizzle v (**-les, -ling, -led**) make a hissing sound like frying fat
sizzled v ▷ **sizzle**
sizzles v ▷ **sizzle**
sizzling v ▷ **sizzle**
skankier adj ▷ **skanky**
skankiest adj ▷ **skanky**
skanky adj (**-kier, -kiest**) (Slang) dirty or unattractive
skate¹ n (pl **-s**) boot with a steel blade or sets of wheels attached to the sole for gliding over ice or a hard surface ▶ v (**-tes, -ting, -ted**) glide on or as if on skates
skate² n (pl **-s**) large marine flatfish
skateboard n (pl **-s**) board mounted on small wheels for riding on while standing up > **skateboarding** n (pl **-s**)
skateboarding n ▷ **skateboard**
skateboardings n ▷ **skateboard**
skateboards n ▷ **skateboard**
skated v ▷ **skate¹**
skates n ▷ **skate¹, ²** ▶ v ▷ **skate¹**
skating v ▷ **skate¹**
skedaddle v (**-les, -ling, -led**) (Informal) run off
skedaddled v ▷ **skedaddle**
skedaddles v ▷ **skedaddle**
skedaddling v ▷ **skedaddle**
skein n (pl **-s**) yarn wound in a loose coil
skeins n ▷ **skein**
skeletal adj ▷ **skeleton**
skeleton n (pl **-s**) framework of bones inside a person's or animal's body ▶ adj reduced to a minimum > **skeletal** adj
skeletons n ▷ **skeleton**
sketch n (pl **-es**) rough drawing ▶ v (**-es, -ing, -ed**) make a sketch (of)
sketched v ▷ **sketch**
sketches n, v ▷ **sketch**
sketchier adj ▷ **sketchy**
sketchiest adj ▷ **sketchy**
sketching v ▷ **sketch**

sketchy adj (**-chier, -chiest**) incomplete or inadequate
skew v (**-s, -ing, -ed**) make slanting or crooked ▶ adj slanting or crooked
skewed v ▷ **skew**
skewer n (pl **-s**) pin to hold meat together during cooking ▶ v (**-s, -ing, -ed**) fasten with a skewer
skewered v ▷ **skewer**
skewering v ▷ **skewer**
skewers n, v ▷ **skewer**
skewing v ▷ **skew**
skews v ▷ **skew**
skewwhiff adj (BRIT) (Informal) slanting or crooked
ski n (pl **-s**) one of a pair of long runners fastened to boots for gliding over snow or water ▶ v (**skis, skiing, skied**) travel on skis > **skier** n (pl **-s**)
skid v (**-s, -dding, -dded**) (of a moving vehicle) slide sideways uncontrollably ▶ n (pl **-s**) skidding
skidded v ▷ **skid**
skidding v ▷ **skid**
skids v, n ▷ **skid**
skied v ▷ **ski**
skier n ▷ **ski**
skiers n ▷ **ski**
skies n ▷ **sky**
skiff n (pl **-s**) small boat
skiffs n ▷ **skiff**
skiing v ▷ **ski**
skilful adj having or showing skill > **skilfully** adv
skilfully adv ▷ **skilful**
skill n (pl **-s**) special ability or expertise > **skilled** adj
skilled adj ▷ **skill**
skillet n (pl **-s**) small frying pan or shallow cooking pot
skillets n ▷ **skillet**
skills n ▷ **skill**
skim v (**-s, -mming, -mmed**) remove floating matter from the surface of (a liquid)
skimmed v ▷ **skim**
skimming v ▷ **skim**
skimp v (**-s, -ing, -ed**) not invest enough time, money, material, etc.
skimped v ▷ **skimp**
skimpier adj ▷ **skimpy**
skimpiest adj ▷ **skimpy**
skimping v ▷ **skimp**
skimps v ▷ **skimp**
skimpy adj (**-pier, -piest**) scanty or insufficient
skims v ▷ **skim**

skin n (pl -s) outer covering of the body ▶ v (-s, -nning, -nned) remove the skin of > **skinless** adj

skinflint n (pl -s) miser
  skinflints n ▷ skinflint

skinhead n (pl -s) youth with very short hair
  skinheads n ▷ skinhead
  skinless adj ▷ skin
  skinned v ▷ skin
  skinnier adj ▷ skinny
  skinniest adj ▷ skinny
  skinning v ▷ skin

skinny adj (-nnier, -nniest) thin
  skins n, v ▷ skin

skint adj (BRIT) (Slang) having no money

skip¹ v (-s, -pping, -pped) leap lightly from one foot to the other ▶ n (pl -s) skipping

skip² n (pl -s) large open container for builders' rubbish
  skipped v ▷ skip¹

skipper n (pl -s) ▶ v (-s, -ing, -ed) captain
  skippered v ▷ skipper
  skippering v ▷ skipper
  skippers n, v ▷ skipper
  skipping v ▷ skip¹
  skips v ▷ skip¹ ▶ n ▷ skip¹, ²

skirl n (pl -s) sound of bagpipes
  skirls n ▷ skirl

skirmish n (pl -es) brief or minor fight or argument ▶ v (-es, -ing, -ed) take part in a skirmish
  skirmished v ▷ skirmish
  skirmishes n, v ▷ skirmish
  skirmishing v ▷ skirmish

skirt n (pl -s) woman's garment hanging from the waist ▶ v (-s, -ing, -ed) border
  skirted v ▷ skirt
  skirting v ▷ skirt
  skirts n, v ▷ skirt
  skis n, v ▷ ski

skit n (pl -s) brief satirical sketch

skite v (-tes, -ting, -ted) ▶ n (pl -s) (AUST & NZ) boast
  skited v ▷ skite
  skites v, n ▷ skite
  skiting v ▷ skite
  skits n ▷ skit

skittish adj playful or lively

skittle n (pl -s) bottle-shaped object used as a target in some games

skittles n ▷ skittle ▶ pl n game in which players try to knock over skittles by rolling a ball at them

skive v (-ves, -ving, -ved) (BRIT) (Informal) evade work or responsibility

skived v ▷ skive
skives v ▷ skive
skiving v ▷ skive
skivvies n ▷ skivvy

skivvy n (pl -vies) (BRIT) female servant who does menial work

skua n (pl -s) large predatory gull
  skuas n ▷ skua
  skulduggeries n ▷ skulduggery

skulduggery n (pl -ries) (Informal) trickery

skulk v (-s, -ing, -ed) move stealthily
  skulked v ▷ skulk
  skulking v ▷ skulk
  skulks v ▷ skulk

skull n (pl -s) bony framework of the head

skullcap n (pl -s) close-fitting brimless cap
  skullcaps n ▷ skullcap
  skulls n ▷ skull

skunk n (pl -s) small black-and-white N American mammal which emits a foul-smelling fluid when attacked
  skunks n ▷ skunk

sky n (pl **skies**) upper atmosphere as seen from the earth

skydiving n (pl -s) sport of jumping from an aircraft and performing manoeuvres before opening one's parachute
  skydivings n ▷ skydiving

skylark n (pl -s) lark that sings while soaring at a great height
  skylarks n ▷ skylark

skylight n (pl -s) window in a roof or ceiling
  skylights n ▷ skylight

skyscraper n (pl -s) very tall building
  skyscrapers n ▷ skyscraper

slab n (pl -s) broad flat piece
  slabs n ▷ slab

slack adj (-er, -est) not tight ▶ n (pl -s) slack part ▶ v (-s, -ing, -ed) neglect one's work or duty > **slacker** n (pl -s) > **slackness** n (pl -es)
  slacked v ▷ slack

slacken v (-s, -ing, -ed) make or become slack
  slackened v ▷ slacken
  slackening v ▷ slacken
  slackens v ▷ slacken
  slacker n, adj ▷ slack
  slackers n ▷ slack
  slackest adj ▷ slack
  slacking v ▷ slack
  slackness n ▷ slack
  slacknesses n ▷ slack

slacks n, v ▷ slack ▶ pl n informal trousers

slag n (pl -s) waste left after metal is smelted ▶ v (-s, -gging, -gged) (foll. by off) (BRIT, AUST & NZ) (Slang) criticize slagged v ▷ slag

slagging v ▷ slag

slags n, v ▷ slag

slain v ▷ slay

slake v (-kes, -king, -ked) satisfy (thirst or desire)

slaked v ▷ slake

slakes v ▷ slake

slaking v ▷ slake

slalom n (pl -s) skiing or canoeing race over a winding course

slaloms n ▷ slalom

slam v (-s, -mming, -mmed) shut, put down, or hit violently and noisily ▶ n (pl -s) act or sound of slamming

slammed v ▷ slam

slamming v ▷ slam

slams v, n ▷ slam

slander n (pl -s) false and malicious statement about a person ▶ v (-s, -ing, -ed) utter slander about ▷ slanderous adj

slandered v ▷ slander

slandering v ▷ slander

slanderous adj ▷ slander

slanders n, v ▷ slander

slang n (pl -s) very informal language ▷ slangy adj (-gier, -giest)

slangier adj ▷ slang

slangiest adj ▷ slang

slangs n ▷ slang

slangy adj ▷ slang

slant v (-s, -ing, -ed) lean at an angle, slope ▶ n (pl -s) slope ▷ slanting adj

slanted v ▷ slant

slanting v, adj ▷ slant

slants v, n ▷ slant

slap n (pl -s) blow with the open hand or a flat object ▶ v (-s, -pping, -pped) strike with the open hand or a flat object

slapdash adj careless and hasty

slaphappy adj (Informal) cheerfully careless

slapped v ▷ slap

slapping v ▷ slap

slaps n, v ▷ slap

slapstick n (pl -s) boisterous knockabout comedy

slapsticks n ▷ slapstick

slash v (-es, -ing, -ed) cut with a sweeping stroke ▶ n (pl -es) sweeping stroke

slashed v ▷ slash

slashes v, n ▷ slash

slashing v ▷ slash

slat n (pl -s) narrow strip of wood or metal

slate¹ n (pl -s) rock which splits easily into thin layers

slate² v (-tes, -ting, -ted) (Informal) criticize harshly

slated v ▷ slate²

slates n ▷ slate¹ ▶ v ▷ slate²

slating v ▷ slate²

slats n ▷ slat

slattern n (pl -s) (Old-fashioned) slovenly woman ▷ slatternly adj

slatternly adv ▷ slattern

slatterns n ▷ slattern

slaughter v (-s, -ing, -ed) kill (animals) for food ▶ n (pl -s) slaughtering

slaughtered v ▷ slaughter

slaughterhouse n (pl -s) place where animals are killed for food

slaughterhouses n ▷ slaughterhouse

slaughtering v ▷ slaughter

slaughters v, n ▷ slaughter

slave n (pl -s) person owned by another for whom he or she has to work ▶ v (-ves, -ing, -ved) work like a slave

slaved v ▷ slave

slaver n (pl -s) person or ship engaged in the slave trade ▶ v [slav-ver] (-s, -ing, -ed) dribble saliva from the mouth

slavered v ▷ slaver

slaveries n ▷ slavery

slavering v ▷ slaver

slavers n, v ▷ slaver

slavery n (pl -ries) state or condition of being a slave

slaves v, n ▷ slave

slaving v ▷ slave

slavish adj of or like a slave

slay v (-s, -ing, slew, slain) kill

slaying v ▷ slay

slays v ▷ slay

sleazes n ▷ sleaze

sleazier adj ▷ sleazy

sleaziest adj ▷ sleazy

sleazy adj (-zier, -ziest) run-down or sordid ▷ sleaze n (pl -s)

sled n (pl -s) ▶ v (-s, -dding, -dded) ▷

sledded v ▷ sled

sledding v ▷ sled

sledge¹ n (pl -s) carriage on runners for sliding on snow ▶ v (-dges, -dging, -dged) travel by sledge

sledge², sledgehammer n (pl -s) heavy hammer with a long handle

sledged v ▷ sledge¹

sledgehammer n ▷ sledge

sledgehammers n ▷ sledge

sledges n ▷ sledge¹, ² ▶ v ▷ sledge¹

sledging v ▷ sledge¹

sleds n, v ▷ **sled**

sleek adj (**-er, -est**) glossy, smooth, and shiny
  sleeker adj ▷ **sleek**
  sleekest adj ▷ **sleek**

sleep n (pl -s) state of rest characterized by
  unconsciousness ▶ v (**-s, -ing, slept**) be in
  or as if in a state of sleep > **sleepy** adj (**-pier,
  -piest**) > **sleepily** adv > **sleepiness** n (pl -es)
  > **sleepless** adj

sleeper n (pl -s) railway car fitted for sleeping
  in
  sleepers n ▷ **sleeper**
  sleepier adj ▷ **sleep**
  sleepiest adj ▷ **sleep**
  sleepily adv ▷ **sleep**
  sleepiness n ▷ **sleep**
  sleepinesses n ▷ **sleep**
  sleeping v ▷ **sleep**
  sleepless adj ▷ **sleep**

sleepout n (pl -s) (NZ) small building for
  sleeping in
  sleepouts n ▷ **sleepout**

sleepover n (pl -s) occasion when a person
  stays overnight at a friend's house
  sleepovers n ▷ **sleepover**
  sleeps n, v ▷ **sleep**
  sleepy adj ▷ **sleep**

sleet n (pl -s) rain and snow or hail falling
  together
  sleets n ▷ **sleet**

sleeve n (pl -s) part of a garment which covers
  the arm > **sleeveless** adj
  sleeveless adj ▷ **sleeve**
  sleeves n ▷ **sleeve**

sleigh n (pl -s) ▶ v (**-s, -ing, -ed**) sledge
  sleighed v ▷ **sleigh**
  sleighing v ▷ **sleigh**
  sleighs n, v ▷ **sleigh**

slender adj (**-er, -est**) slim
  slenderer adj ▷ **slender**
  slenderest adj ▷ **slender**
  slept v ▷ **sleep**

sleuth [slooth] n (pl -s) detective
  sleuths n ▷ **sleuth**

slew¹ v ▷ **slay**

slew² v (**-s, -ing, -ed**) twist or swing round
  slewed v ▷ **slew²**
  slewing v ▷ **slew²**
  slews v ▷ **slew²**

slice n (pl -s) thin flat piece cut from something
  ▶ v (**-ces, -cing, -ced**) cut into slices
  sliced v ▷ **slice**
  slices n, v ▷ **slice**
  slicing v ▷ **slice**

slick adj (**-er, -est**) persuasive and glib ▶ n (pl -s)

patch of oil on water ▶ v (**-s, -ing, -ed**) make
  smooth or sleek
  slicked v ▷ **slick**
  slicker adj ▷ **slick**
  slickest adj ▷ **slick**
  slicking v ▷ **slick**
  slicks n, v ▷ **slick**
  slid v ▷ **slide**

slide v (**-des, -ding, slid**) slip smoothly along (a
  surface) ▶ n (pl -s) sliding
  slides v, n ▷ **slide**
  sliding v ▷ **slide**
  slier adj ▷ **sly**
  sliest adj ▷ **sly**

slight adj (**-er, -est**) small in quantity or extent
  ▶ v (**-s, -ing, -ed**) ▶ n (pl -s) snub > **slightly** adv
  slighted v ▷ **slight**
  slighter adj ▷ **slight**
  slightest adj ▷ **slight**
  slighting v ▷ **slight**
  slightly adv ▷ **slight**
  slights v, n ▷ **slight**

slim adj (**-mmer, -mmest**) not heavy or stout,
  thin ▶ v (**-s, -mming, -mmed**) make or become
  slim by diet and exercise > **slimmer** n (pl -s)

slime n (pl -s) unpleasant thick slippery
  substance
  slimes n ▷ **slime**
  slimier adj ▷ **slimy**
  slimiest adj ▷ **slimy**
  slimmed v ▷ **slim**
  slimmer adj, n ▷ **slim**
  slimmers n ▷ **slim**
  slimmest adj ▷ **slim**
  slimming v ▷ **slim**
  slims v ▷ **slim**

slimy adj (**-mier, -miest**) of, like, or covered
  with slime

sling¹ n (pl -s) bandage hung from the neck to
  support an injured hand or arm ▶ v (**-s, -ing,
  slung**) throw
  slinging v ▷ **sling¹**
  slings n ▷ **sling¹, ²** v ▷ **sling¹**

sling² n (pl -s) sweetened drink with a spirit
  base

slink v (**-s, -ing, slunk**) move furtively or guiltily
  slinkier adj ▷ **slinky**
  slinkiest adj ▷ **slinky**
  slinking v ▷ **slink**
  slinks v ▷ **slink**

slinky adj (**-kier, -kiest**) (of clothes) figure-
  hugging

slip¹ v (**-s, -pping, -pped**) lose balance by sliding
  ▶ n (pl -s) slipping

slip² n (pl -s) small piece (of paper)

slip³ n (pl -s) clay mixed with water used for decorating pottery

slipknot n (pl -s) knot tied so that it will slip along the rope round which it is made
  slipknots n ▷ slipknot
  slipped v ▷ slip¹

slipper n (pl -s) light shoe for indoor wear
  slipperier adj ▷ slippery
  slipperiest adj ▷ slippery
  slippers n ▷ slipper

slippery adj (-rier, -riest) so smooth or wet as to cause slipping or be difficult to hold
  slippier adj ▷ slippy
  slippiest adj ▷ slippy
  slipping v (-ppier, -ppiest) (Informal) slippery

slippy adj (-ppier, -ppiest) (Informal) slippery
  slips n ▷ slip¹, ², ³ v ▷ slip¹

slipshod adj (of an action) careless

slipstream n (pl -s) stream of air forced backwards by a fast-moving object
  slipstreams n ▷ slipstream

slipway n (pl -s) launching slope on which ships are built or repaired
  slipways n ▷ slipway

slit n (pl -s) long narrow cut or opening ▶ v (-s, -tting, slit) make a long straight cut in

slither v (-s, -ing, -ed) slide unsteadily
  slithered v ▷ slither
  slithering v ▷ slither
  slithers v ▷ slither
  slits n, v ▷ slit
  slitting v ▷ slit

sliver [sliv-ver] n (pl -s) small thin piece
  slivers n ▷ sliver

slob n (pl -s) (Informal) lazy and untidy person
  > **slobbish** adj

slobber v (-s, -ing, -ed) dribble or drool
  > **slobbery** adj
  slobbered v ▷ slobber
  slobbering v ▷ slobber
  slobbers v ▷ slobber
  slobbery adj ▷ slobber
  slobbish adj ▷ slob
  slobs n ▷ slob

sloe n (pl -s) sour blue-black fruit
  sloes n ▷ sloe

slog v (-s, -gging, -gged) work hard and steadily ▶ n (pl -s) long and exhausting work or walk

slogan n (pl -s) catchword or phrase used in politics or advertising
  slogans n ▷ slogan
  slogged v ▷ slog
  slogging v ▷ slog
  slogs v, n ▷ slog

sloop n (pl -s) small single-masted ship
  sloops n ▷ sloop

slop v (-s, -pping, -pped) splash or spill ▶ n (pl -s) spilt liquid

slope v (-pes, -ping, -ped) slant ▶ n (pl -s) sloping surface
  sloped v ▷ slope

slopes v, n ▷ slope ▶ pl n hills
  sloping v ▷ slope
  slopped v ▷ slop
  sloppier adj ▷ sloppy
  sloppiest adj ▷ sloppy
  slopping v ▷ slop

sloppy adj (-ppier, -ppiest) careless or untidy

slops v, n ▷ slop ▶ pl n liquid refuse and waste food used to feed animals

slosh v (-es, -ing, -ed) splash carelessly ▶ n (pl -es) splashing sound

sloshed adj (Slang) drunk ▶ v ▷ slosh
  sloshes v, n ▷ slosh
  sloshing v ▷ slosh

slot n (pl -s) narrow opening for inserting something ▶ v (-s, -tting, -tted) make a slot or slots in

sloth [rhymes with both] n (pl -s) slow-moving animal of tropical America

slothful adj lazy or idle
  sloths n ▷ sloth
  slots n, v ▷ slot
  slotted v ▷ slot
  slotting v ▷ slot

slouch v (-es, -ing, -ed) sit, stand, or move with a drooping posture ▶ n (pl -es) drooping posture
  slouched v ▷ slouch
  slouches v, n ▷ slouch
  slouching v ▷ slouch

slough¹ [rhymes with now] n (pl -s) bog

slough² [sluff] v (-s, -ing, -ed) (of a snake) shed (its skin) or (of a skin) be shed
  sloughed v ▷ slough²
  sloughing v ▷ slough²
  sloughs n ▷ slough¹ ▶ v ▷ slough²

sloven n (pl -s) habitually dirty or untidy person
  slovenlier adj ▷ slovenly
  slovenliest adj ▷ slovenly

slovenly adj (-lier, -liest) dirty or untidy
  slovens v ▷ sloven

slow adj (-er, -est) taking a longer time than is usual or expected ▶ v (-s, -ing, -ed) reduce the speed (of) > **slowly** adv > **slowness** n (pl -es)

slowcoach n (pl -es) (Informal) person who moves or works slowly
  slowcoaches n ▷ slowcoach

slowed v ▷ **slow**
slower adj ▷ **slow**
slowest adj ▷ **slow**
slowing v ▷ **slow**
slowly adv ▷ **slow**
slowness n ▷ **slow**
slownesses n ▷ **slow**
slows v ▷ **slow**
slowworm n (pl -s) small legless lizard
slowworms n ▷ **slowworm**
sludge n (pl -s) thick mud
sludges n ▷ **sludge**
slug[1] n (pl -s) land snail with no shell
slug[2] n (pl -s) bullet (Informal)
slug[3] v (-s, -gging, -gged) hit hard ▶ n (pl -s) heavy blow
sluggard n (pl -s) lazy person
sluggards n ▷ **sluggard**
slugged v ▷ **slug**[3]
slugging v ▷ **slug**[3]
sluggish adj slow-moving, lacking energy > **sluggishly** adv > **sluggishness** n (pl -es)
sluggishly adv ▷ **sluggish**
sluggishness n ▷ **sluggish**
sluggishnesses n ▷ **sluggish**
slugs n ▷ **slug**[1, 2, 3] ▷ v ▷ **slug**[3]
sluice n (pl -s) channel carrying off water ▶ v (-ces, -cing, -ced) pour a stream of water over or through
sluiced v ▷ **sluice**
sluices n, v ▷ **sluice**
sluicing v ▷ **sluice**
slum n (pl -s) squalid overcrowded house or area ▶ v (-s, -mming, -mmed) temporarily and deliberately experience poorer places or conditions than usual
slumber v (-s, -ing, -ed) ▶ n (pl -s) (Lit) sleep
slumbered v ▷ **slumber**
slumbering v ▷ **slumber**
slumbers v, n ▷ **slumber**
slummed v ▷ **slum**
slumming v ▷ **slum**
slump v (-s, -ing, -ed) (of prices or demand) decline sharply ▶ n (pl -s) sudden decline in prices or demand
slumped v ▷ **slump**
slumping v ▷ **slump**
slumps v, n ▷ **slump**
slums n, v ▷ **slum**
slung v ▷ **sling**[1]
slunk v ▷ **slink**
slur v (-s, -rring, -rred) pronounce or utter (words) indistinctly ▶ n (pl -s) slurring of words
slurp (Informal) v (-s, -ing, -ed) eat or drink

noisily ▶ n (pl -s) slurping sound
slurped v ▷ **slurp**
slurping v ▷ **slurp**
slurps v, n ▷ **slurp**
slurred v ▷ **slur**
slurries n ▷ **slurry**
slurring v ▷ **slur**
slurry n (pl -ries) muddy liquid mixture
slurs v, n ▷ **slur**
slush n (pl -es) watery muddy substance > **slushy** adj (-shier, -shiest)
slushes n ▷ **slush**
slushier adj ▷ **slush**
slushiest adj ▷ **slush**
slushy adj ▷ **slush**
sly adj (slyer, slyest or slier, sliest) crafty > **slyly** adv > **slyness** n (pl -es)
slyer adj ▷ **sly**
slyest adj ▷ **sly**
slyly adv ▷ **sly**
slyness n ▷ **sly**
slynesses n ▷ **sly**
smack[1] v (-s, -ing, -ed) slap sharply ▶ n (pl -s) sharp slap ▶ adv (Informal) squarely or directly
smack[2] n (pl -s) slight flavour or trace ▶ v (-s, -ing, -ed) have a slight flavour or trace (of)
smack[3] n (pl -s) small single-masted fishing boat
smacked v ▷ **smack**[1, 2]
smacker n (pl -s) (Slang) loud kiss
smackers n ▷ **smacker**
smacking v ▷ **smack**[1, 2]
smacks n ▷ **smack**[1, 2, 3] ▷ v ▷ **smack**[1, 2]
small adj (-er, -est) not large in size, number, or amount ▶ n (pl -s) narrow part of the lower back > **smallness** n (pl -es)
smaller adj ▷ **small**
smallest adj ▷ **small**
smallholding n (pl -s) small area of farming land
smallholdings n ▷ **smallholding**
smallness n ▷ **small**
smallnesses n ▷ **small**
smallpox n (pl -es) contagious disease with blisters that leave scars
smallpoxes n ▷ **smallpox**
smalls n ▷ **small** ▶ pl n (Informal) underwear
smarmier adj ▷ **smarmy**
smarmiest adj ▷ **smarmy**
smarmy adj (-mier, -miest) (Informal) unpleasantly suave or flattering
smart adj (-er, -est) well-kept and neat ▶ v (-s, -ing, -ed) feel or cause stinging pain ▶ n (pl -s) stinging pain > **smartly** adv > **smartness** n (pl -es)

smarted v ▷ smart

smarten v (-s, -ing, -ed) make or become smart

smartened v ▷ smarten

smartening v ▷ smarten

smartens v ▷ smarten

smarter adj ▷ smart

smartest adj ▷ smart

smarting v ▷ smart

smartly adv ▷ smart

smartness n ▷ smart

smartnesses n ▷ smart

smarts v, n ▷ smart

smash v (-es, -ing, -ed) break violently and noisily ▶ n (pl -es) act or sound of smashing

smashed v ▷ smash

smasher n (pl -s) (Informal) attractive person or thing

smashers n ▷ smasher

smashes v, n ▷ smash

smashing adj (Informal) excellent ▶ v ▷ smash

smattering n (pl -s) slight knowledge

smatterings n ▷ smattering

smear v (-s, -ing, -ed) spread with a greasy or sticky substance ▶ n (pl -s) dirty mark or smudge

smeared v ▷ smear

smearing v ▷ smear

smears v, n ▷ smear

smell v (-s, -ing, smelt or -ed) perceive (a scent or odour) by means of the nose ▶ n (pl -s) ability to perceive odours by the nose

smelled v ▷ smell

smellier adj ▷ smelly

smelliest adj ▷ smelly

smelling v ▷ smell

smells v, n ▷ smell

smelly adj (-lier, -liest) having a nasty smell

smelt[1] v (-s, -ing, -ed) extract (a metal) from (an ore) by heating

smelt[2] n (pl smelt) small fish of the salmon family

smelt[3] v ▷ smell

smelted v ▷ smelt[1]

smelter n (pl -s) industrial plant where smelting is carried out

smelters n ▷ smelter

smelting v ▷ smelt[1]

smelts v ▷ smelt[1]

smile n (pl -s) turning up of the corners of the mouth to show pleasure, amusement, or friendliness ▶ v (-les, -ing, -led) give a smile

smiled v ▷ smile

smiles n, v ▷ smile

smiley n (pl -s) symbol depicting a smile or

other facial expression, used in e-mail

smileys n ▷ smiley

smiling v ▷ smile

smirch v (-es, -ing, -ed) ▶ n (pl -es) stain

smirched v ▷ smirch

smirches v, n ▷ smirch

smirching v ▷ smirch

smirk n (pl -s) smug smile ▶ v (-s, -ing, -ed) give a smirk

smirked v ▷ smirk

smirking v ▷ smirk

smirks n, v ▷ smirk

smite v (-tes, -ting, smote, smitten) (Old-fashioned) strike hard

smites v ▷ smite

smith n (pl -s) worker in metal

smithereens pl n shattered fragments

smithies n ▷ smithy

smiths n ▷ smith

smithy n (pl -thies) blacksmith's workshop

smiting v ▷ smite

smitten v ▷ smite

smock n (pl -s) loose overall ▶ v (-s, -ing, -ed) gather (material) by sewing in a honeycomb pattern > **smocking** n (pl -s)

smocked v ▷ smock

smocking v, n ▷ smock

smockings n ▷ smock

smocks n, v ▷ smock

smog n (pl -s) mixture of smoke and fog

smogs n ▷ smog

smoke n (pl -s) cloudy mass that rises from something burning ▶ v (-kes, -king, -ked) give off smoke > **smokeless** adj > **smoker** n (pl -s) > **smoky** adj (-kier, -kiest)

smoked v ▷ smoke

smokeless adj ▷ smoke

smoker n ▷ smok

smokers n ▷ smok

smokes n, v ▷ smoke

smokier adj ▷ smoke

smokiest adj ▷ smoke

smoking v ▷ smoke

smoky adj ▷ smoke

smooch (Informal) v (-es, -ing, -ed) kiss and cuddle ▶ n (pl -es) smooching

smooched v ▷ smooch

smooches v, n ▷ smooch

smooching v ▷ smooch

smooth adj (-er, -est) even in surface, texture, or consistency ▶ v (-s, -ing, -ed) make smooth > **smoothly** adv

smoothed v ▷ smooth

smoother adj ▷ smooth

smoothest adj ▷ smooth

smoothie n (pl -thies) (*Informal*) charming but possibly insincere man
  smoothies n ▷ smoothie
smoothing v ▷ smooth
smoothly adv ▷ smooth
smooths v ▷ smooth
smorgasbord n (pl -s) buffet meal of assorted dishes
  smorgasbords n ▷ smorgasbord
smote v ▷ smite
smother v (-s, -ing, -ed) suffocate or stifle
  smothered v ▷ smother
  smothering v ▷ smother
  smothers v ▷ smother
smoulder v (-s, -ing, -ed) burn slowly with smoke but no flame
  smouldered v ▷ smoulder
  smouldering v ▷ smoulder
  smoulders v ▷ smoulder
smudge v (-ges, -ging, -ged) make or become smeared or soiled ▶ n (pl -s) dirty mark > **smudgy** adj (-gier, -giest)
  smudged v ▷ smudge
  smudges v, n ▷ smudge
  smudgier adj ▷ smudge
  smudgiest adj ▷ smudge
  smudging v ▷ smudge
  smudgy adj ▷ smudge
smug adj (-gger, -ggest) self-satisfied > **smugly** adv > **smugness** n (pl -es)
  smugger adj ▷ smug
  smuggest adj ▷ smug
smuggle v (-les, -ling, -led) import or export (goods) secretly and illegally > **smuggler** n (pl -s)
  smuggled v ▷ smuggle
  smuggler n ▷ smuggle
  smugglers n ▷ smuggle
  smuggles v ▷ smuggle
  smuggling v ▷ smuggle
  smugly adv ▷ smug
  smugness n ▷ smug
  smugnesses n ▷ smug
smut n (pl -s) obscene jokes, pictures, etc. > **smutty** adj (-tier, -ttiest)
  smuts n ▷ smut
  smuttier adj ▷ smut
  smuttiest adj ▷ smut
  smutty adj ▷ smut
snack n (pl -s) light quick meal
  snacks n ▷ snack
snaffle n (pl -s) jointed bit for a horse ▶ v (-les, -ling, -led) (BRIT, AUST & NZ) (*Slang*) steal
  snaffled v ▷ snaffle
  snaffles n, v ▷ snaffle

  snaffling v ▷ snaffle
snag n (pl -s) difficulty or disadvantage ▶ v (-s, -gging, -gged) catch or tear on a point
  snagged v ▷ snag
  snagging v ▷ snag
  snags n, v ▷ snag
snail n (pl -s) slow-moving mollusc with a spiral shell
  snails n ▷ snail
snake n (pl -s) long thin scaly limbless reptile ▶ v (-kes, -king, -ked) move in a winding course like a snake
  snaked v ▷ snake
  snakes n, v ▷ snake
  snakier adj ▷ snaky
  snakiest adj ▷ snaky
  snaking v ▷ snake
snaky adj (-kier, -kiest) twisted or winding
snap v (-s, -pping, -pped) break suddenly ▶ n (pl -s) act or sound of snapping ▶ adj made on the spur of the moment
snapdragon n (pl -s) plant with flowers that can open and shut like a mouth
  snapdragons n ▷ snapdragon
  snapped v ▷ snap
snapper n (pl -s) food fish of Australia and New Zealand with a pinkish body covered with blue spots
  snappers n ▷ snapper
  snappier adj ▷ snappy
  snappiest adj ▷ snappy
  snapping v ▷ snap
  snappish adj ▷ snappy
snappy adj (-ppier, -ppiest) (*also* **snappish**) irritable
  snaps v, n ▷ snap
snapshot n (pl -s) informal photograph
  snapshots n ▷ snapshot
snare n (pl -s) trap with a noose ▶ v (-res, -ring, -red) catch in or as if in a snare
  snared v ▷ snare
  snares n, v ▷ snare
  snaring v ▷ snare
snarl¹ v (-s, -ing, -ed) (of an animal) growl with bared teeth ▶ n (pl -s) act or sound of snarling
snarl² n (pl -s) tangled mess ▶ v (-s, -ing, -ed) make tangled
  snarled v ▷ snarl¹, ²
  snarling v ▷ snarl¹, ²
  snarls n, v ▷ snarl¹, ²
snatch v (-es, -ing, -ed) seize or try to seize suddenly ▶ n (pl -es) snatching
  snatched v ▷ snatch
  snatches v, n ▷ snatch
  snatching v ▷ snatch

snazzier adj ▷ snazzy

snazziest adj ▷ snazzy

snazzy adj (-zzier, -zziest) (Informal) stylish and flashy

sneak v (-s, -ing, -ed) move furtively ▶ n (pl -s) cowardly or underhand person > **sneaky** adj (-kier, -kiest)

sneaked v ▷ sneak

sneakers pl n canvas shoes with rubber soles

sneakier adj ▷ sneak

sneakiest adj ▷ sneak

sneaking adj slight but persistent ▶ v ▷ sneak

sneaks v, n ▷ sneak

sneaky adj ▷ sneak

sneer n (pl -s) contemptuous expression or remark ▶ v (-s, -ing, -ed) show contempt by a sneer

sneered v ▷ sneer

sneering v ▷ sneer

sneers n, v ▷ sneer

sneeze v (-zes, -zing, -zed) expel air from the nose suddenly, involuntarily, and noisily ▶ n (pl -s) act or sound of sneezing

sneezed v ▷ sneeze

sneezes v, n ▷ sneeze

sneezing v ▷ sneeze

snicker n (pl -s) ▶ v (-s, -ing, -ed) ▷ snigger

snickered v ▷ snicker

snickering v ▷ snicker

snickers n, v ▷ snicker

snide adj (-r, -st) critical in an unfair and nasty way

snider adj ▷ snide

snidest adj ▷ snide

sniff v (-s, -ing, -ed) inhale through the nose in short audible breaths ▶ n (pl -s) act or sound of sniffing

sniffed v ▷ sniff

sniffing v ▷ sniff

sniffle v (-les, -ling, -led) sniff repeatedly, as when suffering from a cold ▶ n (pl -s) slight cold

sniffled v ▷ sniffle

sniffles v, n ▷ sniffle

sniffling v ▷ sniffle

sniffs v, n ▷ sniff

snifter n (pl -s) (Informal) small quantity of alcoholic drink

snifters n ▷ snifter

snigger n (pl -s) sly disrespectful laugh, esp. one partly stifled ▶ v (-s, -ing, -ed) utter a snigger

sniggered v ▷ snigger

sniggering v ▷ snigger

sniggers n, v ▷ snigger

snip v (-s, -pping, -pped) cut in small quick strokes with scissors or shears ▶ n (pl -s) (Informal) bargain

snipe n (pl -s) wading bird with a long straight bill ▶ v (-pes, -ping, -ped) (foll. by at) shoot at (a person) from cover

sniped v ▷ snipe

sniper n (pl -s) person who shoots at someone from cover

snipers n ▷ sniper

snipes n, v ▷ snipe

sniping v ▷ snipe

snipped v ▷ snip

snippet n (pl -s) small piece

snippets n ▷ snippet

snipping v ▷ snip

snips v, n ▷ snip

snitch (Informal) v (-es, -ing, -ed) act as an informer ▶ n (pl -es) informer

snitched v ▷ snitch

snitches v, n ▷ snitch

snitching v ▷ snitch

snivel v (-s, -lling, -lled) cry in a whining way

snivelled v ▷ snivel

snivelling v ▷ snivel

snivels v ▷ snivel

snob n (pl -s) person who judges others by social rank > **snobbery** n (pl -ries) > **snobbish** adj

snobberies n ▷ snob

snobbery n ▷ snob

snobbish adj ▷ snob

snobs n ▷ snob

snoek n (pl -s) (S AFR) edible marine fish

snoeks n ▷ snoek

snood n (pl -s) pouch, often of net, loosely holding a woman's hair at the back

snoods n ▷ snood

snook n (pl -s) gesture of contempt

snooker n (pl -s) game played on a billiard table ▶ v (-s, -ing, -ed) leave (a snooker opponent) in a position such that another ball blocks the target ball

snookered v ▷ snooker

snookering v ▷ snooker

snookers n, v ▷ snooker

snooks n ▷ snook

snoop (Informal) v (-s, -ing, -ed) pry ▶ n (pl -s) snooping > **snooper** n (pl -s)

snooped v ▷ snoop

snooper n ▷ snoop

snoopers n ▷ snoop

snooping v ▷ snoop

snoops v, n ▷ snoop

snootier adj ▷ snooty

snootiest adj ▷ snooty
snooty adj (-tier, -tiest) (Informal) haughty
snooze (Informal) v (-zes, -zing, -zed) take a brief light sleep ▶ n (pl -s) brief light sleep
snoozed v ▷ snooze
snoozes v, n ▷ snooze
snoozing v ▷ snooze
snore v (-res, -ring, -red) make snorting sounds while sleeping ▶ n (pl -s) sound of snoring
snored v ▷ snore
snores v, n ▷ snore
snoring v ▷ snore
snorkel n (pl -s) tube allowing a swimmer to breathe while face down on the surface of the water ▶ v (-s, -lling, -lled) swim using a snorkel
snorkelled v ▷ snorkel
snorkelling v ▷ snorkel
snorkels n, v ▷ snorkel
snort v (-s, -ing, -ed) exhale noisily through the nostrils ▶ n (pl -s) act or sound of snorting
snorted v ▷ snort
snorting v ▷ snort
snorts v, n ▷ snort
snot n (pl -s) (Slang) mucus from the nose
snots n ▷ snot
snout n (pl -s) animal's projecting nose and jaws
snouts n ▷ snout
snow n (pl -s) frozen vapour falling from the sky in flakes ▶ v (-s, -ing, -ed) fall as or like snow > **snowy** adj (-wier, -wiest)
snowball n (pl -s) snow pressed into a ball for throwing ▶ v (-s, -ing, -ed) increase rapidly
snowballed v ▷ snowball
snowballing v ▷ snowball
snowballs n, v ▷ snowball
snowboard n (pl -s) board on which a person stands to slide across the snow > **snowboarding** n (pl -s)
snowboarding n ▷ snowboard
snowboardings n ▷ snowboard
snowboards n ▷ snowboard
snowdrift n (pl -s) bank of deep snow
snowdrifts n ▷ snowdrift
snowdrop n (pl -s) small white bell-shaped spring flower
snowdrops n ▷ snowdrop
snowed v ▷ snow
snowflake n (pl -s) single crystal of snow
snowflakes n ▷ snowflake
snowier adj ▷ snow
snowiest adj ▷ snow
snowing v ▷ snow

snowman n (pl -men) figure shaped out of snow
snowmen n ▷ snowman
snowplough n (pl -s) vehicle for clearing away snow
snowploughs n ▷ snowplough
snows n, v ▷ snow
snowshoes pl n racket-shaped shoes for travelling on snow
snowy adj ▷ snow
snub v (-s, -bbing, -bbed) insult deliberately ▶ n (pl -s) deliberate insult ▶ adj (of a nose) short and blunt
snubbed v ▷ snub
snubbing v ▷ snub
snubs v, n ▷ snub
snuff¹ n (pl -s) powdered tobacco for sniffing up the nostrils
snuff² v (-s, -ing, -ed) extinguish (a candle)
snuffed v ▷ snuff²
snuffing v ▷ snuff²
snuffle v (-les, -ling, -led) breathe noisily or with difficulty
snuffled v ▷ snuffle
snuffles v ▷ snuffle
snuffling v ▷ snuffle
snuffs n ▷ snuff¹ ▶ v ▷ snuff²
snug adj (-gger, -ggest) warm and comfortable ▶ n (pl -s) (in Britain and Ireland) small room in a pub > **snugly** adv
snugger adj ▷ snug
snuggest adj ▷ snug
snuggle v (-les, -ling, -led) nestle into a person or thing for warmth or from affection
snuggled v ▷ snuggle
snuggles v ▷ snuggle
snuggling v ▷ snuggle
snugly adv ▷ snug
snugs n ▷ snug

> **sny** n (snys). Sny is a Canadian word for a side channel of a river. This word doesn't contain a vowel, so it can help you to clear an awkward rack. Sny scores 6 points.

so adv to such an extent ▶ conj in order that ▶ interj exclamation of surprise, triumph, or realization
soak v (-s, -ing, -ed) make wet ▶ n (pl -s) soaking > **soaking** n (pl -s) adj
soaked v ▷ soak
soaking v, n, adj ▷ soak
soakings n ▷ soak
soaks v, n ▷ soak
soap n (pl -s) compound of alkali and fat, used with water as a cleaning agent ▶ v (-s, -ing,

-ed) apply soap to > **soapy** adj (-pier, -piest)
soaped v ▷ soap
soapier adj ▷ soap
soapiest adj ▷ soap
soaping v ▷ soap
soaps n, v ▷ soap
soapy adj ▷ soap
soar v (-s, -ing, -ed) rise or fly upwards
soared v ▷ soar
soaring v ▷ soar
soars v ▷ soar
sob v (-s, -bbing, -bbed) weep with convulsive gasps ▶ n (pl -s) act or sound of sobbing
sobbed v ▷ sob
sobbing v ▷ sob
sober adj (-er, -est) not drunk ▶ v (-s, -ing, -ed) make or become sober > **soberly** adv
sobered v ▷ sober
soberer adj ▷ sober
soberest adj ▷ sober
sobering v ▷ sober
soberly adv ▷ sober
sobers v ▷ sober
sobrieties n ▷ sobriety
sobriety n (pl -ties) state of being sober
sobriquet [so-brik-ay] n (pl -s) nickname
sobriquets n ▷ sobriquet
sobs v, n ▷ sob
soccer n (pl -s) football played by two teams of eleven kicking a spherical ball
soccers n ▷ soccer
sociabilities n ▷ sociable
sociability n ▷ sociable
sociable adj friendly or companionable > **sociability** n (pl -ties) > **sociably** adv
sociably adv ▷ sociable
social adj living in a community ▶ n (pl -s) informal gathering > **socially** adv
socialism n (pl -s) political system which advocates public ownership of industries, resources, and transport
socialisms n ▷ socialism
socialist n (pl -s) ▶ adj
socialists n ▷ socialist
socialite n (pl -s) member of fashionable society
socialites n ▷ socialite
socialize v (-zes, -zing, -zed) meet others socially
socialized v ▷ socialize
socializes v ▷ socialize
socializing v ▷ socialize
socially adv ▷ social
socials n ▷ social
societies n ▷ society

society n (pl -ties) human beings considered as a group
sociological adj ▷ sociology
sociologies n ▷ sociology
sociologist n ▷ sociology
sociologists n ▷ sociology
sociology n (pl -gies) study of human societies > **sociological** adj > **sociologist** n (pl -s)
sock[1] n (pl -s) knitted covering for the foot
sock[2] (Slang) v (-s, -ing, -ed) hit hard ▶ n (pl -s) hard blow
socked v ▷ sock[2]
socket n (pl -s) hole or recess into which something fits
sockets n ▷ socket
socking v ▷ sock[2]
socks v ▷ sock[2] ▶ n ▷ sock[1, 2]
sod n (pl -s) (piece of) turf
soda n (pl -s) compound of sodium
sodas n ▷ soda
sodden adj soaked
sodium n (pl -s) (CHEM) silvery-white metallic element
sodiums n ▷ sodium
sods n ▷ sod
sofa n (pl -s) couch
sofas n ▷ sofa
soft adj (-er, -s) easy to shape or cut > **softly** adv
soften v (-s, -ing, -ed) make or become soft or softer
softened v ▷ soften
softening v ▷ soften
softens v ▷ soften
softer adj ▷ soft
softest adj ▷ soft
softly adv ▷ soft
software n (pl -s) computer programs
softwares n ▷ software
softwood n (pl -s) wood of a coniferous tree
softwoods n ▷ softwood
soggier adj ▷ soggy
soggiest adj ▷ soggy
sogginess n ▷ soggy
sogginesses n ▷ soggy
soggy adj (-gier, -ggiest) soaked > **sogginess** n (pl -es)
soigné, fem **soignée** [swah-nyay] adj well-groomed, elegant
soil[1] n (pl -s) top layer of earth
soil[2] v (-s, -ing, -ed) make or become dirty
soiled v ▷ soil
soiling v ▷ soil
soils n ▷ soil[1] ▶ v ▷ soil[2]
soiree [swah-ray] n (pl -s) evening party or gathering

soirees n ▷ soiree

sojourn [soj-urn] n (pl -s) temporary stay ▶ v (-s, -ing, -ed) stay temporarily

sojourned v ▷ sojourn

sojourning v ▷ sojourn

sojourns n, v ▷ sojourn

solace [sol-iss] n, v (-ces, -cing, -ced) comfort in distress

solaced v ▷ solace

solaces v ▷ solace

solacing v ▷ solace

solar adj of the sun

solaria n ▷ solarium

solarium n (pl -riums, -ria) place with beds and ultraviolet lights used for acquiring an artificial suntan

solariums n ▷ solarium

sold v ▷ sell

solder n (pl -s) soft alloy used to join two metal surfaces ▶ v (-s, -ing, -ed) join with solder

soldered v ▷ solder

soldering v ▷ solder

solders n, v ▷ solder

soldier n (pl -s) member of an army ▶ v (-s, -ing, -ed) serve in an army > soldierly adj

soldiered v ▷ soldier

soldiering v ▷ soldier

soldierly adj ▷ soldier

soldiers n, v ▷ soldier

sole¹ adj one and only

sole² n (pl -s) underside of the foot ▶ v (-les, -ling, -led) provide (a shoe) with a sole

sole³ n (pl -s) small edible flatfish

solecism [sol-iss-izz-um] n (pl -s) minor grammatical mistake

solecisms n ▷ solecism

soled v ▷ sole²

solely adv only, completely

solemn adj (-er, -est) serious, deeply sincere > solemnly adv > solemnity n (pl -ties)

solemner adj ▷ solemn

solemnest adj ▷ solemn

solemnities n ▷ solemn

solemnity n ▷ solemn

solemnly adv ▷ solemn

solenoid [sole-in-oid] n (pl -s) coil of wire magnetized by passing a current through it

solenoids n ▷ solenoid

soles n ▷ sole², ³ v ▷ sole²

solicit v (-s, -ing, -ed) request > solicitation n (pl -s)

solicitation n ▷ solicit

solicitations n ▷ solicit

solicited v ▷ solicit

soliciting v ▷ solicit

solicitor n (pl -s) (BRIT, AUST & NZ) lawyer who advises clients and prepares documents and cases

solicitors n ▷ solicitor

solicitous adj anxious about someone's welfare > solicitude n (pl -s)

solicits v ▷ solicit

solicitude n ▷ solicitous

solicitudes n ▷ solicitous

solid adj (-er, -est) (of a substance) keeping its shape ▶ n (pl -s) three-dimensional shape > solidity n (pl -ties) > solidly adv

solidarities n ▷ solidarity

solidarity n (pl -ties) agreement in aims or interests, total unity

solider adj ▷ solid

solidest adj ▷ solid

solidified v ▷ solidify

solidifies v ▷ solidify

solidify v (-fies, -fying, -fied) make or become solid or firm

solidifying v ▷ solidify

solidities n ▷ solid

solidity n ▷ solid

solidly adv ▷ solid

solids n ▷ solid

soliloquies n ▷ soliloquy

soliloquy n (pl -quies) speech made by a person while alone, esp. in a play

soling v ▷ sole²

solipsism n (pl -s) doctrine that the self is the only thing known to exist > solipsist n (pl -s)

solipsisms n ▷ solipsism

solipsist n ▷ solipsism

solipsists n ▷ solipsism

solitaire n (pl -s) game for one person played with pegs set in a board

solitaires n ▷ solitaire

solitary adj alone, single

solitude n (pl -s) state of being alone

solitudes n ▷ solitude

solo n (pl -s) music for one performer ▶ adj done alone ▶ adv by oneself, alone > soloist n (pl -s)

soloist n ▷ solo

soloists n ▷ solo

solos n ▷ solo

solstice n (pl -s) either the shortest (in winter) or longest (in summer) day of the year

solstices n ▷ solstice

solubilities n ▷ soluble

solubility n ▷ soluble

soluble adj able to be dissolved > solubility n (pl -ties)

solution n (pl -s) answer to a problem

solutions n ▷ solution

solvable adj ▷ solve

solve v (-ves, -ving, -ved) find the answer to (a problem) ▷ **solvable** adj

solved v ▷ solve

solvencies n ▷ solvent

solvency n ▷ solvent

solvent adj having enough money to pay one's debts ▶ n (pl -s) liquid capable of dissolving other substances ▷ **solvency** n (pl -cies)

solvents n ▷ solvent

solves v ▷ solve

solving v ▷ solve

sombre adj (-r, -st) dark, gloomy

sombrer adj ▷ sombre

sombrero n (pl -s) wide-brimmed Mexican hat

sombreros n ▷ sombrero

sombrest adj ▷ sombre

some adj unknown or unspecified (Informal) ▶ pron certain unknown or unspecified people or things

somebodies n ▷ somebody

somebody pron some person ▶ n (pl -dies) important person

somehow adv in some unspecified way

someone pron somebody

somersault n (pl -s) leap or roll in which the trunk and legs are turned over the head ▶ v (-s, -ing, -ed) perform a somersault

somersaulted v ▷ somersault

somersaulting v ▷ somersault

somersaults n, v ▷ somersault

something pron unknown or unspecified thing or amount

sometime adv at some unspecified time ▶ adj former

sometimes adv from time to time, now and then

somewhat adv to some extent, rather

somewhere adv in, to, or at some unspecified or unknown place

somnambulism n ▷ somnambulist

somnambulisms n ▷ somnambulist

somnambulist n (pl -s) person who walks in his or her sleep ▷ **somnambulism** n (pl -s)

somnambulists n ▷ somnambulist

somnolent adj drowsy

son n (pl -s) male offspring

sonar n (pl -s) device for detecting underwater objects by the reflection of sound waves

sonars n ▷ sonar

sonata n (pl -s) piece of music in several movements for one instrument with or without piano

sonatas n ▷ sonata

song n (pl -s) music for the voice

songbird n (pl -s) any bird with a musical call

songbirds n ▷ songbird

songs n ▷ song

songster, songstress n (pl -s, -es) singer

songsters n ▷ songster

songstress n ▷ songster

songstresses n ▷ songster

sonic adj of or producing sound

sonnet n (pl -s) fourteen-line poem with a fixed rhyme scheme

sonnets n ▷ sonnet

sonorities n ▷ sonorous

sonority n ▷ sonorous

sonorous adj (of sound) deep or resonant ▷ **sonorously** adv ▷ **sonority** n (pl -ties)

sonorously adv ▷ sonorous

sons n ▷ son

soon adv in a short time

sooner adv rather

soot n (pl -s) black powder formed by the incomplete burning of an organic substance ▷ **sooty** adj (-tier, -tiest)

soothe v (-thes, -thing, -thed) make calm

soothed v ▷ soothe

soothes v ▷ soothe

soothing v ▷ soothe

soothsayer n (pl -s) seer or prophet

soothsayers n ▷ soothsayer

sootier adj ▷ soot

sootiest adj ▷ soot

soots n ▷ soot

sooty adj ▷ soot

sop n (pl -s) concession to pacify someone ▶ v (-s, -pping, -pped) mop up or absorb (liquid)

sophism n ▷ sophistry

sophisms n ▷ sophistry

sophist n (pl -s) person who uses clever but invalid arguments

sophisticate v (-tes, -ting, -ted) make less natural or innocent ▶ n (pl -s) sophisticated person

sophisticated adj having or appealing to refined or cultured tastes and habits ▶ v ▷ **sophisticate** ▷ **sophistication** n (pl -s)

sophisticates v, n ▷ sophisticate

sophisticating v ▷ sophisticate

sophistication n ▷ sophisticated

sophistications n ▷ sophisticated

sophistries n ▷ sophistry

sophistry, sophism n (pl -ries, -s) clever but invalid argument

sophists n ▷ sophistry

sophomore n (pl -s) (US) student in second year at college

sophomores n ▷ sophomore

soporific *adj* causing sleep ▸ *n* (*pl* -s) drug that causes sleep
soporifics *n* ▷ soporific
sopped *v* ▷ sop
soppier *adj* ▷ soppy
soppiest *adj* ▷ soppy
sopping *adj* completely soaked ▸ *v* ▷ sop
soppy *adj* (soppier, soppiest) (*Informal*) oversentimental
soprano *n* (*pl* -s) (singer with) the highest female or boy's voice
sopranos *n* ▷ soprano
sops *n*, *v* ▷ sop
sorbet *n* (*pl* -s) flavoured water ice
sorbets *n* ▷ sorbet
sorcerer *n* (*pl* -s) magician > **sorceress** *n fem* (*pl* -s)
sorcerers *n* ▷ sorcerer
sorceress *n* ▷ sorcerer
sorceresses *n* ▷ sorcerer
sorceries *n* ▷ sorcery
sorcery *n* (*pl* -ries) witchcraft or magic
sordid *adj* (-er, -est) dirty, squalid > **sordidly** *adv* > **sordidness** *n* (*pl* -es)
sordider *adj* ▷ sordid
sordidest *adj* ▷ sordid
sordidly *adv* ▷ sordid
sordidness *n* ▷ sordid
sordidnesses *n* ▷ sordid
sore *adj* (-r, -st) painful ▸ *n* (*pl* -s) painful area on the body ▸ *adv* (*Obs*) greatly > **soreness** *n* (*pl* -es)
sorely *adv* greatly
soreness *n* ▷ sore
sorenesses *n* ▷ sore
sorer *adj* ▷ sore
sores *n* ▷ sore
sorest *adj* ▷ sore
sorghum *n* (*pl* -s) kind of grass cultivated for grain
sorghums *n* ▷ sorghum
sorrel *n* (*pl* -s) bitter-tasting plant
sorrels *n* ▷ sorrel
sorrier *adj* ▷ sorry
sorriest *adj* ▷ sorry
sorrow *n* (*pl* -s) grief or sadness ▸ *v* (-s, -ing, -ed) grieve > **sorrowful** *adj* > **sorrowfully** *adv*
sorrowed *v* ▷ sorrow
sorrowful *adj* ▷ sorrow
sorrowfully *adv* ▷ sorrow
sorrowing *v* ▷ sorrow
sorrows *n*, *v* ▷ sorrow
sorry *adj* (-rier, -riest) feeling pity or regret
sort *n* (*pl* -s) group all sharing certain qualities or characteristics ▸ *v* (-s, -ing, -ed) arrange

according to kind
sorted *v* ▷ sort
sortie *n* (*pl* -s) relatively short return trip
sorties *n* ▷ sortie
sorting *v* ▷ sort
sorts *n*, *v* ▷ sort
sot *n* (*pl* -s) habitual drunkard
sots *n* ▷ sot
soubriquet [so-brik-ay] *n* (*pl* -s) ▷ sobriquet
soubriquets *n* ▷ soubriquet
soufflé [soo-flay] *n* (*pl* -s) light fluffy dish made with beaten egg whites and other ingredients
soufflés *n* ▷ soufflé
sough [rhymes with now] *v* (-s, -ing, -ed) (of the wind) make a sighing sound
soughed *v* ▷ sough
soughing *v* ▷ sough
soughs *v* ▷ sough
sought [sawt] *v* ▷ seek
souk [sook] *n* (*pl* -s) marketplace in Muslim countries, often open-air
souks *n* ▷ souk
soul *n* (*pl* -s) spiritual and immortal part of a human being
soulful *adj* full of emotion
soulless *adj* lacking human qualities, mechanical
souls *n* ▷ soul
sound¹ *n* (*pl* -s) something heard, noise ▸ *v* (-s, -ing, -ed) make or cause to make a sound
sound² *adj* (-er, -est) in good condition > **soundly** *adv*
sound³ *v* (-s, -ing, -ed) find the depth of (water etc.)
sound⁴ *n* (*pl* -s) channel or strait
sounded *v* ▷ sound¹, ³
sounder *adj* ▷ sound²
soundest *adj* ▷ sound²
sounding *v* ▷ sound¹, ³
soundings *pl n* measurements of depth taken by sounding
soundly *adv* ▷ sound²
soundproof *adj* not penetrable by sound ▸ *v* (-s, -ing, -ed) make soundproof
soundproofed *v* ▷ soundproof
soundproofing *v* ▷ soundproof
soundproofs *v* ▷ soundproof
sounds *n* ▷ sound¹, ⁴ ▸ *v* ▷ sound¹, ³
soundtrack *n* (*pl* -s) recorded sound accompaniment to a film
soundtracks *n* ▷ soundtrack
soup *n* (*pl* -s) liquid food made from meat, vegetables, etc. > **soupy** *adj* (-pier, -piest)
soupçon [soop-sonn] *n* (*pl* -s) small amount

soupçons n ▷ soupçon
soupier adj ▷ soup
soupiest adj ▷ soup
soups n ▷ soup
soupy adj ▷ soup
sour adj (-er, -est) sharp-tasting ▶ v (-s, -ing, -ed) make or become sour > sourly adv
> sourness n (pl -s)
source n (pl -s) origin or starting point
sources n ▷ source
soured v ▷ sour
sourer adj ▷ sour
sourest adj ▷ sour
souring v ▷ sour
sourly adv ▷ sour
sourness n ▷ sour
sournesses n ▷ sour
sours v ▷ sour
souse v (-ses, -sing, -sed) plunge (something) into liquid
soused v ▷ souse
souses v ▷ souse
sousing v ▷ souse
soutane [soo-tan] n (pl -s) Roman Catholic priest's cassock
soutanes n ▷ soutane
south n (pl -s) direction towards the South Pole, opposite north ▶ adj to or in the south ▶ adv in, to, or towards the south > southerly adj > southern adj ▷ southward adj, adv
> southwards adv
southerly adj ▷ south
southern adj ▷ south
southerner n (pl -s) person from the south of a country or area
southerners n ▷ southerner
southpaw n (pl -s) (Informal) left-handed person, esp. a boxer
southpaws n ▷ southpaw
souths n ▷ south
southward adj, adv ▷ south
southwards adv ▷ south
souvenir n (pl -s) keepsake, memento
souvenirs n ▷ souvenir
sou'wester n (pl -s) seaman's waterproof hat covering the head and back of the neck
sou'westers n ▷ sou'wester
sovereign n (pl -s) king or queen ▶ adj (of a state) independent > sovereignty n (pl -ties)
sovereigns n ▷ sovereign
sovereignties n ▷ sovereign
sovereignty n ▷ sovereign
soviet n (pl -s) formerly, elected council at various levels of government in the USSR
▶ adj

soviets n ▷ soviet
sow¹ [rhymes with **know**] v (-s, -ing, -ed, sown or -ed) scatter or plant (seed) in or on (the ground)
sow² [rhymes with **cow**] n (pl -s) female adult pig
sowed v ▷ sow¹
sowing v ▷ sow¹
sown v ▷ sow¹
sows n ▷ sow² ▶ v ▷ sow¹

> **sox** pl n. Sox is an informal word for **socks**. This is a good word to remember for when you find an X on your rack without the space or tiles to play a longer word. Sox scores 10 points.

soya n (pl -s) plant whose edible bean is used for food and as a source of oil
soyas n ▷ soya
sozzled adj (BRIT, AUST & NZ) (Slang) drunk
spa n (pl -s) resort with a mineral-water spring
space n (pl -s) unlimited expanse in which all objects exist and move ▶ v (-ces, -cing, -ced) place at intervals
spacecraft, spaceship n (pl -s) vehicle for travel beyond the earth's atmosphere
spacecrafts n ▷ spacecraft
spaced v ▷ space
spaces n, v ▷ space
spaceship n ▷ spacecraft
spaceships n ▷ spacecraft
spacesuit n (pl -s) sealed pressurized suit worn by an astronaut
spacesuits n ▷ spacesuit
spacing v ▷ space
spacious adj having a large capacity or area
spade¹ n (pl -s) tool for digging
spade² n (pl -s) playing card of the suit marked with black leaf-shaped symbols
spades n ▷ spade¹, ²
spadework n (pl -s) hard preparatory work
spadeworks n ▷ spadework
spaghetti n (pl -s) pasta in the form of long strings
spaghettis n ▷ spaghetti
span n (pl -s) space between two points ▶ v (-s, -nning, -nned) stretch or extend across
spangle n (pl -les) small shiny metallic ornament ▶ v (-les, -ling, -led) decorate with spangles
spangled v ▷ spangle
spangles n, v ▷ spangle
spangling v ▷ spangle
spaniel n (pl -s) dog with long ears and silky hair
spaniels n ▷ spaniel

spank v (-s, -ing, -ed) slap with the open hand, on the buttocks or legs ▶ n (pl -s) such a slap
> **spanking** n (pl -s)
 spanked v ▷ spank
spanking adj (Informal) outstandingly fine or smart ▶ v ▷ spank ▶ n ▷ spank
 spankings n ▷ spank
 spanks v, n ▷ spank
 spanned v ▷ span
spanner n (pl -s) tool for gripping and turning a nut or bolt
 spanners n ▷ spanner
 spanning v ▷ span
 spans n, v ▷ span
spar¹ n (pl -s) pole used as a ship's mast, boom, or yard
spar² v (-s, -rring, -rred) box or fight using light blows for practice
spare adj extra ▶ n (pl -s) duplicate kept in case of damage or loss ▶ v (-res, -ring, -red) refrain from punishing or harming
 spared v ▷ spare
 spares n, v ▷ spare
sparing adj economical ▶ v ▷ spare
spark n (pl -s) fiery particle thrown out from a fire or caused by friction ▶ v (-s, -ing, -ed) give off sparks
 sparked v ▷ spark
sparkie n (pl -s) (NZ) (Informal) electrician
 sparkies n ▷ sparkie
 sparking v ▷ spark
sparkle v (-les, -ling, -led) glitter with many points of light ▶ n (pl -s) sparkling points of light
 sparkled v ▷ sparkle
sparkler n (pl -s) hand-held firework that emits sparks
 sparklers n ▷ sparkler
 sparkles v, n ▷ sparkle
sparkling adj (of wine or mineral water) slightly fizzy ▶ v ▷ sparkle
 sparks v, n ▷ spark
 sparred v ▷ spar²
 sparring v ▷ spar²
sparrow n (pl -s) small brownish bird
sparrowhawk n (pl -s) small hawk
 sparrowhawks n ▷ sparrowhawk
 sparrows n ▷ sparrow
 spars n ▷ spar¹ ▶ v ▷ spar²
sparse adj (-r, -st) thinly scattered > **sparsely** adv > **sparseness** n (pl -es)
 sparsely adv ▷ sparse
 sparseness n ▷ sparse
 sparsenesses n ▷ sparse
 sparser adj ▷ sparse

 sparsest adj ▷ sparse
spartan adj strict and austere
 spas n ▷ spa
spasm n (pl -s) involuntary muscular contraction
spasmodic adj occurring in spasms
> **spasmodically** adv
 spasmodically adv ▷ spasmodic
 spasms n ▷ spasm
spastic n (pl -s) person with cerebral palsy ▶ adj suffering from cerebral palsy
 spastics n ▷ spastic
spat¹ n (pl -s) slight quarrel
spat² v ▷ spit¹
spate n (pl -s) large number of things happening within a period of time
 spates n ▷ spate
spatial adj of or in space
spats pl n coverings formerly worn over the ankle and instep ▶ n ▷ spat¹
spatter v (-s, -ing, -ed) scatter or be scattered in drops over (something) ▶ n (pl -s) spattering sound
 spattered v ▷ spatter
 spattering v ▷ spatter
 spatters n, v ▷ spatter
spatula n (pl -s) utensil with a broad flat blade for spreading or stirring
 spatulas n ▷ spatula
spawn n (pl -s) jelly-like mass of eggs of fish, frogs, or molluscs ▶ v (-s, -ing, -ed) (of fish, frogs, or molluscs) lay eggs
 spawned v ▷ spawn
 spawning v ▷ spawn
 spawns n, v ▷ spawn
spay v (-s, -ing, -ed) remove the ovaries from (a female animal)
 spayed v ▷ spay
 spaying v ▷ spay
 spays v ▷ spay
speak v (-s, -ing, spoke, spoken) say words, talk
speaker n (pl -s) person who speaks, esp. at a formal occasion
 speakers n ▷ speaker
 speaking v ▷ speak
 speaks v ▷ speak
spear¹ n (pl -s) weapon consisting of a long shaft with a sharp point ▶ v (-s, -ing, -ed) pierce with or as if with a spear
spear² n (pl -s) slender shoot
 speared v ▷ spear¹
spearhead v (-es, -ing, -ed) lead (an attack or campaign) ▶ n (pl -s) leading force in an attack or campaign
 spearheaded v ▷ spearhead

spearheading v ▷ spearhead
spearheads v, n ▷ spearhead
spearing v ▷ spear¹
spearmint n (pl -s) type of mint
spearmints n ▷ spearmint
spears n ▷ spear¹, ² ▶ v ▷ spear¹
spec n (pl -s) (*Informal*) speculation
special adj distinguised from others of its kind > **specially** adv
specialist n (pl -s) expert in a particular activity or subject
specialists n ▷ specialist
specialities n ▷ speciality
speciality n (pl -ties) special interest or skill
specialization n ▷ specialize
specializations n ▷ specialize
specialize v (-zes, -zing, -zed) be a specialist > **specialization** n (pl -s)
specialized v ▷ specialize
specializes v ▷ specialize
specializing v ▷ specialize
specially adv ▷ special
specie n coins as distinct from paper money
species n (pl species) group of plants or animals that are related closely enough to interbreed naturally
specific adj particular, definite ▶ n (pl -s) drug used to treat a particular disease > **specifically** adv
specifically adv ▷ specific
specification n (pl -s) detailed description of something to be made or done
specifications n ▷ specification
specifics n ▷ specific ▶ pl n particular details
specified v ▷ specify
specifies v ▷ specify
specify v (-fies, -fying, -fied) refer to or state specifically
specifying v ▷ specify
specimen n (pl -s) individual or part typifying a whole
specimens n ▷ specimen
specious [spee-shuss] adj apparently true, but actually false
speck n (pl -s) small spot or particle
speckle n (pl -s) small spot ▶ v (-les, -ling, -led) mark with speckles
speckled v ▷ speckle
speckles n, v ▷ speckle
speckling v ▷ speckle
specks n ▷ speck
specs pl n (*Informal*) ▷ spectacles ▶ n ▷ spec
spectacle n (pl -s) strange, interesting, or ridiculous sight
spectacles n ▷ spectacle ▶ pl n pair of glasses

for correcting faulty vision
spectacles n ▷ spectacle
spectacular adj impressive ▶ n (pl -s) spectacular public show > **spectacularly** adv
spectacularly adv ▷ spectacular
spectaculars n ▷ spectacular
spectate v (-tes, -ting, -ted) watch
spectated v ▷ spectate
spectates v ▷ spectate
spectating v ▷ spectate
spectator n (pl -s) person viewing anything, onlooker
spectators n ▷ spectator
spectra n ▷ spectrum
spectral adj ▷ spectre
spectre n (pl -s) ghost > **spectral** adj
spectres n ▷ spectre
spectroscope n (pl -s) instrument for producing or examining spectra
spectroscopes n ▷ spectroscope
spectrum n (pl -tra) range of different colours, radio waves, etc. in order of their wavelengths
speculate v (-tes, -ting, -ted) guess, conjecture > **speculation** n (pl -s) > **speculative** adj > **speculator** n (pl -s)
speculated v ▷ speculate
speculates v ▷ speculate
speculating v ▷ speculate
speculation n ▷ speculate
speculations n ▷ speculate
speculative adj ▷ speculate
speculator n ▷ speculate
speculators n ▷ speculate
sped v ▷ speed
speech n (pl -es) act, power, or manner of speaking
speeches n ▷ speech
speechless adj unable to speak because of great emotion
speed n (pl -s) swiftness ▶ v (-s, -ing, sped or -ed) go quickly
speedboat n (pl -s) light fast motorboat
speedboats n ▷ speedboat
speeded v ▷ speed
speedier adj ▷ speedy
speediest adj ▷ speedy
speedily adv ▷ speedy
speeding v ▷ speed
speedometer n (pl -s) instrument to show the speed of a vehicle
speedometers n ▷ speedometer
speeds n, v ▷ speed
speedway n (pl -s) track for motorcycle racing
speedways n ▷ speedway

speedwell n (pl -s) plant with small blue flowers
speedwells n ▷ speedwell
speedy adj (-dier, -diest) prompt > **speedily** adv
speleologies n ▷ speleology
speleology n (pl -gies) study and exploration of caves
spell¹ v (-s, -ing, spelt or -ed) give in correct order the letters that form (a word)
spell² n (pl -s) formula of words supposed to have magic power
spell³ n (pl -s) period of time of weather or activity
spellbound adj entranced
spellchecker n (pl -s) (COMPUTING) program that highlights wrongly spelled words in a word-processed document
spellcheckers n ▷ spellchecker
spelled v ▷ spell¹
spelling n (pl -s) way a word is spelt ▷ v ▷ spell¹
spellings n ▷ spelling
spells v ▷ spell¹ ▶ n ▷ spell²,³
spelt v ▷ spell¹
spend v (-s, -ing, spent) pay out (money)
spending v ▷ spend
spends v ▷ spend
spendthrift n (pl -s) person who spends money wastefully
spendthrifts n ▷ spendthrift
spent v ▷ spend
sperm n (pl -s or sperm) male reproductive cell
spermaceti [sper-ma-set-ee] n (pl -s) waxy solid obtained from the sperm whale
spermacetis n ▷ spermaceti
spermatozoa n ▷ spermatozoon
spermatozoon [sper-ma-toe-zoe-on] n (pl -zoa) sperm
spermicide n (pl -s) substance that kills sperm
spermicides n ▷ spermicide
sperms n ▷ sperm
spew v (-s, -ing, -ed) vomit
spewed v ▷ spew
spewing v ▷ spew
spews v ▷ spew
sphagnum n (pl -s) moss found in bogs
sphagnums n ▷ sphagnum
sphere n (pl -s) perfectly round solid object > **spherical** adj
spheres n ▷ sphere
spherical adj ▷ sphere
sphincter n (pl -s) ring of muscle which controls the opening and closing of a hollow organ
sphincters n ▷ sphincter
sphinx n (pl -es) enigmatic person

sphinxes n ▷ sphinx
spice n (pl -s) aromatic substance used as flavouring ▶ v (-ces, -cing, -ced) flavour with spices
spiced v ▷ spice
spices n, v ▷ spice
spicier adj ▷ spicy
spiciest adj ▷ spicy
spicing v ▷ spice
spicy adj (-cier, -ciest) flavoured with spices
spider n (pl -s) small eight-legged creature which spins a web to catch insects for food > **spidery** adj
spiders n ▷ spider
spidery adj ▷ spider
spied v ▷ spy
spiel n (pl -s) speech made to persuade someone to do something
spiels n ▷ spiel
spies v, n ▷ spy
spigot n (pl -s) stopper for, or tap fitted to, a cask
spigots n ▷ spigot
spike n (pl -s) sharp point ▶ v (-kes, -king, -ked) put spikes on > **spiky** adj (-kier, -kiest)
spiked v ▷ spike
spikes n, v ▷ spike ▶ pl n sports shoes with spikes for greater grip
spikier adj ▷ spike
spikiest adj ▷ spike
spiking v ▷ spike
spiky adj ▷ spike
spill¹ v (-s, -ing, spilt or spilled) pour from or as if from a container ▶ n (pl -s) fall > **spillage** n (pl -s)
spill² n (pl -s) thin strip of wood or paper for lighting pipes or fires
spillage n ▷ spill¹
spillages n ▷ spill¹
spilled v ▷ spill¹
spilling v ▷ spill¹
spills n ▷ spill¹,² ▶ v ▷ spill¹
spilt v ▷ spill¹
spin v (-s, -nning, spun) revolve or cause to revolve rapidly ▶ n (pl -s) revolving motion > **spinner** n (pl -s)
spinach n (pl -es) dark green leafy vegetable
spinaches n ▷ spinach
spinal adj of the spine
spindle n (pl -s) rotating rod that acts as an axle
spindles n ▷ spindle
spindlier adj ▷ spindly
spindliest adj ▷ spindly
spindly adj (-lier, -liest) long, slender, and frail

spine n (pl -s) backbone
spineless adj lacking courage
  spines n ▷ spine
spinet n (pl -s) small harpsichord
  spinets n ▷ spinet
  spinier adj ▷ spiny
  spiniest adj ▷ spiny
spinifex n (pl -es) coarse spiny Australian grass
  spinifexes n ▷ spinifex
spinnaker n (pl -s) large sail on a racing yacht
  spinnakers n ▷ spinnaker
  spinner n ▷ spin
  spinners n ▷ spin
spinney n (pl -s) (CHIEFLY BRIT) small wood
  spinneys n ▷ spinney
  spinning v ▷ spin
  spins v, n ▷ spin
spinster n (pl -s) unmarried woman
  spinsters n ▷ spinster
spiny adj (-nier, -niest) covered with spines
spiral n (pl -nier, -niest) continuous curve formed by
  a point winding about a central axis at an
  ever-increasing distance from it ▶ v (-s, -lling,
  -lled) move in a spiral ▶ adj having the form
  of a spiral
  spiralled v ▷ spiral
  spiralling v ▷ spiral
  spirals n, v ▷ spiral
spire n (pl -s) pointed part of a steeple
  spires n ▷ spire
spirit[1] n (pl -s) nonphysical aspect of a person
  concerned with profound thoughts ▶ v (-s,
  -ing, -ed) carry away mysteriously
spirit[2] n (pl -s) liquid obtained by distillation
spirited adj lively ▶ v ▷ spirit[1]
  spiriting v ▷ spirit[1]
  spirits n ▷ spirit[1, 2] ▶ pl n emotional state ▶ v
  ▷ spirit[1]
spiritual adj relating to the spirit ▶ n (pl -s)
  type of religious folk song originating among
  Black slaves in America > **spiritually** adv
  > **spirituality** n (pl -ties)
spiritualism n (pl -s) belief that the spirits of
  the dead can communicate with the living
  > **spiritualist** n (pl -s)
  spiritualisms n ▷ spiritualism
  spiritualist n ▷ spiritualism
  spiritualists n ▷ spiritualism
  spiritualities n ▷ spiritual
  spirituality n ▷ spiritual
  spiritually adv ▷ spiritual
  spirituals n ▷ spiritual
spit[1] v (-s, -tting, spat) eject (saliva or food)
  from the mouth ▶ n (pl -s) saliva
spit[2] n (pl -s) sharp rod on which meat is

skewered for roasting
spite n (pl -s) deliberate nastiness ▶ v (-tes,
  -ting, -ted) annoy or hurt from spite > **spiteful**
  adj > **spitefully** adv
  spited v ▷ spite
  spiteful adj ▷ spite
  spitefully adv ▷ spite
  spites n, v ▷ spite
spitfire n (pl -s) person with a fiery temper
  spitfires n ▷ spitfire
  spiting v ▷ spite
  spits n ▷ spit[1, 2] ▶ v ▷ spit[1]
  spitting v ▷ spit[1]
spittle n (pl -s) fluid produced in the mouth,
  saliva
  spittles n ▷ spittle
spittoon n (pl -s) bowl to spit into
  spittoons n ▷ spittoon
spiv n (pl -s) (BRIT, AUST & NZ) (Slang) smartly
  dressed man who makes a living by shady
  dealings
  spivs n ▷ spiv
splash v (-es, -ing, -ed) scatter liquid on
  (something) ▶ n (pl -es) splashing sound
  splashed v ▷ splash
  splashes v, n ▷ splash
  splashing v, n ▷ splash
splatter v (-s, -ing, -ed) ▶ n (pl -s) splash
  splattered v ▷ splatter
  splattering v ▷ splatter
  splatters v, n ▷ splatter
splay v (-s, -ing, -ed) spread out, with ends
  spreading in different directions
  splayed v ▷ splay
  splaying v ▷ splay
  splays v ▷ splay
spleen n (pl -s) abdominal organ which filters
  bacteria from the blood
  spleens n ▷ spleen
splendid adj (-er, -est) excellent > **splendidly**
  adv > **splendour** n (pl -s)
  splendider adj ▷ splendid
  splendidest adj ▷ splendid
  splendidly adv ▷ splendid
  splendour n ▷ splendid
  splendours n ▷ splendid
splenetic adj spiteful or irritable
splice v (-ces, -cing, -ced) join by interweaving
  or overlapping ends
  spliced v ▷ splice
  splices v ▷ splice
  splicing v ▷ splice
splint n (pl -s) rigid support for a broken bone
splinter n (pl -s) thin sharp piece broken off,
  esp. from wood ▶ v (-s, -ing, -ed) break into

fragments

splintered *v* ▷ splinter
splintering *v* ▷ splinter
splinters *n*, *v* ▷ splinter
splints *n* ▷ splint
split *v* (**-s**, **-tting**, **split**) break into separate pieces ▶ *n* (*pl* **-s**) crack or division caused by splitting
splits *v* ▷ split ▶ *n* ▷ split ▶ *pl n* act of sitting with the legs outstretched in opposite directions
splitting *v* ▷ split
splodge *n* (*pl* **-s**) ▶ *v* (**-ges**, **-ging**, **-ged**) ▷ splotch
splodged *v* ▷ splodge
splodges *n*, *v* ▷ splodge
splodging *v* ▷ splodge
splotch *n* (*pl* **-s**) ▶ *v* (**-ches**, **-ching**, **-ched**) splash, daub
splotched *v* ▷ splotch
splotches *n*, *v* ▷ splotch
splotching *v* ▷ splotch
splurge *v* (**-ges**, **-ging**, **-ged**) spend money extravagantly ▶ *n* (*pl* **-s**) bout of extravagance
splurged *v* ▷ splurge
splurges *v*, *n* ▷ splurge
splurging *v* ▷ splurge
splutter *v* (**-s**, **-ing**, **-ed**) utter with spitting or choking sounds ▶ *n* (*pl* **-s**) spluttering
spluttered *v* ▷ splutter
spluttering *v* ▷ splutter
splutters *v*, *n* ▷ splutter
spoil *v* (**-s**, **-ing**, **-spoilt** or **-ed**) damage
spoiled *v* ▷ spoil
spoiling *v* ▷ spoil
spoils *pl n* booty ▶ *v* ▷ spoil
spoilsport *n* (*pl* **-s**) person who spoils the enjoyment of others
spoilsports *n* ▷ spoilsport
spoilt *v* ▷ spoil
spoke¹ *v* ▷ speak
spoke² *n* (*pl* **-s**) bar joining the hub of a wheel to the rim
spoken *v* ▷ speak
spokes *n* ▷ spoke²
spokesman, spokeswoman, spokesperson *n* (*pl* **-men**, **-women**, **-persons**, **-people**) person chosen to speak on behalf of a group
spokesmen *n* ▷ spokesman
spokespeople *n* ▷ spokesman
spokesperson *n* ▷ spokesman
spokespersons *n* ▷ spokesman
spokeswoman *n* ▷ spokesman
spokeswomen *n* ▷ spokesman
spoliation *n* (*pl* **-s**) plundering
spoliations *n* ▷ spoliation

sponge *n* (*pl* **-s**) sea animal with a porous absorbent skeleton ▶ *v* (**-ges**, **-ging**, **-ged**) wipe with a sponge ▷ **spongy** *adj* (**-gier**, **-giest**)
sponged *v* ▷ sponge
sponger *n* (*pl* **-s**) (*Slang*) person who sponges on others
spongers *n* ▷ sponger
sponges *n*, *v* ▷ sponge
spongier *adj* ▷ sponge
spongiest *adj* ▷ sponge
sponging *v* ▷ sponge
spongy *adj* ▷ sponge
sponsor *n* (*pl* **-s**) person who promotes something ▶ *v* (**-s**, **-ing**, **-ed**) act as a sponsor for ▷ **sponsorship** *n* (*pl* **-s**)
sponsored *v* ▷ sponsor
sponsoring *v* ▷ sponsor
sponsors *n*, *v* ▷ sponsor
sponsorship *n* ▷ sponsor
sponsorships *n* ▷ sponsor
spontaneities *n* ▷ spontaneous
spontaneity *n* ▷ spontaneous
spontaneous *adj* not planned or arranged ▷ **spontaneously** *adv* ▷ **spontaneity** *n* (*pl* **-ties**)
spontaneously *adv* ▷ spontaneous
spoof *n* (*pl* **-s**) mildly satirical parody
spoofs *n* ▷ spoof
spook *n* (*pl* **-s**) (*Informal*) ghost ▷ **spooky** *adj* (**-kier**, **-kiest**)
spookier *adj* ▷ spook
spookiest *adj* ▷ spook
spooks *n* ▷ spook
spooky *adj* ▷ spook
spool *n* (*pl* **-s**) cylinder round which something can be wound
spools *n* ▷ spool
spoon *n* (*pl* **-s**) shallow bowl attached to a handle for eating, stirring, or serving food ▶ *v* (**-s**, **-ing**, **-ed**) lift with a spoon ▷ **spoonful** *n* (*pl* **-s**)
spoonbill *n* (*pl* **-s**) wading bird of warm regions with a long flat bill
spoonbills *n* ▷ spoonbill
spooned *v* ▷ spoon
spoonerism *n* (*pl* **-s**) accidental changing over of the initial sounds of a pair of words, such as *half-warmed fish* for *half-formed wish*
spoonerisms *n* ▷ spoonerism
spoonful *n* ▷ spoon
spoonfuls *n* ▷ spoon
spooning *v* ▷ spoon
spoons *n*, *v* ▷ spoon
spoor *n* (*pl* **-s**) trail of an animal
spoors *n* ▷ spoor

sporadic *adj* intermittent, scattered
> **sporadically** *adv*
  sporadically *adv* ▷ **sporadic**

spore *n* (*pl* -s) minute reproductive body of some plants
  spores *n* ▷ **spore**

sporran *n* (*pl* -s) pouch worn in front of a kilt
  sporrans *n* ▷ **sporran**

sport *n* (*pl* -s) activity for pleasure, competition, or exercise *v* (-s, -ing, -ed) wear proudly > **sporty** *adj* (-tier, -tiest)
  sported *v* ▷ **sport**
  sportier *adj* ▷ **sport**
  sportiest *adj* ▷ **sport**

sporting *adj* of sport ▶ *v* ▷ **sport**

sportive *adj* playful
  sports *n, v* ▷ **sport**

sportsman, sportswoman *n* (*pl* -men, -women) person who plays sports
> **sportsmanlike** *adj* ▷ **sportsmanship** *n* (*pl* -s)
  sportsmanlike *adj* ▷ **sportsman**
  sportsmanship *n* ▷ **sportsman**
  sportsmanships *n* ▷ **sportsman**
  sportsmen *n* ▷ **sportsman**
  sportswoman *n* ▷ **sportsman**
  sportswomen *n* ▷ **sportsman**
  sporty *adj* ▷ **sport**

spot *n* (*pl* -s) small mark on a surface (*Informal*) ▶ *v* (-s, -tting, -tted) notice

spotless *adj* absolutely clean > **spotlessly** *adv*
  spotlessly *adv* ▷ **spotless**

spotlight *n* (*pl* -s) powerful light illuminating a small area
  spotlights *n* ▷ **spotlight**
  spots *n, v* ▷ **spot**
  spotted *v* ▷ **spot**
  spottier *adj* ▷ **spotty**
  spottiest *adj* ▷ **spotty**
  spotting *v* ▷ **spot**

spotty *adj* (-tier, -ttiest) with spots

spouse *n* (*pl* -s) husband or wife
  spouses *n* ▷ **spouse**

spout *v* (-s, -ing, -ed) pour out in a stream or jet (*Slang*) ▶ *n* (*pl* -s) projecting tube or lip for pouring liquids
  spouted *v* ▷ **spout**
  spouting *v* ▷ **spout**
  spouts *v, n* ▷ **spout**

sprain *v* (-s, -ing, -ed) injure (a joint) by a sudden twist ▶ *n* (*pl* -s) such an injury
  sprained *v* ▷ **sprain**
  spraining *v* ▷ **sprain**
  sprains *v, n* ▷ **sprain**
  sprang *v* ▷ **spring**

sprat *n* (*pl* -s) small sea fish

  sprats *n* ▷ **sprat**

sprawl *v* (-s, -ing, -ed) lie or sit with the limbs spread out ▶ *n* (*pl* -s) part of a city that has spread untidily over a large area
  sprawled *v* ▷ **sprawl**
  sprawling *v* ▷ **sprawl**
  sprawls *v* ▷ **sprawl**

spray[1] *n* (*pl* -s) (device for producing) fine drops of liquid ▶ *v* (-s, -ing, -ed) scatter in fine drops

spray[2] *n* (*pl* -s) branch with buds, leaves, flowers, or berries
  sprayed *v* ▷ **spray**[1]
  spraying *v* ▷ **spray**[1]
  sprays *v* ▷ **spray**[1] ▶ *n* ▷ **spray**[1, 2]

spread *v* (-s, -ing, **spread**) open out or be displayed to the fullest extent ▶ *n* (*pl* -s) spreading (*Informal*)
  spreading *v* ▷ **spread**
  spreads *v, n* ▷ **spread**

spreadsheet *n* (*pl* -s) computer program for manipulating figures
  spreadsheets *n* ▷ **spreadsheet**

spree *n* (*pl* -s) session of overindulgence, usu. in drinking or spending money
  sprees *n* ▷ **spree**
  sprier *adj* ▷ **spry**
  spriest *adj* ▷ **spry**

sprig *n* (*pl* -s) twig or shoot
  sprightlier *adj* ▷ **sprightly**
  sprightliest *adj* ▷ **sprightly**
  sprightliness *n* ▷ **sprightly**
  sprightlinesses *n* ▷ **sprightly**

sprightly *adj* (-lier, -liest) lively and brisk
> **sprightliness** *n* (*pl* -es)
  sprigs *n* ▷ **sprig**

spring *v* (-s, -ing, **sprang** or **sprung**) move suddenly upwards or forwards in a single motion, jump ▶ *n* (*pl* -s) season between winter and summer

springboard *n* (*pl* -s) flexible board used to gain height or momentum in diving or gymnastics
  springboards *n* ▷ **springboard**

springbok *n* (*pl* -s) S African antelope
  springboks *n* ▷ **springbok**

springer *n* (*pl* -s) small spaniel
  springers *n* ▷ **springer**
  springier *adj* ▷ **springy**
  springiest *adj* ▷ **springy**
  springing *v* ▷ **spring**
  springs *v, n* ▷ **springs**

springy *adj* (-gier, -giest) elastic

sprinkle *v* (-les, -ling, -led) scatter (liquid or powder) in tiny drops or particles over (something) > **sprinkler** *n* (*pl* -s)

sprinkled v ▷ **sprinkle**
sprinkler n ▷ **sprinkle**
sprinklers n ▷ **sprinkle**
sprinkles v ▷ **sprinkle**
sprinkling v ▷ **sprinkle** ▶ n (pl -s) small quantity or number
sprinklings n ▷ **sprinkling**
sprint n (pl -s) short race run at top speed ▶ v (-s, -ing, -ed) run a short distance at top speed > **sprinter** n (pl -s)
sprinted v ▷ **sprint**
sprinter n ▷ **sprint**
sprinters n ▷ **sprint**
sprinting v ▷ **sprint**
sprints n, v ▷ **sprint**
sprite n (pl -s) elf
sprites n ▷ **sprite**
sprocket n (pl -s) wheel with teeth on the rim, that drives or is driven by a chain
sprockets n ▷ **sprocket**
sprout v (-s, -ing, -ed) put forth shoots ▶ n (pl -s) shoot
sprouted v ▷ **sprout**
sprouting v ▷ **sprout**
sprouts v, n ▷ **sprout**
spruce[1] n (pl -s) kind of fir
spruce[2] adj (-r, -st) neat and smart
sprucer adj ▷ **spruce**[2]
spruces n ▷ **spruce**[1]
sprucest adj ▷ **spruce**[2]
sprung v ▷ **spring**
spry adj (-yer, -yest or **sprier**) (**spriest**) active or nimble
spryer adj ▷ **spry**
spryest adj ▷ **spry**
spud n (pl -s) (Informal) potato
spuds n ▷ **spud**
spume n (pl -s) ▶ v (-mes, -ming, -med) froth
spumed v ▷ **spume**
spumes v, n ▷ **spume**
spuming v ▷ **spume**
spun v ▷ **spin**
spunk n (pl -s) (Informal) courage, spirit > **spunky** adj (-kier, -kiest)
spunkier adj ▷ **spunk**
spunkiest adj ▷ **spunk**
spunks n ▷ **spunk**
spunky adj ▷ **spunk**
spur n (pl -s) stimulus or incentive ▶ v (-s, -rring, -rred) urge on, incite (someone)
spurge n (pl -s) plant with milky sap
spurges n ▷ **spurge**
spurious adj not genuine
spurn v (-s, -ing, -ed) reject with scorn
spurned v ▷ **spurn**

spurning v ▷ **spurn**
spurns v ▷ **spurn**
spurred v ▷ **spur**
spurring v ▷ **spur**
spurs n, v ▷ **spur**
spurt v (-s, -ing, -ed) gush or cause to gush out in a jet ▶ n (pl -s) short sudden burst of activity or speed
spurted v ▷ **spurt**
spurting v ▷ **spurt**
spurts v, n ▷ **spurt**
sputa n ▷ **sputum**
sputnik n (pl -s) early Soviet artificial satellite
sputniks n ▷ **sputnik**
sputter v (-es, -ing, -ed) ▶ n (pl -s) splutter
sputtered v ▷ **sputter**
sputtering v ▷ **sputter**
sputters v, n ▷ **sputter**
sputum n (pl -ta) spittle, usu. mixed with mucus
spy n (pl **spies**) person employed to obtain secret information ▶ v (**spies, spying, spied**) act as a spy
spying v ▷ **spy**
squabble v (-les, -ling, -led) ▶ n (pl -s) (engage in) a petty or noisy quarrel
squabbled v ▷ **squabble**
squabbles v, n ▷ **squabble**
squabbling v ▷ **squabble**
squad n (pl -s) small group of people working or training together
squadron n (pl -s) division of an air force, fleet, or cavalry regiment
squadrons n ▷ **squadron**
squads n ▷ **squad**
squalid adj (-er, -est) dirty and unpleasant
squalider adj ▷ **squalid**
squalidest adj ▷ **squalid**
squall[1] n (pl -s) sudden strong wind
squall[2] v (-s, -ing, -ed) cry noisily, yell ▶ n (pl -s) harsh cry
squalled v ▷ **squall**[2]
squalling v ▷ **squall**[2]
squalls v ▷ **squall**[2] ▶ n ▷ **squall**[1, 2]
squalor n (pl -s) disgusting dirt and filth
squalors n ▷ **squalor**
squander v (-s, -ing, -ed) waste (money or resources)
squandered v ▷ **squander**
squandering v ▷ **squander**
squanders v ▷ **squander**
square n (pl -s) geometric figure with four equal sides and four right angles ▶ adj square in shape ▶ v (-res, -ring, -red) multiply (a number) by itself ▶ adv squarely, directly

squared v ▷ square

squarely adv in a direct way

squares n, v ▷ square

squaring v ▷ square

squash¹ v (-es, -ing, -ed) crush flat ▶ n (pl -es) sweet fruit drink diluted with water > squashy adj (-shier, -shiest)

squash² n (pl -es) marrow-like vegetable

squashed v ▷ squash¹

squashes n ▷ squash¹, ² ▶ v ▷ squash¹

squashier adj ▷ squash¹

squashiest adj ▷ squash¹

squashing v ▷ squash¹

squashy adj ▷ squash¹

squat v (-s, -tting, -tted) crouch with the knees bent and the weight on the feet ▶ n place where squatters live ▶ adj (-tter, -ttest) short and broad

squats v, n ▷ squat

squatted v ▷ squat

squatter n (pl -s) illegal occupier of unused premises ▶ adj ▷ squat

squatters n ▷ squatter

squattest n ▷ squat

squatting v ▷ squat

squaw n (pl -s) (Offens) Native American woman

squawk n (pl -s) loud harsh cry ▶ v (-s, -ing, -ed) utter a squawk

squawked v ▷ squawk

squawking v ▷ squawk

squawks v ▷ squawk

squaws n ▷ squaw

squeak n (pl -s) short shrill cry or sound ▶ v (-s, -ing, -ed) make or utter a squeak > squeaky adj (-kier, -kiest)

squeaked v ▷ squeak

squeakier adj ▷ squeak

squeakiest adj ▷ squeak

squeaking v ▷ squeak

squeaks n, v ▷ squeak

squeaky adj ▷ squeak

squeal n (pl -s) long shrill cry or sound ▶ v (-s, -ing, -ed) make or utter a squeal (Slang)

squealed v ▷ squeal

squealing v ▷ squeal

squeals n, v ▷ squeal

squeamish adj easily sickened or shocked

squeegee n (pl -s) tool with a rubber blade for clearing water from a surface

squeegees n ▷ squeegee

squeeze v (-zes, -zing, -zed) grip or press firmly ▶ n (pl -s) squeezing

squeezed v ▷ squeeze

squeezes v, n ▷ squeeze

squeezing v ▷ squeeze

squelch v (-es, -ing, -ed) make a wet sucking sound, as by walking through mud ▶ n (pl -es) squelching sound

squelched v ▷ squelch

squelches n ▷ squelch

squelching v ▷ squelch

squib n (pl -s) small firework that hisses before exploding

squibs n ▷ squib

squid n (pl -s) sea creature with a long soft body and ten tentacles

squids n ▷ squid

squiggle n (pl -s) wavy line ▶ squiggly adj (-lier, -liest)

squiggles n ▷ squiggle

squigglier adj ▷ squiggle

squiggliest adj ▷ squiggle

squiggly adj ▷ squiggle

squint v (-s, -ing, -ed) have eyes which face in different directions ▶ n (pl -s) squinting condition of the eye ▶ adj crooked (-er, -est)

squinted v ▷ squint

squinter adj ▷ squint

squintest adj ▷ squint

squinting v ▷ squint

squints v, n ▷ squint

squire n (pl -s) country gentleman, usu. the main landowner in a community

squires n ▷ squire

squirm v (-s, -ing, -ed) wriggle, writhe ▶ n (pl -s) wriggling movement

squirmed v ▷ squirm

squirming v ▷ squirm

squirms v, n ▷ squirm

squirrel n (pl -s) small bushy-tailed tree-living animal

squirrels n ▷ squirrel

squirt v (-s, -ing, -ed) force (a liquid) or (of a liquid) be forced out of a narrow opening ▶ n (pl -s) jet of liquid

squirted v ▷ squirt

squirting v ▷ squirt

squirts n, v ▷ squirt

squish v (-es, -ing, -ed) ▶ n (pl -es) (make) a soft squelching sound > squishy adj (-shier, -shiest)

squished v ▷ squish

squishes n, v ▷ squish

squishier adj ▷ squish

squishiest adj ▷ squish

squishing v ▷ squish

squishy adj ▷ squish

squiz n (squizzes). Squiz is an informal word for a look or glance. This is a useful word to remember, both for when you have the most of the tiles to form it and when someone else plays **quiz** which you can then add an S to for a good score. Squiz scores 23 points.

st *interj*. St is a sound people make to request silence or quiet. This is one of two two-letter words beginning with S that do not contain a vowel. It's useful when you want to connect a word beginning with H to one ending in T or vice versa. St scores 2 points.

stab *v* (**-s, -bbing, -bbed**) pierce with something pointed ▶ *n* (*pl* **-s**) stabbing
stabbed *v* ▷ stab
stabbing *v* ▷ stab
stabilities *n* ▷ stable²
stability *n* ▷ stable²
stabilization *n* ▷ stabilize
stabilizations *n* ▷ stabilize
stabilize *v* (**-zes, -zing, -zed**) make or become stable > **stabilization** *n* (*pl* **-s**)
stabilized *v* ▷ stabilize
stabilizer *n* (*pl* **-s**) device for stabilizing a child's bicycle, an aircraft, or a ship
stabilizers *n* ▷ stabilizer
stabilizes *v* ▷ stabilize
stabilizing *v* ▷ stabilize
stable¹ *n* (*pl* **-s**) building in which horses are kept ▶ *v* (**-les, -ling, -led**) put or keep (a horse) in a stable
stable² *adj* (**-r, -st**) firmly fixed or established > **stability** *n* (*pl* **-ties**)
stabled *v* ▷ stable¹
stabler *adj* ▷ stable²
stables *n*, *v* ▷ stable¹
stablest *adj* ▷ stable²
stabling *v* ▷ stable¹
stabs *v*, *n* ▷ stab
staccato [stak-**ah**-toe] *adv* (MUSIC) with the notes sharply separated ▶ *adj* consisting of short abrupt sounds
stack *n* (*pl* **-s**) ordered pile ▶ *v* (**-s, -ing, -ed**) pile in a stack
stacked *v* ▷ stack
stacking *v* ▷ stack
stacks *n*, *v* ▷ stack
stadia *n* ▷ stadium
stadium *n* (*pl* **-diums, -dia**) sports arena with tiered seats for spectators
stadiums *n* ▷ stadium
staff¹ *n* (*pl* **-s**) people employed in an organization ▶ *v* (**-s, -ing, -ed**) supply with personnel
staff² *n* (*pl* **staves**) set of five horizontal lines on which music is written
staffed *v* ▷ staff¹
staffing *v* ▷ staff¹
staffs *n*, *v* ▷ staff¹
stag *n* (*pl* **-s**) adult male deer
stage *n* (*pl* **-s**) step or period of development ▶ *v* (**-ges, -ging, -ged**) put (a play) on stage
stagecoach *n* (*pl* **-es**) large horse-drawn vehicle formerly used to carry passengers and mail
stagecoaches *n* ▷ stagecoach
staged *v* ▷ stage
stages *n*, *v* ▷ stage
stagey *adj* (**-gier, -giest**) overtheatrical
stagger *v* (**-s, -ing, -ed**) walk unsteadily ▶ *n* (*pl* **-s**) staggering
staggered *v* ▷ stagger
staggering *v* ▷ stagger
staggers *v*, *n* ▷ stagger
stagier *adj* ▷ stagey
stagiest *adj* ▷ stagey
staging *v* ▷ stage
stagnant *adj* (of water or air) stale from not moving
stagnate *v* (**-tes, -ting, -ted**) be stagnant > **stagnation** *n* (*pl* **-s**)
stagnated *v* ▷ stagnate
stagnates *v* ▷ stagnate
stagnating *v* ▷ stagnate
stagnation *n* ▷ stagnate
stagnations *n* ▷ stagnate
stags *n* ▷ stag
staid *adj* (**-er, -est**) sedate, serious, and rather dull
staider *adj* ▷ staid
staidest *adj* ▷ staid
stain *v* (**-s, -ing, -ed**) discolour, mark ▶ *n* (*pl* **-s**) discoloration or mark > **stainless** *adj*
stained *v* ▷ stain
staining *v* ▷ stain
stainless *adj* ▷ stain
stains *v*, *n* ▷ stain
staircase, stairway *n* (*pl* **-s**) flight of stairs with a handrail or banisters
staircases *n* ▷ staircase
stairs *pl n* flight of steps between floors, usu. indoors
stairway *n* ▷ staircase
stairways *n* ▷ staircase
stake¹ *n* (*pl* **-s**) pointed stick or post driven into the ground as a support or marker ▶ *v* (**-kes, -king, -ked**) support or mark out with stakes
stake² *n* (*pl* **-s**) money wagered ▶ *v* (**-kes, -king, -ked**) wager, risk
staked *v* ▷ stake¹,²

stakeholder n (pl -s) person who has a concern or interest in something, esp. a business
stakeholders n ▷ stakeholder
stakes v ▷ stake¹, ² ▶ n ▷ stake¹, ²
staking v ▷ stake¹, ²
stalactite n (pl -s) lime deposit hanging from the roof of a cave
stalactites n ▷ stalactite
stalagmite n (pl -s) lime deposit sticking up from the floor of a cave
stalagmites n ▷ stalagmite
stale adj (-r, -st) not fresh > **staleness** n (pl -es)
stalemate n (pl -s) (CHESS) position in which any of a player's moves would put his king in check, resulting in a draw
stalemates n ▷ stalemate
staleness n ▷ stale
stalenesses n ▷ stale
staler adj ▷ stale
stalest adj ▷ stale
stalk¹ n (pl -s) plant's stem
stalk² v (-s, -ing, -ed) follow or approach stealthily
stalked v ▷ stalk²
stalker n (pl -s) person who follows or stealthily approaches a person or an animal
stalkers n ▷ stalker
stalking v ▷ stalk²
stalking-horse n (pl -s) pretext
stalking-horses n ▷ stalking-horse
stalks n ▷ stalk¹ ▶ v ▷ stalk²
stall¹ n (pl -s) small stand for the display and sale of goods ▶ v (-s, -ing, -ed) stop (a motor vehicle or engine) or (of a motor vehicle or engine) stop accidentally
stall² v (-s, -ing, -ed) employ delaying tactics
stalled v ▷ stall¹, ²
stalling v ▷ stall¹, ²
stallion n (pl -s) uncastrated male horse
stallions n ▷ stallion
stalls n ▷ stall¹, ² ▶ v ▷ stall¹, ² ▶ pl n ground-floor seats in a theatre or cinema
stalwart [stawl-wart] adj strong and sturdy ▶ n (pl -s) stalwart person
stalwarts n ▷ stalwart
stamen n (pl -s) pollen-producing part of a flower
stamens n ▷ stamen
stamina n (pl -s) enduring energy and strength
staminas n ▷ stamina
stammer v (-s, -ing, ed) speak or say with involuntary pauses or repetition of syllables ▶ n (pl -s) tendency to stammer
stammered v ▷ stammer
stammering v ▷ stammer

stammers v, n ▷ stammer
stamp n (pl -s) piece of gummed paper stuck to an envelope or parcel to show that the postage has been paid ▶ v (-s, -ing, -ed) bring (one's foot) down forcefully
stamped v ▷ stamp
stampede n (pl -s) sudden rush of frightened animals or of a crowd ▶ v (-des, -ding, -ded) (cause to) take part in a stampede
stampeded v ▷ stampede
stampedes n, v ▷ stampede
stampeding v ▷ stampede
stamping v ▷ stamp
stamps n, v ▷ stamp
stance n (pl -s) attitude
stances n ▷ stance
stanch [stahnch] v (-es, -ing, -ed) ▷ staunch²
stanched v ▷ stanch
stanches v ▷ stanch
stanching v ▷ stanch
stanchion n (pl -s) upright bar used as a support
stanchions n ▷ stanchion
stand v (-s, -ing, stood) be in, rise to, or place in an upright position ▶ n (pl -s) stall for the sale of goods
standard n (pl -s) level of quality ▶ adj usual, regular, or average
standardization n ▷ standardize
standardize v (-zes, -zing, -zed) cause to conform to a standard > **standardization** n (pl -s)
standardized v ▷ standardize
standardizes v ▷ standardize
standardizing v ▷ standardize
standards n ▷ standard
standing adj permanent, lasting ▶ n (pl -s) reputation or status ▶ v ▷ stand
standings n ▷ standing
standoffish adj reserved or haughty
standpipe n (pl -s) tap attached to a water main to provide a public water supply
standpipes n ▷ standpipe
standpoint n (pl -s) point of view
standpoints n ▷ standpoint
stands v, n ▷ stand
standstill n (pl -s) complete halt
standstills n ▷ standstill
stank v ▷ stink
stanza n (pl -s) verse of a poem
stanzas n ▷ stanza
staple¹ n (pl -s) U-shaped piece of metal used to fasten papers or secure things ▶ v (-les, -ling, -led) fasten with staples
staple² adj of prime importance, principal ▶ n

(*pl* **-s**) main constituent of anything
stapled *v* ▷ **staple¹**
stapler *n* (*pl* **-s**) small device for fastening papers together
staplers *n* ▷ **stapler**
staples *n* ▷ **staple¹, ²** ▶ *v* ▷ **staple¹**
stapling *v* ▷ **staple¹**
star *n* (*pl* **-s**) hot gaseous mass in space, visible in the night sky as a point of light ▶ *v* (**-s, -rring, -rred**) feature or be featured in a main role ▶ *adj* leading, famous
starboard *n* (*pl* **-s**) right-hand side of a ship, when facing forward ▶ *adj* of or on this side
starboards *n* ▷ **starboard**
starch *n* (*pl* **-es**) carbohydrate forming the main food element in bread, potatoes, etc., and used mixed with water for stiffening fabric ▶ *v* (**-es, -ing, -ed**) stiffen (fabric) with starch
starched *v* ▷ **starch**
starches *n, v* ▷ **starch**
starchier *adj* ▷ **starchy**
starchiest *adj* ▷ **starchy**
starching *v* ▷ **starch**
starchy *adj* (**-chier, -chiest**) containing starch
stardom *n* (*pl* **-s**) status of a star in the entertainment or sports world
stardoms *n* ▷ **stardom**
stare *v* (**-res, -ring, -red**) look or gaze fixedly (at) ▶ *n* (*pl* **-s**) fixed gaze
stared *v* ▷ **stare**
stares *v, n* ▷ **stare**
starfish *n* (*pl* **-es**) star-shaped sea creature
starfishes *n* ▷ **starfish**
staring *v* ▷ **stare**
stark *adj* (**-er, -est**) harsh, unpleasant, and plain ▶ *adv* completely
starker *adj* ▷ **stark**
starkest *adj* ▷ **stark**
starling *n* (*pl* **-s**) songbird with glossy black speckled feathers
starlings *n* ▷ **starling**
starred *v* ▷ **star**
starrier *adj* ▷ **starry**
starriest *adj* ▷ **starry**
starring *v* ▷ **star**
starry *adj* (**-rrier, -rriest**) full of or like stars
stars *n, v* ▷ **star** ▶ *pl n* astrological forecast, horoscope
start *v* (**-s, -ing, -ed**) take the first step, begin ▶ *n* (*pl* **-s**) first part of something
started *v* ▷ **start**
starter *n* (*pl* **-s**) first course of a meal
starters *n* ▷ **starter**
starting *v* ▷ **start**

startle *v* (**-les, -ling, -led**) slightly surprise or frighten
startled *v* ▷ **startle**
startles *v* ▷ **startle**
startling *v* ▷ **startle**
starts *v, n* ▷ **start**
starvation *n* ▷ **starve**
starvations *n* ▷ **starve**
starve *v* (**-ves, -ving, -ved**) die or suffer or cause to die or suffer from hunger > **starvation** *n* (*pl* **-s**)
starved *v* ▷ **starve**
starves *v* ▷ **starve**
starving *v* ▷ **starve**
stash (*Informal*) *v* (**-es, -ing, -ed**) store in a secret place ▶ *n* (*pl* **-es**) secret store
stashed *v* ▷ **stash**
stashes *v, n* ▷ **stash**
stashing *v* ▷ **stash**
state *n* (*pl* **-s**) condition of a person or thing ▶ *adj* of or concerning the State ▶ *v* (**-tes, -ting, -ted**) express in words
stated *v* ▷ **state**
statehouse *n* (*pl* **-s**) (NZ) publicly-owned house rented to a low-income tenant
statehouses *n* ▷ **statehouse**
statelier *adj* ▷ **stately**
stateliest *adj* ▷ **stately**
stately *adj* (**-lier, -liest**) dignified or grand
statement *n* (*pl* **-s**) something stated
statements *n* ▷ **statement**
stateroom *n* (*pl* **-s**) private cabin on a ship
staterooms *n* ▷ **stateroom**
states *n, v* ▷ **state**
statesman, stateswoman *n* (*pl* **-men, -women**) experienced and respected political leader > **statesmanship** *n* (*pl* **-s**)
statesmanship *n* ▷ **statesman**
statesmanships *n* ▷ **statesman**
statesmen *n* ▷ **statesman**
stateswoman *n* ▷ **statesman**
stateswomen *n* ▷ **statesman**
static *adj* stationary or inactive ▶ *n* (*pl* **-s**) crackling sound or speckled picture caused by interference in radio or television reception
statics *n* ▷ **static**
stating *v* ▷ **state**
station *n* (*pl* **-s**) place where trains stop for passengers ▶ *v* (**-s, -ing, -ed**) assign (someone) to a particular place
stationary *adj* not moving
stationed *v* ▷ **station**
stationer *n* (*pl* **-s**) dealer in stationery
stationeries *n* ▷ **stationery**

stationers n ▷ stationer
stationery n (pl **-ries**) writing materials such as paper and pens
stationing v ▷ station
stations n, v ▷ station
statistic n (pl **-s**) numerical fact collected and classified systematically > **statistical** adj
> **statistically** adv
statistical adj ▷ statistic
statistically adv ▷ statistic
statistician n (pl **-s**) person who compiles and studies statistics
statisticians n ▷ statistician
statistics n ▷ statistic
statuaries n ▷ statuary
statuary n (pl **-ries**) statues collectively
statue n (pl **-s**) large sculpture of a human or animal figure
statues n ▷ statue
statuesque adj (of a woman) tall and well-proportioned
statuette n (pl **-s**) small statue
statuettes n ▷ statuette
stature n (pl **-s**) person's height
statures n ▷ stature
status n (pl **-ses**) social position
statuses n ▷ status
statute n (pl **-s**) written law > **statutory** adj required or authorized by law
statutes n ▷ statute
statutory adj ▷ statute
staunch[1] adj (**-er, -est**) loyal, firm
staunch[2], **stanch** v (**-ches, -ching, -ched**) stop (a flow of blood)
staunched v ▷ staunch[2]
stauncher adj ▷ staunch[1]
staunches v ▷ staunch[2]
staunchest adj ▷ staunch[1]
staunching v ▷ staunch[2]
stave n (pl **-s**) one of the strips of wood forming a barrel
staves n ▷ staff[2]
stay[1] v (**-s, -ing, -ed**) remain in a place or condition ▶ n (pl **-s**) period of staying in a place
stay[2] n (pl **-s**) prop or buttress
stay[3] n (pl **-s**) rope or wire supporting a ship's mast
stayed v ▷ stay[1]
staying v ▷ stay[1]
stays n ▷ stay[1, 2, 3] ▶ v ▷ stay[1] ▶ pl n corset
stead n (pl **-s**) in someone's place
steadfast adj firm, determined > **steadfastly** adv
steadfastly adv ▷ steadfast

steadied v ▷ steady
steadier adj ▷ steady
steadiest adj ▷ steady
steadily adv ▷ steady
steadiness n ▷ steady
steadinesses n ▷ steady
steads n ▷ stead
steady adj (**-dier, -diest**) not shaky or wavering ▶ v (**-dies, -dying, -died**) make steady ▶ adv in a steady manner > **steadily** adv > **steadiness** n (pl **-es**)
steadying v ▷ steady
steak n (pl **-s**) thick slice of meat, esp. beef
steaks n ▷ steak
steal v (**-s, -ing, stole, stolen**) take unlawfully or without permission
stealing v ▷ steal
steals v ▷ steal
stealth n (pl **-s**) secret or underhand behaviour ▶ adj (of technology) able to render an aircraft almost invisible to radar > **stealthy** adj (**-thier, -thiest**) > **stealthily** adv
stealthier adj ▷ stealth
stealthiest adj ▷ stealth
stealthily adv ▷ stealth
stealths n ▷ stealth
stealthy adj ▷ stealth
steam n (pl **-s**) vapour into which water changes when boiled ▶ v (**-s, -ing, -ed**) give off steam
steamed v ▷ steam
steamer n (pl **-s**) steam-propelled ship
steamers n ▷ steamer
steaming v ▷ steam
steamroller n (pl **-s**) steam-powered vehicle with heavy rollers, used to level road surfaces ▶ v (**-s, -ing, -ed**) use overpowering force to make (someone) do what one wants
steamrollered v ▷ steamroller
steamrollering v ▷ steamroller
steamrollers n, v ▷ steamroller
steams n, v ▷ steam
steed n (pl **-s**) (Lit) horse
steeds n ▷ steed
steel n (pl **-s**) hard malleable alloy of iron and carbon ▶ v (**-s, -ing, -ed**) prepare (oneself) for something unpleasant > **steely** adj (**-lier, -liest**)
steeled v ▷ steel
steelier adj ▷ steel
steeliest adj ▷ steel
steeling v ▷ steel
steels n ▷ steel
steely adj ▷ steel
steep[1] adj (**-er, -est**) sloping sharply > **steeply**

adv ▷ **steepness** *n* (*pl* -**es**)
steep² *v* (-**s**, -**ing**, -**ed**) soak or be soaked in liquid
　steeped *v* ▷ **steep²**
　steeper *adj* ▷ **steep¹**
　steepest *adj* ▷ **steep¹**
　steeping *v* ▷ **steep²**
steeple *n* (*pl* -**s**) church tower with a spire
steeplechase *n* (*pl* -**s**) horse race with obstacles to jump
　steeplechases *n* ▷ **steeplechase**
steeplejack *n* (*pl* -**s**) person who repairs steeples and chimneys
　steeplejacks *n* ▷ **steeplejack**
　steeples *n* ▷ **steeple**
　steeply *n* ▷ **steep¹**
　steepness *n* ▷ **steep¹**
　steepnesses *n* ▷ **steep¹**
　steeps *v* ▷ **steep²**
steer¹ (-**s**, -**ing**, -**ed**) direct the course of (a vehicle or ship)
steer² *n* (*pl* -**s**) castrated male ox
steerage *n* (*pl* -**s**) cheapest accommodation on a passenger ship
　steerages *n* ▷ **steerage**
　steered *v* ▷ **steer¹**
　steering *v* ▷ **steer¹**
　steers *v* ▷ **steer¹** ▶ *n* ▷ **steer²**
stein [stine] *n* (*pl* -**s**) earthenware beer mug
　steins *n* ▷ **stein**
stellar *adj* of stars
stem¹ *n* (*pl* -**s**) long thin central part of a plant ▶ *v* (-**s**, -**mming**, -**mmed**) originate from
stem² *v* (-**s**, -**mming**, -**mmed**) stop (the flow of something)
　stemmed *v* ▷ **stem¹, ²**
　stemming *v* ▷ **stem¹, ²**
　stems *v* ▷ **stem¹, ²** ▶ *n* ▷ **stem¹**
stench *n* (*pl* -**es**) foul smell
　stenches *n* ▷ **stench**
stencil *n* (*pl* -**s**) thin sheet with cut-out pattern through which ink or paint passes to form the pattern on the surface below ▶ *v* (-**s**, -**lling**, -**lled**) make (a pattern) with a stencil
　stencilled *v* ▷ **stencil**
　stencilling *v* ▷ **stencil**
　stencils *n*, *v* ▷ **stencil**
stenographer *n* (*pl* -**s**) shorthand typist
　stenographers *n* ▷ **stenographer**
stent *n* (*pl* -**s**) surgical implant used to keep an artery open
stentorian *adj* (of a voice) very loud
　stents *n* ▷ **stent**
step *v* (-**s**, -**pping**, -**pped**) move and set down the foot, as when walking ▶ *n* (*pl* -**s**) stepping

stepladder *n* (*pl* -**s**) folding portable ladder with supporting frame
　stepladders *n* ▷ **stepladder**
　stepped *v* ▷ **step**
steppes *pl n* wide grassy treeless plains in Russia and Ukraine
　stepping *v* ▷ **step**
　steps *pl n* ▷ **stepladder** ▶, *v* ▷ **step**
　stereo *adj* ▷ **stereophonic** ▶ *n* (*pl* -**s**) stereophonic record player
stereophonic *adj* using two separate loudspeakers to give the effect of naturally distributed sound
　stereos *n* ▷ **stereo**
stereotype *n* (*pl* -**s**) standardized idea of a type of person or thing ▶ *v* (-**pes**, -**ping**, -**ped**) form a stereotype of
　stereotyped *v* ▷ **stereotype**
　stereotypes *n*, *v* ▷ **stereotype**
　stereotyping *v* ▷ **stereotype**
sterile *adj* free from germs > **sterility** *n* (*pl* -**ties**)
　sterilities *n* ▷ **sterile**
　sterility *n* ▷ **sterile**
　sterilization *n* ▷ **sterilize**
　sterilizations *n* ▷ **sterilize**
sterilize *v* (-**zes**, -**zing**, -**zed**) make sterile > **sterilization** *n* (*pl* -**s**)
　sterilized *v* ▷ **sterilize**
　sterilizes *v* ▷ **sterilize**
　sterilizing *v* ▷ **sterilize**
sterling *n* (*pl* -**s**) British money system ▶ *adj* genuine and reliable
　sterlings *n* ▷ **sterling**
stern¹ *adj* (-**er**, -**est**) severe, strict > **sternly** *adv* > **sternness** *n* (*pl* -**es**)
stern² *n* (*pl* -**s**) rear part of a ship
　sterna *n* ▷ **sternum**
　sterner *adj* ▷ **stern¹**
　sternest *adj* ▷ **stern¹**
　sternly *adv* ▷ **stern¹**
　sternness *n* ▷ **stern¹**
　sternnesses *n* ▷ **stern¹**
　sterns *n* ▷ **stern²**
sternum *n* (*pl* -**na**, -**nums**) ▷ breastbone
　sternums *n* ▷ **sternum**
steroid *n* (*pl* -**s**) organic compound containing a carbon ring system, such as many hormones
　steroids *n* ▷ **steroid**
stethoscope *n* (*pl* -**s**) medical instrument for listening to sounds made inside the body
　stethoscopes *n* ▷ **stethoscope**
stevedore *n* (*pl* -**s**) person who loads and unloads ships
　stevedores *n* ▷ **stevedore**

stew n (pl -s) food cooked slowly in a closed pot ▸ v (-s, -ing, -ed) cook slowly in a closed pot

steward n (pl -s) person who looks after passengers on a ship or aircraft > **stewardess** n fem (pl -es)

stewardess n ▷ steward

stewardesses n ▷ steward

stewards n ▷ steward

stewed v ▷ stew

stewing v ▷ stew

stews n, v ▷ stew

stick[1] n (pl -s) long thin piece of wood

stick[2] v (-s, -ing, stuck) push (a pointed object) into (something)

sticker n (pl -s) adhesive label or sign

stickers n ▷ sticker

stickier adj ▷ sticky

stickiest adj ▷ sticky

sticking v ▷ stick[2]

stickleback n (pl -s) small fish with sharp spines on its back

sticklebacks n ▷ stickleback

stickler n (pl -s) person who insists on something

sticklers n ▷ stickler

sticks n ▷ stick[1] ▸ v ▷ stick[2]

stickup n (pl -s) (Slang) robbery at gunpoint

stickups n ▷ stickup

sticky adj (-ckier, -ckiest) covered with an adhesive substance

sties n ▷ sty

stiff adj (-er, -est) not easily bent or moved ▸ n (pl -s) (Slang) corpse > **stiffly** adv > **stiffness** n (pl -es)

stiffen v (-s, -ing, -ed) make or become stiff

stiffened v ▷ stiffen

stiffening v ▷ stiffen

stiffens v ▷ stiffen

stiffer adj ▷ stiff

stiffest adj ▷ stiff

stiffly adv ▷ stiff

stiffness n ▷ stiff

stiffnesses n ▷ stiff

stiffs n ▷ stiff

stifle v (-les, -ling, -led) suppress

stifled v ▷ stifle

stifles v ▷ stifle

stifling v ▷ stifle

stigma n (pl -mas, -mata) mark of social disgrace

stigmas n ▷ stigma

stigmata pl n marks resembling the wounds of the crucified Christ ▸ n ▷ stigma

stigmatize v (-zes, -zing, -zed) mark as being shameful

stigmatized v ▷ stigmatize

stigmatizes v ▷ stigmatize

stigmatizing v ▷ stigmatize

stile n (pl -s) set of steps allowing people to climb a fence

stiles n ▷ stile

stiletto n (pl -s) high narrow heel on a woman's shoe

stilettos n ▷ stiletto

still[1] adv now or in the future as before ▸ adj (-er, -est) motionless ▸ n (pl -s) photograph from a film scene ▸ v (-s, -ing, -ed) make still > **stillness** n (pl -es)

still[2] n (pl -s) apparatus for distilling alcoholic drinks

stillborn adj born dead

stilled v ▷ still[1]

stiller adj ▷ still[1]

stillest adj ▷ still[1]

stilling v ▷ still[1]

stillness n ▷ still[1]

stillnesses n ▷ still[1]

stills n ▷ still[1, 2] ▸ v ▷ still[1]

stilted adj stiff and formal in manner

stilts pl n pair of poles with footrests for walking raised from the ground

stimulant n (pl -s) something, such as a drug, that acts as a stimulus

stimulants n ▷ stimulant

stimulate v (-tes, -ting, -ted) act as a stimulus (on) > **stimulation** n (pl -s)

stimulated v ▷ stimulate

stimulates v ▷ stimulate

stimulating v ▷ stimulate

stimulation n ▷ stimulate

stimulations n ▷ stimulate

stimuli n ▷ stimulus

stimulus n (pl -li) something that rouses a person or thing to activity

sting v (-s, -ing, stung) (of certain animals or plants) wound by injecting with poison ▸ n (pl -s) wound or pain caused by or as if by stinging

stingier adj ▷ stingy

stingiest adj ▷ stingy

stinginess n ▷ stingy

stinginesses n ▷ stingy

stinging v ▷ sting

stings v, n ▷ sting

stingy adj (-gier, -giest) mean or miserly > **stinginess** n (pl -es)

stink n (pl -s) strong unpleasant smell ▸ v (-s, -ing, stank or stunk) (stunk) give off a strong unpleasant smell

stinking v ▷ stink

stinks n, v ▷ stink

stint v (-s, -ing, -ed) (foll. by **on**) be miserly with (something) ▶ n (pl -s) allotted amount of work

stinted v ▷ stint

stinting v ▷ stint

stints v, n ▷ stint

stipend [sty-pend] n (pl -s) regular allowance or salary, esp. that paid to a clergyman > **stipendiary** adj receiving a stipend

stipendiary adj ▷ stipend

stipends n ▷ stipend

stipple v (-les, -ling, -led) paint, draw, or engrave using dots

stippled v ▷ stipple

stipples v ▷ stipple

stippling v ▷ stipple

stipulate v (-tes, -ting, -ted) specify as a condition of an agreement > **stipulation** n (pl -s)

stipulated v ▷ stipulate

stipulates v ▷ stipulate

stipulating v ▷ stipulate

stipulation n ▷ stipulate

stipulations n ▷ stipulate

stir v (-s, -rring, -rred) mix up (a liquid) by moving a spoon etc. around in it ▶ n (pl -s) a stirring

stirred v ▷ stir

stirring v ▷ stir

stirrup n (pl -s) metal loop attached to a saddle for supporting a rider's foot

stirrups n ▷ stirrup

stirs v, n ▷ stir

stitch n (pl -es) link made by drawing thread through material with a needle ▶ v (-es, -ing, -ed) sew

stitched v ▷ stitch

stitches n, v ▷ stitch

stitching v ▷ stitch

stoat n (pl -s) small mammal of the weasel family, with brown fur that turns white in winter

stoats n ▷ stoat

stock n (pl -s) total amount of goods available for sale in a shop ▶ adj kept in stock, standard ▶ v (-s, -ing, -ed) keep for sale or future use

stockade n (pl -s) enclosure or barrier made of stakes

stockades n ▷ stockade

stockbroker n (pl -s) person who buys and sells stocks and shares for customers

stockbrokers n ▷ stockbroker

stocked v ▷ stock

stockier adj ▷ stocky

stockiest adj ▷ stocky

stocking n (pl -s) close-fitting covering for the foot and leg ▶ v ▷ stock

stockings n ▷ stocking

stockist n (pl -s) dealer who stocks a particular product

stockists n ▷ stockist

stockpile v (-les, -ling, -led) store a large quantity of (something) for future use ▶ n (pl -s) accumulated store

stockpiled v ▷ stockpile

stockpiles v, n ▷ stockpile

stockpiling v ▷ stockpile

stocks n pl (HIST) instrument of punishment consisting of a wooden frame with holes into which the hands and feet of the victim were locked ▶ n, v ▷ stock

stocktaking n (pl -s) counting and valuing of the goods in a shop

stocktakings n ▷ stocktaking

stocky adj (-ckier, -ckiest) (of a person) broad and sturdy

stodge n (pl -s) (BRIT, AUST & NZ) heavy starchy food

stodges n ▷ stodge

stodgier adj ▷ stodgy

stodgiest adj ▷ stodgy

stodgy adj (-gier, -giest) (of food) heavy and starchy

stoep [stoop] n (pl -s) (S AFR) verandah

stoeps n ▷ stoep

stoic [stow-ik] n (pl -s) person who suffers hardship without showing his or her feelings ▶ adj (also **stoical**) suffering hardship without showing one's feelings > **stoically** adv > **stoicism** [stow-iss-izz-um] n (pl -s)

stoical adj ▷ stoic

stoically adv ▷ stoic

stoicism n ▷ stoic

stoicisms n ▷ stoic

stoics n ▷ stoic

stoke v (-kes, -king, -ked) feed and tend (a fire or furnace) > **stoker** n (pl -s)

stoked v ▷ stoke

stoker n ▷ stoke

stokers n ▷ stoke

stokes v ▷ stoke

stoking v ▷ stoke

stole¹ v ▷ steal

stole² n (pl -s) long scarf or shawl

stolen v ▷ steal

stoles n ▷ stole²

stolid adj (-er, -est) showing little emotion or interest > **stolidly** adv

stolider adj ▷ stolid

stolidest adj ▷ **stolid**

stolidly adv ▷ **stolid**

stomach n (pl -s) organ in the body which digests food ▶ v (-s, -ing, -ed) put up with

stomached v ▷ **stomach**

stomaching v ▷ **stomach**

stomachs n, v ▷ **stomach**

stomp v (-s, -ing, -ed) (Informal) tread heavily

stomped v ▷ **stomp**

stomping v ▷ **stomp**

stomps v ▷ **stomp**

stone n (pl -s) material of which rocks are made ▶ v (-nes, -ning, -ned) throw stones at

stoned adj (Slang) under the influence of alcohol or drugs ▶ v ▷ **stone**

stones n, v ▷ **stone**

stonewall v (-s, -ing, -ed) obstruct or hinder discussion

stonewalled v ▷ **stonewall**

stonewalling v ▷ **stonewall**

stonewalls v ▷ **stonewall**

stoneware n (pl -s) hard kind of pottery fired at a very high temperature

stonewares n ▷ **stoneware**

stonier adj ▷ **stony**

stoniest adj ▷ **stony**

stonily adv ▷ **stony**

stoning v ▷ **stone**

stony adj (-nier, -niest) of or like stone
> **stonily** adv

stood v ▷ **stand**

stooge n (pl -es) actor who feeds lines to a comedian or acts as the butt of his jokes

stooges n ▷ **stooge**

stool n (pl -s) chair without arms or back

stools n ▷ **stool**

stoop v (-s, -ing, -ed) bend (the body) forward and downward ▶ n (pl -s) stooping posture

stooped v ▷ **stoop**

stooping v ▷ **stoop**

stoops v, n ▷ **stoop**

stop v (-s, -pping, -pped) cease or cause to cease from doing (something) ▶ n (pl -s) stopping or being stopped > **stoppage** n (pl -s)

stopcock n (pl -s) valve to control or stop the flow of fluid in a pipe

stopcocks n ▷ **stopcock**

stopgap n (pl -s) temporary substitute

stopgaps n ▷ **stopgap**

stopover n (pl -s) short break in a journey

stopovers n ▷ **stopover**

stoppage n ▷ **stop**

stoppages n ▷ **stop**

stopped v ▷ **stop**

stopper n (pl -s) plug for closing a bottle etc.

stoppers n ▷ **stopper**

stopping v ▷ **stop**

stops v, n ▷ **stop**

stopwatch n (pl -es) watch which can be stopped instantly for exact timing of a sporting event

stopwatches n ▷ **stopwatch**

storage n (pl -s) storing

storages n ▷ **storage**

store v (-res, -ring, -red) collect and keep (things) for future use ▶ n (pl -s) shop

stored v ▷ **store**

stores v, n ▷ **store** ▶ n pl stock of provisions

storey n (pl -s) floor or level of a building

storeys n ▷ **storey**

stories n ▷ **story**

storing v ▷ **store**

stork n (pl -s) large wading bird

storks n ▷ **stork**

storm n (pl -s) violent weather with wind, rain, or snow ▶ v (-s, -ing, -ed) attack or capture (a place) suddenly

stormed v ▷ **storm**

stormier adj ▷ **stormy**

stormiest adj ▷ **stormy**

storming v ▷ **storm**

storms n, v ▷ **storm**

stormy adj (-mier, -miest) characterized by storms

story n (pl -ries) description of a series of events told or written for entertainment

stoup [stoop] n (pl -s) small basin for holy water

stoups n ▷ **stoup**

stout adj (-er, -est) fat ▶ n (pl -s) strong dark beer > **stoutly** adv

stouter adj ▷ **stout**

stoutest adj ▷ **stout**

stoutly adv ▷ **stout**

stouts n ▷ **stout**

stove n (pl -s) apparatus for cooking or heating

stoves n ▷ **stove**

stow v (-s, -ing, -ed) pack or store

stowaway n (pl -s) person who hides on a ship or aircraft in order to travel free

stowaways n ▷ **stowaway**

stowed v ▷ **stow**

stowing v ▷ **stow**

stows v ▷ **stow**

straddle v (-les, -ling, -led) have one leg or part on each side of (something)

straddled v ▷ **straddle**

straddles v ▷ **straddle**

straddling v ▷ **straddle**

strafe v (-fes, -fing, -fed) attack (an enemy) with machine guns from the air

strafed v ▷ strafe
strafes v ▷ strafe
strafing v ▷ strafe
straggle v (-les, -ling, -led) go or spread in a rambling or irregular way > **straggler** n (pl -s) > **straggly** adj (-lier, -liest)
straggled v ▷ straggle
straggler n ▷ straggle
stragglers n ▷ straggle
straggles v ▷ straggle
stragglier adj ▷ straggle
straggliest adj ▷ straggle
straggling v ▷ straggle
straggly adj ▷ straggle
straight adj (-er, -est) not curved or crooked ▶ adv in a straight line ▶ n (pl -s) straight part, esp. of a racetrack > **straighten** v (-s, -ing, -ed)
straightaway adv immediately
straighten v ▷ straight
straightened v ▷ straight
straightening v ▷ straight
straightens v ▷ straighn
straighter adj ▷ straight
straightest adj ▷ straight
straightforward adj honest, frank
straightlaced adj ▷ straitlaced
straights n ▷ straight
strain[1] v (-s, -ing, -ed) cause (something) to be used or tested beyond its limits ▶ n (pl -s) tension or tiredness
strain[2] n (pl -s) breed or race
strained adj not natural, forced ▶ v ▷ strain[1]
strainer n (pl -s) sieve
strainers n ▷ strainer
straining v ▷ strain[1]
strains n ▷ strain[1, 2] ▶ v ▷ strain[1]
strait n (pl -s) position of acute difficulty
straitened adj not having much money
straitjacket n (pl -s) strong jacket with long sleeves used to bind the arms of a violent person
straitjackets n ▷ straitjacket
straitlaced, straightlaced adj prudish or puritanical
straits n ▷ strait ▶ n pl narrow channel connecting two areas of sea
strand[1] v (-s, -ing, -ed) run aground ▶ n (pl -s) (Poetic) shore
strand[2] n (pl -s) single thread of string, wire, etc.
stranded v ▷ strand[1]
stranding v ▷ strand[1]
strands n ▷ strand[1, 2] ▶ v ▷ strand[1]
strange adj (-r, -st) odd or unusual > **strangely** adv > **strangeness** n (pl -es)

strangely adv ▷ strange
strangeness n ▷ strange
strangenesses n ▷ strange
stranger n (pl -s) person who is not known or is new to a place or experience ▶ adj ▷ strange
strangers n ▷ stranger
strangest adj ▷ strange
strangle v (-les, -ling, -led) kill by squeezing the throat > **strangler** n (pl -s)
strangled v ▷ strangle
stranglehold n (pl -s) strangling grip in wrestling
strangleholds n ▷ stranglehold
strangler n ▷ strangle
stranglers n ▷ strangle
strangles v ▷ strangle
strangling v ▷ strangle
strangulation n (pl -s) strangling
strangulations n ▷ strangulation
strap n (pl -s) strip of flexible material for lifting, fastening, or holding in place ▶ v (-s, -pping, -pped) fasten with a strap or straps
strapped n ▷ strap
strapping adj tall and sturdy ▶ v ▷ strap
straps n, v ▷ strap
strata n ▷ stratum
stratagem n (pl -s) clever plan, trick
stratagems n ▷ stratagem
strategic [strat-ee-jik] adj advantageous > **strategically** adv
strategically adv ▷ strategic
strategies n ▷ strategy
strategist n ▷ strategy
strategists n ▷ strategy
strategy n (pl -gies) overall plan > **strategist** n (pl -s)
strathspey n (pl -s) Scottish dance with gliding steps
strathspeys n ▷ strathspey
stratification n ▷ stratified
stratifications n ▷ stratified
stratified adj divided into strata > **stratification** n (pl -s)
stratosphere n (pl -s) atmospheric layer between about 15 and 50 kilometres above the earth
stratospheres n ▷ stratosphere
stratum [strah-tum] n (pl -ta) layer, esp. of rock
straw n (pl -s) dried stalks of grain
strawberries n ▷ strawberry
strawberry n (pl -ries) sweet fleshy red fruit with small seeds on the outside
straws n ▷ straw
stray v (-s, -ing, -ed) wander ▶ adj having strayed ▶ n (pl -s) stray animal

strayed v ▷ stray

straying v ▷ stray

strays v, n ▷ stray

streak n (pl -s) long band of contrasting colour or substance ▶ v (-s, -ing, -ed) mark with streaks > streaker n (pl -s) > streaky adj (-kier, -kiest)

streaked v ▷ streak

streaker n ▷ streak

streakers n ▷ streak

streakier adj ▷ streak

streakiest adj ▷ streak

streaking v ▷ streak

streaks n, v ▷ streak

streaky adj ▷ streak

stream n (pl -s) small river ▶ v (-s, -ing, -ed) flow steadily

streamed v ▷ stream

streamer n (pl -s) strip of coloured paper that unrolls when tossed

streamers n ▷ streamer

streaming v ▷ stream

streamline v (-nes, -ning, -ned) make more efficient by simplifying

streamlined v ▷ streamline

streamlines v ▷ streamline

streamlining v ▷ streamline

streams n, v ▷ stream

street n (pl -s) public road, usu. lined with buildings

streetcar n (us) tram

streetcars n ▷ streetcar

streets n ▷ street

streetwise adj knowing how to survive in big cities

strength n (pl -s) quality of being strong > strengthen v (-s, -ing, -ed)

strengthen v ▷ strength

strengthened v ▷ strength

strengthening v ▷ strength

strengthens v ▷ strength

strengths n ▷ strength

strenuous adj requiring great energy or effort > strenuously adv

strenuously adv ▷ strenuous

streptococci n ▷ streptococcus

streptococcus [strep-toe-kok-uss] n (pl -cocci) bacterium occurring in chains, many species of which cause disease

stress n (pl -es) tension or strain ▶ v (-es, -ing, -ed) emphasize

stressed v ▷ stress

stresses n, v ▷ stress

stressing v ▷ stress

stretch v (-es, -ing, -ed) extend or be extended

▶ n (pl -es) stretching > stretchy adj (-chier, -chiest)

stretched v ▷ stretch

stretcher n (pl -s) frame covered with canvas, on which an injured person is carried

stretchers n ▷ stretcher

stretches v, n ▷ stretch

stretchier adj ▷ stretch

stretchiest adj ▷ stretch

stretching v ▷ stretch

stretchy adj ▷ stretch

strew v (-s, -ing, -ed or strewn) scatter (things) over a surface

strewed v ▷ strew

strewing v ▷ strew

strewn v ▷ strew

strews v ▷ strew

striated adj having a pattern of scratches or grooves

stricken adj seriously affected by disease, grief, pain, etc.

strict adj (-er, -est) stern or severe > strictly adv > strictness n (pl -es)

stricter adj ▷ strict

strictest adj ▷ strict

strictly adv ▷ strict

strictness n ▷ strict

strictnesses n ▷ strict

stricture n (pl -s) severe criticism

strictures n ▷ stricture

stridden v ▷ stride

stride v (-des, -ding, strode, stridden) walk with long steps ▶ n (pl -s) long step

stridencies n ▷ strident

stridency n ▷ strident

strident adj loud and harsh > stridently adv > stridency n (pl -cies)

stridently adv ▷ strident

strides v, n ▷ stride ▶ n pl progress

striding v ▷ stride

strife n (pl -s) conflict, quarrelling

strifes n ▷ strife

strike v (-kes, -king, struck) cease work as a protest ▶ n (pl -s) stoppage of work as a protest

striker n (pl -s) striking worker

strikers n ▷ striker

strikes v, n ▷ strike

striking adj impressive ▶ v ▷ strike

string n (pl -s) thin cord used for tying ▶ v (-s, -ing, strung) provide with a string or strings

stringed adj (of a musical instrument) having strings that are plucked or played with a bow

stringencies n ▷ stringent

stringency n ▷ stringent

stringent [strin-jent] *adj* strictly controlled or enforced > **stringently** *adv* > **stringency** *n* (*pl* -**cies**)

stringently *adv* ▷ **stringent**

stringier *adj* ▷ **stringy**

stringiest *adj* ▷ **stringy**

stringing *v* ▷ **string**

strings *n*, *v* ▷ **string** ▶ *n pl* restrictions or conditions

stringy *adj* (-**gier**, -**giest**) like string

stringybark *n* (*pl* -**s**) Australian eucalyptus with a fibrous bark

stringybarks *n* ▷ **stringybark**

strip[1] *v* (-**s**, -**pping**, -**pped**) take (the covering or clothes) off

strip[2] *n* (*pl* -**s**) long narrow piece

stripe *n* (*pl* -**s**) long narrow band of contrasting colour or substance > **striped**, **stripy**, **stripey** *adj* (-**pier**, -**piest**)

striped *adj* ▷ **stripe**

stripes *n* ▷ **stripe**

stripey *adj* ▷ **stripe**

stripier *adj* ▷ **stripe**

stripiest *adj* ▷ **stripe**

stripling *n* (*pl* -**s**) youth

striplings *n* ▷ **stripling**

stripped *v* ▷ **strip**[1]

stripper *n* (*pl* -**s**) person who performs a striptease

strippers *n* ▷ **stripper**

stripping *v* ▷ **strip**[1]

strips *v* ▷ **strip**[1] ▶ *n* ▷ **strip**[2]

striptease *n* (*pl* -**s**) entertainment in which a performer undresses to music

stripteases *n* ▷ **striptease**

stripy *adj* ▷ **stripe**

strive *v* (-**ves**, -**ving**, **strove**, **striven**) make a great effort

striven *v* ▷ **strive**

strives *v* ▷ **strive**

striving *v* ▷ **strive**

strobe *n* (*pl* -**s**) ▷ **stroboscope**

strobes *n* ▷ **strobe**

stroboscope *n* (*pl* -**s**) instrument producing a very bright flashing light

stroboscopes *n* ▷ **stroboscope**

strode *v* ▷ **stride**

stroke *v* (-**kes**, -**king**, -**ked**) touch or caress lightly with the hand ▶ *n* (*pl* -**s**) light touch or caress with the hand

stroked *v* ▷ **stroke**

strokes *v*, *n* ▷ **stroke**

stroking *v* ▷ **stroke**

stroll *v* (-**s**, -**ing**, -**ed**) walk in a leisurely manner ▶ *n* (*pl* -**s**) leisurely walk

strolled *v* ▷ **stroll**

strolling *v* ▷ **stroll**

strolls *v*, *n* ▷ **stroll**

strong *adj* (-**er**, -**est**) having physical power > **strongly** *adv*

stronger *adj* ▷ **strong**

strongest *adj* ▷ **strong**

stronghold *n* (*pl* -**s**) area of predominance of a particular belief

strongholds *n* ▷ **stronghold**

strongly *adv* ▷ **strong**

strongroom *n* (*pl* -**s**) room designed for the safekeeping of valuables

strongrooms *n* ▷ **strongroom**

strontium *n* (*pl* -**s**) (CHEM) silvery-white metallic element

strontiums *n* ▷ **strontium**

strop *n* (*pl* -**s**) leather strap for sharpening razors

stroppier *adj* ▷ **stroppy**

stroppiest *adj* ▷ **stroppy**

stroppy *adj* (-**pier**, -**piest**) (*Slang*) angry or awkward

strops *n* ▷ **strop**

strove *v* ▷ **strive**

struck *v* ▷ **strike**

structural *adj* ▷ **structure**

structuralism *n* (*pl* -**s**) approach to literature, social sciences, etc., which sees changes in the subject as caused and organized by a hidden set of universal rules > **structuralist** *n* (*pl* -**s**) *adj*

structuralisms *n* ▷ **structuralism**

structuralist *n*, *adj* ▷ **structuralism**

structuralists *n* ▷ **structuralism**

structure *n* (*pl* -**s**) complex construction ▶ *v* (-**res**, -**ring**, -**red**) give a structure to > **structural** *adj*

structured *v* ▷ **structure**

structures *n*, *v* ▷ **structure**

structuring *v* ▷ **structure**

strudel *n* (*pl* -**s**) thin sheet of filled dough rolled up and baked, usu. with an apple filling

strudels *n* ▷ **strudel**

struggle *v* (-**les**, -**ling**, -**led**) work, strive, or make one's way with difficulty ▶ *n* (*pl* -**s**) striving

struggled *v* ▷ **struggle**

struggles *v*, *n* ▷ **struggle**

struggling *v* ▷ **struggle**

strum *v* (-**s**, -**mming**, -**mmed**) play (a guitar or banjo) by sweeping the thumb or a plectrum across the strings

strummed *v* ▷ **strum**

strumming *v* ▷ **strum**

strumpet n (pl -s) (Old-fashioned) prostitute
  strumpets n ▷ strumpet
strums v ▷ strum
strung v ▷ string
strut v (-s, -tting, -tted) walk pompously, swagger ▶ n (pl -s) bar supporting a structure
  struts v, n ▷ strut
  strutted v ▷ strut
  strutting v ▷ strut
strychnine [strik-neen] n (pl -s) very poisonous drug used in small quantities as a stimulant
  strychnines n ▷ strychnine
stub n (pl -s) short piece left after use ▶ v (-s, -bbing, -bbed) strike (the toe) painfully against an object
  stubbed v ▷ stub
  stubbier adj ▷ stubby
  stubbiest adj ▷ stubby
  stubbing v ▷ stub
stubble n (pl -s) short stalks of grain left in a field after reaping ▶ **stubbly** adj (-lier, -liest)
  stubbles n ▷ stubble
  stubblier adj ▷ stubble
  stubbliest adj ▷ stubble
  stubbly adj ▷ stubble
stubborn adj (-er, -est) refusing to agree or give in ▶ **stubbornly** adv ▷ **stubbornness** n (pl -es)
  stubborner adj ▷ stubborn
  stubbornest adj ▷ stubborn
  stubbornly adv ▷ stubborn
  stubbornness n ▷ stubborn
  stubbornnesses n ▷ stubborn
stubby adj (-bbier, -bbiest) short and broad
  stubs n, v ▷ stub
stucco n (pl -oes) plaster used for coating or decorating walls
  stuccoes n ▷ stucco
  stuck v ▷ stick²
stud¹ n (pl -s) small piece of metal attached to a surface for decoration ▶ v (-s, -dding, -dded) set with studs
stud² n (pl -s) male animal, esp. a stallion, kept for breeding
  studded v ▷ stud¹
  studding v ▷ stud¹
student n (pl -s) person who studies a subject, esp. at university
  students n ▷ student
studied adj carefully practised or planned ▶ v ▷ study
  studies v, n ▷ study
studio n (pl -s) workroom of an artist or photographer
  studios n ▷ studio

studious adj fond of study ▶ **studiously** adv
  studiously adv ▷ studious
  studs n ▷ stud¹, ² ▶ v ▷ stud¹
study v (-dies, -dying, -died) be engaged in learning (a subject) ▶ n (pl -dies) act or process of studying
  studying v ▷ study
stuff n (pl -s) substance or material ▶ v (-s, -ing, -ed) pack, cram, or fill completely
  stuffed v ▷ stuff
  stuffier adj ▷ stuffy
  stuffiest adj ▷ stuffy
stuffing n (pl -s) seasoned mixture with which food is stuffed ▶ v ▷ stuff
  stuffings n ▷ stuffing
  stuffs n, v ▷ stuff
stuffy adj (-fier, -fiest) lacking fresh air
stultifying adj very boring and repetitive
stumble v (-les, -ling, -led) trip and nearly fall ▶ n (pl -s) stumbling
  stumbled v ▷ stumble
  stumbles v ▷ stumble
  stumbling v ▷ stumble
stump n (pl -s) base of a tree left when the main trunk has been cut away ▶ v (-s, -ing, -ed) baffle
  stumped v ▷ stump
  stumpier adj ▷ stumpy
  stumpiest adj ▷ stumpy
  stumping v ▷ stump
  stumps n, v ▷ stump
stumpy adj (-pier, -piest) short and thick
stun v (-s, -nning, -nned) shock or overwhelm
  stung v ▷ sting
  stunk v ▷ stink
  stunned v ▷ stun
stunning adj very attractive or impressive ▶ v ▷ stun
  stuns v ▷ stun
stunt¹ v (-ts, -ing, -ed) prevent or impede the growth of ▶ **stunted** adj
stunt² n (pl -s) acrobatic or dangerous action
  stunted v, adj ▷ stunt¹
  stunting v ▷ stunt¹
  stunts v ▷ stunt¹ ▶ n ▷ stunt²
  stupefaction n ▷ stupefy
  stupefactions n ▷ stupefy
  stupefied v ▷ stupefy
  stupefies v ▷ stupefy
stupefy v (-fies, -fying, -fied) make insensitive or lethargic ▶ **stupefaction** n (pl -s)
  stupefying v ▷ stupefy
stupendous adj very large or impressive ▶ **stupendously** adv
  stupendously adv ▷ stupendous

stupid adj (-er, -est) lacking intelligence
> **stupidity** n (pl -ties) > **stupidly** adv
stupider adj ▷ **stupid**
stupidest adj ▷ **stupid**
stupidities n ▷ **stupid**
stupidity n ▷ **stupid**
stupidly adv ▷ **stupid**
stupor n (pl -s) dazed or unconscious state
stupors n ▷ **stupor**
sturdier adj ▷ **sturdy**
sturdiest adj ▷ **sturdy**
sturdily adv ▷ **sturdy**
sturdy adj (-dier, -diest) healthy and robust
> **sturdily** adv
sturgeon n (pl -s) fish from which caviar is
obtained
sturgeons n ▷ **sturgeon**
stutter v (-s, -ing, -ed) speak with repetition
of initial consonants ▶ n (pl -s) tendency to
stutter
stuttered v ▷ **stutter**
stuttering v ▷ **stutter**
stutters v, n ▷ **stutter**
sty n (pl **sties**) pen for pigs
stye n (pl **styes**) inflammation at the base of
an eyelash
styes n ▷ **stye**
style n (pl -s) shape or design ▶ v (-les, -ling,
-led) shape or design
styled v ▷ **style**
styles n, v ▷ **style**
styli n ▷ **stylus**
styling v ▷ **style**
stylish adj smart, elegant, and fashionable
> **stylishly** adv
stylishly adv ▷ **stylish**
stylist n (pl -s) hairdresser
stylistic adj of literary or artistic style
stylists n ▷ **stylist**
stylize v (-zes, -zing, -zed) cause to conform to
an established stylistic form
stylized v ▷ **stylize**
stylizes v ▷ **stylize**
stylizing v ▷ **stylize**
stylus n (pl -**li**, -**luses**) needle-like device on a
record player that rests in the groove of the
record and picks up the sound signals
styluses n ▷ **stylus**
stymie v (-mies, -mieing, -mied) hinder or
thwart
stymied v ▷ **stymie**
stymieing v ▷ **stymie**
stymies v ▷ **stymie**
styptic n (pl -s) ▶ adj (drug) used to stop
bleeding

styptics n ▷ **styptic**
suave [swahv] adj smooth and sophisticated in
manner > **suavely** adv
suavely adv ▷ **suave**
sub n (pl -s) subeditor ▶ v (-s, -bbing, -bbed) act
as a substitute
subaltern n (pl -s) British army officer below
the rank of captain
subalterns n ▷ **subaltern**
subatomic adj of or being one of the particles
which make up an atom
subbed v ▷ **sub**
subbing v ▷ **sub**
subcommittee n (pl -s) small committee
formed from some members of a larger
committee
subcommittees n ▷ **subcommittee**
subconscious adj happening or existing
without one's awareness ▶ n (pl -es)
(PSYCHOANALYSIS) that part of the mind of which
one is not aware but which can influence
one's behaviour > **subconsciously** adv
subconsciouses n ▷ **subconscious**
subconsciously adv ▷ **subconscious**
subcontinent n (pl -s) large land mass that is a
distinct part of a continent
subcontinents n ▷ **subcontinent**
subcontract n (pl -s) secondary contract by
which the main contractor for a job puts
work out to others ▶ v (-s, -ing, -ed) put out
(work) on a subcontract > **subcontractor**
n (pl -s)
subcontracted v ▷ **subcontract**
subcontracting v ▷ **subcontract**
subcontractor n ▷ **subcontract**
subcontractors n ▷ **subcontract**
subcontracts n, v ▷ **subcontract**
subcutaneous [sub-cute-**ayn**-ee-uss] adj under
the skin
subdivide v (-des, -ding, -ded) divide (a part of
something) into smaller parts > **subdivision**
n (pl -s)
subdivided v ▷ **subdivide**
subdivides v ▷ **subdivide**
subdividing v ▷ **subdivide**
subdivision n ▷ **subdivide**
subdivisions n ▷ **subdivide**
subdue v (-dues, -duing, -dued) overcome
subdued v ▷ **subdue**
subdues v ▷ **subdue**
subduing v ▷ **subdue**
subeditor n (pl -s) person who checks and
edits text for a newspaper or magazine
subeditors n ▷ **subeditor**
subject n (pl -s) person or thing being dealt

with or studied ▶ *adj* being under the rule of a monarch or government ▶ *v* (**-s, -ing, -ed**) (*foll. by* **to**) cause to undergo > **subjection** *n* (*pl* **-s**)

subjected *v* ▷ **subject**

subjecting *v* ▷ **subject**

subjection *n* ▷ **subject**

subjections *n* ▷ **subject**

subjective *adj* based on personal feelings or prejudices > **subjectively** *adv*

subjectively *adv* ▷ **subjective**

subjects *n, v* ▷ **subject**

subjugate *v* (**-tes, -ting, -ted**) bring (a group of people) under one's control > **subjugation** *n* (*pl* **-s**)

subjugated *v* ▷ **subjugate**

subjugates *v* ▷ **subjugate**

subjugating *v* ▷ **subjugate**

subjugation *n* ▷ **subjugate**

subjugations *n* ▷ **subjugate**

subjunctive (GRAMMAR) *n* (*pl* **-s**) mood of verbs used when the content of the clause is doubted, supposed, or wished ▶ *adj* in or of that mood

subjunctives *n* ▷ **subjunctive**

sublet *v* (**-s, -letting, -let**) rent out (property rented from someone else)

sublets *v* ▷ **sublet**

subletting *v* ▷ **sublet**

sublimate *v* (**-tes, -ting, -ted**) (PSYCHOL) direct the energy of (a strong desire, esp. a sexual one) into socially acceptable activities > **sublimation** *n* (*pl* **-s**)

sublimated *v* ▷ **sublimate**

sublimates *v* ▷ **sublimate**

sublimating *v* ▷ **sublimate**

sublimation *n* ▷ **sublimate**

sublimations *n* ▷ **sublimate**

sublime *adj* (**-r, -st**) of high moral, intellectual, or spiritual value ▶ *v* (**-mes, -ming, -med**) (CHEM) change from a solid to a vapour without first melting > **sublimely** *adv*

sublimed *v* ▷ **sublime**

sublimely *adv* ▷ **sublime**

sublimer *adj* ▷ **sublime**

sublimes *v* ▷ **sublime**

sublimest *adj* ▷ **sublime**

subliminal *adj* relating to mental processes of which the individual is not aware

subliming *v* ▷ **sublime**

submarine *n* (*pl* **-s**) vessel which can operate below the surface of the sea ▶ *adj* below the surface of the sea

submarines *n* ▷ **submarine**

submerge *v* (**-ges, -ging, -ged**) put or go below the surface of water or other liquid

> **submersion** *n* (*pl* **-s**)

submerged *v* ▷ **submerge**

submerges *v* ▷ **submerge**

submerging *v* ▷ **submerge**

submersion *n* ▷ **submerge**

submersions *n* ▷ **submerge**

submission *n* (*pl* **-s**) submitting

submissions *n* ▷ **submission**

submissive *adj* meek and obedient

submit *v* (**-s, -ting, -tted**) surrender

submits *v* ▷ **submit**

submitted *v* ▷ **submit**

submitting *v* ▷ **submit**

subordinate *adj* of lesser rank or importance ▶ *n* (*pl* **-s**) subordinate person or thing ▶ *v* (**-tes, -ting, -ted**) make or treat as subordinate > **subordination** *n* (*pl* **-s**)

subordinated *v* ▷ **subordinate**

subordinates *n, v* ▷ **subordinate**

subordinating *v* ▷ **subordinate**

subordination *n* ▷ **subordinate**

subordinations *n* ▷ **subordinate**

suborn *v* (**-s, -ing, -ed**) (*Formal*) bribe or incite (a person) to commit a wrongful act

suborned *v* ▷ **suborn**

suborning *v* ▷ **suborn**

suborns *v* ▷ **suborn**

subpoena [sub-pee-na] *n* (*pl* **-s**) writ requiring a person to appear before a law court ▶ *v* (**-nas, -naing, -naed**) summon (someone) with a subpoena

subpoenaed *v* ▷ **subpoena**

subpoenaing *v* ▷ **subpoena**

subpoenas *n, v* ▷ **subpoena**

subs *n, v* ▷ **sub**

subscribe *v* (**-bes, -bing, -bed**) pay (a subscription) > **subscriber** *n* (*pl* **-s**)

subscribed *v* ▷ **subscribe**

subscriber *n* ▷ **subscribe**

subscribers *n* ▷ **subscribe**

subscribes *v* ▷ **subscribe**

subscribing *v* ▷ **subscribe**

subscription *n* (*pl* **-s**) payment for issues of a publication over a period

subscriptions *n* ▷ **subscription**

subsection *n* (*pl* **-s**) division of a section

subsections *n* ▷ **subsection**

subsequent *adj* occurring after, succeeding > **subsequently** *adv*

subsequently *adv* ▷ **subsequent**

subservience *n* ▷ **subservient**

subserviences *n* ▷ **subservient**

subservient *adj* submissive, servile > **subservience** *n* (*pl* **-s**)

subside *v* (**-des, -ding, -ded**) become less

intense
subsided v ▷ subside
subsidence n (pl -s) act or process of subsiding
 subsidences n ▷ subsidence
 subsides v ▷ subside
 subsidiaries n ▷ subsidiary
subsidiary adj of lesser importance ▶ n (pl -ries) subsidiary person or thing
 subsidies n ▷ subsidy
 subsiding v ▷ subside
subsidize v (-izes, -izing, -ized) help financially
 subsidized v ▷ subsidize
 subsidizes v ▷ subsidize
 subsidizing v ▷ subsidize
subsidy n (pl -dies) financial aid
subsist v (-s, -ing, -ed) manage to live
 > **subsistence** n (pl -s)
 subsisted v ▷ subsist
 subsistence n ▷ subsist
 subsistences n ▷ subsist
 subsisting v ▷ subsist
 subsists v ▷ subsist
subsonic adj moving at a speed less than that of sound
substance n (pl -s) physical composition of something
 substances n ▷ substance
substantial adj of considerable size or value
 > **substantially** adv
 substantially adv ▷ substantial
substantiate v (-tes, -ting, -ted) support (a story) with evidence > **substantiation** n (pl -s)
 substantiated v ▷ substantiate
 substantiates v ▷ substantiate
 substantiating v ▷ substantiate
 substantiation n ▷ substantiate
 substantiations n ▷ substantiate
substantive n (pl -s) noun ▶ adj of or being the essential element of a thing
 substantives n ▷ substantive
substitute v (-tes, -ting, -ted) take the place of or put in place of another ▶ n (pl -s) person or thing taking the place of (another)
 > **substitution** n (pl -s)
 substituted v ▷ substitute
 substitutes v, n ▷ substitute
 substituting v ▷ substitute
 substitution n ▷ substitute
 substitutions n ▷ substitute
subsume v (-mes, -ming, -med) include (an idea, case, etc.) under a larger classification or group
 subsumed v ▷ subsume
 subsumes v ▷ subsume
 subsuming v ▷ subsume

subterfuge n (pl -s) trick used to achieve an objective
 subterfuges n ▷ subterfuge
subterranean adj underground
subtitle n (pl -s) secondary title of a book ▶ v (-les, -ling, -led) provide with a subtitle or subtitles
 subtitled v ▷ subtitle
subtitles v, n ▷ subtitle ▶ pl n printed translation at the bottom of the picture in a film with foreign dialogue
 subtitling v ▷ subtitle
subtle adj (-r, -st) not immediately obvious
 > **subtly** adv > **subtlety** n (pl -ties)
 subtler adj ▷ subtle
 subtlest adj ▷ subtle
 subtleties n ▷ subtle
 subtlety n ▷ subtle
 subtly adv ▷ subtle
subtract v (-s, -ing, -ed) take (one number or quantity) from another > **subtraction** n (pl -s)
 subtracted v ▷ subtract
 subtracting v ▷ subtract
 subtraction n ▷ subtract
 subtractions n ▷ subtract
 subtracts v ▷ subtract
subtropical adj of the regions bordering on the tropics
suburb n (pl -s) residential area on the outskirts of a city
suburban adj of or inhabiting a suburb
suburbia n (pl -s) suburbs and their inhabitants
 suburbias n ▷ suburbia
 suburbs n ▷ suburb
subvention n (pl -s) (Formal) subsidy
 subventions n ▷ subvention
 subversion n ▷ subvert
 subversions n ▷ subvert
subversive adj, n ▷ subvert
 subversives n ▷ subvert
subvert v (-s, -ing, -ed) overthrow the authority of > **subversion** n (pl -s)
 > **subversive** adj, n (pl -s)
 subverted v ▷ subvert
 subverting v ▷ subvert
 subverts v ▷ subvert
subway n (pl -s) passage under a road or railway
 subways n ▷ subway
succeed v (-s, -ing, -ed) accomplish an aim
 succeeded v ▷ succeed
 succeeding v ▷ succeed
 succeeds v ▷ succeed
success n (pl -es) achievement of something

attempted
successes n ▷ success

successful adj having success > **successfully** adv

successfully adv ▷ successful

succession n (pl -s) series of people or things following one another in order
successions n ▷ succession

successive adj consecutive > **successively** adv

successively adv ▷ successive

successor n (pl -s) person who succeeds someone in a position
successors n ▷ successor

succinct adj (-er, -est) brief and clear > **succinctly** adv

succincter adj ▷ succinct

succinctest adj ▷ succinct

succinctly adv ▷ succinct

succour v (-s, -ing, -ed) ▶ n (pl -s) help in distress
succoured v ▷ succour

succouring v ▷ succour

succours v, n ▷ succour

succulence n ▷ succulent

succulences n ▷ succulent

succulent adj juicy and delicious ▶ n (pl -s) succulent plant > **succulence** n (pl -s)
succulent n ▷ succulent

succulents n ▷ succulent

succumb v (-s, -ing, -ed) (foll. by to) give way (to something overpowering)
succumbed v ▷ succumb

succumbing v ▷ succumb

succumbs v ▷ succumb

such adj of the kind specified ▶ pron such things

suchlike pron such or similar things

suck v (-s, -ing, -ed) draw (liquid or air) into the mouth ▶ n (pl -s) sucking
sucked v ▷ suck

sucker n (pl -s) (Slang) person who is easily deceived or swindled
suckers n ▷ sucker

sucking v ▷ suck

suckle v (-les, -ling, -led) feed at the breast
suckled v ▷ suckle

suckles v ▷ suckle

suckling n (pl -s) unweaned baby or young animal ▶ v ▷ suckle
sucklings n ▷ suckling

sucks v, n ▷ suck

sucrose [soo-kroze] n (pl -s) chemical name for sugar
sucroses n ▷ sucrose

suction n (pl -s) sucking

suctions n ▷ suction

sudden adj done or occurring quickly and unexpectedly > **suddenly** adv > **suddenness** n (pl -es)
suddenly adv ▷ sudden

suddenness n ▷ suddenness

suddennesses n ▷ suddenness

sudorific [syoo-dor-if-ik] n (pl -s) ▶ adj (drug) causing sweating
sudorifics n ▷ sudorific

suds pl n froth of soap and water, lather

sue v (-ues, -uing, -ued) start legal proceedings against
sued v ▷ sue

suede n (pl -s) leather with a velvety finish on one side
suedes n ▷ suede

sues v ▷ sue

suet n (pl -s) hard fat obtained from sheep and cattle, used in cooking
suets n ▷ suet

suffer v (-s, -ing, -ed) undergo or be subjected to > **sufferer** n (pl -s) > **suffering** n (pl -s) > **sufferance** n (pl -s)
sufferance n ▷ suffer

sufferances n ▷ suffer

suffered v ▷ suffer

sufferer n ▷ suffer

sufferers n ▷ suffer

suffering n, v ▷ suffer

sufferings n ▷ suffer

suffers v ▷ suffer

suffice [suf-fice] v (-ces, -cing, -ced) be enough for a purpose
sufficed v ▷ suffice

suffices v ▷ suffice

sufficiencies n ▷ sufficiency

sufficiency n (pl -cies) adequate amount

sufficient adj enough, adequate > **sufficiently** adv
sufficiently adv ▷ sufficient

sufficing v ▷ suffice

suffix n (pl -es) letter or letters added to the end of a word to form another word, such as -s and -ness in dogs and softness
suffixes n ▷ suffix

suffocate v (-tes, -ting, -ted) kill or be killed by deprivation of oxygen > **suffocation** n (pl -s)
suffocated v ▷ suffocate

suffocates v ▷ suffocate

suffocating v ▷ suffocate

suffocation n ▷ suffocate

suffocations n ▷ suffocate

suffragan n (pl -s) bishop appointed to assist an archbishop

suffragans n ▷ suffragan
suffrage n (pl -s) right to vote in public elections
suffrages n ▷ suffrage
suffragette n (pl -s) (in Britain in the early 20th century) a woman who campaigned militantly for the right to vote
suffragettes n ▷ suffragette
suffuse v (-ses, -sing, -sed) spread through or over (something) > **suffusion** n (pl -s)
suffused v ▷ suffuse
suffuses v ▷ suffuse
suffusing v ▷ suffuse
suffusion n ▷ suffuse
suffusions n ▷ suffuse
sugar n (pl -s) sweet crystalline carbohydrate found in many plants and used to sweeten food and drinks ▶ v (-s, -ing, -ed) sweeten or cover with sugar > **sugary** adj (-rier, -riest)
sugared v ▷ sugar
sugarier adj ▷ sugar
sugariest adj ▷ sugar
sugaring v ▷ sugar
sugars n, v ▷ sugar
sugary adj ▷ sugar
suggest v (-s, -ing, -ed) put forward (an idea) for consideration
suggested v ▷ suggest
suggestible adj easily influenced
suggesting v ▷ suggest
suggestion n (pl -s) thing suggested
suggestions n ▷ suggestion
suggestive adj suggesting something indecent > **suggestively** adv
suggestively adv ▷ suggestive
suggests v ▷ suggest
suicidal adj liable to commit suicide > **suicidally** adv
suicidally adv ▷ suicide
suicide n (pl -s) killing oneself intentionally
suicides n ▷ suicide
suing v ▷ sue
suit n (pl -s) set of clothes designed to be worn together ▶ v (-s, -ing, -ed) be appropriate for
suitabilities n ▷ suitable
suitability n ▷ suitable
suitable adj appropriate or proper > **suitably** adv > **suitability** n (pl -ties)
suitably adv ▷ suitable
suitcase n (pl -s) portable travelling case for clothing
suitcases n ▷ suitcase
suite n (pl -s) set of connected rooms in a hotel
suited v ▷ suit
suites n ▷ suite

suiting v ▷ suit
suitor n (pl -s) (Old-fashioned) man who is courting a woman
suitors n ▷ suitor
suits n, v ▷ suit
sulk v (-s, -ing, -ed) be silent and sullen because of resentment or bad temper ▶ n (pl -s) resentful or sullen mood > **sulky** adj (-kier, -kiest) > **sulkily** adv
sulked v ▷ sulk
sulkier adj ▷ sulk
sulkiest adj ▷ sulk
sulkily adv ▷ sulk
sulking v ▷ sulk
sulks v, n ▷ sulk
sulky adj ▷ sulk
sullen adj (-er, -est) unwilling to talk or be sociable > **sullenly** adv > **sullenness** n (pl -es)
sullener adj ▷ sullen
sullenest adj ▷ sullen
sullenly adv ▷ sullen
sullenness n ▷ sullen
sullennesses n ▷ sullen
sullied v ▷ sully
sullies v ▷ sully
sully v (-lies, -lying, -lied) ruin (someone's reputation)
sullying v ▷ sully
sulphate n (pl -s) salt or ester of sulphuric acid
sulphates n ▷ sulphate
sulphide n (pl -s) compound of sulphur with another element
sulphides n ▷ sulphide
sulphite n (pl -s) salt or ester of sulphurous acid
sulphites n ▷ sulphite
sulphonamide [sulf-**on**-a-mide] n (pl -s) any of a class of drugs that prevent the growth of bacteria
sulphonamides n ▷ sulphonamide
sulphur n (pl -s) (CHEM) pale yellow nonmetallic element
sulphuric, sulphurous adj of or containing sulphur
sulphurous adj ▷ sulphuric
sulphurs n ▷ sulphur
sultan n (pl -s) sovereign of a Muslim country
sultana n (pl -s) kind of raisin
sultanas n ▷ sultana
sultanate n (pl -s) territory of a sultan
sultanates n ▷ sultanate
sultans n ▷ sultan
sultrier n ▷ sultry
sultriest n ▷ sultry
sultry adj (-trier, -triest) (of weather or

climate) hot and humid

sum n (pl -s) result of addition, total
   summaries n ▷ summary
   summarily adv ▷ summary
summarize v (-izes, -izing, -ized) make or be a summary of (something)
   summarized v ▷ summarize
   summarizes v ▷ summarize
   summarizing v ▷ summarize
summary n (pl -ries) brief account giving the main points of something ▶ adj done quickly, without formalities > **summarily** adv
summation n (pl -s) summary
   summations n ▷ summation
summer n (pl -s) warmest season of the year, between spring and autumn > **summery** adj (-rier, -riest)
summerhouse n (pl -s) small building in a garden
   summerhouses n ▷ summerhouse
   summerier adj ▷ summer
   summeriest adj ▷ summer
   summers n ▷ summer
summertime n (pl -s) period or season of summer
   summertimes n ▷ summertime
   summery adj ▷ summer
summit n (pl -s) top of a mountain or hill
   summits n ▷ summit
summon v (-s, -ing, -ed) order (someone) to come
   summoned v ▷ summon
   summoning v ▷ summon
summons n (pl -es) command summoning someone ▶ v (-es, -ing, -ed) order (someone) to appear in court ▶ v ▷ summon
   summonsed n ▷ summons
   summonses v, n ▷ summons
   summonsing v ▷ summons
sumo n (pl -s) Japanese style of wrestling
   sumos n ▷ sumo
sump n (pl -s) container in an internal-combustion engine into which oil can drain
   sumps n ▷ sump
sumptuous adj lavish, magnificent
   > **sumptuously** adv
   sumptuously adv ▷ sumptuous
   sums n ▷ sum
sun n (pl -s) star around which the earth and other planets revolve ▶ v (-s, sunning, sunned) expose (oneself) to the sun's rays
   > **sunless** adj
sunbathe v (-thes, -thing, -thed) lie in the sunshine in order to get a suntan
   sunbathed v ▷ sunbathe

sunbathes v ▷ sunbathe
sunbathing v ▷ sunbathe
sunbeam n (pl -s) ray of sun
   sunbeams n ▷ sunbeam
sunburn n (pl -s) painful reddening of the skin caused by overexposure to the sun
   > **sunburnt, sunburned** adj
   sunburned adj ▷ sunburn
   sunburns n ▷ sunburn
   sunburnt adj ▷ sunburn
sundae n (pl -s) ice cream topped with fruit etc.
   sundaes n ▷ sundae
sundial n (pl -s) device showing the time by means of a pointer that casts a shadow on a marked dial
   sundials n ▷ sundial
sundown n (pl -s) sunset
   sundowns n ▷ sundown
sundries pl n several things of various sorts
sundry adj several, various
sunflower n (pl -s) tall plant with large golden flowers
   sunflowers n ▷ sunflower
sung v ▷ sing
sunk v ▷ sink
sunken v ▷ sink
sunless adj ▷ sun
sunned v ▷ sun
sunnier adj ▷ sunny
sunniest adj ▷ sunny
sunning v ▷ sun
sunny adj (-nnier, -nniest) full of or exposed to sunlight
sunrise n (pl -s) daily appearance of the sun above the horizon
   sunrises n ▷ sunrise
   suns n, v ▷ sun
sunset n (pl -s) daily disappearance of the sun below the horizon
   sunsets n ▷ sunset
sunshine n (pl -s) light and warmth from the sun
   sunshines n ▷ sunshine
sunspot n (pl -s) dark patch appearing temporarily on the sun's surface
   sunspots n ▷ sunspot
sunstroke n (pl -s) illness caused by prolonged exposure to intensely hot sunlight
   sunstrokes n ▷ sunstroke
suntan n (pl -s) browning of the skin caused by exposure to the sun
   suntans n ▷ suntan
sup v (-s, -pping, -pped) take (liquid) by sips
   ▶ n (pl -s) sip

super adj (Informal) excellent

superannuated adj discharged with a pension, owing to old age or illness

superannuation n (pl -s) regular payment by an employee into a pension fund

superannuations n ▷ superannuation

superb adj excellent, impressive, or splendid
> **superbly** adv

superbly adv ▷ superb

superbug n (pl -s) (Informal) bacterium resistant to antibiotics

superbugs n ▷ superbug

supercharged adj (of an engine) having a supercharger

supercharger n (pl -s) device that increases the power of an internal-combustion engine by forcing extra air into it

superchargers n ▷ supercharger

supercilious adj showing arrogant pride or scorn

superconductor n (pl -s) substance which has almost no electrical resistance at very low temperatures

superconductors n ▷ superconductor

superficial adj not careful or thorough
> **superficially** adv > **superficiality** n (pl -ties)

superficialities n ▷ superficial

superficiality n ▷ superficial

superficially adv ▷ superficial

superfluities n ▷ superfluous

superfluity n ▷ superfluous

superfluous [soo-per-flew-uss] adj more than is needed > **superfluity** n (pl -ties)

superhuman adj beyond normal human ability or experience

superimpose v (-ses, -sing, -sed) place (something) on or over something else

superimposed v ▷ superimpose

superimposes v ▷ superimpose

superimposing v ▷ superimpose

superintend v (-s, -ing, -ed) supervise (a person or activity)

superintended v ▷ superintend

superintendent n (pl -s) senior police officer

superintendents n ▷ superintendent

superintending v ▷ superintend

superintends v ▷ superintend

superior adj greater in quality, quantity, or merit ▶ n (pl -s) person of greater rank or status > **superiority** n (pl -ties)

superiorities n ▷ superior

superiority n ▷ superior

superiors n ▷ superior

superlative [soo-per-lat-iv] adj of outstanding quality ▶ n (pl -s) (GRAMMAR) word expressing this

superlatives n ▷ superlative

superman n (pl -men) man with great physical or mental powers

supermarket n (pl -s) large self-service store selling food and household goods

supermarkets n ▷ supermarket

supermen n ▷ superman

supermodel n (pl -s) famous and highly-paid fashion model

supermodels n ▷ supermodel

supernatural adj of or relating to things beyond the laws of nature

supernova n (pl -vae, -vas) star that explodes and briefly becomes exceptionally bright

supernovae n ▷ supernova

supernovas n ▷ supernova

supernumeraries n ▷ supernumerary

supernumerary adj exceeding the required or regular number ▶ n (pl -ries) supernumerary person or thing

superpower n (pl -s) extremely powerful nation

superpowers n ▷ superpower

superscript n (pl -s) ▶ adj (character) printed above the line

superscripts n ▷ superscript

supersede v (-des, -ding, -ded) replace, supplant

superseded v ▷ supersede

supersedes v ▷ supersede

superseding v ▷ supersede

supersonic adj of or travelling at a speed greater than the speed of sound

superstition n (pl -s) belief in omens, ghosts, etc. > **superstitious** adj

superstitions n ▷ superstition

superstitious adj ▷ superstition

superstore n (pl -s) large supermarket

superstores n ▷ superstore

superstructure n (pl -s) structure erected on something else

superstructures n ▷ superstructure

supervene v (-nes, -ning, -ned) occur as an unexpected development

supervened v ▷ supervene

supervenes v ▷ supervene

supervening v ▷ supervene

supervise v (-ses, -sing, -sed) watch over to direct or check > **supervision** n (pl -s)
> **supervisor** n (pl -s) > **supervisory** adj

supervised v ▷ supervise

supervises v ▷ supervise

supervising v ▷ supervise

supervision n ▷ supervise

supervisions n ▷ supervise
supervisor n ▷ supervise
supervisors n ▷ supervise
supervisory adj ▷ supervise
supine adj lying flat on one's back
supped v ▷ sup
supper n (pl -s) light evening meal
suppers n ▷ supper
supping v ▷ sup
supplant v (-s, -ing, -ed) take the place of, oust
supplanted v ▷ supplant
supplanting v ▷ supplant
supplants v ▷ supplant
supple adj (-r, -st) (of a person) moving and bending easily and gracefully > **suppleness** n (pl -es)
supplement n (pl -s) thing added to complete something or make up for a lack ▶ v (-s, -ing, -ed) provide or be a supplement to (something) > **supplementary** adj
supplementary adj ▷ supplement
supplemented v ▷ supplement
supplementing v ▷ supplement
supplements n, v ▷ supplement
suppleness n ▷ supple
supplenesses n ▷ supple
suppler adj ▷ supple
supplest adj ▷ supple
supplicant n (pl -s) person who makes a humble request
supplicants n ▷ supplicant
supplication n (pl -s) humble request
supplications n ▷ supplication
supplied v ▷ supply
supplier n ▷ supply
suppliers n ▷ supply
supplies pl n food or equipment ▶ v ▷ supply
supply v (-lies, -lying, -lied) provide with something required ▶ n (pl -lies) supplying > **supplier** n (pl -s)
supplying v ▷ supply
support v (-s, -ing, -ed) bear the weight of ▶ n (pl -s) supporting > **supportive** adj
supported v ▷ support
supporter n (pl -s) person who supports a team, principle, etc.
supporters n ▷ supporter
supporting v ▷ support
supportive adj ▷ support
supports v, n ▷ support
suppose v (-ses, -sing, -sed) presume to be true
supposed adj presumed to be true without proof, doubtful ▶ v ▷ suppose > **supposedly** adv
supposedly adv ▷ supposed

supposes v ▷ suppose
supposing v ▷ suppose
supposition n (pl -s) supposing
suppositions n ▷ supposition
suppositories n ▷ suppository
suppository n (pl -ries) solid medication inserted into the rectum or vagina and left to melt
suppress v (-es, -ing, -ed) put an end to > **suppression** n (pl -s)
suppressed v ▷ suppress
suppresses v ▷ suppress
suppressing v ▷ suppress
suppression n ▷ suppress
suppressions n ▷ suppress
suppurate v (-tes, -ting, -ted) (of a wound etc.) produce pus
suppurated v ▷ suppurate
suppurates v ▷ suppurate
suppurating v ▷ suppurate
supremacies n ▷ supremacy
supremacy n (pl -cies) supreme power
supreme adj highest in authority, rank, or degree
supremely adv extremely
supremo n (pl -s) (Informal) person in overall authority
supremos n ▷ supremo
sups n, v ▷ sup

> **suq** n (**suqs**). A suq is an open-air marketplace in Arabic-speaking countries. This unusual word can be very useful. Usually, when you have a Q and a U, you will be looking to play words with QU in them. But look out for opportunities to play suq instead. Suq scores 12 points.

surcharge n (pl -s) additional charge
surcharges n ▷ surcharge
surd n (pl -s) (MATHS) number that cannot be expressed in whole numbers
surds n ▷ surd
sure adj (-r, -st) free from uncertainty or doubt ▶ adv, interj (Informal) certainly
surefooted adj unlikely to slip or stumble
surely adv it must be true that
surer adj ▷ sure
surest adj ▷ sure
sureties n ▷ surety
surety n (pl -ties) person who takes responsibility, or thing given as a guarantee, for the fulfilment of another's obligation
surf n (pl -s) foam caused by waves breaking on the shore ▶ v (-s, -ing, -ed) take part in surfing > **surfer** n (pl -s)

surface n (pl -s) outside or top of an object ▶ v (-ces, -cing, -ced) rise to the surface
  surfaced v ▷ surface
  surfaces n, v ▷ surface
  surfacing v ▷ surface
surfboard n (pl -s) long smooth board used in surfing
  surfboards n ▷ surfboard
  surfed v ▷ surf
surfeit n (pl -s) excessive amount
  surfeits n ▷ surfeit
  surfer n ▷ surf
  surfers n ▷ surf
surfing n (pl -s) sport of riding towards the shore on a surfboard on the crest of a wave ▶ v ▷ surf
  surfings n ▷ surfing
  surfs n, v ▷ surf
surge n (pl -s) sudden powerful increase ▶ v (-ges, -ging, -ged) increase suddenly
  surged v ▷ surge
surgeon n (pl -s) doctor who specializes in surgery
  surgeons n ▷ surgeon
  surgeries n ▷ surgery
surgery n (pl -ries) treatment in which the patient's body is cut open in order to treat the affected part > **surgical** adj > **surgically** adv
  surges n, v ▷ surge
  surgical adj ▷ surgery
  surgically adv ▷ surgery
  surging v ▷ surge
  surlier adj ▷ surly
  surliest adj ▷ surly
  surliness n ▷ surly
  surlinesses n ▷ surly
surly adj (-lier, -liest) ill-tempered and rude > **surliness** n (pl -es)
surmise v (-ises, -ising, -ised) ▶ n (pl -s) guess, conjecture
  surmised v ▷ surmise
  surmises n, v ▷ surmise
  surmising v ▷ surmise
surmount v (-s, -ing, -ed) overcome (a problem) > **surmountable** adj
  surmountable adj ▷ surmount
  surmounted v ▷ surmount
  surmounting v ▷ surmount
  surmounts v ▷ surmount
surname n (pl -s) family name
  surnames n ▷ surname
surpass v (-es, -ing, -ed) be greater than or superior to
  surpassed v ▷ surpass
  surpasses v ▷ surpass

  surpassing v ▷ surpass
surplice n (pl -s) loose white robe worn by clergymen and choristers
  surplices n ▷ surplice
surplus n (pl -es) amount left over in excess of what is required
  surpluses n ▷ surplus
surprise n (pl -ses) unexpected event ▶ v (-ses, -sing, -sed) cause to feel amazement or wonder
  surprised v ▷ surprise
  surprises n, v ▷ surprise
  surprising v ▷ surprise
surreal adj bizarre > **surrealist** n (pl -s) adj > **surrealistic** adj
surrealism n (pl -s) movement in art and literature involving the combination of incongruous images, as in a dream
  surrealisms n ▷ surrealism
  surrealist n, adj ▷ surreal
  surrealistic adj ▷ surreal
  surrealists n ▷ surreal
surrender v (-s, -ing, -ed) give oneself up ▶ n (pl -s) surrendering
  surrendered v ▷ surrender
  surrendering v ▷ surrender
  surrenders v, n ▷ surrender
surreptitious adj done secretly or stealthily > **surreptitiously** adv
  surreptitiously adv ▷ surreptitious
surrogate n (pl -s) substitute
  surrogates n ▷ surrogate
surround v (-s, -ing, -ed) be, come, or place all around (a person or thing) ▶ n (pl -s) border or edging
  surrounded v ▷ surround
  surrounding v ▷ surround
surroundings pl n area or environment around a person, place, or thing
  surrounds v, n ▷ surround
surveillance n (pl -s) close observation
  surveillances n ▷ surveillance
survey v (-s, -ing, -ed) view or consider in a general way ▶ n (pl -s) surveying > **surveyor** n (pl -s)
  surveyed v ▷ survey
  surveying v ▷ survey
  surveyor n ▷ survey
  surveyors n ▷ survey
  surveys v, n ▷ survey
survival n (pl -s) condition of having survived
  survivals n ▷ survival
survive v (-ves, -ing, -ved) continue to live or exist after (a difficult experience) > **survivor** n (pl -s)

survived v ▷ survive
survives v ▷ survive
surviving v ▷ survive
survivor n ▷ survive
survivors n ▷ survive
susceptibilities n ▷ susceptible
susceptibility n ▷ susceptible
susceptible adj liable to be influenced or
affected by > susceptibility n (pl -ties)
sushi [soo-shee] n (pl -s) Japanese dish of small
cakes of cold rice with a topping of raw fish
sushis n ▷ sushi
suspect v (-s, -ing, -ed) believe (someone) to be
guilty without having any proof ▶ adj not to
be trusted ▶ n (pl -s) person who is suspected
suspected v ▷ suspect
suspecting v ▷ suspect
suspects v, n ▷ suspect
suspend v (-s, -ing, -ed) hang from a high place
suspended v ▷ suspend
suspenders pl n straps for holding up
stockings
suspending v ▷ suspend
suspends v ▷ suspend
suspense n (pl -s) state of uncertainty while
awaiting news, an event, etc.
suspenses n ▷ suspense
suspension n (pl -s) suspending or being
suspended
suspensions n ▷ suspension
suspicion n (pl -s) feeling of not trusting a
person or thing
suspicions n ▷ suspicion
suspicious adj feeling or causing suspicion
> suspiciously adv
suspiciously adv ▷ suspicious
sustain v (-s, -ing, -ed) maintain or prolong
sustained v ▷ sustain
sustaining v ▷ sustain
sustains v ▷ sustain
sustenance n (pl -s) food
sustenances n ▷ sustenance
suture [soo-cher] n (pl -s) stitch joining the
edges of a wound
sutures n ▷ suture
suzerain n (pl -s) state or sovereign with
limited authority over another self-
governing state > suzerainty n (pl -ties)
suzerains n ▷ suzerain
suzerainties n ▷ suzerain
suzerainty n ▷ suzerain
svelte adj (-r, -st) attractively or gracefully slim
svelter adj ▷ svelte
sveltest adj ▷ svelte
swab n (pl -s) small piece of cotton wool used

to apply medication, clean a wound, etc.
▶ v (-s, -bbing, -bbed) clean (a wound) with
a swab
swabbed v ▷ swab
swabbing v ▷ swab
swabs n, v ▷ swab
swaddle v (-les, -ling, -led) wrap (a baby) in
swaddling clothes
swaddled v ▷ swaddle
swaddles v ▷ swaddle
swaddling v ▷ swaddle
swag n (pl -s) (Slang) stolen property
swagger v (-s, -ing, -ed) walk or behave
arrogantly ▶ n (pl -s) arrogant walk or manner
swaggered v ▷ swagger
swaggering v ▷ swagger
swaggers v, n ▷ swagger
swagman n (pl -men) (AUST HIST) tramp who
carries his belongings in a bundle on his back
swagmen n ▷ swagman
swags n ▷ swag
swain n (pl -s) (Poetic) suitor
swains n ▷ swain
swallow¹ v (-s, -ing, -ed) cause to pass down
one's throat ▶ n (pl -s) swallowing
swallow² n (pl -s) small migratory bird with
long pointed wings and a forked tail
swallowed v ▷ swallow¹
swallowing v ▷ swallow¹
swallows v ▷ swallow¹ ▶ n ▷ swallow¹, ²
swam v ▷ swim
swamp n (pl -s) watery area of land, bog ▶ v (-s,
-ing, -ed) cause (a boat) to fill with water and
sink > swampy adj (-pier, -piest)
swamped v ▷ swamp
swampier adj ▷ swamp
swampiest adj ▷ swamp
swamping v ▷ swamp
swamps n, v ▷ swamp
swampy adj ▷ swamp
swan n (pl -s) large usu. white water bird with
a long graceful neck ▶ v (-s, -nning, -nned)
(Informal) wander about idly
swank (Slang) v (-s, -ing, -ed) show off or boast
▶ n (pl -s) showing off or boasting
swanked v ▷ swank
swankier adj ▷ swanky
swankiest adj ▷ swanky
swanking v ▷ swank
swanks v, n ▷ swank
swanky adj (-kier, -kiest) (Slang) expensive and
showy, stylish
swanned n ▷ swan
swanning n ▷ swan
swans n, v ▷ swan

swap v (**-s, -pping, -pped**) exchange (something) for something else ▶ n (pl **-s**) exchange
swapped v ▷ swap
swapping v ▷ swap
swaps v, n ▷ swap
sward n (pl **-s**) stretch of short grass
swards n ▷ sward
swarm[1] n (pl **-s**) large group of bees or other insects ▶ v (**-s, -ing, -ed**) move in a swarm
swarm[2] v (**-s, -ing, -ed**) (foll. by **up**) climb (a ladder or rope) by gripping with the hands and feet
swarmed v ▷ swarm[1, 2]
swarming v ▷ swarm[1, 2]
swarms v ▷ swarm[1, 2] ▶ n ▷ swarm[1]
swarthier adj ▷ swarthy
swarthiest adj ▷ swarthy
swarthy adj (**-thier, -thiest**) dark-complexioned
swashbuckler n ▷ swashbuckling
swashbucklers n ▷ swashbuckling
swashbuckling adj having the exciting behaviour of pirates, esp. those depicted in films > **swashbuckler** n (pl **-s**)
swastika n (pl **-s**) symbol in the shape of a cross with the arms bent at right angles, used as the emblem of Nazi Germany
swastikas n ▷ swastika
swat v (**-s, -tting, -tted**) hit sharply ▶ n (pl **-s**) sharp blow
swatch n (pl **-es**) sample of cloth
swatches n ▷ swatch
swath [swawth] n (pl **-s**) ▷ swathe
swathe v (**-thes, -thing, -thed**) wrap in bandages or layers of cloth ▶ n (pl **-s**) long strip of cloth wrapped around something (also **swath**)
swathed v ▷ swathe
swathes v, n ▷ swathe
swathing v ▷ swathe
swaths n ▷ swath
swats v, n ▷ swat
swatted v ▷ swat
swatting v ▷ swat
sway v (**-s, -ing, -ed**) swing to and fro or from side to side ▶ n (pl **-s**) power or influence
swayed v ▷ sway
swaying v ▷ sway
sways v, n ▷ sway
swear v (**-s, -ing, swore, sworn**) use obscene or blasphemous language
swearing v ▷ swear
swears v ▷ swear
swearword n (pl **-s**) word considered obscene

or blasphemous
swearwords n ▷ swearword
sweat n (pl **-s**) salty liquid given off through the pores of the skin ▶ v (**-s, -ing, -ed**) have sweat coming through the pores > **sweaty** adj (**-tier, -tiest**)
sweatband n (pl **-s**) strip of cloth tied around the forehead or wrist to absorb sweat
sweatbands n ▷ sweatband
sweated v ▷ sweat
sweater n (pl **-s**) (woollen) garment for the upper part of the body
sweaters n ▷ sweater
sweatier adj ▷ sweat
sweatiest adj ▷ sweat
sweating v ▷ sweat
sweats n, v ▷ sweat
sweatshirt n (pl **-s**) long-sleeved cotton jersey
sweatshirts n ▷ sweatshirt
sweatshop n (pl **-s**) place where employees work long hours in poor conditions for low pay
sweatshops n ▷ sweatshop
sweaty adj ▷ sweat
swede n (pl **-des**) kind of turnip
swedes n ▷ swede
sweep v (**-s, -ing, swept**) remove dirt from (a floor) with a broom ▶ n (pl **-s**) sweeping
sweeping adj wide-ranging ▶ v ▷ sweep
sweeps v, n ▷ sweep
sweepstake n (pl **-s**) lottery in which the stakes of the participants make up the prize
sweepstakes n ▷ sweepstake
sweet adj (**-er, -est**) tasting of or like sugar ▶ n (pl **-s**) shaped piece of food consisting mainly of sugar > **sweetly** adv > **sweetness** n (pl **-es**) > **sweeten** v (**-s, -ing, -ed**)
sweetbread n (pl **-s**) animal's pancreas used as food
sweetbreads n ▷ sweetbread
sweetened v ▷ sweet
sweetener n (pl **-s**) sweetening agent that does not contain sugar
sweeteners n ▷ sweetener
sweetening v ▷ sweet
sweetens v ▷ sweet
sweetheart n (pl **-s**) lover
sweethearts n ▷ sweetheart
sweetly adv ▷ sweet
sweetmeat n (pl **-s**) (Old-fashioned) sweet delicacy such as a small cake
sweetmeats n ▷ sweetmeat
sweetness n ▷ sweet
sweetnesses n ▷ sweet
sweets n ▷ sweet

swell v (**-lls**, **-lling**, **-lled**, **swollen** or **swelled**) expand or increase ▶ n (pl **-s**) swelling or being swollen ▶ adj (**-er**, **-est**) (US) (Slang) excellent or fine
swelled v ▷ swell
sweller adj ▷ swell
swellest adj ▷ swell
swelling n (pl **-s**) enlargement of part of the body, caused by injury or infection ▶ v ▷ swell
swells v, n ▷ swell
swelter v (**-s**, **-ing**, **-ed**) feel uncomfortably hot
sweltered v ▷ swelter
sweltering adj uncomfortably hot ▶ v ▷ swelter
swelters v ▷ swelter
swept v ▷ sweep
swerve v (**-ves**, **-ving**, **-ved**) turn aside from a course sharply or suddenly ▶ n (pl **-s**) swerving
swerved v ▷ swerve
swerves v, n ▷ swerve
swerving v ▷ swerve
swift adj (**-er**, **-est**) moving or able to move quickly ▶ n (pl **-s**) fast-flying bird with pointed wings > **swiftly** adv > **swiftness** n (pl **-es**)
swifter adj ▷ swift
swiftest adj ▷ swift
swiftly adv ▷ swift
swiftness n ▷ swift
swiftnesses n ▷ swift
swifts n ▷ swift
swig n (pl **-s**) large mouthful of drink ▶ v (**-s**, **-gging**, **-gged**) drink in large mouthfuls
swigged v ▷ swig
swigging v ▷ swig
swigs v, n ▷ swig
swill v (**-s**, **-ing**, **-ed**) drink greedily ▶ n (pl **-s**) sloppy mixture containing waste food, fed to pigs
swilled v ▷ swill
swilling v ▷ swill
swills v, n ▷ swill
swim v (**-s**, **-mming**, **swam**, **swum**) move along in water by movements of the limbs ▶ n (pl **-s**) act or period of swimming > **swimmer** n (pl **-s**)
swimmer n ▷ swim
swimmers n ▷ swim
swimming v ▷ swim
swimmingly adv successfully and effortlessly
swims v, n ▷ swim
swindle v (**-les**, **-ling**, **-led**) cheat (someone) out of money ▶ n (pl **-s**) instance of swindling > **swindler** n (pl **-s**)
swindled v ▷ swindle
swindler n ▷ swindle
swindlers n ▷ swindle

swindles v, n ▷ swindle
swindling v ▷ swindle
swine n (pl **-s**) contemptible person
swines n ▷ swine
swing v (**-s**, **-ing**, **swung**) move to and fro, sway ▶ n (pl **-s**) swinging
swingeing [swin-jing] adj punishing, severe
swinging v, n ▷ swing
swings v, n ▷ swing
swipe v (**-ipes**, **-iping**, **-iped**) strike (at) with a sweeping blow ▶ n (pl **-s**) hard blow
swiped v ▷ swipe
swipes v, n ▷ swipe
swiping v ▷ swipe
swirl v (**-s**, **-ing**, **-ed**) turn with a whirling motion ▶ n (pl **-s**) whirling motion
swirled v ▷ swirl
swirling v ▷ swirl
swirls v, n ▷ swirl
swish v (**-es**, **-ing**, **-ed**) move with a whistling or hissing sound ▶ n (pl **-es**) whistling or hissing sound ▶ adj (**-er**, **-est**) (Informal) fashionable, smart
swished v ▷ swish
swisher adj ▷ swish
swishes v, n ▷ swish
swishest adj ▷ swish
swishing v ▷ swish
switch n (pl **-es**) device for opening and closing an electric circuit ▶ v (**-ches**, **-ching**, **-ched**) change abruptly
switchback n (pl **-s**) road or railway with many sharp hills or bends
switchbacks n ▷ switchback
switchboard n (pl **-s**) installation in a telephone exchange or office where telephone calls are connected
switchboards n ▷ switchboard
switched v ▷ switch
switches n, v ▷ switch
switching v ▷ switch
swivel v (**-s**, **-elling**, **-elled**) turn on a central point ▶ n (pl **-s**) coupling device that allows an attached object to turn freely
swivelled v ▷ swivel
swivelling v ▷ swivel
swivels v, n ▷ swivel
swollen v ▷ swell
swoon v (**-s**, **-ing**, **-ed**) ▶ n (pl **-s**) faint
swooned v ▷ swoon
swooning v ▷ swoon
swoons v, n ▷ swoon
swoop v (**-s**, **-ing**, **-ed**) sweep down or pounce on suddenly ▶ n (pl **-s**) swooping
swooped v ▷ swoop

swooping v ▷ swoop

swoops v, n ▷ swoop

swop v (-s, -pping, -pped) ► n (pl -s) ▷ swap

swopped v ▷ swop

swopping v ▷ swop

swops v, n ▷ swop

sword n (pl -s) weapon with a long sharp blade

swordfish n (pl -es) large fish with a very long upper jaw

swordfishes n ▷ swordfish

swords n ▷ sword

swordsman n (pl -men) person skilled in the use of a sword

swordsmen n ▷ swordsman

swore v ▷ swear

sworn v ▷ swear ► adj bound by or as if by an oath

swot (Informal) v (-s, -tting, -tted) study hard ► n (pl -s) person who studies hard

swots v, n ▷ swot

swotted v ▷ swot

swotting v ▷ swot

swum v ▷ swim

swung v ▷ swing

> **swy** n (swys). Swy is an Australian gambling game. This is a very unusual word which doesn't contain a vowel, so it can be useful in helping you to clear a difficult rack. Swy scores 9 points.

sybarite [sib-bar-ite] n (pl -s) lover of luxury > sybaritic adj

sybarites n ▷ sybarite

sybaritic adj ▷ sybarite

sycamore n (pl -s) tree with five-pointed leaves and two-winged fruits

sycamores n ▷ sycamore

sycophancies n ▷ sycophant

sycophancy n ▷ sycophant

sycophant n (pl -s) person who uses flattery to win favour from people with power or influence > sycophantic adj > sycophancy n (pl -cies)

sycophantic adj ▷ sycophant

sycophants n ▷ sycophant

syllabi n ▷ syllabus

syllabic adj ▷ syllable

syllable n (pl -s) part of a word pronounced as a unit > syllabic adj

syllables n ▷ syllable

syllabub n (pl -s) dessert of beaten cream, sugar, and wine

syllabubs n ▷ syllabub

syllabus n (pl -buses, -bi) list of subjects for a course of study

syllabuses n ▷ syllabus

syllogism n (pl -s) form of logical reasoning consisting of two premises and a conclusion

syllogisms n ▷ syllogism

sylph n (pl -s) slender graceful girl or woman > sylphlike adj

sylphlike adj ▷ sylph

sylphs n ▷ sylph

sylvan adj (Lit) relating to woods and trees

symbioses n ▷ symbiosis

symbiosis n (pl -oses) close association of two species living together to their mutual benefit > symbiotic adj

symbiotic adj ▷ symbiosis

symbol n (pl -s) sign or thing that stands for something else > symbolic adj > symbolically adv

symbolic adj ▷ symbol

symbolically adv ▷ symbol

symbolism n (pl -s) representation of something by symbols > symbolist n (pl -s) adj

symbolisms n ▷ symbolism

symbolist n ▷ symbolism

symbolists n ▷ symbolism

symbolize v (-izes, -izing, -ized) be a symbol of

symbolized v ▷ symbolize

symbolizes v ▷ symbolize

symbolizing v ▷ symbolize

symbols n ▷ symbol

symmetrical adj ▷ symmetry

symmetrically adv ▷ symmetry

symmetries n ▷ symmetry

symmetry n (pl -tries) state of having two halves that are mirror images of each other > symmetrical adj > symmetrically adv

sympathetic adj feeling or showing sympathy > sympathetically adv

sympathetically adv ▷ sympathetic

sympathies n ▷ sympathy

sympathize v (-zes, -izing, -ized) feel or express sympathy > sympathizer n (pl -s)

sympathized v ▷ sympathize

sympathizer n ▷ sympathize

sympathizers n ▷ sympathize

sympathizes v ▷ sympathize

sympathizing v ▷ sympathize

sympathy n (pl -thies) compassion for someone's pain or distress

symphonic adj ▷ symphony

symphonies n ▷ symphony

symphony n (pl -nies) composition for orchestra, with several movements > symphonic adj

symposia n ▷ symposium

symposium n (pl -iums, -sia) conference for

discussion of a particular topic

symposiums n ▷ symposium

symptom n (pl -s) sign indicating the presence of an illness > **symptomatic** adj

symptomatic adj ▷ symptom

symptoms n ▷ symptom

> **syn** adv. (**Syn**) is a Scots word for *since*. This is a good word to remember for when you have a shortage of vowels. Syn scores 6 points.

synagogue n (pl -s) Jewish place of worship and religious instruction

synagogues n ▷ synagogue

sync, synch (*Informal*) n (pl -s) synchronization ▶ v (-s, -ing, -ed) synchronize

synced v ▷ sync

synched v ▷ sync

synching v ▷ sync

synchromesh adj (of a gearbox) having a device that synchronizes the speeds of gears before they engage

synchronization n ▷ synchronize

synchronizations n ▷ synchronize

synchronize v (-izes, -izing, -ized) (of two or more people) perform (an action) at the same time > **synchronization** n (pl -s)

synchronized v ▷ synchronize

synchronizes v ▷ synchronize

synchronizing v ▷ synchronize

synchronous adj happening or existing at the same time

synchs n, v ▷ sync

syncing v ▷ sync

syncopate v (-tes, -ting, -ted) (MUSIC) stress the weak beats in (a rhythm) instead of the strong ones > **syncopation** n (pl -s)

syncopated v ▷ syncopate

syncopates v ▷ syncopate

syncopating v ▷ syncopate

syncopation n ▷ syncopate

syncopations n ▷ syncopate

syncope [sing-kop-ee] n (pl -s) (MED) a faint

syncopes n ▷ syncope

syncs n, v ▷ sync

syndicate n (pl -s) group of people or firms undertaking a joint business project ▶ v (-tes, -ting, -ted) publish (material) in several newspapers > **syndication** n (pl -s)

syndicated v ▷ syndicate

syndicates n, v ▷ syndicate

syndicating v ▷ syndicate

syndication n ▷ syndicate

syndications n ▷ syndicate

syndrome n (pl -s) combination of symptoms indicating a particular disease

syndromes n ▷ syndrome

synergies n ▷ synergy

synergy n (pl -gies) potential ability for people or groups to be more successful working together than on their own

synod n (pl -s) church council

synods n ▷ synod

synonym n (pl -s) word with the same meaning as another > **synonymous** adj

synonymous adj ▷ synonym

synonyms n ▷ synonym

synopses n ▷ synopsis

synopsis n (pl -ses) summary or outline

syntactic adj ▷ syntax

syntax n (pl -es) (GRAMMAR) way in which words are arranged to form phrases and sentences > **syntactic** adj

syntaxes n ▷ syntax

syntheses n ▷ synthesis

synthesis n (pl -ses) combination of objects or ideas into a whole

synthesize v (-izes, -izing, -ized) produce by synthesis

synthesized v ▷ synthesize

synthesizer n (pl -s) electronic musical instrument producing a range of sounds

synthesizers n ▷ synthesizer

synthesizes v ▷ synthesize

synthesizing v ▷ synthesize

synthetic adj (of a substance) made artificially > **synthetically** adv

synthetically adv ▷ synthetic

syphilis n (pl -es) serious sexually transmitted disease > **syphilitic** adj

syphilises n ▷ syphilis

syphilitic adj ▷ syphilis

syphon n (pl -s) ▶ v (-s, -ing, -ed) ▷ siphon

syphoned v ▷ syphon

syphoning v ▷ syphon

syphons n, v ▷ syphon

syringe n (pl -s) device for withdrawing or injecting fluids, consisting of a hollow cylinder, a piston, and a hollow needle ▶ v (-ges, -ging, -ged) wash out or inject with a syringe

syringed v ▷ syringe

syringes n, v ▷ syringe

syringing v ▷ syringe

syrup n (pl -s) solution of sugar in water > **syrupy** adj (-pier, -piest)

syrupier adj ▷ syrup

syrupiest adj ▷ syrup

syrups n ▷ syrup

syrupy adj ▷ syrup

system n (pl -s) method or set of methods

> **systematic** *adj* > **systematically** *adv*
systematic *adj* ▷ **system**
systematically *adv* ▷ **system**
systematization *n* ▷ **systematize**
systematizations *n* ▷ **systematize**
systematize *v* (**-izes, -izing, -ized**) organize using a system
systematization *n* (*pl* **-s**) systemizing
systematized *v* ▷ **systematize**

systematizes *v* ▷ **systematize**
systematizing *v* ▷ **systematize**
systemic *adj* affecting the entire animal or body
systems *n* ▷ **system**
systole [**siss**-tol-ee] *n* (*pl* **-s**) regular contraction of the heart as it pumps blood > **systolic** *adj*
systoles *n* ▷ **systole**
systolic *adj* ▷ **systole**

Tt

T is one of the most common consonants in Scrabble. There are only four two-letter words that begin with T, but they are easy to remember as there is one for every vowel except U. Like S, T begins a number of three-letter words that don't use vowels, which are well worth remembering. These are: **thy** (6 points), **try** (6), **tsk** (7), **twp** (8) and **tyg** (7). There are also some useful three-letter words using X: **tax, tix** and **tux** (10 each). If you have an X during a game, remember words like **text** (11), **texts** (12), **textile** (14), **textual** (14) and **texture** (14). The last three of these have seven letters, and so will earn you 50-point bonuses if you use all your tiles to form them.

ta *interj* (*Informal*) thank you

tab *n* (*pl* -s) small flap or projecting label

tabard *n* (*pl* -s) short sleeveless tunic decorated with a coat of arms, worn in medieval times

  tabards *n* ▷ tabard

  tabbies *n* ▷ tabby

tabby *n* (*pl* -bbies) ▶ *adj* (cat) with dark stripes on a lighter background

tabernacle *n* (*pl* -s) portable shrine of the Israelites

  tabernacles *n* ▷ tabernacle

tabla *n* (*pl* -bla, -blas) one of a pair of Indian drums played with the hands

  tablas *n* ▷ tabla

table *n* (*pl* -s) piece of furniture with a flat top supported by legs ▶ *v* (-les, -ling, -led) submit (a motion) for discussion by a meeting

  tabled *v* ▷ table

tableland *n* (*pl* -s) high plateau

  tablelands *n* ▷ tableland

tablespoon *n* (*pl* -s) large spoon for serving food

  tablespoons *n* ▷ tablespoon

tableau [tab-loh] *n* (*pl* -leaux) silent motionless group arranged to represent some scene

  tableaux *n* ▷ tableau

  tabled *v* ▷ table

  tables *n, v* ▷ table

tablet *n* (*pl* -s) pill of compressed medicinal substance

  tablets *n* ▷ tablet

  tabling *v* ▷ table

tabloid *n* (*pl* -s) small-sized newspaper with many photographs and a concise, usu. sensational style

  tabloids *n* ▷ tabloid

taboo *n* (*pl* -s) prohibition resulting from religious or social conventions ▶ *adj* forbidden by a taboo

  taboos *n* ▷ taboo

  tabs *n* ▷ tab

tabular *adj* arranged in a table

tabulate *v* (-tes, -ting, -ted) arrange (information) in a table > **tabulation** *n* (*pl* -s)

  tabulated *v* ▷ tabulate

  tabulates *v* ▷ tabulate

  tabulating *v* ▷ tabulate

  tabulation *n* ▷ tabulate

  tabulations *n* ▷ tabulate

tachograph *n* (*pl* -s) device for recording the speed and distance travelled by a motor vehicle

  tachographs *n* ▷ tachograph

tachometer *n* (*pl* -s) device for measuring speed, esp. that of a revolving shaft

  tachometers *n* ▷ tachometer

tacit [tass-it] *adj* implied but not spoken > **tacitly** *adv*

  tacitly *adv* ▷ tacit

taciturn [tass-it-turn] *adj* habitually uncommunicative > **taciturnity** *n* (*pl* -ties)

  taciturnities *n* ▷ taciturn

  taciturnity *n* ▷ taciturn

tack[1] *n* (*pl* -s) short nail with a large head ▶ *v* (-s, -ing, -ed) fasten with tacks

tack[2] *n* (*pl* -s) course of a ship sailing obliquely into the wind ▶ *v* (-s, -ing, -ed) sail into the wind on a zigzag course

tack[3] *n* (*pl* -s) riding harness for horses

  tacked *v* ▷ tack[1, 2]

  tackier *adj* ▷ tacky[1, 2]

tackies, takkies pl n (sing **tacky**) (S AFR) (Informal) tennis shoes or plimsolls
  tackiest adj ▷ **tacky**[1, 2]
  tacking v ▷ **tack**[1, 2]

tackle v (-les, -ling, -led) deal with (a task) (SPORT) ▶ n (pl -les) (SPORT) act of tackling an opposing player
  tackled v ▷ **tackle**
  tackles v, n ▷ **tackle**
  tackling v ▷ **tackle**
  tacks n ▷ **tack**[1, 2, 3] ▶ v ▷ **tack**[1, 2]

tacky[1] adj (-ckier, -ckiest) slightly sticky

tacky[2] adj (-ckier, -ckiest) (Informal) vulgar and tasteless
  tacky[3] adj ▷ **tackies**

taco [tah-koh] n (pl -s) (MEXICAN COOKERY) tortilla fried until crisp, served with a filling
  tacos n ▷ **taco**

tact n (pl -s) skill in avoiding giving offence > **tactful** adj > **tactfully** adv > **tactless** adj > **tactlessly** adv
  tactful adj ▷ **tact**
  tactfully adv ▷ **tact**

tactic n (pl -s) method or plan to achieve an end > **tactical** adj > **tactician** n (pl -s)
  tactical adj ▷ **tactic**
  tactician n ▷ **tactic**
  tacticians n ▷ **tactic**

tactics pl n art of directing military forces in battle ▶ n ▷ **tactic**

tactile adj of or having the sense of touch
  tactless adj ▷ **tact**
  tactlessly adv ▷ **tact**
  tacts n ▷ **tact**

tadpole n (pl -s) limbless tailed larva of a frog or toad
  tadpoles n ▷ **tadpole**

taffeta n (pl -s) shiny silk or rayon fabric
  taffetas n ▷ **taffeta**

tag[1] n (pl -s) label bearing information ▶ v (-s, -gging, -gged) attach a tag to

tag[2] n (pl -s) children's game where the person being chased becomes the chaser upon being touched ▶ v (-s, -gging, -gged) touch and catch in this game
  tagged v ▷ **tag**[1, 2]
  tagging v ▷ **tag**[1, 2]

tagliatelle n pasta in long narrow strips
  tags n, v ▷ **tag**[1, 2]

tail n (pl -s) rear part of an animal's body, usu. forming a flexible appendage ▶ adj at the rear ▶ v (-s, -ing, -ed) (Informal) follow (someone) secretly > **tailless** adj

tailback n (pl -s) (BRIT) queue of traffic stretching back from an obstruction

tailbacks n ▷ **tailback**

tailboard n (pl -s) removable or hinged rear board on a truck etc.
  tailboards n ▷ **tailboard**
  tailed v ▷ **tail**
  tailing v ▷ **tail**
  tailless adj ▷ **tail**

tailor n (pl -s) person who makes men's clothes ▶ v (-s, -ing, -ed) adapt to suit a purpose
  tailored v ▷ **tailor**
  tailoring v ▷ **tailor**
  tailors n, v ▷ **tailor**

tailplane n (pl -s) small stabilizing wing at the rear of an aircraft
  tailplanes n ▷ **tailplane**

tails adv with the side of a coin uppermost that does not have a portrait of a head on it ▶ pl n (Informal) tail coat ▶ n, v ▷ **tail**

tailspin n (pl -s) uncontrolled spinning dive of an aircraft
  tailspins n ▷ **tailspin**

tailwind n (pl -s) wind coming from the rear
  tailwinds n ▷ **tailwind**

taint v (-s, -ing, -ed) spoil with a small amount of decay, contamination, or other bad quality ▶ n (pl -s) something that taints
  tainted v ▷ **taint**
  tainting v ▷ **taint**
  taints v, n ▷ **taint**

taipan n (pl -s) large poisonous Australian snake
  taipans n ▷ **taipan**

> **taj** n (**tajes**). A taj is a tall conical cap worn by some Muslims. This unusual word can be helpful if you are struggling to use J because there aren't any good opportunities for longer words on the board. Taj scores 10 points.

take v (**takes, taking, took, taken**) remove from a place ▶ n (pl -s) one of a series of recordings from which the best will be used

takeaway n (pl -s) shop or restaurant selling meals for eating elsewhere
  takeaways n ▷ **takeaway**
  taken v ▷ **take**

takeoff n (pl -s) (of an aircraft) act of leaving the ground
  takeoffs n ▷ **takeoff**

takeover n (pl -s) act of taking control of a company by buying a large number of its shares
  takeovers n ▷ **takeover**
  takes v, n ▷ **take**

taking adj charming ▶ v ▷ **take**

takings pl n money received by a shop
  takkies pl n ▷ **tackies**
talc n (pl -s) talcum powder
  talcs n ▷ **talc**
tale n (pl -s) story
talent n (pl -s) natural ability > **talented** adj
  talented adj ▷ **talent**
  talents n ▷ **talent**
  tales n ▷ **tale**
talisman n (pl -s) object believed to have magic power > **talismanic** adj
  talismanic adj ▷ **talisman**
  talismans n ▷ **talisman**
talk v (-s, -ing, -ed) express ideas or feelings by means of speech ▶ n (pl -s) speech or lecture
talkative adj fond of talking
talkback n (pl -s) (NZ) broadcast in which telephone comments or questions from the public are transmitted live
  talkbacks n ▷ **talkback**
  talked v ▷ **talk**
talker n (pl -s) person who talks
  talkers n ▷ **talker**
  talking v ▷ **talk**
  talks v, n ▷ **talk**
tall (-er, -est) adj higher than average
tallboy n (pl -s) high chest of drawers
  tallboys n ▷ **tallboy**
  taller adj ▷ **tall**
  tallest adj ▷ **tall**
  tallied v ▷ **tally**
  tallies v ▷ **tally**
tallow n (pl -s) hard animal fat used to make candles
  tallows n ▷ **tallow**
tally v (-llies, -llying, -llied) (of two things) correspond ▶ n (pl -lies) record of a debt or score
  tallying v ▷ **tally**
talon n (pl -s) bird's hooked claw
  talons n ▷ **talon**
tamarind n (pl -s) tropical tree
  tamarinds n ▷ **tamarind**
tamarisk n (pl -s) evergreen shrub with slender branches and feathery flower clusters
  tamarisks n ▷ **tamarisk**
tambourine n (pl -s) percussion instrument like a small drum with jingling metal discs attached
  tambourines n ▷ **tambourine**
tame adj (-r, -est) (of animals) brought under human control ▶ v (-mes, -ming, -med) make tame > **tamely** adv
  tamed v ▷ **tame**
  tamely adv ▷ **tame**

tamer n (pl -s) person who tames wild animals
  ▶ adj ▷ **tame**
  tamers n ▷ **tamer**
  tames v ▷ **tame**
  tamest adj ▷ **tame**
  taming v ▷ **tame**
tamp v (-s, -ing, -ed) pack down by repeated taps
  tamped v ▷ **tamp**
tamper v (-s, -ing, -ed) (foll. by with) interfere
  tampered v ▷ **tamper**
  tampering v ▷ **tamper**
  tampers v ▷ **tamper**
  tamping v ▷ **tamp**
tampon n (pl -s) absorbent plug of cotton wool inserted into the vagina during menstruation
  tampons n ▷ **tampon**
  tamps v ▷ **tamp**
tan n (pl -s) brown coloration of the skin from exposure to sunlight ▶ v (-s, -nning, -nned) (of skin) go brown from exposure to sunlight
  ▶ adj (-ner, -nest) yellowish-brown
tandem n (pl -s) bicycle for two riders, one behind the other
  tandems n ▷ **tandem**
tandoori adj (of food) cooked in an Indian clay oven
tang n (pl -s) strong taste or smell > **tangy** adj (-gier, -giest)
tangent n (pl -s) line that touches a curve without intersecting it
tangential adj of superficial relevance only > **tangentially** adv
  tangentially adv ▷ **tangential**
  tangents n ▷ **tangent**
tangerine n (pl -s) small orange-like fruit of an Asian citrus tree
  tangerines n ▷ **tangerine**
tangible adj able to be touched > **tangibly** adv
  tangibly adv ▷ **tangible**
  tangier adj ▷ **tang**
  tangiest adj ▷ **tang**
tangle n (pl -les) confused mass or situation ▶ v (-les, -ling, -led) twist together in a tangle
  tangled v ▷ **tangle**
  tangles n, v ▷ **tangle**
  tangling v ▷ **tangle**
tango n (pl -gos) S American dance ▶ v (-goes, -going, -goed) dance a tango
  tangoed v ▷ **tango**
  tangoes v ▷ **tango**
  tangoing v ▷ **tango**
  tangos v ▷ **tango**
  tangs n ▷ **tang**

tangy adj ▷ tang

taniwha [tun-ee-fah] n (pl -s) (NZ) mythical Maori monster that lives in water

taniwhas n ▷ taniwha

tank n (pl -s) container for liquids or gases

tankard n (pl -s) large beer-mug, often with a hinged lid

tankards n ▷ tankard

tanker n (pl -s) ship or truck for carrying liquid in bulk

tankers n ▷ tanker

tanks n ▷ tank

tanned v ▷ tan

tanner adj ▷ tan

tanneries n ▷ tannery

tannery n (pl -ries) place where hides are tanned

tannest adj ▷ tan

tannin n (pl -s) vegetable substance used in tanning

tanning v ▷ tan

tannins n ▷ tannin

tans n, v ▷ tan

tansies n ▷ tansy

tansy n (pl -sies) yellow-flowered plant

tantalize v (-zes, -zing, -zed) torment by showing but withholding something desired > **tantalizing** adj > **tantalizingly** adv

tantalized v ▷ tantalize

tantalizes v ▷ tantalize

tantalizing v, adj ▷ tantalize

tantalizingly adv ▷ tantalize

tantalum n (pl -s) (CHEM) hard greyish-white metallic element

tantalums n ▷ tantalum

tantamount adj equivalent in effect to

tantrum n (pl -s) childish outburst of temper

tantrums n ▷ tantrum

tap[1] v (taps, tapping, -pped) knock lightly and usu. repeatedly ▶ n (pl -s) light knock

tap[2] n (pl -s) valve to control the flow of liquid from a pipe or cask ▶ v (taps, tapping, tapped) listen in on (a telephone call) secretly by making an illegal connection

tape n (pl -s) narrow long strip of material ▶ v (tapes, taping, taped) record on magnetic tape

taped v ▷ tape

taper v (-s, -ing, -ed) become narrower towards one end ▶ n (pl -s) long thin candle

tapered v ▷ taper

tapering v ▷ taper

tapers v, n ▷ taper

tapes n, v ▷ tape

tapestries n ▷ tapestry

tapestry n (pl -tries) fabric decorated with coloured woven designs

tapeworm n (pl -s) long flat parasitic worm living in the intestines of vertebrates

tapeworms n ▷ tapeworm

tapioca n (pl -s) beadlike starch made from cassava root, used in puddings

tapiocas n ▷ tapioca

taping v ▷ tape

tapir [tape-er] n (pl -s) piglike mammal of tropical America and SE Asia, with a long snout

tapirs n ▷ tapir

tapped v ▷ tap[1, 2]

tappet n (pl -s) short steel rod in an engine, transferring motion from one part to another

tappets n ▷ tappet

tapping v ▷ tap[1, 2]

taproot n (pl -s) main root of a plant, growing straight down

taproots n ▷ taproot

taps n, v ▷ tap[1, 2]

tar n (pl -rs) thick black liquid distilled from coal etc. ▶ v (-s, -rring, -rred) coat with tar

taramasalata n (pl -s) creamy pink pâté made from fish roe

taramasalatas n ▷ taramasalata

tarantella n (pl -s) lively Italian dance

tarantellas n ▷ tarantella

tarantula n (pl -s) large hairy spider with a poisonous bite

tarantulas n ▷ tarantula

tardier adj ▷ tardy

tardiest adj ▷ tardy

tardily adv ▷ tardy

tardiness n ▷ tardy

tardinesses n ▷ tardy

tardy adj (-dier, -diest) slow or late > **tardily** adv > **tardiness** n (pl -es)

tare n (pl -s) type of vetch plant

tares n ▷ tare

target n (pl -s) object or person a missile is aimed at ▶ v (-gets, -geting, -geted) aim or direct

targeted v ▷ target

targeting v ▷ target

targets n, v ▷ target

tariff n (pl -s) tax levied on imports

tariffs n ▷ tariff

tarn n (pl -s) small mountain lake

tarnish v (-shes, -shing, -shed) make or become stained or less bright ▶ n (pl -es) discoloration or blemish

tarnished v ▷ tarnish

tarnishes v, n ▷ tarnish

tarnishing v ▷ tarnish

tarns n ▷ tarn

tarot [tarr-oh] n (pl -s) special pack of cards used mainly in fortune-telling

tarots n ▷ tarot

tarpaulin n (pl -s) (sheet of) heavy waterproof fabric

tarpaulins n ▷ tarpaulin

tarragon n (pl -s) aromatic herb

tarragons n ▷ tarragon

tarred v ▷ tar

tarried v ▷ tarry

tarries v ▷ tarry

tarring v ▷ tar

tarry v (tarries, tarrying, tarried) (Old-fashioned) linger or delay

tarrying v ▷ tarry

tars n, v ▷ tar

tarsi n ▷ tarsus

tarsus n (pl -si) bones of the heel and ankle collectively

tart¹ n (pl -s) pie or flan with a sweet filling

tart² adj (-er, -est) sharp or bitter > tartly adv > tartness n (pl -es)

tart³ n (pl -s) (Informal) sexually provocative or promiscuous woman

tartan n (pl -s) design of straight lines crossing at right angles, esp. one associated with a Scottish clan

tartans n ▷ tartan

tartar¹ n (pl -s) hard deposit on the teeth

tartar² n (pl -s) fearsome or formidable person

tartars n ▷ tartar¹,²

tarter adj ▷ tart²

tartest adj ▷ tart²

tartly adv ▷ tart²

tartness n ▷ tart²

tartnesses n ▷ tart²

tartrazine [tar-traz-zeen] n (pl -s) artificial yellow dye used in food etc.

tartrazines n ▷ tartrazine

tarts n ▷ tart¹,³

task n (pl -s) (difficult or unpleasant) piece of work to be done

taskmaster n (pl -s) person who enforces hard work

taskmasters n ▷ taskmaster

tasks n ▷ task

tassel n (pl -s) decorative fringed knot of threads

tassels n ▷ tassel

taste n (pl -s) sense by which the flavour of a substance is distinguished in the mouth ▶ v (-tes, -ting, -ted) distinguish the taste of (a substance)

tasted v ▷ taste

tasteful adj having or showing good taste > tastefully adv

tastefully adv ▷ tasteful

tasteless adj bland or insipid > tastelessly adv

tastelessly adv ▷ tasteless

tastes n, v ▷ taste

tastier adj ▷ tasty

tastiest adj ▷ tasty

tasting v ▷ taste

tasty adj (-tier, -tiest) pleasantly flavoured

tat n (pl -s) (BRIT) tatty or tasteless article(s)

tats n ▷ tat

tattered adj ragged or torn

tattier n ▷ tatty

tattiest n ▷ tatty

tattle v (-les, -ling, -led), n (pl -les) (BRIT, AUST & NZ) gossip or chatter

tattled v ▷ tattle

tattles n ▷ tattle

tattling v ▷ tattle

tattoo¹ n (pl -s) pattern made on the body by pricking the skin and staining it with indelible inks ▶ v (-toos, -tooing, -tooed) make such a pattern on the skin > tattooist n (pl -s)

tattoo² n (pl -s) military display or pageant

tattooed n ▷ tattoo¹

tattooing n ▷ tattoo¹

tattooist n ▷ tattoo¹

tattooists n ▷ tattoo¹

tattoos n ▷ tattoo¹,² ▶ v ▷ tattoo¹

tatty adj (-tier, -tiest) shabby or worn out

taught v ▷ teach

taunt v (-s, -ing, -ed) tease with jeers ▶ n (pl -s) jeering remark

taunted v ▷ taunt

taunting v ▷ taunt

taunts v, n ▷ taunt

taupe adj brownish-grey

taut adj (-er, -est) drawn tight

tauten v (-s, -ing, -ed) make or become taut

tautened v ▷ tauten

tautening v ▷ tauten

tautens v ▷ tauten

tauter adj ▷ taut

tautest adj ▷ taut

tautological adj ▷ tautology

tautologies n ▷ tautology

tautology n (pl -gies) use of words which merely repeat something already stated > tautological adj

tavern n (pl -s) (Old-fashioned) pub

taverns n ▷ tavern

tawdrier adj ▷ tawdry

tawdriest adj ▷ tawdry

tawdry adj (**-drier, -driest**) cheap, showy, and of poor quality

tawnier adj ▷ tawny

tawniest adj ▷ tawny

tawny adj (**-nier, -niest**) yellowish-brown

tax n (pl **-es**) compulsory payment levied by a government on income, property, etc. to raise revenue ▶ v (**-es, -ing, -ed**) levy a tax on ▷ **taxable** adj ▷ **taxpayer** n (pl **-s**)

taxable adj ▷ tax

taxation n (pl **-s**) levying of taxes

taxations n ▷ taxation

taxed v ▷ tax

taxes n, v ▷ tax

taxi n (pl **-s**) car with a driver that may be hired to take people to any specified destination ▶ v (**taxis, taxiing, taxied**) (of an aircraft) run along the ground before taking off or after landing

taxidermies n ▷ taxidermy

taxidermist n ▷ taxidermy

taxidermists n ▷ taxidermy

taxidermy n (pl **-mies**) art of stuffing and mounting animal skins to give them a lifelike appearance ▷ **taxidermist** n (pl **-s**)

taxied v ▷ taxi

taxiing v ▷ taxi

taxing v ▷ tax

taxis n, v ▷ taxi

taxonomic adj ▷ taxonomy

taxonomies n ▷ taxonomy

taxonomist n ▷ taxonomy

taxonomists n ▷ taxonomy

taxonomy n (pl **-mies**) classification of plants and animals into groups ▷ **taxonomic** adj ▷ **taxonomist** n (pl **-s**)

taxpayer n ▷ tax

taxpayers n ▷ tax

te n (**tes**). Te is the seventh note of a musical scale. Although it won't earn you many points on its own, te is extremely useful as it allows you to connect a word beginning with T to one ending in E, or vice versa, which is very helpful as T and E are two of the most common tiles in the game. Te scores 2 points.

tea n (pl **-s**) drink made from infusing the dried leaves of an Asian bush in boiling water

teapot n (pl **-s**) container with a lid, spout, and handle for making and serving tea

teapots n ▷ teapot

teaspoon n (pl **-s**) small spoon for stirring tea

teaspoons n ▷ teaspoon

teach v (**-es, -ing, taught**) tell or show (someone) how to do something ▷ **teaching** n (pl **-s**)

teacher n (pl **-s**) person who teaches, esp. in a school

teachers n ▷ teacher

teaches v ▷ teach

teaching v, n ▷ teach

teachings n ▷ teach

teak n (pl **-s**) very hard wood of an E Indian tree

teaks n ▷ teak

teal n (pl **-s**) kind of small duck

teals n ▷ teal

team n (pl **-s**) group of people forming one side in a game

teams n ▷ team

teamster n (pl **-s**) (US) commercial vehicle driver

teamsters n ▷ teamster

teamwork n (pl **-s**) cooperative work by a team

teamworks n ▷ teamwork

tear¹, teardrop n (pl **-s**) drop of fluid appearing in and falling from the eye

tear² v (**-s, -ing, tore, torn**) rip a hole in ▶ n (pl **-s**) hole or split

tearaway n (pl **-s**) wild or unruly person

tearaways n ▷ tearaway

teardrop n ▷ tear¹

teardrops n ▷ tear¹

tearful adj weeping or about to weep

tearing v ▷ tear²

tears n ▷ tear¹, ² ▶ v ▷ tear²

teas n ▷ tea

tease v (**-ses, -sing, -sed**) make fun of (someone) in a provoking or playful way ▶ n (pl **-s**) person who teases ▷ **teasing** adj, n (pl **-s**)

teased v ▷ tease

teasel, teazel, teazle n (pl **-s**) plant with prickly leaves and flowers

teasels n ▷ teasel

teases v, n ▷ tease

teasing v, adj n ▷ tease

teasings n ▷ tease

teat n (pl **-s**) nipple of a breast or udder

teats n ▷ teat

teazel n ▷ teasel

teazels n ▷ teasel

teazle n ▷ teasel

teazles n ▷ teasel

tech n (pl **-s**) (Informal) technical college

techie (Informal) n (pl **-s**) person who is skilled in the use of technology ▶ adj relating to or skilled in the use of technology

techies n ▷ techie

technetium [tek-neesh-ee-um] n (pl **-s**) (CHEM)

artificially produced silvery-grey metallic element
technetiums n ▷ technetium
technical adj of or specializing in industrial, practical, or mechanical arts and applied sciences > **technically** adv
technicalities n ▷ technicality
technicality n (pl -ties) petty point based on a strict application of rules
technically adv ▷ technical
technician n (pl -s) person skilled in a particular technical field
technicians n ▷ technician
technicolor adj garishly coloured
technique n (pl -s) method or skill used for a particular task
techniques n ▷ technique
techno n (pl -s) type of electronic dance music with a very fast beat
technocracies n ▷ technocracy
technocracy n (pl -cies) government by technical experts > **technocrat** n (pl -s)
technocrat n ▷ technocracy
technocrats n ▷ technocracy
technological adj ▷ technology
technologies n ▷ technology
technologist n ▷ technology
technologists n ▷ technology
technology n (pl -gies) application of practical or mechanical sciences to industry or commerce > **technological** adj > **technologist** n (pl -s)
technos n ▷ techno
techs n ▷ tech
tectonics n study of the earth's crust and the forces affecting it
teddies n ▷ teddy
teddy n (pl -dies) teddy bear
tedious adj causing fatigue or boredom > **tediously** adv
tediously adv ▷ tedious
tedium n (pl -s) monotony
tediums n ▷ tedium
tee n (pl -s) small peg from which a golf ball can be played at the start of each hole
teem[1] v (-s, -ing, -ed) be full of
teem[2] v (-s, -ing, -ed) rain heavily
teemed v ▷ teem[1, 2]
teeming v ▷ teem[1, 2]
teems v ▷ teem[1, 2]
teenage adj ▷ teenager
teenager n (pl -s) person aged between 13 and 19 > **teenage** adj
teenagers n ▷ teenager
teens pl n period of being a teenager

teepee n (pl -s) ▷ tepee
teepees n ▷ teepee
tees n ▷ tee
teeter v (-s, -ing, -ed) wobble or move unsteadily
teetered v ▷ teeter
teetering v ▷ teeter
teeters v ▷ teeter
teeth n ▷ tooth
teethe v (-thes, -thing, -thed) (of a baby) grow his or her first teeth
teethed v ▷ teethe
teethes v ▷ teethe
teething v ▷ teethe
teetotal adj drinking no alcohol > **teetotaller** n (pl -s)
teetotaller n ▷ teetotal
teetotallers n ▷ teetotal
telecommunications n communications using telephone, radio, television, etc.
telegram n (pl -s) formerly, a message sent by telegraph
telegrams n ▷ telegram
telegraph n (pl -s) formerly, a system for sending messages over a distance along a cable ▶ v (-s, -ing, -ed) communicate by telegraph > **telegraphic** adj > **telegraphist** n (pl -s)
telegraphed v ▷ telegraph
telegraphic adj ▷ telegraph
telegraphies n ▷ telegraphy
telegraphing v ▷ telegraph
telegraphist n ▷ telegraph
telegraphists n ▷ telegraph
telegraphs n, v ▷ telegraph
telegraphy n (pl -phies) science or use of a telegraph
telekinesis n (pl -eses) movement of objects by thought or willpower
telekineses n ▷ telekinesis
telemetries n ▷ telemetry
telemetry n (pl -tries) use of electronic devices to record or measure a distant event and transmit the data to a receiver
teleological adj ▷ teleology
teleologies n ▷ teleology
teleology n (pl -gies) belief that all things have a predetermined purpose > **teleological** adj
telepathic adj ▷ telepathy
telepathically adv ▷ telepathy
telepathies n ▷ telepathy
telepathy n (pl -thies) direct communication between minds > **telepathic** adj > **telepathically** adv
telephone n (pl -s) device for transmitting

sound over a distance ▶ v (-nes, -ning, -ned) call or talk to (a person) by telephone > **telephony** n (pl -nies) > **telephonic** adj
telephoned v ▷ telephone
telephones n, v ▷ telephone
telephonic adj ▷ telephone
telephones n ▷ telephone
telephoning v ▷ telephone
telephonist n (pl -s) person operating a telephone switchboard
telephonists n ▷ telephonist
telephony n ▷ telephone
teleprinter n (pl -s) (BRIT) apparatus like a typewriter for sending and receiving typed messages by wire
teleprinters n ▷ teleprinter
telesales n selling of a product or service by telephone
telescope n (pl -s) optical instrument for magnifying distant objects ▶ v (-pes, -ping, -ped) shorten > **telescopic** adj
telescoped v ▷ telescope
telescopes n, v ▷ telescope
telescopic adj ▷ telescope
telescoping v ▷ telescope
televise v (-ses, -sing, -sed) broadcast on television
televised v ▷ televise
televises v ▷ televise
televising v ▷ televise
television n (pl -s) system of producing a moving image and accompanying sound on a distant screen > **televisual** adj
televisions n ▷ television
televisual adj ▷ television
telex n (pl -es) international communication service using teleprinters ▶ v (-es, -ing, -ed) transmit by telex
telexed v ▷ telex
telexes n, v ▷ telex
telexing v ▷ telex
tell v (-s, -lling, told) make known in words
teller n (pl -s) narrator
tellers n ▷ teller
tellies n ▷ telly
telling adj having a marked effect ▶ v ▷ tell
tells v ▷ tell
telltale n (pl -s) person who reveals secrets ▶ adj revealing
telltales n ▷ telltale
tellurium n (pl -s) (CHEM) brittle silvery-white nonmetallic element
telluriums n ▷ tellurium
telly n (pl -lies) (Informal) television
temerities n ▷ temerity

temerity [tim-merr-it-tee] n (pl -ties) boldness or audacity
temp (BRIT) (Informal) n (pl -s) temporary employee, esp. a secretary ▶ v (-s, -ing, -ed) work as a temp
temped v ▷ temp
temper n (pl -s) outburst of anger ▶ v (-s, -ing, -ed) make less extreme
tempera n (pl -s) painting medium for powdered pigments
temperas n ▷ tempera
temperament n (pl -s) person's character or disposition
temperamental adj having changeable moods > **temperamentally** adv
temperamentally adv ▷ temperamental
temperaments n ▷ temperament
temperance n (pl -s) moderation
temperances n ▷ temperance
temperate adj (of climate) not extreme
temperature n (pl -s) degree of heat or cold
temperatures n ▷ temperature
tempered v ▷ temper
tempering v ▷ temper
tempers n, v ▷ temper
tempest n (pl -s) violent storm
tempests n ▷ tempest
tempestuous adj violent or stormy
tempi n ▷ tempo
temping v ▷ temp
template n (pl -s) pattern used to cut out shapes accurately
templates n ▷ template
temple[1] n (pl -s) building for worship
temple[2] n (pl -s) region on either side of the forehead
temples n ▷ temple[1, 2]
tempo n (pl -pi, -pos) rate or pace
temporal adj of time
temporarily adv ▷ temporary
temporary adj lasting only for a short time > **temporarily** adv
temporize v (-zes, -zing, -zed) gain time by negotiation or evasiveness
temporized v ▷ temporize
temporizes v ▷ temporize
temporizing v ▷ temporize
tempos n ▷ tempo
temps n, v ▷ temp
tempt v (-s, -ing, -ed) entice (a person) to do something wrong > **tempter, temptress** n (pl -s, -es)
temptation n (pl -s) tempting
temptations n ▷ temptation
tempted v ▷ tempt

tempter n ▷ **tempt**

tempters n ▷ **tempt**

tempting adj attractive or inviting ▶ v ▷ **tempt**

temptress n ▷ **tempt**

temptresses n ▷ **tempt**

tempts v ▷ **tempt**

ten adj, n (pl -s) one more than nine

tenable adj able to be upheld or maintained

tenacious adj holding fast > **tenaciously** adv
> **tenacity** n (pl -ties)

tenaciously adv ▷ **tenacious**

tenacities n ▷ **tenacious**

tenacity n ▷ **tenacious**

tenancies n ▷ **tenant**

tenancy n ▷ **tenant**

tenant n (pl -s) person who rents land or a
building > **tenancy** n (pl -cies)

tenants n ▷ **tenant**

tench n (pl -es) freshwater game fish of the
carp family

tenches n ▷ **tench**

tend¹ v (-s, -ing, -ed) be inclined

tend² v (-s, -ing, -ed) take care of

tended v ▷ **tend**¹, ²

tendencies n ▷ **tendency**

tendency n (pl -cies) inclination to act in a
certain way > **tendentious** adj biased, not
impartial

tendentious adj ▷ **tendency**

tender¹ adj (-er, -est) not tough > **tenderly** adv
> **tenderness** n (pl -es)

tender² v (-s, -ing, -ed) offer ▶ n (pl -s) such
an offer

tender³ n (pl -s) small boat that brings supplies
to a larger ship in a port

tendered v ▷ **tender**²

tenderer adj ▷ **tender**¹

tenderest adj ▷ **tender**¹

tendering v ▷ **tender**²

tenderize v (-zes, -zing, -zed) soften (meat)
by pounding or treatment with a special
substance

tenderized v ▷ **tenderize**

tenderizes v ▷ **tenderize**

tenderizing v ▷ **tenderize**

tenderly adv ▷ **tender**¹

tenderness n ▷ **tender**¹

tendernesses n ▷ **tender**¹

tenders n ▷ **tender**², ³ ▶ v ▷ **tender**²

tending v ▷ **tend**¹, ²

tendon n (pl -s) strong tissue attaching a
muscle to a bone

tendons n ▷ **tendon**

tendril n (pl -s) slender stem by which a
climbing plant clings

tendrils n ▷ **tendril**

tends v ▷ **tend**¹, ²

tenement n (pl -s) (esp. in Scotland or the US)
building divided into several flats

tenements n ▷ **tenement**

tenet [ten-nit] n (pl -s) doctrine or belief

tenets n ▷ **tenet**

tenner n (pl -s) (BRIT) (Informal) ten-pound note

tenners n ▷ **tenner**

tennis n (pl -es) game in which players use
rackets to hit a ball back and forth over a net

tennises n ▷ **tennis**

tenon n (pl -s) projecting end on a piece of
wood fitting into a slot in another

tenons n ▷ **tenon**

tenor n (pl -s) (singer with) the second highest
male voice ▶ adj (of a voice or instrument)
between alto and baritone

tenors n ▷ **tenor**

tens n ▷ **ten**

tense¹ adj (-r, -st) emotionally strained ▶ v
(-ses, -sing, -sed) make or become tense

tense² n (pl -s) (GRAMMAR) form of a verb
showing the time of action

tensed v ▷ **tense**¹

tenser adj ▷ **tense**¹

tenses n ▷ **tense**² ▶ v ▷ **tense**¹

tensest adj ▷ **tense**¹

tensile adj of tension

tensing v ▷ **tense**¹

tension n (pl -s) hostility or suspense

tensions n ▷ **tension**

tent n (pl -s) portable canvas shelter

tentacle n (pl -s) flexible organ of many
invertebrates, used for grasping, feeding, etc.

tentacles n ▷ **tentacle**

tentative adj provisional or experimental
> **tentatively** adv

tentatively adv ▷ **tentative**

tenterhooks pl n tension

tenth adj, n (pl -s) (of) number ten in a series

tenths n ▷ **tenth**

tents n ▷ **tent**

tenuous adj slight or flimsy > **tenuously** adv

tenuously adv ▷ **tenuous**

tenure n (pl -s) (period of) the holding of an
office or position

tenures n ▷ **tenure**

tepee, teepee [tee-pee] n (pl -s) cone-shaped
tent, formerly used by Native Americans

tepees n ▷ **tepee**

tepid adj (-er, -est) slightly warm

tepider adj ▷ **tepid**

tepidest adj ▷ **tepid**

tequila n (pl -s) Mexican alcoholic drink

tequilas n ▷ tequila
tercentenaries n ▷ tercentenary
tercentenary adj, n (pl -ries) (of) a three hundredth anniversary
term n (pl -s) word or expression ▶ v (-s, -ing, -ed) name or designate
termed v ▷ term
terminal adj (of an illness) ending in death ▶ n (pl -s) place where people or vehicles begin or end a journey > **terminally** adv
terminally adv ▷ terminal
terminals n ▷ terminal
terminate v (-tes, -ting, -ted) bring or come to an end > **termination** n (pl -s)
terminated v ▷ terminate
terminates v ▷ terminate
terminating v ▷ terminate
termination n ▷ terminate
terminations n ▷ terminate
terming v ▷ term
termini n ▷ terminus
terminologies n ▷ terminology
terminology n (pl -gies) technical terms relating to a subject
terminus n (pl -ni, -nuses) railway or bus station at the end of a line
terminuses n ▷ terminus
termite n (pl -s) white antlike insect that destroys timber
termites n ▷ termite
terms n, v ▷ term ▶ pl n conditions
tern n (pl -s) gull-like sea bird with a forked tail and pointed wings
ternary adj consisting of three parts
terns n ▷ tern
terrace n (pl -s) row of houses built as one block ▶ v (-ces, -cing, -ced) form into or provide with a terrace
terraced v ▷ terrace
terraces n, v ▷ terrace ▶ pl n (also **terracing**) tiered area in a stadium where spectators stand
terracing v ▷ terrace
terracotta adj, n (pl -s) (made of) brownish-red unglazed pottery ▶ adj brownish-red
terracottas n ▷ terracotta
terrain n (pl -s) area of ground, esp. with reference to its physical character
terrains n ▷ terrain
terrapin n (pl -s) small turtle-like reptile
terrapins n ▷ terrapin
terraria n ▷ terrarium
terrarium n (pl -raria, -rariums) enclosed container for small plants or animals
terrariums n ▷ terrarium

terrazzo n (pl -s) floor of marble chips set in mortar and polished
terrazzos n ▷ terrazzo
terrestrial adj of the earth
terrible adj very serious > **terribly** adv
terribly adv ▷ terrible
terrier n (pl -s) any of various breeds of small active dog
terriers n ▷ terrier
terries n ▷ terry
terrific adj great or intense
terrified v, adj ▷ terrify
terrifies v ▷ terrify
terrify v (-fies, -fying, -fied) fill with fear > **terrified** adj > **terrifying** adj
terrifying v, adj ▷ terrify
terrine [terr-reen] n (pl -s) earthenware dish with a lid
terrines n ▷ terrine
territorial adj ▷ territory
territories n ▷ territory
territory n (pl -ries) district > **territorial** adj
terror n (pl -s) great fear
terrorism n (pl -s) use of violence and intimidation to achieve political ends > **terrorist** n (pl -s) adj
terrorisms n ▷ terrorism
terrorist n, adj ▷ terrorism
terrorists n ▷ terrorism
terrorize v (-zes, -zing, -zed) force or oppress by fear or violence
terrorized v ▷ terrorize
terrorizes v ▷ terrorize
terrorizing v ▷ terrorize
terrors n ▷ terror
terry n (pl -ries) fabric with small loops covering both sides, used esp. for making towels
terse adj (-r, -st) neat and concise > **tersely** adv
tersely adv ▷ terse
terser adj ▷ terse
tersest adj ▷ terse
tertiary [tur-shar-ee] adj third in degree, order, etc.
tessellated adj paved or inlaid with a mosaic of small tiles
test v (-s, -ing, -ed) try out to ascertain the worth, capability, or endurance of ▶ n (pl -s) critical examination > **testing** adj
testament n (pl -s) proof or tribute
testaments n ▷ testament
testator [test-tay-tor], fem **testatrix** [test-tay-triks] n (pl -s, -xes) maker of a will
testators n ▷ testator
testatrix n ▷ testator

testatrixes n ▷ testator
tested v ▷ test
testes n ▷ testis
testicle n (pl -s) either of the two male reproductive glands
  testicles n ▷ testicle
  testier adj ▷ testy
  testiest adj ▷ testy
  testified v ▷ testify
  testifies v ▷ testify
testify v (-fies, -fying, -fied) give evidence under oath
  testifying v ▷ testify
  testily adv ▷ testy
testimonial n (pl -s) recommendation of the worth of a person or thing
  testimonials n ▷ testimonial
  testimonies n ▷ testimony
testimony n (pl -nies) declaration of truth or fact
  testiness n ▷ testy
  testinesses n ▷ testy
  testing v, adj ▷ test
testis n (pl -tes) testicle
testosterone n (pl -s) male sex hormone secreted by the testes
  testosterones n ▷ testosterone
  tests v, n ▷ test
testy adj (-tier, -tiest) irritable or touchy
  > **testily** adv ▷ **testiness** n (pl -es)
tetanus n (pl -es) acute infectious disease producing muscular spasms and convulsions
  tetanuses n ▷ tetanus
tether n (pl -s) rope or chain for tying an animal to a spot ▶ v (-s, -ing, -ed) tie up with rope
  tethered v ▷ tether
  tethering v ▷ tether
  tethers n, v ▷ tether
  tetrahedra n ▷ tetrahedron
tetrahedron [tet-ra-heed-ron] n (pl -drons, -dra) solid figure with four faces
  tetrahedrons n ▷ tetrahedron
  tetralogies n ▷ tetralogy
tetralogy n (pl -gies) series of four related works
text n (pl -s) main body of a book as distinct from illustrations etc. ▶ v (-s, -ing, -ed) send a text message to (someone) ▶ **textual** adj
textbook n (pl -s) standard book on a particular subject ▶ adj perfect
  textbooks n ▷ textbook
  texted v ▷ text
textile n (pl -s) fabric or cloth, esp. woven
  textiles n ▷ textile

texting v ▷ text
texts n, v ▷ text
textual adj ▷ text
textural adj ▷ texture
texture n (pl -s) structure, feel, or consistency
  > **textured** adj > **textural** adj
  textured v ▷ texture
  textures n ▷ texture
thalidomide [thal-**lid**-oh-mide] n (pl -s) drug formerly used as a sedative, but found to cause abnormalities in developing fetuses
  thalidomides n ▷ thalidomide
thallium n (pl -s) (CHEM) highly toxic metallic element
  thalliums n ▷ thallium
than conj, prep used to introduce the second element of a comparison
thane n (pl -s) (HIST) Anglo-Saxon or medieval Scottish nobleman
  thanes n ▷ thane
thank v (-s, -ing, -ed) express gratitude to
  thanked v ▷ thank
thankful adj grateful
  thanking v ▷ thank
thankless adj unrewarding or unappreciated
thanks pl n words of gratitude ▶ interj polite expression of gratitude ▶ v ▷ thank
that adj, pron used to refer to something already mentioned or familiar, or further away ▶ conj used to introduce a clause ▶ pron used to introduce a relative clause
thatch n (pl -es) roofing material of reeds or straw ▶ v (-ches, -ching, -ched) roof (a house) with reeds or straw
  thatched v ▷ thatch
  thatches n, v ▷ thatch
  thatching v ▷ thatch
thaw v (-s, -ing, -ed) make or become unfrozen ▶ n (pl -s) thawing
  thawed v ▷ thaw
  thawing v ▷ thaw
  thaws n, v ▷ thaw
the adj the definite article, used before a noun
theatre n (pl -s) place where plays etc. are performed
  theatres n ▷ theatre
theatrical adj of the theatre > **theatrically** adv > **theatricality** n (pl -ties)
  theatricalities n ▷ theatrical
  theatricality n ▷ theatrical
  theatrically adv ▷ theatrical
theatricals pl n (amateur) dramatic performances
thee pron (Obs) you
theft n (pl -s) act or an instance of stealing

thefts n ▷ theft
their adj of or associated with them
theirs pron (thing or person) belonging to them
theism [thee-iz-zum] n (pl -s) belief in a God or gods > **theist** n (pl -s) adj > **theistic** adj
theisms n ▷ theism
theist n, adj ▷ theism
theistic adj ▷ theism
theists n ▷ theism
them pron refers to people or things other than the speaker or those addressed
thematic adj ▷ theme
theme n (pl -s) main idea or subject being discussed > **thematic** adj
themes n ▷ theme
themselves pron ▷ they, them
then adv at that time
thence adv from that place or time
theocracies n ▷ theocracy
theocracy n (pl -cies) government by a god or priests > **theocratic** adj
theocratic adj ▷ theocracy
theodolite [thee-odd-oh-lite] n (pl -s) surveying instrument for measuring angles
theodolites n ▷ theodolite
theologian n ▷ theology
theologians n ▷ theology
theological adj ▷ theology
theologically adv ▷ theology
theologies n ▷ theology
theology n (pl -gies) study of religions and religious beliefs > **theologian** n (pl -s)
> **theological** adj > **theologically** adv
theorem n (pl -s) proposition that can be proved by reasoning
theorems n ▷ theorem
theoretical adj based on theory rather than practice or fact > **theoretically** adv
theoretically adv ▷ theoretical
theories n ▷ theory
theorist n ▷ theory
theorists n ▷ theory
theorize v (-zes, -zing, -zed) form theories, speculate
theorized v ▷ theorize
theorizes v ▷ theorize
theorizing v ▷ theorize
theory n (pl -ries) set of ideas to explain something > **theorist** n (pl -s)
theosophical adj ▷ theosophy
theosophies n ▷ theosophy
theosophy n (pl -phies) religious or philosophical system claiming to be based on intuitive insight into the divine nature

> **theosophical** adj
therapeutic [ther-rap-pew-tik] adj curing
therapeutics n art of curing
therapies n ▷ therapy
therapist n ▷ therapy
therapists n ▷ therapy
therapy n (pl -pies) curing treatment
> **therapist** n (pl -s)
there adv in or to that place
thereby adv by that means
therefore adv consequently, that being so
thereupon adv immediately after that
therm n (pl -s) unit of measurement of heat
thermal adj of heat ▶ n (pl -s) rising current of warm air
thermals n ▷ thermal
thermodynamics n scientific study of the relationship between heat and other forms of energy
thermometer n (pl -s) instrument for measuring temperature
thermometers n ▷ thermometer
thermonuclear adj involving nuclear fusion
thermoplastic adj (of a plastic) softening when heated and resetting on cooling
thermosetting adj (of a plastic) remaining hard when heated
thermostat n (pl -s) device for automatically regulating temperature > **thermostatic** adj
thermostatic adj ▷ thermostat
thermostats n ▷ thermostat
therms n ▷ therm
thesaurus [thiss-sore-uss] n (pl -ruses) book containing lists of synonyms and related words
thesauruses n ▷ thesaurus
these adj, pron ▷ this
theses n ▷ thesis
thesis n (pl theses) written work submitted for a degree
thespian n (pl -s) actor or actress ▶ adj of the theatre
thespians n ▷ thespian
they pron refers to: people or things other than the speaker or people addressed
thiamine n (pl -s) vitamin found in the outer coat of rice and other grains
thiamines n ▷ thiamine
thick adj (-er, -est) of great or specified extent from one side to the other > **thickly** adv
thicken v (-s, -ing, -ed) make or become thick or thicker
thickened v ▷ thicken
thickening v ▷ thicken
thickens v ▷ thicken

thicker *adj* ▷ thick
thickest *adj* ▷ thick
thicket *n* (*pl* -s) dense growth of small trees
 thickets *n* ▷ thicket
 thickly *adv* ▷ thick
thickness *n* (*pl* -es) state of being thick
 thicknesses *n* ▷ thickness
thickset *adj* stocky in build
thief *n* (*pl* thieves) person who steals
thieve *v* (-ves, -ving, -ved) steal ▷ thieving *adj*
 thieved *v* ▷ thieve
 thieves *v* ▷ thieve ▶ *n* ▷ thief
 thieving *v*, *adj* ▷ thieve
thigh *n* (*pl* -s) upper part of the human leg
 thighs *n* ▷ thigh
thimble *n* (*pl* -s) cap protecting the end of the
 finger when sewing
 thimbles *n* ▷ thimble
thin *adj* (-nner, -nnest) not thick ▶ *v* (-s, -nning,
 -nned) make or become thin ▷ thinly *adv*
 ▷ thinness *n* (*pl* -es)
thine *pron*, *adj* (*Obs*) (something) of or
 associated with you (thou)
thing *n* (*pl* -s) material object
things *n* ▷ thing ▶ *pl n* possessions, clothes,
 etc.
think *v* (-s, -ing, thought) consider, judge,
 or believe ▷ thinker *n* (*pl* -s) ▷ thinking *adj*,
 n (*pl* -s)
 thinker *n* ▷ think
 thinkers *n* ▷ think
 thinking *v*, *adj*, *n* ▷ think
 thinkings *n* ▷ think
 thinks *v* ▷ think
 thinly *adv* ▷ thin
 thinned *v* ▷ thin
 thinner *adj* ▷ thin
 thinness *n* ▷ thin
 thinnesses *n* ▷ thin
 thinnest *adj* ▷ thin
 thinning *v* ▷ thin
 thins *v* ▷ thin
third *adj* of number three in a series ▶ *n* (*pl* -s)
 one of three equal parts
 thirds *n* ▷ third
thirst *n* (*pl* -s) desire to drink ▶ *v* (-s, -ing, -ed)
 feel thirst ▷ thirsty *adj* (-tier, -tiest) ▷ thirstily
 adv
 thirsted *v* ▷ thirst
 thirstier *adj* ▷ thirst
 thirstiest *adj* ▷ thirst
 thirstily *adv* ▷ thirst
 thirsting *v* ▷ thirst
 thirsts *n*, *v* ▷ thirst
 thirsty *adj* (-tier, -tiest) ▷ thirst

thirteen *adj*, *n* (*pl* -s) three plus ten
 ▷ thirteenth *adj*, *n* (*pl* -s)
 thirteens *n* ▷ thirteen
 thirteenth *n* ▷ thirteen
 thirteenths *n* ▷ thirteen
 thirties *n* ▷ thirty
 thirtieth *n* ▷ thirty
 thirtieths *n* ▷ thirty
thirty *adj*, *n* (*pl* -ties) three times ten
 ▷ thirtieth *adj*, *n* (*pl* -s)
this *adj*, *pron* used to refer to a thing or person
 nearby, just mentioned, or about to be
 mentioned ▶ *adj* used to refer to the present
 time
thistle *n* (*pl* -s) prickly plant with dense flower
 heads
 thistles *n* ▷ thistle
thither *adv* (*Obs*) to or towards that place
thong *n* (*pl* -s) thin strip of leather etc.
 thongs *n* ▷ thong
 thoraces *n* ▷ thorax
 thoracic *adj* ▷ thorax
thorax *n* (*pl* -xes, -races) part of the body
 between the neck and the abdomen
 ▷ thoracic *adj*
 thoraxes *n* ▷ thorax
thorn *n* (*pl* -s) prickle on a plant ▷ thorny *adj*
 (-ier, -iest)
 thornier *adj* ▷ thorn
 thorniest *adj* ▷ thorn
 thorns *n* ▷ thorn
 thorny *adj* ▷ thorn
thorough *adj* complete ▷ thoroughly *adv*
 ▷ thoroughness *n* (*pl* -es)
thoroughbred *n* (*pl* -s) ▶ *adj* (animal) of pure
 breed
 thoroughbreds *n* ▷ thoroughbred
thoroughfare *n* (*pl* -s) way through from one
 place to another
 thoroughfares *n* ▷ thoroughfare
 thoroughly *adv* ▷ thorough
 thoroughness *n* ▷ thorough
 thoroughnesses *n* ▷ thorough
those *adj*, *pron* ▷ that
thou *pron* (*Obs*) you
though *conj* despite the fact that ▶ *adv*
 nevertheless
thought *v* ▷ think ▶ *n* (*pl* -s) thinking
 ▷ thoughtful *adj* considerate
 thoughtful *adj* ▷ thought
thoughtless *adj* inconsiderate
 thoughts *n* ▷ thought
thousand *adj*, *n* (*pl* -s) ten hundred
 thousands *n* ▷ thousand
thousandth *adj*, *n* (*pl* -s) (of) number one

thousand in a series

thousandths n ▷ **thousandth**

thrall n (pl -s) state of being in the power of another person

thralls n ▷ **thrall**

thrash v (-es, -ing, -ed) beat, esp. with a stick or whip

thrashed v ▷ **thrash**

thrashes v ▷ **thrash**

thrashing n (pl -s) severe beating ▶ v ▷ **thrash**

thread n (pl -s) fine strand or yarn ▶ v (-s, -ing, -ed) pass thread through

threadbare adj (of fabric) with the nap worn off

threaded v ▷ **thread**

threading v ▷ **thread**

threads n, v ▷ **thread**

threat n (pl -s) declaration of intent to harm

threaten v (-s, -ing, -ed) make or be a threat to

threatened v ▷ **threaten**

threatening v ▷ **threaten**

threatens v ▷ **threaten**

threats n ▷ **threat**

three adj, n (pl -s) one more than two

threes n ▷ **three**

threesome n (pl -s) group of three

threesomes n ▷ **threesome**

threnodies n ▷ **threnody**

threnody n (pl -dies) lament for the dead

thresh v (-es, -ing, -ed) beat (wheat etc.) to separate the grain from the husks and straw

threshed v ▷ **thresh**

threshes v ▷ **thresh**

threshing v ▷ **thresh**

threshold n (pl -s) bar forming the bottom of a doorway

thresholds n ▷ **threshold**

threw v ▷ **throw**

thrice adv (Lit) three times

thrift n (pl -s) wisdom and caution with money > **thrifty** adj

thrifts n ▷ **thrift**

thrifty adj ▷ **thrif**

thrill n (pl -s) sudden feeling of excitement ▶ v (-s, -ing, -ed) (cause to) feel a thrill > **thrilling** adj

thrilled v ▷ **thrill**

thriller n (pl -s) book, film, etc. with an atmosphere of mystery or suspense

thrillers n ▷ **thriller**

thrilling v, adj ▷ **thrill**

thrills n, v ▷ **thrill**

thrive v (-ves, -ving, -ved or **throve**, **thrived** or **thriven**) flourish or prosper

thrived v ▷ **thrive**

thriven v ▷ **thrive**

thrives v ▷ **thrive**

thriving v ▷ **thrive**

throat n (pl -s) passage from the mouth and nose to the stomach and lungs

throatier adj ▷ **throaty**

throatiest adj ▷ **throaty**

throats n ▷ **throat**

throaty adj (-tier, -tiest) (of the voice) hoarse

throb v (-s, -bbing, -bbed) pulsate repeatedly ▶ n (pl -s) throbbing

throbbed v ▷ **throb**

throbbing v ▷ **throb**

throbs v, n ▷ **throb**

throes pl n violent pangs or pains

thrombosis n (pl -oses) forming of a clot in a blood vessel or the heart

thromboses n ▷ **thrombosis**

throne n (pl -s) ceremonial seat of a monarch or bishop

thrones n ▷ **throne**

throng n (pl -s) ▶ v (-s, -ing, -ed) crowd

thronged v ▷ **throng**

thronging v ▷ **throng**

throngs v, n ▷ **throng**

throstle n (pl -s) song thrush

throstles n ▷ **throstle**

throttle n (pl -s) device controlling the amount of fuel entering an engine ▶ v (-les, -ling, -led) strangle

throttled v ▷ **throttle**

throttles n, v ▷ **throttle**

throttling v ▷ **throttle**

through prep from end to end or side to side of ▶ adj finished

throughout prep, adv in every part (of)

throughput n (pl -s) amount of material processed

throughputs n ▷ **throughput**

throve v ▷ **thrive**

throw v (-s, -ing, **threw**, **thrown**) hurl through the air ▶ n (pl -s) throwing

throwaway adj done or said casually

throwback n (pl -s) person or thing that reverts to an earlier type

throwbacks n ▷ **throwback**

throwing v ▷ **throw**

thrown v ▷ **throw**

throws v, n ▷ **throw**

thrush[1] n (pl -es) brown songbird

thrush[2] n (pl -es) fungal disease of the mouth or vagina

thrushes n ▷ **thrush**[1, 2]

thrust v (-s, -ing, **thrust**) push forcefully ▶ n (pl -s) forceful stab

thrusting v ▷ **thrust**
thrusts v, n ▷ **thrust**
thud n (pl -s) dull heavy sound ▶ v (-s, -dding, -dded) make such a sound
  thudded v ▷ **thud**
  thudding v ▷ **thud**
  thuds n, v ▷ **thud**
thug n (pl -s) violent man, esp. a criminal > **thuggery** n (pl -ries) > **thuggish** adj
  thuggeries n ▷ **thug**
  thuggery n ▷ **thug**
  thuggish adj ▷ **thug**
  thugs n ▷ **thug**
thumb n (pl -s) short thick finger set apart from the others ▶ v (-s, -ing, -ed) touch or handle with the thumb
  thumbed v ▷ **thumb**
  thumbing v ▷ **thumb**
  thumbs n, v ▷ **thumb**
thump n (pl -s) (sound of) a dull heavy blow ▶ v (-s, -ing, -ed) strike heavily
  thumped v ▷ **thump**
  thumping v ▷ **thump**
  thumps n, v ▷ **thump**
thunder n (pl -s) loud noise accompanying lightning ▶ v (-s, -ing, -ed) rumble with thunder > **thunderous** adj > **thundery** (-rier, -riest) adj
thunderbolt n (pl -s) lightning flash
  thunderbolts n ▷ **thunderbolt**
thunderclap n (pl -s) peal of thunder
  thunderclaps n ▷ **thunderclap**
  thundered v ▷ **thunder**
  thunderier adj ▷ **thunder**
  thunderiest adj ▷ **thunder**
  thundering v ▷ **thunder**
  thunderous adj ▷ **thunder**
  thunders v, n ▷ **thunder**
thunderstruck adj amazed
  thundery adj ▷ **thunder**
thus adv therefore
thwack v (-s, -ing, -ed) ▶ n (pl -s) whack
  thwacked v ▷ **thwack**
  thwacking v ▷ **thwack**
  thwacks v, n ▷ **thwack**
thwart v (-s, -ing, -ed) foil or frustrate ▶ n (pl -s) seat across a boat
  thwarted v ▷ **thwart**
  thwarting v ▷ **thwart**
  thwarts v, n ▷ **thwart**
thy adj (Obs) of or associated with you (thou)
thylacine n (pl -s) extinct doglike Tasmanian marsupial
  thylacines n ▷ **thylacine**
thyme [time] n (pl -s) aromatic herb

thymes n ▷ **thyme**
thymi n ▷ **thymus**
thymus n (pl -muses, -mi) small gland at the base of the neck
  thymuses n ▷ **thymus**
thyroid adj, n (pl -s) (of) a gland in the neck controlling body growth
  thyroids n ▷ **thyroid**
thyself pron (Obs) ▷ **thou**

  ti n (**tis**). Ti means the same as **te**. This is a useful word when you want to form words in more than one direction. Ti scores 2 points.

tiara n (pl -s) semicircular jewelled headdress
  tiaras n ▷ **tiara**
tibia n (pl -biae, -bias) inner bone of the lower leg > **tibial** adj
  tibiae n ▷ **tibia**
  tibial adj ▷ **tibia**
  tibias n ▷ **tibia**
tic n (pl -s) spasmodic muscular twitch
tick¹ n (pl -s) mark (✓) used to check off or indicate the correctness of something ▶ v (-s, -ing, -ed) mark with a tick
tick² n (pl -s) tiny bloodsucking parasitic animal
tick³ n (pl -s) (Informal) credit or account
  ticked v ▷ **tick¹**
ticket n (pl -s) card or paper entitling the holder to admission, travel, etc. (CHIEFLY US & NZ) ▶ v (-s, -ing, -ed) attach or issue a ticket to
  ticketed v ▷ **ticket**
  ticketing v ▷ **ticket**
  tickets n, v ▷ **ticket**
ticking n (pl -s) strong material for mattress covers ▶ v ▷ **tick¹**
  tickings n ▷ **ticking**
tickle v (-les, -ling, -led) touch or stroke (a person) to produce laughter ▶ n (pl -s) tickling
  tickled v ▷ **tickle**
  tickles v, n ▷ **tickle**
  tickling v ▷ **tickle**
ticklish adj sensitive to tickling
  ticks v ▷ **tick¹** ▶ n ▷ **tick¹, ², ³**
ticktack n (pl -s) (BRIT) bookmakers' sign language
  ticktacks n ▷ **ticktack**
  tics n ▷ **tic**
  tidal adj ▷ **tide**
tiddler n (pl -s) (Informal) very small fish
  tiddlers n ▷ **tiddler**
  tiddlier adj ▷ **tiddly¹, ²**
  tiddliest adj ▷ **tiddly¹, ²**
tiddly¹ adj (-dlier, -dliest) tiny
tiddly² adj (-dlier, -dliest) (Informal) slightly

drunk

tiddlywink n small plastic disc

tiddlywinks n game in which players try to flip small plastic discs into a cup

tide n (pl -s) rise and fall of the sea caused by the gravitational pull of the sun and moon > **tidal** adj

tides n ▷ tide

tidied v ▷ tidy

tidier adj ▷ tidy

tidies v ▷ tidy

tidiest adj ▷ tidy

tidily adv ▷ tidy

tidiness n ▷ tidy

tidinesses n ▷ tidy

tidings pl n news

tidy adj (-dier, -diest) neat and orderly ▶ v (-dies, -dying, -died) put in order > **tidily** adv > **tidiness** n (pl -es)

tidying v ▷ tidy

tie v (ties, tying, tied) fasten or be fastened with string, rope, etc. ▶ n (pl -s) long narrow piece of material worn knotted round the neck

tied v ▷ tie ▶ adj (BRIT) (of a cottage etc.) rented to the tenant only as long as he or she is employed by the owner

tier n (pl -s) one of a set of rows placed one above and behind the other

tiers n ▷ tier

ties v, n ▷ tie

tiff n (pl -s) petty quarrel

tiffs n ▷ tiff

tiger n (pl -s) large yellow-and-black striped Asian cat

tigers n ▷ tiger

tight adj (-er, -est) stretched or drawn taut > **tightly** adv

tighten v (-s, -ing, -ed) make or become tight or tighter

tightened v ▷ tighten

tightening v ▷ tighten

tightens v ▷ tighten

tighter adj ▷ tight

tightest adj ▷ tight

tightly adv ▷ tight

tightrope n (pl -s) rope stretched taut on which acrobats perform

tightropes n ▷ tightrope

tights pl n one-piece clinging garment covering the body from the waist to the feet

tigress n (pl -es) female tiger

tigresses n ▷ tigress

tiki n (pl -s) (NZ) small carving of a grotesque person worn as a pendant

tikis n ▷ tiki

tikka adj (INDIAN COOKERY) marinated in spices and dry-roasted

tilde n (pl -s) mark (~) used in Spanish to indicate that the letter 'n' is to be pronounced in a particular way

tildes n ▷ tilde

tile n (pl -s) flat piece of ceramic, plastic, etc. used to cover a roof, floor, or wall ▶ v (-les, -ling, -led) cover with tiles > **tiled** adj

tiled v, adj ▷ tile

tiles n, v ▷ tile

tiling n (pl -s) tiles collectively ▶ v ▷ tile

tilings n ▷ tiling

till[1] conj, prep until

till[2] v (-s, -ing, -ed) cultivate (land) > **tillage** n (pl -s)

till[3] n (pl -s) drawer for money, usu. in a cash register

tillage n ▷ till[2]

tillages n ▷ till[2]

tilled v ▷ till[2]

tiller n (pl -s) lever to move a rudder of a boat

tillers n ▷ tiller

tilling v ▷ till[2]

tills v ▷ till[2] ▶ n ▷ till[3]

tilt v (-s, -ing, -ed) slant at an angle ▶ n (pl -s) slope

tilted v ▷ tilt

tilting v ▷ tilt

tilts v, n ▷ tilt

timber n (pl -s) wood as a building material > **timbered** adj

timbered adj ▷ timber

timbers n ▷ timber

timbre [tam-bra] n (pl -s) distinctive quality of sound of a voice or instrument

timbres n ▷ timbre

time n (pl -s) past, present, and future as a continuous whole ▶ v (-mes, -ming, -med) note the time taken by

timed v ▷ time

timeless adj unaffected by time

timelier adj ▷ timely

timeliest adj ▷ timely

timely adj (-lier, -liest) at the appropriate time

timepiece n (pl -s) watch or clock

timepieces n ▷ timepiece

times n, v ▷ time

timeserver n (pl -s) person who changes his or her views to gain support or favour

timeservers n ▷ timeserver

timetable n (pl -s) plan showing the times when something takes place, the departure and arrival times of trains or buses, etc.

timetables n ▷ **timetable**

timid adj (-**er**, -**est**) easily frightened > **timidly** adv > **timidity** n (pl -**dies**)

timider adj ▷ **timid**

timidest adj ▷ **timid**

timidities n ▷ **timid**

timidity n ▷ **timid**

timidly adv ▷ **timid**

timing v ▷ **time**

timorous adj timid

timpani [tim-pan-ee] pl n set of kettledrums > **timpanist** n (pl -**s**)

timpanist n ▷ **timpani**

timpanists n ▷ **timpani**

tin n (pl -**s**) soft metallic element

tincture n (pl -**s**) medicinal extract in a solution of alcohol

tinctures n ▷ **tincture**

tinder n (pl -**s**) dry easily-burning material used to start a fire > **tinderbox** n (pl -**es**)

tinderbox n ▷ **tinder**

tinderboxes n ▷ **tinder**

tinders n ▷ **tinder**

tine n (pl -**s**) prong of a fork or antler

tines n ▷ **tine**

ting n (pl -**s**) high metallic sound, as of a small bell

tinge n (pl -**s**) slight tint ▶ v (-**ges**, -**geing**, -**ged**) give a slight tint or trace to

tinged v ▷ **tinge**

tinges n, v ▷ **tinge**

tinging v ▷ **tinge**

tingle v (-**les**, -**ling**, -**led**) ▶ n (pl -**s**) (feel) a prickling or stinging sensation

tingled v ▷ **tingle**

tingles v, n ▷ **tingle**

tingling v ▷ **tingle**

tings n ▷ **ting**

tinier adj ▷ **tiny**

tiniest adj ▷ **tiny**

tinker n (pl -**s**) travelling mender of pots and pans ▶ v (-**s**, -**ing**, -**ed**) fiddle with (an engine etc.) in an attempt to repair it

tinkered v ▷ **tinker**

tinkering v ▷ **tinker**

tinkers n, v ▷ **tinker**

tinkle v (-**les**, -**ling**, -**led**) ring with a high tinny sound like a small bell ▶ n (pl -**s**) this sound or action

tinkled v ▷ **tinkle**

tinkles v, n ▷ **tinkle**

tinkling v ▷ **tinkle**

tinned adj (of food) preserved by being sealed in a tin

tinnier adj ▷ **tinny**

tinniest adj ▷ **tinny**

tinny adj (-**nier**, -**nniest**) (of sound) thin and metallic

tinpot adj (Informal) worthless or unimportant

tins n ▷ **tin**

tinsel n (pl -**s**) decorative metallic strips or threads

tinsels n ▷ **tinsel**

tint n (pl -**s**) (pale) shade of a colour ▶ v (-**s**, -**ing**, -**ed**) give a tint to

tinted v ▷ **tint**

tinting v ▷ **tint**

tints n, v ▷ **tint**

tiny adj (-**ier**, -**iest**) very small

tip[1] n (pl -**s**) narrow or pointed end of anything ▶ v (-**s**, -**pping**, -**pped**) put a tip on

tip[2] n (pl -**s**) money given in return for service ▶ v (-**s**, -**pping**, -**pped**) give a tip to

tip[3] v (-**s**, -**pping**, -**pped**) tilt or overturn ▶ n (pl -**s**) rubbish dump

tipped v ▷ **tip**[1, 2, 3]

tipping v ▷ **tip**[1, 2, 3]

tipple v (-**les**, -**ling**, -**led**) drink alcohol habitually, esp. in small quantities ▶ n (pl -**s**) alcoholic drink > **tippler** n (pl -**s**)

tippled v ▷ **tipple**

tippler n ▷ **tipple**

tipplers n ▷ **tipple**

tipples v, n ▷ **tipple**

tippling v ▷ **tipple**

tips n, v ▷ **tip**[1, 2, 3]

tipsier adj ▷ **tipsy**

tipsiest adj ▷ **tipsy**

tipster n (pl -**s**) person who sells tips about races

tipsters n ▷ **tipster**

tipsy adj (-**sier**, -**siest**) slightly drunk

tiptoe v (-**toes**, -**toeing**, -**toed**) walk quietly with the heels off the ground

tiptoed v ▷ **tiptoe**

tiptoeing v ▷ **tiptoe**

tiptoes v ▷ **tiptoe**

tiptop adj of the highest quality or condition

tirade n (pl -**s**) long angry speech

tirades n ▷ **tirade**

tire v (-**res**, -**ring**, -**red**) reduce the energy of, as by exertion > **tiring** adj

tired adj (-**er**, -**est**) exhausted ▶ v ▷ **tire**

tireder adj ▷ **tired**

tiredest adj ▷ **tired**

tireless adj energetic and determined

tires v ▷ **tire**

tiresome adj boring and irritating

tiring v, adj ▷ **tire**

tissue n (pl -**s**) substance of an animal body

or plant

tissues *n* ▷ tissue

tit[1] *n* (*pl* **-s**) any of various small songbirds

tit[2] *n* (*pl* **-s**) (*Slang*) female breast

titanic *adj* huge or very important

titanium *n* (*pl* **-s**) (CHEM) strong light metallic element used to make alloys

titaniums *n* ▷ titanium

titbit *n* (*pl* **-s**) tasty piece of food

titbits *n* ▷ titbit

tithe *n* (*pl* **-s**) esp. formerly, one tenth of one's income or produce paid to the church as a tax

tithes *n* ▷ tithe

titian [tish-an] *adj* (of hair) reddish-gold

titillate *v* (**-tes, -ting, -ted**) excite or stimulate pleasurably ▷ **titillating** *adj* ▷ **titillation** *n* (*pl* **-s**)

titillated *v* ▷ titillate

titillates *v* ▷ titillate

titillating *v, adj* ▷ titillate

titillation *n* ▷ titillate

titillations *n* ▷ titillate

titivate *v* (**-tes, -ting, -ted**) smarten up

titivated *v* ▷ titivate

titivates *v* ▷ titivate

titivating *v* ▷ titivate

title *n* (*pl* **-s**) name of a book, film, etc.

titled *adj* aristocratic

titles *n* ▷ title

tits *n* ▷ tit[1, 2]

titter *v* (**-s, -ing, -ed**) laugh in a suppressed way ▶ *n* (*pl* **-s**) suppressed laugh

tittered *v* ▷ titter

tittering *v* ▷ titter

titters *v, n* ▷ titter

titular *adj* in name only

tizzies *n* ▷ tizzy

tizzy *n* (*pl* **-zies**) (*Informal*) confused or agitated state

> **tix** *pl n*. Tix is an informal word for **tickets**. This is a good word if you are struggling to use an X towards the end of a game.

to *prep* indicating movement towards, equality or comparison, etc. ▶ *adv* to a closed position

toad *n* (*pl* **-s**) animal like a large frog

toadied *v* ▷ toady

toadies *n, v* ▷ toady

toads *n* ▷ toad

toadstool *n* (*pl* **-s**) poisonous fungus like a mushroom

toadstools *n* ▷ toadstool

toady *n* (*pl* **-dies**) ingratiating person ▶ *v* (**-dies, -dying, -died**) be ingratiating

toadying *v* ▷ toady

toast[1] *n* (*pl* **-s**) sliced bread browned by heat ▶ *v* (**-s, -ing, -ed**) brown (bread) by heat

toast[2] *n* (*pl* **-s**) tribute or proposal of health or success marked by people raising glasses and drinking together ▶ *v* (**-s, -ing, -ed**) drink a toast to

toasted *v, n* ▷ toast[1, 2]

toaster *n* (*pl* **-s**) electrical device for toasting bread

toasters *n* ▷ toaster

toasting *n, v* ▷ toast[1, 2]

toasts *n, v* ▷ toast[1, 2]

tobacco *n* (*pl* **-os, -oes**) plant with large leaves dried for smoking

tobaccoes *n* ▷ tobacco

tobacconist *n* (*pl* **-s**) person or shop selling tobacco, cigarettes, etc.

tobacconists *n* ▷ tobacconist

tobaccos *n* ▷ tobacco

toboggan *n* (*pl* **-s**) narrow sledge for sliding over snow ▶ *v* (**-s, -ing, -ed**) ride a toboggan

tobogganed *v* ▷ toboggan

tobogganing *v* ▷ toboggan

toboggans *n, v* ▷ toboggan

toccata [tok-kah-ta] *n* (*pl* **-s**) rapid piece of music for a keyboard instrument

toccatas *n* ▷ toccata

today *n* (*pl* **-s**) this day ▶ *adv* on this day

todays *n* ▷ today

toddies *n* ▷ toddy

toddle *v* (**-les, -ling, -led**) walk with short unsteady steps

toddled *v* ▷ toddle

toddler *n* (*pl* **-s**) child beginning to walk

toddlers *n* ▷ toddler

toddles *v* ▷ toddle

toddling *v* ▷ toddle

toddy *n* (*pl* **-dies**) sweetened drink of spirits and hot water

toe *n* (*pl* **-s**) digit of the foot ▶ *v* (**toes, toeing, toed**) touch or kick with the toe

toed *v* ▷ toe

toeing *v* ▷ toe

toes *n, v* ▷ toe

toff *n* (*pl* **-s**) (BRIT) (*Slang*) well-dressed or upper-class person

toffee *n* (*pl* **-s**) chewy sweet made of boiled sugar

toffees *n* ▷ toffee

toffs *n* ▷ toff

tofu *n* (*pl* **-s**) soft food made from soya-bean curd

tofus *n* ▷ tofu

tog *n* (*pl* **-s**) unit for measuring the insulating

power of duvets

toga [**toe**-ga] n (pl **-s**) garment worn by citizens of ancient Rome
togas n ▷ toga

together adv in company ▶ adj (Informal) organized

toggle n (pl **-s**) small bar-shaped button inserted through a loop for fastening
toggles n ▷ toggle
togs n ▷ tog

toil n (pl **-s**) hard work ▶ v (**-s**, **-ing**, **-ed**) work hard
toiled v ▷ toil

toilet n (pl **-s**) (room with) a bowl connected to a drain for receiving and disposing of urine and faeces
toiletries n ▷ toiletry

toiletry n (pl **-ries**) object or cosmetic used to clean or groom oneself
toilets n ▷ toilet
toiling v ▷ toil
toils n, v ▷ toil

token n (pl **-s**) sign or symbol ▶ adj nominal or slight

tokenism n (pl **-s**) policy of making only a token effort, esp. to comply with a law
tokenisms n ▷ tokenism
tokens n ▷ token
told v ▷ tell

tolerable adj bearable > **tolerably** adv
tolerably adv ▷ tolerable

tolerance n (pl **-s**) acceptance of other people's rights to their own opinions or actions > **tolerant** adj > **tolerantly** adv > **toleration** n (pl **-s**)
tolerances n ▷ tolerance
tolerant adj ▷ tolerance
tolerantly adv ▷ tolerance

tolerate v (**-tes**, **-ting**, **-ted**) allow to exist or happen
tolerated v ▷ tolerate
tolerates v ▷ tolerate
tolerating v ▷ tolerate
toleration n ▷ tolerate
tolerations n ▷ tolerate

toll¹ v (**-s**, **-ing**, **-ed**) ring (a bell) slowly and regularly, esp. to announce a death ▶ n (pl **-s**) tolling

toll² n (pl **-s**) charge for the use of a bridge or road
tolled v ▷ toll¹
tolling v ▷ toll¹
tolls n ▷ toll¹, ² ▶ v ▷ toll¹

tom n (pl **-s**) male cat

tomahawk n (pl **-s**) fighting axe of the Native Americans
tomahawks n ▷ tomahawk

tomato n (pl **-es**) red fruit used in salads and as a vegetable
tomatoes n ▷ tomato

tomb n (pl **-s**) grave

tombola n (pl **-s**) lottery with tickets drawn from a revolving drum
tombolas n ▷ tombola

tomboy n (pl **-s**) girl who acts or dresses like a boy
tomboys n ▷ tomboy
tombs n ▷ tomb

tombstone n (pl **-s**) gravestone
tombstones n ▷ tombstone

tome n (pl **-s**) large heavy book
tomes n ▷ tome
tomfooleries n ▷ tomfoolery

tomfoolery n (pl **-ries**) foolish behaviour

tomorrow adv, n (pl **-s**) (on) the day after today
tomorrows n ▷ tomorrow
toms n ▷ tom

ton n (pl **-s**) unit of weight equal to 2240 pounds or 1016 kilograms or, in the US, 2000 pounds or 907 kilograms

tonal adj (MUSIC) written in a key > **tonality** n (pl **-ties**)
tonalities n ▷ tonal
tonality n ▷ tonal

tone n (pl **-s**) sound with reference to its pitch, volume, etc. ▶ v (**-nes**, **-ning**, **-ned**) harmonize (with) > **toneless** adj
toned v ▷ tone
toneless adj ▷ tone
tones n, v ▷ tone

tongs pl n large pincers for grasping and lifting

tongue n (pl **-s**) muscular organ in the mouth, used in speaking and tasting
tongues n ▷ tongue

tonic n (pl **-s**) medicine to improve body tone ▶ adj invigorating
tonics n ▷ tonic

tonight adv, n (pl **-s**) (in or during) the night or evening of this day
tonights n ▷ tonight
toning v ▷ tone

tonnage n (pl **-s**) weight capacity of a ship
tonnages n ▷ tonnage

tonne [**tunn**] n (pl **-s**) unit of weight equal to 1000 kilograms
tonnes n ▷ tonne
tons n ▷ ton

tonsil n (pl **-s**) small gland in the throat
tonsillectomies n ▷ tonsillectomy

tonsillectomy n (pl **-mies**) surgical removal

tonsillitis n (pl -tises) inflammation of the tonsils
tonsillitises n ▷ tonsillitis
tonsils n ▷ tonsil
tonsure n (pl -s) shaving of all or the top of the head as a religious or monastic practice ▷ **tonsured** adj
tonsured adj ▷ tonsure
tonsures n ▷ tonsure
too adv also, as well
took v ▷ take
tool n (pl -s) implement used by hand
tools n ▷ tool
toot n (pl -s) short hooting sound ▶ v (-s, -ing, -ed) (cause to) make such a sound
tooted v ▷ toot
tooth n (pl teeth) bonelike projection in the jaws of most vertebrates for biting and chewing ▷ **toothless** adj
toothless adj ▷ tooth
toothpaste n (pl -s) paste used to clean the teeth
toothpastes n ▷ toothpaste
toothpick n (pl -s) small stick for removing scraps of food from between the teeth
toothpicks n ▷ toothpick
tooting v ▷ toot
toots n, v ▷ toot
top¹ n (pl -s) highest point or part ▶ adj at or of the top ▶ v (-s, -pping, -pped) form a top on
top² n (pl -s) toy which spins on a pointed base
topaz [toe-pazz] n (pl -es) semiprecious stone in various colours
topazes n ▷ topaz
topee, topi [toe-pee] n (pl -s) lightweight hat worn in tropical countries
topees n ▷ topee
topi n ▷ topee
topiaries n ▷ topiary
topiary [tope-yar-ee] n (pl -ries) art of trimming trees and bushes into decorative shapes
topic n (pl -s) subject of a conversation, book, etc.
topical adj relating to current events ▷ **topicality** n (pl -ties)
topicalities n ▷ topical
topicality n ▷ topical
topics n ▷ topic
topis n ▷ topee
topless adj (of a costume or woman) with no covering for the breasts
topmost adj highest or best
topographer n ▷ topography
topographers n ▷ topography

topographical adj ▷ topography
topographies n ▷ topography
topography n (pl -phies) (science of describing) the surface features of a place ▷ **topographer** n (pl -s) ▷ **topographical** adj
topological adj ▷ topology
topologies n ▷ topology
topology n (pl -gies) geometry of the properties of a shape which are unaffected by continuous distortion ▷ **topological** adj
topped n ▷ top¹
topping n (pl -s) sauce or garnish for food ▶ v ▷ top¹
toppings n ▷ topping
topple v (-les, -ling, -led) (cause to) fall over
toppled v ▷ topple
topples v ▷ topple
toppling v ▷ topple
top-notch adj excellent, first-class
tops n ▷ top¹, ² ▶ v ▷ top¹
topsoil n (pl -s) surface layer of soil
topsoils n ▷ topsoil
toque [toke] n (pl -s) small round hat
toques n ▷ toque
tor n (pl -s) high rocky hill
torch n (pl -es) small portable battery-powered lamp ▶ v (-es, -ing, -ed) (Informal) deliberately set (a building) on fire
torched v ▷ torch
torches n, v ▷ torch
torching v ▷ torch
tore v ▷ tear²
toreador [torr-ee-a-dor] n (pl -s) bullfighter
toreadors n ▷ toreador
torment v (-s, -ing, -ed) cause (someone) great suffering ▶ n (pl -s) great suffering ▷ **tormentor** n (pl -s)
tormented v ▷ torment
tormenting v ▷ torment
tormentor n ▷ torment
tormentors n ▷ torment
torments v, n ▷ torment
torn v ▷ tear²
tornado n (pl -s, -es) violent whirlwind
tornadoes n ▷ tornado
tornados n ▷ tornado
torpedo n (pl -es) self-propelled underwater missile ▶ v (-es, -ing, -ed) attack or destroy with or as if with torpedoes
torpedoed v ▷ torpedo
torpedoes n, v ▷ torpedo
torpedoing v ▷ torpedo
torpid adj sluggish and inactive
torpor n (pl -s) torpid state
torpors n ▷ torpor

torque [tork] *n* (*pl* -s) force causing rotation
  torques *n* ▷ torque
torrent *n* (*pl* -s) rushing stream
torrential *adj* (of rain) very heavy
  torrents *n* ▷ torrent
torrid *adj* (-er, -est) very hot and dry
  torrider *adj* ▷ torrid
  torridest *adj* ▷ torrid
  tors *n* ▷ tor
torsion *n* (*pl* -s) twisting of a part by equal
  forces being applied at both ends but in
  opposite directions
  torsions *n* ▷ torsion
torso *n* (*pl* -s) trunk of the human body
  torsos *n* ▷ torso
tort *n* (*pl* -s) (LAW) civil wrong or injury for
  which damages may be claimed
tortilla *n* (*pl* -s) thin Mexican pancake
  tortillas *n* ▷ tortilla
tortoise *n* (*pl* -s) slow-moving land reptile with
  a dome-shaped shell
  tortoises *n* ▷ tortoise
tortoiseshell *n* (*pl* -s) mottled brown shell of
  a turtle, used for making ornaments ▸ *adj*
  having brown, orange, and black markings
  tortoiseshells *n* ▷ tortoiseshell
  torts *n* ▷ tort
tortuous *adj* winding or twisting
torture *v* (-res, -ring, -red) cause (someone)
  severe pain or mental anguish ▸ *n* (*pl* -s)
  severe physical or mental pain > **torturer**
  n (*pl* -s)
  tortured *v* ▷ torture
  torturer *n* ▷ torture
  torturers *n* ▷ torture
  tortures *v*, *n* ▷ torture
  torturing *v* ▷ torture
toss *v* (-es, -ing, -ed) throw lightly ▸ *n* (*pl* -es)
  tossing
  tossed *v* ▷ toss
  tosses *v*, *n* ▷ toss
  tossing *v* ▷ toss
tot[1] *n* (*pl* -s) small child
tot[2] *v* (-s, -tting, -tted) add (numbers) together
total *n* (*pl* -s) whole, esp. a sum of parts ▸ *adj*
  complete ▸ *v* (-s, -lling, -lled) amount to
  > **totally** *adv* > **totality** *n* (*pl* -ties)
totalitarian *adj* of a dictatorial one-party
  government > **totalitarianism** *n* (*pl* -s)
  totalitarianism *n* ▷ totalitarian
  totalitarianisms *n* ▷ totalitarian
  totalities *n* ▷ total
  totality *n* ▷ total
  totalled *v* ▷ total
  totalling *v* ▷ total

totally *adv* ▷ total
  totals *n*, *v* ▷ total
tote[1] *v* (-tes, -ting, -ted) carry (a gun etc.)
tote[2] *n* (*pl* -s) ▷ totalizator
  toted *v* ▷ tote[1]
totem *n* (*pl* -s) tribal badge or emblem
  totems *n* ▷ totem
  totes *v* ▷ tote[1] ▸ *n* ▷ tote[2]
  toting *v* ▷ tote[1]
  tots *n* ▷ tot[1] ▸ *v* ▷ tot[2]
  totted *v* ▷ tot[2]
totter *v* (-s, -ing, -ed) move unsteadily
  tottered *v* ▷ totter
  tottering *v* ▷ totter
  totters *v* ▷ totter
  totting *v* ▷ tot[2]
toucan *n* (*pl* -s) tropical American bird with
  a large bill
  toucans *n* ▷ toucan
touch *v* (-es, -ing, -ed) come into contact
  with ▸ *n* (*pl* -es) sense by which an object's
  qualities are perceived when they come into
  contact with part of the body ▸ *adj* of a non-
  contact version of particular sport
touché [too-shay] *interj* acknowledgement of
  the striking home of a remark or witty reply
touched *adj* emotionally moved ▸ *v* ▷ touch
  touches *v*, *n* ▷ touch
  touchier *adj* ▷ touchy
  touchiest *adj* ▷ touchy
touching *adj* emotionally moving ▸ *v* ▷ touch
touchline *n* (*pl* -s) side line of the pitch in some
  games
  touchlines *n* ▷ touchline
touchstone *n* (*pl* -s) standard by which a
  judgment is made
  touchstones *n* ▷ touchstone
touchy *adj* (-chier, -chiest) easily offended
tough *adj* (-er, -est) strong or resilient ▸ *n* (*pl* -s)
  (*Informal*) rough violent person > **toughness**
  n (*pl* -es)
toughen *v* (-s, -ing, -ed) make or become
  tough or tougher
  toughened *v* ▷ toughen
  toughening *v* ▷ toughen
  toughens *v* ▷ toughen
  tougher *adj* ▷ tough
  toughest *adj* ▷ tough
  toughness *n* ▷ tough
  toughnesses *n* ▷ tough
  toughs *n* ▷ tough
toupee [too-pay] *n* (*pl* -s) small wig
  toupees *n* ▷ toupee
tour *n* (*pl* -s) journey visiting places of interest
  along the way ▸ *v* (-s, -ing, -ed) make a tour

(of)

toured v ▷ tour

touring v ▷ tour

tourism n (pl -s) tourist travel as an industry

tourisms n ▷ tourism

tourist n (pl -s) person travelling for pleasure

tourists n ▷ tourist

touristy adj (Informal) (often derogatory) full of tourists or tourist attractions

tournament n (pl -s) sporting competition with several stages to decide the overall winner

tournaments n ▷ tournament

tourniquet [tour-nick-kay] n (pl -s) something twisted round a limb to stop bleeding

tourniquets n ▷ tourniquet

tours n, v ▷ tour

tousled adj ruffled and untidy

tout [rhymes with **shout**] v (-s, -ing, -ed) seek business in a persistent manner ▶ n (pl -s) person who sells tickets for a popular event at inflated prices

touted v ▷ tout

touting v ▷ tout

touts v, n ▷ tout

tow[1] v (-s, -ing, -ed) drag, esp. by means of a rope ▶ n (pl -s) towing

tow[2] n (pl -s) fibre of hemp or flax

toward n ▷ towards

towards, toward prep in the direction of

towbar n (pl -s) metal bar on a car for towing vehicles

towbars n ▷ towbar

towed v ▷ tow[1]

towel n (pl -s) cloth for drying things

towelling n (pl -s) material used for making towels

towellings n ▷ towelling

towels n ▷ towel

tower n (pl -s) tall structure, often forming part of a larger building

towers n ▷ tower

towing v ▷ tow[1]

town n (pl -s) group of buildings larger than a village

towns n ▷ town

township n (pl -s) small town

townships n ▷ township

towpath n (pl -s) path beside a canal or river, originally for horses towing boats

towpaths n ▷ towpath

tows n ▷ tow[1, 2], v ▷ tow[1]

toxaemia [tox-**seem**-ya] n (pl -s) blood poisoning

toxaemias n ▷ toxaemia

toxic adj poisonous > **toxicity** n (pl -ties)

toxicities n ▷ toxic

toxicity n ▷ toxic

toxicologies n ▷ toxicology

toxicology n (pl -gies) study of poisons

toxin n (pl -s) poison of bacterial origin

toxins n ▷ toxin

toy n (pl -s) something designed to be played with ▶ adj (of a dog) of a variety much smaller than is normal for that breed ▶ v (-s, -ing, -ed) play

toyed v ▷ toy

toying v ▷ toy

toys n, v ▷ toy

trace v (-ces, -cing, -ced) track down and find ▶ n (pl -s) track left by something > **traceable** adj

traceable adj ▷ trace

traced v ▷ trace

tracer n (pl -s) projectile which leaves a visible trail

traceries n ▷ tracery

tracers n ▷ tracer

tracery n (pl -ries) pattern of interlacing lines

traces v, n ▷ trace ▶ pl n strap by which a horse pulls a vehicle

trachea [track-**kee**-a] n (pl -cheae) windpipe

tracheae n ▷ trachea

tracheotomies n ▷ tracheotomy

tracheotomy [track-ee-ot-a-mee] n (pl -mies) surgical incision into the trachea

tracing n (pl -s) traced copy ▶ v ▷ trace

track n (pl -s) rough road or path ▶ v (-s, -ing, -ed) follow the trail or path of

tracked v ▷ track

tracking v ▷ track

tracks n, v ▷ track

tracksuit n (pl -s) warm loose-fitting suit worn by athletes etc., esp. during training

tracksuits n ▷ tracksuit

tract[1] n (pl -s) wide area

tract[2] n (pl -s) pamphlet, esp. a religious one

tractable adj easy to manage or control

traction n (pl -s) pulling, esp. by engine power

tractions n ▷ traction

tractor n (pl -s) motor vehicle with large rear wheels for pulling farm machinery

tractors n ▷ tractor

tracts n ▷ tract[1, 2]

trade n (pl -s) buying, selling, or exchange of goods ▶ v (-des, -ding, -ded) buy and sell > **trader** n (pl -s) > **trading** n (pl -s)

traded v ▷ trade

trademark n (pl -s) (legally registered) name or symbol used by a firm to distinguish its

goods
trademarks n ▷ trademark
trader n ▷ trade
traders n ▷ trade
trades n, v ▷ trade
tradesman n (pl -men) skilled worker
tradesman n ▷ tradesman
tradesmen n ▷ tradesman
trading v, n ▷ trade
tradings n ▷ trad
tradition n (pl -s) body of beliefs, customs, etc. handed down from generation to generation > traditional adj > traditionally adv
traditional adj ▷ tradition
traditionally adv ▷ tradition
traditions n ▷ tradition
traduce v (-ces, -cing, -ced) slander
traduced v ▷ traduce
traduces v ▷ traduce
traducing v ▷ traduce
traffic n (pl -s) vehicles coming and going on a road ▶ v (-fics, -ficking, -ficked) trade, usu. illicitly > trafficker n (pl -s)
trafficked v ▷ traffic
trafficker n ▷ traffic
traffickers n ▷ traffic
trafficking v ▷ traffic
traffics n, v ▷ traffic
tragedian [traj-jee-dee-an], tragedienne [traj-jee-dee-enn] n (pl -s) person who acts in or writes tragedies
tragedians n ▷ tragedian
tragedies n ▷ tragedy
tragedy n (pl -dies) shocking or sad event
tragic adj of or like a tragedy > tragically adv
tragically adv ▷ tragic
tragicomedies n ▷ tragicomedy
tragicomedy n (pl -s) play with both tragic and comic elements
trail n (pl -s) path, track, or road ▶ v (-s, -ing, -ed) drag along the ground
trailed v ▷ trail
trailer n (pl -s) vehicle designed to be towed by another vehicle
trailers n ▷ trailer
trailing v ▷ trail
trails n, v ▷ trail
train v (-s, -ing, -ed) instruct in a skill ▶ n (pl -s) line of railway coaches or wagons drawn by an engine
trained v ▷ train
trainee n (pl -s) person being trained
trainees n ▷ trainee
trainer n (pl -s) person who trains an athlete or sportsman
trainers n ▷ trainer

training v ▷ train
trains v, n ▷ train
traipse v (-pses, -psing, -psed) (Informal) walk wearily
traipsed v ▷ traipse
traipses v ▷ traipse
traipsing v ▷ traipse
trait n (pl -s) characteristic feature
traitor n (pl -s) person guilty of treason or treachery > traitorous adj
traitorous adj ▷ traitor
traitors n ▷ traitor
traits n ▷ trait
trajectories n ▷ trajectory
trajectory n (pl -ries) line of flight, esp. of a projectile
tram n (pl -s) public transport vehicle powered by an overhead wire and running on rails laid in the road
tramlines pl n track for trams
tramp v (-s, -ing, -ed) travel on foot, hike ▶ n (pl -s) homeless person who travels on foot
tramped v ▷ tramp
tramping v ▷ tramp
trample v (-les, -ling, -led) tread on and crush
trampled v ▷ trample
tramples v ▷ trample
trampling v ▷ trample
trampoline n (pl -s) tough canvas sheet attached to a frame by springs, used by acrobats etc. ▶ v (-nes, -ning, -ned) bounce on a trampoline
trampolined v ▷ trampoline
trampolines n, v ▷ trampoline
trampolining v ▷ trampoline
tramps n ▷ tramp
trams n ▷ tram
trance n (pl -s) unconscious or dazed state
trances n ▷ trance
tranche n (pl -s) portion of something large, esp. a sum of money
tranches n ▷ tranche
tranquil adj (-ler, -lest) calm and quiet > tranquilly adv > tranquillity n (pl -ties)
tranquiller adj ▷ tough
tranquillest adj ▷ tough
tranquillities n ▷ tranquil
tranquillity n ▷ tranquil
tranquillize v (-zes, -zing, -zed) make calm
tranquillized v ▷ tranquillize
tranquillizer n (pl -s) drug which reduces anxiety or tension
tranquillizers n ▷ tranquillizer
tranquillizes v ▷ tranquillize
tranquillizing v ▷ tranquillize

tranquilly adv ▷ tranquil

transact v (-s, -ing, -ed) conduct or negotiate (a business deal)
  transacted v ▷ transact
  transacting v ▷ transact

transaction n (pl -s) business deal transacted
  transactions n ▷ transaction
  transacts v ▷ transact

transatlantic adj on, from, or to the other side of the Atlantic

transceiver n (pl -s) transmitter and receiver of radio or electronic signals
  transceivers n ▷ transceiver

transcend v (-s, -ing, -ed) rise above
  > **transcendence** n (pl -s) > **transcendent** adj
  transcended v ▷ transcend
  transcendence n ▷ transcend
  transcendences n ▷ transcend
  transcendent adj ▷ transcend

transcendental adj based on intuition rather than experience
  transcending v ▷ transcend
  transcends v ▷ transcend

transcribe v (-bes, -bing, -bed) write down (something said)
  transcribed v ▷ transcribe
  transcribes v ▷ transcribe
  transcribing v ▷ transcribe

transcript n (pl -s) copy
  transcripts n ▷ transcript

transducer n (pl -s) device that converts one form of energy to another
  transducers n ▷ transducer

transept n (pl -s) either of the two shorter wings of a cross-shaped church
  transepts n ▷ transept

transexual n ▷ transsexual
  transexuals n ▷ transsexual

transfer v (-fers, -ferring, -ferred) move or send from one person or place to another ▶ n (pl -s)
  transferring > **transferable** adj
  transferable adj ▷ transfer

transference n (pl -s) transferring
  transferences n ▷ transference
  transferred v ▷ transfer
  transferring v ▷ transfer
  transfers v, n ▷ transfer

transfiguration n ▷ transfigure
  transfigurations n ▷ transfigure

transfigure v (-res, -ring, -red) change in appearance > **transfiguration** n (pl -s)
  transfigured v ▷ transfigure
  transfigures v ▷ transfigure
  transfiguring v ▷ transfigure

transfix v (-es, -ing, -ed) astound or stun

transfixed v ▷ transfix
  transfixes v ▷ transfix
  transfixing v ▷ transfix

transform v (-s, -ing, -ed) change the shape or character of > **transformation** n (pl -s)
  transformation n ▷ transform
  transformations n ▷ transform
  transformed v ▷ transform

transformer n (pl -s) device for changing the voltage of an alternating current
  transformers n ▷ transformer
  transforming v ▷ transform
  transforms v ▷ transform

transfuse v (-ses, -sing, -sed) give a transfusion to
  transfused v ▷ transfuse
  transfuses v ▷ transfuse
  transfusing v ▷ transfuse

transfusion n (pl -s) injection of blood into the blood vessels of a patient
  transfusions n ▷ transfusion

transgress v (-es, -ing, -ed) break (a moral law) > **transgression** n (pl -s) > **transgressor** n (pl -s)
  transgressed v ▷ transgress
  transgresses v ▷ transgress
  transgressing v ▷ transgress
  transgression n ▷ transgress
  transgressions n ▷ transgress
  transgressor n ▷ transgress
  transgressors n ▷ transgress

transience n ▷ transient
  transiences n ▷ transient

transient adj lasting only for a short time
  > **transience** n (pl -s)

transistor n (pl -s) semiconducting device used to amplify electric currents
  transistors n ▷ transistor

transit n (pl -s) movement from one place to another

transition n (pl -s) change from one state to another > **transitional** adj
  transitional adj ▷ transition
  transitions n ▷ transition

transitive adj (GRAMMAR) (of a verb) requiring a direct object

transitory adj not lasting long
  transits n ▷ transit

translate v (-tes, -ting, -ted) turn from one language into another > **translation** n (pl -s)
  > **translator** n (pl -s)
  translated v ▷ translate
  translates v ▷ translate
  translating v ▷ translate
  translation n ▷ translat

translations n ▷ translat
translator n ▷ translate
translators n ▷ translate
transliterate v (-tes, -ting, -ted) convert to the letters of a different alphabet
> **transliteration** n (pl -s)
transliterated v ▷ transliterate
transliterates v ▷ transliterate
transliterating v ▷ transliterate
transliteration n ▷ transliterate
translucence n ▷ translucence
translucences n ▷ translucent
translucencies n ▷ translucent
translucency n ▷ translucent
translucent adj letting light pass through, but not transparent > **translucence**,
translucency n (pl -cies, -ces)
transmigrate v (-tes, -ting, -ted) (of a soul) pass into another body > **transmigration** n (pl -s)
transmigrated v ▷ transmigrate
transmigrates v ▷ transmigrate
transmigrating v ▷ transmigrate
transmigration n ▷ transmigrate
transmigrations n ▷ transmigrate
transmission n (pl -s) transmitting
transmissions n ▷ transmission
transmit v (-mits, -mitting, -mitted) pass (something) from one person or place to another > **transmittable** adj > **transmitter** n (pl -s)
transmits v ▷ transmit
transmittable adj ▷ transmit
transmitted v ▷ transmit
transmitter n ▷ transmit
transmitters n ▷ transmit
transmitting v ▷ transmit
transmogrified v ▷ transmogrify
transmogrifies v ▷ transmogrify
transmogrify v (-fies, -fying, -fied) (Informal) change completely
transmogrifying v ▷ transmogrify
transmutation n ▷ transmute
transmutations n ▷ transmute
transmute v (-tes, -ting, -ted) change the form or nature of > **transmutation** n (pl -s)
transmuted v ▷ transmute
transmutes v ▷ transmute
transmuting v ▷ transmute
transom n (pl -s) horizontal bar across a window
transoms n ▷ transom
transparencies n ▷ transparency
transparency n (pl -cies) transparent quality
transparent adj able to be seen through, clear

> **transparently** adv
transparently adv ▷ transparent
transpiration n ▷ transpire
transpirations n ▷ transpire
transpire v (-res, -ring, -red) become known
> **transpiration** n (pl -s)
transpired v ▷ transpire
transpires v ▷ transpire
transpiring v ▷ transpire
transplant v (-s, -ing, -ed) transfer (an organ or tissue) surgically from one part or body to another ▶ n (pl -s) surgical transplanting
> **transplantation** n (pl -s)
transplantation n ▷ transplant
transplantations n ▷ transplant
transplanted v ▷ transplant
transplanting v ▷ transplant
transplants n ▷ transplant
transport v (-s, -ing, -ed) convey from one place to another ▶ n (pl -s) business or system of transporting > **transportation** n (pl -s)
transportation n ▷ transport
transportations n ▷ transport
transported v ▷ transport
transporter n (pl -s) large goods vehicle
transporters n ▷ transporter
transporting v ▷ transport
transports v, n ▷ transport
transpose v (-ses, -sing, -sed) interchange two things > **transposition** n (pl -s)
transposed v ▷ transpose
transposes v ▷ transpose
transposing v ▷ transpose
transposition n ▷ transpose
transpositions n ▷ transpose
transsexual, transexual n (pl -s) person of one sex who believes his or her true identity is of the opposite sex
transsexuals n ▷ transsexual
transuranic [tranz-yoor-ran-ik] adj (of an element) having an atomic number greater than that of uranium
transverse adj crossing from side to side
transvestite n (pl -s) person who seeks sexual pleasure by wearing the clothes of the opposite sex > **transvestism** n (pl -s)
transvestism n ▷ transvestite
transvestisms n ▷ transvestite
transvestites n ▷ transvestite
trap n (pl -s) device for catching animals ▶ v (-s, -pping, -pped) catch
trapdoor n (pl -s) door in floor or roof
trapdoors n ▷ trapdoor
trapeze n (pl -s) horizontal bar suspended from two ropes, used by circus acrobats

trapezes n ▷ trapeze

trapezia n ▷ trapezium

trapezium n (pl -ziums, -zia) quadrilateral with two parallel sides of unequal length

trapeziums n ▷ trapezium

trapezoid [trap-piz-zoid] n (pl -s) quadrilateral with no sides parallel

trapezoids n ▷ trapezoid

trapped n ▷ trap

trapper n (pl -s) person who traps animals for their fur

trappers n ▷ trapper

trapping n ▷ trap

trappings pl n accessories that symbolize an office or position

traps n, v ▷ trap

trash n (pl -es) anything worthless > **trashy** adj (-shier, -shiest)

trashes n ▷ trash

trashier adj ▷ trash

trashiest adj ▷ trash

trashy adj ▷ trash

trauma [traw-ma] n (pl -mata, -s) emotional shock > **traumatic** adj > **traumatize** v (-zes, -zing, -zed)

traumas n ▷ trauma

traumata n ▷ trauma

traumatic adj ▷ trauma

traumatized v ▷ trauma

traumatizes v ▷ trauma

traumatizing v ▷ trauma

travail n (pl -s) (Lit) labour or toil

travails n ▷ travail

travel v (-s, -lling, -lled) go from one place to another, through an area, or for a specified distance ▶ n (pl -s) travelling, esp. as a tourist > **traveller** n (pl -s)

travelled v ▷ travel

traveller n ▷ travel

travellers n ▷ travel

travelling v ▷ travel

travelogue n (pl -s) film or talk about someone's travels

travelogues n ▷ travelogue

travels v, n ▷ travel ▶ pl n (account of) travelling

traverse v (-ses, -sing, -sed) move over or back and forth over

traversed v ▷ traverse

traverses v ▷ traverse

traversing v ▷ traverse

travesties n ▷ travesty

travesty n (pl -ties) grotesque imitation or mockery

trawl n (pl -s) net dragged at deep levels behind a fishing boat ▶ v (-s, -ing, -ed) fish with such a net

trawled v ▷ trawl

trawler n (pl -s) trawling boat

trawlers n ▷ trawler

trawling v ▷ trawl

trawls n, v ▷ trawl

tray n (pl -s) flat board, usu. with a rim, for carrying things

trays n ▷ tray

treacheries n ▷ treachery

treacherous adj disloyal > **treacherously** adv

treacherously adv ▷ treacherous

treachery n (pl -ries) wilful betrayal

treacle n (pl -s) thick dark syrup produced when sugar is refined > **treacly** adj (-lier, -liest)

treacles n ▷ treacle

treaclier adj ▷ treacle

treacliest adj ▷ treacle

treacly adj ▷ treacle

tread v (-s, -ing, trod, trodden or trod) set one's foot on ▶ n (pl -s) way of walking or dancing

treading v ▷ tread

treadle [tred-dl] n (pl -s) lever worked by the foot to turn a wheel

treadles n ▷ treadle

treadmill n (pl -s) (HIST) cylinder turned by treading on steps projecting from it

treadmills n ▷ treadmill

treads v, n ▷ tread

treason n (pl -s) betrayal of one's sovereign or country > **treasonable** adj

treasonable adj ▷ treason

treasons n ▷ treason

treasure n (pl -s) collection of wealth, esp. gold or jewels ▶ v (-res, -ring, -red) prize or cherish

treasured v ▷ treasure

treasurer n (pl -s) official in charge of funds

treasurers n ▷ treasurer

treasures n, v ▷ treasure

treasuries n ▷ treasury

treasuring v ▷ treasure

treasury n (pl -ries) storage place for treasure

treat v (-s, -ing, -ed) deal with or regard in a certain manner ▶ n (pl -s) pleasure, entertainment, etc. given or paid for by someone else

treated v ▷ treat

treaties n ▷ treaty

treating v ▷ treat

treatise [treat-izz] n (pl -s) formal piece of writing on a particular subject

treatises n ▷ treatise

treatment n (pl -s) medical care

treatments n ▷ treatment

treats v, n ▷ treat

treaty n (pl -ties) signed contract between states

treble adj triple (MUSIC) ▶ n (pl -s) (singer with or part for) a soprano voice ▶ v (-les, -ling, -led) increase three times > **trebly** adv

trebled v ▷ treble

trebles n, v ▷ treble

trebling v ▷ treble

trebly adv ▷ treble

tree n (pl -s) large perennial plant with a woody trunk > **treeless** adj

treeless adj ▷ tree

trees n ▷ tree

trefoil [tref-foil] n (pl -s) plant, such as clover, with a three-lobed leaf

trefoils n ▷ trefoil

trek n (pl -s) long difficult journey, esp. on foot ▶ v (-s, -kking, -kked) make such a journey

trekked v ▷ trek

trekking v ▷ trek

treks n, v ▷ trek

trellis n (pl -ises) framework of horizontal and vertical strips of wood

trellises n ▷ trellis

tremble v (-les, -ling, -led) shake or quiver ▶ n (pl -les) trembling > **trembling** adj

trembled v ▷ tremble

trembles v, n ▷ tremble

trembling v, adj ▷ tremble

tremendous adj huge > **tremendously** adv

tremendously adv ▷ tremendous

tremolo n (pl -s) (MUSIC) quivering effect in singing or playing

tremolos n ▷ tremolo

tremor n (pl -s) involuntary shaking

tremors n ▷ tremor

tremulous adj trembling, as from fear or excitement

trench n (pl -es) long narrow ditch, esp. one used as a shelter in war

trenchant adj incisive

trencher n (pl -s) (HIST) wooden plate for serving food

trencherman n (pl -men) hearty eater

trenchermen n ▷ trencherman

trenchers n ▷ trencher

trenches n ▷ trench

trend n (pl -s) general tendency or direction

trendier adj ▷ trendy

trendies n ▷ trendy

trendiest adj ▷ trendy

trendiness n ▷ trendy

trendinesses n ▷ trendy

trends n ▷ trend

trendy adj (-dier, -diest) ▶ n (pl -dies) (Informal) consciously fashionable (person) > **trendiness** n (pl -es)

trepidation n (pl -s) fear or anxiety

trepidations n ▷ trepidation

trespass v (-es, -ing, -ed) go onto another's property without permission ▶ n (pl -es) trespassing > **trespasser** n (pl -s)

trespassed v ▷ trespass

trespasser n ▷ trespass

trespassers n ▷ trespass

trespasses v, n ▷ trespass

trespassing v ▷ trespass

tresses pl n long flowing hair

trestle n (pl -s) board fixed on pairs of spreading legs, used as a support

trestles n ▷ trestle

trevallies n ▷ trevally

trevally n (pl -lies) (AUST & NZ) any of various food and game fishes

trews pl n close-fitting tartan trousers

triad n (pl -s) group of three

triads n ▷ triad

trial n (pl -s) investigation of a case before a judge

trials n ▷ trial ▶ pl n sporting competition for individuals

triangle n (pl -s) geometric figure with three sides > **triangular** adj

triangles n ▷ triangle

triangular adj ▷ triangle

tribal adj ▷ tribe

tribalism n (pl -s) loyalty to a tribe

tribalisms n ▷ tribalism

tribe n (pl -s) group of clans or families believed to have a common ancestor > **tribal** adj

tribes n ▷ tribe

tribulation n (pl -s) great distress

tribulations n ▷ tribulation

tribunal n (pl -s) board appointed to inquire into a specific matter

tribunals n ▷ tribunal

tribune n (pl -s) people's representative, esp. in ancient Rome

tribunes n ▷ tribune

tributaries n ▷ tributary

tributary n (pl -ries) stream or river flowing into a larger one ▶ adj (of a stream or river) flowing into a larger one

tribute n (pl -s) sign of respect or admiration

tributes n ▷ tribute

trice n (pl -s) moment

triceps n (pl -pses) muscle at the back of the upper arm tricepses *n* ▷ triceps

trices *n* ▷ trice

trichologies *n* ▷ trichology

trichologist *n* ▷ trichology

trichologists *n* ▷ trichology

trichology [trick-ol-a-jee] *n* (*pl* -gies) study and treatment of hair and its diseases > **trichologist** *n* (*pl* -s)

trick *n* (*pl* -s) deceitful or cunning action or plan ▶ *v* (-s, -ing, -ed) cheat or deceive > **trickery** *n* (*pl* -ries) > **trickster** *n* (*pl* -s)

tricked *v* ▷ trick

trickeries *n* ▷ trick

trickery *n* ▷ trick

trickier *adj* ▷ tricky

trickiest *adj* ▷ tricky

tricking *v* ▷ trick

trickle *v* (-les, -ling, -led) (cause to) flow in a thin stream or drops ▶ *n* (*pl* -s) gradual flow

trickled *v* ▷ trickle

trickles *v*, *n* ▷ trickle

trickling *v* ▷ trickle

tricks *n*, *v* ▷ trick

trickster *n* ▷ trick

tricksters *n* ▷ trick

tricky *adj* (-kier, -kiest) difficult, needing careful handling

tricolour [trick-kol-lor] *n* (*pl* -s) three-coloured striped flag

tricolours *n* ▷ tricolour

tricycle *n* (*pl* -s) three-wheeled cycle

tricycles *n* ▷ tricycle

trident *n* (*pl* -s) three-pronged spear

tridents *n* ▷ trident

tried *v* ▷ try

triennial *adj* happening every three years

tries *v*, *n* ▷ try

trifle *n* (*pl* -s) insignificant thing or amount

trifles *n* ▷ trifle

trifling *adj* insignificant

trigger *n* (*pl* -s) small lever releasing a catch on a gun or machine ▶ *v* (-s, -ing, -ed) (*usu. foll. by off*) set (an action or process) in motion

triggered *v* ▷ trigger

triggering *v* ▷ trigger

triggers *n*, *v* ▷ trigger

trigonometries *n* ▷ trigonometry

trigonometry *n* (*pl* -ries) branch of mathematics dealing with relations of the sides and angles of triangles

trike *n* (*pl* -s) (*informal*) tricycle

trikes *n* ▷ trike

trilateral *adj* having three sides

trilbies *n* ▷ trilby

trilby *n* (*pl* -bies) man's soft felt hat

trill *n* (*pl* -s) (MUSIC) rapid alternation between two notes ▶ *v* (-s, -ing, -ed) play or sing a trill

trilled *v* ▷ trill

trilling *v* ▷ trill

trillion *n* (*pl* -s) one million million, 10^{12}

trillions *n* ▷ trillion

trills *n*, *v* ▷ trill

trilobite [trile-oh-bite] *n* (*pl* -s) small prehistoric sea animal

trilobites *n* ▷ trilobite

trilogies *n* ▷ trilogy

trilogy *n* (*pl* -gies) series of three related books, plays, etc.

trim *adj* (-mmer, -mmest) neat and smart ▶ *v* (-s, -mming, -mmed) cut or prune into good shape ▶ *n* (*pl* -s) decoration

trimaran [trime-a-ran] *n* (*pl* -s) three-hulled boat

trimarans *n* ▷ trimaran

trimmed *v* ▷ trim

trimmer *adj* ▷ trim

trimmest *adj* ▷ trim

trimming *n* (*pl* -s) decoration ▶ *v* ▷ trim

trimmings *n* ▷ trimming ▶ *pl n* usual accompaniments

trims *v*, *n* ▷ trim

trinities *n* ▷ trinity

trinitrotoluene *n* (*pl* -s) TNT

trinitrotoluenes *n* ▷ trinitrotoluene

trinity *n* (*pl* -ties) group of three

trinket *n* (*pl* -s) small or worthless ornament or piece of jewellery

trinkets *n* ▷ trinket

trio *n* (*pl* -s) group of three

trios *n* ▷ trio

trip *n* (*pl* -s) journey to a place and back, esp. for pleasure ▶ *v* (-s, -pping, -pped) (cause to) stumble

tripe *n* (*pl* -s) stomach of a cow used as food

tripes *n* ▷ tripe

triple *adj* having three parts ▶ *v* (-les, -ling, -led) increase three times

tripled *v* ▷ triple

triples *v* ▷ triple

triplet *n* (*pl* -s) one of three babies born at one birth

triplets *n* ▷ triplet

triplicate *adj* tripling

tripling *v* ▷ triple

tripod [tripe-pod] *n* (*pl* -s) three-legged stand, stool, etc.

tripods *n* ▷ tripod

tripos [tripe-poss] *n* (*pl* -poses) final examinations for an honours degree at Cambridge University

triposes *n* ▷ tripos

tripped v ▷ trip

tripper n (pl -s) tourist
trippers n ▷ tripper
tripping v ▷ trip
trips n, v ▷ trip

triptych [trip-tick] n (pl -s) painting or carving on three hinged panels, often forming an altarpiece
triptychs n ▷ triptych

trite adj (of a remark or idea) commonplace and unoriginal

tritium n (pl -s) radioactive isotope of hydrogen
tritiums n ▷ tritium

triumph n (pl -s) (happiness caused by) victory or success ▶ v (-s, -ing, -ed) be victorious or successful

triumphal adj celebrating a triumph

triumphant adj feeling or showing triumph
triumphed v ▷ triumph
triumphing v ▷ triumph
triumphs n, v ▷ triumph

triumvirate [try-umm-vir-rit] n (pl -s) group of three people in joint control
triumvirates n ▷ triumvirate

trivet [triv-vit] n (pl -s) metal stand for a pot or kettle
trivets n ▷ trivet

trivia pl n trivial things or details

trivial adj of little importance > trivially adv
> triviality n (pl -ties)
trivialities n ▷ trivial
triviality n ▷ trivial

trivialize v (-zes, -zing, -zed) make (something) seem less important or complex than it is
trivialized v ▷ trivialize
trivializes v ▷ trivialize
trivializing v ▷ trivialize
trivially adv ▷ trivial

trod v ▷ tread

trodden v ▷ tread

troglodyte n (pl -s) cave dweller
troglodytes n ▷ troglodyte

troika n (pl -s) Russian vehicle drawn by three horses abreast
troikas n ▷ troika

troll n (pl -s) giant or dwarf in Scandinavian folklore

trolley n (pl -s) small wheeled table for food and drink
trolleys n ▷ trolley

trollop n (pl -s) (Old-fashioned) promiscuous or slovenly woman
trollops n ▷ trollop

trolls n ▷ troll

trombone n (pl -s) brass musical instrument with a sliding tube > trombonist n (pl -s)
trombones n ▷ trombone
trombonist n ▷ trombone
trombonists n ▷ trombone

troop n (pl -s) large group ▶ v (-s, -ing, -ed) move in a crowd
trooped v ▷ troop

trooper n (pl -s) cavalry soldier
troopers n ▷ trooper
trooping v ▷ troop

troops n, v ▷ troop ▶ pl n soldiers

trope n (pl -s) figure of speech
tropes n ▷ trope

trophies n ▷ trophy

trophy n (pl -phies) cup, shield, etc. given as a prize

tropic n (pl -s) either of two lines of latitude at 23½°N (tropic of Cancer) or 23½°S (tropic of Capricorn) ▶ pl n part of the earth's surface between these lines

tropical adj of or in the tropics
tropics n ▷ tropic

trot v (-s, -tting, -tted) (of a horse) move at a medium pace, lifting the feet in diagonal pairs ▶ n (pl -s) trotting

troth [rhymes with growth] n (pl -s) (Obs) pledge of devotion, esp. a betrothal
troths n ▷ troth
trots v, n ▷ trot
trotted v ▷ trot

trotter n (pl -s) pig's foot
trotters n ▷ trotter
trotting v ▷ trot

troubadour [troo-bad-oor] n (pl -s) medieval travelling poet and singer
troubadours n ▷ troubadour

trouble n (pl -s) (cause of) distress or anxiety ▶ v (-les, -ling, -led) (cause to) worry > troubled adj > troublesome adj
troubled v, adj ▷ trouble
troubles n, v ▷ trouble

troubleshooter n (pl -s) person employed to locate and deal with faults or problems
troubleshooters n ▷ troubleshooter
troublesome adj ▷ trouble
troubling v ▷ trouble

trough [troff] n (pl -s) long open container, esp. for animals' food or water
troughs n ▷ trough

trounce v (-ces, -cing, -ced) defeat utterly
trounced v ▷ trounce
trounces v ▷ trounce
trouncing v ▷ trounce

troupe [troop] n (pl **-s**) company of performers
> **trouper** n (pl **-s**)
  trouper n ▷ troupe
  troupers n ▷ troupe
  troupes n ▷ troupe

trouser adj of trousers

trousers pl n two-legged outer garment with
legs reaching usu. to the ankles

trousseau [troo-so] n (pl **-seaux, -seaus**) bride's
collection of clothing etc. for her marriage
  trousseaus n ▷ trousseau
  trousseaux n ▷ trousseau

trout n (pl **trout, trouts**) game fish related to
the salmon
  trouts n ▷ trout

trowel n (pl **-s**) hand tool with a wide blade for
spreading mortar, lifting plants, etc.
  trowels n ▷ trowel
  truancies n ▷ truant
  truancy n ▷ truant

truant n (pl **-s**) pupil who stays away from school
without permission > **truancy** n (pl **-cies**)
  truants n ▷ truant

truce n (pl **-s**) temporary agreement to stop
fighting
  truces n ▷ truce

truck[1] n (pl **-s**) railway goods wagon

truck[2] n (pl **-s**) commercial goods

trucker n (pl **-s**) truck driver
  truckers n ▷ trucker
  trucks n ▷ truck[1, 2]

truculence n ▷ truculent
  truculences n ▷ truculent

truculent [truck-yew-lent] adj aggressively
defiant > **truculence** n (pl **-s**)

trudge v (**-dges, -dging, -dged**) walk heavily or
wearily ▶ n (pl **-s**) long tiring walk
  trudged v ▷ trudge
  trudges v, n ▷ trudge
  trudging v ▷ trudge

true adj (**truer, truest**) in accordance with facts
> **truly** adv
  truer adj ▷ true
  truest adj ▷ true

truffle n (pl **-s**) edible underground fungus
  truffles n ▷ truffle

trug n (pl **-s**) (BRIT) long shallow basket used by
gardeners
  trugs n ▷ trug

truism n (pl **-s**) self-evident truth
  truisms n ▷ truism
  truly adv ▷ true

trump[1] n (pl **-s**) ▶ adj (card) of the suit
outranking the others ▶ v (**-s, -ing, -ed**) play a
trump card on (another card)

trump[2] n (pl **-s**) (Lit) (sound of) a trumpet
  trumped v ▷ trump[1]

trumpet n (pl **-s**) valved brass instrument with
a flared tube ▶ v (**-s, -ing, -ed**) proclaim loudly
> **trumpeter** n (pl **-s**)
  trumpeted v ▷ trumpet
  trumpeter n ▷ trumpet
  trumpeters n ▷ trumpet
  trumpeting v ▷ trumpet
  trumpets n, ▷ trumpet
  trumping v ▷ trump[1]

trumps n ▷ trump[1, 2] ▶ pl n suit outranking the
others ▶ v ▷ trump[1]

truncate v (**-tes, -ting, -ted**) cut short
  truncated v ▷ truncate
  truncates v ▷ truncate
  truncating v ▷ truncate

truncheon n (pl **-s**) club carried by a policeman
  truncheons n ▷ truncheon

trundle v (**-les, -ling, -led**) move heavily on
wheels
  trundled v ▷ trundle
  trundles v ▷ trundle
  trundling v ▷ trundle

trunk n (pl **-s**) main stem of a tree

trunks n ▷ trunk ▶ pl n man's swimming shorts

truss v (**-es, -ing, -ed**) tie or bind up ▶ n (pl **-es**)
device for holding a hernia in place
  trussed v ▷ truss
  trusses v, n ▷ truss
  trussing v ▷ truss

trust v (**-s, -ing, -ed**) believe in and rely on ▶ n
(pl **-s**) confidence in the truth, reliability, etc.
of a person or thing
  trusted v ▷ trust

trustee n (pl **-s**) person holding property on
another's behalf
  trustees n ▷ trustee

trustful, trusting adj inclined to trust others
  trustier adj ▷ trusty
  trustiest adj ▷ trusty
  trusting v ▷ trust ▶ adj ▷ trustful

trusts n, v ▷ trust

trustworthy adj reliable or honest

trusty adj (**-tier, -tiest**) faithful or reliable

truth n (pl **-s**) state of being true

truthful adj honest > **truthfully** adv
  truthfully adv ▷ truthful
  truths n ▷ truth

try v (**tries, trying, tried**) make an effort or
attempt ▶ n (pl **tries**) attempt or effort

trying adj (Informal) difficult or annoying ▶ v
▷ try

tryst n (pl **-s**) arrangement to meet
  trysts n ▷ tryst

tsar, czar [zahr] n (pl **-s**) (HIST) Russian emperor
tsars n ▷ tsar

tsk interj. Tsk is a sound people make to show disapproval. This is a useful word because it enables you to play K without using vowels, which is handy if your rack is low on vowel tiles. Tsk scores 7 points.

tsunami n (pl **-mis, -mi**) tidal wave, usu. caused by an earthquake under the sea
tsunamis n ▷ tsunami

tuatara n (pl **-s**) large lizard-like New Zealand reptile
tuataras n ▷ tuatara

tub n (pl **-s**) open, usu. round container

tuba [tube-a] n (pl **-s**) valved low-pitched brass instrument
tubas n ▷ tuba

tubbier adj ▷ tubby

tubbiest adj ▷ tubby

tubby adj (**tubbier, tubbiest**) (of a person) short and fat

tube n (pl **-s**) hollow cylinder

tuber [tube-er] n (pl **-s**) fleshy underground root of a plant such as a potato > **tuberous** adj

tubercle [tube-er-kl] n (pl **-s**) small rounded swelling
tubercles n ▷ tubercle

tubercular adj ▷ tuberculosis

tuberculin n (pl **-s**) extract from a bacillus used to test for tuberculosis
tuberculins n ▷ tuberculin

tuberculosis [tube-berk-yew-lohss-iss] n (pl **-ses**) infectious disease causing tubercles, esp. in the lungs > **tubercular** adj
tuberculoses n ▷ tuberculosis

tuberous adj ▷ tuber

tubers n ▷ tuber

tubes n ▷ tube

tubing n (pl **-s**) length of tube
tubings n ▷ tubing

tubs n ▷ tub

tubular [tube-yew-lar] adj of or shaped like a tube

tuck v (**-s, -ing, -ed**) push or fold into a small space ▶ n (pl **-s**) stitched fold
tucked v ▷ tuck

tucker n (pl **-s**) (AUST & NZ) (Informal) food
tuckers n ▷ tucker
tucking v ▷ tuck
tucks v, n ▷ tuck

tufa [tew-fa] n (pl **-s**) porous rock formed as a deposit from springs
tufas n ▷ tufa

tuffet n (pl **-s**) small mound or seat

tuffets n ▷ tuffet

tuft n (pl **-s**) bunch of feathers, grass, hair, etc. held or growing together at the base
tufts n ▷ tuft

tug v (**-s, -gging, -gged**) pull hard ▶ n (pl **-s**) hard pull
tugged v ▷ tug
tugging v ▷ tug
tugs v, n ▷ tug

tuition n (pl **-s**) instruction, esp. received individually or in a small group
tuitions n ▷ tuition

tulip n (pl **-s**) plant with bright cup-shaped flowers
tulips n ▷ tulip

tulle [tewl] n (pl **-s**) fine net fabric of silk etc.
tulles n ▷ tulle

tumble v (**-les, -ling, -led**) (cause to) fall, esp. awkwardly or violently ▶ n (pl **-s**) fall
tumbled v ▷ tumble

tumbledown adj dilapidated

tumbler n (pl **-s**) stemless drinking glass
tumblers n ▷ tumbler
tumbles v, n ▷ tumble
tumbling v ▷ tumble
tumbrel n ▷ tumbril
tumbrels n ▷ tumbril

tumbril, tumbrel n (pl **-s**) farm cart used during the French Revolution to take prisoners to the guillotine
tumbrils n ▷ tumbril

tumescent [tew-mess-ent] adj swollen or becoming swollen

tummies n ▷ tummy

tummy n (pl **-mies**) (Informal) stomach

tumour [tew-mer] n (pl **-s**) abnormal growth in or on the body
tumours n ▷ tumour

tumuli n ▷ tumulus

tumult n (pl **-s**) uproar or commotion > **tumultuous** [tew-mull-tew-uss] ▶ adj
tumults n ▷ tumult

tumultuous adj ▷ tumult

tumulus n (pl **-li**) burial mound

tun n (pl **-s**) large beer cask

tuna n (pl **-s**) large marine food fish
tunas n ▷ tuna

tundra n (pl **-s**) vast treeless Arctic region with permanently frozen subsoil
tundras n ▷ tundra

tune n (pl **-s**) (pleasing) sequence of musical notes ▶ v (**-nes, -ning, -ned**) adjust (a musical instrument) so that it is in tune > **tuneful** adj > **tunefully** adv > **tuneless** adj > **tuner** n (pl **-s**)
tuned v ▷ tune

tuneful adj ▷ tune
tunefully adv ▷ tune
tuneless adj ▷ tune
tuner n ▷ tune
tuners n ▷ tune
tunes n, v ▷ tune
tungsten n (pl -s) (CHEM) greyish-white metal
tungstens n ▷ tungsten
tunic n (pl -s) close-fitting jacket forming part of some uniforms
tunics n ▷ tunic
tuning v ▷ tune
tunnel n (pl -s) underground passage ▶ v (-s, -lling, -lled) make a tunnel (through)
tunnelled v ▷ tunnel
tunnelling v ▷ tunnel
tunnels n, v ▷ tunnel
tunnies n ▷ tunny
tunny n (pl -nies, -ny) tuna
tuns n ▷ tun
tup n (pl -s) male sheep
tups n ▷ tup
turban n (pl -s) Muslim, Hindu, or Sikh man's head covering, made by winding cloth round the head
turbans n ▷ turban
turbid adj muddy, not clear
turbine n (pl -s) machine or generator driven by gas, water, etc. turning blades
turbines n ▷ turbine
turbot n (pl -s) large European edible flatfish
turbots n ▷ turbot
turbulence n (pl -s) confusion, movement, or agitation > **turbulent** adj
turbulences n ▷ turbulence
turbulent adj ▷ turbulence
tureen n (pl -s) serving dish for soup
tureens n ▷ tureen
turf n (pl -s, turves) short thick even grass ▶ v (-s, -ing, -ed) cover with turf
turfed v ▷ turf
turfing v ▷ turf
turfs n, v ▷ turf
turgid [tur-jid] adj (-er, -est) (of language) pompous
turgider adj ▷ turgid
turgidest adj ▷ turgid
turkey n (pl -s) large bird bred for food
turkeys n ▷ turkey
turmeric n (pl -s) yellow spice obtained from the root of an Asian plant
turmerics n ▷ turmeric
turmoil n (pl -s) agitation or confusion
turmoils n ▷ turmoil
turn v (-s, -ing, -ed) change the position or

direction (of) ▶ n (pl -s) turning > **turner** n (pl -s)
turncoat n (pl -s) person who deserts one party or cause to join another
turncoats n ▷ turncoat
turned v ▷ turn
turner n ▷ turn
turners n ▷ turn
turning n (pl -s) road or path leading off a main route ▶ v ▷ turn
turnings n ▷ turning
turnip n (pl -s) root vegetable with orange or white flesh
turnips n ▷ turnip
turnout n (pl -s) number of people appearing at a gathering
turnouts n ▷ turnout
turnover n (pl -s) total sales made by a business over a certain period
turnovers n ▷ turnover
turnpike n (pl -s) (BRIT) road where a toll is collected at barriers
turnpikes n ▷ turnpike
turns v, n ▷ turn
turnstile n (pl -s) revolving gate for admitting one person at a time
turnstiles n ▷ turnstile
turntable n (pl -s) revolving platform
turntables n ▷ turntable
turnup n (pl -s) turned-up fold at the bottom of a trouser leg
turnups n ▷ turnup
turpentine n (pl -s) (oil made from) the resin of certain trees
turpentines n ▷ turpentine
turpitude n (pl -s) wickedness
turpitudes n ▷ turpitude
turps n turpentine oil
turquoise adj blue-green ▶ n (pl -s) blue-green precious stone
turquoises n ▷ turquoise
turret n (pl -s) small tower
turrets n ▷ turret
turtle n (pl -s) sea tortoise
turtledove n (pl -s) small wild dove
turtledoves n ▷ turtledove
turtleneck n (pl -s) (sweater with) a round high close-fitting neck
turtlenecks n ▷ turtleneck
turtles n ▷ turtle
turves n ▷ turf
tusk n (pl -s) long pointed tooth of an elephant, walrus, etc.
tusks n ▷ tusk
tussle n (pl -s) ▶ v (-les, -ling, -led) fight or

scuffle

tussled v ▷ **tussle**

tussles n, v ▷ **tussle**

tussling v ▷ **tussle**

tussock n (pl -s) tuft of grass

tussocks n ▷ **tussock**

tutelage [tew-till-lij] n (pl -s) instruction or guidance, esp. by a tutor > **tutelary** [tew-till-lar-ee] ▶ adj

tutelages n ▷ **tutelage**

tutelary adj ▷ **tutelage**

tutor n (pl -s) person teaching individuals or small groups ▶ v (-s, -ing, -ed) act as a tutor to

tutored v ▷ **tutor**

tutorial n (pl -s) period of instruction with a tutor

tutorials n ▷ **tutorial**

tutoring v ▷ **tutor**

tutors n, v ▷ **tutor**

tutu n (pl -s) short stiff skirt worn by ballerinas

tutus n ▷ **tutu**

> **tux** n (**tuxes**). Tux is a short form of **tuxedo**. This is a very useful word, as U and T are common tiles, so look for opportunities to play it when you get an X. Tux scores 10 points.

tuxedo n (pl -s) (US & AUST) dinner jacket

tuxedos n ▷ **tuxedo**

twaddle n (pl -s) silly or pretentious talk or writing

twaddles n ▷ **twaddle**

twain n (pl -s) (Obs) two

twains n ▷ **twain**

twang n (pl -s) sharp ringing sound ▶ v (-s, -ing, -ed) (cause to) make a twang

twanged v ▷ **twang**

twanging v ▷ **twang**

twangs n, v ▷ **twang**

tweak v (-s, -ing, -ed) pinch or twist sharply ▶ n (pl -s) tweaking

tweaked v ▷ **tweak**

tweaking v ▷ **tweak**

tweaks v, n ▷ **tweak**

twee adj (Informal) (-r, -st) too sentimental, sweet, or pretty

tweed n (pl -s) thick woollen cloth > **tweedy** adj (-dier, -diest)

tweedier adj ▷ **tweed**

tweediest adj ▷ **tweed**

tweeds n ▷ **tweed** ▶ pl n suit of tweed

tweedy adj ▷ **tweed**

tweer adj ▷ **twee**

tweest adj ▷ **twee**

tweet n (pl -s) ▶ v (-s, -ing, -ed) chirp

tweeted v ▷ **tweet**

tweeter n (pl -s) loudspeaker reproducing high-frequency sounds

tweeters n ▷ **tweeter**

tweeting v ▷ **tweet**

tweets n, v ▷ **tweet**

tweezers pl n small pincer-like tool

twelfth adj, n (pl -s) (of) number twelve in a series

twelfths n ▷ **twelfth**

twelve adj, n (pl -s) two more than ten

twelves n ▷ **twelve**

twenties n ▷ **twenty**

twentieth adj ▷ **twenty**

twentieths n ▷ **twenty**

twenty adj, n (pl -ties) two times ten > **twentieth** adj, n ▷ **twenty**

twerp n (pl -s) (Informal) silly person

twerps n ▷ **twerp**

twice adv two times

twiddle v (-les, -ling, -led) fiddle or twirl in an idle way

twiddled v ▷ **twiddle**

twiddles v ▷ **twiddle**

twiddling v ▷ **twiddle**

twig¹ n (pl -s) small branch or shoot

twig² v (-s, -gging, -gged) (Informal) realize or understand

twigged v ▷ **twig²**

twigging v ▷ **twig²**

twigs n ▷ **twig¹** ▶ v ▷ **twig²**

twilight n (pl -s) soft dim light just after sunset

twilights n ▷ **twilight**

twill n (pl -s) fabric woven to produce parallel ridges

twills n ▷ **twill**

twin n (pl -s) one of a pair, esp. of two children born at one birth ▶ v (-s, -nning, -nned) pair or be paired

twine n (pl -es) string or cord ▶ v (-nes, -ning, -ned) twist or coil round

twined v ▷ **twine**

twines n, v ▷ **twine**

twining v ▷ **twine**

twinge n (pl -s) sudden sharp pain or emotional pang

twinges n ▷ **twinge**

twinkle v (-les, -ling, -led) shine brightly but intermittently ▶ n (pl -les) flickering brightness

twinkled v ▷ **twinkle**

twinkles v, n ▷ **twinkle**

twinkling v ▷ **twinkle**

twinned v ▷ **twin**

twinning v ▷ **twin**

twins n, v ▷ **twin**

twirl v (-s, -ing, -ed) turn or spin around quickly
    twirled v ▷ twirl
    twirling v ▷ twirl
    twirls v ▷ twirl
twist v (-s, -ing, -ed) turn out of the natural position ▸ n (pl -s) twisting
    twisted adj (of a person) cruel or perverted ▸ v ▷ twist
    twister n (pl -s) (BRIT) (Informal) swindler
    twisters n ▷ twister
    twisting v ▷ twist
    twists v, n ▷ twist
twit[1] v (-s, -tting, -tted) poke fun at (someone)
twit[2] n (pl -s) (Informal) foolish person
twitch v (-es, -ing, -ed) move spasmodically ▸ n (pl -es) nervous muscular spasm
    twitched v ▷ twitch
    twitches v, n ▷ twitch
    twitching v ▷ twitch
    twits n ▷ twit[2] ▸ v ▷ twit[1]
    twitted v ▷ twit[1]
twitter v (-s, -ing, -ed) (of birds) utter chirping sounds ▸ n (pl -s) act or sound of twittering
    twittered v ▷ twitter
    twittering v ▷ twitter
    twitters v, n ▷ twitter
    twitting v ▷ twit[1]
two adj, n (pl -s) one more than one
    twos n ▷ two

> **twp** adj. This is a Welsh word that means stupid or daft. This is a useful word because it contains no vowels, and can thus help when you have an awkward rack. Twp scores 8 points.

tycoon n (pl -s) powerful wealthy businessman
    tycoons n ▷ tycoon

> **tyg** n (tygs). A tyg is a cup with more than one handle. This word is useful because it uses no vowels, and can thus help when you are short of them. Tyg scores 7 points.

    tying v ▷ tie
tyke n (pl -s) (BRIT, AUST & NZ) (Informal) small cheeky child
    tykes n ▷ tyke
type n (pl -s) class or category ▸ v (-pes, -ping, -ped) print with a typewriter or word processor
typecast v (-s, -ing, -ed) continually cast (an actor or actress) in similar roles
    typecasted v ▷ typecast
    typecasting v ▷ typecast
    typecasts v ▷ typecast
    typed v ▷ type

    types n, v ▷ type
typewriter n (pl -s) machine which prints a character when the appropriate key is pressed
    typewriters n ▷ typewriter
    typing v ▷ type
typist n (pl -s) person who types with a typewriter or word processor
    typists n ▷ typist
typhoon n (pl -s) violent tropical storm
    typhoons n ▷ typhoon
typhus n (pl -uses) infectious feverish disease
    typhuses n ▷ typhus
typical adj true to type, characteristic
    > **typically** adv
    typically adv ▷ typical
    typified v ▷ typify
    typifies v ▷ typify
typify v (-fies, -fying, -fied) be typical of
    typifying v ▷ typify
    typographer n ▷ typography
    typographers n ▷ typography
    typographical adj ▷ typography
    typographies n ▷ typography
typography n (pl -phies) art or style of printing
    > **typographical** adj ▷ typographer n (pl -s)
tyrannical adj like a tyrant, oppressive
    tyrannies n ▷ tyranny
tyrannize v (-zes, -zing, -zed) exert power (over) oppressively or cruelly > **tyrannous** adj
    tyrannized v ▷ tyrannize
    tyrannizes v ▷ tyrannize
    tyrannizing v ▷ tyrannize
tyrannosaurus [tirr-ran-oh-**sore**-uss] n (pl -es) large two-footed flesh-eating dinosaur
    tyrannosauruses n ▷ tyrannosaurus
    tyrannous n ▷ tyrannize
tyranny n (pl -nies) tyrannical rule
tyrant n (pl -s) oppressive or cruel ruler
    tyrants n ▷ tyrant
tyre n (pl -s) rubber ring, usu. inflated, over the rim of a vehicle's wheel to grip the road
    tyres n ▷ tyre
tyro n (pl -ros) novice or beginner
    tyros n ▷ tyro

> **tzaddiq** n (tzaddiqim, tzaddiqs). A tzaddiq is a Hasidic Jewish leader. This is a fantastic word if you can get the necessary tiles. If someone has played add, you might be able to form it around them; if you can form the whole word using all your tiles you'll earn a 50-point bonus. Tzaddiq scores 27 points.

U

U can be a difficult tile to use effectively. Although there are quite a few two-letter words beginning with U, most of them are quite unusual, and so difficult to remember. Only **up** (4 points) and **us** (2) are immediately obvious, so it's well worth learning words like **ug** (3), **uh** (5), **um** (4), and **un**, **ur** and **ut** (2 each). Three-letter words beginning with U can also be difficult to remember. If you are trying to use a Q, X or Z, bear in mind that there aren't any valid three-letter words with these letters that start with U. Knowing this can save you valuable time. It's also helpful to remember that there aren't any particularly high-scoring two- or three-letter words starting with U.

ubiquities *n* ▷ **ubiquitous**

ubiquitous [yew-**bik**-wit-uss] *adj* being or seeming to be everywhere at once ▷ **ubiquity** *n* (*pl* -**ties**)

ubiquity *n* ▷ **ubiquitous**

udder *n* (*pl* -**s**) large baglike milk-producing gland of cows, sheep, or goats

udders *n* ▷ **udder**

> **ug** *v* (**ugs, ugging, ugged**). Ug is an old word meaning to loathe. The different verb forms of this word can be useful, and remember that if someone plays ug or its inflections, you can put B, L, M or T in front of it to form another valid word. Ug scores 3 points.
>
> **ugh** *interj*. Ugh is a sound that people make when they dislike something or are disgusted by it. Together with uke, this is the highest-scoring three-letter word starting with U. Ugh scores 7 points.

uglier *adj* ▷ **ugly**

ugliest *adj* ▷ **ugly**

ugliness *n* ▷ **ugly**

uglinesses *n* ▷ **ugly**

ugly *adj* (-**lier**, -**liest**) of unpleasant appearance ▷ **ugliness** *n* (*pl* -**es**)

> **uh** *interj*. Uh is a sound that people make when they are unsure about something. This useful little word can help when you are trying to form words in more than one direction. Uh scores 5 points.
>
> **uke** *n* (**ukes**). Uke is a short form of ukulele. Together with ugh, this is the highest-scoring three-letter word

starting with U. Uke scores 7 points.

ukelele *n* ▷ **ukulele**

ukeleles *n* ▷ **ukulele**

ukulele, ukelele [yew-kal-**lay**-lee] *n* (*pl* -**s**) small guitar with four strings

ukuleles *n* ▷ **ukulele**

ulcer *n* (*pl* -**s**) open sore on the surface of the skin or mucous membrane. ▷ **ulceration** *n* (*pl* -**s**)

ulcerated *adj* made or becoming ulcerous

ulceration *n* ▷ **ulcer**

ulcerations *n* ▷ **ulcer**

ulcerous *adj* of, like, or characterized by ulcers

ulcers *n* ▷ **ulcer**

ulna *n* (*pl* -**nae**, -**nas**) inner and longer of the two bones of the human forearm

ulnae *n* ▷ **ulna**

ulnas *n* ▷ **ulna**

ulterior *adj* (of an aim, reason, etc.) concealed or hidden

ultimate *adj* final in a series or process ▷ **ultimately** *adv*

ultimately *adv* ▷ **ultimate**

ultimatum [ult-im-**may**-tum] *n* (*pl* -**s**) final warning stating that action will be taken unless certain conditions are met

ultimatums *n* ▷ **ultimatum**

ultramarine *adj* vivid blue

ultrasonic *adj* of or producing sound waves with a higher frequency than the human ear can hear

ultraviolet *adj*, *n* (*pl* -**s**) (of) light beyond the limit of visibility at the violet end of the spectrum

ultraviolets *n* ▷ **ultraviolet**

ululate [**yewl**-yew-late] *v* (-**tes**, -**ting**, -**ted**) howl

or wail ▷ **ululation** n (pl -s)
ululated v ▷ ululate
ululates v ▷ ululate
ululating v ▷ ululate
ululation n ▷ ululate
ululations n ▷ ululate

um interj. Um is a sound people make when hesitating in speech. If someone plays this word, remember that lots of words end in UM (dictum, podium and rostrum, for example) and look out for chances to play them. Um scores 4 points.

umber adj dark brown to reddish-brown
umbilical adj of the navel
umbrella n (pl -s) portable device used for protection against rain, consisting of a folding frame covered in material attached to a central rod
umbrellas n ▷ umbrella
umpire n (pl -s) official who rules on the playing of a game ▶ v (-res, -ring, -red) act as umpire in (a game)
umpired v ▷ umpire
umpires n, v ▷ umpire
umpiring v ▷ umpire
umpteen adj (Informal) very many
 ▷ **umpteenth** n (pl -s) adj
umpteenth n, adj ▷ umpteen
umpteenths n ▷ umpteen

un pron. Un is a dialect word for one. If someone plays this, remember that you can form lots of words by placing letters after UN. Un scores 2 points.

unable adj lacking the necessary power, ability, or authority to (do something)
unaccountable adj unable to be explained
 ▷ **unaccountably** adv
unaccountably adv ▷ unaccountable
unadulterated adj with nothing added, pure
unanimities n ▷ unanimous
unanimity n ▷ unanimous
unanimous [yew-nan-im-uss] adj in complete agreement ▷ **unanimity** n (pl -ties)
unarmed adj without weapons
unassuming adj modest or unpretentious
unaware adj not aware or conscious
unawares adv by surprise
unbalanced adj biased or one-sided
unbearable adj not able to be endured
 ▷ **unbearably** adv
unbearably adv ▷ unbearable
unbeknown adv without the knowledge of (a person)
unbend v (-s, -ing, unbent) (Informal) become

less strict or more informal in one's attitudes or behaviour ▷ **unbending** adj
unbending v, adj ▷ unbend
unbends v ▷ unbend
unbent v ▷ unbend
unbidden adj not ordered or asked
unborn adj not yet born
unbosom v (-s, -ing, -ed) relieve (oneself) of (secrets or feelings) by telling someone
unbosomed v ▷ unbosom
unbosoming v ▷ unbosom
unbosoms v ▷ unbosom
unbridled adj (of feelings or behaviour) not controlled in any way
unburden v (-s, -ing, -ed) relieve (one's mind or oneself) of a worry by confiding in someone
unburdened v ▷ unburden
unburdening v ▷ unburden
unburdens v ▷ unburden
uncannier adj ▷ uncanny
uncanniest adj ▷ uncanny
uncannily adv ▷ uncanny
uncanny adj (-nnier, -nniest) weird or mysterious ▷ **uncannily** adv
unceremonious adj relaxed and informal
 ▷ **unceremoniously** adv
unceremoniously adv ▷ unceremonious
uncertain adj not able to be accurately known or predicted ▷ **uncertainty** n (pl -ties)
uncertainties n ▷ uncertain
uncertainty n ▷ uncertain
uncle n (pl -s) brother of one's father or mother
unclean adj lacking moral, spiritual, or physical cleanliness
uncles n ▷ uncle
uncomfortable adj not physically relaxed
uncommon adj (-er, -est) not happening or encountered often ▷ **uncommonly** adv
uncommoner adj ▷ uncommon
uncommonest adj ▷ uncommon
uncommonly adv ▷ uncommon
uncompromising adj not prepared to compromise
unconcerned adj lacking in concern or involvement ▷ **unconcernedly** adv
unconcernedly adv ▷ unconcerned
unconditional adj without conditions or limitations
unconscionable adj having no principles, unscrupulous
unconscious adj lacking normal awareness through the senses ▶ n (pl -es) part of the mind containing instincts and ideas that exist without one's awareness
 ▷ **unconsciously** adv ▷ **unconsciousness** n

(pl -es)
unconsciouses n ▷ unconscious
unconsciously adv ▷ unconscious
unconsciousnes n ▷ unconscious
unconsciousnesses n ▷ unconscious
uncooperative adj not willing to help other
people with what they are doing
uncouth adj (-er, -est) lacking in good
manners, refinement, or grace
uncouther adj ▷ uncouth
uncouthest adj ▷ uncouth
uncover v (-s, -ing, -ed) reveal or disclose
uncovered v ▷ uncover
uncovering v ▷ uncover
uncovers v ▷ uncover
unction n (pl -es) act of anointing with oil in
sacramental ceremonies
unctions n ▷ unction
unctuous adj pretending to be kind and
concerned
undecided adj not having made up one's mind
undeniable adj unquestionably true
  > **undeniably** adv
undeniably adv ▷ undeniable
under prep, adv indicating movement to or
position beneath the underside or base ▶ prep
less than
underage adj below the required or standard
age
underarm adj (SPORT) denoting a style of
throwing, bowling, or serving in which the
hand is swung below shoulder level ▶ adv
(SPORT) in an underarm style
undercarriage n (pl -s) landing gear of an
aircraft
undercarriages n ▷ undercarriage
underclass n (pl -es) class consisting of the
most disadvantaged people, such as the
long-term unemployed
underclasses n ▷ underclass
undercoat n (pl -s) coat of paint applied before
the final coat
undercoats n ▷ undercoat
undercover adj done or acting in secret
undercurrent n (pl -s) current that is not
apparent at the surface
undercurrents n ▷ undercurrent
undercut v (-cuts, -cutting, -cut) charge less
than (a competitor) to obtain trade
undercuts v ▷ undercut
undercutting v ▷ undercut
underdog n (pl -s) person or team in a weak or
underprivileged position
underdogs n ▷ underdog
underdone adj not cooked enough

underestimate v (-tes, -ting, -ted) make too
low an estimate of
underestimated v ▷ underestimate
underestimates v ▷ underestimate
underestimating v ▷ underestimate
underfoot adv under the feet
undergarment n (pl -s) any piece of
underwear
undergarments n ▷ undergarment
undergo v (-goes, -going, -went, -gone)
experience, endure, or sustain
undergoes v ▷ undergo
undergoing v ▷ undergo
undergone v ▷ undergo
undergraduate n (pl -s) person studying in a
university for a first degree
undergraduates n ▷ undergraduate
underground adj occurring, situated, used,
or going below ground level ▶ n (pl -s) electric
passenger railway operated in underground
tunnels
undergrounds n ▷ underground
undergrowth n (pl -s) small trees and bushes
growing beneath taller trees in a wood or
forest
undergrowths n ▷ undergrowth
underhand adj sly, deceitful, and secretive
underlain v ▷ underlie
underlay v ▷ underlie
underlie v (-lies, -lying, -lay, -underlain)
lie or be placed under > **underlying** adj
fundamental or basic
underlies v ▷ underlie
underline v (-s, -ning, -d) draw a line under
underlined v ▷ underline
underlines v ▷ underline
underling n (pl -s) subordinate
underlings n ▷ underling
underlining v ▷ underline
underlying v, adj ▷ underlie
undermine v (-nes, -ning, -ned) weaken
gradually
undermined v ▷ undermine
undermines v ▷ undermine
undermining v ▷ undermine
underneath prep, adv under or beneath ▶ adj, n
(pl -s) lower (part or surface)
underneaths n ▷ underneath
underpants pl n man's undergarment for the
lower part of the body
underpass n (pl -es) section of a road that
passes under another road or a railway line
underpasses n ▷ underpass
underpin v (-pins, -pinning, -pinned) give
strength or support to

underpinned v ▷ underpin
underpinning v ▷ underpin
underpins v ▷ underpin
underprivileged adj lacking the rights and advantages of other members of society
underrate v (-tes, -ting, -ted) not realize the full potential of > underrated adj
underrated v, adj ▷ underrate
underrates v ▷ underrate
underrating v ▷ underrate
underseal n (pl -s) (CHIEFLY BRIT) coating of tar etc. applied to the underside of a motor vehicle to prevent corrosion
underseals n ▷ underseal
underside n (pl -s) bottom or lower surface
undersides n ▷ underside
understand v (-s, -ing, -stood) know and comprehend the nature or meaning of > understandable adj > understandably adv
understandable adj ▷ understand
understandably adj ▷ understand
understanding n (pl -s) ability to learn, judge, or make decisions ▸ adj kind and sympathetic ▸ v ▷ understand
understandings n ▷ understanding
understands v ▷ understand
understate v (-tes, -ting, -ted) describe or represent (something) in restrained terms > understatement n (pl -s)
understated v ▷ understate
understatement n ▷ understate
understatements n ▷ understate
understates v ▷ understate
understating v ▷ understate
understood v ▷ understand
understudied v ▷ understudy
understudies n, v ▷ understudy
understudy n (pl -dies) actor who studies a part in order to be able to replace the usual actor if necessary ▸ v (-dies, -dying, -died) act as an understudy for
understudying v ▷ understudy
undertake v (-takes, -taking, -took, -taken) agree or commit oneself to (something) or to do (something)
undertaken v ▷ undertake
undertaker n (pl -s) person whose job is to prepare corpses for burial or cremation and organize funerals
undertakers n ▷ undertaker
undertakes v ▷ undertake
undertaking n (pl -s) task or enterprise ▸ v ▷ undertake
undertakings n ▷ undertaking
undertone n (pl -s) quiet tone of voice

undertones n ▷ undertone
undertook v ▷ undertake
undertow n (pl -s) strong undercurrent flowing in a different direction from the surface current
undertows n ▷ undertow
underwear n (pl -s) clothing worn under the outer garments and next to the skin
underwears n ▷ underwear
underwent v ▷ undergo
underworld n (pl -s) criminals and their associates
underworlds n ▷ underworld
underwrite v (-writes, -writing, -wrote, -written) accept financial responsibility for (a commercial project)
underwriter n (pl -s) person who underwrites (esp. an insurance policy)
underwriters n ▷ underwriter
underwrites v ▷ underwrite
underwriting v ▷ underwrite
underwritten v ▷ underwrite
underwrote v ▷ underwrite
undesirable adj not desirable or pleasant, objectionable ▸ n (pl -s) objectionable person
undesirables n ▷ undesirable
undid v ▷ undo
undo v (-does, -doing, -did, -done) open, unwrap > undone adj
undoes v ▷ undo
undoing n (pl -s) cause of someone's downfall ▸ v ▷ undo
undoings n ▷ undoing
undone v, adj ▷ undo
undoubted adj certain or indisputable > undoubtedly adv
undoubtedly adv ▷ undoubted
undue adj greater than is reasonable, excessive > unduly adv
undulate v (-tes, -ting, -ted) move in waves > undulation n (pl -s)
undulated v ▷ undulate
undulates v ▷ undulate
undulating v ▷ undulate
undulation n ▷ undulate
undulations n ▷ undulate
unduly adv ▷ undue
undying adj never ending, eternal
unearth v (-s, -ing, -ed) reveal or discover by searching
unearthed v ▷ unearth
unearthing v ▷ unearth
unearthly adj ghostly or eerie
unearths v ▷ unearth
unease n (pl -s) feeling of anxiety

uneases n ▷ unease
uneasier adj ▷ uneasy
uneasiest adj ▷ uneasy
uneasily adv ▷ uneasy
uneasiness n ▷ uneasy
uneasinesses n ▷ uneasy
uneasy adj (**-sier, -siest**) (of a person) anxious or apprehensive > **uneasily** adv > **uneasiness** n (pl **-es**)
unemployed adj out of work > **unemployment** n (pl **-s**)
unemployment n ▷ unemployed
unemployments n ▷ unemployed
unequivocal adj completely clear in meaning > **unequivocally** adv
unequivocally adv ▷ unequivocal
unerring adj never mistaken, consistently accurate
unexceptionable adj beyond criticism or objection
unfailing adj continuous or reliable > **unfailingly** adv
unfailingly adv ▷ unfailing
unfair adj (**-er, -est**) not right, fair, or just > **unfairly** adv > **unfairness** n (pl **-es**)
unfairer adj ▷ unfair
unfairest adj ▷ unfair
unfairly adv ▷ unfair
unfairness n ▷ unfair
unfairnesses n ▷ unfair
unfaithful adj having sex with someone other than one's regular partner > **unfaithfulness** n (pl **-es**)
unfaithfulness n ▷ unfaithful
unfaithfulnesses n ▷ unfaithful
unfeeling adj without sympathy
unfit adj unqualified or unsuitable
unflappabilities n ▷ unflappable
unflappability n ▷ unflappable
unflappable adj (Informal) not easily upset > **unflappability** n (pl **-ties**)
unfold v (**-s, -ing, -ed**) open or spread out from a folded state
unfolded v ▷ unfold
unfolding v ▷ unfold
unfolds v ▷ unfold
unforgettable adj impossible to forget, memorable
unfortunate adj unlucky, unsuccessful, or unhappy > **unfortunately** adv
unfortunately adv ▷ unfortunate
unfrock v (**-s, -ing, -ed**) deprive (a priest in holy orders) of his or her priesthood
unfrocked v ▷ unfrock
unfrocking v ▷ unfrock

unfrocks v ▷ unfrock
ungainlier adj ▷ ungainly
ungainliest adj ▷ ungainly
ungainly adj (**-lier, -liest**) lacking grace when moving
ungodlier adj ▷ ungodly
ungodliest adj ▷ ungodly
ungodly adj (**-lier, -liest**) (Informal) unreasonable or outrageous
ungrateful adj not grateful or thankful
unguarded adj not protected
unguent [ung-gwent] n (pl **-s**) (Lit) ointment
unguents n ▷ unguent
unhand v (**-s, -ing, -ed**) (Old-fashioned or lit) release from one's grasp
unhanded v ▷ unhand
unhanding v ▷ unhand
unhands v ▷ unhand
unhappier adj ▷ unhappy
unhappiest adj ▷ unhappy
unhappily adv ▷ unhappy
unhappiness n ▷ unhappy
unhappinesses n ▷ unhappy
unhappy adj (**-ppier, -ppiest**) sad or depressed > **unhappily** adv > **unhappiness** n (pl **-es**)
unhealthier adj ▷ unhealthy
unhealthiest adj ▷ unhealthy
unhealthy adj (**-thier, -thiest**) likely to cause poor health
unhinge v (**-ges, -ging, -ged**) derange or unbalance (a person or his or her mind)
unhinged v ▷ unhinge
unhinges v ▷ unhinge
unhinging v ▷ unhinge
unicorn n (pl **-s**) imaginary horselike creature with one horn growing from its forehead
unicorns n ▷ unicorn
unification n ▷ unify
unifications n ▷ unify
unified v ▷ unify
unifies v ▷ unify
uniform n (pl **-s**) special identifying set of clothes for the members of an organization, such as soldiers ▶ adj regular and even throughout, unvarying > **uniformly** adv > **uniformity** n (pl **-ties**)
uniformities n ▷ uniform
uniformity n ▷ uniform
uniformly adv ▷ uniform
uniforms n ▷ uniform
unify v (**-fies, -fying, -fied**) make or become one > **unification** n (pl **-s**)
unifying v ▷ unify
unilateral adj made or done by only one person or group > **unilaterally** adv

unilaterally adv ▷ **unilateral**

unimpeachable adj completely honest and reliable

uninterested adj having or showing no interest in someone or something

union n (pl -s) uniting or being united

unionist n (pl -s) member or supporter of a trade union

unionists n ▷ **unionist**

unionization n ▷ **unionize**

unionizations n ▷ **unionize**

unionize v (-zes, -zing, -zed) organize (workers) into a trade union > **unionization** n (pl -s)

unionized v ▷ **unionize**

unionizes v ▷ **unionize**

unionizing v ▷ **unionize**

unions n ▷ **union**

unique [yoo-**neek**] adj being the only one of a particular type > **uniquely** adv

uniquely adv ▷ **unique**

unisex adj designed for use by both sexes

unison n (pl -s) complete agreement

unisons n ▷ **unison**

unit n (pl -s) single undivided entity or whole

unitary adj consisting of a single undivided whole

unite v (-tes, -ting, -ted) make or become an integrated whole

united v ▷ **unite**

unites v ▷ **unite**

unities n ▷ **unity**

uniting v ▷ **unite**

units n ▷ **unit**

unity n (pl -ties) state of being one

universal adj of or typical of the whole of mankind or of nature > **universally** adv > **universality** n (pl -ties)

universalities n ▷ **universal**

universality n ▷ **universal**

universally adv ▷ **universal**

universe n (pl -s) whole of all existing matter, energy, and space

universes n ▷ **universe**

universities n ▷ **university**

university n (pl -ties) institution of higher education with the authority to award degrees

unkempt adj (of the hair) not combed

unknown adj not known ▶ n (pl -s) unknown person, quantity, or thing

unknowns n ▷ **unknown**

unleaded adj (of petrol) containing less tetraethyl lead, in order to reduce environmental pollution

unless conj except under the circumstances that

unlike adj dissimilar or different ▶ prep not like or typical of

unlikely adj improbable

unload v (-s, -ing, -ed) remove (cargo) from (a ship, truck, or plane)

unloaded v ▷ **unload**

unloading v ▷ **unload**

unloads v ▷ **unload**

unmask v (-s, -ing, -ed) remove the mask or disguise from

unmasked v ▷ **unmask**

unmasking v ▷ **unmask**

unmasks v ▷ **unmask**

unmentionable adj unsuitable as a topic of conversation

unmistakable, unmistakeable adj not ambiguous, clear > **unmistakably, unmistakeably** adv

unmistakably adv ▷ **unmistakable**

unmistakeable adj ▷ **unmistakable**

unmistakeably adv ▷ **unmistakable**

unmitigated adj not reduced or lessened in severity etc.

unmoved adj not affected by emotion, indifferent

unnatural adj strange and frightening because not usual

unnerve v (-ves, -ving, -ved) cause to lose courage, confidence, or self-control

unnerved v ▷ **unnerve**

unnerves v ▷ **unnerve**

unnerving v ▷ **unnerve**

unnumbered adj countless

unorthodox adj (of ideas, methods, etc.) unconventional and not generally accepted

unpack v (-s, -ing, -ed) remove the contents of (a suitcase, trunk, etc.)

unpacked v ▷ **unpack**

unpacking v ▷ **unpack**

unpacks v ▷ **unpack**

unparalleled adj not equalled, supreme

unpick v (-s, -ing, -ed) undo (the stitches) of (a piece of sewing)

unpicked v ▷ **unpick**

unpicking v ▷ **unpick**

unpicks v ▷ **unpick**

unpleasant adj not pleasant or agreeable > **unpleasantly** adv > **unpleasantness** n (pl -s)

unpleasantly adv ▷ **unpleasant**

unpleasantness n ▷ **unpleasant**

unpleasantnesses n ▷ **unpleasant**

unprintable adj unsuitable for printing for reasons of obscenity or libel

unprofessional *adj* contrary to the accepted code of a profession > **unprofessionally** *adv*
unprofessionally *adv* ▷ **unprofessional**
unqualified *adj* lacking the necessary qualifications
unravel *v* (-vels, -velling, -velled) reduce (something knitted or woven) to separate strands
unravelled *v* ▷ **unravel**
unravelling *v* ▷ **unravel**
unravels *v* ▷ **unravel**
unremitting *adj* never slackening or stopping
unrequited *adj* not returned
unrest *n* (*pl* -s) rebellious state of discontent
unrests *n* ▷ **unrest**
unrivalled *adj* having no equal
unroll *v* (-s, -ing, -ed) open out or unwind (something rolled or coiled) or (of something rolled or coiled) become opened out or unwound
unrolled *v* ▷ **unroll**
unrolling *v* ▷ **unroll**
unrolls *v* ▷ **unroll**
unrulier *adj* ▷ **unruly**
unruliest *adj* ▷ **unruly**
unruly *adj* (-lier, -liest) difficult to control or organize
unsavoury *adj* distasteful or objectionable
unscathed *adj* not harmed or injured
unscrupulous *adj* prepared to act dishonestly, unprincipled
unseat *v* (-s, -ing, -ed) throw or displace from a seat or saddle
unseated *v* ▷ **unseat**
unseating *v* ▷ **unseat**
unseats *v* ▷ **unseat**
unsettled *adj* lacking order or stability
unsightlier *adj* ▷ **unsightly**
unsightliest *adj* ▷ **unsightly**
unsightly *adj* (-lier, -liest) unpleasant to look at
unsociable *adj* ▷ **unsocial**
unsocial *adj* (also **unsociable**) avoiding the company of other people
unsound *adj* unhealthy or unstable
unstable *adj* (-r, -st) lacking stability or firmness
unstabler *adj* ▷ **unstable**
unstablest *adj* ▷ **unstable**
unsuitable *adj* not right or appropriate for a particular purpose > **unsuitably** *adv*
unsuitably *adv* ▷ **unsuitable**
unsuited *adj* not appropriate for a particular task or situation
unswerving *adj* firm, constant, not changing

unthinkable *adj* out of the question, inconceivable
untidier *adj* ▷ **untidy**
untidiest *adj* ▷ **untidy**
untidily *adv* ▷ **untidy**
untidiness *n* ▷ **untidy**
untidinesses *n* ▷ **untidy**
untidy *adj* (-dier, -diest) messy and disordered > **untidily** *adv* > **untidiness** *n* (*pl* -es)
untie *v* (-ties, -tying, -tied) open or free (something that is tied)
untied *v* ▷ **untie**
unties *v* ▷ **untie**
until *conj* up to the time that ▶ *prep* in or throughout the period before
untimelier *adj* ▷ **untimely**
untimeliest *adj* ▷ **untimely**
untimely *adj* (-lier, -liest) occurring before the expected or normal time
unto *prep* (Old-fashioned) to
untold *adj* incapable of description
untouchable *adj* above reproach or suspicion ▶ *n* (*pl* -s) member of the lowest Hindu caste in India
untouchables *n* ▷ **untouchable**
untoward *adj* causing misfortune or annoyance
untrue *adj* (-r, -st) incorrect or false
untruer *adj* ▷ **untrue**
untruest *adj* ▷ **untrue**
untruth *n* (*pl* -s) statement that is not true, lie
untruths *n* ▷ **untruth**
untying *v* ▷ **untie**
unusual *adj* uncommon or extraordinary > **unusually** *adv*
unusually *adv* ▷ **unusual**
unutterable *adj* incapable of being expressed in words > **unutterably** *adv*
unutterably *adv* ▷ **unutterable**
unvarnished *adj* not elaborated upon
unwieldier *adj* ▷ **unwieldy**
unwieldiest *adj* ▷ **unwieldy**
unwieldy *adj* (-dier, -diest) too heavy, large, or awkward to be easily handled
unwind *v* (-s, -ing, unwound) relax after a busy or tense time
unwinding *v* ▷ **unwind**
unwinds *v* ▷ **unwind**
unwitting *adj* not intentional > **unwittingly** *adv*
unwittingly *adv* ▷ **unwitting**
unwonted *adj* out of the ordinary
unworthier *adj* ▷ **unworthy**
unworthiest *adj* ▷ **unworthy**
unworthy *adj* (-thier, -thiest) not deserving

or worthy
unwound v ▷ unwind
unwrap v (-s, -pping, -pped) remove the
wrapping from (something)
   unwrapped v ▷ unwrap
   unwrapping v ▷ unwrap
   unwraps v ▷ unwrap
unwritten adj not printed or in writing
up prep, adv indicating movement to or
position at a higher place ▶ adv indicating
readiness, intensity or completeness, etc.
▶ adj of a high or higher position ▶ v (-s,
-pping, -pped) increase or raise ▶ adv (also
upwards) from a lower to a higher place,
level, or condition
upbeat adj (Informal) cheerful and optimistic
▶ n (pl -s) (MUSIC) unaccented beat
   upbeats n ▷ upbeat
upbraid v (-s, -ing, -ded) scold or reproach
   upbraided v ▷ upbraid
   upbraiding v ▷ upbraid
   upbraids v ▷ upbraid
upbringing n (pl -s) education of a person
during the formative years
   upbringings n ▷ upbringing
update v (-tes, -ting, -ted) bring up to date
   updated v ▷ update
   updates v ▷ update
   updating v ▷ update
upend v (-s, -ing, -ed) turn or set (something)
on its end
   upended v ▷ upend
   upending v ▷ upend
   upends v ▷ upend
upfront adj open and frank ▶ adv, adj (of
money) paid out at the beginning of a
business arrangement
upgrade v (-des, -ding, -ded) promote (a
person or job) to a higher rank
   upgraded v ▷ upgrade
   upgrades v ▷ upgrade
   upgrading v ▷ upgrade
upheaval n (pl -s) strong, sudden, or violent
disturbance
   upheavals n ▷ upheaval
   upheld v ▷ uphold
uphill adj sloping or leading upwards ▶ adv up
a slope ▶ n (pl -s) (S AFR) difficulty
   uphills n ▷ uphill
uphold v (-s, -ing, upheld) maintain or defend
against opposition > **upholder** n (pl -s)
   upholder n ▷ uphold
   upholders n ▷ uphold
   upholding v ▷ uphold
   upholds v ▷ uphold

upholster v (-s, -ing, -ed) fit (a chair or
sofa) with padding, springs, and covering
> **upholsterer** n (pl -s)
   upholstered v ▷ upholster
   upholsterer n ▷ upholster
   upholsterers n ▷ upholster
   upholsteries n ▷ upholstery
   upholstering v ▷ upholster
   upholsters v ▷ upholster
upholstery n (pl -ries) soft covering on a chair
or sofa
upkeep n (pl -s) act, process, or cost of keeping
something in good repair
   upkeeps n ▷ upkeep
upland adj of or in an area of high or relatively
high ground ▶ **uplands** pl n area of high or
relatively high ground
   uplands pl n ▷ upland
uplift v (-s, -ing, -ed) raise or lift up ▶ n (pl -s)
act or process of improving moral, social, or
cultural conditions > **uplifting** adj
   uplifted v ▷ uplift
   uplifting v, adj ▷ uplift
   uplifts v, n ▷ uplift
upload v (-s, -ing, -ed) transfer (data or a
program) from one's own computer into the
memory of another computer
   uploaded v ▷ upload
   uploading v ▷ upload
   uploads v ▷ upload
upon prep on
   upped v ▷ up
upper adj higher or highest in physical
position, wealth, rank, or status ▶ n (pl -s)
part of a shoe above the sole
uppermost adj highest in position, power, or
importance ▶ adv in or into the highest place
or position
   uppers n ▷ upper
   upping v ▷ up
uppish, uppity adj (BRIT) (Informal) snobbish,
arrogant, or presumptuous
   uppity adj ▷ uppish
upright adj vertical or erect ▶ adv vertically or
in an erect position ▶ n (pl -s) vertical support,
such as a post > **uprightness** n (pl -s)
   uprightness n ▷ upright
   uprightnesses n ▷ upright
   uprights n ▷ upright
uprising n (pl -s) rebellion or revolt
   uprisings n ▷ uprising
uproar n (pl -s) disturbance characterized by
loud noise and confusion
uproarious adj very funny > **uproariously** adv
   uproariously adv ▷ uproarious

uproars n ▷ uproar

uproot v (-s, -ing, -ed) pull up by or as if by the roots

uprooted v ▷ uproot

uprooting v ▷ uproot

uproots v ▷ uproot

ups v ▷ up

upset adj emotionally or physically disturbed or distressed ▶ v (-s, -tting, upset) tip over ▶ n (pl -s) unexpected defeat or reversal > **upsetting** adj

upsets v, n ▷ upset

upsetting v, adj ▷ upset

upshot n (pl -s) final result or conclusion

upshots n ▷ upshot

upstage adj at the back half of the stage ▶ v (-ges, -ging, -ged) (Informal) draw attention to oneself from (someone else)

upstaged v ▷ upstage

upstages v ▷ upstage

upstaging v ▷ upstage

upstairs adv to or on an upper floor of a building ▶ n upper floor

upstanding adj of good character

upstart n (pl -s) person who has risen suddenly to a position of power and behaves arrogantly

upstarts n ▷ upstart

upstream adv, adj in or towards the higher part of a stream

upsurge n (pl -s) rapid rise or swell

upsurges n ▷ upsurge

uptake n (pl -s) (Informal) quick or slow to understand or learn

uptakes n ▷ uptake

uptight adj (Informal) nervously tense, irritable, or angry

upturn n (pl -s) upward trend or improvement > **upturned** adj facing upwards

upturned adj ▷ upturn

upturns n ▷ upturn

upward adj directed or moving towards a higher place or level

upwards adv ▷ up

> **ur** interj. Ur is a sound people make when hesitating in speech. If someone plays this, you may be able to use it to form words that begin with UR. Ur is also handy for connecting words beginning with U to those ending in R. Ur scores 2 points.

uranium n (pl -s) (CHEM) radioactive silvery-white metallic element, used chiefly as a source of nuclear energy

uraniums n ▷ uranium

urban adj of or living in a city or town

urbane adj (-r, -st) characterized by courtesy, elegance, and sophistication > **urbanity** n (pl -ties)

urbaner adj ▷ urbane

urbanest adj ▷ urbane

urbanities n ▷ urbane

urbanity n ▷ urbane

urbanization n ▷ urbanize

urbanizations n ▷ urbanize

urbanize v (-zes, -zing, -zed) make (a rural area) more industrialized and urban > **urbanization** n (pl -s)

urbanized v ▷ urbanize

urbanizes v ▷ urbanize

urbanizing v ▷ urbanize

urchin n (pl -s) mischievous child

urchins n ▷ urchin

urethra [yew-reeth-ra] n (pl -rae) canal that carries urine from the bladder out of the body

urethrae n ▷ urethra

urge n (pl -s) strong impulse, inner drive, or yearning ▶ v (-urges, -urging, -urged) plead with or press (a person to do something)

urged v ▷ urge

urgencies n ▷ urgent

urgency n ▷ urgent

urgent adj requiring speedy action or attention > **urgency** n (pl -cies) > **urgently** adv

urgently adv ▷ urgent

urges n, v ▷ urge

urging v ▷ urge

urinal n (pl -s) sanitary fitting used by men for urination

urinals n ▷ urine

urinary adj ▷ urine

urinate v (-tes, -ting, -ted) discharge urine > **urination** n (pl -s)

urinated v ▷ urinate

urinates v ▷ urinate

urinating v ▷ urinate

urination n ▷ urinate

urinations n ▷ urinate

urine n (pl -s) pale yellow fluid excreted by the kidneys to the bladder and passed as waste from the body > **urinary** adj

urines n ▷ urine

urn n (pl -s) vase used as a container for the ashes of the dead

urns n ▷ urn

ursine adj of or like a bear

us pron ▷ we

usable adj able to be used

usage n (pl -s) regular or constant use

usages n ▷ usage

use v (**-ses, -sing, -sed**) put into service or action ▶ n (pl **-s**) using or being used > **user** n (pl **-s**) > **useful** adj > **usefully** adv > **usefulness** n (pl **-es**) > **useless** adj > **uselessly** adv > **uselessness** n (pl **-es**)

used adj second-hand ▶ v ▷ use

useful adj ▷ use

usefully adv ▷ use

usefulness n ▷ use

usefulnesses n ▷ use

useless adj ▷ use

uselessly adv ▷ use

uselessness n ▷ use

uselessnesses n ▷ use

user n ▷ use

username n (pl **-s**) (COMPUTERS) name entered into a computer for identification purposes

usernames n ▷ username

users n ▷ use

uses v, n ▷ use

usher n (pl **-s**) official who shows people to their seats, as in a church ▶ v (**-s, -ing, -ed**) conduct or escort

ushered v ▷ usher

usherette n (pl **-s**) female assistant in a cinema who shows people to their seats

usherettes n ▷ usherette

ushering v ▷ usher

ushers n, v ▷ usher

using v ▷ use

usual adj of the most normal, frequent, or regular type

usually adv most often, in most cases

usurer n ▷ usury

usurers n ▷ usury

usuries n ▷ usury

usurp [yewz-zurp] v (**-s, -ing, -ed**) seize (a position or power) without authority > **usurpation** n (pl **-s**) > **usurper** n (pl **-s**)

usurpation n ▷ usurp

usurpations n ▷ usurp

usurped v ▷ usurp

usurper n ▷ usurp

usurpers n ▷ usurp

usurping v ▷ usurp

usurps v ▷ usurp

usury n (pl **-ries**) practice of lending money at an extremely high rate of interest > **usurer** [yewz-yoor-er] ▶ n (pl **-s**)

> **ut** n (**uts**). Ut is a musical note. This unusual word is useful for connecting words beginning with U to those ending with T. Ut scores 2 points.

ute [yoot] n (pl **-s**) (AUST & NZ) (Informal) utility truck

utensil n (pl **-s**) tool or container for practical use

utensils n ▷ utensil

uteri n ▷ uterus

uterine adj ▷ uterus

uterus [yew-ter-russ] n (pl **uteri**) womb > **uterine** adj

utes n ▷ ute

utilitarian adj useful rather than beautiful

utilitarianism n (pl **-s**) (ETHICS) doctrine that the right action is the one that brings about the greatest good for the greatest number of people

utilitarianisms n ▷ utilitarianism

utilities n ▷ utility

utility n (pl **-ties**) usefulness ▶ adj designed for use rather than beauty

utilization n ▷ utilize

utilizations n ▷ utilize

utilize v (**-zes, -zing, -zed**) make practical use of > **utilization** n (pl **-s**)

utilized v ▷ utilize

utilizes v ▷ utilize

utilizing v ▷ utilize

utmost, uttermost adj, n (pl **-s**) (of) the greatest possible degree or amount

utmosts n ▷ utmost

utopia [yew-tope-ee-a] n (pl **-s**) any real or imaginary society, place, or state considered to be perfect or ideal > **utopian** adj

utopian adj ▷ utopia

utopias n ▷ utopia

utter¹ v (**-s, -ing, -ed**) express (something) in sounds or words

utter² adj total or absolute > **utterly** adv

utterance n (pl **-s**) something uttered

utterances n ▷ utterance

uttered v ▷ utter¹

uttering v ▷ utter¹

utterly adv ▷ utter²

uttermost adj, n (pl **-s**) ▷ utmost

uttermosts n ▷ uttermost

utters v ▷ utter¹

uvula [yew-view-la] n (pl **-s**) small fleshy part of the soft palate that hangs in the back of the throat > **uvular** adj

uvular adj ▷ uvula

uvulas n ▷ uvula

uxorious [ux-or-ee-uss] adj excessively fond of or dependent on one's wife

Vv

If you have a V on your rack, the first thing to remember is that there are no valid two-letter words beginning with V. In fact, there are no two-letter words that end in V either, so you can't form any two-letter words using V. Remembering this will stop you wasting time trying to think of some. While V is useless for two-letter words, it does start some good three-letter words. **Vex** and **vox** (13 points each) are the best of these, while **vaw, vow** and **vly** (9 each) are also useful.

vac n (**vacs**). Vac is a short form of vacuum cleaner. This word can prove useful when you have a V but not much space to play it in. Remember that if you have the letters for vac, you might be able to form **cave** using an E that is already on the board. Vac scores 8 points.

vacancies n ▷ vacancy

vacancy n (pl -cies) unfilled job

vacant adj (of a toilet, room, etc.) unoccupied > **vacantly** adv

vacantly adv ▷ vacant

vacate v (-tes, -ting, -ted) cause (something) to be empty by leaving

vacated v ▷ vacate

vacates v ▷ vacate

vacating v ▷ vacate

vacation n time when universities and law courts are closed

vacations n ▷ vacation

vaccinate v (-tes, -ting, -ted) inject with a vaccine > **vaccination** n (pl -s)

vaccinated v ▷ vaccinate

vaccinates v ▷ vaccinate

vaccinating v ▷ vaccinate

vaccination n ▷ vaccinate

vaccinations n ▷ vaccinate

vaccine n (pl -s) substance designed to cause a mild form of a disease to make a person immune to the disease itself

vaccines n ▷ vaccine

vacillate [vass-ill-late] v (-tes, -ting, -ted) keep changing one's mind or opinions > **vacillation** n (pl -s)

vacillated v ▷ vacillate

vacillates v ▷ vacillate

vacillating v ▷ vacillate

vacillation n ▷ vacillate

vacillations n ▷ vacillate

vacua n ▷ vacuum

vacuous adj not expressing intelligent thought > **vacuity** n (pl -ties)

vacuum n (pl -cuums, -cua) empty space from which all or most air or gas has been removed ▶ v (-s, -ing, -ed) clean with a vacuum cleaner

vacuumed v ▷ vacuum

vacuuming v ▷ vacuum

vacuums n ▷ vacuum

vagabond n (pl -s) person with no fixed home, esp. a beggar

vagabonds n ▷ vagabond

vagaries n ▷ vagary

vagary [vaig-a-ree] n (pl -ries) unpredictable change

vagina [vaj-jine-a] n (pl -s) (in female mammals) passage from the womb to the external genitals > **vaginal** adj

vaginal adj ▷ vagina

vaginas n ▷ vagina

vagrancies n ▷ vagrancy

vagrancy n ▷ vagrant

vagrant [vaig-rant] n (pl -s) person with no settled home ▶ adj wandering > **vagrancy** n (pl -cies)

vagrants n ▷ vagrant

vague adj (-guer, -guest) not clearly explained > **vaguely** adv

vaguely adv ▷ vague

vaguer adj ▷ vague

vaguest adj ▷ vague

vain adj (-er, -est) excessively proud, esp. of one's appearance

vainer adj ▷ vain

vainest adj ▷ vain

vainglorious adj (Lit) boastful

valance [val-lenss] n (pl -s) piece of drapery round the edge of a bed
  valances n ▷ valance
vale n (pl -s) (Lit) valley
valediction n (pl -s) farewell speech
  valedictions n ▷ valediction
valedictory [val-lid-**dik**-tree] adj (of a speech, performance, etc.) intended as a farewell
valence [**vale**-ence] n (pl -s) molecular bonding between atoms
  valences n ▷ valence
  valencies n ▷ valency
valency n (pl -cies) power of an atom to make molecular bonds
valentine n (pl -s) (person to whom one sends) a romantic card on Saint Valentine's Day, 14th February
  valentines n ▷ valentine
valerian n (pl -s) herb used as a sedative
  valerians n ▷ valerian
  vales n ▷ vale
valet n (pl -s) man's personal male servant
  valets n ▷ valet
valetudinarian [val-lit-yew-din-**air**-ee-an] n (pl -s) person with a long-term illness
  valetudinarians n ▷ valetudinarian
valiant adj brave or courageous
valid adj (-er, -est) soundly reasoned > **validity** n (pl -ies)
validate v (-tes, -ting, -ted) make valid > **validation** n (pl -s)
  validated v ▷ validate
  validates v ▷ validate
  validating v ▷ validate
  validation n ▷ validate
  validations n ▷ validate
  valider adj ▷ valid
  validest adj ▷ valid
  validities n ▷ valid
  validity n ▷ valid
valise [val-**leez**] n (pl -s) (Old-fashioned) small suitcase
  valises n ▷ valise
valley n (pl -s) low area between hills, often with a river running through it
  valleys n ▷ valley
valour n (pl -s) (Lit) bravery
  valours n ▷ valour
valuable adj having great worth
valuables pl n valuable personal property
valuation n (pl -s) assessment of worth
  valuations n ▷ valuation
value n (pl -s) importance, usefulness ▶ pl moral principles ▶ v (-ues, -uing, -ued) assess the worth or desirability of > **valueless** adj

> **valuer** n (pl -s)
  valued v ▷ value
  valueless adj ▷ value
  valuer n ▷ value
  valuers n ▷ value
  values n, v ▷ value
  valuing v ▷ value
valve n (pl -s) device to control the movement of fluid through a pipe > **valvular** adj
  valves n ▷ valve
  valvular adj ▷ valve
vamp[1] n (pl -s) (Informal) sexually attractive woman who seduces men
vamp[2] v (-s, -ing, -ed) make (a story, piece of music, etc.) seem new by inventing additional parts
  vamped v ▷ vamp[2]
  vamping v ▷ vamp[2]
vampire n (pl -s) (in folklore) corpse that rises at night to drink the blood of the living
  vampires n ▷ vampire
  vamps n, v ▷ vamp[1, 2]
van[1] n (pl -s) motor vehicle for transporting goods
van[2] n (pl -s) ▷ vanguard
vanadium n (pl -s) (CHEM) metallic element, used in steel
  vanadiums n ▷ vanadium
vandal n (pl -s) person who deliberately damages property > **vandalism** n (pl -s) > **vandalize** v (-zes, -zing, -zed)
  vandalism n ▷ vandal
  vandalisms n ▷ vandal
  vandalize n ▷ vandal
  vandalized n ▷ vandal
  vandalizes n ▷ vandal
  vandalizing v ▷ vandal
  vandals n ▷ vandal
vane n (pl -s) flat blade on a rotary device such as a weathercock or propeller
  vanes n ▷ vane
vanguard n (pl -s) unit of soldiers leading an army
  vanguards n ▷ vanguard
vanilla n (pl -s) seed pod of a tropical climbing orchid, used for flavouring
  vanillas n ▷ vanilla
vanish v (-es, -ing, -ed) disappear suddenly or mysteriously
  vanished v ▷ vanish
  vanishes v ▷ vanish
  vanishing v ▷ vanish
  vanities n ▷ vanity
vanity n (pl -ies) (display of) excessive pride
vanquish v (-es, -ing, -ed) (Lit) defeat

(someone) utterly
vanquished v ▷ **vanquish**
vanquishes v ▷ **vanquish**
vanquishing v ▷ **vanquish**
vans n ▷ **van¹, ²**
vantage n (pl -s) position that gives one an overall view
vantages n ▷ **vantage**
vapid adj (-er, -est) lacking character, dull
vapider adj ▷ **vapid**
vapidest adj ▷ **vapid**
vaporize v ▷ **vapour**
vaporized v ▷ **vapour**
vaporizer n ▷ **vapour**
vaporizers n ▷ **vapour**
vaporizes v ▷ **vapour**
vaporizing v ▷ **vapour**
vaporous adj ▷ **vapour**
vapour n (pl -s) moisture suspended in air as steam or mist > **vaporize** v (-zes, -zing, -zed) > **vaporizer** n (pl -s) > **vaporous** adj
vapours n ▷ **vapour**
variabilities n ▷ **variable**
variability n ▷ **variable**
variable adj not always the same, changeable ▶ n (pl -s) (MATHS) expression with a range of values > **variability** n (pl -ties)
variables n ▷ **variable**
variant adj differing from a standard or type ▶ n (pl -s) something that differs from a standard or type
variants n ▷ **variant**
variation n (pl -s) something presented in a slightly different form
variations n ▷ **variation**
varied v, adj ▷ **vary**
variegated adj having patches or streaks of different colours > **variegation** n (pl -s)
variegation n ▷ **variegate**
variegations n ▷ **variegate**
varies adj ▷ **vary**
varieties n ▷ **variety**
variety n (pl -ies) state of being diverse or various
various adj of several kinds > **variously** adv
variously adv ▷ **various**
varnish n (pl -es) solution of oil and resin, put on a surface to make it hard and glossy ▶ v (-es, -ing, -ed) apply varnish to
varnished v ▷ **varnish**
varnishes n, v ▷ **varnish**
varnishing v ▷ **varnish**
vary v (-ries, -rying, -ried) change > **varied** adj
varying v ▷ **vary**
vascular adj (BIOL) relating to vessels

vase n (pl -s) ornamental jar, esp. for flowers
vasectomies n ▷ **vasectomy**
vasectomy n (pl -mies) surgical removal of part of the vas deferens, as a contraceptive method
vases n ▷ **vase**
vassal n (pl -s) (HIST) man given land by a lord in return for military service > **vassalage** n (pl -s)
vassalage n ▷ **vassal**
vassalages n ▷ **vassal**
vassals n ▷ **vassal**
vast adj (-er, -est) extremely large > **vastly** adv > **vastness** n (pl -es)
vaster adj ▷ **vast**
vastest adj ▷ **vast**
vastly adv ▷ **vast**
vastness n ▷ **vast**
vastnesses n ▷ **vast**
vat n (pl -s) large container for liquids
vats n ▷ **vat**
vaudeville n (pl -s) variety entertainment of songs and comic turns
vaudevilles n ▷ **vaudeville**
vault¹ n (pl -s) secure room for storing valuables
vault² v (-s, -ing, -ed) jump over (something) by resting one's hand(s) on it. ▶ n such a jump
vaulted adj having an arched roof ▶ v ▷ **vault²**
vaulting v ▷ **vault²**
vaults n, v ▷ **vault¹, ²**
vaunt v (-s, -ing, -ed) describe or display (success or possessions) boastfully > **vaunted** adj
vaunted adj, v ▷ **vaunt**
vaunting v ▷ **vaunt**
vaunts v ▷ **vaunt**

> **vaw** n (**vaws**). Vaw is a letter of the Hebrew alphabet. This is a very unusual word that can be useful when you are short of options. If you have the tiles for vaw, look out for opportunities to play **wave** or **wavy** using an E or Y that is already on the board. Vaw scores 9 points.

veal n (pl -s) calf meat
veals n ▷ **veal**
vector n (pl -s) (MATHS) quantity that has size and direction, such as force
vectors n ▷ **vector**
veer v (-s, -ing, -ed) change direction suddenly
veered v ▷ **veer**
veering v ▷ **veer**
veers v ▷ **veer**

> **veg** n (**veges**). Veg is a short form of **vegetable**. If someone plays this, look

out for opportunities to form **vegan** or **vegetate** from it. Veg scores 7 points.

vegan [vee-gan] n (pl -s) person who eats no meat, fish, eggs, or dairy products ▶ adj suitable for a vegan > **veganism** n (pl -s)
 veganism n ▷ vegan
 veganisms n ▷ vegan
 vegans n ▷ vegan
vegetable n (pl -s) edible plant ▶ adj of or like plants or vegetables
 vegetables n ▷ vegetable
vegetarian n (pl -s) person who eats no meat or fish ▶ adj suitable for a vegetarian > **vegetarianism** n (pl -s)
 vegetarianism n ▷ vegetarian
 vegetarianisms n ▷ vegetarian
 vegetarians n ▷ vegetarian
vegetate v (-tes, -ting, -ted) live a dull boring life with no mental stimulation
 vegetated v ▷ vegetate
 vegetates v ▷ vegetate
 vegetating v ▷ vegetate
vegetation n (pl -s) plant life of a given place
 vegetations n ▷ vegetation
vehemence n ▷ vehement
 vehemences n ▷ vehement
vehement adj expressing strong feelings > **vehemence** n (pl -s) > **vehemently** adv
 vehemently adv ▷ vehement
vehicle n (pl -s) machine, esp. with an engine and wheels, for carrying people or objects > **vehicular** adj
 vehicles n ▷ vehicle
 vehicular adj ▷ vehicle
veil n (pl -s) piece of thin cloth covering the head or face ▶ v (-s, -ing, -ed) cover with or as if with a veil
 veiled adj disguised ▶ v ▷ veil
 veiling v ▷ veil
 veils n, v ▷ veil
vein n (pl -s) tube that takes blood to the heart > **veined** adj
 veined adj ▷ vein
 veins n ▷ vein
veld, veldt n (pl -s) high grassland in southern Africa
 velds n ▷ veld
veldskoen, velskoen n (pl -s) (S AFR) leather ankle boot
 veldskoens n ▷ veldskoen
 veldts n ▷ veld
vellum n (pl -s) fine calfskin parchment
 vellums n ▷ vellum
 velocities n ▷ velocity
velocity n (pl -ties) speed of movement in a

given direction
velour, velours [vel-loor] n (pl -s) fabric similar to velvet
 velours n ▷ velour
 velskoen n ▷ veldskoen
 velskoens n ▷ veldskoen
velvet n (pl -s) fabric with a thick soft pile
velveteen n (pl -s) cotton velvet
 velveteens n ▷ velveteen
 velvetier adj ▷ velvety
 velvetiest adj ▷ velvety
 velvets n ▷ velvet
velvety adj (-tier, -tiest) soft and smooth
venal adj easily bribed
vend v (-s, -ing, -ed) sell > **vendor** n (pl -s)
 vended v ▷ vend
vendetta n (pl -s) prolonged quarrel between families, esp. one involving revenge killings
 vendettas n ▷ vendetta
 vending v ▷ vend
 vendor n ▷ vend
 vendors n ▷ vend
 vends v ▷ vend
veneer n (pl -s) thin layer of wood etc. covering a cheaper material
 veneers n ▷ veneer
venerable adj worthy of deep respect
venerate v (-tes, -ting, -ted) hold (a person) in deep respect > **veneration** n (pl -s)
 venerated v ▷ venerate
 venerates v ▷ venerate
 venerating v ▷ venerate
 veneration n ▷ venerate
 venerations n ▷ venerate
vengeance n (pl -s) revenge
 vengeances n ▷ vengeance
vengeful adj wanting revenge
venial [veen-ee-al] adj (of a sin or fault) easily forgiven
venison n (pl -s) deer meat
 venisons n ▷ venison
venom n (pl -s) malice or spite > **venomous** adj
 venomous adj ▷ venom
 venoms n ▷ venom
venous adj (ANAT) of veins
vent[1] n (pl -s) outlet releasing fumes or fluid ▶ v (-s, -ing, -ed) express (an emotion) freely
vent[2] n (pl -s) vertical slit in a jacket
 vented v ▷ vent[1]
ventilate v (-tes, -ting, -ted) let fresh air into > **ventilation** n (pl -s) > **ventilator** n (pl -s)
 ventilated v ▷ ventilate
 ventilates v ▷ ventilate
 ventilating v ▷ ventilate
 ventilation n ▷ ventilate

ventilations *n* ▷ ventilate
ventilator *n* ▷ ventilate
ventilators *n* ▷ ventilate
venting *v* ▷ vent¹
ventral *adj* relating to the front of the body
ventricle *n* (*pl* -s) (ANAT) one of the four cavities of the heart or brain
ventricles *n* ▷ ventricle
ventriloquism *n* ▷ ventriloquist
ventriloquisms *n* ▷ ventriloquist
ventriloquist *n* (*pl* -s) entertainer who can speak without moving his or her lips, so that a voice seems to come from elsewhere ▷ **ventriloquism** *n* (*pl* -s)
ventriloquists *n* ▷ ventriloquist
vents *n*, *v* ▷ vent¹, ²
venture *n* (*pl* -s) risky undertaking, esp. in business ▸ *v* (-res, -ring, -red) do something risky
ventured *v* ▷ venture
ventures *n*, *v* ▷ venture
venturesome *adj* daring
venturing *v* ▷ venture
venue *n* (*pl* -s) place where an organized gathering is held
venues *n* ▷ venue
veracious *adj* ▷ veracity
veracities *n* ▷ veracity
veracity *n* (*pl* -ties) habitual truthfulness ▷ **veracious** *adj*
veranda *n* ▷ verandah
verandah, veranda *n* (*pl* -s) open porch attached to a house
verandahs *n* ▷ verandah
verandas *n* ▷ verandah
verb *n* (*pl* -s) word that expresses the idea of action, happening, or being
verbal *adj* spoken ▷ **verbally** *adv*
verbalize *v* (-s, -ing, -ed) express (something) in words
verbalized *v* ▷ verbalize
verbalizes *n* ▷ verbalize
verbalizing *v* ▷ verbalize
verbally *adv* ▷ verbal
verbatim [verb-bait-im] *adv*, *adj* word for word
verbena *n* (*pl* -s) plant with sweet-smelling flowers
verbenas *n* ▷ verbena
verbiage *n* (*pl* -s) excessive use of words
verbiages *n* ▷ verbiage
verbose [verb-bohss] *adj* (-r, -st) speaking at tedious length ▷ **verbosity** *n* (*pl* -ties)
verboser *adj* ▷ verbose
verbosest *adj* ▷ verbose
verbosities *n* ▷ verbose

verbosity *n* ▷ verbose
verbs *n* ▷ verb
verdant *adj* (Lit) covered in green vegetation
verdict *n* (*pl* -s) decision of a jury
verdicts *n* ▷ verdict
verdigris [ver-dig-riss] *n* (*pl* -es) green film on copper, brass, or bronze
verdigrises *n* ▷ verdigris
verdure *n* (*pl* -s) (Lit) flourishing green vegetation
verdures *n* ▷ verdure
verge *n* (*pl* -s) grass border along a road
verger *n* (*pl* -s) (C OF E) church caretaker
vergers *n* ▷ verger
verges *n* ▷ verge
verifiable *adj* ▷ verify
verification *n* ▷ verify
verifications *n* ▷ verify
verified *v* ▷ verify
verifies *v* ▷ verify
verify *v* (-fies, -fying, -fied) check the truth or accuracy of ▷ **verifiable** *adj* ▷ **verification** *n* (*pl* -s)
verifying *v* ▷ verify
verily *adv* (Obs) in truth
verisimilitude *n* (*pl* -s) appearance of being real or true
verisimilitudes *n* ▷ verisimilitude
veritable *adj* rightly called, without exaggeration ▷ **veritably** *adv*
veritably *adv* ▷ veritable
verities *n* ▷ verity
verity *n* (*pl* -ies) true statement or principle
vermicelli [ver-me-chell-ee] *n* (*pl* -s) fine strands of pasta
vermicellis *n* ▷ vermicelli
vermiform *adj* shaped like a worm
vermilion *adj* orange-red
vermin *pl n* (*pl* -s) animals, esp. insects and rodents, that spread disease or cause damage ▷ **verminous** *adj*
verminous *adj* ▷ vermin
vermins *n* ▷ vermin
vermouth [ver-muth] *n* (*pl* -s) wine flavoured with herbs
vermouths *n* ▷ vermouth
vernacular [ver-nak-yew-lar] *n* (*pl* -s) most widely spoken language of a particular people or place
vernaculars *n* ▷ vernacular
vernal *adj* occurring in spring
vernier [ver-nee-er] *n* (*pl* -s) movable scale on a graduated measuring instrument for taking readings in fractions
verniers *n* ▷ vernier

veronica n (pl **-s**) plant with small blue, pink, or white flowers
  veronicas n ▷ **veronica**
verruca [ver-**roo**-ka] n (pl **-s**) wart, usu. on the foot
  verrucas n ▷ **verruca**
versatile adj having many skills or uses
  > **versatility** n (pl **-ties**)
  versatilities n ▷ **versatile**
  versatility n ▷ **versatile**
verse n (pl **-s**) group of lines forming part of a song or poem
  verses n ▷ **verse**
versification n (pl **-s**) writing in verse
  versifications n ▷ **versification**
version n (pl **-s**) form of something, such as a piece of writing, with some differences from other forms
  versions n ▷ **version**
verso n (pl **-s**) left-hand page of a book
  versos n ▷ **verso**
versus prep in opposition to or in contrast with
vertebra n (pl **-rae**) one of the bones that form the spine > **vertebral** adj
  vertebrae n ▷ **vertabra**
  vertebral adj ▷ **vertebra**
vertebrate n, adj (pl **-s**) (animal) having a spine
  vertebrates n ▷ **vertebrate**
vertex n (pl **-texes, -tices**) (MATHS) point on a geometric figure where the sides form an angle
  vertexes n ▷ **vertex**
vertical adj straight up and down ▶ n (pl **-s**) vertical direction
  verticals n ▷ **vertical**
  vertices n ▷ **vertex**
  vertiginous adj ▷ **vertigo**
vertigo n (pl **-s**) dizziness, usu. when looking down from a high place > **vertiginous** adj
  vertigoes n ▷ **vertigo**
vervain n (pl **-s**) plant with spikes of blue, purple, or white flowers
  vervains n ▷ **vervain**
verve n (pl **-s**) enthusiasm or liveliness
  verves n ▷ **verve**
very adv more than usually, extremely ▶ adj absolute, exact
vesicle n (pl **-s**) (BIOL) sac or small cavity, esp. one containing fluid
  vesicles n ▷ **vesicle**
vespers pl n (RC CHURCH) (service of) evening prayer
vessel n (pl **-s**) ship
  vessels n ▷ **vessel**

vest n (pl **-s**) undergarment worn on the top half of the body ▶ v (**-s, -ing, -ed**) (foll. by **in** or **with**) give (authority) to (someone)
  vested v ▷ **vest**
vestibule n (pl **-s**) small entrance hall
  vestibules n ▷ **vestibule**
vestige [**vest**-ij] n (pl **-s**) small amount or trace
  > **vestigial** adj
  vestiges n ▷ **vestige**
  vestigial adj ▷ **vestige**
  vesting v ▷ **vest**
vestments pl n priest's robes
  vestries n ▷ **vestry**
vestry n (pl **-ies**) room in a church used as an office by the priest or minister
  vests n, v ▷ **vest**
vet[1] n (pl **-s**) ▷ **veterinary surgeon** ▶ v (**-s, -tting, -tted**) check the suitability of
vet[2] n (pl **-s**) (US, AUST & NZ) military veteran
vetch n (pl **-es**) climbing plant with a beanlike fruit used as fodder
  vetches n ▷ **vetch**
veteran n (pl **-s**) person with long experience in a particular activity, esp. military service
  ▶ adj long-serving
  veterans n ▷ **veteran**
veterinary adj concerning animal health
veto n (pl **-es**) official power to cancel a proposal ▶ v (**-es, -ing, -ed**) enforce a veto against
  vetoed v ▷ **veto**
  vetoes n, v ▷ **veto**
  vetoing v ▷ **veto**
  vets n, v ▷ **vet**[1, 2]
  vetted v ▷ **vet**[1]
  vetting v ▷ **vet**[1]
vex v (**-es, -ing, -ed**) frustrate, annoy
vexation n (pl **-s**) something annoying
  > **vexatious** adj
  vexations n ▷ **vexation**
  vexatious adj ▷ **vexation**
  vexed v ▷ **vex**
  vexes v ▷ **vex**
  vexing v ▷ **vex**
via prep by way of
  viabilities n ▷ **viable**
  viability n ▷ **viable**
viable adj able to be put into practice
  > **viability** n (pl **-ties**)
viaduct n (pl **-s**) bridge over a valley
  viaducts n ▷ **viaduct**
vial n (pl **-s**) ▷ **phial**
  vials n ▷ **vial**
viands pl n (Obs) food
vibes pl n (Informal) emotional reactions

between people

vibrant [vibe-rant] *adj* vigorous in appearance, energetic

vibraphone *n* (*pl* -s) musical instrument with metal bars that resonate electronically when hit

vibraphones *n* ▷ vibraphone

vibrate *v* (-tes, -ting, -ted) move back and forth rapidly ▷ **vibration** *n* (*pl* -s)

vibrated *v* ▷ vibrate

vibrates *v* ▷ vibrate

vibrating *v* ▷ vibrate

vibration *n* ▷ vibrate

vibrations *n* ▷ vibrate

vibrato *n* (*pl* -s) (MUSIC) rapid fluctuation in the pitch of a note

vibrator *n* (*pl* -s) device that produces vibratory motion, used for massage or as a sex aid ▷ **vibratory** *adj*

vibrators *n* ▷ vibrate

vibratos *n* ▷ vibrato

vicar *n* (*pl* -s) (C OF E) member of the clergy in charge of a parish

vicarage *n* (*pl* -s) vicar's house

vicarages *n* ▷ vicarage

vicarious [vick-air-ee-uss] *adj* felt indirectly by imagining what another person experiences ▷ **vicariously** *adv*

vicariously *adv* ▷ vicarious

vicars *n* ▷ vicar

vice[1] *n* (*pl* -s) immoral or evil habit or action

vice[2] *n* (*pl* -s) tool with a pair of jaws for holding an object while working on it

vice[3] *adj* serving in place of

viceregal *adj* ▷ viceroy

viceroy *n* (*pl* -s) governor of a colony who represents the monarch ▷ **viceregal** *adj*

viceroys *n* ▷ viceroy

vices *n* ▷ vice[1, 2]

vicinities *n* ▷ vicinity

vicinity [viss-in-it-ee] *n* (*pl* -ties) surrounding area

vicious *adj* cruel and violent ▷ **viciously** *adv*

viciously *adv* ▷ vicious

vicissitudes [viss-iss-it-yewds] *pl n* changes in fortune

victim *n* (*pl* -s) person or thing harmed or killed

victimization *n* ▷ victimize

victimizations *n* ▷ victimize

victimize *v* (-zes, -zing, -zed) punish unfairly ▷ **victimization** *n* (*pl* -s)

victimized *v* ▷ victimize

victimizes *v* ▷ victimize

victimizing *v* ▷ victimize

victims *n* ▷ victim

victor *n* (*pl* -s) person who has defeated an opponent, esp. in war or in sport

victories *n* ▷ victory

victorious *adj* ▷ victory

victors *n* ▷ victor

victory *n* (*pl* -ries) winning of a battle or contest ▷ **victorious** *adj*

victuals [vit-tals] *pl n* (Old-fashioned) food and drink

vicuña [vik-koo-nya] *n* (*pl* -s) S American animal like the llama

vicuñas *n* ▷ vicuña

video *n* (*pl* -s) ▷ **video cassette (recorder)** ▶ *v* (-s, -ing, -ed) record (a TV programme or event) on video ▶ *adj* relating to or used in producing television images

videoed *v* ▷ video

videoing *v* ▷ video

videos *n, v* ▷ video

videotext *n* (*pl* -s) means of representing on a TV screen information that is held in a computer

videotexts *n* ▷ videotext

vie *v* (vies, vying, vied) compete (with someone)

vied *v* ▷ vie

vies *v* ▷ vie

view *n* (*pl* -s) opinion or belief ▶ *v* (-s, -ing, -ed) think of (something) in a particular way

viewdata *n* (*pl* -as) ® videotext service linking users to a computer by telephone

viewdatas *n* ▷ viewdatas

viewed *v* ▷ view

viewer *n* person who watches television

viewers *n* ▷ viewer

viewfinder *n* (*pl* -s) window on a camera showing what will appear in a photograph

viewfinders *n* ▷ viewfinder

viewing *v* ▷ view

views *n, v* ▷ view

vigil [vij-ill] *n* (*pl* -s) night-time period of staying awake to look after a sick person, pray, etc.

vigilance *n* ▷ vigilant

vigilances *n* ▷ vigilant

vigilant *adj* watchful in case of danger ▷ **vigilance** *n* (*pl* -s)

vigilante [vij-ill-ant-ee] *n* (*pl* -s) person, esp. as one of a group, who takes it upon himself or herself to enforce the law

vigilantes *n* ▷ vigilante

vigils *n* ▷ vigil

vignette [vin-yet] *n* (*pl* -s) concise description of the typical features of something

vignettes *n* ▷ vignette

vigorous adj ▷ vigour
vigorously adv ▷ vigour
vigour n (pl -s) physical or mental energy
> **vigorous** adj > **vigorously** adv
vigours n ▷ vigour
viking n (pl -s) (HIST) seafaring raider and
settler from Scandinavia
vikings n ▷ viking
vile (-r, -st) adj very wicked > **vilely** adv
> **vileness** n (pl -s)
vilely adv ▷ vile
vileness n ▷ vile
vilenesses n ▷ vile
viler adj ▷ vile
vilest adj ▷ vile
vilification n ▷ vilify
vilifications n ▷ vilify
vilified v ▷ vilify
vilifies v ▷ vilify
vilify v (-fies, -fying, -fied) attack the character
of > **vilification** n (pl -s)
vilifying v ▷ vilify
villa n (pl -s) large house with gardens
village n (pl -s) small group of houses in a
country area > **villager** n (pl -s)
villager n ▷ village
villagers n ▷ village
villages n ▷ village
villain n (pl -s) wicked person > **villainous** adj
> **villainy** n (pl -nies)
villainies n ▷ villain
villainous adj ▷ villain
villains n ▷ villain
villas n ▷ villa
villein [vill-an] n (pl -s) (HIST) peasant bound in
service to his lord
villeins n ▷ villein
villiany n ▷ villian

vim n (vims). Vim means vigour or
energy. This word can be helpful when
you're stuck with unpromising letters,
and gives a reasonable score for a
three-letter word. Vim scores 8 points.

vinaigrette n (pl -s) salad dressing of oil and
vinegar
vinaigrettes n ▷ vinaigrette
vindicate v (-tes, -ting, -ted) clear (someone)
of guilt > **vindication** n (pl -s)
vindicated v ▷ vindicate
vindicates v ▷ vindicate
vindicating v ▷ vindicate
vindication n ▷ vindicate
vindications n ▷ vindicate
vindictive adj maliciously seeking revenge
> **vindictiveness** n (pl -es) > **vindictively** adv

vindictively adv ▷ vindictive
vindictiveness n ▷ vindictive
vindictivenesses n ▷ vindictive
vine n (pl -s) climbing plant, esp. one
producing grapes
vinegar n (pl -s) acid liquid made from wine,
beer, or cider > **vinegary** adj
vinegars n ▷ vinegar
vinegary adj ▷ vinegar
vines n ▷ vine
vineyard [vinn-yard] n (pl -s) plantation of
grape vines, esp. for making wine
vineyards n ▷ vineyard
vino [vee-noh] n (pl -s) (Informal) wine
vinos n ▷ vino
vintage n (pl -s) wine from a particular harvest
of grapes ▶ adj best and most typical
vintages n ▷ vintage
vintner n (pl -s) dealer in wine
vintners n ▷ vintner
vinyl [vine-ill] n (pl -s) type of plastic, used in
mock leather and records
vinyls n ▷ vinyl
viol [vie-oll] n (pl -s) early stringed instrument
preceding the violin
viola¹ [vee-oh-la] n (pl -s) stringed instrument
lower in pitch than a violin
viola² [vie-ol-la] n (pl -s) variety of pansy
violas n ▷ viola¹, ²
violate v (-tes, -ting, -ted) break (a law or
agreement) > **violation** n > **violator** n
violated v ▷ violate
violates v ▷ violate
violating v ▷ violate
violation n ▷ violate
violations n ▷ violate
violator n ▷ violate
violators n ▷ violate
violence n (pl -s) use of physical force, usu.
intended to cause injury or destruction
> **violent** adj > **violently** adv
violences n ▷ violence
violent adj ▷ violence
violently adv ▷ violent
violet n (pl -s) plant with bluish-purple flowers
▶ adj bluish-purple
violets n ▷ violet
violin n (pl -s) small four-stringed musical
instrument played with a bow. > **violinist**
n (pl -s)
violinist n ▷ violin
violinists n ▷ violin
violins n ▷ violin
viols n ▷ viol
viper n (pl -s) poisonous snake

vipers n ▷ viper

virago [vir-**rah**-go] n (pl -**goes**, -**gos**) aggressive woman

viragoes n ▷ virago

viragos n ▷ virago

viral adj of or caused by a virus

virgin n (pl -s) person, esp. a woman, who has not had sexual intercourse ▶ adj not having had sexual intercourse > **virginity** n (pl -**ties**)

virginal adj like a virgin ▶ n early keyboard instrument like a small harpsichord

virginities n ▷ virgin

virginity n ▷ virgin

virgins n ▷ virgin

virile adj having the traditional male characteristics of physical strength and a high sex drive > **virility** n (pl -**ties**)

virilities n ▷ virile

virility n ▷ virile

virologies n ▷ virology

virologies n ▷ virology

virology n (pl -**gies**) study of viruses

virtual adj having the effect but not the form of > **virtually** adv practically, almost

virtually adv ▷ virtual

virtue n (pl -s) moral goodness

virtues n ▷ virtue

virtuosi n ▷ virtuoso

virtuosities n ▷ virtuoso

virtuosity n ▷ virtuoso

virtuoso n (pl -**sos**, -**si**) person with impressive esp. musical skill > **virtuosity** n (pl -**ies**)

virtuosos n ▷ virtuoso

virtuous adj morally good > **virtuously** adv

virtuously adv ▷ virtuous

virulent [vir-**yew**-lent] adj very infectious

virus n (pl -**es**) microorganism that causes disease in humans, animals, and plants

viruses n ▷ virus

visa n (pl -s) permission to enter a country, granted by its government and shown by a stamp on one's passport

visage [**viz**-zij] n (pl -s) (Lit) face

visages n ▷ visage

visas n ▷ visa

viscera [**viss**-er-a] pl n large abdominal organs

visceral [**viss**-er-al] adj instinctive

viscid [**viss**-id] adj sticky

viscose n (pl -s) synthetic fabric made from cellulose

viscoses n ▷ viscose

viscosities n ▷ viscous

viscosity n ▷ viscous

viscount [**vie**-count] n (pl -s) British nobleman ranking between an earl and a baron

viscountess [**vie**-count-iss] n (pl -**es**) woman holding the rank of viscount in her own right

viscountesses n ▷ viscountess

viscounts n ▷ viscount

viscous adj thick and sticky > **viscosity** n (pl -**ties**)

visibilities n ▷ visibility

visibility n (pl -**ties**) range or clarity of vision

visible adj able to be seen > **visibly** adv

visibly adv ▷ visible

vision n (pl -s) ability to see

visionaries n ▷ visionary

visionary adj showing foresight ▶ n (pl -**ries**) visionary person

visions n ▷ vision

visit v (-s, -ing, -ed) go or come to see ▶ n instance of visiting > **visitor** n (pl -s)

visitation n (pl -s) formal visit or inspection

visitations n ▷ visitation

visited v ▷ visit

visiting v ▷ visit

visitor n ▷ visit

visitors n ▷ visit

visits v ▷ visit

visor [**vize**-or] n (pl -s) transparent part of a helmet that pulls down over the face

visors n ▷ visor

vista n (pl -s) (beautiful) extensive view

vistas n ▷ vista

visual adj done by or used in seeing

visualization n ▷ visualize

visualizations n ▷ visualize

visualize v (-zes, -zing, -zed) form a mental image of > **visualization** n (pl -s)

visualized v ▷ visualize

visualizes v ▷ visualize

visualizing v ▷ visualize

vital adj essential or highly important > **vitally** adv

vitalities n ▷ vitality

vitality n (pl -**ties**) physical or mental energy

vitally adv ▷ vital

vitals pl n bodily organs necessary to maintain life

vitamin n (pl -s) one of a group of substances that are essential in the diet for specific body processes

vitamins n ▷ vitamin

vitiate [**vish**-ee-ate] v (-**tes**, -**ting**, -**ted**) spoil the effectiveness of

vitiated v ▷ vitiate

vitiates v ▷ vitiate

vitiating v ▷ vitiate

viticulture n (pl -s) cultivation of grapevines

viticultures n ▷ viticulture

vitreous adj like or made from glass

vitriol n (pl -s) language expressing bitterness and hatred > **vitriolic** adj
vitriolic adj > vitriol
vitriols n > vitriol

vituperation n > vituperative
vituperations n > vituperative
vituperative [vite-tyew-pra-tiv] adj bitterly abusive > **vituperation** n (pl -s)

viva¹ interj long live (a person or thing)
viva² n (pl -s) (BRIT) examination in the form of an interview

vivace [viv-**vah**-chee] adv (MUSIC) in a lively manner

vivacious adj full of energy and enthusiasm > **vivacity** n (pl -ties)
vivacities n > vivacious
vivacity n > vivacious
vivas n > viva²

vivid adj (-er, -est) very bright > **vividly** adv > **vividness** n (pl -es)
vivider adj > vivid
vividest adj > vivid
vividly adv > vivid
vividness n > vivid
vividnesses n > vivid

vivisection n (pl -s) performing surgical experiments on living animals > **vivisectionist** n (pl -s)
vivisectionist n > vivisection
vivisectionists n > vivisection
vivisections n > vivisection

vixen n (pl -s) female fox
vixens n > vixen

vizier [viz-**zeer**] n (pl -s) high official in certain Muslim countries
viziers n > vizier

vizor n (pl -s) > visor
vizors n > vizor

> **vly** n (**vlys**). Vly is a South African word meaning an area of low marshy ground. This is a good word to remember because it doesn't contain any vowels, making it useful when you are short of vowel tiles. Vly scores 9 points.

vocabularies n > vocabulary
vocabulary n (pl -ries) all the words that a person knows

vocal adj relating to the voice

vocalist n (pl -s) singer
vocalists n > vocalist
vocalization n > vocalize
vocalizations n > vocalize
vocalize v (-zes, -zing, -zed) express with or use the voice > **vocalization** n (pl -s)
vocalizes v > vocalize
vocalizes v > vocalize
vocalizing v > vocalize
vocally adv > vocal

vocals pl n singing part of a piece of pop music > **vocally** adv

vocation n (pl -s) profession or trade
vocational adj directed towards a particular profession or trade
vocations n > vocation

vociferous adj shouting, noisy

vodka n (pl -s) (Russian) spirit distilled from potatoes or grain
vodkas n > vodka

vogue n (pl -s) popular style
vogues n > vogue

voice n (pl -s) (quality of) sound made when speaking or singing ▸ v (-ces, -cing, -ced) express verbally > **voiceless** adj
voiced v > voice
voiceless adj > voice
voices n, v > voice
voicing v > voice

void adj not legally binding ▸ n (pl -s) empty space ▸ v (-s, -ing, -ed) make invalid
voided v > void
voiding v > void
voids n, v > void

voile [voyl] n (pl -s) light semitransparent fabric
voiles n > voile

volatile adj liable to sudden change, esp. in behaviour > **volatility** n (pl -ties)
volatilities n > volatile
volatility n > volatile

volcanic adj > volcano

volcano n (pl -noes, -nos) mountain with a vent through which lava is ejected > **volcanic** adj
volcanoes n > volcano
volcanos n > volcano

vole n (pl -s) small rodent
voles n > vole

volition n (pl -s) ability to decide things for oneself
volitions n > volition

volley n (pl -s) simultaneous discharge of ammunition ▸ v (-s, -ing, -ed) discharge (ammunition) in a volley
volleyball n (pl -s) team game where a ball is hit with the hands over a high net
volleyballs n > volleyball
volleyed v > volley
volleying v > volley

volleys *n, v* ▷ volley

volt *n (pl -s)* unit of electric potential

voltage *n (pl -s)* electric potential difference expressed in volts

voltages *n* ▷ voltage

voltmeter *n* instrument for measuring voltage

voltmeters *n* ▷ voltmeter

volts *n* ▷ volt

volubilities *n* ▷ voluble

volubility *n* ▷ voluble

voluble *adj* talking easily and at length
> **volubility** *n (pl -ties)* > **volubly** *adv*

volubly *adv* ▷ voluble

volume *n (pl -s)* size of the space occupied by something

volumes *n* ▷ volume

volumetric *adj* relating to measurement by volume

voluminous *adj* (of clothes) large and roomy

voluntaries *n* ▷ voluntary

voluntarily *adv* ▷ voluntary

voluntary *adj* done by choice ▶ *n (pl -ries)* organ solo in a church service > **voluntarily** *adv*

volunteer *n (pl -s)* person who offers voluntarily to do something ▶ *v (-s, -ing, -ed)* offer one's services

volunteered *v* ▷ volunteer

volunteering *v* ▷ volunteer

volunteers *n, v* ▷ volunteer

voluptuaries *n* ▷ voluptuary

voluptuary *n (pl -ries)* person devoted to sensual pleasures

voluptuous *adj* (of a woman) sexually alluring through fullness of figure

volute *n (pl -s)* spiral or twisting turn, form, or object

volutes *n* ▷ volute

vomit *v (-s, -ing, -ed)* eject (the contents of the stomach) through the mouth ▶ *n (pl -s)* matter vomited

vomited *v* ▷ vomit

vomiting *v* ▷ vomit

vomits *v, n* ▷ vomit

voodoo *n (pl -s)* religion involving ancestor worship and witchcraft, practised by Black people in the West Indies, esp. in Haiti.

voodoos *n* ▷ voodoo

voracious *adj* craving great quantities of food
> **voraciously** *adv* > **voracity** *n (pl -ties)*

voraciously *adv* ▷ voracious

voracities *n* ▷ voracious

voracity *n* ▷ voracious

vortex *n (pl -texes, -tices)* whirlpool

vortexes *n* ▷ vortex

vortices *n* ▷ vortex

vote *n (pl -s)* choice made by a participant in a shared decision, esp. in electing a candidate ▶ *v (-tes, -ting, -ted)* make a choice by a vote
> **voter** *n (pl -s)*

voted *v* ▷ vote

voter *n* ▷ vote

voters *n* ▷ vote

votes *n, v* ▷ vote

voting *v* ▷ vote

votive *adj* done or given to fulfil a vow

vouch *v (-es, -ing, -ed)* give one's personal assurance about

vouched *v* ▷ vouch

voucher *n (pl -s)* ticket used instead of money to buy specified goods

vouchers *n* ▷ voucher

vouches *v* ▷ vouch

vouching *v* ▷ vouch

vouchsafe *v (-fes, -fing, -fed)* (Old-fashioned) give, entrust

vouchsafed *v* ▷ vouchsafe

vouchsafes *v* ▷ vouchsafe

vouchsafing *v* ▷ vouchsafe

vow *n (pl -s)* solemn and binding promise ▶ *pl* formal promises made when marrying or entering a religious order ▶ *v (-s, -ing, -ed)* promise solemnly

vowed *v* ▷ vow

vowel *n (pl -s)* speech sound made without obstructing the flow of breath

vowels *n* ▷ vowel

vowing *v* ▷ vow

vows *n, v* ▷ vow

> **vox** *n (voces)*. Vox means a voice or sound. Along with **vex**, this is the highest-scoring three-letter word beginning with V. Vox scores 13 points.

voyage *n (pl -s)* long journey by sea or in space ▶ *v (-ges, -ging, -ged)* make a voyage
> **voyager** *n (pl -s)*

voyaged *v* ▷ voyage

voyager *n* ▷ voyage

voyagers *n* ▷ voyager

voyages *n, v* ▷ voyage

voyaging *v* ▷ voyage

voyeur *n (pl -s)* person who obtains pleasure from watching people undressing or having sex > **voyeurism** *n (pl -s)*

voyeurism *n* ▷ voyeur

voyeurisms *n* ▷ voyeur

voyeurs *n* ▷ voyeur

> **vug** *n (vugs)*. A vug is a small cavity in a rock. This is a very unusual word

that can be useful when you have an uninspiring combination of letters. Vug scores 7 points.

vulcanize v (-zes, -zing, -zed) strengthen (rubber) by treating it with sulphur

vulcanized v ▷ vulcanize

vulcanizes v ▷ vulcanize

vulcanizing v ▷ vulcanize

vulgar adj (-er, -est) showing lack of good taste, decency, or refinement > **vulgarly** adv > **vulgarity** n (pl -ies)

vulgarer adj ▷ vulgar

vulgarest adj ▷ vulgar

vulgarian n (pl -s) vulgar (rich) person

vulgarians n ▷ vulgarian

vulgarities n ▷ vulgar

vulgarities n ▷ vulgar

vulgarly adv ▷ vulgar

vulnerabilities n ▷ vulnerable

vulnerability n ▷ vulnerable

vulnerable adj liable to be physically or emotionally hurt > **vulnerability** n (pl -s)

vulpine adj of or like a fox

vulture n (pl -s) large bird that feeds on the flesh of dead animals

vultures n ▷ vulture

vulva n (pl -vae) woman's external genitals

vulvae n ▷ vulva

vying v ▷ vie

Ww

W is a useful tile to have on your rack as it earns 4 points on its own and produces a number of high-scoring short words. There are, however, only two two-letter words begin with W: **we** and **wo** (5 points each). If you know this, though, you won't waste time looking for others. There are lots of everyday three-letter words that earn good scores: **wax** (13) with its two old-fashioned variants **wex** and **wox** (also 13 each) and **way, who, why, wow** and **wry** (9 each). Don't forget **wok** (10) either, which can be as useful on the Scrabble board as in the kitchen!

wackier adj ▷ wacky
wackiest adj ▷ wacky
wackiness n ▷ wacky
wackinesses n ▷ wacky
wacky adj (-ckier, -ckiest) (Informal) eccentric or funny > **wackiness** n (pl -es)
wad n (pl -s) small mass of soft material
waddies n ▷ waddy
wadding n (pl -s) soft material used for padding or stuffing
waddings n ▷ wadding
waddle v (-les, -ling, -led) walk with short swaying steps ▶ n (pl -s) swaying walk
waddled v, n ▷ waddle
waddles v ▷ waddle
waddling v ▷ waddle
waddy n (pl -ies) heavy wooden club used by Australian Aborigines
wade v (-des, -ding, -ded) walk with difficulty through water or mud
waded v ▷ wade
wader n (pl -s) long-legged water bird ▶ pl angler's long waterproof boots
waders n ▷ wader
wades v ▷ wade
wadi [wod-dee] n (pl -s) (in N Africa and Arabia) river which is dry except in the wet season
wading v ▷ wade
wadis n ▷ wadi
wads n ▷ wad
wafer n (pl -s) thin crisp biscuit
wafers n ▷ wafer
waffle¹ (Informal) v (-les, -ling, -led) speak or write in a vague wordy way ▶ n (pl -s) vague wordy talk or writing
waffle² n (pl -s) square crisp pancake with a gridlike pattern

waffled v ▷ waffle¹
waffles v, n ▷ waffle¹, ²
waffling v ▷ waffle¹
waft v (-s, -ing, -ed) drift or carry gently through the air ▶ n (pl -s) something wafted
wafted v ▷ waft
wafting v ▷ waft
wafts v, n ▷ waft
wag v (-s, -gging, -gged) move rapidly from side to side ▶ n (pl -s) wagging movement
wage n (pl -s) (often pl) payment for work done, esp. when paid weekly ▶ v (-ges, -ging, -ged) engage in (an activity)
waged v ▷ wage
wager n, v (-s, -ing, -ed) bet on the outcome of something
wagered v ▷ wager
wagering v ▷ wager
wagers n, v ▷ wager
wages n, v ▷ wage
wagged v ▷ wag
wagging v ▷ wag
waggle v (-les, -ling, -led) move with a rapid shaking or wobbling motion
waggled v ▷ waggle
waggles v ▷ waggle
waggling v ▷ waggle
waggon n ▷ wagon
waggons n ▷ wagon
waging v ▷ wage
wagon, waggon n (pl -s) four-wheeled vehicle for heavy loads
wagons n ▷ wagon
wags v ▷ wag
wagtail n (pl -s) small long-tailed bird
wagtail n ▷ wagtails
wahoo n (pl -s) food and game fish of tropical

seas

wahoos n ▷ wahoo

waif n (pl -s) young person who is, or seems, homeless or neglected

waifs n ▷ waif

wail v (-s, -ing, -ed) cry out in pain or misery ▸ n (pl -s) mournful cry

wailed v ▷ wail

wailing v ▷ wail

wails v, n ▷ wail

wain n (pl -s) (Poetic) farm wagon

wains n ▷ wain

wainscot, wainscoting n (pl -s) wooden lining of the lower part of the walls of a room

wainscoting n ▷ wainscot

wainscotings n ▷ wainscot

wainscots n ▷ wainscot

waist n (pl -s) part of the body between the ribs and hips

waistband n (pl -s) band of material sewn on to the waist of a garment to strengthen it

waistbands n ▷ waistband

waistcoat n (pl -s) sleeveless garment which buttons up the front, usu. worn over a shirt and under a jacket

waistcoats n ▷ waistcoat

waistline n (pl -s) (size of) the waist of a person or garment

waistlines n ▷ waistline

waists n ▷ waist

wait v (-s, -ing, -ed) remain inactive in expectation (of something) ▸ n (pl -s) act or period of waiting

waited v ▷ wait

waiter n (pl -s) man who serves in a restaurant etc. > **waitress** n fem (pl -es)

waiters n ▷ waiter

waiting v ▷ wait

waitress n ▷ waiter

waitresses n ▷ waiter

waits v, n ▷ wait

waive v (-ves, -ving, -ved) refrain from enforcing (a claim, right, etc.)

waived v ▷ waive

waiver n (pl -s) act or instance of voluntarily giving up a claim, right, etc.

waivers n ▷ waiver

waives v ▷ waive

waiving v ▷ waive

waka n (pl -s) (NZ) Maori canoe

wakas n ▷ waka

wake¹ v (-kes, -king, woke, woken) rouse from sleep or inactivity ▸ n (pl -s) vigil beside a corpse the night before the funeral > **wakeful** adj

wake² n (pl -s) track left by a moving ship

wakeful adj ▷ wake¹

waken v (-s, -ing, -ed) wake

wakened v ▷ waken

wakening v ▷ waken

wakens v ▷ waken

wakes n ▷ wake¹, ²

waking v ▷ wake¹

walk v (-s, -ing, -ed) move on foot with at least one foot always on the ground ▸ n (pl -s) act or instance of walking > **walker** n (pl -s)

walkabout n (pl -s) informal walk among the public by royalty etc.

walkabouts n ▷ walkabout

walked v ▷ walk

walker n ▷ walk

walkers n ▷ walk

walking v ▷ walk

walkout n (pl -s) strike

walkouts n ▷ walkout

walkover n (pl -s) easy victory

walkovers n ▷ walkover

walks v, n ▷ walk

wall n (pl -s) structure of brick, stone, etc. used to enclose, divide, or support ▸ v (-s, -ing, -ed) enclose or seal with a wall or walls

wallabies n ▷ wallaby

wallaby n (pl -bies) marsupial like a small kangaroo

wallaroo n (pl -s) large stocky Australian kangaroo of rocky regions

wallaroos n ▷ wallaroo

walled v ▷ wall

wallet n (pl -s) small folding case for paper money, documents, etc.

wallets n ▷ wallet

walleye n (pl -s) fish with large staring eyes (also **dory**)

walleyes n ▷ walleye

wallflower n (pl -s) fragrant garden plant

wallflowers n ▷ wallflower

wallies n ▷ wally

walling v ▷ wall

wallop (Informal) v (-s, -ing, -ed) hit hard ▸ n (pl -s) hard blow

walloped v ▷ wallop

walloping (Informal) n thrashing ▸ adj large or great ▸ v ▷ wallop

wallops v, n ▷ wallop

wallow v (-s, -ing, -ed) revel in an emotion ▸ n (pl -s) act or instance of wallowing

wallowed v ▷ wallow

wallowing v ▷ wallow

wallows v, n ▷ wallow

wallpaper n (pl -s) decorative paper to cover

interior walls

wallpapers n ▷ wallpaper

walls n, v ▷ wall

wally n (pl -ies) (BRIT) (Slang) stupid person

walnut n (pl -s) edible nut with a wrinkled shell

walnuts n ▷ walnut

walrus n (pl -ruses, -rus) large sea mammal with long tusks

walruses n ▷ walrus

waltz n (pl -es) ballroom dance ▶ v (-zes, -zing, -zed) dance a waltz

waltzed v ▷ waltz

waltzes n, v ▷ waltz

waltzing v ▷ waltz

wampum [wom-pum] n (pl -s) shells woven together, formerly used by Native Americans for money and ornament

wampums n ▷ wampum

wan [rhymes with swan] adj (-nner, -nnest) pale and sickly looking

wand n (pl -s) thin rod, esp. one used in performing magic tricks

wander v (-s, -ing, -ed) move about without a definite destination or aim ▶ n (pl -s) act or instance of wandering > **wanderer** n (pl -s)

wandered v ▷ wander

wanderer n ▷ wander

wanderers n ▷ wander

wandering v ▷ wander

wanderlust n (pl -s) great desire to travel

wanderlusts n ▷ wanderlust

wanders v, n ▷ wander

wands n ▷ wand

wane v (-nes, -ning, -ned) decrease gradually in size or strength

waned v ▷ wane

wanes v ▷ wane

wangle v (-les, -ling, -led) (Informal) get by devious methods

wangled v ▷ wangle

wangles v ▷ wangle

wangling v ▷ wangle

waning v ▷ wane

wanner adj ▷ wan

wannest adj ▷ wan

want v (-s, -ing, -ed) need or long for ▶ n (pl -s) act or instance of wanting

wanted adj sought by the police ▶ v ▷ want

wanting adj lacking ▶ v ▷ want

wanton adj (-er, -est) without motive, provocation, or justification

wantoner adj ▷ wanton

wantonest adj ▷ wanton

wants v, n ▷ want

war n (pl -s) fighting between nations ▶ adj of, like, or caused by war ▶ v (-s, -rring, -rred) conduct a war > **warring** adj

waratah n (pl -s) Australian shrub with crimson flowers

waratahs n ▷ waratah

warble v (-les, -ling, -led) sing in a trilling voice

warbled v ▷ warble

warbler n (pl -s) any of various small songbirds

warblers n ▷ warbler

warbles v ▷ warble

warbling v ▷ warble

ward n (pl -s) room in a hospital for patients needing a similar kind of care

warden n (pl -s) person in charge of a building and its occupants

wardens n ▷ warden

warder n (pl -s) prison officer > **wardress** n fem (pl -es)

warders n ▷ warder

wardress n ▷ warder

wardresses n ▷ warder

wardrobe n (pl -s) cupboard for hanging clothes in

wardrobes n ▷ wardrobe

wardroom n (pl -s) officers' quarters on a warship

wardrooms n ▷ wardroom

wards n ▷ ward

ware n (pl -s) articles of a specified type or material ▶ pl goods for sale

warehouse n (pl -s) building for storing goods prior to sale or distribution

warehouses n ▷ warehouse

wares n ▷ ware

warfare n (pl -s) fighting or hostilities

warfares n ▷ warfare

warhead n (pl -s) explosive front part of a missile

warheads n ▷ warhead

warier adj ▷ wary

wariest adj ▷ wary

warily adv ▷ wary

wariness n ▷ wary

warinesses n ▷ wary

warlike adj of or relating to war

warlock n (pl -s) man who practises black magic

warlocks n ▷ warlock

warm adj (-er, -est) moderately hot ▶ v (-s, -ing, -ed) make or become warm > **warmly** adv

warmed v ▷ warm

warmer adj ▷ warm

warmest adj ▷ warm

warming v ▷ warm

warmly adv ▷ warm

warmonger n (pl **-s**) person who encourages war

warmongers n ▷ warmonger

warms v ▷ warm

warmth n (pl **-s**) mild heat

warmths n ▷ warmth

warn v (**-s, -ing, -ed**) make aware of possible danger or harm

warned v ▷ warn

warning n (pl **-s**) something that warns ▶ v ▷ warn

warnings n ▷ warning

warns v ▷ warn

warp v (**-s, -ing, -ed**) twist out of shape ▶ n (pl **-s**) state of being warped

warped v ▷ warp

warping v ▷ warp

warps v, n ▷ warp

warrant n (pl **-s**) (document giving) official authorization ▶ v (**-s, -ing, -ed**) make necessary

warranted v ▷ warrant

warranties n ▷ warranty

warranting v ▷ warrant

warrants n, v ▷ warrant

warranty n (pl **-ties**) (document giving) a guarantee

warred v ▷ war

warren n (pl **-s**) series of burrows in which rabbits live

warrens n ▷ warren

warrigal (AUST) n (pl **-s**) dingo ▶ adj wild

warrigals n ▷ warrigal

warring v ▷ war

warrior n (pl **-s**) person who fights in a war

warriors n ▷ warrior

wars n, v ▷ war

warship n (pl **-s**) ship designed and equipped for naval combat

warships n ▷ warship

wart n (pl **-s**) small hard growth on the skin

warts n ▷ wart

wary [ware-ree] adj (**-rier, -riest**) watchful or cautious ▶ **warily** adv > **wariness** n (pl **-es**)

was v ▷ be

wash v (**-es, -ing, -ed**) clean (oneself, clothes, etc.) with water and usu. soap (Informal) ▶ n (pl **-es**) act or process of washing > **washable** adj

washable adj ▷ wash

washed v ▷ wash

washer n (pl **-s**) ring put under a nut or bolt or in a tap as a seal

washers n ▷ washer

washes v, n ▷ wash

washing n (pl **-s**) clothes to be washed ▶ v ▷ wash

washings n ▷ washing

washout n (pl **-s**) (Informal) complete failure

washouts n ▷ washouts

wasp n (pl **-s**) stinging insect with a slender black-and-yellow striped body

waspish adj bad-tempered

wasps n ▷ wasp

wastage n (pl **-s**) loss by wear or waste

wastages n ▷ wastage

waste v (**-tes, -ting, -ted**) use pointlessly or thoughtlessly ▶ n (pl **-s**) act of wasting or state of being wasted ▶ pl desert ▶ adj rejected as worthless or surplus to requirements

wasted v ▷ waste

wasteful adj extravagant > **wastefully** adv

wastefully adv ▷ waste

waster, wastrel n (pl **-s**) layabout

wasters n ▷ waster

wastes v, n ▷ waste

wasting v ▷ waste

wastrel n ▷ waster

wastrels n ▷ waster

watch v (**-es, -ing, -ed**) look at closely ▶ n (pl **-es**) portable timepiece for the wrist or pocket > **watchable** adj > **watcher** n (pl **-s**)

watchable adj ▷ watch

watchdog n (pl **-s**) dog kept to guard property

watchdogs n ▷ watchdog

watched v ▷ watch

watcher n ▷ watch

watchers n ▷ watch

watches v, n ▷ watch

watchful adj vigilant or alert > **watchfully** adv

watchfully adv ▷ watchful

watching v ▷ watch

watchman n (pl **-men**) man employed to guard a building or property

watchmen n ▷ watchman

watchword n (pl **-s**) word or phrase that sums up the attitude of a particular group

watchwords n ▷ watchword

water n (pl **-s**) clear colourless tasteless liquid that falls as rain and forms rivers etc. ▶ v (**-s, -ing, -ed**) put water on or into > **watery** adj (**-rier, -riest**)

watercolour n (pl **-s**) paint thinned with water

watercolours n ▷ watercolour

watercourse n (pl **-s**) bed of a stream or river

watercourses n ▷ watercourse

watercress n (pl **-es**) edible plant growing in clear ponds and streams

watercresses n ▷ watercress

watered v ▷ water

waterfall n (pl **-s**) place where the waters of a

river drop vertically
waterfalls n ▷ waterfall
waterfront n (pl -s) part of a town alongside a
body of water
waterfronts n ▷ waterfront
waterier adj ▷ watery
wateriest adj ▷ watery
watering v ▷ water
watermark n (pl -s) faint translucent design in
a sheet of paper
watermarks n ▷ watermark
watermelon n (pl -s) melon with green skin
and red flesh
watermelons n ▷ watermelon
waterproof adj not letting water through ▶ n
(pl -s) waterproof garment ▶ v (-s, -ing, -ed)
make waterproof
waterproofed v ▷ waterproof
waterproofing v ▷ waterproof
waterproofs n, v ▷ waterproof
waters n ▷ water
watershed n (pl -s) important period or factor
serving as a dividing line
watersheds n ▷ watershed
watersider n (pl -s) (NZ) person employed to
load and unload ships
watersiders n ▷ watersider
waterskiing n (pl -s) sport of riding over water
on skis towed by a speedboat
waterskiings n ▷ waterskiing
watertight adj not letting water through
watery adj ▷ water
watt [wott] n (pl -s) unit of power
wattage n (pl -s) electrical power expressed
in watts
wattages n ▷ wattage
wattle [wott-tl] n (pl -s) branches woven over
sticks to make a fence making fences
wattles n ▷ wattle
watts n ▷ watt
wave v (-ves, -ving, -ved) move the hand to and
fro as a greeting or signal ▶ n (pl -s) moving
ridge on water > **wavy** adj (-vier, -viest)
waved v ▷ wave
wavelength n (pl -s) distance between the
same points of two successive waves
wavelengths n ▷ wavelength
waver v (-s, -ing, -ed) hesitate or be irresolute
> **waverer** n (pl -s)
wavered v ▷ waver
waverer n ▷ waver
waverers n ▷ waver
wavering v ▷ waver
wavers v ▷ waver
waves v, n ▷ wave

wavier adj ▷ wave
waviest adj ▷ wave
waving v ▷ wave
wavy adj ▷ wave
wax¹ n (pl -es) solid shiny fatty or oily
substance used for sealing, making candles,
etc. ▶ v (-es, -ing, -ed) coat or polish with wax
> **waxy** adj (-xier, -xiest)
wax² v (-es, -ing, -ed) increase in size or
strength
waxed v ▷ wax¹, ²
waxen adj made of or like wax
waxes n, v ▷ wax¹, ²
waxier adj ▷ wax
waxiest adj ▷ wax
waxing v ▷ wax¹, ²
waxwork n (pl -s) lifelike wax model of a
(famous) person ▶ pl place exhibiting these
waxworks n ▷ waxwork
waxy adj ▷ wax¹
way n (pl -s) manner or method
wayfarer n (Lit) traveller
wayfarers n ▷ wayfarer
waylaid v ▷ waylay
waylay v (-lays, -laying, -laid) lie in wait for
and accost or attack
waylaying v ▷ waylay
waylays v ▷ waylay
ways n ▷ way
wayside adj, n (pl -s) (situated by) the side of
a road
waysides n ▷ wayside
wayward adj erratic, selfish, or stubborn
> **waywardness** n (pl -es)
waywardness n ▷ wayward
waywardnesses n ▷ wayward
we pron (used as the subject of a verb) the speaker
or writer and one or more others
weak adj (-er, -est) lacking strength
weaken v (-s, -ing, -ed) make or become weak
weakened v ▷ weaken
weakening v ▷ weaken
weakens v ▷ weaken
weaker adj ▷ weak
weakest adj ▷ weak
weakling n feeble person or animal
weaklings n ▷ weakling
weakly adv feebly
weakness n (-es) being weak
weaknesses n ▷ weakness
weal n (pl -s) raised mark left on the skin by
a blow
weals n ▷ weal
wealth n (pl -s) state of being rich > **wealthy**
adj (-thier, -thiest)

wealthier adj ▷ wealth
wealthiest adj ▷ wealth
wealthy adj ▷ wealth
wean v (-s, -ing, -ed) accustom (a baby or young mammal) to food other than mother's milk
  weaned v ▷ wean
  weaning v ▷ wean
  weans v ▷ wean
weapon n (pl -s) object used in fighting
  weaponries n ▷ weapon
weaponry n (pl -ries) weapons collectively
  weapons n ▷ weapon
wear v (-s, -ing, wore, worn) have on the body as clothing or ornament ▶ n (pl -s) clothes suitable for a particular time or purpose
  > **wearer** n (pl -s)
  wearer n ▷ wear
  wearers n ▷ wear
  wearied v ▷ weary
  wearier adj ▷ weary
  wearies v ▷ weary
  weariest adj ▷ weary
  wearily adv ▷ weary
  weariness n ▷ weary
  wearinesses n ▷ weary
  wearing v ▷ wear
wearisome adj tedious
  wears n, v ▷ wear
weary adj (-rier, -riest) tired or exhausted ▶ v (-ries, -rying, -ried) make or become weary
  > **wearily** adv > **weariness** n (pl -es)
  wearying v ▷ weary
weasel n (pl -s) small carnivorous mammal with a long body and short legs
  weasels n ▷ weasel
weather n (pl -s) day-to-day atmospheric conditions of a place ▶ v (-s, -ing, -ed) (cause to) be affected by the weather
weathercock, weathervane n device that revolves to show the direction of the wind
  weathercocks n ▷ weathercock
  weathered v ▷ weather
  weathering v ▷ weather
  weathers v, n ▷ weather
  weathervanes n ▷ weathervane
weave v (-s, -ing, wove or weaved, woven or weaved) make (fabric) by interlacing (yarn) on a loom ▶ **weaver** n (pl -s)
  weaved v ▷ weave
  weaver n ▷ weave
  weavers n ▷ weave
  weaves v ▷ weave
web n (pl -s) net spun by a spider > **webbed** adj
  webbed adj ▷ web

webbing n (pl -s) strong fabric woven in strips
  webbings n ▷ web
webcam n (pl -s) camera that transmits images over the Internet
  webcams n ▷ webcam
webcast n (pl -s) broadcast of an event over the Internet
  webcasts n ▷ webcast
weblog n (pl -s) person's online journal (also blog)
  weblogs n ▷ weblog
  webs n ▷ web
website n (pl -s) group of connected pages on the World Wide Web
  websites n ▷ website
wed v (-s, -dding, -dded or wed) marry
  wedded v ▷ wed
wedding n (pl -s) act or ceremony of marriage ▶ v ▷ wed
  weddings n ▷ wedding
wedge n (pl wedges) piece of material thick at one end and thin at the other ▶ v (-ges, -ging, -ged) fasten or split with a wedge
  wedged v ▷ wedge
  wedges n, v ▷ wedge
  wedging v ▷ wedge
wedlock n (pl -s) marriage
  wedlocks n ▷ wedlock
wee adj (-r, -st) (BRIT, AUST & NZ) (Informal) small or short
weed n (pl -s) plant growing where undesired (Informal) ▶ v (-s, -ing, -ed) clear of weeds
  weeded v ▷ weed
  weedier adj ▷ weedy
  weediest adj ▷ weddy
  weeding v ▷ weed
  weeds n, v ▷ weed ▶ pl n (Obs) widow's mourning clothes
weedy adj (-dier, -diest) (Informal) (of a person) thin and weak
week n (pl -s) period of seven days, esp. one beginning on a Sunday
weekday n (pl -s) any day of the week except Saturday or Sunday
  weekdays n ▷ weekday
weekend n (pl -s) Saturday and Sunday
  weekends n ▷ weekend
  weeklies n ▷ weekly
weekly adj, adv happening, done, etc. once a week ▶ n (pl -lies) newspaper or magazine published once a week
  weeks n ▷ week
weep v (-s, -ing, wept) shed tears
  weepier adj ▷ weepy
  weepiest adj ▷ weepy

weeping v ▷ weep

weeps v ▷ weep

weepy adj (-pier, -piest) liable to cry

weer adj ▷ wee

weest adj ▷ wee

weevil n (pl -s) small beetle which eats grain etc.

weevils n ▷ weevil

weft n (pl -s) cross threads in weaving

wefts n ▷ weft

weigh v (-s, -ing, -ed) have a specified weight

weighbridge n (pl -s) machine for weighing vehicles by means of a metal plate set into the road

weighbridges n ▷ weighbridge

weighed v ▷ weigh

weighing v ▷ weigh

weighs v ▷ weigh

weight n (pl -s) heaviness of an object ▶ v (-s, -ing, -ed) add weight to ▶ weightless adj > weightlessness n

weighted v ▷ weight

weightier adj ▷ weighty

weightiest adj ▷ weighty

weightily adv ▷ weighty

weighting v ▷ weight ▶ n (pl -s) (BRIT) extra allowance paid in special circumstances

weightings n ▷ weighting

weightless adj ▷ weight

weightlessness n ▷ weight

weights n, v ▷ weight

weighty adj (-tier, -tiest) important or serious > weightily adv

weir n (pl -s) river dam

weird (-er, -est) adj strange or bizarre

weirder adj ▷ weird

weirdest adj ▷ weird

weirdo n (pl -s) (Informal) peculiar person

weirdos n ▷ weirdo

weirs n ▷ weir

welch v (-es, -ing, -ed) ▷ welsh

welched v ▷ welch

welches v ▷ welch

welching v ▷ welch

welcome v (-mes, -ming, -med) greet with pleasure ▶ n (pl -s) kindly greeting ▶ adj received gladly

welcomed v ▷ welcome

welcomes v, n ▷ welcome

welcoming v ▷ welcome

weld v (-s, -ing, -ed) join (pieces of metal or plastic) by softening with heat ▶ n (pl -s) welded joint > welder n (pl -s)

welded v ▷ weld

welder n ▷ weld

welders n ▷ weld

welding v ▷ weld

welds v, n ▷ weld

welfare n (pl -s) wellbeing

welfares n ▷ welfare

well¹ adv (better, best) satisfactorily ▶ adj in good health ▶ interj exclamation of surprise, interrogation, etc.

well² n (pl -s) hole sunk into the earth to reach water, oil, or gas ▶ v (-s, -ing, -ed) flow upwards or outwards

wellbeing n (pl -s) state of being well, happy, or prosperous

wellbeings n ▷ wellbeing

welled v ▷ well²

wellies pl n (BRIT & AUST) (Informal) wellingtons

welling v ▷ well²

wellingtons pl n (BRIT & AUST) high waterproof rubber boots

wells n, v ▷ well²

welsh v (-es, -ing, -ed) fail to pay a debt or fulfil an obligation

welshed v ▷ welsh

welshes v ▷ welsh

welshing v ▷ welsh

welt n (pl -s) raised mark on the skin produced by a blow

welter n (pl -s) jumbled mass

welters n ▷ welter

welterweight n (pl -s) boxer weighing up to 147lb (professional) or 67kg (amateur)

welterweights n ▷ welterweight

welts n ▷ welt

wen n (pl -s) cyst on the scalp

wench n (pl -es) (facetious) young woman

wenches n ▷ wench

wend v (-s, -ing, -ed) go or travel

wended v ▷ wend

wending v ▷ wend

wends v ▷ wend

wens n ▷ wen

went v ▷ go

wept v ▷ weep

were v form of the past tense of be used after we, you, they, or a plural noun ▷ be

werewolf n (pl -wolves) (in folklore) person who can turn into a wolf

werewolves n ▷ werewolf

west n (pl -s) (direction towards) the part of the horizon where the sun sets ▶ adj to or in the west ▶ adv in, to, or towards the west ▶ westerly adj ▶ westward adj, adv > westwards adv

westerly adj ▷ west

western adj of or in the west ▶ n (pl -s) film or

story about cowboys in the western US

westernize v (-zes, -zing, -zed) adapt to the customs and culture of the West

westernized v ▷ westernize

westernizes v ▷ westernize

westernizing v ▷ westernize

westerns n ▷ western

wests n ▷ west

westward adj ▷ west

westwards adv ▷ west

wet adj (-tter, -ttest) covered or soaked with water or another liquid (BRIT) (Informal) ▶ n moisture or rain (BRIT) (Informal) ▶ v (-s, -tting, wet or wetted) make wet

wetland n (pl -s) area of marshy land

wetlands n ▷ wetland

wetted v ▷ wet

wetter adj ▷ wet

wettest adj ▷ wet

wetting v ▷ wet

> **wex** n (**wexes**). Wex is an old word for wax. This gives a very good score for a three-letter word, and is a good one to look for when you have an X. Wex scores 13 points.

whack v (-s, -ing, -ed) strike with a resounding blow ▶ n (pl -s) such a blow

whacked adj exhausted ▶ v ▷ whack

whacking adj (Informal) huge ▶ v ▷ whack

whacks v, n ▷ whack

whale n (pl -s) large fish-shaped sea mammal

whaler n ship or person involved in whaling

whalers n ▷ whaler

whales n ▷ whale

whaling n (pl -s) hunting of whales for food and oil

whalings n ▷ whaling

wharf n (pl **wharves, wharfs**) platform at a harbour for loading and unloading ships

wharfie n (pl -s) (AUST) person employed to load and unload ships

wharfies n ▷ wharfie

wharfs n ▷ wharf

wharves n ▷ wharf

what pron which thing ▶ interj exclamation of anger, surprise, etc. ▶ adv in which way, how much

whatnot n (pl -s) (Informal) similar unspecified things

whatnots n ▷ whatnot

whatsoever adj at all

wheat n (pl -s) grain used in making flour, bread, and pasta ▶ wheaten adj

wheatear n (pl -s) small songbird

wheatears n ▷ wheatear

wheaten adj ▷ wheat

wheats n ▷ wheat

wheedle v (-les, -ling, -led) coax or cajole

wheedled v ▷ wheedle

wheedles v ▷ wheedle

wheedling v ▷ wheedle

wheel n (pl -s) disc that revolves on an axle ▶ v (-s, -ing, -ed) push or pull (something with wheels)

wheelbarrow n (pl -s) shallow box for carrying loads, with a wheel at the front and two handles

wheelbarrows n ▷ wheelbarrow

wheelbase n (pl -s) distance between a vehicle's front and back axles

wheelbases n ▷ wheelbase

wheelchair n (pl -s) chair mounted on wheels for use by people who cannot walk

wheelchairs n ▷ wheelchair

wheeled v ▷ wheel

wheeling v ▷ wheel

wheels n, v ▷ wheel

wheeze v (-zes, -zing, -zed) breathe with a hoarse whistling noise ▶ n (pl -s) wheezing sound (Informal) > **wheezy** adj (-zier, -ziest)

wheezed v ▷ wheeze

wheezes v, n ▷ wheeze

wheezier adj ▷ wheeze

wheeziest adj ▷ wheeze

wheezing v ▷ wheeze

wheezy adj ▷ wheeze

whelk n (pl -s) edible snail-like shellfish

whelks n ▷ whelk

whelp n (pl -s) pup or cub ▶ v (-s, -ing, -ed) (of an animal) give birth

whelped v ▷ whelp

whelping v ▷ whelp

whelps n, v ▷ whelp

when adv at what time? ▶ conj at the time that ▶ pron at which time

whence adv, conj (Obs) from what place or source

whenever adv, conj at whatever time

where adv in, at, or to what place? ▶ pron in, at, or to which place ▶ conj in the place at which

whereabouts n present position ▶ adv at what place

whereas conj but on the other hand

whereby pron by which

wherefore (Obs) adv why ▶ conj consequently

whereupon conj at which point

wherever conj, adv at whatever place

wherewithal n (pl -s) necessary funds, resources, etc.

wherewithals n ▷ wherewithals

whet v (**-s, -tting, -tted**) sharpen (a tool)

whether conj used to introduce an indirect question or a clause expressing doubt or choice

whets v ▷ whet

whetstone n (pl **-s**) stone for sharpening tools

whetstones n ▷ whetstone

whetted v ▷ whet

whetting v ▷ whet

whey [way] n (pl **-s**) watery liquid that separates from the curd when milk is clotted

wheys n ▷ whey

which adj, pron used to request or refer to a choice from different possibilities ▶ pron used to refer to a thing already mentioned

whichever adj, pron any out of several

whiff n (pl **-s**) puff of air or odour

whiffs n ▷ whiff

whig n (pl **-s**) member of a British political party of the 18th–19th centuries that sought limited reform

whigs n ▷ whig

while conj at the same time that ▶ n (pl **-s**) period of time

whiles n ▷ while

whilst conj while

whim n (pl **-s**) sudden fancy

whimper v (**-s, -ing, -ed**) cry in a soft whining way ▶ n (pl **-s**) soft plaintive whine

whimpered v ▷ whimper

whimpering v ▷ whimper

whimpers v, n ▷ whimper

whims n ▷ whim

whimsical adj unusual, playful, and fanciful

whimsies n ▷ whimsy

whimsy n (pl **-ies**) capricious idea

whin n (pl **-s**) (BRIT) gorse

whine n (pl **-s**) high-pitched plaintive cry ▶ v (**-nes, -ning, -ned**) make such a sound > **whining** n, adj (pl **-s**)

whined v ▷ whine

whines n, v ▷ whine

whinge (BRIT, AUST & NZ) (Informal) v (**-ges, -geing, -ged**) complain ▶ n (pl **-s**) complaint

whinged v ▷ whinge

whingeing v ▷ whinge

whinges v, n ▷ whinge

whining v, n adj ▷ whine

whinings n ▷ whine

whinnied v ▷ whinny

whinnies v, n ▷ whinny

whinny v (**-nnies, -nnying, -nnied**) neigh softly ▶ n (pl **-nnies**) soft neigh

whinnying v ▷ whinny

whins n ▷ whin

whip n (pl **-s**) cord attached to a handle, used for beating animals or people ▶ v (**-s, -pping, -pped**) strike with a whip, strap, or cane

whipped v ▷ whip

whippet n (pl **-s**) racing dog like a small greyhound

whippets n ▷ whippet

whipping v ▷ whip

whips v, n ▷ whip

whir v ▷ whirr

whirl v (**-s, -ing, -ed**) spin or revolve ▶ n (pl **-s**) whirling movement

whirled v ▷ whirl

whirling v ▷ whirl

whirlpool n (pl **-s**) strong circular current of water

whirlpools n ▷ whirlpool

whirls v, n ▷ whirl

whirlwind n (pl **-s**) column of air whirling violently upwards in a spiral ▶ adj much quicker than normal

whirlwinds n ▷ whirlwind

whirr, whir n (pl **-s**) prolonged soft buzz ▶ v (**-s, -rring, -rred**) (cause to) make a whirr

whirred v ▷ whirr

whirring v ▷ whirr

whirrs n, v ▷ whirr

whirs n ▷ whirr

whisk v (**-s, -ing, -ed**) move or remove quickly ▶ n (pl **-s**) egg-beating utensil

whisked v ▷ whisk

whisker n (pl **-s**) any of the long stiff hairs on the face of a cat or other mammal ▶ pl hair growing on a man's face

whiskers n ▷ whisker

whiskey n (pl **-s**) Irish or American whisky

whiskeys n ▷ whiskey

whiskies n ▷ whisky

whisking v, vb ▷ whisk

whisks n ▷ whisk

whisky n (pl **-ies**) spirit distilled from fermented cereals

whisper v (**-s, -ing, -ed**) speak softly, without vibration of the vocal cords ▶ n (pl **-s**) soft voice (Informal)

whispered v ▷ whisper

whispering v ▷ whisper

whispers v, n ▷ whisper

whist n (pl **-s**) card game in which one pair of players tries to win more tricks than another pair

whistle v (**-les, -ling, -led**) produce a shrill sound, esp. by forcing the breath through pursed lips ▶ n (pl **-s**) whistling sound > **whistling** n, adj (pl **-s**)

whistled v ▷ whistle

whistles v, n ▷ whistle

whistling v, n ▷ whistle

whistlings n ▷ whistle

whists n ▷ whist

whit n (pl -s) not the slightest amount

white adj (-r, -st) of the colour of snow ▶ n (pl -s) colour of snow > **whiteness** n (pl -es) > **whitish** adj

whitebait n (pl -s) small edible fish

whitebaits n ▷ whitebait

whiten v (-s, -ing, -ed) make or become white or whiter

whitened v ▷ whiten

whiteness n ▷ white

whitenesses n ▷ white

whitening v ▷ whiten

whitens v ▷ whiten

whiter adj ▷ white

whites n ▷ white

whitest adj ▷ white

whitewash n (pl -es) substance for whitening walls ▶ v (-es, -ing, -ed) cover with whitewash

whitewashed v ▷ whitewash

whitewashes n, v ▷ whitewash

whitewashing v ▷ whitewash

whither adv (Obs) to what place

whiting n (pl -s) edible sea fish

whitings n ▷ whiting

whitish adj ▷ white

whittle v (-les, -ling, -led) cut or carve (wood) with a knife

whittled v ▷ whittle

whittles v ▷ whittle

whittling v ▷ whittle

whiz v ▷ whizz

whizz, whiz v (-es, -ing, -ed) make a loud buzzing sound (Informal) ▶ n (pl -es) loud buzzing sound (Informal)

whizzed v ▷ whizz

whizzes n, v ▷ whizz

whizzing v ▷ whizz

who pron which person

whodunnit, whodunit [hoo-dun-nit] n (pl -s) (Informal) detective story, play, or film

whodunnits n ▷ whodunnit

whoever pron any person who

whole adj containing all the elements or parts ▶ n (pl -s) complete thing or system > **wholly** adv

wholefood n (pl -s) food that has been processed as little as possible

wholefoods n ▷ wholefood

wholehearted adj sincere or enthusiastic

wholemeal adj (of flour) made from the whole wheat grain

wholes n ▷ whole

wholesale adj, adv dealing by selling goods in large quantities to retailers > **wholesaler** n (pl -s)

wholesaler n ▷ wholesale

wholesalers n ▷ wholesale

wholesome adj physically or morally beneficial

wholly adv ▷ whole

whom pron ▷ who

whoop v, n (pl -s) shout or cry to express excitement

whoopee interj (Informal) cry of joy

whoops n ▷ whoop

whopper n (pl -s) (Informal) anything unusually large > **whopping** adj

whoppers n ▷ whopper

whopping adj ▷ whopper

whore [hore] n (pl -s) prostitute

whores n ▷ whore

whorl n (pl -s) ring of leaves or petals

whorls n ▷ whorl

whose pron of whom or of which

why adv for what reason ▶ pron because of which

wick n (pl -s) cord through a lamp or candle which carries fuel to the flame

wicked (-er, -est) adj morally bad > **wickedly** adv > **wickedness** n (pl -es)

wickedly adv ▷ wicked

wickedness n ▷ wicked

wickednesses n ▷ wicked

wicker adj made of woven cane > **wickerwork** n (pl -s)

wickerwork n ▷ wicker

wickerworks n ▷ wicker

wicket n (pl -s) set of three cricket stumps and two bails

wickets n ▷ wicket

wicks n ▷ wick

wide adj (-r, -st) large from side to side ▶ adv to the full extent > **widely** adv

widely adv ▷ wide

widen v (-s, -ing, -ed) make or become wider

widened v ▷ widen

widening v ▷ widen

widens v ▷ widen

wider adj ▷ wide

widespread adj affecting a wide area or a large number of people

widest adj ▷ wide

widgeon n (pl -s) ▷ wigeon

widgeons n ▷ widgeon

widow n (pl -s) woman whose husband is dead

and who has not remarried ▷ **widowed** *adj*
▷ **widowhood** *n* (*pl* -s)
widowed *adj* ▷ **widow**
widower *n* (*pl* -s) man whose wife is dead and
who has not remarried
widowers *n* ▷ **widower**
widowhood *n* ▷ **widow**
widowhoods *n* ▷ **widow**
widows *n* ▷ **widow**
width *n* (*pl* -s) distance from side to side
widths *n* ▷ **width**
wield *v* (-s, -ing, -ed) hold and use (a weapon)
wielded *v* ▷ **wield**
wielding *v* ▷ **wield**
wields *v* ▷ **wield**
wife *n* (*pl* **wives**) woman to whom a man is
married
wig *n* (*pl* -s) artificial head of hair
wigeon *n* (*pl* -s) duck found in marshland
wigeons *n* ▷ **wigeon**
wiggle *v* (-les, -ling, -led) move jerkily from
side to side ▶ *n* (*pl* -les) wiggling movement
wiggled *v* ▷ **wiggle**
wiggles *v*, *n* ▷ **wiggle**
wiggling *v* ▷ **wiggle**
wigs *n* ▷ **wig**
wigwam *n* (*pl* -s) Native American's tent
wigwams *n* ▷ **wigwam**
wild *adj* (-er, -est) (of animals) not tamed or
domesticated ▷ **wildly** *adv* ▷ **wildness** *n* (*pl*
-es)
wildcat *n* (*pl* -s) European wild animal like a
large domestic cat
wildcats *n* ▷ **wildcat**
wildebeest *n* (*pl* -s) gnu
wildebeests *n* ▷ **wildebeest**
wilder *adj* ▷ **wild**
wilderness *n* (*pl* -es) uninhabited uncultivated
region
wildernesses *n* ▷ **wilderness**
wildest *adj* ▷ **wild**
wildlife *n* (*pl* -s) wild animals and plants
collectively
wildlifes *n* ▷ **wildlife**
wildly *adv* ▷ **wild**
wildness *n* ▷ **wild**
wildnesses *n* ▷ **wild**
wilds *pl n* desolate or uninhabited place
wiles *pl n* tricks or ploys
wilful *adj* headstrong or obstinate ▷ **wilfully**
adv
wilfully *adv* ▷ **wilful**
wilier *adj* ▷ **wily**
wiliest *adj* ▷ **wily**
will[1] *v* (*past* **would**) used as an auxiliary to form

the future tense or to indicate intention,
ability, or expectation
will[2] *n* (*pl* -s) strong determination ▶ *v* (-s,
-ing, -ed) use one's will in an attempt to do
(something)
willed *v* ▷ **will**[2]
willing *adj* ready or inclined (to do something)
▶ *v* ▷ **will**[2] ▷ **willingly** *adv* ▷ **willingness** *n*
(*pl* -es)
willingly *adv* ▷ **willing**
willingness *n* ▷ **willing**
willingnesses *n* ▷ **willing**
willow *n* (*pl* -s) tree with thin flexible branches
willowier *adj* ▷ **willowy**
willowiest *adj* ▷ **willowy**
willows *n* ▷ **willow**
willowy *adj* (-wier, -wiest) slender and graceful
willpower *n* (*pl* -s) ability to control oneself
and one's actions
willpowers *n* ▷ **willpower**
wills *n*, *v* ▷ **will**[2]
wilt *v* (-s, -ing, -ed) (cause to) become limp or
lose strength
wilted *v* ▷ **wilt**
wilting *v* ▷ **wilt**
wilts *v* ▷ **wilt**
wily *adj* (-lier, -liest) crafty or sly
wimp *n* (*pl* -s) (*Informal*) feeble ineffectual
person
wimple *n* (*pl* -s) garment framing the face,
worn by medieval women and now by nuns
wimples *n* ▷ **wimple**
wimps *n* ▷ **wimp**
win *v* (-s, -nning, **won**) come first in (a
competition, fight, etc.) ▶ *n* (*pl* -s) victory, esp.
in a game ▷ **winner** *n* (*pl* -s)
wince *v* (-ces, -cing, -ced) draw back, as if in
pain ▶ *n* (*pl* -s) wincing
winced *v* ▷ **wince**
winces *v*, *n* ▷ **wince**
winch *n* (*pl* -es) machine for lifting or hauling
using a cable or chain wound round a drum
▶ *v* (-es, -ing, -ed) lift or haul using a winch
winched *v* ▷ **winch**
winches *n*, *v* ▷ **winch**
winching *v* ▷ **winch**
wincing *v* ▷ **wince**
wind[1] *n* (*pl* -s) current of air ▶ *v* (-s, -ing, -ed)
render short of breath ▷ **windy** *adj* (-dier,
-diest)
wind[2] *v* (-s, -ing, **wound**) coil or wrap around
winded *v* ▷ **wind**[1]
windfall *n* (*pl* -s) unexpected good luck
windfalls *n* ▷ **windfall**
windier *adj* ▷ **wind**[1]

windiest adj ▷ wind¹
winding v ▷ wind¹, ²
windlass n (pl -es) winch worked by a crank
 windlasses n ▷ windlass
windmill n (pl -s) machine for grinding or
 pumping driven by sails turned by the wind
 windmills n ▷ windmill
window n (pl -s) opening in a wall to let in
 light or air
 windows n ▷ window
windpipe n (pl -s) tube linking the throat and
 the lungs
 windpipes n ▷ windpipe
winds n, v ▷ wind¹, ²
windscreen n (pl -s) front window of a motor
 vehicle
 windscreens n ▷ windscreen
windsock n (pl -s) cloth cone on a mast at an
 airfield to indicate wind direction
 windsocks n ▷ windsock
windsurfing n (pl -s) sport of riding on water
 using a surfboard propelled and steered by
 a sail
 windsurfings n ▷ windsurfing
windward adj, n (pl -s) (of or in) the direction
 from which the wind is blowing
 windwards n ▷ windward
windy adj ▷ wind¹
wine n (pl -s) alcoholic drink made from
 fermented grapes
 wines n ▷ wine
wing n (pl -s) one of the limbs or organs of a
 bird, insect, or bat that are used for flying ▶ pl
 sides of a stage ▶ v (-s, -ing, -ed) fly ▷ **winged**
 adj
 winged v, adj ▷ wing
winger n (pl -s) (SPORT) player positioned on the
 side of the pitch
 wingers n ▷ winger
 winging v ▷ wing
 wings n, v ▷ wing
wink v (-s, -ing, -ed) close and open (an eye)
 quickly as a signal ▶ n (pl -s) winking
 winked v ▷ wink
 winking v ▷ wink
winkle n (pl -s) shellfish with a spiral shell
 winkles n ▷ winkle
 winks v, n ▷ wink
winner n ▷ win
 winners n ▷ win
winning adj gaining victory ▶ v ▷ win
winnings pl n sum won, esp. in gambling
winnow v (-s, -ing, -ed) (pl -s) separate (chaff
 from (grain)
 winnowed v ▷ winnow

winnowing v ▷ winnow
winnows v, n ▷ winnow
winsome adj (-r, -st) charming or winning
 winsomer adj ▷ winsome
 winsomest adj ▷ winsome
winter n (pl -s) coldest season ▶ v (-s, -ing, -ed)
 spend the winter
 wintered v ▷ winter
 wintering v ▷ winter
 winters n, v ▷ winter
 wintrier adj ▷ wintry
 wintriest adj ▷ wintry
wintry adj (-rier, -riest) of or like winter
wipe v (-pes, -ping, -ped) clean or dry by
 rubbing ▶ n (pl -s) wiping
 wiped v ▷ wipe
 wipes v, n ▷ wipe
 wiping v ▷ wipe
wire n (pl -s) thin flexible strand of metal (Obs)
 ▶ v (-res, -ring, -red) equip with wires
 wired v ▷ wire
wirehaired adj (of a dog) having a stiff wiry
 coat
wireless n (pl -es) (Old-fashioned) ▷ **radio** ▶ adj
 (of a computer network) connected by radio
 rather than by cables or fibre optics
 wirelesses n ▷ wireless
 wires n, v ▷ wire
 wirier adj ▷ wiry
 wiriest adj ▷ wiry
wiring n (pl -s) system of wires ▶ v ▷ wire
 wirings n ▷ wiring
wiry adj (-rier, -riest) lean and tough
wisdom n (pl -s) good sense and judgment
 wisdoms n ▷ wisdom
wise¹ adj (-r, -st) having wisdom > **wisely** adv
wise² n (pl -s) (Obs) manner
wiseacre n (pl -s) person who wishes to seem
 wise
 wiseacres n ▷ wiseacre
wisecrack (Informal) n (pl -s) clever, sometimes
 unkind, remark ▶ v (-s, -ing, -ed) make a
 wisecrack
 wisecracked v ▷ wisecrack
 wisecracking v ▷ wisecrack
 wisecracks n, v ▷ wisecrack
 wisely adv ▷ wise¹
 wiser adj ▷ wise¹
 wises n ▷ wise²
 wisest adj ▷ wise¹
wish v (-es, -ing, -ed) want or desire ▶ n (pl -es)
 expression of a desire
wishbone n (pl -s) V-shaped bone above the
 breastbone of a fowl
 wishbones n ▷ wishbone

wished v ▷ wish
wishes v, n ▷ wish
wishful adj too optimistic
wishing v ▷ wish
wisp n (pl -s) light delicate streak > wispy adj (-pier, -piest)
wispier adj ▷ wisp
wispiest adj ▷ wisp
wisps n ▷ wisp
wispy adj ▷ wisp
wisteria n (pl -s) climbing shrub with blue or purple flowers
wisterias n ▷ wisteria
wistful adj sadly longing > wistfully adv
wistfully adv ▷ wistful
wit n (pl -s) ability to use words or ideas in a clever and amusing way
witch n (pl -es) person, usu. female, who practises (black) magic
witchcraft n (pl -s) use of magic
witchcrafts n ▷ witchcraft
witches n ▷ witch
withdraw v (-drawing, -drew, -drawn) take or move out or away > withdrawal n (pl -s)
withdrawal n ▷ withdraw
withdrawals n ▷ withdraw
withdrawn adj unsociable ▶ v ▷ withdraw
withdraws v ▷ withdraw
withdrew v ▷ withdraw
wither v (-s, -ing, -ed) wilt or dry up
withered v ▷ wither
withering adj (of a look or remark) scornful ▶ v ▷ wither
withers v ▷ wither ▶ pl n ridge between a horse's shoulder blades
withheld v ▷ withhold
withhold v (-s, -ing, -held) refrain from giving
withholding v ▷ withhold
withholds v ▷ withhold
within prep, adv in or inside
without prep not accompanied by, using, or having
withstand v (-s, -ing, -stood) oppose or resist successfully
withstanding v ▷ withstand
withstands v ▷ withstand
withstood v ▷ wwithstand
witless adj foolish
witness n (pl -es) person who has seen something happen ▶ v (-es, -ing, -ed) see at first hand
witnessed v ▷ witness

witnesses n, v ▷ witness
witnessing v ▷ witness
wits n ▷ wit
witter v (-s, -ing, -ed) (CHIEFLY BRIT) chatter pointlessly or at unnecessary length
wittered v ▷ witter
wittering v ▷ witter
witters v ▷ witter
witticism n (pl -s) witty remark
witticisms n ▷ witticism
wittier adj ▷ witty
wittiest adj ▷ witty
wittily adv ▷ witty
wittingly adv intentionally
witty adj (-ttier, -ttiest) clever and amusing > wittily adv
wives n ▷ wife

> **wiz** n (wizzes). Wiz is a short form of **wizard**. This is the highest-scoring three-letter word beginning with W, and can be especially useful when there isn't much room to manoeuvre. Wiz scores 15 points.

wizard n (pl -s) magician > wizardry n (pl -ies)
wizardries n ▷ wizard
wizardry n ▷ wizard
wizards n ▷ wizard
wizened [wiz-zend] adj shrivelled or wrinkled

> **wo** n (wos). Wo is an old-fashioned spelling of **woe**. This unusual word is handy for joining words ending in W to those beginning in O. Wo scores 5 points.

woad n (pl -s) blue dye obtained from a plant, used by the ancient Britons as a body dye
woads n ▷ woad
wobbegong n (pl -s) Australian shark with brown-and-white skin
wobbegongs n ▷ wobbegong
wobble v (-les, -ling, -led) move unsteadily ▶ n (pl -s) wobbling movement or sound > wobbly adj (-lier, -liest)
wobbled v ▷ wobble
wobbles v, n ▷ wobble
wobblier adj ▷ wobble
wobbliest adj ▷ wobble
wobbling v ▷ wobble
wobbly adj ▷ wobble
wodge n (pl -s) (Informal) thick lump or chunk
wodges n ▷ wodge
woe n (pl -s) grief
woebegone adj looking miserable
woeful adj extremely sad > woefully adv
woefully adv ▷ woeful
woes n ▷ woe

wok n (pl -s) bowl-shaped Chinese cooking pan, used for stir-frying
  woke v ▷ **wake¹**
  woken v ▷ **wake¹**
  woks n ▷ **wok**
wold n (pl -s) high open country
  wolds n ▷ **wold**
wolf n (pl **wolves**) wild predatory canine mammal ▶ v eat ravenously
wolverine n (pl -s) carnivorous mammal of Arctic regions
  wolverines n ▷ **wolverine**
  wolves n ▷ **wolf**
woman n (pl **women**) adult human female > **womanhood** n (pl -s)
  womanhood n ▷ **woman**
  womanhoods n ▷ **woman**
womanish adj effeminate
  womanizer n ▷ **womanizing**
  womanizers n ▷ **womanizing**
womanizing n (pl -s) practice of indulging in casual affairs with women > **womanizer** n (pl -s)
  womanizings n ▷ **womanizing**
womanly adj having qualities traditionally associated with a woman
womb n (pl -s) hollow organ in female mammals where babies are conceived and develop
wombat n (pl -s) small heavily-built burrowing Australian marsupial
  wombats n ▷ **wombat**
  wombs n ▷ **womb**
  women n ▷ **woman**
  won v ▷ **win**
wonder v (-s, -ing, -ed) be curious about ▶ n (pl -s) wonderful thing ▶ adj spectacularly successful > **wonderment** n (pl -s)
  wondered v ▷ **wonder**
wonderful adj very fine > **wonderfully** adv
  wonderfully adv ▷ **wonderful**
  wondering v ▷ **wonder**
  wonderment n ▷ **wonder**
  wonderments n ▷ **wonder**
  wonders v, n ▷ **wonder**
wondrous adj (Old-fashioned) wonderful
  wonkier adj ▷ **wonky**
  wonkiest adj ▷ **wonky**
wonky adj (-kier, -kiest) (BRIT, AUST & NZ) (Informal) shaky or unsteady
wont [rhymes with **don't**] adj accustomed ▶ n (pl -s) custom
  wonts n ▷ **wont**
woo v (-s, -ing, -ed) try to persuade (Old-fashioned)

wood n (pl -s) substance trees are made of, used in carpentry and as fuel > **woody** adj (-dier, -diest)
woodbine n (pl -s) honeysuckle
  woodbines n ▷ **woodbine**
woodcock n (pl -s) game bird
  woodcocks n ▷ **woodcook**
woodcut n (pl -s) (print made from) an engraved block of wood
  woodcuts n ▷ **woodcut**
wooded adj covered with trees
wooden adj made of wood
  woodier adj ▷ **wood**
  woodiest adj ▷ **wood**
woodland n (pl -s) forest
  woodlands n ▷ **woodland**
  woodlice n ▷ **woodlouse**
woodlouse n (pl -**lice**) small insect-like creature with many legs
woodpecker n (pl -s) bird which searches tree trunks for insects
  woodpeckers n ▷ **woodpecker**
  woods n ▷ **wood**
woodwind adj, n (pl -s) (of) a type of wind instrument made of wood
  woodwinds n ▷ **woodwind**
woodworm n insect larva that bores into wood
  woodworms n ▷ **woodworm**
  woody adj ▷ **wood**
  wooed v ▷ **woo**
woof¹ n (pl -s) cross threads in weaving
woof² n (pl -s) barking noise made by a dog
woofer n (pl -s) loudspeaker reproducing low-frequency sounds
  woofers n ▷ **woofer**
  woofs n ▷ **woof¹, ²**
  wooing v ▷ **woo**
wool n (pl -s) soft hair of sheep, goats, etc. > **woollen** adj
  woollen adj ▷ **wool**
  woollier adj ▷ **woolly**
  woolliest adj ▷ **woolly**
woolly adj (-llier, -lliest) of or like wool ▶ n knitted woollen garment
  wools n ▷ **wool**
woomera n (pl -s) notched stick used by Australian Aborigines to aid the propulsion of a spear
  woomeras n ▷ **woomera**
  woos v ▷ **woo**
  woozier adj ▷ **woozy**
  wooziest adj ▷ **woozy**
woozy adj (-zier, -ziest) (Informal) weak, dizzy, and confused

word n (pl **-s**) smallest single meaningful unit of speech or writing ▶ v (**-s**, **-ing**, **-ed**) express in words
worded v ▷ word
wordier adj ▷ wordy
wordiest adj ▷ wordy
wording n (pl **-s**) choice and arrangement of words ▶ v ▷ word
wordings n ▷ wording
words n, v ▷ word
wordy adj (**-dier**, **-diest**) using too many words
wore v ▷ wear
work n (pl **-s**) physical or mental effort directed to making or doing something ▶ pl factory (Informal) ▶ adj of or for work ▶ v (**-s**, **-ing**, **-ed**) (cause to) do work > **workable** adj > **worker** n (pl **-s**)
workable adj ▷ work
workaholic n (pl **-s**) person obsessed with work
workaholics n ▷ workaholic
worked v ▷ work
worker n ▷ work
workers n ▷ work
workhorse n (pl **-s**) person or thing that does a lot of dull or routine work
workhorses n ▷ workhorse
workhouse n (pl **-s**) (in England, formerly) institution where the poor were given food and lodgings in return for work
workhouses n ▷ workhouse
working v ▷ work
workman n (pl **-men**) manual worker
workmanship n (pl **-s**) skill with which an object is made
workmanships n ▷ workmanship
workmen n ▷ workman
works n, v ▷ work
workshop n (pl **-s**) room or building for a manufacturing process
workshops n ▷ w
worktop n (pl **-s**) surface in a kitchen, used for food preparation
worktops n ▷ worktop
world n (pl **-s**) the planet earth ▶ adj of the whole world
worldlier adj ▷ worldly
worldliest adj ▷ worldly
worldly adj (**-ier**, **-iest**) not spiritual
worlds n ▷ world
worm n (pl **-s**) small limbless invertebrate animal ▶ pl illness caused by parasitic worms in the intestines ▶ v (**-s**, **-ing**, **-ed**) rid of worms > **wormy** adj (**-mier**, **-miest**)
wormed v ▷ worm

wormier adj ▷ worm
wormiest adj ▷ worm
worming v ▷ worm
worms n, v ▷ worm
wormwood n (pl **-s**) bitter plant
wormwoods n ▷ wormwood
wormy adj ▷ worm
worn v ▷ wear
worried v, adj ▷ worry
worries n, v ▷ worry
worry v (**-ies**, **-ying**, **-ied**) (cause to) be anxious or uneasy ▶ n (pl **-ies**) (cause of) anxiety or concern > **worried** adj > **worrying** adj, n
worrying v, adj ▷ worry
worse adj, adv ▷ bad, badly
worsen v (**-s**, **-ing**, **-ed**) make or grow worse
worsened v ▷ worsen
worsening v ▷ worsen
worsens v ▷ worsen
worship v (**-s**, **-pping**, **-pped**) show religious devotion to ▶ n (pl **-s**) act or instance of worshipping > **worshipper** n (pl **-s**)
worshipful adj worshipping
worshipped v ▷ worship
worshipper n ▷ worship
worshippers n ▷ worship
worshipping v ▷ worship
worships v, n ▷ worship
worst adj, adv ▷ bad, badly ▶ n worst thing
worsted [wooss-tid] n (pl **-s**) type of woollen yarn or fabric
worsteds n ▷ worsted
worth prep having a value of ▶ n (pl **-s**) value or price > **worthless** adj
worthier adj ▷ worthy
worthiest adj ▷ worthy
worthily adv ▷ worthy
worthiness n ▷ worthy
worthinesses n ▷ worthy
worthless adj ▷ worth
worths n ▷ worth
worthwhile adj worth the time or effort involved
worthy adj (**-thier**, **-thiest**) deserving admiration or respect ▶ n (Informal) notable person > **worthily** adv > **worthiness** n (pl **-es**)
would v ▷ will¹
wound¹ n (pl **-s**) injury caused by violence ▶ v (**-s**, **-ing**, **-ed**) inflict a wound on
wound² v ▷ wind²
wounded v ▷ wound¹
wounding v ▷ wound¹
wounds n, v ▷ wound¹
wove v ▷ weave
woven v ▷ weave

wow interj exclamation of astonishment ▶ n (pl -s) (Informal) astonishing person or thing
wows n ▷ wow

wowser n (pl -s) (AUST & NZ) (Slang) puritanical person
wowsers n ▷ wowser

wox n (woxes). Wox is an old past tense of the verb **wax**. This gives a good score for a three-letter word, and is a good one to look for when you have an X. Wox scores 13 points.

wrack n (pl -s) seaweed
wracks n ▷ wrack

wraith n (pl -s) ghost
wraiths n ▷ wraith

wrangle v (-les, -ling, -led) argue noisily ▶ n (pl -s) noisy argument
wrangled v ▷ wrangle
wrangles v, n ▷ wrangle
wrangling v ▷ wrangle

wrap v (-s, -pping, -pped) fold (something) round (a person or thing) so as to cover ▶ n (pl -s) garment wrapped round the shoulders
wrapped v ▷ wrap

wrapper n (pl -s) cover for a product
wrappers n ▷ wrapper

wrapping n (pl -s) material used to wrap ▶ v ▷ wrap
wrappings n ▷ wrapping
wraps v, n ▷ wrap

wrasse n (pl -s) colourful sea fish
wrasses n ▷ wrasse

wrath [roth] n (pl -s) intense anger > **wrathful** adj
wrathful adj ▷ wrath
wraths n ▷ wrath

wreak v (-s, -ing, -ed) cause (chaos)
wreaked v ▷ wreak
wreaking v ▷ wreak
wreaks v ▷ wreak

wreath n (pl -s) twisted ring or band of flowers or leaves used as a memorial or tribute
wreathed adj surrounded or encircled
wreaths n ▷ wreath

wreck v (-s, -ing, -ed) destroy ▶ n (pl -s) remains of something that has been destroyed or badly damaged, esp. a ship > **wrecker** n (pl -s)
wreckage n (pl -s) wrecked remains
wreckages n ▷ wreckage
wrecked v ▷ wreck
wrecker n ▷ wreck
wreckers n ▷ wreck
wrecking v ▷ wreck
wrecks v, n ▷ wreck

wren n (pl -s) small brown songbird

wrench v (-es, -ing, -ed) twist or pull violently ▶ n (pl -es) violent twist or pull
wrenched v ▷ wrench
wrenches v, n ▷ wrench
wrenching v ▷ wrench
wrens n ▷ wren

wrest v (-s, -ing, -ed) twist violently
wrested v ▷ wrest
wresting v ▷ wrest

wrestle v (-les, -ling, -led) fight, esp. as a sport, by grappling with and trying to throw down an opponent > **wrestler** n (pl -s) > **wrestling** n (pl -s)
wrestled v ▷ wrestle
wrestler n ▷ wrestle
wrestlers n ▷ wrestle
wrestles v ▷ wrestle
wrestling v, n ▷ wrestle
wrestlings n ▷ wrestle
wrests v ▷ wrest

wretch n (pl -es) despicable person

wretched [retch-id] adj (-er, -est) miserable or unhappy > **wretchedly** adv > **wretchedness** n (pl -es)
wretcheder adj ▷ wretched
wretchedest adj ▷ wretched
wretchedly adv ▷ wretched
wretchedness n ▷ wretched
wretchednesses n ▷ wretched
wretches n ▷ wretch

wrier adj ▷ wry
wriest adj ▷ wry

wriggle v (-les, -ling, -led) move with a twisting action ▶ n (pl -s) wriggling movement
wriggled v ▷ wriggle
wriggles v, n ▷ wriggle
wriggling v ▷ wriggle

wright n (pl -s) maker
wrights n ▷ wright

wring v (-s, -ing, wrung) twist, esp. to squeeze liquid out of
wringing v ▷ wring
wrings v ▷ wring

wrinkle n (pl -s) slight crease, esp. one in the skin due to age ▶ v (-les, -ling, -led) make or become slightly creased > **wrinkly** adj (-lier, -liest)
wrinkled v ▷ wrinkle
wrinkles n, v ▷ wrinkle
wrinklier adj ▷ wrinkle
wrinkliest adj ▷ wrinkle
wrinkling v ▷ wrinkle
wrinkly adj ▷ wrinkle

wrist n (pl -s) joint between the hand and

the arm
 wrists n ▷ **wrist**
wristwatch n (pl **-es**) watch worn on the wrist
 wristwatches n ▷ **wristwatch**
writ n (pl **-s**) written legal command
write v (**-tes, -ting, wrote, written**) mark paper
etc. with symbols or words > **writing** n (pl **-s**)
writer n (pl **-s**) author
 writers n ▷ **writer**
writhe v (**-thes, -thing, -thed**) twist or squirm
in or as if in pain
 writhed v ▷ **writhe**
 writhes v ▷ **writhe**
 writhing v ▷ **writhe**
 writing v, n ▷ **write**
 writings n ▷ **write**
 writs n ▷ **writ**
 written v ▷ **write**
wrong adj incorrect or mistaken ▶ adv in a
wrong manner ▶ n (pl **-s**) something immoral
or unjust ▶ v (**-s, -ing, -ed**) treat unjustly
> **wrongly** adv > **wrongful** adj > **wrongfully**
adv
 wrongdoer n ▷ **wrongdoing**
 wrongdoers n ▷ **wrongdoing**

wrongdoing n (pl **-s**) immoral or illegal
behaviour > **wrongdoer** n (pl **-s**)
 wrongdoings n ▷ **wrongdoing**
 wronged v ▷ **wrong**
 wrongful adj ▷ **wrong**
 wrongfully adv ▷ **wrong**
 wronging v ▷ **wrong**
 wrongly adv ▷ **wrong**
 wrongs n, v ▷ **wrong**
 wrote v ▷ **write**
wrought [rawt] v (Lit) ▷ **work** ▶ adj (of metals)
shaped by hammering or beating
 wrung v ▷ **wring**
wry adj (**wrier, wriest** or **wryer**) (**wryest**) drily
humorous > **wryly** adv
 wryer adj ▷ **wry**
 wryest adj ▷ **wry**
 wryly adv ▷ **wry**

> **wye** n (**wyes**). Wye is the letter Y. If you
> have W and Y on your rack, look for an
> E on the board that will allow you to
> play this especially if you can land on
> a bonus square as a result. Wye scores
> 9 points.

Xx

Worth 8 points on its own, X is one of the best tiles in the game. It doesn't, however, start many two- and three-letter words. There are only two valid two-letter words, **xi** and **xu** (9 points each), beginning with X, and only one three-letter word, **xis.** Therefore, if you have an X on your rack and need to play short words, you're probably better off thinking of words that end in X or have X in them rather than those that start with X.

xebec n (**xebecs**). A xebec is an Algerian ship. This is a good high-scoring word. If you have an X, you'll probably only need one E as well as B and C to play it, as there is likely to be an available E on the board already. Xebec scores 16 points.

xenon n (pl -s) (CHEM) colourless odourless gas found in very small quantities in the air
xenons n ▷ xenon

xenophobia [zen-oh-**fobe**-ee-a] n (pl -s) fear or hatred of people from other countries
xenophobias n ▷ xenophobia

    xi n (**xis**). Xi is the 14th letter of the Greek alphabet. The plural of this word is the only three-letter word that starts with X. Xi scores 9 points.

xoanon n (**xoanons**) A xoanon is a primitive carving of a god. If you have all the tiles for the plural, and are able to place them all on the board, you'll earn a 50-point bonus. Xoanon scores 13 points.

    xu n (**xu**). The xu is a unit of currency in Vietnam. The plural form of this word is the same as its singular, so be sure to challenge anyone who adds an S to it! Xu scores 9 points.

xylem [**zy**-lem] n (pl -s) plant tissue that conducts water and minerals from the roots to all other parts
xylems n ▷ xylem

xylophone [**zile**-oh-fone] n (pl -s) musical instrument made of a row of wooden bars played with hammers
xylophones n ▷ xylophone

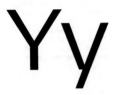

Yy

Y is a useful tile to have on your rack. It's worth 4 points on its own, and so often gives you good scores. There are only four two-letter words beginning with Y, but these are easy to remember as there's one for every vowel except I: **ya**, **ye**, **yo** and **yu** (5 points each). There are quite a few useful three-letter words: **yew** (9) and **yob** (8) and remember that yob was originally **boy** backwards: if you can't fit in yob, you may be able to use boy instead. And while his half-brother the **zo** (or **dzo** or **dso** or **zho**) gets all the attention, don't forget that the **yak** (10) earns quite a decent score!

ya *interj* (S AFR) yes

yabbies *n* ▷ yabby

yabby *n* (*pl* -bbies) (AUST) small freshwater crayfish

yacht [yott] *n* (*pl* -s) large boat with sails or an engine, used for racing or pleasure cruising > **yachting** *n* (*pl* -s) > **yachtsman** *n* (*pl* -men) > **yachtswoman** *n* (*pl* -women)

   yachting *n* ▷ yacht

   yachtings *n* ▷ yacht

   yachts *n* ▷ yacht

   yachtsman *n* ▷ yacht

   yachtsmen *n* ▷ yacht

   yachtswoman *n* ▷ yacht

   yachtswomen *n* ▷ yacht

yak¹ *n* (*pl* -s) Tibetan ox with long shaggy hair

yak² *v* (yaks, yakking, yakked) (Slang) talk continuously about unimportant matters

yakka *n* (*pl* -s) (AUST & NZ) (Informal) work

   yakkas *n* ▷ yakka

   yakked *v* ▷ yak²

   yakking *v* ▷ yak²

   yaks *n* ▷ yak¹ ▶ *v* ▷ yak²

yam *n* (*pl* -s) tropical root vegetable

   yams *n* ▷ yam

yank *v* (-s, -ing, -ed) pull or jerk suddenly ▶ *n* (*pl* -s) sudden pull or jerk

   yanked *v* ▷ yank

   yanking *v* ▷ yank

   yanks *v*, *n* ▷ yank

yap *v* (-s, -pping, -pped) bark with a high-pitched sound (Informal) ▶ *n* (*pl* -s) high-pitched bark

   yapped *v* ▷ yap

   yapping *v* ▷ yap

   yaps *v* ▷ yap

yard¹ *n* (*pl* -s) unit of length equal to 36 inches or about 91.4 centimetres > **yardstick** *n* (*pl* -s) standard against which to judge other people or things

yard² *n* (*pl* -s) enclosed area, usu. next to a building and often used for a particular purpose

   yards *n* ▷ yard¹,²

   yardstick *n* ▷ yard¹

   yardsticks *n* ▷ yard¹

yarmulke [yar-mull-ka] *n* (*pl* -s) skullcap worn by Jewish men

   yarmulkes *n* ▷ yarmulke

yarn *n* (*pl* -s) thread used for knitting or making cloth

   yarns *n* ▷ yarn

yashmak *n* (*pl* -s) veil worn by a Muslim woman to cover her face in public

   yashmaks *n* ▷ yashmak

yaw *v* (-s, -ing, -ed) (of an aircraft or ship) turn to one side or from side to side while moving

   yawed *v* ▷ yaw

   yawing *v* ▷ yaw

yawl *n* (*pl* -s) two-masted sailing boat

   yawls *n* ▷ yawl

yawn *v* (-s, -ing, -ed) open the mouth wide and take in air deeply, often when sleepy or bored ▶ *n* (*pl* -s) act of yawning > **yawning** *adj*

   yawned *v* ▷ yawn

   yawning ▷ yawn

   yawns *v*, *n* ▷ yawn

   yaws *v* ▷ yaw

ye [yee] *pron* (Obs) you

year *n* (*pl* -s) time taken for the earth to make

one revolution around the sun, about 365 days

yearling n (pl -s) animal between one and two years old
yearlings n ▷ **yearling**

yearly adj, adv (happening) every year or once a year

yearn v (-s, -ing, -ed) want (something) very much ▷ **yearning** n (pl -s) adj
yearned v ▷ **yearn**
yearning n, v ▷ **yearn**
yearnings n ▷ **yearn**
yearns v ▷ **yearn**
years n ▷ **year**

yeast n (pl -s) fungus used to make bread rise and to ferment alcoholic drinks > **yeasty** adj
yeasts n ▷ **yeast**

yebo interj (S AFR) (Informal) yes

yell v (-s, -ing, -ed) shout or scream in a loud or piercing way ▷ n (pl -s) loud cry of pain, anger, or fear
yelled v ▷ **yell**
yelling v ▷ **yell**

yellow n (pl -s) the colour of gold, a lemon, etc. ▷ adj (-er, -est) of this colour ▷ v (-s, -ing, -ed) make or become yellow
yellowed v ▷ **yellow**
yellower adj ▷ **yellow**
yellowest adj ▷ **yellow**

yellowhammer n (pl -s) European songbird with a yellow head and body
yellowhammers n ▷ **yellowhammer**
yellowing v ▷ **yellow**
yellows n, v ▷ **yellow**
yells v, n ▷ **yell**

yelp v (-s, -ing, -ed) ▷ n (pl -s) (give) a short sudden cry
yelped v ▷ **yelp**
yelping v ▷ **yelp**
yelps v, n ▷ **yelp**

yen² n (pl **yen**) monetary unit of Japan
yen² n (pl **yen**) (Informal) longing or desire

yeoman [yo-man] n (pl -**men**) (HIST) farmer owning and farming his own land
yeomen n ▷ **yeoman**

yes interj expresses consent, agreement, or approval

yesterday adv, n (pl -s) (on) the day before today
yesterdays n ▷ **yesterday**

yet conj nevertheless, still ▷ adv up until then or now

yeti n (pl **yetis**) large apelike creature said to live in the Himalayas
yetis n ▷ **yeti**

yew n (pl -s) evergreen tree with needle-like leaves and red berries
yews n ▷ **yew**

yex v (**yexes**, **yexing**, **yexed**). Yex is a Scots word that means to hiccup or cough. This word gives you a good score, and the verb forms offer the chance to expand it if someone else plays it, or if you get the chance later on. Yex scores 13 points.

yield v (-s, -ing, -ed) produce or bear ▷ n (pl -s)
yielded v ▷ **yield**
yielding adj submissive ▷ v ▷ **yield**
yields v, n ▷ **yield**

yo interj. Yo is an informal greeting. This is useful for connecting words ending in Y with ones beginning in O. Yo scores 5 points.

yob n (pl -s) (Slang) bad-mannered aggressive youth

yobbo n (pl -**bboes** or -**bbos**) yob
yobboes n ▷ **yobbo**
yobbos n ▷ **yobbo**
yobs n ▷ **yob**

yodel v (-s, -lling, -lled) sing with abrupt changes between a normal and a falsetto voice
yodelled v ▷ **yodel**
yodelling v ▷ **yodel**
yodels v ▷ **yodel**

yoga n (pl -s) Hindu method of exercise and discipline aiming at spiritual, mental, and physical wellbeing
yogas n ▷ **yoga**
yoghurt n ▷ **yogurt**
yoghurts n ▷ **yogurt**

yogi n (pl -s) person who practises yoga
yogis n ▷ **yogi**

yogurt, yoghurt n (pl -s) slightly sour custard-like food made from milk that has had bacteria added to it, often sweetened and flavoured with fruit
yogurts n ▷ **yogurt**

yok n (**yoks**). A yok is a noisy laugh. This unusual word is useful if there isn't much space on the board, as there's likely to be an O available to form it around. Yok scores 10 points.

yoke n (pl -s) wooden bar put across the necks of two animals to hold them together (Lit) ▷ v (-**kes**, -**king**, -**ked**) put a yoke on
yoked v ▷ **yoke**

yokel n (pl **yokels**) (Offens) person who lives in the country and is usu. simple and old-fashioned

yokels n ▷ yokel
yokes n, v ▷ yoke
yoking v ▷ yoke
yolk n (pl -s) yellow part of an egg that provides food for the developing embryo
yolks n ▷ yolk
yonder adj, adv (situated) over there
yonks pl n (Informal) very long time
yore n (pl -s) (Lit) a long time ago
yores n ▷ yore
you pron refers to: the person or people addressed
young adj in an early stage of life or growth
 ▶ pl n young people in general
youngster n (pl -s) young person
youngsters n ▷ youngster
your adj of, belonging to, or associated with you ▶ **yourself** pron
yours pron something belonging to you
yourself pron ▷ your
youth n (pl -s) time of being young ▷ **youthful** adj ▷ **youthfulness** n (pl -es)
youthful adj ▷ youth
youthfulness adj ▷ youth
youthfulnesses adj ▷ youth
youths n ▷ youth
yowl v, n (pl -s) (produce) a loud mournful cry

yowls n ▷ yowl
yttrium [it-ree-um] n (pl -s) (CHEM) silvery metallic element used in various alloys
yttriums n ▷ yttrium

yu n (**yus**). Yu is a Chinese word that means precious jade. This word is good for connecting words ending in Y with ones beginning in U. Yu scores 5 points.

yucca n (pl -s) tropical plant with spikes of white leaves
yuccas n ▷ yucca
yuckier adj ▷ yucky
yuckiest adj ▷ yucky
yucky adj (-ckier, -ckiest) (Slang) disgusting, nasty

yuk interj. Yuk is a noise people make to express disgust or dislike. This funny little word is worth remembering as it give a good score and uses an unpromising combination of letters. Yuk scores 10 points.

yuppie n (pl -s) young highly-paid professional person, esp. one who has a materialistic way of life ▶ adj typical of or reflecting the values of yuppies
yuppies n ▷ yuppie

Zz

Scoring the same as Q but easier to use, Z is the most valuable tile in Scrabble. There is only one two-letter word beginning with Z, **zo** (11 points), but remembering this will save you wasting time looking for others. There some very good three-letter words starting with Z, however. These include another variant of **zo**, **zho** (15), as well as **zax** and **zex** (19 each), **zap** (14), **zip** (14) and **zoo** (12).

zanier adj ▷ zany
zaniest ▷ zany

> **zanja** n (**zanjas**). A zanja is an irrigation canal. This unusual word is very useful because of its combination of J and Z. As there are many As in the game, if you are lucky enough to get J and Z together, you may well be able to play this somewhere. Zanja scores 21 points.
>
> **zanjero** n (**zanjeros**). A zanjero is a supervisor of irrigation canals. If you can use all your tiles to play zanjero, you'll earn a 50-point bonus. Zanjero scores 23 points.

zany [zane-ee] adj (**-nier, -niest**) comical in an endearing way
zap v (**-s, -pping, -pped**) (Slang) kill (by shooting)
zapped v ▷ zap
zapping v ▷ zap
zaps v ▷ zap

> **zax** n (**zaxes**). A zax a small axe for cutting slates. This is great word combining X and Z. If you get a Z late in the game, check if X has already been played, and whether there is an opportunity to form zax or **zex**. Zax scores 19 points.

zeal n (pl **-s**) great enthusiasm or eagerness
zealot [zel-lot] n (pl **-s**) fanatic or extreme enthusiast
zealots n ▷ zealot
zealous [zel-luss] adj extremely eager or enthusiastic > **zealously** adv
zealously adv ▷ zealous
zeals n ▷ zeal
zebra n (pl **-s**) black-and-white striped African animal of the horse family

zebras n ▷ zebra
zebu [zee-boo] n (pl **-s**) Asian ox with a humped back and long horns
zebus n ▷ zebu

> **zed** n (**zeds**). Zed is the letter Z. This is a handy word when you have a Z but no space or letters for a longer word. Zed scores 13 points.
>
> **zee** n (**zees**). Zee is the American pronunciation of the letter Z. This word can be very useful because E is the most common tile in Scrabble, so keep it in mind if you draw a Z. Zee scores 12 points.

zenith n (pl **-s**) highest point of success or power
zeniths n ▷ zenith
zephyr [zef-fer] n (pl **-s**) soft gentle breeze
zephyrs n ▷ zephyr
zeppelin n (pl **-s**) (HIST) large cylindrical airship
zeppelins n ▷ zeppelin
zero n (pl **-ros, -roes**) (symbol representing) the number o ▶ adj having no measurable quantity or size
zeroes n ▷ zero
zeros n ▷ zero
zest n (pl **-s**) enjoyment or excitement
zests n ▷ zest

> **zeuxite** n (**zeuxites**). Zeuxite is a mineral. This unusual word is great if you have the letters for it. If you can use all of your tiles to play zeuxite, you'll get a 50-point bonus. Zeuxite scores 23 points.
>
> **zex** n (**zexes**). Zex means the same as **zax**. If you get a Z late in the game, check if X has already been played, and whether there is an opportunity to form zax. Zex scores 19 points.

zho n (**zhos**) Zho is one of several spelling for a Tibetan animal bred from yaks and cattle. The other forms are **dso, dzo** and **zo**, and it's worth remembering all of them. Zho scores 15 points.

zigzag n (pl -s) line or course having sharp turns in alternating directions ▶ v (**-zags, -zagging, -zagged**) move in a zigzag ▶ adj formed in or proceeding in a zigzag
zigzagged v ▷ zigzag
zigzagging v ▷ zigzag
zigzags n, v ▷ zigzag

zinc n (pl -s) (CHEM) bluish-white metallic element used in alloys and to coat metal
zincs n ▷ zinc

zing n (pl -s) (Informal) quality in something that makes it lively or interesting
zings n ▷ zing

zip n (pl -s) fastener with two rows of teeth that are closed or opened by a small clip pulled between them ▶ v (**-s, -pping, -pped**) fasten with a zip
zipped v ▷ zip
zipping v ▷ zip
zips n, v ▷ zip

zircon n (pl -s) mineral used as a gemstone and in industry

zirconium n (pl -s) (CHEM) greyish-white metallic element that is resistant to corrosion
zirconiums n ▷ zirconium
zircons n ▷ zircon

zit n (**zits**). A zit is a pimple. This nasty little word can be very useful during a game, especially when there's not much space left on the board. Zit scores 12 points.

zither n (pl -s) musical instrument consisting of strings stretched over a flat box and plucked to produce musical notes
zithers n ▷ zither

zo n (**zos**). Zo is one of several spelling for a Tibetan animal bred from yaks and cattle. The other forms are **dso, dzo** and **zho**, and it's worth remembering all of them. If someone plays zo and you have a D, remember that you can form dzo from it. Zo is the

only two-letter word beginning with Z, and scores 11 points.

zodiac n (pl -s) imaginary belt in the sky within which the sun, moon, and planets appear to move, divided into twelve equal areas, called signs of the zodiac, each named after a constellation
zodiacs n ▷ zodiac
zombi n ▷ zombie

zombie, zombi n (pl -s) person who appears to be lifeless, apathetic, or totally lacking in independent judgment
zombies n ▷ zombie
zombis n ▷ zombie
zonal adj ▷ zone

zone n (pl -s) area with particular features or properties ▶ v (**-nes, -ning, -ned**) divide into zones > **zonal** adj
zoned v ▷ zone
zones n, v ▷ zone
zoning v ▷ zone

zoo n (pl -s) place where live animals are kept for show
zoological adj ▷ zoology
zoologies n ▷ zoology
zoologist n ▷ zoology
zoologists n ▷ zoology

zoology n (pl -gies) study of animals > **zoologist** n (pl -s) > **zoological** adj

zoom v (**-s, -ing, -ed**) move or rise very rapidly
zoomed v ▷ zoom
zooming v ▷ zoom
zooms v ▷ zoom
zoos n ▷ zoo

zootaxy n (**zootaxies**). Zootaxy is the scientific classification of animals. If you're lucky enough to have the letters for this word, you can earn a 50-point bonus by using all of your tiles to form it. Zootaxy scores 26 points.

zucchini [zoo-keen-ee] n (pl -**ni, -nis**) (US & AUST) courgette
zucchinis n ▷ zucchini

zulu n (pl -s) member of a tall Black people of southern Africa
zulus n ▷ zulu

zygote n (pl -s) fertilized egg cell
zygotes n ▷ zygote

NOTES

NOTES

NOTES

NOTES

NOTES

NOTES

NOTES

NOTES

NOTES

NOTES

NOTES

NOTES

NOTES

NOTES

NOTES

NOTES

NOTES